Admiralty Record®

Volume 11

PUBLISHED ADMIRALTY OPINIONS OF
THE SUPREME COURT OF THE UNITED STATES AND
THE UNITED STATES COURTS OF APPEALS ISSUED DURING
THE CALENDAR YEAR

2023

Cite as: 11 Adm. R. ____

REPORTED BY KIRK N. AURANDT, ESQ.
MEMBER OF THE BAR IN LOUISIANA AND PENNSYLVANIA

ADMIRALTY RECORD PUBLISHING COMPANY, L.L.C.
MANDEVILLE, LOUISIANA, U.S.A.

ISSN 2334-5411
ISBN 979-8-9964295-0-9

Admiralty record: published admiralty opinions of the Supreme Court of the United States and the United States Courts of Appeals issued during the calendar year ... Mandeville, Louisiana, U.S.A.: Admiralty Record Publishing Company, LLC, 2014-

KF1104.A75
ISSN: 2334-5411

https://lccn.loc.gov/2014200303

PREFACE

Volume 11 of the Admiralty Record® reports the published admiralty opinions of the Supreme Court of the United States and the United States Courts of Appeals that were issued during the calendar year 2023. The opinions reported are the original majority, concurring, and dissenting opinions of the Court, with only minor changes in formatting to better suit a dual-column presentation. The pagination found in the Court's original opinion is indicated by the number contained inside of black brackets, *see, e.g.*, **[—15—]**. The pagination found in the official Reporter is indicated by the number contained inside of black braces, *see, e.g.*, **{–15–}**. Also, where applicable, I have added parallel citations to opinions reported in this Volume and in prior Volumes of the Admiralty Record®.

The decision to select an opinion to appear in Volume 11 of the Admiralty Record® was made solely by me following an examination of those opinions that each of the above-named courts designated for publication in 2023. Every effort has been made to ensure inclusion of all 2023 federal appellate court admiralty opinions that were designated for publication; however, to the extent that a relevant admiralty opinion has been inadvertently overlooked or otherwise mistakenly omitted, the error is regretted and is solely my own. A few opinions from appeals in civil cases that technically may not have fallen under a federal district court's admiralty or maritime jurisdiction have been reported if they touched upon admiralty matters or were otherwise deemed to be of potential interest to the admiralty practitioner. Additionally, several opinions from criminal cases involving maritime crimes and civil cases arising under the Federal Employers' Liability Act have been included.

To assist the reader in locating those opinions from 2023 involving subject matters of interest, I have prepared an Index to the opinions. I have also prepared Tables of Authority, which supply page references to the cases, statutes, and rules cited in each opinion. Prior to relying upon any of the opinions reported herein, the reader is reminded to verify the current status of any particular case as valid precedent by checking the case with a reliable citator.

I hope that the Admiralty Record® will continue to be a valuable and ready reference source for not only the admiralty practitioner, but for anyone who is interested in reading the published admiralty opinions of the federal appellate courts.

KIRK N. AURANDT, ESQ.

This page intentionally left blank

Table of Contents[1]

(Cases arranged chronologically by Court)

[1] In 2023, there were no published admiralty opinions from the United States Courts of Appeals for the Third, Sixth, and Tenth Circuits.

This page intentionally left blank

Supreme Court of the United States

Supreme Court of the United States

No. 156, Orig.

NEW YORK
VS.
NEW JERSEY

On Cross-Motions for Judgment on the Pleadings

Decided: April 18, 2023

Citation: 598 U.S. 218, 143 S.Ct. 918, 11 Adm. R. 2 (2023).

[—220—] {–921–} JUSTICE KAVANAUGH delivered the opinion of the Court: {–922–}

Under Article I, § 10, of the Constitution, each State possesses the sovereign authority to enter into a compact with another State, subject to Congress's approval. In 1953, New York and New Jersey exercised that authority and entered into the Waterfront Commission Compact. The Compact created a bistate agency to perform certain regulatory [—221—] and law-enforcement functions at the Port of New York and New Jersey. In 2018, after concluding that the decades-old Compact had outlived its usefulness, New Jersey sought to withdraw from the Compact. New York opposes New Jersey's withdrawal and contends that the Compact does not allow either State to unilaterally withdraw. We hold that New Jersey may unilaterally withdraw from the Waterfront Commission Compact notwithstanding New York's opposition.

I

In 1951, New York and New Jersey began a joint investigation of organized crime at the Port of New York and New Jersey, a commercial port that spans the border of the two States. To address corruption within the labor force on both sides of the Port, each State enacted legislation to form the Waterfront Commission Compact. See 1953 N. J. Laws p. 1511; 1953 N. Y. Laws p. 2417. New York and New Jersey obtained Congress's approval of the Compact in 1953, consistent with the Compact Clause of the Constitution. President Eisenhower signed the Compact. See 67 Stat. 541; U. S. Const., Art. I, § 10, cl. 3.

The Compact established a bistate agency known as the Waterfront Commission of New York Harbor. The Commission consists of two members, one appointed by the Governor of New York and the other by the Governor of New Jersey. Through the Compact, New York and New Jersey delegated to the Commission their sovereign authority to conduct regulatory and law-enforcement activities at the Port. For example, the Compact authorizes the Commission to oversee mandatory employment licensing for waterfront workers and to conduct law-enforcement investigations at the Port.

Under the Compact, New York and New Jersey must agree if they want to make any "[a]mendments and supplements." Art. XVI(1), 67 Stat. 557. The Compact also recognizes Congress's authority to "alter, amend, or repeal" the Compact. Art. XVI, § 2, *ibid.* But the Compact does not [—222—] address each State's power to unilaterally withdraw: It neither expressly allows nor expressly proscribes unilateral withdrawal. {–923–}

The Compact and Commission have operated for 70 years. But as the decades have passed, circumstances at the Port have changed. In 1953, roughly 70% of waterfront employees worked on the New York side of the Port. But by 2018, according to New Jersey, more than 80% of work hours occurred on the New Jersey side, and more than 80% of the Port's cargo flowed through the New Jersey side. New Jersey also came to view the Commission as ill-equipped to handle 21st-century security challenges and as a source of over-regulation that impedes job growth.

In 2018, the New Jersey Legislature passed and Governor Christie signed a law to withdraw New Jersey from the Waterfront Commission Compact. See 2017 N. J. Laws p. 2102. The statute required the New Jersey Governor to give 90 days' notice of the State's intention to withdraw. Upon withdrawal, the Commission would dissolve, and the New Jersey State Police would take over the Commission's law-enforcement functions on the New Jersey side of the Port.

The day after enactment of the withdrawal statute, the Commission sued in Federal

District Court to stop New Jersey from unilaterally withdrawing from the Compact. The District Court ruled that New Jersey could not unilaterally withdraw. *Waterfront Comm'n of N. Y. Harbor* v. *Murphy*, 429 F. Supp. 3d 1 (NJ 2019). But the U. S. Court of Appeals for the Third Circuit reversed and ruled in New Jersey's favor, determining that state sovereign immunity barred the Commission's lawsuit. *Waterfront Comm'n of N. Y. Harbor* v. *Governor of New Jersey*, 961 F. 3d 234, 8 Adm. R. 82 (2020).

In 2021, in the wake of the Third Circuit's decision, Acting Governor Oliver announced New Jersey's intent to unilaterally withdraw from the Compact. Before the expected date of withdrawal, New York moved in this Court for leave to file a bill of complaint and for a temporary order preventing **[—223—]** New Jersey's withdrawal. This Court temporarily enjoined New Jersey from withdrawing from the Compact pending final disposition of this case. The Court later granted New York's motion for leave to file a bill of complaint and allowed the parties to file cross-motions for judgment on the pleadings. In this Court, the United States also participated as *amicus curiae* in support of New Jersey's unilateral withdrawal from the Compact.

II

The question presented is straightforward: Does the Waterfront Commission Compact allow New Jersey to unilaterally withdraw from the Compact notwithstanding New York's opposition? The answer is yes.

The interpretation of the Waterfront Commission Compact—an interstate compact approved by Congress—presents a federal question. See *Cuyler* v. *Adams*, 449 U. S. 433, 438 (1981). To resolve the dispute over whether each State may unilaterally withdraw, we "begin by examining the express terms of the Compact as the best indication of the intent of the parties." *Tarrant Regional Water Dist.* v. *Herrmann*, 569 U. S. 614, 628 (2013).

Some interstate compacts expressly allow, prohibit, or limit unilateral withdrawal.[1] But this Compact does not address **{-924-}** withdrawal. The Compact mentions neither "withdrawal" nor "termination" in any relevant context. The Compact provides for amendments, which require both States to agree. See Art. XVI(1), 67 Stat. 557. But unilat- **[—224—]** eral withdrawal does not constitute an amendment to the Compact and thus does not implicate the amendment provision. The Compact also authorizes Congress to "alter, amend, or repeal" the Compact. See Art. XVI, § 2, *ibid.* But Congress did not retain an *exclusive* right to terminate the Compact.

Because the Compact's text does not address whether a State may unilaterally withdraw, we look to background principles of law that would have informed the parties' understanding when they entered the Compact. This Court has long explained that interstate compacts "are construed as contracts under the principles of contract law." *Tarrant*, 569 U. S., at 628; see also *Alabama* v. *North Carolina*, 560 U. S. 330, 359 (2010) (Kennedy, J., concurring in part and concurring in judgment); *Texas* v. *New Mexico*, 482 U. S. 124, 128–129 (1987); *Green* v. *Biddle*, 8 Wheat. 1, 92 (1823). To that end, the Court has looked to "background principles of contract law" to interpret compacts that are silent on a particular issue. *Mississippi* v. *Tennessee*, 595 U. S. ——, —— (2021); see *Tarrant*, 569 U. S., at 628, 633.

To be sure, background rules of contract interpretation may not override a compact's terms. *Alabama*, 560 U. S., at 351–352. This Court has said that a compact "is not just a contract," but also "a federal statute enacted by Congress" that preempts contrary state law.

[1] See, *e. g.,* Central Interstate Low-Level Radioactive Waste Compact, Art. VII(d), 99 Stat. 1870 (1986) (expressly allowing unilateral withdrawal); Snake River Compact, Art. XII, 64 Stat. 33 (1950) (expressly providing that the compact will remain in force unless terminated by both state legislatures and consented to by Congress); New York-New Jersey Port Authority Compact, Art. 21, 42 Stat. 179 (1921) (expressly allowing unilateral withdrawal within two years of the compact's formation); Delaware River Basin Compact, Art. 1, § 1.6(a), 75 Stat. 691 (1961) (expressly allowing unilateral termination only after 100 years).

Id., at 351; see *Tarrant*, 569 U. S., at 627, n. 8. But when the compact does not speak to a disputed issue, background contract-law principles have informed the Court's analysis.

Under the default contract-law rule at the time of the Compact's 1953 formation, as well as today, a contract (like this Compact) that contemplates "continuing performance for an indefinite time is to be interpreted as stipulating only for performance terminable at the will of either party." 1 R. Lord, Williston on Contracts § 4:23, p. 570 (4th ed. 2022); see also, *e. g.*, Restatement (Second) of Contracts § 33, Com- **[—225—]** ment *d*, p. 94 (1979); 1 S. Williston, Law of Contracts § 38, p. 59 (1920); *Compania Embotelladora Del Pacifco, S. A.* v. *Pepsi Cola Co.*, 976 F. 3d 239, 245 (CA2 2020); *In re Miller's Estate*, 90 N. J. 210, 219, 447 A. 2d 549, 554 (1982); *Zimco Restaurants, Inc.* v. *Bartenders and Culinary Workers Union, Local 340*, 165 Cal. App. 2d 235, 240 (1958); *Fulghum* v. *Selma*, 238 N. C. 100, 103–104, 76 S. E. 2d 368, 370–371 (1953); *Bailey* v. *S. S. Stafford, Inc.*, 178 App. Div. 811, 815, 166 N. Y. S. 79, 82 (1917). Parties to a contract that calls for ongoing and indefinite performance generally need not continue performance after the contractual relationship has soured, or when the circumstances that originally motivated the agreement's formation have changed, for example. See *Delta Servs. & Equip., Inc.* v. *Ryko Mfg. Co.*, 908 F. 2d 7, 11 (CA5 1990); **{-925-}** *Jespersen* v. *Minnesota Min. & Mfg. Co.*, 183 Ill. 2d 290, 295, 700 N. E. 2d 1014, 1017 (1998).

That default contract-law rule—that contracts calling for ongoing and indefinite performance may be terminated by either party—supports New Jersey's position in this case. Through the Waterfront Commission Compact, New York and New Jersey delegated their sovereign authority to the Commission on an ongoing and indefinite basis. And the Compact contemplates the Commission's exercise of that authority on an ongoing and indefinite basis. The default contract-law rule therefore "speaks in the silence of the Compact" and indicates that either State may unilaterally withdraw. *New Jersey* v. *New York*, 523 U. S. 767, 784 (1998).

Principles of state sovereignty likewise support New Jersey's position. "The background notion that a State does not easily cede its sovereignty has informed our interpretation of interstate compacts." *Tarrant*, 569 U. S., at 631. Here, the Compact involves the delegation of a fundamental aspect of a State's sovereign power—its ability to protect the people, property, and economic activity within its borders—to a bistate agency. The nature of that delegation **[—226—]** buttresses our conclusion that New York and New Jersey did not permanently give up, absent the States' joint consent or congressional action to terminate the Compact, their authority to withdraw from the Compact and to exercise those sovereign police powers at the Port as each State sees fit.

We draw further guidance from the fact that, as is undisputed, New York and New Jersey never intended for the Compact and Commission to operate forever. See Brief for New York 19, 26; Brief for New Jersey 33, n. 8; Tr. of Oral Arg. 69, 100–101. Given that the States did not intend for the agreement to be perpetual, it would not make much sense to conclude that each State implicitly conferred on the other a perpetual veto of withdrawal.

In sum, background principles of contract law, reinforced here by principles of state sovereignty and the fact that the States did not intend for the Compact to operate forever, indicate that New Jersey may unilaterally withdraw from the Waterfront Commission Compact. To be clear, the contract-law rule that we apply today governs compacts (like this Compact) that are silent as to unilateral withdrawal and that exclusively call for ongoing performance on an indefinite basis. But that rule does not apply to other kinds of compacts that do not exclusively call for ongoing performance on an indefinite basis—such as compacts setting boundaries, apportioning water rights, or otherwise conveying property interests. Both New York and New Jersey agree that States may not unilaterally withdraw from compacts that are silent as to withdrawal and that set boundaries, apportion water rights, or otherwise convey property interests. See Brief for New York 3–4, 30, 38; Brief for New Jersey 27–29; Tr. of Oral Arg. 30, 44, 55.

III

New York advances several additional arguments in support of its view that the Compact nonetheless should be read to prohibit unilateral withdrawal. But none is persuasive. **[—227—]**

First, New York invokes the history of compacts before 1953. In New York's view, many pre-1953 compacts were silent on unilateral withdrawal but nonetheless were understood to forbid it. New York says that when States at that time wanted to allow unilateral withdrawal, the compacts would expressly provide for it. And New **{–926–}** York adds that we should interpret the 1953 Compact in light of that practice.

As New York acknowledges, however, many of those pre-1953 compacts concerned boundaries and water-rights allocation. See Brief for New York 3–4, 30; Tr. of Oral Arg. 30, 33. Those compacts, as we have explained, are not governed by the default contract-law rule authorizing unilateral withdrawal. New York offers no persuasive evidence that the background understanding of withdrawal from boundary and water-rights compacts also applied to compacts that exclusively call for ongoing performance on an indefinite basis by an interstate agency. Indeed, just three years before the Compact here was formed, the United States explained to this Court that a compacting State could unilaterally withdraw from a compact that was silent as to withdrawal and that required an ongoing and indefinite exercise of sovereign authority. See Brief for United States in *West Virginia ex rel. Dyer* v. *Sims*, O. T. 1950, No. 147, pp. 23–24, 26–27. In addition, New York overlooks that some compacts, including one formed three years before this Compact, expressly prohibited unilateral withdrawal. See Snake River Compact, Art. XII, 64 Stat. 33; see also, *e. g.*, Goose Lake Basin Compact, Arts. V, VII(B), 98 Stat. 292 (1984). That language would have been unnecessary if New York were correct about the pre-1953 practice.

In short, New York identifies no clear historical practice in support of its view that compacts calling for ongoing and indefinite performance and that were silent on withdrawal were understood as of 1953 to prohibit unilateral withdrawal. **[—228—]**

Second, New York invokes international treaty law. According to New York, international law generally prohibits a signatory nation's unilateral withdrawal from a treaty absent express language otherwise. But to the extent that international treaty practice is relevant here, it is equivocal. Scholars have "long debated" whether nations may unilaterally withdraw from treaties that do not expressly authorize withdrawal. L. Helfer, Exiting Treaties, 91 Va. L. Rev. 1579, 1592 (2005). And although the Vienna Convention on the Law of Treaties (to which the United States is not a party) provides that nations generally may not withdraw from a treaty absent express authorization, the Convention acknowledges that the nature of the treaty may nonetheless imply a right of withdrawal. Art. 56(1), May 23, 1969, 1155 U. N. T. S. 331; see also J. Brierly, The Law of Nations 240 (4th ed. 1949).

Third, New York points out that New York and New Jersey have resolved Commission-related disputes in the decades since 1953. According to New York, that practice suggests that the Compact prohibits unilateral withdrawal. But the States' past success in resolving disputes says little about whether New York or New Jersey could unilaterally withdraw if and when either State wanted to do so.

Fourth, New York argues that allowing New Jersey to withdraw would have sweeping consequences for interstate compacts generally. But our decision today only addresses a compact that (i) is silent on unilateral withdrawal; (ii) calls for ongoing and indefinite performance; and (iii) does not set boundaries, apportion water rights, or otherwise convey property interests. Moreover, for any current and future compacts, States can propose language expressly allowing or prohibiting unilateral withdrawal if they wish to do so.

* * *

New Jersey may unilaterally withdraw from the Waterfront Commission Compact notwithstanding New York's op- **[—229—]** position. We therefore grant New Jersey's motion **{–927–}** for judgment on the pleadings and deny New York's cross-motion.

It is so ordered.

Supreme Court of the United States

No. 21-1168

MALLORY
vs.
NORFOLK S. RY. CO.

On Writ of Certiorari to the Supreme Court of Pennsylvania, Eastern District

Decided: June 27, 2023

Citation: 600 U.S. 122, 143 S.Ct. 2028, 11 Adm. R. 7 (2023).

[—125—] {-2031-} **JUSTICE GORSUCH** announced the judgment of the Court and delivered the opinion of the Court with respect to Parts I and III–B, and an opinion with respect to Parts II, III–A, and IV, in which **JUSTICE THOMAS, JUSTICE SOTOMAYOR,** and **JUSTICE JACKSON** join. **{-2032-}**

Imagine a lawsuit based on recent events. A few months ago, a Norfolk Southern train derailed in Ohio near the Pennsylvania border. Its cargo? Hazardous chemicals. Some poured into a nearby creek; some burst into flames. In the aftermath, many residents reported unusual symptoms.[1] Suppose an Ohio resident sued the train conductor seeking compensation for an illness attributed to the accident. Suppose, too, that the plaintiff served his complaint on the conductor across the border in Pennsylvania. Everyone before us agrees a Pennsylvania court could hear that lawsuit consistent with the Due Process Clause of the Fourteenth Amendment. The court could do so even if the conductor was a Virginia resident who just happened to be passing through Pennsylvania when the process server caught up with him.

Now, change the hypothetical slightly. Imagine the same Ohio resident brought the same suit in the same Pennsylvania state court, but this time against Norfolk Southern. Assume, too, the company has fled paperwork consenting to appear in Pennsylvania courts as a condition of registering to do business in the Commonwealth. Could a Pennsylvania court hear that case too? You might think so. But today, **[—126—]** Norfolk Southern argues that the Due Process Clause entitles it to a more favorable rule, one shielding it from suits even its employees must answer. We reject the company's argument. Nothing in the Due Process Clause requires such an incongruous result.

I

Robert Mallory worked for Norfolk Southern as a freight-car mechanic for nearly 20 years, first in Ohio, then in Virginia. During his time with the company, Mr. Mallory contends, he was responsible for spraying boxcar pipes with asbestos and handling chemicals in the railroad's paint shop. He also demolished car interiors that, he alleges, contained carcinogens.

After Mr. Mallory left the company, he moved to Pennsylvania for a period before returning to Virginia. Along the way, he was diagnosed with cancer. Attributing his illness to his work for Norfolk Southern, Mr. Mallory hired Pennsylvania lawyers and sued his former employer in Pennsylvania state court under the Federal Employers' Liability Act, 35 Stat. 65, as amended, 45 U. S. C. §§ 51–60. That law creates a workers' compensation scheme permitting railroad employees to recover damages for their employers' negligence. See *Norfolk Southern R. Co.* v. *Sorrell*, 549 U. S. 158, 165–166 (2007). **{-2033-}**

Norfolk Southern resisted Mr. Mallory's suit on constitutional grounds. By the time he fled his complaint, the company observed, Mr. Mallory resided in Virginia. His complaint alleged that he was exposed to carcinogens in Ohio and Virginia. Meanwhile, the company itself was incorporated in Virginia and had its headquarters there too.[2] On these facts, Norfolk Southern submitted, any effort by a Pennsylvania court to exercise personal jurisdiction over it would offend the Due Process Clause of the Fourteenth Amendment. **[—127—]**

[1] See U. S. Environmental Protection Agency, East Palestine, Ohio Train Derailment (June 21, 2023), https://www.epa.gov/east-palestine-oh-train-derailment.

[2] After Mr. Mallory commenced this suit, Norfolk Southern relocated its headquarters to Georgia. See Brief for Respondent 5.

Mr. Mallory saw things differently. He noted that Norfolk Southern manages over 2,000 miles of track, operates 11 rail yards, and runs 3 locomotive repair shops in Pennsylvania. He also pointed out that Norfolk Southern has registered to do business in Pennsylvania in light of its "'regular, systematic, [and] extensive'" operations there. 266 A. 3d 542, 562 (Pa. 2021); see 15 Pa. Cons. Stat. § 411(a) (2014). That is significant, Mr. Mallory argued, because Pennsylvania requires out-of-state companies that register to do business in the Commonwealth to agree to appear in its courts on "any cause of action" against them. 42 Pa. Cons. Stat. § 5301(a) (2)(i), (b) (2019); see 266 A. 3d, at 564. By complying with this statutory scheme, Mr. Mallory contended, Norfolk Southern had consented to suit in Pennsylvania on claims just like his.

Ultimately, the Pennsylvania Supreme Court sided with Norfolk Southern. Yes, Mr. Mallory correctly read Pennsylvania law. It requires an out-of-state firm to answer any suits against it in exchange for status as a registered foreign corporation and the benefits that entails. *Id.*, at 561–563. But, no, the court held, Mr. Mallory could not invoke that law because it violates the Due Process Clause. *Id.*, at 564–568. In reaching this conclusion, the Pennsylvania Supreme Court acknowledged its disagreement with the Georgia Supreme Court, which had recently rejected a similar due process argument from a corporate defendant. *Id.*, at 560, n. 13 (citing *Cooper Tire & Rubber Co.* v. *McCall*, 312 Ga. 422, 863 S. E. 2d 81 (2021)).

In light of this split of authority, we agreed to hear this case and decide whether the Due Process Clause of the Fourteenth Amendment prohibits a State from requiring an out-of-state corporation to consent to personal jurisdiction to do business there. 596 U. S. ––– (2022).[3] **[—128—]**

II.

The question before us is not a new one. In truth, it is a very old question—and one this Court resolved in *Pennsylvania Fire Ins. Co. of Philadelphia* v. *Gold Issue Mining & Milling Co.*, 243 U. S. 93 (1917). There, the Court unanimously held that laws like Pennsylvania's comport with the Due Process Clause. Some background helps explain why the Court reached the result it did.

Both at the time of the founding and the Fourteenth Amendment's adoption, the Anglo-American legal tradition recognized that a tribunal's competence was generally constrained only by the "territorial limits" of the sovereign that created it. J. Story, **{-2034-}** Commentaries on the Conflict of Laws § 539, pp. 450–451 (1834) (Story); see also *United States* v. *Union Pacific R. Co.*, 98 U. S. 569, 602–603 (1879). That principle applied to all kinds of actions, but cashed out differently based on the object of the court's attention. So, for example, an action *in rem* that claimed an interest in immovable property was usually treated as a "*local*" action that could be brought only in the jurisdiction where the property was located. 3 W. Blackstone, Commentaries on the Laws of England 117–118, 294 (1768). Meanwhile, an *in personam* suit against an individual "for injuries that might have happened any where" was generally considered a "*transitory*" action that followed the individual. *Id.*, at 294. All of which meant that a suit could be maintained by anyone on any claim in any place the defendant could be found. Story § 538, at 450.

American courts routinely followed these rules. Chief Justice Marshall, for one, was careful to distinguish between local and transitory actions in a case brought by a Virginia plaintiff against a Kentucky defendant based on a fraud perpetrated in Ohio. *Massie* v. *Watts*, 6 Cranch 148, 162–163 **[—129—]** (1810). Because the action was a transitory one that followed the individual, he

[3] The Pennsylvania Supreme Court did not address Norfolk Southern's alternative argument that Pennsylvania's statutory scheme as applied here violates this Court's dormant Commerce Clause doctrine. See 266 **[—128—]** A. 3d, at 559–560, nn. 9, 11. Nor did we grant review to consider that question. Accordingly, any argument along those lines remains for consideration on remand.

held, the suit could be maintained "wherever the [defendant] may be found." *Id.*, at 158, 161–163; see also, *e. g.*, *Livingston* v. *Jefferson*, 15 F. Cas. 660, 663–664 (No. 8,411) (CC Va. 1811) (opinion of Marshall, C. J.); *Peabody* v. *Hamilton*, 106 Mass. 217, 220–221 (1870); *Bissell* v. *Briggs*, 9 Mass. 462, 468–470 (1813).

This rule governing transitory actions still applies to natural persons today. Some call it "tag" jurisdiction. And our leading case applying the rule is not so old. See *Burnham* v. *Superior Court of Cal., County of Marin*, 495 U. S. 604 (1990). The case began with Dennis Burnham's business trip to California. *Id.*, at 608 (plurality opinion). During his short visit, Mr. Burnham's estranged wife served him with a summons to appear in California state court for divorce proceedings. *Ibid.* This Court unanimously approved the state court's exercise of personal jurisdiction over Mr. Burnham as consistent with the Due Process Clause—and did so even though the Burnhams had spent nearly all their married life in New Jersey and Mr. Burnham still resided there. See *id.*, at 607–608, 616–619; *id.*, at 628 (White, J., concurring in part and concurring in judgment); *id.*, at 635–639 (Brennan, J., concurring in judgment); *id.*, at 640 (Stevens, J., concurring in judgment).

As the use of the corporate form proliferated in the 19th century, the question arose how to adapt the traditional rule about transitory actions for individuals to artificial persons created by law. Unsurprisingly, corporations did not relish the prospect of being haled into court for any claim anywhere they conducted business. "No one, after all, has ever liked greeting the process server." *Ford Motor Co.* v. *Montana Eighth Judicial Dist. Court*, 592 U. S. —, — (2021) (Gorsuch, J., concurring in judgment). Corporations chartered in one State sought the right to send their sales agents and products freely into other States. At the same time, when confronted with lawsuits in those other States, some firms sought to hide behind their foreign character **[—130—]** and deny their presence to defeat the court's jurisdiction. *Ibid.*; see Brief for Petitioner 13–15; see also R. Jackson, What Price "Due Process"?, 5 N. Y. L. Rev. 435, 438 (1927) (describing this as the asserted right to "both be and not be"). **{-2035-}**

Lawmakers across the country soon responded to these stratagems. Relevant here, both before and after the Fourteenth Amendment's ratification, they adopted statutes requiring out-of-state corporations to consent to in-state suits in exchange for the rights to exploit the local market and to receive the full range of benefits enjoyed by in-state corporations. These statutes varied. In some States, out-of-state corporate defendants were required to agree to answer suits brought by in-state plaintiffs. See, *e. g.*, N. Y. Code Proc. § 427 (1849); 1866 Wis. Laws ch. 1, § 86.1; Md. Ann. Code, Art. 26, § 211 (1868); N. C. Gen. Stat., ch. 17, § 82 (1873). In other States, corporations were required to consent to suit if the plaintiff's cause of action arose within the State, even if the plaintiff happened to reside elsewhere. See, *e. g.*, Iowa Code, ch. 101, § 1705 (1851); 1874 Tex. Gen. Laws p. 107; 1881 Mich. Pub. Acts p. 348. Still other States (and the federal government) omitted both of these limitations. They required all out-of-state corporations that registered to do business in the forum to agree to defend themselves there against any manner of suit. See, *e. g.*, Act of Feb. 22, 1867, 14 Stat. 404; 1889 Nev. Stats. p. 47; S. C. Rev. Stat., Tit. 7, ch. 45, § 1466 (1894); Conn. Gen. Stat. § 3931 (1895). Yet another group of States applied this all-purpose-jurisdiction rule to a subset of corporate defendants, like railroads and insurance companies. See, *e. g.*, 1827 Va. Acts ch. 74, p. 77; 1841 Pa. Laws p. 29; 1854 Ohio Laws p. 91; Ill. Comp. Stat., ch. 112, § 68 (1855); Ark. Stat., ch. 76, § 3561 (1873); Mo. Rev. Stat., ch. 119, Art. 4, § 6013 (1879). Mr. Mallory has collected an array of these statutes, enacted between 1835 and 1915, in **[—131—]** his statutory appendix. See App. to Brief for Petitioner 1a–274a.[4]

[4] Norfolk Southern and the dissent observe that *some* state courts applied these laws narrowly. Brief for Respondent 43–44; *post*, at 173–175, and n. 4 (Barrett, J., dissenting). But, as we will see in a moment, *others* did not. Part III, *infra*. Even state courts that adopted narrowing constructions of their laws did so by invoking statutory interpretation principles and discretionary doctrines. Notably, neither Norfolk Southern nor the dissent has identified a *single* case (or any other source) from

III

A

Unsurprisingly, some corporations challenged statutes like these on various grounds, due process included. And, ultimately, one of these disputes reached this Court in *Pennsylvania Fire*.

That case arose this way. Pennsylvania Fire was an insurance company incorporated under the laws of Pennsylvania. In 1909, the company executed a contract in Colorado to insure a smelter located near the town of Cripple Creek owned by the Gold Issue Mining & Milling Company, an Arizona corporation. **{-2036-}** *Gold Issue Min. & Milling Co.* v. *Penn-* **[—132—]** *sylvania Fire Ins. Co. of Phila.*, 267 Mo. 524, 537, 184 S. W. 999, 1001 (1916). Less than a year later, lightning struck and a fire destroyed the insured facility. *Ibid.* When Gold Issue Mining sought to collect on its policy, Pennsylvania Fire refused to pay. So, Gold Issue Mining sued. But it did not sue where the contract was formed (Colorado), or in its home State (Arizona), or even in the insurer's home State (Pennsylvania). Instead, Gold Issue Mining brought its claim in a Missouri state court. *Id.*, at 534, 184 S. W., at 1000. Pennsylvania Fire objected to this choice of forum. It said the Due Process Clause spared it from having to answer in Missouri's courts a suit with no connection to the State. *Id.*, at 541, 184 S. W., at 1002.

The Missouri Supreme Court disagreed. It first observed that Missouri law required any out-of-state insurance company "desiring to transact any business" in the State to file paperwork agreeing to (1) appoint a state official to serve as the company's agent for service of process, and (2) accept service on that official as valid in any suit. *Id.*, at 543, 184 S. W., at 1003 (internal quotation marks omitted). For more than a decade, Pennsylvania Fire had complied with the law, as it had "desir[ed] to transact business" in Missouri "pursuant to the laws thereof." *Id.*, at 545, 184 S. W., at 1003. And Gold Issue Mining had served process on the appropriate state official, just as the law required. See *id.*, at 535, 184 S. W., at 1000.

As to the law's constitutionality, the Missouri Supreme Court carefully reviewed this Court's precedents and found they "clearly" supported "sustain[ing] the proceeding." *Id.*, at 569, 576, 184 S. W., at 1010, 1013; see *id.*, at 552–576, 601, 184 S. W., at 1005–1013, 1020–1021. The Missouri Supreme Court explained that its decision was also supported by "the origin, growth, and history of transitory actions in England, and their importation, adoption, and expansion" in America. *Id.*, at 578–586, 184 S. W., at 1013–1016. It stressed, too, **[—133—]** that the law had long permitted suits against individuals in any jurisdiction where they could be found, no matter where the underlying cause of action happened to arise. What sense would it make to treat a fictitious corporate person differently? See *id.*, at 588–592, 600, 184 S. W., at 1016– 1018, 1020. For all these reasons, the court concluded, Pennsylvania Fire "ha[d] due process of law, regardless of the place, state or nation where the cause of action arose." *Id.*, at 576, 184 S. W., at 1013.

Dissatisfied with this answer, Pennsylvania Fire turned here. Writing for a unanimous Court, Justice Holmes had little trouble dispatching the company's due process

---

this period holding that all-purpose jurisdiction premised on a consent statute violates the Due Process Clause. Indeed, some of the decisions they cite presumed just the opposite. See, *e. g., Camden Rolling Mill Co.* v. *Swede Iron Co.*, 32 N. J. L. 15, 17–18 (1866) (a law like Pennsylvania's "could be judicially adopted" consistent with due process if clearly expressed); *Sawyer* v. *North Am. Life Ins. Co.*, 46 Vt. 697, 706–707 (1874) (similar). Nothing in this body of case law, then, comes close to satisfying Norfolk Southern's burden of establishing that consent statutes like Pennsylvania's "'offen[d] some principle of justice so rooted in the traditions and conscience of our people as to be ranked'" among those secured by the Due Process Clause. *Medina* v. *California*, 505 U. S. 437, 445–448 (1992). In saying this much, we hardly suggest, as the dissent supposes, that the practice of States or their courts is irrelevant. *Post*, at 173, n. 3. Our point is simply that Norfolk Southern has not met *its burden* of showing that original and historic understandings of due process foreclose consent statutes.

argument. Under this Court's precedents, there was "no doubt" Pennsylvania Fire could be sued in Missouri by an out-of-state plaintiff on an out-of-state contract because it had agreed to accept service of process in Missouri on any suit as a condition of doing business there. *Pennsylvania Fire*, 243 U. S., at 95. Indeed, the Court thought the matter so settled by existing law that the case "hardly" presented an "open" question. *Ibid.* The Court acknowledged that the outcome might have been different if the corporation had never appointed an agent for service of process in Missouri, given this Court's earlier decision in *Old Wayne Mut. Life Assn. of Indianapolis* v. *McDonough*, 204 U. S. 8 (1907). But the Court thought that *Old Wayne* had "left untouched" the principle that due process allows a corporation to be sued on any claim in a State where it has appointed an agent to receive whatever suits may come. 243 U. S., at 95–96. The Court found it unnecessary to say more because the company's objections had been resolved **{–2037–}** "at length in the judgment of the court below." *Id.*, at 95.

That assessment was understandable. Not only had the Missouri Supreme Court issued a thoughtful opinion. Not only did a similar rule apply to transitory actions against individuals. Other leading judges, including Learned Hand **[—134—]** and Benjamin Cardozo, had reached similar conclusions in similar cases in the years leading up to *Pennsylvania Fire*. See *Smolik* v. *Philadelphia & Reading Coal & Iron Co.*, 222 F. 148, 150–151 (SDNY 1915) (Hand, J.); *Bagdon* v. *Philadelphia & Reading Coal & Iron Co.*, 217 N. Y. 432, 436–437, 111 N. E. 1075, 1076–1077 (1916) (Cardozo, J.). In the years following *Pennsylvania Fire*, too, this Court reaffirmed its holding as often as the issue arose. See, *e. g.*, *Louisville & Nashville R. Co.* v. *Chatters*, 279 U. S. 320, 325–326 (1929); *Neirbo Co.* v. *Bethlehem Shipbuilding Corp.*, 308 U. S. 165, 175 (1939); see also *Robert Mitchell Furniture Co.* v. *Selden Breck Constr. Co.*, 257 U. S. 213, 215–216 (1921); *Wuchter* v. *Pizzutti*, 276 U. S. 13, 20 (1928).

B

Pennsylvania Fire controls this case. Much like the Missouri law at issue there, the Pennsylvania law at issue here provides that an out-of-state corporation "may not do business in this Commonwealth until it registers with" the Department of State. 15 Pa. Cons. Stat. § 411(a). As part of the registration process, a corporation must identify an "office" it will "continuously maintain" in the Commonwealth. § 411(f); see also § 412(a)(5). Upon completing these requirements, the corporation "shall enjoy the same rights and privileges as a domestic entity and shall be subject to the same liabilities, restrictions, duties and penalties . . . imposed on domestic entities." § 402(d). Among other things, Pennsylvania law is explicit that "qualification as a foreign corporation" shall permit state courts to "exercise general personal jurisdiction" over a registered foreign corporation, just as they can over domestic corporations. 42 Pa. Cons. Stat. § 5301(a)(2)(i).

Norfolk Southern has complied with this law for many years. In 1998, the company registered to do business in Pennsylvania. Acting through its Corporate Secretary as a **[—135—]** "duly authorized officer," the company completed an "Application for Certificate of Authority" from the Commonwealth "[i]n compliance with" state law. App. 1–2. As part of that process, the company named a "Commercial Registered Office Provider" in Philadelphia County, agreeing that this was where it "shall be deemed . . . located." *Ibid.* The Secretary of the Commonwealth approved the application, conferring on Norfolk Southern both the benefits and burdens shared by domestic corporations—including amenability to suit in state court on any claim. *Id.*, at 1. Since 1998, Norfolk Southern has regularly updated its information on file with the Secretary. In 2009, for example, the company advised that it had changed its Registered Office Provider and would now be deemed located in Dauphin County. *Id.*, at 6; see 15 Pa. Cons. Stat. § 4144(b) (1988). All told, then, Norfolk Southern has agreed to be found in Pennsylvania and answer any suit there for more than 20 years.

Pennsylvania Fire held that suits premised on these grounds do not deny a defendant due process of law. Even Norfolk Southern does not seriously dispute that much. It concedes that it registered to do business in Pennsylvania, that it established an office there to receive service of process, and that in doing so it understood it would be amenable to suit on any claim. **{-2038-}** Tr. of Oral Arg. 62; *post*, at 150–151 (Alito, J., concurring in part and concurring in judgment); *post*, at 148 (Jackson, J., concurring). Of course, Mr. Mallory no longer lives in Pennsylvania and his cause of action did not accrue there. But none of that makes any more difference than the fact that Gold Issue Mining was not from Missouri (but from Arizona) and its claim did not arise there (but in Colorado). See *Pennsylvania Fire*, 267 Mo., at 537, 184 S. W., at 1001. To decide this case, we need not speculate whether any other statutory scheme and set of facts would suffice to establish consent to suit. It is enough to **[—136—]** acknowledge that the state law and facts before us fall squarely within *Pennsylvania Fire*'s rule. See *post*, at 150–153 (opinion of Alito, J.).

In the proceedings below, the Pennsylvania Supreme Court seemed to recognize that *Pennsylvania Fire* dictated an answer in Mr. Mallory's favor. Still, it ruled for Norfolk Southern anyway. It did so because, in its view, intervening decisions from this Court had "implicitly overruled" *Pennsylvania Fire*. See 266 A. 3d, at 559, 567. But in following that course, the Pennsylvania Supreme Court clearly erred. As this Court has explained: "If a precedent of this Court has direct application in a case," as *Pennsylvania Fire* does here, a lower court "should follow the case which directly controls, leaving to this Court the prerogative of overruling its own decisions." *Rodriguez de Quijas* v. *Shearson/American Express, Inc.*, 490 U. S. 477, 484 (1989). This is true even if the lower court thinks the precedent is in tension with "some other line of decisions." *Ibid.*[5]

IV

Now before us, Norfolk Southern candidly asks us to do what the Pennsylvania Supreme Court could not—overrule **[—137—]** *Pennsylvania Fire*. Brief for Respondent 36–38. To smooth the way, Norfolk Southern suggests that this Court's decision in *International Shoe Co.* v. *Washington*, 326 U. S. 310 (1945), has already done much of the hard work for us. That decision, the company insists, seriously undermined *Pennsylvania Fire*'s foundations. Brief for Respondent 34–36. We disagree. The two precedents sit comfortably side by side. See *post*, at 152–153 (opinion of Alito, J.).

A

Start with how Norfolk Southern sees things. On the company's telling, echoed by the dissent, *International Shoe* held that the Due Process Clause tolerates two (and only two) types of personal jurisdiction over a corporate defendant. First, "specific jurisdiction" permits suits that "'arise out of or relate to'" a corporate defendant's activities in the forum State. *Ford Motor Co.*, 592 U. S., at ____ – ____. Second, "general **{-2039-}** jurisdiction" allows all kinds of suits against a corporation, but only in States where the corporation is incorporated or has its "principal place of business." *Id.*, at ___. After *International Shoe*, Norfolk Southern insists, no other bases for personal jurisdiction over a corporate defendant are permissible. Brief for Respondent 13–15; see *post*, at 164–166 (Barrett, J., dissenting).

But if this account might seem a plausible summary of some of our *International Shoe* jurisprudence, it oversimplifies matters. Here

---

[5] The dissent stresses that Pennsylvania's statute does not use the word "consent" in describing the jurisdictional consequences of registration. When the dissent finally comes around to addressing *Pennsylvania Fire* at the end of its opinion, it fleetingly seeks to distinguish the decision along the same lines—stressing that words like "agent" and "jurisdiction" do not appear "in Norfolk Southern's registration paperwork." *Post*, at 167, 179, and n. 8. But, as the dissent itself elsewhere acknowledges, "'[a] variety of legal arrangements have been taken to represent express or implied consent to'" personal jurisdiction consistent with due process. *Post*, at 167. And neither *Pennsylvania Fire*, nor our later decisions applying it, nor our precedents approving other forms of consent to personal jurisdiction have ever imposed some sort of "magic words" requirement. See *infra*, at 145–146; *Pennsylvania Fire*, 243 U. S., at 95; *Neirbo Co.*, 308 U. S., at 175.

is what really happened in *International Shoe.* The State of Washington sued a corporate defendant in state court for claims based on its in-state activities even though the defendant had *not* registered to do business in Washington and had *not* agreed to be present and accept service of process there. 326 U. S., at 312–313. Despite this, the Court held that the suit against the company comported with due process. In doing so, the Court reasoned that the Fourteenth Amendment "permit[s]" suits **[—138—]** against a corporate defendant that has not agreed to be "presen[t] within the territorial jurisdiction of a court," so long as "the quality and nature of the [company's] activity" in the State "make it reasonable and just" to maintain suit-there. *Id.*, at 316, 319–320. Put simply, even without agreeing to be present, the out-of-state corporation was still amenable to suit in Washington consistent with "'fair play and substantial justice'"—terms the Court borrowed from Justice Holmes, the author of *Pennsylvania Fire. International Shoe,* 326 U. S., at 316 (citing *McDonald* v. *Mabee,* 243 U. S. 90, 91–92 (1917)).

In reality, then, all *International Shoe* did was stake out an *additional* road to jurisdiction over out-of-state corporations. *Pennsylvania Fire* held that an out-of-state corporation that *has* consented to in-state suits in order to do business in the forum is susceptible to suit there. *International Shoe* held that an out-of-state corporation that *has not* consented to in-state suits may also be susceptible to claims in the forum State based on "the quality and nature of [its] activity" in the forum. 326 U. S., at 319. Consistent with all this, our precedents applying *International Shoe* have long spoken of the decision as asking whether a state court may exercise jurisdiction over a corporate defendant "'that *has not consented* to suit in the forum.'" *Goodyear Dunlop Tires Operations, S. A.* v. *Brown,* 564 U. S. 915, 927–928 (2011) (emphasis added); see also *Daimler AG* v. *Bauman,* 571 U. S. 117, 129 (2014). Our precedents have recognized, too, that "express or implied consent" can continue to ground personal jurisdiction—and consent may be manifested in various ways by word or deed. See, *e. g., Insurance Corp. of Ireland* v. *Compagnie des Bauxites de Guinee,* 456 U. S. 694, 703 (1982); *BNSF R. Co.* v. *Tyrrell,* 581 U. S. 402, 415, 5 Adm. R. 2, 7 (2017). See also *post,* at 152–153 (opinion of Alito, J.).[6] **[—139—]**

That Norfolk Southern overreads *International Shoe* finds confirmation in that decision's emphasis on "'fair play and substantial justice.'" 326 U. S., at 316. Sometimes, *International Shoe* said, the nature of a company's in-state activities will support jurisdiction over a nonconsenting **{-2040-}** corporation when those activities "give rise to the liabilities sued on." *Id.*, at 317. Other times, it added, suits "on causes of action arising from dealings entirely distinct from [the company's] activities" in the forum State may be appropriate. *Id.*, at 318. These passages may have pointed the way to what (much) later cases would label "specific jurisdiction" over claims related to in-forum activities and "general jurisdiction" in places where a corporation is incorporated or headquartered. See, *e. g., Helicopteros Nacionales de Colombia, S. A.* v. *Hall,* 466 U. S. 408, 414–415, and nn. 8–9 (1984). But the fact remains that *International Shoe* itself eschewed any "mechanical or quantitative" test and instead endorsed a flexible approach focused on "the fair and orderly administration of the laws which it was the purpose of the due process clause to insure." 326 U. S., at 319. Unquestionably, too, *International Shoe* saw this flexible standard as expanding—not contracting—state court jurisdiction. See *Daimler,* 571 U. S., at 128, and n. 6. As we later put the point: "The immediate effect of [*International Shoe*] was to increase the ability of the state courts to obtain personal jurisdiction over nonresident defendants." *Shaffer* v. *Heitner,* 433 U. S. 186, 204 (1977).

Given all this, it is no wonder that we have already turned aside arguments very much like Norfolk Southern's. In *Burnham,* the

6 Because *International Shoe* allowed a suit against a corporation that had *not* registered to do business in the forum State, if it disturbed anything it was only this Court's decision in *Old Wayne,* not *Pennsylvania* **[—139—]** *Fire.* See *supra,* at 133; *Perkins* v. *Benguet Consol. Mining Co.,* 342 U. S. 437, 443–444 (1952).

defendant contended that *International Shoe* implicitly overruled the traditional tag rule holding that individuals physically served in a State are subject to suit there for claims of any kind. 495 U. S., at 616 (plurality opinion). **[—140—]** This Court rejected that submission. Instead, as Justice Scalia explained, *International Shoe* simply provided a "novel" way to secure personal jurisdiction that did nothing to displace other "traditional ones." *Id.*, at 619. What held true there must hold true here. Indeed, seven years *after* deciding *International Shoe*, the Court cited *Pennsylvania Fire* approvingly. *Perkins* v. *Benguet Consol. Mining Co.*, 342 U. S. 437, 446, n. 6 (1952).[7]

B

Norfolk Southern offers several replies, but none persuades. The company begins by pointing to this Court's decision in *Shaffer*. There, as the company stresses, the Court indicated that "`prior decisions . . . inconsistent with'" *International Shoe* "`are overruled.'" Brief for Respondent 35 (quoting *Shaffer*, 433 U. S., at 212, n. 39); *post*, at 177–178 (opinion of Barrett, J.). True as that statement may be, however, it only poses the question whether *Pennsylvania Fire* is "inconsistent **{-2041-}** with" *International Shoe*. And, as we have seen, it is not. Instead, the latter decision expanded upon the traditional grounds of personal jurisdiction recog- **[—141—]** nized by the former. This Court has previously cautioned litigants and lower courts against (mis)reading *Shaffer* as suggesting that *International Shoe* discarded every traditional method for securing personal jurisdiction that came before. See *Burnham*, 495 U. S., at 620–622 (plurality opinion); cf. *Daimler*, 571 U. S., at 126, 132–133. We find ourselves repeating the admonition today.[8]

Next, Norfolk Southern appeals to the spirit of our age. After *International Shoe*, it says, the "primary concern" of the personal jurisdiction analysis is "[t]reating defendants fairly." Brief for Respondent 19 (internal quotation marks omitted). And on the company's telling, it would be "unfair" to allow Mr. Mallory's suit to proceed in Pennsylvania because doing so would risk unleashing "`local prejudice'" against a company that is "not `local' in the eyes of the community." *Id.*, at 19–21.

But if fairness is what Norfolk Southern seeks, pause for a moment to measure this suit against that standard. When Mr. Mallory brought his claim in 2017, Norfolk Southern had registered to do business in Pennsylvania for many years. It had established an office for receiving service of process. It had done so pursuant to a statute that gave the company the right to do business in-state in return for agreeing to answer any suit against it. And the company had taken full advantage of its opportunity to do business in the Commonwealth, boasting of its presence this way: **[—142—] {-2042-}**

---

[7] Norfolk Southern and the dissent observe that, today, few States continue to employ consent statutes like Pennsylvania's. Brief for Respondent 22; *post*, at 172–173, 177, n. 6. Surely, too, some States may see strong policy reasons for proceeding differently than Pennsylvania has. See, *e. g.*, *State ex rel. Am. Central Life Ins. Co.* v. *Landwehr*, 300 S. W. 294, 297 (1927) (abandoning construction of Missouri law at issue in *Pennsylvania Fire* based on "the legislative policy in th[e] state"); cf. *Cooper Tire*, 312 Ga., at 437, 863 S. E. 2d, at 92 (Bethel, J., concurring) (suggesting Georgia's consent scheme "creates a disincentive for foreign corporations to" do business in-state and conflicts with the State's claim to be " `business-friendly' "). But the meaning of the Due Process Clause is not measured by the latest popularity poll, nor does it come with some desuetude rule against a traditional practice like consent-based jurisdiction long held consistent with its demands. See *Ownbey* v. *Morgan*, 256 U. S. 94, 110–111 (1921).

[8] Taking up the *Shaffer* baton from the company, the dissent insists that *International Shoe* "`cast . . . aside'" consent statutes in favor of a minimum contacts analysis. *Post*, at 175–176. But, as we have seen, nothing in *International Shoe* purported to address, let alone condemn, consent statutes. Even the dissent ultimately acknowledges, as it must, that "`a variety of legal arrangements'" can signal consent to jurisdiction after *International Shoe*, and these arrangements *can* include state laws requiring consent to suit in exchange "for access to [a State's] markets." *Post*, at 167, 168; see also *Neirbo Co.*, 308 U. S., at 175 (calling this form of consent "*real* consent" (emphasis added)).

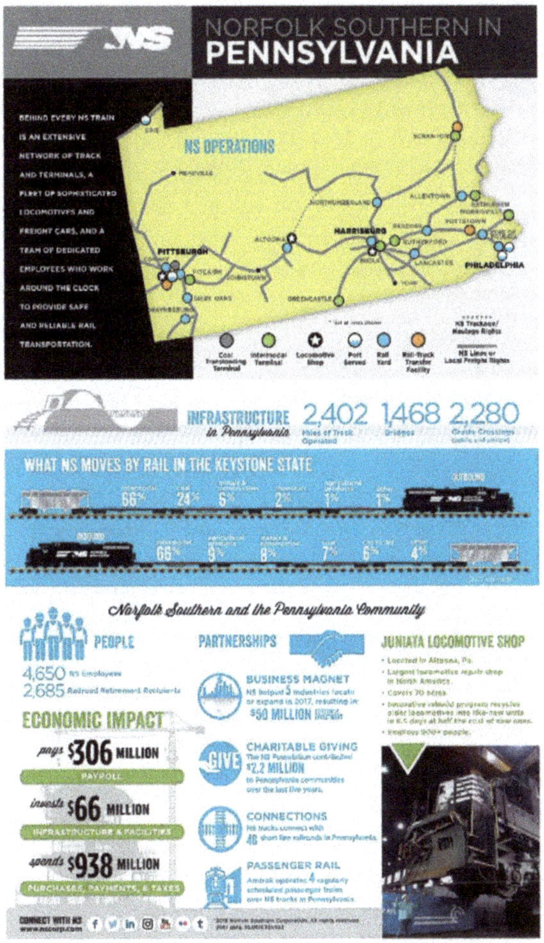

[—143—]

Norfolk Southern Corp., State Fact Sheets–Pennsylvania (2018), https://nscorp.com/content/dam/nscorp/get-to-knowns/about-ns/state-fact-sheets/pa-state-fact-sheet.pdf.

All told, when Mr. Mallory sued, Norfolk Southern employed nearly 5,000 people in Pennsylvania. It maintained more than 2,400 miles of track across the Commonwealth. Its 70-acre locomotive shop there **{–2043–}** was the largest in North America. Contrary to what it says in its brief here, the company even proclaimed itself a proud part of "the Pennsylvania Community." *Ibid.* By 2020, too, Norfolk Southern managed more miles of track in Pennsylvania than in any other State. Brief for Public Citizen as *Amicus Curiae* 21. And it employed more people in Pennsylvania than it did in Virginia, where its headquarters was located. *Ibid.* Nor are we conjuring these statistics out of thin air. The company *itself* highlighted its "intrastate activities" in the proceedings below. 266 A. 3d, at 560, 563 (discussing the firm's "extensive operations in Pennsylvania," including "2,278 miles of track," "eleven rail yards," and "three locomotive repair shops"). Given all this, on what plausible account could *International Shoe*'s concerns with "fair play and substantial justice" require a Pennsylvania court to turn aside Mr. Mallory's suit? See *post*, at 153–154 (opinion of Alito, J.).[9] **[—144—]**

Perhaps sensing its arguments from fairness meet a dead end, Norfolk Southern ultimately heads in another direction altogether. It suggests the Due Process Clause separately prohibits one State from infringing on the sovereignty of another State through exorbitant claims of personal jurisdiction. Brief for Respondent 16–19; see *post*, at 168–171 (opinion of Barrett, J.). And, in candor, the company is half right. Some of our personal jurisdiction cases have discussed the federalism implications of one State's assertion of jurisdiction over the corporate residents of another. See, *e. g.*, *Bristol-Myers Squibb Co.* v. *Superior Court of Cal., San Francisco Cty.*, 582 U. S. 255, 263 (2017). But that neglects an important part of the story. To date, our personal jurisdiction cases have never found a

[9] The dissent does not dispute the company's extensive in-state contacts but replies that counsel for Mr. Mallory abandoned any reliance on them at oral argument. *Post*, at 179–180, and n. 9. In support of its claim, however, the dissent shears from context two sentences counsel uttered in response to a question about "why [Mr. Mallory] sue[d] in Philadelphia." Tr. of Oral Arg. 48. In reply, counsel explained that Mr. Mallory "used to live . . . in Pennsylvania" and "his lawyers are from there." *Id.*, at 48–49. Counsel then agreed that "*[t]hose* contacts" would not establish jurisdiction and pointed this Court to Norfolk Southern's "consent" to suit in Pennsylvania. *Id.*, at 49 (emphasis added). All in all, it was a prosaic response to a simple question about why Mr. Mallory filed suit where he did. Nor, contrary to the dissent's suggestion, are we alone in discussing the company's in-state contacts; the lower court, the company, *and* the dissent all point to them too. See 266 A. 3d, at 547; Brief for Respondent 16–21; *post*, at 165–166.

Due Process Clause problem sounding in federalism when an out-of-state defendant submits to suit in the forum State. After all, personal jurisdiction is a *personal* defense that may be waived or forfeited. See *Insurance Corp. of Ireland*, 456 U. S., at 704–705; see also *post*, at 156 (opinion of Alito, J.); *post*, at 147–148 (opinion of Jackson, J.).

That leaves Norfolk Southern one final stand. It argues that it has not *really* submitted to proceedings in Pennsylvania. Brief for Respondent 11–13; see *post*, at 167–168, 170 (opinion of Barrett, J.). The company does not dispute that it has filed paperwork with Pennsylvania seeking the right to do business there. It does not dispute that it has established an office in the Commonwealth to receive service of process on any claim. It does not dispute that it appreciated the jurisdictional consequences attending these actions and proceeded anyway, presumably because it thought the benefits outweighed the costs. But, in the name of the Due Process Clause, Norfolk Southern insists **{-2044-}** we should dismiss all that as a raft of meaningless formalities.[10] **[—145—]**

Taken seriously, this argument would have us undo not just *Pennsylvania Fire* but a legion of precedents that attach jurisdictional consequences to what some might dismiss as mere formalities. Consider some examples we have already encountered. In a typical general jurisdiction case under *International Shoe*, a company is subject to suit on any claim in a forum State only because of its decision to file a piece of paper there (a certificate of incorporation). The firm is amenable to suit even if all of its operations are located elsewhere and even if its certificate only sits collecting dust on an office shelf for years thereafter. See, *e. g.*, *Goodyear*, 564 U. S., at 924. Then there is the tag rule. The invisible state line might seem a trivial thing. But when an individual takes one step off a plane after flying from New Jersey to California, the jurisdictional consequences are immediate and serious. See *Burnham*, 495 U. S., at 619 (plurality opinion).

Consider, too, just a few other examples. A defendant who appears "specially" to contest jurisdiction preserves his defense, but one who forgets can lose his. See *York* v. *Texas*, 137 U. S. 15, 19–21 (1890). Failing to comply with certain pre-trial court orders, signing a contract with a forum selection clause, accepting an in-state benefit with jurisdictional strings attached—all these actions as well can carry with them profound consequences for personal jurisdiction. See *Insurance Corp. of Ireland*, 456 U. S., at 703–706 (collecting cases); see also *post*, at 147–148 (opinion of Jackson, J.). **[—146—]**

The truth is, under our precedents a variety of "actions of the defendant" that may seem like technicalities nonetheless can "amount to a legal submission to the jurisdiction of a court." *Insurance Corp. of Ireland*, 456 U. S., at 704–705; see also Brief for Stephen E. Sachs as *Amicus Curiae* 10. That was so before *International Shoe*, and it remains so today. Should we overrule them all? Taking Norfolk Southern's argument seriously would require just that. But, tellingly, the company does not follow where its argument leads or even acknowledge its implications. Instead, Norfolk Southern asks us to pluck out and overrule just one longstanding precedent that it happens to dislike. We decline the invitation. *Post*, at 152–

[10] While the dissent joins Norfolk Southern in this argument, it wavers. At points, the dissent seems to insist that laws like Pennsylvania's "mak[e] no sense." *Post*, at 167–168. But the closest the dissent comes to identifying authority for the notion that laws like these are impermissible are **[—145—]** two cases that did not involve personal jurisdiction or purport to interpret the Due Process Clause. *Post*, at 170 (citing *Home Ins. Co.* v. *Morse*, 20 Wall. 445 (1874); *Barron* v. *Burnside*, 121 U. S. 186 (1887)). The dissent's observation that one of those cases in turn cited *Lafayette Ins. Co.* v. *French*, 18 How. 404 (1856), hardly helps—that decision *approved* a consent-to-suit regime for out-of-state corporations under the Full Faith and Credit Clause. *Id.*, at 405–407. At other points, however, and as we have seen, the dissent rightly acknowledges that a "'variety of legal arrangements [may] represent express or implied consent'" to personal jurisdiction consistent with due process, and these arrangements can include requiring at least some companies to consent to suit in exchange "for access to [a State's] markets." *Post*, at 167, 168.

153 (opinion of Alito, J.). There is no fair play or substantial justice in that.[11] **{–2045–}**

* * *

Not every case poses a new question. This case poses a very old question indeed—one this Court resolved more than a century ago in *Pennsylvania Fire*. Because that decision remains the law, the judgment of the Supreme Court of Pennsylvania is vacated, and the case is remanded.

It is so ordered. **[—147—]**

(Reporter's Note: Concurring opinion follows on p. 18).

---

[11] While various separate writings accompany this opinion, it should be apparent a majority of the Court today agrees that: Norfolk Southern consented to suit in Pennsylvania. *Supra*, at 134–136; *post*, at 151 (opinion of Alito, J.). *Pennsylvania Fire* therefore controls this case. *Supra*, at 135–136; *post*, at 151–152 (opinion of Alito, J.). *Pennsylvania Fire*'s rule for consent-based jurisdiction has not been overruled. *Supra*, at 136–138; *post*, at 152–153 (opinion of Alito, J.). *International Shoe* governs where a defendant has not consented to exercise of jurisdiction. *Supra*, at 138; *post*, at 152–153 (opinion of Alito, J.). Exercising jurisdiction here is hardly unfair. *Supra*, at 141–143; *post*, at 153–154 (opinion of Alito, J.). The federalism concerns in our due process cases have applied only when a defendant has not consented. *Supra*, at 144; *post*, at 156 (opinion of Alito, J.). Nor will this Court now overrule *Pennsylvania Fire*. *Supra*, at 144–146; *post*, at 152 (opinion of Alito, J.).

[—147—] **{-2045-}** JUSTICE JACKSON, concurring:

I agree with the Court that this case is straightforward under our precedents. I write separately to say that, for me, what makes it so is not just our ruling in *Pennsylvania Fire Ins. Co. of Philadelphia* v. *Gold Issue Mining & Milling Co.*, 243 U. S. 93 (1917). I also consider our ruling in *Insurance Corp. of Ireland* v. *Compagnie des Bauxites de Guinee*, 456 U. S. 694 (1982), to be particularly instructive.

In *Insurance Corp. of Ireland*, this Court confirmed a simple truth: The due process "requirement of personal jurisdiction" is an individual, waivable right. *Id.*, at 703. The requirement exists, we said, to ensure that the forum State has sufficient contacts with a defendant, such that "'the maintenance of the suit [does] not offend "traditional notions of fair play and substantial justice."'" *Ibid.* (quoting *International Shoe Co.* v. *Washington*, 326 U. S. 310, 319 (1945)). We noted further that the interstate federalism concerns informing that right are "ultimately a function of the individual liberty interest" that this due process right preserves. 456 U. S., at 703, n. 10. Because the personal-jurisdiction right belongs to the defendant, however, we explained that a defendant can choose to "subject [itself] to powers from which [it] may otherwise be protected." *Ibid.* When that happens, a State can exercise jurisdiction over the defendant consistent with the Due Process Clause, even if our personal-jurisdiction cases would normally preclude the State from subjecting a defendant to its authority under the circumstances presented. *Ibid.*

Waiver is thus a critical feature of the personal-jurisdiction analysis. And there is more than one way to waive personal-jurisdiction rights, as *Insurance Corp. of Ireland* also clarified. A defendant can waive its rights by explicitly or implicitly consenting to litigate future disputes in a particular State's courts. *Id.*, at 703–704. A defendant might also fail to follow specific procedural rules, and end up waiving the right to object to personal jurisdiction as a **[—148—]** consequence. *Id.*, at 705–706. Or a defendant can voluntarily invoke certain benefits from a State that are conditioned on submitting to the State's jurisdiction. *Id.*, at 704 (citing *Adam* v. *Saenger*, 303 U. S. 59, 67–68 (1938)).

Regardless of whether a defendant relinquishes its personal-jurisdiction rights expressly or constructively, the basic teaching of *Insurance Corp. of Ireland* is **{-2046-}** the same: When a defendant chooses to engage in behavior that "amount[s] to a legal submission to the jurisdiction of the court," the Due Process Clause poses no barrier to the court's exercise of personal jurisdiction. 456 U. S., at 704–705.

In my view, there is no question that Norfolk Southern waived its personal-jurisdiction rights here. As the Court ably explains, Norfolk Southern agreed to register as a foreign corporation in Pennsylvania in exchange for the ability to conduct business within the Commonwealth and receive associated benefits. *Ante*, at 134–135; see also *post*, at 151 (Alito, J., concurring in part and concurring in judgment). Moreover, when Norfolk Southern made that decision, the jurisdictional consequences of registration were clear. See 42 Pa. Cons. Stat. § 5301(a)(2)(i) (1981) (expressly linking "qualification as a foreign corporation under the laws of th[e] Commonwealth" to the "exercise [of] general personal jurisdiction"); 266 A. 3d 542, 569 (Pa. 2021) (acknowledging that "foreign corporations are given reasonable notice" of the jurisdictional implications of registration).

Nor was Norfolk Southern compelled to register and submit itself to the general jurisdiction of Pennsylvania courts simply because its trains passed through the Commonwealth. See, *e. g.*, 15 Pa. Cons. Stat. § 403(a)(11) (2014); 1972 Pa. Laws pp. 1154–1155. Registration is required when corporations seek to conduct *local* business in a "regular, systematic, or extensive" way. 266 A. 3d, at 562–563 (internal quotation marks omitted). Norfolk Southern apparently deemed registration worthwhile and opted in. **[—149—]**

Under *Insurance Corp. of Ireland*, the due process question that this case presents is easily answered. Having made the choice to register and do business in Pennsylvania despite the jurisdictional consequences (and having thereby voluntarily relinquished the due process rights our general-jurisdiction precedents afford), Norfolk Southern cannot be heard to complain that its due process rights are violated by having to defend itself in Pennsylvania's courts. Whether Pennsylvania could have asserted general jurisdiction over Norfolk Southern *absent* any waiver, see *post*, at 165–166 (Barrett, J., dissenting), is beside the point.

In other areas of the law, we permit States to ask defendants to waive individual rights and safeguards. See, *e. g.*, *Brady* v. *United States*, 397 U. S. 742, 748 (1970) (allowing plea bargains to waive a defendant's trial rights and the right against self-incrimination); *Barker* v. *Wingo*, 407 U. S. 514, 529, 536 (1972) (waiver of speedy trial rights). Moreover, when defendants do so, we respect that waiver decision and hold them to that choice, even though the government could not have otherwise bypassed the rules and procedures those rights protect. Insisting that our general-jurisdiction precedents preclude Pennsylvania from subjecting corporations to suit within its borders—despite their waiver of the protections those precedents entail—puts the personal-jurisdiction requirement on a pedestal. But there is nothing "unique about the requirement of personal jurisdiction [that] prevents it from being . . . waived like other [individual] rights." *Insurance Corp. of Ireland*, 456 U. S., at 706.

In short, *Insurance Corp. of Ireland* makes clear that the personal-jurisdiction requirement is an individual, waivable right, and I agree with the Court that Norfolk Southern waived that right by choosing to register as a foreign corporation under the circumstances presented in this case. Therefore, I perceive no due **{–2047–}** process problem with the registration statute at issue here. **[—150—]**

(Reporter's Note: Opinion concurring in part and concurring in the judgment follows on p. 20).

[—150—] {-2047-} JUSTICE ALITO, concurring in part and concurring in the judgment:

The sole question before us is whether the Due Process Clause of the Fourteenth Amendment is violated when a large out-of-state corporation with substantial operations in a State complies with a registration requirement that conditions the right to do business in that State on the registrant's submission to personal jurisdiction in any suits that are brought there. I agree with the Court that the answer to this question is no. *Assuming* that the Constitution allows a State to impose such a registration requirement, I see no reason to conclude that such suits violate the corporation's right to "`fair play and substantial justice.'" *International Shoe Co.* v. *Washington*, 326 U. S. 310, 316 (1945).

I am not convinced, however, that the Constitution permits a State to impose such a submission-to-jurisdiction requirement. A State's assertion of jurisdiction over lawsuits with no real connection to the State may violate fundamental principles that are protected by one or more constitutional provisions or by the very structure of the federal system that the Constitution created. At this point in the development of our constitutional case law, the most appropriate home for these principles is the so-called dormant Commerce Clause. Norfolk Southern appears to have asserted a Commerce Clause claim below, but the Pennsylvania Supreme Court did not address it. See 266 A. 3d 542, 559–560, nn. 9, 11 (2021). Presumably, Norfolk Southern can renew the challenge on remand. I therefore agree that we should vacate the Pennsylvania Supreme Court's judgment and remand the case for further proceedings.

I.

When Virginia resident Robert Mallory initiated this suit, Norfolk Southern Railway Company, a railroad that was at that time incorporated and headquartered in Virginia, had long operated rail lines and conducted related business in **[—151—]** Pennsylvania. Consistent with Pennsylvania law, the company had registered as a "foreign" corporation, most recently in 1998. 15 Pa. Cons. Stat. § 411(a) (2014); App. 1–2. Then, as now, Pennsylvania law expressly provided that "qualification as a foreign corporation" was a "sufficient basis" for Pennsylvania courts "to exercise general personal jurisdiction" over an out-of-state company. 42 Pa. Cons. Stat. § 5301(a)(2)(i) (2019). Norfolk Southern is a sophisticated entity, and we may "presum[e]" that it "acted with knowledge" of state law when it registered. *Commercial Mut. Accident Co.* v. *Davis*, 213 U. S. 245, 254 (1909). As a result, we may also presume that by registering, it consented to all valid conditions imposed by state law.

I do not understand Norfolk Southern to challenge this basic premise. Tr. of Oral Arg. 62 (acknowledging that "the railroad understood by fling [registration paperwork] that it was subject to [Pennsylvania's general jurisdiction] law"). Instead, Norfolk Southern argues that giving force to the company's consent would violate the Fourteenth Amendment's Due Process Clause. See *Power Mfg. Co.* v. *Saunders*, 274 U. S. 490, 496–497 (1927).

That argument is foreclosed by our precedent. We addressed this question more than a century ago in *Pennsylvania Fire Ins. Co. of Philadelphia* v. *Gold Issue Mining & Milling Co.*, 243 U. S. 93 (1917). There, an Arizona mining company sued a Pennsylvania **{-2048-}** insurance company in a Missouri court, alleging claims arising from events in Colorado. *Id.*, at 94. The Pennsylvania insurance company had "obtained a license to do business in Missouri," and so had complied with a Missouri statute requiring the company to execute a power of attorney consenting to service of process on the state insurance superintendent in exchange for licensure. *Ibid.* The Missouri Supreme Court had previously construed such powers of attorney as consent to jurisdiction in Missouri for all claims, including those arising from transactions outside the State. *Gold Issue Mining & Milling Co.* **[—152—]** v. *Pennsylvania Fire Ins. Co. of Philadelphia*, 267 Mo. 524, 549–550, 184 S. W. 999, 1003–1005 (1916) (citing *State ex rel. Pacific Mut. Life Ins. Co.* v. *Grimm*, 239 Mo. 135, 159–171, 143 S. W. 483, 490–494 (1911)). Because the insurance company had executed the power of attorney to obtain its license, the court held that Missouri had jurisdiction over the company in that suit. 267 Mo., at 610, 184 S. W., at 1024. We affirmed in a brief opinion, holding that the construction of Missouri's statute and its application to the Pennsylvania insurance company under the circumstances of the case did not violate due process. *Pennsylvania Fire*, 243 U. S., at 95.

The parallels between *Pennsylvania Fire* and the case before us are undeniable. In both, a large company incorporated in one State was actively engaged in business in another State. In connection with that business, both companies took steps that, under the express terms or previous authoritative construction of state law, were understood as consent to the State's jurisdiction in suits on all claims, no matter where the events underlying the suit took place. In both cases, an out-of-state plaintiff sued the out-of-state company, alleging claims unrelated to the company's forum-state conduct. And in both, the out-of-state company objected, arguing that holding it to the terms of its consent would violate the Fourteenth Amendment's Due Process Clause. In *Pennsylvania Fire*, we held that there was no due process violation in these circumstances. Given the near-complete overlap of material facts, that holding, unless it has been overruled, is binding here.

Norfolk Southern has not persuaded me that *Pennsylvania Fire* has been overruled. While we have infrequently invoked that decision's due process holding, we have never expressly overruled it. Nor can I conclude that it has been impliedly overruled. See *post*, at 177–178 (BARRETT, J., dissenting). Norfolk Southern cites the *International Shoe* line of cases, but those cases involve constitutional limits on jurisdiction over *non-consenting* corporations. See *Inter-* **[—153—]** *national Shoe*, 326 U. S., at 317; *Goodyear Dunlop Tires Operations, S. A.* v. *Brown*, 564 U. S. 915, 927–928 (2011); *Daimler AG* v. *Bauman*, 571 U. S. 117, 129 (2014); *BNSF R. Co.* v. *Tyrrell*, 581 U. S. 402, 415, 5 Adm. R. 2, 7 (2017) (declining to consider defendant's alleged consent because court below did not reach it). Consent is a separate basis for personal jurisdiction. *Insurance Corp. of Ireland* v. *Compagnie des Bauxites de Guinee*, 456 U. S. 694, 703 (1982); *Burger King Corp.* v. *Rudzewicz*, 471 U. S. 462, 472, n. 14 (1985); *J. McIntyre Machinery, Ltd.* v. *Nicastro*, 564 U. S. 873, 880–881 (2011) (plurality opinion). *Pennsylvania Fire*'s holding, insofar as it is predicated on the out-of-state company's consent, is not "inconsistent" with *International Shoe* or its progeny. **{–2049–}** *Shaffer* v. *Heitner*, 433 U. S. 186, 212, n. 39 (1977).

Nor would I overrule *Pennsylvania Fire* in this case, as Norfolk Southern requests. At the least, *Pennsylvania Fire*'s holding does not strike me as "egregiously wrong" in its application here. *Ramos* v. *Louisiana*, 590 U. S. —, — (2020) (Kavanaugh, J., concurring in part). Requiring Norfolk Southern to defend against Mallory's suit in Pennsylvania, as opposed to in Virginia, is not so deeply unfair that it violates the railroad's constitutional right to due process. *International Shoe*, 326 U. S., at 316. The company has extensive operations in Pennsylvania, 266 A. 3d, at 562–563; see also *ante*, at 141–143; has availed itself of the Pennsylvania courts on countless occasions, Brief for Academy of Rail Labor Attorneys as *Amicus Curiae* 4–5 (collecting cases); and had clear notice that Pennsylvania considered its registration as consent to general jurisdiction, 15 Pa. Cons. Stat. § 411(a); 42 Pa. Cons. Stat. § 5301(a)(2)(i). Norfolk Southern's "conduct and connection with [Pennsylvania] are such that [it] should reasonably anticipate being haled into court there." *World-Wide Volkswagen Corp.* v. *Woodson*, 444 U. S. 286, 297 (1980).

If having to defend this suit in Pennsylvania seems unfair to Norfolk Southern, it is only because it is hard to see Mal- **[—154—]** lory's decision to sue in Philadelphia as anything other than the selection of a venue that is reputed to be especially favorable to tort plaintiffs.[1] But we have never held that the Due Process Clause protects against forum shopping. Perhaps for that understandable

[1] See, *e. g.*, U. S. Chamber of Commerce Institute for Legal Reform, Nuclear Verdicts: Trends, Causes, and Solutions 20 (2022); M. Behrens & C. Silverman, Litigation Tourism in Pennsylvania: Is Venue Reform Needed? 22 Widener L. J. 29, 30–31 (2012).

reason, no party has suggested that we go so far.

For these reasons, I agree that *Pennsylvania Fire* controls our decision here, but I stress that it does so due to the clear overlap with the facts of this case.

II

A

While that is the end of the case before us, it is not the end of the story for registration-based jurisdiction. We have long recognized that the Constitution restricts a State's power to reach out and regulate conduct that has little if any connection with the State's legitimate interests. This principle, an "obviou[s]" and "necessary result" of our constitutional order, is not confined to any one clause or section, but is expressed in the very nature of the federal system that the Constitution created and in numerous provisions that bear on States' interactions with one another. *New York Life Ins. Co.* v. *Head*, 234 U. S. 149, 161 (1914).[2]

The dissent suggests that we apply this principle through the Due Process Clause of the Fourteenth Amendment, *post*, **[—155—]** at 169–171, and there is support for this **{-2050-}** argument in our case law, if not in the ordinary meaning of the provision's wording. By its terms, the Due Process Clause is about procedure, but over the years, it has become a refuge of sorts for constitutional principles that are not "procedural" but would otherwise be homeless as the result of having been exiled from the provisions in which they may have originally been intended to reside. This may be true, for example, with respect to the protection of substantive rights that might otherwise be guaranteed by the Fourteenth Amendment's Privileges and Immunities Clause. See *McDonald* v. *Chicago*, 561 U. S. 742, 754–759 (2010) (plurality opinion); *id.*, at 808–812 (Thomas, J., concurring in part and concurring in judgment). And in a somewhat similar way, our due process decisions regarding personal jurisdiction have often invoked respect for federalism as a factor in their analyses.

In our first decision holding that the Fourteenth Amendment's Due Process Clause protects a civil defendant from suit in certain fora, the Court proclaimed that "no State can exercise direct jurisdiction and authority over persons or property without its territory." *Pennoyer* v. *Neff*, 95 U. S. 714, 722 (1878). "The several States," the Court explained, "are of equal dignity and authority, and the independence of one implies the exclusion of power from all others." *Ibid.* The Court warned that, in certain circumstances, a State's exercise of jurisdiction over non-residents would be "an encroachment upon the independence of [another] State" and a "usurpation" of that State's authority. *Id.*, at 723. And the Court noted that this was not a newly-developed doctrine, but reflected "well-established principles of public law" that "ha[d] been frequently expressed . . . in opinions of eminent judges, and . . . carried into adjudications in numerous cases." *Id.*, at 722, 724; see, *e. g.*, *D'Arcy* v. *Ketchum*, 11 How. 165, 176 (1851); *Picquet* v. *Swan*, 19 F. Cas. 609, 612 (No. 11,134) (CC Mass. 1828) (Story, J.). **[—156—]**

Our post-*International Shoe* decisions have continued to recognize that constitutional restrictions on state court jurisdiction "are more than a guarantee of immunity from inconvenient or distant litigation," but reflect "territorial limitations" on state power. *Hanson* v. *Denckla*, 357 U. S. 235, 251 (1958); see also *World-Wide Volkswagen*, 444 U. S., at 292 (in addition to "protect[ing] the defendant against the burdens of litigating in a distant or inconvenient forum," due process "acts to ensure that the States, through their courts, do not reach out beyond the limits imposed on them by their status as coequal sovereigns in a federal system"); *id.*, at 293 ("The sovereignty

[2] See, *e. g.*, *Florida* v. *Georgia*, 17 How. 478, 494 (1855); *Bonaparte* v. *Tax Court*, 104 U. S. 592, 594 (1882); *Huntington* v. *Attrill*, 146 U. S. 657, 669 (1892); *Alaska Packers Assn.* v. *Industrial Accident Comm'n of Cal.*, 294 U. S. 532, 540 (1935); *Baldwin* v. *G. A. F. Seelig, Inc.*, 294 U. S. 511, 521–523 (1935); *BMW of North America, Inc.* v. *Gore*, 517 U. S. 559, 571–572, and n. 16 (1996); *State Farm Mut. Automobile Ins. Co.* v. *Campbell*, 538 U. S. 408, 422 (2003).

of each State . . . implie[s] a limitation on the sovereignty of all of its sister States—a limitation express or implicit in both the original scheme of the Constitution and the Fourteenth Amendment"); *J. McIntyre Machinery*, 564 U. S., at 884 (plurality opinion) (if a "State were to assert jurisdiction in an inappropriate case, it would upset the federal balance, which posits that each State has a sovereignty that is not subject to unlawful intrusion by other States"). And we have recognized that in some circumstances, "federalism interest[s] may be decisive" in the due process analysis. *Bristol-Myers Squibb Co.* v. *Superior Court of Cal., San Francisco Cty.*, 582 U. S. 255, 263 (2017).

Despite these many references to federalism in due process decisions, there is a significant obstacle to addressing those concerns through the Fourteenth Amendment **{-2051-}** here: we have never held that a State's assertion of jurisdiction unconstitutionally intruded on the prerogatives of another State when the defendant had consented to jurisdiction in the forum State. Indeed, it is hard to see how such a decision could be justified. The Due Process Clause confers a right on "person[s]," Amdt. 14, § 1, not States. If a person voluntarily waives that right, that choice should be honored. See *Insurance Corp. of Ireland*, 456 U. S., at 703; *ante*, at 148 (JACKSON, J., concurring). **[—157—]**

B

1

The federalism concerns that this case presents fall more naturally within the scope of the Commerce Clause.[3] "By its terms, the Commerce Clause grants Congress the power `[t]o regulate Commerce . . . among the several States.'" *Raymond Motor Transp., Inc.* v. *Rice*, 434 U. S. 429, 440 (1978) (quoting Art. I, § 8, cl. 3). But this Court has long held that the Clause includes a negative component, the so-called dormant Commerce Clause, that "prohibits state laws that unduly restrict interstate commerce." *Tennessee Wine and Spirits Retailers Assn.* v. *Thomas*, 588 U. S. ——, —— – —— (2019); see, *e. g.*, *Cooley* v. *Board of Wardens of Port of Philadelphia ex rel. Soc. for Relief of Distressed Pilots*, 12 How. 299, 318–319 (1852); *Willson* v. *Black Bird Creek Marsh Co.*, 2 Pet. 245, 252 (1829).

While the notion that the Commerce Clause restrains States has been the subject of "thoughtful critiques," the concept is "deeply rooted in our case law," *Tennessee Wine*, 588 U. S., at ——, and vindicates a fundamental aim of the Constitution: fostering the creation of a national economy and avoiding the every-State-for-itself practices that had weakened the country under the Articles of Confederation. See *Hughes* v. *Oklahoma*, 441 U. S. 322, 325–326 (1979); *Healy* v. *Beer Institute*, 491 U. S. 324, 335–336 (1989). The Framers "might have thought [that other provisions] would fill that role," but "at this point in the Court's history, no **[—158—]** provision other than the Commerce Clause could easily do the job." *Tennessee Wine*, 588 U. S., at ——.[4]

[3] Analyzing these concerns under the Commerce Clause has the additional advantage of allowing Congress to modify the degree to which States should be able to entertain suits involving out-of-state parties and conduct. If Congress disagrees with our judgment on this question, it "has the authority to change the . . . rule" under its own Commerce power, subject, of course, to any other relevant constitutional limit. *South Dakota* v. *Wayfair, Inc.*, 585 U. S. ——, —— – —— (2018); see also *Southern Pacific Co.* v. *Arizona ex rel. Sullivan*, 325 U. S. 761, 769–770 (1945).

[4] In the past, the Court recognized that the Import-Export Clause, Art. I, § 10, cl. 2, and the Privileges and Immunities Clause, Art. IV, § 2, might restrict state regulations that interfere with the national economy. See, *e. g.*, *Brown* v. *Maryland*, 12 Wheat. 419, 445–449 (1827) (reading Import-Export Clause to prohibit state laws imposing duties on "importations from a sister State"); *Almy* v. *California*, 24 How. 169, 175 (1861) (applying Import-Export Clause to invalidate state law taxing gold and silver shipments between States); *Toomer* v. *Witsell*, 334 U. S. 385, 396, and n. 26 (1948) (observing that the Privileges and Immunities

In its negative aspects, the Commerce Clause serves to "mediate [the States'] {-2052-} competing claims of sovereign authority" to enact regulations that affect commerce among the States. *National Pork Producers Council* v. *Ross*, 598 U. S. 356, 376 (2023). The doctrine recognizes that "one State's power to impose burdens on . . . interstate market[s] . . . is not only subordinate to the federal power over interstate commerce, but is also constrained by the need to respect the interests of other States." *BMW of North America, Inc.* v. *Gore*, 517 U. S. 559, 571 (1996) (citing *Gibbons* v. *Ogden*, 9 Wheat. 1, 194–196 (1824)). It is especially appropriate to look to the dormant Commerce Clause in considering the constitutionality of the authority asserted by Pennsylvania's registration scheme. Because the right of an out-of-state corporation to do business in another State is based on the **[—159—]** dormant Commerce Clause, it stands to reason that this doctrine may also limit a State's authority to condition that right. See *Granholm* v. *Heald*, 544 U. S. 460, 472 (2005); *H. P. Hood & Sons, Inc.* v. *Du Mond*, 336 U. S. 525, 539 (1949).

2

This Court and other courts have long examined assertions of jurisdiction over out-of-state companies in light of interstate commerce concerns.[5] Consider *Davis* v. *Farmers Co-operative Equity Co.*, 262 U. S. 312 (1923), a case very much like the one now before us. In *Davis*, a Kansas company sued a Kansas railroad in Minnesota on a claim that was "in no way connected with Minnesota." *Id.*, at 314. Jurisdiction over the railroad was based on its compliance with a state statute regulating the in-state activities of out-of-state corporations: the railroad maintained a soliciting agent in Minnesota, and the Minnesota Supreme Court had interpreted state law as compelling out-of-state carriers, as a "condition of maintaining a soliciting agent," to "submit to suit" in Minnesota on any "cause of action, wherever it may have arisen." *Id.*, at 315.

The Minnesota Supreme Court upheld jurisdiction against the railroad, but we reversed, holding that Minnesota's condition "impos[ed] upon interstate commerce a serious and unreasonable burden, which renders the statute obnoxious to the [C]ommerce [C]lause." *Ibid.* "By requiring from interstate carriers general submission to suit," Minnesota's stat- **[—160—]** ute "unreasonably obstruct[ed], and unduly burden[ed], interstate commerce." **{-2053-}** *Id.*, at 317.[6]

Although we have since refined our Commerce Clause framework, the structural constitutional principles underlying these decisions are unchanged, and the Clause remains a vital constraint on States' power over out-of-state corporations.

C

In my view, there is a good prospect that Pennsylvania's assertion of jurisdiction here—

Clause guarantees out-of-state citizens the right to do business in a State on equal terms with state citizens (citing *Ward* v. *Maryland*, 12 Wall. 418 (1871))). But the Court has since narrowed the scope of these provisions. See *Woodruff* v. *Parham*, 8 Wall. 123, 136–137 (1869) (holding that the Import-Export Clause applies only to international trade); *Western & Southern Life Ins. Co.* v. *State Bd. of Equalization of Cal.*, 451 U. S. 648, 656 (1981) (observing that "the Privileges and Immunities Clause is inapplicable to corporations" (citing *Hemphill* v. *Orloff*, 277 U. S. 537, 548–550 (1928))). Whether or not these restrictive interpretations are correct as an original matter, they are entrenched. Unless we overrule them, we must look elsewhere if "a national economic union unfettered by state-imposed limitations on commerce" is to be preserved. *Healy*, 491 U. S., at 336.

[5] See, *e. g., Atchison, T. & S. F. R. Co.* v. *Wells*, 265 U. S. 101, 103 (1924); *Michigan Central R. Co.* v. *Mix*, 278 U. S. 492, 494–495 (1929); *Denver & Rio Grande Western R. Co.* v. *Terte*, 284 U. S. 284, 287 (1932); *Baltimore & Ohio R. Co.* v. *Kepner*, 314 U. S. 44, 50–51 (1941); *Moss* v. *Atlantic Coast Line R. Co.*, 157 F. 2d 1005, 1007 (CA2 1946); *Kern* v. *Cleveland, C., C. & St. L. R. Co.*, 204 Ind. 595, 601–604, 185 N. E. 446, 448–449 (1933); *Hayman* v. *Southern Pacific Co.*, 278 S. W. 2d 749, 753 (Mo. 1955); *White* v. *Southern Pacific Co.*, 386 S. W. 2d 6, 7–9 (Mo. 1965).

[6] Because we resolved the case under the Commerce Clause, we declined to consider the railroad's Fourteenth Amendment challenges. *Davis* v. *Farmers Co-operative Equity Co.*, 262 U. S. 312, 318 (1923).

over an out-of-state company in a suit brought by an out-of-state plaintiff on claims wholly unrelated to Pennsylvania—violates the Commerce Clause.

Under our modern framework, a state law may offend the Commerce Clause's negative restrictions in two circumstances: when the law discriminates against interstate commerce or when it imposes "undue burdens" on interstate commerce. *South Dakota* v. *Wayfair, Inc.*, 585 U. S. ––, –– (2018). Discriminatory state laws are subject to "`a virtually *per se* rule of invalidity.'" *Ibid.* (quoting *Granholm*, 544 U. S., at 476). "[O]nce a state law is shown to discriminate against interstate commerce `either on its face or in practical effect,'" the law's proponent must "demonstrate both that the statute `serves a legitimate local purpose,' and that this purpose could not be served as well by available nondiscriminatory means." *Maine* v. *Taylor*, 477 U. S. 131, 138 (1986). Justification of a discriminatory law faces a "high" bar to overcome the presumption of invalidity. *New Energy Co. of Ind.* v. *Limbach*, 486 U. S. 269, 278 (1988). Laws that "`even-handedly'" regulate to advance "`a legitimate local public interest'" are subject to a looser standard. *Wayfair*, 585 U. S., at ––. These laws will be upheld "`unless the burden imposed on [interstate] commerce is clearly excessive **[—161—]** in relation to the putative local benefits.'" *Ibid.* In these circumstances, "`the question becomes one of degree,'" and "`the extent of the burden that will be tolerated will . . . depend on the nature of the local interest involved.'" *Raymond Motor Transp.*, 434 U. S., at 441. See also *Pike* v. *Bruce Church, Inc.*, 397 U. S. 137, 142 (1970).

There is reason to believe that Pennsylvania's registration-based jurisdiction law discriminates against out-of-state companies.[7] But at the very least, the law imposes a "significant burden" on interstate commerce by "[r]equiring a foreign corporation . . . to defend itself with reference to all transactions," including those with no forum connection. *Bendix Autolite Corp.* v. *Midwesco Enterprises, Inc.*, 486 U. S. 888, 893 (1988); see, *e. g.*, *Davis*, 262 U. S., at 315–317 (burden in these circumstances **{–2054–}** is "serious and unreasonable," "heavy," and "undu[e]"); *Michigan Central R. Co.* v. *Mix*, 278 U. S. 492, 495 (1929) (burden is "heavy"); *Denver & Rio Grande Western R. Co.* v. *Terte*, 284 U. S. 284, 287 (1932) (burden is "serious"); *Atchison, T. & S. F. R. Co.* v. *Wells*, 265 U. S. 101, 103 (1924) (jurisdiction "interfered unreasonably with interstate commerce").

The foreseeable consequences of the law make clear why this is so. Aside from the operational burdens it places on out-of-state companies, Pennsylvania's scheme injects intolerable unpredictability into doing business across state borders. Large companies may be able to manage the patch- **[—162—]** work of liability regimes, damages caps, and local rules in each State, but the impact on small companies, which constitute the majority of all U. S. corporations, could be devastating.[8] Large companies may resort to creative corporate structuring to limit their amenability to suit. Small companies may prudently choose not to enter an out-of-state market due to the increased risk of remote litigation. Some companies may forgo registration altogether, preferring to risk the consequences rather than expand their exposure to general jurisdiction. "No one benefits from this `efficient breach' of corporate-registration laws": corporations must manage their added risk, and plaintiffs face challenges in serving unregistered

[7] See, *e. g.*, J. Preis, The Dormant Commerce Clause as a Limit on Personal Jurisdiction, 102 Iowa L. Rev. 138–140 (2016). A state law discriminates against interstate commerce if its "`practical effect'" is to disadvantage out-of-state companies to the benefit of in-state competitors. *Maine* v. *Taylor*, 477 U. S. 131, 138 (1986); see *United Haulers Assn., Inc.* v. *Oneida-Herkimer Solid Waste Management Authority*, 550 U. S. 330, 338 (2007). Pennsylvania's law seems to discriminate against out-of-state companies by forcing them to increase their exposure to suits on all claims in order to access Pennsylvania's market while Pennsylvania companies generally face no reciprocal burden for expanding operations into another State.

[8] Congressional Research Service, M. Keightley & J. Hughes, Pass-Throughs, Corporations, and Small Businesses: A Look at Firm Size 4–5 (2018) (in 2015, 62% of S corporations and 55% of C corporations had fewer than fve employees).

corporations. Brief for Tanya Monestier as *Amicus Curiae* 16. States, meanwhile, "would externalize the costs of [their] plaintiff-friendly regimes." Brief for Stephen E. Sachs as *Amicus Curiae* 26.

Given these serious burdens, to survive Commerce Clause scrutiny under this Court's framework, the law must advance a "'legitimate local public interest'" and the burdens must not be "'clearly excessive in relation to the putative local benefits.'" *Wayfair*, 585 U. S., at ——. But I am hard-pressed to identify any *legitimate local* interest that is advanced by requiring an out-of-state company to defend a suit brought by an out-of-state plaintiff on claims wholly unconnected to the forum State. A State certainly has a legitimate interest in regulating activities conducted within its borders, which may include providing a forum to redress harms that occurred within the State. *State Farm Mut. Automobile Ins. Co.* v. *Campbell*, 538 U. S. 408, 422 (2003); *BMW of North America*, 517 U. S., at 568–569; *Hess* v. *Pawloski*, 274 U. S. 352, 356 (1927). A State also may have an **[—163—]** interest "in providing its residents with a convenient forum for redressing injuries inflicted by out-of-state actors." *Burger King*, 471 U. S., at 473. But a State generally does *not* have a legitimate local interest in vindicating the rights of non-residents harmed by out-of-state actors through conduct outside the State. See, *e. g.*, *Edgar* v. *MITE Corp.*, 457 U. S. 624, 644 (1982). With no legitimate local interest served, "there is nothing to be weighed . . . to sustain the law." *Ibid.* And even if some legitimate local interest could be identified, I am skeptical that any local benefits of the State's assertion of jurisdiction in these circumstances could overcome the serious burdens on interstate commerce that it imposes. See, *e. g.*, *id.*, at 643–646; *Raymond Motor Transp.*, 434 U. S., at 444–446. **{-2055-}**

* * *

Because *Pennsylvania Fire* resolves this case in favor of petitioner Mallory and no Commerce Clause challenge is before us, I join the Court's opinion as stated in Parts I and III–B, and agree that the Pennsylvania Supreme Court's judgment should be vacated and the case remanded for further proceedings.

(Reporter's Note: Dissenting opinion follows on p. 27).

[—163—] {-2055-} JUSTICE BARRETT, with whom THE CHIEF JUSTICE, JUSTICE KAGAN, and JUSTICE KAVANAUGH join, dissenting:

For 75 years, we have held that the Due Process Clause does not allow state courts to assert general jurisdiction over foreign defendants merely because they do business in the State. *International Shoe Co.* v. *Washington*, 326 U. S. 310, 317 (1945). Pennsylvania nevertheless claims general jurisdiction over all corporations that lawfully do business within its borders. As the Commonwealth's own courts recognized, that flies in the face of our precedent. See *Daimler AG* v. *Bauman*, 571 U. S. 117, 139–140 (2014).

The Court finds a way around this settled rule. All a State must do is compel a corporation to register to conduct [—164—] business there (as every State does) and enact a law making registration sufficient for suit on any cause (as every State could do). Then, every company doing business in the State is subject to general jurisdiction based on implied "consent"—not contacts. That includes suits, like this one, with no connection whatsoever to the forum.

Such an approach does not formally overrule our traditional contacts-based approach to jurisdiction, but it might as well. By relabeling their long-arm statutes, States may now manufacture "consent" to personal jurisdiction. Because I would not permit state governments to circumvent constitutional limits so easily, I respectfully dissent.

I

A

Personal jurisdiction is the authority of a court to issue a judgment that binds a defendant. If a defendant submits to a court's authority, the court automatically acquires personal jurisdiction. *Insurance Corp. of Ireland* v. *Compagnie des Bauxites de Guinee*, 456 U. S. 694, 703 (1982). But if a defendant *contests* the court's authority, the court must determine whether it can nevertheless assert coercive power over the defendant. That calculus turns first on the statute or rule defining the persons within the court's reach. See *World-Wide Volkswagen Corp.* v. *Woodson*, 444 U. S. 286, 290 (1980). It depends next on the Due Process Clause, which guards a defendant's right to resist the judicial authority of a sovereign to which it has an insufficient tie. *International Shoe*, 326 U. S., at 316. The Clause has the companion role of ensuring that state courts "do not reach out beyond the limits imposed on them by their status as coequal sovereigns in a federal system." *World-Wide Volkswagen*, 444 U. S., at 291–292.

Our precedent divides personal jurisdiction into two categories: specific and general. Both are subject to the demands of the Due Process Clause. Specific jurisdiction, as [—165—] its name suggests, allows a state court to adjudicate specific claims against a defendant. When a defendant "purposefully avails itself of the privilege of conducting activities within the forum State," *Hanson* v. *Denckla*, 357 U. S. 235, 253 (1958), that State's courts may adjudicate claims that "`arise out of or relate to the defendant's contacts' with the forum," {-2056-} *Ford Motor Co.* v. *Montana Eighth Judicial Dist. Court*, 592 U. S. ——, —— (2021) (quoting *Bristol-Myers Squibb Co.* v. *Superior Court of Cal., San Francisco Cty.*, 582 U. S. 255, 262 (2017)).

General jurisdiction, by contrast, allows a state court to adjudicate "`any and all claims' brought against a defendant." *Ford Motor*, 592 U. S., at —— (quoting *Goodyear Dunlop Tires Operations, S. A.* v. *Brown*, 564 U. S. 915, 919 (2011)). This sweeping authority exists only when the defendant's connection to the State is tight—so tight, in fact, that the defendant is "`at home'" there. *Ford Motor*, 592 U. S., at ——. An individual is typically "at home" in her domicile, *Goodyear*, 564 U. S., at 924, and a corporation is typically "at home" in both its place of incorporation and principal place of business, *Daimler*, 571 U. S., at 137. Absent an exceptional circumstance, general jurisdiction is cabined to these locations. *Id.*, at 139.

B

This case involves a Pennsylvania statute authorizing courts to exercise general jurisdiction over corporations that are not "at home" in the Commonwealth. All foreign corporations must register to do business in Pennsylvania, 15 Pa. Cons. Stat. § 411(a) (2014), and all registrants are subject to suit on "any cause" in the Commonwealth's courts, 42 Pa. Cons. Stat. §§ 5301(a)(2)(i), (b) (2019). Section 5301 thus purports to empower Pennsylvania courts to adjudicate any and all claims against corporations doing business there.

As the Pennsylvania Supreme Court recognized, this statute "clearly, palpably, and plainly violates the Constitution." **[—166—]** 266 A. 3d 542, 565–566 (2021). Look no further than *BNSF R. Co.* v. *Tyrrell*, a case with remarkably similar facts—and one that the Court conspicuously ignores. 581 U. S. 402, 5 Adm. R. 2 (2017). There, we assessed whether Montana's courts could exercise general jurisdiction over the BNSF railroad. No plaintiff resided in Montana or suffered an injury there. Like Mallory, one of the plaintiffs alleged that the railroad exposed him to toxic substances that caused his cancer. *Id.*, at 406, 5 Adm. R. at 2. Like Norfolk Southern, BNSF had tracks and employees in the forum, but it was neither incorporated nor headquartered there. *Id.*, at 406–407, 5 Adm. R. at 3. We rejected Montana's assertion of general jurisdiction over BNSF because "in-state business . . . does not suffice to permit the assertion of general jurisdiction over claims . . . that are unrelated to any activity occurring in [the State]." *Id.*, at 414, 5 Adm. R. at 7. *Daimler* and *Goodyear*, we explained, could not have made that any clearer. *BNSF*, 581 U. S., at 414, 5 Adm. R. at 7.

The same rule applies here. The Pennsylvania statute announces that registering to do business in the Commonwealth "shall constitute a sufficient basis" for general jurisdiction. § 5301(a). But as our precedent makes crystal clear, simply doing business is *insufficient*. Absent an exceptional circumstance, a corporation is subject to general jurisdiction only in a State where it is incorporated or has its principal place of business. *Ford Motor*, 592 U. S., at —; *Daimler*, 571 U. S., at 139; *Goodyear*, 564 U. S., at 924. Adding the antecedent step of registration does not change that conclusion. If it did, "every corporation would be subject to general jurisdiction in every state in which it registered, and *Daimler's* ruling would be **{-2057-}** robbed of meaning by a back-door thief." *Brown* v. *Lockheed Martin Corp.*, 814 F. 3d 619, 640 (CA2 2016).

II

A

The Court short-circuits this precedent by characterizing this case as one about consent rather than contacts-based **[—167—]** jurisdiction. Consent is an established basis for personal jurisdiction, which is, after all, a waivable defense. "A variety of legal arrangements have been taken to represent express or implied consent to the personal jurisdiction of the court," including contract, stipulation, and in-court appearance. *Insurance Corp. of Ireland*, 456 U. S., at 703–704. Today, the Court adds corporate registration to the list.

This argument begins on shaky ground, because Pennsylvania itself does not treat registration as synonymous with consent. Section 5301(a)(2)(i) baldly asserts that "qualification as a foreign corporation" in the Commonwealth is a sufficient hook for general jurisdiction. The *next* subsection (invoked by neither Mallory nor the Court) permits the exercise of general jurisdiction over a corporation based on "[c]onsent, to the extent authorized by the consent. " § 5301(a)(2)(ii). If registration were actual consent, one would expect to see some mention of jurisdiction in Norfolk Southern's registration paperwork—which is instead wholly silent on the matter. App. 1–7. What Mallory calls "consent" is what the Pennsylvania Supreme Court called "compelled submission to general jurisdiction by legislative command." 266 A. 3d, at 569. Corporate registration triggers a statutory repercussion, but that is not "consent" in a conventional sense of the word.

To pull § 5301(a)(2)(i) under the umbrella of consent, the Court, following Mallory, casts it as setting the terms of a bargain: In exchange for access to the Pennsylvania market, a corporation must allow the Commonwealth's courts to adjudicate any and all claims against it, even those (like Mallory's) having nothing to do with Pennsylvania. Brief for Petitioner 27–28. Everyone is charged with knowledge of the law, so corporations are on notice of the deal. By registering, they agree to its terms.

While this is a clever theory, it falls apart on inspection. The Court grounds consent in a corporation's choice to register with knowledge (constructive or actual) of the jurisdic- **[—168—]** tional consequences. *Ante*, at 134–135, 144 ("proceed[ing] anyway" in light of "the jurisdictional consequences attending these actions"); *ante*, at 151 (Alito, J., concurring in part and concurring in judgment) (basing "consent" on "presume[d]" knowledge of state law); *ante*, at 149 (Jackson, J., concurring) ("register[ing] and do[ing] business in Pennsylvania despite the jurisdictional consequences"). But on that logic, *any* long-arm statute could be said to elicit consent. Imagine a law that simply provides, "any corporation doing business in this State is subject to general jurisdiction in our courts." Such a law defies our precedent, which, again, holds that "in-state business . . . does not suffice to permit the assertion of general jurisdiction." *BNSF*, 581 U. S., at 414, 5 Adm. R. at 7. Yet this hypothetical law, like the Pennsylvania statute, gives notice that general jurisdiction is the price of doing business. And its "notice" is no less "clear" than Pennsylvania's. *Ante*, at 153 (opinion of Alito, J.). So on the Court's reasoning, corporations that choose to do business in the State impliedly consent to general jurisdiction. The result: A State could defeat the Due Process Clause by adopting a law at odds with the Due Process Clause.

That makes no sense. If the hypothetical statute overreaches, then Pennsylvania's **{-2058-}** does too. As the United States observes, "[i]nvoking the label `consent' rather than `general jurisdiction' does not render Pennsylvania's long-arm statute constitutional." Brief for United States as *Amicus Curiae* 4. Yet the Court takes this route without so much as acknowledging its circularity.

B

While our due process precedent permits States to place reasonable conditions on foreign corporations in exchange for access to their markets, there is nothing reasonable about a State extracting consent in cases where it has "no connection whatsoever." 266 A. 3d, at 566; *Bristol-Myers*, 582 U. S., at 263; see *Lafayette Ins. Co.* v. *French*, 18 How. 404, 407 (1856). **[—169—]** The Due Process Clause protects more than the rights of defendants—it also protects interstate federalism. We have emphasized this principle in case after case. For instance, in *Hanson* v. *Denckla*, we stressed that "restrictions" on personal jurisdiction "are more than a guarantee of immunity from inconvenient or distant litigation. They are a consequence of territorial limitations on the power of the respective States." 357 U. S., at 250–251. In *World-Wide Volkswagen*, we explained that "[e]ven if the defendant would suffer minimal or no inconvenience from being forced to litigate before the tribunals of another State . . . the Due Process Clause, acting as an instrument of interstate federalism, may sometimes act to divest the State of its power to render a valid judgment." 444 U. S., at 294. And in *Bristol-Myers*, we reinforced that "this federalism interest may be decisive." 582 U. S., at 263; see also, *e. g.*, *Ford Motor*, 592 U. S., at ——; *Asahi Metal Industry Co.* v. *Superior Court of Cal., Solano Cty.*, 480 U. S. 102, 113, 115 (1987); *International Shoe*, 326 U. S., at 317. A defendant's ability to waive its objection to personal jurisdiction reflects that the Clause protects, first and foremost, an individual right. But when a State announces a blanket rule that ignores the territorial boundaries on its power, federalism interests are implicated too.

Pennsylvania's effort to assert general jurisdiction over every company doing business within its borders infringes on the sovereignty of its sister States in a way no less "exorbitant" and "grasping" than attempts we have previously rejected.[1] *Daimler*, 571 U. S., at

[1] This case provides a "textbook example" of overreach at the expense of other States. 266 A. 3d 542, 567 (Pa. 2021). Virginia has considerable connections to Mallory's suit: Mallory lives in Virginia, Norfolk Southern is a Virginia corporation, Mallory's injuries arose—at least in part—from his

121–122, 138–139. Condi- [—170—] tions on doing in-state business cannot be "inconsistent with those rules of public law which secure the jurisdiction and authority of each State from encroachment by all others." *Lafayette*, 18 How., at 407; *St. Clair* v. *Cox*, 106 U. S. 350, 356 (1882). Permitting Pennsylvania to impose a blanket claim of authority over controversies with no connection to the Commonwealth intrudes on the prerogatives of other States—domestic and foreign—to adjudicate the rights of their citizens and enforce their own laws. See *Ford Motor*, 592 U. S., at —— - ——; *Daimler*, 571 U. S., at 141–142.

The plurality's response is to fall back, yet again, on "consent." **{-2059-}** *Ante*, at 144, 146, n. 11. In its view, because a defendant can *waive* its personal jurisdiction right, a State can never overreach in demanding its *relinquishment. Ibid.*; see also *ante*, at 156 (opinion of Alito, J.); *ante*, at 147–149 (opinion of Jackson, J.). That is not how we treat rights with structural components. The right to remove a case to federal court, for instance, is primarily personal—it secures for a non-resident defendant a federal forum thought to be more impartial. See The Federalist No. 80, p. 478 (C. Rossiter ed. 1961) (A. Hamilton). At the same time, however, it serves federal interests by ensuring that federal courts can vindicate federal rights. See, *e. g.*, *Georgia* v. *Rachel*, 384 U. S. 780, 804–805 (1966). Recognizing this dual role, we have rejected efforts of States to require defendants to relinquish this (waivable) right to removal as a condition of doing business. See *Home Ins. Co.* v. *Morse*, 20 Wall. 445, 453, 456–458 (1874) (citing *Lafayette*, 18 How., at 407); *Barron* v. *Burnside*, 121 U. S. 186, 196–198 (1887) ("[W]hile the right to remove a suit might be waived," a statute may not require a foreign corporation "to forfeit [its] rights at all times and on all occasions, whenever the case might be presented"). The same logic applies here. Pennsylvania's power grab in- [—171—] fringes on more than just the rights of defendants—it upsets the proper role of the States in our federal system.

III

A

The plurality attempts to minimize the novelty of its conclusion by pointing to our decision in *Burnham* v. *Superior Court of Cal., County of Marin*, 495 U. S. 604 (1990). There, we considered whether "tag jurisdiction"—personal service upon a defendant physically present in the forum State—remains an effective basis for general jurisdiction after *International Shoe*. *Burnham*, 495 U. S., at 607 (opinion of Scalia, J.). We unanimously agreed that it does. *Id.*, at 619, 622; *id.*, at 628 (White, J., concurring in part and concurring in judgment); *id.*, at 628–629 (Brennan, J., concurring in judgment); *id.*, at 640 (Stevens, J., concurring in judgment). The plurality claims that registration jurisdiction for a corporation is just as valid as the "tag jurisdiction" that we approved in *Burnham*. But in drawing this analogy, the plurality omits any discussion of *Burnham*'s reasoning.

In *Burnham*, we acknowledged that tag jurisdiction would not satisfy the contacts-based test for general jurisdiction. Nonetheless, we reasoned that tag jurisdiction is "both firmly approved by tradition and still favored," making it "one of the continuing traditions of our legal system that define[s] the due process standard of `traditional notions of fair play and substantial justice.'" *Id.*, at 619 (opinion of Scalia, J.) (quoting *International Shoe*, 326 U. S., at 316); see also 495 U. S., at 635–637 (Brennan, J., concurring in judgment) (a jurisdictional rule that reflects "our common understanding *now*, fortified by a century of judicial practice, . . . is entitled to a strong presumption that it comports with due process"). *Burnham* thus permits a longstanding and still-accepted basis for jurisdiction to pass *International Shoe*'s test. [—172—]

General-jurisdiction-by-registration flunks both of these prongs: It is neither "firmly approved by tradition" nor "still favored." 495

employment in Virginia, and he was diagnosed with cancer there. See *ante*, at 126; Tr. of Oral Arg. 39. Pennsylvania, by contrast, "has no legitimate interest in a controversy with no connection to the Commonwealth [—170—] that was filed by a non-resident against a foreign corporation." 266 A. 3d, at 567.

U. S., at 622 (opinion of Scalia, J.). Thus, the plurality's analogy to tag jurisdiction is superficial at best. **{–2060–}**

Start with the second prong. In *Burnham*, "[w]e [did] not know of a single state . . . that [had] abandoned in-state service as a basis of jurisdiction." *Id.*, at 615. Here, as Mallory concedes, Pennsylvania is the *only* State with a statute treating registration as sufficient for general jurisdiction. Tr. of Oral Arg. 47. Indeed, quite a few have jettisoned the jurisdictional consequences of corporate registration altogether—and in no uncertain terms. See, *e. g.*, *Chavez* v. *Bridgestone Americas Tire Operations, LLC*, 2022–NMSC–006, ¶¶1, 53–54, 503 P. 3d 332, 336, 349 ("Reliance upon outdated legal fictions . . . would be absurd and, as explained above, inconsistent with contemporary understandings of due process"); *Genuine Parts Co.* v. *Cepec*, 137 A. 3d 123, 137 (Del. 2016) ("[W]e no longer live in a time where foreign corporations cannot operate in other states unless they somehow become a resident"); see also *DeLeon* v. *BNSF R. Co.*, 392 Mont. 446, 453, n. 1, 426 P. 3d 1, 7, n. 1 (2018) (listing States with statutes that do not permit the practice).[2] With the Pennsylvania Legislature standing alone, the plurality does not even attempt to describe this method of securing general jurisdiction as "still favored," *Burnham*, 495 U. S., at 622 (opinion of Scalia, J.), or reflective of "our common understanding now," *id.*, at 635–637 (Brennan, J., concurring in judgment) (emphasis deleted). Quite the op- **[—173—]** posite: The plurality denigrates "the spirit of our age"—reflected by the vast majority of States—and appeals to its own notions of fairness. *Ante*, at 141–143.

The past is as fatal to the plurality's theory as the present. *Burnham*'s tradition prong asks whether a method for securing jurisdiction was "shared by American courts at the crucial time"—"1868, when the Fourteenth Amendment was adopted." 495 U. S., at 611 (opinion of Scalia, J.). But the plurality cannot identify a *single* case from that period supporting its theory.[3] In fact, the evidence runs in the opposite direction. Statutes that required the appointment of a registered agent for service of process were far more modest than Pennsylvania's.[4] And even when a statute was written **{–2061–}** more broadly, state courts generally understood it to implicitly limit jurisdiction to suits with a connection to the forum. **[—174—]** The state reporters are replete with examples of judicial decisions that stood by the then-prevailing rule: Compliance with a registration law did not subject a foreign corporation to suit on *any*

[2] The plurality offers only one other State that (through its Supreme Court) has treated foreign corporate registration as adequate support for general jurisdiction following *Daimler* and *Goodyear*. See *Cooper Tire & Rubber Co.* v. *McCall*, 312 Ga. 422, 436–437, 863 S. E. 2d 81, 92 (2021). There, a judicial precedent, not a long-arm statute, maintained that registration justified general jurisdiction. Applying the consent theory, the Georgia Supreme Court held that corporations that choose to do business in the State are on notice of the jurisdictional consequences of its case law. *Id.*, at 434, 863 S. E. 2d, at 90.

[3] The plurality argues that the uniform practice of state courts at the time of ratification is inapposite because no state court held that general-jurisdiction-by-registration violates the Fourteenth Amendment. *Ante*, at 131, n. 4. This approach reflects a misunderstanding of *Burnham*. The inquiry is not whether courts rejected a process for obtaining jurisdiction as unconstitutional. It is whether courts *actually used*—and continue to use—the challenged process. 495 U. S., at 622 (opinion of Scalia, J.); see also *Hurtado* v. *California*, 110 U. S. 516, 528 (1884) ("[A] process of law . . . must be taken to be due process of law" if it "has been immemorially the actual law of the land"). Registration jurisdiction falls short on both fronts.

[4] Many States expressly limited their statutes to disputes with *a connection to the State*. See, *e. g.*, Ind. Code § 25–2 (1852) (foreign corporations must consent to actions "arising out of any transaction in this State"), App. to Brief for Petitioner 47a; Conn. Gen. Stat. § 7–389 (1866) (foreign insurance companies must appoint an in-state agent to accept process "in all suits before any court in this state, for any liability incurred by such company or association in this state"), App. to Brief for Petitioner 18a; Md. Code Ann. § 26–211 (1868) (foreign corporation may be sued by nonresident "when the cause of action has arisen, or the subject of the action shall be situate[d] in this state"), App. to Brief for Petitioner 90a; S. C. Code Ann. § 13–1–422(2) (1873) (nonresident may sue a foreign corporation "when the cause of action shall have arisen, or the subject of the action shall be situated, within this State"), App. to Brief for Petitioner 227a.

cause in a State, but only those related to the forum. *Smith* v. *Mutual Life Ins. Co. of N. Y.*, 96 Mass. 336, 340–343 (1867); see also, *e. g.*, *Camden Rolling Mill* v. *Swede Iron Co.*, 32 N. J. L. 15, 18 (1866) (rejecting a statutory construction that would "place within the jurisdiction of our courts, all the corporations of the world"); *Newell* v. *Great W. R. Co. of Canada*, 19 Mich. 336, 345–346 (1869) (legislature "could never have intended . . . to make our tribunals, maintained by the people of Michigan, the arbiters of differences in which our citizens have no interest"); *Sawyer* v. *North Am. Life Ins. Co.*, 46 Vt. 697, 707 (1874) (broadly worded statute did not reach a corporate "party not a resident, on a cause of action which did not accrue here"); *Central R. & Banking Co.* v. *Carr*, 76 Ala. 388, 393 (1884) (collecting cases).[5] Our cases from this era articulate the same line. See, *e. g.*, *Lafayette*, 18 How., at 407 (statutory consent to suit may reach "contracts made and to be performed within that State"); *St. Clair*, 106 U. S., at 356–357 (statutory consent permitted for suits "arising out of [a foreign corporation's] transactions in the State"); *Old Wayne Mut. Life Assn. of Indianapolis* v. *McDonough*, 204 U. S. 8, 21 (1907) ("[I]t cannot be held that the company agreed that service of process . . . would alone be sufficient to bring it into court in respect of *all* business transacted by it, no matter where"); *Simon* v. *Southern R. Co.*, 236 U. S. 115, 130 (1915) ("statutory consent of a foreign corporation to be sued does not extend to causes of action arising in other states"). Although "plaintiffs typi- **[—175—]** cally did not sue defendants in fora that had no rational relation to causes of action," *Genuine Parts*, 137 A. 3d, at 146, courts repeatedly turned them away when they did.

B

Sidestepping *Burnham*'s logic, the plurality seizes on its bottom-line approval of tag jurisdiction. According to the plurality, tag jurisdiction (based on physical presence) and registration jurisdiction (based on deemed consent) are essentially the same thing—so by blessing one, *Burnham* blessed the other. See *ante*, at 125–126, 139–140. The plurality never explains why they are the same, even though—as we have just discussed—more than a century's worth of law treats them as distinct. See also *Burnham*, 495 U. S., at 610, n. 1 (opinion of Scalia, J.) (corporations "have never fi[t] comfortably in a jurisdictional regime based primarily upon `de facto power over the defendant's person'"); *International Shoe*, 326 U. S., at 316–317. The plurality's rationale seems to be that if a person is subject **{-2062-}** to general jurisdiction anywhere she is present, then a corporation should be subject to general jurisdiction anywhere it does business. See *ante*, at 125–126, 129–130, 132–134, 139–140, 145. That is not only a non sequitur—it is "contrary to the historical rationale of *International Shoe*." *Wenche Siemer* v. *Learjet Acquisition Corp.*, 966 F. 2d 179, 183 (CA5 1992).

Before *International Shoe*, a state court's power over a person turned strictly on "service of process within the State" (presence) "or [her] voluntary appearance" (consent). *Pennoyer* v. *Neff*, 95 U. S. 714, 733 (1878). In response to changes in interstate business and transportation in the late 19th and early 20th centuries, States deployed new legal fictions designed to secure the presence or consent of nonresident individuals and foreign corporations. For example, state laws required nonresident drivers to give their "implied consent" to be sued for their in-state accidents as a condition of using the road. *Hess* v. *Pawloski*, 274 U. S. 352, **[—176—]** 356 (1927); *World-Wide Volkswagen*, 444 U. S., at 296, n. 11. And foreign corporations, as we have discussed, were required by statute to "consent" to the appointment of a resident agent, so that the company could then be constructively "present" for in-state service. *Mutual Reserve Fund Life Assn.* v. *Phelps*, 190 U. S. 147, 158–159 (1903); see *St. Clair*, 106 U. S., at 356.

[5] Mallory cannot find an example of an exercise of registration jurisdiction without a forum connection until 1882. See *Johnston* v. *Trade Ins. Co.*, 132 Mass. 432, 434–435. But even that example ignores Massachusetts's rejection of registration jurisdiction for cases with no connection to the forum in 1867—the year it ratified the Fourteenth Amendment. See *Smith*, 96 Mass., at 340–343.

As Justice Scalia explained, such extensions of "consent and presence were purely fictional" and can no longer stand after *International Shoe. Burnham*, 495 U. S., at 618; see also, *e. g.*, *Shaffer* v. *Heitner*, 433 U. S. 186, 202–203 (1977) (*International Shoe* abandoned "both the fictions of implied consent to service on the part of a foreign corporation and of corporate presence"); *McGee* v. *International Life Ins. Co.*, 355 U. S. 220, 222 (1957) (*International Shoe* "abandoned `consent,' `doing business,' and `presence' as the standard for measuring the extent of state judicial power over [foreign] corporations"); *International Shoe*, 326 U. S., at 318. The very point of *International Shoe* was to "cast . . . aside" the legal fictions built on the old territorial approach to personal jurisdiction and replace them with its contacts-based test. *Burnham*, 495 U. S., at 618 (opinion of Scalia, J.); *id.*, at 630 (Brennan, J., concurring in judgment) (*International Shoe* abandoned the previous " `patchwork of legal and factual fictions' "). In *Burnham*, we upheld tag jurisdiction because it is not one of those fictions—it *is* presence. By contrast, Pennsylvania's registration statute is based on deemed consent. And this kind of legally implied consent is one of the very fictions that our decision in *International Shoe* swept away. See 326 U. S., at 318; *Ford Motor*, 592 U. S., at —— (Gorsuch, J., concurring in judgment).

C

Neither Justice Alito nor the plurality seriously contests this history. Nor does either deny that Mallory's theory would gut *Daimler*. Instead, they insist that we al- **[—177—]** ready decided this question in a pre-*International Shoe* precedent: *Pennsylvania Fire Ins. Co. of Philadelphia* v. *Gold Issue Mining & Milling Co.*, 243 U. S. 93 (1917).

In *Pennsylvania Fire*, an Arizona corporation sued a Pennsylvania corporation in Missouri for a claim arising from an insurance contract issued in Colorado and protecting property in Colorado. *Id.*, at 94. The defendant maintained that the Missouri court lacked personal jurisdiction **{-2063-}** over it because the plaintiff 's claim had no connection to the forum. *Id.*, at 94–95. But in compliance with Missouri law, the defendant company had previously filed "a power of attorney consenting that service of process upon the superintendent [of the State's insurance department] should be deemed personal service upon the company." *Id.*, at 94. The Missouri Supreme Court construed that power of attorney as express consent to personal jurisdiction in Missouri in any case whatsoever, and this Court held that "the construction did not deprive the defendant of due process of law." *Id.*, at 95.[6]

The Court asserts that *Pennsylvania Fire* controls our decision today. I disagree. The case was "decided before this Court's transformative decision on personal jurisdiction in *International Shoe*," *BNSF*, 581 U. S., at 412, 5 Adm. R. at 5, and we have already stated that "prior decisions [that] are inconsistent with this standard . . . are overruled," *Shaffer*, 433 U. S., at 212, n. 39. *Pennsylvania Fire* fits that bill. Time and **[—178—]** again, we have reinforced that "`doing business' tests"—like those "framed before specific jurisdiction evolved in the United States"—are not a valid basis for general jurisdiction. *Daimler*, 571 U. S., at 140, n. 20. The only innovation of Pennsylvania's statute is to make "doing business" synonymous with "consent." If *Pennsylvania Fire* endorses that trick, then *Pennsylvania Fire* is no longer good law.

The plurality tries to get around *International Shoe* by claiming that it did no more than expand jurisdiction, affecting

[6] The plurality praises the Missouri Supreme Court's "carefu[l]" and "thoughtful opinion." *Ante*, at 132–133. Only a decade later, however, the same court unanimously concluded that it had misinterpreted the reach of the statute and overruled this aggressive approach. *State ex rel. Am. Central Life Ins. Co.* v. *Landwehr*, 318 Mo. 181, 190–192, 300 S. W. 294, 297–298 (1927) (requiring a connection to Missouri); *State ex rel. Phoenix Mut. Life Ins. Co. of Hartford* v. *Harris*, 343 Mo. 252, 258–260, 121 S. W. 2d 141, 145–146 (1938). This remains the rule in Missouri today: Compliance with its registration statute does not constitute consent to general jurisdiction. *State ex rel. Norfolk Southern R. Co.* v. *Dolan*, 512 S. W. 3d 41, 52–53, and n. 11 (Mo. 2017).

nothing that came before it.[7] *Ante*, at 138–139. That is as fictional as the old concept of "corporate presence" on which the plurality relies. We have previously abandoned even "ancient" bases of jurisdiction for incompatibility with *International Shoe*. *Shaffer*, 433 U. S., at 211–212 (repudiating *quasi in rem* jurisdiction). And we have repeatedly reminded litigants not to put much stock in our pre-*International Shoe* decisions. *Shaffer*, 433 U. S., at 212, n. 39; see also *BNSF*, 581 U. S., at 412, 5 Adm. R. at 5. *Daimler* itself reinforces that pre-*International Shoe* decisions "should not attract heavy reliance today." 571 U. S., at 138, n. 18. Over and over, we have reminded litigants that *International Shoe* is "canonical," "seminal," "pathmarking," and even "momentous"—to give just a few examples. *Ford Motor*, 592 U. S., at ––; *Bristol-Myers*, 582 U. S., at 262; *Daimler*, 571 U. S., at 128; *Goodyear*, 564 U. S., at 919. Yet the Court acts as if none of this ever happened. **{-2064-}**

In any event, I doubt *Pennsylvania Fire* would control this case even if it remained valid. *Pennsylvania Fire* distinguished between express consent (that is, consent "actually . . . conferred by [the] document") and deemed consent (inferred from doing business). 243 U. S., at 95–96; see **[—179—]** also *Neirbo Co.* v. *Bethlehem Shipbuilding Corp.*, 308 U. S. 165, 175 (1939) (basing jurisdiction on "finding an *actual* consent" (emphasis added)). As Judge Learned Hand emphasized in a decision invoked by the plurality, without "express consent," the normal rules apply. *Smolik* v. *Philadelphia & Reading Coal & Iron Co.*, 222 F. 148, 150–151 (SDNY 1915).

The express power of attorney in *Pennsylvania Fire* "made service on the [insurance] superintendent the equivalent of . . . a corporate vote [that] had accepted service in this specific case." 243 U. S., at 95. Norfolk Southern, by contrast, "executed no document like the power of attorney there." Brief for Respondent 31; see App. 1–7. The Court makes much of what Norfolk Southern did write on its forms, *ante*, at 135: It named a "Commercial Registered Office Provider," App. 1, 6, it notified Pennsylvania of a merger, *id.*, at 3–5, and it paid $70 to update its paperwork, *id.*, at 6. None of those documents use the word "agent," nothing hints at the word "jurisdiction," and (as the Pennsylvania Supreme Court explained) nothing about that registration is "voluntary." 266 A. 3d, at 570, and n. 20.[8] Consent in *Pennsylvania Fire* was contained in the document itself; here it is deemed by statute. If "mere formalities" matter as much as the plurality says they do, it should respect this one too. *Ante*, at 144.

IV

By now, it should be clear that the plurality's primary approach to this case is to look past our personal jurisdiction precedent. Relying on a factsheet downloaded from the internet, for instance, the plurality argues that Norfolk Southern is such a "part of 'the Pennsylvania Community,'" and **[—180—]** does so much business there, that its "presence" in Pennsylvania is enough to require it to stand for suits having nothing to do with the Commonwealth. *Ante*, at 141–143; see also *ante*, at 153–154 (opinion of Alito, J.).[9] In *Daimler*, however, we roundly rejected the plaintiff's request that we "approve the exercise of general jurisdiction in every State

[7] While *International Shoe* expanded the bases for *specific* jurisdiction, it did no such thing for *general* jurisdiction. On the contrary, *International Shoe* itself recognized that *general* jurisdiction for a corporation exists in its "'home' or principal place of business." 326 U. S. 310, 317 (1945). That line has remained constant.

[8] I agree with the Court that no "magic words" are necessary to establish valid consent. *Ante*, at 136, n. 5. But when the statutory scheme itself distinguishes between actual "consent" and registration, §§ 5301(a)(2)(i), (ii), and when the Pennsylvania Supreme Court sees a difference between the two, it is quite a stretch to treat them as one and the same.

[9] Mallory, by contrast, chooses to rest his case for jurisdiction on registration and registration alone. Tr. of Oral Arg. 49 ("We're relying on consent and consent alone. Without consent, we don't prevail"). Apparently dissatisfied with this concession, the plurality finds its own facts and develops its own argument. That is not how we usually do things. See *United States* v. *Sineneng-Smith*, 590 U. S. ––, –– – –– (2020).

in which a corporation `engages in a substantial, continuous, and systematic course of business.'" 571 U. S., at 138. The established test—which the plurality barely acknowledges—is whether the corporation is "at home" in the State. "A corporation that operates in many places," and must therefore register in just as many, "can scarcely be deemed at home in all of them." *Id.*, at 140, n. 20.

* * *

Critics of *Daimler* and *Goodyear* may be happy to see them go. See, *e. g.*, **{–2065–}** *Ford Motor*, 592 U. S., at —— (Alito, J., concurring in judgment); *id.*, at —— – —— (Gorsuch, J., joined by Thomas, J., concurring in judgment); *BNSF*, 581 U. S., at 416, 5 Adm. R. at 8 (Sotomayor, J., concurring in part and dissenting in part). And make no mistake: They are halfway out the door. If States take up the Court's invitation to manipulate registration, *Daimler* and *Goodyear* will be obsolete, and, at least for corporations, specific jurisdiction will be "superfluous." *Daimler*, 571 U. S., at 140; see *Goodyear*, 564 U. S., at 925. Because I would not work this sea change, I respectfully dissent.

This page intentionally left blank

United States Court of Appeals for the First Circuit

United States Court of Appeals
for the First Circuit

No. 21-1886

RELENTLESS, INC.
VS.
UNITED STATES DEPT. OF COMMERCE***

Appeal from the United States District Court for the District of Rhode Island

Decided: March 16, 2023

****Vacated by Relentless, Inc. v. U.S. Dept. of Commerce,* **No. 21-1886, 2024 WL 3647769 (1st Cir. Jul. 31, 2024).*****

Citation: 62 F.4th 621, 11 Adm. R. 38 (1st Cir. 2023).

Before **KAYATTA, LIPEZ,** and **THOMPSON,** Circuit Judges.

[—3—] {-624-} KAYATTA, Circuit Judge:

Charged with promoting the sustainability of the nation's fisheries, the National Marine Fisheries Service requires vessels fishing for herring on certain fishing trips to carry monitors on board. Although the government trains and certifies these monitors, it does not always pay them for their work. Instead, the vessel owners must procure and pay for certain monitors by contracting with private entities. Owners of two fishing vessels that harvest herring—plaintiffs Relentless Inc., Huntress Inc., and Seafreeze Fleet LLC—challenge the agency's authority to promulgate this requirement. The district court granted summary judgment for the government, reasoning that the rule is a permissible exercise of agency authority under the statute governing fishery stocks and conservation, that its promulgation followed proper procedures, and that it does not violate the Constitution. On appeal, **{-625-}** plaintiffs renew their attacks. Because we agree with the district court that the rule is a permissible exercise of the agency's authority and is otherwise lawful, we affirm. Our reasoning follows.

I.

A.

Atlantic herring fishing is regulated under the Magnuson-Stevens Fishery Conservation and Management Act (the "MSA"), which was enacted to respond to the threat of overfishing **[—4—]** and to promote conservation. 16 U.S.C. §§ 1801 et seq. The MSA established eight regional councils that manage the various "fisheries" (defined as "one or more stocks of fish which can be treated as a unit") in their respective regions. *Id.* §§ 1802(13)(A), 1852(a). The councils accomplish this task primarily by promulgating fishery management plans, which specify the conservation measures "necessary and appropriate" to prevent overfishing, to protect fish stocks, and to promote the sustainability of each fishery. *Id.* §§ 1852–1853. The MSA sets out elements that fishery management plans shall include, such as a description of the fishery and the optimal yield for the fishery, *id.* § 1853(a), as well as several elements that plans may include, such as requirements that vessels subject to the plan obtain permits, *id.* § 1853(b). Fishery management plans must also comply with ten "National Standards" set out in the MSA that identify broad goals and priorities such as minimizing cost, taking communities into account, prioritizing efficiency, and using the best scientific information available. *Id.* § 1851(a).

The Secretary of Commerce is tasked with reviewing each fishery management plan or amendment and publishing it along with implementing regulations for notice and comment. *Id.* § 1854(a)– b). The Secretary has delegated these responsibilities to the National Marine Fisheries Service (NMFS or the "Agency"), a division of the National Oceanic and Atmospheric Administration **[—5—]** (NOAA). Regional councils submit plans and amendments to NMFS, which publishes them for notice and comment while undertaking its own review to ensure that the plans are consistent with the MSA, its National Standards, and "any other applicable law." *Id.* § 1854(a)(1). The Agency must then approve, disapprove, or partially approve the plan or amendment. *Id.* § 1854(a)(3). Once a plan or amendment is approved, the Agency works with the regional council and completes a notice and comment procedure to issue implementing regulations. *Id.* § 1854(b).

B.

The New England Fishery Management Council ("New England Council") regulates fisheries in the Atlantic Ocean seaward of Maine, New Hampshire, Massachusetts, Rhode Island, and Connecticut. *Id.* § 1852(a)(1)(A). This includes the Atlantic herring fishery. The New England Council implemented the current fishery management plan for Atlantic herring in 2000. The plan includes an annual catch limit and restrictions on the location and timing of herring fishing. 50 C.F.R. § 648.200. The Atlantic herring fishery is subject to monitoring, including by government-funded observers using Standardized Bycatch Reporting Methodology **[—6—]** (SBRM) to measure bycatch (fish unintentionally caught) on fishing trips.[1] *Id.* § 648.11(m). **{-626-}**

In 2013, the New England Council began a process to provide for the use of industry-funded monitoring to reduce uncertainty around catch estimates. In 2017, the Council approved an Omnibus Amendment, which both provided general guidelines for industry-funded monitoring in all of its fishery management plans and specifically provided for the owners of herring vessels to bear the expense of contracting for some of the monitors engaged on their vessels. Magnuson-Stevens Fishery Conservation and Management Act Provisions; Fisheries of the Northeastern United States; Industry-Funded Monitoring, 85 Fed. Reg. 7414, 7414 (Feb. 7, 2020). The Agency approved the amendment in 2018. It published the final rule implementing the amendment and the **[—7—]** industry-funded monitoring program for the herring fishery in 2020. 85 Fed. Reg. at 7414.

The rule implementing industry-funded monitoring for the herring fishery (the "Final Rule" or "Rule") does not require monitors on all vessels. Rather, it sets a target percentage (50%) of herring trips to be monitored. *Id.* at 7417. Observer coverage required under the SBRM program, which is fully paid for by the government, counts toward this target. Additional monitoring, up to a target of 50%, is covered by industry-funded monitoring (so if SBRM observers are placed on 10% of trips, industry would be asked to pay for monitoring on an additional 40% of trips). *Id.* The Rule requires the Council to reexamine the monitoring coverage targets after two years to consider the results of increased monitoring, if any, and determine whether to make adjustments. 50 C.F.R. § 648.11(m)(1)(ii)(F). The government bears the administrative expenses associated with the program, including the training and certification of monitors. 85 Fed. Reg. at 7415.

The Rule specifies how industry-funded monitoring will work in practice. Vessels must "declare into" a fishery before beginning a fishing trip, meaning they contact NMFS and announce the species of fish they intend to harvest. 50 C.F.R. § 648.11(m)(2). When a vessel declares into the herring fishery, the Agency then informs it whether a monitor will be required for that trip. *Id.* § 648.11(m)(3). Trips may receive a waiver of the **[—8—]** monitor requirement under several circumstances: if a monitor is not available, if the vessel is carrying certain fishing gear only and does not intend to carry fish, or if the vessel

[1] The MSA requires that all fishery management plans "establish a standardized reporting methodology to assess the amount and type of bycatch occurring in the fishery." 16 U.S.C. § 1853(a)(11). The New England Council, along with the Mid-Atlantic Council, developed an SBRM omnibus amendment in 2015 that implements this requirement. Magnuson-Stevens Fishery Conservation and Management Act Provisions; Fisheries of the Northeastern United States; Standardized Bycatch Reporting Methodology Omnibus Amendment, 80 Fed. Reg. 37,182 (June 30, 2015); 50 C.F.R. § 648.18. The methodology in that omnibus amendment, which is primarily implemented through the Northeast Fisheries Observer Program placement of observers on vessels, applies to several fisheries, including the herring fishery. 50 C.F.R. § 648.18. Although the SBRM has been heavily litigated, *see Oceana, Inc. v. Ross*, 920 F.3d 855, 859–60 (D.C. Cir. 2019), it is not at issue in this appeal.

intends to catch less than 50 metric tons of herring on the trip. *Id.* § 648.11(m)(1)(ii)(D)–(E), (4)(ii). Vessels using certain types of gear are exempt from the requirement to carry a monitor altogether if they use electronic monitoring and portside sampling instead. *Id.* § 648.11(m)(1)(iii).

When a nonexempt vessel that does not meet the criteria for a waiver declares into the herring fishery, the Agency will inform the vessel whether it needs to carry a monitor for that trip. If so, the vessel must contact one of the private entities that provide certified monitors, and pay that entity its resulting fees and expenses. *Id.* § 648.11(m)(4). If the vessel cannot find a **{-627-}** monitor after contacting all available providers, it may ask for a waiver. *Id.*

The precise cost of the industry-funded monitoring program to vessels participating in the herring fishery is unclear. In its notice publishing the Final Rule, the Agency cautioned that "the economic impact of industry-funded monitoring coverage on the herring fishery is difficult to estimate," because it would vary with "sampling costs, fishing effort, SBRM coverage, price of herring, and participation in other fisheries." 85 Fed. Reg. at 7420. The agency also noted that the Environmental Assessment **[—9—]** estimated "industry's cost for at-sea monitoring coverage at $710 per day," although this figure would "largely depend on negotiated costs between vessels and monitoring service providers." *Id.* The Agency further acknowledged that the Rule could reduce vessel returns-to-owner (gross profits minus fixed and operational costs) by around 20%. In total, the New England Council recognized in its amendment adopting the herring plan that "the impacts of [the Rule] on fishery-related businesses and human communities are negative and result from reductions in returns-to-owner."

C.

Plaintiffs participate in the herring fishery using small-mesh bottom trawl gear. They also participate in the mackerel, butterfish, and squid fisheries. Able to freeze fish at sea, their vessels make longer trips, but also have less processing capacity per day (125,000 pounds of fish per day, they state, which equals approximately 57 metric tons) and higher overhead costs than other herring vessels. Plaintiffs' style of fishing also means that they can choose what to catch at sea, so they often declare into multiple fisheries before leaving the dock in order to catch whatever they encounter on the trip.

Plaintiffs assert that due to their unique fishing style, they are disproportionately burdened by carrying monitors, because they make longer trips (during which they may not even **[—10—]** catch herring) and therefore need to pay a monitor for more days at sea. They also claim that they cannot avail themselves of any of the exceptions to having to carry monitors under the Rule because of their style of fishing. In particular, they focus on the exemption for trips taking less than 50 metric tons of herring. While most herring trips only last 2–4 days, the vessels claim, their trips last 10–14 days. So although they may catch less than 50 metric tons of herring every 2–4 days, they might catch far more herring in a single trip, and thus cannot use the exemption that is available for shorter trips despite having a similar catch per day..

Plaintiffs therefore have a strong incentive to challenge the Rule. They argue that it is not authorized by the MSA, is arbitrary and capricious in violation of the Administrative Procedure Act (APA), violates the National Standards set forth in the MSA, violates the Regulatory Flexibility Act ("RFA"), and violates the Commerce Clause. Defendants (the Agency, along with the Secretary of Commerce, NOAA, and the Administrators of the Agency) disagree on all counts.

The district court granted summary judgment for the Agency. The court found that the MSA is ambiguous regarding authorization for industry-paid monitors, and that under *Chevron U.S.A., Inc. v. Natural Resources Defense Council, Inc.*, 467 U.S. 837 (1984), the Agency's interpretation is entitled to deference. **[—11—]** It further found that the Rule does not violate any of the National Standards found in the MSA, and also does not violate the RFA because the Agency issued a regulatory flexibility analysis {-628-} that indicates it considered plaintiffs' concerns, satisfying the statute's procedural require-ments.[2] Finally, the court found that the Rule does not violate the Commerce Clause, because it does not force plaintiffs to enter the market for monitors.

II.

We review the district court's grant of summary judgment de novo. *Lovgren v. Locke*, 701 F.3d 5, 20 (1st Cir. 2012). Judicial review of agency actions under the MSA is governed by the APA. *Id.*; 16 U.S.C. § 1855(f). We may set aside an agency action only if it is "arbitrary, capricious, an abuse of discretion, or otherwise not in accordance with law." *Lovgren*, 701 F.3d at 20 (quoting 5 U.S.C. § 706(2)(A)). Our review is limited to the administrative record. *Id.*

At issue here, principally, is the interpretation of the MSA. Plaintiffs challenge the Agency's authoritative interpretation of the statute as granting it the power to enact the Rule. In considering such a challenge, we employ "the familiar *Chevron* two-step analysis." *Bais Yaakov of Spring Valley v. ACT,* **[—12—]** *Inc.*, 12 F.4th 81, 86 (1st Cir. 2021). "First, always, is the question whether Congress has directly spoken to the precise question at issue. If the intent of Congress is clear, that is the end of the matter . . . ." *Id.* (quoting *Chevron*, 467 U.S. at 842). Second, "[i]f the statute is silent or ambiguous with respect to the specific issue, the question for the court is whether the agency's answer is based on a permissible construction of the statute." *Bais Yaakov*, 12 F.4th at 86 (quoting *Chevron*, 467 U.S. at 843).

In determining whether a statute has clearly spoken to the question at issue, we "apply the 'ordinary tools of statutory construction.'" *Flock v. U.S. Dep't of Transp.*, 840 F.3d 49, 55 (1st Cir. 2016) (quoting *City of Arlington v. FCC*, 569 U.S. 290, 296 (2013)). Further, "a reviewing court should not confine itself to examining a particular statutory provision in isolation." *Nat'l Ass'n of Home Builders v. Defs. of Wildlife*, 551 U.S. 644, 666 (2007) (quoting *FDA v. Brown & Williamson Tobacco Corp.*, 529 U.S. 120, 132 (2000)). Rather, "the words of a statute must be read in their context and with a view to their place in the overall statutory scheme." *Id.* (quoting *Brown & Williamson*, 529 U.S. at 132–33). If, after using these tools, we find that there is still relevant ambiguity, "we typically interpret it as granting the agency leeway to enact rules that are reasonable in light of the **[—13—]** text, nature, and purpose of the statute." *Cuozzo Speed Techs. v. Lee*, 579 U.S. 261, 277 (2016).

With these principles in mind, we turn to plaintiffs' challenges to the Agency's authority under the MSA to promulgate the Rule. Plaintiffs argue generally that the MSA does not authorize the Rule, and specifically that other provisions of the MSA establishing fee programs make clear that the Agency has no authority to require industry-funded monitoring in this instance. They further argue that the legislative history and definitions in the MSA support their position.

A.

Plaintiffs' primary contention is that the MSA does not authorize industry-funded **{-629-}** monitoring and that the Agency therefore exceeded its statutory authority in promulgating the Rule. This argument faces an uphill textual climb. Congress expressly provided that fishery management plans may "require that one or more observers be carried on board a vessel of the United States engaged in fishing for species that are subject to the plan, for the purpose of collecting data necessary for the conservation and management of the fishery." 16 U.S.C. § 1853(b)(8).

But, say plaintiffs, "at-sea monitors"—as the term is used in the industry-funded monitoring program—are something entirely different than the "observers" authorized by section 1853(b)(8). We disagree. The statutory definition of **[—14—]** "observers" in the MSA is quite broad and includes "any person required or authorized to be carried on a vessel for

[2] The district court also found that the Rule did not violate the APA because the comment periods for an amendment and its implementing rule overlapped. Plaintiffs do not challenge this finding on appeal.

conservation and management purposes by regulations or permits under this [Act]." 16 U.S.C. § 1802(31). This certainly includes at-sea monitors, who are authorized by regulation to be carried on a vessel to collect data for conservation purposes. 50 C.F.R. § 648.11(m)(1)(i) (requiring at-sea monitors to be carried on Atlantic herring vessels); *id.* § 648.2 (defining "observer or monitor" as "any person authorized by NMFS to collect . . . operational fishing data [or] biological data . . . for conservation and management purposes"). The narrow differentiation in the notice promulgating the Final Rule, which at one point notes that at-sea monitors, "in contrast to observers," would not collect whole specimens, 85 Fed. Reg. at 7418, does not mean that at-sea monitors do not form a subset of "observers." Rather, it simply acknowledges that the set of observers is broader than that subset. In short, the MSA explicitly provides for the placement of at-sea monitors on fishing vessels.

Plaintiffs are thus left to argue that Congress somehow conditioned the Agency's right to require monitors on the Agency paying for the cost of the monitors. And this is indeed plaintiffs' most prominently presented argument: Because the statute, they contend, contains no language allowing the Agency to **[—15—]** force plaintiffs to pay for those monitors, the Agency lacks the authority to require any such payments (meaning there will be no monitors on board unless the government pays for the monitors). There are two defects with this argument.

1.

First, the "default norm" as "manifest without express statement in literally hundreds of regulations, is that the government does not reimburse regulated entities for the cost of complying with properly enacted regulations, at least short of a taking. If this statute needs clarification on this point, then so too do hundreds of others." *Goethel v. U.S. Dep't of Com.*, 854 F.3d 106, 117–18, 5 Adm. R. 21, 30 (1st Cir. 2017) (Kayatta, J., concurring). When Congress says that an agency may require a business to do "X," and is silent as to who pays for "X," one expects that the regulated parties will cover the cost of "X."

Plaintiffs insist that the requirement to pay for a monitor does not fall into this default norm because it is not a "traditional regulatory cost" and differs from an ordinary instance of requiring a regulated party to bear its own costs. The daily salary of a monitor, they assert, differs from the cost inflicted by other regulatory requirements, such as those mandating permits or particular fishing equipment, in both type (because it pays for a credentialed individual, rather than a thing or a piece of gear) and degree (because it is larger). Moreover, **[—16—]** they argue, the compliance cost the MSA inflicts (and that the **{-630-}** Agency should try to reduce per the statute) is represented by the room fishers make available on their vessels to physically host observers—something far short of paying an at-sea monitor's salary.

To a regulated party, paying the expenses of a credentialed at-sea monitor may well seem different than paying, for example, a vendor who provides fishing gear mandated by a regulation,[3] or for an EPA-required scrubber or monitoring device on a smoke stack.[4] But plaintiffs offer no authority indicating that these differences are material to the question of who pays. To the extent they also argue that the monitors present a different type of costs because they are "federal officers," we disagree. *See infra*, Section II.B. We therefore see no reason why the default rule does not apply: When Congress expressly authorized **[—17—]**

[3] *See* 16 U.S.C. § 1853(b)(4) (allowing fishery management plans to "prohibit, limit, condition, or require the use of specified types and quantities of fishing gear"); 50 C.F.R. § 622.188 (requiring certain types of gear in order to possess South Atlantic snapper-grouper).

[4] *See* 42 U.S.C. § 7412(d)(2) (requiring EPA to promulgate standards "requir[ing] the maximum degree of reduction in emissions of the hazardous air pollutants subject to this section"); 40 C.F.R. § 61.122 (defining emission standard from kilns at elemental phosphorous plants, and noting that compliance will be shown if certain scrubbers are installed and operated); *id.* § 61.126 (requiring owner or operator of source "using a wet-scrubbing emission control device" to "install, calibrate, maintain, and operate a monitoring device").

plans promulgated under the MSA to require vessels to carry an observer, it presumed that the vessels' owners would bear the cost of compliance, much like an SEC requirement to submit independently audited financials imposes on the regulated entity the cost of paying an independent accountant. *See* 15 U.S.C. § 77aa (25)–(27).

Nor are we persuaded that the cost of an at-sea monitor is different than other compliance costs because it may be greater than fees imposed elsewhere in the statute. The vessels decry that they may be subject to costs of up to 20% of returns-to-owner, while in other fishery programs, fees for observers are capped at 2% or 3%. But the fact that costs of complying with one regulatory requirement are greater than the costs of complying with another regulatory requirement does not mean that the former is unlawful.[5] Nor do we have here any costs that are so great as to cause us to think that Congress without so stating did not presume that they would be borne by the regulated entities. **[—18—]**

2.

Adding belt to suspenders, the government points out that the statutory support for its position need not rely only on the implication raised by the default norm. Section 1858(g)(1)(D) in the MSA allows the Agency to suspend or revoke the license of any vessel if any "payment required for observer services provided to or contracted by the owner or operator [of the vessel] . . . has not been paid and is overdue." 16 U.S.C. § 1858(g)(1)(D). This **{-631-}** penalty would make no sense if Congress did not anticipate that owners and/or operators of the vessels would be paying the observers.

Plaintiffs concede that Congress expected that some vessels would have to pay for monitors, but they argue that that expectation was limited to payments required in a few specific instances elsewhere in the MSA in which Congress expressly authorized the imposition of monitor costs on vessels (more on these instances later). But the provision penalizing the nonpayment of observers appears in a general part of the MSA applicable to all fisheries and fishery management plans, rather than in the specific provisions creating particular fee programs. If Congress had meant to apply this provision only to certain fee programs, it likely would have included it in the sections creating those programs. Or it would have cross-referenced the specific statutes creating fee programs in the penalty provision. *See Silva* **[—19—]** *v. Garland*, 27 F.4th 95, 103–04 (1st Cir. 2022) (interpreting statutory language broadly, rather than as limited by other statutes, when potentially limiting statutes were not cross-referenced in the broader statute).

The D.C. Circuit, which recently considered a similar challenge to the very same Rule, relied on just such reasoning in rejecting plaintiffs' position that the penalty provisions apply only to a few statutorily specified fee programs. *Loper Bright Enters. v. Raimondo*, 45 F.4th 359, 368, 10 Adm. R. 488, 492 (D.C. Cir. 2022) (reasoning that "the penalties in a broadly applicable section of the [MSA] appear to recognize the possibility of industry-contracted and funded observers beyond [a single] context"). That court sensibly observed that "[i]f Congress had intended for penalties associated with industry-funded monitoring to apply only in in the foreign fishing context, the court would expect that Congress in the penalty provisions would have specifically referenced foreign vessels or included a cross-reference to the foreign fishing provision." *Id.*, 10 Adm. R. at 492.

---

[5] It is not clear that the plaintiffs will face a 20% reduction in their returns-to-owner. The Final Rule states that the monitoring program "has the potential to reduce annual [returns-to-owner] . . . up to 20 percent." But that figure represents an estimate across all types of fishing equipment; the New England Council's Omnibus Amendment shows that for small-mesh bottom trawl vessels, the type of gear Relentless uses, median returns to owner were expected to be reduced only by 5.4%. Applied only to vessels that take more than 50 metric tons of herring per trip, returns to owner could be reduced even less, by a median of 2.5%.

B.

In an effort to rebut the clear textual support for the Agency's lawful authority to require the vessel owners to pay for at-sea monitors, plaintiffs point to other sections of the MSA that expressly authorize the imposition of fees to be paid to the government to cover certain observer costs. Plaintiffs ask us to **[—20—]** reason that because Congress expressly authorized the imposition of fees in three instances, its failure to do so in the instance of observer costs under section 1853(b)(8) must mean that no such costs can be imposed on plaintiffs. They also suggest that to read the MSA as authorizing industry-funded monitoring would render those other fee provisions superfluous, a result we usually try to avoid.

The instances to which plaintiffs point in which the MSA expressly provides for payments of a cost by the vessels are as follows: First, section 1853a authorizes and sets requirements for Limited Access Privilege Programs (LAPPs) to be created in certain fisheries. To support a LAPP, a Council may "provide . . . for a program of fees paid by limited access privilege holders that will cover the costs of management, data collection and analysis, and enforcement activities." 16 U.S.C. § 1853a(e)(2). Second, section 1862(a) allows the North Pacific Council to prepare a "fisheries research plan" for any fishery within its jurisdiction except a salmon fishery. Such plans may require that observers be stationed on vessels, and "establish[] a system . . . of fees." *Id.* § 1862(a)(1)–(2). Third, section 1827(d) imposes fees "in an amount sufficient to cover **{-632-}** all of the costs of providing an observer aboard that vessel" on foreign fishing vessels in certain circumstances which may result in the incidental taking of billfish. *Id.* § 1827(d). Plaintiffs contend that these **[—21—]** are the only instances in which industry vessels may be required to pay for observers.

This argument falters at the threshold because this is not a case in which the agency need rely only on the default presumption that a regulated party presumably bears its own costs. To the contrary, as we have described in Part II.A.2 of this opinion, the statutory text provides affirmative confirmation that Congress presumed that vessel owners would bear the cost of complying with monitoring requirements. So plaintiffs' effort to use these examples to negate reliance on statutory silence is inapt, or at least insufficient. In any event, the three instances to which plaintiffs point do not present apples-to-apples comparators from which one can infer that anything mentioned in those instances but not in the general observer provision was intentionally omitted from the latter.

First and foremost, no money is paid into government coffers under the industry-funded monitoring program. Instead, vessels are required to obtain and pay for a service from a nongovernmental source, just as they would have to pay for a certain type of fishing gear. As the *Loper Bright* court explained, the fact that Congress instituted a "different funding mechanism" in the North Pacific fishery and for LAPPs, where funds are collected by the Agency and deposited into the Treasury, does not indicate **[—22—]** that Congress intended to preclude the entirely different mechanism of industry-funded monitoring. 45 F.4th at 367–68, 10 Adm. R. at 491–92.

Moreover, the North Pacific and LAPP programs are further distinguishable because the fees fund agency programs that include more than direct observer costs. *See, e.g.*, 16 U.S.C. § 1854(d)(2)(A) (allowing fee "to recover the actual costs directly related to the management, data collection, and enforcement of any limited access privilege program," without limiting fee to payment for observers); Fisheries of the Northeastern United States; Amendment 17 to the Atlantic Surfclam and Ocean Quahog Fishery Management Plan, 81 Fed. Reg. 38,969, 38971 (June 15, 2016) (in responding to comment regarding cost recovery program for LAPP, noting that recoverable costs through fee "would include the costs of issuing and renewing ITQ permits, processing cage tag transfers, and tracking cage tag usage"); 16 U.S.C. § 1862(b)(2)(A) (providing that fees not exceed "the combined cost" of stationing observers, "inputting collected data," and assessing the necessity of a risk-sharing pool); Groundfish Fisheries of the

Exclusive Economic Zone off Alaska and Pacific Halibut Fisheries; Observer Program, 77 Fed. Reg. 23,326, 23,339 (April 18, 2012) (explaining that in North Pacific fee program which was eventually adopted, "[o]bserver fees would not be linked to the actual level of observer coverage for individual vessels and plants," but rather "each participant" would pay the **[—23—]** same percentage regardless of when it carried observers). In the industry-funded monitoring program at issue here, by contrast, the Agency must pay its own administrative costs and vessels only pay for observers they actually carry. As for the third instance—fees imposed on foreign vessels for observer costs—the placement of observers is authorized under a different provision than the one relied on by the Agency, because section 1853(b)(8) authorizes observers only on board "vessel[s] of the United States." But even putting that aside, one can easily see why Congress might opt for a direct fee rather than **{–633–}** relying on foreign owners to arrange for observers themselves. With treaties, international agreements, and foreign relations at stake, it makes sense that Congress would have opted for extra specificity.[6] **[—24—]**

Plaintiffs also contend that the costs under the Final Rule are actually fees paid to the Agency. To build this argument, they claim that privately contracted monitors are government employees or agents. To that end, plaintiffs describe the monitors engaged by private companies as "federal officers." To justify this relabeling, the plaintiffs point to a penalty provision which provides that interfering with an "observer" or "data collector" is prohibited by federal law, 16 U.S.C. § 1857(1)(L), as well as a decision upholding a conviction for sexually harassing an at-sea monitor in violation of this law. *See United States v. Cusick*, No. 11-cr-10066, 2012 WL 442005, at *6 (D. Mass. Feb. 9, 2012). But, establishing that Congress intended to deter the harassment of monitors falls well short of establishing that Congress intended to turn those monitors into "federal officers." And the MSA expressly distinguishes the provision that prohibits assaulting "any observer" or "data collector," 16 U.S.C. § 1857(1)(L), from a provision prohibiting similar actions against "officer[s]," *id.* § 1857(1)(D)-(F).

C.

Finally, plaintiffs argue that the legislative history confirms their preferred interpretation of the statute. They note that amendments to the MSA enacted in 1990, which added the fee provisions for observers in the North Pacific, indicated that "nothing in [that] section should be construed as affecting the **[—25—]** rights and responsibilities of other Regional Fishery Management Councils." H.R. Rep. No. 101-393, at 31 (1989). We have already explained why the industry-funded monitoring program at issue here does not impose a fee. And in rejecting plaintiffs' challenge to the observer rule, we do not (nor did the Agency) rely on any contention that anything in that section altered another Council's rights and responsibilities by granting new authority to require plaintiffs to carry observers on board. To the contrary, the Councils already had that authority, as acknowledged in the very legislative history on which plaintiffs rely. *See* H.R. Rep. No. 101-393, at 28 (1989) (stating that "the Councils already have -- and have used -- such authority" to require that observers be carried on board).[7]

---

[6] In their reply brief, plaintiffs also point to section 1821(h)(6), which provides that if there are insufficient appropriations to station an observer on each foreign vessel, the Secretary shall "establish a reasonable schedule of fees that certified observers or their agents shall be paid" by foreign fishing vessel operators. 16 U.S.C. § 1821(h)(6). As an initial matter, this argument was raised for the first time on reply, and absent exceptional circumstances we consider it waived. *See Gottlieb v. Amica Mut. Ins.*, 57 F.4th 1, 11 (1st Cir. 2022). Even if we were to consider this argument, we would not find that this provision renders the Agency's interpretation unreasonable. It makes sense that Congress would provide more detail in a sensitive area (foreign relations) where it wanted to ensure observer coverage, rather than leaving such coverage to the discretion of the Agency or a regional Council. Such a provision does not suggest that Congress did not delegate authority to the Agency to require industry-funded monitoring in other instances. *See Loper Bright*, 45 F.4th at 367–68, 10 Adm. R. at 491–92.

[7] The Agency also points to regulations that implement industry-funded monitoring in other fisheries. *See, e.g.*, 50 C.F.R. § 648.11(k)(4)-(5) (sea

***

In sum, we have no trouble finding that the Agency's interpretation of its authority **{-634-}** to require at-sea monitors who are paid for by owners of regulated vessels does not "exceed[] the bounds of the permissible." *Barnhardt v. Walton*, 535 U.S. 212, 218 (2002). We need not decide whether we classify this conclusion as a product of *Chevron* step one or step two. Congress expressly authorized NMFS to require vessels to carry monitors. And at the **[—26—]** very least, it is certainly reasonable for the Agency to conclude that its exercise of that authority is not contingent on its payment of the costs of compliance.

III.

Having found that the MSA authorizes the adoption of a rule requiring vessels to procure at their expense the services of an at-sea monitor, we now consider plaintiffs' other challenges to the Agency's decision process and procedure in adopting the Rule.

A.

Plaintiffs argue that the Rule is arbitrary and capricious because it allows for waivers for trips on which a vessel plans to catch less than 50 metric tons of herring. This exemption benefits mostly small mesh bottom trawlers and single midwater trawlers that make short trips and plan on catches of less than 50 metric tons of herring. Plaintiffs point out that their larger scale operation, having the capacity to freeze and hold more fish, catches around 50 metric tons per day but may harvest many more tons than that on a per-trip basis. Hence, the waiver is practically unavailable to them. The result, they argue, is that plaintiffs would have to pay for an at-sea monitor on a single 14-day trip in which they catch 343 metric tons of herring, but a hypothetical smaller boat catching 49 metric tons on each of seven back-to-back 2-day trips (for a total of the same 343 metric tons) would not have to pay for a monitor at all. Additionally, **[—27—]** the flexibility to stay at sea for longer means that plaintiffs declare into multiple fisheries before leaving the dock, which means they may declare that they will catch herring but not actually take any herring. Thus, not only can they not use the exemption, but they may be forced to pay for a herring monitor on a trip where no herring is caught. Plaintiffs argue that these features render the Rule and the exemptions arbitrary and capricious.

"The scope of review under the 'arbitrary and capricious' standard is narrow and a court is not to substitute its judgment for that of the agency." *Sorreda Transp., LLC v. DOT*, 980 F.3d 1, 3 (1st Cir. 2020) (quoting *Motor Vehicle Mfrs. Ass'n v. State Farm Mut. Auto. Ins. Co.*, 463 U.S. 29, 43 (1983)). Under this deferential standard, "[a]n agency rule is arbitrary and capricious if the agency lacks a rational basis for adopting it -- for example, if the agency relied on improper factors, failed to consider pertinent aspects of the problem, offered a rationale contradicting the evidence before it, or reached a conclusion so implausible that it cannot be attributed to a difference of opinion **[—28—]** or the application of agency expertise." *Associated Fisheries of Me., Inc. v. Daley*, 127 F.3d 104, 109 (1st Cir. 1997).

Here, the Agency expressly considered plaintiffs' objections and rejected them. It stated:

> In an effort to minimize the economic impact of industry-funded monitoring, the Council explicitly considered measures to address Seafreeze's concern about disproportional impacts on its vessels, including considering alternatives for coverage waivers for trips when landings would be less than 20-percent herring or less than 50 mt of herring per **{-635-}** day. Ultimately, the Council determined that the potential for a relatively high herring catches per trip aboard those vessels warranted additional monitoring and chose the 50 mt per trip threshold.

85 Fed. Reg. at 7426. The Agency also found it highly unlikely that plaintiffs would be paying as much as they claimed for trips that did not

scallop vessels required to carry observers must arrange and pay for those observers).

take herring, based on cost estimates contained in the Environmental Assessment. *Id.* So plaintiffs cannot argue that the Agency failed to consider their objections.[8] Nor do they develop any contention that the explanation given by the agency relied on any factors prohibited by Congress or ran counter to the available evidence.

And the rationale given by the Agency -- "that the potential for a relatively high herring catches per trip aboard those vessels warranted additional monitoring" -- does not strike **[—29—]** us as "so implausible that it cannot be attributed to a difference in view or the applicable agency expertise." *Associated Fisheries of Me.*, 127 F.3d at 109. To the contrary, determinations as to whether monitoring will be more effective on a per-trip basis or per-day basis seem squarely within the expertise of the Agency. Although we agree that the Agency could have provided a more thorough explanation than it did, we do not find the per-trip waiver to be arbitrary and capricious on its face. Certainly, one can see why monitoring per trip rather than per day may be easier to administer, and why plaintiffs' uncertainty about how much herring they will decide to catch might counsel for including a monitor rather than not. *See id.* at 111 ("Whether or not we, if writing on a pristine page, would have reached the same set of conclusions is not the issue. What matters is that the administrative judgment, right or wrong, derives from the record, possesses a rational basis, and evinces no mistake of law.")

B.

Plaintiffs further contend that the Rule violates several National Standards contained in the MSA. All fishery management plans must be consistent with ten National Standards, which "are broadly worded statements of the MSA's objectives for all fishery conservation and management measures." *Lovgren*, 701 F.3d at 32. "The purposes of the national standards are many, and can be in tension with one another." *Id.* As such, "we will uphold **[—30—]** a regulation against a claim of inconsistency with a 'national standard' under § 1851 if the [Agency] had a 'rational basis' for it." *Id.* (quoting *Or. Trollers Ass'n v. Gutierrez*, 452 F.3d 1104, 1119 (9th Cir. 2006)).

First, plaintiffs allege that the Rule violates National Standard One (which requires plans to "prevent overfishing while achieving, on a continuing basis, the optimum yield from each fishery," 16 U.S.C. § 1851(a)(1)) because it disproportionately burdens them although they take less bycatch and herring than other types of trawlers, and because it allows boats taking more herring to harvest without monitors. The government counters that the purpose of the industry-funded monitoring requirement -- more accurately tracking catch -- will allow better calibration of regulation, and thus furthers the goals of National Standard One. We agree that the rule implementing industry-funded monitoring is consistent with the Standard for this reason. The district court also pointed out that plaintiffs' argument here relates to the distribution of herring catch between vessels, not the optimum yield for the fishery as a whole. This mismatch between plaintiffs' complaint and the actual **{-636-}** subject of the Standard further renders their challenge under National Standard One unavailing.

Second, plaintiffs allege that the Rule violates National Standard Two, which requires that plans "be based upon **[—31—]** the best scientific information available," 16 U.S.C. § 1851(a)(2), because it burdens them without "scientific evidence of clear increase in Atlantic herring stocks" as a result of the Rule. But they do not actually allege that the Agency ignored specific scientific data or point to better data available. "If no one proposed anything better, then what is available is the best." *Massachusetts ex rel. Div. of Marine Fisheries v. Daley*, 170 F.3d 23, 30 (1st Cir. 1999). National Standard Two does not require the Agency to wait to regulate because it does not have certain data. *See* 50 C.F.R. § 600.315(e)(2) ("The fact that scientific information concerning a fishery is incomplete

[8] Plaintiffs presented no evidence that their hypothetical scenarios actually occur.

does not prevent the preparation or implementation of an FMP."). Nor does it prohibit an agency from regulating in the face of some uncertainty about the effects of its chosen rule. *See Coastal Conservation Ass'n v. U.S. Dep't of Com.*, 846 F.3d 99, 109, 5 Adm. R. 185, 190 (5th Cir. 2017) (explaining that where economic impacts of rule were uncertain because they depended on the choices of several parties, "[t]he National Standards [did] not require analysis of unpredictable, and thus unavailable, data"). Where, as here, plaintiffs point to no data they say should have been considered or relied upon -- and where the very purpose of the Rule is to gather better data to be used in future fishery management -- we find that the regulation complies with National Standard Two. *See Massachusetts ex rel. Div. of Marine Fisheries*, 170 F.3d at 30; **[—32—]** *see also Coastal Conservation Ass'n*, 846 F.3d at 109, 5 Adm. R. at 190 (finding that National Standard Two was not violated where no one pointed to data that Secretary had ignored, and citing cases doing the same).

The Rule also does not violate National Standard Six (which requires the Agency to account for "variations among, and contingencies in, fisheries, fishery resources, and catches," 16 U.S.C. § 1851(a)(6)). The regulations implementing this National Standard focus on maintaining flexibility to adjust to uncertainty or changed circumstances. 50 C.F.R. § 600.335; *see J.H. Miles & Co. v. Brown*, 910 F. Supp. 1138, 1155 (E.D. Va. 1995) ("National Standard Six, on its face, dictates flexibility on the part of fishery managers. It suggests that the Secretary and his designees must be prepared to address uncertainties or changes that might arise."). Plaintiffs' challenge has nothing to do with flexibility to adjust to changing circumstances, but rather protests that the Rule does not adequately take their unique style of fishing or community into account. As with their challenge based on National Standard One, this mismatch between what the Standard requires and the nature of Plaintiffs' challenge renders their complaints unavailing. We do not see anything in the National Standard that requires the Agency to change its regulations to eliminate all differential impacts on all of the varied types of vessels. *See Ace Lobster Co. v. Evans*, 165 F. Supp. 2d 148, 182 (D.R.I. 2001) ("There is no requirement in national standard 6 or anywhere else **[—33—]** in the statute that defendant finely attune its regulations to each and every fishing vessel in the offshore fishery.").

Finally, the Rule does not violate National Standards Seven and Eight, which require the Agency to consider fishery resources and cost burdens. *See* 16 U.S.C. § 1851(a)(7) (plans "shall, where practicable, minimize costs and avoid unnecessary duplication"); *id.* § 1851(a)(8)) (plans shall "utiliz[e] economic and social **{-637-}** data . . . to (A) provide for the sustained participation of such communities, and (B) to the extent practicable, minimize adverse economic impacts on such communities"). Plaintiffs argue that the Rule violates these standards because their boats bear heavier regulatory burdens than other boats. As a result, they claim, National Standard Seven "has been completely ignored," and National Standard Eight "has been violated in the same way" because "Appellants are not more damaging" to the fishery, but their community bears the brunt of severe impacts.

Our precedent suggests that "the required analysis of alternatives and impacts [under National Standard 8] is subject to a rule of reason, for study could go on forever." *Little Bay Lobster Co. v. Evans*, 352 F.3d 462, 470 (1st Cir. 2003). "About the best a court can do is ask whether the [Agency] has examined the impacts of, and alternatives to, the plan [it] ultimately adopts and whether a challenged failure to carry the analysis **[—34—]** further is clearly unreasonable, taking account of the usual considerations . . . ." *Id.* Moreover, we are mindful that "the plain language of [National Standard] 8 and its advisory guidelines make clear that these obligations are subordinate to the MSA's overarching conservation goals." *Lovgren*, 701 F.3d at 35.

Here, the Agency has done what is required under National Standards Seven and Eight. The National Standards require consideration, not adoption, of alternatives; they also require the Agency to minimize costs "where practicable," not to eliminate cost burdens entirely. The Agency considered various coverage targets to meet its goal of gathering additional data, balanced those targets with costs, and selected a 50% monitoring target. Similarly, it adopted a waiver for boats taking less than 50 metric tons of herring per trip, after considering and rejecting Relentless' proposed alternative waiver. 85 Fed. Reg. at 7425–26. The New England Council's Omnibus Amendment also considered in detail the economic impacts to industry participants using various gear types. The Agency explained how exemptions for vessels catching below a certain weight threshold per trip would minimize cost impacts. 85 Fed. Reg. at 7430. Nothing in our prior opinions suggests that the National Standards require that cost and community impacts, even those disproportionately borne by some regulated parties, must be eliminated or distributed exactly **[—35—]** evenly under National Standards Seven and Eight among those who employ different methods of fishing.

Plaintiffs' challenges under each of the National Standards boil down to arguments that the Rule burdens them more heavily than it burdens others without a clear enough justification, or without adopting an alternative they suggested. But they have not proffered the types of evidence or argument under which courts have found that agency actions violate the National Standards. For example, they do not argue that the differential treatment of different fishers under the Rule was based not on scientific data, but on political compromise. *See Hadaja, Inc. v. Evans*, 263 F. Supp. 2d 346, 354 (D.R.I. 2003); *Hall v. Evans*, 165 F. Supp. 2d 114, 136 (D.R.I. 2001). They also cannot show that no reason was given either for the Rule itself or for the scope of the exceptions. *See Massachusetts ex rel. Div. of Marine Fisheries*, 170 F.3d at 31–32; *Hall*, 165 F. Supp. 2d at 137–38. The Agency gave reasons for adopting the Rule and the waivers; the fact that those reasons were unsatisfactory to these plaintiffs does not mean that the Rule violates the National Standards.

This is not to say that the Rule, or the Agency's explanation for it, is a model of **{-638-}** clarity. Plaintiffs point out several features of the Rule (for example, the hypothetical ability of a boat to take more overall herring with no monitoring under the structure of the exemptions) that might cause one to wonder if **[—36—]** the Agency could have tailored the rule more precisely or chosen a different alternative. But adoption of the Rule, and consideration of alternatives, was the Agency's prerogative; it met its obligations to respond to comments and explain the reason for the Rule's adoption and structure. Plaintiffs' criticisms that the Rule does not account for peculiarities of their specific businesses under all hypothetical scenarios do not convince us that the Rule violates the National Standards.

C.

Plaintiffs also contend that the Rule violates the RFA, which requires agencies to consider the effects of their actions on small businesses. *Associated Fisheries of Me.*, 127 F.3d at 110, 116. Agencies must publish interim and final regulatory flexibility analyses in the Federal Register along with Notices of Proposed Rulemaking, and make them available for comment in the same way. 5 U.S.C. §§ 603–04. These analyses are reviewable under the APA in a similar manner to final agency actions. *Id.* § 611.

Here, the Final Rule states that the Agency considered the impact of the Rule on small businesses, and, to address that impact, set the monitoring target at 50% of trips (rather than 75% or 100%) and allowed waivers on certain types of trips. 85 Fed. Reg. at 7429–30. Plaintiffs argue that the Agency nonetheless violated the RFA because it did not consider the effect of its actions on, or include recommendations to assist, businesses that **[—37—]** freeze catch at sea like themselves. They also argue that the Agency did not adequately respond to comments in response to the RFA, did not consider data regarding a drop in fishermen, and did not make a plan to ensure monitors are allocated fairly across the fleet.

The RFA "does not alter the substantive mission of the agencies" but creates "procedural obligations." *Little Bay Lobster*, 352 F.3d at 470–71. The Agency met those here. The Agency explained potential impacts on small businesses and accordingly described how it mitigated those impacts, largely by setting the monitoring coverage target at 50% and by setting a weight threshold for monitored trips that would exempt many small businesses from the requirement to carry a monitor. 85 Fed. Reg. at 7429–30. The Agency also explained why it disagreed that small businesses would be forced out of fishing. Finally, as discussed above, it explained why it did not adopt alternative measures that Relentless suggested. 75 Fed. Reg. at 7426. Plaintiffs' suggestion that the Agency could have done more to respond to their specific concerns is not without some appeal. But the RFA only required the Agency to consider and respond to comments and to evaluate the impact of its action on small businesses. It did so here. *See Little Bay Lobster*, 352 F.3d at 471 (noting that "there is no requirement as to the amount of detail with which specific comments need to be discussed," and that "[t]he agency's obligation **[—38—]** is simply to make a reasonable good faith effort to address comments and alternatives.")

D.

Finally, plaintiffs claim that, by forcing them "to participate in the market" for at-sea monitors, the Rule is an unconstitutional exercise of Congress's commerce power under the Supreme Court's decision in *NFIB v. Sebelius*, 567 U.S. 519 (2012). That case, plaintiffs argue, held that Congress **{-639-}** cannot force individuals to become active in a market in which they do not already participate. They argue that because Congress has forced them to become unwilling participants in the market for at-sea monitors, the Rule is unconstitutional since it is beyond the power of the Commerce Clause.

We reject this contention. Plaintiffs harvest a national resource for economic gain. But no one is forcing plaintiffs to participate in any market. Rather, they choose to engage in an activity that has long been subject to regulation. In so doing, they can hardly complain about complying with the otherwise lawful regulations that govern the manner in which they engage in that activity merely because compliance requires some **[—39—]** payment to another person, whether a seller of nets or life preservers, or a seller of monitoring services.[9]

IV.

For the foregoing reasons, we hold that the rule requiring plaintiffs to bear the costs of complying with on-board monitor regulation is authorized by Congress and is otherwise immune to plaintiffs' assorted procedural and substantive challenges. We therefore *affirm* the judgment of the district court.

******(Reporter's Note: Vacated by Relentless, Inc. v. U.S. Dept. of Commerce, No. 21-1886, 2024 WL 3647769 (1st Cir. Jul. 31, 2024)).******

[9] To the extent plaintiffs challenge the Rule as violating constitutional controls on taxing, appropriations, and spending, U.S. Const. art. I, §§ 1, 7, 8, those challenges are referenced only in passing, are undeveloped, and are therefore waived. *See United States v. Zannino*, 895 F.2d 1, 17 (1st Cir. 1990). Similarly, any potential Fourth Amendment argument was not raised in the briefing on appeal, and is therefore waived.

United States Court of Appeals
for the First Circuit

No. 21-1648

GREAT LAKES INS. SE
vs.
ANDERSSON

Appeal from the United States District Court for the District of Massachusetts

Decided: April 19, 2023

Citation: 66 F.4th 20, 11 Adm. R. 51 (1st Cir. 2023).

Before **BARRON,** Chief Judge, **HOWARD** and **MONTECALVO,** Circuit Judges.

[—2—] {–22–} MONTECALVO, Circuit Judge:

This maritime insurance case from Massachusetts arises on interlocutory appeal pursuant to 28 U.S.C. § 1292(a)(3) from the district court's grant of judgment on the pleadings in favor of the plaintiff-insurer, Great Lakes Insurance SE (GLI). The defendant, Martin Andersson, asserted that GLI engaged in unfair claim settlement practices in violation of Massachusetts General Laws chapters 176D and 93A. The district court ruled that Andersson's claim was barred by the choice-of-law provision of the marine insurance policy he purchased from GLI. For the reasons that follow, we conclude that the choice-of-law provision is ambiguous as to what law applies to the statutorily based claim that is at issue. Consistent with the applicable principles of interpretation we construe this ambiguity against the drafter -- GLI -- and conclude that Andersson's Massachusetts state law claim is not subject to the choice-of-law provision. Accordingly, we reverse.

I. Background

As this question comes to us on appeal from a motion for judgment on the pleadings, "[w]e view the facts contained in the pleadings in the light most favorable to the nonmovant and draw all reasonable inferences in his favor." *Zipperer v. Raytheon Co.*, 493 F.3d 50, 53 (1st Cir. 2007). These facts may be supplemented by reference to "documents 'fairly incurporated' in the pleadings" and "facts susceptible to judicial notice." **[—3—]** *Sevelitte v. Guardian Life Ins. Co. of Am.*, 55 F.4th 71, 76 (1st Cir. 2022) (citation omitted). **{–23–}**

GLI issued an insurance policy to Andersson which provided hull and machinery coverage for his forty-seven-foot catamaran sailing vessel, the *Melody*. The effective dates of the policy were from December 21, 2018, to December 21, 2019. The policy included the following choice-of-law provision, (which is directly at issue in this case):

> It is hereby agreed that any dispute arising hereunder shall be adjudicated according to well established, entrenched principles and precedents of substantive United States Federal Admiralty law and practice but where no such well established, entrenched precedent exists, this insuring agreement is subject to the substantive laws of the State of New York.[1] **[—4—]**

On December 16, 2019, the *Melody* was traveling to the Port of Boca Chica in the

[1] We are aware that this choice-of-law provision is currently before the Supreme Court in *Great Lakes Ins. SE v. Raiders Retreat Realty Co.*, 47 F.4th 225, 10 Adm. R. 88 (3d Cir. 2022), *cert. granted*, __ S. Ct. __, 2023 WL 2357327 (U.S. March 6, 2023) (No. 22-500). The Third Circuit held that prior to applying New York law the district court should have considered whether applying New York law would contravene the forum state's "strong public policy," including protecting insureds from "bad faith and unfair trade practices by insurance companies." *Raiders Retreat Realty Co.*, 47 F.4th at 230-33, 10 Adm. R. at 90-93. The Supreme Court granted limited review as to whether "[u]nder federal admiralty law, can a choice of law clause in a maritime contract be rendered unenforceable if enforcement is contrary to the 'strong public policy' of the state whose law is displaced?" *Raiders Retreat Realty Co.*, 47 F.4th 225, *cert. granted*, __ S. Ct. __, 2023 WL 2357327 (U.S. March 6, 2023) (No. 22-500); Petition for Cert. at i, *Raiders Retreat Realty Co.*, 47 F.4th 225, 10 Adm. R. 88 (3d Cir. 2022), *cert. granted*, __ S. Ct. __, 2023 WL 2357327 (U.S. March 6, 2023) (No. 22-500), 2022 WL 17361673, at *i. This question is not raised by the instant appeal, and we do not delve into public policy here.

Dominican Republic when it struck a breakwater and became stranded. The vessel was severely damaged, and Andersson notified GLI of the incident. GLI began investigating the incident and put Andersson in touch with a marine surveyor. The marine surveyor informed Andersson that the vessel was a "constructive total loss." Thereafter, on December 27, 2019, GLI reserved the right to deny coverage.

Andersson informed GLI that salvage of the vessel would cost $50,000, or, alternatively, Andersson could give title of the vessel and its contents to the salvor in exchange for the salvor's services. On January 2, 2020, the marine surveyor determined that the *Melody* "ha[d] very little residual value and a high salvage cost," and so GLI did not object to Andersson "transferring title to the vessel in exchange for salvage." Accordingly, Andersson and the salvor executed a contract requiring the salvor to remove the *Melody* from the breakwater, and title of the *Melody* was transferred to the salvor. The salvor agreed that it would retain the vessel and provide access to it upon request. In a January 16, 2020 letter, Andersson informed GLI that the right of access to the vessel would expire on February 10, 2020. Andersson also told GLI that the vessel's global positioning system (GPS) device was taken by the surveyor on GLI's behalf. **[—5—]**

On January 28, 2020, Andersson asked GLI for confirmation that it had received his January 16th letter. GLI confirmed receipt and indicated that "[w]e have asked our surveyors for comments." On February 19, 2020, Andersson inquired when the GPS device would be returned to him, to which GLI responded that Andersson should contact the surveyor directly. Andersson did so, and the surveyor informed him that the GPS device was not received from the salvor. The surveyor told Andersson that "[b]eyond the meeting you and I **{-24-}** had with the salvors on the beach when I was there, we have had no further involvement with salvors. Once we reported to [GLI,] our file was closed."

On February 27, 2020, GLI brought a declaratory judgment action to determine whether there was coverage under the policy. GLI alleged that coverage was unavailable because Andersson breached the policy by 1) failing to keep the *Melody* in seaworthy condition; and 2) travelling outside the navigational limits that were permitted under the policy.

Andersson filed an answer and counterclaim alleging, inter alia, a statutorily based claim for violations of chapter 176D, section 3(9) and chapter 93A, section 9(3A) of the Massachusetts General Laws, which -- taken together -- prohibit unfair or deceptive acts or practices in the business of insurance. Specifically, chapter 176D, section 3(9) "regulates the insurance business and identifies 'unfair claim settlement practices.'" **[—6—]** *Rawan v. Cont'l Cas. Co.*, 136 N.E.3d 327, 335 (Mass. 2019). "A violation of . . . c[h.] 176D amounts to an unfair or deceptive act or practice for purposes of claims made under . . . c[h.] 93A." *Id.*

Andersson alleged that GLI violated chapters 176D and 93A by failing to obtain or inspect the GPS device from the *Melody*, resulting in loss of access to the GPS device and an incomplete investigation into the course taken by the vessel. Andersson further alleged that GLI "failed to affirm or deny the claim promptly after the surveyor's report was received on or about January 2nd" and instead "misrepresented the status of its claims decision . . . so that it could proactively file a declaratory judgment action[.]"

After answering the counterclaim, GLI moved for judgment on the pleadings pursuant to Federal Rule of Civil Procedure 12(c). GLI contended that Andersson's unfair trade and settlement practices claim under Massachusetts law was barred by the policy's choice-of-law provision. Specifically, GLI argued that the policy's choice-of-law provision dictated that any issue not governed by an entrenched rule of federal admiralty law was governed by New York law. Thus, GLI pressed, Andersson's Massachusetts state law claim failed as a matter of law. Andersson's retort was that the choice-of-law provision limited the application of New York law to disputes that concern **[—7—]** interpretation of the policy itself, but not to claims entirely separate and distinct from a breach of the policy (hereinafter, "extracontractual claim(s)"). Thus, Andersson maintained, his Massachusetts state law claim remained viable because it was an extracontractual claim that did not concern disputes about the proper interpretation of the contract.

The district court rejected Andersson's position. It ruled that pursuant to the choice-of-law provision, New York law governed and barred Andersson's Massachusetts counterclaim. The district court reasoned that, in the absence of well-established admiralty law, New York law applied to all claims, including extracontractual claims, arising from and related to performance under the policy. Therefore, because New York law does not provide for a chapters 176D and 93A claim, the district court dismissed Andersson's counterclaim. This timely appeal ensued.[2] **[—8—] {-25-}**

II. Analysis

"We review the district court's judgment on the pleadings de novo." *Rezende v. Ocwen Loan Servicing, LLC*, 869 F.3d 40, 42 (1st Cir. 2017). The non-moving party's well-pleaded facts are accepted as true, and all reasonable inferences are drawn in the non-movant's favor. *Id.* "Judgment on the pleadings is proper 'only if the uncontested and properly considered facts conclusively establish the movant's entitlement to a favorable judgment.'" *Zipperer*, 493 F.3d at 53 (quoting *Aponte-Torres v. Univ. of P.R.*, 445 F.3d 50, 54 (1st Cir. 2006)).

From this posture, we consider whether the choice-of-law provision in the policy requires the application of New York law to extracontractual claims arising between the parties outside the scope of federal admiralty law, thereby barring Andersson's Massachusetts state law claim. The parties agreed, in the policy itself, that

> any dispute arising hereunder shall be adjudicated according to well established, entrenched principles and precedents of substantive United States Federal Admiralty law and practice but where no such well established, entrenched precedent exists, this insuring agreement is subject to the substantive laws of the State of New York. **[—9—]**

As an initial matter, Andersson does not contest that the choice-of-law provision is valid and enforceable.[3] He also concedes that entrenched principles of admiralty law would control an extracontractual claim if such precedent existed.

Thus, Andersson's challenge centers on the proper interpretation of the choice-of-law

---

[2] Andersson appealed three orders of the district court: 1) an order granting GLI's motion to strike Andersson's jury demand; 2) an order denying Andersson's motion to reconsider the order striking the jury demand; and 3) an order granting GLI's motion for judgment on the pleadings. In response to an order to show cause as to why the challenged orders were not appealable on an interlocutory basis, Andersson notified this court that he would not pursue an appeal of the denial of his motion for reconsideration. Andersson never withdrew his appeal of the order granting GLI's motion to strike his jury demand but failed to brief the issue. As such, this issue is waived for purposes of appeal. *See Sonoran Scanners, Inc. v. Perkinelmer, Inc.*, 585 F.3d 535, 545 n.7 (1st Cir. 2009).

Therefore, the only order properly before this court on appeal is the district court's order granting GLI's motion for judgment on the pleadings because it is an appealable interlocutory order **[—8—]** pursuant to 28 U.S.C. § 1292(a)(3). That order conclusively determined that GLI is not liable for unfair trade and claim settlement practices under Massachusetts law, and GLI does not dispute the propriety of this appeal. *See Doyle v. Huntress, Inc.*, 419 F.3d 3, 6-7 (1st Cir. 2005).

[3] GLI devotes a substantial portion of its brief to the argument that the choice-of-law provision is enforceable pursuant to a two-part test articulated by the Fifth Circuit in *Stoot v. Fluor Drilling Servs., Inc.*, 851 F.2d 1514 (5th Cir. 1988). Even setting aside the fact that *Stoot* is not binding on this court, GLI's argument is misplaced in this regard because *Stoot* presupposes that the parties' choice-of-law provision applies to the claims at issue. Whether Andersson's Massachusetts state law claim falls within the scope of the choice-of-law provision is the question at the very heart of this case.

provision when faced with an extracontractual claim that is not governed by entrenched principles of admiralty law. Andersson maintains that the second, disjunctive clause of the choice-of-law provision -- which states that "this insuring agreement is subject to the substantive laws of the State of New York" -- "narrowed the application of New York law to the insuring agreement[,]" and not to extracontractual claims. He thus asserts that his statutory extracontractual claim does not fall within the ambit of the choice-of-law provision.

A. Andersson's statutorily based counterclaim is extracontractual.

Because Andersson does not dispute that contract-related claims fall within the scope of the choice-of-law provision, the **[—10—]** first issue we must resolve is whether **{-26-}** Andersson's counterclaim is, in fact, extracontractual. Andersson alleged that GLI, in handling his insurance claim, engaged in unfair or deceptive acts that amounted to unfair claim settlement practices in violation of chapters 176D and 93A.

The conduct prohibited by chapter 176D, such as "[f]ailing to adopt and implement reasonable standards for the prompt investigation of claims" or "[r]efusing to pay claims without conducting a reasonable investigation based upon all available information[,]" can be entirely separate and distinct from the breach of an insurance policy. Mass. Gen. Laws ch. 176D, § 3(9)(c), (d). Even if an "insurer eventually pays the claim and honors the contract, its method of conducting the claims settlement process, and the payment strategy it adopts, can implicate liability under c[h.] 176D, and thus under c[h.] 93A." *Schwartz v. Travelers Indem. Co.*, 740 N.E.2d 1039, 1043 (Mass. App. Ct. 2001).

As pleaded, contract violations are not at the core of Andersson's chapters 176D and 93A claim. Andersson never alleges that GLI violated chapter 176D by breaching, or taking actions forbidden by, the contract. *See Ne. Data Sys., Inc. v. McDonnell Douglas Comput. Sys. Co.*, 986 F.2d 607, 609 (1st Cir. 1993) (holding that chapter 93A claims "amount[ed] to embroidered 'breach of contract claims'" where the supporting allegations were **[—11—]** based on actions that broke or were forbidden by the contract). Rather, Andersson's allegations -- taken in the light most favorable to him -- are not duplicative of a breach of contract claim based on the policy. Thus, Andersson's claim is extracontractual.

B. The plain language of the choice-of-law provision is not broad enough to unambiguously encompass an extracontractual claim.

Having established the nature of Andersson's claim, we must now address the exact scope of the choice-of-law provision. There is no federal maritime rule governing construction of marine insurance contracts, *see Littlefield v. Acadia Ins. Co.*, 392 F.3d 1, 6 (1st Cir. 2004), and under New York or Massachusetts law, the relevant rules of contract interpretation are essentially the same.[4] **[—12—]**

We begin with the actual language of the policy and give the words their plain and ordinary meaning. *See Jalbert ex rel. F2 Liquidating Tr. v. Zurich Servs. Corp.*, 953

---

[4] We recognize that courts have taken different approaches to determining the scope of a valid choice-of-law provision. Some courts view the scope of a choice-of-law provision as a matter of contract interpretation subject to the law chosen in the provision. *See Bunker Holdings, Ltd. v. Green Pac. A/S*, 346 F. App'x 969, 973 (4th Cir. 2009); *Odin Shipping Ltd. v. Drive Ocean V MV*, 221 F.3d 1348 (9th Cir. 2000) (unpublished table decision). Others determine the scope of the choice-of-law provision pursuant to the laws of the forum state. *See Schwan's Sales Enters., Inc. v. SIG Pack, Inc.*, 476 F.3d 594, 597-98 (8th Cir. 2007); *Fin. One Pub. Co. v. Lehman Brothers Special Fin., Inc.*, 414 F.3d 325, 333 (2d Cir. 2005). This court has not had occasion to undertake this particular analysis beyond noting that "[g]iving effect to [a choice-of-law] provision for the purpose of determining whether it . . . should be given effect obviously would be putting the barge before the tug." *DeNicola v. Cunard Line Ltd.*, 642 F.2d 5, 7 n.2 (1st Cir. 1981). Fortunately, we need not wade into these murky waters any further as there are no differences between applying **[—12—]** New York or Massachusetts law to the scope determination, and the parties agree as much.

F.3d 143, 150 (1st Cir. 2020) (applying Massachusetts law); *Ali v. Fed. Ins. Co.*, 719 F.3d 83, 90 (2d Cir. 2013) (applying New York law). The choice-of-law provision first provides that "any dispute arising hereunder" is subject to entrenched admiralty principles. Andersson's chapters 176D and 93A claim is a "dispute arising hereunder," and there is no "well established, **{-27-}** entrenched principles and precedent of substantive United States Federal Admiralty law" governing unfair trade and claim settlement practices. Absent admiralty precedent, the choice-of-law provision does not specifically dictate what law applies to a "dispute arising hereunder," but instead proceeds to state that "this insuring agreement is subject to the substantive laws of New York."

This differential in wording employed by GLI in the choice-of-law provision -- "any dispute arising hereunder" versus "this insuring agreement" -- creates ambiguity because it is subject to more than one reasonable interpretation. *See Scottsdale Ins. Co. v. Torres*, 561 F.3d 74, 77 (1st Cir. 2009) (applying Massachusetts law); *Aronstein v. Mass. Mut. Life Ins. Co.*, 15 F.4th **[—13—]** 527, 534 (1st Cir. 2021) (applying New York law). Indeed, two distinct classes of claims are arguably contemplated in the choice-of-law provision. The first clause encompasses "any dispute arising hereunder," which could include contract-related and extracontractual claims. But, the second clause is limited to "this insuring agreement," which could be limited to contract-related claims. Only these contract-related claims are specifically subjected to New York law. It is entirely unclear whether extracontractual claims -- even if they may be said to "arise[] hereunder" -- are also subject to New York law.

Although GLI urges us to ignore the differential wording, a canon of construction refutes this attempt. "Every word in an insurance contract must be presumed to have been employed with a purpose and must be given meaning and effect whenever practicable." *Valley Forge Ins. Co. v. Field*, 670 F.3d 93, 99 (1st Cir. 2012) (quoting *Bos. Gas Co. v. Century Indem. Co.*, 910 N.E.2d 290, 304 (Mass. 2009)); *see Nomura Home Equity Loan, Inc., Series 2006-FM2, by HSBC Bank USA, Nat'l Ass'n v. Nomura Credit & Cap., Inc.*, 92 N.E.3d 743, 748 (N.Y. 2017) ("[A] contract must be construed in a manner which gives effect to each and every part, so as not to render any provision 'meaningless or without force or effect.'" (quoting *Ronnen v. Ajax Elec. Motor Corp.*, 671 N.E.2d 534, 536 (N.Y. 1996))). The term "this insuring agreement" should be given meaning and effect apart from the term **[—14—]** "any dispute arising hereunder." Using both terms makes the scope of the choice-of-law provision ambiguous.

C. Any ambiguity in the policy must be construed in favor of Andersson.

Because the plain language of the choice-of-law provision is not broad enough to unambiguously encompass extracontractual claims, "any ambiguities must be construed in favor of the insured." *Clark Sch. for Creative Learning, Inc. v. Phila. Indem. Ins. Co.*, 734 F.3d 51, 55 (1st Cir. 2013) (applying Massachusetts law); *see J.P. Morgan Sec. Inc. v. Vigilant Ins. Co.*, 183 N.E.3d 443, 447 (N.Y. 2021). While both Massachusetts and New York law recognize this rule of construction, "[u]nder New York law, courts must first examine extrinsic evidence of the parties' intent before turning to doctrinal presumptions." *Aronstein*, 15 F.4th at 534 (applying New York law). However, "if the extrinsic evidence does not yield a conclusive answer as to the parties' intent, a court may apply other rules of contract construction[.]" *Parks Real Est. Purchasing Grp. v. St. Paul Fire & Marine Ins. Co.*, 472 F.3d 33, 43 (2d Cir. 2006) (cleaned up) (applying New York law).

Here, extrinsic evidence of the parties' intent will not aid our analysis of **{-28-}** the policy's boilerplate choice-of-law provision. *See Kolbe v. BAC Home Loans Servicing, LP*, 738 F.3d 432, 440 (1st Cir. 2013) ("Because uniform contracts are **[—15—]** interpreted uniformly across cases whenever it is reasonable to do so, extrinsic evidence about what a particular party intended or expected when signing the contract is generally irrelevant.") Thus, we proceed directly to the rules of contract construction. *See Sharon Steel Corp. v. Chase Manhattan Bank, N.A.*, 691 F.2d 1039, 1048

(2d Cir. 1982) ("There are no adjudicative facts relating to the parties to the litigation for a jury to find[,] and the meaning of [the] boilerplate provision[] is, therefore, a matter of law rather than fact."). When, as here, there are "competing plausible interpretations of the insurance policy 'doubts as to the intended meaning of the words must be resolved against the insurance company that employed them.'" *Performance Trans., Inc. v. Gen. Star Indem. Co.*, 983 F.3d 20, 28 (1st Cir. 2020) (quoting *Surabian Realty Co. v. NGM Ins. Co.*, 971 N.E.2d 268, 271 (Mass. 2012)); *see Lend Lease (US) Const. LMB Inc. v. Zurich Am. Ins. Co.*, 71 N.E.3d 556, 560 (N.Y. 2017) ("Of course, where the policy may be reasonably interpreted in two conflicting manners, its terms are ambiguous, and any ambiguity must be construed in favor of the insured and against the insurer." (cleaned up)). Doing so leads to the inescapable conclusion that *only* contract-related claims are subject to the substantive laws of New York. Extracontractual claims do not fall within the scope of the second clause of the choice-of-law provision. **[—16—]**

Having already determined that Andersson's chapters 176D and 93A claim, as pleaded, is extracontractual and forms a cause of action independent from the insuring agreement, it does not fall within the scope of the choice-of-law provision.

III. Conclusion

For the reasons stated above, the judgment of the district court is reversed.

United States Court of Appeals for the First Circuit

No. 22-1359

IN RE G&J FISHERIES, INC.

Appeal from the United States District Court for the District of Massachusetts

Decided: May 2, 2023

Citation: 67 F.4th 20, 11 Adm. R. 57 (1st Cir. 2023).

Before **KAYATTA, LYNCH,** and **HOWARD,** Circuit Judges.

[—3—] {-23-} LYNCH, Circuit Judge:

When Appellant Eduino Costa, a commercial fisherman who alleged he was injured while serving on a vessel owned by Appellee G&J Fisheries, Inc. ("G&J"), failed to file a claim as required under Supplemental Rule F of the Federal Rules of Civil Procedure, G&J moved for entry of default judgment. The district court allowed G&J's motion and denied Costa's request for leave to file a late claim. *In re G&J Fisheries, Inc.* (*In re G&J I*), 570 F. Supp. 3d 8, 11-12 (D. Mass. 2021). The district court thereafter entered a judgment of exoneration for G&J. *In re G&J Fisheries, Inc.* (*In re G&J II*), 598 F. Supp. 3d 18, 22 (D. Mass. 2022). Our review of these orders is for abuse of discretion. Costa has not met his burden to show such abuse. We affirm.

I.

Costa worked as a deckhand aboard the commercial fishing vessel F/V GEORGES BANKS, owned and operated by G&J, during a scallop fishing trip that started on or about June 9, 2017. Costa did not file any claim of injury in the thirty-five months following that voyage.

Three years later, on June 12, 2020, Costa sued G&J in Massachusetts Superior Court, alleging that he had been injured on or about June 15, 2017, on the F/V GEORGES BANKS and that G&J was liable for unseaworthiness and Jones Act negligence, 46 U.S.C. § 30104, and seeking maintenance and cure. Costa alleged that he "worked at least six trips as a deckhand" aboard G&J's vessel "in **[—4—]** 2016 and for some time in 2017." Costa's state court complaint also named as defendant Elizabeth & Niki Fishing Corporation ("E&N"), owner of the commercial fishing vessel F/V ELIZABETH & NIKI, on which Costa allegedly worked as a deckhand for over thirty years. Costa alleged that on multiple occasions aboard the F/V GEORGES BANKS and the F/V ELIZABETH & NIKI, he "was required to perform . . . extremely dangerous [tasks]" and "unsafely ordered . . . to perform work which was beyond his physical and medical capacity to perform."

After receiving written notice of Costa's state court action, G&J filed a complaint in the U.S. District Court for the District of Massachusetts on September 16, 2020, seeking "exoneration from liability for any and all injuries, damages, and losses of any kind arising from the voyage ending on or about June 16, 2017, including personal injuries allegedly sustained by Costa," "pursuant to 46 U.S.C. §§ 30501-12 . . . and Supplemental Admiralty Rule F of the **{-24-}** Federal Rules of Civil Procedure."[1] *See* 46 U.S.C. § 30529(a) (formerly 46 U.S.C. § 30511(a)) (providing that a vessel owner can "bring a civil action in a district court of the United States for limitation of liability" after receiving "written notice of a claim"). **[—5—]**

The Supreme Court has described the exoneration-from-liability process as follows:

> The district court secures the value of the vessel or owner's interest, marshals claims, and enjoins the prosecution of other actions with respect to the claims. In these proceedings, the court, sitting without a jury, adjudicates the claims. The court determines whether the vessel owner is liable and whether the owner may limit liability. The court then

[1] On January 6, 2021, E&N also filed such a complaint in federal district court seeking "exoneration from, or limitation of, any liability [it] may face by reason of Mr. Costa's alleged injury" aboard the F/V GEORGES BANKS.

> determines the validity of the claims, and if liability is limited, distributes the limited fund among the claimants.

Lewis v. Lewis & Clark Marine, Inc., 531 U.S. 438, 448 (2001) (citing Fed. R. Civ. P. Supp. R. F). When such a federal court exoneration action is filed, Rules F(4)-(5) of the Supplemental Rules for Admiralty or Maritime Claims of the Federal Rules of Civil Procedure set forth clear requirements for notice and for potential claimants to file claims in the district court by a certain date:

> [T]he [district] court shall issue a notice to all persons asserting claims with respect to which the complaint seeks limitation, admonishing them *to file their respective claims* with the clerk of the court and to serve on the attorneys for the plaintiff a copy thereof on or before a date to be named in the notice. . . . *For cause shown, the court may enlarge the time within which claims may be filed.*

Fed. R. Civ. P. Supp. R. F(4) (emphasis added). There is no dispute that such notice was provided here. **[—6—]**

Supplemental Rule F(5) specifies when a claim must be filed and the claim's contents and differentiates between a "claim" and an "answer":

> Claims shall be filed and served on or before the date specified in the notice provided for in subdivision (4) of this rule. *Each claim shall specify the facts upon which the claimant relies in support of the claim, the items thereof, and the dates on which the same accrued. If a claimant desires to contest either the right to exoneration from or the right to limitation of liability the claimant shall file and serve an answer* to the complaint unless the claim has included an answer.

Id. F(5) (emphasis added). The Rule, by its terms, sets certain requirements for every claim.

In response to G&J's exoneration complaint, the district court issued an order on October 13, 2020, enjoining "any and all lawsuits, causes of action, and claims against Plaintiffs and their property arising from the Incident" pursuant to Supplemental Rule F(3). The order further directed the issuance of notice pursuant to Supplemental Rule F(4) and required that any claimants must "file their respective claims . . . on or before November 18, 2020 or be defaulted." The formal notice issued two days later. It reiterated that "[a]ll persons having claims for injuries, losses, or damages must file a Claim, as provided by Supplemental Rule F(4)" and that "[a]ny Claimant desiring to contest [G&J's] right to exoneration from or right **{-25-}** to limitation of liability must **[—7—]** also file an answer to the Limitation Complaint, as required by Supplemental Rule F(5)."[2]

Costa responded to the exoneration action on November 17, 2020. He filed only an answer to G&J's complaint. He did not, by his own admission, "file a pleading specifically entitled a 'claim.'" Nor did he attach to his federal filing a copy of his state court complaint. Costa and G&J commenced discovery.[3]

Nearly eight months later, Costa still had not filed a claim nor, in G&J's view, had he adequately responded to discovery. On July 8, 2021, G&J filed a motion for entry of default as to all persons who failed to file claims by the November 18 deadline. The next day, E&N filed a claim and answer, albeit late. On July 22, 2021, Costa filed a "limited opposition" to entry of default, in which he argued that

---

[2] The district court's first notice contained a November 4 deadline for the filing of claims, contrary to the court's order, which set a deadline of November 18. The court issued a second notice on October 21, changing the deadline to November 18, consistent with the court's order.

[3] After Costa's counsel did not agree to an April 2021 date for Costa's deposition, the parties agreed that Costa would be deposed on July 7, 2021. Costa, his counsel, G&J's counsel, E&N's counsel, an interpreter, and a court reporter met in Costa's counsel's New Bedford office for the deposition on that date. But Costa's counsel refused to produce Costa for deposition, citing a need to consolidate Costa's case with the E&N exoneration action, so that Costa would only be deposed once.

default should not be entered [—8—] because his state court complaint was referenced in G&J's exoneration complaint and his answer.

On July 27, 2021, G&J filed a reply in support of its motion for entry of default.[4] G&J argued that Costa was in default because he had never filed a claim in district court, as required by Supplemental Rule F(5), and because neither Costa's answer nor his state court complaint counted as a claim under the "plain terms" of that Rule. G&J contended that, by failing to properly file a claim, Costa avoided Supplemental Rule F's requirements.[5]

G&J further argued that the court should not grant Costa [—9—] leave to file a late claim because Costa's failure to timely file was not due to excusable neglect. Rather, G&J alleged, Costa's "failure to file a claim was and is [a] deliberate" gambit "to leave his options open to craft a fictitious claim *ad hoc* after obtaining discovery." In support of this assertion, G&J cited Costa's {-26-} decision not to submit to a deposition and Costa's unsigned and "conclusory" answers to interrogatories. Further, G&J appended Costa's medical records, which showed that Costa had degenerative back problems well before the date of the accident on or about June 15, 2017, and that as of July 19, 2017 (the date of the medical examination), those problems were "not related to accident or injury." G&J also noted that "Costa's counsel is experienced in maritime cases and knows he is required to file a claim under Supplemental Admiralty Rule F(5)."

On July 30, 2021, Costa filed a sur-reply arguing that he "properly preserved his Claim by defending and filing an Answer as a Claimant and properly described as his affirmative defense that the negligence of [G&J] was the cause of his injury." Costa also requested "leave to file a late claim to preserve his rights" if the district court "f[ound] that this [a]ffirmative [d]efense lacks sufficient specificity under the circumstances."

On August 4, 2021, G&J responded to Costa's sur-reply, emphasizing that "Costa's bare and conclusory affirmative defenses [did] not pass as a claim"; that "Costa [did] nothing to explain [—10—] how he ha[d] failed to file a claim at this eleventh hour"; that Costa "appear[ed] to suggest that engaging [in] discovery excuse[d]" him from filing a claim; and that Costa, "despite ample opportunity and warning, ha[d] failed to demonstrate a meritorious claim through evidence or affidavit that would warrant declining entry of default against him."

In a memorandum and order issued November 5, 2021, the district court held that Costa's answer did not amount to a claim under Supplemental Rule F and denied Costa leave to file a late claim. *See In re G&J I*, 570 F. Supp. 3d at 11-12. The district court noted that it "[was] unaware of any caselaw construing an answer as a claim under Rule F to save a claimant from default judgment and Costa cites none." *Id.* at 11. The district court also emphasized that Costa referred to his own pleadings "as an answer, an answer and pleadings, or pleadings" -- not a claim. *Id.*

---

[4] G&J attached nine exhibits to its filings below: (1) a page from Costa's counsel's website describing the firm's expertise in maritime litigation; (2) claims under Supplemental Rule F(5) that Costa's firm timely filed in other limitation actions; (3) Costa's answers to G&J's first set of interrogatories; (4) the two notices of Costa's deposition and related correspondence; (5) a statement on the record regarding the attempted July 7 deposition of Costa; (6) Costa's medical records from a visit dated July 19, 2017, in which the physician's assistant noted that Costa "present[ed] . . . with a 1 year history of severe back pain . . . not related to accident or injury"; (7) the complaint against G&J and E&N that Costa filed in state court; (8) further correspondence regarding the July 7 deposition; and (9) Costa's supplemental answers to G&J's first set of interrogatories.

[5] Costa made the following allegations in his state court complaint: that, on or about June 15, 2017, he "sustained a severe and painful traumatic injury" aboard the F/V GEORGES BANKS when the vessel's captain "ordered [him] . . . to go to the wheelhouse to man the helm and finish cutting scallops"; that when he stepped on the main stairwell's first step, "while carrying the heavy basket full of scallops in an unsafe, awkward and ergonomically unsafe posture," he heard his lower back "pop" and felt "immediate intense [back] pain"; and that he then "fell face forward on to the stairwell constructed of diamond plate steel."

The district court applied our excusable neglect standard, which requires analysis of the "totality of the circumstances," including such factors as "(1) the explanation for the delay, (2) whether the non-movant will be prejudiced and (3) whether the party requesting relief acted in good faith." *Id.* (first citing *Nansamba v. N. Shore Med. Ctr., Inc.*, 727 F.3d 33, 38-39 (1st Cir. 2013); and then citing *Rivera-Velázquez v. Hartford Steam Boiler Inspection & Ins. Co.*, 750 F.3d 1, 4 (1st Cir. 2014)). **[—11—]** The district court stated that under this standard, "'[a]t a bare minimum' the party seeking to alter the judgment 'must offer a convincing explanation as to why the neglect was excusable.'" *Id.* (quoting *Nansamba*, 727 F.3d at 39). The district court concluded that Costa "provided no such explanation" as to why the neglect was excusable; that Costa's argument "[was] impossible to reconcile with the plain language of Rule F, as well as clear precedent requiring claimants to file claims, rather than answers"; and that Costa's counsel's failure "to admit to this oversight . . . undermine[d] his good faith." *Id.* at 11-12. The district court noted that Costa was represented by counsel who were "experienced practitioners who recently filed claims in other limitation proceedings governed by Rule F." *Id.* at 11. The district court granted G&J's motion for entry of default.[6] *Id.* at 12. **{-27-}**

G&J then moved the district court to enter final judgment pursuant to its November 5, 2021 ruling. Costa filed an opposition **[—12—]** to G&J's motion again seeking permission to file a late claim but failing to attach one.

The district court entered final judgment for G&J on April 14, 2022. *In re G&J II*, 598 F. Supp. 3d at 22. Costa filed a timely appeal.

II.

We review for abuse of discretion the district court's denial of permission to file late claims in an exoneration action. *See Lloyd's Leasing Ltd. v. Bates*, 902 F.2d 368, 371 (5th Cir. 1990); *Tex. Gulf Sulphur Co. v. Blue Stack Towing Co.*, 313 F.2d 359, 363 (5th Cir. 1963). To prevail, the appellant must meet the "heavy burden" of showing an abuse of discretion. *Thibeault v. Square D Co.*, 960 F.2d 239, 242-43 (1st Cir. 1992). Abuse of discretion is found in only the "rare[st]" of instances. *Tex. Gulf Sulphur Co.*, 313 F.2d at 363. "[A]n appellate court must defer to the lower court's 'sound judgment,' so long as its decision falls within its 'wide discretion,' and is not 'manifestly erroneous.'" *United States v. Tsarnaev*, 142 S. Ct. 1024, 1040 (2022) (citations omitted) (first quoting *United States v. Abel*, 469 U.S. 45, 54 (1984); then quoting *id.*; and then quoting *Gen. Elec. Co. v. Joiner*, 522 U.S. 136, 142 (1997)). Here, while the district court could have reached a different result, the result **[—13—]** it reached was within its wide discretion and was not manifestly erroneous.

District courts applying Supplemental Rule F(4) have "discretion 'to allow . . . late claims'" for cause shown. *In re Urbelis*, No. 15-cv-12358, 2018 WL 701350, at *4 (D. Mass. Feb. 2, 2018) (quoting *Golnoy Barge Co. v. M/T SHINOUSSA*, 980 F.2d 349, 351 (5th Cir. 1993) (per curiam)). For cause, district courts may extend the time to file a claim under Supplemental Rule F: "[S]o long as the limitation proceeding is pending and undetermined, and the rights of the parties are not adversely affected, the court will freely grant permission to file late claims . . . upon a showing of the reasons therefor." *Lloyd's Leasing Ltd.*, 902 F.2d at 371 (alteration and omission in original) (quoting *Tex. Gulf Sulphur Co.*, 313 F.2d at 362); *see also*

[6] Costa then filed an interlocutory appeal and moved to stay the district court proceedings while this appeal was pending. The district court found that the interlocutory appeal provided no basis for a stay of the action because (1) Costa made "no effort to meet [his] burden" and (2) the court was "skeptical that he would be able to do so if he tried." *In re G&J II*, 598 F. Supp. 3d at 21. Costa voluntarily dismissed his interlocutory appeal after this court issued a show cause order on June 9, 2022, directing Costa to either voluntarily dismiss the interlocutory appeal or show cause why it should not be dismissed as being duplicative of his subsequent appeal.

Schoenbaum, *Admiralty and Maritime Law* § 15.6 n.18 (6th ed. 2022 update).[7]

This court has not previously addressed the issue of abuse of discretion in a district court's denial of permission to file a late claim under Supplemental Rule F(4).[8] **[—14—] {-28-}**

If a claimant "fail[s] to offer any evidence to support their reasons for filing their claims after the notice date," then a district court does not abuse its discretion in "refus[ing] to permit the [filing of] late claims." *In re River City Towing Servs., Inc.*, 420 F.3d 385, 388 (5th Cir. 2005). Costa has provided no such evidence.

III.

Costa argues that (1) "his answer and the other pleadings taken [in context] should have been construed as a claim for purposes of Rule F(5)";[9] and (2) under *Texas Gulf Sulphur Co.* and "basic principles of admiralty law," the district court "should have granted Costa permission to file his claim late." We address each argument in turn and hold that, on the particular facts of this case and arguments presented by Costa, the district court did not abuse its discretion.

A. Costa's Answer and Other Pleadings Are Not a Claim Under Supplemental Rule F(5)

The text of Supplemental Rule F(5) clearly **[—15—]** differentiates between a claim and an answer. A claim "shall specify the facts upon which the claimant relies in support of the claim, the items thereof, and the dates on which the same accrued." Fed. R. Civ. P. Supp. R. F(5). Under the Rule, an answer is clearly different from a claim and serves a different purpose. An answer may be filed "[i]f a claimant desires to contest either the right to exoneration from or the right to limitation of liability." *Id.* A claim can be accompanied by an answer, but an answer alone is not a claim. *See id.* Supplemental Rule F(5) makes clear that Costa's answer is not a claim. Like the district court, we are unaware of any caselaw construing an answer like Costa's as a claim under Supplemental Rule F to save a claimant from default judgment. *See In re G&J I*, 570 F. Supp. 3d at 11; *see also In re Tappan Zee Constructors, LLC*, No. 17-cv-00168, 2018 WL 1183711, *2-3 (N.D.N.Y. Mar. 6, 2018) (refraining from construing answer as claim under Rule F); *In re Carnival Corp.*, No. 05-cv-21633, 2006 WL 8432012, at *2 (S.D. Fla. Jan. 6, 2006) (rejecting claimant's argument that "the state court complaint, attached to her motion to dismiss, can be construed as her claim"). Costa relies on *White v. Sabatino*, 415 F. Supp. 2d 1163 (D. Haw. 2006), to argue that his answer should be construed as a claim. But *White* is easily distinguishable. In *White*, the district court found the claimant satisfied Supplemental Rule F's requirements where the plaintiff had filed a complaint in a separate action, filed an **[—16—]** answer in the limitation action, and then the two cases were consolidated. The court reasoned that the "[c]omplaint, [a]nswer, and consolidation of the two cases [were] sufficient to satisfy the aim of Rule F(5)." *Id.* at 1180. Thus, in *White*, unlike here, the cases were consolidated, such that the claimant's complaint was part of the same action as the limitation proceeding.

Further, the differentiation between a claim and an answer in Supplemental Rule F(5) is consistent with other admiralty rules. Under Supplemental Rule C(6), "a person who asserts a right of possession or any ownership interest in the property that is the subject of [an in rem] action must file a verified statement of right or

---

[7] "[R]elief from a tardy claim is not a matter of right. It depends upon an equitable showing." *Tex. Gulf Sulphur Co.*, 313 F.2d at 363.

[8] We note that federal appellate courts have rarely found abuse of discretion. Such abuse has been found in situations not like this one, such as when the notice was not published in the claimant's geographical area. *See, e.g., Sagastume v. Lampsis Navigation Ltd.*, 579 F.2d 222, 224 (2nd Cir. 1978); *Jappinen v. Can. S.S. Lines, Ltd.*, 417 F.2d 189, 190–91 (6th Cir. 1969); *see* **[—14—]** *also Lloyd's Leasing Ltd.*, 902 F.2d at 371 (discussing these cases).

One circuit has commented that the "cause" required by Supplemental Rule F(4) "is minimal; an explanation rather than a justification for the delay will suffice." *Alter Barge Line, Inc. v. Consol. Grain & Barge Co.*, 272 F.3d 396, 397 (7th Cir. 2001) (per curiam).

[9] Costa does not make clear what other pleadings he contends amount to a claim.

interest," and such person "must serve an answer within 21 days after filing the statement of interest or right." Fed. R. Civ. P. Supp. R. C(6)(a). The filing of this statement "is a prerequisite to the right to {-29-} file an answer and defend on the merits." *United States v. One Dairy Farm*, 918 F.2d 310, 311 (1st Cir. 1990) (quoting *United States v. Fourteen (14) Handguns*, 524 F. Supp. 395, 397 (S.D. Tex. 1981)) (discussing earlier version of the Rule). The same logic applies to Supplemental Rule F(5): a potential claimant lacks standing to file an answer in a limitation proceeding if they have not properly filed a claim in district court. *See Am. River Transp. Co. v. United States*, 728 F.3d 839, 844, 1 Adm. R. 378, 381 (8th Cir. 2013) (holding that government lacked standing to [—17—] move to dismiss limitation proceeding because it failed to first file a claim under Supplemental Rule F(5)).

The district court reasonably concluded that Costa's answer did not specify the facts as required by Supplemental Rule F(5).[10] His answer only references the civil suit he filed in Bristol County Superior Court without any further detail; admits that "he was injured aboard the F/V GEORGES BANKS on a voyage that ended on or about June 16, 2017," and that he "was on the F/V GEORGES BANKS on a scalloping voyage on June 15, 2017"; and raises affirmative defenses, including that G&J "failed to exercise due care, including the failures to properly inspect, maintain and equip the F/V GEORGES BANKS Vessel."

In response to a vessel owner's limitation action, a claimant cannot merely point to their state court complaint to satisfy Supplemental Rule F(5)'s claim requirement. *See In re Carnival Corp.*, 2006 WL 8432012, at *2. Surely the drafters of Supplemental Rule F, knowing that a state court complaint could [—18—] provide notice to a vessel owner to file a federal action for limitation of liability, would have explicitly provided that a state court complaint could substitute for the claim provision if they so intended. But Supplemental Rule F(5) does not make any exception to the requirement that a claim be filed in federal court in a limitation action, even where there is a state court complaint. Costa could have filed a proper claim in response to the district court's notice, but he chose not to do so. It was insufficient to merely refer the federal court to a case pending on a state court docket. Such an argument, if accepted, would lead to obvious inefficiencies and burdens on the federal courts, which Supplemental Rule F(5) was meant to avoid.

B. The District Court Did Not Abuse Its Discretion in Denying Costa Leave to File a Late Claim

Costa argues that the district court applied the wrong legal standard in evaluating his motion for leave to file a late claim under Supplemental Rule F(4). He takes issue with the district court's conclusion that "[c]ase law suggests that Rule F, like Fed. R. Civ. P. Rule 60(b)(1), sets a standard of 'excusable neglect' in allowing a late claim." *In re G&J I*, 570 F. Supp. 3d at 11. Costa also argues that the district court "fail[ed] to fully assess all of the relevant factors." We disagree on both points. There was no error in the use of the excusable neglect standard. *See* {-30-} *In re Urbelis*, 2018 WL 701350, at *5 n.5 (noting [—19—] that "[t]he case law suggests" that an excusable neglect standard applies); *see also Nansamba*, 727 F.3d at 38-39; *Rivera-Velázquez*, 750 F.3d at 4. Though Supplemental Rule F(4) does not use the term "excusable neglect," *cf.* Fed. R. Civ. P. 60(b)(1), the standard for a district court to grant the filing of late claims "upon a showing of the reasons therefor" under the Rule is effectively one of excusable neglect, *Tex. Gulf Sulphur Co.*, 313 F.2d at 362. Like a

---

[10] This case is unlike *United States v. 1 Street A-1*, 885 F.2d 994 (1st Cir. 1989). In *1 Street A-1*, this court construed a timely filed verified answer containing all the information required of a claim to have fulfilled the function of a claim under an earlier version of Supplemental Rule C(6). *See id.* at 999-1000. Costa's citation to this case only in his reply brief is insufficient to avoid waiver of the argument. And even if this argument were not waived, it does not help Costa because his answer did *not* contain all the information required of a claim under Supplemental Rule F(5). Costa's answer, for example, did not "specify the facts upon which" he relied in support of his claim, as Supplemental Rule F(5) requires.

showing of excusable neglect under Rule 60(b)(1), "a showing of the reasons therefor," *id.*, under Rule F(4) encompasses a showing of "inadvertence, mistake, or carelessness, as well as [] intervening circumstances beyond the party's control," *Nansamba*, 727 F.3d at 38 (alteration in original) (quoting *Pioneer Inv. Servs. Co. v. Brunswick Assocs. Ltd. P'ship*, 507 U.S. 380, 388 (1993)). The district court did assess the record. Thus, the district court did not abuse its discretion in finding there was not excusable neglect.

As the district court found, Costa "careless[ly]" made no attempt to remedy his failure to file a claim for a "full year since his initial filling." *In re G&J I*, 570 F. Supp. 3d at 12. Instead, he asserted that there was no failure on his part at all, and that he "believed that his rights were sufficiently protected under" his answer. *Id.* at 11. The district court found that argument "impossible to reconcile with the plain language of Rule **[—20—]** F."[11] *Id.* Costa's argument that the district court's entry of default against him is inconsistent with the Jones Act's purpose of providing liberal recovery for injured seamen is unavailing. The Jones Act does not exempt Costa or any other seaman from complying with Supplemental Rule F's requirements for timely filing a claim in a limitation action.

The district court did not abuse its discretion in finding that Costa's counsel "failed to present a convincing excuse for [their] error," particularly because they "were experienced practitioners" in maritime litigation. *Id.* In the district court and in state court, Costa was represented by counsel who specialize in maritime law and thus should be familiar with Supplemental Rule F(5)'s requirement that a claim -- not just an answer -- be filed in a limitation action. In limitation actions contemporaneous to this one, Costa's counsel timely filed claims under Supplemental Rule F(5). *See id.* For example, one of Costa's attorneys filed a claim against G&J on behalf of a different personal injury claimant in another case pending before the same district court roughly three weeks before the claim in this case was due. And at oral argument, Costa's counsel acknowledged that "our office has **[—21—]** filed claims in exoneration actions." Costa's representation by counsel experienced in maritime litigation makes especially troubling his failure to submit any evidence explaining why he failed to timely file claims. *Cf. In re River City Towing Servs., Inc.*, 420 F.3d at 388.

Further, Costa's approach clearly harms the efficient administration of admiralty rules by the federal courts, and G&J has argued it has harmed its defense of the case. The courts "ha[ve] a 'strong institutional interest in ensuring that litigants honor court orders' so that [the courts] may efficiently administer [their] docket[s]." *United States v. 2008 33' Contender Model Tournament Vessel*, 990 F.3d 725, 727 (1st Cir. 2021) (quoting *Tower Ventures, Inc. v. City of Westfield*, 296 F.3d 43, 47 (1st Cir. 2002)). The failure to file a **{–31–}** claim as required by Supplemental Rule F also caused delay, which G&J argues harmed its defense of the case as memories of events became stale. And Costa has consistently failed to commit to specific information underlying his alleged injury. G&J argues that Costa "seeks to take advantage of faded memories, missing witnesses and massaged evidence," thereby disrupting G&J's ability to adequately defend the case.

We *affirm*.

---

[11] Further, as E&N filed its own late claim immediately after G&J moved for default, Costa was reminded of the need to file a claim and nonetheless took no steps in the ensuing four months to file a claim before the district court ruled on G&J's motion.

United States Court of Appeals
for the First Circuit

No. 20-2129

UNITED STATES
VS.
ANDINO-RODRÍGUEZ

Appeal from the United States District Court for the District of Puerto Rico

Decided: August 21, 2023

Citation: 79 F.4th 7, 11 Adm. R. 64 (1st Cir. 2023).

Before **KAYATTA, LYNCH,** and **THOMPSON,** Circuit Judges.

[—3—] {-12-} THOMPSON, Circuit Judge:

Experience has taught us drugs are trafficked in many ways, with drug runners using assorted transportation methods and various concealment techniques to move their narcotics. Today's drug-trafficking case comes by sea, via the Black Wolfpack, a boat that ferried cocaine smugglers and their product between Caribbean islands. Specifically, the players in this scheme undertook voyages from Puerto Rico to St. Thomas to acquire and package bricks of cocaine for transport back to Puerto Rico, where they would then receive compensation for their efforts. That came to an end in January 2018, though, when federal agents intercepted the Black Wolfpack off the coast of St. Thomas and, with it, four of the trafficking enterprise's participants.

What resulted was a multi-defendant indictment charging drug conspiracy crimes. While four co-conspirators entered guilty pleas, our appellants -- co-defendants Katerin Martínez-Alberto ("Martínez") and Alexandria Andino-Rodríguez ("Andino") -- each exercised their trial rights. Following a joint eight-day jury trial, both were convicted for their roles in the trafficking venture.

Now, in these consolidated appeals, Martínez and Andino, alleging trial and sentencing errors, ask us to reverse what happened below. But for reasons we'll explain, we affirm in toto. **[—4—]**

BACKGROUND

Facts

Drawing from the record to tell this tale -- and doing so in the light most favorable to the jury's verdict, *see, e.g., United States v. Ciresi*, 697 F.3d 19, 23 (1st Cir. 2012) (citing *United States v. Mitchell*, 596 F.3d 18, 20 n.1 (1st Cir. 2010)) -- we begin by laying out the facts of the drug-trafficking scheme in which our appellants were embroiled, providing a good bit of saga up front in order to facilitate the gentle reader's understanding of how this all transpired. We will fill in more detail later, when additional factual and procedural particulars become necessary to our analysis.

Back on January 27, 2018, in the Crown Bay Marina in St. Thomas, a Customs and Border Protection ("CBP") marine interdiction agent had eyes on the Black Wolfpack, a vessel suspected of trafficking drugs to and from Puerto Rico.[1] Walking **{-13-}** towards the Black Wolfpack, carrying luggage, boxes, and a cooler, were two men and two women, later identified as Maximiliano Figueroa-Benjamín ("Maximiliano"), Emiliano Figueroa-Benjamín **[—5—]** ("Emiliano"),[2] Martínez, and Andino. All aboard, the Black Wolfpack departed the St. Thomas marina towards Puerto Rico, but, about halfway through what became a hazardous return journey,[3] it was intercepted

[1] Information had been relayed to CBP by the FBI after it learned from a source of information that a vessel would soon depart Puerto Rico for St. Thomas, pick up cocaine there, then return with the kilos to Puerto Rico. As a result, the CBP agent was called into action "to be on the lookout" that day.

[2] Given these first two co-defendants have the same last name, we use their first names to avoid confusion, no disrespect intended.

[3] The weather that day wasn't exactly ideal for a leisure trip between the islands: Agents testified the waves were between 10 and 15 feet high (some of the worst one agent had seen), forcing the experienced seafaring agents to debate the safety of pursuing the Black Wolfpack before ultimately deciding to give chase.

and escorted back to St. Thomas by law enforcement.

Over the course of their searches that day, federal agents seized from the Black Wolfpack several items, including the four individuals' identifications as well as their cell phones.[4] Also found and retrieved inside a hidden compartment were 55 bundles of what was believed (and subsequently confirmed) to be cocaine. Two days later, agents further searched the Black Wolfpack, this time finding 56 bundles of suspected cocaine under a table bolted to the vessel's floor.[5] Among the 111 total bundles seized, there were various stickers and insignia affixed to the **[—6—]** bricks, including stickers with crowns and $100 bills on them. All told, the total weight of the 111 cocaine bricks was 132 kilograms, with a street value of $20k-22k per brick (for a grand total of more than $2 million in value).

To better understand the scope of what led to this moment at sea, let us travel back to 2017 to walk through what happened over the course of the charged conspiracy. Because while January 27, 2018 was the first time this group got caught, it was not their first rodeo.

We introduce you to two names, new to our recounting but central to the enterprise: Bernardo Coplin-Benjamín ("Coplin") and José Javier Resto-Miranda ("Resto").[6] It was Coplin who, around March of 2017, came up with the grand idea to buy a boat that would move drugs from St. Thomas to Puerto Rico, and in anticipation of that goal Coplin asked his friend and **{-14-}** associate, **[—7—]** Resto, for his help. In time, Coplin followed up and purchased a boat: the Wasikoki.

In preparation to set sail on their trafficking venture, Coplin and Resto did some reconnaissance. To get a read on the planned route, length of the trip, and fuel costs, Coplin asked another individual (whose identity is irrelevant here) to captain a test run. Aboard that April 2017 Wasikoki trial outing were Coplin, Andino (a close friend of Resto, who brought her into the enterprise), and Maximiliano.

Thereafter, with the route settled, a basic plan was hatched: Resto, Maximiliano, Martínez (another of Resto's friends and recruits), and Andino would make a trip on the Wasikoki to St. Thomas, with the women playing the roles of "fillers" to erect a facade of two couples out on a leisure ride (Resto told them they'd be paid $3,000 apiece for their participation); the group would pick up the cocaine; and they'd return to Puerto Rico with it. Come May 2017, they headed out to sea. Upon their arrival in St. Thomas, Maximiliano picked up the cocaine from his contact there, and he and Resto stashed the vacuum-sealed and greased bundles in a hidden compartment on the Wasikoki. But then they hit a snag: The Wasikoki had technical problems. Resto (as captain on this voyage) decided the journey would have to be abandoned -- as he told his companions aboard the vessel, it wasn't worth the risk of undertaking the drug run on the Wasikoki when she was struggling **[—8—]** with mechanical issues and might break down. Resto gave the kilos to Maximiliano, who returned them to his contact. Emptyhanded, the Wasikoki and its crew then made the return voyage back to Puerto Rico.

---

[4] Andino and Maximiliano consented to the searches of their phones. Martínez did not, but after the seizure of her phone from the arrested Black Wolfpack, federal agents extracted the information used by the government in its prosecution case. The record suggests warrants were obtained for the search of and extraction from each of the phones, but it is not crystal clear. Regardless, no one has challenged the propriety of the searches on appeal.

[5] Of the various federal agencies involved, the FBI was designated the seizing agency.

[6] With respect to Coplin, we note that he also was indicted, then pled guilty and was sentenced. In the wake of all that, he filed a timely appeal. *See United States v. Coplin-Benjamin*, No. 21-1737. To be clear: We discuss Coplin here based only on the evidence offered at the joint trial of Martínez and Andino, and we do so solely for the purpose of fleshing out the trafficking scheme as it relates to their involvement and issues raised by them in *this* appeal. We offer no take whatsoever on the facts or merits of Coplin's appeal.

As for Resto, the only co-conspirator to testify at Martínez and Andino's trial, he has an important role to play in our factual recitation, and he also figures prominently in one of the appellate issues we'll be chasing down in the pages to come.

The Wasikoki's mechanical issues were persistent, as it turned out, so in May 2017, Resto helped Coplin acquire a new boat: the Black Wolfpack, which Resto registered in his name.

In late July or early August of 2017, Resto, Maximiliano, and Andino (no Martínez this time) climbed aboard the Black Wolfpack and made another trip to Crown Bay Marina in St. Thomas to pick up cocaine. Once there, Maximiliano went to meet with the supplier while Resto and Andino went to an apartment on St. Thomas to help get the cocaine ready for its journey to Puerto Rico, including by putting the coke into packages, some of which had crowns on the seal. More on this later. For context, all the reader need file away for now is that Andino made another trip, then helped package the kilos for transport home to Puerto Rico, where, at Coplin's house, she received $7,000 for her efforts. Also worth noting now, for purposes of explaining Resto's role in all of this, is that Resto got $35,000 and complained he "thought it should be more."

The Black Wolfpack set sail for St. Thomas yet again in September 2017, this time with Andino, Maximiliano, Resto, and his girlfriend (who is not a co-defendant here) aboard, and under the **[—9—]** pretext that they were bringing aid in the wake of Hurricane Irma. Andino again participated in preparing the cocaine for transportation, then got back aboard the Black Wolfpack to head back to Puerto Rico, where she, as before, was paid $7,000 for her efforts. Resto, again disappointed by his "unfair" payout ($20,000 this time), confronted Coplin, urging that he should be paid more as captain. Coplin's response was to tell Resto "to deal with it" -- "this [was] the way that it was going to be done." Displeased and feeling like the risk/benefit balance was not "a good deal" for him, Resto then "distanced" himself from the group.

A couple of months later, text messages between Martínez and Andino reflected an **{–15–}** upcoming November 4, 2017 trip. Indeed, Crown Bay Marina paperwork bears Andino's registration of the Black Wolfpack on that same date. Further proof of that particular voyage -- telling photos. There's a November 4 selfie of Martínez and Andino that was found on Maximiliano's phone during the search following that January 27, 2018 seizure -- it shows the women aboard the Black Wolfpack with the cooler they used to transport the cocaine from its packaging site back to the vessel. And Maximiliano is in another picture from his phone -- he's steering the Black Wolfpack, and Martínez and Andino are standing in close proximity. Meanwhile, Martínez's phone contained a November 4 photo showing crown-sticker and $100-bill-sticker bundles. **[—10—]**

And St. Thomas got another November 2017 visit from the Black Wolfpack, this time on the 17th. Marina registration papers for that day once more show Andino's signature, and Maximiliano's phone has a November 19 photo showing him, Andino, Martínez, and another individual at the cocaine-packaging site (an apartment) with that telltale cooler used to move the kilos (as Resto attested at trial) behind them.

Fast forward to January 2018, back to the events we started with. Now, Resto had not been participating in this drug-trafficking enterprise for a few months, but he was asked to join for that January 2018 trip. He declined, instead going to Alaska, where he would renew his asbestos removal license (he'd worked in Alaska over the years, he explained at trial). Resto later learned of his four associates getting busted when Coplin called him and broke the news that Martínez, Andino, Maximiliano, and Emiliano had been arrested in St. Thomas.[7]

Procedural History

In the wake of the January 2018 seizures and arrests, a second superseding indictment ultimately issued charging Martínez, Andino,

[7] A few weeks after that, Resto returned to Puerto Rico and met up with Andino, who was out on pretrial release, during which meeting she told Resto the January 2018 crew had actually noticed they were being followed as they left St. Thomas, and Andino had suggested they throw away their phones, but Maximiliano rejected that suggestion because his phone was new and had been pricey.

Maximiliano, and Emiliano, and later Coplin and Resto, **[—11—]** with conspiracy to possess with the intent to distribute a controlled substance in violation of 21 U.S.C. § 846 (Count One) and conspiracy to import controlled substances into the U.S. in violation of 21 U.S.C. § 963 (Count Two) (said conduct beginning on a date unknown, but not later than 2017, and continuing until a date unknown, but not earlier than January 27, 2018).

Over time, each of Martínez and Andino's co-defendants entered guilty pleas.[8] For their part, Martínez and Andino, as we noted earlier, proceeded jointly to trial, at which both defendants were found guilty[9] **{-16-}** and later sentenced (concurrent 120-month terms of imprisonment, to be followed by concurrent five-year terms of supervised release, for each defendant). Appellants timely and separately appealed, and here we are. **[—12—]**

DISCUSSION

The appellate contentions pressed by Martínez and Andino are discrete ones with no overlap as between each appellant. Martínez presses three challenges on appeal, each arising from a different moment during trial.[10] In sum, she argues the district court committed errors (1) regarding Resto's trial testimony, (2) in making an evidentiary ruling, and (3) when it delivered jury instructions. As for Andino, she says the district court erred when it denied her the minor participant adjustment she sought. Proceeding chronologically, let's test the waters.

Martínez

Resto: Recross-Examination and the Motion to Strike

Martínez's first argument zeroes in on Resto, the coconspirator turned cooperating witness, and a couple of aspects of the district court's handling of his testimony. The thrust of her argument, as we understand it to be, is that two of the district **[—13—]** court's rulings -- its denial of recross of Resto and, later, its grant of the government's motion to strike some of Resto's testimony -- denied her the opportunity to impeach Resto's testimony and credibility in violation of her Sixth Amendment Confrontation Clause rights. To navigate her claims, we first provide some preliminary guiding principles, then wade into the transcripts of the waning days of the trial to explicate the sequence of events and rulings.

It's axiomatic that "[t]he Confrontation Clause of the Sixth Amendment guarantees criminal defendants the right to cross-examine witnesses who testify against them." *United States v. Maldonado-Peña*, 4 F.4th 1, 31 (1st

---

[8] The important plea to note right off the bat is Resto's. As relevant to this appeal, Resto's plea included: him copping to conspiring with his co-defendants to distribute between 15 and 50 kilos of cocaine; his understanding that his sentencing range would be no less than ten years' imprisonment and at least five years' supervised release; and his agreement that the parties would recommend that minimum term to the sentencing court. And Resto signed a cooperation agreement, too, in which he signaled, among other things, his willingness to provide truthful testimony at a future trial.

[9] The government met its case burden using: the agents that intercepted and searched the Black Wolfpack; the agents who extracted the data from the defendants' cell phones; the forensic chemist who tested the seized cocaine; and a cooperating Resto, who testified pursuant to a cooperation agreement. It also adduced photos and video evidence of the searches, the cocaine, and business records from the marina in St. Thomas, along with the relevant photos, text exchanges, and voice messages retrieved from the defendants' phones.

[10] Below, Martínez made a Rule 29 motion challenging the government's evidence as to her knowing participation in the conspiracy. The district court denied it. While Martínez's appellate papers at times suggest that the evidence as to her conspiracy participation and knowledge wasn't sufficient, we do not understand her to be advancing a sufficiency-of-the-evidence challenge here. Nor did the government. To the extent she may have intended to mount such a challenge before us, we deem it waived. *See, e.g., Rodríguez v. Mun. of San Juan*, 659 F.3d 168, 175-76 (1st Cir. 2011) (deeming waived arguments offered with no citations or analysis); *United States v. Zannino*, 895 F.2d 1, 17 (1st Cir. 1990) (urging that litigants are required to develop their own arguments rather than "leaving the court to do counsel's work").

Cir. 2021) (quoting *United States v. Casey*, 825 F.3d 1, 23-24 (1st Cir. 2016)), *cert. denied Rivera-Alejandro v. United States*, 142 S. Ct. 729 (2021), and *cert. denied Rivera-George v. United States*, 142 S. Ct. 1184 (2022), and *cert. denied Rivera-Alejandro v. United States*, 142 S. Ct. 1185 (2022). It allows defendants to "test the believability of a witness and the truth of his testimony." *Id.* (quoting *United States v. Rivera-Donate*, 682 F.3d 120, 126 (1st Cir. 2012)). "This right is not without limits, however; the district court wields considerable discretion to impose 'reasonable limits' on cross-examination." *Id.* (quoting *Casey*, 825 F.3d at 24); *see also United States v. Kenrick*, 221 F.3d 19, 33 (1st Cir. 2000) (en banc) (acknowledging the district court's **{-17-}** extensive discretion when it **[—14—]** comes to controlling recross-examination), *abrogated on other grounds by Loughrin v. United States*, 573 U.S. 351 (2014). Importantly, "[w]hen a witness's credibility is at issue, the trial court may limit cross-examination as long as the court allows sufficient leeway to establish a reasonably complete picture of the witness' veracity, bias, and motivation." *Maldonado-Peña*, 4 F.4th at 31 (quoting *Rivera-Donate*, 682 F.3d at 126). For our part, we employ a two-step analysis: We first "review de novo whether a defendant was afforded a reasonable opportunity to impeach a witness, and [second,] for abuse of discretion limitations the trial court imposed on that opportunity." *Id.* (quoting *Casey*, 825 F.3d at 24); *see also United States v. Pérez-Ruiz*, 353 F.3d 1, 11 (1st Cir. 2003) ("In the first instance, Confrontation Clause challenges are reviewed de novo in order to verify that the trial court afforded the defendant a reasonable opportunity to impeach adverse witnesses. When that constitutional threshold is crossed, we examine the trial court's restrictions on the manner and extent of cross-examination for abuse of discretion.").

Initial guidance in place, we turn back to our case to see how things played out below.

On trial days six and seven (of eight), defense counsel -- first for Andino, then for Martínez -- conducted their cross-examinations of Resto. As relevant here, both counsel probed **[—15—]** Resto's cooperation agreement. Martínez's counsel went further and explored Resto's purchase and possession of a gun in Alaska, which he admitted to, as well as his drug-dealing business in Alaska. He also acknowledged that his plea agreement did not include a charge of possession of a weapon in furtherance of drug trafficking, nor did his sentencing guidelines recommendation include any points provided for possession of a firearm.[11] About the propriety of his gun ownership, Resto testified his having it was legal in Alaska, but Martínez's counsel countered by asking, "[I]sn't it true that even if you buy a weapon . . . you have to register the weapon with the police department closest to your home[?]"

Following cross-examination by both defense counsel, the government briefly redirected, and during the redirect, Resto testified there was no connection between his gun ownership and his selling drugs in Alaska. Thereafter, the district court excused Resto from the stand.

Needing to take care of several procedural housekeeping matters, the court, outside the presence of the jury, held a sidebar at which Andino's attorney represented that he had intended to recross-examine Resto regarding aspects of his testimony **[—16—]** concerning his cooperation with the government and benefits he might have derived from that cooperation. He made a particularized proffer indicating he would have recrossed on "three specific moments in which [Resto] was promised by the agents that he was going to get specific considerations": (1) the FBI's statements to Resto which showed they made promises to him including bail and staying in Alaska; (2) the timing of when Resto began to cooperate; and (3) Resto's misstatements about what he said during his FBI interview. Martínez's counsel, without elaboration, "join[ed] brother counsel's objection." The district court denied the request, indicating that all those proposed topics had already been

[11] The terms of Resto's plea agreement provided the agreement bound only "the United States Attorney's office for the District of Puerto Rico and the defendant."

covered **{–18–}** (or should have been covered) during cross-examination.[12]

On the next and final day of the trial, the government, returning to the topic of Resto's cross-examination, moved to strike the testimony about Resto's Alaskan gun possession, argued that whether Resto had registered the gun was irrelevant to his credibility, and even if he may have run afoul of a registration requirement, he hadn't been convicted of any such violation. After **[—17—]** hearing from each side, the district court granted the motion on the grounds that Martínez's attorney, when asked, was unable to cite any firearm ownership law Resto had purportedly violated. The district court, finding that the gun-in-Alaska questioning could mislead the jury, instructed the jury to disregard all of it.

On appeal, Martínez's argument takes aim at these two events -- the denial of recross-examination and the grant of the motion to strike -- and argues the district court's striking of Resto's gun testimony concerning his possession of the gun while dealing cocaine, "exacerbated by the court's denial of [her] opportunity to recross him," had the effect of depriving her "of the constitutionally required threshold level of inquiry," robbing her of "sufficient leeway to establish a reasonably complete picture of the witness's veracity, bias, and motivation." More specifically, she argues, the gun evidence could have been used to show Resto's bias given that the government could have charged him, but, favorable to him, didn't (*see supra* note 8),[13] or could have enhanced his sentence, but, again favorable to him, didn't, **[—18—]** based on firearm possession (*see* 18 U.S.C. § 924(c)),[14] thereby casting doubt on Resto's credibility. As she puts it, "[Resto's] credibility was at the core of the government's case against Martínez," and the court's double-barreled rulings impinged upon her ability to attack that credibility.[15] Our bottom line takeaway from her argument boils down to this: Martínez asserts that being denied recross and then being unable to argue anything about the gun at all, because the little gun evidence there was had gotten stricken, impacted her ability to effectively attack Resto's credibility "by exploring the benefits he derived from his cooperation."

The government offers a fulsome retort to Martínez's arguments which we'll weave into our analysis as we go along.

We open by acknowledging our agreement with Martínez's top line assertion: **{–19–}** The opportunity to recross a witness can **[—19—]** implicate the Confrontation Clause. *See, e.g., Pérez-Ruiz*, 353 F.3d at 10-11. And that's where we'll start our review, doing so with fresh eyes. *Id.* at 11 (arraying our court's review as starting with the de novo consideration of the confrontation-driven challenge, then, once "that constitutional threshold is crossed," moving to abuse-of-discretion scrutinization of the trial court's restrictions on cross).

Reasonable Opportunity to Impeach

Taking a look at the record, it clearly reflects, as the government contends, that the

---

[12] No strictly new topics came up during redirect that would have, as we sometimes say, opened the door to new lines of inquiry Martínez's trial counsel couldn't have had an opportunity (or reason) to ask about up until that door was opened. *See generally, e.g., United States v. Tetioukhine*, 725 F.3d 1, 10 (1st Cir. 2013) (discussing what can suffice "to open the door to further cross-examination"). Martínez has not argued otherwise.

[13] Martínez does not pursue her trial-stage theory based on Resto having committed a crime by failing to register his gun in Alaska.

[14] We note Resto was not charged as a felon in possession of a firearm, presumably because his presentence report reflects that he had no known criminal history.

[15] We pause to make an observation. To the extent Martínez intends her arguments contesting the combination of rulings to be something akin to a violation of the cumulative error doctrine, *see, e.g., United States v. Baptiste*, 8 F.4th 30, 39 (1st Cir. 2021) ("The cumulative-error doctrine holds that errors not individually reversible can become so cumulatively."), at the end of our analysis of these claims, we find no error and as we've said before, "[b]ecause we find no merit to the individual claims, as a matter of course there can be no cumulative error," *United States v. Bulger*, 816 F.3d 137, 160 n.25 (1st Cir. 2016) (citing *United States v. Brown*, 669 F.3d 10, 28 (1st Cir. 2012)).

district court gave Martínez a reasonable opportunity to confront and impeach Resto.

As mentioned, cross-examination commenced on trial day six, a day after the government completed its direct (with the government briefly "reopen[ing]" direct to show a few pictures). And as far as cross-examinations go, it went smoothly, with the district court allowing nearly all lines of inquiry, many of which prompted responses from Resto that reasonably could tend to cast doubt on his credibility. For example, Resto agreed that he had repeatedly lied to federal agents -- even up to four days before the trial started -- and that he was never charged with a separate crime based on these lies. The jury learned through his testimony that it was only after his attorney advised him to stop lying that Resto fully began to cooperate. The cross also focused on Resto's signed cooperation agreement with the government and the benefits **[—20—]** that he derived from it, including the possibility of a reduced sentence. Indeed, even in the wake of some sustained objections over the course of the two-day cross-examination, the record is clear "that the defense got its main point[s] across." *Maldonado-Peña*, 4 F.4th at 34-35; *Pérez-Ruiz*, 353 F.3d at 11 (finding it "crystal clear" that an appellant had "ample opportunity to confront [the witness's] testimony" when the district court gave defense counsel a recess after the direct had concluded and "did nothing to limit the length of [the ensuing] (and skillfully conducted) cross-examination"); *see also Cruz-Rivera*, 14 F.4th at 52 (spying no confrontation issue when defense counsel had explored the witness's bias through a cooperation agreement and reduced sentence -- and leaned on the same during closing argument).

Recross-Examination Request

What remains, then, at step two, is for us to resolve whether the denial of recross-examination of Resto constituted an abuse of discretion. *See Maldonado-Peña*, 4 F.4th at 31; *Casey*, 825 F.3d at 24. "The abuse-of-discretion standard is not 'appellant-friendly.'" *United States v. Marino*, 833 F.3d 1, 7 (1st Cir. 2016). We have said that "[t]he touchstone of abuse of discretion review . . . is reasonableness." *Id.* at 10 (quoting *United States v. Vargas–Dávila*, 649 F.3d 129, 130 (1st Cir. 2011)). This means that we will affirm only if "no reasonable person could **[—21—]** agree with the ruling." *United States v. Rivera-Carrasquillo*, 933 F.3d 33, 44 (1st Cir. 2019).

The short of it is that contrary to Martínez's claim, and as the government contends, the district court's ruling was not an abuse of its extensive discretion. Recall first that it was Andino's attorney, not Martínez's, who put any meat on the bones of the objection he made to the court's recross ruling. And here, Martínez does not even mention that three-point proffer Andino's attorney made to the court. Instead, Martínez's brief shifts back to talking about the exclusion of the gun testimony and how the earlier denial of recross prevented defense counsel from probing **{-20-}** Resto's disclaimer of any connection between the gun and his drug dealing in Alaska.[16]

But not only is this rear-view-mirror approach untenable in light of basic preservation principles, crucially, that's not how our review of her claim works. Our examination of her allegations of error focuses on the district court judge's reasonableness assessment of the evidentiary ruling at the time the decision was made. *See United States v. Brown*, 669 F.3d 10, **[—22—]** 22 (1st Cir. 2012) (instructing that "[i]mplicit in [the abuse of discretion] standard is the requirement that we not indulge in review by hindsight but consider what evidence was before the trial judge at the time").

Accordingly, on these facts, we cannot characterize the district court's denial of recross as an abuse of discretion. *See, e.g., Maldonado-Peña*, 4 F.4th at 31; *Kenrick*, 221 F.3d at 33.

---

[16] We understand her argument on why she believes the court erred to go like this -- now knowing the district court would later strike Resto's gun testimony, she would have us consider that future ruling alongside the recross ruling to strengthen her contention that the court abused its discretion when it denied her the opportunity to recross. Creative -- give her that. Yet she cites nothing to support such a proposition.

Strike Motion

We turn now to the motion to strike, which generally gets abuse-of-discretion review.[17] *See, e.g., United States v. Sabetta*, 373 F.3d 75, 82 (1st Cir. 2004); *United States v. Houlihan*, 92 F.3d 1271, 1297 (1st Cir. 1996).

Think back to the basic progression that led to the motion to strike: defense counsel suggested during cross that Resto had broken an Alaska law by possessing a gun and failing to register it; the motion to strike was filed a day later; when asked, Martínez's counsel could not provide the court with the Alaska law Resto supposedly broke. In the exchanges that followed, the court, Martínez's attorney, and the government debated whether the gun testimony should be stricken, with Martínez's counsel **[—23—]** urging that Resto's apparent belief that he should have registered the gun goes to credibility. The exchange also touched on the point that, according to the defense, Resto derived a benefit from his cooperation because he wasn't charged under § 924(c) as possessing a firearm in furtherance of drug trafficking.[18] For example, in response to Martínez's counsel's assertion that "the drugs were drugs that were sent from Puerto Rico" to Alaska, the court replied, "His testimony was that he had that gun because of his business of sending drugs to Alaska and selling them, but it has nothing to do with transporting drugs from St. Thomas to Puerto Rico." Counsel said, "That's a classic 924(c), possession of a firearm in furtherance of a drug trafficking crime," and the court responded that it had "nothing to do with this case," that "he has to have actively employed the firearm in furtherance of this drug crime."

The government, for its part, maintained that there was "zero connection" between Resto's gun possession and the facts of the **{-21-}** instant case on trial, and the government "looked into the possibility of a 924(c) and determined [it] was an unprovable charge" because "there was no direct linkage to drug trafficking," **[—24—]** so Resto wasn't "obtaining a benefit by [the government] not charging him with 924(c)."

Trying to pin it all down, the court squarely asked Martínez's counsel, "Whether or not the [g]overnment brought a 924(c), how does that go to [Resto's] credibility?" In response, Martínez's counsel revisited Resto's testimony regarding Alaska's law about purchasing and registering guns, having previously asked Resto, "And isn't it true that . . . you have to register the weapon . . .?" and Resto answered, "That is correct." The district court said, "[B]ut that's beside the point." Martínez's counsel replied, "But that goes to his credibility. He says that he knows the law." Said the district court in response: "But that is not the law. . . . I don't care if the witness says that it is. The witness can say that opening that door is against the law, and it isn't. I am going to strike the testimony." And strike it he did, saying the cross-examination concerning the gun had been improperly misleading.

Martínez's point here, as she frames it, continues her central thesis that striking the gun testimony had the effect of denying her the opportunity to impeach Resto, in a constitutional sense, and to challenge his credibility.

We take her argument to be either that Resto's shipping cocaine to himself from Puerto Rico to Alaska was part of the Puerto Rico conspiracy or that it was a separate but supportably **[—25—]** chargeable § 924(c) crime to possess the gun in furtherance of the Alaskan drug trafficking (perhaps it's both). Thus, she again urges that Resto's gun possession while dealing drugs and lack of consequences for it, coupled with his

[17] Strictly speaking, Martínez never argues that the grant of the motion was an abuse of discretion, instead specifically stating that the ruling as it related to the misleading gun-registration-law testimony was not something she was actually challenging on appeal. But this, we note, was the basis for the motion to strike and its eventual granting.

[18] For inquiring minds, the relevant portion of § 924(c) here lays out the penalties for "any person who, during and in relation to any . . . drug trafficking crime . . . for which the person may be prosecuted in a court of the United States, uses or carries a firearm, or who, in furtherance of any such crime, possesses a firearm." 18 U.S.C. § 924(c)(1)(A).

cooperation, could have been used to establish bias for impeachment purposes. Further, she says, granting the motion to strike "cannot be deemed harmless" because Resto was basically the star witness and the case hinged on his credibility. Regardless of which § 924(c) angle is the primary play here, and assuming her argument is preserved,[19] we conclude, contrary to Martínez's assertion, that any error was harmless.[20] **[—26—]** **{-22-}**

"Harmlessness turns on things like the importance of the testimony to the case, the cumulativeness of the testimony, the presence or absence of other evidence corroborating or contradicting the testimony, the extent of permitted cross-examination, and the overall strength of the government's case." *George*, 761 F.3d at 56 (citing *Earle*, 488 F.3d at 546). And "[w]e will affirm a conviction if the 'contested . . . statements . . . were at best cumulative of other compelling proof that [the defendant] committed the charged [crime].'" *Earle*, 488 F.3d at 546 (quoting *United States v. Bartelho*, 129 F.3d 663, 670 (1st Cir. 1997)).

Here, our review of the above-described list of harmlessness considerations prompts our conclusion that any error regarding Martínez's ability to probe Resto's credibility was indeed harmless. As the government points out, even without Resto's gun testimony in the evidentiary mix, Martínez had, as we've already described, plenty of tools available to her to impeach Resto's credibility -- her counsel was still able to use **[—27—]** the defense's effective cross-examinations during closing arguments, hammering home for the jury's benefit Resto's potential bias, motives, and truthfulness issues on points apart from the gun testimony. For example, the jury heard Resto readily cop to wanting the best possible deals, and cooperation was one way to get a better sentence. And another benefit of Resto's cooperation was the drug quantity stipulation he secured -- 15 to 50 kilos of cocaine as opposed to the significantly higher quantity he actually trafficked based on the evidence the jury heard. His pattern of lying to agents (but not being charged for doing so) and minimizing his involvement in the trafficking scheme was likewise probed during Resto's testimony, then used during closing arguments. Also during closings, defense counsel was able to highlight Resto's plea and cooperation agreements for the jury and counseled the jury to "consider . . . immensely" how much to trust Resto based on his testimony because his plea deal meant that he was on "un dedo pillao" (a short leash) with the government.

Aside from this effective dissection of Resto's credibility, the record reflects that the jury heard and saw ample evidence establishing Martínez's knowing involvement in the drug-smuggling enterprise -- and

[19] Martínez's counsel's answer to the district court's § 924(c) question did not directly posit any analysis of how such a charge not being brought impacts Resto's credibility, but, because it makes no difference to our outcome and we think enough lies latent in the record exchanges to give texture to the argument, we will bypass waiver.

[20] Our harmlessness inquiry can go one of two ways, with us inquiring whether: (1) any error was harmless beyond a reasonable doubt, *see United States v. George*, 761 F.3d 42, 56 (1st Cir. 2014) (sidestepping whether an evidentiary ruling offended an appellant's confrontation rights "because even if an error occurred (something we do not decide), that error was harmless beyond a reasonable doubt" (citing *United States v. Earle*, 488 F.3d 537, 542 (1st Cir. 2007) (instructing that "[i]f a constitutional error has occurred, we must order a new trial unless the government has shown that any error was 'harmless' beyond a reasonable doubt"))); or (2) any error was harmless in that it did not affect Martínez's substantial rights, *see* Fed. R. Civ. P. 61 ("At every stage of the proceeding, the court must disregard all errors and defects that do not affect any party's substantial rights."); *see also Tersigni v. Wyeth*, 817 F.3d 364, 369 (1st Cir. 2016) ("We may affirm in spite of an erroneous evidentiary ruling if the error was harmless, meaning that 'it is highly probable **[—26—]** that the error did not affect the outcome of the case.'" (quoting *McDonough v. City of Quincy*, 452 F.3d 8, 19-20 (1st Cir. 2006))).

While we grant (and have examined how) a recross issue does tap into constitutional confrontation issues, it is not clear (and Martínez does not say) why the motion to strike necessarily follows suit. Because the government carries the burden here, *see Earle*, 488 F.3d at 542, and because we would find harmlessness under either approach, we follow the government's lead and apply the "harmless beyond a reasonable doubt" lens.

corroborating Resto's telling of the tale, to boot. Consider, for example (this list of evidence is non-exhaustive): **[—28—]**

- The day the 28-foot Black Wolfpack (with 111 kilos stashed on it) was intercepted at sea, Martínez was aboard;

- The evidence extracted from her cell phone included text messages from Martínez saying she was "working" and "rich" during the January 2018 trip to St. Thomas;

- November 3, 2017 text messages between Martínez and Andino showed Martínez responding to Andino's "[w]e're leaving tomorrow early" message with "[o]kay. We're ready";

- Then, Martínez's cell phone took a November 4, 2017 picture of cocaine bricks -- the same day Andino registered the Black Wolfpack at the marina in St. Thomas; and

- Martínez appears in a November 19, 2017 photograph at the St. Thomas apartment where the cocaine had been packaged.

As the government argued to the jury in closing, "[Y]ou don't need Mr. Resto to tell **{-23-}** you the story, the phones an[d] the documents tell you the story already."

Taking everything into account, in view of our case law's harmlessness considerations (like strength of the government's case, corroborative or contradictory evidence, cumulativeness, the extent of permitted cross-examination), and even if Martínez's motion-to-strike arguments have some merit, on this record, any error in granting the motion was harmless beyond a reasonable doubt. *See George*, 761 F.3d at 56; *Earle*, 488 F.3d at 542. **[—29—]**

The Foot

On the heels of her Resto-based asseverations comes Martínez's argument that the district court committed error by denying her request to (literally) put her foot in evidence, i.e., showing it to the jury so, as she tells it, the jury could compare that evidence to the government's photographic evidence. As the record and resulting appellate arguments bear out, this request produced a somewhat distinctive evidentiary situation. We begin again with the specifics of what happened below.

Journey back with us to the close of trial proceedings, to when, before bringing the jury in for final instructions, the district court asked defense counsel whether either of the defendants would testify. Martínez and Andino each said no. And the record reflects the defense had no witnesses it wished to call, either. But counsel for Martínez stated he did want to present "one piece of evidence": an in-court exhibition of Martínez's foot. The idea was for the jury to compare her foot to (what Martínez says is) a foot that appears in the government's Exhibit 88.[21] [22] The district court hesitated, querying how anyone would

[21] Exhibit 88 was a photograph extracted from Martínez's phone depicting cocaine bundles with crown stickers and $100-bill stickers affixed to them. The photograph was taken on November 4, 2017. On the bottom right side of the photograph, there is a dark and blurry shape. According to Martínez, that shape is a foot.

[22] This, we gather from the record exchanges, was the basic gist of the proffer -- the in-court foot display, as direct evidence, would prompt a comparison to Exhibit 88 that would rebut **[—30—]** what Martínez says was the government's argument that it is her foot in Exhibit 88 and is evidence of her presence and knowledge while aboard the Black Wolfpack. (Our review finds no basis for the assertion that the government advanced such an Exhibit 88 argument, as we'll soon get to.) This proffer could have been cleaner, but for purposes of our review, we need not grapple with it. *See* Fed. R. Evid. 103(a)(2); *see also Kelley v. Airborne Freight Corp.*, 140 F.3d 335, 347 (1st Cir. 1998) (cautioning that a court cannot "assess the importance of [] excluded evidence," absent compliance with Fed. R. Evid. 103(a)(2), when the proponent of the evidence "[a]t no time . . . ma[d]e an offer of proof that described the basic contours of the evidence [it] planned to introduce"); *Earle v. Benoit*, 850 F.2d 836, 847 (1st Cir. 1988) (declining to review a claim when the proponent of the evidence never made an offer of proof describing the substance of the proposed

[—30—] "know it's her foot" in the photo and why this should be probed outside of closing arguments, then reasoning Martínez's counsel couldn't argue Exhibit 88 did not depict Martínez's foot unless she testified about it.

Martínez's counsel tried to clarify by stressing

> all we are going to show the jury is Ms. Martínez-Alberto's foot. I'm going to request that a screen shot be taken, and that be Defense Exhibit 2, and that is all that we are planning on doing. We're not going to ask any questions, we're not {-24-} making any statements, that is all that we're going to do in this case, Your Honor.

The district court's response was to say Martínez would need to testify as to whether the exhibit depicts her foot. And when in response Martínez's counsel asked if he could ask his client one question -- "Is the foot that appears on Exhibit 88 your foot?" -- the district court again reasoned that Martínez couldn't [—31—] just show her foot to the jury; she'd need to testify, and she could be subject to cross-examination if she did. And so, counsel for Martínez said, "We have no evidence."[23]

Before us, Martínez says it was error for the district court to deny her the opportunity to show her foot to the jurors. Specifically, she urges it was incorrect to conclude that Martínez would open herself up to cross-examination if she showed her foot since doing so isn't testimonial -- and this error was not harmless, she says, in that "[t]he evidence of Martínez's knowledge of the conspiracy was not overwhelming," "[t]he photograph showing the foot next to the bricks of cocaine was the most compelling evidence of knowledge," and the government "extensively relied upon it" to argue she knew about and was involved in the conspiracy.

The government parries by offering a variety of reasons why the district court was right to reject Martínez's request. For instance, the government posits that Martínez failed to lay [—32—] any foundation for the evidence (her foot), and that because of this failure, it would render this evidentiary offer irrelevant. Moreover, according to the government, Martínez's characterization of Exhibit 88 and how the government used it at trial is off. Contrary to her insistence otherwise, says the government, that photo wasn't used to identify her foot and thus prove her knowledge of the conspiracy or her presence on the Black Wolfpack (whether by the purported foot itself or its proximity to the cocaine or, perhaps, the suggestion that she was the one who took the photo); rather, Exhibit 88 was used to show that Martínez's phone took a November 4, 2017 photo that showed logos on cocaine bundles, and those matched later images of similarly packaged and stickered cocaine bundles that were seized from the Black Wolfpack in January 2018.

We will review for abuse of discretion the foot-as-evidence issue.[24] *See, e.g., United States v. Vázquez-Soto*, 939 F.3d 365, 373 (1st Cir. 2019); *United States v. Zaccaria*, 240 F.3d 75, 78 (1st Cir. 2001) (stating abuse-of-discretion review applies to district court

evidence, reasoning that "the offer of proof device exists" for instances in which "a court refuses to receive evidence and yet the same is needed to elucidate [a] proponent's claim for admissibility, that the offer of proof device exists").

[23] The district court pointed out the possible risk of Martínez taking the stand to testify about Exhibit 88 and her foot in that it might open her up to cross-examination on topics beyond "the foot." *See, e.g., Johnson v. United States*, 318 U.S. 189, 195 (1943) (explaining that "[t]he case of an accused who voluntarily takes the stand and the case of an accused who refrains from testifying are of course vastly different" -- a "voluntary offer of testimony upon any fact is a waiver as to all other relevant facts, because of the necessary connection between all" (quoting 8 Wigmore, Evidence § 2276(2) (3d ed. 1940))). We note this, but need not opine on it given our outcome.

[24] Our review of the record suggests Martínez did not lodge an objection to the court's ruling, but it is not clear. So we stick with abuse-of-discretion review for this argument. *See, e.g., United States v. Rosado-Pérez*, 605 F.3d 48, 54 & n.2 (1st Cir. 2010) (opting to conduct abuse-of-discretion review even when the appellants "did not always clearly object" and hadn't "preserved every concern they raise[d] on appeal").

rulings admitting or excluding evidence and, in **[—33—]** so doing, noting that "[e]very trial presents a blend of idiosyncratic circumstances," so "presiding judges must be afforded some leeway in making evidentiary rulings"). And from our vantage **{-25-}** point, this issue's resolution turns on the fundamentals of introducing evidence. Martínez's counsel ran afoul of those fundamentals relative to the proposed display of his client's foot in a way that undercuts her argument on appeal: the failure to proffer a proper evidentiary foundation.

"District courts 'have wide discretion in deciding whether an adequate foundation has been laid for the admission of evidence.'" *United States v. Velazquez-Fontanez*, 6 F.4th 205, 221 (1st Cir.) (quoting *Veranda Beach Club Ltd. P'ship v. W. Sur. Co.*, 936 F.2d 1364, 1371 (1st Cir. 1991)), *cert. denied*, 142 S. Ct. 500 (2021), and *cert. denied sub nom. Resto-Figueroa v. United States*, 142 S. Ct. 1164 (2022); *see also Gomez v. Rivera Rodríguez*, 344 F.3d 103, 117 (1st Cir. 2003) (instructing that "the determination of whether a party has built a proper foundation is left principally to the sound discretion of the presider").[25] **[—34—]**

And when, as here, an evidentiary dispute arises, and when tendering an evidentiary proffer to the court in support of admissibility, "the most important procedural rule is that the proponent of an item of evidence must ordinarily lay the foundation before formally offering the item into evidence." Edward J. Imwinkelreid, *Evidentiary Foundations*, § 1.02[1] (10th ed. March 2018). "At a bare minimum, the requisite foundation demands something more than intuitive judgments emanating from broad generalities." *Gomez*, 344 F.3d at 117; *see also Kissinger v. Lofgren*, 836 F.2d 678, 683 (1st Cir. 1988) (explaining that a proper foundation for evidence requires its proponent to provide "'evidence sufficient to support a finding' that the evidence is what the proponent claims it to be" (quoting 5 J. Weinstein & M. Berger, *Weinstein's Evidence*, ¶ 901(a))); Fed. R. Evid. 104(b).

Important here, building a proper evidentiary foundation involves demonstrating the relevance of the proffered evidence. *See* Fed. R. Evid. 401 (providing that evidence is relevant if "(a) it has any tendency to make a fact more or less probable than it would be without the evidence; and (b) the fact is of consequence in determining the action"); Fed. R. Evid. 402 **[—35—]** (relevant evidence is admissible). "In general, with respect to an item of real evidence, a foundation must be presented establishing that the item is relevant, its identity, and that its condition has not materially changed." *Test for Relevant Evidence*, Courtroom Handbook on Federal Evidence, Ch. 5 Rule 401 (2023). "With respect to an item used demonstratively or illustratively, the foundation must establish that the item depicts relevant information that is or will be proven by other, substantive evidence; that it is accurate; and that it will probably aid the trier of fact in understanding the evidence." *Id.* And relevance must be "determined in the context of the facts and arguments in a particular case." **{-26-}** *Sprint/United Mgmt. Co. v. Mendelsohn*, 552 U.S. 379, 387 (2008); *see also* Advisory Committee's Notes on Fed. R. Evid. 401, 28 U.S.C. App., p. 864 ("Relevancy is not an inherent characteristic of any item of evidence but exists only as a relation between an item of evidence and a matter properly provable in the case. Does the item of evidence tend to prove the matter sought to be proved?").

---

[25] This is a good moment to revisit Martínez's depiction of the district court's ruling as being based on the foot-display as testimonial and thus triggering cross-examination, very cause-and-effect style. Certainly, the record reflects some debate about whether Martínez would testify and whether she'd then be subject to cross as a result. But the record also can be fairly read to reflect the district court's more threshold confusion and concern about the proposed evidence having no foundation, nothing to actually get it *into* evidence -- unless, for example, Martínez testified about it. Indeed, on balance, the record shows the **[—34—]** district court grappling with the totality of the idiosyncratic situation, wrestling with logistics (Martínez was the only possible defense witness; there was no one else to call to talk about her foot) and the customary, gateway questions swirling around foundation.

So, what would the relevance of Martínez's in-court foot display be? Her suggestion, recall, is that her in-court display would tend to rebut what she characterizes as the government's suggestion that it is her foot in Exhibit 88, making her in-court display relevant inasmuch as it could tend to disprove her knowledge, presence, and participation in the scheme. To do this, **[—36—]** though, she needed to foundationally connect these evidentiary dots -- and she did not.

We explain, starting with Exhibit 88 itself. To admit this picture (showing cocaine bundles with crown stickers and $100-bill stickers affixed to them) into evidence, the government called the special agent who conducted the extraction that led to the discovery of the photograph on Martínez's phone. As pertinent here, when the government showed Exhibit 88 to the agent, he testified that he recognized it because the "image [was] part of the extraction that [he] performed of the phone." After Exhibit 88 was admitted, the government continued:

> [Government]: So this was an image that you found, correct, on this phone?
>
> [Agent]: Correct.
>
> [Government]: And this phone belonged to [Martínez].
>
> [Agent]: Correct.

In response to the government's further questioning, the agent testified as to Exhibit 88-1, "the report performed of the telephone extraction." As the agent confirmed, the report captures information about Exhibit 88. Looking at the extraction and metadata report, the agent explained (in some technical detail not necessary to get into here) that the photo (Exhibit 88) was taken on November 4, 2017 at 9:49 p.m. using Martínez's phone. Over an **[—37—]** objection unrelated to any issue on appeal, Exhibit 88 was admitted in full.

The next day, Resto was questioned by the government about the process he and his crew undertook when packaging their kilos. Resto was asked whether the wrapping pictured in Exhibit 88 (which was on display for this line of questioning) was what was done to the kilos of cocaine he and his partners would transport, and he confirmed, "That is correct[, t]his is how they [were] received" and then wrapped by his team.

Having studied the record and the Exhibit 88-related exchanges closely, we agree with the government that in her efforts to convince the court to permit the in-court display of her foot (and still before us), Martínez mischaracterized the government's use of and reliance on its Exhibit 88 at trial. The record reflects that Exhibit 88 was not introduced by the government for the purpose of identifying Martínez or to intimate that the blurry shape at the bottom of the photo is Martínez's foot. Rather, the significance of Exhibit 88, as the government set forth in the foundation it laid for admissibility, was in its timing and what it showed: A November 4, 2017 photo on Martínez's phone, aligning with the Black Wolfpack's November 4, 2017 trafficking journey, showing cocaine bundles with stickers that matched those appearing on bundles seized after the January 2018 arrests. The fact that **[—38—]** a foot might be in the photo was of no moment to the government's case.

Thus, the significance of the display of Martínez's foot -- whether exhibiting her foot directly to the jury, putting it on the **{-27-}** court's projector, or taking a screenshot so the jury could get a good look at it -- to permit the jury to contrast it with "the foot" in Exhibit 88 rested on a faulty relevancy premise to begin with. Martínez has not shown how her proposed foot evidence (a) has any tendency to make a fact of import here more or less probable than it would be without the evidence, and (b) why the foot evidence is of consequence in determining some action of consequence to the government's case or to her defense.[26] *See*

[26] Nothing in Martínez's briefing reasonably explains how her proposed foot evidence implicates her knowledge or any other rational theory of defense. For instance, if the jury made a determination that "the foot" in Exhibit 88 was not her foot, she doesn't explicate why such a finding would somehow demonstrate her ignorance of the drug smuggling activity on January 27, 2018. *See, e.g., United States v. Andino-Morales*, 73 F.4th 24, 42 (1st Cir. 2023) (citing *Zannino*, 895 F.2d at 17);

Fed. R. Evid. 401 (providing that evidence is relevant if "(a) it has any tendency to make a fact more or less probable than it would be without the evidence; and (b) the fact is of consequence in **[—39—]** determining the action"); Fed. R. Evid. 402 (relevant evidence is admissible).[27]

Indeed, on the record before us and bearing in mind the above-recapped guiding principles of relevancy, we do not see -- and Martínez has not shown -- why a direct-evidence-showing of her foot would be relevant.[28] Accordingly, we cannot say it was an abuse of discretion to exclude the display of Martínez's foot.

Jury Instructions

Martínez's third and final appellate argument is of the instructional variety, and it has two dimensions: The district court committed error when it failed to instruct the jury to consider the charges against Martínez and Andino separately, and in the instructions it did issue, it impermissibly and repeatedly referred to the defendants as a single unit. We begin our inspection of this assertion by setting the instructional scene, then we'll drill down on these arguments. **[—40—]**

In the lead-up to trial, the district court issued an order directing the parties to submit proposed jury instructions. The government filed proposed instructions; neither Martínez nor Andino followed suit. In time, the district court gave counsel its proposed jury instructions and verdict forms for their review, some changes were made during the charging conference, the instructions were redistributed to all counsel at the end of trial day seven, and then, at the close of evidence, the district court read the instructions to the jury.

Throughout the instructions, the district court referred to Martínez and Andino as "the defendants," and "they," "their," and "them," too. One example of many such instances came when the district court instructed the jury that, "Even if the Defendants **{-28-}** were not part of the agreement at the very start, they can be found guilty of conspiracy if the Government proves that they willfully joined the agreement later." This phrasing occurs throughout the instructions. Later, the district court did instruct that the jury could not "find the Defendants guilty unless [the jury found] beyond a reasonable doubt that each of them participated in the conspiracies as charged with at least one other person, whether a Defendant or not." Additionally, each defendant had her own verdict form. The district court separately identified each form ("There are two verdict forms; one for each Defendant.") and read each form to the jury. Martínez's verdict form directed the jury **[—41—]** to determine whether Martínez was guilty or not guilty for conspiring to possess with the intent to distribute and import cocaine, and did not mention Andino; Andino's form communicated the same directive, likewise never mentioning Martínez.

Debuting her concerns about the instructional phase, Martínez focuses on two aspects of what happened during the jury charge. First, she says the district court failed to issue an instruction to the jury directing it to consider each defendant separately and not think of them as a group. Second, she argues the district court's consistent and repeated reference to the defendants as a unit constituted prejudicial error because there was more extensive evidence against Andino than Martínez. Indeed, Martínez urges that the district court's error was not putting the terms

Díaz-Alarcón v. Flández-Marcel, 944 F.3d 303, 313 (1st Cir. 2019) (noting that "developing a sustained argument out of . . . legal precedents is a litigant's job, not ours" (internal quotations and citation omitted)).

[27] And, moreover, absent her testimony, Martínez offered no avenue for adducing that her foot, as it would have appeared that day at trial in 2019, resembled or was similar to how her foot would have looked on or around the date that picture was taken in 2017 -- a piece of the foundational puzzle.

[28] And at any rate, other evidence supported the government's position that Martínez was a knowing member of this conspiracy: Resto's testimony (regarding recruiting and working with her, for instance); her own text-message statements -- on dates when the Black Wolfpack was in St. Thomas -- about working and being rich while "not in PR"; and a picture of some bricks taken by her phone while in St. Thomas. And recall, Martínez does not mount a sufficiency-of-the-evidence challenge on appeal.

"each of" before every mention of "the defendants" throughout, instead doing so only once -- that "each of them participated in the conspiracies" line we mentioned -- and even that was against the backdrop of many more instructions that group them together as one entity. And Martínez further argues the separate jury verdict forms shouldn't impact our calculus at all since they are not instructions, but rather are a mere end-of-the-process formality that could not undo the damage that had already been done during the instructional phase.

For its part, the government disagrees entirely, maintaining that a whole-picture view of the jury charge plainly **[—42—]** demonstrates the jury was told to consider Martínez and Andino separately to determine guilt as to each individual woman.

Martínez correctly owns that there was no objection to the final instructions below, which contain the offending language she now protests on appeal. Given this concession, and assuming, contrary to the government's assertion, the argument is not waived, *see United States v. Clough*, 978 F.3d 810, 823 (1st Cir. 2020) ("We need not linger over [appellant's] contentions because he waived this claim by failing to request such an instruction below."), our review of these contentions is, at best, for plain error,[29] *see United States v. Cruz-Ramos*, 987 F.3d 27, 39 (1st Cir. 2021) (explaining that an appellant "must run the usually lethal gauntlet of plain-error review" on his instructional-error claim when he did not raise the issue below). This requires Martínez to "make the difficult showing that the judge erred and clearly [or obviously] so, and that the error also affected [her] substantial rights -- but even then we can still affirm if [she] does not show as well that the error seriously harmed the fairness, integrity, or public perception of [her] trial." *Id.*; *see also United States v. Bauzo-Santiago*, 867 F.3d 13, 22-23 & 23 n.8 (1st Cir. 2017). "This standard is exceedingly difficult to **{-29-}** satisfy in jury **[—43—]** instruction cases: '[T]he plain error hurdle, high in all events, nowhere looms larger than in the context of alleged instructional errors.'" *United States v. González-Vélez*, 466 F.3d 27, 35 (1st Cir. 2006) (quoting *United States v. Paniagua-Ramos*, 251 F.3d 242, 246 (1st Cir. 2001)).

"When applying the plain error standard in the context of jury instructions, [this court] look[s] at the instructions as a whole to ascertain the extent to which they adequately explain the law without confusing or misleading the jury." *Bauzo-Santiago*, 867 F.3d at 23 (quoting *United States v. Candelario-Santana*, 834 F.3d 8, 27 (1st Cir. 2016)) (cleaned up); *see also United States v. Padilla-Galarza*, 990 F.3d 60, 83-84 (1st Cir. 2021) (observing that this review of jury instructions "is context-dependent and must take into account the jury instructions as a whole"); *United States v. Vega*, 813 F.3d 386, 396–97 (1st Cir. 2016) (concluding on plain-error review that, "read[] against the backdrop of the charge as a whole," the jury instructions were sufficient, even if not "letter perfect" (quoting *Paniagua-Ramos*, 251 F.3d at 246-47)). Given all of this, we've said this lens of review "is cold comfort to most defendants pursuing claims of instructional error." *Mitchell*, 596 F.3d at 25 (quoting *United States v. Gómez*, 255 F.3d 31, 37 (1st Cir. 2001)).

The stage set, we proceed to our plain-error review, mindful that "a reversal on instruction-error grounds is 'a remedy **[—44—]** that is granted sparingly.'" *United States v. Takesian*, 945 F.3d 553, 566 (1st Cir. 2019) (quoting *United States v. Gelin*, 712 F.3d 612, 620 (1st Cir. 2013)). We won't hide the ball: Martínez's instructional-error arguments cannot withstand the "exceedingly difficult to satisfy" plain-error scrutiny, *González-Vélez*, 466 F.3d at 35, and that is because we discern no clear or obvious error.

Martínez says the district court should have included an (unrequested) instruction that the jury consider the defendants separately, and its failure to do so -- coupled with its repeated lumping together of "the defendants" during the jury charge -- is an error that was plain.

[29] When a party fails to object to a jury instruction, Federal Rules of Criminal Procedure, Rule 30(d) "precludes appellate review" except for plain error.

But in looking at these arguments "against the backdrop of the charge as a whole," *Vega*, 813 F.3d at 396–97 (quoting *Paniagua-Ramos*, 251 F.3d at 246-47), it's clear they were sufficient and no clear or obvious error lies.

True, the district court did not say "each defendant" or place "each of" before "the defendants" throughout the jury charge. But these standard instructions, again, read in context and as a whole, had the effect of appropriately directing the jury to consider Martínez and Andino separately. Early in the instructions, setting the stage and tone, the district court told the jury that (emphasis ours)

> [t]he presumption of innocence alone may be sufficient to raise a reasonable doubt and to require the acquittal of *a Defendant*. The Defendants before you, Katerin **[—45—]** Martínez-Alberto and Alexandria Andino-Rodríguez, have had the benefit of the presumption of innocence throughout the trial and you are not to convict them of the charges against them unless you are persuaded of their guilt of these charges beyond a reasonable doubt.

Later, the district court was clear that the jury could not "find the Defendants guilty unless [it found] beyond a reasonable doubt that *each* of them participated in the conspiracies as charged with at least one other person . . . ." (Emphasis added.) We also note that the jury had before it the defendants' indictment -- the charging document that spells out the counts against each defendant -- which the district court **{–30–}** referenced throughout its instructions and gave to the jury (the government having redacted Maximiliano and Emiliano from it) for its use during deliberations. Add to that (as the government points out) the separate jury verdict forms canvassed thoroughly during the jury charge. Remember, the district court told the jury, "There are two verdict forms; one for each Defendant," then walked through each form for the jury's benefit, with Martínez's verdict form being entirely unique to her and the charges against her, never mentioning Andino, who had her own jury verdict form.[30] And as for Martínez's assertion that any **[—46—]** consideration of an extraneous document like a jury verdict form should not be part of our decisional calculus, we believe the district court's careful review of the purpose and operation of the forms would have clarified any possible ambiguity in the jurors' minds about their decision-making responsibilities towards each defendant.

And despite Martínez's protestations to the contrary, our case law does not favor her position given our standard of review here. We've described a plain (i.e., clear or obvious) error as being one that is "'indisputable' in light of controlling law." *United States v. Rabb*, 5 F.4th 95, 101 (1st Cir. 2021) (quoting *United States v. Jones*, 748 F.3d 64, 70 (1st Cir. 2014)). While some of the cases to which Martínez points flag steps that *may* be taken during the jury charge to dispel the risk of prejudice, like issuing an instruction that the jury give separate **[—47—]** consideration to each defendant, we are unaware of any controlling

---

[30] For example, the district court read into the record:

> [A]s to Ms. Martínez-Alberto, the verdict reads as follows:
>
> "As to the charge in Count One of the indictment, conspiring to possess with intent to distribute cocaine, we, the jury, unanimously find the Defendant, Katerin **[—46—]** Martínez-Alberto," and then there is a place for you to check "guilty" or "not guilty".
>
> And as to the charge in Count Two of the indictment, "Conspiring to import cocaine into the customs territory of the United States from a place outside the customs territory of the United States, but within the United States, we, the jury unanimously find the Defendant Katerin Martínez-Alberto," and again, you have a place to check "guilty" or "not guilty".
>
> . . .
>
> There is a place for the jury foreperson to sign and date the verdict.

The district court then did the same with Andino's verdict form.

law that affirmatively obligates courts to issue this specific instruction in order to avoid committing clear and obvious error. And when, as here, a full-picture review of the instructional phase shows the jury was sufficiently clear on its task to consider the defendants and the evidence against each separately, there is no indispensable need for such a requirement.[31] **{-31-}**

In all, in view of our context-dependent reviewing parameters, Martínez has not shown plain error. *See, e.g., Padilla-Galarza*, 990 F.3d at 83-84; *Bauzo-Santiago*, 867 F.3d at 23; *Vega*, 813 F.3d at 396–97. **[—48—]**

Andino

We come now to Andino and the sole issue she raises on appeal, a sentencing challenge. Andino says the district court committed reversible error when it denied her request for a mitigating role adjustment pursuant to the federal sentencing guidelines, and that error resulted in the improper calculation of her guidelines sentencing range. Having carefully reviewed the sentencing record, we are unconvinced. Before we explain why that is so, we offer a little contextual primer on the sentencing framework in which Andino's appellate contention operates and the lens through which we must review it.

Andino's sentencing challenge is based upon the guidelines' available downward adjustments for a defendant who played a mitigating role in an offense. Specifically, section 3B1.2 of the guidelines allows a court to decrease a defendant's offense level by four levels if she is deemed a minimal participant, two levels if she is deemed a minor participant, and three levels if the case falls somewhere in between. *See* U.S.S.G. § 3B1.2; *see also United States v. De la Cruz-Gutiérrez*, 881 F.3d 221, 225, 6 Adm. R. 2, 3–4 (1st Cir. 2018) (tracking some of the evolution of this reduction). "Adjustments under this section apply to defendants whose role in the offense make them 'substantially less culpable than the average participant in the criminal activity.'" *United States v. Mendoza-Maisonet*, 962 F.3d 1, 23 (1st Cir. 2020) (quoting **[—49—]** U.S.S.G. § 3B1.2 cmt. n.3(A)). A defendant "who [is] plainly among the least culpable of those involved in the conduct of a group" is considered a minimal participant. U.S.S.G. § 3B1.2 cmt. n.4. Alternatively, a minor participant is one "who is less culpable than most other participants in the criminal activity, but whose role could not be described as minimal." *Id.* cmt. n.5.

Now, our method of review for Andino's mitigating-role argument. Zooming out for the basics, we review procedural reasonableness challenges like Andino's "under a multifaceted abuse-of-discretion standard whereby we afford de novo review to the sentencing court's interpretation and application of the sentencing guidelines, assay the court's factfinding for clear error, and evaluate its judgment calls for abuse of discretion." *Mendoza-Maisonet*, 962 F.3d at 20 (quoting *United States v. Arsenault*, 833 F.3d 24, 28 (1st Cir. 2016)).

Narrowing our focus to the sort of mitigating role adjustment issue we're confronted with in this case, we emphasize that "[t]he defendant seeking the mitigating role adjustment 'bears the burden of proving, by a preponderance of the evidence, that [she] is entitled to the

[31] Were Martínez's jury instruction challenge preserved (thereby triggering a more appellant-friendly standard of review), this might have been a closer call. As we've said, when it comes to jury instructions in multi-defendant trials, the best practice is for district courts to take care to instruct in the clearest possible terms as to each individual defendant -- one way to do so is to proactively issue instructions to avoid the spillover prejudice Martínez is concerned about here. *See, e.g., United States v. Simon*, 12 F.4th 1, 44 (1st Cir. 2021) (relying on the district court's "prudent[]" instruction to the jury "to treat each defendant individually and to weigh separately the evidence as to each defendant" to combat the risk of prejudice), *cert. denied sub nom. Kapoor v. United States*, 142 S. Ct. 2811 (2022), and *cert. denied sub nom. Lee v. United States*, 142 S. Ct. 2812 (2022); *González-Vélez*, 466 F.3d at 35-36 (relying in part on the district court having "explicitly stat[ed] that, '[T]he evidence pertaining to each defendant should be considered separately and individually'" to conclude "the instructions did not constitute error as to the finding of guilt").

downward adjustment.'" *Id.* at 23 (quoting *United States v. Arias-Mercedes*, 901 F.3d 1, 5 (1st Cir. 2018)). We've often warned that, "[b]ecause determining one's role in an offense is a fact-specific inquiry, 'we rarely reverse a district court's decision regarding whether to apply a minor **[—50—]** role adjustment.'" *De la Cruz-Gutiérrez*, 881 F.3d at 225-26, 6 Adm. R. at 4 (quoting *United States v. Bravo*, 489 F.3d 1, 11 (1st Cir. 2007)); *see also United States v. Valenzuela*, 849 F.3d 477, 489 (1st Cir. 2017) (reviewing the district court's decision to impose a minor participant reduction for clear error because "[r]ole-in-the-offense determinations are notoriously fact-sensitive" (quoting *United States v. Montes-Fosse*, 824 F.3d 168, 172 (1st Cir. 2016))); *United States v. Pérez*, 819 F.3d 541, 546, 4 Adm. R. 20, 21 (1st Cir. 2016) ("[B]attles over a defendant's status . . . **{-32-}** will almost always be won or lost in the district court." (second alteration in original)). Indeed, "[a] defendant will 'only prevail on appeal by demonstrating that the district court's determination as to his role in the offense was clearly erroneous.'" *De la Cruz-Gutiérrez*, 881 F.3d at 226, 6 Adm. R. at 4 (quoting *United States v. González-Soberal*, 109 F.3d 64, 74 (1st Cir. 1997)). And our "clear-error standard is demanding and will be satisfied 'only if, upon whole-record review, an inquiring court forms a strong, unyielding belief that a mistake has been made.'" *Mendoza-Maisonet*, 962 F.3d at 20 (quoting *United States v. Montañez-Quiñones*, 911 F.3d 59, 66 (1st Cir. 2018)) (cleaned up). What's more, if the record supports at least two plausible inferences, the district court's choice among these **[—51—]** alternatives cannot be clearly erroneous. *See De la Cruz-Gutiérrez*, 881 F.3d at 227, 6 Adm. R. at 5.[32]

All of this to say, "the standard is highly deferential, and reversal is rare." *United States v. Ruiz*, 999 F.3d 742, 750 (1st Cir. 2021) (citing *Mendoza-Maisonet*, 962 F.3d at 23).

With this guidance in tow, we turn to the opposing views presented at the presentencing regarding Andino's role in the trafficking operation. After the trial concluded and before the sentencing hearing, a probation officer produced Andino's presentence report ("PSR"). The report came up with an initial offense level of 36 pursuant to U.S.S.G. § 2D1.1(a) and the application of a two-level reduction according to the safety valve criteria under U.S.S.G. § 5C1.2, cmt. n.2.[33] The probation officer posited that "Ms. Andino is entitled to a mitigating role **[—52—]** adjustment" and thus reduced her base offense level by three levels (meaning she was less culpable than other participants in the offense but had more than a minimal role) and then reduced it an additional two levels for being a minor participant.

The government objected to the probation officer's application of the two mitigating role adjustments, however the probation officer stood by his initial determination, stating Andino's role in the offense "seems to be small when compared to that of some of her co-conspirators within the overall drug importation scheme." The probation officer did not dispute the events (being present in meetings, signing marina forms, helping wrap and clean the kilos), but argued a closer look at those activities reveals the role of a minor participant. Andino's sentencing memorandum adopted the probation officer's reasoning, and in turn proposed to the district court an 87-month sentence, the lower bound of the sentencing range once adjusted for the safety valve and both mitigating role adjustments.

---

[32] *See also* U.S.S.G. Notes: "The determination whether to apply subsection (a) or subsection (b), or an intermediate adjustment, is based on the totality of the circumstances and involves a determination that is heavily dependent upon the facts of the particular case."

[33] The safety valve provision limits the application of mandatory minimum sentences for certain drug offenders who qualify under a list of factors included in 18 U.S.C. § 3553(f). *See also* U.S.S.G. § 5C1.2. We have found "Congress's purpose in enacting the provision was to 'mitigate the harsh effect of mandatory minimum sentences' on first-time, low-level offenders in drug trafficking schemes." *United States v. Padilla-Colón*, 578 F.3d 23, 30 (1st Cir. 2009) (citing *United States v. Ortiz-Santiago*, 211 F.3d 146, 150 (1st Cir. 2000)); *see* H.R. Rep. No. 103-460 (1994). After Andino's safety valve interview, the government determined she satisfied the statutory requirements and therefore agreed to the application of this two-level adjustment.

In its ensuing formal objection, the government applied the five-factor assessment {-33-} listed in section 3B1.2 cmt. n.3 (C) to the facts of Andino's case,[34] concluding from this exercise that [—53—] Andino was no mere mule or smokescreen within the trafficking enterprise. Based on this telling of the story, the government asked for 120 months' imprisonment.

With this point of contention looming, the parties headed into the sentencing hearing. Once there, the district court, after considering arguments from both sides, disagreed with the probation officer and Andino's position, ultimately finding Andino ineligible for any mitigating role adjustment. To justify its decision, the court went through the five mitigating role adjustment factors (*see supra* note 34) and matched Andino's conduct to each factor. The district court noted Andino had sailed to St. Thomas on several occasions, well aware of her role as a "filler" to cover up the true nature of the voyage. Prior to at least one trip to St. Thomas, Andino met at Coplin's home to coordinate and plan the next criminal venture. Andino's role while in St. Thomas -- registering the Black Wolfpack at the Crown Bay Marina and assisting in the packaging of several kilos of cocaine -- demonstrated her willing participation in the commission of the crime. And lastly, as the final factor, the district court observed that Andino received $7,000 for her participation in a single trip from which the court inferred Andino stood to benefit from the criminal activity. [—54—]

With all the facts on the table, the district court concluded Andino did not play a minor role in the operations of the Black Wolfpack and denied the mitigating role adjustments she requested. From there, the court landed on a total offense level of 34, which, when bundled with her criminal history category of I, yielded a guideline range of 151-188 months. After noting that range was greater than necessary to achieve the goals of sentencing and, consequently, adding a downward variance, the district court's tabulations concluded with the pronouncement of a 120- month sentence of imprisonment and a five-year term of supervised release.

Now we assess whether the district court clearly erred in its decision to deny Andino this adjustment. Remember, Andino had the burden of proving her entitlement to the requested adjustment, *Mendoza-Maisonet*, 962 F.3d at 23, and we defer to the district court's factual determinations as to whether she carried that burden unless we form "a strong, unyielding belief that a mistake has been made," *id.* at 20 (quoting *Montañez-Quiñones*, 911 F.3d at 66). Viewed under this exacting lens, we spy no such mistake and conclude Andino's sentencing claim must fail.

Andino's arguments in support of her overall sentencing challenge share intertwined theses and themes: She carried her burden of showing she was an inessential "smokescreen" who played a tiny, non-leadership role in the trafficking scheme and was thus [—55—] far less blameworthy than most of her smuggling cohorts, and the district court committed error in ignoring some evidence and misconstruing other evidence to reach the opposite conclusion. We tease all of this out as we go.

Let's start with Andino's argument that the court's denial of her requested adjustment {-34-} was clearly erroneous[35] because "she was less culpable than most codefendants; the only exception being codefendant . . . Martínez-Alberto."

For starters, our case law is clear that all parties engaged in a criminal enterprise can be "located on a continuum." *Arias-Mercedes*, 901 F.3d at 8. Those who are primarily responsible

[34] These five non-exhaustive factors are: (i) the degree to which the defendant understood the scope of the criminal activity; (ii) the degree to which the defendant participated in planning or organizing; (iii) the degree to which the defendant exercised decision-making authority; (iv) the nature and extent of the [—53—] defendant's participation; and (v) the degree to which the defendant stood to benefit. *See* U.S.S.G. § 3B1.2, cmt. n.3 (C).

[35] A quick aside to acknowledge the possibility that Andino's counsel conceded at argument before us that there was no clear error in the district court's findings. But because it's not entirely clear and it's similarly unclear how sweeping the concession would be, we'll proceed to our analysis.

stand on one end, and the least culpable participants, described here as being Martínez, stand at the opposite end. When a defendant "stands somewhere in the middle," as Andino seems to concede is where she falls on this continuum, a district court may reasonably infer the defendant is "not substantially less culpable than the average participant." *Id.* This fundamentally undercuts much of her argument.

Another problem with this asseveration is that it asks us to simply take a different view of the same facts that were **[—56—]** before the district court to reach Andino's preferred outcome.[36] This is not a winning approach. *See Pérez*, 819 F.3d 546, 4 Adm. R. at 21–22 (dismissing appellant's arguments based on the same facts considered by the district court); *Mendoza-Maisonet*, 962 F.3d at 24 (rejecting appellant's argument that the district court failed to accurately interpret the facts within the record). And despite Andino's disagreement with the inferences drawn by the district court, when "the record supports at least two permissible inferences, 'the sentencing court's choice among supportable alternatives cannot be clearly erroneous.'" *De la Cruz-Gutiérrez*, **[—57—]** 881 F.3d at 227, 6 Adm. R. at 5 (quoting *Pérez*, 819 F.3d at 546, 4 Adm. R. at 21). That is what we have here.

Next consider Andino's supposition that because other co-defendants had greater organizing roles, the court erroneously inferred she took part in planning the crime based on testimony placing Andino at a meeting to plan an operation. Not so. Instead, when the district court considered these facts, it reasonably viewed Andino's presence at the meeting as evidence "establish[ing] that Ms. Andino possessed some degree of decision-making authority or that she was sufficiently trusted to be part of the coordination efforts." Similarly, Andino argues the $7,000 payout for her role in the operation was insignificant considering other participants received over $20,000. When the district court considered testimony stating Andino received **{-35-}** thousands of dollars for her efforts and $7,000 for a single trip, it inferred "the financial benefits for participating in the criminal activity were significant." We are left with two sides of the same story, and no reason to find the district court clearly erred in determining she hadn't carried her burden -- "the fact that someone else might have been more culpable than [Andino] does not necessarily mean that [Andino's] participation was minor [or minimal]." *De la Cruz-Gutiérrez*, 881 F.3d at 226, 6 Adm. R. at 5 (third alteration in original); *see also Mendoza-Maisonet*, 962 F.3d at 24-25. **[—58—]**

Then there's Andino's argument that the district court relied too heavily upon the government's position, did not consider the arguments made by the probation officer, and failed to support its decision for denying Andino's adjustment with evidence in the record. Andino bases this claim on the addendum to the PSR where the probation officer stood by and doubled down on his determination that Andino was deserving of a minor role. But despite Andino's insistence that "the sentencing [c]ourt did not consider them and ultimately sided with the government's version of the facts," the court

---

[36] And another quick aside on the topic of what, exactly, was before the district court with respect to Andino because, in her papers and at oral argument, Andino devoted some attention to her safety valve interview and the role she thinks it should have played in sentencing. In her interview, Andino provided information about her knowledge and participation in the criminal enterprise. She says this was presented at sentencing and should have been considered by the court in determining her role in the offense.

Here's the thing. When the district court clearly stated it would not use this information, opting instead to "strictly determine her role in the offense based on what was testified at trial," Andino did not object. That means our review of this question is for plain error. *See United States v. Pupo*, 995 F.3d 23, 29 (1st Cir. 2021). But Andino failed to cite any case law that requires district courts to consider safety valve interviews or explain how the information produced in her interview would help her case. Truth be told, she made no mention of the plain-error review this aspect of her argument was up against, let alone attempt to meet the onerous four-part burden. For these reasons, this aspect of Andino's argument is waived. *See Cruz-Ramos*, 987 F.3d at 40 (collecting examples of waiver arising when appellants fail to attempt to meet the demanding burden of plain-error review).

made clear it had reviewed the parties' submissions (including the defense's sentencing memorandum, which relies upon the probation officer's reasoning in the addendum to the PSR) and went on to reference the probation officer's perspective throughout the sentencing hearing. Notably, the district court concluded that the "probation officer did not correctly apply the guideline computations, and the pre-sentence investigation report does not reflect the components of Ms. Andino's offenses, or consider their nature and circumstances." In other words, and contrary to Andino's argument otherwise, the court considered both the probation officer's and the government's views before making a "choice among supportable alternatives," and we "cannot [find this] clearly erroneous." *De la Cruz-Gutiérrez*, 881 F.3d at 227, 6 Adm. R. at 5 (quoting *Pérez*, 819 F.3d at 546, 4 Adm. R. at 21); *see also Mendoza-Maisonet*, 962 F.3d at 24 (acknowledging the district court hadn't **[—59—]** explained its decision to deny a minimal participation reduction, but "infer[ring] that it sided with the [g]overnment's arguments and therefore decided not to apply the reduction").

And Andino also invokes the guidelines' commentaries, alleging that the district court's failure to follow these commentaries amounted to an incorrect application of the guidelines. *See, e.g., United States v. Carrasco-Mateo*, 389 F.3d 239, 243-44 (1st Cir. 2004) ("The Sentencing Commission's commentary, including the application notes, is binding on the courts as long as it does not conflict either with the sentencing guidelines themselves or with some statutory provision."). Like the arguments that came before it, this one also fails to move the needle. Section 3B1.2, cmt. n.3 (C) establishes the now familiar non-exhaustive list of factors, but also informs us that a defendant "who is simply being paid to perform certain tasks should be considered for an adjustment under this guideline," and an adjustment remains a possibility even for a defendant who "performs an essential or indispensable role in the criminal activity." However, we've observed that "[t]he commentary does not indicate that every such offender is entitled to a mitigating role adjustment; it merely instructs that every such offender 'should be considered for a mitigating role adjustment.'" *Arias-Mercedes*, 901 F.3d at 9 (quoting U.S.S.G. App. C, Amend. 794). While Andino's circumstances could be found to meet this commentary's **[—60—]** parameters, the record shows that the district court considered Andino's role in the offense and found it undeserving of a mitigating role adjustment. And when, as we've observed, someone participates "in a **{–36–}** hazardous voyage at sea" to move a significant volume of drugs, "it ordinarily will not be clear error for the sentencing court to refuse [her] a mitigating role adjustment." *Id.* at 8 (citing *Pérez*, 819 F.3d at 546, 4 Adm. R. at 22). This is an example of that ordinary no-clear-error case.

And so, seeing no clear error in the district court's determination that Andino did not carry her burden to demonstrate she was entitled to the downward adjustment she sought, we affirm here as well.

CONCLUSION

Having reasoned through all of the issues leading to the across-the-board affirmance we previewed at the outset, we now make it official: Based on the foregoing, we *affirm*.

United States Court of Appeals
for the First Circuit

No. 21-1737

UNITED STATES
vs.
COPLIN-BENJAMIN

Appeal from the United States District Court for the District of Puerto Rico

Decided: August 21, 2023

Citation: 79 F.4th 36, 11 Adm. R. 85 (1st Cir. 2023).

Before **KAYATTA, HOWARD,** and **THOMPSON,** Circuit Judges.

[—2—] {-38-} HOWARD, Circuit Judge:

On August 8, 2019, Bernardo Coplin-Benjamin pleaded guilty to (1) conspiracy to possess with the intent to distribute a controlled substance in violation of 21 U.S.C. § 846 and (2) conspiracy to import a controlled substance into the United States in violation of 21 U.S.C. § 963. The district court sentenced him to 262 months' imprisonment. On appeal, Coplin challenges both the procedural and substantive reasonableness of his sentence. For the following reasons, we affirm.

I.

Because this appeal follows a straight guilty plea without a plea agreement, we glean the relevant facts from the unchallenged portions of the presentence investigation **{-39-}** report (PSR) and the sentencing hearing. *See United States v. Rivera–González*, 776 F.3d 45, 47 (1st Cir. 2015); *United States v. Dávila-González*, 595 F.3d 42, 45 (1st Cir. 2010).

On January 27, 2018, federal agents intercepted a vessel named the "Black Wolfpack" that was suspected of transporting drugs from St. Thomas, United States Virgin Islands, to Fajardo, Puerto Rico. The individuals on the vessel at the time were identified as Maximiliano Figaro-Benjamín, Emiliano Figaro-Benjamín, Katerín Martínez-Alberto, and Alexandria Andino-Rodríguez.

During multiple searches of the Black Wolfpack, agents found approximately 132 kilograms of cocaine (worth about three **[—3—]** million dollars) hidden in bundles in multiple locations on the vessel. Agents also found a WhatsApp chat on Maximiliano Figaro-Benjamín's phone between him and Coplin discussing the drug trafficking venture. The messages showed them discussing the distribution of 130 kilograms of cocaine as well as details like the number of packages, cost per package, estimated departure date, and a meeting in St. Thomas. The messages showed that Coplin had spoken directly to the narcotics supplier in St. Thomas to discuss the price per kilogram of cocaine transported. Additional discovery showed that Coplin was in regular communication with the key individuals from the January 27, 2018, seizure throughout the duration of the vessel's trip and thereafter.

Coplin was arrested on February 22, 2019. On August 8, 2019, he entered a straight guilty plea for conspiracy to possess with the intent to distribute a controlled substance and conspiracy to import a controlled substance.

Several of Coplin's co-defendants opted to proceed to trial. The testimony at trial revealed details about the drug trafficking conspiracy and the acts preceding the St. Thomas-Puerto Rico trip in which the Black Wolfpack was seized. A codefendant named Javier Resto-Miranda testified that he would buy drugs from Coplin to sell in Alaska and that, during the course of these dealings, "the idea came up of purchasing a vessel to buy drugs in St. Thomas and bring them to Puerto Rico." Resto **[—4—]** indicated that Coplin had had the idea and asked to put the vessel in Resto's name. The vessel was purchased but ultimately seized. However, Coplin had another vessel, named Wasikoki. Coplin again talked about the possibility of trafficking drugs from St. Thomas to Puerto Rico, this time with the Wasikoki. Resto testified that Coplin "asked [him] to get somebody who could take [them] to St. Thomas so [they] could learn about the route, how much gas would be needed, how much fuel, how much time." He said they arrived in St. Thomas and Coplin asked Resto to propose to the captain doing a test run with two kilograms of cocaine. On one trip, Resto called Coplin for guidance on how to proceed when a boat didn't work properly, and Coplin advised him to wait and check later.

Coplin later gave Resto $30,000 to purchase the Black Wolfpack vessel. Resto testified that before every trip, Coplin would plan, would meet with the members of the conspiracy, and would tell Resto "what had to be done." He testified that Coplin was the one to pay the other co-defendants and that he gave them money for gas, food, and supplies for the trip. Resto also testified that Coplin and his business partner would count the money at Coplin's home.

Based on this testimony and the other facts outlined in the PSR, the probation officer classified Coplin as a leader of a criminal activity involving five or more participants and therefore added a four-level **{-40-}** enhancement. Coupled with a base **[—5—]** level offense of 36 and multiple other calculations not relevant on appeal, the total offense level was 39. The recommended guideline range was 262 to 327 months' imprisonment.

Coplin filed a written objection to the PSR, arguing "that he does not deserve to be labeled as a leader in this case as he was not in charge of the overall operation and was not putting his own money to develop . . . the drug venture." He did not challenge the underlying factual allegations and testimony. He also argued at his sentencing hearing that he should receive a downward adjustment for cooperating with the government and that the government's proposed sentence for Coplin was disproportionate to those of coconspirators, among other arguments not relevant on appeal. The district court denied Coplin's objections, found that he was a leader and not a supervisor, and did not give him credit for cooperation with the government. The court sentenced Coplin to 262 months' imprisonment.

II.

The key arguments Coplin advances on appeal are (1) that he was a "supervisor" and not a "leader," so the district court should not have applied the four-level leadership enhancement; (2) that the court failed to consider factors set out in 18 U.S.C. § 3553 regarding his cooperation with the government; and (3) that **[—6—]** his sentence was substantively unreasonable given that he received a much longer sentence than several co-defendants.[1]

We review claims of sentencing errors in two steps: "We first examine any claims of procedural error. If the sentence clears these procedural hurdles, we then consider any claim that questions its substantive reasonableness." *United States v. McKinney*, 5 F.4th 104, 107 (1st Cir. 2021) (quoting *United States v. Ilarraza*, 963 F.3d 1, 7 (1st Cir. 2020)). The first two arguments Coplin advances are claims of procedural error, *see United States v. Laureano-Pérez*, 797 F.3d 45, 80 (1st Cir. 2015), so we begin there, taking each in turn.

A. [—7—]

Coplin first challenges the district court's imposition of a four-level enhancement based on Coplin's role as a leader of the criminal activity. "We review the imposition of this particular sentencing enhancement, and any

[1] During oral argument, Coplin's counsel also advanced an argument (not included in his briefing on appeal) that the base offense level of 36 was incorrect because it was based on the offense involving at least 150 but less than 450 kilograms of cocaine, whereas agents only seized 132 kilograms on the Black Wolfpack. Counsel suggested that this discrepancy was "overlooked" by everyone and asked for review for clear error based on a miscarriage of justice even though arguments raised for the first time at oral argument are considered waived. *See, e.g., United States v. Leoner-Aguirre*, 939 F.3d 310, 319 (1st Cir. 2019). However, the circumstances here contradict counsel's argument. The district court transcript makes clear that defense counsel, the prosecutor, and the district judge all discussed this issue at the sentencing hearing. The government's position at sentencing was that there was evidence of other trips in the drug trafficking conspiracy involving additional kilograms of cocaine beyond the 132 seized on the Black Wolfpack. The district judge agreed with this offense level calculation and denied defense counsel's objection to it. It is therefore clear that this issue was not merely "overlooked," and Coplin's counsel on appeal has not advanced any other argument that the calculation was incorrect.

predicate factual findings, for clear error." *United States v. Ahmed*, 51 F.4th 12, 28 (1st Cir. 2022) (quoting *United States v. Appolon*, 695 F.3d 44, 70 (1st Cir. 2012)). "Where the raw facts are susceptible to competing inferences, **{-41-}** the sentencing court's choice between those inferences cannot be clearly erroneous." *McKinney*, 5 F.4th at 107 (quoting *United States v. McCormick*, 773 F.3d 357, 359 (1st Cir. 2014)). "Given this deferential standard of review, battles over a defendant's role in the offense 'will almost always be won or lost in the district court.'" *United States v. Meléndez-Rivera*, 782 F.3d 26, 29 (1st Cir. 2015) (quoting *United States v. Graciani*, 61 F.3d 70, 75 (1st Cir. 1995)).

The federal Sentencing Guidelines provide for a four-level enhancement "[i]f the defendant was an organizer or leader of a criminal activity that involved five or more participants or was otherwise extensive." U.S.S.G. § 3B1.1(a). By contrast, the guidelines provide for only a three-level enhancement "[i]f the defendant was a manager or supervisor (but not an organizer or leader) and the criminal activity involved five or more participants or was otherwise extensive." *Id.* at § 3B1.1(b). These enhancements require both a status determination of whether **[—8—]** the defendant acted as an "organizer or leader" or "manager or supervisor," as well as a determination of the scope of the criminal activity -- i.e., "that the criminal activity met either the numerosity or the extensiveness benchmarks established by the [G]uideline[s]." *Ahmed*, 51 F.4th at 28 (alterations in original) (quoting *United States v. Hernández*, 964 F.3d 95, 101 (1st Cir. 2020)). On appeal, Coplin focuses solely on the status determination rather than the scope of criminal activity. He argues that he was merely a supervisor and not a leader, therefore warranting a three-level increase instead of four.[2]

In making the determination of whether someone is an "organizer or leader" or merely a "manager or supervisor," courts should consider "the exercise of decision making authority, the nature of participation in the commission of the offense, the recruitment of accomplices, the claimed right to a larger share of the fruits of the crime, the degree of participation in planning or organizing the offense, the nature and scope of the illegal **[—9—]** activity, and the degree of control and authority exercised over others." U.S.S.G. § 3B1.1 cmt. n.4. "This list is 'representative rather than exhaustive,' and 'proof of each and every factor' is not necessary to establish that a defendant acted as an organizer or leader." *United States v. Rivera*, 51 F.4th 47, 52 (1st Cir. 2022) (quoting *United States v. Tejada-Beltran*, 50 F.3d 105, 111 (1st Cir. 1995)). For the enhancement to apply, the defendant "must have led or organized at least one other criminal *actor* -- and not just a criminal *activity* -- on at least one occasion." *Ahmed*, 51 F.4th at 28 (emphases in original).

In conducting this assessment, the district court recited many of the undisputed facts from the PSR regarding codefendant Resto's testimony. The court noted that Resto testified that Coplin initiated the conspiracy with the idea of purchasing a vessel to buy drugs in St. Thomas and bring them to Puerto Rico. Resto testified that Coplin twice directed him to buy vessels **{-42-}** and gave him $30,000 to buy the second vessel, which was the Black Wolfpack. He further testified that Coplin initiated and directed several trips, including asking Resto to go St. Thomas to learn more details about the route and asking him to propose running a test trip with two kilograms of cocaine. Resto indicated that, before every trip, Coplin would plan, meet with the coconspirators, tell them what they needed to do, and give them petty cash for food, gas, and supplies. Coplin and his

[2] The government argues that Coplin has waived this argument on appeal given that Coplin's discussion of this issue is just over a page and contains no standard of review or citations to case law. We have repeatedly held that "issues adverted to in a perfunctory manner, unaccompanied by some effort at developed argumentation, are deemed waived." *United States v. Zannino*, 895 F.2d 1, 17 (1st Cir. 1990). We need not here determine whether the brevity of Coplin's argument constituted waiver, given that it fails on the merits. However, we reiterate that "[i]t is not enough merely to mention a possible argument in the most skeletal way, leaving the court to do counsel's work, create the ossature for the argument, and put flesh on its bones." *Id.*

business partner counted [—10—] the money in Coplin's home, and Coplin was the one to pay codefendants.

On appeal, Coplin does not advance any argument that these findings are inaccurate or that they fail to show that he led or organized at least one coconspirator on at least one occasion. *Cf. Hernández*, 964 F.3d at 102-05 (concluding organizer enhancement was warranted where defendant instructed coconspirator on one occasion). Rather, Coplin points to the existence of another "leader that was paying for everything and that was providing the strategic overview of the operation" as the sole basis for finding that Coplin "had a smaller part and played a role akin to a manager." But the Sentencing Guidelines and our case law make clear that the existence of another leader -- even one superior to Coplin in the scheme's hierarchy -- does not foreclose the possibility of Coplin also acting as a leader. *See Appolon*, 695 F.3d at 70; *United States v. Casas*, 356 F.3d 104, 129 (1st Cir. 2004) ("The mere fact that [the defendant] was subordinate to [a coconspirator] does not establish, without more, that [he] was not an organizer or leader of the conspiracy."); U.S.S.G. § 3B1.1 cmt. n.4 ("There can, of course, be more than one person who qualifies as a leader or organizer of a criminal association or conspiracy."). Standing alone, this argument therefore cannot invalidate the district court's finding that Coplin was a leader himself. Coplin advances no other arguments [—11—] in support of his contention, and the district court's factual findings regarding Coplin's role in the conspiracy certainly support the inference that Coplin was indeed a leader. The district court therefore did not clearly err in applying the four-level enhancement.

B.

Coplin's second procedural argument is that the district court failed to consider his cooperation with the government under 18 U.S.C. § 3553.

Preserved claims of procedural sentencing error are reviewed under an abuse of discretion standard. *United States v. Viloria-Sepulveda*, 921 F.3d 5, 8 (1st Cir. 2019) (citing *Gall v. United States*, 552 U.S. 38, 55 (2007)). Coplin raised the governmental cooperation argument before the district court, so it is preserved.

Under 18 U.S.C. § 3553, a sentencing court must consider "the nature and circumstances of the offense and the history and characteristics of the defendant" in determining the appropriate sentence. 18 U.S.C. § 3553(a)(1). This broad provision includes as a factor "the defendant's cooperation with the government." *United States v. Landrón-Class*, 696 F.3d 62, 77 (1st Cir. 2012). We have thus held that a sentencing court has discretion under § 3553 to consider a defendant's cooperation with the government [—12—] even if the government has not made a U.S.S.G. § 5K1.1 motion for a downward departure in sentencing. *Id.*

Here, however, there is no indication that the district court failed to consider the defendant's cooperation with the government. During the sentencing hearing, **{-43-}** defense counsel raised the issue of cooperation at the outset, and the government attorney responded in depth. The government's position, reiterated on appeal before this court, was that although the defendant had met with the government on three different occasions, he had not substantially assisted the government and had not identified any coconspirators by name until the third interview. After hearing these arguments, among others, the district court did not apply any downward adjustments for cooperation with the government.

It is true that the district court did not explicitly mention Coplin's cooperation in discussing the imposed sentence. But "a sentencing court is not required to address frontally every argument advanced by the parties, nor need it dissect every factor made relevant by 18 U.S.C. § 3553." *Landrón-Class*, 696 F.3d at 78 (quoting *United States v. Turbides–Leonardo*, 468 F.3d 34, 40–41 (1st Cir.2006)); *see also United States v. Dixon*, 449 F.3d 194, 205 (1st Cir. 2006) (a sentencing court "is not required to address [the § 3553(a)] factors, one by one, in some sort of rote incantation"). "When a defendant has identified potentially mitigating sentencing factors and those factors are thoroughly

[—13—] debated at sentencing, the fact that the court 'did not explicitly mention them during the sentencing hearing suggests they were unconvincing, not ignored.'" *United States v. Díaz-Lugo*, 963 F.3d 145, 152 (1st Cir. 2020) (quoting *United States v. Lozada-Aponte*, 689 F.3d 791, 793 (1st Cir. 2012)). Here, the district court heard arguments by both parties on the issue of governmental cooperation and explicitly noted that it had "considered the . . . sentencing factors set forth in Title 18, United States Code, Section 3553(a)." We therefore find Coplin's argument that the court failed to consider this factor unavailing.

C.

We next turn to Coplin's claim that his sentence was substantively unreasonable due to the disparity between his sentence and those of two co-defendants.

We review preserved challenges to the substantive reasonableness of a sentence for abuse of discretion. *See Viloria-Sepulveda*, 921 F.3d at 8 (citing *Gall*, 552 U.S. at 55). Coplin raised this argument before the district court, so it is preserved.

Under § 3553(a)(6), courts are directed to consider "the need to avoid unwarranted sentence disparities among defendants with similar records who have been found guilty of similar conduct." 18 U.S.C. § 3553(a)(6); *see also United States v. Reyes-Santiago*, 804 F.3d 453, 467 (1st Cir. 2015). This provision is "primarily aimed at national disparities, rather than those **[—14—]** between co-defendants," but a sentence may nevertheless be "substantively unreasonable because of the disparity with the sentence given to a codefendant." *Reyes-Santiago*, 804 F.3d at 467 (first quoting *United States v. Rivera-Gonzalez*, 626 F.3d 639, 648 (1st Cir. 2010); and then quoting *United States v. Reverol-Rivera*, 778 F.3d 363, 366, 3 Adm. R. 36, 38 (1st Cir. 2015)).

To establish a well-founded claim of sentencing disparity, a defendant must "compare apples to apples." *Id.* at 467. Where "material differences between the defendant and the proposed comparator suffice to explain the divergence," a sentencing disparity claim is unlikely to prevail. *United States v. Demers*, 842 F.3d 8, 15 (1st Cir. 2016); *see also Reyes-Santiago*, 804 F.3d at 467 ("We have routinely rejected disparity claims ... because complaining defendants typically fail to acknowledge material differences between their own circumstances and those of their more leniently punished confederates."). **{-44-}**

Here, Coplin compares his sentence of 262 months to the 60-month sentence and 120-month sentence of coconspirators Katerín Martínez-Alberto and Alexandria Andino-Rodríguez, respectively. Coplin notes that both the coconspirators proceeded to trial whereas he pleaded guilty and calls it "foul play" that his sentence then exceeded theirs by more than a decade. But Coplin fails to address key ways in which he is not similarly situated to these co-defendants. Chiefly, as the district court found, Coplin **[—15—]** was a *leader* of the conspiracy and not a mere participant like Martínez and Andino. *Cf. Reverol-Rivera*, 778 F.3d at 366, 3 Adm. R. at 38 (noting "differences in culpability can justify disparate sentences among co-defendants"); *United States v. Rivera–Maldonado*, 194 F.3d 224, 236 (1st Cir. 1999) (finding a leader and subordinates were not similarly situated). These co-defendants therefore are not fair comparators, and we cannot find an unwarranted sentencing disparity here.

Furthermore, the court sentenced Coplin on the lowest end of the guideline range, which, as we have explained above, was properly calculated. "A challenge to the substantive reasonableness of a sentence is particularly unpromising when the sentence imposed comes within the confines of a properly calculated [guideline sentencing range]," "particularly . . . where, as here, the sentence is at the nadir of the range." *Demers*, 842 F.3d at 15.

Based on the foregoing, we find that the district court did not abuse its discretion in imposing a 262-month sentence.

III.

For the reasons above, the sentence is ***affirmed***.

United States Court of Appeals
for the First Circuit

No. 16-2089

UNITED STATES
VS.
DÁVILA-REYES

Appeal from the United States District Court for the District of Puerto Rico

Decided: October 5, 2023

Citation: 84 F.4th 400, 11 Adm. R. 91 (1st Cir. 2023) (en banc).

Before **BARRON,** Chief Judge, and **LYNCH, LIPEZ, HOWARD, THOMPSON, KAYATTA, GELPI,** and **MONTECALVO,** Circuit Judges.

[—3—] {-402-} **BARRON,** Chief Judge:

In these consolidated appeals, Jeffri Dávila-Reyes and José Reyes-Valdivia challenge their 2016 convictions for violating the Maritime Drug Law Enforcement Act, 46 U.S.C. §§ 70501 *et seq.* ("MDLEA"), despite their having pleaded guilty unconditionally to the underlying charges. The charges were set forth in a single indictment that was handed up in the District of Puerto Rico in 2015. The indictment alleged that the defendants, each of whom is a national of Costa Rica, had violated the MDLEA by trafficking drugs "on the high seas ... and within the jurisdiction of this court" while on board a "covered vessel," 46 U.S.C. § 70503(a), which includes any "vessel subject to the jurisdiction of the United States," 46 U.S.C. § 70503(e)(1). The indictment alleged that the vessel was "subject to the jurisdiction of the United States" because it was "without nationality." 46 U.S.C. § 70502(c)(1)(A).

A panel of this Court vacated the defendants' convictions and ordered the underlying charges dismissed. The panel did so based on the defendants' contention that Congress had no power under the Felonies Clause of the U.S. Constitution to criminalize their charged conduct because they were foreign nationals who were aboard a foreign vessel on the high seas at the time of that conduct. *See* U.S. Const. art. I, § 8, cl. 10 (granting Congress the power "[t]o define and punish Piracies and Felonies committed on the high Seas, and Offences against the Law of **[—4—]** Nations"). The defendants based their contention that the vessel was foreign on the ground that even if the vessel was "without nationality," 46 U.S.C. § 70502(c)(1)(A), for purposes of the MDLEA it was not stateless for purposes of international law. *See United States v. Dávila-Reyes*, 23 F.4th 153, 195 (1st Cir. 2022).

The government petitioned for rehearing en banc. We granted the petition and vacated the panel's ruling. We now affirm the defendants' convictions, albeit on narrow, record-based grounds that bypass many of the broader questions of international and federal constitutional law that the defendants ask us to resolve. Because those questions touch on sensitive issues of U.S. foreign relations and national power that have implications far beyond this specific statutory context, it is prudent for us to resolve them only in a case that, unlike this one, requires that we do so.

We do address, however, a threshold legal question about the MDLEA that itself has broad significance: Does 46 U.S.C. § 70503(e)(1), which establishes that a "vessel subject to the jurisdiction of the United States" is a "covered vessel," limit the subject matter jurisdiction of federal courts under Article III of the Constitution? *See* U.S. Const. art. III, § 2, cl. 1. We conclude, in accord with an earlier ruling of this Court, *see United States v. González*, 311 F.3d 440 (1st Cir. 2002), that **[—5—]** § 70503(e)(1) does not set such a limit and that the provision instead merely limits the substantive reach of the MDLEA. **{-403-}**

I.

A.

The MDLEA applies to drug trafficking on the high seas only if that conduct occurs aboard a "covered vessel." 46 U.S.C. § 70503(a). Section 70503(e)(1) provides that a "covered vessel" includes a "vessel subject to the jurisdiction of the United States."

A U.S. vessel is a "covered vessel." *See* 46 U.S.C. § 70503(e)(1). But § 70502(c)(1) provides in subsection (A) that a vessel is also "subject to the jurisdiction of the United States" if it is "without nationality." Section 70502(d)(1) then states that:

> the term "vessel without nationality" includes:
>
> (A) a vessel aboard which the master or individual in charge makes a claim of registry that is denied by the nation whose registry is claimed;
> (B) a vessel aboard which the master or individual in charge fails, on request of an officer of the United States authorized to enforce applicable provisions of United States law, to make a claim of nationality or registry for that vessel;
> (C) a vessel aboard which the master or individual in charge makes a claim of registry and for which the claimed nation of registry does not affirmatively and unequivocally **[—6—]** assert that the vessel is of its nationality[.][1]

B.

A criminal complaint from the District of Puerto Rico was issued against the defendants on November 9, 2015. It stated that the defendants were "in violation of Title 46, United States Code, Section 70503(a)(1), 70504(b)(1), and 70506(a) and (b)."[2] An affidavit from a law enforcement officer attached to the complaint recounted the following facts.

On or about October 29, 2015, a maritime patrol aircraft's crew identified a "go fast" vessel in international waters about 30 nautical miles southeast of San Andrés Island, **[—7—]** Colombia. The crew reported observing persons on the vessel throwing packages and fuel barrels into the water.

The crew noted that a cloud of white powder was seen escaping from one of the packages. The crew "also observed what was believed to be a Costa Rica flag painted on the port bow of the go fast" vessel.

The United States Coast Guard dispatched a Boarding Team to intercept the vessel. The Boarding Team commenced "Right to Approach" questioning of the vessel's crew.

The vessel's master claimed that the vessel was of Costa Rican nationality. He did not provide the members of the Boarding **{-404-}** Team any Costa Rican registration documents,[3] and the Boarding Team did not identify any "further indicia of nationality."

The Boarding Team proceeded to contact the government of Costa Rica to inquire about the vessel. The government of Costa Rica was unable to "affirmatively and unequivocally assert," § 70502(d)(1)(C), that the vessel was registered with that country. The Boarding Team "determined" that the vessel was "without nationality."

The Boarding Team found trace amounts of cocaine after searching the vessel and arrested the three people on board -- specifically, the two defendants in these consolidated appeals, **[—8—]** Dávila-Reyes and Reyes-Valdivia, and a third crew member. The three individuals were taken to the United States's military base at Guantánamo Bay, Cuba before they were transported to Puerto Rico, where they were held pending charges.

---

[1] 46 U.S.C. § 70502(d)(1) was amended on December 23, 2022. *See* James M. Inhofe National Defense Authorization Act for Fiscal Year 2023, Pub. L. No. 117-263, § 11519, 136 Stat. 2395, 4142 (2022). That amendment, which added § 70502(d)(1)(D), is not relevant to this case.

[2] 46 U.S.C. § 70504(b)(1) states: "Venue. -- A person violating section 70503 ... shall be tried in the district in which such offense was committed."

46 U.S.C. § 70506(a) states: "Violations. -- A person violating paragraph (1) of section 70503(a) of this title shall be punished as provided in section 1010 of the Comprehensive Drug Abuse Prevention and Control Act of 1970 (21 U.S.C. 960). However, if the offense is a second or subsequent offense as provided in section 1012(b) of that Act (21 U.S.C. 962(b)), the person shall be punished as provided in section 1012 of that Act (21 U.S.C. 962)."

46 U.S.C. § 70506(b) states: "Attempts and conspiracies. -- A person attempting or conspiring to violate section 70503 of this title is subject to the same penalties as provided for violating section 70503."

[3] The affidavit makes no reference to a "claim of registry" having been made.

C.

Dávila-Reyes, Reyes-Valdivia, and the third member of the vessel's crew were indicted in the District of Puerto Rico on November 23, 2015. The indictment charged each of the three crew members with two counts of violating the MDLEA while "on board a vessel subject to the jurisdiction of the United States, as defined in Title 46, United States Code, Section 70502(c)(1) (A)." The indictment did not further specify the ground for so deeming the vessel.

D.

Reyes-Valdivia moved on February 1, 2016, to dismiss the charges. The motion relied on various constitutional grounds.

Reyes-Valdivia's motion first contended that the charges must be dismissed because Congress lacked the power under the Felonies Clause to criminalize the underlying conduct. The motion argued that the Felonies Clause does not empower Congress to make it a crime for a foreign national to engage in drug trafficking outside the "territorial jurisdiction" of the United States while aboard a foreign vessel. The motion further contended that § 70502(d)(1)(C)'s definition of a "vessel without nationality" **[—9—]** "extends jurisdiction over vessels that are not in fact stateless under international law, where the claimed nation of registry fails to unequivocally confirm registry." The motion then asserted that, "[b]ecause the MDLEA's statelessness provision is significantly broader than international law's concept of statelessness, the statute's assertion of jurisdiction over stateless vessels is an invalid exercise of Congress's Article I powers" in that it extends the reach of the MDLEA to persons who are aboard vessels on the high seas that are foreign rather than stateless for purposes of international law.

The motion separately contended that the charges must be dismissed pursuant to the Due Process Clause of the Fifth Amendment. *See* U.S. Const. amend. V. The motion argued that § 70502(d)(1) (A) and § 70502(d)(1)(C) are void for vagueness because neither provision explains the steps that a nation must take either to "den[y]" or "affirmatively and unequivocally assert that the vessel is of its nationality."

The motion also took aim at the charges for two additional reasons under the Due Process Clause. First, the motion contended that the indictment violated the Due Process Clause because the MDLEA does not require the government to bear the **{–405–}** burden of affirmatively proving that the vessel in question was stateless under international law. Second, the motion contended that the indictment violated the Due Process Clause because it did **[—10—]** not allege the drugs that the defendants were charged with trafficking were "destined for the United States" and so did not allege any "nexus" between the defendants' allegedly unlawful conduct and the United States.[4]

Dávila-Reyes joined Reyes-Valdivia's motion. The government opposed Dávila-Reyes and Reyes-Valdivia's joint motion and attached to its brief in opposition decisions from the District of Puerto Rico that had rejected challenges to the MDLEA like those that the defendants' joint motion advanced.

The District Court denied the motion in a two-page order. The District Court explained that it had "reviewed, considered and analyzed the applicable statutes, case law and the opinions by other judges" attached to the government's opposition to the motion to dismiss the indictment and "agree[d] with their analyses and conclusions."

E.

On March 25, 2016, the government filed a motion pursuant to 46 U.S.C. § 70504(a), which provides: "Jurisdiction of the United States with respect to a vessel subject to this chapter is not an element of an offense. Jurisdictional

[4] The motion also contended that the MDLEA charges could not be justified under the Treaties Clause, *see* U.S. Const. art. II, § 2, cl. 2, but neither the defendants nor the government address this argument on appeal and so we need not consider the issue.

issues arising under this chapter are preliminary questions of law to be determined [—11—] solely by the trial judge." The motion asked the District Court to "find, as a matter of law, that the vessel in question was subject to the jurisdiction of the United States, as defined in Title 46, United States Code, Sections 70502(c)(1)(A) and (d)(1)(C)." The motion also requested that the District Court, "prior to the beginning of testimony in this case, preliminarily [instruct] the jury pursuant to Title 46, United States Code, Section[s] 70502(c)(1)(A) and (d)(1) (C) that the suspect vessel carrying the [d]efendants was a vessel [w]ithout [n]ationality and therefore subject to the jurisdiction of the United States."

To support the motion, the government attached an affidavit from the leader of the Boarding Team. The affidavit stated that the master of the vessel initially "claimed ... that there was no nationality for the vessel," then "later tried to change the claim [of the vessel's nationality] to Costa Rica." The affidavit stated that "a Costa Rican flag [was] painted on the bow" of the vessel. The motion itself asserted that there was no "name, hailing port, or registration numbers on the [vessel's] hull" and that "the vessel was not flying any flag."

In further support of the motion, the government attached a certification from the United States Department of State. Under 46 U.S.C. § 70502(d) (2), such a certification is in and of itself conclusive proof as to the response of a country that has been contacted for purposes of determining that a vessel [—12—] is "without nationality" under § 70502(d)(1)(C). The certification explained that the vessel was located by law enforcement 30 nautical miles southeast of San Andrés Island, Colombia; that law enforcement suspected the vessel of illicit drug trafficking because the crew was jettisoning unknown packages in an area where drug trafficking was common; that the master made a claim of Costa Rican nationality; that no registration documents were present on the vessel; and {-406-} that Costa Rica, when contacted, "could not confirm the vessel's registry." The certification concluded that, "[a]ccordingly, the Government of the United States determined the vessel was "without nationality in accordance with 46 U.S.C. § 70502(d)(1)(C), rend[er]ing the vessel subject to the jurisdiction of the United States, pursuant to 46 U.S.C. § 70502(c)(1)(A)."

F.

Before the defendants responded to the government's § 70504(a) motion or the District Court ruled on it, all three defendants on April 4, 2016, pleaded guilty to violating the MDLEA.[5] Each defendant admitted in his respective plea agreement to:

> [k]nowingly and intentionally combining, conspiring, confederating and agreeing with others, to commit an offense defined in Title [—13—] 46, United States Code, Section 70503, that is: to possess with intent to distribute five (5) kilograms or more of a mixture or substance containing a detectable amount of cocaine, a Schedule II, Narcotic Drug Controlled Substance, on board a vessel subject to the jurisdiction of the United States, as defined in Title 46, United States Code, Section 70502(c)(1) (A).

Each defendant also "adopt[ed]" as part of his plea agreement the Government's Version of the Facts, which was attached to the plea agreement. Thus, by signing the plea agreement, each defendant agreed that, as to the Government's Version of the Facts, "the facts therein are accurate in every respect and, had the matter proceeded to trial, that the United States would have proven those facts beyond a reasonable doubt." The Government's Version of the Facts stated in relevant part:

> A U.S. Coast Guard ... Boarding Team approached the vessel and commenced Right to Approach ... questioning. The master claimed Costa Rican nationality for the vessel but provided no registration paperwork and there was no indicia of nationality on the vessel. The government of Costa Rica was

[5] The third crew member entered into substantially the same plea agreement as Dávila-Reyes and Reyes-Valdivia but, because he did not appeal his conviction, his case is not before us.

approached and responded that it could neither confirm nor refute the registry of the suspect vessel. The vessel was determined to be one without nationality.

Dávila-Reyes was sentenced to 120 months of imprisonment on August 2, 2016, and his judgment of conviction was entered that same day. Reyes-Valdivia was sentenced to 70 months of **[—14—]** imprisonment on August 5, 2016, and his judgment of conviction was also entered that day.[6]

G.

Dávila-Reyes and Reyes-Valdivia each filed a timely notice of appeal from the "judgment" that the District Court had entered in each of their respective cases. Dávila-Reyes's and Reyes- Valdivia's appeals were consolidated.

In the defendants' briefing to the panel, the defendants challenged the judgments that the District Court had entered against them under the Felonies Clause and the Due Process Clause. In addition, Dávila-Reyes raised a new argument: Congress **{-407-}** lacked the power under the Constitution to criminalize his charged conduct because the vessel that he was aboard was not on the high seas and was instead within the territorial waters of Colombia.

The two defendants contended in their briefing to the panel that they had not waived the constitutional claims that they were raising on appeal by entering unconditional guilty pleas in the District Court. They argued that § 70503(e)(1), in referencing the "jurisdiction of the United States," establishes a limitation **[—15—]** on the subject matter jurisdiction of courts. On that basis, they contended that they were entitled to raise their various claims on appeal despite their unconditional guilty pleas because the claims implicated the question of whether the District Court had subject matter jurisdiction under Article III to enter the judgments against them.

After the parties filed their briefs with the panel, but before oral argument to the panel, the government filed a letter under Federal Rule of Appellate Procedure 28(j) about *Class v. United States*, — U.S. —, 138 S. Ct. 798, 200 L.Ed.2d 37 (2018). There, the Supreme Court of the United States held that an unconditional guilty plea does not necessarily waive a constitutional challenge to the defendant's statute of conviction. The government argued in the letter that, notwithstanding *Class*, the defendants were barred from raising their challenges on appeal by their unconditional guilty pleas.

The defendants responded with their own Rule 28(j) letter. They contended in their letter that *Class* established that they had not waived their claims by entering their unconditional guilty pleas.

The panel heard oral argument in the defendants' appeals on March 7, 2018. Then, on January 15, 2019, the panel ordered the parties to submit supplemental briefing to address two questions: **[—16—]**

> 1. What is the basis for deeming appellants' vessel "a Vessel without nationality" under 4[6] U.S.C. § 70502(d)(1) given that none of the clauses of 46 U.S.C. § 70502(d)(1) appears to apply by its terms? As background, we note that the statements of fact presented in appellants' plea agreements report that the master of appellants' vessel declared Costa Rican nationality, not Costa Rican registry. That declaration renders § 70502(d)(1)(B) inapplicable, and clauses (A) and (C) refer only to claims of registry.
>
> 2. Assuming that the circumstances do not permit deeming appellants' vessel

[6] Reyes-Valdivia also appealed his sentence. The panel affirmed his sentence in its original opinion. That holding was vacated when that opinion was withdrawn, so Reyes-Valdivia's sentencing appeal remains before us. *United States v. Dávila-Reyes*, 937 F.3d 57, 63-64, 7 Adm. R. 76, 79–81 (1st Cir. 2019). But Reyes-Valdivia is no longer in custody, and so his sentencing challenge is now moot. *See United States v. Suarez-Reyes*, 910 F.3d 604, 606 (1st Cir. 2018).

> one "without nationality" pursuant to any clause of 46 U.S.C. § 70502(d)(1), what other jurisdictional basis supports this prosecution by United States authorities under United States law against appellants -- citizens of Costa Rica who were detained in international waters on a vessel claimed to be of Costa Rican nationality?

The parties submitted briefing on the questions.

H.

In September 2019, the panel -- in its original opinion, which the panel later withdrew when issuing its subsequent opinion -- rejected the challenges that Dávila-Reyes and Reyes-Valdivia had brought under the Felonies Clause and the Due Process Clause to the "judgments" entered against them. *See United States v. Dávila-Reyes*, 937 F.3d 57, 62-64, 7 Adm. R. 76, 78–81 (1st Cir. 2019) (*Dávila-Reyes I*). The panel relied on *Class* to hold that the defendants' guilty pleas did not "foreclose their right to challenge the constitutionality of the MDLEA." *Id.* at 61, 7 Adm. R. at 78. But the panel ruled against the defendants on the merits based on **{-408-}** *United States v.* **[—17—]** *Cardales*, 168 F.3d 548 (1st Cir. 1999), "and the cases reiterating its approach." *Dávila-Reyes I*, 937 F.3d at 63, 7 Adm. R. at 80.

The panel explained that those precedents established that the MDLEA was a valid assertion of the United States's protective jurisdiction under international law, given the United States's interest in protecting itself from the baleful effects of drug trafficking. *Id.* at 62-63, 7 Adm. R. 78–80. The panel explained that this was so no matter the basis under § 70502(c) (1)(A) of the MDLEA for determining that a defendant was on a "vessel without nationality" on which the government was relying. Thus, the panel explained, this was so notwithstanding the defendants' contention that the MDLEA (per § 70502(d)(1)(C)) permitted a vessel to be so deemed even when it was not stateless for purposes of international law.[7] *Id.*, 7 Adm. R. 78–80.

Dávila-Reyes and Reyes-Valdivia petitioned for rehearing en banc from the panel's ruling in October 2019. The petition contended that the defendants' convictions ran afoul of the Felonies Clause and the Due Process Clause. The petition contended on that basis that *Cardales* should be overruled. **[—18—]**

While the petition was pending, our court, sitting en banc, decided *United States v. Aybar-Ulloa*, 987 F.3d 1, 9 Adm. R. 10 (1st Cir. 2021). In that case, we rejected the defendant's contention that the Felonies Clause did not empower Congress to criminalize his conduct, which involved alleged drug trafficking on the high seas while aboard a vessel "without nationality" under § 70502(c)(1) (A).

Aybar-Ulloa did not rely in so holding, as *Cardales* and the panel in *Dávila-Reyes I* had, on the United States's assertion of protective jurisdiction under international law. *Aybar-Ulloa* relied instead on the ground that Congress had the power under the Felonies Clause to make it a crime for a foreign national to engage in drug trafficking on the high seas while aboard a vessel that was stateless under international law. *Id.* at 4-5, 9 Adm. R. at 11–13. *Aybar-Ulloa* explained that the MDLEA conviction at issue there did not exceed Congress's Felonies Clause power because the defendant in that case did not dispute that he was a foreign national who was aboard a vessel at the time of his drug trafficking that was both on the high seas and stateless for purposes of international law. *Id.* at 5-6, 9 Adm. R. at 12–14.

Following our en banc decision in *Aybar-Ulloa*, the panel in Dávila-Reyes's and Reyes-Valdivia's cases construed the pending petition for rehearing en banc as a petition for panel rehearing, granted the petition, and vacated the panel's September 2019 **[—19—]** opinion. The panel explained that it had "concluded that the en banc decision in [*Aybar-Ulloa*] has

[7] The panel did not appear to address Dávila-Reyes' contention that Congress lacked the power to criminalize his conduct because the vessel that he was aboard was not on the high seas. The defendants did not raise the contention in the petition for rehearing en banc that they filed after the panel's original opinion issued. Thus, the argument has been abandoned, and we need not address it here.

diminished the force of this circuit's precedent on the protective principle such that the panel ... deem[ed] it appropriate to address appellants' contention that the government improperly deemed their vessel stateless." *United States v. Dávila-Reyes*, No. 16-2089, 2021 WL 5276369 (1st Cir. Mar. 17, 2021).

The panel issued a new decision in January 2022 that vacated the defendants' convictions and dismissed the charges against them. *See United States v. Dávila-Reyes*, 23 F.4th 153 (1st Cir. 2022) (*Dávila-Reyes II*). A majority of the panel explained that *Class* allowed the defendants to press their **{-409-}** constitutional claims despite their unconditional guilty pleas. *Id.* at 162-164. Then, the majority turned to the merits.

The majority reasoned that Congress lacks the power under the Felonies Clause to criminalize a foreign national's drug trafficking in international waters unless the United States's assertion of regulatory jurisdiction over that foreign national would be permissible under international law. *Id.* at 173-83. The majority then explained that, although *Aybar-Ulloa* held that international law permits the United States to assert such regulatory jurisdiction when the foreign national is aboard a vessel on the high seas that is stateless under international law, a vessel cannot be deemed stateless under international law merely **[—20—]** because, as § 70502(d)(1)(C) provides, a foreign nation whose nationality the vessel's master claims for the vessel "fail[s] to supply an 'affirmative and unequivocal' confirmation of nationality." *Id.* at 186-95 (cleaned up). And, the majority concluded, the defendants' charges and convictions necessarily depended on the application of § 70502(d)(1)(C) -- and on no other basis -- to deem the vessel that they were aboard at the time of their MDLEA violations to be "without nationality" under § 70502(c)(1)(A). *Id.* at 162-65.

In so holding, the majority acknowledged that the government had argued in its supplemental briefing to the panel that the defendants' vessel "could have been deemed without nationality based on ... jurisdictional theories" other than application of § 70502(d)(1)(C). *Id.* at 164-65. These alternative bases included that the vessel's master "fail[ed] to produce registration paperwork or otherwise substantiate his verbal claim of nationality." *Id.* at 164. But the majority concluded that "it [was] simply too late for the government to proffer alternative bases for jurisdiction" because those bases were "not the basis on which the government relied to arrest and prosecute appellants, and to obtain their guilty pleas." *Id.* at 164-65.

Thus, the majority explained, the defendants' charges and convictions exceeded Congress's power, including under the Felonies Clause, because a vessel deemed to be "without **[—21—]** nationality" under § 70502(c)(1)(A) solely by application of § 70502(d)(1)(C) is not stateless under international law. *Id.* at 194-95. Accordingly, the panel ordered the defendants' convictions vacated and the charges against them dismissed. *Id.* at 195.

Then-Chief Judge Howard issued an opinion concurring in the judgment. *Id.* at 195-96 (Howard, C.J., concurring in the result). He explained that the MDLEA provides that a vessel is "without nationality" under § 70502(c)(1)(A) when, as § 70502(d)(1)(C) provides, "the master or individual in charge makes a claim of registry and for which the claimed nation of registry does not affirmatively and unequivocally assert that the vessel is of its nationality." *Id.* But, he concluded, the master of the vessel in question in Dávila-Reyes and Reyes-Valdivia's cases had made a claim of Costa Rican "nationality" rather than Costa Rican "registry." *Id.* Then-Chief Judge Howard explained that as a result the conclusive presumption of a vessel being "without nationality" that § 70502(d)(1)(C) sets forth had no application in the defendants' cases and that, for that statutory reason alone, the defendants' convictions must be vacated and the charges against them in the indictment dismissed.[8] *Id.* at 196. **[—22—] {-410-}**

[8] Then-Chief Judge Howard noted that the defendants' statutory contention arguably was waived because the defendants did not brief the statutory argument until ordered to by the panel. But he **[—22—]** suggested that the supplemental briefing may have been sufficient to "bypass [this] appellate waiver." *Dávila-Reyes II*, 23 F.4th at 196 n.65.

Following the panel's decision, the United States petitioned for rehearing en banc. We granted the petition in July 2022; vacated the panel's February 2022 opinion; ordered supplemental briefing, which the parties then supplied; and heard oral argument.

II.

The defendants seek to challenge their convictions on various grounds despite their unconditional guilty pleas. Thus, we confront a threshold question: Did the defendants' guilty pleas waive the various challenges that they seek to have us address? Insofar as we conclude that the defendants' guilty pleas did not, we then also confront one further threshold question: What standard of review applies to each of the challenges that the defendants bring on appeal?

The defendants contend to us, as they did to the panel, that their unconditional guilty pleas did not waive their challenges because the challenges concern whether their vessel was "subject to the jurisdiction of the United States" under the MDLEA. The defendants contend that this requirement in the MDLEA places a limit on a federal court's subject matter jurisdiction and thus a federal court's jurisdiction under Article III of the United **[—23—]** States Constitution. In consequence, the defendants contend, their challenges take aim at the Article III jurisdiction of the District Court and so are both not waivable by an unconditional guilty plea and subject to de novo (rather than plain error) review whether their challenges were raised below or not.

The defendants also contend, in the alternative, that their guilty pleas did not waive their challenges for a different reason. Here, they rely on *Class*.

We explain in Part III why we reject the defendants' Article III-based ground for both permitting their challenges to their convictions to go forward despite their unconditional guilty pleas and reviewing those challenges de novo even if the challenges were not raised below. We then address in Part IV the defendants' *Class*-based ground for permitting their challenges to go forward. There, we explain that, even assuming that under *Class* the defendants' challenges are not waived, we must reject them, either because they have no merit under de novo review or because they **[—24—]** are subject to the plain error standard of review and cannot meet it.[9]

III.

The defendants contend that their challenges take aim at the subject matter jurisdiction of the District Court because the challenges take aim at the basis for concluding that their vessel was "subject to the jurisdiction of the United States" for purposes of the MDLEA. This phrase appears in several sections of the MDLEA, although the defendants and the government focus chiefly on its use in § 70502(c)(1) and § 70504 of the MDLEA. The defendants' and the government's contentions are best understood, however, to **{-411-}** be addressing the use of the phrase in § 70503(e)(1). That provision is the operative one, as it provides that a "vessel subject to the jurisdiction of the United States" is a "covered **[—25—]** vessel" and so the type of vessel that a person must be "on board" to violate the MDLEA under § 70503(a).[10]

We may assume that the defendants are right to contend that their various challenges on appeal implicate § 70503(e)(1), because we agree with the government that, even if the challenges do, the challenges do not implicate the subject matter jurisdiction of the District Court, because § 70503(e)(1) does not impose a

---

[9] The government separately contends that both Dávila-Reyes's and Reyes-Valdivia's appeals are barred by the waiver of appeal contained in each of their plea agreements. We note that Reyes-Valdivia's appeal waiver was predicated on his receipt of a sentence of no more than 57 months of imprisonment. Because he received a 70-month prison sentence, that waiver appears to be unenforceable. In any event, we may assume for present purposes that neither waiver is a bar to these appeals because the defendants' challenges to their indictment and convictions fail on other grounds.

[10] To be clear, our analysis would be no different if we treated the parties as addressing § 70502(c)(1) or § 70504 rather than § 70503(e)(1).

limitation on a court's subject matter jurisdiction. Accordingly, we reject the defendants' Article III-based arguments as to both whether their guilty pleas waived their challenges and why the standard of review that applies to those challenges is de novo regardless of whether the challenges were raised below.

A.

The defendants acknowledge up front that, in *United States v. González*, 311 F.3d 440 (1st Cir. 2002), a panel of this court held that § 70503(e)(1) does not establish a limitation on a court's subject matter jurisdiction. But the defendants contend that *González* was wrong to so hold -- as some other circuits have also concluded, *see United States v. Miranda*, 780 F.3d 1185, 1191-97, 3 Adm. R. 676, 679–86 (D.C. Cir. 2015); *United States v. Tinoco*, 304 F.3d 1088, 1106 **[—26—]** (11th Cir. 2002); *United States v. Bustos-Useche*, 273 F.3d 622, 626 (5th Cir. 2001) -- and that we should overrule that precedent.

The Second Circuit has comprehensively reviewed the relevant post-*González* precedent, however, and sided with *González. See United States v. Prado*, 933 F.3d 121, 132-51, 7 Adm. R. 92, 97–114 (2nd Cir. 2019). We conclude that the Second Circuit's reasoning is persuasive.

1.

Congress vested "*courts* of the United States" (emphasis added) with "original jurisdiction ... of all offenses against the laws of the United States" in 18 U.S.C. § 3231. Thus, the defendants need to show that § 70503(e)(1) of the MDLEA, by referring to the "jurisdiction of the *United States*" (emphasis added), limits the otherwise operative grant of subject matter jurisdiction to federal courts over federal criminal prosecutions that 18 U.S.C. § 3231 sets forth. *See Prado*, 933 F.3d at 134-35, 7 Adm. R. at 99–100.

The Supreme Court has explained in a case that post-dates *González* that "[i]f the Legislature clearly states that a threshold limitation on a statute's scope shall count as jurisdictional," then the limitation concerns the Article III subject matter jurisdiction of the courts. *Arbaugh v. Y&H Corp.*, 546 U.S. 500, 515 (2006). But the Court went on to say in that case that "when Congress does not rank a statutory limitation on coverage as jurisdictional," the limitation does not concern the **[—27—]** Article III subject matter jurisdiction of the courts. *Id.* at 516.

Here, of course, the provision in question does use the word "jurisdiction." But, as *Prado* emphasized, 933 F.3d at 132, and *González* itself noted, "[t]he term 'jurisdiction' is notoriously malleable and is used in a variety of contexts ... that have nothing whatever to do with the court's subject matter jurisdiction," 311 F.3d at 443 (emphasis **{-412-}** removed). We therefore find it telling that, as *Arbaugh* acknowledges, Congress knows how to write statutes that provide for or limit the subject matter jurisdiction of courts by expressly referring to cases or controversies heard by the courts themselves. *See, e.g.*, 28 U.S.C. § 1331 ("The district courts shall have original jurisdiction of all civil actions arising under the Constitution, laws, or treaties of the United States."); 7 U.S.C. § 2707(e)(3) ("[T]he several district courts of the United States are hereby vested with jurisdiction to entertain such suits [that pertain to orders of the Egg Board] regardless of the amount in controversy."); 16 U.S.C. § 814 ("United States district courts shall only have jurisdiction of cases [concerning suits regarding the use of eminent domain to obtain land to construct a dam or certain public waterways] when the amount claimed by the owner of the property to be condemned exceeds $3,000."). **[—28—]**

This past legislative practice is telling because the provision at issue here does not refer to courts having "jurisdiction" over "actions," "suits," or their equivalent. It refers only to a "vessel" being "subject to ... jurisdiction" and to "the United States" -- rather than a court -- having "jurisdiction" over the vessel. Thus, § 70503(e)(1) does not by using the term "jurisdiction" impose a limitation on the Article III subject matter jurisdiction of courts. It instead defines the scope of the regulatory jurisdiction that Congress is asserting through the MDLEA.

Section 70503(b) supports the same understanding. That section, titled "Extension beyond *territorial* jurisdiction," (emphasis added), clarifies that the substantive prohibition that is set forth in § 70503(a) -- the provision that invokes the phrase "covered vessel" -- "applies even though the act is committed outside *the territorial jurisdiction of the United States*" (emphasis added). Because the phrase "jurisdiction of the United States" in § 70503(b) clearly is not referring to the jurisdiction of a court, we see no reason to read that same phrase in § 70503(e)(1) to be doing so. *See Prado*, 933 F.3d at 142-44, 7 Adm. R. at 106–08.

Other sections of Title 46 of the United States Code, we note, also use the phrase "jurisdiction of the United States" in contexts that make clear that those sections are not referring to the power of courts to adjudicate disputes. *See Prado*, 933 F.3d **[—29—]** at 143 n.12, 7 Adm. R. at 106 n.12 (collecting statutes). By contrast, § 70505 of the MDLEA states that "[a] failure to comply with international law does not divest a court of jurisdiction and is not a defense to a proceeding under this chapter." Given that § 70503(e)(1) refers only to the "jurisdiction of the United States" over a "vessel," we see no basis for reading it as if it, like § 70505, were referring to the "jurisdiction" of a "court" over a "proceeding."

In sum, the MDLEA's statutory text provides no support for the conclusion that Congress intended the phrase "subject to the jurisdiction of the United States" in § 70503(e)(1) to impose a limitation on the subject matter jurisdiction of courts. Nor do we see any basis for concluding that Congress's use of the phrase constitutes the kind of clear statement required by *Arbaugh* to impose such a limitation. Accordingly, we see no basis for breaking with our ruling in *González*.

2.

We recognize that the D.C. Circuit, in concluding otherwise in *Miranda*, noted that the phrase " [j]urisdiction of the United States" also appears in § 70504(a) of the MDLEA, which is titled "Jurisdiction and venue." 780 F.3d at 1196, 3 Adm. R. at 684. The D.C. Circuit concluded from the inclusion of that phrase in a provision so titled that the phrase as it **{-413-}** appears in § 70503(e)(1) must be a limitation on the subject matter jurisdiction of courts, **[—30—]** notwithstanding that § 70503(e)(1) is not similarly titled.[11] We are not persuaded.

The precursor to § 70504(a), which bore the same title to which the D.C. Circuit gave such interpretive weight, was 46 U.S.C. app. § 1903(f) (1996). That provision, however, had a companion provision, 46 U.S.C. app. § 1903(d) (1996). And that companion provision was titled "Claim of failure to comply with international law; standing; *jurisdiction of court*." (emphasis added).

Thus, the relevant statutory history reveals that the "Jurisdiction and venue" title to which the D.C. Circuit gave such import made no reference to the "jurisdiction of court" at a time when the title to a companion provision expressly did. That makes it difficult to conclude that the "Jurisdiction and venue" title demonstrates that the phrase "jurisdiction of the United States" was intended to set a limit on the "jurisdiction of court[s]."

Congress did later drop "jurisdiction of court" from the title of the companion provision, which now appears in the MDLEA as § 70505. But Congress made that title change as part of a 2006 effort to "reorganize[] and restate[]" the MDLEA and so to "codif[y] existing law rather than creat[e] new law." *Miranda*, **[—31—]** 780 F.3d at 1196, 3 Adm. R. at 684 (quoting H.R. Rep., No. 109-170, at 2 (2005)). We thus do not see how we may infer from the change to the title of § 70505 that Congress intended the phrase "jurisdiction of the United States" in § 70503(e)(1) to set a subject matter limitation on the jurisdiction of a court, given that § 70503(e)(1) itself makes no mention of courts at all.

---

[11] Neither the Eleventh Circuit in *Tinoco* nor the Fifth Circuit in *Bustos-Useche* presents any arguments that *Miranda* did not rely on in determining that § 70503(e)(1) implicates the subject matter jurisdiction of courts.

3.

The D.C. Circuit also concluded in *Miranda* that the phrase "jurisdiction of the United States" in § 70503(e)(1) must be construed to limit the Article III subject matter jurisdiction of courts for another reason. The D.C. Circuit reasoned that Congress would have wanted the question of whether a vessel was "subject to the jurisdiction of the United States" to be non-waivable "in order to minimize the extent to which the MDLEA's application might otherwise cause friction with foreign nations" by ensuring that the defendants were properly subject to prosecution in the United States "in every case -- and at every level of review." 780 F.3d at 1193-94, 3 Adm. R. at 682.

But the relevant statutory text, as we have explained, is to the contrary, and nothing in the legislative history shows that the text does not mean what it appears to say. *Prado*, 933 F.3d at 139-40, 7 Adm. R. at 103–05. In fact, § 70505 appears to reflect a contrary congressional understanding to the one posited in *Miranda*: It provides that "[a] failure to comply with international law does **[—32—]** not divest a court of jurisdiction and is not a defense to a proceeding under this chapter."

4.

The D.C. Circuit did also imply that the constitutional avoidance canon supports construing the provision of the MDLEA at issue to limit the Article III subject matter jurisdiction of courts. The D.C. Circuit explained that, if § 70503(e)(1) establishes an element of the crime, rather than a limitation on the subject matter jurisdiction of courts, then the statute may run afoul of **{–414–}** the Sixth Amendment to the United States Constitution. *See Miranda*, 780 F.3d at 1195-96, 3 Adm. R. at 683–84; *see also González*, 311 F.3d at 444.

The notion is that, if § 70503(e)(1) were not construed to establish a limitation on the subject matter jurisdiction of a court, then that provision of the MDLEA would establish an element of the offense that would have to be proved to a jury beyond a reasonable doubt. *See Torres v. Lynch*, 578 U.S. 452, 467 (2016) ("Both [the substantive and jurisdictional] elements [of a crime] must be proved to a jury beyond a reasonable doubt."). Section 70504(a), however, provides that the determination as to whether a vessel is "subject to the jurisdiction of the United States" need be made only by a court -- rather than a jury. And this determination, we have held, need be made only by a preponderance of the evidence rather than beyond a reasonable **[—33—]** doubt. *United States v. Matos-Luchi*, 627 F.3d 1, 5 (1st Cir. 2010) (holding that a vessel may be shown to be "without nationality" by "a preponderance of the evidence").

The defendants do not themselves invoke the constitutional avoidance canon in pressing their Article III-based arguments to us, however. And seemingly for good reason. The canon applies only if there is an ambiguity in the relevant respect, *see Nielsen v. Preap*, 139 S. Ct. 954, 972 (2019) (constitutional avoidance is "irrelevant" if text of statute is clear); *Jennings v. Rodriguez*, 138 S. Ct. 830, 842 (2018) (cautioning that the canon of constitutional avoidance "comes into play only when, after the application of ordinary textual analysis, the statute is found to be susceptible of more than one construction" (quoting *Clark v. Martinez*, 543 U.S. 371, 385 (2005))), and, as we have explained, there is none here.

Moreover, a majority of a panel of this court has held that even if § 70503(e)(1) does not implicate the Article III jurisdiction of a court, no Sixth Amendment issue arises. *United States v. Vilches-Navarrete*, 523 F.3d 1, 19-23 (1st Cir. 2008) (Lynch and Howard, JJ., concurring). And, despite the law of the circuit established by that ruling, neither defendant makes any argument to us as to why we should reconsider our precedent on that score. **[—34—]**

B.

For all these reasons, we decline to depart from our holding in *González* that § 70503(e)(1) merely sets a limit on the scope of the conduct that the MDLEA itself criminalizes. As a result, we reject the defendants' Article III-jurisdiction-based argument for contending both that their unconditional guilty pleas did not waive the challenges to their convictions that they make on appeal and that we must review all those challenges de novo regardless of whether they were raised below.

IV.

The defendants separately contend that, in consequence of *Class*, their unconditional guilty pleas did not waive the challenges that they now advance on appeal. *Class* concerned a defendant who had entered an unconditional guilty plea and then appealed his conviction on the ground that the statute under which he was convicted violated the Constitution. The Supreme Court allowed the defendant's challenge to proceed, as against a claim that the challenge had been waived by his unconditional guilty plea, because the defendant was pressing a challenge to "'the very power of the State' to prosecute" him. *Class*, 138 S. Ct. at 803 (quoting **{-415-}** *Blackledge v. Perry*, 417 U.S. 21, 30 (1974)); *see also Menna v. New York*, 423 U.S. 61 (1975).

Class made clear the limited nature of this exception to the usual rule that an unconditional guilty plea waives challenges **[—35—]** to the defendant's conviction. It explained that the exception applies only to a challenge to the "constitutionality of the statute of conviction," 138 S. Ct. at 803, and then only when the challenge "does not in any way deny that [the defendant] engaged in the conduct to which he admitted" and does not "contradict the terms of the indictment or the written plea agreement," *id.* at 804-05. Moreover, the Court explained the challenge must, "'judged on its face' based upon the existing record," be of the sort that, if successful, "would extinguish the government's power to 'constitutionally prosecute' the defendant." *Id.* at 806 (quoting *United States v. Broce*, 488 U.S. 563, 575 (1989)).

Dávila-Reyes and Reyes-Valdivia contend that *Class* encompasses their challenges on appeal, while the government disagrees. The government contends that the defendants are challenging the MDLEA's constitutionality only as it has been applied to them in their specific cases and that such as-applied constitutional challenges do not fall within *Class*. The government further contends that *Class* does not apply here because the defendants' challenges on appeal necessarily seek to deny what the defendants admitted in pleading guilty unconditionally, given that in so pleading the defendants admitted both that they were aboard "a vessel subject to the jurisdiction of the United States" and to certain facts that bear on that very determination. But, as we will explain, even if we were to assume that *Class* permits the **[—36—]** defendants to raise any or all their challenges on appeal despite their unconditional guilty pleas, the challenges still would fail under the standard of review that we conclude applies to each of those challenges.

A.

We begin with the defendants' constitutional claim that Congress has no power under the Felonies Clause to criminalize their charged conduct. The defendants do not spell out the claim as clearly as they might, but we understand it to come to us in two distinct variants.

The first variant tracks the Felonies Clause-based challenge that the defendants made in their motion to dismiss the indictment that they filed in the District Court. Like that challenge, we understand this variant also to take aim at the indictment and to do so on the ground that it sets forth charges that are asserted to be beyond Congress's power to authorize under the Felonies Clause.

The second variant, by contrast, does not depend on an any assertion that the indictment itself is defective because it sets forth charges that exceed Congress's power under the Felonies Clause. This variant of the challenge contends instead that, even if the indictment is unassailable, the convictions cannot stand because the nature of the post-indictment record is such that it **[—37—]** shows that the convictions violate the Felonies Clause. We consider each variant of the Felonies Clause-based claim in turn.

1.

The indictment-focused variant depends on the following chain of logic. The Felonies Clause does not give Congress the power to criminalize drug trafficking by persons on a vessel on the high seas if the United States would not have regulatory **{-416-}** jurisdiction over those persons under international law. Because international law does not permit the United States to exercise regulatory jurisdiction over foreign nationals engaged in drug trafficking on the high seas while aboard foreign vessels, the United States could criminalize the defendants' charged conduct under the Felonies Clause only if the defendants were aboard a vessel on the high seas that was stateless under international law. A vessel may not be deemed stateless under international law, however, simply because the nation to which the vessel's master has claimed that it belongs fails to "affirmatively and unequivocally assert," § 70502(d)(1)(C), that the vessel is registered with that nation. Yet, the indictment charged that the vessel that the defendants were aboard was "without nationality" under § 70502(c)(1)(A) solely based on the operation of § 70502(d)(1)(C). Thus, the indictment necessarily charged the defendants with violating the MDLEA on a basis that is not constitutional, given that § 70502(d)(1)(C) provides that "a **[—38—]** vessel aboard which the master or individual in charge makes a claim of registry and for which the claimed nation of registry does not affirmatively and unequivocally assert that the vessel is of its nationality" is a vessel that is "without nationality" for the purposes of the MDLEA.

Because the defendants advanced this exact claim in their motion to dismiss the indictment, it is preserved, such that our review of the challenge is de novo. *See United States v. Savarese*, 686 F.3d 1, 6 (1st. Cir 2012). But the government contends that the challenge nonetheless fails, and we agree. The reason is simple: The indictment cannot be read, even on de novo review, to rely exclusively on § 70502(d)(1)(C) in charging the defendants with having been aboard a "vessel without nationality" under § 70502(c)(1)(A). Thus, the challenge rests on a faulty premise about the basis for the indictment's charge that the defendants were on a vessel that was "without nationality."

The indictment states with respect to whether the defendants were aboard a "vessel subject to the jurisdiction of the United States" only that they were aboard a vessel "as defined in Title 46, United States Code, Section 70502(c)(1)(A)." The indictment thus makes no reference to § 70502(d)(1)(C), let alone solely to that provision. Nor does the indictment refer to any other provision of the MDLEA that bears on the question of whether **[—39—]** the vessel was "subject to the jurisdiction of the United States" because it was "without nationality."

In addition, the indictment alleges no facts that could be understood to limit to § 70502(d)(1)(C) the permissible bases for finding the vessel in question to be "without nationality" under § 70502(c)(1)(A). For example, the indictment makes no reference to any facts that implicate § 70502(d)(1)(C), such as to the master of the vessel having made a "claim of registry" (or even a "claim of nationality") or the United States having attempted unsuccessfully to confirm the vessel's registration with another country.

Moreover, the defendants do not dispute that a vessel may be shown to be a "vessel without nationality" under § 70502(c)(1)(A) -- the one "jurisdictional" provision of the MDLEA that the indictment does mention -- through means other than the application of § 70502(d)(1)(C). Nor do we see how the defendants could do so.

As a panel of this court explained in *Matos-Luchi*, the use of the word "includes" in § 70502(d)(1) makes clear that "the listed examples" set forth in that section "do not exhaust the scope of [§] 70502(d)" in defining a "vessel without nationality." 627 F.3d at 4. Moreover, **{-417-}** *Matos- Luchi* explained that a vessel may be determined to be "without nationality" under § 70502(c)(1)(A) through a means other than application of any of the subsection of **[—40—]** § 70502(d)(1) -- namely, when a vessel is not "entitled to fly[] the flag of a State." 627 F.3d at 6 (quoting *Molvan v. Att'y-Gen. for Palestine*, [1948] A.C. 351 (P.C.) 369-

70) (cleaned up). And *Matos-Luchi* also described that standard as a proper one for determining whether a vessel is stateless for purposes of international law. *See id.*; *see also United States v. Rosero*, 42 F.3d 166, 171 (3d Cir. 1994) ("Under international law, 'ships have the nationality of the State whose flag they are entitled to fly.'" (quoting Convention on the High Seas of 1958 art. 5(1), Apr. 29, 1958, 13 U.S.T. 2312, 450 U.N.T.S. 11) (cleaned up)).

Because the defendants do not contend that *Matos-Luchi* was wrong on any of these counts, they fail to explain why the indictment on its face would not permit the government to show that the defendants' vessel was not authorized to fly the flag of any state and so was "without nationality" under § 70502(c)(1)(A) -- and stateless under international law -- for reasons independent of the vessel being the kind of vessel that § 70502(d)(1)(C) describes. *See United States v. Stepanets*, 879 F.3d 367, 372 (1st Cir. 2018) ("[T]he government need not recite all of its evidence in the indictment." (quoting *United States v. Innamorati*, 996 F.2d 456, 477 (1st Cir. 1993))). Thus, we conclude that, even on de **[—41—]** novo review, the first variant of the defendants' Felonies Clause-based challenge fails.[12]

2.

We turn, then, to the other variant of the defendant's Felonies Clause-based challenge. Here, the defendants contend that, even if the indictment is not dependent on § 70502(d)(1)(C), their convictions still violate the Felonies Clause. We are not persuaded by this variant of the defendants' Felonies Clause-based challenge, however, given the standard of review that we conclude applies to it.

a.

The defendants do not dispute that, as we held in *United States v. Ríos-Rivera*, 913 F.3d 38, 41-43 (1st Cir. 2019), a constitutional claim that is raised on appeal pursuant to *Class* is subject to review only for plain error if it was not raised below. Thus, our review of the second variant of the defendants' Felonies Clause-based claim is only for plain error if this variant is being raised for the first time on appeal.

To determine whether this variant of the claim is being newly raised, as the government contends it is, we must attend to **[—42—]** the fact that, in pressing this variant of the Felonies Clause-based challenge, the defendants are necessarily taking issue with the import that the government ascribes to the admissions that the defendants made in pleading guilty. That is because the government contends that those admissions provide a basis independent of § 70502(d)(1)(C) for deeming the defendants' vessel to be both "without nationality" under § 70502(c)(1)(A) and stateless under international law.

In particular, the government contends that under our decision in *Matos-Luchi* the factual admissions that the defendants made in pleading guilty in and of themselves suffice to show that the defendants' vessel was not "entitled to fly[] the flag of **{-418-}** a State," 627 F.3d at 6, and so was both "without nationality" under the MDLEA and stateless under international law for reasons independent of the operation of § 70502(d)(1)(C). Those admissions are that the sole basis for claiming the vessel had a foreign nationality was the oral claim of that nationality made by the vessel's master and that this oral claim of foreign nationality for the vessel was wholly uncorroborated.

Thus, the government contends, to succeed on their Felonies Clause-based challenge, the defendants need to do more than show that § 70502(d)(1)(C) does not provide a basis for deeming a vessel to be stateless under international law. The government contends that the defendants also need to explain why **[—43—]** the factual admissions regarding the wholly uncorroborated nature of the oral claim of the vessel's foreign nationality that the defendants made in pleading guilty do not themselves provide an independent basis

[12] The dissent does not take issue with any aspect of the description of the indictment that we have set forth above or with the proposition that a vessel may be deemed to be "without nationality" under § 70502(c)(1)(A) on a ground other than § 70502(d)(1)(C).

under *Matos-Luchi* for deeming their vessel "without nationality" as a statutory matter and stateless as an international law matter. Otherwise, the government contends, the defendants will have failed to show that the convictions violate the Felonies Clause because the defendants will have failed to show that the vessel was not in fact stateless under international law.

But, in challenging the indictment in the District Court under the Felonies Clause, the defendants obviously did not purport to address the legal significance under *Matos-Luchi* of any of the factual admissions that they made in their plea agreements regarding the wholly uncorroborated nature of the oral claim of the vessel's foreign nationality to which the government now directs our attention. Indeed, at that time, those factual admissions had not even been made by the defendants, as the defendants had not at that time entered into any plea agreements. Rather, at that time, the defendants were merely taking aim at the indictment itself on the ground that the indictment was dependent solely on § 70502(d)(1)(C) based on what the indictment alone provided. Nor did the defendants at any other time or in any other filing in the District Court make any argument as to the legal **[—44—]** import of the facts to which they admitted by entering into their plea agreements.

For these reasons, we conclude that the government is right that our review of the defendants' Felonies Clause-based challenge to the merits of their convictions is only for plain error insofar as that challenge does not take aim only at the indictment and instead addresses the relevance under *Matos-Luchi* of the defendants' post-indictment factual admissions. *See Ríos-Rivera*, 913 F.3d at 41-43; *cf. United States v. Caraballo-Rodriguez*, 480 F.3d 62, 68-76 (1st Cir. 2007) (applying plain error review to a challenge to the factual basis for a plea predicated on a challenge to the scope of the statute of conviction). And, as we will explain, we conclude that the defendants have failed to satisfy the second prong of the plain error standard with respect to that aspect of the challenge, given our reasoning in *Matos-Luchi* about when a vessel may be deemed to be "without nationality" under the MDLEA and stateless for international law purposes. *See United States v. Pérez-Rodríguez*, 13 F.4th 1, 16 (1st Cir. 2021) (explaining that, to satisfy the plain error standard, the defendant must show not only that "an error occurred" but also that the error "was clear or obvious," "affected the[ir] substantial rights" and "seriously impaired the fairness, **[—45—]** integrity, or public reputation of judicial proceedings" (quoting *United States v. Duarte*, 246 F.3d 56, 60 (1st Cir. 2001))). **{-419-}**

b.

We begin with the defendants' contention that the government is wrong to contend based on *Matos-Luchi* that the factual admissions in the plea agreements concerning the wholly uncorroborated nature of the oral claim of the vessel's foreign nationality provide a basis for deeming the defendants' vessel to be "without nationality" under § 70502(c)(1)(A) other than by the operation of § 70502(d)(1)(C). The government's contention on that score proceeds as follows.

The government points out that the defendants, in admitting to the Government's Version of the Facts through the plea agreements, necessarily admitted both that their vessel had no registration paperwork and that the vessel had no other indicia of nationality on board.[13] The government then contends that -- at least when those factual admissions are considered alongside the defendants' admission that Costa Rica could not confirm the vessel's registry -- the post-indictment record shows that there is a factual basis for finding under *Matos-Luchi* that the **[—46—]** defendants' vessel was "without nationality" under § 70502(c)(1)(A). It thus follows, according to the government, that at the time of their pleas their vessel could have been deemed to have been "without

[13] The fact that the vessel's master originally claimed the vessel had no nationality before asserting that it had Costa Rican nationality does not appear in the Government's Version of the Facts to which the defendants agreed when entering their guilty pleas. We thus do not consider that fact in addressing the merits of the defendants' challenges to their convictions.

nationality" under § 70502(c)(1)(A) solely based on § 70502(d)(1)(C).

The defendants' admissions in pleading guilty establish that there is no corroboration whatsoever for the oral claim of the vessel's foreign nationality, even though that oral claim supplies the sole basis for the defendants' contention that the vessel has such a nationality. In consequence, it is not clear or obvious that on the record as it stood at the time of the pleas the defendants' vessel could be deemed to have been "without nationality" under § 70502(c)(1)(A) solely based on § 70502(d)(1)(C) and not also based on the rationale set forth in *Matos-Luchi*.[14]

Matos-Luchi explained in relevant part that "[u]nder international law, every vessel must sail under the flag of one and only one state; those that sail under no flag or more than one **[—47—]** flag enjoy no legal protection." 627 F.3d at 5. *Matos-Luchi* further explained that "[b]y custom, a vessel claims nationality by flying the flag of the nation with which it is affiliated or carrying papers showing it to be registered with that nation." *Id.*

True, *Matos-Luchi* did also explain that "[w]ithout a flag or papers, a vessel may also traditionally make an oral claim of nationality when a proper demand is made," while noting that the MDLEA recognized as much in its provision defining what constitutes a "vessel without nationality." *Id.* But *Matos-Luchi* then went on to note that "[a]lthough enforcement jurisdiction presumptively lies with the flag state, '[i]t is not enough that a vessel have **{-420-}** a nationality; she must claim it *and be in a position to provide evidence of it*.'" *Id.* at 6 (citation omitted) (emphasis added) (quoting Andrew W. Anderson, *Jurisdiction over Stateless Vessels on the High Seas: An Appraisal Under Domestic and International Law*, 13 J. Mar. L. & Com. 323, 341 (1982)).

Moreover, *Matos-Luchi* added that the MDLEA follows this approach "energetically." *Id.* at 6. It explained in that regard that, because " [p]ractically every vessel, including the legendary Flying Dutchman, has links with some country[,] ... the stateless vessel concept in the MDLEA and in international law is designed *prudentially*." *Id.* And so, according to *Matos-Luchi*, under both § 70502(c)(1)(A) and international law, "[t]he **[—48—]** controlling question is whether at the point at which the authorities confront the vessel, it bears the insignia or papers of a national vessel or its master is prepared to make an affirmative and *sustainable* claim of nationality." *Id.* (emphasis added); *see also Miranda*, 780 F.3d at 1197-98, 3 Adm. R. at 685–86 (affirming finding that a vessel was "without nationality" when factual admissions accompanying guilty pleas included that the vessel was not registered with a foreign nation, did not fly the flag of any nation, and carried no registration paperwork).

The defendants do contend that these statements from *Matos-Luchi* regarding the "controlling question" in determining whether a vessel is "without nationality" under the MDLEA are nonbinding dicta. But we do not see why that matters on plain error review, at least given the well-considered nature of the dicta. *See United States v. Cortés-Medina*, 819 F.3d 566, 570 (1st Cir. 2016) (holding that a decision was not plainly erroneous when it was supported by dicta in our circuit precedent).

The defendants separately contend that, in any event, two precedents demonstrate that an oral claim of nationality is, even when wholly uncorroborated, enough to ensure that a vessel has a nationality and so is not "without nationality" under **[—49—]** § 70502(c)(1)(A). But, in the face of *Matos-Luchi*, neither precedent suffices to show that is clearly or obviously so.

[14] The affidavits filed in support of the criminal complaint and the government's motion requesting that the District Court declare the vessel to be "subject to the jurisdiction of the United States" both included references to a Costa Rican flag painted on the vessel's hull. But the defendants cannot now assert that fact to corroborate the claim that the vessel was of Costa Rican nationality, because that assertion would contradict the statement in the Government's Version of the Facts that "there was no indicia of nationality on the vessel." *See Class*, 138 S. Ct. at 804.

The first case is *Rosero*, 42 F.3d 166, which the defendants assert rejects the kind of "totality of the evidence" test that they contend would have to be endorsed to deem their vessel "without nationality" solely based on the uncorroborated nature of the vessel's master's oral claim of nationality. But *Rosero* is an out-of-circuit ruling that also pre-dates key changes that were made to the MDLEA by the time of *Matos-Luchi*. *Rosero* thus addressed only the validity of jury instructions[15] that permitted a finding beyond a reasonable doubt that a vessel is "without nationality" under the MDLEA. *Id.* at 171-72. As a result, it did not purport to address the question that we confront here: Are the facts in question sufficient to show by a preponderance of the evidence that the vessel at issue was a "vessel without nationality" under § 70502(c)(1)(A)? *See Matos-Luchi*, 627 F.3d at 5.

Moreover, *Rosero* concerned a challenge to jury instructions that allowed the jury to engage in "an unstructured weighing of the totality of the evidence." 42 F.3d at 172. *Rosero* **[—50—]** thus addressed whether a vessel may be deemed "without nationality" under the MDLEA based on jury instructions **{-421-}** that invited the jury to consider all the evidence without instructing the jury about what would make a vessel "without nationality." As a result, *Rosero* did not address whether (as *Matos-Luchi* reasoned) a vessel is "without nationality" because, insofar as a sustainable claim of nationality cannot be made, the vessel is not authorized to fly the flag of the nation to which it is claimed to belong.

The other precedent that the defendants point to is one of our own: *United States v. Potes*, 880 F.2d 1475 (1st Cir. 1989). But we do not agree with the defendants that *Potes* holds that, contrary to *Matos-Luchi*'s dicta, a bare claim of nationality in and of itself suffices to demonstrate that a vessel is not a vessel "without nationality" under § 70502(c)(1)(A), even absent the application of a provision like § 70502(d)(1)(C). *See Potes*, 880 F.2d at 1478-79.

Like *Rosero*, *Potes* concerned only the earlier version of the MDLEA. It thus addressed the standard for showing that a vessel was "without nationality" beyond a reasonable doubt rather than merely by a preponderance of the evidence. *See Matos-Luchi*, 627 F.3d at 5. Moreover, while *Potes* held that the record there did not suffice to support a determination that sufficient proof of the "vessel without nationality" requirement had been provided, the vessel at issue in that case was flying a foreign flag. 880 **[—51—]** F.2d at 1478. *Potes* thus does not address whether, per the reasoning in *Matos-Luchi*, a vessel in circumstances like those presented here may be deemed by a preponderance of the evidence to be "without nationality" under § 70502(c)(1)(A) for reasons independent of the application of § 70502(d)(1)(C).

c.

Of course, if it were clear or obvious that the *Matos-Luchi*-based ground for deeming the defendants' vessel to be "without nationality" under § 70502(c)(1)(A) of the MDLEA could not suffice to show that the vessel was also stateless under international law, then the defendants might still prevail in challenging the constitutionality of their convictions under the Felonies Clause. In that event, we would have to address how § 70502(d)(1)(C) fares under the Felonies Clause to determine whether the challenge could succeed.

But our review of whether the defendants' vessel is not only "without nationality" for purposes of § 70502(c)(1)(A) under *Matos-Luchi* but also stateless for purposes of international law under that same precedent is itself only for plain error. After all, in purporting to counter the government's reliance on *Matos-Luchi*, the defendants are again necessarily challenging the legal import of the factual admissions that they made in their guilty pleas. Yet, the

[15] The version of the MDLEA under which *Rosero* was decided made the question of whether a vessel was subject to the regulatory jurisdiction of the United States an issue for the jury. 42 F.3d at 171-72. The current version of the MDLEA makes regulatory jurisdiction issues "preliminary questions of law to be determined solely by the trial judge." 46 U.S.C. § 70504(a).

defendants made no argument below that the facts that they admitted to in pleading guilty could not suffice under **[—52—]** *Matos-Luchi* to render their vessel stateless under international law.

Moreover, *Matos-Luchi* is clear that its analysis is not limited to the statutory question addressed above about when a vessel is "without nationality" under § 70502(c)(1)(A) of the MDLEA. That analysis also applies to the international law question of when a vessel is stateless. *Matos-Luchi*, 627 F.3d at 6; *see also Rosero*, 42 F.3d at 171 (interpreting the predecessor of § 70502(c)(1)(A) to describe vessels that are both "without nationality" as a statutory matter and "stateless under international law"). Thus, here, too, the defendants cannot show that it is clear or obvious that the government's *Matos-Luchi*-based defense of the convictions -- and thus the government's defense of the convictions on a ground independent of § 70502(d)(1)(C) -- is mistaken. As a result, **{-422-}** the Felonies Clause-based challenge fails for that reason alone.

d.

As a fallback, the defendants contend that they need not show that the government's *Matos-Luchi*-based theory is clearly or obviously wrong to succeed on the Felonies Clause-based challenge to their convictions, even assuming that the indictment itself is sound. They contend that is so because the government is engaged in impermissible "jurisdiction switching" in relying on the *Matos-Luchi* theory to defend the convictions on appeal. The defendants **[—53—]** argue in that contention that § 70502(d)(1)(C) is the only jurisdictional provision on which the government relied below. For that reason, they contend, it is also the only jurisdictional provision that the government may put in play on appeal.

The dissent then goes on to contend not only that the defendants are right on this score but also that it follows that the only Felonies Clause-based challenge before us is the defendants' challenge to § 70502(d)(1)(C). And, the dissent proceeds to argue, because the defendants also challenged that provision below under the Felonies Clause in moving to dismiss the indictment, the challenge is preserved, thereby making our review of that challenge on appeal de novo rather than for plain error.[16] **[—54—]**

For reasons that we will next explain, we do not find this line of argument to be persuasive. And that is so even if we were to excuse its late-breaking nature.[17]

To start, the only jurisdictional provision of the MDLEA to which the plea agreements refer is § 70502(c)(1)(A), not § 70502(d)(1)(C). Yet that provision "includes" as a ground for a vessel to be "without nationality" the one that is laid out in *Matos-Luchi*: The person making the oral claim of nationality for the vessel on which the vessel's claim to being foreign depends is not "in a position to provide evidence" of its claimed nationality. 627 F.3d at 6 (quoting Andrew W. Anderson, *Jurisdiction over Stateless Vessels on the High Seas: An*

[16] In making the claim of "jurisdiction switching," neither the defendants nor the dissent contends that the defendants reasonably but mistakenly thought in pleading guilty that their vessel was being deemed stateless only based on § 70502(d)(1)(C). The defendants and the dissent contend instead only that the plea agreements must be construed to bar the government from arguing that the defendants' vessel is "without nationality" under the MDLEA and stateless under international law on any basis other than § 70502(d)(1)(C). Thus, the aim of the contention is not to explain why the pleas must be vacated for not having been knowingly and voluntarily made, such that we need not resolve whether § 70502(d)(1)(C) comports with the Felonies Clause to overturn the convictions. The aim instead is to show that we must decide whether § 70502(d)(1)(C) comports with that Clause to resolve the defendants' Felonies Clause-based challenge because the government gave up reliance on any other jurisdictional theory.

[17] As we will explain, the defendants raised this concern about "jurisdiction switching" only in their briefing to the en banc court, which they submitted only after the panel majority had *sua sponte* raised and relied on the ground that the government could not switch jurisdictional theories. *See Dávila-Reyes II*, 23 F.4th at 164-65.

Appraisal Under Domestic and International Law, 13 J. Mar. L. & Com. 323, 341 (1982)).

Moreover, the plea agreements incorporated the Government's Version of the Facts, which included facts concerning the lack of any indicia of nationality aboard the defendants' vessel. Yet those facts are relevant only to the *Matos-Luchi*-based ground that § 70502(c)(1)(A) includes and not to the **[—55—]** § 70502(d)(1)(C)-based ground that the plea agreements do not mention. **{–423–}**

These features of the plea agreements warrant attention because, although we construe ambiguities in plea agreements in favor of defendants, *United States v. Newbert*, 504 F.3d 180, 185 (1st Cir. 2007), we are not free to read the plea agreements "ex silentio, to include a waiver by the government," *United States v. Anderson*, 921 F.2d 335, 338 (1st Cir. 1990). For, "[w]hile the government must be held to the promises it made in a plea agreement, it will not be bound to those it did not make." *Id.* (cleaned up) (quoting *United States v. Fentress*, 792 F.2d 461, 464 (4th Cir. 1986)). And, here, the nature of the plea agreements is such that we could find the claimed waiver only by reading them silently to include it.

Indeed, with respect to the MDLEA's jurisdictional requirement, the plea agreements mirrored the indictment, which itself referred only to § 70502(c)(1)(A) and alleged no facts that impliedly made it dependent on § 70502(d)(1)(C) alone. Given that even the dissent acknowledges that the indictment cannot be construed to be predicated solely on § 70502(d)(1)(C), we find it hard to see how the government may be understood to have "intentional[ly] relinquished" or "affirmatively disclaimed" reliance on any "jurisdictional" provision other than § 70502(d)(1)(C) merely by having entered into plea agreements **[—56—]** that reference only the same more encompassing "jurisdictional" provision that the indictment itself did. *United States v. Carrasco-De-Jesús*, 589 F.3d 22, 26 (1st Cir. 2009).

The dissent does make much of the criminal complaint that preceded the indictment. But, like the indictment, the complaint also does not refer to § 70502(d)(1)(C) or to facts that bear only on its applicability. And, ultimately, the dissent itself does not contend that the criminal complaint locked the government into relying on that theory alone.

The dissent is right that the defendants chose to "focus[]" on § 70502(d)(1)(C) in their motion to dismiss the indictment. *See* dissent, *infra*, at 7. But the defendants obviously cannot narrow the indictment -- and thereby preclude the government from asserting a ground for determining the vessel's nationality that the indictment on its face does not exclude -- merely by choosing to challenge the indictment on a limited ground.

So, in the end, the asserted waiver must be found in the government's post-indictment filings. But we cannot agree that in them the government waived any or all grounds for deeming the vessel to be "without nationality" other than the one that § 70502(d)(1)(C) recognizes.

The government's brief in opposition to the defendants' motion to dismiss the indictment did cite to § 70502(d)(1)(C). **[—57—]** But it did so only twice - - and then without at either point identifying that provision as supplying the sole basis for deeming the defendants' vessel stateless. The brief instead referred to that provision in explaining *Matos-Luchi*'s holding that "the MDLEA's definition of a 'vessel without nationality' provided a non-exhaustive list of possible circumstances that would qualify a particular vessel, while acknowledging that customary international law may encompass additional types of vessels" (citing 627 F.3d at 7).[18]

The paragraph of the government's response to the motion that directly followed that discussion, moreover, set out the same facts that the defendants' plea agreements later included -- that the vessel's master claimed their vessel had Costa Rican nationality, that

[18] The brief's other reference to § 70502(d)(1)(C) was made in restating the defendant's contention that that provision was unconstitutionally vague.

Costa Rica could not confirm {-424-} that claim, that the defendants did not present registration paperwork, and that the vessel was devoid of indicia of nationality. And it was only *after* having recounted all those facts -- the last two of which concern the *Matos-Luchi*-based predicate rather than the § 70502(d)(1)(C)-based one -- that the government asserted without **[—58—]** reference to any one jurisdictional theory that "*[t]herefore*, the vessel was without nationality" (emphasis added).

The government thereafter filed a motion of its own in which it requested that the District Court find that the defendants' vessel was "subject to the jurisdiction of the United States." But that filing, too, did not purport at any point to commit the government to relying only on the § 70502(d)(1)(C)-based theory for deeming the defendants' vessel "without nationality" under the MDLEA, regardless of what the indictment charged or the record showed in that regard.

True, the motion pointed to facts that would satisfy § 70502(d)(1)(C). But, in support of the conclusion that there was "ample evidence" that the vessel was subject to the jurisdiction of the United States "as defined in Title 46, United States Code, Sections 70502(c)(1)(A) *and* (d)(1)(C)" (emphasis added), the motion listed facts that bear on the *Matos-Luchi*-based theory (which itself falls under § 70502(c)(1)(A)) no less than on the § 70502(d)(1)(C)-based one. We therefore do not understand the motion, in requesting that the District Court "find as a matter of law that the vessel in question was subject to the jurisdiction of the United States" on the statutory grounds, to have amounted to a waiver by the government of its right to rely on a *Matos-* **[—59—]** *Luchi*-based ground for so finding insofar as § 70502(c)(1)(A) encompasses that ground.

The dissent does contend that the State Department Certification attached to the government's motion to establish jurisdiction locked the government into proceeding on a § 70502(d)(1)(C)-based theory alone. The dissent emphasizes that the certification states that "the Government of the United States determined the vessel was without nationality in accordance with 46 U.S.C. § 70502(d)(1)(C), rendering the vessel subject to the jurisdiction of the United States, pursuant to 46 U.S.C. § 70502(c)(1)(A)."

But the certification was only one of the evidentiary attachments to the motion, and in purporting to support the jurisdictional basis provided for in § 70502(d)(1)(C), the certification does not purport to disclaim all others. Indeed, as we have explained, the certification was attached to a motion that itself recited facts elsewhere supported in the record that were relevant not only to the § 70502(d)(1)(C)-based theory but also to the *Matos-Luchi*-based one.

Nor is this a case in which a district court ruling established that the only jurisdictional ground in play was narrower than the grounds encompassed by the indictment and supported by the admitted facts. The defendants pleaded guilty to the charges set forth in the indictment before the District Court **[—60—]** had passed on the government's jurisdictional motion. And, in doing so, they entered into plea agreements that, like the indictment, conspicuously did not mention -- with respect to whether the vessel was "subject to the jurisdiction of the United States" -- § 70502(d)(1)(C). Instead, the plea agreements mentioned only the facially more encompassing § 70502(c)(1)(A).

Finally, it is worth noting that, while the defendants now press the "jurisdiction switching" point to fend off the government's *Matos-Luchi*-based defense of the convictions, the defendants did not make this point in their oral argument to the panel, where the *Matos-Luchi* theory was {-425-} raised, nor did they raise it in their supplemental briefing to the panel. And that is so even though the defendants submitted their supplemental brief *after* the government had advanced the *Matos-Luchi*-based theory for deeming their vessel "without nationality" in its own supplemental brief. If indeed the parties to the plea agreements had agreed that the government precluded itself from relying on a theory of jurisdiction supported by the admitted facts, one would have expected the defendants themselves -- rather than judges who were not party to the agreement -- to have been the ones to raise that interpretation of the agreements.

In fact, the defendants chose at that time to take on the merits of the theory without asserting any waiver. And, they argued, too, that in pleading guilty they were not making any **[—61—]** admissions at all regarding the legal basis for deeming their vessel "without nationality" under the MDLEA precisely because that question was reserved to the District Court by § 70504(a) of the MDLEA. As the defendants put it, "the guilty plea conceding factual guilt does not resolve the antecedent question of the [United States'] ability to assert jurisdiction over appellants' vessel."

Thus, it was only in the panel opinion -- and not in any filing that the defendants themselves had made up to that point -- that the notion first appeared of the government having agreed in the plea agreements to be barred from relying on a *Matos-Luchi*-based theory to defend the convictions even if the indictment encompassed it and the record supported it. *See Dávila-Reyes II*, 23 F.4th at 164-65. So, while the dissent contends that our conclusion that the *Matos-Luchi* theory of jurisdiction remained available to the government after the plea agreements were struck is "patently absurd," the dissent does not dispute that the contention originated with the panel rather than the defendants themselves. It would thus appear that what the dissent contends is self-evident about the plea agreements was not self-evident to the actual parties to those plea agreements. In our view, then, if a gloss is being retroactively imposed on the record, it is the gloss that would attribute to the government an intentional waiver of the *Matos-Luchi*-based theory. But, as no authority establishes **[—62—]** that the government must be understood in these circumstances to have intentionally (though silently) made such a waiver, *cf. Caraballo-Rodriguez*, 480 F.3d at 75 (explaining that "a novel interpretation of the [relevant] statute" advanced by the government in response to a challenge to the factual basis of a plea "cannot be said to be plainly erroneous" even when the court had "found no ... cases discussing the theory"), we cannot accept the contention that one was made.

B.

Having explained that the defendants' Felonies Clause-based claim fails in all its variants, we move on to the defendants' remaining claims. The first of those claims is that the indictment does not charge a crime that comports with the Due Process Clause because a key aspect of § 70502(d)(1)(A) and § 70502(d)(1)(C) is void for vagueness.

But here, again, we are not persuaded that there is any basis for concluding, even on de novo review, that the indictment is dependent on the application of § 70502(d)(1)(C) in alleging that the defendants violated the MDLEA while aboard a vessel "without nationality" under § 70502(c)(1)(A). And, as we have explained, there is no basis on plain error review for concluding that the record at the time of the judgments of conviction **{–426–}** was such that § 70502(d)(1)(C) provided the sole means of determining the defendants' vessel to have been "without nationality." Nor, **[—63—]** as we also have explained, can we conclude that the government waived the *Matos-Luchi*-based theory that it advances in defending the convictions. Thus, we must reject this constitutional claim because it rests on the unfounded premise that § 70502(d)(1)(C) supplies the sole basis for deeming the defendants' vessel to be "without nationality" under § 70502(c)(1)(A). We add only that, because the defendants at no point developed an argument below or to us as to how § 70502(d)(1)(A) might apply to their case, we must reject this challenge as it relates to that provision as well.

C.

We next must address the defendants' claim under the Due Process Clause in which they target a supposed failure by the government to establish any nexus between the defendants' allegedly unlawful conduct and the United States. The defendants have developed this challenge only insofar as they contend that they were aboard a vessel with foreign nationality. They have not developed any argument as to why there must be such a nexus even if the vessel was stateless under international law.

As we have explained, however, we cannot conclude, even on de novo review, that the indictment charged the defendants with being on a vessel that could be deemed "subject to the jurisdiction of the United States" only on grounds that would fail to show that the vessel was stateless under international law. And, as we have also explained, there is no basis, on plain error review, for **[—64—]** concluding that the record as it stood at the time of the defendants' convictions only supports a ground for deeming their vessel to have been "subject to the jurisdiction of the United States" that clearly or obviously would not suffice to permit the vessel to be deemed stateless under international law. Finally, for the reasons given above, the government may not be understood to have waived all jurisdictional theories save for the one based on § 70502(d)(1)(C). Thus, this constitutional claim fails, too.

D.

There remains only to address the defendants' claim that the government violated the Due Process Clause by failing to bear the burden of showing that the defendants' vessel was stateless under international law. But, as best we can tell, the premise for this claim is that the sole basis for deeming the vessel to be "without nationality" under § 70502(c)(1)(A) is by operation of § 70502(d)(1). Thus, this constitutional claim fails for the same reasons that the other claims we have addressed fail -- it rests on a premise that cannot be sustained as to the indictment, even on de novo review, or as to the record at the time of the judgments of conviction, under plain error review, and the government did **[—65—]** not intentionally relinquish reliance on all jurisdictional theories save for the one based on § 70502(d)(1)(C).[19] **{-427-}**

V.

For the reasons given above, the judgments of the District Court are ***affirmed***.

–Dissenting Opinion Follows–

(Reporter's Note: Dissenting opinion follows on p. 113).

[19] We note that we must also reject the defendants' sole, purely statutory challenge -- that the government improperly relied on § 70502(d)(1)(C) to establish that their vessel was "without nationality" because § 70502(d)(1)(C) references only a claim of "registry" and defendants made a claim of nationality. The reason is by now familiar. The defendants cannot show, even on de novo review, that the indictment is premised solely on § 70502(d)(1)(C), and they cannot show, on plain error review, that it is clear or obvious from the state of the record at the time that the defendants entered their guilty pleas that § 70502(d)(1)(C) provided the sole basis for deeming the vessel "without nationality." Nor can the defendants show that the government waived all "jurisdictional" theories other than the § 70502(d)(1)(C)-based one.

[—66—] {-427-} LIPEZ, THOMPSON, and **MONTECALVO,** Circuit Judges, dissenting:

It is a basic principle of plea agreements, derived from contract law, that the parties' written agreement embodies their commitments to each other and governs their expectations. Today, in their effort to avoid important and complex issues concerning the United States' authority to prosecute foreign nationals encountered on vessels in international waters, our colleagues in the majority have done serious damage to the reliability of plea agreements. Stymied by the content of appellants' agreements and the proceedings leading to their pleas, the majority adopts a view of the record inappropriately favorable to the government and justifies the analysis with an indefensible application of the plain-error doctrine. We cannot accept the resulting perversion of the plea process and, for that reason among others, dissent from the majority's decision.

I.

Using the majority's terminology, we wish to make clear that our disagreement with our colleagues' analysis does not arise from their treatment of the so-called "first variant" of appellants' constitutional claim, a dichotomy imposed by the majority. We recognize that the indictment itself does not specify the basis on which the government was alleging that the defendants were on board a vessel without nationality. Nor are we saying that the criminal complaint that initiated appellants' prosecution **[—67—]** necessarily fixed the boundaries for the indictment and confined the government to showing that appellants' vessel was stateless pursuant to 46 U.S.C. § 70502(d)(1)(C). However, we *are* saying that when the government reduces the broad terms of an indictment to a specific theory of prosecution and relies on that theory to obtain guilty pleas, the government cannot later justify those convictions with a different rationale when it discovers that its chosen theory is flawed.

The majority's "second variant" analysis, however, endorses just such an unfair substitution. As we shall describe, appellants had no reason in the district court proceedings to challenge any basis for deeming their vessel "without nationality" other than by operation of § 70502(d)(1)(C). The majority nonetheless latches onto the omission of any such challenge to avoid appellants' claim that their convictions violate the Felonies Clause because Congress lacked authority to deem their vessel without nationality based on that provision. In other words, the majority addresses appellants' challenge to their convictions under the false pretense that, at the time appellants signed plea agreements, the government was relying on alternative theories for deeming their vessel stateless.

Put even more bluntly, the majority performs a sleight-of-hand to allow the government to ambush appellants with a theory of jurisdiction under the Maritime Drug Law Enforcement Act **[—68—]** ("MDLEA") that was not the one used to secure their guilty pleas. As set forth in detail in Section II below, the government consistently premised its assertion that appellants' vessel was stateless solely on the failure of Costa Rica to "affirmatively and unequivocally" confirm nationality pursuant to **{-428-}** 46 U.S.C. § 7052(d)(1)(C). Appellants, in turn, consistently argued that § 70502(d)(1)(C) is unconstitutional and in conflict with international law. That same claim of constitutional invalidity is at the forefront of this appeal from appellants' convictions.

Now, the government insists that we should uphold the prosecution, regardless of the validity of § 70502(d)(1)(C), because the facts included in appellants' plea agreements establish that their vessel was "without nationality" *apart from* § 70502(d)(1)(C). The government thus asks us to treat the litigation history and appellants' reasonable understanding of their plea agreements as irrelevant. The majority condones that strategy and dwells on one alternative theory in particular: that Reyes-Valdivia's oral claim of Costa Rican nationality when confronted on his vessel was ineffective because it was not substantiated by other indicia of nationality.

Indefensibly, however, the majority contrives a procedural default that does not exist. The government never changed course in its theory of the prosecution from the time of the criminal complaint through the entry of appellants' guilty **[—69—]** pleas; it invoked § 70502(d)(1)(C), implicitly or explicitly, at every stage. Nor did any facts change during the course of the proceedings. The affidavit attached to the Criminal Complaint that *preceded* the indictment contained a "Summary of the Investigation" that included the following information:

> The master claimed Costa Rican nationality for the vessel but provided no registration paperwork. The Boarding Team reported no further indicia of nationality. The government of Costa Rica was approached to either confirm or deny vessel registry. Costa Rica responded that it could not confirm nor refute the registry of the suspect vessel. The vessel was determined to be one without nationality.

Affidavit in Support of Criminal Complaint, *United States v. Reyes-Valdivia*, No. 3:15-cr-00721-FAB (D.P.R. Nov. 9, 2015), ECF No. 1-1, at 3-4.[20] These facts, which also appear in the plea agreements, give rise to jurisdiction under § 70502(d)(1)(C).[21] The government recited these same facts repeatedly throughout the subsequent proceedings to support jurisdiction under § 70502(d)(1)(C). *See infra* Section II. There was simply no new argument that appellants **[—70—]** failed to make, and the majority's plain-error analysis thus depends on altering the assumptions underlying the plea agreements, contrary to basic principles of plea bargaining and contract law.

Of course, the majority's ability to rely on plain error is essential to the decision to affirm appellants' convictions without addressing their constitutional challenge to § 70502(d)(1)(C). That is so because the majority relies primarily on dicta contained in a single decision of a divided panel of our court -- which in turn cited only a single authority -- for the proposition that Reyes-Valdivia's oral claim of nationality was inadequate on its own to establish that appellants' vessel was not stateless. *See United States v. Matos-Luchi*, 627 F.3d 1, 5 (1st Cir. 2010). The **{-429-}** adequacy of an oral claim of nationality under international law is one of the issues at the heart of the merits of this case -- relevant to the constitutionality of § 70502(d)(1)(C) -- and a subject the majority desperately wants to avoid. *See United States v. Dávila-Reyes* (*Dávila-Reyes II*), 23 F.4th 153, 187-93 (1st Cir. 2022). Only plain-error review allows the majority to give *Matos-Luchi*'s dicta dispositive effect without considering its correctness and, hence, to avoid dealing with the difficult constitutional questions posed by this appeal.

It is no surprise that, to establish MDLEA jurisdiction, the government chose to rely on the government of Costa Rica's **[—71—]** statement that it could neither confirm nor refute Reyes-Valdivia's claim of nationality -- a straightforward method under the MDLEA for deeming a vessel stateless. Now what the government wants us to do, and what the majority has agreed to do, is to uphold the convictions based on a different rationale anchored only in the dicta from *Matos-Luchi*. That retroactive change-of-course is unfair to appellants and harmful to the plea-bargaining process.

II.

The en banc majority's analysis rests on the view that the government never relinquished any theory for deeming appellants' vessel "without nationality" that could be supported by the facts incorporated into appellants' plea agreements. Brushing aside the well-established law that ambiguities in plea agreements must be construed in favor of defendants, *see infra*, the majority instead credits the government with silently preserving a theory of jurisdiction appellants

---

20 All subsequent citations in this opinion to the district court's docket will use the short-form "*Reyes-Valdivia*, ECF No. ___ (filing date)."

21 Section 70502(d)(1)(C) defines a "vessel without nationality" to include any vessel "aboard which the master or individual in charge makes a claim of registry and for which the claimed nation of registry does not affirmatively and unequivocally assert that the vessel is of its nationality." 46 U.S.C. § 70502(d)(1)(C).

had no reason to contemplate during the plea-bargaining process -- thereby condoning the government's introduction of a new construction of the plea agreements.

In fact, a fair reading of the record shows that, from the outset of appellants' prosecutions, and consistently throughout, the government relied exclusively on 46 U.S.C. § 70502(d)(1)(C) to support jurisdiction over appellants and their **[—72—]** vessel. As recounted above, that approach was previewed in the affidavit attached to the Criminal Complaint, which stated that the "vessel was determined to be one without nationality" after the master claimed Costa Rican nationality and that "Costa Rica responded that it could not confirm nor refute the registry of the suspect vessel." *Reyes-Valdivia*, ECF No. 1-1, at 3-4. Although -- as we have acknowledged -- the theory of statelessness reflected in the pre-indictment affidavit did not prevent the government from developing other jurisdictional rationales post-indictment, the government's version of the facts and theory of jurisdiction did not change.

Each time the government defended the jurisdictional foundation for the prosecution -- in its response to appellants' motion to dismiss the indictment (dated Feb. 16, 2016), in its own motion in support of jurisdiction (dated Mar. 25, 2016), at the change-of-plea hearing (held on Apr. 4, 2016), and in the plea agreements themselves (filed on Apr. 4, 2016) -- the government presented the same facts originally set forth in the Criminal Complaint (filed in Nov. 2015) and never stated that it was proceeding on alternative theories of jurisdiction, one statutory and one non-statutory. Appellants focused on § 70502(d)(1)(C) in their motion to dismiss the indictment. In that motion, after noting that the MDLEA prohibits drug activity by individuals on a vessel subject to U.S. jurisdiction, appellants stated: "*As* **[—73—]** *relevant here*, a 'vessel subject to the jurisdiction of the United States' includes ... 'a vessel **{–430–}** aboard which the master or individual in charge makes a claim of registry and for which the claimed nation of registry does not affirmatively and unequivocally assert that the vessel is of its nationality.' [46 U.S.C.] § 70502(c)(1)(A), (d)(1)(C)." *Reyes-Valdivia*, ECF No. 29, at 3 (Feb. 1, 2016) (emphasis added).

In its response, the government did not contest appellants' assumption that the "relevant" provision was § 70502(d)(1)(C). The response addressed appellants' multiple statutory-based arguments by asserting, inter alia, that the MDLEA is within Congress's authority under the Constitution; that "drug trafficking, as criminalized by the MDLEA, is properly within the scope of the Felonies Clause"; that the MDLEA does not require a nexus between the drug activity and the United States; that the MDLEA is consistent with international law; and that § 70502(d)(1) is not unconstitutionally vague. *See Reyes-Valdivia*, ECF No. 38, at 3-8, 11-13 (Feb. 16, 2016). The government also noted the applicability of the protective principle of international law. *See id.* at 17. The government repeated, nearly verbatim, the facts that had appeared in the Criminal Complaint:

> In this case, the Defendants made a claim of Costa Rican nationality over the vessel. The United States approached the government of Costa Rica and they responded that they could not confirm or deny the nationality of the **[—74—]** vessel. Furthermore, the Defendants failed to present any registration paperwork supporting their claim and there were no other indicators of nationality, such as a flag, on the vessel. Therefore, the vessel was without nationality.

Id. at 11.

Although the response cited *Matos-Luchi* seven times, none of those references invoked the dicta on the need to substantiate an oral claim of nationality. *See id.* at 8, 11, 12, 15, 16. Indeed, the government distinguished appellants' case from one cited by appellants in which "the [g]overnment [had] attempted to proceed on two theories of jurisdiction" and had "failed to provide any evidence that ... the alleged flagging nation" had denied the claim of registry. *Id.* at 16 (discussing *United States v. Potes*, 880 F.2d 1475 (1st Cir. 1989)). The government asserted that, by contrast, in this case it "ha[d] been consistent in its theory of jurisdiction and provided all [d]efendants in discovery statements by the boarding team and pilots that prove the master's claim of Costa Rican nationality, the lack of other indicia of nationality, and the fact that the U.S. Coast Guard Seventh District Commander permitted the vessel to be treated as one without nationality." *Id.* The government, in other words, emphasized that it had provided appellants with the facts, first reported in the Criminal Complaint and now reproduced in their response to the motion to dismiss, that appellants understood as premising jurisdiction solely on **[—75—]** § 70502(d)(1)(C) -- an understanding the government did not dispute in its response to the motion to dismiss.

But even if the government's response left ambiguity in its theory of jurisdiction, any lack of clarity was dispelled when the government later filed its motion in support of jurisdiction. The connection between the government's consistently reported facts and § 70502(d)(1)(C) was drawn explicitly in the Department of State Certification that was submitted as an attachment to the government's motion. The Certification, signed by a U.S. Coast Guard Commander, reported that the master of the vessel "made a claim of Costa Rican nationality," that the United States government "requested that the [g]overnment of the Republic of Costa Rica confirm **{-431-}** the registry or nationality of the suspect vessel," and that "the [g]overnment of the Republic of Costa Rica replied that it could not confirm [the] vessel's registry." *Reyes-Valdivia*, ECF No. 46-2, at 1 (Mar. 25, 2016). The Certification then expressly linked those facts to the assertion of jurisdiction: "*Accordingly*, the [g]overnment of the United States determined the vessel was without nationality *in accordance with 46 U.S.C. § 70502(d)(1)(C)*, rendering the vessel subject to the jurisdiction of the United States, pursuant to 46 U.S.C. § 70502(c)(1)(A)." *Id.* (emphases added). Significantly, this motion, with its attached Certification, also gives important context for the government's earlier reference, in its response to appellants' **[—76—]** motion to dismiss, to "the fact that the U.S. Coast Guard Seventh District Commander permitted the vessel to be treated as one without nationality." *Reyes-Valdivia*, ECF No. 38, at 16. The Certification specifies that the U.S. Coast Guard Commander gave that permission "in accordance with 46 U.S.C. § 70502(d)(1)(C)."

The Certification language also reveals a significant flaw in the government's attempt to obscure its chosen theory of jurisdiction by insisting that it always relied on § 70502(c)(1)(A) separately from § 70502(d)(1)(C), thereby giving notice that it was contemplating other rationales for deeming the vessel "without nationality." Section 70502(c)(1)(A) of the MDLEA states generally that "a vessel without nationality" is "subject to the jurisdiction of the United States." 46 U.S.C. § 70502(c)(1)(A). Section 70502(d)(1)(C) specifies one way in which the United States may deem a "vessel without nationality" -- namely, if the master "makes a claim of registry and for which the claimed nation of registry does not affirmatively and unequivocally assert that the vessel is of its nationality." 46 U.S.C. § 70502(d)(1)(C). These two provisions plainly operate in tandem when cited together, as the government consistently did in this case. And, when those provisions were combined with the facts offered by the government, the general allegations of the indictment concerning jurisdiction -- that appellants' vessel was "subject to the jurisdiction of the United States" because it was **[—77—]** "without nationality" -- were reduced to the specific version of the crime the government was charging.

The Certification sets forth that specific theory in unambiguous terms: appellants' boat was subject to United States jurisdiction as a "vessel without nationality" under § 70502(c)(1)(A) *because* the circumstances satisfied the requirements of § 70502(d)(1)(C).[22] As noted above, the

[22] As the panel majority opinion explained, it does not matter that § 70502(d)(1)(C) by its terms applies when there has been a "claim of registry" but, in this case, Reyes-Valdivia made a claim of Costa Rican nationality. *See Dávila-Reyes II*, 23 F.4th at 165-69. Both the government and appellants assumed that § 70502(d)(1)(C) applied to Reyes-Valdivia's claim of nationality until the panel

government had emphasized in its response to appellants' motion to dismiss that it "ha[d] been consistent in its theory of jurisdiction," thus giving appellants no reason to believe that it was invoking any theory of statelessness other than § 70502(d)(1)(C). Put simply, the unmistakable import of the government's representations in the district court is that the government relied consistently -- and exclusively -- on the theory of statelessness that appellants have consistently challenged. **{-432-}**

The government attempts to step away from that acknowledgment by pointing out that it had no opportunity to press **[—78—]** other theories of statelessness because appellants pleaded guilty before the district court ruled on its motion in support of jurisdiction. Nowhere in that motion, however, does the government indicate that it was planning to argue that the vessel could be deemed "without nationality" on the ground that appellants did not substantiate Reyes-Valdivia's oral assertion of Costa Rican nationality with documentary or visual indicia of nationality. There is no reference in the motion to the *Matos-Luchi* dicta on which the majority relies. Indeed, as described above, the motion included the Certification as an attachment and, referring to the Certification's contents, the government asserted that the Coast Guard Commander "certified that the Government of Costa Rica was approached and could neither confirm nor deny registry of the go-fast vessel, *thereby enabling the United States to treat the vessel as one without nationality pursuant to Section 70502(d)[(1)](C).*" *Reyes-Valdivia*, ECF No. 46, at 4 (emphasis added). It is clear from this motion -- filed a week before appellants moved to change their pleas -- that the government was adhering to its "consistent" reliance on § 70502(d)(1)(C).

Critical, of course, is what admissions appellants understood they were making at the time they signed their plea agreements. We have recognized that, in construing plea agreements, "[t]he touchstone is the 'defendant's reasonable understanding.'" *United States v. Gardner*, 5 F.4th 110, 114 (1st **[—79—]** Cir. 2021) (quoting *United States v. Conway*, 81 F.3d 15, 17 (1st Cir. 1996)); *see generally United States v. Gall*, 829 F.3d 64, 72 n.6 (1st Cir. 2016) (citing cases for the general proposition that a court's construction of a plea agreement should align with the reasonable expectations of the parties). If there is any uncertainty about the scope of defendants' pleas, the consequence of the imprecision "must fall upon the government," *United States v. Newbert*, 504 F.3d 180, 185 (1st Cir. 2007), "not only because ambiguities in contracts are traditionally interpreted against the drafter, but also because plea agreements implicate broader societal interests, some of constitutional magnitude," *id.* at 185 n.3 (citation omitted).

At the change-of-plea hearing, when asked to "give a brief explanation of the theory to be presented to prove each Defendant guilty if a trial were to be held," the prosecutor stated, in relevant part:

> The vessel was tracked by aircraft and eventually came to a stop. The U.S. Coast Guard boarding team approached the vessel and commenced right of approach questioning.
>
> The master claimed Costa Rican nationality for the vessel but provided no registration[] paperwork, and there was no indicia of nationality on the vessel.
>
> The Government of Costa Rica was approached. They responded they could neither confirm nor refute the registry of [the] suspect vessel.
>
> The vessel was determined to be one without nationality. **[—80—]**

Reyes-Valdivia, ECF No. 117, at 25-26 (Oct. 3, 2016). These same facts -- reiterating Reyes-Valdivia's claim of nationality and Costa Rica's failure to confirm or deny his claim -- were incorporated into the plea agreements themselves. Hence, a reasonable defendant would conclude that the plea agreements' inclusion of the same facts used consistently by the government to support jurisdiction based

suggested otherwise in a request for supplemental briefing. Whether § 70502(d)(1)(C) covers claims of nationality is a distinct question from whether, in the particular circumstances of this case, that provision was the basis on which the government asserted MDLEA jurisdiction.

solely on § 70502(d)(1) (C) meant that the government was relying solely on that provision as the jurisdictional foundation for their guilty pleas. It is *not* reasonable to attribute to appellants an awareness of a different **{-433-}** theory of statelessness that they also needed to challenge. Given the government's handling of the case from inception to pleas, the majority's resort to plain-error review of a different jurisdictional rationale is unfathomable.[23]

The majority makes much of the fact that the government's version of the relevant events includes information that is not part of the § 70502(d)(1)(C) requirements, specifically that the vessel had no registration paperwork or other indicia of Costa **[—81—]** Rican nationality on board. However, the government's report that no evidence of nationality was found on the vessel -- in the same sentence reporting the master's oral claim of nationality -- does not indicate, or even suggest, that the government was setting forth a theory of jurisdiction independent of § 70502(d)(1)(C). The factual statement does not declare that the vessel was determined to be without nationality because no corroborating evidence was found. Nor does the government preface the report of its inquiry to Costa Rica with language -- such as "In addition" - - to indicate that § 70502(d)(1)(C) was a second, independent basis for deeming the vessel "without nationality." Rather, the sequence of facts in the statement confirms that the vessel was determined to be without nationality, per the Certification, "in accordance with 46 U.S.C. § 70502(d)(1)(C)."

The majority's use of the government's reference to the lack of corroboration to infer an unarticulated alternative theory of statelessness is thus unjustified from a commonsense reading of the factual statement. That approach is especially unacceptable given our obligation to impose the burden of any ambiguity in plea agreements on the government. Absent some explicitly stated connection between those non-essential facts and a non-statutory theory of jurisdiction, the inclusion in the plea agreements of the same facts that had informed every phase of the prosecution simply does not show -- or even suggest -- that the government is **[—82—]** relying on any basis other than § 70502(d)(1)(C) to deem appellants' vessel without nationality. We do not know why the government placed those facts in the plea agreements. Perhaps the government wanted to eliminate any possibility that appellants could reassert their earlier claim that the vessel bore indicia of nationality.[24] What we *do* know, however, is that the government did not communicate a connection between those facts and the non-statutory theory of statelessness attributable to the dicta in *Matos-Luchi.* **{-434-}**

There is not even a hint in the provisions of the plea agreements that the government was relying on multiple theories of jurisdiction. It is irrelevant that the agreements do not expressly cite to § 70502(d)(1)(C). As explained above, the unelaborated reference in the agreements to § 70502(c)(1)(A) serves to identify the pertinent category of vessels "subject to United States jurisdiction" -- i.e., vessels "without nationality" **[—83—]** -- but it

---

[23] The government also makes a somewhat different plain-error argument in its en banc briefing, asserting that appellants failed to argue that their guilty pleas lacked a factual foundation. However, putting aside the statutory-language problem first noted by the panel, *see supra*, Reyes-Valdivia and Dávila-Reyes have not contested that the facts stated by the government satisfy the requirements of § 70502(d)(1)(C) and thus provide a statutory foundation for their guilty pleas. Their claim challenges the authority of the government to rely on § 70502(d)(1)(C).

[24] Appellants argued to us that "[p]hotos of the vessel clearly show the civil ensign of Costa Rica painted, albeit vertically, on the port and starboard sides of the ship's bow." *See Dávila-Reyes II*, 23 F.4th at 164 n.20 (quoting Appellants' Supp. Br. at 18 n.4). That assertion is supported by a statement attached as an exhibit to the government's motion in support of jurisdiction, in which a U.S. Customs Boarding Officer reported that a marine patrol had spotted a vessel "with a Costa Rican flag painted on the bow." *Id.* As the panel majority observed, however, appellants necessarily gave up the claim that their vessel bore indicia of Costa Rican nationality when they pled guilty based on the "Government's Version of the Facts" incorporated into their plea agreements. *Id.*

does not identify the specific basis on which appellants' vessel fit within that category. *Id.* It is the factual statement incorporated into the plea agreements, detailing the government's compliance with § 70502(d)(1)(C) in the same way the government had been doing throughout the proceedings, that provides the necessary, specific basis for that finding. There is simply no room for debate about the theory of jurisdiction on which the plea agreements -- and thus the guilty pleas -- rested.

On appeal, too, the government maintained its focus on § 70502(d)(1)(C). *See Dávila-Reyes II*, 23 F.4th at 163 n.18. Its appellate brief linked § 70502(c)(1)(A) and § 70502(d)(1)(C) in the way we have emphasized -- i.e., citing them as a single invocation of jurisdiction -- when it stated: "The absence of an assertion by the Costa Rican government rendered the Appellants' boat a 'vessel without nationality,' [46 U.S.C.] *§ 70502(d)(1), and thus* a 'vessel subject to the jurisdiction of the United States,' *id.* § 70502(c)(1)(A)." *Id.* (alteration in original) (emphases added). This framing again clearly reveals the government's view that appellants' vessel was subject to United States jurisdiction *because* the circumstances matched one of the definitions of a stateless vessel listed in § 70502(d)(1).

In its supplemental en banc brief, the government argues at length that the examples of vessels without nationality listed in § 70502(d)(1)(A)-(C) are "non-exhaustive" and that the **[—84—]** government can establish that a vessel is "without nationality" in various ways.[25] The government asserts that, if appellants had not pleaded guilty, it "would have been prepared" to prove that the vessel both fell within § 70502(d)(1)(C) *and* "otherwise qualified as a stateless vessel under international law." But the question here is not what theory the government *could have* used; the question is what rationale it *did* use to secure the guilty pleas.[26]

Notably, even in its motion on jurisdiction, when the government was required to make clear to the court the jurisdictional basis for the prosecution, the government **[—85—] {-435-}** ultimately and only asked the district court to make a finding and instruct the jury "pursuant to Title 46, United States Code, Section 70502(c)(1)(A) *and (d)(1)(C)* that the suspect vessel carrying the Defendants was a vessel Without Nationality and therefore subject to the jurisdiction of the United States." *Reyes-Valdivia*, ECF No. 46, at 5 (emphasis added). There was no alternative request for the court to instruct the jury or make a finding of jurisdiction under general principles of international law based on the lack of corroboration of Reyes-Valdivia's oral claim. Given the definitive pronouncements by the government seeking court validation of § 70502(d)(1)(C) as the basis for its assertion of jurisdiction over the vessel, it is absurd for the majority to validate the government's contention that it was proceeding under alternative theories. And it is simply preposterous to say that appellants should have understood that their plea agreements left the door open to theories of statelessness other than § 70502(d)(1)(C).

[25] In December 2022, a fourth type of vessel was added to the list in § 70502(d)(1): "a vessel aboard which no individual ... claims to be the master or is identified as the individual in charge, and that has no other claim of nationality or registry under paragraph (1) or (2) of subsection (e)." 46 U.S.C. § 70502(d)(1)(D). The pertinent paragraphs of subsection (e) refer to documents "evidencing the vessel's nationality" and "flying [a] nation's ensign or flag." *Id.* § 70502(e)(1), (2).

[26] Unsurprisingly, the government's assertion that it could have demonstrated that appellants' vessel "otherwise qualified" as "without nationality" relies, in part, on a report that Reyes-Valdivia initially told a Coast Guard Boarding Officer that appellants' vessel had no nationality. In other words, the government highlights that Reyes-Valdivia had admitted a fact that would be decisive in establishing that the vessel was "without nationality" apart from the requirements of § 70502(d)(1)(C). But that fact was not in the Criminal Complaint or the Department of State's official attestation of jurisdiction. And, critically, it was not in the government's recitation of facts at appellants' change of plea hearing, in the "Government's Version of the Facts" incorporated into their plea agreements, or in appellants' Presentence Investigation Reports. As the majority also recognizes, at least implicitly, the government cannot now retrieve a fact it plainly chose to abandon.

Indeed, the majority's view of the record depends on drawing meaning from what the government did *not* say. In effect, the majority holds that, because the government did not promise to rely only on § 70502(d)(1)(C), any theory of jurisdiction that could be supported by the facts in appellants' plea agreements remained on the table -- regardless of whether the government had specifically invoked such alternatives during the proceedings that **[—86—]** culminated with appellants' guilty pleas. As we have described, the government never told appellants or the district court that it was relying on the *Matos-Luchi* dicta as a basis for jurisdiction over appellants' vessel, while it repeatedly relied expressly on § 70502(d)(1)(C). For the majority, the government's singular reliance on that statutory provision does not matter. Our colleagues, for example, discount the State Department's certification that appellants' vessel was determined to be without nationality "in accordance with 46 U.S.C. § 70502(d)(1)(C)" by observing that "the certification does not purport to disclaim all other[]" theories of jurisdiction. In other words, the government may retroactively introduce the non-statutory *Matos-Luchi* rationale because it never promised not to do so.

We cannot emphasize enough that the question at this juncture is not what theories the government could have offered to support jurisdiction, but what theory informed appellants' decision to plead guilty. As should be clear by now, the plea agreements incorporated the facts consistently cited by the government to establish that appellants' vessel was "without nationality" pursuant to § 70502(d)(1)(C): the claim of nationality and the failure of Costa Rica to "affirmatively and unequivocally" confirm nationality. That theory of jurisdiction, and that theory alone, should determine the validity of appellants' convictions. **[—87—]**

III.

The majority acknowledges that appellants argued in their motion to dismiss the indictment that the government had deemed their vessel to be "without nationality" based solely, and unconstitutionally, on § 70502(d)(1)(C).[27] Our colleagues thus **{-436-}** realize that they cannot say that appellants failed to preserve the argument that their convictions must be vacated because § 70502(d)(1)(C) is unconstitutional. Hence, needing to find a rationale for the application of plain error, the majority contends that appellants failed to timely argue against theories for deeming their vessel stateless that are *not* based on § 70502(d)(1)(C). And, because the government's oft-repeated version of the facts supports a determination of statelessness pursuant to the dicta in *Matos-Luchi*, the majority concludes that there is no clear or obvious error and that appellants' convictions are properly affirmed.

This contrived use of plain error -- i.e., the disregard of the government's singular reliance on § 70502(d)(1)(C) -- is **[—88—]** contrary to our obligation to "hold prosecutors ... to 'the most meticulous standards of both promise and performance'" in effectuating a plea agreement. *United States v. Lessard*, 35 F.4th 37, 42 (1st Cir. 2022) (quoting *United States v. Clark*, 55 F.3d 9, 12 (1st Cir. 1995)). As we indicated above, our colleagues' reasoning permits the government to retroactively expand the jurisdictional foundation for appellants' guilty pleas. That is not the way ordinary contracts work, and it is the principles of contract law that govern plea agreements. *See generally Garza v. Idaho*, — U.S. —, 139 S. Ct. 738, 744, 203 L.Ed.2d 77 (2019) ("[P]lea bargains are essentially contracts." (quoting *Puckett v. United States*, 556 U.S. 129, 137, 129 S.Ct. 1423, 173 L.Ed.2d 266 (2009))); *see also United States v. Brown*, 31 F.4th 39, 50 (1st Cir. 2022) ("Traditional principles of contract law guide

[27] The majority notes that appellants argued that "[a] vessel may not be deemed stateless under international law ... simply because the nation to which the vessel's master has claimed that it belongs fails to 'affirmatively and unequivocally assert,' § 70502(d)(1)(C), that the vessel is registered with that nation." The majority further observes that appellants construed the indictment to "charge[] that the vessel that the defendants were aboard was 'without nationality' under § 70502(c)(1)(A) *solely based on the operation of § 70502(d)(1)(C)*." (Emphasis added.)

our interpretation of the terms and performance of a plea agreement."). We find especially troubling the unilateral revision of a contractual agreement when the result is to disfavor the party who gave up "a panoply of constitutional rights." *United States v. Tanco-Pizarro*, 873 F.3d 61, 65 (1st Cir. 2017) (quoting *United States v. Almonte-Nunez,* 771 F.3d 84, 89 (1st Cir. 2014)).

As we have demonstrated, at the time they negotiated and signed their plea agreements, appellants had no reason to evaluate whether to plead guilty based on theories of MDLEA jurisdiction other than § 70502(d)(1)(C). The facts giving rise to jurisdiction under that provision were undisputed. But there *were* factual and **[—89—]** legal issues relevant to the *Matos-Luchi* dicta on which the majority relies to affirm appellants' convictions. Indeed, appellants gave up the contention that their vessel bore indicia of nationality when they signed plea agreements that included the fact that the vessel lacked any such display. *See supra* note 24. If the government was not relying solely on jurisdiction under § 70502(d)(1)(C), surely appellants were entitled to explicit notice of such other theory or theories before agreeing to give up competing facts and arguments, and ultimately pleading guilty.

To justify appellants' prosecutions based on jurisdictional theories unspecified when they agreed to admit guilt is not only unfair in this case but also troubling as a precedent for plea agreements more generally. If the government is permitted to support convictions by superimposing a new rationale on plea agreements that were so clearly premised on different understandings, the concept of plea agreements as contracts -- whose linchpin is the reasonable expectations of the parties -- will be grievously eroded.

The government made its choice to rely on § 70502(d)(1)(C) when it obtained appellants' acquiescence to facts the government had consistently invoked to deem **{-437-}** their vessel "without nationality" under that specific provision. The panel majority concluded that the government's chosen theory is unconstitutional. Hence, in effect, the en banc majority is **[—90—]** holding that the government may unilaterally renegotiate the deal it struck with a defendant when flaws are identified in the original agreement. The majority's approach is not restricted to proceedings under the MDLEA and thus could be used to the government's advantage whenever it chooses. The harm to the plea-bargaining process from the majority's holding is severe and indefensible.

As described above, however, the majority maintains that appellants should have realized that the facts in the plea agreements, along with citation to the MDLEA provision that generally authorizes jurisdiction over vessels "without nationality," preserved jurisdictional theories that the government never specifically invoked. In other words, according to the majority, appellants should have challenged theories on which the government did not rely because the government never pledged to forego reliance on them at a later juncture. To bolster their position that plain error thus applies to the *Matos-Luchi*-based theory, our colleagues repeatedly and pointedly say that the claim of "jurisdiction switching" -- their term -- was voiced by appellants "only in their briefing to the en banc court, which they submitted only after the panel majority had raised and relied on the theory sua sponte." Hence, our colleagues say, "if a gloss is being retroactively imposed on the record, it is the gloss that **[—91—]** would attribute to the government an intentional waiver of the *Matos-Luchi*-based theory."

But we are not arguing that the government *waived* reliance on *Matos-Luchi*. Rather, the government is precluded from switching jurisdictional gears because of ordinary contract principles and the particular importance of adhering to those principles in the context of plea-bargaining. As explained above, appellants have focused on the validity of their prosecutions based on § 70502(d)(1)(C) because that was the sole jurisdictional rationale specifically relied upon by the government throughout the proceedings in the district court. The panel majority's statement that the government could not reconceive the plea agreements retroactively was -- and is -- merely an inescapable conclusion based on contract law and our obligation to honor a defendant's reasonable understanding of his plea agreement. Even if appellants in their en banc briefs had not repeated the panel's objection to new theories of jurisdiction, it would be wrong for us to ignore the government's attempt to ambush appellants with an alternative basis for deeming their vessel "without nationality."

To the extent this contractual constraint on the government's ability to change course operates like a waiver, that limitation is simply a function of the way contracts and plea-bargaining work. The inclusion of facts extraneous to § 70502(d)(1)(C) in the plea agreements cannot, without some **[—92—]** linkage to a specified jurisdictional theory, open the door to the government's permissible reliance on such an alternative to validate an otherwise impermissible prosecution. At most, those stray facts create an ambiguity that precedent tells us must be resolved in appellants' favor. Certainly, the obligation to deal forthrightly with defendants who will be giving up important constitutional rights cannot be met with plea agreements that sub silentio -- at best -- or deceptively -- at worst -- enlarge the government's end of the bargain.

Yet, our colleagues attempt to justify their choice to rely on a contrived plain-error analysis by discrediting the ways in **{-438-}** which appellants responded to the government's shift in strategy. First, the majority notes that appellants have not sought to vacate their pleas as unknowing and involuntary in light of the government's assertion that the plea agreements covered rationales for deeming their vessel "without nationality" other than § 70502(d)(1)(C). Second, the majority observes that, in the supplemental brief requested by the panel in early 2019, appellants responded to the government's *Matos-Luchi*-based argument on its merits rather than asserting that the argument had been waived.

This turning of the tables on appellants is another example of the remarkable lengths the majority is traveling to justify avoiding appellants' constitutional challenge to § 70502(d)(1)(C). Appellants admitted that the government's facts **[—93—]** establish their vessel's statelessness pursuant to § 70502(d)(1)(C), and they necessarily concede that, if § 70502(d)(1)(C) is constitutional, their pleas and convictions would stand (assuming their other challenges to the MDLEA also failed).[28] In other words, appellants do not dispute that their pleas were knowing and voluntary based on the only ground relied upon by the government to secure them. It is patently absurd to suggest that, rather than challenging the constitutional legitimacy of the government's actual theory of jurisdiction, they should be seeking to undo their pleas -- more than seven years later and after Reyes-Valdivia served his entire sentence -- based on a counterfactual version of the record.

The majority also suggests that, by arguing against the merits of the *Matos-Luchi* alternative, appellants gave up the argument that their plea agreements were reasonably understood to establish their vessel's statelessness only via § 70502(d)(1)(C). But the majority ignores and thereby distorts the significance of appellants' substantive rebuttal to the *Matos-Luchi* dicta. Appellants addressed *Matos-Luchi* on the merits only when responding to a series of questions posed to both parties by the panel, including whether there were other possible theories of **[—94—]** jurisdiction to support the prosecution given that, by its terms, § 70502(d)(1)(C) refers only to claims of registry, not -- as occurred here -- to claims of nationality. *See supra* note 22. The government relied heavily on *Matos-Luchi* in its response, even asserting -- contrary to the reality described in Section II above -- that "[b]efore the Appellants pleaded guilty, the Government's primary basis for determining that their vessel was 'subject to the jurisdiction of the United States' under 46 U.S.C. § 70502(c)(1) was that it bore no indicia of nationality and its master did not support his verbal claim of Costa Rican nationality." Appellants' response sensibly covered the possibility that our court would allow a post-conviction switch in jurisdictional theory based

[28] As described in the majority opinion, appellants also presented multiple arguments alleging violations of the Due Process Clause of the Constitution.

on *Matos-Luchi* in disregard of appellants' reasonable understanding of the plea agreements -- a step the majority has, in fact, lamentably taken.[29] **[—95—]** **{-439-}**

IV.

Under *Class v. United States*, — U.S. —, 138 S. Ct. 798, 200 L.Ed.2d 37 (2018), Reyes-Valdivia and Dávila-Reyes are entitled to challenge their convictions on the ground that Congress exceeded its constitutional authority when it enacted § 70502(d)(1)(C) as a basis for designating a vessel "without nationality." As the panel majority opinion shows, that challenge is legally complex - - requiring us to examine, inter alia, the Constitution's language, the Founding generation's understanding of that language, the legislative history of the MDLEA, our circuit's precedent on the protective principle, and the principles of international law governing vessels traveling on the high seas. Indeed, our court is now ruling on appellants' challenge for the third time, reflecting the difficulty of the issues and the undeveloped nature of our precedent. Twice, the panel confronted the merits of appellants' claims, once after a pause of more than a year for completion of the en banc proceedings in *United States v. Aybar-Ulloa*, 987 F.3d 1, 9 Adm. R. 10 (1st Cir. 2021) (en banc), a case that presented overlapping issues concerning the United States' authority to prosecute foreign nationals accused of drug-trafficking on the high seas. Now, for the first time, the court's dispositive ruling avoids seriously engaging with any aspect of the merits of appellants' claim. **[—96—]**

The majority's justification for that avoidance depends on a non-existent plain-error scenario and a deeply problematic misuse of the plain-error standard. The plain-error doctrine sets a high threshold for remedying errors on appeal to "keep[] parties from hiding problems below" that could have "been fixed then and there." *United States v. Romero*, 906 F.3d 196, 205 n.4 (1st Cir. 2018); *see also Puckett*, 556 U.S. at 134, 129 S.Ct. 1423 ("[T]he contemporaneous-objection rule prevents a litigant from 'sandbagging' the court -- remaining silent about his objection and belatedly raising the error only if the case does not conclude in his favor." (quoting *Wainwright v. Sykes*, 433 U.S. 72, 89, 97 S.Ct. 2497, 53 L.Ed.2d 594 (1977))). Ignoring that rationale for the plain-error doctrine, the majority uses plain error as a convenient off-ramp. The government consistently relied on § 70502(d)(1)(C) to support the prosecutions, and appellants have consistently challenged the prosecutions as unconstitutional based on the government's reliance on that provision. Appellants never hid the ball, leaving no justification for invoking the plain-error rubric to avoid their claims. It is the government, abetted by the majority, that seeks to change the terms of the plea bargain.

The majority's sidestepping of substantial issues of great import based on a contrived procedural ground is particularly disconcerting at this late stage of the case. At no point during the case's lengthy history in our court was there a suggestion **[—97—]** that the case should end because of a procedural default. Of course, that history would not justify ignoring a true procedural impediment to the en banc court's reaching the merits. But the procedural impediment on which the majority relies is an artifice in the name of constitutional avoidance with severe consequences for the practice of plea-bargaining. Nor should we forget the impact on the two individuals directly affected by the majority's dogged avoidance of the merits. Reyes-Valdivia and Dávila-Reyes, Costa Rican nationals who plausibly claimed Costa Rican nationality for their vessel, have

[29] The majority's plain-error analysis relying on *Matos-Luchi* is disturbing beyond the disregard of appellants' understanding of their plea agreements. At a minimum, the en banc court should be considering whether *Matos-Luchi*'s dicta aligns with international law. If international law does require corroboration of an oral claim of nationality to establish a vessel's foreign status, appellants' prosecutions at least would be within Congress's authority under the Felonies Clause, even if improper given the government's sole reliance on § 70502(d)(1)(C) to obtain the guilty pleas. If *Matos-Luchi* is wrong, however, the prosecutions would be unconstitutional unless sustainable under § 70502(d)(1)(C) or our court's precedent on the protective principle -- issues the majority also refuses to address.

vigorously pressed **{–440–}** their constitutional challenge to § 70502(d)(1)(C), and they deserve to know -- after more than seven years -- whether they were lawfully prosecuted. Although Reyes-Valdivia completed his sentence, Dávila-Reyes remains incarcerated.

Constitutional avoidance is an important principle. But it is not properly used here to escape confronting appellants' challenge to § 70502(d)(1)(C). Indeed, as an intermediate appellate court, we could perform an important service by exploring "the broader questions of international and constitutional law" acknowledged by the majority and attempting to crystalize the issues in a way that would be useful to the Supreme Court if it chose to review our decision. We do not minimize the "sensitive issues of U.S. foreign relations and national power" implicated by appellants' challenge to § 70502(d)(1)(C), but we cannot sidestep **[—98—]** such questions because of their sensitivity and import when properly raised. If we answer them incorrectly, the Supreme Court will tell us. In addition, with their avoidance, our colleagues forsake their obligation to address and clarify multiple unresolved issues in our own law on MDLEA prosecutions, including the role of the protective principle and the validity of the *Matos-Luchi* dicta as a basis for deeming a vessel "without nationality." These recurring issues deserve our attention now.

Moreover, the dance the majority performs to avoid appellants' serious constitutional challenge undermines the Supreme Court's decision in *Class* to forgo the usual finality of unconditional guilty pleas to protect criminal defendants from prosecutions -- and, perhaps most importantly, imprisonments -- that the United States lacks authority to pursue. *See Class*, 138 S.Ct. at 805 (holding that an unconditional guilty plea does not bar a direct appeal where the defendant's claims "call into question the [g]overnment's power to 'constitutionally prosecute' him" (quoting *United States v. Broce*, 488 U.S. 563, 575, 109 S.Ct. 757, 102 L.Ed.2d 927 (1989))). Accordingly, we dissent and, based on the analysis set forth in the panel majority opinion, *see* Appendix, conclude that appellants' convictions should be reversed.[30]

(Reporter's Note: The Appendix referenced above and in footnote 30 is omitted).

---

[30] The majority suggests that, if appellants' contentions did not otherwise fail, their claims may be waived. The panel majority explained why appellants' plea agreements do not bar their appeals and why, pursuant to *Class*, their guilty pleas do not foreclose their constitutional claims. Those explanations are contained in Section III of the panel majority opinion. *See* Appendix.

United States Court of Appeals for the First Circuit

No. 22-1700

CIARAMETARO
vs.
CITY OF GLOUCESTER

Appeal from the United States District Court for the District of Massachusetts

Decided: November 28, 2023

Citation: 87 F.4th 83, 11 Adm. R. 125 (1st Cir. 2023).

Before **KAYATTA, LIPEZ,** and **RIKELMAN,** Circuit Judges.

[—3—] {-84-} KAYATTA, Circuit Judge: **{-85-}**

Thomas Ciarametaro, the Harbormaster of the City of Gloucester, Massachusetts, claims that several Gloucester city officials (the "City Officials") violated his First Amendment rights because they retaliated against him for his expert testimony in a maritime tort dispute between several Gloucester fishermen and the United States Coast Guard. The district court granted summary judgment to the City Officials. In so ruling, the district court concluded that qualified immunity shielded the City Officials -- in their personal capacities -- from Ciarametaro's First Amendment retaliation claims. Ciarametaro appeals only that conclusion. Because we agree that the City Officials are entitled to qualified immunity, we affirm.

I.

A.

In reviewing the grant of a motion for summary judgment dismissing Ciarametaro's claims, we accept the facts in the light most favorable to him, and we draw all reasonable inferences on his behalf. *See Potvin v. Speedway LLC*, 891 F.3d 410, 413–14 (1st Cir. 2018).

As Harbormaster, Ciarametaro regulates and maintains the Gloucester waterfront. His duties include enforcing local maritime ordinances, responding to boating emergencies, maintaining harbor facilities, and cooperating with state and federal maritime agencies. Ciarametaro also owns a private **[—4—]** consulting firm called Five Fathoms Consulting, which provides, among other things, "marine investigation and expert witness" services.[1]

In January 2018, counsel for two Gloucester fishermen (and the estate of a third fisherman) approached Ciarametaro in his capacity as the owner of Five Fathoms Consulting. The fishermen were suing a Gloucester fishing captain and the United States Coast Guard, alleging that both parties negligently sank the fishermen's stranded vessel during a botched rescue attempt. *See* Complaint at 3–7, *Lane v. Powell*, No. 17–12356–PBS (D. Mass. Nov. 30, 2017). The fishermen asked Ciarametaro to testify on their behalf as an expert witness in the case (the "*Lane* case").

Before accepting the offer, Ciarametaro contacted Charles Payson, the then-City Solicitor of Gloucester. According to Ciarametaro, Payson stated that he had "no problem" with the expert witness arrangement, given that neither Ciarametaro nor the Harbormaster's Office had been involved in the *Lane* accident. Payson then **{-86-}** recommended that Ciarametaro speak to the Massachusetts State Ethics Commission. Ciarametaro alleges that he did so. He also alleges that the Commission's representative advised him that testifying in the *Lane* case would present "no **[—5—]** legal or ethical conflict." Shortly thereafter, Ciarametaro accepted the expert witness assignment.

Ciarametaro filed his expert report in June 2019. The report criticized the actions of both the rescuing fishing captain and the Coast Guard. Ciarametaro wrote that "everything about [the defendant-fishing captain's tow of the plaintiffs' vessel] was improper from the start." He also described the Coast Guard

[1] The parties agree that Gloucester officials may pursue outside employment that does not interfere with their public duties.

response as plagued by a "significant breakdown in communication . . . up and down the chain of command." Trial on the *Lane* case was scheduled for July 2020.

On April 6, 2020, James Destino -- the then-Chief Administrative Officer of Gloucester -- learned from the president of the Massachusetts Lobstermen's Association ("MLA") that Ciarametaro was an expert witness in the *Lane* case. Destino then called Ciarametaro, expressing concern that the latter's testimony in *Lane* would strain Gloucester's relationships with the fishing community, harm Ciarametaro's reputation, and cost Ciarametaro his job. During the call, Destino and Ciarametaro discussed the risk that the public would look askance at Gloucester's harbormaster testifying against a Gloucester fishing captain. In a follow-up text exchange later that day, Destino wrote that he did not want to see Ciarametaro's "good reputation in town . . . [compromised]." The pair discussed how Ciarametaro could **[—6—]** "extricate" himself from the *Lane* case, and Ciarametaro agreed to try to withdraw as an expert witness.

After the April 6 call with Destino, Ciarametaro texted Sefatia Theken, the then-Mayor of Gloucester. Ciarametaro wrote that he "[understood] the public perception" of his testimony in the *Lane* case. He also emphasized that he was "working . . . to recuse [himself]" from the case.[2] Theken wrote back that the *Lane* case was a "big conflict" that could undermine the fishing community's trust in the Harbormaster's Office. Theken also left Ciarametaro a voice message, in which she berated him in crude terms, threatened his job, demanded that he recuse himself from *Lane*, and warned that he was "losing the trust of the fishermen." In an email exchange with Ciarametaro and several other City Officials on April 7, Theken reiterated that she did not want to "los[e] the trust" of local fishermen or risk a "conflict" between Ciarametaro's public and private duties. In the same email exchange, Payson added that Ciarametaro's involvement in *Lane* "sends a clear message to the fishing community that if you stop and help a fellow fisherman you could be liable for negligence." **[—7—]**

On April 9, Theken received a letter from the executive director of the MLA. The letter stated that the MLA's members had a "lack of faith within the port of Gloucester," with "many commercial fishermen [questioning] the reliability and position individual harbormasters have taken on [the *Lane* case]." The letter went on to say that "commercial fishermen need a champion now more than ever[,] and not an anti-fisherman authority working against them[.]" **{-87-}**

Despite the City Officials' newly reinforced concerns, and his prior indications that he would try to withdraw as a witness, Ciarametaro remained an expert witness in the *Lane* case. Starting in April 2020, the City Officials allegedly began a campaign of retaliation against Ciarametaro. He claims that the City Officials created a hostile work environment by excluding him from important policymaking meetings and subjecting him to repeated verbal abuse. For example, Ciarametaro claims that Theken called him a "fraud" and an "asshole" and suggested to others that her relatives should "brea[k] [Ciarametaro's] kneecaps." He also alleges that the City Officials reduced his compensation by denying him permission to work on overtime details, and by withholding a previously agreed-upon pay raise that Ciarametaro expected to receive after the Harbormaster's Office merged with the Gloucester Shellfish Department. Ciarametaro further alleges that the City Officials interfered with his management of the Harbormaster's **[—8—]** Office, particularly by harassing one of Ciarametaro's part-time administrative clerks and accusing her of "f*****g everyone in the [Harbormaster's Office]."

Finally, Ciarametaro alleges that the City Officials conspired to conjure a pretext for firing him. For example, he alleges that Theken admitted to working with Holly Dougwillo -- Gloucester's Human Resources Director -- to

---

[2] In a separate email to Theken -- also dated April 6 -- Ciarametaro suggested that recusal "may not be . . . simple at this point," and asked Theken to advise him on how to proceed. He did not retract his previous statements that he would attempt to withdraw from the case.

"fis[h] for wrongdoing" in his personnel files. And he alleges that Destino told the other City Officials that "the goal is to get rid of [Ciarametaro] . . . Human Resources has been building a file against him, he's done."

B.

In February 2021, Ciarametaro sued the City of Gloucester and the City Officials (i.e., Theken, Destino, Payson, and Dougwillo) in Massachusetts state court. The complaint, as later amended, includes three counts. Count I is a tort claim for intentional infliction of emotional distress. Count II is a First Amendment retaliation claim under 42 U.S.C. § 1983. Count III is a civil rights claim under the Massachusetts Civil Rights Act. The City and the City Officials timely removed the case to the U.S. District Court for the District of Massachusetts.

The district court granted summary judgment to the defendants on all counts. As relevant here, the district court held that Counts II and III failed as against the City Officials **[—9—]** in their personal capacities because it was not "clearly established" that Ciarametaro's speech "enjoyed First Amendment protection." The district court held that the City Officials were therefore entitled to qualified immunity.

Ciarametaro timely appealed, challenging only the district court's qualified immunity finding as to the City Officials. Ciarametaro argues that by retaliating against him for his expert testimony in *Lane*, the defendants violated his clearly established First Amendment rights. He does not argue that the City Officials are liable for damages even if their alleged retaliation were constitutionally permissible. Nor does he argue that even if some form of retaliation were legally permissible, the specific nature of the City Officials' retaliation nevertheless violated his First Amendment rights.

II.

A.

Qualified immunity shields public officials from personal liability for "actions taken while performing discretionary functions." *Lynch v. City of Boston*, 180 F.3d 1, 13 (1st Cir. 1999). The goal of qualified immunity is to "give[] government officials breathing room to make reasonable but **{-88-}** mistaken judgments about open legal questions." *Ashcroft v. al-Kidd*, 563 U.S. 731, 743 (2011). To achieve that goal, a court will grant qualified immunity unless it is "sufficiently clear **[—10—]** 'that every reasonable official would [have understood] that what he [was] doing violate[d]'" the plaintiff's rights. *Reichle v. Howards*, 566 U.S. 658, 664 (2012) (first alteration in the original) (quoting *Ashcroft*, 563 U.S. at 741). Qualified immunity therefore protects "all but the plainly incompetent or those who knowingly violate the law." *Malley v. Briggs*, 475 U.S. 335, 341 (1986).

To surmount qualified immunity, a plaintiff must show that 1) the official "violated a statutory or constitutional right," and 2) the ostensibly violated right was "clearly established" at the time of the challenged conduct. *Ashcroft*, 563 U.S. at 735. The plaintiff must point to controlling authority, or a "robust consensus" of persuasive authority, clearly demonstrating the "violative nature of [the defendant's] particular conduct." *Id.* at 741–42 (internal citations and quotations omitted). That authority need not be "directly on point," but a plaintiff also may not "define clearly established law at a high level of generality." *Id.* at 741–42. Instead, the plaintiff must identify authority that is sufficiently analogous to "place[] the statutory or constitutional question beyond debate." *Id.* at 741.

B.

To determine whether a public employer violates an employee's First Amendment rights by retaliating against him on **[—11—]** account of his speech, we employ a three-step standard. *See Davignon v. Hodgson*, 524 F.3d 91, 100 (1st Cir. 2008).

The first step is to determine whether the public employee "spoke as a citizen on a matter of public concern." *Id.* The second step requires balancing the value of the employee's speech -- both to himself and to the public -- against the government employer's legitimate interest in "preventing unnecessary disruptions and inefficiencies in carrying out its public service mission." *Guilloty Perez v. Pierluisi*, 339 F.3d 43, 52 (1st Cir. 2003) (quoting *O'Connor v. Steeves*, 994 F.2d 905, 915 (1st Cir. 1993)); *see also Garcetti v. Ceballos*, 547 U.S. 410, 420 (2006) (noting the need to respect both the "individual and societal interests" in the public employee's speech and the ability of the public employer to "perform [its] important public functions."). This balancing inquiry is known as *Pickering* balancing. *See Pickering v. Bd. of Ed. of Twp. High Sch. Dist. 205, Will Cnty.*, 391 U.S. 563, 568 (1968) (articulating the original version of the balancing test).

If an employee's speech satisfies the first two steps, then it is protected speech under the First Amendment. *See Rosaura Bldg. Corp. v. Municipality of Mayaguez*, 778 F.3d 55, 66–67 (1st Cir. 2015). The analysis then proceeds to the third step, which asks whether the protected speech was a "substantial or motivating **[—12—]** factor in the adverse employment decision." *Curran v. Cousins*, 509 F.3d 36, 45 (1st Cir. 2007).

As to step one, for purposes of summary judgment, the City Officials do not meaningfully dispute that Ciarametaro spoke as a private citizen on a matter of public concern. So, we can proceed to step two (the *Pickering* analysis), within the context of a qualified immunity defense. We ask whether, at the time of the City Officials' alleged retaliation, the law clearly **{-89-}** established that the value of Ciarametaro's speech outweighed the municipality's interest in the efficient provision of public services by the Harbormaster's Office. For the following reasons, we find that it did not.[3] The City Officials are therefore entitled to qualified immunity, and we need not address step three of the First Amendment retaliation analysis.

III.

A.

We start by analyzing the City Officials' *Pickering* interest in the efficient provision of public services. At the outset, Ciarametaro asserts that there is "no evidence that [his **[—13—]** testimony] was disruptive to the [Harbormaster's Office] or the [City]." But an employer need not "allow events to unfold to the extent that the . . . destruction of working relationships is manifest before taking action." *Curran*, 509 F.3d at 49 (quoting *Connick v. Myers*, 461 U.S. 138, 152 (1983)). Instead, to assess the employer interests implicated by Ciarametaro's speech, the relevant question is whether the City Officials were reasonably concerned that Ciarametaro's expert testimony would disrupt relationships between commercial fishermen and the Harbormaster's Office. *Id.* (quoting *Waters v. Churchill*, 511 U.S. 661, 673 (1994)) ("[R]easonable [employer] predictions of disruption" receive significant weight under *Pickering*); *see also Kinney v. Weaver*, 367 F.3d 337, 364 (5th Cir. 2004) (en banc) ("The key limitation on preemptive action . . . is that [an employer's] predictions of disruption must be *reasonable*.").

Ciarametaro's brief concedes that the City Officials were, in fact, "concerned" that his speech was causing local fishermen to "question the continued successes of the fleet in Gloucester." City Officials expressed such concerns immediately upon learning about Ciarametaro's involvement in the *Lane* case in April 2020. In his phone call with Ciarametaro, Destino emphasized the public perception risks of the City Harbormaster testifying against a local fisherman. Theken wrote in a text message to Ciarametaro that the testimony created a "big conflict" that could **[—14—]** drive the fishing community to "lose trust" in the Harbormaster's Office. And Payson stated

[3] Our analysis of Ciarametaro's federal claim under section 1983 applies equally to his state claim under the Massachusetts Civil Rights Act. The Massachusetts Supreme Judicial Court has made clear that the "[f]ederal system of immunity for discretionary functions under [section] 1983" also applies to claims brought under the Massachusetts Civil Rights Act. *Duarte v. Healy*, 537 N.E.2d 1230, 1232 (Mass. 1989).

in an email that Ciarametaro's *Lane* testimony sent a "clear message" to the fishing community that the Harbormaster may not support them in a similar tort suit.

The City Officials' concerns about the disruptive impact of Ciarametaro's testimony were certainly reasonable. Indeed, the organization representing many local fishermen -- the MLA -- expressly told Theken that those fishermen considered the Harbormaster's Office to be "anti-fisherman." Given that blunt language, the City Officials could reasonably predict that Ciarametaro's testimony risked undermining his ability to "[p]romote the City as a hospitable port of call." Ciarametaro himself was aware of this risk. In his text messages with Theken, Ciarametaro acknowledged that his testimony threatened the "public perception" of his department.[4] **{-90-}**

This is therefore not a case like *Mihos v. Swift*, 358 F.3d 91 (1st Cir. 2004), in which the plaintiff alleged that the content of his speech -- rather than concerns about the impact of that speech on his job performance -- provoked his employer's retaliatory pique. *Id.* at 103–08. Here, Ciarametaro acknowledges that the City Officials were concerned about his testimony **[—15—]** alienating an important local industry. In sum, the defendants' side of the *Pickering* scale bears substantial weight.

B.

Were we required to decide finally whether the City Officials violated Ciarametaro's First Amendment rights, we would now need to balance the City's foregoing interests against the interests of Ciarametaro and the public in his *Lane* testimony. *Garcetti*, 547 U.S. at 420. This would be a delicate and "fact-intensive" inquiry. *Fabiano v. Hopkins*, 352 F.3d 447, 457 (1st Cir. 2003).

But we need not undertake this inquiry. This is because the outcome of such a difficult and fact-bound analysis "can rarely be considered 'clearly established,' at least in the absence of closely corresponding factual or legal precedent." *Frazier v. Bailey*, 957 F.2d 920, 931 (1st Cir. 1992). And Ciarametaro identifies no "closely corresponding" precedent clearly establishing that the City Officials -- at the time of their actions -- could not restrict his expert testimony to preserve relationships with the Gloucester fishing community.

In his brief, Ciarametaro indirectly cites to *Rankin v. McPherson*, 483 U.S. 378 (1987), where the Supreme Court noted that it is "clearly established that a State may not discharge an employee on a basis that infringes that employee's constitutionally protected interest in freedom of speech." *Id.* at **[—16—]** 383. This simply begs the question. Ciarametaro's citation to *Rankin* tautologically presumes that his speech was protected. But whether and how clearly Ciarametaro's speech was protected in the first place is the crux of this entire dispute.

In a supplemental letter to the court, Ciarametaro points to *Swartzwelder v. McNeilly*, 297 F.3d 228 (3d Cir. 2002). But *Swartzwelder* is plainly distinguishable on its facts. That case involved a sweeping police department policy that required "the vast rank and file" of officers to obtain approval before giving expert opinion testimony. 297 F.3d at 231–32, 237 (quoting *United States v. Nat'l Treasury Emp. Union*, 513 U.S. 454, 472 (1995)). The breadth of that prior restraint invited a "tailoring requirement," *id.* at 236, which the police department's broad policy could not satisfy, *id.* at 241. By contrast, this case involves a town responding to specific testimony by a specific official. Hence, it does not present the overbreadth defect that took center stage in *Swartzwelder*.

In the same letter, Ciarametaro also cites to *Brady v. Tamburini*, 518 F. Supp. 3d 570 (D.R.I. 2021). *Brady* is a district court case, and district court decisions "do not necessarily settle constitutional standards or prevent repeated claims of qualified immunity." *Camreta v. Greene*, 563 U.S. 692, 709 n.7 (2011). In any event, *Brady* is inapposite.

[4] At oral argument, Ciarametaro's counsel conceded that these text messages reflected Ciarametaro's belief that his testimony could disrupt the relationship between the Harbormaster's Office and the fishing community.

There, a police department disciplined a detective for comments he made to a newspaper **[—17—]** reporter. 518 F. Supp. 3d at 577. The district court concluded that *Pickering* balancing favored the officer, because the department "presented no evidence" that the officer's speech actually or potentially disrupted department operations. *Id.* at 586. That is not the case here, where the City Officials had ample reason to believe that **{-91-}** Ciarametaro's speech threatened relationships with commercial fishermen.

Our own review also reveals no case clearly establishing that Ciarametaro's speech was categorically entitled to First Amendment protection. *See Elder v. Holloway*, 510 U.S. 510, 512 (1994) ("[A]ppellate review of qualified immunity dispositions is to be conducted in light of all relevant precedents . . . ."). In fact, several appellate cases have held that a public employee's judicial testimony was *not* protected under *Pickering* when the testimony criticized third parties with whom the public employer wished to maintain a strong working relationship. *See, e.g., Worrell v. Henry*, 219 F.3d 1197, 1208 (10th Cir. 2000) (district attorney could withdraw an offer of employment to serve as the coordinator of a drug task force, because the offeree's past testimony on behalf of a criminal defendant risked relationships with a cooperating agency); *Tedder v. Norman*, 167 F.3d 1213, 1215 (8th Cir. 1999) (director of a law enforcement training center could demote his deputy, because the deputy's prior testimony in an excessive force case threatened relationships between the **[—18—]** training center and the law enforcement agencies it trained); *cf. Gilchrist v. Citty*, 173 Fed. App'x 675, 685 (10th Cir. 2006) (forensic lab could demote an analyst who previously gave faulty testimony because, among other things, further testimony could threaten the lab's credibility in court).

To be clear, we need not (and therefore do not) decide whether the value of Ciarametaro's speech outweighed the City Officials' interests under *Pickering* balancing. We hold only that the City Officials could have reasonably concluded that it did not. And even if the City Officials' reasoning was "mistaken, it would not have been egregiously so . . . . [A]ccordingly, qualified immunity is available." *See Wagner v. City of Holyoke*, 404 F.3d 504, 509 (1st Cir. 2005).

IV.

For the foregoing reasons, the judgment of the district court is *affirmed*.

United States Court of Appeals for the First Circuit

No. 22-1844

ST ENG'G MARINE, LTD.
VS.
THOMPSON, MACCOLL & BASS, LLC

Appeal from the United States District Court for the District of Maine

Decided: December 6, 2023

Citation: 88 F.4th 27, 11 Adm. R. 131 (1st Cir. 2023).

Before **RIKELMAN, SELYA,** and **HOWARD,** Circuit Judges.

[—2—] {-30-} SELYA, Circuit Judge:

Following a bench trial, the district court found that a law firm, defendant-appellant Thompson, MacColl & Bass, LLC, P.A. (TM&B), had breached its duty of care in advising its quondam client, plaintiff-appellee ST Engineering Marine, Ltd. (STEM), about the viability of a maritime lien. The district court further found that TM&B's negligence was the actual and proximate cause of STEM's loss and awarded STEM damages in the amount of $261,839.04. TM&B appeals. Affording due deference to the district court's findings of fact, we affirm.

I

We briefly rehearse the relevant facts and travel of the case. In 2013, STEM owned the *M/V Nova Star*. At that time, it entered into a bareboat charter agreement for the vessel with Nova Star Cruises Ltd. (NSC). NSC assumed responsibility for all aspects of the vessel's operations and associated costs (including providing and paying for bunker fuel). It hired the shipmanagement company Fleetpro Ocean Inc. (Fleetpro) to operate the *M/V Nova Star* as its agent.

In June of 2015, Fleetpro contacted Bunkers International Corporation (BIC), a firm that arranged the delivery of fuel for charterers, to supply fuel for the *M/V Nova Star*. Fleetpro proceeded to send BIC purchase orders for two sales. Each purchase order laid out the details of the particular sale, listed Fleetpro "AS AGENTS FOR" NSC, and listed BIC as the "Supplier." **[—3—]**

BIC thereafter engaged Sprague Operating Resources, LLC (Sprague) to supply fuel to the vessel. Neither the vessel's owner, its master, nor Fleetpro had any involvement in the selection of Sprague as the fuel vendor.

Withal, Sprague supplied fuel to the *M/V Nova Star* on two separate occasions. At the end of each delivery, the master and chief engineer of the vessel signed or stamped the fuel receipts. Sprague sent an invoice to BIC after each delivery ($147,354.92 for the first delivery and $149,719.68 for the second delivery). In turn, BIC sent invoices to NSC "and/or Master, Owners, Operators, Charterers, Managers, Managing Agents" for $156,460.73 and $157,729.23. Fleetpro paid BIC, but BIC filed for bankruptcy without paying Sprague.

Months later, the *M/V Nova Star* was arrested at the instance of a company asserting **{-31-}** a maritime lien for unpaid services. In the ensuing melee, several other entities (including Sprague) purposed to assert maritime liens on the vessel. Pertinently, Sprague alleged that it had acquired its maritime lien of $297,074.60 upon supplying the *M/V Nova Star* with fuel.

With its vessel embroiled in numerous legal actions, STEM turned to TM&B for legal advice. STEM asked TM&B to analyze the flurry of lien claims and assess the validity of each claim so that STEM could decide which claims should be resisted (that is, bonded but not paid) and which claims should be settled. In mid- **[—4—]** November 2015, a TM&B attorney and STEM's president and in-house counsel exchanged multiple emails. The attorney advised that Sprague's lien should be honored and its claim paid. In one of his November 16, 2015, emails, the attorney added:

> Dear All,
>
> I have reviewed the lien claims and have requested back-up documents from

the claimants. Once we get the back-up documents, I will provide my comments on the bona fide nature of the lien claims.

. . . Sprague Energy is the provider of bunker on the order of [BIC] . . . . Sprague has attached to its complaint copies of the bunker receipts for its two deliveries, both signed by the Master. I understand that BIC is the bunker trader that filed for bankruptcy protection . . . .

If BIC was acting as agent or broker for the ship and ordered bunkers for the ship from Sprague and then filed in bankruptcy, the fact that Fleetpro paid BIC would not help us in the lien claim filed by the innocent provide[r] that actually delivered the bunkers. Our recourse is to file a claim in the BIC bankruptcy proceeding for the amount paid to Sprague. [STEM] would in effect step into the position of Sprague claiming against BIC.

Acting on TM&B's advice, STEM proceeded to settle Sprague's claim for $267,366. It then filed a counterpart claim in the BIC bankruptcy proceeding for an equivalent sum. But in the end, STEM recovered only $5,526.96 as a result of its bankruptcy claim.

In September of 2020, STEM sued TM&B for professional negligence. STEM alleged that TM&B had advised it that Sprague possessed a valid maritime lien on the *M/V Nova Star* and that the **[—5—]** only way to extinguish the lien was by paying Sprague for the fuel it had supplied. In providing this advice, STEM alleged, TM&B fell below the standard of care that it owed to STEM and was negligent. As STEM saw the matter, TM&B negligently failed to advise it that the governing law was "unsettled generally and in a state of transition"; that there was no controlling decision on the issue in the District of Maine; that further investigation into Sprague's claim was needed; that STEM could try to provide security to obtain the release of the *M/V Nova Star* while contesting Sprague's lien claim; and that there were legal arguments that could be made to defeat Sprague's claim. Because it paid Sprague "as a direct and proximate result" of TM&B's negligent advice, STEM averred, it was entitled to recover damages from TM&B.

TM&B denied that its legal advice fell below the applicable standard of care but it did not deny that it had advised STEM that Sprague had a valid lien. Pretrial discovery ensued, followed by a three-day bench trial. The district court ruled in favor of STEM. See *ST Eng'g Marine, Ltd. v. Thompson, MacColl & Bass, LLC*, 633 F. Supp. 3d 354, 365 (D. Me. 2022). In the process, the court found that Sprague was a subcontractor. *See id.* at 357. It then **{-32-}** found that "STEM, Nova Star Cruises, and Fleetpro did not control the selection or performance of Sprague, nor did they have **[—6—]** other dealings with Sprague apart from the routine acceptance of the delivery." *Id.* at 357-58.

In its conclusions of law, the court held that TM&B breached the duty of care that it owed to STEM. *See id.* at 361. The most recent First Circuit case concerning maritime liens at the time TM&B advised STEM (November of 2015) was *Cianbro Corp. v. George H. Dean, Inc.*, 596 F.3d 10 (1st Cir. 2010), which established that "a subcontractor who was not directly ordered to provide necessaries can assert a lien if 'it can be shown that an entity authorized to bind the ship controlled the selection of the subcontractor and/or its performance.'" *ST Eng'g Marine*, 633 F. Supp. 3d at 358 (quoting *Cianbro*, 596 F.3d at 17). Nevertheless, TM&B predicated its advice on the older case of *Tramp Oil & Marine, Ltd. v. M/V Mermaid I*, 805 F.2d 42 (1st Cir. 1986), and failed to "account for *Cianbro*'s analysis of the issue." *ST Eng'g Marine*, 633 F. Supp. 3d at 359-60. The court further concluded that — by not conducting legal research beyond *Tramp Oil* and by not rereading any of the cases cited and/or relied upon in *Cianbro* — TM&B furnished advice based on an "erroneous interpretation of the controlling law at the time." *Id.* at 361. TM&B — the district court determined — thereby failed to exercise due diligence in investigating Sprague's lien claim and, thus, breached the professional duty that it owed to STEM. *See id.* **[—7—]**

The district court proceeded to find that this breach of duty proximately caused STEM's loss: "it is more likely than not that STEM would have been able to prove in the underlying arrest proceeding that BIC was not acting as an agent of STEM, Nova Star Cruises, or Fleetpro." *Id.* at 365. So, STEM proved "by a preponderance of the evidence that it would have prevailed in the arrest proceeding on Sprague's maritime lien claim but for TM&B's negligent advice." *Id.* The court concluded its decision by ordering TM&B to pay STEM $261,839.04 in damages. *See id.*

This timely appeal ensued.

II

When a district court conducts a bench trial, we review de novo its legal conclusions. *See United States v. 15 Bosworth St.*, 236 F.3d 50, 53 (1st Cir. 2001). This review encompasses "determinations about the sufficiency of the evidence." *Aadland v. Boat Santa Rita II, Inc.*, 42 F.4th 34, 41, 10 Adm. R. 21, 24 (1st Cir. 2022) (quoting *15 Bosworth St.*, 236 F.3d at 53). The district court's factual findings are, of course, reviewed for clear error. *See id.*, 10 Adm. R. at 24; *see also* Fed. R. Civ. P. 52(a)(6) ("Findings of fact, whether based on oral or other evidence, must not be set aside unless clearly erroneous, and the reviewing court must give due regard to the trial court's opportunity to judge the witnesses' credibility."). The clear error standard is deferential and, where it applies, we will not overturn a factual finding unless — on the **[—8—]** whole of the record — we are "left with the definite and firm conviction that a mistake has been committed." *United States v. U.S. Gypsum Co.*, 333 U.S. 364, 395 (1948).

Although the parties do not raise the question, "we have an obligation to inquire into our subject matter jurisdiction *sua sponte*." *One & Ken Valley Hous. Grp. v. Me. St. Hous. Auth.*, 716 F.3d 218, 224 (1st Cir. 2013). Here, that inquiry reduces to a determination as to whether we are sitting in diversity jurisdiction or in admiralty jurisdiction. **{-33-}**

STEM's cause of action sounds in legal malpractice (a tort arising under the common law). STEM is a business entity organized under the laws of Singapore and has its principal place of business there. TM&B is a professional services company organized under Maine law, which maintains its principal place of business in Portland, Maine. The matter in controversy comfortably exceeds the sum of $75,000.

Although questions of maritime law linger at the margins, those questions are subordinate to the alleged malpractice and the resulting injury. Put another way, the alleged negligent act and resulting injury, in combination, do not comprise the stuff needed to trigger admiralty jurisdiction. For a tort claim to come within admiralty jurisdiction, it "must satisfy conditions both of location and of connection with maritime **[—9—]** activity." *Jerome B. Grubart, Inc. v. Great Lakes Dredge & Dock Co.*, 513 U.S. 527, 534 (1995).

Here, the location requirement has not been satisfied. The alleged tort (the allegedly negligent advice) occurred on land. And as we have recently explained, "[w]hen . . . the 'injury suffered' is on 'land,'" it must be shown "that 'a vessel on navigable water' caused the tort." *Rhode Island v. Shell Oil Prods. Co.*, 35 F.4th 44, 61, 10 Adm. R. 10, 19 (1st Cir. 2022) (quoting *Jerome B. Grubart, Inc.*, 513 U.S. at 534). STEM suffered its injury on land, and it was an attorney's advice — not a vessel on navigable waters — that is alleged to have caused the tort.

Given this collocation of facts, we hold that this lawsuit arises in diversity jurisdiction. *See* 28 U.S.C. § 1332(a)(2). The case simply does not present the conditions required to invoke admiralty jurisdiction.

This determination, in turn, controls our choice of law. Because the case is in a federal court by virtue of diversity jurisdiction, state law supplies the substantive rules of decision. *See Erie R.R. Co. v. Tompkins*, 304 U.S. 64, 78 (1938); *Conformis, Inc. v. Aetna, Inc.*, 58 F.4th 517, 528 (1st Cir. 2023). The parties agree that the law of Maine controls, and we accept that reasonable agreement. *See Borden v. Paul Revere Life Ins. Co.*, 935 F.2d 370, 375 (1st Cir. 1991). We caution, though, that when we address the questions of maritime law that are embedded in **[—10—]** this controversy, we look to federal maritime law and precedents — as Maine courts would likewise do. *See, e.g., Offshore Logistics, Inc. v. Tallentire*, 477 U.S. 207, 223 (1986) (explaining that state law is constrained by what some have called the reverse-*Erie* doctrine, "which requires that the substantive remedies afforded by the States conform to governing federal maritime standards").

A

Under Maine law, a plaintiff seeking to prove attorney malpractice "must show (1) a breach by the defendant of the duty owed to the plaintiff to conform to a certain standard of conduct; and (2) that the breach of that duty proximately caused an injury or loss to the plaintiff." *Brooks v. Lemieux*, 157 A.3d 798, 802 (Me. 2017) (quoting *Pawlendzio v. Haddow*, 148 A.3d 713, 715 (Me. 2016)). TM&B challenges the district court's determination that it breached the duty of care that it owed to STEM. It also challenges the district court's determination that any such breach was an actual and proximate cause of the injury to STEM. We address these challenges separately. **{-34-}**

B

We start with the district court's determination regarding breach of duty. In Maine, the duty of care owed by an attorney to his client is the use of "such skill, prudence and diligence as is reasonable according to the standards of ordinarily **[—11—]** competent lawyers performing similar services under like conditions." *Pawlendzio*, 148 A.3d at 715 (quoting *Sohn v. Bernstein*, 279 A.2d 529, 532 (Me. 1971)).

TM&B argues that the district court erred in concluding that it breached the duty it owed to STEM. In TM&B's view, it exercised reasonable skill, prudence, and diligence when it advised STEM that Sprague had a valid lien claim.

Notably, TM&B does not contest the district court's determination that its advice to STEM was predicated on *Tramp Oil*. It continues to argue that *Tramp Oil* was (and is) the most relevant precedent. Building on this foundation, it argues that the advice that it provided to STEM was correct. In the process, it takes issue with the district court's conclusion that *Cianbro*, not *Tramp Oil*, is controlling. *See ST Eng'g Marine*, 633 F. Supp. 3d at 360.

We review for clear error the district court's finding that TM&B breached its duty of care to STEM. *See Fairest-Knight v. Marine World Distribs., Inc.*, 652 F.3d 94, 98 (1st Cir. 2011). Embedded within this clear-error review is a legal determination as to what was in November of 2015 the most recent and relevant law, when viewed through the eyes of a reasonably skillful, prudent, and diligent attorney. We review this embedded question of law de novo. *See Aadland*, 42 F.4th at 41, 10 Adm. R. at 24.

For a start, we discern no clear error in the district court's determination that TM&B breached its duty of care to STEM. **[—12—]** The record, fairly read, supports a finding that the legal research that TM&B's attorney conducted in examining Sprague's lien claim was not carried out with sufficient care and attention as would be expected of a reasonably skillful, prudent, and diligent lawyer. So, too, the fact that the TM&B attorney did not alert STEM to the unsettled nature of maritime lien law in the First Circuit supports the district court's finding of negligence. Had he conducted a more careful and attentive canvass of the case law, he would have identified at least three reasons why a cloud of uncertainty hung over the *Tramp Oil* dicta upon which he relied. Given this cloud of uncertainty, a reasonably skillful, prudent, and diligent attorney would have explicitly hedged his advice, apprising STEM of the unsettled nature of the law in this area.

First, a reasonably skillful, prudent, and diligent attorney would have understood that the statements in *Tramp Oil* were dicta. There, Logos Shipping APS, a charterer of a vessel, asked J&L Bunkers A/S (J&L) to arrange fuel for the chartered vessel. *See Tramp Oil*, 805 F.2d at 44. J&L then contacted Tramp Oil and Marine, Ltd. (Tramp), a fuel broker. *See id.* Tramp contracted with Exxon International

(Exxon), which caused Colonial Oil Industries, Inc. (Colonial) to supply the fuel to the vessel. *See id.* Once the fuel was supplied, Tramp paid Exxon in full — but did so without any authorization from the owner or charterer of the vessel. *See id.* at 44-45. After J&L failed to repay Tramp **[—13—]** in full, Tramp claimed that it had acquired a maritime lien. *See id.* at 44. By paying Exxon, Tramp asserted it had made an "advance" on behalf of the vessel. *Id.* at 45. And pursuant to the rule of advances, it professed to have acquired the lien that Exxon had previously held. *See id.*

We rejected Tramp's contention, explaining that Tramp had acted without authorization from either the vessel's owner **{-35-}** or any other person with proper authority. *See id.* at 45-46. We added, as an aside, that "[n]o one disputes that Exxon and Colonial, as direct suppliers of the fuel to the [vessel], would be entitled to a maritime lien. Fuel is unquestionably a 'necessary' within the meaning of the Act, and it was furnished upon the order of someone with authority to do so."[1] *Id.* at 44. Later in the opinion, we wrote that "Tramp's payment was used to satisfy an outstanding lien claim." *Id.* at 45. In other words, we implied that both Exxon and Colonial had valid and outstanding lien claims.

As a reasonably skillful, prudent, and diligent attorney would have realized, these last two statements were plainly dicta. *See Lake Charles Stevedores, Inc. v. Professor Vladimir Popov MV*, **[—14—]** 199 F.3d 220, 230 (5th Cir. 1999) (reaching this conclusion). In *Tramp Oil*, we were not asked to address the viability of these lien claims. Accordingly, our statement that "[n]o one disputes that Exxon and Colonial . . . would be entitled to a maritime lien," 805 F.2d at 44, was not intended to be read as a general pronouncement of law. Seen in this light, a reasonably skillful, prudent, and diligent attorney would have understood that it would not be safe to rely on the *Tramp Oil* dicta as binding pronouncements.

Second, we discern no clear error in the district court's finding that the TM&B attorney failed to conduct adequate legal research. *See ST Eng'g Marine*, 633 F. Supp. 3d at 361. In reaching this conclusion, we think that the district court must have regarded the TM&B attorney's primary misstep as failing to conduct research with an adequate level of care and attention. The record supports a conclusion that — had TM&B's attorney read the relevant case law with the requisite degree of care and attention — he would have discovered that the other courts of appeals that had addressed the matter all had departed from his reading of *Tramp Oil*'s dicta when determining the circumstances in which a direct supplier of a necessary acquires a maritime lien.

On TM&B's reading, *Tramp Oil* stands for the proposition that as long as a supplier provides a necessary to a vessel and does so pursuant to an order that was initially issued by a **[—15—]** vessel's owner or a person authorized by the owner, the supplier is entitled to a maritime lien. This is true, TM&B asserts, even if the order is relayed through multiple layers of intermediaries, each of whom passes along the entire order for a traditional necessary that originated from the vessel.

A reasonably skillful, prudent, and diligent attorney conducting adequate legal research would have realized that — by November of 2015 — the courts of appeals had moved away from this interpretation of the provision in the Commercial Instruments and Maritime Liens Act (CIMLA), which states that "a person providing necessaries to a vessel on the order of the owner or a person authorized by the owner . . . has a maritime lien on the vessel." 46 U.S.C. § 31342(a). Those courts had held — contrary to *Tramp Oil*'s dicta — that, in order to be considered to have provided a necessary "on the order of the owner or a person authorized by the owner," a supplier must do more than simply deliver a necessary. Some

[1] The Act discussed in *Tramp Oil* (and in effect at that time) was the Federal Maritime Lien Act, the predecessor to the Commercial Instruments and Maritime Liens Act (CIMLA), 46 U.S.C. §§ 31301-31343. The CIMLA was in effect at all times relevant to the case at hand.

additional connection with a person authorized to bind the vessel must be shown.

To be sure, this essential connection can be forged in a variety of ways. One way is **{-36-}** through privity of contract with the owner or a person authorized by the owner. *Cf. Farwest Steel Corp. v. Barge Sea-Span 241*, 828 F.2d 522, 525-26 (9th Cir. 1987) (holding that subcontractor — who lacked privity of contract with owner or person authorized by owner — did not have claim to lien **[—16—]** when general repair contractor who hired him failed to pay him for his services). Another way is by showing that the supplier has been explicitly "nominated by the owner" of the vessel to provide a necessary, *Marine Fuel Supply & Towing, Inc. v. M/V Ken Lucky*, 869 F.2d 473, 475 (9th Cir. 1988), and demonstrating that the necessary has been directly "sold to" a person with authority to bind the vessel, *id.* at 477 (emphasis in original). A third way is by involvement with an owner or a person authorized by the owner in a manner that was "significant and ongoing during the pertinent transaction." *Galehead, Inc. v. M/V Anglia*, 183 F.3d 1242, 1245 (11th Cir. 1999).

Although these three ways differ from each other, there is a common denominator: all of the relevant case law teaches that merely being the supplier of a necessary does not suffice to acquire a maritime lien. The short of it is that, among the decided cases, the general trend as of November of 2015 was pointing away from *Tramp Oil*'s dicta.

Third, had TM&B's attorney conducted more careful and attentive research — as a reasonably skillful, prudent, and diligent attorney would have done — he would have understood that our most recent case on maritime liens, *Cianbro*, cast *Tramp Oil*'s dicta in grave doubt. In *Cianbro*, the Hornbeck entities contracted with the Cianbro Corporation (C-Corp.) to convert their two sulfur tankers into multi-purpose supply vessels. *See* 596 F.3d at 12. **[—17—]** C-Corp., in turn, contracted with Hub Technologies, Inc. (Hub) to fabricate certain steel components that were to be used in the conversion work. *See id.* Hub then subcontracted with Dean Steel (Dean) to perform some of the initial cutting work on the steel. *See id.* at 13. C-Corp. shipped raw steel directly to Dean, and Dean returned the cut material to Hub, which fabricated the components that C-Corp. had ordered. *See id.* After Hub failed to pay Dean and filed for bankruptcy, Dean claimed maritime liens on the vessels. *See id.* The district court rejected Dean's claim, holding that it failed to satisfy several of the requirements for a maritime lien. *See id.* at 14.

We upheld the district court's decision. *See id.* at 18. Among other things, we rejected Dean's claim that it had acted "on the order of the owner or a person authorized by the owner," as required by CIMLA. *Id.* at 16-18. Dean's claim that C-Corp. had the authority to bind the vessels' owners, we explained, "would strain the language and purpose of the Maritime Lien Act." *Id.* at 17. In addition, we determined, that Dean's claims fared no better under the Fifth Circuit's analysis of CIMLA and its so-called middleman line of cases.[2] *See* **{-37-}** *id.* Dean was unable to show "that

---

[2] In *Lake Charles Stevedores*, 199 F.3d at 228-29, the Fifth Circuit differentiated between the general contractor/subcontractor line of cases and the middleman line of cases in assessing whether a supplier of a necessary has acted "on the order of the owner or a person authorized by the owner." The former line of cases involves instances in which an owner or agent **[—18—]** of a vessel hires a general contractor to complete a task and the contractor solicits subcontractors for assistance in completing the work. *See id.* at 229. A subcontractor lacking privity of contract with the "owner or a person authorized by the owner" can acquire a lien if "it can be shown that an entity authorized to bind the ship controlled the selection of the subcontractor and/or its performance." *Id.*

In contrast, the middleman line of cases involves instances in which an owner or agent of a vessel employs a broker to find a third party to complete a job that it needs done. *See id.* at 229 ("The primary distinguishing characteristic between a general contractor and a middle-man . . . is that a general contractor can be expected to supply the necessary itself, whereas a middle-man is not expected to do so."). In such cases, a court must assess "the nature of the relationship between each pair of entities that are involved in the transaction at issue (e.g., agent vs. independent contractor)" in determining whether a supplier lacking privity can acquire a lien. *Id.* at

[—18—] an entity authorized to bind the ship controlled [its] selection . . . and/or its performance." *Id.* (quoting *Lake Charles Stevedores*, 199 F.3d at 229).

Had TM&B's attorney given due weight to *Cianbro* — we think it reasonable to conclude, as did the district court — that he would have had second thoughts about the persuasive force of *Tramp Oil*'s dicta. Although our discussion of the middleman line of cases in *Cianbro* was not a model of clarity, it is apparent that the *Cianbro* court concluded that a supplier does not acquire a maritime lien simply by virtue of providing a necessary. Some additional connection with a person authorized to bind the vessel must be shown. *Cianbro*'s narrow reading of the term "on the order **[—19—]** of the owner or a person authorized by the owner" is consistent with both our favorable citation to Fifth Circuit precedent and our steadfast adherence to the "well-established precept that the requirements for the allowance of a maritime lien are strictly construed." *Cianbro*, 596 F.3d at 14.

TM&B's contrary contentions are unconvincing. It conspicuously avoids any consideration of whether Sprague would qualify for a maritime lien under the analysis put forth in *Lake Charles Stevedores*, 199 F.3d at 230, the most pertinent Fifth Circuit precedent. When analyzing whether a middleman qualifies for a maritime lien, what is crucial "is not whether an intermediary can be expected to supply the necessaries itself that distinguishes instances in which the actual suppliers have liens, but it is rather the nature of the relationship between each pair of entities that are involved in the transaction at issue (e.g., agent vs. independent contractor)." *Id.*

TM&B avoids this analysis for two obvious reasons. For one thing, the analysis undermines TM&B's overarching argument that a supplier acquires a lien merely by virtue of providing the necessary. For another thing, the analysis paves the conceptual path for understanding why TM&B's advice that Sprague had a valid lien claim was incorrect. After all, the nature of the relationship between Sprague and the only three entities authorized to bind the *M/V Nova Star* (STEM, NSC, and Fleetpro) was **[—20—]** not one of agency — and the district court so found. *See ST Eng'g Marine*, 633 F. Supp. 3d at 357. It follows inexorably that — under the test articulated in *Lake Charles Stevedores* — Sprague did not have a valid lien claim.

At oral argument, TM&B placed great emphasis on the Ninth Circuit's decision in *Ken Lucky*, 869 F.2d at 473. But that decision offers scant support for TM&B's reading of the law. There, as in this case, an intermediary was used in ordering the fuel. *See id.* at 476. Even so, the role of that intermediary did not factor into the *Ken Lucky* court's analysis because the lien challenger admitted that the fuel was ordered by and sold to a person with authority to bind the vessel. *See id.* at 477. Here, by contrast, Sprague sold the fuel to BIC, which was not authorized to bind the vessel. **{-38-}**

Nor does TM&B's reliance on the legislative history of CIMLA gain it any headway. This history, it argues, demonstrates that "American companies like Sprague that supply traditional necessaries directly to foreign vessels on an order that originated from the vessel were the intended beneficiaries of the Lien Act." Whether or not such a reading of the legislative history is correct — a matter on which we take no view — we do not rely on legislative history alone to interpret statutory text.[3] *See, e.g., Chamber of* **[—21—]** *Com. of U.S. v. Whiting*, 563 U.S. 582, 599 (2011) ("Congress's 'authoritative statement is the statutory text, not the legislative history.'") (quoting *Exxon Mobil Corp. v. Allapattah Servs., Inc.*, 545 U.S. 546, 568 (2005)).

That ends this aspect of the matter. We hold that, by November of 2015, *Tramp Oil*'s dicta

---

230. It is this test — and not "whether an intermediary can be expected to supply the necessaries itself" — that determines whether a supplier has a valid lien claim. *Id.*

[3] To the extent that *Tramp Oil* relied on legislative history, at least one other court of appeals has thrown shade on its **[—21—]** analysis. *See Triton Marine Fuels Ltd. v. M/V Pacific Chukotka*, 575 F.3d 409, 418 (4th Cir. 2009) ("*Tramp Oil* relies on a misreading of the FMLA's legislative history.").

as to how a direct supplier of a necessary could acquire a maritime lien were on life support. Here, moreover, the record supports the district court's finding that TM&B's attorney failed to conduct adequate legal research — research that, when properly evaluated, would have exposed the frailty of *Tramp Oil*'s dicta. The record also supports a finding that TM&B's attorney did not appropriately counsel his client about the cloud of uncertainty that hovered over Sprague's lien claim.[4] **[—22—]** We thus decline to disturb the district court's conclusion that TM&B failed to exercise "such skill, prudence and diligence as is reasonable according to the standards of ordinarily competent lawyers performing similar services under like conditions." *Pawlendzio*, 148 A.3d at 715. Thus, we hold that the district court did not clearly err when it found that TM&B breached the professional duty that it owed to STEM. *See ST Eng'g Marine*, 633 F. Supp. 3d at 361.

Let us be perfectly clear. An attorney is not an insurer, liable for professional negligence simply because his advice proves to be incorrect. The standard of care expected of an ordinarily competent attorney is not omniscience. Instead, it is the exercise of a reasonable level of skill, prudence, and diligence in conducting research and advising his or her client. The district court's finding that TM&B's performance undershot this standard was not clearly erroneous. *Cf. Cumpiano v. Banco Santander P.R.*, 902 F.2d 148, 152 (1st Cir. 1990) (explaining that when reviewing for clear error, "we ought not to upset findings of fact or conclusions drawn therefrom unless, on the whole of the record, **{-39-}** we form a strong, unyielding belief that a mistake has been made"). **[—23—]**

C

Our voyage is not yet finished. What remains is for us to examine the district court's finding that the negligence of TM&B's attorney proximately caused STEM's loss.

We begin with first principles. "[I]n a legal malpractice case, once a plaintiff demonstrates that the defendant attorney was negligent, the plaintiff must show that that negligence actually and proximately caused his or her injury." *Wheeler v. White*, 714 A.2d 125, 127 (Me. 1998). To prove causation, "a plaintiff must demonstrate that he or she would have achieved a more favorable result but for the defendant's alleged legal malpractice." *Niehoff v. Shankman & Assocs. Legal Ctr., P.A.*, 763 A.2d 121, 124 (Me. 2000). "[T]he plaintiff typically proves that the attorney's professional negligence caused injury to the plaintiff by presenting evidence of what would have happened in the underlying action had the attorney not been negligent." *Reppucci v. Nadeau*, 238 A.3d 994, 999 (Me. 2020) (quoting *Brooks*, 157 A.3d at 804).

TM&B strives to convince us that the district court clearly erred in finding that it was more likely than not that STEM would have prevailed in contesting Sprague's lien claim but for TM&B's advice. TM&B suggests that this finding was clearly erroneous in two ways. First, it contends that Sprague's lien was valid: the finding that Sprague was not selected or controlled by **[—24—]** STEM, NSC, or Fleetpro was not, as TM&B sees it, based on sufficient evidence. Second, TM&B contends that the district court should not have regarded the advice that TM&B gave to STEM

[4] Maine's highest court has not spelled out what standard of care a reasonably skillful, prudent, and diligent attorney owes to his client when confronted with an area of law that is unsettled. Some jurisdictions hold that an attorney fulfills his duty of care by conducting adequate legal research and exercising reasonable judgment when dealing with an unsettled area of law. *See, e.g., Kempf v. Magida*, 832 N.Y.S.2d 47, 49 (N.Y. App. Div. 2007). Other jurisdictions require an attorney to alert his client that there is an unsettled question of law and inform his client as to any adverse outcome that could arise should the law subsequently be decided contrary to his view. This requirement stems from the attorney's obligation to afford his client "the opportunity to assess the risk" and make an educated decision. *Williams v. Ely*, 668 N.E.2d 799, 806 (Mass. 1996). For present purposes, we need not make an "informed prophecy" as to which rule the Maine Supreme Judicial Court would adopt. *Blinzler v. Marriott Int'l, Inc.*, 81 **[—22—]** F.3d 1148, 1151 (1st Cir. 1996). In this instance, TM&B failed to satisfy either standard.

concerning Sprague's maritime lien claim as dispositive.

Neither contention moves the needle. The district court did not clearly err when it found the allegations that Sprague put forth in its complaint — including that BIC was authorized to bind the vessel — to be just that: allegations made "after-the-fact" and "on information and belief." *ST Eng'g Marine*, 633 F. Supp. 3d at 364. Allegations are not evidence, and the district court was at liberty to find — as it did — that the revealed facts discredited Sprague's allegations.

So, too, the district court did not clearly err in affording little weight to STEM's allegation in the BIC bankruptcy proceeding that BIC was paid as an intermediary. *See id.* at 364-65. This allegation was riddled with factual errors and it shed little light on whether STEM, NSC, or Fleetpro agreed that BIC would operate as an agent on their behalf. Similarly, the district court did not commit clear error when it rejected TM&B's claim that the language in the Fleetpro purchase order directing BIC to coordinate the delivery of fuel with the vessel's master signified that BIC was an agent of STEM, NSC, or Fleetpro. *See id.* at 365. Nothing in this purchase order suffices to prove that BIC had an agency relationship with STEM, NSC, or Fleetpro. In fact — and as **[—25—]** the district court found, *see id.* — this purchase order listed Fleetpro "AS AGENTS FOR" NSC and BIC as the "Supplier," thus dispelling any notion that either BIC or Sprague was acting as an agent for STEM, NSC, or Fleetpro, *id.* at 357.

Nor did the district court clearly err when it rejected the claim that Sprague's fuel delivery receipts evinced the fact that those in charge of the vessel knew that Sprague was asserting a lien. These receipts, as the district court found, "reflect **{-40-}** nothing more than the vessel's acceptance of the deliveries." *Id.* at 365.

TM&B's contention that its advice was not the actual cause of STEM's loss is equally unavailing. In support, TM&B claims that the conditional nature of its advice in one of its November 16, 2015, emails "did not . . . foreclose the possibility that BIC might not have been authorized to pass along an order on behalf of the vessel." It also claims that STEM's conduct obstructed TM&B's ability to evaluate the asserted liens.

None of these claims withstand scrutiny. The record supports a conclusion that TM&B was focused only on whether the order that BIC placed with Sprague "originated" with the vessel; and whether the fuel was actually delivered. Yet those two factors alone were not sufficient to determine whether Sprague had a valid maritime lien. *See supra* Part II(B). Although TM&B hedged its advice regarding BIC on the assumption that BIC was acting as an **[—26—]** agent or a broker, this advice was faulty in the first instance. The conditional nature of TM&B's advice thus fails to shield it from liability. By like token, even if STEM assumed responsibility for collecting documents that would have been of relevance in analyzing Sprague's lien claim, that fact would not discharge TM&B of its responsibility for the advice that it provided. And the fact that STEM, not TM&B, opted to pursue expedited settlement of the lien claim does not change the equation.

We thus hold that the district court did not clearly err when it determined that STEM had proven by a preponderance of evidence that it would have prevailed in the arrest proceedings on Sprague's maritime lien claim but for TM&B's errant advice.

III

We need go no further. For the reasons elucidated above, the judgment of the district court is

Affirmed.

United States Court of Appeals
for the First Circuit

No. 23-1359

GREAT LAKES INS. SE
vs.
ANDERSSON

Appeal from the United States District Court for the District of Massachusetts

Decided: December 22, 2023

Citation: 89 F.4th 212, 11 Adm. R. 140 (1st Cir. 2023).

Before **GELPÍ**, **HOWARD** and **RIKELMAN**, Circuit Judges.

[—2—] {-214-} GELPÍ, Circuit Judge:

Defendant-Appellee Martin Andersson ("Andersson") purchased an insurance policy ("policy") for his vessel, the *Melody* ("vessel"), from Plaintiff-Appellant Great Lakes Insurance SE ("Great Lakes") in November 2018. In December 2019, the vessel ran aground off the coast of the Dominican Republic. Great Lakes brought a declaratory judgment action to determine coverage under the policy and Andersson filed counterclaims for breach of contract and equitable estoppel. Great Lakes moved for summary judgment on its declaratory judgment claim and Andersson moved for partial summary judgment on his breach of contract claim. Great Lakes' motion was denied, and Andersson was granted partial summary judgment on his breach of contract claim. Great Lakes now appeals the denial of its motion for summary judgment, and entry of summary judgment in Andersson's favor, claiming the district court erred as a matter of law in refusing to apply the policy's definition of seaworthiness.[1] We affirm. **[—3—] {-215-}**

I. Background

A. Facts[2]

In November 2018, Andersson purchased an insurance policy from Great Lakes which afforded $365,000 in first party property damage coverage for his vessel and covered Florida, the Bahamas, and the Caribbean.[3] The policy was issued in December 2018. The policy's seaworthiness warranty stated that "[i]t is warranted that the Scheduled Vessel is seaworthy at all times during the duration of this insuring agreement. Breach of this warranty will void this insuring agreement from its inception." The policy defined "seaworthy" as:

> [F]it for the Scheduled Vessel's intended purpose. Seaworthiness applies not only to the physical condition of the hull, but to all its parts, equipment and gear and includes the responsibility of assigning an adequate crew. For the Scheduled Vessel to be seaworthy, it and its crew must be reasonably proper and suitable for its intended use.

The policy defined "Scheduled Vessel" as:

> [T]he vessel described on the declaration page, including machinery, electrical equipment, sails, masts, spars, rigging, and all other equipment normally required for the operation and maintenance of the vessel and situate on

[1] This interlocutory appeal is properly before us pursuant to 28 U.S.C. § 1292(a)(3) because it determines the rights and liabilities of the parties to an admiralty case. *See Great Lakes Ins. SE v. Andersson*, 66 F.4th 20, 22, 11 Adm. R. 51, 51 (1st Cir. 2023) (stating interlocutory appeal in admiralty law is properly before the court pursuant to 28 U.S.C. § 1292(a)(3)); *United States v. Nature's Way Marine, L.L.C.*, 904 F.3d 416, 419 n.5, 6 Adm. R. 258, 259 n.5 (5th Cir. 2018) (exercising jurisdiction over appeal from ruling of partial summary judgment). In a previous decision, we held that the policy's choice of law provision does not bar Andersson from bringing an unfair-settlement-practices counterclaim under Massachusetts law. *See Andersson*, 66 F.4th at 22, 11 Adm. R. at 51. This appeal does not involve that claim, so we omit any further reference to it.

[2] The relevant facts for review of summary judgment are undisputed, except as noted. *See Underwriters at Lloyd's v. Labarca*, 260 F.3d 3, 5 (1st Cir. 2001).

[3] Great Lakes claims that Andersson chose the locations, whereas Andersson claims the broker chose the locations with little input from him and that his language barrier prevented him from specifying the correct locations.

> the Scheduled Vessel, which would normally be sold with the vessel. This does not include **[—4—]** spare parts of the Scheduled Vessel, the Scheduled Vessel's life raft, tender or dinghy unless the same has been declared on the declaration page, nor does it include any items being stored on premises other than on board the Scheduled Vessel.

Andersson alleges that he intended to pick up the vessel in Grenada after it was repaired and sail to Aruba before he ended his journey in Sint Maarten.[4] It is unclear whether there were, or were not, any paper charts on the vessel at the time of the policy's inception.[5]

On December 14, 2019, Andersson left Aruba for Sint Maarten having checked the weather forecasts for the intended route without issue. The intended route was around the southeastern tip of Aruba, then northeast to clear the Venezuelan Islands. Andersson then planned to head east toward Grenada and then north to Sint Maarten. After rounding the southeastern tip of Aruba and attempting to head northeast, the winds increased and caused his crewmember to become seasick. Andersson headed more northward, attempting to avoid damage from the waves and ease his crewmember's seasickness. Eventually, the winds pushed Andersson northwesterly toward the Dominican Republic, at which point he realized his radio **[—5—]** transmitter was broken. He called the agent who sold him the vessel who suggested Andersson dock in Boca Chica, Dominican Republic, for repairs. **{-216-}**

On December 17, 2019, within the policy's period of coverage, while waiting to dock in Boca Chica, the vessel ran aground on a breakwater. It is undisputed that at the time the vessel left for its voyage, the same had updated paper charts onboard for the Leeward Islands, the Windward Islands, and Aruba, all of which were on Andersson's intended course from Aruba to Sint Maarten. The vessel also had electronic charts on its Garmin GPS for the Dominican Republic which were outdated and did not show the breakwater.[6] More current charts that were available, but not on board, in December 2018 did show the breakwater. The other GPS onboard, the Raymarine, did not have charts for the Dominican Republic. It is also undisputed that the vessel lacked up-to-date paper charts for Florida, the Bahamas, and the Western Caribbean during the trip from Aruba to Sint Maarten.

B. Procedural History

Following the breakwater incident, Andersson requested coverage and Great Lakes filed a declaratory judgment to determine whether the loss of the vessel was covered by the policy, claiming **[—6—]** the vessel was unseaworthy due to the lack of up-to-date paper charts for Florida, the Bahamas, the Western Caribbean, and the Dominican Republic. Thereafter, before judgment, Great Lakes denied coverage claiming Andersson neglected to maintain the vessel in a seaworthy condition per federal admiralty law and the policy. Andersson counterclaimed, alleging a claim of breach of contract and a claim of equitable estoppel. As to the breach of contract claim, Andersson alleged that the vessel was seaworthy at all times, maintaining up-to-date paper charts for its intended voyage. Great Lakes moved for summary judgment on its declaratory judgment claim, alleging that the lack of updated paper charts for Florida, the Bahamas, the Western Caribbean, and the Dominican Republic rendered the vessel unseaworthy. Andersson filed a motion for partial summary judgment on the breach of contract claim.

The district court held a summary judgment motion hearing on December 19, 2022, before issuing its order on March 21, 2023. The

---

[4] While commonly referred to as Saint Martin, we chose to provide the island's proper Dutch name, Sint Maarten.

[5] Great Lakes claims that at the inception of the policy, the only current paper charts on the vessel were for the Leeward Islands, Windward Islands, and Aruba. Andersson, however, claims that there is no evidence that any paper charts were on the vessel at the inception of the policy.

[6] Andersson disputes the fact that the Garmin was never updated, however, it is undisputed that the Garmin did not show the breakwater and that updated Garmin charts did.

district court denied Great Lakes' motion for summary judgment and granted Andersson's motion for partial summary judgment. The district court determined that Great Lakes had not proven that the vessel was unseaworthy under federal admiralty law and the policy. The district court granted Andersson's motion for summary judgment as to his breach of contract claim, and denied Great Lakes motion for summary judgment as to its declaratory judgment claim. **[—7—]**

II. Discussion[7]

Great Lakes makes a single argument on appeal: The district court erred as a matter of law by refusing to enforce the policy's express definition of seaworthiness. But in making this argument, Great Lakes also relies on the absolute implied warranty of seaworthiness, which it contends was incorporated into the policy. Great Lakes claims that the policy's express warranty of seaworthiness is at least coextensive with the implied warranty of **{-217-}** seaworthiness based in federal admiralty law, and that the district court erred by interpreting this implied warranty too narrowly. But even if the implied warranty of seaworthiness does not require a vessel to carry up-to-date charts for every single location that could be navigated under the policy's coverage area, Great Lakes argues that the policy's plain language imposes such a requirement. Because the policy's express warranty requires a vessel to have adequate "parts, equipment and gear" to be seaworthy, Great Lakes asserts that the district court violated fundamental principles of **[—8—]** contract interpretation by finding that the policy did not require the vessel to have the charts on board.

Ultimately, we must determine whether either warranty required the vessel to carry up-to-date charts for all geographic areas covered by the policy in order to be considered seaworthy. We begin with the implied warranty of seaworthiness. Like the district court, we find no precedent to suggest that the implied warranty imposes such a requirement. Therefore, we proceed to the express terms of the policy.

A. Standard of Review

A district court's summary judgment ruling is reviewed de novo. *O'Neill v. Baker*, 210 F.3d 41, 46 (1st Cir. 2000). In this case, Andersson filed a cross-motion for summary judgment, but "[t]he presence of [the same] neither dilutes nor distorts this standard of review." *Mandel v. Bos. Phx., Inc.*, 456 F.3d 198, 205 (1st Cir. 2006). "[W]e must scrutinize the record in the light most favorable to the summary judgment loser . . . ." *All. of Auto. Mfrs. v. Gwadosky*, 430 F.3d 30, 34 (1st Cir. 2005).

B. Absolute Implied Warranty of Seaworthiness

Under admiralty law, there is an absolute implied warranty applicable to all marine insurance contracts.[8] *See* **[—9—]** *Labarca*, 260 F.3d at 7. The absolute implied warranty requires that the insured vessel be seaworthy at the inception of the policy. *See* Schoenbaum, *supra*, at 505-06; *Emps. Ins. of Wausau v. Occidental Petroleum Corp.*, 978 F.2d 1422, 1431-32 (5th Cir. 1992). If the vessel is not

---

[7] Great Lakes and Andersson both make references to "charts," "paper charts," and "electronic charts" in their briefs. Throughout the discussion, we use the terms "charts" and "paper charts." However, regardless of the term used, our ruling applies to any type of chart.

[8] Under American federal admiralty law, there are two distinct implied warranties that attach to all time hull policies: the absolute implied warranty that attaches at inception, and the continuing implied warranty that is recognized at the commencement **[—9—]** of each individual voyage the vessel takes. *See* Thomas J. Schoenbaum, *Admiralty and Maritime Law* 505-07 (6th ed. 2018 & Supp. 2023). Both Great Lakes and Andersson refer to, and seem to accept, both implied warranties in their briefs. The district court also utilized both implied warranties in its summary judgment order. However, Great Lakes stated that this appeal pertains only to "the first warranty, the absolute warranty of seaworthiness that applies at the inception of every policy of marine insurance" as its argument concerns the vessel's seaworthiness at the time of the inception of the policy, not its continuing seaworthiness. Therefore, we omit discussion on the second implied warranty of seaworthiness and focus only on the absolute implied warranty.

seaworthy at the policy's inception, then the policy is void. *See* Schoenbaum, *supra*, at 507. The insurer bears the burden of proving the unseaworthiness. *See Cont'l Ins. Co. v. Lone Eagle Shipping Ltd. (Liber.),* 952 F. Supp. 1046, 1067 (S.D.N.Y. 1997). "[S]eaworthiness can be established by demonstrating that the vessel was well-maintained." *Carib Resorts, Inc. v. Watkins Underwriters at Lloyds, Syndicate No. 457,* No. 16-25024-CV-GRAHAM/SIMONTON, 2018 WL 8048755, at *16 (S.D. Fla. Mar. 20, 2018) (citing *Great Lakes Reinsurance (UK) PLC v. Kan-Do, Inc.*, No. 8:12-cv-2923-T-33TGW, 2014 WL 12573013, at *5 (M.D. Fla. June 16, 2014)). "[A] finding of unseaworthiness is **[—10—]** not affected by whether the **{–218–}** owner was or was not negligent or at fault." *Labarca,* 260 F.3d at 8.

The cases considering the issue find that the absolute implied warranty concerns whether the physical condition of the vessel and its equipment are sufficient for the vessel's intended use. *See Michalic v. Cleveland Tankers, Inc.*, 364 U.S. 325, 331 (1960) (discussing whether a worn grip on a wrench rendered the vessel unseaworthy); *Martinez v. Sea Land Servs., Inc.*, 763 F.2d 26, 27-28 (1st Cir. 1985) (determining a summary judgment ruling was erroneous because seaworthiness extends to a plastic sleeve covering a box); *Axis Reinsurance Co. v. Resmondo,* No. 8:08-cv-569-T-33TBM, 2009 WL 1537903, *4 (M.D. Fla. June 2, 2009) (determining whether fractured gimbal ring rendered vessel unseaworthy at inception); *Royal Ins. Co. of Am. v. Deep Sea Int'l,* No. 02 Civ. 3175 (KMW)(FM), 2006 WL 8454021, *6-8 (S.D.N.Y. Mar. 24, 2006) (discussing repair and maintenance of the vessel in regard to absolute implied warranty). "A vessel is unseaworthy if it is not fit and 'is unable to withstand the perils of an ordinary voyage.'" *Home Ins. Co. v. Pan Am. Grain Mfg. Co., Inc.*, 397 F.3d 12, 13 n.2 (1st Cir. 2005) (quoting *Unseaworthy, Black's Law Dictionary* (6th ed. 1990)); *Hubbard v. Faros Fisheries, Inc.*, 626 F.2d 196, 199 (1st Cir. 1980) ("[T]emporary and unforeseeable malfunction or failure of a piece of equipment under proper and expected use is sufficient to **[—11—]** establish . . . unseaworthiness . . . ."); *cf. United States v. Rivera,* 131 F.3d 222, 233 n.16 (1st Cir. 1997) (Torruella, J., concurring) ("The warranty of seaworthiness provides that the owner of a vessel owes an absolute duty to seamen to provide a ship's hull, gear, appliances, ways, and appurtenances which are reasonably fit for their intended purpose, *Mitchell v. Trawler Racer, Inc.*, 362 U.S. 539, 80 S. Ct. 926, 4 L.Ed.2d 941 (1960), as well as to appoint a competent master and a crew adequate in their number and competent for their duty, *Usner v. Luckenbach Overseas Corp.*, 400 U.S. 494, 91 S. Ct. 514, 27 L.Ed.2d 562 (1971).").

To make the vessel seaworthy under the absolute implied warranty, Andersson was not required to keep up-to-date paper charts on board for every covered location from the inception of the policy. Great Lakes contends that the district court "refuse[d] to consider whether the lack of current, updated charts rendered the [v]essel unfit for its 'intended purpose' at the inception of the [p]olicy." This is simply incorrect. The district court did consider this in the context of the absolute implied warranty of seaworthiness when it found that "there are no cases in which the court held that a lack of up-to-date maps voids an insurance policy from its inception under the [f]irst [w]arranty; the [c]ourt found none where the argument was even made." In addition, the district court found that Great Lakes was **[—12—]** not claiming a deficiency in the physical condition of the vessel, therefore the absolute implied warranty does not apply.

As noted above, the absolute implied warranty has been interpreted by caselaw to pertain to the physical condition of the vessel. There have been no cases that have determined out-of-date paper charts to be a violation of the absolute implied warranty of seaworthiness. In addition, Great Lakes' argument that up-to-date paper charts for any location the vessel could navigate during the entirety of the policy coverage area are required on the vessel at the inception of the policy is simply unreasonable. It is difficult to ascertain how Andersson could predict exactly where his vessel would dock in every port in the Caribbean if the dock were not on his intended voyage, let alone account for the **{–219–}** myriad of updates that might occur over the course of the policy. Therefore, the absolute implied warranty, which attaches at the inception of the policy and renders the policy void if the vessel was unseaworthy, does not support Great Lakes' argument that up-to-date charts for every location that could be navigated under the entirety of the coverage area are required when the policy attaches to deem a vessel seaworthy.

The cases that Great Lakes cites do not alter this conclusion. Although the existence of up-to-date paper charts may go to a breach of the continuing implied warranty of seaworthiness, not at issue here, the cases that Great Lakes cites do not stand **[—13—]** for the proposition that a vessel must have up-to-date paper charts from the policy's inception to satisfy the absolute implied warranty of seaworthiness. Crucially, the cases cited analyze only whether the party responsible for that breach met the privity or knowledge portion associated with that continuing implied warranty, not the absolute implied warranty, or had knowledge of the condition pursuant to the Carriage of Goods by Sea Act.[9] **[—14—]**

C. Express Warranty of Seaworthiness

We next consider whether the policy's express seaworthiness warranty required Andersson to carry the charts in question. Under New York law, which governs the policy here, "the [c]ourt should interpret an insurance contract 'to give effect to the intent of the parties as expressed in the clear language of the contract.'" *Royal Indem. Co. v. Deep Sea Int'l*, 619 F. Supp. 2d 14, 18 (S.D.N.Y. 2007) (quoting *Parks Real Estate Purchasing Grp. v. St. Paul Fire & Marine Ins. Co.*, 472 F.3d 33, 42 (2d Cir. 2006)). "An insurance policy should be read in light of common speech and the reasonable expectations of a businessperson." *Pepsico, Inc. v. Winterthur Int'l Am. Ins. Co.*, 788 N.Y.S.2d 142, 144 (N.Y. App. Div. 2004) (internal quotation marks and citation omitted). Each provision should be given "full meaning and effect." *LaSalle Bank Nat'l Ass'n v. Nomura Asset Cap. Corp.*, 424 F.3d 195, 206 (2d Cir. 2005) **{-220-}** (quoting *Shaw Grp., Inc. v. Triplefine Int'l Corp.*, 322 F.3d 115, 121 (2d Cir. 2003)). In addition, "[t]he rule that insurance policies are to be construed in favor of the insured is most rigorously applied in construing the meaning of exclusions incorporated into a policy of insurance or provisions seeking to narrow the insurer's liability." *Ingersoll Milling Mach. Co. v. M/V Bodena*, 829 F.2d 293, 306 (2d Cir. 1987). These insurance policies "are to be accorded a strict and narrow construction." *Pioneer Tower Owners Ass'n v. State Farm Fire &* **[—15—]** *Cas. Co.*, 908 N.E.2d 875, 877 (N.Y. 2009). "Every clause or word is deemed to have some meaning." *Mazzaferro v. RLI Ins. Co.*, 50 F.3d 137, 140 (2d Cir. 1995).

---

[9] *See Cont'l Ins. Co.*, 952 F. Supp. at 1070; *Union Oil of Cal. v. M/V Point Dover*, 756 F.2d 1223, 1229 (5th Cir. 1985) (analyzing whether the failure to keep up-to-date charts and maps breached the continuing implied warranty based on actual knowledge); *Dir. Gen. of India Supply Mission for & ex rel. President of Union of India v. S.S. Maru*, 459 F.2d 1370, 1371 (2d Cir. 1972) (considering whether the defendant could successfully raise the defense of the shipowner's negligence under the Carriage of Goods by Sea Act); *The W.W. Bruce*, 94 F.2d 834, 837 (2d Cir. 1938) ("The burden of proving *the exercise of due diligence* to make the ship seaworthy is upon the owner . . . ." (emphasis added)); *The Maria*, 91 F.2d 819, 824 (4th Cir. 1937) (asking whether the shipowner exercised "due diligence" under the continuing implied warranty); *Matter of Complaint of Supreme Towing Co. Inc.*, No. 07-9231, 2010 WL 11561150, at *22 (E.D. La. Aug. 12, 2010) ("Having established that the CAPT. BRENNAN was unseaworthy, and that the CAPT. BRENNAN's unseaworthy condition was the proximate cause of its allision with Well #14, the Court must now determine whether Supreme Towing had privity or knowledge of the CAPT. BRENNAN's unseaworthy condition."); *In re TT Boat Corp.*, No. CIV A 98-494, 1999 WL 223165, at *10–11 (E.D. La. Apr. 14, 1999) (analyzing under 46 U.S.C. § 183(a) whether the captain possessed knowledge of the lack of up-to-date charts that led to the vessel's unseaworthiness); *Complaint of Thebes Shipping, Inc.*, 486 F. Supp. 436, 438 (S.D.N.Y. 1980) (discussing COGSA's due diligence standard); *Complaint of Delphinus Maritima, S.A.*, 523 F. Supp. 583, 593 (S.D.N.Y. 1981) ("Having brought this action, the initial burden was on the vessel owner to show no fault on its part or if there was fault, that the fault was without personal knowledge." (citing *Tug Ocean Prince, Inc. v. United States*, 584 F.2d 1151, 1155 (2d Cir. 1978))).

Great Lakes argues that insurance contracts, just like other contracts, must be read as a whole, giving meaning to each clause and provision. The insurance policy at issue here includes a seaworthiness warranty provision, the definition of seaworthiness, and the definition of a scheduled vessel, detailed above. Ultimately, Great Lakes argues that the district court failed to follow New York law when it did not interpret these provisions to have required Andersson to carry the charts in question. Narrowly interpreting the policy, as required under New York law, and considering the language used by Great Lakes leaves its argument baseless.

Although Great Lakes primarily objects to the district court's failure to rely on the policy's language, it concedes that the district court did quote part of the policy's definition of seaworthiness. Great Lakes nonetheless contends that the district court "neutered" the policy's express definition of seaworthy when it did not include up-to-date paper charts in its interpretation of the language "parts, equipment and gear." However, this is not so. The district court simply found that Great Lakes' interpretation was not supported by the express terms of the policy, precedent, or common sense. To construe the express **[—16—]** warranty in such a way would be to require a vessel to have and maintain updated paper charts for every location in the area where it could navigate at all times from the time the policy commences which, as we stated above, is completely unreasonable and unsupported by admiralty caselaw. Further, interpreting the policy in this manner would render the policy void from its inception whether the vessel ran aground or not. In addition, the district court compared this case to that of *Acadia Ins. Co. v. Hansen*, which had a similar express warranty of seaworthiness. *See* 2022 U.S. Dist. LEXIS 75760 (E.D.N.Y. 2022). The court determined there that "the applicable measure for a breach of express warranty of seaworthiness is whether the vessel was fit for its *voyage intended* when it embarked." *Id.* at *91. The district court used this holding to clarify that an express warranty of seaworthiness concerns whether the vessel was equipped for its specific intended course, not for every location that could be navigated under the entirety of the policy coverage area at its inception, rendering Great Lakes' argument meritless.

Great Lakes argues that the district court should have taken a closer look at the policy's language. But doing so only confirms that the district court reached the correct outcome. First, nowhere in the express terms of the policy are charts required or mentioned, nor do they qualify under the definition of a "Scheduled Vessel." Narrowly construing the policy's definition **[—17—]** of "Scheduled Vessel," charts cannot be recognized as an included element. Charts are not "machinery, electrical equipment, sails, masts, spars, or rigging."[10] And although charts are arguably

[10] Machinery is defined as "machines in general or as a functioning unit," "the working parts of a machine," or "the means or system by which something is kept in action or a desired result is obtained." Electrical is "of, relating to, or operated by electricity" which by its terms excludes paper charts when in reference to equipment. Sails are "an extent of fabric (such as canvas) by means of which wind is used to propel a ship through water" or "the sails of a ship." A mast is "a long pole or spar rising from the keel or deck of a ship and supporting the yards, booms, and rigging" or "a slender vertical or nearly vertical structure (such as an upright post in various cranes)." A spar is "a stout pole" or "a stout rounded usually wood or metal piece (such as a mast, boom, gaff, or yard) used to support rigging." Rigging is "lines and chains used aboard a ship especially in working sail and supporting masts and spars." *Machinery*, Merriam-Webster Online Dictionary, https://www.merriam-webster.com/dictionary/machinery (last visited Dec. 21, 2023); *Electrical*, Merriam-Webster Online Dictionary, https://www.merriam-webster.com/dictionary/electrical (last visited Dec. 21, 2023); *Sail*, Merriam-Webster Online Dictionary, https://www.merriam-webster.com/dictionary/sail (last visited Dec. 21, 2023); *Mast*, Merriam-Webster Online Dictionary, https://www.merriam-webster.com/dictionary/mast (last visited Dec. 21, 2023); *Spar*, Merriam-Webster Online Dictionary, https://www.merriam-webster.com/dictionary/spar (last visited on Dec. 21, 2023); *Rigging*, Merriam-Webster Online Dictionary, https://www.merriam-webster.com/dictionary/rigging (last visited Dec. 21, 2023); *cf. Merriam-Webster's Collegiate Dictionary*, (11th ed. 2020); *Merriam-Webster's Collegiate Dictionary* (11th ed. 2003) (providing the same

{-221-} "equipment normally required for the operations and maintenance of the vessel," they are not "normally . . . sold with the vessel," and therefore do not qualify as part of the "Scheduled Vessel." In the definition of seaworthiness, it is not clearly stated that **[—18—]** charts are considered "parts, equipment or gear" and Great Lakes has provided no caselaw, as discussed above, to support that interpretation. Insurance contracts are to be construed against the insurer, further weakening Great Lakes' argument that "charts" should be read into the policy. *See Ingersoll Milling Mach. Co.*, 829 F.2d at 306-07 (construing the meaning of provisions seeking to narrow insurer's liability in favor of the insured).

Second, at no point do the express terms of the policy warranty require a higher standard at any particular time, most notably not at the inception of the agreement. The warranty provision of seaworthiness only requires that the 1) "[s]cheduled [v]essel" 2) must be "seaworthy" 3) "at all times" 4) "during the duration of [the] insuring agreement." The only mention of the inception of the policy is in the warranty where it notes that the policy would be void from its inception if the vessel was not seaworthy "at all times." What the policy does not do is require that the vessel itself must be seaworthy in the specific sense that it maintain updated charts for every location that could be navigated under the entirety of the policy coverage area, from the inception of the policy. Therefore, the argument that updated paper charts are required on board at the inception of the policy for every area covered by the policy is unsupported by the express language of the policy. **[—19—]**

Third, even if it were to be determined that updated paper charts were included in "parts, equipment and gear," there is a difference in language used in the definition of seaworthiness between the vessel's intended "purpose" and intended "use." As the definition states, "[f]or the Scheduled Vessel to be seaworthy, it . . . must be reasonably proper and suitable for its intended use." Intended "use" is not defined or limited in the policy language. The intended "use" of the vessel could change daily depending on the journey embarked upon or the activities pursued, requiring different "parts, equipment and gear" for each "use." In addition, the **{-222-}** two different phrases within the provision, "intended use" and "intended purpose," are to be given their own full effect and meaning, per New York law. See *LaSalle Bank Nat'l Ass'n*, 424 F.3d at 206; *Theater Guild Prods., Inc. v. Ins. Corp. of Ir.*, 267 N.Y.S.2d 297, 300-01 (N.Y. App. Div. 1966).

In addition to its main argument that the policy language was not applied, Great Lakes also argues that affirmation of the district court order would render a vessel unseaworthy in a tort liability sense due to a lack of updated charts, but seaworthy in an insurance dispute even with the lack of updated charts. This argument fails. We see nothing to suggest that a vessel would be liable in tort for failing to carry paper charts for routes it never intended to sail. **[—20—]**

Great Lakes lastly attempts to argue that the district court order gave no reasonable basis for asserting that Great Lakes could not expressly enforce the definition of seaworthiness provided in *Labarca*, which Great Lakes claims to have mirrored in its own policy. Rather, *Labarca* stands for the proposition that we have outlined above: that a vessel's seaworthiness depends upon whether it is "reasonably fit for [its] intended use[,]" which itself turns upon the circumstances. *Labarca*, 260 F.3d at 7 (quoting *Trawler Racer, Inc.*, 362 U.S. at 550). We have never held, nor do we now, that this finding turns upon one irrelevant facet of a vessel's voyage that bears no connection to whether it is reasonably fit for its intended use. The notion that Great Lakes was relying on *Labarca*, which therefore means charts for every location that could be navigated under the entirety of the policy coverage area are included in the determination of seaworthiness at a policy's inception, is unsupported and fails as this is not what *Labarca* held.

---

definitions for each term with the omission of "such" in the parentheticals).

When we narrowly construe the policy, read it as a whole, and give meaning to each of its words and provisions, we conclude it cannot reasonably be read to require updated paper charts for every location that could be navigated under the entirety of the policy coverage area to be on board at the inception of the policy. In addition, there is no precedent supporting the claim that updated paper charts for every location that could be navigated **[—21—]** under the entirety of the policy coverage area are required to have been on board the vessel at the inception of the policy. Therefore, Great Lakes' arguments fail and the district court's order in favor of Andersson for partial summary judgment was warranted.

III. Conclusion

The district court's order finding Andersson to be covered by the policy is

Affirmed.

This page intentionally left blank

United States Court of Appeals for the Second Circuit

United States Court of Appeals
for the Second Circuit

No. 18-2974

IN RE M/V MSC FLAMINIA

Appeal from the United States District Court for the Southern District of New York

Decided: June 30, 2023

Citation: 72 F.4th 430, 11 Adm. R. 150 (2d Cir. 2023).

Before **CHIN**, **CARNEY**, and **MENASHI**, Circuit Judges.

[—7—] {-436-} **CARNEY**, Circuit Judge: **{-437-}**

Deltech Corp. ("Deltech"), a chemical manufacturer, joins here with Stolt-Nielsen USA, Inc., and Stolt Tank Containers B.V. (together, "Stolt"), a shipping concern, to challenge the district court's determination that they alone bear liability for damages caused by an explosion and fire that took place in June 2012 aboard the ocean-going vessel M/V MSC Flaminia. Two weeks into the Flaminia's trip from New Orleans Terminal across the Atlantic, toward Belgium, three tanks of 80% grade of the chemical divinylbenzene (DVB-80)—manufactured by Deltech and shipped by Stolt—exploded. The explosion and ensuing fire killed several members of the ship's crew, injured others, and damaged the ship and its cargo.

In the first phase of a three-part proceeding in the United States District Court for the Southern District of New York (Forrest, *J.*), the district court addressed the causes of the explosion. It determined that the conditions in which the tanks of DVB-80 were kept at New Orleans Terminal and then stowed onboard were two of the primary causes of the explosion. Together, these conditions resulted in the chemical undergoing a process known as auto-polymerization; this in turn caused the tanks to emit a cloud of vapor that ultimately ignited and exploded when the crew's firefighting efforts generated a fateful spark. *See In re M/V MSC FLAMINIA*, No. 12-cv-8892, 2018 WL 526549 (KBF), at *30-31 (S.D.N.Y. Jan. 23, 2018) ("*Phase I*").

In the second phase, the district court addressed the parties' respective liability for cargo loss and damage. (Separately, claims for death and bodily injury had largely been settled.) The district court found Deltech and Stolt, together, wholly responsible **[—8—]** for the cargo losses: Deltech, at a 55% level, and Stolt, at 45%. *In re M/V MSC FLAMINIA*, 339 F. Supp. 3d 185, 229–30 (S.D.N.Y. 2018) ("*Phase II*"). As detailed below, it exonerated other parties to the shipping transaction. It is the latter rulings that Deltech and Stolt challenge in this interlocutory appeal.[1] In a **{-438-}** third phase and final phase, the court will award damages. *Id.* at 191.

On review, we affirm in part and reverse in part. We AFFIRM the district court's ruling that Deltech and Stolt are liable for the explosion's resulting damages under a failure-to-warn theory pursuant to Section 4(3) of the Carriage of Goods by Sea Act ("COGSA"), 46 U.S.C. § 30701 (note); we REVERSE, however, the district court's determination that Deltech and Stolt are strictly liable for the damages under Section 4(6) of COGSA. We also AFFIRM the district court's conclusion that the carrier and related shipowner interests—MSC Mediterranean Shipping Company S.A. ("MSC"), Container Schiffahrts-GMBH & Co., KG MSC "FLAMINIA" ("Conti"), and NSB Niederelbe Schiffahrtsgesellschaft MBH & Co. KG ("NSB")—were not negligent in relation to the shipment, and that New Orleans Terminal too was not negligent. We also AFFIRM the district court's determination that Stolt has not stated a claim against its subcontractor, the documentation provider BDP International, Inc. ("BDP"): we agree that Stolt failed to show that BDP's breach in processing the shipment's waybill was a contributing cause of the damages. Finally, we AFFIRM the district court's determination that MSC, Conti, and NSB are entitled to indemnification for their losses by Stolt and Deltech. **[—9—]**

[1] The courts of appeals generally have jurisdiction over appeals from "[i]nterlocutory decrees of such district courts or the judges thereof determining the rights and liabilities of the parties to admiralty cases in which appeals from final decrees are allowed." 28 U.S.C. § 1292(a)(3).

BACKGROUND[2]

On July 1, 2012, the Flaminia departed New Orleans Terminal, loaded with cargo and bound for Antwerp, Belgium. Fourteen days into its journey across the Atlantic, a major explosion occurred in one of its holds, causing the tragic deaths of several crew members, serious bodily injury to others, and substantial damage to both the ship and the cargo of numerous shippers.

Phase I of the court proceedings regarding the resulting losses examined the conditions in which Deltech's DVB-80 was manufactured and shipped and considered the physical cause or causes of the explosion. After an extensive bench trial, the district court, by a preponderance of the evidence, concluded that a spark that ignited a cloud of vapor rising from three tanks of DVB-80 stored in one of the Flaminia's holds—Hold 4—caused the explosion. The spark was generated by the crew in their efforts to fight what they perceived to be a fire in that hold. The cloud of vapor, in turn, was the result of DVB-80 undergoing a chemical process called auto-polymerization and reaching thermal runaway. When DVB-80 auto-polymerizes, it can be dangerous because the reaction generates heat and is self-perpetuating.

In Phase II, the district court considered liability for the explosion, fire, and physical damage. The district court explained that the DVB-80 onboard the Flaminia was manufactured by Deltech in its Baton Rouge, Louisiana, plant. Stolt—Deltech's regular non-vessel operating common carrier ("NVOCC")[3]—made shipping **[—10—]** **{-439-}** arrangements for the DVB-80 on behalf of Deltech. To enable the shipment, it provided three large shipping tanks (also known as "ISO containers"),[4] which were filled with the DVB-80 at the Baton Rouge plant. Stolt also procured space for the shipment aboard an ocean-going vessel; arranged for a trucker to transport the tanks to a suitable shipping terminal; and was responsible for certain aspects of documenting the shipment. Applying a preponderance of the evidence standard, the district court found Deltech and Stolt together exclusively liable for the damages that resulted when the shipped DVB-80 exploded both under a strict-liability theory (in the COGSA regime) and under a failure-to-warn theory (also in the COGSA regime), with damages for the lost and damaged cargo to be apportioned in the projected Phase III. *See Phase II*, 339 F. Supp. 3d at 194–95.

In contrast, the district court found appellees not liable for the losses. Appellees are primarily other parties who had a role in delivering the DVB-80 shipment to Deltech customers in Antwerp. Key among them are:

- **MSC Mediterranean Shipping Company S.A.** ("MSC"): the charterer of the Flaminia;

- **Conti 11 Container Schiffahrts-GMBH & Co., KG MSC "FLAMINIA"** ("Conti"): the owner of the Flaminia;

- **NSB Niederelbe Schiffahrts-gesellschaft MBH & Co. KG** ("NSB"): the operator of the Flaminia; **[—11—]**

[2] Unless otherwise noted, the facts set forth in this background section are drawn from the district court's two thorough opinions. We note any relevant disagreements among the parties.

[3] As the district court explained, "Stolt played two roles with regard to the DVB cargo at issue here. First, it acted as an NVOCC, and in that capacity was Deltech's shipping agent and arranged for transport aboard the Flaminia. Stolt also arranged for truck transport . . . from Deltech to [New Orleans Terminal]." *Phase II*, 339 F. Supp. 3d at 205. NVOCCs "typically assist **[—10—]** a cargo shipper with making necessary arrangements for the booking of any pre-carriage (such as transport by truck to an ocean terminal), as well as the booking for ocean carriage. Ocean carriage is provided by a 'vessel operating common carrier' who either owns a vessel outright or charters space on vessels for the transportation of cargo. NVOCCs are middlemen acting between the shipper and the ocean carrier." *Id.* at 205 n.31.

[4] "ISO containers" are large shipping containers meeting standards set by the International Organization for Standardization ("ISO"). *See* https://www.iso.org/home.html (last visited June 29, 2023).

• **Chemtura Corp.** ("Chemtura"): the owner and shipper of the chemical, diphenylamine ("DPA"), which was stored at high temperatures on the Flaminia in tanks next to the DVB-80 containers;[5]

• **BDP International, Inc.** ("BDP"): a Stolt subcontractor that prepared shipping documents for the three DVB-80 tanks and was the subject of a contract claim by Stolt;

• **New Orleans Terminal** ("the Terminal" or "NOT"): where a trucker retained by Stolt delivered Deltech's DVB-80 to await loading onto the Flaminia.

In the Phase I and II proceedings, the parties asserted many claims and counterclaims, as the district court ably described, discussed, and resolved in its comprehensive prior opinions. Only the following five are before us now:

(1) Strict liability: Was the district court correct in concluding that both Deltech and Stolt are strictly liable to Conti and NSB under COGSA?

(2) Failure-to-warn negligence: Did the district court err in concluding that both Deltech and Stolt are liable to Conti and NSB under a failure-to-warn negligence theory pursuant to COGSA? **{-440-}**

(3) Non-negligence of carrier interests: Did the district court err in finding that MSC, Conti, and NSB (these three together, the "carrier" interests) did not act negligently and therefore do not bear partial responsibility for the losses? **[—12—]**

(4) Breach of contract claim: Did the district court err in ruling that Stolt's breach of contract claim against BDP is not actionable?

(5) Indemnification: Did the district court err in concluding that Stolt and Deltech breached the Sea Waybills and must indemnify MSC, Conti, and NSB for their losses?

In answering these questions, we adopt the district court's uncontested description of the setting for the applicable legal regimes:

> This action concerns claims based on contracts for the carriage of goods by sea and torts that occurred at sea. As such, the contracts at issue are maritime contracts and the torts are maritime torts within the admiralty jurisdiction of the Court pursuant to 28 U.S.C. § 1333(1). And with admiralty jurisdiction comes the application of substantive admiralty law. Absent a relevant statute, the general maritime law, as developed by the judiciary, applies.

Phase II, 339 F. Supp. 3d at 229 n.91 (alterations, citations, and internal quotation marks omitted). Various additional statutory and international regulatory regimes also bear on the parties' claims. We discuss those below as they become relevant.

To enable us to address the liability arguments, we turn first to a more in-depth review of the accident's causation as determined by the district court.

I. The Properties of DVB-80

DVB-80 is a chemical compound that is used in water purification. When exposed to heat, DVB-80 molecules can become unstable, causing them to react, link together, and form a polymer chain. This bonding of two or more simple molecules to form larger molecules with repeating structural units is called polymerization. When DVB-80 polymerizes, it releases heat. The polymerization process can thus become self-sustaining and can even accelerate without the addition of any more

[5] In a Nondispositive Stipulation dated April 27, 2020, Stolt and Deltech withdrew their respective appeals insofar as they renewed claims against defendants-counter-claimants-appellees Chemtura Corporation, Chemtura Italy S.R.L., and Chemtura Europe GmbH, and third-party defendant-appellee Rubicon, LLC (collectively, the "Chemtura Appellees"). *See* Order, Dkt. 376, *In re M/V MSC Flaminia*, No. 18-2974 (2d Cir. Apr. 28, 2020).

heat. That phenomenon is called auto-polymerization. **[—13—]**

When the heat generated by DVB-80's polymerization exceeds the heat that the reaction loses to the environment, the rate of polymerization increases exponentially, and the reaction is said to have reached "thermal runaway." *Phase I*, 2018 WL 526549 at *8. At that stage, the temperature increases rapidly, building pressure in any tank in which it is stored. Eventually, any pressure-release valve found on the tank starts to vent a white vapor resembling the smoke that is generated by an ordinary fire. Unlike ordinary smoke, however, the cloud resulting from DVB-80 in thermal runaway can explode in certain conditions if exposed to an ignition source and a specific amount of oxygen.

When it stores DVB-80, Deltech uses an additive called p-tert-butylcatechol (commonly known as "TBC") to inhibit polymerization. *See Phase II*, 339 F. Supp. 3d at 196. TBC, combined with the oxygen that is dissolved in the liquid DVB-80 and that is inside empty storage tanks, impedes polymerization, making DVB-80 relatively safe for transport in tanks, at least under ordinary conditions. Even TBC-treated DVB-80 is heat-sensitive, however. A storage tank's exposure to heat causes its contents to consume oxygen more quickly and reduces TBC's effectiveness. Like untreated DVB-80, then, TBC-treated DVB-80 requires careful "handling and storage" at **{-441-}** each step of transport and delivery. *Id.* at 200. Deltech developed its shipment protocols accordingly, and then in 2006, not long after it had begun shipping its DVB-80 overseas, it refined its protocols after a few of its shipments underwent auto-polymerization. *Id.* at 197.[6] **[—14—]**

In 2012, when it engaged Stolt to handle the Antwerp-bound shipment, Deltech protocols included: (1) generally shipping from the Port of New York (Newark) during the summer months, when temperatures at New Orleans Terminal, which is nearest to the Deltech plant, are especially high; and (2) avoiding exposure of tanks filled with DVB-80 to more than 15 to 20 days of average external temperatures between 75 to 85 degrees Fahrenheit. One Deltech employee explained that shipping from Newark in the summer months offered three important safety advantages: "(1) a cooler port of departure, (2) therefore cooler temperatures preceding vessel loading (*e.g.*, at the terminal), and (3) a shorter ocean voyage." *Id.* at 201. Confirming that statement, data cited by the district court showed that "the maximum number of days in transit from [New Orleans Terminal] to Antwerp is 31 days, with a median of 16; from Newark, the maximum days in transit is 13 days with a median of 9.5." *Id.* at 197.

II. The DVB-80 Shipment Loaded onto the Flaminia

In March or April 2012, Deltech made what the district court called the "fateful decision" to make at least one shipment of its DVB-80 to customers in Europe from New Orleans Terminal, contrary to its protocols. *Id.* at 201–02. Either intentionally, or (as alleged by Deltech) because of an internal "miscommunication," Deltech slated the Antwerp shipment at issue here to be sent from New Orleans Terminal in June. *Id.* at 210.

On June 8, 2012, Deltech requested that Stolt make the arrangements for the shipment, and Stolt duly began to do so. On June 11, Stolt sent Deltech its booking confirmation and contacted MSC to reserve space aboard a suitable vessel.

On June 21, Stolt supplied Deltech with three ISO tanks for the shipment, and Deltech personnel filled the tanks with Deltech's TBC-treated DVB-80 later that day. Under Stolt's direction, the tanks were then trucked to New

[6] Deltech experienced two auto-polymerization incidents involving overseas shipments of DVB-80 in 2006. *Phase II*, 339 F. Supp. 3d at 197. It also had five other shipments with "polymerization issues" that year, but the district court found that those incidents were not analogous to the incident aboard the Flaminia. *See Phase I*, 2018 WL 526549, at *16 (finding only the "Chauncy" and "Grangemouth" incidents "useful" and "support[ing] the view that the Flaminia DVB80 cargo would have completed the voyage safely under normal conditions").

Orleans Terminal that same **[—15—]** day.[7] And there, for about ten days, they sat on the dock, in direct sunlight and in average ambient temperatures of 85 degrees Fahrenheit and a high of 96–98 degrees.

Finally, on July 1, they were loaded onto the Flaminia along with the ship's other cargo. The Deltech tanks were stored below deck in Hold 4, which was flanked by the ship's wing tanks holding heated fuel oil. The tanks also sat alongside three heat-producing containers of the chemical DPA, manufactured and shipped by Chemtura. **{-442-}**

The Flaminia departed New Orleans at 10:00 a.m. on July 1. Two weeks later, on July 14, while the vessel was at sea, the three DVB-80 tanks exploded and a firestorm erupted. By then, Deltech's DVB-80 shipment had been in transit from the Baton Rouge factory for a total 23 days, many of them—if not all—in hot conditions.

III. Warnings About Handling DVB-80

In preparation for the shipment, Deltech, Stolt, and BDP created several different documents that served as contracts among the parties to the shipment, guidance for the treatment of the shipment, or sometimes both. The documents were also used to arrange and track the tanks' transport and manage their safety. Each contained some kind of warning and instructions related to the safe handling of DVB-80.

June 8 Booking Request: Deltech's June 8 booking request to Stolt included the following brief specifications: (1) "Please secure a booking with temperature monitoring to load DVB 80%"; (2) "Container to be stowed 'in stack' or below deck to avoid exposure to direct sunlight. Do not stow near heat sources[]"; and (3) "If container is **[—16—]** greater than 27 C, the Iso-Container cannot be shipped." *Phase II*, 339 F. Supp. 3d at 202 n.17.

Straight Bill of Lading & Material Safety Data Sheet: Deltech developed and used a Straight Bill of Lading, which it gave to Boasso, the trucking concern Stolt engaged to transport the filled tanks to New Orleans Terminal. The Straight Bill of Lading advised: "SEE ATTACHED MATERIAL SAFETY DATA SHEET FOR EMERGENCY RESPONSE INFORMATION. PRODUCT IS HEAT SENSITIVE! DO NOT APPLY HEAT TO CONVEYANCE DURING TRANSIT. IF PRODUCT TEMPERATURE EXCEEDS 100°F, CONTACT DELTECH IMMEDIATELY." *Id.* at 203 n.22.

With the Straight Bills of Lading, Deltech gave Boasso a Material Safety Data Sheet. Of all of the Deltech shipping documents, this contained the most detailed and explicit instructions and warnings about DVB-80. It provided: "Closed containers of DVB (80%) may build up explosive pressures when exposed to the heat of fires. Closed containers of DVB (80%) exposed to heat may begin to polymerize in an exothermic manner leading to auto acceleration and rapid pressure increase and explosion potential." *Id.* The Material Safety Data Sheet also directed stowage in a "cool area or refrigerated tank away from high temperatures, hot pipes or direct sunlight" and cautioned the shipper to "[a]void excessive heat and keep away from open flames or ignition sources." *Id.* It further instructed the shipper to "[m]aintain temperature below 80°F (27°C)." *Id.* Stolt also received the Material Safety Data Sheet but, the district court found, Stolt did not enter the warnings it contained into Stolt's internal information systems.[8] **[—17—]**

Boasso provided the Straight Bills of Lading and Material Safety Data Sheet to the management of New Orleans Terminal.

[7] The record suggests that the tanks were filled and left Baton Rouge for New Orleans Terminal earlier than expected because of some unforeseen circumstances, including an emergency medical need of a Deltech employee. *See Phase II*, 339 F. Supp. 3d at 215–16.

[8] *See Phase II*, 339 F. Supp. 3d at 208 ("A significant gap in Stolt's internal procedures, and causally linked to the incident here, was its failure to populate the AS/400 database with sufficient information regarding handling DVB80 during transport as to product characteristics. **[—17—]** . . . Information from the [Material Safety Data Sheet] was thus rendered irrelevant, and that irrelevancy was carried forward into future cargo shipments.").

Terminal management testified that it did not transmit the documents to MSC,[9] **{-443-}** however, and that it had "filed [them] away" by the time the DVB-80 tanks were loaded onto the Flaminia. *Id.* at 220.[10] This, however, was not a departure from any ordinary protocol: the district court found that the Terminal stores cargo simply according to the information associated with the cargo's internationally recognized UN number and class.[11] All "Class 9" cargo,[12] such as the DVB and DPA, "are treated similarly and interchangeably for storage in the yard." *Id.* at 221. **[—18—]**

Express Bill of Lading Instructions, Master Bill of Lading Instructions & Sea Waybills: Deltech provided "Express Bill of Lading Instructions" to its freight forwarder, Panalpina,[13] as well as to BDP. BDP was charged with using the Express Bill of Lading Instructions to create "Master Bill of Lading Instructions" ("MBLI") for the vessel charterer (MSC). MSC, in turn, was expected to use the MBLI to draft Sea Waybills,[14] which would govern the relationship between Stolt, Deltech, MSC, and MSC's subcontractors, Conti and NSB.

Deltech's Express Bill of Lading Instructions called for the following warnings to be included on the MBLI: "DO NOT STOW NEAR HEAT SOURCES. STOW ABOVE DECK FOR TEMPERATURE MONITORING." *Id.* at 203-04 n.23.[15] The MBLI that BDP sent to MSC included the heat warning, and BDP was expected to ensure that MSC reproduced the warning on its Sea Waybills. The draft Sea Waybills then created by MSC, however, and ostensibly based on the MBLI, omitted this warning. **{-444-}**

Dangerous Goods Declarations: Finally, Stolt prepared and sent draft and final versions of Dangerous Goods Declarations ("DGDs") to MSC, disclosing certain safety information regarding DVB-80's dangerous characteristics. The DGDs contained the UN code and class number for DVB-80—UN 3082, class 9—which identified the cargo **[—19—]** as an environmentally hazardous substance and implied a general need for care. The DGDs gave no additional warnings or instructions. *Id.* at 214–15.

---

9 MSC is a partial owner of New Orleans Terminal, but the entities' roles here are separate. *See Phase II*, 339 F. Supp. 3d at 220-21 (explaining that New Orleans Terminal is responsible for processing and storage at the Terminal, whereas MSC is responsible for stowage aboard the vessel).

10 Thus, neither the Straight Bills of Lading nor the Material Safety Data Sheet ever reached MSC.

11 The UN number is part of an international tracking convention overseen by the United Nations and in widespread use. UN numbers convey categorical information about the nature of a shipment. *Phase II*, 339 F. Supp. 3d at 199. Similarly, the International Maritime Dangerous Goods ("IMDG") Code categorizes dangerous goods into classes based on the type of risk presented by the goods. The Convention for the Safety of Life at Sea ("SOLAS"), which has been ratified by the United States, incorporates the IMDG Code by amendment. *See In re M/V DG Harmony*, 533 F.3d 83, 88 (2d Cir. 2008). SOLAS provides that the "carriage of dangerous goods in packaged form shall be in compliance with the relevant provisions of the IMDG Code." *Phase II*, 339 F. Supp. 3d at 199 (quoting SOLAS, Ch. VII, Reg. 3 (5th ed. 2009)).

12 Class 9 is used to identify "miscellaneous and environmentally hazardous" substances. *Phase II*, 339 F. Supp. 3d at 199. DVB-80 is a Class 9 substance; its UN number is UN 3082. The IMDG Code does not require UN 3082 items to be stowed at a distance from any other substances or from the vessel structure, nor does it require ventilation when the cargo is stowed below deck. *Id.* at 233.

13 A freight forwarder facilitates the movement of cargo and assists in processing a client's export and import documentation related to shipments being transported under arrangements made by a common carrier, either a non-vessel operating common carrier ("NVOCC") or a vessel-operating common carrier. *See* 46 U.S.C. § 40102(19); *Prima U.S. Inc. v. Panalpina, Inc.*, 223 F.3d 126, 129 (2d Cir. 2000).

14 A sea waybill is a nonnegotiable contract of carriage. *See Royal & Sun All. Ins., PLC v. Ocean World Lines, Inc.*, 612 F.3d 138, 141 n.3 & n.5 (2d Cir. 2010); *see also* 1 T. Schoenbaum, 1 Admiralty & Mar. Law § 10:11 (6th ed. 2022).

15 This of course was in tension with the booking request instructions from Deltech to Stolt, requesting temperature monitoring but asking for either in-stack or below-deck stowage to avoid direct sunlight. *See Phase II*, 339 F. Supp. 3d at 202 n.17.

IV. The Explosion

At approximately 5:42 am on July 14, 2012, the smoke alarm sounded on the Flaminia. Hold 4 was identified as the trigger for the alarm. The ship's Chief Officer deployed a system designed to suppress a fire by releasing CO_2 into the hold. At three times between 6:42 am and 8:06 am, the crew released CO_2 into Hold 4, where Deltech's DVB-80 tanks were stored. A few minutes after the third release, a small explosion occurred. A "large amount of dense black smoke" and flames were then seen billowing from the direction of Hold 4, according to one witness. *Phase I*, 2018 WL 526549, at *28. The district court determined by a preponderance of evidence that one of the crew's actions—either opening the man-lid entrance to Hold 4 or inserting firehoses to send water into the hold—created a spark that ignited the vapor in Hold 4 and triggered the primary, deadly explosion.

V. The District Court's Findings

A. Phase I: Conclusions on Causation

Based on evidence presented at the Phase I trial, the district court reached several conclusions. Preliminarily, it found no deficiencies in Deltech's manufacturing process or the process of loading the tanks of DVB-80 aboard the Flaminia. It determined that the DVB-80 was adequately oxygenated while the three tanks were being filled, and that the DVB-80 contained more than enough TBC to "ensure complete inhibition" of polymerization on a typical voyage. *Id.* at *8 n.13. Because the chemical was "sufficiently oxygenated and chilled," the district court estimated that "under normal transit time and temperature conditions," it would have arrived safely in Antwerp. *Id.* at *12. **[—20—]**

It then concluded that each of the following was a "substantial contributing factor" to the DVB-80's auto-polymerization and the subsequent explosion:

> [1] The decision to ship the DVB-80 out of NOT, which necessitated a longer voyage than would have a more northeastern port and exposed it to undesirable conditions;
>
> [2] The fact that the DVB-80 was left still on the dock at NOT for 10 days in the sun, in hot weather, and next to a number of tanks of heated DPA;
>
> [3] The placement of the DVB-80 in Hold 4, where it was stored next to containers of heated DPA and near the ship's heated fuel tanks; and
>
> [4] The lack of proper ventilation, leading to hotter-than-typical ambient temperatures in Hold 4.

Id. at *30–31 (footnote omitted).

B. Phase II: Conclusions on Responsibility

In its Phase II decision, the district court determined that Deltech bore the greatest responsibility for the explosion. *See Phase II*, 339 F. Supp. 3d at 194. It pointed to two critical decisions made by Deltech in conflict with its preexisting safety protocols. First, Deltech authorized shipment of DVB-80 to be made from New Orleans in late June. *Id.* Second, it authorized filling the ISO containers several days earlier than necessary for the expected **{-445-}** embarkation date of June 30 or July 1, "resulting in the containers sitting stagnant in the hot New Orleans sun." *Id.* In the district court's estimation, these two decisions "were by far the most critical." *Id.* On this basis, it assigned Deltech 55% liability on both strict liability and failure-to-warn theories.

The district court additionally found that Stolt, as Deltech's NVOCC dealing with the many parties to the shipment, was liable for the losses under a strict liability theory, for failure-to-warn, for general negligence, and because it breached its contractual obligations to several parties. *Id.* at 194–95. Stolt possessed "extensive information regarding the heat-sensitive nature of [DVB-80]," the court found, but it **[—21—]** failed to share that information with MSC, the vessel charterer. *Id.* at 195. It also failed to share with MSC the information that the ISO containers of DVB-80 had been filled early and then sat in the sun for days in advance of loading. The district court found that Stolt bore responsibility for the early loading of the DVB-80 into the tanks, for arranging for early transport to New Orleans Terminal, and for leaving the tanks to sit in the open air at NOT. *Id.*

The district court found that BDP, Stolt's documentation agent, bore no liability for damages. Although it found that BDP failed to meet its contractual obligation to Stolt to "ensure certain information was contained on the Master Bill of Lading Instructions," the district court determined that the breach did not lead to any loss because "no participant in the chain of events would have acted on the information BDP failed to include." *Id.*

MSC (the vessel's time charterer) was also not liable, the district court ruled, because MSC lacked sufficient information about the conditions that the tanks of DVB had been exposed to pre-shipment. Rather, MSC acted in accordance with "industry practice, its [own] prior practices, and the reasonable (versus unreasonable) expectations of the parties," the district court decided. *Id.* Further, "MSC's [on-board] stowage plan was consistent with industry practice and reasonable under normal circumstances." *Id.* Absent more specific warnings—and none were provided by Stolt—MSC acted reasonably.

The district court found that Conti (the ship owner) and NSB (the ship operator) bore no legal responsibility for the disaster. Conti provided a seaworthy vessel, the court ruled, and NSB's crew was properly trained. The crew's reaction to the smoke in Hold 4—speedily mounting efforts to fight what they understood to be a fire in the hold—was reasonable even if in doing so the crew inadvertently sparked the main explosion. *Id.* at 195–96. Additionally, Chemtura—the shipper of the DPA cargo that **[—22—]** was stored next to Deltech's DVB-80 tanks—bore no responsibility for any losses, the court ruled. *Id.* at 196. Chemtura managed its shipment according to protocol.

Finally, the district court determined that MSC, Conti, and NSB were entitled to full indemnification from Stolt and Deltech. *Id.* at 245. Under the Sea Waybills' "dangerous goods clause" (Clause 15), Stolt and Deltech had an obligation to "fully inform the Carrier"—MSC—"in writing of the precise and accurate details" of dangerous goods as well as any "special precautions or handling required" for their transport. *Id.* Stolt and Deltech breached that obligation, the court found, and therefore were required under the Sea Waybills' dangerous goods clause to indemnify MSC and its subcontractors—Conti, and NSB—for their damages arising from the transport of DVB. *Id.* at 245–46.

This appeal followed. **{-446-}**

DISCUSSION

After a bench trial, we review the district court's findings of fact for clear error and conclusions of law *de novo*. *Vasquez v. GMD Shipyard Corp.*, 582 F.3d 293, 297 (2d Cir. 2009). Because rulings on negligence are ultimately conclusions of law, the rule in this circuit has long been to consider them *de novo*. *See Ching Sheng Fishery Co. v. United States*, 124 F.3d 152, 157 (2d Cir. 1997) ("[U]nder the decisions of this circuit, a district court's finding on the issue of negligence—as distinguished from the evidentiary facts on which the finding is based—is not entitled to the benefit of the 'unless clearly erroneous' rule, but instead is reviewed *de novo*."); *see also Payne v. United States*, 359 F.3d 132, 135 (2d Cir. 2004) (describing this circuit's "long-held" rule of *de novo* review for negligence determinations). While this rule has been met with "nearly unanimous disagreement by the other circuits and commentators," in practice it is "not so different" from the other circuits' more deferential standard of review. *In re City of New* **[—23—]** *York*, 522 F.3d 279, 282 (2d Cir. 2008); *cf. Payne*, 359 F.3d at 137 (remarking that we have "severely undercut our rule over the years"). Indeed, because the determination of negligence is "so bound up with the specific and complex facts of each individual case," we will not disturb a district court's negligence finding unless it "manifests an incorrect conception of the applicable law." *In re City of New York*, 522 F.3d at 282 (internal quotation marks omitted). Even in this circuit, "the question of the existence of negligence . . . has become primarily one for the factfinder to determine." *Payne*, 359 F.3d at 137. We have explained that this is because "the issue today is only very rarely whether the trial court has applied the correct *legal* standard. For, under present law, such standards are . . . unlikely to be determinative." *Id.* Instead, the issue is typically whether the defendant exercised appropriate conduct and behaved how a "reasonable person" ought to have behaved given the specific facts and circumstances of the individual case. *Id.* Thus, even where the question involves a legal judgment about what a party reasonably ought to have known, "a fact-sensitive, 'calibrated' analysis" is appropriate. *DG Harmony*, 533 F.3d at 95. These principles hold when we exercise our maritime jurisdiction as well. *See id.*

While negligence is ultimately a legal determination, "[a]ttributions of fault among the various parties are considered factual determinations and therefore are reviewed under the clearly erroneous standard." *Contship Containerlines, Ltd. v. PPG Indus., Inc.*, 442 F.3d 74, 77 (2d Cir. 2006) (citing *Ching Sheng Fishery*, 124 F.3d at 157 ("A district court's finding on issues of causation and on its allocation of fault among negligent parties continues to be subject only to clearly erroneous review.")).

I. No Strict Liability Recovery Against Stolt and Deltech

The district court held that Stolt and Deltech were strictly liable for the loss arising from the explosion aboard the Flaminia. The district court took great care with its factual rulings in this difficult case; this legal determination, however, was error. **[—24—]**

The Carriage of Goods by Sea Act ("COGSA"), 46 U.S.C. § 30701 (note), applies to all contracts for carriage of goods by sea.[16] It thus governs the relationships of at least some of the parties before us. **{-447-}**

As most relevant here, COGSA provides that a "shipper" of "inflammable, explosive, or dangerous" goods "shall be liable for all damages and expenses directly or indirectly arising out of or resulting from such shipment" when the "carrier" does not have knowledge of the "nature and character" of the goods. COGSA § 4(6); *see DG Harmony*, 533 F.3d at 92–94 (applying COGSA's strict liability provision); *Senator Linie Gmbh & Co. KG v. Sunway Line, Inc.*, 291 F.3d 145, 168–70 (2d Cir. 2002) (same).[17] Strict liability will not attach to the shipper, however, when the carrier knows that a particular type of cargo in its charge is dangerous. *See DG Harmony*, 553 F.3d at 93 (holding that "notice of *any* aspect of the cargo's dangerousness" is sufficient to defeat the carrier's ability to recover in strict liability (emphasis added)).[18] There is no dispute **[—25—]** here that MSC, as the charterer of the vessel, is a "carrier" under COGSA. The question is whether Stolt and Deltech are strictly liable.

The district court reasoned that "generalized knowledge regarding a type of cargo" and its dangerousness is insufficient to warn of its "*particular* contents and chemical sensitivities." *Phase II*, 339 F. Supp. 3d at 240 (emphasis added). Because MSC could not have known that the DVB-80 stored in the tanks it loaded onto the Flaminia had been exposed to

---

16 COGSA was published at 46 U.S.C. app. §§ 1300–1315 until 2006, when it was recodified at 46 U.S.C. § 30701 (note). For clarity, we refer to COGSA's sections as they appear in the recodification, which mirrors the section numbering used in the original statute. *See* An Act of Apr. 16, 1936, ch. 229, §§ 1-16, 49 Stat. 1207.

17 Section 4(6) is an exception to COGSA's general rule requiring proof of negligence for shipper liability. *See* 46 U.S.C. § 30701 (note) § 4(3) ("The shipper shall not be responsible for loss or damage sustained by the carrier or the ship arising or resulting from any cause without the act, fault, or neglect of the shipper, his agents, or his servants."); *see also Contship Containerlines*, 442 F.3d at 78.

18 This principle does not convey that *no* liability will attach to the shipper, of course; it is only to highlight that the special rules of strict liability will not apply when the carrier has sufficient notice of the nature of the cargo. *See Contship Containerlines*, 442 F.3d at 77 (explaining that a carrier with general knowledge of a cargo's dangerousness may "ultimately prevail [] depending on the particulars of what it and the shipper knew and their respective duties" even if it is prevented from prevailing on strict liability).

the specific dangerous conditions that we have described, the court ruled that Deltech and Stolt both were strictly liable to MSC for the loss.

As we held in *Contship Containerlines*, however, a carrier's entitlement to recovery in strict liability requires overcoming a very high hurdle: "[A] carrier cannot invoke strict liability if it knows that a cargo poses a danger and requires gingerly handling or stowage, and nevertheless exposes the cargo to the general condition that triggers the known danger, regardless of whether the carrier is aware of the *precise characteristics* of the cargo." 442 F.3d at 77 (emphasis added). Thus, recovery on a strict liability theory is unavailable to a party with "notice of the general dangerousness" of the cargo it agreed to transport. *DG Harmony*, 533 F.3d at 93. The strict liability analysis is "binary," *Contship Containerlines*, 442 F.3d at 77, and the notice threshold is relatively modest: the carrier's knowledge can be "incomplete" or reflect an "underestimation of the danger" and yet still preclude recovery in strict liability, *DG Harmony*, 533 F.3d at 94.

Here, MSC did not have specific knowledge of the conditions to which the DVB-80 tanks were exposed at New Orleans **{-448-}** Terminal. It did, however, have prior experience shipping DVB-80, and MSC was aware, at least at the corporate level, that DVB-80 generally was heat sensitive. In particular, the record showed that MSC had shipped DVB-80 cargo many times before June 2012 and had received transport documents, including other DGDs and Straight Bills of Lading, that warned of the chemical's heat sensitivity. The manager of MSC's Dangerous Cargo Department conceded that he, **[—26—]** "and therefore MSC," had previously "reviewed information that DVB should not be loaded onto a vessel if [its] temperature was above 27 [degrees Celsius]." *Phase II*, 339 F. Supp. 3d at 219 (internal quotation marks omitted).[19]

On this record, in our view it was incorrect to conclude broadly that MSC was not on notice as to "any aspect of the cargo's dangerousness." MSC's experience with DVB-80 and its management's general knowledge of the chemical's heat sensitivity surpasses the low threshold that precludes a recovery in strict liability. Our holding closely aligns with our conclusion in *DG Harmony* that recovery in strict liability was not available where the ship-owning interests did not know "the precise characteristics of the cargo, but they knew that [the cargo] was an unstable substance that became vulnerable to combustion when heated . . . [and] exposed [the cargo] to the general condition—heat—that induces such combustion." 533 F.3d at 93 (internal quotation marks omitted).

For reasons explained below, however, the district court correctly concluded that MSC's high-level knowledge of DVB-80's dangerousness was not sufficient to establish that the carrier was negligent in its stowage and handling of the specific tanks of DVB-80 aboard the Flaminia. We turn to that issue in Part III. **[—27—]**

II. Negligent Failure to Warn by Stolt and Deltech

The district court determined that Stolt and Deltech were liable to Conti and NSB for losses caused by the explosion under a negligent failure-to-warn theory in the COGSA regime.[20] We agree.

---

[19] At oral argument, counsel for MSC acknowledged that MSC had knowledge of the general characteristics of DVB—including that the chemical "can polymerize if exposed to heat over time." Oral Argument at 21:53–22:12. Counsel advised that it was instead "the degree of danger that MSC didn't know about." *Id.* This is not enough to create an entitlement to strict liability recovery.

[20] The district court also determined that Chemtura was not negligent in its shipping of DPA and therefore not liable for damages here because it did not have a duty to warn that its containers of DPA had been heated as part of its fill and loading process. Chemtura labeled the DPA according to the IMDG Code, and it was not reasonably foreseeable to Chemtura that the DPA would be stored next to containers of DVB-80 that, as here, had been exposed to unusual conditions making those containers particularly sensitive to heat. *See Phase II*, 339 F. Supp. 3d at 236-37. For the reasons stated by the district court, *id.* at 223-24, we too conclude that Chemtura was not negligent in its labelling of

Under COGSA's general rule of shipper liability, a "shipper shall not be responsible for loss or damage sustained by the carrier or the ship arising or resulting from any cause without the act, fault, or neglect of the shipper, his agents, or his servants." 46 U.S.C. § 30701 (note) § 4(3). We have recognized that "[a] shipper's failure to adequately inform a carrier of the foreseeable dangers posed by cargo can constitute" such "fault[] or neglect" and may give rise to a negligent failure-to-warn claim. **{-449-}** *Contship Containerlines*, 442 F.3d at 78. To prevail on this type of claim, a "plaintiff must show that the shipper had a duty to warn because the cargo presented dangers about which the carrier could not reasonably be expected to know." *DG Harmony*, 533 F.3d at 94; *see also Contship Containerlines*, 442 F.3d at 78. That showing, in turn, depends on whether it "would have been reasonable to expect the carrier to know of the *specific type and degree of danger* posed by the cargo at issue." *DG Harmony*, 533 F.3d at 95 (emphasis in original). Generally, the shipper is in the best position to know of the relevant dangers and to provide an effective warning; absent prior or independent knowledge of the **[—28—]** nature of the cargo or the particular shipment, the carrier is entitled to rely on the warnings given by the shipper without conducting further inquiries. *See DG Harmony*, 533 F.3d at 95 (explaining that when the dangerousness of cargo is not readily apparent, "a carrier may rely on the shipper's attestations as to the cargo's characteristics" because carriers and their agents "often must make quick and complex stowage decisions about diverse containerized cargoes" and therefore should not be expected to have "encyclopedic knowledge beyond" those attestations (citation omitted)).

Consistent with the principles enunciated in *DG Harmony*, the district court correctly concluded that Stolt and Deltech bore a duty to warn of the "particular heat sensitivities of the DVB[-80]" in the tanks loaded onto the Flaminia. *Phase II*, 339 F. Supp. 3d at 239. Under the circumstances presented here, it would have been unreasonable to expect MSC, Conti, and NSB either together or individually to know of the specific type and degree of danger posed by this cargo of DVB-80. The risk-producing circumstances—the early filling of the tanks and the long period outside in the heat at NOT, in particular—were neither apparent on visual inspection nor described in the tanks' accompanying documentation.

Further, Stolt and Deltech each had material information about the DVB-80 tanks that neither communicated to MSC. In particular, Deltech informed Stolt of the dangerous nature of generic DVB-80 but failed to ensure that the information was shared with each party in the shipping process chain. Deltech also "failed to effectively ensure that the necessary monitoring, including checking the temperature prior to loading, would occur." *Id.* at 237. As for Stolt, the district court concluded that Stolt did not warn other players of the dangers of a generic DVB-80 cargo or of this shipment in particular: Stolt gave no hint to MSC that the tanks of DVB-80 onboard the Flaminia had been delivered early to New Orleans Terminal and sat there day after day, exposed to the sun. **[—29—]**

Deltech and Stolt failed to notify MSC, Conti, and NSB that originating the shipment at New Orleans in June ran contrary to Deltech's safety protocols and risked DVB-80's stability by lengthening the summertime voyage. They also failed to arrange for the necessary temperature monitoring before loading. Stolt further breached its duty to warn by omitting heat warnings from the DGDs that it delivered to the carrier entities and failing to highlight or even note in the DGDs that the tanks had been filled early and sat outside at NOT. MSC could not be expected to know that the three tanks had been exposed to such conditions, and therefore presented a higher risk of danger, without an express warning from Deltech or Stolt. The tanks thus posed a "specific type and degree of danger" that was not adequately reflected in Stolt's and Deltech's warnings. *See DG Harmony*, 533 F.3d at 95; *see also Phase II*, 339 F. Supp. 3d at 195 (describing the conditions to which the DVB-80

---

the containers of DPA. After withdrawing their appeals with respect to claims against Chemtura, however, neither Deltech nor Stolt presses for contribution from Chemtura. *See supra* n.5.

was exposed as creating "ticking time **{-450-}** bombs"). We therefore find no error in the district court's ruling that Stolt and Deltech breached their respective duties to the later participants in the shipment chain.

None of Stolt and Deltech's arguments to the contrary is persuasive. First, striving to fend off this conclusion, Stolt and Deltech contend that MSC's substantial prior experience with the chemical DVB-80 excused them from providing MSC with any further warning. MSC was adequately aware of the chemical's characteristics, they urge, to appreciate the risk presented by these tanks and their shipment in the summer months. We are not persuaded. It is true that a carrier's general knowledge of the nature of a cargo can be sufficient to defeat its claim for the shipper's strict liability, but a failure-to-warn claim turns on whether "it would have been reasonable to expect the carrier to know of *the specific type and degree of danger* posed by the cargo at issue." *DG Harmony*, 533 F.3d at 95. Conducting the "reasonable awareness inquiry"—in contrast to the "binary" strict liability assessment—"requires a fact-sensitive, 'calibrated' analysis **[—30—]** of the cargo's dangerousness and the extent to which that risk was different from risks commonly encountered by carriers." *Id.*

We are convinced that Stolt and Deltech bore a duty to warn other participants in the transportation chain of the particular characteristics of the tanks of DVB-80 that were left outside at New Orleans Terminal and later stowed aboard the Flaminia. We see no reasonable basis to expect the carrier, MSC (and through MSC, the other ship owning interests), to know of the specific degree of danger posed by the cargo as a result of its early loading and careless storage ashore. In *Senator Linie Gmbh*, we explained that "[i]n contrast to a carrier, which typically is in the position of taking aboard its vessel a large quantity and variety of cargoes, a shipper can be expected to have greater access to and familiarity with goods and their manufacturers before those goods are placed in maritime commerce." 291 F.3d at 169. The shipper, therefore, is often the party "in a better position to ascertain ahead of time the dangerous nature of shipped goods." *Id.*

Such is the case here. MSC had experience with DVB-80 and general information about DVB-80 was available in its databases, it is true. But to require MSC to "associate[e] the chemical properties it may know somewhere within its organization with a shipment of three discrete tanks," *Phase II*, 339 F. Supp. 3d at 238, would unreasonably allocate risk and burden among the parties—particularly when critical characteristics of those specific tanks were out of the ordinary. Stolt and Deltech, on the other hand, knew of not only the general dangerousness and heat sensitivity of DVB-80, but also the specific handling and stowage conditions that made the DVB-80 in the tanks aboard the Flaminia particularly hazardous.

Second, Stolt and Deltech resist the conclusion that they were negligent under Section 4(3) of COGSA by arguing that MSC failed in its "duty to listen" to those warnings that Deltech *did* provide. We decide that, even if MSC had such a duty, it **[—31—]** committed no breach: it "listened" to the information conveyed in the DGDs. Section 5.1.1.3.1 of the IMDG Code, which the parties here had an obligation to follow,[21] **{-451-}** requires a carrier to "receive[] a shipping paper" from the offeror of the dangerous good that contains certain information about the cargo before carrying it. 49 C.F.R. § 176.24(a); *see also id.* § 172.200(a) (imposing on "each person who offers a hazardous material for transportation" the requirement to properly "describe the hazardous material on the shipping paper").

[21] The U.S. Department of Transportation has promulgated regulations that incorporate the IMDG Code by reference. *See* 49 C.F.R. § 171.7. These regulations impose obligations on shippers and carriers of dangerous goods. *See id.* § 171.2(e) ("No person may *offer* or *accept* a hazardous material for transportation in commerce unless the hazardous material is properly classed, described, packaged, marked, labeled, and in condition for shipment as required by or authorized by applicable requirements of this subchapter[.]" (emphasis added)). SOLAS, which the United States has ratified, also requires compliance with the IMDG Code. *See Phase II*, 339 F. Supp. 3d at 198–99.

The district court reasonably found that in 2012, the "shipping paper" that the cargo shipping industry used "as the central repository of information relating to safe handling and transport of dangerous cargo" was the DGD. *Phase II*, 339 F. Supp. 3d at 214. By regulation, a carrier is entitled generally to "rely on information provided by the offeror of the hazardous material . . . unless the carrier knows . . . that the information provided by the offeror . . . is incorrect." 49 C.F.R. § 171.2(f). Here, Stolt provided DGDs to MSC showing the UN number and class for DVB-80—and nothing more. *Phase II*, 339 F. Supp. 3d at 214. The DGDs did not warn MSC that DVB-80 could auto-polymerize when exposed to high temperatures, and they did not inform MSC that these tanks of DVB-80 in particular had been exposed to conditions that put the DVB-80 at a higher risk of auto-polymerization. The district court determined based on the trial record that it was industry custom for a carrier to rely on the shipper's DGDs to create a stowage plan. Stolt and Deltech have not shown that this factual finding was clearly erroneous, and there is no basis for finding that MSC **[—32—]** unreasonably relied on the DGDs here with respect to the tanks of DVB it stowed aboard the Flaminia.

Stolt and Deltech argue that MSC ignored—that it failed to "listen" to—the heat warning on the Master Bill of Lading Instructions. The district court concluded based on the evidence at trial that the MBLI was a "transport document," *i.e.*, not the type of document used "to convey necessary and critical safety information about a dangerous good," and therefore that Stolt and Deltech could not rely on it to escape liability. *Id.* at 238. We agree that the warning contained in the MBLI was insufficient to put MSC on notice of the specific type and degree of danger posed by DVB-80 once loaded onto the Flaminia. The MBLI's warning called for above-deck temperature monitoring because of heat sensitivity, certainly, but it did not disclose the temperature at which DVB-80 becomes unstable (27 degrees Celsius) or alert MSC to any of the natural consequences of overheating, including the auto-polymerization and explosion that happened here. Apart from those basic inadequacies, it also did not disclose that the tanks of DVB-80 had been filled early and had already been exposed to long days of heat. The general heat warning presented in the MBLI was insufficient to place MSC on reasonable notice of the dangerousness of the cargo that it agreed to carry for Stolt and Deltech. MSC did not breach any obligation to "listen" or by its actions relieve Stolt and Deltech of liability under a failure-to-warn theory.[22] **[—33—] {-452-}**

III. MSC's Lack of Negligence

The district court concluded that MSC was not negligent in its stowage and handling of the DVB-80. Deltech and Stolt challenge that conclusion. While the question is closer than the two we have just discussed, on *de novo* review, we are persuaded by the district court's analysis. We reiterate that while our review is *de novo*, we remain mindful of the "specific and complex facts" that form the basis of the district court's negligence determination, *In re*

[22] We additionally find no merit in Stolt's argument that the district court's order should be reversed because it failed to make a legal determination as to causation, the second element of the failure-to-warn claim. To prevail on a failure-to-warn claim, a plaintiff must show that the "absent warning, if given, would have impacted stowage." *DG Harmony*, 533 F.3d at 94 (quoting *Contship Containerlines*, 442 F.3d at 78). Stolt argues on appeal that the district court "made no finding as to whether an adequate warning, if given, *would* have impacted MSC's stowage decision and averted the loss." Stolt Br. at 45. But the district court did, in fact, make factual findings to support the legal determination that had MSC properly been warned about the temperature risks, the need for temperature monitoring, and the DVB-80's early arrival at the **[—33—]** terminal, MSC would not have loaded the DVB-80 onto the Flaminia. The court expressly held that "Stolt's failure to effectively inform MSC *resulted in* the DVB cargo being stowed aboard the Flaminia, and the crew being blind to that fact." *Phase II*, 339 F. Supp. 3d at 239 (emphasis added). The court also found that "[h]ad the temperature been checked on June 30 or July 1 when the product was loaded, [it] is persuaded that the DVB cargo would have been pulled from the Flaminia." *Id.* at 237. We are convinced that these findings by the district court adequately establish causation.

City of New York, 522 F.3d at 282, and therefore apply a "fact-sensitive, 'calibrated' analysis" on review, *DG Harmony*, 533 F.3d at 95.

MSC's rights and obligations as the carrier are governed by COGSA.[23] COGSA provides that "[t]he carrier shall properly and carefully load, handle, stow, carry, keep, care for, and discharge the goods carried." 46 U.S.C. § 30701 (note) § 3(2). Under the COGSA regime, a carrier is not liable for failing to store or stow cargo as suited for special conditions of which it was not aware. *See, e.g., DG Harmony*, 533 F.3d at 95 ("[T]he shipper had an obligation to inform the carrier of special requirements **[—34—]** regarding stowage location, and to make such special arrangements in advance of stowage[.]"); *O'Connell Mach. Co. v. M.V. Americana*, 797 F.2d 1130, 1134 (2d Cir. 1986) (same); *Tenneco Resins, Inc. v. Davy Int'l AG*, 881 F.2d 211, 213–14 (5th Cir. 1989) (holding that a carrier was not required to protect cargo from rain absent special instructions).

The district court correctly determined that MSC did not breach its duty of care in its stowage or general handling of the DVB-80 tanks because MSC's handling of the cargo was proper assuming "normal voyage conditions" and because Stolt and MSC never provided any special instruction or warning regarding the heightened dangerousness of this cargo. *Phase II*, 339 F. Supp. 3d at 235. Stolt gave MSC three sets of documents regarding the July 1 shipment: on June 20, the preliminary DGDs; on June 25, the MBLI; and on June 26, the final DGDs. Of these three, only **{-453-}** the MBLI contained any heat warning at all.

The district court concluded that, consistent with industry practice, the DGDs—not the MBLI or any combination of documents—were the "central repository of information relating to the safe handling and transport" of the ship's cargo, and that it was reasonable for MSC to rely on the DGDs for accurate information regarding the type of hazard posed by the DVB-80.[24] *Phase II*, 339 F. Supp. 3d at 214. It further found that "MSC's practice, and industry practice, was to use DGDs as the primary source of safe handling information for dangerous goods." *Id.* The only special instructions provided—to stow the DVB-80 "above deck for temperature monitoring"—were in the MBLI, which MSC did not receive until June 25, far too late for MSC to use in creating **[—35—]** its stowage plan. Additionally, the district court found that the MBLI "is neither designed nor used in the industry to provide a vessel with special handling instructions for dangerous goods." *Id.* at 213. While an alleged tortfeasor cannot "rely *solely* upon its adherence to industry standards, customs, or practices as a *per se* defense to a negligence claim," *Berretta v. Tug Vivian Roehrig, LLC*, 259 F. App'x 343, 344–45 (2d Cir. 2007) (summary order), a court may properly consider custom or standard practice in the industry as a "useful measure in assessing the standard of care," *In re City of New York*, 522 F.3d at 285 (citation omitted). Indeed, "[c]ourts will not lightly presume an entire industry negligent." *Id.* (citing *Spancrete Ne. Inc. v. Occupational Safety & Health Rev. Comm'n*, 905 F.2d 589, 594 (2d Cir. 1990)). Here, the district court's factual findings regarding MSC's practice and industry custom

[23] "By its terms, COGSA governs bills of lading for the carriage of goods 'from the time when the goods are loaded on to the time when they are discharged from the ship.'" *Norfolk S. Ry. Co. v. Kirby*, 543 U.S. 14, 29 (2004) (quoting COGSA § 1(e)); *see also Herod's Stone Design v. Mediterranean Shipping Co., S.A.*, 846 F. App'x 37, 39 (2d Cir. 2021) (summary order) (same). COGSA also gives shippers and carriers the option to extend by contract COGSA's coverage to include periods of handling on land. *See Kirby*, 543 U.S. at 29 (citing COGSA § 7). Deltech, Stolt, and MSC have done so here. Clause 6.1 of the Sea Waybills makes COGSA the applicable legal regime as a matter of contract "throughout the entire time the [DVB-80 tanks] are in [MSC's] custody, including before loading and after discharge." Exs. at 3635, 3640; *see also Phase II*, 339 F. Supp. 3d at 240 n.97.

[24] While "COGSA does not require a shipper to use any particular method . . . to inform a carrier of the dangerous properties of its cargo" in order to defeat a strict liability claim, *Chem One, Ltd. v. M/V RICKMERS GENOA*, 502 F. App'x 66, 71 (2d Cir. 2012) (summary order), a district court may properly consider the method used to convey safety information when determining whether a shipper or carrier acted negligently in carrying out its respective duties, *see id.* at 73.

were well supported by the record and not clearly erroneous.

In any case, even if MSC should have relied on the MBLI, MSC did not receive it until after the DVB-80 was loaded into tanks and after the tanks had already sat stagnant in the sun at New Orleans Terminal for four days, at which point it was far too late to alter existing stowage plans. At trial, MSC offered testimony that providing instructions for stowage on June 25 through the MBLI was too close to the July 1 loading date for MSC to make alternative loading arrangements. *See Phase II*, 339 F. Supp. 3d at 213 (finding that special handling instructions must be received "further in advance of the cargo so that proper arrangements can be made"). This circumstance made the temperature monitoring instruction on the MBLI functionally useless absent concurrent instructions forbidding shipment when the carrier could not adhere to the instructions. Apart from the general heat warning on the MBLI—which did not reveal the temperature at which DVB-80 became unstable or advise that the chemical could auto-polymerize above such a temperature—Stolt never requested, either at the time of booking or at any point thereafter, special stowage, segregation, or handling of the DVB **[—36—]** cargo. *Id.* And of course, the MBLI did not inform MSC that the tanks had been filled early, had sat in the sun at the Terminal, or that these conditions increased the risk that the DVB-80 inside the tanks would auto-polymerize and cause an explosion. **{-454-}**

Based on these factual findings, we decide that a carrier in 2012 could exercise reasonable care by relying on the information it received from a shipper at the time of booking and that it was provided by the cargo's DGDs to plan safe stowage. As the district court observed, "[i]t would have been impractical for carriers to have had multiple pieces of paper relating to handling dangerous goods, the primary use of which was different . . . and then to have had to compare them to each other and/or to a DGD." *Phase II*, 339 F. Supp. 3d at 214. We therefore find no error in the district court's determination that MSC met its standard of care with respect to its stowage of the DVB-80 cargo aboard the Flaminia. Stolt had the requisite knowledge and authority but made no arrangements for special stowage and gave MSC no precise temperature instructions, either at the time of booking or in the DGDs. Employees from both Stolt and Deltech testified that to provide such special instructions would be standard practice for certain cargos. *See, e.g.*, Joint App'x at 8231–32 (testimony of Deltech employee); *id.* at 4556–60 (testimony of Stolt employee); *see also id.* at 3108 ("MSC . . . expect[s] that any special requests will be made by the customer before or at the time of booking . . . ."). In this setting, it was reasonable for MSC to stow the DVB-80 tanks below deck in Hold 4, next to Chemtura's heated DPA tanks and near the ship's heated bunker tanks.[25] **[—37—]**

The evidence presented at trial also supports the conclusion that neither Stolt nor Deltech expected the DVB-80 to be stored above-deck or that MSC (or the ship's crew)

---

[25] We agree with the district court that MSC's stowage of the DVB-80 tanks next to the heated DPA containers and near the ship's fuel tanks did not breach its duty to properly stow the cargo under COGSA. Even assuming that the MBLI's vague heat warning was sufficient to put MSC on notice of this particular cargo's heat sensitivity, MSC's handling of the tanks was adequate. The district court found that MSC's policy called for stowing *all* dangerous goods as if they **[—37—]** were heat sensitive, which meant stowing this cargo away from bunker tanks and motors. Hold 4, while adjacent to the ship's wing tanks containing heated fuel oil, had been approved for dangerous goods by the vessel's classification society. With respect to stowage next to the heated DPA containers, Chemtura never informed MSC that its containers could radiate heat and MSC had no reason to know of this fact. Indeed, DPA, like DVB-80, was Class 9 cargo and the IMDG Code does not have any separation requirements for cargo within this class. Additionally, the IMDG Code does not treat cargo itself as a heat source. *See* Joint App'x at 3337 (quoting IMDG Code § 7.1.1.15). While the district court found that the DPA containers and the ship's fuel tanks increased the temperature in Hold 4, *see Phase I*, 2018 WL 526549, at *26, this fact is insufficient to find that MSC breached its duty of care in the stowage of the DVB-80 tanks, which it reasonably assumed were safe for transport under normal conditions.

would monitor the chemical's temperature during the voyage. *See Phase II*, 339 F. Supp. 3d at 208 n.36 (finding that "Stolt did not charge Deltech extra" for obtaining temperature monitoring and did not request temperature monitoring when booking the cargo with MSC); *id.* at 211 n.40 (concluding that "above deck stowage was not a Deltech requirement" based on testimony from Deltech's president, Robert Elefante, that "whether the [DVB-80] was stored above or below deck ultimately did not matter so long as the ISO containers were kept away from a heat source"); *id.* at 223 n.76 (finding that above-deck stowage was not included in Deltech's operative shipping protocols at the time of the incident and noting the testimony of Zachary Levine, Deltech's VP of Commercial Operations, that "storage of the DVB ISO containers *below deck* was acceptable to Deltech" (emphasis added)). In other words, the DVB-80's stowage below deck **{-455-}** in Hold 4 was entirely foreseeable to Stolt and Deltech.

Stolt and Deltech's expectation that the DVB might be stowed either below or above deck was consistent with the IMDG Code, as well.[26] Deltech and Stolt properly identified DVB-80 as an "Environmentally Hazardous Substance[], Liquid, NOS [Not **[—38—]** Otherwise Specified] UN 3082, Class 9." *Phase II*, 339 F. Supp. 3d at 214. Cargo with this classification is considered to be vessel stowage category A. *See* Joint App'x at 3335. "Stowage category A means the material may be stowed 'on deck' or 'under deck' on a cargo vessel or on a passenger vessel." 49 C.F.R. § 172.101(k)(1). The IMDG Code does not require that UN 3082 cargo, if placed below deck, be stowed in a ventilated area. We therefore identify no error in the district court's finding that MSC treated the tanks exactly as specified by the IMDG Code.

Absent a booking request for on-deck stowage and temperature monitoring, MSC's stowage of the three DVB-80 tanks below deck in Hold 4 was both reasonable and foreseeable to Stolt and Deltech. Therefore, the district court's determination that MSC did not breach its duty of care by stowing the DVB-80 below deck does not "manifest[] an incorrect conception of the applicable law." *In re City of New York*, 522 F.3d at 282 (quoting *Esso Standard Oil S.A. v. S.S. Gasbras Sul*, 387 F.2d 573, 580 (2d Cir. 1967)).[27] **[—39—]**

IV. Conti and NSB's Lack of Negligence

The district court concluded that NSB and Conti were not negligent in hiring or training the crew on the Flaminia and that the crew acted reasonably when confronted with the vapor generated under-deck by Deltech's DVB-80. Stolt and Deltech challenge this conclusion, arguing that the crew should have known that the vapor was not smoke caused by a fire and that moving the manhole covers could generate

[26] As discussed, *supra* n.21, carriage of dangerous goods must conform to the IMDG Code's requirements for stowage.

[27] The district court also held that the COGSA fire exception protected MSC. That exception protects the carrier from responsibility for damage caused by fire, unless the fire is the "actual fault" of the carrier. COGSA § 4(2)(b). As a general matter, a shipper can recover against a carrier "merely by showing that the carrier received the [shipper's] goods in sound condition and delivered them damaged." *Asbestos Corp. Ltd. v. Compagnie De Navigation Fraissinet et Cyprien Fabre*, 480 F.2d 669, 672 (2d Cir. 1973). The carrier thus normally bears the burden of proof to show that it exercised due diligence. *Id.* COGSA's fire exception shifts the burden of proof to the shipper, requiring it to "prove that the carrier's negligence caused the fire or prevented its extinguishment." *In re Ta Chi Nav. Corp., S.A.*, 677 F.2d 225, 229 (2d Cir. 1982); *see also Asbestos Corp.*, 480 F.2d at 672–73. Because Stolt and Deltech have not proved that MSC stowed the DVB-80 negligently, the district court correctly concluded that the explosion aboard the Flaminia was not the "actual fault" of MSC. *Ta Chi*, 677 F.2d at 229. The facts here are unlike those at issue in *In re Liberty Shipping Corp., Motor Ship Don Jose Figueras*, 509 F.2d 1249, 1252 (9th Cir. 1975), where the Ninth Circuit held that the fire was the "actual fault" of the carrier because the carrier "permitt[ed] the vessel to put to sea without having properly trained the master and crew in the use of fire-fighting equipment." *Id.* In that case, there was evidence of "owner **[—39—]** neglect and actual fault constituting failure to exercise the due diligence required by COGSA." *Id.* Not so here.

a potentially catastrophic spark. On review, we agree with the district court.

When the district court's findings of fact are "premised upon credibility determinations, we grant particularly strong deference to those findings." *United States v. Mendez*, 315 F.3d 132, 135 (2d Cir. 2002); *see also* **{-456-}** *Phoenix Global Ventures, LLC v. Phoenix Hotel Assocs., Ltd.*, 422 F.3d 72, 76 (2d Cir. 2005) (deferring to district court's factual findings, "particularly those involving credibility determinations"). Here, the district court's concluded that Conti and NSB were not negligent in their firefighting conduct because they responded appropriately based on their belief that a fire had broken out in Hold 4. This determination rested largely on the testimony of Captain Brian Hall, an expert in shipboard firefighting, with over 20 years of relevant experience. *See Phase II*, 339 F. Supp. 3d at 226 n.83. The district court found Captain Hall's testimony persuasive, calling the Captain "knowledgeable, consistent, and logical"; it "relie[d] heavily on his opinions." *Id.* We accordingly afford strong deference to those of the district court's findings that were premised on Captain Hall's testimony.

Captain Hall testified that the captain, officers, and crew aboard the Flaminia were "appropriately trained and drilled in firefighting procedures and equipment, and were in compliance with applicable regulations." *Id.* at 227. He gave his view that it was **[—40—]** reasonable for the crew to believe that opening the man-lid when confronted with an already-oxygenated fire would not have caused an explosion. Relying on this testimony, the district court found that, under the circumstances as the crew reasonably perceived, opening the man-lid would not initiate oxygenation because, "the presence of the smoky cloud indicated that any fire was already oxygenated." *Id.* at 235. Thus, "there was reason to assume that opening a man[-]lid and placing a hose into the Hold could assist in addressing what was believed to be a fire," according to the district court. *Id.* We identify no error in the district court's finding on the basis of Captain Hall's testimony that the crew aboard the Flaminia was not negligent in opening the man-lid. We reject Stolt and Deltech's contentions to the contrary.

The district court also determined that Conti and NSB did not act negligently by failing to release more carbon dioxide ("CO_2") into Hold 4. The district court found that, "while the [carbon dioxide] system was not perfectly designed or installed, it worked appropriately." *Id.* at 228. It also concluded that it was not unreasonable for the crew to believe that they were dealing with a fire, rather than a DVB-80 vapor cloud.[28] Neither Stolt nor Deltech have demonstrated persuasively that these conclusions are erroneous. We therefore affirm the district court's determination that the crew's conduct did not make Conti and NSB liable for the loss. **[—41—]**

V. New Orleans Terminal's Lack of Negligence

The district court concluded that the Terminal was not negligent under federal maritime law because its actions—permitting stowage of the DVB-80 tanks in the open air in the terminal yard—was "consistent with its own prior practice as well as industry practice." *Id.* at 195. We find no error in this determination and the parties identify none persuasively.

The district court found that "[n]one of [New Orleans Terminal's] processes or procedures are confidential" and its storage handling is conducted "literally out in **{-457-}** the open—if a shipper is sending cargo out of New Orleans, he can expect that at some point it will arrive at [New Orleans Terminal's] yard; if the

[28] Separately, the district court concluded that NSB and Conti, like MSC, are entitled to the protections of the "fire exemptions" in COGSA and the Limitation of Shipowner's Liability Act (the "Limitation Act"). Because the fire did not result from the "actual fault" or negligence of MSC, NSB, or Conti, the district court was correct that these defenses are available to these three parties. *See* 46 U.S.C. § 30701 (note) §§ 4(2)(b),(q) (COGSA "fire exemptions"); 46 U.S.C. § 30522 (Limitation Act "loss by fire" provision, earlier codified at 46 U.S.C. § 30504). *See* n.27, *supra*.

shipper has not made other arrangements, it is entirely foreseeable that the cargo will sit in that yard, stagnant, under the New Orleans sun." *Id.* at 221. Deltech and Stolt did not instruct or even imply in the booking with New Orleans Terminal that the cargo should be stored in any other manner. *Id.* Further, they failed to ensure that the external temperature gauge on each tank of DVB-80 was checked prior to its loading onto the Flaminia. *Id.*

Stolt and Deltech insist nonetheless that the Terminal was negligent in its handling and storage of the DVB-80. They argue primarily that New Orleans Terminal fell below the applicable standard of care when it failed to heed the warnings that appeared on the Straight Bills of Lading and Materials Safety Data Sheet, to the effect that the DVB-80 cargo was heat sensitive and should not be stored in direct sunlight.

The evidence showed that New Orleans Terminal's longstanding practice is to recognize only those handling and storage instructions that it receives at the time of booking from the carrier (here, MSC), and not the delivery agent (here, Boasso). For this reason, New Orleans Terminal neither noted nor followed the warnings contained in the Straight Bills of Lading and Material Safety Data Sheet, which were delivered to it **[—42—]** by Boasso. Rather, those documents were "filed away," *id.* at 220, and used just to identify the source of the shipment and the UN cargo type.

It was established at trial that New Orleans Terminal provides information to the general public about how it processes cargo. It was incumbent on Stolt and Deltech, arranging for the dangerous shipment—especially when the shipment was contrary to Deltech's protocols insofar as it was slated for a summer loading in New Orleans rather than Newark—to inform themselves about how the Terminal operated and align the safety measures they took accordingly. They, not the Terminal, were in the best position to identify the risks and take steps to secure appropriate storage at the Terminal. Absent such measures, it was entirely foreseeable to both Deltech and Stolt that the tanks would sit "in the open sun at [New Orleans Terminal], adjacent to other UN number 3082, Class 9 cargo." *Id.* at 221. Having failed to inform themselves of NOT's procedures and to take direct measures for special handling of the DVB-80 cargo, Stolt and Deltech cannot transform New Orleans Terminal's handling of the cargo in accordance with its published practices into the Terminal's negligence merely by delivering otherwise ordinary transit documents. Accordingly, we find no error in the district court's determination that the Terminal was not negligent.

VI. No Recovery Against BDP

In addition to the tort claims discussed above, Stolt sued its subcontractor BDP for breach of contract to obtain indemnification and/or contribution for Stolt's damage liability. Below, Stolt argued that BDP's handling of the shipment documentation was a cause of the accident and, at the very least, deprived Stolt of a defense to the tort and contract claims brought by the other parties to this action. On appeal, Stolt presses only the second theory. **[—43—]**

It was BDP's role to process documents related to the shipment for Stolt: the district court referred to BDP as Stolt's "Documentation Department." *Phase II*, 339 F. Supp. 3d at 195. It is undisputed that BDP failed to obtain from MSC a Sea Waybill that included the correct stowage instructions and that, in this way, BDP breached its contractual obligations **{–458–}** to Stolt. The district court nevertheless determined that BDP's breach is not actionable because it was not this breach that caused harm resulting in Stolt's liability, nor did this breach deprive Stolt of any real defense. We are persuaded that this conclusion is correct.

When BDP transmitted the draft of Stolt's multipage Sea Waybill to MSC in the form of the MBLI, it included the following instruction: "DO NOT STOW NEAR HEAT SOURCES. STOW ABOVE DECK FOR TEMPERATURE MONITORING." *Id.* at 204 n.25. But when MSC prepared a proof copy of the Sea Waybill based on the MBLI and sent it back to BDP, the document omitted the heat warning. BDP failed to notice this omission. As a result, the final Sea Waybills between Deltech, Stolt, and MSC did not include the MBLI's instruction regarding DVB-80's heat sensitivity or the direction to store the cargo above deck. *Id.* at 217. On the face of it, this could have been a crucial omission. The instruction, while somewhat vague, was the only explicit warning of DVB-80's heat sensitivity received by MSC.

The evidence at trial indicated, however, that none of the parties—including MSC, Stolt, and Deltech—would have considered this stowage instruction to be operative, and that MSC would not (and arguably could not) have acted on it even if it had been included in the Sea Waybills. *See id.* at 243 ("[There] is insufficient evidence that had that language been preserved, MSC here would have acted differently or had different legal responsibilities to do so."). The evidence presented at trial demonstrated that MSC's Sea Waybills did not "play any operational function in the stowage plan" for the Flaminia, as that task had "been completed by the time these documents [were] **[—44—]** issue[d]," *Phase II*, 339 F. Supp. 3d at 223, but were used only as contract of carriage (i.e., maritime contracts that formalized the relationships among the parties), *see id.* at 241. Instead, special requests for stowage were expected to be communicated to MSC prior to or at the time of booking. Joint App'x at 3108. Deltech's booking requests to Stolt called for stowage *either* "in stack" *or* "below deck," since either would "avoid exposure to direct sunlight." *Phase II*, 339 F. Supp. 3d at 202 n.17. MSC followed this instruction by storing the DVB-80 in Hold 4.[29]

On appeal, Stolt maintains that had BDP ensured that MSC had included the instructions on the Sea Waybills, Stolt could at least have raised MSC's breach as a defense to its own breach and thereby averted or diminished its own liability. Stolt asserts that in a scenario in which BDP had ensured that the Sea Waybills included this explicit language directing temperature monitoring and stowage above decks, "Stolt would not have been liable to MSC and NSB/Conti under the Master contracts, and Stolt would have had valid contractual bases to assert claims against MSC." Stolt Reply Br. 56.

This argument has some force. Even were we to assume that Stolt could have asserted a breach of contract action against MSC for failing to adhere to the Sea Waybills, however, Stolt does not explain how MSC's subsequent hypothetical breach would have excused, prevented, or superseded its own. In other words, Stolt **{–459–}** does not explain how the inclusion of the heat warning on the Sea Waybills would have adequately warned MSC of the specific degree of danger posed by the DVB-80 cargo **[—45—]** aboard the Flaminia such that it could have defended against the carrier interests' failure-to-warn claim.

Stolt bore an affirmative obligation, independent of the documentation responsibilities it delegated to BDP, to warn MSC of the dangerousness of the DVB-80—an obligation placed squarely on Stolt by both COGSA and the Sea Waybills. The district court ruled that Stolt breached Clause 15.1[30] of the Sea Waybills by failing to warn MSC of three important and interrelated facts: (1) the three tanks were loaded with DVB-80 early at the Deltech plant; (2) it delivered tanks filled

[29] The evidence presented at trial was consistent with the district court's earlier determination that BDP was entitled to summary judgment on Stolt's claim that BDP's breach was a proximate cause of the loss aboard the Flaminia. *See In re M/V MSC Flaminia*, No. 12-cv-8892, 2017 WL 3738726, at *6 (S.D.N.Y. Aug. 30, 2017). Even though BDP's omission of the heat warning amounts to a breach of contract, the district court concluded that its relationship to the explosion was too attenuated to be considered a proximate cause of the loss.

[30] Clause 15.1 provides that when the "merchant" (Stolt and Deltech) "delivers Goods of a dangerous or hazardous nature to the Carrier" (MSC), Stolt and Deltech "shall fully inform [MSC] in writing of the precise and accurate details of the Goods, and special precautions or handling required for the Goods." *Phase II*, 339 F. Supp. 3d at 245. The operative Sea Waybills identify MSC as the carrier, Stolt "on behalf of" Deltech as the shipper, and Stolt as the consignee. *Id.* at 241.

with DVB-80 that would auto-polymerize in hot conditions; and (3) it deposited those tanks outside in the terminal yard in New Orleans to sit stagnant and heat up for the many days until vessel departure. *Phase II*, 339 F. Supp. 3d at 246. The heat warning that was omitted from the Sea Waybills—the same warning that MSC *did* receive on the MBLI—would not have adequately warned MSC of any of these three conditions.

The district court also decided that Stolt breached its obligation under Clause 15.1 to "fully inform" MSC by failing in the DGDs to warn of the risk that DVB-80 would auto-polymerize under certain conditions. *Id.* at 247. This was crucial, the court found, because it was the DGDs on which carriers in general and MSC in particular rely, rather than the Material Safety Data Sheet or MBLI. *Id.* Acting on behalf of Deltech, Stolt therefore breached its fundamental duty to warn when at booking it failed to request special handling and sent MSC DGDs in which no heat warning was provided. Even a heat warning in the Sea Waybills, then, would not have excused Stolt's separate **[—46—]** material breach in the deficient DGDs.[31] Stolt's failure to explain this deficiency only heightens our conviction that any failure by MSC that Stolt may now hypothesize—a speculative failure to heed the Sea Waybill's hypothetical instructions to stow the DVB-80 above deck and to monitor temperature—would not excuse Stolt's more profound breach. Therefore, BDP's failure to include the instructions on the Sea Waybill did not deprive Stolt of any real defense and warrants no practical effect in the allocation of liability between those two parties.

VII. MSC, Conti, and NSB's Entitlement to Indemnification by Stolt and Deltech

The district court held that the terms of the Sea Waybills require Stolt **{–460–}** and Deltech to indemnify MSC, as well as its subcontractors Conti, and NSB, for their losses. Under Clause 15.2 of the Sea Waybills, the "Merchant" (here, Stolt and Deltech) agrees to indemnify the "carrier" (MSC) and its "subcontractors" (Conti and NSB) for "all loss, damage, delay, personal injury, death or expenses . . . arising from such [dangerous or hazardous] Goods and/or from the breach of clause 15.1." *Phase II*, 339 F. Supp. 3d at 245–46 (quoting Sea Waybills Cl. 15.2) Because we agree with the district court's rulings that Stolt and Deltech breached Clause 15.1 and that MSC, Conti, and NSB were not negligent, we find no error in the district court's further holding that MSC and its **[—47—]** subcontractors are entitled to be indemnified by Stolt and Deltech: the loss or damage to MSC, Conti, and NSB indisputably arose at least in part from that breach.

As discussed above, we determine that the district court did not err in concluding that Stolt and Deltech violated Clause 15.1 of the Sea Waybills.[32] Clause 15.1 required them each to "fully inform [MSC] in writing of the precise and accurate details of the [DVB-80], and the special precautions or handling required for the [DVB-80]." *Id.* at 245. Deltech and Stolt failed to inform MSC that the temperature of the DVB-80 should be checked and monitored before loading onboard and that the chemical should not be loaded if its temperature exceeded 27 degrees Celsius. Deltech and Stolt also did not fully inform MSC of the hazardous or potentially dangerous

---

[31] Stolt arranged the booking with MSC on June 11, the date when (according to the district court) it would have been appropriate for Stolt to request special stowage. On June 20, Stolt sent the draft DGDs to MSC. MSC did not develop its stowage plan for the Flaminia until June 28. *See Phase II*, 339 F. Supp. 3d at 202–04. Therefore, MSC's hypothetical breach (developing a stowage plan that ignored the Sea Waybill) would not provide Stolt with a valid excuse for its failure to perform adequately under the contract, nor would it have provided Stolt with a valid contractual claim against MSC, since Stolt's own breach occurred prior to MSC's hypothetical one. *See Harsco Corp. v. Segui*, 91 F.3d 337, 348 (2d Cir. 1996) (requiring adequate performance of the contract by the claimant for a successful breach of contract claim).

[32] Based on the information in the MBLI, MSC prepared the three Sea Waybills—one for each tank—and provided them to BDP. The Sea Waybills, alongside a 2011 service contract between Stolt and MSC (the terms of which are not at issue here) governed the contractual relationship between Deltech, Stolt, and MSC. *See Phase II*, 339 F. Supp. 3d at 209.

characteristics of this particular shipment of DVB-80—the now-familiar, troubling facts that the tanks were filled early, sat stagnant in steamy New Orleans for ten days, and thus were significantly more susceptible to auto-polymerization during the voyage. *Id.* at 246–47.

Because Stolt and Deltech breached Clause 15.1, we agree with the district court that they must indemnify MSC and its subcontractors, Conti and NSB, pursuant to Clause 15.2 of the Sea Waybills.[33] **[—48—]**

CONCLUSION

We have considered the parties' remaining arguments and find in them no basis for any additional reversal. Accordingly, the district court's order is **REVERSED** in part, to the extent that the district court determined that Deltech and Stolt were strictly liable under Section 4(6) of the Carriage of Goods at Sea Act. The district court's order is otherwise **AFFIRMED** in part, insofar as it ruled as follows:

(1) Stolt and Deltech were liable under a failure-to-warn theory.

(2) MSC was not negligent in its stowage and handling of the DVB-80 shipment.

(3) NSB and Conti were not negligent in hiring or training the crew on the Flaminia, and the crew acted reasonably.

(4) New Orleans Terminal was not negligent in its handling of the shipment. **{-461-}**

(5) BDP's breach is not actionable by Stolt because the breach did not proximately cause the resulting harm and did not deprive Stolt of a defense.

(6) The Sea Waybills require Stolt and Deltech to indemnify MSC, Conti, and NSB for their losses.

The case is **REMANDED** for further proceedings consistent with this Opinion.

(Reporter's Note: Opinion concurring in part and dissenting in part follows on p. 171).

[33] Because we also agree with the district court that MSC, Conti, and NSB were not negligent, *see* above Parts III–IV, we do not reach the question addressed by our dissenting colleague with regard to the enforceability of Clause 15.2 of the Sea Waybills in light of the Harter Act, 46 U.S.C. § 30701, *et seq.* *See* Diss. Op. at 6–9.

[—1—] {-461-} MENASHI, Circuit Judge, concurring in part and dissenting in part:

I join Parts I, II, IV, and V of the court's opinion. For the reasons the court states, the district court erred when it decided that Deltech and Stolt could be held strictly liable under the Carriage of Goods by Sea Act ("COGSA"), 46 U.S.C. § 30701 note.[1] But the district court did not err when it held that Deltech and Stolt were negligent under COGSA on a failure-to-warn theory or when it held that Conti, NSB, and NOT were not negligent for those entities' respective actions.

I disagree with the court about three issues. First, the district court erred in holding that MSC was not negligent. Second, the district court erred when it concluded that Stolt's breach-of-contract claim against BDP is not actionable because BDP did not cause any harm to Stolt. Third, MSC is not entitled to full indemnification from Deltech and Stolt.

I

The district court concluded that MSC was not negligent at all. That was erroneous. Even if Deltech and Stolt had duties to provide additional warnings and failed to discharge those duties, MSC received information concerning the stowage of DVB-80 but failed to heed those warnings. The instructions for the Master Bill of Lading ("MBLI") explained that the DVB-80 was to be stowed away from heat sources. *In re M/V MSC Flaminia*, 339 F. Supp. 3d 185, 204 n.25 (S.D.N.Y. 2018) ("The Master Bill of Lading Instructions provided the following heat warning: 'DO NOT STOW NEAR HEAT SOURCES. STOW ABOVE DECK FOR TEMPERATURE MONITORING.'") There is no doubt that **[—2—]** MSC received those instructions; it relied on the instructions to generate the Sea Waybills. Had MSC complied with the instructions, the DVB-80 might not have autopolymerized and exploded. That is because, in addition to the early filling of the tanks and the tanks' stowage at the NOT dock, the district court identified two factors that "substantially contributed" to the autopolymerization: "[t]he placement of [the tanks] in Hold 4, where it was stored next to the containers of heated DPA and near the ship's heated fuel tanks" and the "hotter-than-typical ambient temperatures in Hold 4." *Id.* at 192 (quoting *In re M/V MSC Flaminia*, No. 12-CV-8892, 2018 WL 526549, at *30-31 (S.D.N.Y. Jan. 23, 2018)). The DVB-80 would not have been exposed to those conditions had MSC heeded the warnings provided in the MBLI.

In concluding that MSC's failure to heed the warnings contained in the MBLI was not negligent, the district court focused almost entirely on the method by which Stolt communicated information about the proper stowage of DVB-80. The district court identified "the DGD as the locus of critical information and warnings about the dangers of goods" and concluded that "Stolt's DGDs were defective." *Id.* at 238. It is correct that the DGDs were defective, but the district court's emphasis on those documents was misplaced. "COGSA does not require a shipper to use any particular method ... to inform a carrier of the dangerous properties of its cargo." **{-462-}** *Chem One, Ltd. v. M/V Rickmers Genoa*, 502 F. App'x 66, 71 (2d Cir. 2012). The district court even acknowledged that "other shippers and NVOCCs had included handling instructions on bills of lading or other non-DGD documents," *Flaminia*, 339 F. Supp. 3d at 219, indicating that maritime custom does not make it reasonable to rely solely on the DGDs. *See The Innocenta*, 13 F. Cas. 64, 65 (S.D.N.Y. 1879) ("[T]o make a custom of the port, the rule must be so generally known and **[—3—]** acknowledged and acted upon, as virtually to be applied by the whole of that part of the business community which it would affect."). Because neither COGSA nor maritime custom permits a carrier to ignore information other than that contained in the DGDs, MSC was not entitled to disregard the warning because it was not presented on a particular form. I would reverse the district court's decision that MSC was not negligent.

The court responds that, "even if MSC should have relied on the MBLI, MSC did not receive it until after the DVB-80 was loaded

[1] Unless otherwise noted, I use the same abbreviations as the opinion of the court.

into tanks and after the tanks had already sat stagnant in the sun at New Orleans Terminal for four days, at which point it was far too late to alter existing stowage plans." *Ante* at 35. The court concludes that the MBLI's warnings were "functionally useless absent concurrent instructions forbidding shipment when the carrier could not adhere to the instructions." *Id.* But MSC received the MBLI on June 25—days before "MSC develop[ed] its stowage plan for the cargo aboard the Flaminia" on June 28 and well before the Flaminia even arrived at NOT to receive the cargo on June 30. *Flaminia*, 339 F. Supp. 3d at 204. The loading was not complete until July 1. *Id.*

In another part of its opinion, the court holds that Stolt failed to provide MSC with "material information about the DVB-80 tanks," specifically that "the tanks of DVB-80 onboard the Flaminia had been delivered early to New Orleans Terminal and sat there day after day, exposed to the sun." *Ante* at 28. If that holding is correct—and I believe it is—then it means that MSC could have acted to prevent risks even after the DVB-80 was loaded into tanks and sat out in the sun. MSC could have, for example, monitored the temperature of the DVB-80 or stowed it away from heat sources—as the MBLI directed. **[—4—]**

Even if MSC could not have changed its stowage plan in response to the MBLI—despite the fact that the stowage plan had not yet been developed—MSC could have contacted Stolt or Deltech to determine the risks of failing to follow the heat warning. Because MSC did not do anything to heed the heat warning it received from the shipper, I would hold that it was negligent.

On remand, the district court would need to determine whether and to what extent MSC's breach of its duty of care gives rise to liability. Assuming the resultant damage flowed directly from MSC's breach and was within the scope of the risk of MSC's negligent act, *see In re Kinsman Transit Co.*, 338 F.2d 708, 724 (2d Cir. 1964) (Friendly, J.) ("The weight of authority in this country rejects the limitation of damages to consequences foreseeable at the time of the negligent conduct when the consequences are 'direct,' and the damages, although other and greater than expectable, is of the same general sort that was risked."), the district court would need to apportion fault between Deltech, Stolt, and MSC in the first instance. *See Derdiarian v. Felix Contracting Corp.*, 51 N.Y.2d 308, 315 (1980) (noting that "[b]ecause questions concerning what is foreseeable and what is normal may be the subject of varying inferences, as is the question of negligence itself, **{-463-}** these issues generally are for the fact finder to resolve" except "where only one conclusion may be drawn from the established facts"). I would remand for the district court to make that determination.

II

The district court erred when it concluded that Stolt's breach-of-contract claim against BDP was not actionable because the breach did not cause harm. BDP's breach did in fact harm Stolt because, had the Sea Waybills contained terms requiring the stowage of DVB-80 **[—5—]** away from heat sources, MSC's conduct in this case—its stowing of the DVB-80 near heat and its lack of temperature monitoring—would have constituted a contractual breach of the Sea Waybills. MSC's contractual breach would render it liable to Stolt for its lack of proper stowage, and the other terms of the Sea Waybills—including the indemnity provision—could not be invoked against Stolt and Deltech after MSC's breach. *See U.W. Marx, Inc. v. Koko Contracting, Inc.*, 124 A.D.3d 1121, 1122 (N.Y. App. Div. 3d Dep't 2015) (explaining that one party's "prior material breach" relieves the other party of its duty to "perform[] its remaining obligations under the contract").

BDP argues that MSC would never have agreed to include such a provision in the Sea Waybills. That argument fails for several reasons. First, there is evidence that MSC had previously permitted stowage instructions to be included in sea waybills. In early June 2012 Deltech shipped a container of DVB-80 on the MSC Marianna. The sea waybill issued for that shipment contained the exact warning at issue in this case: "DO NOT STOW NEAR HEAT SOURCES. STOW ABOVE DECK FOR TEMPERATURE MONITORING." Exs. 5346-

47. The same warning appeared on a sea waybill issued by MSC to Deltech in February 2012 for a shipment of DVB-63. *See* Ex. 5351. Second, the relevant comparator for causation-of-damages purposes is the state of affairs in which BDP *had* performed its duties; it was BDP's obligation to *secure* Sea Waybills with the appropriate stowage instructions, and doing so would have altered MSC's legal obligations. Third, even if BDP's obligation was solely to seek—rather than to *secure*—the inclusion of Deltech's stowage instructions in the Sea Waybills, the proper and adequate performance of BDP's duties required it to inform Stolt of MSC's refusal to accept the stowage conditions. *See Flaminia*, 339 F. Supp. 3d at 242 (noting that "[p]roper and adequate performance" of BDP's "document processing duties" was "implicit **[—6—]** in [its] agreement" with Stolt). Such notice could have either prevented the voyage altogether or prompted renewed negotiation between MSC and Stolt regarding the conditions of stowage.

In any event, the district court's conclusion was based on the premise that MSC would not have "had different legal responsibilities" if the stowage instructions had been contained in the Sea Waybills. *Id.* at 243. Because that premise is incorrect, I would reverse on this issue.

III

The district court concluded that the terms of the Sea Waybills required Deltech and Stolt to indemnify MSC, Conti, and NSB for the losses those entities sustained. That was erroneous because the Sea Waybills' indemnification provision is partially unenforceable under the Harter Act, 46 U.S.C. § 30704.

Clause 15.1 of the Sea Waybills provides that when Deltech or Stolt deliver "Goods of a dangerous or hazardous nature" to MSC, Deltech and Stolt need to "fully inform [MSC] in writing of the precise and accurate details of the Goods, and special **{-464-}** precautions or handling required for the Goods." *Flaminia*, 339 F. Supp. 3d at 245 (quoting Sea Waybills cl. 15.1). In turn, Clause 15.2 provides that Deltech and Stolt "shall be fully liable for and shall indemnify, hold harmless and defend [MSC] ... for all loss, damage, delay, personal injury, death or expenses including fines and penalties, and all reasonable legal expenses and costs caused to [MSC] ... arising from such Goods and/or from the breach of clause 15.1, whether or not [MSC] was aware of the nature of such goods." *Id.* at 245-46 (quoting Sea Waybills cl. 15.2). The district court held that, because Deltech and Stolt breached Clause 15.1, the breach triggered the obligation to indemnify MSC, Conti, and NSB under Clause 15.2. **[—7—]**

The Harter Act provides, in relevant part, that "[a] carrier may not insert into any bill of lading or shipping document a provision avoiding its liability for loss or damage arising from negligence or fault in loading, stowage, custody, care, or proper delivery." 46 U.S.C. § 30704. Clause 15.2 provides MSC with an indemnity against its own negligence and is therefore a "provision avoiding liability for loss or damage arising from negligence." *See Flaminia*, 339 F. Supp. 3d at 245.

In reaching that conclusion, this court's decision in *Gibbs v. United States*, 599 F.2d 36 (2d Cir. 1979), is instructive. In that case, we construed a contractual provision that provided as follows:

> The Contractor shall save harmless and indemnify the Postal Service and its officers, agents, representatives, and employees from all claims, loss, damage, actions, causes of action, expense and/or liability resulting from, brought for, or on account of any personal injury or property damage received or sustained by any person, persons, or property growing out of, occurring, or attributable to any work performed under or related to this contract, regardless of whether such claims, loss, damage, actions, cause[s] of action[], expense and/or liability may be attributable to the fault, failure, or negligence of the Contractor.

Id. at 40.

In concluding that this language provided the Postal Service with an indemnity against its own negligence, this court emphasized three textual points that resemble the terms of Clause 15.2. First, the contract required that the contractor "save harmless and indemnify" the Postal Service. That language, this court said, "show[s] an intent to encompass indemnification for the indemnitee's negligence." *Id.* **[—8—]** Clause 15.2 similarly provides that Deltech "shall indemnify" MSC and hold it harmless.

Second, the contract in *Gibbs* referred to "all claims" that might arise out of the work performed under the contract. This court observed that this language "on its face" covered claims arising out of the government's negligence. *Id.* Clause 15.2's language is similarly comprehensive, requiring Deltech to indemnify MSC for "all loss, damage, delay, personal injury, death or expenses including fines and penalties, and all reasonable legal expenses and costs caused to" MSC arising from the dangerous goods. *Flaminia*, 339 F. Supp. 3d at 245 (quoting Sea Waybills cl. 15.2).

Third, the contract in *Gibbs* provided for indemnification "regardless of whether" the damage to the government "may be attributable to the fault, failure, or negligence of the Contractor." *Gibbs*, 599 F.2d at 40. While this court did not explain why that language implied that the indemnity extended even to liability arising out of the government's own negligence, the most likely reason is that, by untethering liability from the contractor's fault, the language **{-465-}** evinced an intent to provide as broad an indemnity as possible. Clause 15.2 works similarly because it states that MSC is entitled to indemnification regardless of "whether or not the Merchant was aware of the nature" of the dangerous goods. *Flaminia*, 339 F. Supp. 3d at 245-46 (quoting Sea Waybills cl. 15.2). For that reason, Clause 15.2 evinces an intent to give a very broad indemnity that encompasses damages arising from MSC's own negligence.

MSC argues that the Harter Act cannot apply because COGSA is incorporated into the Sea Waybills—a contract—and so displaces the Harter Act. That argument cannot succeed because COGSA applies here only as a matter of contract. Because a contract cannot **[—9—]** displace a statute, the Harter Act would govern even if there were a conflict between the two statutes. But there is no conflict: As COGSA itself makes clear, it "shall [not] be construed as superseding ... any other law[s] which would be applicable in the absence of this Act, insofar as they relate to the duties, responsibilities, and liabilities of the ship or carrier prior to the time when the goods are loaded on or after the time they are discharged from the ship." 46 U.S.C. § 30701 note. Because the Harter Act "relate[s] to the duties, responsibilities, and liabilities of the ... carrier prior to the time when the goods are loaded on ... the ship," COGSA would not displace the Harter Act to the extent it would have governed prior to loading. 46 U.S.C. § 30704; *see also English Elec. Valve Co., Ltd. v. M/V Hoegh Mallard*, 814 F.2d 84, 87 (2d Cir. 1987) (stating that "while COGSA defines a carrier's liability 'from the time when the goods are loaded on to the time when they are discharged from the ship,'" the Harter Act applies before loading and after discharge).

Because the contract's language allows MSC to avoid its "liability for loss or damage arising from negligence or fault in loading, stowage, custody, care, or proper delivery," it is void under the Harter Act to the extent that the indemnity extends to pre-loading and post-discharge conduct. 46 U.S.C. § 30704. Because MSC's principal negligence occurred prior to the loading of the vessel, I would remand for the district court to revisit the allocation of fault. As the district court found, MSC developed its stowage plan on June 28, 2012, days before the ship was loaded. *See Flaminia*, 339 F. Supp. 3d at 204. The stowage plan disregarded the warnings provided in the MBLI. *See id.* at 213. Because the development of the stowage plan occurred prior to loading, the Harter Act prohibits MSC from being indemnified from the consequences to the extent that act was negligent. **[—10—]**

* * *

I agree with the court that the district court erred when it concluded that Deltech and Stolt were liable under a strict liability theory, and I agree that the district court did not err when it concluded (1) that those parties were liable on a negligent-failure-to-warn theory and (2) that Conti, NSB, and NOT were not negligent.

However, the district court did err when it concluded that MSC was not negligent even though it disregarded the instructions on the MBLI. It erred when it held that Stolt could not recover from BDP for breach of contract. And it erred when it concluded that Deltech and Stolt were required to indemnify MSC, Conti, and NSB under Clause 15.2 of the Sea Waybills for MSC's negligent actions performed prior to loading. For those reasons, I dissent in part.

United States Court of Appeals
for the Second Circuit

No. 21-1083

UNITED STATES
VS.
ANTONIUS

Appeal from the United States District Court for the Southern District of New York

Decided: July 10, 2023

Citation: 73 F.4th 82, 11 Adm. R. 176 (2d Cir. 2023).

Before **CALABRESI**, **LYNCH**, and **ROBINSON**, Circuit Judges.

[—3—] **{-84-}** **CALABRESI**, Circuit Judge:

Defendants–Appellants Steven Antonius, Shervington Lovell, and Argemiro Zapata-Castro ("Appellants") appeal their respective convictions, which were entered after each pled guilty to conspiring to violate the Maritime Drug Law Enforcement Act ("MDLEA"). Appellants, along with other co-conspirators and undercover informants of the United States Drug Enforcement Administration ("DEA"), planned for the shipment of cocaine from Guyana to the Netherlands. The plan included a series of steps. First, two boats, each carrying approximately 600 kilograms of cocaine, were to meet off the coast of Barbados. There, the second boat would transfer its contraband to the first. Next, the first boat, now carrying 1,200 kilograms of cocaine, would set sail for Europe, where it **[—4—]** would meet a third boat at a location between the coast of Ireland and the Azores Islands. The cocaine on the first boat would then be transferred to the third boat. The third boat, disguised as a fishing vessel with a crew wearing fisherman's uniforms, would deliver the cocaine to the Netherlands—its final destination. At no point did Appellants plan for the drugs to be delivered to the United States or to travel in United States waters.

Each of the Appellants played a leadership role in the drug-trafficking conspiracy. They attended planning meetings in the Spring and Summer of 2018, which took place in Guyana and Jamaica. During these meetings Appellants, their co-conspirators, and the undercover DEA informants discussed the logistics, route, and cost of the cocaine shipment, as well as the supplies, financing, and amount of cocaine they would each contribute to the endeavor. Appellants also communicated by radio, using code names for their operation.

Zapata-Castro agreed to procure the first boat—the one which was to make the **{-85-}** transoceanic journey. Zapata-Castro also agreed to provide the crew and three months' worth of rations. Antonius and Lovell agreed to supply the cocaine and to contribute to transportation expenses. Antonius contributed €135,000 and Lovell contributed $100,000-worth of Guyanese currency to the endeavor. **[—5—]** Antonius and Zapata-Castro were to decide the coordinates of the location where the first and second boats would meet off the coast of Barbados. They both also rallied their co-conspirators to consolidate their collective cocaine shipments into a single voyage, as initial discussions had contemplated multiple trips. Using his connections in the Netherlands, Antonius additionally arranged for the third boat and its crew to be disguised as a fishing operation and to meet the first at a point between the coast of Ireland and the Azores Islands.

Despite Appellants' grand plans, the cocaine did not make it very far. On July 27, 2018, the United States Coast Guard intercepted the first boat—the one procured by Zapata-Castro—hundreds of miles off the coast of Barbados. The boat did not display any country's flag. Members of the Coast Guard boarded the vessel, where its captain informed them that the vessel could not claim any nationality and that the mission of the voyage was trafficking drugs. The Coast Guard did not locate any documentation on board the vessel that indicated that it was registered with a particular nation. After a search, the Coast Guard discovered over 600 kilograms of cocaine hidden in duffel bags stored beneath **[—6—]**

wooden planks and covered by mattresses.[1] The Coast Guard arrested the boat's six crew members.[2] None of the Appellants were on board.

Antonius, Lovell, and Zapata-Castro were not United States citizens. In fact, other than Antonius, who had been to the United States once on vacation in 2014, they had not set foot on United States soil until they were extradited to be prosecuted in this case. The vessel did not originate in the United States, was not bound for the United States, and was not intercepted in United States waters.

Appellants were arrested in Jamaica on October 25, 2018. On November 8, 2018, the United States government charged each Appellant with one count of conspiracy to violate the MDLEA by attempting to ship 624 kilograms of cocaine from Guyana to the Netherlands in violation of the MDLEA, 46 U.S.C. §§ 70503 **[—7—]** and 70506(b). On November 30, 2018, Appellants were extradited to the Southern District of New York.

Appellants filed a motion to dismiss, arguing that charging them under the MDLEA violated their Fifth Amendment right to due process because (1) they were never on board a vessel that was subject to United States jurisdiction and (2) there was no nexus between their alleged criminal conduct and the United States. While **{-86-}** the motion was pending, this Court decided *United States v. Alarcon Sanchez*, 972 F.3d 156, 8 Adm. R. 42 (2d Cir. 2020), which held that foreign, land-based conspirators who planned to transport drugs from Colombia to Australia without traveling through United States waters—but who had minor contact with the United States as part of their efforts to further the conspiracy—could be prosecuted under the MDLEA. The district court asked the parties for supplemental briefing in light of that decision. Largely based on *Alarcon Sanchez*, the district court denied Appellants' joint motion to dismiss.

Each Appellant subsequently pled guilty. Antonius was sentenced to twelve years' imprisonment; Lovell was sentenced to eleven years' imprisonment; and Zapata-Castro was sentenced to thirteen years' imprisonment. Though each Appellant's plea agreement included an appeal waiver, the government conceded **[—8—]** that they were not foreclosed from appealing the issues presented in their motions to dismiss.

On appeal, all three Appellants again claim that their prosecution under the MDLEA denied them due process because their conduct lacked a nexus to the United States. They additionally argue, for the first time on appeal, that as applied to their case, Congress exceeded its authority under Article I of the Constitution in enacting the MDLEA.

DISCUSSION

We affirm the decision of the district court. Appellants' conviction under the MDLEA did not violate their due process rights, nor did Congress overstep its powers under Article I when it enacted the MDLEA, as applied to the facts of Appellants' case.

I. The MDLEA

The MDLEA prohibits knowingly or intentionally distributing, or possessing with intent to distribute, a controlled substance

[1] The Coast Guard also recovered a magazine with thirty rounds of ammunition.

[2] Four of the crew members pled guilty to conspiring to distribute, or possess with intent to distribute, 500 or more grams of cocaine while onboard a vessel subject to the jurisdiction of the United States. *See, e.g.*, Gonzalez Plea Tr. at 5, *United States v. Gonzalez, et al.*, No. 1:18-cr-00601-PGG (S.D.N.Y. 2021) (ECF No. 120). These four crew members were each sentenced to a five-year term of imprisonment. Torres Judgment at 2, *id.* (ECF No. 236); Monasterio Judgment at 2, *id.* (ECF No. 239); Gonzalez Judgment at 2, *id.* (ECF No. 459); Maikel Judgment at 2, *id.* (ECF No. 496). Two of the crew members pled guilty to conspiring to violate maritime drug laws. One of these crew members was sentenced to a two-year term of imprisonment and the other was sentenced to time served. Roopwah Judgment at 2, *id.* (ECF No. 238); Sucre Judgment at 2, *id.* (ECF No. 312).

"[w]hile on board a covered vessel." 46 U.S.C. § 70503(a). **[—9—]**

While the MDLEA's substantive prohibition contains "the locational limitation of 'on board a covered vessel,'" we held in *Alarcon Sanchez* that persons who are "not themselves . . . on board the covered vessel" may nevertheless be prosecuted under the MDLEA's attempt-and-conspiracy provision, 46 U.S.C. § 70506, for knowingly and intentionally conspiring to violate the MDLEA with others who were on board a covered vessel. *See* 972 F.3d at 164–65, 8 Adm. R. at 46–48. Thus, Appellants concede that the MDLEA, as written, covers them. Their arguments are that—as applied to them—such MDLEA prosecutions violate the Constitution.

A "covered vessel" is one that is "subject to the jurisdiction of the United States." 46 U.S.C. § 70503(e)(1). The United States has jurisdiction over "a vessel without nationality." *Id.* § 70502(c)(1)(A). A vessel lacks a nationality where, as here, the captain or "individual in charge fails, on request of an officer of the United States authorized to enforce applicable provisions of United States law, to make a claim of nationality or registry for that vessel." *Id.* § 70502(d)(1)(B).

The MDLEA explicitly gives the United States jurisdiction over offenses committed "outside the territorial jurisdiction of the United States." *Id.* § 70503(b). Additionally, where "the offense was . . . committed upon the high **[—10—]** seas, or elsewhere outside the jurisdiction of any particular State or district," an individual in violation of Section 70503 "may be tried in any [United States] district." *Id.* § 70504(b)(2). Whether the vessel in question is subject to the jurisdiction of the **{-87-}** United States is not an element of the offense; rather, it is a preliminary question for the trial judge to determine and it is the government's burden to show that the United States had jurisdiction over the vessel. *Id.* § 70504(a); *United States v. Prado*, 933 F.3d 121, 129–30, 7 Adm. R. 92, 94–96 (2d Cir. 2019).

The parties do not seriously dispute that the vessel used in the drug-trafficking operation was stateless, that the vessel in question and those on board it were subject to the jurisdiction of the United States, or that the Appellants in this case were co-conspirators with those actually on board the vessel.

II. Due Process

At issue in the instant case, therefore, is whether due process permits the MDLEA to be used to prosecute conspirators in drug-trafficking schemes who are not citizens of the United States, who act exclusively on foreign soil, who do not utilize contacts or resources in the United States, and who were not on board the seized vessel. **[—11—]**

Appellants argue that allowing such individuals to be prosecuted under the MDLEA would be fundamentally unfair because, in their view, the law requires a nexus between Appellants' actions and the United States but, here, no nexus existed. Appellants support their argument by asserting that "[n]one of the conduct, the meetings, or the alleged instrumentalities of the offense occurred in or had any relation to the United States" nor did Appellants "inten[d] to have contact with the United States, or to cause any harm to the interests of the United States." Appellants' Br. at 19–20.

The government counters that under our Circuit's case law, no nexus is required to bring MDLEA prosecutions against persons involved in trafficking drugs on stateless vessels. The government further argues that, even were it required to show nexus, it could do so because the aim of its prosecution was to curtail drug trafficking on the high seas, which specifically threatens the security and societal well-being of the United States—and that this is nexus enough.

The district court agreed with the government. It did "not read the MDLEA, its legislative history, or relevant case law as requiring a nexus to the United States beyond this nation's compelling interest in 'curtailing international drug trafficking on the high seas.'" *United States v. Cardona-Cardona*, 500 F. Supp. **[—12—]** 3d 123, 135 (S.D.N.Y. 2020) (quoting *Alarcon Sanchez*, 972 F.3d at 169, 8

Adm. R. at 51). The district court also explained that Appellants had fair warning that they might be subject to prosecution in the United States because they knew that their conduct was criminal and would therefore subject them to prosecution *somewhere*. *Id.* at 136.

Generally, "[i]n order to apply extraterritorially a federal criminal statute to a defendant consistently with due process, there must be a sufficient nexus between the defendant and the United States, so that such application would not be arbitrary or fundamentally unfair." *United States v. Epskamp*, 832 F.3d 154, 168 (2d Cir. 2016) (quoting *United States v. Yousef*, 327 F.3d 56, 111 (2d Cir. 2003)) (alteration in original). When individuals who are not United States citizens act on foreign soil, nexus is present where "the aim of [the] activity is to cause harm inside the United States or to U.S. citizens or interests." *Id.* (quoting *United States v. Al Kassar*, 660 F.3d 108, 118 (2d Cir. 2011)).

But in the context of the MDLEA, we have held that no showing of nexus is required for the prosecution of individuals accused of trafficking drugs who are actually on board a stateless vessel. This is so **{–88–}** "because such prosecutions are not arbitrary, since any nation may exercise jurisdiction over stateless vessels, **[—13—]** and they are not unfair, since persons who traffic drugs may be charged with knowledge that such activity is illegal and may be prosecuted somewhere." *United States v. Van Der End*, 943 F.3d 98, 106, 7 Adm. R. 123, 127 (2d Cir. 2019).

Van Der End, however, deliberately left open the question of whether proof of nexus was constitutionally required to determine whether "persons who are not on board a vessel without nationality may be prosecuted for violating the MDLEA." *Id.* at 105 n.4, 7 Adm. R. at 127 n.4. A year later, when confronted with that very question in *Alarcon-Sanchez*, we considered the differences between "seafaring defendants" who "had forfeited their protections under international law and were therefore fair game for any nation to 'subject them to their laws'" and land-based conspirators who were "obviously subject" to the "jurisdiction and laws" of the country in which their actions in advancing the conspiracy took place. 972 F.3d at 168–69, 8 Adm. R. at 50 (quoting *Van Der End*, 943 F.3d at 105, 7 Adm. R. at 127). Ultimately, we declined to decide whether nexus was required in such circumstances. We instead held that the due process rights of the particular land-based conspirators in *Alarcon Sanchez* were not violated even assuming *arguendo* that a nexus requirement applied. *Id.*, 8 Adm. R. at 50–51. **[—14—]**

For the same reason, we need not decide whether proof of nexus with the United States must be established in cases involving land-based conspirators using stateless vessels on the high seas to traffic drugs. That is because, even assuming a nexus requirement, the harm caused by drug trafficking on the high seas threatens the societal well-being of the United States. In enacting the MDLEA, Congress explicitly found that "trafficking in controlled substances aboard vessels is a serious international problem, is universally condemned, and presents a specific threat to the security and societal well-being of the United States." 46 U.S.C. § 70501. As we explained in *Alarcon Sanchez*, conspiring to traffic controlled substances presents the same threat to the security and societal well-being of the United States and, therefore, constitutes a sufficient nexus. *See* 972 F.3d at 169, 8 Adm. R. at 51; *see also Epskamp*, 832 F.3d 154, 168 ("For non-citizens acting entirely abroad, a jurisdictional nexus exists when the aim of that activity is to cause *harm* inside the United States or *to U.S.* citizens or *interests*." (quoting *Al Kassar*, 660 F.3d at 118) (emphasis added)).

Appellants argue that our nexus determination in *Alarcon Sanchez* should not be adopted in this case because the facts in that case meaningfully differ from the facts here. Appellants point out that in *Alarcon Sanchez*, the actions of some **[—15—]** of the defendants in furtherance of the conspiracy involved contact with the United States. And, in *Alarcon Sanchez*, we did mention that the conspirators in that case "us[ed] a U.S.-registered vessel and procur[ed] false visas in the United States." 972 F.3d at 169, 8 Adm. R. at 51. But our decision did not rest on these connections with the United States. Rather, our decision in *Alarcon Sanchez* depended on our determination that international drug trafficking on the high seas is inherently related to the specific interests of the United States and thus constituted adequate nexus. *Id.*, 8 Adm. R. at 51.[3] **{-89-}**

Our holding in *Alarcon Sanchez* also made clear that Appellants had adequate warning that their actions could be prosecuted in the United States. In *Alarcon Sanchez*, we held that the conspirators need not have understood that their conduct would subject them to prosecution in the United States *specifically*, as long as they knew their actions were criminal and could subject them to **[—16—]** prosecution *somewhere*. *Id.*, 8 Adm. R. at 51. We explained that the conspirators' prosecution under the MDLEA was "neither arbitrary nor fundamentally unfair" because they "were aware that their scheme to transport cocaine on the high seas was illegal and could result in their criminal prosecution 'somewhere.'" *Id.*, 8 Adm. R. at 51 (quoting *Al Kassar*, 660 F.3d at 119). They, therefore, "were not ensnared by a trap laid for the unwary." *Al Kassar*, 660 F.3d at 119.

It is certainly plausible—and even likely—that Appellants never expected to be subject to prosecution by the United States even though they may have expected to be subject to prosecution by Guyana or Jamaica, where their actions to further the conspiracy took place, or by the Netherlands, the planned destination for the contraband. But because Appellants understood that their efforts to traffic drugs would subject them to criminal liability in some jurisdiction, our case law clearly holds that they had notice consistent with due process to be prosecuted under the MDLEA in the United States. *See, e.g.*, *Alarcon Sanchez*, 972 F.3d at 169, 8 Adm. R. at 51; *Epskamp*, 832 F.3d at 168–69.[4] **[—17—]**

As we held in *Alarcon Sanchez*, we conclude here that, "in light of the conspiracy's nexus to United States interests in eliminating drug trafficking on the high seas, and the fair warning we ascribe to those that participate in such conspiracies, . . . due process was not offended by defendants' MDLEA prosecutions." 972 F.3d at 169, 8 Adm. R. at 51.[5]

III. Article I

Appellants claim that applying the MDLEA to their foreign, land-based activities is an

---

[3] Recently, a district court in the District of Puerto Rico similarly recognized that "[p]recedent from sister jurisdictions suggests that the MDLEA extends to extraterritorial conspiracies (*i.e.* defendants who plan drug-trafficking ventures but never leave the country of origin)," when evaluating whether foreign, land-based defendants could be prosecuted under the MDLEA for planning to traffic drugs from Colombia to Portugal. *United States v. Serrano*, 618 F. Supp. 3d 70, 71–72 (D.P.R. 2022) (citing *Alarcon-Sanchez*, 972 F.3d at 165, 8 Adm. R. at 47–48; *United States v. Ballestas*, 795 F.3d 138, 145, 3 Adm. R. 698, 701 (D.C. Cir. 2015)) (ultimately holding that the defendants' motion to dismiss was not ripe for adjudication).

[4] Moreover, no specific proof is required to establish that perpetrators of international illegal drug trafficking know that their conduct is criminal. *See, e.g.*, *Van Der End*, 943 F.3d at 106, 7 Adm. R. at 127–28 ("[W]e have little trouble concluding that those who participate in international drug trafficking **[—17—]** activity are aware that such conduct is illegal."). Even so, the record supports that Appellants knew their conduct was illegal. They used code names for the vessels they planned to use to transport the drugs, and they planned for the crew on the final boat which would deliver the cocaine to the shores of the Netherlands to disguise themselves as fishermen.

At oral argument, Appellants argued that the fact that it was a *DEA informant* who arranged for the co-conspirators to use a stateless vessel, thereby subjecting the vessel to the jurisdiction of the United States, should suffice to establish that Appellants had not intended to be subject to United States jurisdiction. That argument is foreclosed by *Alarcon Sanchez*. In that case, it was "[a]t the direction of Homeland Security[] [that] the cooperating source" arranged use of the drug vessel, and yet the foreign, land-based conspirators were still subject to the MDLEA's reach. *Alarcon Sanchez*, 972 F.3d at 160, 8 Adm. R. at 43.

[5] We reserve for another day the question of whether foreign, land-based conspirators trafficking drugs not destined for the United States may be prosecuted under the MDLEA if they specifically planned to use a vessel that had been properly registered with a foreign nation, but where the crew defied that plan.

invalid exercise of congressional power under Article I. Appellants did not raise this argument before the district court. We nevertheless **[—18—]** choose to consider **{–90–}** it,[6] and review the district court's decision for plain error. Fed. R. Crim. P. 52(b). Plain-error review requires that we determine whether (1) there was an error, (2) the error was clear or obvious and not subject to reasonable dispute, (3) the error affected Appellants' substantial rights, and (4) the error seriously affected the fairness, integrity, or public reputation of the judicial proceedings. *United States v. Marcus*, 560 U.S. 258, 262 (2010).

The Constitution's Define and Punish Clause gives Congress the power to "define and punish Piracies and Felonies committed on the high Seas, and Offences against the Law of Nations." U.S. Const. art. I, § 8, cl. 10. This Clause grants Congress three individual powers: (1) to define and punish piracy, (2) to define and punish felonies committed on the high seas, and (3) to define and punish offenses against the Law of Nations. *Alarcon Sanchez*, 972 F.3d at 169–70, 8 Adm. R. at 51. We conclude that the district court did not err when it held that Appellants may be prosecuted under the MDLEA because doing so does not exceed Congress's power to punish felonies on the high seas. **[—19—]**

Appellants reason that they could only have been constitutionally subject to the MDLEA as a result of Congress's power to punish offenses against the Law of Nations. They argue that, because they were never physically on the high seas themselves, Congress's power to punish felonies on the high seas cannot subject them to prosecution under the MDLEA. Appellants further claim that, because their crime does not concern piracy, the congressional power to punish piracy also cannot provide Congress the means to subject them to the MDLEA's reach. And, relying on an Eleventh Circuit case, *United States v. Bellaizac-Hurtado*, 700 F.3d 1245 (11th Cir. 2012), they contend that the congressional power to punish offenses against the Law of Nations does not allow Congress to punish drug trafficking because drug trafficking is "not a violation of customary international law." *Id.* at 1258.

Appellants' reasoning is misguided. They are incorrect that only the congressional power to punish offenses against the Law of Nations applies to the prosecution of their conduct. Instead, we have held that punishing drug trafficking on the high seas "falls squarely within [Congress's] constitutional power to punish *felonies* on the high seas," including the punishment of conspirators on land. *Alarcon Sanchez*, 972 F.3d at 170, 8 Adm. R. at 51 (emphasis added). In so **[—20—]** holding, our Court considered, and rejected, the same argument Appellants make here: that because Congress's power to punish felonies "contains locational language: the high seas," "the MDLEA cannot constitutionally be construed to reach [the] conduct" of a defendant who was not personally "on the high seas in connection with the charged conspiracy." *Id.* at 167, 8 Adm. R. at 48–49. Thus, just as *Alarcon Sanchez* decides Appellants' due process challenge, that case decides their Article I challenge.

Moreover, the case Appellants rely on, *Bellaizac-Hurtado* and its sequela, are in fact consistent with our precedent. In *Bellaizac-Hurtado*, the defendants were in *Panamanian* waters and not on the high seas. 700 F.3d at 1248–49. And for that reason only, Congress's ability to punish felonies on the high seas was held not to have been the source of its power to proscribe their conduct as it can, and does, here. Indeed, the Eleventh Circuit has since explained (by summary order) that where the MDLEA has been invoked under the congressional power to punish felonies on the high seas, as here, "the assertion **{–91–}** of jurisdiction over stateless vessels on the high seas in no way transgresses recognized principles of international law." *United States v. Macias*, 654 F. App'x 458, 461 (11th Cir. 2016) (quoting *United States v. Marino–Garcia*, 679 F.2d 1373, 1382 (11th Cir. 1982)). **[—21—]**

[6] *See United States v. Bodnar*, 37 F.4th 833, 843 (2d Cir. 2022).

Furthermore, when we read the language of the MDLEA to cover land-based conspirators in *Alarcon Sanchez*, we noted that the Necessary and Proper Clause of the Constitution allows the application of the MDLEA to land-based conspirators. 972 F.3d at 167–68, 8 Adm. R. at 49. And we there held that it is "necessary and proper for Congress to confer federal jurisdiction over all conspirators, both those who go on the seas and those who remain on land." *Id.* at 167, 8 Adm. R. at 49. That is because "prosecuting MDLEA conspirators who *are not* on the high seas is a means that is rationally related to the legitimate end of prosecuting MDLEA conspirators who *are* on the high seas." *Id.*, 8 Adm. R. at 49 (emphasis added).

To hold otherwise, moreover, would be to encourage a sentencing scheme that punishes only the lowest-level members of the conspiracy—those who physically transport the drugs on the high seas—while the masterminds on land—usually with more power, money, and resources—operate free from the MDLEA's reach. *See id.* at 166, 8 Adm. R. at 48 (declining to read "the attempt-and-conspiracy provision" in a way that "would immunize" foreign land-based conspirators—who are often "the higher-ups that engineered the shipment in the first place"—because such a reading would "undercut[] Congress's findings on the scope and gravity of the threat posed by drug trafficking aboard vessels"). And this would **[—22—]** contradict the "long [-]recognized" common-law principle that "persons who intentionally direct or facilitate the crimes physically executed by others must be held accountable for their actions." *United States v. Hoskins*, 902 F.3d 69, 77 (2d Cir. 2018).

Lastly, Appellants have raised one claim that was not addressed in *Alarcon Sanchez*—that Congress exceeded its Article I powers by expanding the definition of "stateless vessel" in the MDLEA beyond its internationally recognized definition. Appellants, however, acknowledged at oral argument that they know of no authority to support this claim.

Appellants originally relied on a decision of the First Circuit for support in their briefing. But that decision has since been withdrawn. *See United States v. Dávila-Reyes*, 23 F.4th 153 (1st Cir. 2022), *withdrawn by*, 38 F.4th 288 (2022) (granting rehearing en banc). And, the First Circuit had recognized even in its withdrawn decision the constitutionality of the provision under which Appellants were prosecuted—specifically, that Congress's passage of § 70502(d)(1)(B), deeming a vessel stateless "when the individual in charge of a **[—23—]** vessel fails to make a claim of nationality," is "clearly consistent with international law." *Id.* at 186–87.[7]

Moreover, our own Court's law is clear. We have long read the United Nations Convention on the High Seas to indicate that a vessel "which does not sail under the flag of one state to whose jurisdiction it has submitted" is "a stateless vessel" and "may not claim the protection of international **{–92–}** law and does not have the right to travel the high seas with impunity." *United States v. Pinto-Mejia*, 720 F.2d 248, 260 (2d Cir. 1983).

Since no authority supports Appellants' argument that Congress exceeded its Article I powers by extending the MDLEA to foreign, land-based conspirators orchestrating the trafficking of drugs aboard a stateless vessel, the district court did not err, let alone commit plain error, when it held Appellants could be prosecuted under the MDLEA.

CONCLUSION [—24—]

We have considered all of Appellants' other arguments and find them to be without merit. We **AFFIRM** the decision of the district court.

---

[7] Indeed, even had *Dávila-Reyes* remained good law in the First Circuit, it would be inapposite. The panel opinion in *Dávila-Reyes* held that Congress overstepped its Article I powers when it passed § 70502(d)(1)(C), which deemed stateless those vessels whose captains make "a claim of nationality recognized by international law," but where "the identified country neither confirms or denies that claim." 23 F.4th at 187. And that is not the statutory mechanism for determining statelessness at issue in the instant case.

United States Court of Appeals
for the Second Circuit

No. 22-1189

NEW YORK
vs.
RAIMONDO

Appeal from the United States District Court for the Southern District of New York

Decided: October 13, 2023

Citation: 84 F.4th 102, 11 Adm. R. 183 (2d Cir. 2023).

Before **WESLEY** and **PARK,** Circuit Judges.*

* Circuit Judge Rosemary S. Pooler, who was a member of the panel, passed away on August 10, 2023. Judge Pooler participated in the consideration and decision of this case and had initial responsibility for the opinion of the Court. The two remaining members of the panel have determined to issue this opinion. *See* 28 U.S.C. § 46(d); 2d Cir. IOP E(b).

[—3—] {-104-} **WESLEY,** Circuit Judge:

The federal government uses a fishery management plan to conserve and manage summer flounder, also known as fluke, off the Eastern Seaboard. Under the Magnuson-Stevens Fishery Conservation and Management Act (the "MSA"), 16 U.S.C. §§ 1801 *et seq.*, that fishery management plan must account for ten "national standards." Each national standard prioritizes a different objective: **[—4—]** from preventing overfishing, to using accurate scientific data, to promoting efficiency, to protecting existing fishing communities, and more.

Eleven states participate in the summer flounder fishery. The fishery management plan includes annual commercial quotas for each state, which determine how much summer flounder that state's fishermen can catch. One of those states, New York, brought this action against the National Marine Fisheries Service (the "NMFS")—the federal agency responsible for the summer flounder fishery—and several related federal entities. New York argues that in setting the current quotas, the NMFS failed to account for the long-term **{-105-}** movement of summer flounder northward, closer to New York's shores. New York claims the quotas violate several of the MSA's national standards as well as the Administrative Procedure Act (the "APA"), 5 U.S.C. §§ 701 *et seq.* The district court rejected that argument; it granted summary judgment to the NMFS.

We conclude that in setting each state's summer flounder quotas, the NMFS properly weighed the relevant statutory considerations. We therefore affirm the judgment of the district court. **[—5—]**

BACKGROUND

Summer flounder are a sought-after commercial fish. Their habitat spans the Eastern Seaboard, but during winter months they concentrate in offshore waters managed by the federal government through the NMFS.[1] Commercial fishermen in eleven coastal states, from Maine to North Carolina, fish these waters.

The NMFS regulates the commercial summer flounder catch through a fishery management plan. Congress, through the MSA, requires the fishery management plan to account for ten national standards. Those national standards are set forth in full below, but at a high level, they seek to conserve and manage the fishery for future generations. *See* 16 U.S.C. § 1802(5) (defining "conservation and management"); *id.* § 1851(a) (requiring "conservation and management" measures to comport with the ten national standards).

The summer flounder fishery incorporates a quota system designed to prevent overfishing. Each state is allocated a quota percentage of the total summer flounder catch for the year. Any summer flounder that are "landed" (brought **[—6—]** ashore) in a state count towards that state's annual quota—regardless of where those fish were caught. For example,

[1] "The federal government is responsible for regulation of the 'exclusive economic zone'—waters from three to 200 miles from shore." *New York v. Atl. States Marine Fisheries Comm'n*, 609 F.3d 524, 527 (2d Cir. 2010). By contrast, states "retain primary authority over the conservation and management of fisheries within the 'territorial sea'—waters within three miles of shore, as well as in rivers and estuaries." *Id.*

fishermen from Virginia catch summer flounder near Long Island, New York, "land" those fish back in Virginia, and those fish count towards Virginia's quota.

The NMFS first incorporated quotas into the fishery management plan in 1992, with a slight adjustment in 1993 (the "1993 Allocation Rule"). At that time, each state's quota was based on how much summer flounder that state had landed from 1980 through 1989. From 1993 onward, New York received authorization for approximately 7% of each year's total catch. States with higher historical landings received higher quotas: for example, Virginia received approximately 21% of each year's total catch.[2]

Since 1993, however, summer flounder populations have shifted steadily northward, closer to the coast of New York. In response, NMFS undertook a rulemaking process to reassess and potentially revise the quota system. It completed that process in 2020, when it promulgated a new rule (the "2020 **[—7—]** Allocation Rule") that New York now challenges. *See* 85 Fed. Reg. 80,661 (Dec. 14, 2020) (codified at 50 C.F.R. § 648.102(c)(1)). **{-106-}**

The 2020 Allocation Rule retains each state's original quota from the 1993 Allocation Rule—but only up to the first 9.55 million pounds of summer flounder caught. *See* 50 C.F.R. § 648.102(c)(1)(i). Past that point, the 2020 Allocation Rule subjects any additional catch to a new, evenly divided, "surplus" quota—by which every state receives approximately 12% of any additional catch during a good fishing year.[3] *See id.* § 648.102(c)(1)(ii). Consequently, under the 2020 Allocation Rule, New York is entitled to its historical 7% of the first 9.55 million pounds of coastwide catch, and 12% of any surplus beyond that.

New York filed comments regarding the 2020 Allocation Rule; it protested that it should receive a higher quota percentage because summer flounder populations had relocated closer to its own shores. New York claimed that the NMFS had ignored scientific evidence showing the summer flounder movement. **[—8—]** The NMFS rejected New York's comments and explained why the quotas crafted in the 2020 Allocation Rule were preferrable.

After the NMFS finalized the 2020 Allocation Rule, New York filed this action against the NMFS and related federal entities. New York maintained its argument that the 2020 Allocation Rule, as well as annual implementation rules promulgated thereunder,[4] fail to account for the summer flounder's long-term relocation. New York claimed that by doing so, the NMFS disregarded four of the MSA's ten national standards—which required the agency to use the "best scientific data available" and to promote efficiency and fairness among fishermen.

The United States District Court for the Southern District of New York (Vyskocil, *J.*) denied New York's motion for summary judgment and granted the defendants' cross-motion. The district court concluded it was "clear from the administrative record that NMFS appropriately considered all the ten national standards and, in exercising its discretion to formulate the 2020 Allocation Rule, **[—9—]** did not violate the MSA." *New*

---

[2] The exact baseline quotas are as follows: Maine 0.04756%; New Hampshire 0.00046%; Massachusetts 6.82046%; Rhode Island 15.68298%; Connecticut 2.25708%; New York 7.64699%; New Jersey 16.72499%; Delaware 0.01779%; Maryland 2.03910%; Virginia 21.31676%; North Carolina 27.44584%. *See* 58 Fed. Reg. 49,937, 49,940 (Sept. 24, 1993) (codified at 50 C.F.R. § 625.20).

[3] The exceptions are Maine, New Hampshire, and Delaware, who receive only a *de minimis* amount of the surplus quota. These three states do not participate substantially in the summer flounder catch.

[4] Each year, NMFS adopts a "Specifications Rule," which announces that year's coastwide quota and then, based on the 2020 Allocation Rule, calculates the distribution of that quota among the states. *See* 50 C.F.R. § 648.102(c). New York has also challenged the most recent Specifications Rule, but the parties agree that the validity of the 2020 Allocation Rule will determine the validity of any derivative Specifications Rule. *See New York v. Raimondo*, 594 F. Supp. 3d 588, 597 (S.D.N.Y. 2022).

York v. Raimondo, 594 F. Supp. 3d 588, 599 (S.D.N.Y. 2022). New York appealed.

DISCUSSION

A. Standard of Review

"On appeal from a grant of summary judgment involving a claim brought under the [APA], we review the administrative record *de novo* without according deference to the decision of the district court." *Town of Southold v. Wheeler*, 48 F.4th 67, 77, 10 Adm. R. 59, 64 (2d Cir. 2022) (quoting *Karpova v. Snow*, 497 F.3d 262, 267 (2d Cir. 2007)). Nevertheless, our review in this case is narrow, and deferential to the NMFS's expertise as an agency. *See id.*, 10 Adm. R. at 65. That is because MSA provides that courts review NMFS rulemakings under the APA's arbitrary and capricious standard. *See* 16 U.S.C. § 1855(f). Under that standard, an agency need only "examine the relevant data and articulate a satisfactory explanation for its action including a rational connection between the facts found **{–107–}** and the choice made." *Motor Vehicle Mfrs. Ass'n v. State Farm Mut. Auto. Ins.*, 463 U.S. 29, 43 (1983) (citation and internal quotation marks omitted); *see* 5 U.S.C. § 706(2)(A). **[—10—]**

B. Validity of the 2020 Allocation Rule

Fishery management plans "shall be consistent with" the MSA's ten national standards. 16 U.S.C. § 1851(a). Those standards are:

> (1) Conservation and management measures shall prevent overfishing while achieving, on a continuing basis, the optimum yield from each fishery for the United States fishing industry.
>
> (2) Conservation and management measures shall be based upon the best scientific information available.
>
> (3) To the extent practicable, an individual stock of fish shall be managed as a unit throughout its range, and interrelated stocks of fish shall be managed as a unit or in close coordination.
>
> (4) Conservation and management measures shall not discriminate between residents of different States. If it becomes necessary to allocate or assign fishing privileges among various United States fishermen, such allocation shall be (A) fair and equitable to all such fishermen; (B) reasonably calculated to promote conservation; and (C) carried out in such manner that no particular individual, corporation, or other entity acquires an excessive share of such privileges.
>
> (5) Conservation and management measures shall, where practicable, consider efficiency in the utilization of fishery resources; except that no such measure shall have economic allocation as its sole purpose.
>
> (6) Conservation and management measures shall take into account and allow for variations among, and contingencies in, fisheries, fishery resources, and catches.
>
> (7) Conservation and management measures shall, where practicable, minimize costs and avoid unnecessary duplication. **[—11—]**
>
> (8) Conservation and management measures shall, consistent with the conservation requirements of this chapter (including the prevention of overfishing and rebuilding of overfished stocks), take into account the importance of fishery resources to fishing communities by utilizing economic and social data that meet the requirements of paragraph (2), in order to (A) provide for the sustained participation of such communities, and (B) to the extent practicable, minimize adverse economic impacts on such communities.
>
> (9) Conservation and management measures shall, to the extent practicable, (A) minimize bycatch and (B) to the extent bycatch cannot be avoided, minimize the mortality of such bycatch.

(10) Conservation and management measures shall, to the extent practicable, promote the safety of human life at sea.

Id.

The ten national standards encompass disparate concerns. There is, consequently, a "necessary tension" among them. *All. Against IFQs v. Brown*, 84 F.3d 343, 349–50 (9th Cir. 1996). The national standards' expansive text and structure reflect that Congress intended for the NMFS to use "discretion and judgment" to reconcile this tension when managing the fishery. *Id.* The MSA gives the NMFS rulemaking flexibility to react to dynamic natural conditions and account for multiple stakeholders. One national standard does not trump the others; incremental adjustments to a fishery management plan are acceptable. *See Massachusetts v. E.P.A.*, 549 U.S. 497, 524 (2007). **[—12—] {-108-}**

C. Validity of the 2020 Allocation Rule

New York contends that by failing to allocate a higher quota to New York, the 2020 Allocation Rule ignores the northward movement of the summer flounder population and is therefore inconsistent with National Standards 2, 4, 5, and 7.

i. National Standard 2: Best Scientific Information Available

National Standard 2 provides that "[c]onservation and management measures shall be based upon the best scientific information available." 16 U.S.C. § 1851(a)(2). New York ties its appeal to National Standard 2 and notes that the NMFS acknowledged that the "best scientific information available" showed summer flounder populations had shifted northward toward New York. In New York's view, its quota must therefore reflect its increased proximity to the summer flounder populations. New York argues that by keeping each state's baseline quota unchanged from the 1993 Allocation Rule, and by evenly splitting each state's surplus quota during good fishing years, the 2020 Allocation Rule is not "based upon" the recent concentration of summer flounder near New York and other northern states. **[—13—]**

We disagree. New York is correct that the phrase "based upon" implies the agency must use (and not merely consider) the location of summer flounder populations when crafting the fishery management plan. "In its plain meaning, 'based on' means 'having as the foundation' or 'arising from.'" *Env't Def. v. E.P.A.*, 369 F.3d 193, 203 (2d Cir. 2004). However, the agency did use these fish location data. The new surplus quotas in the 2020 Allocation Rule are based, to some degree, on the northward movement of summer flounder. As the NMFS explained, the surplus quotas are meant to "generally" shift fishing rights during good fishing years. 85 Fed. Reg. at 80,663. They "reduce the proportion of quota for states at the southern end of summer flounder distribution (North Carolina, Virginia, and New Jersey) and increase allocation for many northern states, including New York." *Id.* New York's quota increases from 7% to 12% during surplus periods, while states now farther away from the summer flounder see corresponding decreases in their quotas. The agency explained that it introduced the surplus quotas to "reflect[] the shift of the center of summer flounder biomass." *Id.* Accordingly, the 2020 Allocation Rule is "based upon" the shifted location of the summer flounder—and New York can catch a higher percentage of fish under **[—14—]** the current rule than the previous rule—just not to a degree that New York would prefer.

Moreover, the NMFS can base its rule upon multiple sets of "scientific information." The MSA does not restrict National Standard 2 to encompass fish location data alone; other types of scientific information may merit greater consideration.[5] Here, the primary data that

[5] The MSA requires the Secretary of Commerce to establish advisory guidelines based on the national standards. These guidelines lack the force of law but "assist in the development" of fishery management plans. 16 U.S.C. § 1851(b). For National Standard 2, the guidelines state that scientific data should include "biological, ecological, environmental, economic, and sociological scientific information." 50 C.F.R. § 600.315(a). Historical data, such as landings data, may be useful so long as they

the NMFS employed were landings data: statistics showing which fishing communities landed summer flounder in previous years. New York does not dispute that landings data have remained the same since the 1993 Allocation Rule, or that landings data remain the **{–109–}** "best" information available to determine which fishing communities depend on the summer flounder today. NMFS has prioritized landings data over fish location data when allocating state quotas. That is a choice rooted in the agency's technical expertise—for which it enjoys substantial deference. *See Env't Def.*, 369 F.3d at 204. **[—15—]**

ii. National Standards 4, 5, and 7: Fairness and Efficiency

New York also contends the 2020 Allocation Rule violates National Standards 4, 5, and 7. National Standard 4 provides that "[c]onservation and management measures shall not discriminate between residents of different States" and that allocation of fishing privileges shall be "fair and equitable to all such fishermen." 16 U.S.C. § 1851(a)(4). National Standards 5 and 7 call for such measures, "where practicable," to "consider efficiency in the utilization of fishery resources" and to "minimize costs and avoid unnecessary duplication." *Id.* §§ 1851(a)(5), (7). Similar to its previous argument, New York says it is unfair and inefficient to allocate higher quotas to states that are farther away from summer flounder populations.

We disagree with this argument as well. The NMFS articulated why it balanced the national standards the way it did, and why it rejected the location-based rule that New York seeks. Regarding the fairness and equity concerns in National Standard 4, the NMFS explained why it found it would be unfair to reduce baseline quotas for communities in states who have become economically dependent, over time, on fishing for summer flounder. In doing so, the NMFS explicitly balanced National Standard 4 against National Standard 8, which **[—16—]** requires management measures to "take into account the importance of fishery resources to fishing communities" and "minimize adverse economic impacts on such communities" where practicable. 16 U.S.C. § 1851(a)(8). By including ten standards, the MSA contemplates that other fishery management considerations—here, the inertia of fishing industries established over decades—can outweigh equitability concerns that flow from the transitory movement of the summer flounder. "The [NMFS] is allowed, under this authority, to sacrifice the interests of some groups of fishermen, for the benefit as the [NMFS] sees it of the fishery as a whole." *All. Against IFQs*, 84 F.3d at 350.

As for the efficiency and cost concerns in National Standards 5 and 7, the NMFS reasoned that southern states' operations involve longer trips and larger vessels built in reliance on their higher quotas. A location-based rule, the agency explained, would ignore the "substantial variability in the mobility of each state's fleet" and the "traditional areas of operation for each state's fleet." 85 Fed. Reg. at 80,663. Put differently, it would not necessarily be efficient for a southern state to scrap its existing (longer-range) fleet just for a northern state to expand its (shorter-range) fleet. That is a policy judgment the agency was entitled to draw based on **[—17—]** the landings data it reviewed. *See F.C.C. v. Prometheus Radio Project*, 141 S. Ct. 1150, 1158 (2021).

* * *

The NMFS adopted a rule that sought to "balance preservation of historical state access and infrastructure at recent quota levels, with the intent to provide equitability among states when the stock and quota are at higher levels." 85 Fed. Reg. at 80,663. We cannot say that this adjustment to the previous rule—the result of balancing ten different national standards—lacked a rational basis articulated in the administrative record. *See State Farm*, 463 U.S. at 43. We therefore **{–110–}** conclude the NMFS did not violate the MSA or the APA when it set summer flounder quotas through the 2020 Allocation Rule.

---

are "evaluated for [their] relevance to inform the current situation." *Id.* § 600.315(a)(6)(v)(B).

CONCLUSION

We have considered New York's remaining arguments and find them to be without merit. Accordingly, we **AFFIRM** the judgment of the district court.

United States Court of Appeals
for the Second Circuit

No. 22-766

EZRASONS, INC.
VS.
TRAVELERS INDEM. CO.

Appeal from the United States District Court for the Southern District of New York

Decided: December 26, 2023

Citation: 89 F.4th 388, 11 Adm. R. 189 (2d Cir. 2023).

Before **LEVAL**, **CHIN**, and **NATHAN**, Circuit Judges.

[—2—] {-391-} LEVAL, Circuit Judge:

This is an appeal by plaintiff Ezrasons, Inc. (the "Insured") from the grant of summary judgment by the United States District Court for the Southern District of New York (Lorna G. Schofield, *J.*), in favor **{-392-}** of defendant **[—3—]** The Travelers Indemnity Company ("Travelers"),[1] the insurer under a marine cargo insurance policy (the "Policy"). The Insured, which is engaged in the garment trade, suffered a loss of insured goods of a value, according to the Insured, exceeding $600,000 while the goods were stored in a warehouse owned and operated by Chamad Warehouse, Inc.,[2] in Marion, North Carolina. The warehouse was consumed by fire on August 14, 2019. Travelers paid the Insured $250,000, but declined to pay more based on its contention that the Policy's coverage was limited to $250,000, because the warehouse building where the goods were destroyed was not an "Approved Location" under the Policy. If the warehouse qualified as an "Approved Location," the coverage limit would be $600,000. **[—4—]**

The Insured brought this action originally in the New York State courts in March 2021 to recover the higher amount. Travelers removed the case to the United States District Court on grounds of diversity of citizenship. 28 U.S.C. § 1441(b). The parties submitted a joint letter to the district court stating their shared belief that the case could "be resolved as a matter of law without need for a factfinder's determination as to material facts . . . [and that it was] appropriate to cross-move for summary judgment without exchanging discovery . . . ." App'x at 374. Both parties then moved for summary judgment. The district court agreed with Travelers and ruled that the warehouse was unambiguously not within the Policy's definition of an "Approved Location."

In our view, the Policy was ambiguous as to whether the warehouse where the destruction occurred was an "Approved Location." Furthermore, the district court erroneously excluded admissible evidence by which the Insured sought to prove that the warehouse was an "Approved Location." Finally, because the extrinsic evidence available to aid in resolving the ambiguity does not furnish a basis for preferring either possible meaning, New York law dictates that the ambiguity should be resolved in favor of the **[—5—]** insured. We accordingly vacate the district court's judgment and remand with instructions to enter judgment in favor of the Insured.

BACKGROUND

Many of the facts are not in dispute. The Policy provided coverage for "goods and/or merchandise while temporarily detained in warehouses and/or processing locations" within the contiguous United States and Canada. App'x at 135, 513. The maximum limit of coverage depended on whether the loss occurred at an "Approved Location." In the part

[1] Apparently, it is unclear which of the companies within the Travelers complex is the insurer. The company named as defendant in the complaint is The Travelers Indemnity Company. Defendant, however, asserts in its brief that the Insurer is in fact Travelers Property Casualty Company of America. Appellee's Br. at 41. In any event, it appears, at least at this stage, that nothing turns on which of the Travelers companies is party to the contract of insurance. We refer to defendant as "Travelers."

[2] It is not clear whether the name of the warehousing company is "Chamad Warehouse, Inc." or "Chamad, Inc.," *see* App'x at 557, but neither party has raised any argument that would be affected by the difference. We will refer to the company simply as "Chamad."

of the Policy where "Approved Locations" were listed, two were specified: One of the two, the pertinent one, was "CHAMAD WAREHOUSE, INC. 371 Branch Street[,] Marion, NC 28752" (with a coverage limit of $600,000). App'x at 137. Under a subsection entitled "Unnamed Domestic Locations," the agreement provided **{-393-}** that "goods and/or merchandise in any <u>public warehouse or processing center</u> not listed above" (i.e., not "Approved Locations") will be covered only up to $250,000. App'x at 138.

It is undisputed that "371 Branch Street," the address listed in the Policy as the address of an "Approved Location," was renumbered to "56 **[—6—]** Branch Street," so that, with the parties' agreement, we read the Policy as if it said "CHAMAD WAREHOUSE, INC., 56 Branch Street."

It is also undisputed that Chamad operates its warehousing business in three warehouse buildings situated on a 19.03-acre parcel of land. Travelers has not rebutted the Insured's evidence that the lot is surrounded by a continuous chain link fence. One side of the irregularly shaped parcel borders Branch Street, where one of its three warehouses with the address 56 Branch Street is located. A second warehouse on the parcel, the one that burned, fronts on Virginia Road. There is evidence that, at least for some purposes, this warehouse was known as 1386 Virginia Road.

The Insured consigned its goods to Chamad for storage. There is no evidence that, prior to the fire, there was any communication between the Insured and Chamad as to which of the three warehouses would be, or was being, used for the storage. The Insured, furthermore, submitted the unrebutted affidavit of Chamad President Steve Guffey, stating that goods entrusted to Chamad are stored in any of the three warehouses. Chamad placed the Insured's goods in the warehouse that fronts on Virginia Road, where they were destroyed by a fire. **[—7—]**

In presenting and disputing their cross motions for summary judgment, the parties submitted evidence bearing on whether the destroyed warehouse came within the Policy's specification of an "Approved Location." Travelers cited the report of the Marion Fire Department with respect to its response to the fire, stating that the fire occurred at 1386 Virginia Road. It also cited the satellite map maintained by the McDowell County Tax Assessor showing rooftop views of Chamad's 19.03-acre parcel, with street-address numbers added to individual rooftops. On that document, the warehouse fronting on Branch Street has the number "56" superimposed on its rooftop. The warehouse fronting on Virginia Road has the number "1386" superimposed on its rooftop.

The Insured submitted a Deed of Trust by which Chamad had conveyed the 19.03-acre parcel in trust for the benefit of a lending bank, as security for its indebtedness. The deed, naming Chamad as Grantor and giving its address as 56 Branch Street, conveyed to the Trustee all of Grantor's right, title, and interest in the 19.03 acres of "Real Property . . . commonly known as 56 Branch St, Marion, NC 28752" "together with all existing or **[—8—]** subsequently erected or affixed buildings . . . ." App'x at 444.[3] In addition, the Insured **{-394-}** submitted the sworn declaration of its President Guffey stating that "[t]he Chamad Warehouse is located at 56 Branch Street, Marion, North Carolina."

---

[3] The Insured also cited newspaper articles that refer to the warehouse fire as taking place at "Chamad Warehouse." App'x at 461–79. Travelers argues that this evidence was inadmissible hearsay. We are inclined to disagree. Hearsay is defined in Rule 801 of the Federal Rules of Evidence as a declarant's statement made otherwise than while testifying in the current trial or hearing, which is offered by a party to prove the truth of what was asserted in the statement. Fed. R. Evid. 801(c). The newspaper evidence was offered not to prove that the warehouse on Virginia Road was owned and operated by Chamad, but to prove that it was known as part of the Chamad Warehouse. In any event, we make no ruling on the question because these newspaper articles play no role in our decision to grant judgment to the Insured. Our reasoning would be the same regardless of whether this evidence had been offered.

The district court denied the Insured's motion for summary judgment and granted Travelers' motion. *Ezrasons, Inc. v. Travelers Indem. Co.*, No. 21-3165, 2022 WL 768366 (S.D.N.Y. Mar. 14, 2022). The court reasoned that the fire occurred at 1386 Virginia Road, which unambiguously is not 56 Branch Street.[4] *Id.* at *3. Explaining that the Policy is unambiguous in naming the **[—9—]** Branch Street address, and not 1386 Viginia Road, as an "Approved Location," it ruled that the Insured's evidence seeking to show that 56 Branch Street was the address of all three warehouses must be rejected because it impermissibly relied on extrinsic or parol evidence to create ambiguity in an unambiguous agreement. *Id.*

This appeal followed.

DISCUSSION

I. Standard of review.

A district court's grant of summary judgment is reviewed by a court of appeals de novo, "construing the evidence in the light most favorable to the party against whom summary judgment was granted and drawing all reasonable inferences in that party's favor." *Bey v. City of New York*, 999 F.3d 157, 164 (2d Cir. 2021) (citing *Sista v. CDC Ixis N. Am., Inc.*, 445 F.3d 161, 168–69 (2d Cir. 2006)).

Summary judgment should be granted only if "there is no genuine dispute as to any material fact and the movant is entitled to judgment as a matter of law." Fed. R. Civ. P. 56(a). A genuine dispute as to a material fact **[—10—]** "exists and summary judgment is therefore improper 'where the evidence is such that a reasonable jury could decide in the non-movant's favor.'" *Lucente v. County of Suffolk*, 980 F.3d 284, 296 (2d Cir. 2020) (quoting *Beyer v. County of Nassau*, 524 F.3d 160, 163 (2d Cir. 2008)). "[S]ummary judgment should usually be denied" if the "resolution of a dispute turns on the meaning of an ambiguous term or phrase." *Dish Network Corp. v. Ace Am. Ins. Co.*, 21 F.4th 207, 212 (2d Cir. 2021) (quoting *Fed. Ins. Co. v. Am. Home Assurance Co.*, 639 F.3d 557, 567 (2d Cir. 2011)).

When parties cross-move for summary judgment, as done here, each motion is analyzed separately, "in each case construing the evidence in the light most favorable to the non-moving party." *Schwebel v. Crandall*, 967 F.3d 96, 102 (2d Cir. 2020). "[T]he fact that both sides have moved for summary judgment does not mean that the court" is required to enter judgment "for one side or the other." *Schwabenbauer v. Bd. of Educ. of City Sch. Dist. of City of Olean*, 667 F.2d 305, 313 (2d Cir. 1981); *see also Morales v. Quintel Ent., Inc.*, 249 F.3d 115, 121 (2d Cir. 2001). **[—11—]**

II. New York law as to ambiguity in insurance policies.

Under New York law,[5] an insurance policy is a contract, and unambiguous **{–395–}** provisions are given their plain and ordinary meaning. *Universal Am. Corp. v. Nat'l Union Fire Ins. Co. of Pittsburgh, Pa.*, 25 N.Y.3d 675, 680 (2015). Whether or not a term of a contract is ambiguous is a question of law that is reviewed by the appellate court de novo. *Dish Network Corp.*, 21 F.4th at 212 (quoting *Duane Reade, Inc. v. St. Paul Fire & Marine Ins. Co.*, 600 F.3d 190, 201 (2d Cir. 2010)); *see also Donohue v. Cuomo*, 38 N.Y.3d 1, 13 (2022).

Ambiguity exists "where [a contract's] terms are subject to more than one reasonable interpretation." *Universal Am. Corp.*, 25 N.Y.3d at 680. "[T]he test to determine whether an insurance contract is ambiguous focuses on

[4] The district court's first reason for its judgment was that the "Approved Location" listed in the Policy is 371 Branch Street and neither party contends that the fire occurred at 371 Branch Street. *Id.* at *3. Travelers, however, as noted above, agrees that 371 Branch Street was renumbered to 56 Branch **[—9—]** Street and that the Policy should therefore be read as if it said "56 Branch Street." We accordingly reject that reason for granting judgment to Travelers.

[5] We apply New York state law to this case because the parties' briefs both assume New York state law governs and such "implied consent is . . . sufficient to establish the applicable choice of law." *Trikona Advisers Ltd. v. Chugh*, 846 F.3d 22, 31 (2d Cir. 2017) (quoting *Arch Ins. Co. v. Precision Stone, Inc.*, 584 F.3d 33, 39 (2d Cir. 2009)).

the reasonable expectations of the average insured upon reading the policy and employing common speech . . . ." *Id.* (quoting *Mostow v. State Farm Ins. Cos.*, 88 N.Y.2d 321, 326–27 (1996)). **[—12—]**

Ordinarily, in assessing whether a contract is ambiguous, a court looks within only the four corners of the document; extrinsic or parole evidence is usually "not admissible to create an ambiguity in a written agreement which is complete and clear and unambiguous upon its face." *Donohue*, 38 N.Y.3d at 12–13 (quoting *W.W.W. Assocs., Inc. v. Giancontieri*, 77 N.Y.2d 157, 163 (1990)). However, contractual ambiguities come in two forms – patent and latent. *See* 2 Couch on Ins. 3d § 21:12. Latent ambiguities present an exception to the rule that courts must look within the four corners of a document to determine ambiguity. "A patent ambiguity appears on the face of the instrument while a latent ambiguity is raised by evidence[.]" *Petrie v. Trs. of Hamilton Coll.*, 158 N.Y. 458, 464 (1899). Latent ambiguities occur when, although the words of the contract appear on their face to have a clear meaning, the evidence shows that they could apply to different facts, objects, or circumstances. *Id.*; *see also Teig v. Suffolk Oral Surgery Assocs.*, 2 A.D.3d 836, 837 (N.Y. 2d Dep't 2003) ("Even where an agreement seems clear on its face, a 'latent ambiguity' may exist by reason of 'the ambiguous or obscure state of extrinsic circumstances to which the words of the instrument refer'" (quoting *Lerner v. Lerner*, 120 A.D.2d 243, 247 (N.Y. 2d Dep't 1986))); *Morgan Stanley Grp. Inc. v. New Eng.* **[—13—]** *Ins. Co.*, 225 F.3d 270, 276 (2d Cir. 2000) ("[A] contract may be ambiguous when applied to one set of facts but not another."). If a person contracts for value to bequeath "my house to my daughter," the contract appears to be unambiguous on its face. *See Petrie*, 158 N.Y. at 463. Nonetheless, if application of the terms of the contract to the facts reveals that the person making the commitment had two houses (or two daughters) and nothing in the terms of the contract clarifies which house (or daughter) was intended, the contract presents a latent ambiguity which cannot be interpreted without making resort to extrinsic evidence. *See id.*

An example of latent ambiguity, familiar to many law students, is the story from *Raffles v. Wichelhaus*, [1864] 159 Eng. Rep. 375 (Exch.), of a cargo of cotton contracted to be delivered from Bombay to Liverpool aboard the ship Peerless. When the cargo arrived in Liverpool aboard a **{-396-}** ship named Peerless, the consignee refused to accept delivery, contending that the contract called for delivery on board another ship Peerless that had arrived in Liverpool from Bombay two months earlier. *Id.* While the contract appeared **[—14—]** unambiguous on its face, application of its terms to real world facts revealed ambiguity.[6] *Id.*

Interpretation of an unambiguous contract is for the court without a role for the factfinder. *See Universal Am. Corp.*, 25 N.Y.3d at 680. However, if the contract is ambiguous, then relevant extrinsic evidence should be admitted and considered by the factfinder to resolve the ambiguity. *State v. Home Indem. Co.*, 66 N.Y.2d 669, 671 (1985); *Dish Network Corp.*, 21 F.4th at 212; *see also In re Van Vliet*, 181 A.D. 879, 880 (N.Y. 2d Dep't 1918), *aff'd* 224 N.Y. 572 (1918) (applying this principle in the context of a latent ambiguity). When the resolution of a contract depends on an ambiguous term or phrase, summary judgment should usually be denied and the ambiguity submitted to the factfinder for resolution by resort to the extrinsic evidence. *Dish Network Corp.*, 21 F.4th at 212. But, "if the tendered extrinsic evidence is itself conclusory and will not resolve the equivocality of the language of the contract, the issue remains a question of law for the court" and there is no role **[—15—]** for the factfinder in interpreting the contract. *Home Indem. Co.*, 66 N.Y.2d at 671.

When dealing with insurance policies, it is a "fundamental" principle of New York law that

[6] The court found that mutual mistake between the parties meant there had been no meeting of the minds sufficient to form a contract. Neither party contends that here. Further, adopting such an interpretation here would contravene the policy preferences of New York law to award judgment to the insured in cases such as these. *See, e.g.*, *Fed. Ins. Co. v. Int'l Bus. Machs. Corp.*, 18 N.Y.3d 642, 646 (2012).

ambiguities should be interpreted against the insurer and in favor of the insured. *Thomas J. Lipton, Inc. v. Liberty Mut. Ins. Co.*, 34 N.Y.2d 356, 361 (1974); *Int'l Bus. Machs.*, 18 N.Y.3d at 646 (citing *Breed v. Ins. Co. of N. Am.*, 46 N.Y.2d 351, 353 (1978)). This presumption, however, is used only "as a matter of last resort," after making use of all other available tools to resolve the ambiguity. *U.S. Fire Ins. Co. v. Gen. Reins. Corp.*, 949 F.2d 569, 573 (2d Cir. 1991) (quoting *Schering Corp. v. Home Ins. Co.*, 712 F.2d 4, 10 n.2 (2d Cir. 1983)). When that presumption is invoked by the insured, the insurer bears the burden of showing that the insured's interpretation is unreasonable. *Haber v. St. Paul Guardian Ins. Co.*, 137 F.3d 691, 697–98 (2d Cir. 1998).

We accordingly first determine whether there is an ambiguity, either patent or latent, in the terms of the Policy that prevents deciding the dispute solely on the basis of the terms of the contract without reference to extrinsic factors. If so, we assess whether the parties provided admissible extrinsic evidence that could resolve the ambiguity. If they have not, then New York **[—16—]** law dictates that the ambiguity should be decided in favor of the insured, as a matter of law, provided the insured's interpretation is reasonable. If they have, then we must remand so that the extrinsic evidence may be considered by the factfinder.

III. Is the Policy ambiguous?

Each side contends, in support of its motion for summary judgment, that the **{-397-}** Policy unambiguously supports its side of the dispute.

A

The Insured contends that, in naming CHAMAD WAREHOUSE, INC., 56 Branch Street as an "Approved Location," the Policy unambiguously so identifies the entire 19.03-acre parcel, including the three warehouses on it. This is for two reasons: First, the "Approved Location" designation gives the company name as its focus. Accordingly what is identified is not merely a single building, but all that is part of Chamad Warehouse, Inc., at 56 Branch Street, which is the entirety of the 19.03-acre parcel. Second, it argues that because the address of the 19.03-acre parcel is 56 Branch Street, so identified by the deed in the public land records, that designation refers to any and all Chamad warehouses on the 19.03 acres. **[—17—]**

We reject the argument. When one considers that there is a Chamad warehouse that is publicly identified as bearing the address 56 Branch Street, the designation could also be reasonably read to identify only that warehouse as an "Approved Location."

B

Travelers similarly contends that the Policy unambiguously names only the warehouse physically located at 56 Branch Street as an "Approved Location," and not the other two warehouses, which are physically located at different parts of the 19.03-acre parcel, and in particular not the warehouse identified in public documents as located at 1386 Virginia Road. It argues that, if the warehouse fronting on Virginia Road is known as 1386 Virginia Road, it cannot also have as an address 56 Branch Street, but cites no rule of law or evidence of usage to support that proposition, especially as to a circumstance where there is evidence reasonably supporting the use of both addresses.

It contends that the term "Location" unambiguously means a single building and not a parcel containing multiple buildings. We find no merit in the argument. The word "Location," without further explanation, does not **[—18—]** communicate that it necessarily means a single building, as opposed to two or more buildings on the same parcel of land. Travelers has pointed to nothing in the Policy (or in application documents) specifying that a "Location," as used in the term "Approved Location," must be an individual building and cannot refer to multiple buildings at the same address. While it is true that an address such as 56 Branch Street, particularly in an urban context, often identifies nothing other than a single building, there is nothing unusual, particularly in the case of business companies or other institutions, in the use of a street address to identify an entire campus or parcel that includes multiple buildings. In fact, it is surely often the case that the additional buildings can have no other address (other than a subdivision of the same address) because no other part of the parcel touches on an identifiable street or road. The affidavit of Frank Harten, a Managing Director of Travelers, implicitly acknowledges that it is not unusual that companies in the warehousing business are identified by a single address that includes multiple warehouse buildings. He testified that in such cases, Travelers will "identify each building under the warehouse schedule as 111 Smith Street, **[—19—]** Building #1, 111 Smith Street, Building #2, and 111 Smith Street, Building #3." App'x at 553.

We can certainly understand why it might be important to an insurer such as Travelers to know exactly which building is being used as the warehouse in deciding **{-398-}** whether to insure warehoused goods and on what terms. If the terms of the Policy told the Insured that a "Location" submitted for Travelers' approval must be a single building, and that when insurance is sought classifying multiple buildings as Approved Locations, each building must be separately identified, the inclusion of such terms would likely dispel the ambiguity that inhabits the present Policy. It would be an easy matter for Travelers to insert such a clarifying limitation into the documentation of a policy. But it did not do so. It drafted an ambiguous policy as to the scope of Approved Locations. Upon considering the Insured's evidence, including Chamad's Deed of Trust, which gives Chamad's address and that of the entire 19.03-acre parcel, including the buildings on it, as 56 Branch Street, the Policy can reasonably be read as giving "Approved Location" status to all three warehouses on the parcel located at 56 Branch Street. **[—20—]**

It is not always easy to distinguish between patent ambiguity and latent ambiguity. While both parties argue that the Policy is patently unambiguous, each undercuts that argument by relying on extrinsic evidence to support its contention about what is meant by its reference to "56 Branch Street." In any event, this case has much in common with the case of the ship Peerless. The words of the contract did not make clear what warehouse or warehouses come within the scope of its reference to 56 Branch Street. When one looks at all of the contextual facts, they could as easily support the Insured's argument as Travelers', and vice versa. By looking solely at the terms of the Policy without reference to external facts, it is not clear whether the pertinent "Approved Location" includes only the warehouse building located at 56 Branch Street, or all three warehouse buildings on the parcel located at 56 Branch Street. By reason of the latent ambiguity, it was error of the district court to decline to consider the extrinsic evidence. When a contract is ambiguous, whether patently or latently, refusal to consider the extrinsic evidence could easily lead a court to construe the contract to mean something that neither side intended at the time of contracting. **[—21—]**

In support of its decision not to consider the extrinsic evidence, the district court cited the opinion of the New York Court of Appeals in *Donohue v. Cuomo*, 38 N.Y. 3d 1, 13 (2022), for the proposition that that extrinsic evidence "is not admissible to create an ambiguity in a written agreement which is complete and clear and unambiguous upon its face." *Ezrasons*, 2022 WL 768366, at *3 (quoting *Donohue*, 38 N.Y.3d at 13). We believe this was an oversimplification and a misinterpretation of the quoted passage from *Donohue*, rendering it misleading. Notwithstanding the ordinary rule that extrinsic evidence cannot be used to vary the terms of a contract whose meaning is clear, it has long been accepted in New York law that an exception to this principle arises in the relatively rare circumstances where the application of the contract terms to the facts encounters a latent ambiguity that leaves the meaning of the contract unclear. *See Petrie*, 158 N.Y. at 463–64. The *Donohue* opinion did not purport to overturn this rule of New York law which is both long established and rooted in logic. The *Donohue* court made no suggestion that the circumstance it dealt with was one of latent ambiguity, such as arises when the meaning of a vital term of the contract cannot be determined because, upon consideration of extrinsic evidence, that term **[—22—]** could refer to one thing or another. An agreement can appear to be "complete and clear and unambiguous on its face," *Ezrasons*, 2022 WL 768366, at *3 (quoting **{-399-}** *Donohue*, 38 N.Y.3d at 13), but its apparently clear language may nonetheless conceal a latent ambiguity that becomes apparent when one seeks to apply its terms to the facts. If so, it becomes necessary to consider extrinsic evidence to understand the meaning of the contract. *See Petrie*, 158 N.Y. at 463–64. For these reasons we reject Travelers' argument that the unambiguous terms of the Policy require affirmance of the district court's grant of summary judgment to it.

C

Travelers further argues that "substantially similar" policy language has been held to unambiguously support Travelers' interpretation by courts within our circuit. Appellee's Br. at 26. We disagree. The cases Travelers cites do not support its argument. In *LaptopPlaza, Inc. v. Starr Indemnity & Liability Co.*, 697 F. App'x 20, 20–21 (2d Cir. 2017) (summary order), this court found that goods stored in a trailer abutting a warehouse were not "detained in warehouses" as required for the policy coverage to attach. In *Royal Insurance Co. of America v. Sportswear Group, LLC*, 85 F. Supp. 2d 275, 277, 280 (S.D.N.Y. **[—23—]** 2000), the district court for the Southern District of New York similarly found that goods that were stolen while sitting outdoors were not covered by a policy that covered only goods "stored in warehouses." The fact that a separate part of the policy referenced goods stored "at the approved locations" did not negate the policy requirement that goods must be stored "in warehouses." *Id.* at 280–81. We would make the same ruling as made in *Royal Insurance Co.* if the goods in our case had been stored in a truck or on the ground on the Branch Street property, rather than in a warehouse as unambiguously required by this Policy.

Those two cases do nothing for the insurer's argument. They rule merely that a policy's requirement that the covered goods be stored in a warehouse is not satisfied where goods are stored outside of the warehouse.

Nor are we persuaded by the Insurer's citation to *Starr Indemnity & Liability Co. v. Brightside Corp.*, 388 F. Supp. 3d 304, 339–40 (S.D.N.Y. 2019). In that case, the terms of the policy required that approved locations be on the "schedule on file with [the] underwriters." *Id.* at 338. The question was whether coverage extended to new locations of which the insured notified the insurer, but which had not been added by the insurer to the "schedule on file **[—24—]** with [the] underwriters," or included only those which the insurer had added to "the schedule," as the policy specified. *Id.* at 340. The question was answered by the unambiguous terms of the policy, which limited approved locations to those that had been added to the schedule. *Id.* The court ruled that because the policy specified that in order to be covered as approved locations, the locations must be on "the schedule," the insured's mere notification to the insurer of the locations did not make them approved locations. *Id.* The insured's argument, which the court rejected, was akin to our Insured's arguing that a location should be viewed as approved under this Policy merely because the Insured had submitted the location to the Insurer requesting approval. Such an argument has no merit. That case sheds no light on ours. Again, here there is no question that "CHAMAD WAREHOUSE, INC., 56 Branch Street" is properly on the list of Approved Locations. Our question is what that meant.

IV. *Can the extrinsic evidence submitted by the parties resolve the ambiguity?*

When a contract is ambiguous, we must determine whether extrinsic evidence **{-400-}** provided by the parties can resolve the ambiguity. *Home Indem. Co.*, 66 N.Y.2d at 671. If one or both parties offer extrinsic evidence that is capable **[—25—]** of resolving the ambiguity as to the meaning of the contract given its bearing on the facts, there is an issue of material fact to be resolved by the factfinder, which will dictate the interpretation of the contract. *Id.* at 671–72. Summary judgment is inappropriate in such a case. If there is no extrinsic evidence available, or the evidence is conclusory or incapable of resolving the ambiguity, then there is no role for the factfinder as to the meaning of the contract. *Id.*

In our case, both parties have offered admissible extrinsic evidence in support of their respective contentions on how the disputed issue of material fact should be resolved.

A

With regards to the address of the warehouse, Travelers submitted evidence that 56 Branch Street can refer to the warehouse building at that address and that the warehouse destroyed by fire is, at least for some purposes, designated by the address 1386 Virginia Road. The Insured submitted evidence that Chamad's 19.03-acre parcel in its entirety bears the address 56 Branch Street. Neither side, however, has submitted evidence that effectively rebuts the other side's documentary evidence. Addresses do not **[—26—]** necessarily denote only a single building and can be ambiguous in that an address can both describe a single building and a larger plot containing multiple buildings, all of which can have the same address. "Location," the word used in the Policy, is even less precise as to what it does or does not mean. The facts that the building at the Branch Street entrance to the parcel is for some purposes known as 56 Branch Street and that the building destroyed by fire is for some purposes known as 1386 Virginia Road do not rebut the Insured's evidence that the address of the 19.03-acre parcel and all buildings on it is 56 Branch Street. In this case, the aggregate of the extrinsic evidence offered by the parties is incapable of resolving the ambiguity because it furnishes no rational or logical basis for preferring one meaning over the other. A jury deciding the case would not find answers in the parties' extrinsic evidence.

B

Travelers next argues that the declarations of Frank Harten are competent extrinsic evidence showing that Travelers did not intend for the warehouse fronting Virginia Road to be part of an "Approved Location," because "Travelers was neither asked to approve the Virginia Road **[—27—]** Warehouse nor afforded the opportunity to underwrite that location." App'x at 184. According to Travelers, this extrinsic evidence resolves the ambiguity in its favor.

In his first declaration (dated August 12, 2021), Harten stated that he has "personal knowledge concerning the comprehensive underwriting process performed by Travelers in cases where an insured requests to have specific warehouse locations approved by Travelers and added to a marine cargo policy[.]" App'x at 184. He described the extensive processes by which Travelers "develop[s] rates [for the particular warehouse] based on projections of future losses" by "obtain[ing] data about past losses and then us[ing] probabilities to predict whether future losses will be higher, lower or the same . . . ." App'x at 186. An "essential component" of the process is the receipt of a "COPE" report from ISO (the Insurance Services Office), which furnishes information relating to the "physical **C**onstruction features of the **{-401-}** warehouse location . . . , the contents and operations of the **O**ccupancy inside the warehouse location, the public and private fire **P**rotection available . . . , and the **E**xternal exposures adjacent to or nearby to the location." App'x at 186–87 (emphases in original). Travelers also "requests this type of **[—28—]** information directly from the insured/its broker, and underwriters will then compare that information against the information that is contained on the ISO Loss Report." App'x at 187. It also collects information by "enter[ing] the Travelers Risk Control Portal to see if Travelers ever inspected the specific warehouse location in the past," and, if so, retrieving the inspection report and providing it to the underwriter. App'x at 187. It will "utilize certain proprietary programs and systems to evaluate flood, wind, and earthquake risks." *Id.* Based on careful evaluation of all this information, it will:

> make a decision if the location is insurable . . . [and] will determine rate/premiums, terms and conditions, deductible and limits . . . [as well as] decide if coverage will be granted for flood, wind and earthquake . . . . The underwriter will view each location separately and may have different rates,

terms and conditions or will even exclude flood at one location.

App'x at 187. "Unlike the Virginia Road Warehouse, Travelers was advised about the Branch Street Warehouse which was underwritten per the guidelines above." App'x at 188. He concluded, "The Virginia Road Warehouse was not a location submitted or approved by Travelers, which is why it falls into the classification of an 'Unnamed Domestic Location' which carries a lower insurance limit." App'x at 188. **[—29—]**

We are not persuaded by these arguments. We find, for several reasons, that Harten's declaration gives little or no support to them. To the extent that it tells that Travelers never conducted the elaborate inquiries and evaluations that assist in making an informed decision to insure a particular warehouse and on what terms, concerning the warehouse that burned, and that Travelers never intended to underwrite it, what Travelers did or did not do on its own in agreeing to the Policy language is irrelevant to what the Insured could reasonably understand to be the meaning of the Policy. Harten did not assert that these facts or intentions were communicated by Travelers to the Insured. *See Home Indem. Co.*, 66 N.Y.2d at 671–72.

To the extent that Harten does make statements about the contents of negotiating exchanges between Travelers and the Insured, which might be relevant to interpreting ambiguities of the Policy—such as Harten's statements that Travelers was not "asked [by the Insured] to approve the Virginia Road Warehouse," App'x at 184, and that "[t]he Virginia Road Warehouse was not a location submitted . . . [to] Travelers, which is why it falls into the classification of an 'Unnamed Domestic Location," App'x at 188—these assertions are to no effect because Harten, so far as his declaration **[—30—]** reveals, had no personal knowledge of the exchanges between Travelers and the Insured that resulted in their agreement on the Policy. App'x at 184. He is therefore not a competent witness on that subject, so that his testimony that the Insured did not request "Approved Location" status for the Virginia Road warehouse must be disregarded. *See* Fed. R. Civ. P. 56(c)(4). ("An affidavit or declaration used to support or oppose a motion [for summary judgment] must be made on personal knowledge, set out facts that would be admissible in evidence, and show that the affiant or declarant is competent to testify on the matters stated."). Nor did Harten's declarations include business records, which, depending on what they say, **{-402-}** might have furnished a competent source for his contentions.

The same is true of his further assertions that Travelers "was never afforded the opportunity to underwrite the Virginia Road Warehouse." App'x at 184, 188. This assertion is similarly beyond Harten's testimonial competence because it depends on the content of exchanges between Travelers and the Insured of which Harten had no personal knowledge.

Going further, Travelers' assertion that giving Approved status to the warehouse adjacent to Virginia Road would be unreasonable and unfair to **[—31—]** Travelers because Travelers never had the opportunity to assess its insurability is also logically unpersuasive. Granting that Travelers could make a better-informed insurance decision if it knew exactly in which warehouse building or buildings the insured goods would be stored, several paths were open to it. It needed only to tell its Insured that it would grant "Approved Location" status only to an individual warehouse located at 56 Branch Street, and that, if there was a possibility that the goods would be housed in other Chamad warehouse buildings, the Insured needed to so specify or run the risk of having coverage limited to the maximum for Unnamed Locations. Alternatively, Travelers could have simply worded its Policy to make this clear. Either avenue would have given Travelers the information permitting it to make an informed assessment of the risks attending the warehouse on Virginia Road or else limit its coverage responsibility to a level it was willing to accept without investigating the additional warehouses' insurance worthiness. There is no basis for Travelers' claim that it was denied the opportunity to make an informed decision or that interpreting the Policy to cover the warehouse fronting on Virginia Road would be unfair to it. **[—32—]**

Interpreting the Policy to include within "Approved Locations" any warehouses located at the address furnished by the Insured results solely from Travelers having written its Policy in an ambiguous manner that admits of that understanding. Travelers cannot fairly ask its insureds to bear the brunt of ambiguities that it wrote into its Policy. To the extent Travelers contends that so interpreting its Policy subjects it to unfairness, it is far less unfair than it would be for the court to rule that the Insured must bear the brunt of Travelers having misled it by presenting it with an ambiguous Policy, failing to warn that, despite the absence of anything in the Policy saying so, Approved status with its elevated limits will apply only to individually identified buildings and not to buildings reasonably identified by their collective addresses.[7]

We therefore reject Travelers' arguments based on the contention that it was denied the opportunity to assess the insurability of the warehouse **[—33—]** fronting on Virginia Road and would be subjected to unfairness by our reading the Policy that it wrote to say what it reasonably appears to say.

C

For such intractable circumstances, the law of New York furnishes a solution. When a contract of insurance is ambiguous and the evidence furnishes no basis for resolving the ambiguity, New York law provides that the court's decision must favor the insured over the insurer as **{-403-}** long as the insured's interpretation is reasonable. *See, e.g., Haber*, 137 F.3d at 697–98; *Thomas J. Lipton, Inc.*, 34 N.Y.2d at 361; *Int'l Bus. Machs.*, 18 N.Y.3d at 646 (citing *Breed*, 46 N.Y.2d at 353). As 56 Branch Street is the address of Chamad and of the 19.03-acre parcel on which sat the warehouse that suffered the fire, there is nothing unreasonable about the Insured's interpretation of the Policy's identification of the relevant "Approved Location" "CHAMAD WAREHOUSE, INC., 56 Branch Street" as covering the Chamad warehouse fronting on Virginia Road. Because the Insured's interpretation of an ambiguity in the Policy is reasonable and unrebutted, judgment must be awarded to the Insured. **[—34—]**

It is, of course, theoretically possible that, if the case were remanded for discovery and trial, Travelers might find and present evidence that would support its contentions. But, as noted above, both parties agreed to have the court hear cross-motions for summary judgment without prior discovery proceedings. Either party could have insisted on the opportunity to take discovery before being obliged to defend against the other side's motion for summary judgment. *See* Fed. R. Civ. P 56(d) ("If a nonmovant shows by affidavit or declaration that, for specified reasons, it cannot present facts essential to justify its opposition, the court may: (1) defer considering the motion or deny it; (2) allow time to obtain affidavits or declarations or to take discovery; or (3) issue any other appropriate order."). Both sides instead made the strategic decision to face the other side's motion for summary judgment without discovery. As a consequence of that decision, Travelers, like the Insured, faced the risk that, if the record on the other side's motion showed the other side's entitlement to summary judgment, summary judgment would be granted, conclusively foreclosing any opportunity to take discovery. For the reasons described above, that is what the record showed. Under New York law's requirement that unresolved ambiguities in a contract **[—35—]** of insurance be resolved against the insurer, the Insured showed entitlement to judgment.

CONCLUSION

For the foregoing reasons, the district court's grant of summary judgment to Travelers is VACATED and this case is REMANDED with directions to enter

[7] Travelers argues, in addition, that being a large company experienced in the garment trade, the Insured should have understood that only a specifically identified warehouse would serve as an "Approved Location." The argument has no merit as Travelers submitted no evidence to support the contention that this was the custom of the trade.

judgment in favor of the Insured. Costs to the Insured.

This page intentionally left blank

United States Court of Appeals for the Fourth Circuit

United States Court of Appeals
for the Fourth Circuit

No. 23-1059

SOUTH CAROLINA STATE PORTS AUTH.
vs.
NATIONAL LABOR RELATIONS BD.

On Petition for Review of an Order of the National Labor Relations Board

Decided: July 28, 2023

Citation: 75 F.4th 368, 11 Adm. R. 202 (4th Cir. 2023).

Before **DIAZ,** Chief Judge, **NIEMEYER,** Circuit Judge, and **MOTZ,** Senior Circuit Judge.

[—4—] **{-372-}** **DIAZ,** Chief Judge: **{-373-}**

A collective-bargaining agreement between the International Longshoremen's Association (ILA) and the United States Maritime Alliance (USMX), an association of carriers and other employers, earmarks all container loading and unloading work on the East and Gulf Coasts for the union's members. So when USMX-affiliated ships docked at a new South Carolina terminal that used non-union lift operators, the union sued USMX and its carrier-members for damages. Soon enough, USMX's carrier-members stopped calling at that terminal.

We're asked to determine whether the ILA's lawsuit—and a separate provision of its contract with USMX—violate the National Labor Relations Act, 29 U.S.C. § 151 *et seq*. The National Labor Relations Board held that they don't, and the South Carolina State Ports Authority petitioned for review.

We agree with the Board and deny the petition.

I.

A.

First, some historical context. Before the "container revolution," longshore workers would transfer loose ("break-bulk") cargo piece-by-piece from pier to ship. *Am. Trucking Ass'ns v. NLRB*, 734 F.2d 966, 968 (4th Cir. 1984), *aff'd sub nom. NLRB v. Int'l Longshoremen's Ass'n (ILA II)*, 473 U.S. 61 (1985). But "[a]s might be expected, moving cargo in this break-bulk manner proved expensive and inefficient." **[—5—]**

A more economical method emerged in the mid-1950s with the "containership," a vessel made to transport large containers of cargo. *Id.* at 969. Since containers didn't need to be packed and unpacked at the pier, the new ships could be "loaded or unloaded in a fraction of the time required for a conventional ship." *NLRB v. Int'l Longshoremen's Ass'n (ILA I)*, 447 U.S. 490, 494–95 (1980). And since the containerships spent less time in port and could make more frequent journeys, fewer ships were needed to carry a given volume of cargo. *Id.* at 495.

But as "containerization" streamlined the shipping industry, it also "threatened the jobs of longshoremen by dramatically increasing their productivity." **{-374-}** *Id.* at 496. Because containers could be hooked up to trucks and driven to their destinations, shippers were no longer bound to the ports closest to their customers. They "could now call at ports with cheaper non-union labor, then truck the goods the extra distance, and save money." *Bermuda Container Line Ltd. v. Int'l Longshoremen's Ass'n*, No. 97 CIV. 1257, 1997 WL 795766, at *5 (S.D.N.Y. Dec. 29, 1997). The result was "wide job loss in the longshore industry, and widespread upheaval and acrimony in the management-labor relationship in the industry." *Id.*

B.

In the face of these technological developments, the ILA has sought to maintain its members' traditional work through collective bargaining. The ILA and its constituent local units represent "longshoremen, clerks, checkers, and maintenance employees working on ships and terminals" on the East and Gulf Coasts "from Maine to Texas." J.A. 433–34. **[—6—]** Local 1422, an intervenor here, represents members working at the Port of Charleston, South Carolina.

The ILA has negotiated a series of collective-bargaining agreements—known as "Master Contracts"—with USMX, a multi-employer association of shipping carriers and longshore companies. The current Master Contract, effective from 2018 to 2024, contains several provisions relevant to this appeal.

First, Article I, Section 3 provides that the Master Contract is a "full and complete agreement" between the ILA and USMX on all issues

> relating to the employment of longshore employees on container and ro-ro [roll on/roll off] vessels and container and ro-ro terminals in all ports from Maine to Texas at which ships of USMX carriers and carriers that are subscribers to this Master Contract may call.

J.A. 434.

Second, Appendix A to the Master Contract (the "Containerization Agreement") recognizes the "existing work jurisdiction of ILA employees" and bars USMX from contracting out that work to non-union members. It reads, in part:

> 1. Management and the Carriers recognize the existing work jurisdiction of ILA employees covered by their agreements with the ILA over all container work which historically has been performed by longshoremen and all other ILA crafts at container waterfront facilities. Carriers, direct employers and their agents covered by such agreements agree to employ employees covered by their agreements to perform such work which includes, but which is not limited to:
>
> (a) the loading and discharging of containers on and off ships
> (b) the receipt of cargo
> (c) the delivery of cargo
> (d) the loading and discharging of cargo into and out of containers
> (e) the maintenance and repair of containers
> (f) the inspection of containers at waterfront facilities (TIR men). **[—7—]**
>
> 2. Management, the Carriers, the direct employers and their agents shall not contract out any work covered by this agreement. Any violations of this provision shall be considered a breach of this agreement.
>
> * * *
>
> 9. Violations of Agreement: This Agreement defines the work jurisdiction of employees and prohibits the subcontracting out of any of the work covered hereby. It is understood that the provisions of this Agreement are to be rigidly **{–375–}** enforced in order to protect against the further reduction of the work force. . . . The parties agree that the enforcement of these provisions is especially important and that any violation of such other provisions is of the essence of the Agreement.

J.A. 484–85 (cleaned up).

Finally, Article VII, Section 7 of the Master Contract deals with the anomalous "hybrid labor model" historically used by ports in Wilmington, North Carolina; Charleston, South Carolina; and Savannah, Georgia. Under the hybrid model, non-union employees operate lift equipment to load and unload the containerships and ILA members perform the rest of the longshore work.

It's not clear from the record why the hybrid model arose at these ports. And while the hybrid model seems to violate the no-subcontracting provision (included in all past Master Contracts), the ILA has never sought to enforce the contract's terms against those ports.

The ILA and USMX negotiated Section 7 in 2012 and 2013 to address the hybrid model and kept the provision in their current contract without further discussion. It reads:

Section 7. Port Authorities.

(a) USMX and the ILA shall conduct a study to determine how the business model currently used by port authorities in the Ports of Charleston, SC, Savannah, GA, and Wilmington, NC, could be altered to permit work **[—8—]** currently performed by state employees to be performed by Master Contract-bargaining-unit employees in a more productive, efficient, and competitive fashion. USMX and the ILA will use this study to meet with these port authorities in an effort to convince them to employ Master Contract-bargaining-unit employees.

(b) USMX agrees to formally notify any port authority contemplating the development of or intending to develop a new container handling facility that USMX members may be prohibited from using that new facility if the work at that facility is not performed by Master Contract bargaining-unit employees.

J.A. 449.

USMX and the ILA never conducted the study described in Section 7(a). And they disagree about Section 7(b)'s intended purpose and application. ILA and Local 1422 officials involved in the negotiations believed that Section 7(b) requires USMX carrier-members to refrain from doing business at any new facility where ILA members don't perform all the longshore work. But USMX's former counsel testified that the language was meant to be a compromise, acknowledging the ILA's issues with the hybrid model without binding USMX.

C.

The South Carolina State Ports Authority operates three terminals at the Port of Charleston: the North Charleston Terminal, the Wando Welch Terminal, and the new Hugh K. Leatherman, Sr. Terminal. The North Charleston and Wando Welch Terminals use the hybrid labor model, and USMX carrier-members have long docked at those terminals. The Ports Authority isn't a party to the Master Contract.

In 2020, the Ports Authority announced that it planned to operate the Leatherman Terminal using the same hybrid model. Under the Master Contract's Section 7(b), USMX **[—9—]** notified the Ports Authority that "USMX members may be prohibited from using the new facility . . . if the work at that facility is not performed by Master Contract bargaining-unit employees." J.A. 531. Several USMX carrier-members sent **{–376–}** similar letters to the Ports Authority. Then things fell apart.

USMX, the ILA, the Ports Authority, and the State of South Carolina met several times over the ensuing months but couldn't agree on a work arrangement for the new terminal. At one meeting, the ILA proposed that the existing hybrid terminals be "redline[d]" and allowed to keep using non-union labor, but that all longshore work at the new terminal be performed by ILA members. J.A. 549. The State and the Ports Authority responded that they weren't bound by Section 7(b) and were free to use non-union lift workers at the new terminal just as they had at the older Charleston terminals.

The State and the Ports Authority then filed an unfair labor practice charge with the National Labor Relations Board against the ILA, USMX, and Local 1422. They claimed that the ILA and USMX violated Section 8(e) of the National Labor Relations Act, *see* 29 U.S.C. § 158(e), by agreeing to a "hot cargo" provision—a provision barring an employer from doing business with another party—in Section 7(b) of the Master Contract.

Undeterred by the failed discussions, the Ports Authority began operating the Leatherman Terminal using the hybrid model. Two USMX carrier-members sent ships to the Leatherman Terminal, and the ILA promptly sued them (and USMX) in New Jersey state court.

Among other claims, the ILA alleged that USMX and the carrier-members breached Article I, Section 3 of the Master Contract and Sections 1, 2, and 9 of the Containerization

[—10—] Agreement by docking at Leatherman. Its complaint didn't mention Section 7(b). And while the ILA sought $300 million in damages, the union didn't ask for injunctive relief like assigning union employees to the work. J.A. 529.

Soon after the ILA filed its lawsuit, at least five USMX carrier-members contacted the Ports Authority and demanded to be reassigned from the Leatherman Terminal to the Wando Welch Terminal. One threatened to redirect its vessels to the Port of Savannah, Georgia. The Ports Authority agreed to reassign the vessels, and USMX carrier-members eventually stopped sending ships to the Leatherman Terminal.

The State, the Ports Authority, and USMX then filed more unfair labor practice charges against the ILA and Local 1422, claiming that the ILA's lawsuit also violated the National Labor Relations Act.

II.

A.

The Board's General Counsel consolidated both sets of charges and an Administrative Law Judge ("ALJ") held a hearing and issued a decision.

First, the ALJ rejected the Ports Authority's argument that Section 7(b) of the Master Contract was an illegal "hot cargo" provision. The section's language was facially valid, the ALJ held, because it didn't require USMX to stop doing business with the Ports Authority—it only required USMX to notify the Ports Authority that it "may be prohibited" from using a hybrid facility. J.A. 942. [—11—]

The ALJ acknowledged that the ILA and USMX had debated the provision's meaning and that union officials believed it to bar USMX carrier-members from calling at Leatherman. But he found that the evidence "establishe[d] disagreement, rather than agreement," so it didn't demonstrate a meeting of the minds on the issue. J.A. 943.

Next, however, the ALJ held that the ILA's lawsuit against USMX and the carrier-members **{-377-}** violated the National Labor Relations Act. Rejecting the ILA's argument that the lawsuit had a lawful "work preservation" goal, the ALJ found that the ILA used the Master Contract "as a sword to achieve an unlawful, secondary object"—the acquisition of "all the container work at the Leatherman Terminal, as well as at any future container-handling facilities." J.A. 948–49. And the ALJ further found that the ILA intended its lawsuit to make USMX cease doing business at Leatherman Terminal, violating Section 8(b)(4)(ii)(B) of the Act.

B.

The State, the Ports Authority, and the ILA filed exceptions to the Board's rulings. A three-member panel issued its own opinion, finding for the ILA on both issues.

The Board quickly dismissed the challenge to Section 7(b) of the Master Contract, unanimously affirming the ALJ's ruling "for the reasons stated by the judge." J.A. 1328.

But the Board disagreed that the ILA's lawsuit had an illegal work-acquisition objective. Instead, the Board found, the ILA lawfully sought to preserve its traditional work and jobs—"the loading and unloading generally at East and Gulf Coast ports"—against the technological changes wrought by containerization. J.A. 1332. While the lawsuit may have had the "secondary *effect*" of causing ships to bypass the Port of [—12—] Charleston, that effect was still "incidental to a lawful primary purpose." *Id.* The Board also disagreed with the ALJ's requirement that the ILA show a threat of job losses in Charleston—if such a showing was required, it was measured coastwide and "satisfied by the history of containerization and its effect on the number of longshoremen." J.A. 1333.

Board Member John F. Ring dissented on the lawsuit issue. Rejecting the majority's coastwide definition of the "work" being preserved, Ring instead posited that "the work in question is the operation of the lift-equipment work at the Leatherman Terminal, and USMX and its carrier-members do not have the power to give that work to ILA-represented employees." J.A. 1334. The ILA's real beef was with the Ports Authority, he continued, and its lawsuit had the unlawful secondary *objective* (rather than a secondary *effect*) of pressuring the Ports Authority to assign lift-equipment work at Leatherman to union members.

The Ports Authority petitioned for review of the Board's decision under 29 U.S.C. § 160(f), and the Board is the respondent before us. The State of South Carolina intervened on the Ports Authority's behalf, and the ILA and Local 1422 intervened for the Board. USMX, also an intervenor, sides with the Ports Authority on the lawsuit issue, but with the ILA on the Section 7(b) issue.

III.

The Ports Authority advances two issues on appeal. First, it argues, the ILA's lawsuit against USMX and its carrier-members had the illegal aim of obtaining the lift work at Leatherman Terminal—work that ILA members had never performed and USMX **[—13—]** was powerless to award. Second, the Ports Authority claims that the Master Contract's Section 7(b) represents a tacit unlawful agreement that USMX's carrier-members won't call at new terminals unless ILA members perform all the longshore work there.

Because the Board's rulings for the union are supported by substantial evidence and aren't illogical or inconsistent with the National Labor Relations Act, we deny the Ports Authority's petition for review. **{-378-}**

A.

Our review of a Board decision is "limited." *Tecnocap, LLC v. NLRB*, 1 F.4th 304, 312 (4th Cir. 2021). We will uphold the Board's findings of fact if they're supported by substantial evidence, "even though we might have reached a different result had we heard the evidence in the first instance." *Id.* at 313.

Under this standard, we can't "displace the [Board's] choice between two fairly conflicting views" of the evidence. *NLRB v. Pepsi Cola Bottling Co. of Fayetteville*, 258 F.3d 305, 310 (4th Cir. 2001). And when factual findings "rest upon credibility determinations," we accept them absent "exceptional circumstances"—for example, when a credibility determination is unreasonable or contradictory. *Eldeco, Inc. v. NLRB*, 132 F.3d 1007, 1011 (4th Cir. 1997).

We will also uphold the Board's legal interpretations if they're "rational and consistent with the Act," even if the Board's reading isn't "the best way to read the statute." *Tecnocap*, 1 F.4th at 313. But we don't give "special deference . . . to the Board's interpretation of collective bargaining contracts" (though we're "mindful of the Board's **[—14—]** considerable experience" in interpreting such agreements). *Bonnell/Tredegar Indus. v. NLRB*, 46 F.3d 339, 343 (4th Cir. 1995).

B.

The primary issue is whether the ILA's lawsuit against USMX and its carrier-members violates the Act. Since the First Amendment protects a union's right to access the courts, the Board may determine that a union's lawsuit constitutes an unfair labor practice only if it is baseless or "has an objective that is illegal under federal law." *Bill Johnson's Rests., Inc. v. NLRB*, 461 U.S. 731, 738 n.5, 743 (1983).

No one asserts that the ILA's lawsuit is baseless. So we're left to determine whether it has an illegal objective under the Act. We conclude that it doesn't.

Section 8(b)(4)(ii)(B) of the Act makes it an unfair labor practice for a union "to threaten, coerce, or restrain any person engaged in commerce," where "an object" of the union's coercive conduct is to force that person to "cease doing business with any other person." 29 U.S.C. § 158(b)(4)(ii)(B). Section 8(e) prohibits unions and employers from agreeing to "cease doing business with any other person," and Section 8(b)(4)(ii)(A) prohibits unions from pressuring employers into such agreements. *Id.* § 158(b)(4)(ii)(A), (e).

These provisions exempt "primary" activity—that is, a "union's efforts [] directed at its own employer on a topic . . . that the employer can control." *ILA II*, 473 U.S. at 81. An activity has a "secondary" purpose, by contrast, if it is "directed at affecting the business relations of neutral employers and [is] 'tactically calculated' to achieve union objectives outside the primary employer-employee relationship." *Id.; see also Nat'l Woodwork Mfrs.* **[—15—]** *Ass'n v. NLRB*, 386 U.S. 612, 623 (1967) (explaining that a secondary boycott is characterized by "pressure tactically directed toward a neutral employer in a labor dispute not his own.").

The Supreme Court has emphasized that secondary *purposes* are distinct from secondary *effects*: If a union has "no forbidden secondary purpose to disrupt the business relations of a neutral employer," any "extra-unit effects, no matter how severe, are irrelevant to the analysis." *ILA II*, 473 U.S. at 79 (cleaned up). **{-379-}**

Preserving work for bargaining-unit members is a lawful, primary object.[1] *ILA I*, 447 U.S. at 504. A union's activity must pass two tests to be considered work-preserving. First, the activity "must have as its objective the preservation of work traditionally performed by employees represented by the union." *Id.* And second, the "contracting employer must have the power to give the employees the work in question" (the "right of control" test). *Id.*

The Ports Authority claims that the ILA's lawsuit violates several of the Act's prohibitions on activities with secondary purposes. In the Ports Authority's view, the union's lawsuit aims to "coerc[e] neutral parties (USMX and its carrier-members) to pressure [the Ports Authority] to give ILA members the lift-equipment jobs." Petitioner's **[—16—]** Br. at 3. But the Board found that the lawsuit met both requirements to be considered lawful work preservation:

> (1) the lawsuit's objective was the preservation of work traditionally performed by employees represented by ILA, and (2) USMX and its carrier members had the power to give the employees the work in question, and therefore, are primary employers.

J.A. 1331. We address each finding in turn.

1.

a.

First, the parties dispute whether the ILA's lawsuit seeks to preserve the union's historic work jurisdiction or to acquire new work. To decide this question, "the first and most basic question is: What is the 'work' that the [activity] allegedly seeks to preserve?" *ILA I*, 447 U.S. at 505.

The Board looked to the Master Contract and found that the "work" was all container work historically performed by ILA members "in all ports from Maine to Texas." J.A. 1331–32. But the Ports Authority argues that the work is narrower, encompassing only "the lift-equipment jobs at the Port's Leatherman Terminal" that are performed by non-union employees. Petitioner's Br. at 32.

We're guided by a pair of 1980s Supreme Court cases that also involved the ILA. These cases were about challenges to the ILA's Rules on Containers, which gave union longshore workers the right to load and unload containers that would otherwise be packed or unpacked within fifty miles of the port. *ILA I*, 447 U.S. at 499. **[—17—]**

---

[1] Several circuits have referred to the work-preservation doctrine as a "defense" available to a union facing charges of an unfair labor practice. *See, e.g., Int'l Longshore & Warehouse Union v. NLRB*, 978 F.3d 625, 637, 8 Adm. R. 334, 341 (9th Cir. 2020); *Loc. 32B-32J, SEIU v. NLRB*, 68 F.3d 490, 494 (D.C. Cir. 1995); *Nat'l Mar. Union of Am. v. Com. Tankers Corp.*, 457 F.2d 1127, 1134 (2d Cir. 1972). At oral argument, the Board agreed that the doctrine could be characterized as a defense, giving the union the burden of proving it applies. Assuming the burden is on the union, we find—as we'll explain—that the ILA met it here.

After several shipping companies contracted with third parties who used non-ILA labor to pack and unpack cargo within the 50-mile radius, the ILA assessed damages against the shipping companies. *Id.* at 502. The shipping companies stopped working with the third parties, and the third parties filed unfair labor charges with the Board. *Id.*

The Board found the charges substantiated, defining the "work" as "the off-pier stuffing and stripping of containers" and determining that the ILA members hadn't traditionally performed that work. *Id.* at 506. **{-380-}**

But the Court rejected that formulation of the "work" in *ILA I*. After sketching the history of containerization, the Court explained that the Board needed to perform "a careful analysis of the traditional work patterns that the parties are allegedly seeking to preserve" in the face of "technological displacement." *Id.* at 507.

The Board had "focused on the work done by the employees of the charging parties . . . after the introduction of containerization." *Id.* But it should have focused "on the work of the bargaining unit employees"—the ILA longshore workers—"not on the work of other employees who may be doing the same or similar work." *Id.* The Court remanded to the Board "to evaluate the relationship between traditional longshore work and the work which the Rules attempt to assign to ILA members." *Id.* at 509.

Five years later in *ILA II*, the Court held that the Rules on Containers—and the ILA's attempts to enforce them—were lawfully aimed at work preservation, articulating two principles relevant here.

First, the Court noted that in cases involving work displaced by innovation, "the place where work is to be done . . . is seldom relevant to the definition of the work itself." **[—18—]** *ILA II*, 473 U.S. at 77. The Court therefore defined the work as "simply 'the work of loading and unloading containers,'" not just at the ports or within the fifty-mile range covered by the collective-bargaining agreements. *Id.* at 77 n.17. And second, the Court reiterated that "extra-unit effects, no matter how severe, are irrelevant to the analysis." *Id.* at 79 (cleaned up).

Finding that the Rules on Containers were "motivated entirely by the longshoremen's understandable desire to preserve jobs" in the face of dwindling longshore work, the Court concluded that harmful effects on non-union workers weren't alone sufficient to find an improper secondary objective. *Id.*

Given the Court's directive to focus "on the work of the bargaining unit employees," *ILA I*, 447 U.S. at 507, we hold that the Board here rationally determined that the "work in question is the loading and unloading generally at East and Gulf Coast ports." J.A. 1332. The Master Contract defines the ILA's existing work jurisdiction in similarly broad strokes.[2] And the Contract controls "in all ports from Maine to Texas," J.A. 434, reflecting that it was "designed to preserve the work of ILA employees in the coast-wide bargaining unit," *Bermuda Container Line Ltd. v. Int'l Longshoremen's Ass'n*, 192 F.3d 250, 257 (2d Cir. 1999). **[—19—]**

The Ports Authority would prefer to define the work as only the lift-equipment work at Leatherman Terminal. But that view ignores two takeaways from the *ILA* cases: (1) it focuses on "the place where work is to be done," which is "seldom relevant"; and (2) it focuses on "extra-unit effects," not the work of bargaining-unit employees. *ILA II*, 473 U.S. at 77, 79.

It's true that "ILA-represented employees have never performed the lift-equipment work at any terminal of the Port of Charleston," Petitioner's Br. at 33—the Board recognized as much, *see* J.A. 1327. But as the Board explained, the *ILA* cases **{-381-}** instruct us to "look beyond the locus of a dispute and consider traditional work patterns" more broadly. J.A. 1332; *see also Bermuda Container*, 192 F.3d at

[2] *See* J.A. 484 ("Management and the Carriers recognize the existing work jurisdiction of ILA employees covered by their agreements with the ILA over all container work which historically has been performed by longshoremen and all other ILA crafts at container waterfront facilities.").

257 (declining to "narrow the employment relationship to include only employees of Maher terminals"); *Int'l Longshore & Warehouse Union v. NLRB,* 978 F.3d 625, 639–40, 8 Adm. R. 334, 343 (9th Cir. 2020) (rejecting a Board order as overly "preoccupied with the precise location of the disputed work" where it "made prior performance of electrical M&R work" at a particular facility "a talisman"). It would defang the parties' collective-bargaining agreement to hold that the union couldn't enforce it at a new location just because no one, union or otherwise, had "historically" worked there.

The Ports Authority relies on *Marrowbone Development Co. v. District 17, United Mine Workers of America,* 147 F.3d 296 (4th Cir. 1998), but that case is distinguishable. *Marrowbone* involved a newly certified local union of mineworkers that sought work at a particular mining site. *Id.* at 298–299. Although members of other locals had performed **[—20—]** such work, we looked narrowly at the (lack of) work historically performed *by the new local* to determine that it sought to acquire, not preserve, work. *Id.* at 302.

But in *Marrowbone,* the new local—as the "exclusive bargaining representative" of the mine's employees—was the relevant "bargaining unit." *Id.* at 298, 303 (citing *ILA I,* 447 U.S. at 507); *see also* J.A. 946 n.29 (ALJ drawing same distinction). We emphasized that given the site-specific nature of the mining work, only the members of the new local would be "directly affected by the dispute"—any effects on members of other locals "would be by and large incidental." *Marrowbone,* 147 F.3d at 303.

Here, by contrast, the ILA (not Local 1422) is the relevant bargaining unit. The ILA negotiated the Master Contract and filed the lawsuit to benefit its coastwide constituents. And as we'll explain, the "work" of loading and unloading containers isn't tethered to a single location, unlike the work at the Marrowbone mine—so it's not the case that the ILA's lawsuit will have only "incidental" effects across the coastwide unit. We therefore agree with the ALJ that *Marrowbone* is inapt.

At oral argument, the Ports Authority and USMX suggested that Section 7(a) of the Master Contract effectively excludes the hybrid-model ports—Charleston, Savannah, and Wilmington—from the ILA's work jurisdiction. But while that section acknowledges the reality that non-union employees currently perform the lift work at those ports, it doesn't suggest that the union meant to forever surrender its claim to that work.[3] **[—21—]**

As the ALJ put it, the "origin and rationale for [the hybrid model] is not clear from the record, but there is no indication the parties intended to carve out, individually or collectively, these three South Atlantic ports from the multi-port bargaining unit." J.A. 948 n.32. No party challenged this finding. So giving due deference to the agency, we decline to find that Section 7(a) represents any kind of tacit agreement to exclude the lift work at hybrid ports from the Master Contract's jurisdiction.

In all, we conclude that the Board and ALJ rationally defined "the work in question" as longshore work throughout the **{-382-}** ILA's coastwide jurisdiction, not just the lift work at Leatherman Terminal.

b.

Next, we consider whether the challenged activity (the lawsuit) sought to preserve that work. The Board found that although this case arose some 40 years after the *ILA* cases, it follows in their lineage: The ILA is still "seeking to preserve the traditional work of unit employees in the face of the technological advances affecting the coastal units," including at Leatherman Terminal. J.A. 1332. And the union is trying to do so by enforcing its coastwide Containerization Agreement—the

[3] To be clear, we express no view on the merits of USMX's potential waiver defense in the New Jersey lawsuit. We only observe that a union may still claim work preservation (Continued) **[—21—]** when its traditional work is performed at a new location within the jurisdiction of its collective-bargaining agreement.

Rules on Containers' direct descendant, *see* J.A. 1328 n.9—against employers that breach its terms by choosing hybrid ports for their **[—22—]** longshore work.[4] Though its lawsuit against USMX had the effect of diverting ships away from Leatherman, the key word is *effect*—and "extra-unit effects, no matter how severe, are irrelevant to the analysis." *ILA II*, 473 U.S. at 79 (cleaned up).

None of the Ports Authority's arguments undermine this conclusion. First, the Ports Authority contends that the *ILA* cases are inapt because "the lift-equipment work at Leatherman Terminal does not involve any technological change." Petitioner's Br. at 35–36; *see also* Dissent at 44 (contending that the "historic loss of work because of containerization" is "long past for this case"); J.A. 1341 (dissenting member arguing that the Board's opinion is stuck "back in the 1960s or 1970s").

But we decline to disregard history, especially where the Court has demanded a "careful analysis of the *traditional* work patterns that the parties are allegedly seeking to preserve." *ILA I*, 447 U.S. at 507 (emphasis added). And we see no reason why the passage of time should negate the bargain the ILA negotiated in the (aptly named) Containerization Agreement.

As the Board explains, "The lift work arose from and was enabled by containerization." Respondent's Br. at 48. Before containerization, cranes were mounted **[—23—]** on ships and operated by union employees. J.A. 269–72. The rise of containers made specially designed shoreside cranes, like those operated by the state employees in Charleston, a better option. *Id.* So the ILA negotiated its containerization agreements to combat the loss of this traditional work. J.A. 272–73; *see also* J.A. 484 (defining work jurisdiction to include "the loading and discharging of containers on and off ships"). Indeed, no one disputes that at non-hybrid ports, ILA members perform all the lift work.

It's true that at terminals in the Port of Charleston, non-union employees have operated the shoreside cranes since the early days of containerization. But *ILA I* warns against "focusing on the work as performed, after the innovation took place, by the employees who allegedly have displaced the longshoremen's work." 447 U.S. at 508. Such a focus would **{-383-}** "foreclose[]—by definition—any possibility that the longshoremen could negotiate an agreement" to keep loading or unloading cargo as the work evolved. *Id.*

The Ports Authority also argues that this isn't a situation "where the ILA workforce is genuinely threatened" by the "continued use of state-employees to perform the lift-equipment work." Petitioner's Br. at 37 (cleaned up); *see also Nat'l Woodwork*, 386 U.S. at 630–31 (suggesting that workers boycotting to "acquire new job tasks when their own jobs are not threatened" may be an unfair labor practice). But even if such a showing of genuine threat is required, it's satisfied by "the history of containerization and its effect on the number of longshoremen." J.A. 1333.

Like its predecessors, the Master Contract aims "to preserve jobs against the steadily dwindling volume of cargo work." *ILA II*, 473 U.S. at 79 (cleaned up). The Leatherman Terminal contributes to that "dwindling" by assigning to non-union workers jobs **[—24—]** earmarked for the union by contract. As the ILA argues, moreover, the lower labor costs of hybrid-model ports could draw cargo away from fully union ports, threatening other bargaining-unit jobs. *See* ILA's Br. at 13, 34–35; *cf.* J.A. 92–93 (Ports Authority president

[4] To support its view that the ILA seeks to acquire, not preserve work, the dissent cites several comments from ILA officials expressing a "desire to 'have all of the work . . . that is performed by nonbargaining workers to be brought under the ILA[’s] jurisdiction." Dissent at 49 (citing J.A. 260). These remarks aren't smoking guns, however. It's no secret that the ILA isn't a fan of the hybrid model—but doesn't follow that the ILA isn't entitled to sue to enforce its collective-bargaining agreement. And more broadly, in nearly *all* work-preservation cases, a union is seeking work not currently assigned to it. Our inquiry is whether that aim is lawful work preservation considering the union's traditional work patterns.

testifying that "[a] deviation from [the hybrid model] would put us at a competitive disadvantage . . . relative to any new terminal or any facility that had to operate a more expensive model"); Gov. McMaster's Amicus Br. at 10 (heralding the "efficiency of the Port's hybrid model").[5]

Finally, the Ports Authority notes that the ILA has, for decades, "acquiesced in the Port of Charleston's use of state employees to perform the lift-equipment work." Petitioner's Br. at 39; *see also* Gov. McMaster's Amicus Br. at 10 (noting "settled expectations" that Leatherman would also use the hybrid model). But while that might serve as a defense for USMX in the New Jersey breach-of-contract lawsuit, it doesn't bear on whether the lawsuit itself has an unlawful work-acquisition object.

The Board rationally found the ILA's lawsuit against USMX to have a valid work-preservation purpose. We therefore find that it passes *ILA I*'s first prong. **[—25—]**

2.

ILA I's second prong asks whether USMX has the "right to control" the relevant work's assignment. 447 U.S. at 512. The answer largely turns on how we define the work. *Id.* at 512 n.27.

The Board, viewing the "work" on a coastwide scale, found that USMX's carrier-members controlled the work because they could "bypass the Port of Charleston entirely and call on other [fully union] ports." J.A. 1332. But USMX and the Ports Authority again urge us to focus on the lift-equipment work at the port of Charleston, which the Ports Authority exclusively controls. Because we agree with the Board's broader work definition, it follows that USMX and its carrier-members have the right to control it.

In *American Trucking,* we held that shipping companies had the "right to control **{-384-}** the container work sought by the longshoremen" because they owned or leased the containers and controlled where they went. 734 F.2d at 978. That holding applies here.

As the ALJ put it, "the USMX carrier-members, like the carrier-members in *ILA I* and *II*, own or lease their containers, and, therefore, determine what ports they call on, which ultimately gives the carriers the right to control who performs the lift-equipment work on their containers." J.A. 948. That's because "[i]n the longshore industry, containers (and other sorts of cargo) *are* the work." ILA's Br. at 44. If no ships dock at a terminal, there's no longshore work to be done there. So where USMX's carrier-members choose to send their ships is the whole ballgame.

The Ports Authority and USMX rely on a West-Coast longshore case holding that the Port of Portland—not the carriers or third-party terminal operator—controlled the **[—26—]** "reefer work" of "plugging in, unplugging, and monitoring refrigerated shipping containers." *Hooks ex rel. NLRB v. Int'l Longshore & Warehouse Union*, 905 F. Supp. 2d 1198, 1201, 1211 (D. Or. 2012), *aff'd in relevant part*, 544 F. App'x 657, 658 (9th Cir. 2013) (unpublished); *accord Int'l Longshore & Warehouse Union v. NLRB*, 705 F. App'x 1, 3 (D.C. Cir. 2017) (per curiam). But *Hooks* is distinguishable.

In that case—a jurisdictional scuffle between two unions—the Board determined that the "work in dispute" was site-specific reefer work at one terminal in Portland. *See Int'l Bhd. of Elec. Workers, Loc. 48*, 358 N.L.R.B. 903, 904 (2012). One union expressly sought reassignment of the reefer work, threatening to picket the terminal operator "or take other economic action if the disputed work was not assigned to its members." *Id.* at 905.

[5] Much of Governor McMaster's amicus brief details the potential economic impact of ruling in the ILA's favor. The State of Maryland, in turn, argues in its amicus brief supporting the Board that "union labor provides tremendous benefits for workers" and their communities. Md.'s Amicus Br. at 12. While these arguments may have normative force, it's "not our function as a court of review to weigh the economic cost" of a collective bargaining agreement. *Am. Trucking*, 734 F.2d at 979.

ILA's lawsuit, by contrast, seeks damages from USMX and its carrier-members for breaching the Master Contract—not injunctive relief like work reassignment. We accept that USMX, like the terminal operator in *Hooks*, can't control who operates the cranes (or plugs in the reefers) at a specific terminal. But USMX and its carrier-members *can* control whether they send their containers to a terminal whose labor model doesn't comply with their contractual obligations. And under *American Trucking*, that's what matters.

The Ports Authority also claims this case is like *NLRB v. Enterprise Association of Pipefitters*, 429 U.S. 507 (1977), which preceded *ILA I* and *II*. There, a subcontractor entered into two conflicting agreements: one with a union, promising that pipe threading and cutting would be performed onsite; and one with a general contractor, agreeing to use units with pre-cut pipes on a construction project. *Id.* at 511–1. Relying on the first agreement, the union members refused to install the units at the jobsite. *Id.* at 512–13. **[—27—]**

The Court found that while the agreement was valid, the boycott wasn't. The union members were exerting pressure on a subcontractor with "no power to award the [jobsite cutting and threading work] to the union," the Court held, when their real problem was with the (neutral) general contractor. *Id.* at 513, 521–523.

Following the dissenting Board member's lead, the Ports Authority argues that USMX is analogous to the subcontractor in *Pipefitters*. Like the subcontractor, the Ports Authority contends, USMX has no power to assign the lift work at Leatherman to union members.[6] And while USMX could direct its carrier-members to avoid **{-385-}** hybrid ports, the subcontractor likewise could have walked away from its deal with the general contractor—but the general contractor (like the Ports Authority) would still control the work.

But that analogy doesn't fit. In *Pipefitters*, the "work" was confined to cutting and threading pipes at one specific site. 429 U.S. at 529–30. The subcontractor could have walked away from the deal with the general contractor—but the union members would have gone home empty-handed too.

Here, as we've discussed, the "work" is the loading and unloading of containers along the coastwide bargaining unit. And USMX's carrier-members *can* unilaterally give that work to union members by "simply refus[ing] to supply their containers" to ports using non-ILA labor. *Int'l Longshoremen's Ass'n v. NLRB*, 613 F.2d 890, 913 (D.C. Cir. 1979), *aff'd*, *ILA I*, 447 U.S. 490 (1980); *see also id.* n.192 (finding *Pipefitters* "inapplicable to the instant cases"). **[—28—]**

In other words, USMX has all the "power to settle the dispute with the union" by avoiding terminals that would violate the Master Contract. *Pipefitters*, 429 U.S. at 522. "It is difficult to imagine a more forceful demonstration of control." *Int'l Longshoremen's Ass'n*, 613 F.2d at 913.

Since USMX and its carrier-members control where the containers go, the Board rationally concluded they also control the relevant work—the loading and unloading of containers along the East Coast. Finding that the union has satisfied *ILA I*'s right-of-control test as well, we hold that the ILA's lawsuit had a legitimate work-preservation objective.

We therefore deny the Ports Authority's petition on this issue.

IV.

The ALJ separately held (and the Board affirmed) that Section 7(b) of the Master Contract wasn't a prohibited agreement to stop doing business—known as a "hot cargo" clause—with the Ports Authority. The Ports Authority contends that the Board erred in concluding that the provision didn't violate Section 8(e) of the Act, which makes it an unfair labor practice for a union and employer to form an agreement, "express or implied,

6 True enough, and the Board readily concedes the point.

whereby such employer . . . agrees to cease . . . doing business with any other person." 29 U.S.C. § 158(e).

In the Ports Authority's view, the ILA and USMX had an "implied agreement not to do business with new container-handling terminals that did not exclusively employ ILA members"—an agreement that became reality when carriers asked not to dock at Leatherman Terminal. Petitioner's Br. at 56–57. **[—29—]**

The Board responds that the provision doesn't require USMX carrier-members to boycott Leatherman; it only requires them to give notice that they "may be prohibited" from calling there. Respondent's Br. at 25 (cleaned up). And while the Ports Authority argues that extrinsic evidence shows the contracting parties made an unlawful agreement, the Board and the ILA say that the evidence in fact shows "a dispute, not an agreement," about the provision's meaning. ILA's Br. at 54 (cleaned up); *see also* Petitioner's Br. at 29–30. We agree with the Board and the ILA.

The Board evaluates whether a contractual clause violates Section 8(e) in two steps. *See Gen. Teamsters, Loc. 982*, 181 N.L.R.B. 515, 517 (1970). First, the Board determines whether the clause's meaning is clear. *Id.* If it is, the Board will determine whether it's valid under Section 8(e). *Id.* But if the clause is ambiguous, the Board can then "consider extrinsic evidence **{-386-}** to determine whether the clause was intended to be administered in a lawful or unlawful manner." *Id.*

In conducting this analysis, the ALJ first found that the meaning of Section 7(b) was clear: It didn't "require USMX or its carrier-members to boycott the Leatherman Terminal or to cease doing business with [the Ports Authority] or any other employer or person." J.A. 942. The ALJ's reasoning was sound.

The plain text of Section 7(b) requires USMX to "notify" port authorities that their members "may be prohibited" from using terminals staffed by non-union workers. J.A. 449. As the ALJ explained, "The word 'may' is ordinarily construed to mean permissive and discretionary," while "shall" connotes a requirement. J.A. 1350; *see also Kingdomware Techs., Inc. v. United States*, 579 U.S. 162, 171–72 (2016) ("Unlike the word **[—30—]** 'may,' which implies discretion, the word 'shall' usually connotes a requirement."). And elsewhere in the contract, the parties used "shall" and "may" to differentiate terms. *See* J.A. 942 (listing examples). We therefore agree that Section 7(b) doesn't bind USMX to a particular plan—so the ALJ (and Board) correctly concluded that the provision isn't "clearly unlawful on its face." *Id.*

The Ports Authority contends that the provision is at least ambiguous and that we should examine extrinsic evidence that "reveals the parties' intentions." Petitioner's Br. at 52–53. But even if we consider the extrinsic evidence, it doesn't change our view.

First, the Ports Authority notes that ILA President Harold Daggett testified that Section 7(b) was meant to stop carriers from docking at "any new terminal that comes online, if it's not 100 percent ILA." J.A. 295. But USMX's former counsel Donato Caruso testified that he negotiated for the term "may" because he "didn't want to give the impression that USMX agreed . . . with the Union's position." J.A. 314.

The ALJ credited Caruso over Daggett "because Caruso's recollection and testimony were more logical and consistent with the other evidence." J.A. 935 n.16. Giving due deference to the agency's credibility findings, *see Eldeco*, 132 F.3d at 1011, substantial evidence establishes that USMX and the ILJ didn't come to a tacit unlawful agreement when they negotiated Section 7(b).

The Ports Authority points to a series of communications from USMX carrier-members indicating that they wouldn't dock at Leatherman unless the terminal was fully union-staffed. As the ALJ noted, however, the carrier-members weren't speaking for USMX, but for the individual shipping companies. And even if the statements could be **[—31—]** attributed to USMX, none establish a bilateral agreement between ILA and USMX that ships couldn't call at Leatherman. *See Loc. 27, Sheet Metal Workers Int'l Ass'n*, 321 N.L.R.B. 540,

541 n.3 (1996) ("solely unilateral" conduct by a union "to enforce an unlawful interpretation of a facially lawful contract clause does not violate Sec. 8(e) because such conduct does not constitute an 'agreement'" (cleaned up)). To the contrary, the statements note the carriers' concerns about "risk," "challenges," and "uncertainty," J.A. 117, 540, 651—all suggesting "disagreement, rather than agreement" about what Section 7(b) meant. J.A. 943.

We agree that USMX and the ILA haven't made an agreement that violates Section 8(e), so we deny the Ports Authority's petition on this issue too. **{-387-}**

V.

The Board rationally held that the ILA's lawsuit against USMX sought to preserve its coastwide jurisdiction over loading and unloading work, so it didn't violate the Act. And the Board and ALJ correctly concluded that Section 7(b) of the Master Contract didn't constitute an illegal hot-cargo provision, whether by its text or by tacit agreement.

The South Carolina State Ports Authority's petition for review is therefore

DENIED.

(Reporter's Note: Dissenting opinion follows on p. 215).

[—32—] {-387-} NEIMEHYER, Circuit Judge, dissenting, except as to Part IV:

In its effort to coerce the South Carolina State Ports Authority to hire union workers to operate the state-owned cranes at the new Leatherman Terminal in the Port of Charleston, the International Longshoremen's Association ("ILA") sued the United States Maritime Alliance, whose members are customers of the Port, to effect a boycott by Maritime Alliance members' ships of the new terminal. This was an unfair labor practice under § 8(b) of the National Labor Relations Act ("NLRA"), as so found by the Administrative Law Judge ("ALJ"), and I would reverse the National Labor Relations Board and remand, directing it to provide relief to the Ports Authority.

After the State of South Carolina spent $1.5 billion building the new terminal to handle increased demand, the Ports Authority staffed the new terminal in accordance with the practice that it had followed at the port's two other terminals for 50 years — "a hybrid" division of labor in which the work of operating the state-owned cranes is performed by state employees and the remaining longshore work is performed by members of the ILA local union. The ILA, which represents longshoremen on the East Coast and Gulf Coast, has long wanted to displace the port's state employees with union workers, as it has also wanted to do at the Ports of Wilmington, North Carolina, and Savannah, Georgia, which likewise use the hybrid division of labor. As an ILA officer specifically stated, the ILA wanted "100 percent" of the work at the new terminal. Indeed, he stated that they "were interested in consuming all the jobs" and told the Ports Authority, "as you try to grow your business, I have to try to grow mine as well." **[—33—]**

Consequently, before the opening of the new terminal, the ILA negotiated with the State and the Ports Authority in an attempt to displace the hybrid model and acquire new work for union workers. When the discussions yielded no change, the ILA took further steps to achieve its goal. After the new terminal opened and cargo ships began calling at it, the ILA sued the United States Maritime Alliance — a multi-employer association of container carriers — and two of its members whose ships had called at the new terminal, alleging that, by doing so, they were violating the collective bargaining agreement between the ILA and the Maritime Alliance. The ILA sought $300 million in damages. It also made clear that the same fate would befall any other Maritime Alliance carrier whose ships called at the new terminal. In response to that suit, Maritime Alliance carriers immediately stopped calling at the new terminal, causing the Ports Authority extensive damages, which are ongoing.

In response to this ILA activity, the Ports Authority and the Maritime Alliance brought an unfair labor practice charge against the ILA, alleging that it was attempting to enforce the collective bargaining agreement in a coercive manner so as to force Maritime Alliance carriers to cease calling at the new terminal, thus **{-388-}** effecting a boycott in violation of § 8(b) of the NLRA. Separately, the Ports Authority brought an additional unfair labor practice charge against both the ILA and the Maritime Alliance, alleging that a provision of their collective bargaining agreement violates § 8(e) of the NLRA.

Section 8(b) prohibits unions "from engaging in secondary activities whose object is to force one employer [here, the Maritime Alliance] to cease doing business with another [here, the Ports Authority]." *NLRB v. Int'l Longshoremen's Ass'n (ILA I)*, 447 U.S. 490, **[—34—]** 503 (1980); *see also* 29 U.S.C. § 158(b)(4)(ii)(B). And § 8(e) "makes unlawful those collective-bargaining agreements in which the employer [here, the Maritime Alliance] agrees to cease doing business with any other person [here, the Ports Authority]." *ILA I*, 447 U.S. at 503–04; *see also* 29 U.S.C. § 158(e). Unions can, however, avoid liability under those provisions if they show, as an affirmative defense, that the primary objective of their activity is the *preservation* of work historically done by the bargaining unit, not the *acquisition* of union work. *See National Woodwork Mfrs. Ass'n v. NLRB*, 386 U.S. 612, 630 (1967); *see also ILA I*, 447 U.S. at 504.

The majority concludes that because ILA workers perform "the loading and unloading generally at East and Gulf ports," *ante* at 18, as described without exception in the Master Contract between the ILA and the Maritime Alliance, the ILA's efforts at the Port of Charleston were intended merely to preserve such work for union workers. This conclusion, however, is fundamentally flawed because it fails to focus on the work performed by the relevant bargaining unit, Local 1422, as required. *See ILA I*, 447 U.S. at 507 (requiring the analytical focus to be on "whether an agreement seeks no more than to preserve the work *of bargaining unit members*" (emphasis added)); *Marrowbone Dev. Co. v. Dist. 17, United Mine Workers of Am.*, 147 F.3d 296, 302–03 (4th Cir. 1998) (same). Moreover, the majority's premise for making this argument is inaccurate. While ILA workers do *generally* operate the cranes in East Coast and Gulf Coast ports, the undisputed facts of record show a longstanding exception to that generalization — they have *never* operated cranes in the Ports of Charleston, Wilmington, and Savannah, each of which has *always* operated with a hybrid division of labor. Thus, the ILA's effort to bring about **[—35—]** change in the Port of Charleston to eliminate the hybrid model in favor of 100% ILA work was clearly an effort *to acquire* work, which, as it was attempted, was illegal, and not the lawful effort *to preserve* work. The record shows further that the ILA faced no loss or threatened loss of work in the Port of Charleston from the opening of the new terminal. Moreover, as the ALJ found, there is no record evidence that the opening of the new terminal caused or threatened to cause loss of work at any other port on the East Coast or Gulf Coast.

I agree with the ALJ in this case, as well as the dissenting member of the National Labor Relations Board ("NLRB" or the "Board"), both of whom concluded that the ILA committed an unfair labor practice in violation of § 8(b). I would therefore grant the Ports Authority's petition for review, reverse, and remand to require the Board to provide relief to the Ports Authority.

I

In the spring of 2021, the Ports Authority opened the Hugh K. Leatherman, Sr., Terminal in the Port of Charleston, operating the new terminal with the same hybrid **{-389-}** division of labor that had been in use at the port for some 50 years. Under the hybrid model, state employees operate the state-owed cranes at the port and ILA workers perform all other longshore work. The state employees are not represented by the ILA, and the Ports Authority has no agreement with the ILA governing the terms and conditions of the Ports Authority's employment of crane operators. This hybrid model is also in use at the Ports of Wilmington and Savannah. **[—36—]**

The vast majority of container ships that call at the Port of Charleston are owned by carriers who are members of the United States Maritime Alliance, which represents the carriers in negotiating collective bargaining agreements with the ILA. The most recent "Master Contract" between the ILA and the Maritime Alliance became effective in 2018 and will continue to 2024.

The Master Contract provides the terms and conditions for union longshore work in all the ports on the East Coast and Gulf Coast — "from Maine to Texas." It requires that all Maritime Alliance members' cargo be loaded and unloaded exclusively by ILA longshore workers. While the Master Contract contains no explicit exception for crane operators in the Ports of Charleston, Savannah, and Wilmington, the parties agree that the crane operators in those ports have never been union workers. And the Master Contract recognizes this in Article VII, § 7(a)–(b):

> (a) [The Maritime Alliance] and the ILA shall conduct a study to determine how the *business model currently used by port authorities in the Ports of Charleston, SC, Savannah, GA, and Wilmington, NC could be altered* to permit work currently performed by state employees to be performed by Master Contract-bargaining-unit employees in a more productive, efficient, and competitive fashion. *[The Maritime Alliance] and the ILA will use this study to meet with these port authorities in an effort to convince*

them to employ Master Contract-bargaining-unit employees.

(b) [The Maritime Alliance] agrees to formally notify any port authority contemplating the development of or intending to develop a new container handling facility that [Maritime Alliance] members may be prohibited from using that new facility if the work at that facility is not performed by Master Contract-bargaining-unit employees.

(Emphasis added). **[—37—]**

The study contemplated by § 7(a) was never conducted, and no action has ever been taken before the ILA's activities in this case with respect to the Maritime Alliance members' right to call at these three ports. Even so, the representatives of the ILA and the Maritime Alliance disagree over the meaning of § 7. The ILA asserts that it precludes Maritime Alliance carriers from calling at the new terminal in the Port of Charleston unless the terminal is staffed "100 percent ILA," while the Maritime Alliance asserts that § 7 was intended merely to cabin the hybrid model to those ports using the hybrid model.

Despite the long and consistent history of the hybrid model's being used at the three ports, the ILA has been intent on changing the model and acquiring 100% of the work at those ports. Before the new terminal in the Port of Charleston opened, the ILA met with representatives of the State of South Carolina and the Ports Authority in an effort to persuade the Ports Authority to make the change at the new terminal. As the ALJ noted, the ILA representative stated that the ILA "[was] interested in consuming all the jobs at the Leatherman Terminal" and that the ILA **{-390-}** representative "opposed the use of the hybrid operating model throughout his 24-year career as a union officer." The representative also stated that with the opening of the new terminal, the ILA decided to focus on combatting the use of the hybrid model at the Port of Charleston because "Charleston just happened to be the 'first terminal up at bat.'"

When negotiations between the ILA and the Ports Authority failed and the new terminal opened using the hybrid model, the ILA pursued a different course and filed an action against the Maritime Alliance and two member carriers who had called at the new terminal, alleging that they violated the Master Agreement between the ILA and the **[—38—]** Maritime Alliance. The ILA sought $300 million in damages, intending to deter other carriers from calling at the new terminal. That effort proved effective. Thereafter, no Maritime Alliance carriers called at the new terminal, causing the State and the Ports Authority substantial damages, as it presently operates at only 10% capacity.

The Ports Authority filed two unfair labor practice charges against the ILA. In the first, it alleged that by employing the ILA's interpretation of Article VII, § 7 of the Master Contract, the ILA illegally attempted to require Maritime Alliance carriers to refrain from dealing with the Ports Authority at its new terminal, in violation of § 8(e) of the NLRA. In the second charge, the Ports Authority alleged that the ILA filed suit against the Maritime Alliance and its member carriers with the unlawful objective of forcing Maritime Alliance carriers to cease doing business with the Ports Authority and thereby to coerce the Ports Authority to assign union workers to state-owned cranes, in violation of §§ 8(b) and 8(e).

After a two-day trial in June 2021, the ALJ dismissed the first unfair practice charge because the language of § 7 did not *require* the Maritime Association to refrain from calling at the new terminal but merely required the Maritime Alliance members to *warn* the Ports Authority that they *may* not be able to use the new terminal if it used the hybrid model. With respect to the second charge, however, the ALJ found that the ILA's action in filing suit against the Maritime Alliance was an illegal effort to create a secondary boycott with the purpose of *acquiring new work*, not *preserving existing work*. The ALJ drew on the Supreme Court's distinction in *National Woodwork* between contractual provisions employed as a "'sword' to reach out and acquire new work" and provisions employed as a "'shield' to retain work traditionally performed by Union employees." (Quoting *National* **[—39—]** *Woodwork*, 386 U.S. at 630). The ALJ concluded that the ILA had used its suit to enforce the Master Contract as a "sword" to acquire new work because "a condition precedent to finding a lawful work preservation object is evidence of an actual or anticipated threat to [bargaining] unit jobs." He found both (1) that the ILA had not adduced sufficient evidence to support its claim that the new terminal in the Port of Charleston threatened existing ILA jobs, and (2) that there was concrete evidence of the ILA's "desire to obtain all the container work at the Leatherman Terminal, as well as at any future container-handling facilities." Both findings supported a conclusion that the purpose of the ILA's activities was to acquire work.

While the NLRB affirmed the ALJ's dismissal of the first charge, it reversed the ALJ's finding of an unfair labor practice with respect to the second charge by a 2-to-1 vote. The panel majority concluded both that the ALJ took too narrow a view "of the work preservation defense" and that the object of the ILA's lawsuit was **{-391-}** actually work preservation. It found that the primary object of the suit was to force the Maritime Alliance members to give longshore work to ILA members by avoiding the Leatherman Terminal in favor of facilities staffed completely by ILA workers, and that any secondary effects on the Port of Charleston were unintended — and thus permissible. With respect to the ALJ's conclusion that there was no job loss or threat thereof, the majority said that the ILA was merely pursuing job preservation, a conclusion it took to be supported by the history of containerization and its effect on longshoremen, citing *NLRB v. Int'l Longshoremen's Ass'n (ILA II)*, 473 U.S. 61, 79 (1985). It also concluded that the ILA's activity was not a secondary effort directed at the Ports Authority but rather was legitimately directed at the **[—40—]** Maritime Alliance and its carriers because the carriers had "the power to give the employees the work in question, and therefore, are primary employers."

From the NLRB's order of December 16, 2022, dismissing the Ports Authority's charges against the ILA, the Ports Authority filed this petition for review.

II

Section 8(b) of the NLRA forbids "forcing or requiring any person . . . to cease doing business with any other person." 29 U.S.C. § 158(b)(4)(ii)(B). And § 8(e) of the NLRA forbids any employer from entering "into any contract or agreement . . . whereby such employer ceases or refrains or agrees to cease . . . doing business with any other person." *Id.* § 158(e). The general principles implemented by these provisions are not complex or even unique to labor law. While the NLRA allows union activities "having the object of pressuring the employer for agreements regulating relations between [the employer] and [its] own employees," it prohibits "'secondary' objectives" — that is, the "use of the boycott to further [a union's] aims by involving an employer in disputes not [that employer's] own." *National Woodwork*, 386 U.S. at 620. As the *National Woodwork* Court noted:

> The congressional design in enacting § 8(b)(4)(A) is therefore crucial to the determination of the scope of §§ 8(e) and 8(b)(4)(B). Senator Taft said of its purpose:
>
> > This provision makes it unlawful to resort to a *secondary boycott to injure the business of a third person who is wholly unconcerned in the disagreement between an employer and his employees.*
>
> * * * **[—41—]**
>
> And the Senate Committee Report carefully characterized the conduct prohibited by § 8(b)(4)(A) in the same terms:
>
> > Thus, it would not be lawful for a union to engage in [a] strike against employer A for the purpose of forcing that employer to cease doing business with employer B; nor would it be lawful for a union to

> boycott employer A because employer A uses or otherwise deals in the goods of or does business with employer B (with whom the union has a dispute).

Id. at 624–25 (emphasis added). Thus, in enacting §§ 8(b) and 8(e), "Congress intended to reach only agreements with *secondary* objectives." *ILA I*, 447 U.S. at 504 (emphasis added). In other words, § 8(b) does not prohibit the kinds of activities described where those activities are directed toward achieving primary union objectives, and "[a]mong the primary purposes protected by the [NLRA] is 'the purpose of *preserving* for the contracting employees themselves work traditionally done by them.'" *Id.* (emphasis added) (quoting **{-392-}** *NLRB v. Enterprise Ass'n of Steam, Hot Water, Hydraulic Sprinkler, Pneumatic Tube, Ice Mach. & Gen. Pipefitters of N.Y. (Pipefitters)*, 429 U.S. 507, 517 (1977)). Thus, if a union's activity is directed at preserving "work traditionally performed by [bargaining unit employees]" and if the target of the union action has the "right of control" over that work — *i.e.*, the right to decide who performs the work — then the union activity is permitted even where it would otherwise violate the letter of § 8. *Id.* Because § 8(b) facially prohibits union activities "requiring any person . . . to cease doing business with any other person," 29 U.S.C. § 158(b)(4)(ii)(B), the union carries the burden of establishing the affirmative defense that its activities are nonetheless permissible on the ground that they (1) have the purpose of *preserving* for its employees the work traditionally done by them, rather than **[—42—]** acquiring new work, and (2) are *directed at the employer with the right to control the work, see ILA I*, 447 U.S. at 504; *Marrowbone*, 147 F.3d at 302.

I conclude that the ILA's activities clearly fall under § 8(b) and that the ILA did not carry its burden to avoid liability. The intent of its conduct in filing suit against the Maritime Alliance was *to gain* union work, not to preserve it, as the ILA failed to show any loss or threatened loss of work caused by the opening of the new terminal in the Port of Charleston. Furthermore, its effort was not directed against the employer it was seeking to persuade — the Ports Authority — but against customers of the Ports Authority, *i.e.*, the Maritime Alliance and its members. Those entities had no control over the Ports Authority's employees, except to bring collateral pressure on the Ports Authority with a boycott, and thus the ILA's activity was secondary. In pursuing these activities, the ILA violated § 8(b) and thus committed an unfair labor practice, as charged by the Ports Authority. I address in turn the ILA's failure to demonstrate each of the two requirements of the affirmative defense.

A

With respect to the first requirement, the NLRB and the ILA contend that the ILA is entitled to the benefit of its Master Contract, which has as its purpose "to preserve traditional work and the jobs of union employees in the face of the technological advances [such as containerization] affecting the coastal units." While this assertion is true enough, it gains the ILA nothing unless it also shows that the opening of the new terminal in the Port of Charleston threatened a loss of work from technological advances and that its **[—43—]** actions were directed toward preserving that work. To fill that gap in its reasoning, the Board and the ILA argue that when more cargo — and therefore work — is directed to the Port of Charleston or the other two ports using the hybrid model, work is being pulled away from all other ports, which use only ILA workers. First, this analysis is too broad and is inconsistent with the focused analysis required for determining whether work is being preserved or acquired. As our court held in *Marrowbone*, "regardless of whether the agreement is national in scope, in determining whether it preserves or acquires work, the analysis must focus on the work of the local employees and not those elsewhere." 147 F.3d at 303 (citing *ILA I*, 447 U.S. at 507 (noting that "the Board must focus on the work of the bargaining unit employees, not on the work of other employees who may be doing the same or similar work")). The NLRB and ILA's argument focusing on all coastal units is thus legally irrelevant. **{-393-}**

Second, even the broad argument that the NLRB and the ILA make lacks support in the record. The record lacks any evidence to show that the new terminal caused the diversion of cargo in a manner that resulted in loss of union work, and the ILA only offered the thought that "discretionary cargo work *might* migrate from ILA-controlled ports to Charleston" (emphasis added), which the ALJ characterized as "vague speculation."

Moreover, without any apparent logic, both the NLRB and the majority also describe the ILA's impetus in this case as being the loss of traditional work performed by union workers emanating from the containerization of cargo in the 1950s. But there is no factual or logical basis to conclude that the ILA's effort to obtain the crane-operating work at the new terminal in the Port of Charleston is an effort to preserve work lost by **[—44—]** containerization. Both of the first two terminals in the Port of Charleston, as well as the new terminal, handle containerized cargo, and the division of labor has always been that state employees operate the state-owned cranes, and the union workers perform the other longshore work. Simply, the issue is not whether there was a historic loss of work because of containerization — that issue is long past for this case — but whether the union can change the post-containerization settled status quo of the hybrid model's use at the Port of Charleston to obtain 100% ILA work at the new terminal.

Not only have the NLRB and the ILA not shown a loss or threatened loss of work at other ports, they have not even shown any loss or threatened loss of work by Local 1422 within the Port of Charleston, the burden that they must carry. The cranes in the Port of Charleston were *always* operated by state employees and *never* by union workers, and the record shows that the hybrid division of work that existed before the opening of the new terminal continued thereafter without change. The ALJ found, and no one challenges on appeal, that after the new terminal opened, the same division of work and the same proportion of workers were used at the new terminal as had been used at the other two terminals in the port. There was no transfer of workers from the other two terminals to the new one, but rather the new terminal was staffed by new employees, in the same proportion that had always existed in the port *i.e.*, the status-quo hybrid model. As the ALJ found, "There is no evidence that the work performed by state employees at the Leatherman Terminal differed in any way from the other Port of Charleston terminals. The same is true regarding the work of [union] members performed there." **[—45—]**

Both the NLRB and the ILA, perhaps recognizing that the undisputed facts show no loss or threatened loss of jobs anywhere, argue with some futility that the ILA need not show "a specific loss or threat of loss of jobs" because of the "unique" context of longshore work, citing *ILA I*, *ILA II*, and *American Trucking Ass'ns v. NLRB*, 734 F.2d 966 (4th Cir. 1984). But this position is conclusively refuted by the very sources that the NLRB and ILA cite, and their argument simply amounts to a concession of error. *ILA I* was, of course, a maritime shipping case — decided much closer in time to the immediate aftereffects of containerization — and yet even in that case, the Supreme Court expressly reaffirmed the requirement that a union make a precise showing of there being *an actual or imminent threat to bargaining-unit jobs*. In other words, the requirement of a rigorous showing was imposed by the Supreme Court in a case that took place within precisely the same "unique maritime context" as this dispute. Thus, the maritime context of this case in no way relieves the ILA of the requirement **{-394-}** that its activity be directed at *preserving work traditionally performed* by the relevant bargaining unit of the union. As the Supreme Court stated:

> Identification of the work at issue in a complex case of technological displacement requires a *careful analysis of the traditional work patterns* that the parties are allegedly seeking to preserve, and of *how the agreement seeks to accomplish that result* under the changed circumstances created by the technological advance. The analysis must take into account "all the surrounding circumstances," including the nature of

> the work *both before and after the innovation*. . . . Whatever its scope, . . . the inquiry must be *carefully focused*: to determine whether an agreement seeks *no more than* to preserve the work of bargaining unit members, the Board must focus on the work of the bargaining unit employees . . . .

ILA I, 447 U.S. at 507 (emphasis added) (quoting *National Woodwork*, 386 U.S. at 644). **[—46—]**

The Board's conclusions to the contrary are owed deference only if they are "supported by substantial evidence." *Universal Camera Corp. v. NLRB*, 340 U.S. 474, 493 (1951) (quoting 29 U.S.C. § 160(e)). Yet, there is no evidence in this case supporting the proposition that any ILA jobs were lost or threatened by the use of the hybrid model at the new terminal and were therefore in need of preservation.

This case closely resembles a course of conduct explicitly described as impermissible by the Supreme Court in *Pipefitters*. In that case, an agreement required that unionized workers perform threading and cutting of pipes themselves while on the job, rather than working with pre-threaded and pre-cut pipes. *Pipefitters*, 429 U.S. at 511–12. The Court held that the union's actions in furtherance of that contract — a boycott of a neutral subcontractor without authority to control whether the right kinds of pipes were ordered for the job site — were illegal. *Id.* at 520–21, 528–31. The Court explained that while the union's activity was *partially* premised on permissible primary objectives, it was also clearly partially premised on impermissible secondary objectives — it was enough that "*an* object" of the union's activities was an illegal secondary objective. *Id.* at 528 (emphasis added); *see also id.* at 529–30 n.16 (stating that if a union were to attempt to capture work it had previously acquiesced to non-union workers' performing, such conduct would serve "not to preserve, but to aggrandize, its own position and that of its members," concluding that "[s]uch activity is squarely within the statute" and thus prohibited).

In this case, the impermissible secondary objective motivating the ILA's suit against the Maritime Alliance was to obtain *new work* by means of a boycott of the Ports Authority's new terminal. **[—47—]**

B

To satisfy the second part of the *ILA I* test for demonstrating a defense of an alleged § 8(b) violation, the ILA must show that the Maritime Alliance had the "right of control" over the work at issue. *ILA I*, 447 U.S. at 504. To meet that test, the Board and the ILA argue that the boycott effected in this case was not secondary, as prohibited by § 8(b), but primary, because the Maritime Alliance had the *right of control* over the crane-operating work in the Port of Charleston. They make this claim on the basis that the Maritime Alliance carriers have discretion as to where their ships call, and thus they can, in exercising that discretion, offload ships at ports staffed solely by ILA workers. **{-395-}** The majority adopts the same reasoning, describing the Maritime Alliance members as having the power to "unilaterally give [the] work to union members." *Ante* at 27. But the ILA's coercing the Maritime Alliance members to exercise this power is precisely what § 8(b) prohibits as an illegal secondary boycott. *See National Woodwork*, 386 U.S. at 627 (noting Congress's concern with the "dangerous practice of unions" to widen industrial conflict by creating coercive pressures on neutral employers) (cleaned up). Rather than dealing with the Ports Authority directly with respect to the work that the Ports Authority controls, the ILA brought pressure against the Ports Authority's customers in an attempt to coerce the Ports Authority. This is secondary activity and is illegal.

It must be recalled that, as an undisputed matter, the crane operators at the Port of Charleston are employees of the Ports Authority, hired and paid by it. Neither those employees nor the Ports Authority are under any contract with the ILA with respect to **[—48—]** crane-operating work. The crane workers are thus neither employees of the Maritime Alliance carriers nor under their control, as required for the ILA's actions to be lawful. The Maritime Alliance carriers were contractual strangers to the crane operators employed by the Ports Authority. While it would indeed be primary conduct for the ILA to deal directly with and bring pressure on the Ports Authority about the assignment of union workers to crane operation, it was secondary conduct for them to seek to achieve that result through a coercive suit against the Maritime Alliance. The determining fact focuses on whether there was a contractual relationship between the Maritime Alliance carriers and the port workers. As the Supreme Court made clear:

> Whether an agreement is a lawful work preservation agreement depends on "whether, under all the surrounding circumstances, the Union's objective was preservation of work for bargaining unit employees, or whether the agreement was tactically calculated to satisfy union objectives elsewhere. . . . The touchstone is whether the agreement or its maintenance is addressed to *the labor relations of the contracting employer vis-à-vis his own employees.*"

ILA I, 447 U.S. at 504 (emphasis added) (cleaned up) (quoting *National Woodwork*, 386 U.S. at 644–45). The Court explained that "if the contracting employer has *no power to assign the work*, it is reasonable to infer that the agreement has a secondary objective, that is, to influence whoever does have such power over the work." *Id.* at 504–05 (emphasis added). Of course, in this case, it was the Ports Authority that had the right to assign the work.

Not only does the argument that the Board and the ILA make with respect to the right of control fly in the face of controlling Supreme Court precedent, the ILA's own statements and testimony fairly concede that the Ports Authority is the relevant employer. **[—49—]** First, the complaint in the ILA's lawsuit against the Maritime Alliance states that a Maritime Alliance ship "went to the Leatherman Terminal even though it knew that the non-bargaining unit employees who were *not covered* by the Master Contract *would be hired* to unload its containers." Moreover, in previously negotiating with and attempting to persuade the Ports Authority, the ILA by its actions acknowledged that it was the Ports Authority that would assign the employees and that it was the Ports Authority whom had to persuade to use union workers. But then, when those negotiations failed, the ILA sought to bring secondary pressure on the Ports Authority by **{-396-}** intimidating Maritime Alliance carriers, who otherwise would call at the new terminal, thereby forcing them not to do so and thus effecting a secondary boycott — the exact course of conduct that Congress prohibited when it enacted § 8(b).

III

Finally, *ILA II* instructs that an absence of unlawful secondary purposes is essential to a defense against charges under § 8(b). 473 U.S. at 82. But the record here shows clearly, by undisputed evidence, that the ILA's purpose was to acquire new work, not to preserve existing work. An ILA representative acknowledged at trial that the very origin of Article VII in the Master Contract was the ILA's desire to "have all of the work . . . that is performed by nonbargaining workers to be brought under the ILA jurisdiction." An ILA vice president also testified that the purpose of Article VII of the Master Contract was to establish that, with respect to new terminals, the "jobs would be bargaining unit workers . . . or else those [carriers] would be prohibited from coming into those terminals." The ILA **[—50—]** representative also testified that the ILA was interested in "consuming all the jobs," and that in doing so it was trying to "grow" its business. The goal of *growing* union work through secondary pressure renders the ILA's activity illegal and an unfair labor practice under § 8(b).

* * *

For the reasons given, I would grant the Ports Authority's petition for review and reverse the NLRB's order and remand with instructions to grant relief to the State and the Ports Authority.

United States Court of Appeals
for the Fourth Circuit

No. 21-2184

NORTH CAROLINA COASTAL FISHERIES REFORM GROUP
vs.
CAPT. GASTON LLC

Appeal from the United States District Court for the Eastern District of North Carolina, at Greenville

Decided: August 7, 2023

Citation: 76 F.4th 291, 11 Adm. R. 223 (4th Cir. 2023).

Before **RICHARDSON** and **RUSHING**, Circuit Judges, and **LYDON**, District Judge.*

* The Hon. Sherri A. Lydon, United States District Judge for the District of South Carolina, sitting by designation.

[—3—] {-293-} **RICHARDSON**, Circuit Judge: **{-294-}**

Fisheries Reform Group alleges that shrimp trawlers operating in North Carolina's Pamlico Sound are violating the Clean Water Act by engaging in two types of unpermitted activity: throwing bycatch overboard and disturbing sediment with their trawl nets. But these activities do not violate the Clean Water Act. The Act forbids the unpermitted discharge of a pollutant. Returning bycatch to the ocean is not discharging a pollutant, so throwing it overboard without a permit is not forbidden by the Act. Likewise, because the trawl nets merely kick up sediment already present in the Sound, their use does not discharge any pollutants either. Accordingly, we affirm the district court's dismissal of Fisheries' complaint.

I. Background

Defendants are commercial shrimpers in Pamlico Sound, a coastal estuary in North Carolina. Shrimpers harvest shrimp by dragging trawl nets along the ocean's floor. The nets trap shrimp. But, along the way, the nets also stir up sediment, which later resettles on the ocean floor. They also inadvertently snare other fish and marine organisms. These other fish and marine organisms, many of which the trawlers cannot legally keep, are known as "bycatch." Trawlers throw the bycatch overboard, returning it to the ocean.

Fisheries Reform Group seeks to change or limit the way trawlers discard bycatch and disturb sediment. To do so, it sued under the Clean Water Act's citizen-suit provision, alleging that these shrimpers are violating the Act and must obtain Clean Water Act permits—on top of the fishing permits already required—to engage in commercial shrimping. The district court dismissed the suit for failure to state a claim, holding that the **[—4—]** Act does not regulate bycatch and that disturbing sediment with trawl nets does not violate the Act.

II. Discussion

We affirm the district court's decision that Fisheries Reform Group fails to plausibly allege that shrimp trawlers are violating the Clean Water Act by either (1) throwing their bycatch back into Pamlico Sound, or (2) disturbing sediment on the Sound's floor with their trawl nets, thereby causing it to resettle.

The Clean Water Act is a comprehensive scheme to reduce water pollution **{-295-}** in the United States. *See generally* 33 U.S.C. § 1251 *et seq.* Among other things, it prohibits "the discharge of any pollutant by any person" "[e]xcept as in compliance with" the Act.[1] § 1311(a). To comply with the Act, would-be polluters can obtain permits that authorize

[1] "[A] discharge of a pollutant occurs when five elements exist: (1) a pollutant must be (2) added (3) to navigable waters (4) from (5) a point source." *U.S. Pub. Rsch. Grp. v. Atl. Salmon of Me., LLC*, 215 F. Supp. 2d 239, 246 (D. Me. 2002) (internal quotation marks omitted). The parties do not dispute that Pamlico Sound is part of the navigable waters. Nor do they dispute that the shrimp boats are "a point source," which the Act defines to include "any . . . vessel or other floating craft." § 1362(14). So we focus on whether a pollutant was added.

them to discharge pollutants. Two such permits are relevant here. First, the Environmental Protection Agency can issue National Pollutant Discharge Elimination System permits, which authorize "the discharge of any pollutant" so long as certain conditions prescribed by the EPA are satisfied. § 1342(a)(1). Second, the Army Corps of Engineers can issue permits under § 1344 authorizing the discharge of "dredged or fill material into the **[—5—]** navigable waters at specified disposal sites."[2] § 1344(a). Fisheries alleges that because the shrimpers are operating without these permits, they are violating the Act.

A. Fisheries' bycatch claim fails

Fisheries claims that the shrimpers are violating the Clean Water Act's prohibition on the "discharge" of "pollutants" by putting bycatch back into Pamlico Sound without a Clean Water Act permit. Bycatch, they argue, is a pollutant. A "pollutant" is defined to "mean[ ]," among other things, "biological materials."[3] § 1362(6). "Biological materials" is not further defined, but Fisheries argues that it encompasses all animal matter, including the marine organisms that make up bycatch. *See, e.g., Biological*, American Heritage Dictionary of the English Language (1976) ("Of, pertaining to, caused by, or affecting life or living organisms."); *Material*, American Heritage Dictionary of the English Language (1976) ("The substance or substances out of which a thing is or may be constructed.").

So, relying on § 1362's literal language, Fisheries asserts that bycatch is a "pollutant" because it is within what it claims is the ordinary meaning of "biological materials." And a "discharge of a pollutant" is defined to include "any addition of any pollutant to navigable waters from any point source." § 1362(12). Putting these definitions **[—6—]** together, Fisheries argues that dumping bycatch back into the ocean from a boat after it was hauled onboard by nets plausibly amounts to an addition to the ocean. On this theory, discharging bycatch without a permit would violate the Act.

That sounds plausible. And, viewed in isolation, we might well agree. Faced with a statute, we typically determine the text's meaning based on the ordinary understanding of the language. And considering only the statutory text, Fisheries makes a plausible case for why returning **{-296-}** bycatch to the ocean fits within the ordinary meaning of a "discharge" of "biological materials."[4]

Yet, in appropriate cases, we have been instructed to consider, as a background rule, other legal interests that contextually inform our understanding of a statute's meaning. For example, the rule of lenity teaches that we must resolve ambiguities in criminal statutes in favor of the criminal defendant. Other examples of background interpretive principles or rules of construction abound: constitutional avoidance, presumptions against implied repeal, liberal constructions to benefit Indians or soldiers, or the presumptions against retroactive or extraterritorial application.

---

[2] Both the EPA and the Corps can delegate their authority to issue permits to the individual states if certain conditions are met. *See* §§ 1342(b), 1344(g), (h). For simplicity's sake, we refer only to the EPA and the Corps in this opinion.

[3] The Act's definition of "pollutant" reads, in part: "The term 'pollutant' means dredged spoil, solid waste, incinerator residue, sewage, garbage, sewage sludge, munitions, chemical wastes, biological materials, radioactive materials, heat, wrecked or discarded equipment, rock, sand, cellar dirt and industrial, municipal, and agricultural waste discharged into water." § 1362(6).

[4] Indeed, the Sixth Circuit essentially agrees with Fisheries' expansive definition of "biological materials" in the Act. *See Nat'l Cotton Council of Am. v. E.P.A.*, 553 F.3d 927, 937–38 (6th Cir. 2009); *Nat'l Wildlife Fed'n v. Consumers Power Co.*, 862 F.2d 580, 583 (6th Cir. 1988). Meanwhile the Ninth Circuit has limited its reading of "biological materials" to "waste material of a human or industrial process," *Ass'n to Protect Hammersley, Eld, & Toten Inlets v. Taylor Res., Inc.*, 299 F.3d 1007, 1016 (9th Cir. 2002), but we have good reason to doubt its logic since it reached its conclusion by misapplying the linguistic canon of *ejusdem generis*, *see id.* (applying *ejusdem generis* even though the Act's definition of pollutant is not an illustrative list and "biological materials" is not a catchall phrase following more-specific enumerated categories).

These background principles influence our **[—7—]** reading of a statute, sometimes even moving us to interpret a provision differently than we might otherwise.

Recently, the Supreme Court formalized another background principle: the major-questions doctrine. *West Virginia v. EPA*, 142 S. Ct. 2587, 2608–14 (2022); *see also Biden v. Nebraska,* 143 S. Ct. 2355, 2372–75 (2023). This background rule requires clear congressional authorization for agency action in "extraordinary cases" when the "history and breadth" and "economic and political significance" of the action at issue gives us "'reason to hesitate before concluding that Congress' meant to confer such authority" to act on the agency. *West Virginia*, 142 S. Ct. at 2608 (quoting *FDA v. Brown & Williamson Tobacco Corp.*, 529 U.S. 120, 159–60 (2000). The doctrine's boundaries remain hazy,[5] but the Supreme Court's cases provide helpful guideposts.

As its name suggests, the major-questions doctrine applies only when the question at issue—*i.e.*, the authority the agency is claimed to have—is a major one. That is, the question must have significant political and economic consequences. *See, e.g., Nebraska,* **[—8—]** 143 S. Ct. at 2372–73 (finding a major question where the Secretary of Education sought to free 43 million borrowers from their obligations to repay **{-297-}** $430 billion in student loans); *West Virginia*, 142 S. Ct. at 2604 (applying the major-questions doctrine when agency plan would have worked an "aggressive transformation in the domestic energy industry"); *Util. Air Regulatory Grp. v. EPA*, 573 U.S. 302, 328 (2014) (holding that the authority to regulate "millions of small sources—including retail stores, offices, apartment buildings, shopping centers, schools, and churches" was a major question).

But that is not all. The Court has highlighted several other hallmarks that should send us searching for clear authorization from Congress before adopting an "expansive construction of the statute," *West Virginia*, 142 S. Ct. at 2608 (quoting *Brown & Williamson*, 529 U.S. at 160), that would generate an "[e]xtraordinary grant[ ] of regulatory authority," *id.* at 2609. One such hallmark is when the Act's structure indicates that Congress did not mean to regulate the issue in the way claimed. *See, e.g., Util. Air*, 573 U.S. at 321–22; *Brown & Williamson*, 529 U.S. 138–39; *Nebraska*, 143 S. Ct. at 2373–74. Likewise, we might draw the same inference when there is a different, "distinct regulatory scheme" already in place to deal with the issue which would conflict with the agency's newly asserted authority. *See Brown & Williamson*, 529 U.S. at 143–46.

Similarly, we are more hesitant to recognize new-found powers in old statutes against a backdrop of an agency failing to invoke them previously. *See West Virginia*, 142 S. Ct. at 2610; *Nat'l Fed'n of Indep. Bus. v. Dep't of Labor,* 142 S. Ct. 661, 666 (2022). Or when the asserted power raises federalism concerns. *See Solid Waste Agency of N. Cook Cnty. v. U.S. Army Corps of Engineers*, 531 U.S. 159, 172–73, 174 (2001); *see also* **[—9—]** *Alabama Ass'n of Realtors v. Dep't of Health & Hum. Servs.*, 141 S. Ct. 2485, 2489 (2021). And the Court has said that we should be skeptical when the asserted authority falls outside the agency's traditional expertise, *see West Virginia,* 142 S. Ct. at 2609, 2612–13, or is found in an

[5] One ongoing debate is whether the major-questions doctrine is a clear-statement rule. Some believe that it is. *See* Cass R. Sunstein, *There Are Two "Major Questions" Doctrines*, 73 Admin. L. Rev. 475, 483–84 (2021); *see also West Virginia*, 142 S. Ct. at 2616–17, 2619 (Gorsuch, J., concurring). But clear-statement rules sit uncomfortably with our commitment to textualism. *See* Antonin Scalia, *A Matter of Interpretation* 27–29 (1997) (arguing that substantive interpretive canons "load the dice for or against a particular result"); *see also Nebraska*, 143 S. Ct. at 2376 (Barrett, J., concurring). So academics and the Supreme Court have rightfully plumbed the analytical foundations of clear-statement rules. *See* Stephen E. Sachs, *The Law of Interpretation*, 130 Harv. L. Rev. 1079, 1122–28 (2017); *Nebraska*, 143 S. Ct. at 2377 (Barrett, J., concurring); *see also* Tr. of Oral Arg. 59–60, *Ysleta del Sur Pueblo v. Texas*, No. 20-493 (Feb. 22, 2022) (Justice Kagan asking if the Court should "just toss . . . out" the substantive canons of interpretation). Yet, whatever its analytical foundation, an inferior court must simply apply the major-questions doctrine.

"ancillary provision." *Whitman v. Am. Trucking Ass'ns, Inc.*, 531 U.S. 457, 468 (2001); *West Virginia*, 142 S. Ct. at 2610. While these indicators are non-exhaustive and need not be present in every major-questions case, they are among the things that cause us to hesitate and look for clear congressional authorization before proceeding.

1. The major-questions doctrine applies to Fisheries' claim

In this context, these factors demand that we seek clear authorization from Congress before holding that the shrimpers need a Clean Water Act permit to return their bycatch to the Pamlico Sound. In other words, whether returning bycatch qualifies as a "discharge" of a "pollutant" under the Act is a major question, so the major-questions doctrine applies to Fisheries' suit.

To start, Congress has erected a "distinct regulatory scheme" to address the bycatch problem. *See Brown & Williamson*, 529 U.S. at 143–46. This scheme leaves regulating bycatch to the states and the National Marine Fisheries service—not the EPA.

Congress created this scheme when it passed the Magnuson-Stevens Act of 1976, just four years after it passed the Clean Water Act. *See* 16 U.S.C. §§ 1801, 1851. Under the Act, Congress maintained the *states'* primary authority over *state* waters like Pamlico Sound. *See* § 1856(a). Fisheries **{-298-}** in state waters generally remain within the control of the **[—10—]** state unless it shirks its duty.[6] By contrast, within *federal* waters (generally between 3 and 200 nautical miles from shore), *federal* authorities must create plans to address the problem of bycatch. *See generally* Sustainable Fisheries Act, Pub. L. No. 104-297, 106 Stat. 66; *see also* 16 U.S.C. §§ 1851(a)(9), 1853(a)(11), 1881d, 1865. But even in federal waters, the job of regulating fisheries falls within the authority, and expertise, of the National Marine Fisheries Service and Regional Fishery Management Councils, not the EPA. This distinct regulatory scheme suggests that we should expect clear authorization from Congress before finding that it was effectively displaced by the Clean Water Act. *See West Virginia*, 142 S. Ct. at 2612–13; *Brown & Williamson*, 529 U.S. at 144; *Train v. Colorado Pub. Interest Rsch. Grp., Inc.*, 426 U.S. 1, 23–25 (1976).

Adopting Fisheries' interpretation would upset the Magnuson-Stevens Act's federal-state balance and raise significant federalism concerns. And Congress must be explicitly clear if it wishes to "alter[ ] the federal-state framework by permitting federal **[—11—]** encroachment upon a traditional state power." *Solid Waste Agency*, 531 U.S. at 172–73, 174; *see also Sackett v. EPA*, 143 S. Ct. 1322, 1341 (2023). This principle has played an important role in interpreting the Clean Water Act, leading the Supreme Court to reject an expansive interpretation of the Act because it "would result in a significant impingement of the States' traditional and primary power over land and water use." *Solid Waste Agency*, 531 U.S. at 174.

So too here. Congress has repeatedly confirmed that states have the primary authority to regulate fishing in their waters. Section 1251(b) of the Clean Water Act

---

[6] This federal scheme only reaches fisheries, and therefore bycatch, in state waters if, after notice and comment, the Secretary of Commerce concludes that "any State has taken any action, or omitted to take any action, the results of which will substantially and adversely affect the carrying out of [a fishery management plan implemented under the Act.]" § 1856(b)(1)(B); *see also* § 1856(a).

North Carolina has not shirked its duties to regulate bycatch in state waters. It has had a detailed fishery-management plan for shrimp since 2006. North Carolina Dept. of Envt'l and Nat. Res., *North Carolina Fishery Management Plan: Shrimp* (2006). One of the original plan's stated goals was to minimize bycatch. *Id.* at 2–3. The Division of Marine Fisheries amended the plan in 2015, and again in 2022. North Carolina Dept. of Envt'l and Nat. Res., *North Carolina Shrimp Fishery Management Plan Amendment 1,* (2015); North Carolina Dept. of Envt'l and Nat. Res., *North Carolina Shrimp Fishery Management Plan Amendment 2* (2022). A goal of the 2022 Amendment was to "[r]educe bycatch of non-target species." *See Amendment 2,* at 2. In furtherance of that goal, the Amendment included an extensive assessment of the bycatch issue and regulations intended to reduce bycatch. *See id.* at 32–50, 114–292.

contains a states'-rights-saving clause: "It is the policy of the Congress to recognize, preserve, and protect the primary responsibilities and rights of States . . . to plan the development and use (including restoration, preservation, and enhancement) of land and water resources."[7] **{-299-}** 33 U.S.C. § 1251(b). Likewise, Congress has declared that states have "title to and ownership of the lands beneath navigable waters within the boundaries of the respective States, and the natural resources within such lands and waters" and "the right and power to manage, administer, lease, develop, and use the said lands and natural resources," 43 U.S.C. § 1311(a), including "fish, shrimp . . . and other marine animal and **[—12—]** plant life." § 1301(e). Congress has also said that "it is in the public interest for each State to continue to regulate the taking for any purpose of fish and wildlife within its boundaries." Act of May 11, 2005, Pub. L. No. 109-13, 119 Stat. 231, § 6036(b)(1). Accordingly, we must read the Clean Water Act—especially when it comes to fisheries—against a backdrop where Congress has time-and-time again confirmed that primary authority resides with the states. We thus demand "exceedingly clear language" from Congress to upend this delicate federal-state balance. *Sackett*, 143 S. Ct. at 1341.

Given this balance under the existing regulatory scheme, it is unsurprising that the EPA has never sought the authority to regulate bycatch in the fifty years since the Clean Water Act was passed. Indeed, the EPA does not even seek it now. Instead, Fisheries tries to foist this authority on it.[8] The EPA's own lack of confidence that it has this authority also suggests that this is a major-questions case. *Cf. West Virginia*, 142 S. Ct. at 2610 ("'[J]ust as established practice may shed light on the extent of power conveyed by general **[—13—]** statutory language, so the want of assertion of power by those who presumably would be alert to exercise it, is equally significant in determining whether such power was actually conferred.'" (quoting *FTC v. Bunte Bros., Inc.*, 312 U.S. 349, 253 (1941))).

The authority that Fisheries seeks for the EPA would have significant political and economic consequences. *West Virginia*, 142 S. Ct. at 2608. Interpreting the Act to require the EPA to regulate bycatch would give it power over "a significant portion of the American economy." *See Brown & Williamson*, 529 U.S. at 159. Almost every commercial or recreational fishermen in America would be subject to the EPA's new regulatory control. Anyone who fishes from a boat using live bait, or by chumming, or who—after catching a fish—releases it back into the ocean, would

[7] Along with the saving clause, the Act also contains a list of "categories of sources" for which EPA must promulgate standards that limit the discharge of pollutants. *See* 33 U.S.C. § 1316(b). This list lacks any mention of bycatch or commercial fishing, despite targeting adjacent industries. *See id.* (identifying "canned and preserved seafood processing" as a type of source). The combination of these two provisions further suggests that the statute does not impliedly regulate bycatch. *See Gonzales v. Oregon*, 546 U.S. 243, 272 (2006) ("In the face of the [Controlled Substance Act's] silence on the practice of medicine generally and its recognition of state regulation of the medical profession it is difficult to defend the Attorney General's declaration that the statute impliedly criminalizes physician-assisted suicide.").

[8] This fact makes our case different from other major-questions cases. In those cases, an agency asserted broad, nationwide power, resting its authority on a provision that did not clearly authorize such an assertion. Under those circumstances, "both separation of powers principles and a practical understanding" of how Congress legislates led the Court to seek clear congressional authorization. *West Virginia*, 142 S. Ct. at 2609.

Here, the EPA is not asserting such a power. In fact, it's not asserting anything since this is a citizen suit between private parties. But Fisheries is suing precisely because the EPA has not acted. Their suit is designed to compel EPA action.

If we sided with Fisheries, the immediate consequence would be to simply ban the shrimpers from throwing their bycatch into Pamlico Sound. That might sound like a small effect; yet the consequences would be vast. For, if we adopted Fisheries' reading of the statute and held that bycatch falls within the Act's definition of pollutant, then that same reading would force the EPA to regulate not just all bycatch, but virtually all fishing, through the Act's permitting scheme. The economic and separation-of-powers stakes of our ruling thus mirror those at play in other major-questions cases.

violate the Clean Water Act unless they first obtained **{-300-}** a Clean Water Act permit alongside their ordinary fishing permits.

For example, under Fisheries' proposed reading, when my daughter fishes on a boat by casting a hooked mud minnow into the sea, she has discharged a pollutant. She has taken a biological material (the minnow) and added it to the navigable waters (the sea) from a point source (the boat). And because she has done so without a permit, she faces crushing consequences. *See Sackett*, 143 S. Ct. at 1330 (noting the crushing criminal and civil consequences for even inadvertent violations of the Clean Water Act). So too if she—like most any fisherman—returns a fish that she caught, whether because she was targeting certain species, practicing catch and release, or complying with local harvesting limits or **[—14—]** bans.[9] At argument, Fisheries sought to assure me that the EPA would not exercise its discretion to lock her up or take her allowance. *See* Oral Arg. at 7:50–9:30. Small comfort.

My daughter is not the only one who should be concerned. The economic and social consequences would be enormous. Fishing in America generates hundreds of billions of dollars, employs millions of people, and provides recreational sport for millions more.[10] *See Nebraska*, 143 S. Ct. at 2373 (noting that $469 to $519 billion is "ten times the economic impact" that has triggered the major questions doctrine (internal quotation marks omitted)). As Congress has recognized, "[c]ommercial and recreational fishing constitutes a major source of employment and contributes significantly to the economy of the Nation." 16 U.S.C. § 1801(a); *see also* 16 U.S.C. § 742a ("[T]he fish, shellfish, and wildlife resources of the Nation make a material contribution to our national economy and food supply."). Forcing virtually every fisherman to risk punishment or obtain a permit from the EPA—separate from the existing state and federal schemes—would work an enormous effect. *See Sackett*, 143 S. Ct. at 1335–36.[11] **[—15—]**

To recap, Fisheries is attempting to force the EPA to regulate bycatch, something that the agency itself has never sought to do and for which it lacks the relevant expertise. In doing so, Fisheries seeks to vastly expand the EPA's regulatory authority in a way that would upset the federal-state balance by intruding on states' authority to manage fisheries in their own waters and essentially moot the established scheme to regulate bycatch in federal waters. This sea-change would have an enormous impact on the recreational and commercial fishing industries; industries which Congress has specifically sought to protect. "Given these circumstances," **{-301-}** "this is a major questions case." *West Virginia*, 142 S. Ct. at 2610.

2. Fisheries has not identified clear authorization from Congress to support its reading of the Clean Water Act

Because the major-questions doctrine applies, Fisheries must identify "clear congressional authorization" to regulate bycatch under § 1311 of the Clean Water Act. *See West Virginia*, 142 S. Ct. at 2609. Neither "vague terms" nor "oblique or elliptical language" will suffice. *Id.* (quoting *Whitman*, 531 U.S. at 468). Yet that is all Fisheries offers. It points only to the Act's definitional section

[9] In 2020, recreational anglers took an estimated 199 million fishing trips and caught 1 billion fish, 65% of which—650 million fish—were returned to the ocean. (And even these large numbers exclude fish caught to be put back in the ocean as bait.) National Marine Fisheries Service, 2020 Fisheries of The United States 12–13 (May 2022).

[10] *See, e.g.*, National Marine Fisheries Service, Fisheries Economics of the United States 2020 (Feb. 2023); National Marine Fisheries Service, Fisheries Economics of the United States 2016 (Dec. 2016).

[11] At oral argument, Fisheries suggested in passing that the EPA could create a *de minimis* exception that would alleviate such concerns. It did not identify a source of authority for this proposition, and it does not appear that there is one. *See N.W. Env't Advocates v. EPA*, 537 F.3d 1006, 1020–22 (9th Cir. 2008). Fisheries also suggested the **[—15—]** EPA might use a general permit to cover these discharges. But it again failed to provide any authority for the EPA to do so. Given that Fisheries only referred to this possibility in passing, we need not definitively decide whether the EPA could, or would, promulgate a general permit here.

defining "pollutant" to include "biological materials" and "discharge" to include "any addition." But the Supreme Court has made clear that this kind of language does not provide the required clear authorization. **[—16—]**

To start, the Supreme Court has twice rejected the idea that literal readings of the broad terms in the Clean Water Act's definitional section—§ 1362—supply clear authorization to regulate something under the Act. In *Train v. Colorado Public Interest Research Group Inc.*, 426 U.S. 1 (1976), the Court held that the meaning of "radioactive materials" under § 1362(6) did not include nuclear materials regulated under the Atomic Energy Act. *Train*, 426 U.S. at 7–8, 25. Those nuclear materials are certainly within the literal meaning of "radioactive materials" in § 1362(6). But, to the Court, that did not clearly indicate that Congress intended the Clean Water Act to displace the Atomic Energy Commission's authority to regulate certain effluents discharged from nuclear power plants. *Id.* at 23–25. Similarly, in *Solid Waste Agency of Northern Cook County v. U.S. Army Corps of Engineers*, 531 U.S. 159 (2001), the Court acknowledged that certain isolated wetlands arguably fell within the literal meaning of "waters of the United States"—the term that § 1362(7) used to define "navigable waters," the Clean Water Act's jurisdictional hook. *Id.* at 172–73. But that literalism, the Court instructed, was not a clear authorization for the agency to regulate those wetlands. *Id.*

This approach is not unique to the Clean Water Act, either. In *Utility Air Regulatory Group v. EPA*, 573 U.S. 302 (2014), the Court discarded the idea that Congress had clearly authorized the EPA to regulate greenhouse gases under a specific provision of the Clean Air Act just because they fell within a literal interpretation of the Act's definition of "air **[—17—]** pollutant."[12] *Id.* at 315–16, 319–21. Similarly, in *FDA v. Brown & Williamson Tobacco Corp.*, 529 U.S. 120 (2000), the Court denied the FDA authority to regulate tobacco products under the Food, Drug, and Cosmetic Act even though those products fell within that statute's expansive definitions of "drug," "device," and "combination products."[13] *Id.* at 125–26. **{-302-}** Those broad definitions were too "cryptic" to qualify as clear congressional authorization. *Id.* at 160.

Each of these cases demonstrates that an expansive, vaguely worded definition is not akin to clear congressional authorization. So, in a major-questions case, more is required before holding that the agency has been granted the asserted power. Yet Fisheries cannot point to anything else. The sole basis for its reading is the Act's use of "biological materials" and "discharge." But, under the major-questions doctrine, it does not follow that the Clean Water Act *clearly* regulates returning bycatch to the ocean simply because bycatch falls within the literal definition of "biological materials" and returning it might be **[—18—]** understood as a "discharge."[14] *Cf.*

---

[12] The Clean Air Act defines "air pollutant" as "any air pollution agent or combination of such agents, including any physical, chemical, biological, radioactive . . . substance or matter which is emitted into or otherwise enters the ambient air." 42 U.S.C. § 7602(g).

[13] The Food, Drug, and Cosmetic Act defines "drug" to include "articles (other than food) intended to affect the structure or any function of the body." 21 U.S.C. § 321(g)(1)(C). It defines "device" to include "an instrument, apparatus, implement, machine, contrivance, implant, in vitro reagent, or other similar or related article . . . intended to affect the structure or any function of the body." § 321(h)(1)(C). "Combination products" are "products that constitute a combination of a drug, device, or biological product." 21 U.S.C. § 353(g)(1).

[14] Discharge is defined as an "addition," *see* § 1362(12), but that does not clearly encompass throwing bycatch overboard. "Addition" means "a thing or part added; increase." *Addition*, Webster's New World Dictionary (3d College ed. 1988). But bycatch adds nothing to the water that was not already there. When shrimp trawlers haul their nets out of the water, the nets are (ideally) full of shrimp and other fish (bycatch). The trawlers keep the shrimp, and throw the bycatch overboard, returning it to the water. So there is no "increase" of anything. As the Second Circuit colorfully put it, "[i]f one takes a ladle of soup from a pot, lifts it above the pot, and pours it back into the pot, one has not 'added' soup or anything else to the pot (beyond, perhaps, a *de minimis* quantity of airborne dust that fell into the ladle)." *Catskill Mountains Chapter of Trout Unlimited, Inc. v. City of New York*, 273 F.3d 481,

Util. Air, 573 U.S. at 319 (explaining that a "sweeping" act-wide definition "is not a command to regulate").

The simple truth is that, although there is a "plausible textual basis" for Fisheries' reading, § 1362(6)'s statement that "pollutant means . . . biological materials" and § 1362(12)'s statement that "discharge . . . means addition" fall short of the clear congressional authorization needed when the major-questions doctrine applies. *See West Virginia*, 142 S. Ct. at 2609. So we must reject Fisheries' proposed interpretation and hold that § 1311 of the Clean Water Act does not regulate returning bycatch to state waters. The district court thus properly dismissed Fisheries' bycatch claim.

B. Fisheries' sediment claim fails

Fisheries also alleges that the shrimp trawlers are violating § 1311(a) of the Act by employing trawl nets in the Pamlico Sound without a permit. According to Fisheries, these nets disturb the Sound's floor, causing sediment to temporarily suspend in the water. Disturbing this sediment, Fisheries says, amounts to the unpermitted discharge of a **[—19—]** pollutant. To prevail, Fisheries must leap at least three hurdles: (1) the disturbed sediment must be a pollutant; (2) that pollutant must be added to the water; and (3) that addition must come from a point source. *See* §§ 1311, 1362(11); *U.S. Pub. Rsch. Grp.*, 215 F. Supp. 2d at 246.

Fisheries has two theories of victory. Its first theory is that the sediment that the trawl nets disturb is "dredged spoil," and thus a "pollutant." If that is right, and if the shrimpers add that "dredged spoil" to the water from a point source, then they would need a § 1344 permit from the U.S. Army Corps of Engineers to lawfully use their nets.

Fisheries' second theory is that, even if the disturbed sediment is not dredged **{-303-}** spoil, it at least consists of rock and sand, which separately qualify as pollutants. If so—and again if that rock and sand is added to the water from a point source—then the trawlers would need a § 1342 permit from the EPA to lawfully use their nets.[15]

Fisheries' first theory fails at the first hurdle: it has not identified a *pollutant*. True, the Clean Water Act's definition of "pollutant" includes "dredged spoil." § 1362(6). But the trawlers' stirred-up sediment cannot be understood as dredged spoil. While the Act does not define "dredged spoil," plain language makes at least one thing clear: it must be dredged. The verb dredge means "[t]o clear out with a dredge; remove sand, silt, mud, etc., from the bottom of." *See Dredge*, American College Dictionary (1970). It generally refers **[—20—]** to an act meant "to enlarge or clean out (a river channel, harbor, etc.)." *Dredge*, Webster's New World Dictionary (2d coll. ed. 1968). In other words, dredged spoil is the accumulated result of some excavation or land-altering activity. *See* 33 C.F.R. § 323.2(c) (defining dredged material as "material that is excavated or dredged from waters of the United States."). It is not the temporary, incidental disturbance caused by a shrimp net.[16]

492 (2d Cir. 2001). Extending that analogy here, Fisheries asks us to believe that taking a ladle of soup from a pot, lifting it above the pot, removing some vegetables, and pouring the ladle back into the pot is an addition. That unintuitive understanding of discharge cannot provide clear congressional authorization.

[15] Fisheries wins if it succeeds on either theory. But the two theories are mutually exclusive since an activity cannot require both types of permits. *See Coeur Alaska, Inc. v. Se. Alaska Conservation Council*, 557 U.S. 261, 274 (2009) ("[I]f the Corps has authority to issue a permit for a discharge under [§ 1344], then the EPA lacks the authority to do so under [§ 1342].").

[16] Even if it were, Fisheries' claim might still fail. Take the second hurdle: Fisheries must show that the trawlers "discharged"—that is, *added*—a pollutant. Fisheries argues that, by stirring up sediment, the trawlers are *transforming* the ocean floor into "dredged spoil," and that this transformation constitutes the "addition" of a pollutant even if no new material is added to the water. But we need not decide whether this kind of "transformation" amounts to an "addition," and thus a "discharge."

Consider also the third hurdle: the alleged addition must come from a "point source." A point source is "any discernible, confined and discrete conveyance, including but not limited to any pipe,

This reading of "dredged spoil" also reflects the structure of the Clean Water Act. The Act sends most would-be dischargers of pollutants to the EPA to obtain a permit. *See* § 1342. But, for would-be dischargers of dredged spoil and other dredged material, the Act has a different plan. Would-be dredgers must go to the Army Corps of Engineers for their permit. *See* § 1344. The Corps specializes in—as one might expect—engineering. It oversees construction and land-alteration projects. This specialization sets it apart from the EPA. And the fact that this type of pollutant is singled out for Corps jurisdiction suggests that dredged spoil, as the term is used in the Clean Water Act, is the product of excavation and similar land-altering activities. **[—21—]**

So too does the fact that the only other type of discharge handled by the Corps is the discharge of "fill material." Discharges of fill material usually occur during construction projects. *See* 40 C.F.R. § 232.2. As this demonstrates, the Corps has jurisdiction over activities that alter the water's floor through excavation (discharge of dredged materials) and construction (discharge of fill materials). If you are not **{-304-}** performing one of those activities, you are not dredging or filling. So the shrimpers are not dredging—and thus cannot be creating dredged spoil—simply because their nets temporarily kick up sediment as they trawl for the day's catch. And that means that they do not need to obtain a permit from the Corps.

Fisheries second theory—that trawling discharges rock and sand—fails at the second hurdle: no pollutant is *added*. The Clean Water Act expressly identifies both rock and sand as pollutants. § 1362(6). Yet, even if the disturbed sediment is a "pollutant," the shrimpers did not "discharge" it. Discharging a pollutant requires its "addition" to navigable waters. § 1362(12). But, if a pollutant is already present in the body of water, moving that pollutant around inside that same body of water is not discharging it—nothing is added. *L.A. Cnty. Flood Control Dist. v. Nat. Res. Def. Council, Inc.*, 568 U.S. 78, 82–83 (2013). So the shrimpers do not need a Clean Water Act permit to stir up already-present rock and sand with their nets.

* * *

"[I]n certain extraordinary circumstances, both separation of powers principles and a practical understanding of legislative intent make us 'reluctant to read into ambiguous statutory text' the delegation claimed to be lurking there" absent "clear congressional **[—22—]** authorization" for the power claimed. *West Virginia*, 142 S. Ct. at 2609 (quoting *Util. Air*, 573 U.S. at 324). This is such a circumstance. Though the Clean Water Act's includes the term "biological materials" in its definition of "pollutant," that is not clear authorization for the EPA to regulate bycatch under the Act. So Fisheries Reform Group's first claim—that shrimpers are violating the Clean Water Act by discarding bycatch overboard without a § 1342 permit—was properly dismissed.

Fisheries' second claim—that shrimpers are violating the Act by using trawl nets without a permit—fares no better. The shrimpers are not "dredging" the Pamlico Sound with their nets, so they cannot be discharging "dredged spoil." And the dirt and sand that their nets kick up is not "added"—and thus not "discharged"—into the Sound.

Because Fisheries has not plausibly stated a claim for relief, the decision of the district court is thus

AFFIRMED.

---

ditch, channel, tunnel, conduit, well, discrete fissure, container, rolling stock, concentrated animal feeding operation, or vessel or other floating craft, from which pollutants are or may be discharged." § 1362(14). While the boat itself constitutes a point source, the net is the cause of the alleged discharge here. And it is unclear how the net constitutes a point source. *See id.* But we need not decide either question today.

This page intentionally left blank

United States Court of Appeals for the Fifth Circuit

United States Court of Appeals
for the Fifth Circuit

No. 22-40124

PORT OF CORPUS CHRISTI AUTH. OF NUECES COUNTY, TEX.
VS.
THE PORT OF CORPUS CHRISTI

Appeal from the United States District Court for the Southern District of Texas

Decided: January 6, 2023

Citation: 57 F.4th 432, 11 Adm. R. 234 (5th Cir. 2023).

Before **HIGGINBOTHAM, SOUTHWICK,** and **HIGGINSON,** Circuit Judges.

[—1—] {-433-} SOUTHWICK, Circuit Judge:

The Port of Corpus Christi Authority of Nueces County, Texas (a governmental entity), sued The Port of Corpus Christi, L.P. (a private entity) and Kenneth Berry in state court. The claims were for trespass **{-434-}** and encroachment on its submerged land that resulted from dredge operations occurring in a ship channel. The defendants removed the case, but the district court remanded, holding there was no basis for removal either under the federal officer removal statute or due to a federal question. We AFFIRM. **[—2—]**

FACTUAL AND PROCEDURAL BACKGROUND

Kenneth Berry owns Berry Island, which lies in the La Quinta Ship Channel near Corpus Christi, Texas. He also owns a company named The Port of Corpus Christi, L.P. When there is no reason to distinguish them, we refer to Kenneth Berry and his company collectively as the "Berry Parties." Berry's The Port of Corpus Christi, L.P., was sued in state court by the Port of Corpus Christi Authority of Nueces County, Texas ("Port Authority"), for service mark dilution and infringement in April 2018. The Port Authority is a creature of Texas statute. *See* Texas Special District Local Laws Code Ch. 5016.[1] In February 2022, the Port Authority filed its Second Amended Petition, added Kenneth Berry as a party, and asserted claims for trespass under Texas common law. We do not address the merits of either claim.

In this case, much of the discussion concerns a permit issued by the United States Army Corps of Engineers ("Corps"). Neither of the Berry Parties is the permittee. Instead, the permit was issued to Moda Ingleside Oil Terminal, LLC, which is also known as Enbridge Ingleside Oil Terminal, LLC ("Moda/Enbridge"). The permit authorized improvements to the company's facilities, including construction of what appears to be five new barge docks for the oil terminal. The permit allowed Moda/Enbridge to "conduct maintenance dredging operations" pursuant to specified terms and **[—3—]** conditions for compliance with federal regulations. Dredging involves the removal of sea bottom from a subsurface location to a Dredge Material Placement Area ("DMPA"). The Corps' permit required Moda/Enbridge to deposit the dredged spoil on Berry Island, an approved DMPA. After the spoil is deposited, the solid particles settle, and the liquid decants through a piping system back into Corpus Christi Bay.

Under the permit, Moda/Enbridge was required to enter into "a land use agreement with the Port of Corpus Christi as outlined in Attachment A." The district court found it unclear what "Port of Corpus Christi" referenced — Berry's company or the governmental entity. We find some clarity is provided by Attachment A, labeled "Mitigation

---

[1] The Port Authority was formerly known as the Nueces County Navigation District No. 1; the legislature adopted the current name in 1981. *See* Texas Special District Local Laws Code § 5016.0002. It is a centenarian "governmental agency and body politic incorporated with governmental powers and existing under the laws of the State of Texas . . . . After an election on October 31, 1922, it was created under Article 3, Section 52 of the Constitution and the General Laws of the State of Texas. . . . [In 1931, it] was duly converted to a Navigation District operating under Article 16, Section 59, of the Constitution of the State of Texas (Conservation and Reclamation) and the laws applicable thereto." *Meaney v. Nueces Cnty. Nav. Dist. No. 1*, 222 S.W.2d 402, 404 (Tex. Civ. App. — San Antonio, 1949, writ ref'd) (quotation marks omitted).

Plan." The lengthy attachment describes the planned improvements to the Moda/Enbridge terminal. Primarily, though, it outlines mitigation objectives and tasks. It refers several times to the "PCCA," which it identifies as the "Port of Corpus Christi Authority." It also has this reference: "The permittee [Moda/Enbridge] is negotiating a land use agreement with PCCA, owners of the submerged **{-435-}** land." The district court found only one land use agreement in the record, an easement between Moda/Enbridge and the Berry Parties, and it allowed the dredged spoil to be placed on Berry Island. For purposes of our analysis, we accept that the permit and its attachments are referring to the Berry company as a party to the land use agreement.

The permit granted to Moda/Enbridge expresses these limitations:

a. This permit does not obviate the need to obtain other Federal, state, or local authorizations required by law.
b. This permit does not grant any property rights or exclusive privileges.
c. This permit does not authorize any injury to the property or rights of others. **[—4—]**

The permit also states the federal government in no way "assume[s] any liability for . . . [d]amages to persons, property, or to other permitted or unpermitted activities or structures caused by the activity authorized by this permit."

In its Second Amended Petition, the Port Authority alleged the dredging operations on Berry Island resulted in physical trespasses and encroachments on its submerged land. Specifically, the petition added one count for Texas common law trespass, sought a temporary restraining order, and sought a temporary and permanent injunction. The Port Authority claimed "the dredge placement activities on Berry Island have in the past resulted, and in the future are practically certain to result, in suspended solids and other materials encroaching upon Plaintiff's submerged land," which adjoins Berry Island in the La Quinta Ship Channel. The Port Authority complained of sand, clay, and large, loose concrete or stones — called "rip rap" — that the defendants placed onto the Port Authority's submerged land, as well as a dredge pipe affixed over their land. These "obstructions" create "sandbars and islands that can be viewed above the low tide water line," which interfere with their "use of the submerged area in conjunction with the Corpus Christi Ship Channel and the La Quinta Ship Channel."

On February 14, 2022, after the Port Authority filed its Second Amended Petition raising the DMPA issues, the Berry Parties removed the case to the United States District Court for the Southern District of Texas. The Port Authority's complaint expressly disclaimed any issue regarding permit compliance, and it stated its claim exclusively in terms of Texas common law trespass. Nonetheless, in an amended Notice of Removal filed on February 23, 2022, the Berry Parties asserted federal jurisdiction on these grounds: (1) Federal Officer Removal Jurisdiction under 28 U.S.C. § 1442(a); (2) Federal Question Jurisdiction under 28 U.S.C. § 1331; and (3) Admiralty/Maritime Jurisdiction under 28 U.S.C. § 1333(1). **[—5—]**

The district court granted the Port Authority's motion to remand. It held federal-officer jurisdiction does not exist because the Berry Parties do not hold any federal permits, are not operating "under" the direction of any federal officer, and are not acting in the interest of the federal government. As to federal-question jurisdiction, the court held that the presence of federal dredging permits does not displace or preempt state tort law. Further, the Port Authority's requested remedy of money damages to pay for remediation does not require federal oversight. Finally, as to admiralty or maritime jurisdiction, the court concluded that "[w]ithout a separate basis for jurisdiction, an admiralty or maritime claim is not removable," and the cases to the contrary on which the Berry Parties relied are "no longer authoritative." **{-436-}**

The Berry Parties appealed, and the district court denied their motion to stay the remand during the appeal. On the same day as the Berry Parties' notice of appeal, Moda/Enbridge filed a notice of intervention in the Texas state court proceeding. The parties disagree about whether the case has been remanded.

DISCUSSION

The Berry Parties raise three issues on appeal. First, they seek reversal of the district court's order denying removal for their failure to demonstrate they are entitled to remove under the federal officer removal statute. Second, and in the alternative, they seek reversal of the district court's order denying removal for failure to demonstrate that the Port Authority's claims raise a federal question. Third, they argue this case arises under maritime and admiralty jurisdiction, which the district court determined they abandoned for failure to address the argument in a response at the district court level. **[—6—]**

An order to remand a case to state court is generally nonreviewable. 28 U.S.C. § 1447(d). Even so, when removal is sought under Section 1442 or 1443, the remand "shall be reviewable by appeal or otherwise." *Id.* The district court's remand order is reviewed *de novo*, "without a thumb on the remand side of the scale." *Latiolais v. Huntington Ingalls, Inc.*, 951 F.3d 286, 290, 8 Adm. R. 155, 156 (5th Cir. 2020) (en banc) (quotation marks and citation omitted). Federal officer removal differs from other removal doctrines because "it is not narrow or limited." *Texas v. Kleinert*, 855 F.3d 305, 311 (5th Cir. 2017) (quotation marks and citations omitted). Because part of the district court's order granting remand turned on federal officer removal under Section 1442, we review the district court's order in its entirety. *See BP P.L.C. v. Mayor & City Council of Balt.*, 141 S. Ct. 1532, 1542–43 (2021).

I. Federal officer removal

We begin with the federal officer removal statute. We recently reexamined our caselaw regarding the statute. *See Latiolais*, 951 F.3d 286, 8 Adm. R. 155. In *Latiolais*, we declared that in order to remove under Section 1442(a), the defendant must show "(1) it has asserted a colorable federal defense, (2) it is a 'person' within the meaning of the statute, (3) that has acted pursuant to a federal officer's directions, and (4) the charged conduct is connected or associated with an act pursuant to a federal officer's directions." *Id.* at 296, 8 Adm. R. at 161.

The district court applied that test and focused primarily on the third element. The district court found the defendants were not acting pursuant to any federal authority. The district court stated the Berry Parties "appear[ed] to assume that they have demonstrated the first three elements by simply referencing the [Corps'] DMPA permit." The Port Authority, in response to the notice of removal, argued the defendants did not meet their burden to establish the third element and disputed their assumptions under the first and fourth elements. **[—7—]**

The Port Authority and the district court relied heavily on *Watson v. Philip Morris Cos. Inc.*, 551 U.S. 142 (2007). The *Watson* Court concentrated on the language of the second and third elements in holding that a party does not come within the scope of the federal officer removal statute by mere compliance with federal regulations. *Id.* at 151–52. Specifically, the Court stated that

> precedent and statutory purpose make clear that the private person's "acting under" must involve an effort to assist, or to help carry out, the duties or tasks **{-437-}** of the federal superior. In our view, the help or assistance necessary to bring a private person within the scope of the statute does not include simply complying with the law.

Id. at 152 (emphasis omitted) (citations omitted). Further, the Court considered a similar, though distinguishable, situation as the one here:

> The question before us is whether the fact that a federal regulatory agency directs, supervises, and monitors a company's activities in considerable detail brings that company within the scope of the italicized language ("*acting*

under" an "*officer*" of the United States) and thereby permits removal. We hold that it does not.

Id. at 145 (emphasis in original).

The district court determined that "[d]elegation of federal governmental authority is what triggers the statute, not the status of being regulated and therefore subject to federal authority wielded by others." Relying on *Watson*, the district court found that "[n]othing in the materials of record demonstrates that either Defendant has acted to help or assist any federal officer or agency." The district court also found the Berry Parties had not demonstrated they are federal permittees. The only permittee of record was Moda/Enbridge. In reaching its decision, the district court did not consider the other three elements in *Latiolais*. **[—8—]**

On appeal, the Berry Parties rely on one of our decisions that considered the third element in some detail. *See St. Charles Surgical Hosp., L.L.C. v. Louisiana Health Serv. & Indem. Co.*, 990 F.3d 447 (5th Cir. 2021). There, we examined "the *relationship* between the removing party and the relevant federal officer," which requires "courts to determine whether the federal officer exert[s] a sufficient level of subjection, guidance, or control over the private actor." *Id.* at 455 (emphasis in original) (quotation marks and citation omitted).

The Berry Parties assert that Moda/Enbridge's permit with the Corps establishes this causal "relationship" between the Berry Parties and the Corps. Further, they contend they are not merely complying with the law but, instead, are carrying out the duties or tasks of the federal authority. The problem here is there is no federal endeavor involved with this permit, *i.e.*, there is no task or duty of a federal officer or agency the Berry Parties are carrying out. It is true the Corps authorized Moda/Enbridge to dredge and dump spoil on Berry Island. The permit, though, is allowing a private company to improve its berths for barges in a manner consistent with federal law.

The Berry Parties argue that "more attenuated relations" than theirs with the federal government have allowed appeal under Section 1442. They cite a series of cases demonstrating the difference between a private party acting under federal authority and one merely being regulated. The Port Authority, though, correctly summarizes that these opinions "dealt with a private party performing a government task delegated to it by the government, typically through a contract." The cases the Berry Parties cite are readily distinguishable:

- *Latiolais* involved a federal contractor hired by the U.S. Navy to build and refurbish the Navy's own vessels. 951 F.3d at 289, 8 Adm. R. at 155. Because the **[—9—]** alleged negligence occurred "during the refurbishment of the USS *Tappahannock*" pursuant to a federal contract, the private entity was acting "pursuant to directions of the U.S. Navy" and the "civil action relate[d] **{–438–}** to an act under color of federal office." *Id.* at 296, 8 Adm. R. at 161.

- *St. Charles* vacated a remand order where "the Office of Personnel Management . . . contracted with BCBS for administration of claims under federal health insurance plans," one of the Office's own governmental obligations. 990 F.3d at 451, 455.

- *Zeringue* held that "Crane's provision of parts in an effort to assist the Navy's construction of [Navy] vessels satisfies the 'acting under' requirement." *Zeringue v. Crane Co.*, 846 F.3d 785, 792, 5 Adm. R. 193, 196–97 (5th Cir. 2017). There, "the Navy directed Crane to build parts, and, had Crane not done so, the Navy would have had to build those parts instead." *Id.*, 5 Adm. R. at 197.

- *Humphries* dealt with a private party that "constructed and operated [a] federal facility" and thus asserted the "government contractor defense." *Humphries v. Elliott Co.*, 760 F.3d 414, 415 (5th Cir. 2014) (quotation marks and citation omitted).

- *Thornburg* held a bankruptcy trustee was "acting under" a federal officer because he was "appointed pursuant to federal law by the U.S. Trustee for the purpose of assisting the U.S. Trustee with especially heavy Chapter 13 bankruptcy caseloads" and was "tasked with carrying out the provisions of the Bankruptcy Code." *Bell v. Thornburg*, 743 F.3d 84, 89 (5th Cir. 2014).

The Berry Parties must show their activities "involve an effort to assist, or to help carry out, the duties or tasks of the federal superior." *Watson*, 551 U.S. at 152 (emphasis omitted). Acting consistently with a federal permit that authorized and set conditions for making improvements to the berths for barges at a private oil terminal is not carrying out a federal officer's tasks or duties. Because they do not satisfy the requirement of assisting or carrying out the duties of a federal officer, we need not consider **[—10—]** the other elements for federal officer removal. The district court did not err in denying removal on the basis of the federal officer removal statute.

II. Federal question jurisdiction

In the alternative, the Berry Parties contend this case arises under federal law because "any challenge to their operations constitutes a collateral attack on the [Corps'] authority pursuant to federal statutes — the Rivers and Harbors Act and Clean Water Act — and associated federal regulations."

The district courts have "original jurisdiction of all civil actions arising under the Constitution, laws, or treaties of the United States." 28 U.S.C. § 1331. Removal based on federal-question jurisdiction is permitted by 28 U.S.C. § 1441(a). Unlike federal officer removal under Section 1442, removal based on federal question is "strictly construed against removal," with doubts resolved in favor of remand in recognition of the interests of comity with state court jurisdiction. *Leffall v. Dallas Indep. Sch. Dist.*, 28 F.3d 521, 524 (5th Cir. 1994); *see also Shamrock Oil & Gas Corp. v. Sheets*, 313 U.S. 100, 108–09 (1941). "'[T]he mere presence of a federal issue in a state cause of action does not automatically confer federal-question jurisdiction.'" *Singh v. Duane Morris LLP*, 538 F.3d 334, 338 (5th Cir. 2008) (quoting *Merrell Dow Pharms. Inc. v. Thompson*, 478 U.S. 804, 813 (1986)).

In addition, "[a] plaintiff is the master of his complaint and may allege only state law causes of action, even when federal remedies might also exist." **{-439-}** *Hood ex rel. Miss. v. JP Morgan Chase & Co.*, 737 F.3d 78, 89 (5th Cir. 2013) (quotation marks and citation omitted). "[A] *defendant* cannot, merely by injecting a federal question into an action that asserts what is plainly a state-law claim, transform the action into one arising under federal law, thereby selecting the forum in which the claim shall be litigated." *Id.* (emphasis in original) (quotation marks and citation omitted). Moreover, "it is the **[—11—]** character of the action and not the defense which determines whether there is federal question jurisdiction." *Thurston Motor Lines, Inc. v. Jordan K. Rand, Ltd.*, 460 U.S. 533, 535 (1983).

The Port Authority's complaint alleges state-law trespass claims that do not implicate any federal law. When the claim is based on state law, a federal issue can be a basis for federal jurisdiction, but the federal issue is not automatically a sufficient basis:

> Only in a special and small category of cases will federal jurisdiction exist when state law creates the cause of action. That limited category of federal jurisdiction only exists where (1) resolving a federal issue is necessary to resolution of the state-law claim; (2) the federal issue is actually disputed; (3) the federal issue is substantial; and (4) federal jurisdiction will not disturb the balance of federal and state judicial responsibilities.

Board of Comm'rs v. Tennessee Gas Pipeline Co., 850 F.3d 714, 721–22 (5th Cir. 2017) ("*Tennessee Gas*") (quotation marks and footnotes omitted). In *Tennessee Gas*, we held the plaintiffs' state-law claims for negligence and nuisance properly relied on standards and duties of care that arose from federal law, and those federal standards created the necessary federal-question jurisdiction. *Id.* at 722-23.

The district court here determined the defendants' arguments "for finding a federal question embedded in the Port Authority's trespass claim [were] based on the premise that Defendants' actions were authorized, prescribed, and [were] perpetually regulated by the [Corps] pursuant to federal statutes and regulations." The defendants relied on the Rivers and Harbors Act, the Clean Water Act, "a host of federal regulations," and the Corps' Navigation Servitude. The district court rejected the argument, holding the Corps "has not exercised any right of condemnation or otherwise **[—12—]** assumed jurisdiction over the Port Authority's property rights" or their interests.

To resolve the claims here, the Texas law of trespass needs to be applied to these facts because the relevant duties and standards are not created by federal law. As defined in Texas law, a trespass is an "(1) entry (2) onto the property of another (3) without the property owner's consent or authorization." *See Environmental Processing Sys., L.C. v. FPL Farming Ltd.*, 457 S.W.3d 414, 419 (Tex. 2015). The Rivers and Harbors Act, the Clean Water Act, and other referenced federal statutes and regulations are irrelevant to the Port Authority's complaint.

We agree with the district court that the Port Authority's complaint "disclaims any issue regarding permit compliance, stating its claim exclusively in terms of Texas state law: common law trespass." The Port Authority did not allege a violation of either the Clean Water Act or the Rivers and Harbors Act. These laws do not "create[] the cause of action" and are not necessary to the Port Authority's "right to relief." *See Empire Healthchoice Assur., Inc. v. McVeigh*, 547 U.S. 677, 690 (2006). Also important, the Clean Water Act's federal permit program does not preempt all state common law causes of action. *See* **{-440-}** *International Paper Co. v. Ouellette*, 479 U.S. 481, 497–98 (1987).

Finally, the Berry Parties argue the remedies sought by the Port Authority implicate federal law because they seek to impose injunctive remedies against the Corps. Actually, such relief is not requested.

There is no federal issue raised by the Port Authority under any of the theories suggested by the Berry Parties. **[—13—]**

III. Admiralty/maritime jurisdiction

The Berry Parties also argue this case arises under maritime and admiralty jurisdiction. The district court determined the defendants abandoned this basis for removal because they did not address it in their response or sur-reply to the Port Authority's motion to remand. The Berry Parties contend this basis for removal is not waived because these arguments were "incorporated by reference from the Removal" pursuant to Rule 10(c) of the Federal Rules of Civil Procedure. Even so, the Berry Parties failed to address the Port Authority's citations to cases holding that maritime cases filed in state court cannot be removed to federal court, unless an independent basis for federal jurisdiction exists. *See Barker v. Hercules Offshore, Inc.*, 713 F.3d 208, 220, 1 Adm. R. 206, 213 (5th Cir. 2013).

We agree there was insufficient briefing on this issue in district court. The arguments presented on appeal are also thin. Essentially, the argument rests on the fact that Berry Island is in "navigable water." That is it. That is not nearly enough.

AFFIRMED.

United States Court of Appeals
for the Fifth Circuit

No. 22-30105

MEXICAN GULF FISHING CO.
vs.
UNITED STATES DEPT. OF COMMERCE

Appeal from the United States District Court for the Eastern District of Louisiana

Decided: February 23, 2023

Citation: 60 F.4th 956, 11 Adm. R. 240 (5th Cir. 2023).

Before **RICHMAN,** Chief Judge, and **ELROD** and **OLDHAM,** Circuit Judges.*

* CHIEF JUDGE RICHMAN concurs in the judgment and joins Parts II.A.1.a, II.B.1, and III of the majority opinion. JUDGE OLDHAM concurs in the judgment and joins the majority opinion except as to its reliance on *Chevron USA Inc. v. Natural Resources Defense Council, Inc.*, 467 U.S. 837 (1984).

[—2—] {-960-} ELROD, Circuit Judge:

The shores of the Gulf of Mexico are home to many charter boats. These modest vessels range in size from thirty to forty feet, and usually serve small businesses. When a charter-boat captain is not using the ship for personal recreation, he or she charters a trip for six to eight passengers, for sight-seeing or some similar purpose. This is the type of boat a few friends **{-961-}** might reserve for a fishing trip off the Galveston coast. And although recreational fishing is one of a charter boat's primary uses, the number of fish caught by anglers aboard a charter boat is relatively small; charter-boat fishing accounts for an estimated 0.20% of annual fishing in the Gulf of Mexico. This appeal concerns a regulation issued by the United States Department of Commerce that requires charter-boat owners to, at their own expense, install onboard a vessel monitoring system that continuously transmits the boat's GPS location to the Government, regardless of whether the vessel is being used for commercial or personal purposes.

We conclude that, in promulgating this regulation, the Government committed multiple independent Administrative Procedure Act violations, and very likely violated the Fourth Amendment. We are therefore compelled **[—3—]** to hold unlawful and set aside the regulation, reverse the judgment of the district court, and render judgment for the Appellants.

I

A

The Government issued the subject regulation pursuant to the Magnuson-Stevens Fishery Conservation and Management Act of 1976. That law and subsequent amendments are codified at 16 U.S.C. ch. 38. Together, the laws apply within the United States' exclusive economic zone, which extends two hundred nautical miles from each coastal state's seaward boundary. *Id.* § 1802(11). Chapter 38's stated purpose is, among other things, "to conserve and manage the fishery resources found off the coasts of the United States." *Id.* § 1801(b)(1). In pursuit of this goal, the Magnuson-Stevens Act creates supervisory bodies called fishery management councils that have jurisdiction in defined regions. *Id.* § 1852(a)(1). The body with jurisdiction in the Gulf of Mexico is called the Gulf Council. *Id.* § 1852(a)(1)(E).

The Act directs the regional councils to create and administer fishery management plans, 16 U.S.C. § 1852(h)(1), whose purpose is to "achieve and maintain, on a continuing basis, the optimum yield from each fishery." *Id.* § 1801(b)(4). It further requires that all management plans contain certain provisions, *id.* § 1853(a), and gives the regional councils discretion to include others, *id.* § 1853(b). Among other things, a management plan may require fishing vessels to obtain a for-hire permit. *Id.* § 1853(b)(1).[1] Also, all plans must accord with codified national standards. *See id.* § 1851. With respect to **[—4—]** the Magnuson-Stevens Act, the Department of Commerce has

[1] And in fact, the Gulf region management plans include such a requirement. *See, e.g.*, 50 C.F.R. § 622.20 (requiring a permit for Gulf reef fish); *see generally* 50 C.F.R. ch. VI, Pt. 622 (Fisheries of the Caribbean, Gulf of Mexico, and South Atlantic) (requiring permits for other fisheries).

delegated regulatory authority to the National Oceanic and Atmospheric Administration, and NOAA regulates fisheries through the National Marine Fisheries Service (one of its subagencies).

B

NMFS and NOAA proposed the regulation at issue on October 26, 2018. *See* Fisheries of the Caribbean, Gulf of Mexico, and South Atlantic; Electronic Reporting for Federally Permitted Charter Vessels and Headboats[2] in Gulf of Mexico Fisheries, 83 Fed. Reg. 54069. The proposed rule contained three substantive components. **{–962–}**

First, as mentioned above, the proposed rule would require charter-boat owners to install NMFS-approved Vessel Monitoring System hardware and software that transmit the vessel's GPS location "at least once per hour, 24 hours a day, every day of the year." 83 Fed. Reg. at 54076 (the GPS-tracking requirement). Further, "[a]s a condition of authorized fishing . . . a vessel owner . . . must allow NMFS [and] the U.S. Coast Guard . . . access to the vessel's position data obtained from the VMS or GPS." *Id.* at 54077. There are limited exceptions for when the vessel is in port or out of the water.

Second, the rule would require charter-boat owners to submit a report to NMFS before offloading any fish, detailing "all fish harvested and discarded, and any other information requested by the [Science and Research Director of NMFS]." 83 Fed. Reg. at 54076 (the business-information requirement). The rule does not define "other information," but it does note **[—5—]** that reports should include "information about the permit holder, vessel, location fished, fishing effort, discards, and socio-economic data." *Id.* at 54071.

Third, the rule would require that, before a charter-boat owner may take a boat out to sea, he or she must submit a trip declaration to NMFS, indicating the purpose of the trip, such as for-hire, fishing recreational, or non-fishing. 83 Fed. Reg. at 54071 (the trip-declaration requirement). In the event of a for-hire trip, the owner must "report the expected trip completion date, time, and landing location." *Id.*

After notice and comment, NOAA and NFMS published the Final Rule on July 21, 2020. *See* Fisheries of the Caribbean, Gulf of Mexico, and South Atlantic; Electronic Reporting for Federally Permitted Charter Vessels and Headboats in Gulf of Mexico Fisheries, 85 Fed. Reg. 44005. The Final Rule adopted the GPS-tracking and trip-declaration requirements as initially proposed, but modified the description of the business-information requirement. As before, the latter rule did not define "other information," and the preamble explained that reports should include "information about the permit holder, vessel, location fished, fishing effort, discards, and socio-economic data." *Id.* at 44005. But in response to a comment concerning these data, the Final Rule gave the following additional information: "NMFS will require the reporting of five economic values per trip: The charter fee, the fuel price and estimated amount of fuel used, number of paying passengers, and the number of crew for each trip." *Id.* at 44011.

As promulgated by the Final Rule, the three requirements are codified in NOAA regulations as follows: 50 C.F.R. § 622.26(b)(5) (GPS-tracking requirement); *id.* § 622.26(b)(1) (business-information requirement); and *id.* § 622.26(b)(6) (trip-declaration requirement). **[—6—]**

C

Appellants (Plaintiffs below) are captains of charter boats operating in the Gulf of Mexico with federal for-hire permits, and their companies. They filed a class-action complaint in the Eastern District of Louisiana in August of 2020, naming as defendants the Department of Commerce, NOAA, NMFS, and related federal officials. The district court certified the class on June 2, 2021. The parties then filed cross summary judgment motions. The district court granted the Government's motion and

[2] Fees for a headboat are assessed per-person, whereas fees for a charter boat are assessed per-trip. Unlike charter boats, headboats can carry as many as 70–80 passengers. Larger and more heavily-regulated that charter boats, headboats are not at issue here.

denied Plaintiffs' motion, leading to this appeal. *See Mexican Gulf Fishing Co. v. U.S. Dept. of Commerce*, 587 F. Supp. 3d 428 (E.D. La. 2022).

The business-information and trip-declaration requirements went into effect on January 5, 2021, but NMFS delayed implementation of the GPS-tracking requirement. **{-963-}** The effective date was set for March 1, 2022, and Appellants sought a stay of that requirement in the district court, but the motion was denied. Appellants then moved for an injunction pending appeal. A motions panel of this court denied that motion in an unpublished, *per curiam* order. All three requirements are therefore in effect.

II

The focus of Appellants' challenge is the GPS-tracking requirement. Appellants maintain that this requirement violates the Fourth Amendment, exceeds the authority granted by the Magnuson-Stevens Act, and is arbitrary and capricious in violation of the Administrative Procedure Act. We begin with statutory authorization, consider the merits of the constitutional question (but do not reach them), and proceed to arbitrary-and-capricious review.

A

The logically antecedent question is whether the Magnuson-Stevens Act authorizes NOAA and NMFS to issue the GPS-tracking requirement. **[—7—]** *See* 5 U.S.C. § 706(2)(C) (court must set aside agency action if it is "in excess of statutory . . . authority"). This question invokes the analytical framework set forth in *Chevron USA Inc. v. Natural Resources Defense Council, Inc.*, 467 U.S. 837 (1984). The familiar framework proceeds in two steps. "At step one, we ask whether Congress has directly spoken to the precise question at issue, in which case we must give effect to the unambiguously expressed intent of Congress and reverse an agency's interpretation that fails to conform to the statutory text." *Huawei Technologies USA, Inc. v. FCC*, 2 F.4th 421, 433 (5th Cir. 2021) (internal quotation marks and citation omitted). This inquiry uses "authoritative Supreme Court decisions" and "conventional standards of statutory interpretation." *Chamber of Commerce v. U.S. Dept. of Labor*, 885 F.3d 360, 369 (5th Cir. 2018). "If the statute is silent or ambiguous as to the specific issue, we proceed to step two and ask whether 'the agency's answer is based on a permissible construction of the statute.'" *Huawei Technologies*, 2 F.4th at 433 (quoting *Alenco Comms., Inc. v. FCC*, 201 F.3d 608, 619 (5th Cir. 2000)). But if "the statute's text is unambiguous, we need not proceed to Step Two of *Chevron*." *Western Refining Southwest, Inc. v. FERC*, 636 F.3d 719, 727 (5th Cir. 2011).[3] **[—8—]**

1

a

In keeping with the above, the first inquiry is whether, based on traditional principles of statutory construction, the Magnuson-Stevens Act authorizes the GPS-tracking **{-964-}** requirement. It is undisputed that no provision explicitly allows the Government to demand reporting of GPS information. Rather, the Government defends the requirement primarily by reference to 16.U.S.C.

[3] The concurring opinion would jettison the *Chevron* framework and simply apply the traditional tools of statutory construction to analyze the issues presented. Indeed, the opinion conjures up *Chevron* as "the Lord Voldemort of administrative law." *Post* at 30 (quoting *Aposhian v. Wilkinson*, 989 F.3d 890, 896 (10th Cir. 2021) (Tymkovich, C.J., dissenting)). To be sure, *Chevron* has become something of the-precedent-who-must-not-be-named—left unmentioned by the Supreme Court in two recent decisions addressing the reasonableness of agency action. *See generally American Hospital Assn. v. Becerra*, 142 S. Ct. 1896 (2022); *Becerra v. Empire Health Foundation, for Valley Hospital Medical Center*, 142 S. Ct. 2354 (2022). And we recognize that the concurring judge and many other distinguished jurists—as well as some who are less distinguished, *see Cargill v. Garland*, 57 F.4th 447, 464–69 (5th Cir. 2023) (*en banc*)—have questioned *Chevron*'s consistency with our duty to say what the law is. But lest we not forget, "fear of a name increases fear of the thing itself." J.K. Rowling, *Harry Potter and the Sorcerer's Stone* 298 (1998). We therefore name *Chevron*, and apply its precedent—until and unless it is overruled by our highest Court.

§ 1853(b)(4). That paragraph authorizes NMFS to include a provision within a fishery management plan that mandates the use of particular equipment: "[A fishery management plan may] prohibit, limit, condition, or require the use of specified types and quantities of fishing gear, fishing vessels, or equipment for such vessels, including devices which may be required to facilitate enforcement of the provisions of this chapter." A VMS device is "equipment," the Government says, and so NMFS may require it.

Assuming *arguendo* that a VMS device is equipment, this argument fails because the Government does not demonstrate that such a device facilitates the enforcement of the Magnuson-Stevens Act. As the Appellants observe, "no provision of the MSA requires 24-hour GPS tracking of charter-boat operators." To be sure, it could be possible that the GPS-tracking requirement facilitates the enforcement of *other* provisions. In this regard, the Government says that the GPS-tracking requirement is necessary to enforce the Act's data-collection provisions. *See* 16 U.S.C. § 1853(a)(5) (requiring that fishery management plans "specify the pertinent data which shall be submitted to the Secretary with respect to commercial, recreational, [and] charter fishing");[4] *id.* § 1851(a)(2) (mandating that "conservation and **[—9—]** management measures shall be based upon the best scientific information available"); *id.* § 1801(a)(8) (finding as a matter of fact that "[t]he collection of reliable data is essential to the effective conservation, management, and scientific understanding of the fishery resources of the United States"). According to the Government, the GPS data "will help validate [fishing] effort and aid with enforcement of the reporting requirements." 85 Fed. Reg. at 44012. It also contends that the data "improves the accuracy and reliability of fishery data by providing trip validation—in other words, corroborating whether a vessel has left the dock."

Cutting against this argument is the fact that charter-boat owners are already required to report all of the information that the Government says the GPA-tracking requirement is designed to collect. That is, before going on a trip, charter-boat owners must tell the Government the type of trip (fishing or otherwise), and if it is a fishing trip, they must also tell the Government where they are going, how long they expect the trip will take, and when and where they expect to return. 50 C.F.R. § 622.26(b)(6). And they must report "all fish harvested and discarded," as well as other commercial information. *Id.* § 622.26(b)(1). What is more, the record lacks any evidence that charter-boat owners fail to accurately report their trips. Indeed, when asked at oral argument to identify one instance in which NOAA or NMFS documented inaccurate trip reporting, counsel for the Government failed to do so.

However, an agency is not necessarily required to show evidence of an actual violation before it takes steps to detect or enforce a violation. And in a self-reporting regulatory scheme, the Government surely **{-965-}** has some interest in verifying the accuracy of self-reported data. The problem for NOAA and **[—10—]** NFMS, though, is that the GPS-tracking requirement does not conceivably enforce any statutory data-collection requirements. The data the Government demands does not communicate the location or duration of fishing, nor does it communicate the number and type of fish caught, or the equipment used to catch those fish. *See* 16 U.S.C. § 1853(a)(5). It only communicates a particular charter boat's exact location. Because that information does not further the enforcement of any provision of the Magnuson-Stevens Act, and based on the record before us, a VMS device is not "equipment" whose use the Government may mandate. 16 U.S.C. § 1853(b)(4).

---

[4] The data to be submitted includes, but is not limited to, "information regarding the type and quantity of fishing gear used, catch by species in numbers of fish or weight thereof, areas in which fishing was engaged in, time of fishing, number of hauls, economic **[—9—]** information necessary to meet the requirements of this chapter, and the estimated processing capacity of, and the actual processing capacity utilized by, United States fish processors." 16 U.S.C. § 1853(a)(5).

b

The Government also argues that the GPS-tracking requirement is authorized under two catchall provisions. The first provision requires fishery management plans to "contain the conservation and management measures . . . which are necessary and appropriate for the conservation and management of the fishery." 16 U.S.C. § 1853(a)(1)(A). And the second provision authorizes plans to "prescribe such other measures, requirements, or conditions and restrictions as are determined to be necessary and appropriate for the conservation and management of the fishery." *Id.* § 1853(b)(14).

As an initial matter, we stress that the adjectives *necessary* and *appropriate* limit the authorization contained in this provision. *See Gulf Fishermens Assn. v. NMFS*, 968 F.3d 454, 465 (5th Cir. 2020) ("The grant of authority to promulgate necessary regulations cannot expand the scope of the provisions the agency is tasked with carry[ing] out.") (internal citations omitted). For this reason, the rule is authorized by the Magnuson-Stevens Act only if it is necessary and appropriate, which at a minimum requires that its benefits reasonably outweigh its costs. *National Grain & Feed Assn. v. OSHA*, 866 F.2d 717, 733 (5th Cir. 1988); *see also Texas Independent Ginners v. Marshall*, **[—11—]** 630 F.2d 398, 411 n.44 (5th Cir. 1980) (explaining that the "expected costs" must be "reasonably related to the expected benefits").

These principles in mind, we must reject the Government's position because the asserted benefits from the GPS-tracking requirement do not bear any reasonable relationship to the undisputed costs. Start with the costs. The Final Rule found that installation of a VMS device would cost $3,000, with an additional $40 to $75 per month in service fees. *See* 85 Fed. Reg. at 44013. These are significant fees for charter-boat owners, for they primarily operate small businesses, with roughly $26,000 per year in net income. *See* 86 Fed. Reg. at 12165. And in addition to the financial cost, of course, the regulation imposes a massive privacy cost; demanding that charter-boat owners transmit their exact location to the Government, every hour of every day forever, regardless of why they are using the vessel.

What benefits does the Government point to in response? Next to nothing. It observes that "NMFS is charged with the conservation and management of the Nation's fisheries." That is certainly true, but the Government fails to connect the GPS-tracking requirement with any legitimate conservation purpose. By the Government's own telling, the only other purpose served by the requirement is to "verify whether a vessel is at the dock" and to "determine when a fishing trip was taken, and the length of that trip." 83 Fed. Reg. at 54071; 85 Fed. Reg. at 44009.[5] Perhaps **{-966-}** such information might **[—12—]** justify the inordinate costs imposed, if the Government truly needed it. But the Government already *has* this information. Indeed, at oral argument, counsel for the Government denied any awareness of inaccuracies in charter-boat owners' reporting of this same information in accordance with preexisting reporting requirements. In light of this fact, the benefit the Government obtains from receiving duplicative information is minimal, if not zero.

As a result, the Government has failed to show that the GPS-tracking requirement is necessary and appropriate for the conservation and management of the fishery. To be sure, a "strict cost-benefit analysis" is not required. *National Grain & Feed Assn.*, 866 F.2d at 733. Likewise, "we cannot say that the cost of compliance is unreasonable if the [regulation] in fact alleviates a grave danger." *Asbestos*

[5] The full explanation to the cost concern is as follows: "[R]equiring each Gulf for-hire vessel be equipped, at a minimum, with archivable vessel location tracking (cellular VMS) best balances the need to collect and report timely information with the need to minimize the cost and time burden to the industry. The vessel location tracking system is an additional mechanism that verifies vessel activity without a report having to be completed by the vessel operators. The vessel location tracking system will allow NMFS to independently determine whether the vessel leaves the dock. This will help validate effort and aid with enforcement of the reporting requirements." 85 Fed. Reg. at 44009, 44012.

Information Assn. North America v. OSHA, 727 F.2d 415, 424 (5th Cir. 1984). But here, the uncontroverted record shows that the regulation gives no meaningful benefit, let alone alleviates some great danger. Also, a necessary-and-appropriate condition requires more than just consideration of financial costs. It requires an analysis of the costs to constitutionally protected privacy interests too. *See Michigan v. EPA*, 576 U.S. 743, 752 (2015) ("[C]ost includes more than the expense of complying with regulations; *any disadvantage* could be termed a cost.") (emphasis added). Here, the Government failed to account for this crucial "cost of compliance . . . before deciding whether [the] regulation [was] appropriate and necessary." *Id.* at 751. As such, it did not "operate within the bounds of reasonable interpretation." *Id.* For these reasons, we must conclude that the expected costs associated with the GPS-tracking requirement are not "reasonably related" to its expected benefits. *Texas Independent Ginners*, 630 F.2d at 411.

* * *

The record before us does not demonstrate that a VMS device, when used as required by the regulation, is "equipment . . . which . . . facilitate[s] **[—13—]** enforcement" of the Magnuson-Stevens Act, 16.U.S.C. § 1853(b)(4), or that such a device is "necessary and appropriate for the conservation and management of the fishery." *Id.* § 1853(a)(1)(A), (b)(14). Accordingly, on these facts, we hold that the Act does not authorize NOAA and NMFS to promulgate the GPS-tracking requirement.

2

We reach the holding above according to the statute's plain and unambiguous language. But, as explained above, the Government urges a broad reading of the Magnuson-Stevens Act—one that authorizes the GPS-tracking requirement even on the record before us. We therefore assume *arguendo* that it is ambiguous whether the relevant provisions mean what the Government says they mean. Even so, we are required to construe them against authorizing the Final Rule because to do otherwise would raise grave constitutional concerns. *See, e.g., Hersh v. United States*, 553 F.3d 743, 754–55 (5th Cir. 2008) ("Where an otherwise acceptable construction **{-967-}** of a statute would raise serious constitutional problems, the Court will construe the statute to avoid such problems unless such construction is plainly contrary to the intent of Congress.") (quoting *Edward J. DeBartolo Corp. v. Fla. Gulf Coast Building & Constr. Trades Council*, 485 U.S. 568, 575 (1988)); *see also* Antonin Scalia & Bryan A. Garner, *Reading Law: The Interpretation of Legal Texts* 250 (2012).

a

To begin, the requirement that charter boats transmit their GPS location to the Government appears to be a search, and no warrant authorizes that search. In most circumstances, "a warrantless search is presumed to be unreasonable." *United States v. Riley*, 968 F.2d 422, 424 (5th Cir. 1992). But the Government invokes the closely-regulated-industry doctrine as an exception to that general rule. Beginning in the 1970s, the Supreme Court held that some industries "have such a history of government oversight that no **[—14—]** reasonable expectation of privacy exists." *Marshall v. Barlow's, Inc.*, 436 U.S. 307, 313 (1978). For such an industry, the threshold for whether a search is reasonable for purposes of the Fourth Amendment is much lower. *New York v. Burger*, 482 U.S. 691, 702–03 (1987). Here, the district court held that "the fishing industry" is closely regulated and concluded under *Burger* that the GPS-tracking requirement does not violate the Fourth Amendment.

Appellants and several *amici* vigorously dispute that the exception applies here. First, they contend that the Supreme Court's decision in *City of Los Angeles v. Patel*, 576 U.S. 409 (2015), which held that the hotel industry is not closely regulated, changed the standard. *Patel* explained that the Court has recognized only four industries as being closely regulated: liquor sales, firearms dealing, mining, and the operation of an automobile junkyard. 576 U.S.

at 424.[6] The Court explained its holding as follows: "Simply listing these industries refutes petitioners' argument that hotels should be counted among them. Unlike [each of the four], nothing inherent in the operation of hotels poses a *clear and significant risk to the public welfare.*" *Id.* (emphasis added). Appellants and the *amici* argue that *Patel* requires that an industry be "intrinsically dangerous," in order to be pervasively regulated.

Since *Patel,* this argument has been raised several times. Among courts of appeals, it seems only the Sixth, Seventh, and Eighth Circuits have considered the issue. The Sixth and Seventh Circuits rejected the argument, instead holding that the extent to which an industry is dangerous is just a factor to be considered in the closeness analysis. *Liberty Coins, LLC v. Goodman,* 880 F.3d 274, 284–85 (6th Cir. 2018); *Owner-Operator Independent Drivers Ass'n v. U.S. Dept. of Treasury,* 840 F.3d 879, 894 (7th Cir. 2016). The Eighth **[—15—]** Circuit did not address the question at length, but seemed to say dangerousness is now a requirement. *Calzone v. Olson,* 931 F.3d 722, 724 (8th Cir. 2019) ("But in the case of commercial property that is involved in a closely regulated industry whose operation 'poses a clear and significant risk to the public welfare,' the property **{-968-}** owner has a reduced expectation of privacy."). This court has said that the closeness analysis turns in part on "whether the industry would pose a threat to the public welfare if left unregulated," *Zadeh v. Robinson,* 928 F.3d 457, 465 (5th Cir. 2019), but was not directly confronted with the argument Appellants present here.

We now hold the Government has the better reading of *Patel.* Appellants fail to identify any textual or historical reason why the Fourth Amendment distinguishes between industries that pose a clear and significant risk to the public welfare, and those that do not. For this reason, we now join our sister Sixth and Seventh Circuits, and conclude that *Patel* "simply recognized that the industries the Court had deemed closely regulated in the past . . . were intrinsically dangerous." *Liberty Coins,* 880 F.3d at 284. *Patel* did not establish a new requirement for the closely-regulated-industry test.

b

Appellants next argue that the district court conducted its analysis too broadly. Specifically, they say the relevant industry is charter-boat fishing or recreational fishing, not commercial fishing. The district court disagreed, assessing whether the general fishing industry is closely regulated, and concluding that it is. This was error.

Dissenting in *Burger,* Justice Brennan warned that if the question of whether an industry is closely regulated is asked too broadly, "few businesses will escape such a finding." 482 U.S. at 721. The Supreme Court carried that warning forward in *Patel,* reiterating that "[t]he clear import of our cases it that the closely regulated industry . . . is the exception." 576 U.S. at 524 **[—16—]** (quoting *Barlow's,* 436 U.S. at 313). Loose application of this doctrine will "permit what has always been a narrow exception to swallow the rule." *Id.*

Because this exception is narrow, federal courts must not define the industry at issue at too high a level of generality. Indeed, in *Zadeh,* this court was careful to explain that pervasive regulation within a subset of an industry does not necessarily extend to the whole industry. 928 F.3d at 466 ("We conclude, then, that the medical industry as a whole is not a closely regulated industry for purposes of *Burger*. Still, even if the medical profession at large cannot be said to fall within these *Burger* factors, it is possible that a subset, such as those who prescribe controlled substances, would do so."). Other circuit courts regularly make the same distinction. *See, e.g., United States v. Herrera,* 444 F.3d 1238, 1243–45 (10th Cir. 2006) (although the motor carrier industry may be a closely regulated industry, the exception does not apply to a man in a pickup truck); *McLaughlin v. Kings Island,* 849 F.2d 990, 994

[6] *Colonnade Catering Corp. v. United States,* 397 U.S. 72 (1970) (liquor sales); *United States v. Biswell,* 406 U.S. 311 (1972) (firearms dealing); *Donovan v. Dewey,* 452 U.S. 594 (1981) (mining); *New York v. Burger,* 482 U.S. 691 (1987) (operation of a junkyard).

(6th Cir. 1988) (although some industries covered by OSHA may be closely regulated, the exception does not apply to all such industries).

Here, the district court erred by failing to consider whether the *charter boat fishing industry* is closely regulated. Indeed, all of the cases the district court cited for the proposition that fishing is a closely regulated industry specifically deal with *commercial* fishing.[7] As an initial matter, the Government appears to take as granted that the commercial fishing industry is closely regulated. We are not so sure. True, the Government cites several decisions **{–969–}** from two of our sister circuits that answered the question in the affirmative. *Lovgren v. Byrne*, 787 F.2d 857, 865 & n.8 (3d Cir. 1986); *Balelo v. Baldridge*, **[—17—]** 724 F.2d 753, 764–67 (9th Cir. 1984) (*en banc*); *United States v. Kaiyo Maru No. 53*, 699 F.2d 989, 994–97 (9th Cir. 1983). But all of these decisions pre-date *Burger*, which was the zenith of this doctrine, after which the Supreme Court has never again recognized an industry as closely regulated. Moreover, we have never directly considered the question, and do not address it here.

We do not address the general fishing industry because the relevant subject here is the charter boat fishing industry. As the *amici* States explain, federal statutes and regulations distinguish between fishing and charter-boat fishing, as well as between commercial and recreational fishing. On the latter point, the record shows that charter-boat fishing is more recreational than it is commercial in many respects.

The Government offers two unavailing responses. First, it contends that "courts have never approached *Burger* with Plaintiffs' self-serving level of granularity," but it neither cites authorities for this proposition nor tries to distinguish Appellants' arguments. Its only other claim is that "charter fishing is distinct from recreational fishing." That may well be true, but it does not follow that the subject of this analysis should be the general fishing industry. If anything, the legal distinctions the Government cites emphasize the need to precisely identify the scope of the industry at issue.

c

Turning to the merits, we have understood the closely related industry inquiry to turn on several factors: "The history of warrantless searches in the industry, how extensive the regulatory scheme is, whether other states have similar schemes, and whether the industry would pose a threat to the public welfare if left unregulated." *Zadeh*, 928 F.3d at 465 (citing *Burger*, 482 U.S. at 704 and *Patel*, 576 U.S. at 424). Applying the factors to the proper subject, we conclude that the charter boat fishing industry is not closely regulated. **[—18—]**

As an initial matter, the record shows there are significant differences between the charter-boat fishing industry and the general commercial fishing industry. As previously stated, charter-boat fishing accounts for only .20% of annual fishing in the Gulf of Mexico. In addition, charter boats are typically owned by small businesses, and are commonly used both for non-fishing commercial purposes, like sightseeing or personal recreation. In short, the charter boat fishing industry is different in kind and degree from the commercial-fishing industry.

Those general differences in mind, we now directly address the factors listed above. First, the record is devoid of any evidence of history of warrantless searches within the charter boat fishing industry. *Zadeh*, 928 F.3d at 465. To be sure, the Government points to some evidence of a tradition of warrantless searches with respect to the commercial fishing industry. But it fails to connect that history to the particular industry at issue here. After all, it is "the effect of such regulation upon an owner's expectation of privacy," that really matters, not history for its own sake. *Burger*, 482 U.S. at 701. Here, there is simply no evidence that a pattern of

[7] *Lovgren v. Byrne*, 787 F.3d 857, 860 (3d Cir. 1986); *Balelo v. Baldrige*, 724 F.2d 753, 765 (9th Cir. 1984); *United States v. Kaiyo Maru No. 53*, 699 F.2d 989, 997 (9th Cir. 1983); *United States v. Raub*, 637 F.2d 1205, 1209 (9th Cir. 1980) ("Commercial fishing has a long history of being a closely regulated industry.").

warrantless searches within the commercial fishing industry ever extended down to charter boats, such that it would alter the expectation of privacy in this context. Likewise, the Government offers no evidence that States employ regulatory schemes respecting the charter boat fishing industry. *Zadeh*, 928 F.3d at 465. **{-970-}**

Finally, there is no evidence in the record that the charter boat fishing industry "would pose a threat to the public welfare if left unregulated." *Id.* at 465. The Government responds that, if left unregulated, the fishing industry would pose a serious risk of overfishing and depleting a critical food supply. 16 U.S.C. § 1801 ("A national program for the conservation and management of the fishery resources of the United States is necessary to prevent overfishing."). But this makes the same mistake as before: it considers the risk of the general fishing industry, instead of considering the risk of the **[—19—]** particular charter-boat fishing industry. And the only evidence presented here shows that charter-boat fishing does *not* pose an overfishing risk because it accounts for a small percentage of total fishing within the Gulf of Mexico.

We reiterate the Supreme Court's instruction that "the closely regulated industry . . . is the exception," not the rule. *Patel*, 576 U.S. at 524. Our highest Court has recognized only four industries as closely regulated, and none since 1987. And in the dozens of cases we have considered in this area of the law, our court has extended the doctrine only twice: to the coal mining industry, *Marshall v. Texoline Co.*, 612 F.2d 935, 938 (5th Cir. 1980), and to the commercial trucking industry, *United States v. Fort*, 248 F.3d 475, 480 (5th Cir. 2001). We must be tremendously cautious in extending this doctrine, lest we "permit what has always been a narrow exception to swallow the rule." *Patel*, 576 U.S. at 524. That caution is needed to ensure that future recognition of a closely regulated industry, if any, will be consistent with the original public meaning of the Fourth Amendment. (Or perhaps, for state penal laws, consistent with the original public meaning of the Fourteenth Amendment. *See New York State Rifle & Pistol Assn. v. Bruen*, 142 S. Ct. 2111, 2162–63 (2022) (Barrett, J., concurring)). The legitimacy of any categorical exception to that Amendment rests, of course, on the exception's accordance with constitutional text, history, and tradition—as interpreted and explained by our highest Court. *See, e.g.*, *Atwater v. City of Lago Vista*, 532 U.S. 318, 326 (2001) ("In reading the [Fourth] Amendment, we are guided by 'the traditional protections against unreasonable searches and seizures afforded by the common law at the time of the framing' . . . .") (quoting *Wilson v. Arkansas*, 514 U.S. 927, 931 (1995)).

Here, the Government presents no evidence whatsoever tending to show that the charter boat fishing industry is closely regulated. On the contrary, all the pertinent evidence suggests the opposite. We therefore decline **[—20—]** to expand the narrow exception, and conclude that the charter-boat fishing industry is not closely regulated.

* * *

In light of our holding immediately above, the constitutionality of the GPS-tracking requirement turns on whether charter-boat owners have a legitimate expectation of privacy to the whole of their movements while at sea, and, if so, whether the regulation violates that expectation. *Byrd v. United States*, 138 S. Ct. 1518, 1526 (2018); *Katz v. United States*, 389 U.S. 347, 351–52 (1967). We have serious concerns that the GPS requirement violates the Fourth Amendment in this circumstance, given the Supreme Court's instruction that members of the public have a "reasonable expectation of privacy in the whole of their movements." *Carpenter v. United States*, 138 S. Ct. 2206, 2217 (2018); *see United States v. Jones*, 565 U.S. 400, 413 (2012) (Sotomayor, J., concurring); *id.* at 430 (Alito, J., concurring in **{-971-}** the judgment). Ultimately, we need not address the merits of this question because, as explained above, the requirement violates the APA for other, non-constitutional reasons. But to the extent that it is ambiguous whether the provisions at issue should be accorded the broad reading advanced by the Government, our interpretation is further supported by the obligation to construe texts to avoid "serious constitutional problems." *Hersh*, 553 F.3d at

754 (quoting *Edward J. DeBartolo Corp.*, 485 U.S. at 575).[8] **[—21—]**

B

Next, Appellants present two arguments for why the GPS-tracking requirement is arbitrary and capricious. First, that NOAA and NMFS failed to address privacy concerns expressed in public comments. And second, that the agencies did not adequately justify the GPS-monitoring requirement's costs and benefits. We agree on both counts.[9]

The APA instructs courts to set aside agency action that is "arbitrary, capricious, an abuse of discretion, or otherwise not in accordance with law." 5 U.S.C. § 706(2)(A). "Arbitrary and capricious review focuses on whether an agency articulated a rational connection between the facts found and the decision made." *ExxonMobil Pipeline Co. v. U.S. Dept. of Transportation*, 867 F.3d 564, 571 (5th Cir. 2017) (internal quotation marks and citation omitted). "In reviewing that explanation, we must consider whether the decision was based on a consideration of the relevant factors and whether there has been a clear error of judgment." *Texas v. EPA*, 983 F.3d 826, 835 (5th Cir. 2020) (quoting *Motor Vehicle Mfrs. Assn. of U.S. v. State Farm Mut. Auto. Ins. Co.*, 463 U.S. 29, 43 (1983)).

In turn, to determine whether the agency considered the relevant factors, the court must decide whether the agency addressed any "significant points . . . raised by the public comments." *Huawei Technologies*, 2 F.4th at 449 (quoting *Carlson v. Postal Regulatory Commn.*, 938 F.3d 337, 344 (D.C. Cir. 2019)). "Comments are 'significant,' and thus require response, only if they raise points 'which, if true . . . and which, if adopted, would require a **[—22—]** change in an agency's proposed rule.'" *Id.* (quoting *City of Portland v. EPA*, 507 F.3d 706, 714–15 (D.C. Cir. 2007) (alteration in original)).

1

Appellants contend that the Final Rule failed to address Fourth Amendment concerns expressed in several public comments. At least three individuals submitted an identical comment expressing this concern. The relevant text of these comments is as follows:

> There are versions of the eVTRs [electric vessel trip reporting] that provide all transiting details from the time the vessel leaves the dock, fishes and returns back to the dock. Start and end time are already recorded on the eVTR. *Providing all confidential transiting details* **{–972–}** *is a violation of our 4th Amendment right to privacy and not necessary to manage the fishery.* Such details are considered confidential by NOAA and utilized by other agencies not associated with management of the fishery. This is a dangerous precedent. Fish have tails, they move and with the climatic shift and movement of our fish into new areas over the last several years utilizing such historical data for fishery management purposes is flawed and can be misused to deny us access to the fishery. Therefore to require detailed GPS data for vessels utilized by the for hire community is not necessary for fishery management purposes, flawed if used for fishery management purposes due to the climatic shift of our stocks and is also a violation of our 4th Amendment rights. Therefore, I can't recommend mandatory use of GPS other than what is presently required by NOAA.

[8] We reiterate that our opinion does not answer the Fourth Amendment question on the merits. In addition, nothing in our discussion of the pervasively regulated industry doctrine is intended to call into question reasonable and historical regulatory practices on government land. *See, e.g.*, *United States v. Williams*, 617 F.2d 1063, 1077–79 (5th Cir. 1980) (*en banc*) (warrantless searches of vessels at sea).

[9] Our holding in Part II.A is sufficient to demand that we render judgment for the Appellants. As such, our conclusions in Parts II.B.1, II.B.2, and III should be understood as independently sufficient alternative holdings. In the Fifth Circuit, "alternative holdings are binding precedent and not obiter dictum." *Jarkesy v. SEC*, 34 F.4th 446, 459 n.9 (5th Cir. 2022) (quoting *Texas v. United States*, 809 F.3d 134, 178 n.158 (5th Cir. 2015)).

(emphasis added). NOAA and NMFS interpreted these comments to be expressing a concern relating to the handling of proprietary data. The Final Rule responded to this point, assuring the public that "data submitted to NMFS under the Gulf For-hire Reporting Amendment shall be confidential and shall not be disclosed." 85 Fed. Reg. at 44010. **[—23—]**

The district court dismissed this claim, reasoning that the comments cited above did not clearly state their privacy concerns. An agency "need not sift pleadings and documents to identify arguments that are not stated with clarity by a petitioner." *Mexican Gulf Fishing Co.*, 587 F. Supp. 3d at 466 (quoting *Huawei Technologies*, 2 F.4th at 449). Having addressed the data-confidentiality issue, the district court concluded, NMFS "was not required to dig for another basis of generalized Fourth Amendment concerns." *Id.*

However, we must agree with the Appellants because the personal-privacy concern is clear from the face of these comments. Indeed, the comments explicitly asserted that the proposed rule violated their "4th Amendment right to privacy." To be sure, an agency need not respond to issues stated unclearly. *Huawei Technologies*, 2 F.4th at 449. But neither must a comment be written by a legal or technical expert in order to put an agency on notice of a particular concern. In short, the requirement for an agency to respond to significant issues raised by public comments would be utterly toothless if it could ignore comments like those presented here. *See Texas v. Biden*, 10 F.4th 538, 554 n.4 ("[T]he opportunity to comment is meaningless unless the agency responds to significant points raised by the public.") (quoting *Sherley v. Sebelius*, 689 F.3d 776, 784 (D.C. Cir. 2012)).

Moreover, the personal-privacy concern is obvious from the invocation of the Fourth Amendment. The Supreme Court's corpus of Fourth Amendment case law on warrantless government surveillance is legion. *Carpenter v. United States*, 138 S. Ct. 2206 (2018); *United States v. Jones*, 565 U.S. 400 (2012); *Kyllo v. United States*, 533 U.S. 27 (2001); *United States v. Knotts*, 460 U.S. 276 (1983); *Smith v. Maryland*, 442 U.S. 735 (1979); *Alderman v. United States*, 394 U.S. 165 (1969); *Katz v. United States*, 389 U.S. 347 (1967); *McDonald v. United States*, 335 U.S. 451 (1948); *Goldstein v. United States*, 316 U.S. 114 (1942). The assertion that the Government failed to identify this particular concern from the public comments borders on incredible. **[—24—]**

The Government responds that its interpretation of the public comments need only **{-973-}** be "reasonable." That is true, but the standard of review does not grant the Government free license to interpret comments in a manner that ducks the hard questions. Indeed, too much deference would essentially allow the Government to bury its head in the sand. The Administrative Procedure Act demands more than this.

Having determined that the public comments raised a significant issue, we must now determine whether the Government sufficiently addressed that issue. We are compelled to conclude in the negative because, as all agree, the Government did not address the issue at all. *See, e.g., Carlson*, 938 F.3d at 345–48; *Hewitt v. Commr. of IRS*, 21 F.4th 1336, 1353 (11th Cir. 2021). Nor is there any doubt that the personal-privacy issue is significant for purposes of the APA. If the GPS-tracking requirement violates the Fourth Amendment—and we have grave concerns that it might—that constitutional issue surely "would require a change" in the proposed rule. *Huawei Technologies*, 2 F.4th at 449 (quoting *City of Portland*, 507 F.3d at 715). The Final Rule violates the APA for this additional reason.

2

Last, Appellants argue that the GPS-tracking requirement is arbitrary and capricious because NOAA and NMFS failed to justify the costs the rule would impose on the charter-boat fishing industry. In this regard, a regulation is arbitrary and capricious if the agency "failed to consider an important aspect of the problem." *State Farm*, 463 U.S. at 43. This includes, of course, considering the costs and benefits associated with the regulation. *See, e.g., Michigan*, 576 U.S. at 751. In other words, the agency's "reasons and policy choices" must "satisfy minimum standards of rationality." *Pub. Citizen v. EPA*, 343 F.3d 449, 455 (5th Cir. 2003). **[—25—]**

This argument succeeds for the same reason that the necessary-and-appropriate provisions do not authorize the GPS-tracking requirement: the Government has failed to demonstrate that it would obtain meaningful benefits from the GPS data. *Supra* Part II.A.1.b. The data only tells the Government what it already knows: when a charter boat embarks on a trip, how long it is gone, and when it returns. Although the Government stresses the value of verifying this information, verification is entirely duplicative where, as here, the Government offers no evidence that the preexisting reporting is inaccurate. And, as explained above, it is unclear from this record what, if anything, GPS data would tell the Government about where fishing occurs, how long fishing occurs, and what equipment is used for fishing. Those insignificant benefits do not bear a rational relationship to the serious financial and privacy costs imposed. As a result, the GPS-tracking requirement is arbitrary and capricious. *Pub. Citizen*, 343 F.3d at 455.

* * *

In summary, the GPS-tracking requirement is unlawful for several independently sufficient reasons. First, because the unambiguous language of the Magnuson-Stevens Act does not authorize the regulation. And the need to interpret regulations against creating constitution problems lends further support to our construction of that language. Second, because the Government failed to respond to public comments expressing concerns of personal-privacy violations stemming from GPS surveillance. And third, because the Government failed to rationally consider the associated costs and benefits.[10] **[—26—] {-974-}**

III

Appellants' final argument concerns a different component of the Final Rule: the business-information requirement. Appellants contend that this requirement violates the APA because the final version is not a "logical outgrowth" of the proposed rule. *Huawei Technologies*, 2 F.4th at 447 (quoting *National Lifeline Assn. v. FCC*, 921 F.3d 1102, 1115 (D.C. Cir. 2019)). In this regard, the Government must "adequately frame the subjects for discussion," such that "the affected party 'should have anticipated' the agency's final course in light of the initial notice." *Id.* at 447 (quoting *National Lifeline Assn.*, 921 F.3d at 1115); *see also CSX Transp., Inc. v. Surface Transp. Bd.*, 584 F.3d 1076, 1080 (D.C. Cir. 2009) (explaining that members of the public need not "divine [the agency's] unspoken thoughts") (internal quotation marks and citation omitted).

The Proposed and Final Rule describe the business-information requirement in the same manner: reports must include "all fish harvested and discarded, and any other information requested by the [Science and Research Director of NMFS]." 83 Fed. Reg. at 54076; 85 Fed. Reg. at 44017. Neither version defines *other information*. Both versions explain that the report must include "information about the permit holder, vessel, location fished, fishing effort, discards, and socio-economic data." 83 Fed. Reg. at 54071; 85 Fed. Reg. at 44005. The only difference is that the Final Rule also specifies five entries that will be required: "NMFS will require the reporting of five economic values per trip: The charter fee, the fuel price and estimated amount of fuel used, number of paying passengers, and the number of crew for each trip." 85 Fed. Reg. at 44011. **[—27—]**

The Final Rule did not provide "fair notice" because it required the reporting of an entirely

[10] Appellants offer two final arguments respecting the GPS-tracking requirements: (i) that the requirement constitutes "forced commerce" because it instructs charter-boat owners to install a VMS device at their own expense, and (ii) that the district court's interpretation of the necessary-and-appropriate provisions within the Magnuson-Stevens Act constitute a delegation of regulatory power without an "intelligible principle." *See* **[—25—]** *Gundy v. United States*, 139 S. Ct. 2116, 2123 (2019). Because we conclude that the GPS-tracking requirement is unlawful on other grounds, we do not reach these arguments.

different category of data than the data described in the Proposed Rule. *Texas Assn. of Manufacturers v. U.S. Consumer Product Safety Commn.*, 989 F.3d 368, 381 (5th Cir. 2021). The Proposed Rule gave notice of the potential obligation to report socio-economic data. The adjective *socio-economic* means "that derives from both social and economic factors; that combines both factors to provide an indication of a person's or a group's effective social situation, especially as a *socio-economic class*." 15 *The Oxford English Dictionary* 915 (2d ed. reprint 1991); *see also Webster's Third New International Dictionary* at 2163 ("[O]f, relating to, or involving a combination of social and economic factors. *Specif*; of or relating to income and social position considered as a single factor."). As such, this word limits the noun *data* to items that are both social and economic in nature.

None of the data listed in the Final Rule—charter fee, the fuel price and estimated amount of fuel used, number of paying passengers, and the number of crew for each trip—are socio-economic in essence. Rather, they are all purely economic. Indeed, that is how the regulation describes them, using the label "economic values." 85 Fed. Reg. at 44011. The Government argues that socio-economic data necessarily include economic factors, and thus that Appellants were on notice the Final Rule may demand reporting of such **{-975-}** factors. But that argument would rewrite the rule to say "social or economic data" instead of "socio-economic data."

As understood by Appellants, socio-economic is "a broad term that encompasses age, marital status, income, race, religion, sexual preference, health status, and political affiliation to name a few." This argument better comports with the language's plain meaning. If an ordinary person were asked about her socio-economic status, she would instinctively report her education, annual income, occupation, and the like. To be sure, some socio-economic data—like annual income—is more focused on the economic **[—28—]** component than on the social component. But the reason annual income is properly classified as socio-economic is that it furthers that word's meaning. That is, a person's annual income informs that person's "effective social situation." 15 *The Oxford English Dictionary* 915. The data the Government seeks to collect go only to charter-boat owners' business operations. They do not relate to "income and social position considered as a single factor," *Webster's Third New International Dictionary* 2163, and so cannot be properly characterized as socio-economic in nature.

When the Government said it may require reporting of socio-economic data, the public was entitled to take that statement at face value. To be sure, an agency need not "spell out with particularity the proposed meaning" of every term in a proposed rule. *United Steelworkers of America, AFL-CIO-CLC v. Schuylkill Metals Corp.*, 828 F.2d 314, 318 (5th Cir. 1987). But here, the Government expressly contradicted itself by including a requirement that was not within the scope of the obligations set forth in the Proposed Rule. As such, we must reject the contention that the public "should have anticipated the agency's final course in light of the initial notice." *Huawei Technologies*, 2 F.4th at 447 (quoting *Natl. Lifeline Assn.*, 921 F.3d at 1115).

The Government also points to several comments submitted by members of the public that expressed concern that economic data might be required, arguing that these comments support its assertion that the public was on notice that the Final Rule might require the reporting of purely economic values. Several commenters did indeed address economic reporting, but the Government draws the wrong inference from this fact. These comments show only that a few members of the public happened to "divine" the Government's "unspoken thoughts." *CSX Transp.*, 584 F.3d at 1080. Comments such as these do not satisfy the Government's obligation to afford the general public an opportunity to respond to clearly stated proposals. Indeed, we have expressly rejected that reasoning. *See Tex. Assn. of Manufacturers*, **[—29—]** 989 F.3d at 383 ("The fact that one commenter suggested that data above the 95th percentile is too unstable for rulemaking does not relieve the Commission of its burden to provide notice and an opportunity to comment on the clearly articulated justification for its use of such data.").

The Government gave notice that it would require reporting of socio-economic data, but ultimately required the reporting of five purely economic data points. We are therefore compelled to hold that, in promulgating a requirement that is different in kind than the proposed requirement, the Government did not adequately frame the subjects for discussion. *Huawei Technologies*, 921 F.3d at 1115. It therefore did not provide an opportunity for interested persons to participate in rulemaking, and in so doing violated the APA. 5 U.S.C. § 553(b)(2), (b)(3).

IV

In conclusion, two components of the Final Rule are unlawful. First, the Magnuson-Stevens **{–976–}** Act does not authorize the Government to issue the GPS-tracking requirement. In addition, that rule violates the Administrative Procedure Act because it is arbitrary and capricious, in turn because the Government failed to address Fourth Amendment issues when considering it and failed to rationally consider the associated costs and benefits. Second, the business-information requirement violates the APA because the Government did not give fair notice that it would require the type of data specified in the Final Rule.

We therefore HOLD UNLAWFUL and SET ASIDE the Final Rule, REVERSE the judgment of the district court, and RENDER judgment for the Appellants.

(Reporter's Note: Opinion concurring in part follows on p. 254).

[—30—] {-976-} **OLDHAM**, Circuit Judge, concurring in part:

I join the court, except as to its invocation of *Chevron*. That's for two reasons. First, the Supreme Court has directed us to use "the traditional tools of statutory interpretation" in lieu of *Chevron*. *Am. Hosp. Ass'n v. Becerra*, 142 S. Ct. 1896, 1906 (2022). In two cases just last Term, both of which directly implicated *Chevron* and the "reasonableness" *vel non* of an agency's statutory interpretation, the Court did not even cite the case. *See ibid.*; *Becerra v. Empire Health Found., for Valley Hosp. Med. Ctr.*, 142 S. Ct. 2354 (2022). Second, it's unclear how "the Lord Voldemort of administrative law" comports with our legal history and tradition. *Aposhian v. Wilkinson*, 989 F.3d 890, 896 (10th Cir. 2021) (Tymkovich, C.J., dissenting); *see also Buffington v. McDonough*, 143 S. Ct. 14, 16–19 (2022) (Gorsuch, J., dissenting from the denial of certiorari); *Baldwin v. United States*, 140 S. Ct. 690, 691–94 (2020) (Thomas, J., dissenting from the denial of certiorari); Aditya Bamzai, *The Origins of Judicial Deference to Executive Interpretation*, 126 Yale L.J. 908 (2017). Accordingly, I'd use the Supreme Court's instructions and the traditional tools of statutory interpretation to hold the GPS-tracking requirement violates the unambiguous text of the Magnuson-Stevens Act.

United States Court of Appeals
for the Fifth Circuit

No. 22-30416

NEWBOLD
VS.
KINDER MORGAN SNG OPERATOR, L.L.C.

Appeal from the United States District Court for the Western District of Louisiana

Decided: March 14, 2023

Citation: 65 F.4th 175, 11 Adm. R. 255 (5th Cir. 2023).

Before WIENER, STEWART, and ENGELHARDT, Circuit Judges.

[—1—] {-177-} ENGELHARDT, Circuit Judge:

Two years after an unfortunate single-boat accident, one of the boat's two occupants died as a result of his injuries. The boat in which he was a passenger had struck a warning sign that was totally submerged at the time of the allision between the boat and sign. His estate and survivors sued the companies responsible for the sign in question. The district court granted summary judgment to the Defendants on the ground that the incident occurred on water governed by Louisiana law rather than federal. The parties [—2—] agree that if Louisiana law governs, the claims are barred. At issue in this appeal is whether or not the allision occurred in "navigable" waters such that federal law governs. For the reasons that follow, we hold that the allision occurred on non-navigable waters and thus AFFIRM the decision of the district court.

Factual Background

On April 16, 2020, John Andrew Newbold and his nephew Jason Rodgers went fishing in the D'Arbonne Wildlife Refuge. As they were making their way back to the boat launch after a largely unsuccessful day, Newbold and Rodgers noticed a clear channel of water off to one side and decided to make one last go at fishing for the day. They turned into the swath and Rodgers, who was operating the boat, accelerated down the center. The boat then struck a submerged object and Newbold, who was sitting on a bench in the front of the boat, was ejected. Newbold hit his head on the boat's propeller, which left two large gashes on the left side of his head. Roughly two years later, Newbold died of those injuries.

It was later determined that the clear swath of water was atop a right-of-way granted to the Southern Natural Gas Company for two natural gas pipelines. Those pipelines, which are operated by Kinder Morgan,[1] cross Bayou D'Arbonne. The {-178-} rights-of-way are mowed regularly and the land above which the allision occurred had been dry roughly 67 percent of the time in the past 30 years, according to an expert report prepared on behalf of the Defendants. The submerged item which the boat struck is believed to have been a sign warning boaters not to anchor or dredge above the pipeline. The sign was subsequently replaced after it was damaged by a hurricane, but at [—3—] the time of the allision the sign was roughly 15 feet high. According to the Defendants' expert report, due to seasonal flooding, the sign has been submerged for roughly seven percent of the time across the past 30 years.

Procedural History

Through a curator,[2] Newbold, joined by his children (collectively, "Plaintiffs"), filed a petition for damages against Kinder Morgan and Southern Natural Gas in Louisiana state court. The Defendants then removed to the Western District of Louisiana under diversity jurisdiction. After roughly a year of litigation in the district court, the Defendants filed a motion for summary judgment in which they sought dismissal on the grounds that Louisiana's Recreational Use Statute ("RUS") provided them immunity from tort liability on the uncontested facts. The Plaintiffs conceded that, if applicable, the RUS would bar recovery. They submitted, however, that "the location of the

[1] Collectively, Kinder Morgan and Southern Natural Gas will be referred to as "Defendants."

[2] At the time the petition was filed and removed, Newbold was alive but incapacitated. As has been noted, Newbold passed away during the pendency of litigation. His children, who were already in the suit, carried the suit forward and amended it to include a survival action.

allision was navigable in fact and in law." Finding no material issue of fact on this issue, the district court held that the location was not navigable and thus granted summary judgment to the Defendants. This appeal followed.

Standard of Review

"We review a grant of summary judgment de novo, viewing all the evidence in the light most favorable to the nonmoving party and drawing all reasonable inferences in that party's favor." *Parm v. Shumate*, 513 F.3d 135, 142 (5th Cir. 2007) (citing *Crawford v. Formosa Plastics Corp.*, 234 F.3d 899, 902 (5th Cir. 2000)). "The court shall grant summary judgment if the **[—4—]** movant shows that there is no genuine dispute as to any material fact and the movant is entitled to judgment as a matter of law." Fed. R. Civ. P. 56(a).

Discussion

"It is well established that the Commerce Clause of the United States Constitution gives the federal government a 'dominant servitude' over the navigable waters of the United States." *Parm*, 513 F.3d at 142-43 (quoting *United States v. Cherokee Nat. of Okla.*, 480 U.S. 700, 704 (1987)). Congress has exercised that power in part to declare that "[t]he creation of any obstruction not affirmatively authorized by Congress[] to the navigable capacity of any of the waters of the United States is prohibited." 33 U.S.C. § 403. Louisiana law, however, provides that "[a]n owner, lessee, or occupant of premises owes no duty of care to keep such premises safe ... for ... fishing ... or boating or to give warning of any hazardous conditions ... whether the hazardous condition ... is one normally encountered ... or one created by the placement of structures." LA. REV. STAT. § 9:2791. Louisiana courts have noted, however, that "an injury which occurs on a navigable waterway ... is not **{-179-}** subject to a defense under" this statute. *Buras v. United Gas Pipeline Co.*, 598 So. 2d 397, 400 (La. Ct. App. 1992). As such, the parties agree that if the injury occurred in navigable water, summary judgment was unwarranted; if, conversely, the injury occurred in non-navigable water, summary judgment is appropriate.

We have elsewhere noted that "[t]he navigational servitude does not burden land that is only submerged when the river floods." *Parm*, 513 F.3d at 143. The location of the allision is on such land. Any flood waters on land unburdened by the navigational servitude are by definition not navigable for purposes of federal law and summary judgment would therefore be appropriate. However, the Plaintiffs posit three independent grounds by **[—5—]** which they suggest an exception to this general rule may be found. Each are addressed in turn.

I. Whether, due to rights procured by the Army Corps of Engineers, the navigational servitude for the Refuge is 65 feet above mean sea level.

The first ground on which the Plaintiffs claim that the allision took place on navigable water is that the "navigational servitude" for the Refuge is alleged to be 65 feet above the mean sea level ("MSL"). The allision is claimed to have occurred at 55 feet above MSL. As part of the Comprehensive Conservation Plan for the Refuge, the Army Corps of Engineers "has the right to permanently flood those lands lying below 65 feet above MSL and to flood on a seasonal basis any land lying between 65 feet above MSL and 70 feet above MSL." As such, Plaintiffs assert that the navigational servitude for the land of the Refuge is now 65 feet above MSL. At no point do the Plaintiffs assert that the Corps has, in fact, permanently flooded the Refuge, though the Comprehensive Conservation Plan notes that seasonal flooding may reach as high as 70 feet above MSL at times (a rise which the Plaintiffs attribute to the Corps' work). In response, the Defendants contend simply that "[t]he right to flood a national wildlife refuge, and not doing so, does not create navigable waters where none exist."

Any water burdened by the navigational servitude is by definition navigable, and federal law would therefore apply. "The so-called navigational servitude extends 'laterally to the entire water surface and bed of a navigable waterway, which includes all the land and waters below the ordinary high water mark.' A river's ordinary high water mark is set at 'the line of the shore established by the fluctuations of water.'" *Parm*, 513 F.3d at 143 (quoting 33 C.F.R. § 329.11(a)) (internal citation omitted). In other words, the navigational servitude relates to actualities – "the waters below the ordinary high water mark," "the line of the shore," and so forth, *id.* – rather than **[—6—]** potentialities. Should the Corps permanently flood the Refuge, the water there would likely be navigable. But as the parties agree that the Corps has not in fact permanently flooded the refuge, the water may not be said to be navigable under this theory.

II. Whether the allision occurred below the ordinary high-water mark of the Bayou D'Arbonne.

The district court reasoned that the location of the allision is above the ordinary high-water mark of the Bayou D'Arbonne because "[t]he area ... is dry 67% of the time." What's more, the district court suggested that "[t]he fact that the area has vegetation at all shows it is outside of the navigable waters of Bayou D'Arbonne." This latter ground, the Plaintiffs suggest, "defies over a century of jurisprudence and is inconsistent with the tests established by the Corps, and state **{-180-}** and federal courts." Instead, Plaintiffs submit that the ordinary high-water mark "is found at the line below which the water is so consistently present that it changes the soil and destroys the terrestrial vegetation and agricultural value of the land." The channel in which the allision occurred, an expert employed by the Plaintiffs concluded, is a "semi-permanently flooded" area which "is not ... suitable for agriculture, grazing, or growing and harvesting desirable or marketable hardwood timber." Thus, Plaintiffs submit, the location of the allision is below the ordinary high-water mark of the Bayou.

Any water below the ordinary high-water mark of a navigable waterbody is navigable. "A river's ordinary high water mark is set at 'the line of the shore established by the fluctuations of water.' It is ascertained by 'physical characteristics such as a clear, natural line impressed on the bank; ... changes in the character of the soil; destruction of terrestrial vegetation; ... or other appropriate means that consider the characteristics of the surrounding areas.'" *Parm*, 513 F.3d at 143 (quoting 33 C.F.R. § 329.11(a)) **[—7—]** (internal citation omitted). None of these characteristics – clear banks, changes in soil, destruction of vegetation and so on – is dispositive in itself. Instead, they are markers which direct courts to the type of characteristics worth evaluating: namely, "physical characteristics" which "consider the characteristics of the surrounding areas." A vegetation-based test may not be useful, for example, in a desert area in which vegetation is scarce; likewise, a vegetation-based test may be difficult to apply in a swampy area in which vegetation coincides with standing water. The D'Arbonne National Wildlife Refuge, in which the relevant location sits, is "17,421 acres of deep overflow swamp, bottomland hardwood forest, and mixed pine/hardwood uplands" which is held by the United States for the "conservation, maintenance, and management of wildlife, resources thereof, and its habitat thereon."

Plaintiffs suggest that we follow the test laid out in *Borough of Ford City v. United States*, in which the Third Circuit held that the ordinary high-water mark should be determined by finding "the land upon which the waters have visibly asserted their dominion, the value of which for agricultural purposes has been destroyed." 345 F.2d 645, 648 (3d Cir. 1965). "[T]he vegetation test for a navigable stream's ordinary high-water mark means not that within such line all vegetation has been destroyed by the water covering the soil but that the soil has been covered by water for sufficient periods of time to destroy its value for agricultural purposes." *Id.* As noted in that very case, however: "The vegetation test is useful where there is no clear, natural line impressed on the bank. If there is a clear line, as shown by erosion, and other easily recognized characteristics such as shelving, change in the character of the soil, destruction of terrestrial vegetation, and litter, it determines the line of ordinary high-water." *Id.* at 648.

Here, the location of the allision is on land that is dry 67 percent of the time, where vegetation is not destroyed and the land is not bare, as evidenced by the need to mow it with some regularity. More significantly, the Bayou **[—8—]** D'Arbonne *does* have an "unvegetated channel" which is some 597 feet wide at the location where the boat split off to fish near the sign. The sign was located 58 feet away from the unvegetated channel. The unvegetated channel is a neat, natural line by which the ordinary high-water mark may be established. Within the channel, there is no vegetation; outside of it, there is.

In *United States v. Harrell*, the Eleventh Circuit rejected a definition of the **{-181-}** navigational servitude that would have extended it "laterally over the entire area covered by the ordinary high waters of the stream, including tributaries that might not otherwise be considered navigable and areas *adjacent to the low water channel that revert to a swampy or even a dry condition as the waters recede*." 926 F.2d 1036, 1043 (11th Cir. 1991) (emphasis in original opinion). The court there called the proposed definition "ludicrous" and cited favorably the district court's assertion that such a definition "would recognize no horizontal limits to the bed of a navigable river in those areas where the banks are relatively low and flat." *Id.* (internal quotation marks and citation omitted). That language applies equally here. The unvegetated channel establishes the ordinary high-water mark of the Bayou; water outside of that channel is not navigable.

III. Whether the location is navigable in fact.

Alternatively, the Plaintiffs suggest that "there is a question of material fact as to whether the location of allision is susceptible of being used in its ordinary condition as a highway for commerce." To be clear, there is no allegation that the channel *is* currently being used for commercial purposes; the nearest evidence of that is that the boat in which Mr. Newbold was a passenger was able to traverse the channel, but "[n]either navigation nor commerce encompass recreational fishing." *Parm*, 513 F.3d at 143 (citations omitted). Instead, the Plaintiffs suggest that the channel has the *potential* to be used for commerce, and that it *may* be used either presently or **[—9—]** in the future for commerce in manners as yet apparently unknown to either the Plaintiffs or the court. As possible evidence for this, Plaintiffs note that the very placement of the sign suggests that the Defendants "expected water levels to be frequently high enough for boats to regularly travel through the area."[3]

In 1870, the Supreme Court declared that the term "navigable" refers to "every stream or body of water, susceptible of being made, in its natural condition, a highway for commerce, even though that trade be nothing more than the floating of lumber in rafts or logs." *The Daniel Ball*, 77 U.S. 557, 560 (1870). The Supreme Court has also made clear that "[t]he extent of existing commerce is not the test" for navigability. *United States v. Utah*, 283 U.S. 64, 82 (1931). Instead, while "[t]he evidence of the actual use of streams, and especially of extensive and continued use for commercial purposes may be most persuasive, ... where conditions ... explain the infrequency or limited nature of such use, the susceptibility to use as a highway of commerce may still be satisfactorily proved." *Id.* As a later Supreme Court decision summarized, "lack of commercial traffic [is not] a bar to a conclusion of navigability where personal or private use by boats demonstrates the availability of the stream for the simpler types of commercial navigation." *United States v. Appalachian Elec. Power Co.*, 311 U.S. 377, 416 (1940) (citing *Utah*, 283 U.S. at 82).

Finally, "[n]avigability, in the sense of the law, is not destroyed because the water course is interrupted by occasional natural obstructions or portages; nor need the navigation be open at all **{-182-}** seasons of the year, or at all **[—10—]** stages of the water." *Econ. Light & Power Co. v. United States*, 256 U.S. 113, 122 (1921). "Indeed, there are but few of our fresh-water rivers which did not

[3] At oral argument, Defendants' counsel suggested that the sign was not intended for boaters traversing the seasonally-flooded right-of-way but was instead designed to warn boaters on the Bayou D'Arbonne itself not to anchor over the pipeline. Given the posture of the case, we assume as correct Appellant's position on the matter.

originally present serious obstructions to an uninterrupted navigation. ... the vital and essential point is whether the natural navigation of the river is such that it affords a channel for useful commerce. If this be so the river is navigable in fact." *The Montello*, 87 U.S. 430, 443 (1874).

The Plaintiffs here fail to present even slight evidence concerning a commercial purpose for the channel in question. The closest they get is noting that the presence of the sign evinces expected boat traffic in the channel. The forms of evidence which convinced the Supreme Court that particular bodies of water are navigable are illustrative as to why this is insufficient. The Supreme Court has found navigability in fact on the basis of: (1) accounts of "large interstate commerce" involving "vessels from seventy to one hundred feet in length, with twelve feet beam, [which] drew when loaded two to two and one-half feet of water," *The Montello*, 87 U.S. at 441, (2) evidence that a channel had previously been used to support the fur trade, *Econ. Light & Power Co.*, 256 U.S. at 117, (3) evidence that a relevant section of the Colorado river had been used for "a large number of enterprises, with boats of various sorts, including rowboats, flatboats, steamboats, motorboats, barges and scows, some being used for exploration, some for pleasure, some to carry passengers and supplies, and others in connection with prospecting, surveying, and mining operations," *Utah*, 283 U.S. at 82, and (4) evidence of "two keelboats operating in 1881, eight in 1882, and eight together with a small steamboat in 1883 .... [which] carried iron ore and pig iron, as well as produce and merchandise," *Appalachian Electric Power Co.*, 311 U.S. at 411–12. No evidence of the sort exists here. If the channel in question, in its ordinary condition, has potential commercial value such that it may be called "navigable," Plaintiffs have not carried their burden to "satisfactorily prove[]" as much. *See Utah*, 283 U.S. at 82. Thus, **[—11—]** the water in which the allision occurred was not navigable and summary judgment was proper.

Conclusion

The district court's judgment is AFFIRMED.

United States Court of Appeals
for the Fifth Circuit

No. 22-20345

CORPORATIVO GRUPO
vs.
MARFIELD LTD.

Appeal from the United States District Court for the Southern District of Texas

Decided: March 24, 2023

Citation: 64 F.4th 603, 11 Adm. R. 260 (5th Cir. 2023).

Before **WIENER, STEWART,** and **ENGELHARDT,** Circuit Judges.

[—2—] {-605-} WIENER, Circuit Judge: **{-606-}**

Plaintiff-Appellant Corporativo Grupo R SA DE C.V. ("Grupo R") appeals some of the district court's findings of fact and conclusions of law following a January 2022 bench trial. Grupo R asserts that the district court erred by (1) incorrectly interpreting and applying vessel mortgage recordation requirements under Panamanian law and (2) recognizing specific lien claims by parties who failed to obtain substitute security following the judicial sale of a vessel. We AFFIRM.

I. Factual Background

In 2008, Intervenors-Appellees Caterpillar Financial Services Asia Pte Ltd ("Caterpillar") and Eksportfinans ASA ("Eksportfinans") provided a loan to Marfield Limited Incorporated ("Marfield") for the construction of an offshore construction vessel named the M/V CABALLO MAYA ("MAYA"). To secure payment of this loan, Marfield executed and delivered a First Preferred Naval Mortgage to Eksportfinans and a Second Preferred Naval Mortgage to Caterpillar on December 19, 2008. As further security for outstanding sums owed to Caterpillar, Marfield executed a Third Preferred Naval Mortgage on April 17, 2014, encumbering the whole of the MAYA. The MAYA was flagged in Panama, so all three of those mortgages were submitted to the Panama Maritime Authority Directorate General of Public Registry of Property of Vessels ("PMA"), which is the central office for the recordation of Panamanian ship mortgages. The PMA reviewed all three mortgages twice and accepted them for recordation.

In 2012, Caterpillar and Intervenor-Appellee the Norwegian Government ("Norway") provided a loan to Shanara Maritime International S.A. ("Shanara") for construction of another offshore construction vessel named the M/V CABALLO MARANGO ("MARANGO"). To secure this **[—3—]** loan, Shanara executed and delivered a First Preferred Naval Mortgage to Caterpillar and Norway on February 9, 2012. The following year, KFW IPEX-Bank GmbH ("KFW") provided a loan to Shanara to finance the acquisition of cranes for installation aboard the MARANGO. To secure payment of this loan, Shanara executed and delivered a Second Preferred Naval Mortgage to KFW on January 24, 2013. The MAYA was also flagged in Panama, so both mortgages were submitted to the PMA, which reviewed the mortgages twice and accepted them for recordation.

Once construction of the MAYA and MARANGO was completed, Marfield and Shanara chartered the vessels to Oceanografia S.A. de C.V. ("Oceanografia") for use in Mexico. The MAYA and the MARANGO were chartered there until early 2014, when the Mexican government seized the vessels in conjunction with its criminal investigation of Oceanografia. On February 28, 2014, Marfield and Shanara terminated their bareboat charters of the vessels with Oceanografia, and the vessels remained in the Mexican government's custody. Shanara and Marfield could not generate revenue on the vessels and began to fall behind on their loan payments to Intervenors-Appellees Caterpillar, Norway, KFW, and Eksportfinans (collectively, the "Lenders"). Shortly after that, bankruptcy proceedings were commenced against Oceanografia in Mexico, and, on **{-607-}** April 10, 2014, the Mexican government separately seized the MAYA and MARANGO in connection with the bankruptcy.

In early 2014, Grupo R, a Mexican conglomerate in the oil, gas, and energy sector, initiated discussions with Marfield and

Shanara to purchase the MAYA and MARANGO. On March 21, 2014, the parties entered into purchase agreements for the vessels. Shanara and Marfield were subsequently unable to obtain the release of the vessels from the Mexican government, which violated the deadlines set forth in the purchase agreements. Since the agreements are governed by English Law and contain **[—4—]** a London Maritime Arbitration Association dispute resolution clause, Grupo R initiated a London arbitration against Shanara and Marfield. Grupo R prevailed, and on May 30, 2019, a London Arbitration Panel entered awards of $5,000,000 against Marfield and $5,000,000 against Shanara.

From the initial arrest of the vessels until December 2017, the Lenders executed a number of amendments to the original loan agreements to reaffirm Marfield's and Shanara's payment obligations, which remained unfulfilled. On July 10, 2015, the Lenders, Marfield, and Shanara executed two Standstill Agreements in which Shanara and Marfield admitted that their cancellation of the Oceanografia charters constituted "materially adverse" events of default under their respective loan agreements. To avoid the imposition of liens over the MAYA and MARANGO, Caterpillar provided additional financing to Marfield and Shanara in the form of four "protective advances," or loans. In return, Marfield and Shanara executed four Preferred Naval Mortgages in favor of Caterpillar to secure the outstanding amounts due, then registered those mortgages with the PMA. The PMA reviewed each of the mortgages twice, then accepted them for recordation. Since 2014, Shanara and Marfield have made no loan payments to the Lenders on any of the nine mortgages issued.

II. Proceedings Below

On May 30, 2019, Grupo R filed suit in the U.S. District Court for the Southern District of Texas seeking to attach the MAYA and MARANGO under the Texas Civil Practice and Remedies Code Section 61.001, *et seq*. Grupo R requested that the court attach the vessels so they could be sold at judicial auction to satisfy Grupo R's arbitration awards. Grupo R attached a Certificate of Ownership and Encumbrance to its Complaint, identifying the First, Second, and Third Preferred mortgages over the MAYA and the **[—5—]** MARANGO. At the time, the MAYA and MARANGO had been released from Mexican seizure and were located in Galveston, Texas.

The district court granted Grupo R's motion to attach the MAYA and MARANGO on June 4, 2019. Shortly thereafter, the Lenders moved to intervene in the case to assert their rights, seeking judgment against Marfield and Shanara *in personam* and the MAYA and MARANGO *in rem*. The Lenders caused the vessels to be re-arrested pursuant to Rule C of the Supplemental Rules for Admiralty or Maritime Claims and Asset Forfeiture Actions.[1] Marfield and Shanara then filed an answer and counterclaim against the Lenders for declaratory judgment, fraud, and wrongful arrest.

On April 22, 2020, the district court ordered the United States Marshals Service to put the MAYA and MARANGO up for sale at a judicial auction. At the auction, the MAYA was sold to Karadeniz Holding **{-608-}** for the price of $1,700,000, which the district court confirmed on January 7, 2021. Caterpillar, which had been authorized by the court to credit bid the amount of its debt, was the successful high bidder on the MARANGO for $5,000,000. The court ordered Caterpillar to file a security bond in the amount of $4.95 million to confirm the sale of the MARANGO. Caterpillar filed the security bond on November 15, 2021, but Grupo R objected to its language. Grupo R expressed concern that the security bond would prevent Grupo R from collecting against the bond if the Lenders' mortgages were ruled unenforceable against third parties like Grupo R. The district court directed Caterpillar to amend the bond in open court to assuage Grupo R's concerns, and the parties executed an amended bond (the "Amended Bond"). **[—6—]**

On January 4, 2022, Grupo R, Marfield, and Shanara filed a stipulation of various facts,

[1] FED. R. CIV. P. SUPP. R. C.

agreeing that the London arbitration awards were subject to enforcement and recognition under the New York Convention. The district court then entered an order and judgment recognizing and confirming the London arbitration awards. With this resolved, the parties could proceed to trial.

On January 18, 2022, a three-day bench trial commenced to determine the priority of the Lenders' foreign ship mortgages and Grupo R's state-created liens, as well as the enforceability of the Lenders' mortgages. At trial, Marfield and Shanara presented testimony from the parties' corporate representatives, while the Lenders and Grupo R presented testimony from two Panamanian law experts, Jorge Loaiza for Grupo R, and Margareth Mosquera for Lenders. On June 7, 2022, the court issued its findings of fact and conclusions of law, holding, in relevant part, that (1) Marfield and Shanara are in default under the loan agreements; and (2) the Lenders' preferred ship mortgages related to said default outrank Grupo R's state-created liens arising from Grupo R's attachment of the MAYA and MARANGO under Texas state law. Grupo R timely appealed.[2]

III. Standard of Review

Following a bench trial, the district court's findings of fact are reviewed for clear error and its conclusions of law are reviewed *de novo*.[3] "So **[—7—]** long as the 'district court's account of the evidence is plausible in light of the record viewed in its entirety,' its findings must be affirmed, even if the court of appeals might 'have weighed the evidence differently.'"[4]

The district court's determination of foreign law pursuant to Rule 44.1 of the Federal Rules of Civil Procedure is a question of law subject to *de novo* review.[5] When determining an issue of foreign law **{–609–}** under Rule 44.1, "the court may consider any relevant material or source, including testimony, whether or not submitted by a party or admissible under the Federal Rules of Evidence."[6] Although treated as a question of fact at trial, on appeal, "[t]he court's determination must be treated as a ruling on a question of law."[7]

IV. Discussion

Grupo R makes two primary arguments on appeal. First, it asserts that the district court erred by incorrectly applying and interpreting Panamanian law in its determination of the relative priority of the parties' lien claims. Second, Grupo R contends that the district court erred by recognizing Caterpillar's and KFW's lien claims in connection with the credit sale of the **[—8—]** MARANGO when they failed to obtain substitute security following the sale. These arguments are discussed in turn below.

A. *Relative priority of the Lenders' mortgages as to Grupo R's state-created liens*

On appeal, the parties dispute whether the Lenders' liens created by the nine ship mortgages take priority over Grupo R's liens that arose from the attachment of the MAYA and MARANGO under Texas state law. The relative priorities of the Lenders' and Grupo R's rights determine how the proceeds from the judicial sale of the MAYA and MARANGO

---

[2] Marfield and Shanara are no longer parties to this case because the MAYA and MARANGO were sold before trial and final judgment. Marfield and Shanara expressly waived the opportunity to file briefs on behalf of those vessels in a letter to this court dated November 14, 2022. *See* Letter from Robert E. Booth in re: Cause No. 22-20345, November 14, 2022.

[3] *See Barto v. Shore Constr., LLC*, 801 F.3d 465, 471, 3 Adm. R. 415, 416 (5th Cir. 2015) (quoting *Becker v. Tidewater, Inc.*, 586 F.3d 358, 365 (5th Cir. 2009)); *Beatriz Ball, L.L.C. v. Barbagallo Co.*, **[—7—]** *L.L.C.*, 40 F.4th 308, 315 (5th Cir. 2022) (citing *Preston Expl. Co., L.P. v. GSF, L.L.C.*, 669 F.3d 518 (5th Cir. 2012)).

[4] *Bates Energy Oil & Gas, L.L.C. v. Complete Oil Field Services, L.L.C.*, No. 20-50952, 2021 WL 4840961 (5th Cir. Oct. 15, 2021) (citing *Anderson v. Bessemer City*, 470 U.S. 564, 574 (1985)).

[5] *See Iracheta v. Holder*, 730 F.3d 419, 423 (5th Cir. 2013); *Banco de Credito Indus., S.A. v. Tesoreria Gen.*, 990 F.2d 827, 832-33 (5th Cir. 1993); FED. R. CIV. P. 44.1.

[6] FED. R. CIV. P. 44.1.

[7] *Id.*; *see also Access Telecom, Inc. v. MCI Telecommunications Corp.*, 197 F.3d 694, 713 (5th Cir. 1999) (citing FED. R. CIV. P. 44.1); *Perez & Compania v. M/V Mexico I*, 826 F.2d 1449, 1450 (5th Cir. 1987).

should have been allocated.[8] The law of the forum provides the relative rankings of the liens, while Panamanian law governs the substance of the liens.[9] The ranking of liens in the United States, from highest priority to lowest priority, is as follows:

1. ***Custodia legis* expenses;**
2. Seamen's liens for wages;
3. Salvage and general average liens;
4. Tort liens;
5. **Preferred ship mortgage liens;**
6. Liens for necessaries under CIMLA;
7. **State-created liens that are maritime in nature;**
8. Maritime liens for penalty/forfeiture for violation of federal statutes;
9. Perfected non-maritime liens;
10. Attachment liens; **[—9—]**
11. Maritime liens in bankruptcy.[10]

"Once competing liens have been ranked according to class, the top priority liens will of course be paid first."[11] Moreover, "[i]f the funds are insufficient to pay the next lower ranked class in full, the available funds will be distributed among claimants in that class according to rules operating within that class."[12]

Under this ranking regime, Grupo R's rights are classified as "state-created liens that are maritime in nature," while the Lenders' liens are classified as "preferred ship mortgages." Grupo R's liens arose when it caused the MAYA and MARANGO to be attached under Texas state law. **{-610-}** The Lenders' mortgage liens, on the other hand, arose when Shanara and Marfield failed to pay the mortgages over the MAYA and MARANGO, which had been executed in Panama and registered with the PMA.[13] The Commercial Instruments and Maritime Liens Act ("CIMLA"), 46 U.S.C. § 31301 *et seq.*, defines a preferred ship mortgage as a:

> mortgage . . . established as a security on a foreign vessel if the mortgage . . . was executed under the laws of the foreign country under whose laws the ownership of the vessel is documented and has been registered under those laws in a public register at the port of registry of the vessel or at a central office.[14] **[—10—]**

The parties do not dispute that the Lenders' preferred ship mortgage liens outrank Grupo R's state-created maritime attachment liens, and the district court confirmed those rankings in its findings of fact and conclusions of law.[15] The threshold issue on appeal is whether the Lenders' mortgages are valid and enforceable against third parties like Grupo R, allowing Lenders to exercise their priority over the proceeds of the judicial sale of the MAYA and MARANGO.

B. *Validity and enforceability of the preferred ship mortgages under CIMLA and Panamanian law*

Grupo R and the Lenders agree that CIMLA and Panamanian law are implicated in the resolution of this lawsuit. At trial, it was undisputed that (1) the Vessels are registered under Panama's flag; (2) the PMA is the public register or central office charged with recording vessel mortgages in Panama; and (3) all nine of the Lenders' mortgages were recorded with the PMA, reviewed and accepted by the PMA before their recordation, and reviewed again by the PMA when it issued certificates confirming the mortgages' compliance with Panamanian law.

[8] *United States v. (One) 1 254 Ft. Freighter, M/V ANDORIA*, 570 F. Supp. 413, 415 (E.D. La. 1983), *aff'd*, 768 F.2d 597 (5th Cir. 1985).

[9] *Banco de Credito Indus.*, 990 F.2d at 832.

[10] *M/V ANDORIA*, 570 F. Supp. at 415.

[11] *Id.* at 415 (citing *Rayon Y. Celanese Peruana v. M/V PHGH*, 471 F. Supp. 1363 (S.D. Ala. 1979)); *see also* G. Varian, *Rank and Priority of Maritime Liens*, 47 Tul. L. Rev. 751 (1973); G. Gilmore and C. Black, The Law of Admiralty, 596 (2d ed. 1975).

[12] *M/V ANDORIA*, 570 F. Supp. at 415.

[13] 46 U.S.C. § 31301(6)(B).

[14] *Id.*

[15] Grupo R acknowledges the ranking of KFW's preferred ship mortgage lien in relation to its state-created lien but contends that KFW waived its respective "preferred ship mortgage" ranking by failing to seek substitute security following Caterpillar's credit bid for the MARANGO. This is a separate issue that is discussed further below.

Under CIMLA, "a mortgage on a foreign vessel is preferred so long as it was properly (1) executed and (2) recorded under the laws of the nation in which the foreign vessel is registered."[16] For a preferred ship mortgage, CIMLA provides a cause of action in federal court "[o]n default of any term **[—11—]** of the preferred mortgage."[17] The mortgagee may bring a civil action or an admiralty action *in personam* against the mortgagor or guarantors to recover a deficiency.[18] The mortgagee may also "enforce the preferred mortgage lien in a civil action in rem for . . . a foreign vessel."[19] As noted above, the parties agree that each of the Lender's mortgages was executed in Panama and registered with the PMA. Accordingly, the Lenders' mortgages are properly classified as "preferred ship mortgages" under CIMLA.

The Lenders contend that the inquiry should end here, asserting that CIMLA **{-611-}** "does not require Lenders to affirmatively establish all facets of Panama law before their mortgages can be recognized as preferred ship mortgages." However, Grupo R takes the position that these preferred ship mortgages are unenforceable against third parties—such as Grupo R—because they fail to meet the substantive requirements for vessel mortgages under Panamanian law. This highly technical argument is discussed further below.

The parties agree that Article 260 of Law No. 55 of 2008, the Commercial Maritime Law of Panama, governs the substantive mortgage recordation requirements under Panamanian law. The Panamanian government has apparently not issued an official English translation of the full text of Article 260 from the original Spanish version. The parties' Panamanian law experts, Loaiza and Mosquera, offered their own competing English translations of Article 260 at trial and in their expert declarations. Grupo R also pointed out that in 2011, the PMA published a "Merchant **[—12—]** Marine Circular MMC-11" in English, which refers to Article 260 and includes a translation of the mortgage recordation requirements. On appeal, the parties dispute the meaning of Article 260's third clause ("Clause 3"), which in its original form states:

> Las fechas de pago del capital o cumplimiento de las obligaciones garantizadas e intereses, o la forma de determinar dichas fechas, salvo que la hipoteca se haya constituido para garantizar obligaciones exigibles a requerimiento, futuras o sujetas a condición suspensiva.

Loaiza's translation of Clause 3 of Article 260 is as follows:

> <u>Dates of repayment of principal</u>, or for satisfaction of the secured obligations, <u>and of interest</u>, or the method to determine such dates, unless the mortgage has been granted to secure obligations payable on demand, in the future or of conditional compliance. (emphasis in original).

Mosquera's translation of Clause 3 is as follows:

> The maturity dates of principal or of compliance with the guaranteed obligations and interest or the form to determine said dates, unless the mortgage is executed as security for obligations repayable on demand, obligations subject to suspensive condition or future obligations.

The Merchant Marine Circular MMC-11's translation of Clause 3 is as follows:

> The dates for the payment of the capital of fulfilment of the secured obligation and interest, or the method used to determine said dates, except if the mortgage is created to secure obligation payable on

---

[16] *Caterpillar Fin. Servs. Corp. v. IZTACCIHUATL*, 510 F. Supp. 3d 404 (E.D. La. 2020) (citing *Governor & Co. of the Bank of Scotland v. Maria S.J.*, No. 98-1187, 1999 WL 130632, at *2 (E.D. La. Mar. 10, 1999)); *see also* 46 U.S.C. § 31301(6)(B).

[17] 46 U.S.C. § 31325(b)(1).

[18] 1 Schoenbaum, Admiralty & Mar. Law § 9:5 (6th ed. 2020) (citing 46 U.S.C. § 31325(b)(2)).

[19] 46 U.S.C. § 31325(b)(1).

demand, future obligations or obligations subject to precedent conditions.

On appeal, the parties dispute whether the phrase "[l]as fechas de pago del capital" in the original version means "loan repayment schedule," thereby requiring each registered mortgage to include a loan repayment schedule. **[—13—]**

Grupo R asserts that all nine of the Lenders' preferred ship mortgages are invalid and unenforceable against third parties because they do not include loan repayment schedules or their corresponding payment dates. At trial, Loaiza testified that "las fechas" literally translates to the plural phrase "the dates," and that none of the preferred ship mortgages include dates of repayment of the loan interest or principal. Loaiza contended at trial that that a strict interpretation of Clause 3 is warranted because Article 9 of the Panamanian Civil Code states: "[w]hen the meaning of the law is clear, its literal word will not be neglected on the pretext of consulting **{-612-}** its intent."[20] Loaiza asserts that the Lenders improperly attempted to add "maturity date" into Clause 3 when the literal translation does not support this. Grupo R claims that "[i]f the Panama legislature had intended Article 260, Clause 3 to be satisfied by the inclusion of a mortgage's maturity date alone, they would have signaled that by writing the term 'fecha de vencimiento' into Clause 3's text." Relying on *Mobile Marine Sales, Ltd. v. M/V Prodromos*,[21] a case from another circuit, Grupo R contends that the review and certification of the nine mortgages by the PMA is of little persuasive significance as to their validity.

The Lenders agree that none of the preferred mortgages include loan repayment schedules, but they dispute whether Clause 3 requires such schedules at all. Mosquera took issue with Loaiza's strict interpretation of Clause 3, analogizing it to the Spanish translation of the idiom "it's raining cats and dogs." At trial, Mosquera testified that, although Loaiza's translation of Clause 3 is technically correct, it does not reflect the true **[—14—]** meaning of Clause 3 under Panamanian law. Mosquera testified that the inclusion of the loan maturity dates in each of the preferred ship mortgages was sufficient under Clause 3, because "the maturity date is actually the date of repayment of the capital and interest of any debt." Mosquera further testified that inclusion of the maturity date is an acceptable and often-used way to satisfy the "dates of repayment of principal, or for satisfaction of the secured obligations, and of interest, or the method to determine such dates" under Clause 3. Mosquera explained that some lenders may choose to include a loan repayment schedule, but that most lenders opt to include only the loan maturity date.

The Lenders alternatively contend that Grupo R had actual and constructive knowledge of the preferred ship mortgages and has not shown that it was prejudiced by the exclusion of loan repayment schedules from the preferred ship mortgages. The Lenders point out that Grupo R acknowledged that all nine mortgages were recorded with the PMA and available for review before initiating this lawsuit. The Lenders also point out that that Grupo R attached Certificates of Ownership and Encumbrance for the MAYA and MARANGO to the initial complaint, and these certificates contained information about the mortgages on the vessels. The Lenders thus contend that Grupo R had both actual and constructive knowledge of the preferred ship mortgages prior to initiating this lawsuit and that the primary purpose of mortgage registration—alerting third parties to the preferred ship mortgages—was achieved.

Under Rule 44.1 of the Federal Rules of Civil Procedure, "[f]ederal courts are competent to make determinations of foreign law."[22] Although **[—15—]** treated as a question of fact at trial, "[t]he court's determination [of foreign

[20] Loaiza relied on his own English interpretation of Article 9 in support of this assertion.

[21] 776 F.2d 85, 89 (3d Cir. 1985) ("The certification of due registration by the Public Registry is of limited persuasiveness.").

[22] *United States v. One Afghan Urial Ovis Orientalis Blanfordi Fully Mounted Sheep*, 964 F.2d 474, 477 (5th Cir. 1992) (citing FED. R. CIV. P. 44.1).

law] must be treated as a ruling on a question of law" on appeal.[23] To determine whether a mortgage is valid under foreign law, a court may consider "any relevant material or source, including testimony, whether or **{–613–}** not submitted by a party or admissible under the Federal Rules of Evidence."[24] "Courts frequently accept affidavits from foreign-law experts to guide their analyses of foreign law."[25] When there are conflicting opinions offered by experts on foreign law, "it is not the credibility of the experts that is at issue, it is the persuasive force of the opinions they expressed."[26]

The district court ultimately held that the Lenders' preferred ship mortgages are valid and enforceable under Panamanian law. The court considered testimony from both Loaiza and Mosquera at trial, as well as these experts' corresponding declarations. The court pointed out that Loaiza had contributed to the 2019 and 2021 editions of the *Maritime Law Desk Handbook*, in which he described Clause 3's requirement as "the terms for the payment of principal and interest, **or of the maturity date** or dates for compliance of the obligation secured by the mortgage, except in the case of mortgages granted to secure obligations payable on demand, future or conditional obligations, when such stipulations are not required."[27] Acknowledging its **[—16—]** authority to make determinations of foreign law pursuant to Rule 44.1, the court stated that it was "not persuaded that a Panama Maritime Court would invalidate [Lenders'] mortgages." The court explained that "the credibility and persuasive force of the opinion of [Lenders'] expert, Margareth Mosquera, are greater than that of Plaintiff's expert, Jorge Loaiza."

The district court directed the allocation of proceeds of the MAYA and the MARANGO pursuant to its conclusions regarding the liens' relative priorities. The proceeds from judicial sale of the MAYA were to be allocated as follows: (1) $63,243.90 to Grupo R and $663,745.12 to Caterpillar for their *custodia legis* lien claims; and (2) any remaining proceeds to Eksportfinans for its First Preferred Vessel Mortgage over the MAYA. The proceeds from the credit sale of the MARANGO were to be allocated to Grupo R in the amount of $63,243.90 for its *custodia legis* lien claims, and the remainder of the Amended Security Bond released to Norway, KFW, and Caterpillar.

Here, the district court sufficiently weighed the experts' competing interpretations of Panamanian law and applied the correct meaning of Clause 3. Both Loaiza and Mosquera are highly experienced and well-credentialed experts in the field of Panamanian law, but the persuasive force of Loaiza's testimony was diminished during the district court proceedings. As noted above, he admitted to publishing a passage in a well-known maritime law treatise in which he endorsed Mosquera's proposed interpretation of Clause 3. During trial, Loaiza testified that this interpretation **{–614–}** of Clause 3 only **[—17—]** applies to mortgages that are payable on demand or call for a single "balloon" payment, but he does not offer any evidentiary support for this position.

When considered together, Loaiza's, Mosquera's, and the PMA's translations of Clause 3 do not appear to preclude enforceability solely because a loan repayment schedule was omitted. Grupo R's position

---

23 *Id.*; *see also Access Telecom*, 197 F.3d at 713 (citing FED. R. CIV. P. 44.1); *Perez*, 826 F.2d at 1450.

24 *Banco de Credito Indus.*, 990 F.2d at 833 n.12 (quoting FED. R. CIV. P. 44.1).

25 *IZTACCIHUATL*, 510 F. Supp. 3d at 410 (citing *McGee v. Arkel Int'l, LLC*, 671 F.3d 539, 546–47 (5th Cir. 2012) (considering affidavits from experts on Iraqi law); *Authenment v. Ingram Barge Co.*, 878 F. Supp. 2d 672, 682 (E.D. La. 2012) (considering affidavit of expert on English law).

26 *Itar-Tass Russian News Agency v. Russian Kurier, Inc.*, 153 F.3d 82, 92 (2d Cir. 1998) (internal citation omitted).

27 CHRISTIAN BREITZKE, JONATHAN S. LUX, MARITIME LAW DESK HANDBOOK, Part II. Flag and Registration of Vessels and Mortgages of Vessels (Wolters Kluwer 2019, **[—16—]** 2021) (emphasis added). This text was not introduced into the record as an exhibit, but the district court was authorized to consider it under Rule 44.1 of the Federal Rules of Civil Procedure. FED. R. CIV. P. 44.1. During trial, Loaiza testified that he authored this portion of the treatise.

appears to ignore the phrase "o cumplimiento de las obligaciones garantizadas e intereses," or, as Loaiza translated it, "or for satisfaction of the secured obligations." According to Mosquera, the PMA and Panamanian attorneys interpret this phrase to mean "maturity date." Thus, it appears that there are two different avenues to achieve compliance with Clause 3: provide a loan repayment schedule *or* provide the maturity date of the loan in question.

We are also not convinced that compliance with Article 260's highly technical requirements is dispositive in this case. We previously held that it is "well established that the validity of a mortgage is dependent only on the existence of a debt actually secured by the mortgage and not on the description of the debt contained in the instrument."[28] Further, other circuits have explained that foreign law plays a more limited role in determining the validity and enforceability of foreign mortgages under CIMLA.[29] In *M/V Prodromos*, the Third Circuit explained that "the stringent procedural requirements for perfecting domestic ship mortgages are not **[—18—]** imposed on foreign ship mortgages . . . to provide a simplified procedure for enforcing mortgages without destroying substantive rights."[30] In fact, Grupo R's heavy reliance on *M/V Prodromos* appears to work against it because the Third Circuit ultimately held that the mortgagees' failure to include a technical requirement—the vessel's navigation license number—did not render the mortgage invalid under Panamanian law.[31]

We conclude that the district court correctly held that the nine preferred ship mortgages at issue are enforceable under CIMLA and Panamanian law, and that the Lenders' preferred ship mortgage liens enjoy priority over Grupo R's state-created maritime attachment liens.

C. *Whether Caterpillar and KFW waived their respective lien positions in relation to the credit sale of the MARANGO*

Grupo R's second primary contention on appeal is that KFW and Caterpillar waived their respective lien positions in relation to the judicial sales of the MAYA and the MARANGO. Grupo R asserts that "Caterpillar made use of a procedural tactic that allowed it to purchase the MARANGO via credit bid, such that no actual **{-615-}** monies were provided." Grupo R claims that this provided an unfair benefit to Caterpillar because it was never required to exchange or place any money in the court's registry to stand as the *res*, or substitute security, for the MARANGO after the sale. Grupo R asserts that, by failing to seek substitute security, KFW forfeited its *in rem* **[—19—]** lien claim against the MARANGO, and that Caterpillar forfeited its *custodia legis* claim against the MARANGO.

Grupo R claims that, by moving for substitute security following the MARANGO's credit sale, it was the only party to preserve its lien claims. Grupo R insists that the Amended Security Bond responded only to Grupo R's claims and made no exception for Caterpillar's *custodia legis* costs, which arose as a separate claim. Grupo R claims that, as a result, Caterpillar was not entitled to reduce the Amended Security Bond by the amount of its *custodia legis* lien claim. Grupo R further contends that any judgment KFW may now possess exists solely *in personam* against Shanara, as it no longer has a valid lien claim against the Amended Security Bond.

---

[28] *Tropicana Shipping, S.A. v. Empresa Nacional "Elcano" de la Marina Mercante,* 366 F.2d 729, 733 (5th Cir. 1966) (emphasis added); *see also Merchants Nat. Bank of Mobile v. Ward Rig No. 7, Off. No. 547149,* 634 F.2d 952, 958 (5th Cir. 1981) (citing *Tropicana Shipping* for this same proposition); *State Bank & Tr. Co. v. Lil Al M/V,* No. CV 16-5053, 2018 WL 6326448, at *3 (E.D. La. Dec. 4, 2018).

[29] *Oil Shipping (Bunkering) B.V. v. Sonmez Denizcilik Ve Ticaret A.S.*, 10 F.3d 1015, 1023 (3d Cir. 1993) (holding that the Ship Mortgage Act—CIMLA's precursor—"specifically speaks to a limited role for foreign law by making the preferred status of foreign mortgages dependent only on their compliance with the execution and registration requirements of the applicable foreign law").

[30] 776 F.2d at 89.

[31] *Id.* at 92.

The Lenders counter that it would be absurd to require Caterpillar to lodge security for its own *custodia legis* claim. Moreover, the Lenders contend that KFW's claim against the MARANGO is subject to a stipulation of payment amounts between Caterpillar and KFW under an intercreditor agreement, obviating the need for substitute security. In support, the Lenders reference Rule E(5)(a) of the Supplemental Rules for Admiralty or Maritime Claims, which states that "[w]henever process of maritime attachment and garnishment or process *in rem* is issued the execution of such process shall be stayed, or the property released, on the giving of security, to be approved by the court or clerk, or by stipulation of the parties."[32]

The district court agreed with the Lenders, holding that their interpretation of Supplemental Rule E(5)(a) was correct. The court further held that the intercreditor agreement containing a stipulation of payment between KFW and Caterpillar was sufficient to secure KFW's lien claim against the MARANGO. That court likened the stipulation to a "letter of undertaking," **[—20—]** which "is customary in the maritime industry" and "is the functional equivalent of a bond for the purpose of securing a claim against a vessel." The district court also noted that Grupo R did not offer any authority for its assertion that a secured creditor's failure to seek substitute security constitutes lien claim forfeiture.

We perceive no merit in Grupo R's alternative arguments and therefore affirm for the same reasons provided by the district court.

V. Conclusion

For the reasons detailed above, we AFFIRM the district court's findings of fact and conclusions of law with regard to (1) the validity, enforceability, and relative priority of the parties' liens following the judicial sale of the MAYA and MARANGO, and (2) the status of Caterpillar's and KFW's lien positions following the credit sale of the MARANGO.

---

32 FED. R. CIV. P. SUPP. R. E(5)(a).

United States Court of Appeals
for the Fifth Circuit

No. 22-30168

GANPAT
vs.
EASTERN PAC. SHIPPING

Appeal from the United States District Court for the Eastern District of Louisiana

Decided: April 28, 2023

Citation: 66 F.4th 578, 11 Adm. R. 269 (5th Cir. 2023).

Before **JONES, HO,** and **WILSON,** Circuit Judges.

[—1—] {-579-} HO, Circuit Judge: **{-580-}**

Litigating in a foreign country can be fraught with peril. The basic procedural and substantive protections guaranteed litigants in American courts are often taken for granted here—yet sharply limited or missing entirely before tribunals in foreign lands.

This case provides a vivid illustration: An individual brings tort and contract claims in federal court in Louisiana against a foreign corporation. In response, the corporation evades service and brings a countersuit in India, **[—2—]** before a court where the individual lacks counsel and is instead forced to take legal advice from the corporation's own attorneys.

Predictably, the corporation's attorneys act in direct conflict with the individual's interests. The corporation's attorneys not only pressure him to settle—they even manage to convince the foreign court to place him in prison, based on a bizarre claim that the individual does not object to imprisonment without bail while the case is pending.

In response to these alarming developments abroad, the federal district court in Louisiana unsurprisingly enters an anti-suit injunction to prevent the foreign corporation from litigating the same issues simultaneously before the court in India.

Our circuit precedents have long authorized district courts to enter anti-suit injunctions like the one entered here. *See, e.g.*, *Bethell v. Peace*, 441 F.2d 495, 498 (5th Cir. 1971). And our review of such anti-suit injunctions is limited to abuse of discretion. *See Kaepa, Inc. v. Achilles Corp.*, 76 F.3d 624, 626 (5th Cir. 1996). Finding no abuse, we affirm.

I.

Kholkar Vishveshwar Ganpat, a citizen of India, worked as a crew member on the *Stargate*, a merchant ship managed by the Singapore-based shipping company Eastern Pacific. When the *Stargate* stopped at Savannah, Georgia, in spring 2017, Eastern Pacific allegedly failed to stock up on anti-malarial medicine, despite warnings that the supply was low. Ganpat then contracted malaria in Gabon, the *Stargate*'s next stop—and a predictably high-risk area for malaria. When the *Stargate* arrived at Rio de Janeiro, the stop after Gabon, Ganpat went to the hospital, where his gangrenous toes—a complication of malaria—were amputated. **[—3—]**

In December 2018, Ganpat brought suit against Eastern Pacific in the Eastern District of Louisiana, alleging tort claims under the Jones Act and general maritime law, as well as contract claims arising from a collective bargaining agreement.

Eastern Pacific waived objections to personal jurisdiction and venue. However, "[o]ver a period of approximately two and a half years, [Ganpat] attempted multiple times to perfect service upon Eastern Pacific," but the corporation "did not accept service, and, instead, filed several motions to dismiss [Ganpat's] claims . . . for insufficient service of process." *Ganpat v. E. Pac. Shipping, PTE. LTD*, No. CV 18-13556, 2022 WL 1015027, at *1 (E.D. La. Apr. 5, 2022). Ganpat thus did not perfect service on the company until August 2021.

In March 2020—after Ganpat brought his complaint and Eastern Pacific consented to federal court jurisdiction, but before Ganpat perfected service—Eastern Pacific **{-581-}** sued Ganpat in Goa, India. In the Indian suit, Eastern Pacific sought an anti-suit injunction to prevent Ganpat from litigating in American court.[1]

The Indian court enjoined Ganpat from continuing his lawsuit in the United States. The court then issued an arrest warrant against Ganpat when he failed to comply.[2] Police officers, accompanied by the court bailiff and an **[—4—]** Eastern Pacific attorney, subsequently arrested Ganpat and brought him before the court.

As Ganpat's uncontradicted testimony shows, the post-arrest hearing was procedurally stacked against him. *See id.* at *3. Eastern Pacific had multiple lawyers. He had none. *See id.* What's worse, the judge instructed one of the Eastern Pacific attorneys to advise Ganpat. *See id.* In response, the Eastern Pacific lawyer took Ganpat aside and pressured him to settle. The lawyer then lied to the judge, absurdly claiming that Ganpat opposed his own release on bail. *See id.* Ganpat was then placed in a prison for violent criminals, where he was strip searched and held in a cramped cell. *See id.*[3]

In August 2021, back in the Eastern District of Louisiana, Ganpat sought an anti-suit injunction to prohibit Eastern Pacific from prosecuting its Indian suit against him. Finding the Indian litigation vexatious and oppressive, and determining that it need not show comity to the Indian court that had attempted to enjoin the American suit, the district court granted the injunction in favor of Ganpat. Eastern Pacific now appeals the district court's grant of the anti-suit injunction.

II.

We review the district court for abuse of discretion. "Under this deferential standard, findings of fact are upheld unless clearly erroneous, **[—5—]** whereas legal conclusions are subject to broad review and will be reversed if incorrect." *Kaepa*, 76 F.3d at 626 (cleaned up).

Our standard for the grant of an anti-suit injunction weighs the vexatiousness of the foreign litigation against considerations of comity. *See id.* at 627; *Karaha Bodas Co. v. Perusahaan Pertambangan Minyak Dan Gas Bumi Negara*, 335 F.3d 357, 366 (5th Cir. 2003). In this case, the vexatiousness of the foreign suit is severe—the comity considerations are, by contrast, weak. Accordingly, we see no basis to conclude that the district **{-582-}** court abused its discretion in granting the anti-suit injunction.

A.

Our circuit precedents authorize district courts to grant anti-suit injunctions "to prevent vexatious or oppressive litigation." *Kaepa*, 76 F.3d at 627. Three factors help courts determine whether to enjoin foreign litigation as vexatious: "(1) 'inequitable hardship' resulting from the foreign suit; (2) the foreign suit's ability to 'frustrate and delay the speedy and efficient determination of the cause'; and

---

[1] Strangely, the dissent characterizes Ganpat as evasive and inept. *See post*, at 16, 23. Yet it was Eastern Pacific that was evasive and coercive. Ganpat simply declined to dismiss the pre-existing American suit when Eastern Pacific foisted papers on him that would have had that effect. *See Ganpat*, 2022 WL 1015027, at *3. Eastern Pacific, by contrast, sought to slow down the American suit by repeatedly refusing service. *See id.* at *1. And Eastern Pacific aimed to thwart American jurisdiction by coercing Ganpat into dropping his suit. *See id.* at *3. Eastern Pacific's whole course of conduct thus "smacks of cynicism, harassment, and delay." *Kaepa*, 76 F.3d at 628.

[2] The dissent claims that Ganpat was "jailed for his *continued refusal* to participate in the legal proceedings." *Post*, at 16. But Ganpat was actually jailed because he refused to **[—4—]** be bullied into dropping the American suit. As the factual findings of the district court indicate, Eastern Pacific and the Indian court demanded that Ganpat sign papers acknowledging the American suit was "stopped." *Ganpat*, 2022 WL 1015027, at *3. Had Ganpat given in and signed these papers, he would not have gone to jail. *See id.*

[3] The dissent does not dispute that the Indian judge instructed the attorney of Eastern Pacific, the opposing party, to advise Ganpat. Nor does the dissent dispute that the Eastern Pacific attorney then claimed that Ganpat opposed his own release on bail. And the dissent does not deny—how could it?—that this is a bizarre way for a court of law to proceed.

(3) the extent to which the foreign suit is duplicitous of the litigation in the United States." *Karaha Bodas*, 335 F.3d at 366 (footnotes omitted).

The district court here found that the Indian suit was vexatious and oppressive under our precedents.

First, the district court correctly concluded that the Indian litigation would result in inequitable hardship. As the district court noted, Ganpat "has already been jailed once for violating the ex parte antisuit injunction, and . . . faces a real possibility of being sent back to jail and having his property seized, as Eastern Pacific . . . seeks to have the Indian court enforce sixteen **[—6—]** counts of contempt against [Ganpat]." *Ganpat*, 2022 WL 1015027, at *8 n.104.[4]

Indeed, this is as strong a case of inequitable hardship as the previous cases where we have upheld injunctive relief. Under our caselaw, "unwarranted inconvenience [and] expense" can suffice to constitute hardship meriting an anti-suit injunction. *Kaepa*, 76 F.3d at 627. *See also In re Unterweser Reederei, Gmbh*, 428 F.2d 888, 896 (5th Cir. 1970) ("[A]llowing simultaneous prosecution of the same action in a foreign forum thousands of miles away would result in 'inequitable hardship.'"), *rev'd on other grounds by M/S Bremen v. Zapata Off-Shore Co.*, 407 U.S. 1 (1972); *Bethell*, 441 F.2d at 498 ("[T]he court was within its discretion in relieving the plaintiff of expense and vexation of having to litigate in a foreign court."). If unwarranted inconvenience and expense present sufficient hardship to support an anti-suit injunction, surely jailtime and seizure of property also suffice.

The second vexatiousness factor—"the foreign suit's ability to 'frustrate and delay the speedy and efficient determination'" of the American suit, *Karaha Bodas*, 335 F.3d at 366—likewise favors the injunction. The Indian court has sought to prevent Ganpat from litigating in the United States, even though the American suit was filed first. This "attempt to enjoin [Ganpat] effectively translates into an attempt to enjoin the [American] court itself and to interfere with the sovereign actions of the [United States]." *Id.* at 372. **[—7—]**

When a foreign court tries to keep an American court from hearing a case, that frustrates the American litigation. We have reversed a district court injunction where the foreign litigation was "ineffective in curtailing the ability of . . . U.S. courts[] to enforce" the rights of the plaintiff. *Id.* at 369. There, an American court could enforce the plaintiff's rights regardless of what the foreign court did, so there was no frustration of American litigation. *See id.* Here, by contrast, the Indian court seeks to prevent the American litigation from proceeding. The district court's injunction **{-583-}** is thus "necessary to protect the court's jurisdiction." *MacPhail v. Oceaneering Intern., Inc.*, 302 F.3d 274, 277 (5th Cir. 2002).

The Indian litigation imposes a hardship on Ganpat while frustrating the American litigation, and that is ample justification to find the Indian litigation vexatious and oppressive. Accordingly, we need not consider the third vexatiousness factor, "the extent to which the foreign suit is duplicitous of the litigation in the United States." *Karaha Bodas*, 335 F.3d at 366. *See Bethell*, 441 F.2d at 498 (upholding an anti-suit injunction on the basis of the "expense and vexation of having to litigate in a foreign court" without analyzing whether the foreign suit was duplicative).

In any event, we agree with the district court that the Indian suit is indeed duplicative. The Indian suit rests on "the same or similar legal bases" as the American suit. *Karaha Bodas*, 335 F.3d at 370. Eastern Pacific seeks to establish in Indian court by declaratory judgment the very same legal theory it raises as an affirmative defense in U.S. court—namely, that an employment agreement limits its liability to Ganpat.[5] **[—8—]**

[4] The dissent claims that "any future threat of Ganpat's being jailed is wholly speculative." *Post*, at 22. But the likelihood of Ganpat's future arrest—not to mention the prospective seizure of his property—is the kind of factual issue on which we defer to the district court. *See Kaepa*, 76 F.3d 624 at 626.

[5] The dissent invokes *MacPhail*, where we vacated the injunction in part because the foreign

Accordingly, all three relevant factors indicate that the Indian litigation is vexatious and oppressive.

B.

Although our anti-suit injunction test "focuses on the potentially vexatious nature of foreign litigation, it by no means excludes the consideration of principles of comity." *Kaepa*, 76 F.3d at 627. That said, the comity considerations are not overly strict. "We decline . . . to require a district court to genuflect before a vague and omnipotent notion of comity every time that it must decide whether to enjoin a foreign action." *Id.*

Our precedents make clear that comity concerns are at a minimum where—as here—"no public international issue is implicated by the case" and "the dispute has been long and firmly ensconced within the confines of the United States judicial system." *Id.*

To begin with, no public international issues are implicated in this case. As in *Kaepa*, where we upheld the injunction, this case involves "a private party engaged in a . . . dispute with another private party." *Id.* In *Karaha Bodas*, by contrast, substantial comity concerns militated against the injunction. *See* 335 F.3d at 371–74. That's because the anti-suit injunction posed significant ramifications for a treaty to which the United States was a signatory, and one of the parties to the foreign case was a foreign state-owned enterprise. *See id.* at 373 ("[A]n injunction here is likely . . . to demonstrate an assertion of authority not contemplated by the [treaty]."); *see id.* at 372; ("[The defendant company] is wholly owned by the [foreign government]."); *id.* at 374 (upholding the district court injunction could result in **[—9—]** "diplomatic[]" problems). Here, no party is a government entity, and the injunction has no obvious consequences for international relations.[6] **{-584-}**

In addition, Ganpat's case has long been ensconced in the American judicial system. Under our precedent, a case becomes ensconced in the United States when a party consents to American jurisdiction and appears in the case. *See Kaepa*, 76 F.3d at 627 (suit ensconced in the United States when defendant "consented to jurisdiction in Texas" and "appeared in an action brought in Texas"). In April 2019, Eastern Pacific appeared and waived objections to personal jurisdiction and venue. Only in March 2020, almost a year after Ganpat's suit had already become ensconced within the United States, did Eastern Pacific file its Indian lawsuit against Ganpat.

Despite the fact that the American suit was well underway before the Indian litigation began, the Indian court sought to enjoin the American **[—10—]** litigation. It would be strange to "require a district court to

suit was not duplicative. *See* 302 F.3d at 277–78. There, however, the similarity between the two suits was merely factual: the legal theories at issue in the two suits were different. *See id.* Here, by contrast, the legal theories at issue in the two suits are the same.

[6] The dissent points to the fact that "India, Singapore, and Liberia are all signatories of the 2006 Maritime Labour Convention." *Post*, at 23. The dissent then proceeds to argue that "any decision regarding Ganpat's claims will . . . necessarily implicate an international treaty." *Post*, at 24. There are two fatal problems with this argument.

First, as the dissent concedes, "the United States is not a signatory to the [Maritime Labour Convention]." *Post*, at 24 n.19. In *Karaha Bodas*, we reversed an anti-suit injunction that affected a United States treaty. *See* 335 F.3d at 373–74. The problem there was that enjoining the foreign litigation would "demonstrate an assertion of authority not contemplated by" a treaty to which the United States was party. *Id.* at 373. *See also id.* at 359–60 ("Given . . . the responsibilities of the United States under that treaty, we conclude that the district court abused its discretion."). Here, by contrast, there is no such problem.

Second, no party has argued that granting Ganpat relief under American law would cause India to violate its obligations under the 2006 Maritime Labour Convention. Eastern Pacific merely points out that an Indian legal regime, enacted pursuant to a treaty, regulates some of the relationships in this case. But the fact that India has its own "regulatory regime," *post*, at 23, does not mean that "public international issues" are in play. *Karaha Bodas*, 335 F.3d at 371. All it means is that there is a run-of-the-mill choice-of-law question—a question outside the scope of this appeal.

genuflect," *Kaepa*, 76 F.3d at 627, before a foreign court that refuses to respect the American court. In light of the "not-insubstantial" vexatiousness of the Indian litigation and the "scant" comity interests at stake, *Karaha Bodas*, 335 F.3d at 371, the district court was well within its discretion to grant the injunction.

III.

The dissent points out that an anti-suit injunction is an "extraordinary remedy." *Post*, at 14. That is true enough. *See Karaha Bodas*, 335 F.3d at 363. Yet this extraordinary remedy was amply warranted by the extraordinary conduct of Eastern Pacific and the Indian court toward Ganpat. The dissent also makes several arguments that misconstrue our anti-suit injunction precedents. And it is to these arguments that we now turn.

A.

The dissent first argues that this court errs by failing to employ the traditional four-part preliminary injunction test—including the requirement of irreparable injury. *Post*, at 17.

But the international anti-suit injunction precedents in our circuit do not require a showing of irreparable injury. When affirming an international anti-suit injunction, we have never discussed the traditional four-part test. *See Unterweser*, 428 F.2d at 895–96; *Bethell*, 441 F.2d at 497–99; *Kaepa*, 76 F.3d at 626–29. Nor have we ever reversed an anti-suit injunction on the basis that the district court failed to apply the traditional preliminary injunction test, including the irreparable injury prong. *See MacPhail* 302 F.3d **[—11—]** at 277–78; *Karaha Bodas*, 335 F.3d at 364 ("[T]he suitability of such relief ultimately depends on considerations unique to antisuit injunctions.").[7] **{-585-}**

We recognize that other federal courts are currently split on anti-suit injunctions—some circuits such as ours take a more permissive approach, while others take a more restrictive approach. *See* Kathryn E. Vertigan, *Foreign Antisuit Injunctions: Taking A Lesson from the Act of State Doctrine*, 76 GEO. WASH. L. REV. 155, 164–73 (2007). But even the more restrictive circuits do not necessarily require analysis of the traditional four-part test for injunctive relief. *See Quaak v. Klynveld Peat Marwick Goerdeler Bedrijfsrevisoren*, 361 F.3d 11, 17–18 (1st Cir. 2004) (rejecting the Fifth Circuit's more permissive approach and adopting the more restrictive approach); *id.* at 19 ("The lower court applied the traditional four-part test for preliminary injunctions. Because this generic algorithm provides an awkward fit in cases involving international antisuit injunctions, district courts have no obligation to employ it in that context.") (citation omitted).

B.

The dissent also argues that "[t]his case bears the hallmarks of those [cases] in which we vacated antisuit injunctions." *Post*, at 20. In particular, the dissent emphasizes two issues: Ganpat is an alien, and the underlying facts involve few contacts with the United States. **[—12—]**

But only twice has this circuit vacated an international anti-suit injunction in a published opinion. *See MacPhail*, 302 F.3d at 278; *Karaha Bodas*, 335 F.3d at 375–76. And neither case makes the nationality of the party seeking the injunction, or the contacts with the United States, part of its anti-suit injunction analysis. *See MacPhail*, 302 F.3d at 277–78; *Karaha Bodas*, 335 F.3d at 366–74.

Our precedents do not ask whether the party seeking the injunction is a foreigner—or whether the underlying facts were related to the American forum. Rather, our precedents

[7] Of our circuit's five published anti-suit injunction cases, four do not so much as mention the four-part test. *See Unterweser*, 428 F.2d at 895–96; *Bethell*, 441 F.2d at 497–99; *Kaepa*, 76 F.3d at 626–28; *MacPhail* 302 F.3d at 277–78. *Karaha Bodas* briefly alludes to the "four prerequisites to the issuance of a traditional preliminary injunction"—but only because the district court and the parties had discussed them. *See* 335 F.3d at 364. And *Karaha Bodas* ultimately concludes that international anti-suit injunctions are "unique." *Id.*

weigh the vexatiousness of the foreign litigation against considerations of comity.

If we were undertaking an analysis of personal jurisdiction or venue, contacts with the United States would surely be an appropriate consideration. *See, e.g., Douglass v. Nippon Yusen Kabushiki Kaisha*, 46 F.4th 226, 235, 10 Adm. R. 206, 211 (5th Cir. 2022) (en banc) ("[T]he Fifth Amendment due process test for personal jurisdiction requires . . . 'minimum contacts' with the United States."); 28 U.S.C. § 1391(b) (establishing venue where "a substantial part of the events or omissions giving rise to the claim occurred" or where "defendant is subject to the court's personal jurisdiction").

But Eastern Pacific waived its objections to both personal jurisdiction and venue. Only the merits of the anti-suit injunction are at issue in this appeal.

C.

Finally, the dissent argues that the injunction is overbroad: "It purports to bind [Eastern Pacific] India, which"—unlike Eastern Pacific—"is not a party to the U.S. action." *Post*, at 26. But the Federal Rules permit issuance of an injunction against "persons who are in active concert or participation" with parties, as well as against parties themselves. FED. R. CIV. P. 65(d)(2)(C). "[An] injunction not only binds **{-586-}** the parties defendant **[—13—]** but also those identified with them in interest . . . or subject to their control. . . . [D]efendants may not nullify a decree by carrying out prohibited acts through aiders and abettors, although they were not parties to the original proceeding." *United States v. Jenkins*, 974 F.2d 32, 36 (5th Cir. 1992) (quoting *Regal Knitwear Co. v. NLRB*, 324 U.S. 9, 14 (1945)).

As the district court found, "[Eastern Pacific] India is a subsidiary of Eastern Pacific . . . [and] is 99.99% owned by Eastern Pacific." *Ganpat*, 2022 WL 1015027, at *12. The district court also found "complete identity of interests and positions" between Eastern Pacific and Eastern Pacific India. *Id.* "The district court did not err in finding that it was necessary to bind" Eastern Pacific India. *Jenkins*, 974 F.2d at 36.

* * *

The district court was well within its discretion to conclude that the vexatiousness of the Indian litigation outweighed any comity concerns. We accordingly affirm the anti-suit injunction.

(Reporter's Note: Dissenting opinion follows on p. 275).

[—14—] {-586-} **JONES**, Circuit Judge, dissenting:

This circuit, to be sure, takes a more permissive approach to foreign antisuit injunctions than many of our sister circuits. *See Kaepa, Inc. v. Achilles Corp.*, 76 F.3d 624, 626–27 (5th Cir. 1996).[1] Nonetheless, a foreign antisuit injunction is "an extraordinary remedy" fraught with "unique" concerns regarding international comity. *Karaha Bodas Co. v. Perusahaan Pertambangan Minyak Dan Gas Bumi Negara*, 335 F.3d 357, 363, 364 (5th Cir. 2003). Yet the district court wheeled out this extraordinary remedy so that a sailor from India can sue a Singaporean ship management company under the Jones Act, claiming that he got malaria in Africa after his Liberian-flagged vessel docked briefly in Savannah, Georgia and received insufficient anti- **[—15—]** malaria pills. The district court's decision and the majority's basis for affirming deviate severely from our precedent. I respectfully dissent. **{-587-}**

A. Background

It is just as inaccurate for the majority to assert that Ganpat's being sued in India, in a court located one hour from his home, is "fraught with peril," as it is to conclude that he is entitled to the potential windfall of a Jones Act recovery. The majority's criticisms of the Indian court procedures, which derive from English law, may be required to sustain their result but are unsupported by the facts.

Ganpat alleges he contracted malaria because the Liberian-flagged vessel on which he sailed was insufficiently supplied with anti-malaria pills at port in Savannah, Georgia. Falling ill at sea after docking in Africa, he was treated in Brazil, some toes were removed, and he went back home to Goa, India. Eastern Pacific Shipping India (EPS India), an Indian entity that oversaw the execution of Ganpat's seafarer employment agreement (SEA), coordinated and furnished Ganpat's medical care in Brazil and his continued care in India. In December 2018, Ganpat sued Eastern Pacific Shipping (EPS), the Singaporean ship manager for the vessel, in the New Orleans federal district court, but he failed to make proper service of process for twenty-seven months (until August 2021). The majority has no basis in the record to assert that EPS "continually evaded service of process," as EPS had every right to rely on being served according to the letter of American law and international protocol.[2]

EPS and EPS India sued Ganpat in Goa fifteen months after the U.S. suit was filed and was going nowhere. These entities sought a declaration **[—16—]** enforcing his employment

[1] This approach is probably wrong and should be reconsidered at an appropriate time. *See, e.g.*, *Kaepa*, 76 F.3d at 629–34 (Garza, J., dissenting); *Goss Int'l Corp. v. Man Roland Druckmaschinen Aktiengesellschaft*, 491 F.3d 355, 359–60 (8th Cir. 2007) ("The First, Second, Third, Sixth, and District of Columbia Circuits have adopted the 'conservative approach,' under which a foreign antisuit injunction will issue only if the movant demonstrates (1) an action in a foreign jurisdiction would prevent United States jurisdiction or threaten a vital United States policy, and (2) the domestic interests outweigh concerns of international comity."); *id.* at 360 (adopting the conservative approach because it "(1) recognizes the rebuttable presumption against issuing international antisuit injunctions, (2) is more respectful of principles of international comity, (3) compels an inquiring court to balance competing policy considerations, and (4) acknowledges that issuing an international antisuit injunction is a step that should be taken only with care and great restraint and with the recognition that international comity is a fundamental principle deserving of substantial deference." (internal quotation marks and citation omitted)).

Our precedents commence with *In re Unterweser Reederei, GmbH,* 428 F.2d 888, 890 (5th Cir. 1970), which approved a federal district court's antisuit injunction to prevent litigation in London in an admiralty dispute, while disregarding, as against "public policy," the parties' forum selection clause. *Id.* at 894. Holding that in the modern era, such clauses are to be enforced between sophisticated parties, the Supreme Court overturned this court's decision. *M/S Bremen v. Zapata Off-Shore Co.*, 407 U.S. 1, 92 S. Ct. 1907 (1972). The Supreme Court's ruling gravely undermined the basis for the injunction. *See also Kaepa*, 76 F.3d at 633 n.13 (Garza, J., dissenting) (distinguishing *Unterweser* and *Bethell v. Peace*, 441 F.2d 495 (5th Cir. 1971), from modern cases).

[2] The majority erroneously imply that waiver of jurisdiction and venue require a defendant also to waive correct service of process.

contract, which is based on Liberian and Indian law. They obtained a temporary injunction order (in March 2020, on *forum non conveniens grounds*) to prevent Ganpat from pursuing the American suit. Ganpat admits that he repeatedly evaded service by the Indian court and was ultimately held in contempt. At the court hearing in March 2021, the Indian court offered Ganpat a court-appointed lawyer, but he rejected the offer because he did not want to pay the expense. A lawyer for EPS then spoke with Ganpat, who was accompanied by his father and brother-in-law, in an apparent attempt to negotiate his acceptance of the contracted-for injury payment. Upon reentering the courtroom, Ganpat admitted, he *refused* "three or four additional times" the judge's demand that he "sign the papers, take a bond, or hire a lawyer." *Ganpat v. Eastern Pacific Shipping, Pte. Ltd.*, 2022 WL 1015027, *3 (E.D. La. Apr. 5, 2022). He was thus jailed for his *continued refusal* to participate in the legal proceedings, not, as the majority contends, because he "refused to be bullied into dropping the American suit." The next day, he obtained counsel and bonded out. He has been represented by counsel since and has not again been threatened with jail.[3]

Ganpat further ignored the Indian court's order by pursuing the U.S. litigation in his many fruitless attempts to serve EPS properly. His efforts culminated in the U.S. district court's April 2022 antisuit injunction against both EPS and the non-party to that case, EPS India.[4] **[—17—] {-588-}**

The district court described EPS's Indian suit as a "stratagem," and the majority imply without any record evidence that the Indian legal system lacks legal protection for Ganpat. When this tortured procedural history is considered in toto, it is more accurate to describe the district court's rulings as an attempt to compel domestic jurisdiction over a suit with highly tenuous domestic connections.

B. Standard for Foreign Antisuit Injunctions

Antisuit injunctions in this circuit are described as a subspecies of injunctions. *Karaha Bodas*, 335 F.3d at 364. The majority discounts that Ganpat, like any movant for equitable relief, must ultimately satisfy a four-part test and show a likelihood of success on the merits.[5] The fact that unique considerations affect the propriety of foreign court antisuit injunctions should not detract from the recognition that equitable relief requires an extraordinary justification. Consequently, our cases explain the need to weigh preventing "vexatious or oppressive litigation" and "protecting the court's jurisdiction" against deference to principles of international comity. *See, e.g., id.* at 366; *see also Kaepa*, 76 F.3d at 627; *MacPhail v. Oceaneering Int'l*, 302 F.3d 274, 277 (5th Cir. 2002).[6] Elaborating on what is vexatious, we have identified: (1) inequitable hardship resulting from the foreign suit; **[—18—]** (2) the foreign suit's ability to frustrate and delay the speedy and efficient determination of the cause; and (3) the extent to which the foreign suit is duplicitous of the U.S. litigation. *Karaha Bodas*, 335 F.3d at 366. And *Karaha Bodas* clarified that this inquiry goes to the first traditional factor: likelihood of success on the merits. *Id.* at 364 & n.19. Ultimately, the unique aspects of foreign antisuit injunctions must relate to the challenging tests for equitable relief.

[3] He admits as well that his American lawyer provided the money to hire the Indian lawyer.

[4] The district court speedily denied EPS's *forum non conveniens* motion to dismiss despite the lack of any substantial connection of this litigation to the United States. EPS and EPS India, unlike Ganpat, have complied with the foreign antisuit injunction order, and the Indian litigation is in limbo pending this dispute.

[5] *See Karaha Bodas*, 335 F.3d at 364 & n.19 (asserting that the court's anti-suit injunction standard acts as a substitute for the traditional standard's "likelihood of success" prong but intimating that the remaining factors of the traditional standard may be applicable); *see also MWK Recruiting, Inc. v. Jowers*, 833 F. App'x 560, 562 (5th Cir. 2020) (per curiam).

[6] The factors to be weighed seem to compress a four-factor test articulated by this court in *Unterweser, i.e.*, whether the foreign litigation would (1) frustrate a policy of the U.S. forum; (2) be vexatious or oppressive; (3) threaten the issuing court's in rem or quasi in rem jurisdiction; or (4) cause prejudice or offend other equitable principles. *See* 428 F.2d at 890.

The majority opinion, unfortunately, reduces this "extraordinary remedy" essentially to a routine order under a routine multifactor test. The majority's analysis finds "inequitable hardship" if Ganpat must endure litigating the Indian lawsuit; and it finds "frustration" of the American litigation because the "Indian court has sought to prevent Ganpat from litigating in the United States, even though the American suit was filed first." With these sole prerequisites, the majority declares it unnecessary to consider "the extent to which the foreign suit is duplicitous of the litigation in the United States." *Karaha Bodas*, 335 F.3d at 366. But the majority then endorses the district court's statement that the Indian suit rests on "the same or similar legal bases." Each of these findings is incorrect, as is the majority's minimization of international comity concerns and its further refusal to apply traditional equitable principles. A look at our previous case law concerning foreign antisuit injunctions readily demonstrates the majority's departure from the underlying standards we have used.

1. "Vexatiousness"

First, contrary to the majority's dismissive math, half of the antisuit injunctions **{-589-}** issued in this circuit have been vacated on appeal. Of this **[—19—]** circuit's six opinions covering antisuit injunctions, three upheld and three vacated district court orders.[7]

Our cases share several common themes, and they uniformly point toward rejecting the district court's injunction in this case. Where we have upheld antisuit injunctions, the defendant in the foreign proceeding was a United States citizen or company[8]; the facts giving rise to the dueling actions bore a substantial relationship to the United States forum[9]; and the dueling actions involved identical parties and nearly identical, if not identical claims.[10] In contrast, where this court vacated antisuit injunctions, the **[—20—]** defendant in the foreign proceeding was a foreigner[11]; the facts underlying the actions were largely unrelated to the United States forum[12]; the parties were not identical[13]; and, though the dueling cases arose out of the same

[7] Those cases in which we have upheld antisuit injunctions are *Unterweser*, 428 F.2d 888 (5th Cir. 1970), *rev'd by M/S Bremen*, 407 U.S. 1, 92 S. Ct. 1907 (1972); *Bethell*, 441 F.2d 495 (5th Cir. 1971); and *Kaepa*, 76 F.3d 624 (5th Cir. 1996). Those cases in which we have vacated antisuit injunctions are *MacPhail*, 302 F.3d 274 (5th Cir. 2002); and *Karaha Bodas*, 335 F.3d 357 (5th Cir. 2003). The most recent such case vacating an injunction is well reasoned but unpublished. *MWK Recruiting*, 833 F. App'x 560 (5th Cir. 2020) (per curiam).

[8] *Unterweser*, 428 F.2d at 889; *Bethell*, 441 F.2d at 496; *Kaepa*, 76 F.3d at 625.

[9] *Unterweser*, 428 F.2d at 889 (ship docked in Florida after accident in Gulf of Mexico while transporting drilling barge from Louisiana to Italy); *Bethell*, 441 F.2d at 496 (contract signed in Florida by Florida residents while defendant was acting in capacity as Florida real estate broker, which gave rise to fiduciary duties under Florida law); *Kaepa*, 76 F.3d at 625–26 (Japanese company contracted with U.S. company and agreed to litigate disputes in United States).

[10] *Unterweser*, 428 F.2d at 889 (U.S. company sued German company in federal district court for damages; German company then sued U.S. company in England for moneys due under towage contract and for breach of contract); *Kaepa*, 76 F.3d at 625–26 (U.S. company sued Japanese company in federal district court for fraudulent and negligent inducement as well as breach of contract; Japanese company sued U.S. company in Japan on identical claims); *see also Bethell*, 441 F.2d at 496 (Florida real estate broker sued owners in Bahamas to enforce contract to sell property and to quiet title; Texas co-owner sued real estate broker in federal district court for fraud and declaratory judgment as to validity of the contract); *id.* at 498–99 (narrowing scope of injunction because it "attempt[ed] to affect rights between [real estate broker] and co-owners who were not parties to the [U.S.] action").

[11] *MacPhail*, 302 F.3d at 276 & n.2; *Karaha Bodas*, 335 F.3d at 360.

[12] *MacPhail*, 302 F.3d at 275–76 (injuries in South China Sea resulted in settlement agreement between U.S. company and Australian that was signed in Australia and confirmed by Australian court); *Karaha Bodas*, 335 F.3d at 360–61 (arbitration award from Switzerland arising out of failed construction contract between Caymanian company and state-owned Indonesian company).

[13] *Karaha Bodas*, 335 F.3d at 362. *But see MacPhail*, 302 F.3d at 277 (identical parties).

underlying facts, they involved different legal claims.[14]

This case bears the hallmarks of those in which we vacated antisuit injunctions. First, all parties are foreign to the United States. The only connection this case has to the United States, besides Ganpat's lawyer, **{-590-}** is Ganpat's allegation that EPS, a Singaporean ship manager, failed to supply the *M/V Stargate,* a Liberian-flagged vessel, with enough anti-malaria medication while briefly in port at Savannah, Georgia. Ganpat has remained in India since his repatriation. He couldn't even be bothered to personally attend the dispositive hearing on the district court's antisuit injunction. The court permitted him to appear by Zoom from India.

Even more significant, the parties to each action are *not* the same and the cases involve *different* legal claims. In the New Orleans district court, **[—21—]** Ganpat sued only EPS for damages under the Jones Act, the collective bargaining agreement, and general maritime law. In India, EPS and EPS India filed suit for a declaration that Ganpat's damages are limited by the SEA Ganpat executed with Ventnor Navigation, Inc. through Ventnor's authorized representative, EPS India.[15] But EPS India is not a party to the U.S. litigation.

Although the majority assert that it is unnecessary to discuss whether the parties' claims in each case are "duplicitous," they go on to endorse the district court's finding that the cases rest on the same or similar legal claims. What the majority means is thus unclear. But the inquiry into legal overlap between the domestic and foreign proceedings has been a basic and indispensable feature of previous cases. Indubitably, the parties here are proceeding on distinct legal claims. Ganpat has no recourse to the Jones Act's remedies in Indian courts. And although EPS in the district court asserted as an affirmative defense that the SEA limited Ganpat's damages, these actions "share the same or similar legal bases" only to the extent that the resolution of one case *may* serve "as the basis for a plea of res judicata" in the other case. *Ganpat,* 2022 WL 1015027 at *10, *11. Res judicata is hard to imagine, however, because any rejection of the SEA by the district court (were that to occur) is unlikely to be enforced against *EPS India,* a nonparty over which the district court lacked jurisdiction, via its judgment solely against EPS.

The district court reasoned otherwise by asserting simply that the SEA is at issue in both the U.S. and Indian fora. Such a superficial factual analogy has been repeatedly rejected by this court because "the duplicative factor [relating to vexatiousness] is about *legal,* not *factual,* similarity." **[—22—]** *MWK Recruiting, Inc. v. Jowers,* 833 F. App'x 560, 564 (5th Cir. 2020) (per curiam) (emphasis in original); *see also Karaha Bodas,* 335 F.3d at 370; *Kaepa,* 76 F.3d at 626 ("mirror-image" claims in foreign suit and U.S. suit). *MacPhail,* in fact, rejected the exact argument made by the district court here, holding the assertion of a *defense* in U.S. proceedings that serves as the basis for a *claim* in foreign proceedings does not render the actions duplicitous. 302 F.3d at 277. And indeed, preventing these parties from proceeding on different claims in the U.S. and India makes no sense. The district court is powerless to compel a complete resolution of the three parties' dispute before its bench; and the parties are prevented from going forward in India's dispositive litigation with EPS India. The majority's analysis thus evades what should be a *sine qua non* to justify a foreign antisuit injunction.[16] **{-591-}**

[14] *MacPhail,* 302 F.3d at 277 (U.S. action sought damages from maritime tort claim, whereas Australian action sought specific performance of settlement agreement); *Karaha Bodas,* 335 F.3d at 361 (U.S. action sought confirmation of award, whereas Indonesian action sought annulment of award); *see also MWK Recruiting,* 833 F. App'x at 564 (rejecting use of the "logical relationship test" to determine duplicative claims).

[15] That agreement is governed by Liberian and Indian law and covered work on the *M/V Stargate,* which EPS managed.

[16] Contrary to the majority's assertion, this court has never found that "inconvenience [and] expense" alone can justify a foreign anti-suit injunction. By that standard, *any* foreign suit could be enjoined. The inconvenience and expense of foreign litigation is instead only "unwarranted"

Properly applying our precedents to the facts at hand, it seems plain that Ganpat does not suffer "inequitable hardship" from being involved in parallel litigation, a course his actions foreordained. Parallel proceedings, alone, are insufficient to show vexation or oppression. *Karaha Bodas*, 335 F.3d at 372 & n.59; *see also MWK Recruiting*, 833 F. App'x at 564. The Indian court is doubtlessly a *forum conveniens.* And any future threat of Ganpat's being jailed is wholly speculative, as he has obtained counsel in India. *Karaha Bodas*, 335 F.3d at 368–69 (no inequitable hardship where asserted harm was speculative). It is likewise speculative that the Indian suit could have frustrated or delayed the district court's proceedings. The district court certainly had means to defend its jurisdiction that fell short of requiring EPS and EPS India to abandon the Indian action entirely. *See id.* at **[—23—]** 361–62 (district court required the plaintiff in foreign case to withdraw application for antisuit injunction and prohibited plaintiff from taking any substantive action in foreign case, but it allowed plaintiff to "take any ministerial steps necessary to maintain the cause of action."). And it was Ganpat, not EPS or the Indian court, who delayed his American case for over two years with inept dithering about proper service of process. Finally, the current posture of these cases prevents either court from fully resolving the three parties' differences, and this means the legal claims cannot be substantially similar. It was error to deem the pendency of the Indian lawsuit "vexatious and oppressive" to Ganpat.

2. Comity

On the other side of the equitable ledger, international comity concerns here decidedly outweigh the need to "prevent vexatious or oppressive litigation" and "to protect the court's jurisdiction."[17] To begin, India, Singapore, and Liberia are all signatories of the 2006 Maritime Labour Convention (MLC).[18] That treaty embodies "as far as possible all up-to-date standards of existing international maritime labour Conventions and Recommendations, as well as the fundamental principles to be found in other international labour Conventions." MLC, 2006, preamble. In accordance with its duties under the treaty, India promulgated a complex regulatory regime that governs the relationship among EPS, EPS India, and Ganpat. For instance, EPS India exists because Indian law prevents a foreign company from employing Indian nationals to work on a foreign flagged ship without **[—24—]** the involvement of a locally licensed placement service. Consequently, any decision regarding Ganpat's claims will, as in *Karaha Bodas*, necessarily implicate an international treaty and foreign states' rules promulgated thereunder.[19] **{-592-}**

Comity concerns, however, do not only arise where public international relations are at stake. Such a holding would place this court's precedent well outside the norm. Indeed, even circuits friendly to this court's approach to antisuit injunctions acknowledge there are "international-comity concerns inherent in enjoining a party from pursuing claims in a foreign court." *1st Source Bank v. Neto*, 861 F.3d 607, 613 (7th Cir. 2017).[20] Those inherent

---

where the foreign action is duplicative of the domestic action. *Kaepa*, 76 F.3d at 627–28.

[17] *Karaha Bodas* makes clear that while "notions of comity do not wholly dominate our analysis," the court must still weigh the "need to defer to principles of international comity." 335 F.3d at 366; *see also Kaepa*, 76 F.3d at 627.

[18] *Ratifications of MLC, 2006*, International Labour Organization https://www.ilo.org/dyn/normlex/en/f?p=NORMLEXPUB:11300:0::NO::P11300_INSTRUMENT_ID:312331 (last visited Apr. 13, 2023).

[19] Although the United States is not a signatory to the MLC, surely U.S. courts ought to proceed carefully before ignoring treaties and foreign statutes, especially those governing employment relationships. Yet the majority seem to deride this aspect of comity. *See, e.g., Goss Int'l*, 491 F.3d at 366 (vacating injunction because "[i]nternational comity requires us to give deference to the Japanese courts to interpret Japanese laws").

[20] As the Sixth Circuit observed, an antisuit injunction in and of itself "conveys the message, intended or not, that the issuing court has so little confidence in the foreign court's ability to adjudicate a given dispute fairly and efficiently that it is unwilling even to allow the possibility." *Gau Shan Co. v. Bankers Trust Co.*, 956 F.2d 1349, 1355 (6th Cir. 1992).

concerns are on full display here. In March 2020, seventeen months *before* service was perfected in the district court, the Indian court determined that it had jurisdiction over the dispute and the parties, was a convenient forum, and should temporarily enjoin Ganpat from his U.S. litigation. In April 2022, two years *after* the Indian court's order, the district court issued its foreign antisuit injunction in the face of Ganpat's ongoing disregard of the Indian court's order.[21] Had Ganpat instead litigated on the merits in the Indian court, this case might have been concluded already, albeit **[—25—]** on terms he might not have found attractive. But as noted above, the district court's injunction forced EPS and EPS India to dismiss the Indian action. In short, the district court's actions not only clashed "with the general principle that a sovereign country has the competence to determine its own jurisdiction and grant the kinds of relief it deems appropriate," but also "effectively attempt[ed] to arrest the judicial proceedings of another foreign sovereign." *Karaha Bodas*, 335 F.3d at 371, 372–73. The fact that the Eastern District of Louisiana maintains absolutely zero factual connection to the dispute only exacerbates the violation of comity.

The *MacPhail* case provides an excellent parallel. There, an Australian citizen suffered injuries while working in the South China Sea. 302 F.3d at 275. Three years later, he brought a general maritime tort claim against an American company in federal district court. *Id.* at 276. The company proffered a prior settlement agreement between the parties as a defense. *Id.* When the district court rejected the agreement as unenforceable, the company brought an action in Australia seeking specific performance of the agreement. *Id.* at 277. The district court issued an antisuit injunction, and the company appealed. *Id.* This court first held that the actions were not duplicitous: Although both actions arose "out of facts contemplated" by the agreement, the actions did not involve identical claims. *Id.* It also held that the foreign action was not vexatious considering the Australian citizen had previously resorted to Australia's courts to confirm the agreement. *Id.* And it rejected the contention that the antisuit injunction was necessary to protect the district court's jurisdiction because the Australian court established "prima facie jurisdiction" before the federal district court and nothing prevented the Australian citizen from opposing the validity of the agreement in the Australian courts. *Id.* at 277–78. The court consequently vacated the antisuit injunction. *Id* at 278. **[—26—]**

Like *MacPhail*, the case at hand bears almost no relationship to the United States. The claims at issue in the domestic **{-593-}** and foreign litigation are not identical. And though the district court here assumed jurisdiction over the case earlier than the Indian court, the domestic case lay dormant for years due to Ganpat's dilatory conduct. In the meantime, the Indian court established jurisdiction and preliminarily found itself to be a *forum conveniens*. The significant international comity interests at issue here, which were not present in *McPhail*, go well beyond those inherent in enjoining foreign litigation and further weigh in favor of vacating the antisuit injunction.

3. Equitable Considerations

As a final instance of abuse, the district court failed to balance the equities traditionally important to granting injunctive relief, as it should have done after finding Ganpat had shown a likelihood of success on the merits. Moreover, the district court failed to "narrowly tailor" the injunction "to remedy the specific action" that gave rise to its order. *John Doe #1 v. Veneman*, 380 F.3d 807, 818 (5th Cir. 2004). The injunction purports to bind EPS India, which is not a party to the U.S. action. Though Rule 65 of the Federal Rules of Civil Procedure permits a court to bind non-parties "who are in active concert or participation with" a party against whom an injunction is issued, the district court must first find that the non-party is "so identified in interest with those named in the decree that it would be reasonable to conclude that their rights and interests have been represented and

[21] Indeed, the district court's course of conduct greenlit Ganpat's contempt by allowing him to continue prosecuting the U.S. action in apparent defiance of the Indian court's order.

adjudicated in the original injunction proceeding." *Harris Cnty. v. CarMax Auto Superstores, Inc.*, 177 F.3d 306, 314 (5th Cir. 1999) (citation omitted). Despite the fact that EPS India is a wholly owned subsidiary of EPS, EPS India may have different obligations to Ganpat and might have claims EPS is unable to assert. For instance, Ganpat has argued the SEA does not govern his relationship with EPS. Consequently, it was an abuse of discretion to bind EPS India. *See Bethell*, 441 F.2d at 498 (scope of injunction **[—27—]** overbroad where it "attempts to affect rights between" defendant in U.S. action and those "who were not parties to the" district court action). The court also brazenly required EPS and EPS India to dismiss the Indian action, as opposed to requiring them, for example, to ask the Indian court to abandon its injunction. *See Karaha Bodas*, 335 F.3d at 361. The injunction's terms are abusive, especially if the Indian statute of limitations could prevent EPS and EPS India from refiling their claim.

Returning to the theme that injunctive relief is to be sparingly granted, and only when the balance of hardships clearly weighs in favor of the movant and against the respondent,[22] I believe the foregoing discussion demonstrates the legal and factual errors underpinning the district court's foreign antisuit injunction. I respectfully dissent.

---

[22] *See Karaha Bodas*, 335 F.3d at 363–64 & n.19; *see also MacPhail*, 302 F.3d at 277–78; *MWK Recruiting*, 833 F. App'x at 562, 564–65.

United States Court of Appeals
for the Fifth Circuit

No. 22-20281

NOBLE HOUSE, L.L.C.
vs.
CERTAIN UNDERWRITERS AT LLOYD'S, LONDON

Appeal from the United States District Court for the Southern District of Texas

Decided: May 1, 2023

Citation: 67 F.4th 243, 11 Adm. R. 282 (5th Cir. 2023).

Before **HIGGINBOTHAM, SMITH,** and **ENGELHARDT,** Circuit Judges.

[—1—] {-246-} ENGELHARDT, Circuit Judge: **{-247-}**

Plaintiff-appellant Noble House, L.L.C. ("Noble House") appeals a judgment of dismissal, without prejudice, based on *forum non conveniens*, granted in favor of defendant-appellee Certain Underwriters at Lloyd's, London ("Underwriters"). The district court ruled that the parties' insurance policy contained an enforceable forum-selection clause requiring litigation in the courts of England and Wales and that a return-jurisdiction clause was not required. We AFFIRM. **[—2—]**

I. Factual and Procedural Background

On August 20, 2018, Noble House's yacht lost its port-side rudder while entering a channel in the Bahamas. The following day, Noble House advised Underwriters, its insurer, of the casualty, which was allegedly covered by its marine-insurance policy. Noble House purchased the policy from Underwriters by way of a Texas-based insurance broker on February 1, 2018. The policy contained a forum-selection clause that selected the courts of England and Wales. Attached to the policy was a cover note with its own forum-selection clause that selected any court of competent jurisdiction within the United States. Allegedly, the cover note was not prepared by Underwriters, but by Noble House's own insurance broker.[1] Approximately two months after the casualty, on October 19, 2018, Underwriters issued a letter advising that coverage "may not exist." Underwriters has not yet denied coverage.

Noble House sued to recover its damages, first in the United States District Court for the Southern District of Florida on October 12, 2020. Months later, on March 2, 2021, that district court granted Underwriters' motion to dismiss for lack of personal jurisdiction and dismissed the case without prejudice.

Then, Noble House filed the instant suit in the United States District Court for the Southern District of Texas on November 1, 2021. Underwriters moved to dismiss on *forum non conveniens* grounds. On March 23, 2022, after hearing argument, the district court granted Underwriters' motion and dismissed all claims without prejudice. Noble House filed a motion for reconsideration, which the court denied. This appeal followed. **[—3—]**

II. Standard of Review

Underwriters filed its motion to dismiss on *forum non conveniens* grounds, requesting that the court enforce the mandatory forum-selection clause selecting the courts of England and Wales and dismiss the action. We apply "a mixed standard of review for post-*Atlantic Marine* [*forum non conveniens*] rulings involving [forum-selection clauses]." *Weber v. PACT XPP Techs., AG*, 811 F.3d 758, 768 (5th Cir. 2016). First, we review the district court's interpretation of the forum-selection clause and the court's assessment of that clause's enforceability *de novo*. *Id.* Second, we review the district court's balancing of the *Atlantic Marine* private- and public-interest factors for abuse of discretion. *Id.*

III. The Applicable Framework

"[T]he appropriate way to enforce a forum-selection clause pointing to a … foreign forum

[1] At oral argument, Underwriters discussed the preparation of the cover note, which, it conceded, was a fact not in the record.

is through the doctrine of *forum non conveniens*," *Atl. Marine*, 571 U.S. at 60, "under which a court may decline to exercise its jurisdiction and dismiss a **{-248-}** case that is otherwise properly before it so that the case can be adjudicated in another forum." *PCL Civ. Constructors, Inc. v. Arch Ins. Co.*, 979 F.3d 1070, 1073 (5th Cir. 2020). The parties dispute which *forum non conveniens* framework applies. "Usually, a court applying th[e] doctrine must determine whether there is an adequate alternative forum and, if so, decide which forum is best-suited to the litigation by considering a variety of private- and public-interest factors and giving deference to the plaintiff's choice of forum." *Barnett v. DynCorp Int'l, L.L.C.*, 831 F.3d 296, 300 (5th Cir. 2016) (citing *DTEX, LLC v. BBVA Bancomer, S.A.*, 508 F.3d 785, 794-95 (5th Cir. 2007)). So, to obtain a *forum non conveniens* dismissal under this framework, "a party must demonstrate (1) the existence of an available and adequate alternative forum and (2) that the balance of relevant private and public interest factors favor dismissal." *Vasquez v.* **[—4—]** *Bridgestone/Firestone, Inc.*, 325 F.3d 665, 671 (5th Cir. 2003) (citing *Alpine View Co. v. Atlas Copco AB*, 205 F.3d 208, 221-22 (5th Cir. 2000)). It is this "usual" analysis that Noble House says controls.

But Noble House is wrong. Its reliance on *Vasquez* is misplaced. *Vasquez* and its progeny address the *forum non conveniens* inquiry where no forum-selection clause exists. As Underwriters correctly explains, the presence of a mandatory, enforceable forum-selection clause simplifies the "usual" analysis in two ways. *Barnett*, 831 F.3d at 300. "First, the plaintiff's choice of forum merits no weight" because, by contracting for a specific forum, "the plaintiff has effectively exercised its 'venue privilege' before a dispute arises." *Atl. Marine*, 571 U.S. at 63. Second, the private-interest factors "weigh entirely in favor of the preselected forum"; so, the "district court may consider arguments about public-interest factors only." *Id.* at 64. "Hence, a valid forum-selection clause controls the *forum non conveniens* inquiry 'in all but the most unusual cases.'" *Barnett*, 831 F.3d at 300 (quoting *Atl. Marine*, 571 U.S. at 66) (alteration omitted). "This harmonizes with the [Supreme] Court's guidance that contractually selected forums often 'figure centrally in the parties' negotiations' and become part of those parties' 'settled expectations' – so if a plaintiff disregards such a contractual commitment, 'dismissal works no injustice.'" *Id.* (quoting *Atl. Marine*, 571 U.S. at 66 & n.8) (alterations omitted).

We apply a "strong presumption" in favor of enforcing mandatory forum-selection clauses. *Weber*, 811 F.3d at 773 (citing *Haynsworth*, 121 F.3d at 962-63). "The presumption of enforceability may be overcome, however, by a clear showing that the clause is 'unreasonable' under the circumstances." *Weber*, 811 F.3d at 773 (quoting *Haynsworth*, 121 F.3d at 963). We've stated: **[—5—]**

> Unreasonableness potentially exists where (1) the incorporation of the forum selection clause into the agreement was the product of fraud or overreaching; (2) the party seeking to escape enforcement will for all practical purposes be deprived of his day in court because of the grave inconvenience or unfairness of the selected forum; (3) the fundamental unfairness of the chosen law will deprive the plaintiff of a remedy; or (4) enforcement of the forum selection clause would contravene a strong public policy of the forum state.

Haynsworth, 121 F.3d at 963 (citing *Carnival Cruise Lines, Inc. v. Shute*, 499 U.S. 585, 595 (1991), and **{-249-}** *M/S Bremen v. Zapata Off-Shore Co.*, 407 U.S. 1, 12-13, 15, 18 (1972)) (internal quotation marks omitted). "The party resisting enforcement on these grounds bears a 'heavy burden of proof.'" *Id.* (quoting *Bremen*, 407 U.S. at 17). Federal law determines the clause's enforceability. *See id.* at 962. If the forum-selection clause is both mandatory and enforceable, the court must decide whether, under *Atlantic Marine*'s balancing test, the case "is one of the rare cases in which the public-interest [*forum non conveniens*] factors favor keeping a case despite the existence of a valid and enforceable [forum-selection clause]." *Weber*, 811 F.3d at 775-76. We review the "unreasonableness" inquiry *de novo* and the

Atlantic Marine inquiry for abuse of discretion. *Weber*, 811 F.3d at 776.

Here, although there are arguably two forum-selection clauses at play, one foreign and one domestic,[2] the district court concluded that the forum- **[—6—]** selection clause selecting the courts of England and Wales controls. Noble House does not dispute this conclusion in its opening brief.[3] Nor does Noble House dispute that the foreign forum-selection clause is mandatory. Only the foreign forum-selection clause's enforceability is contested, which is addressed under the "unreasonable under the circumstances" framework – not the usual "available and adequate" framework.[4]

IV. The mandatory clause is not "unreasonable under the circumstances," and is therefore enforceable.

To Noble House, the courts of England and Wales do not provide "available and adequate" fora because it fears its claims would be time-barred if litigated there.[5] So, says Noble House, the foreign forum-selection clause is "unreasonable under the circumstances" because it would be "'deprived of [its] day in court' due to a shortened statute of limitation[s] in England that would be invalid under Texas law and because enforcement of the forum selection clause would violate the public policy **{-250-}** of Texas." Under **[—7—]** *de novo* review, Noble House does not carry its "heavy burden of proof" to show that the clause selecting the courts of England and Wales is unreasonable under the circumstances.

A. The law does not reward a plaintiff for violating a forum-selection clause.

Noble House's fear that its claims would be time-barred under the foreign fora's statutes of limitations is not novel. Both the Supreme Court and this Court have acknowledged the risk of time-barred claims in the forum-selection-clause context. Unfortunately for Noble House, controlling caselaw affords it no sympathy.

It is no secret that dismissal under *forum non conveniens* "makes it possible for plaintiffs to lose out completely[] through the running of the statute of limitations in the forum finally deemed appropriate." *Atl. Marine*, 571 U.S. at 66 n.8 (alteration omitted). But dismissal of a suit "when the plaintiff has violated a contractual obligation by filing suit in a forum other than the one specified in a valid forum-selection clause ... work[s] no injustice on the plaintiff." *Id.* That is why we have said: "[T]hat an action may be time-barred in the chosen forum does not make a forum-selection clause unreasonable." *Barnett*, 831 F.3d at 309 n.14.

---

[2] Noble House's insurance policy details that: "This Insurance shall be governed by and construed in accordance with the law of England and Wales and each party agrees to submit to the exclusive jurisdiction of the courts of England and Wales." The attached cover note provides: "It is agreed that in the event of the failure of the Underwriters hereon to pay any amount claimed to be due hereunder, the Underwriters hereon, at the request of the Assured (or Reinsured), will submit to the jurisdiction of a Court of competent jurisdiction within the United States." Importantly, the cover note states that it "is intended for use as evidence that insurance described herein has been effected against **[—6—]** which a policy(ies) will be issued and that *in the event of any inconsistency therewith the terms and conditions and provisions of the policy(ies) prevail.*"

[3] In its reply brief, Noble House raises, for the first time, that it disputes that the foreign forum-selection clause controls. But "[a]rguments raised for the first time in a reply brief are waived." *Dixon v. Toyota Motor Credit Corp.*, 794 F.3d 507, 508 (5th Cir. 2015) (citing *Unida v. Levi Strauss & Co.*, 986 F.2d 970, 976 n. 4 (5th Cir. 1993)).

[4] Even if this Court were to rely on the "available and adequate" standard, as Noble House suggests, Noble House's argument that the courts of England and Wales are not "available and adequate" fails. By contracting for those courts' exclusive jurisdiction, it necessarily agreed that such courts are available and adequate. *See Atl. Marine,* 571 U.S. at 63 (noting that a forum-selection clause "represents the parties' agreement as to the most proper forum") (quoting *Stewart Org., Inc. v. Ricoh Corp.*, 487 U.S. 22, 31 (1988)).

[5] That the statute of limitations has run is a non-jurisdictional affirmative defense, *see Flagg v. Stryker Corp.*, 819 F.3d 132, 143 (5th Cir. 2016) (Haynes, J., concurring in part), not a jurisdictional pre-requisite. Accordingly, we need not resolve whether the claims are time-barred at this juncture.

We have already considered a statute-of-limitations concern in the forum-selection-clause context. *Id.* In *Barnett*, we said that such consideration "would create a large loophole for the party seeking to avoid enforcement of the forum selection clause." *Id.* (quoting *Trafigura Beheer B.V. v. M/T PROBO ELK*, 266 F. App'x. 309, 312 n.4 (5th Cir. 2007) (per curiam) (unpublished)). That is because the plaintiff "could simply postpone its cause of action until the statute of limitations has run in the chosen forum and then file its action in a more convenient forum." *Id.* (quoting *Trafigura*, 266 F. App'x at 312 n.4). The law cannot promote such **[—8—]** gamesmanship. So, "absent some compelling and countervailing reason," the arms-length agreement choosing that forum-selection clause "should be honored by the parties and enforced by the courts." *Bremen*, 407 U.S. at 12; *see also Stewart Org., Inc. v. Ricoh Corp.,* 487 U.S. 22, 33 (1988) (Kennedy, J., concurring) ("[E]nforcement of valid forum-selection clauses, bargained for by the parties, protects their legitimate expectations and furthers vital interests of the justice system."). Noble House offers no compelling reason justifying its filing in Texas or why its action could not be filed timely in the foreign fora. Its violation of the clause should not be rewarded. It occasioned its own predicament by failing to timely file its claim in the contractually-specified forum. *See Trafigura*, 266 F. App'x at 312. And it will be held to its bargain.

B. The "unreasonableness" factors weigh in favor of enforcement.

Even if this Court's jurisprudence were sympathetic to Noble House's position, Noble House fails to show that the operative forum-selection clause is unreasonable under the circumstances and, consequently, unenforceable. Noble House's "showing" of unreasonableness is a simple insertion of a two-columned table submitted to the district court. One column lists the four factors pertinent to the unreasonableness analysis. *See Haynsworth*, 121 F.3d at 963. The other column lists alleged evidence in support of each factor. Instead of addressing the evidence in support of unreasonableness, Noble House argues that the district court's alleged failure to articulate its rationale for dismissal on the **{-251-}** record results in an abuse of discretion. Noble House confuses the applicable standard of review at this juncture. We review *de novo* the district court's conclusion that the forum-selection clause was enforceable. *PCL*, 979 F.3d at 1073. And the record does not support that the operative forum-selection clause was unreasonable under the circumstances. **[—9—]**

First, there is no evidence that the forum-selection clause was the product of fraud or overreaching. Noble House contends the following is evidence of fraud or overreaching: "i. placement of the forum selection clause deep within a voluminous document, ii. the lack of noticeable headers calling attention to the clause, iii. the presence of a forum selection clause selecting United States, [and] iv. [n]o endorsements or forms that supersede the forum selection clause in the Cover Note." This "evidence" falls short. To its first two points, the document is approximately 50 pages, with plenty of line and page breaks, and Noble House is presumed to have read the contract to which it agreed. To its third point, there is an express clause stating that the provisions in the policy supersede that in the cover note. And finally, to its fourth point, at the district court's hearing on Underwriters' motion to dismiss, Noble House admitted that it does not argue that the foreign forum-selection clause was fraudulently inserted.

Second, there is no evidence that Noble House will for all practical purposes be deprived of its day in court because of the grave inconvenience or unfairness of the selected forum. Noble House relies on its oft-repeated refrain that it is deprived of a remedy because its claims are time-barred due to the shorter foreign statutes of limitations. But "[w]hen parties agree to a forum-selection clause, they waive the right to challenge the preselected forum as inconvenient or less convenient for themselves or their witnesses, or for their pursuit of the litigation." *Atl. Marine*, 571 U.S. at 64. Any grave inconvenience or unfairness of the selected forum Noble House "would suffer by being forced to litigate in the contractual forum as it agreed to do was clearly foreseeable at the time of contracting." *Bremen*, 407 U.S. at 17-18. Because the applicable foreign statutes of limitations were certainly foreseeable at the time the parties executed the policy, their enforcement is not unfair. **[—10—]**

Moreover, "[a] chosen forum is not fundamentally unfair merely because its law is less generous than, or because the result might differ from that under, the forum state's law." *Barnett*, 831 F.3d at 308 n.14 (citing *Haynsworth*, 121 F.3d at 969). That a shorter statute of limitations applies abroad does not make the foreign fora unfair. To be sure, "American courts repeatedly have recognized [English courts] to be fair and impartial." *Haynsworth*, 121 F.3d at 967. Noble House's deprivation of a day in court is the result of a self-inflicted problem (a failure to timely file where no evidence suggests it was prevented from timely filing), not the result of a grave inconvenience or unfairness due to the fora. Aside from the running of the statute of limitations, Noble House points to no other inconvenience or unfairness.

Third, there is no evidence that the fundamental unfairness of the chosen law will deprive the plaintiff of a remedy. Again, Noble House argues that it is deprived of a remedy "by virtue of a shortened statute of limitations permissible under English law." Noble House does not argue that there are no causes of action available under English law that would allow it to seek the same relief requested here. *See Weber*, 811 F.3d at 774. Rather, as Noble House seemingly concedes, it is its procedural **{-252-}** error, not the underlying substantive law, that may deny it a remedy. Courts enforce a forum-selection clause unless the contracted forum accords the plaintiff *no* remedies whatsoever. *Id.* at 774 & n.24; *see also Barnett*, 831 F.3d at 308 n.14. That's because "[i]t is the *availability* of a remedy that matters, not predictions of the likelihood of a win on the merits." *Weber*, 811 F.3d at 774 (emphasis in original). Noble House's failure to point to a substantive law that bars its claim for relief is fatal.

Fourth, there is no evidence that enforcement of the forum-selection clause would contravene a strong public policy of the forum state. Noble House states that "Texas has a strong public policy of regulating insurance" **[—11—]** because: (1) "the public policy of the State of Texas is reflected in its statutes"; (2) there is a statute providing that insurance contracts sold to citizens or inhabitants of Texas are governed by Texas law, TEX. INS. CODE § 21.42; (3) Texas residents must consent to the transfer of a suit involving an insurance contract, TEX. INS. CODE § 982.305; (4) Texas may regulate insurance; and (5) Texas has a strong interest in protecting its citizens against "overbearing tactics of insurance underwriters." The district court found this unconvincing. So do we.

Even assuming it were true that Texas has a strong public policy of regulating insurance, this Court has already explained that the Supreme Court, "rejecting as a 'parochial concept' the idea that 'notwithstanding solemn contracts all disputes must be resolved under our laws and in our courts,' held that federal courts presumptively must enforce forum selection clauses in international [contracts]." *Haynsworth*, 121 F.3d at 962 (quoting *Bremen*, 407 U.S. at 9) (alteration in original omitted). And public policy "weighs strongly in favor" of this presumption. *Id.* Tellingly, Noble House fails to cite a case where enforcement of a forum-selection clause contravened state public policy. *Cf. id.* ("Since *The Bremen*, the [Supreme] Court has consistently followed this rule [that federal courts presumptively must enforce forum-selection clauses] and, in fact, has enforced every forum selection clause in an international contract that has come before it."). And when asked at oral argument if such a case existed, Noble House conceded that it was not aware of such a case. As the record stands, there is insufficient evidence that enforcement of the foreign forum-selection clause would contravene Texas public policy.

Noble House bears the heavy burden of establishing that a *forum non conveniens* dismissal is unwarranted. *Weber*, 811 F.3d at 767. It has not overcome our strong presumption in favor of enforcing forum-selection **[—12—]** clauses. *Id.* at 775. The operative forum-selection clause, then, is enforceable. The district court did not err.

C. Noble House forfeited any argument regarding the *Atlantic Marine* factors.

Once we find that the forum-selection clause is enforceable, as here, we then "review for abuse of discretion the district court's use of *Atlantic Marine*'s balancing test" of public-interest factors. *Weber*, 811 F.3d at 766.

Noble House does not argue that the district court misapplied the public-interest factors. In fact, absent from Noble House's briefing is any reference to the *Atlantic Marine* public-interest factors. Its failure to address the public-interest factors results in forfeiture of the argument on appeal. *See PCL*, 979 F.3d at 1074 (citing *United States v. Young*, 872 F.3d 742, 747 (5th Cir. 2017)). **{–253–}**

V. A return-jurisdiction clause or total waiver of any statute-of-limitations defenses is not necessary.

Finding that the foreign forum-selection clause was enforceable, the district court dismissed the action without mention of a return-jurisdiction clause. Prior to dismissal, the court prompted Underwriters' express commitment that it would "not count the pendency of this action against any statute of limitation argument that's made in the future." Noble House contends that a "return-jurisdiction clause" was mandatory and that "a total waiver of any statute of limitations defenses [or laches defenses] is ... a valid prerequisite for transfer to a foreign jurisdiction pursuant to *forum non conveniens*." Noble House's position lacks merit.

"A return jurisdiction clause remedies th[e] concern [that the identified forum will remain available or that defendants will submit to its jurisdiction] by permitting parties to return to the dismissing court should **[—13—]** the lawsuit become impossible in the foreign forum." *Vasquez*, 325 F.3d at 675. "The 'failure to include a return jurisdiction clause in an f.n.c. [*i.e., forum non conveniens*] dismissal constitutes a *per se* abuse of discretion.'" *Vasquez*, 325 F.3d at 675 (quoting *Robinson v. TCI/US West Communications, Inc.*, 117 F.3d 900, 907-08 (5th Cir. 1997)). "This is because, as [this] [C]ourt has repeatedly made clear, 'courts must take measures, as part of their dismissals in [*forum non conveniens*] cases, to ensure that defendants will not attempt to evade the jurisdiction of the foreign courts.'" *Rajet Aeroservicios S.A. de C.V. v. Castillo Cervantes*, 801 F. App'x 239, 244 (5th Cir. 2020) (unpublished) (per curiam) (quoting *Baris v. Sulpicio Lines, Inc.*, 932 F.2d 1540, 1551 (5th Cir. 1991)). "Such measures often include agreements between the parties to litigate in another forum, to submit to service of process in that jurisdiction, to waive the assertion of any limitations defenses, to agree to discovery, and to agree to the enforceability of the foreign judgment." *Baris*, 932 F.2d at 1551 (citations omitted). "A return-jurisdiction clause assists in preventing defendants from circumventing these measures and ensures plaintiffs have the opportunity to proceed with the action in one of the forums." *Rajet Aeroservicios*, 801 F. App'x at 244.

The existence of a mandatory, enforceable forum-selection clause swallows the purpose of a return-jurisdiction clause whole. *See Baris*, 932 F.2d at 1551. As noted, an agreement is one of the express "measures" to ensure that defendants will not attempt to evade the jurisdiction of the foreign courts. *See Baris*, 932 F.2d at 1551. By agreement, Noble House and Underwriters are contractually bound to litigate their dispute in the courts of England and Wales. Accordingly, there is no concern that Underwriters will "attempt to evade jurisdiction of the foreign courts" or flout the litigation procedure and outcome. The clause ensures that Noble House will have the opportunity to proceed with the action in the foreign fora. *See Rajet Aeroservicios*, 801 F. App'x at 244. Moreover, should Underwriters evade the **[—14—]** jurisdiction of the foreign courts, Noble House has a remedy in a breach-of-contract action, a protection which does not exist in the *forum non conveniens* context where there is no forum-selection clause. The parties' agreement to proceed with the action in the selected fora obviates the need for a return-jurisdiction clause. *See Baris*, 932 F.2d at 1551.

A "total waiver of any statute of limitations defense" or laches defenses is similarly unnecessary. First, while such a waiver is one of the many "measures" provided to "ensure" that defendants will not evade the jurisdiction of foreign **{–254–}** courts, none of those measures is mandatory. *See id.* (listing examples of protective measures that a court may often – but not "must" – utilize). Again, the primary concern that a defendant will evade jurisdiction is not present where the parties willingly submitted to foreign fora by agreement. So, waiver as a protective measure is redundant, gratuitous, and serves no purpose. Although not required, the district court confirmed that Underwriters' statute-of-limitations defense did not encompass the time period including "the duration of the pendency of this action." This exceeds what was expected of the court to ensure Underwriters would not "evade" jurisdiction. Accordingly, the district court did not err.

VI. Conclusion

For the foregoing reasons, the district court did not err when it: (1) concluded that the foreign forum-selection clause is enforceable; or (2) failed to include a return-jurisdiction clause and total waiver of any statute-of-limitations defenses. We AFFIRM the district court's judgment of dismissal.

United States Court of Appeals
for the Fifth Circuit

No. 21-60752

HUNTINGTON INGALLS, INC.
vs.
DIRECTOR, OFFICE OF WORKERS' COMPENSATION PROGRAMS

Petition for Review of the Order of the Benefits Review Board

Decided: June 6, 2023

Citation: 70 F.4th 245, 11 Adm. R. 289 (5th Cir. 2023).

Before **STEWART, ELROD,** and **GRAVES,** Circuit Judges.

[—1—] {-246-} ELROD, Circuit Judge:

The Longshore and Harbor Workers' Compensation Act provides covered employees with "the right to choose an **{-247-}** attending physician authorized by the Secretary to provide medical care under this chapter." 33 U.S.C. § 907(b). The question here is whether audiologists are "physicians" under § 907(b) of the LHWCA. In this matter of first impression, we hold that they are. **[—2—]**

I

First, the facts. Although "nothing recounted in this Part has much bearing on the rest of our decision"—given that the dispositive issue is purely a legal one—"a recitation of the facts and proceedings below at least shows how the question presented arose." *Kisor v. Wilkie*, 139 S. Ct. 2400, 2408–09 (2019).

From 2003 to 2009, Clarence Jones worked at Huntington Ingalls Incorporated as a sheet-metal mechanic. After leaving the company, Jones complained of hearing loss. In April 2014, Jones selected and met with an audiologist. Audiologists are health care professionals who identify, assess, and manage disorders of hearing, balance, and other neural systems. Jones's selected audiologist administered a hearing test that generated an audiogram, a chart that shows how well one hears sounds in terms of frequency and intensity. The audiogram indicated a 17.2% binaural hearing impairment under the American Medical Association's *Guide to the Evaluation of Permanent Impairment*. Jones presented the audiogram and the results of a completed hearing-loss questionnaire to Huntington Ingalls's claims adjuster. In May 2014, the company filed a report recognizing Jones's claim.

Upon recognizing Jones's claim, the company scheduled Jones for another audiogram. This time, Huntington Ingalls wanted Jones to be evaluated by its own preferred audiologist. Jones complied. The company's preferred audiologist completed an audiogram and determined that Jones's level of hearing impairment was not 17.2%, but rather 0% (albeit with "mild high frequency sensorineural hearing loss"). The company took the position that it would accept liability for medical benefits, but only as to the results of the audiogram completed by the company's own selected audiologist.

In March 2015, Jones filed a formal claim for compensation under the Longshore and Harbor Workers' Compensation Act. 33 U.S.C. § 901. In **[—3—]** response, Huntington Ingalls reiterated its position that it would authorize Jones to schedule an appointment to be fitted with hearing aids, but only from its preferred audiologist. Jones requested instead that his original audiologist conduct the fitting. The company again refused, and the claim proceeded.

In 2016, an administrative law judge denied Jones's LHWCA claim for compensation and medical benefits, holding that Jones did not prove causation by a preponderance of the evidence. Jones moved for reconsideration, but the administrative law judge again denied his claim.

Jones appealed this decision to the Department of Labor's Benefits Review Board. In October 2017, the Board unanimously affirmed as to the denial of compensation benefits. But the Board reversed and remanded to the District Director regarding medical benefits, based on the Company's earlier stipulation to pay for Jones's hearing aids. Critical to the present dispute, the Board held that although Jones was eligible for that medical benefit, he did not "have a statutory or regulatory right to choose [his] own audiologist[]."

Jones moved for reconsideration. In July 2021, by a two-to-one vote, the Board reversed its initial decision on whether Jones could choose his own audiologist. The Board held instead that "an audiologist is a **{-248-}** 'physician' such that Claimant is permitted his initial choice of audiologist pursuant to Section 7(b) of the [LHWCA] as a matter of statutory construction." The Company timely petitioned this court for review. We have jurisdiction under 33 U.S.C. § 921(c).

II

The sole question presented by this appeal is whether an audiologist is a "physician" as that word is used in § 907(b) of the LHWCA. We review the Benefits Review Board's ruling on that matter of law *de novo*. *Grant v. Dir., Off. of Worker's Comp. Programs*, 502 F.3d 361, 363 (5th Cir. 2007). As **[—4—]** is always true when we first interpret of one of Congress's laws, "we start with the statutory text." *Tanzin v. Tanvir*, 141 S. Ct. 486, 489 (2020).

The LHCWA provides that if a covered employee is injured, his or her employer must "furnish such medical, surgical, and other attendance or treatment . . . for such period as the nature of the injury or the process of recovery may require." 33 U.S.C. § 907(a). And a claimant under the LHWCA "shall have the right to choose an attending *physician* authorized by the Secretary to provide medical care under this chapter as hereinafter provided." *Id.* § 907(b) (emphasis added).

A

The term "physician" in § 907(b), which was added in 1972, is not provided with a statutory definition. *See* Act of Oct. 27, 1972, Pub. L. No. 92-576, 86 Stat. 1251, 1254. Dictionaries published in or around 1972 may then shed some light on the meaning of the term "physician" at the time it was codified in the LHWCA. *See Bostock v. Clayton County*, 140 S. Ct. 1731, 1740 (2020) (consulting dictionary definitions published around the time that the law being examined was enacted). *Webster's Third* provides that a physician is:

1. a person skilled in the art of healing : one duly authorized to treat disease : a doctor of medicine — often distinguished from *surgeon*
2. one who restores (as a troubled spirit or the body politic) : one exerting a remedial or salutary influence <a ~ of the soul> <nature as a ~>
3. *obs* : NATURAL PHILOSOPHER, PHYSICIST

Webster's Third New International Dictionary 1707 (1966).

The second and third definitions can safely be discarded for overbreadth and obsolescence, respectively. Under the second definition, anyone who restores the troubled spirit or exerts a remedial influence is a **[—5—]** "physician." This cannot be what Congress meant. After all, the barista at my preferred coffee shop restores my tired spirit and remedies my fatigue. Is she a physician? The linguistic context of the word "physician" is that the Act requires employers to "furnish such medical, surgical, and other attendance or treatment [of injured employees] . . . for such period as the nature of the injury or the process of recovery may require." 33 U.S.C. § 907(a). As helpful as the coffee she brews may be, my barista does not provide me with medical, surgical, or other similar treatment. To call her a "physician" would thus be an inappropriate reading of that word outside the semantic context in which it appears within the statute. *Cf. Bond v. United States*, 572 U.S. 844, 870–71 (2014) (Scalia, J., concurring in the judgment) ("When, for example, 'draft,' a word of many meanings, is one of the words used in a definition of 'breeze,' we know it has nothing to do with military conscription or beer.").

The third definition may also be set aside. Under that meaning, which *Webster's* **{-249-}** *Third* notes specifically to be obsolete, an entirely different profession with similar linguistic origin is identified: physicists.[1] This does not apply to the case at hand.

We turn then to the primary definition listed in *Webster*'s. At its start, the definition provides a broad sense of the word. It says that a physician is **[—6—]** "a person skilled in the art of healing: one duly authorized to treat disease." This reading would undoubtedly include audiologists, as audiology is "a clinical profession devoted to the diagnosis and treatment of hearing and balance disorders." Brad A. Stach & Virginia Ramachandran, *Clinical Audiology: An Introduction* xiii (3d ed. 2022). But the definition continues, also offering a narrower sense of the word. The more restrictive portion of the definition says that somebody is a physician only if he or she is "a doctor of medicine — often distinguished from *surgeon*." Webster's Third New International Dictionary 1707 (1966). If that more restrictive conception controls, then audiologists are not physicians. Although the work of audiologists often intertwines with that of otolaryngologists—the medical doctors who study the ears, nose, and throat—audiologists are not themselves doctors of medicine. *See Doctor of Audiology Program Overview*, The University of Mississippi Medical Center, Degree Programs, https://www.umc.edu/graduateschool/Degree-Programs/Doctor-of-Audiology/Program-Overview.html.

The duality within the primary definition—having both a broad and narrow sense—is not unique to *Webster*'s understanding of the word. *The American Heritage Dictionary*, another reputable text published shortly after the adoption of the relevant amendment to the LHWCA, confirms these two distinct meanings:

1. A person licensed to practice medicine; medical doctor.
2. A person who heals or exerts a healing influence.

The American Heritage Dictionary 936 (2d College ed. 1976). The first sense is narrower and more technical, covering only those who practice medicine. The second sense is broader and sweeps in those who heal, even if they are not medical doctors. **[—7—]**

Dictionaries thus leave us with genuine ambiguity. Based on the education they receive and the role that they play in identifying and treating hearing disorders, audiologists can fairly be described as "skilled in the art of healing." Webster's Third New International Dictionary 1707 (1966). And the technical, post-graduate education they receive makes them "duly authorized to treat disease" related to hearing. *Id.* However, audiologists are not themselves medical doctors. Their work complements that of medical doctors, where the medical doctors and audiologists play important but distinct roles.

B

But dictionaries are not the only item in our interpretive toolkit: we can turn as well to the structure of the LHWCA. As Justice Thomas once explained **{–250–}** when writing for the Court, "The plainness or ambiguity of statutory language is determined by reference to the language itself, the specific context in which that language is used, and the broader context of the statute as a whole." *Robinson v. Shell Oil Co.*, 519 U.S. 337, 341 (1997). Section 907(b) is the specific part of the law at issue in this case, but the very next section seems to equate audiologists with physicians who have a certification in otolaryngology. That part of the LHWCA, amended relevantly in 1984, says

[1] As *Merriam-Webster*'s etymological researchers explain:

> Medical experts are called *physicians* because the word *physic* originally referred to both the practice of medicine and to natural science. As scientific fields matured, *physic* as it applied to healing was phased out in favor of *medicine*. *Physicist* was coined to refer to someone who studies "physics," and *physician* was left with its association with medical doctors.

Why Is a Medical Expert Called a 'Physician'?, Merriam-Webster: Word History (June 2, 2020), https://www.merriam-webster.com/words-at-play/why-is-a-medical-expert-called-a-physician.

that in calculating payments for permanent partial disability, "[a]n audiogram shall be presumptive evidence of the amount of hearing loss sustained as of the dater thereof, only if (i) such audiogram was administered by a licensed or certified audiologist or a physician who is certified in otolaryngology." 33 U.S.C. § 908(c)(13)(C).

It would be structurally odd for § 908 and § 907 to treat audiologists differently in this regard. If an audiologist can perform the audiogram that is necessary to determine *quantitively* the amount of disability for § 908, then an audiologist would also seem able to use that audiogram for purposes of a **[—8—]** § 907 as a diagnostic tool in determining *qualitatively* that care is necessary. And if claimants were not free to choose their own audiologists but were able to choose their own otolaryngologist, then that otolaryngologist would likely need to refer the claimant to an audiologist anyway for an audiogram and the fitting of hearing aids. This additional step adds delay for claimants and costs for the employers ultimately responsible for their medical care.

Our job is not to design efficient statutes, though. "[O]ur task is confined to deciding cases and controversies, which requires us to apply the law as Congress has written it." *Cargill v. Garland*, 57 F.4th 447, 472 (5th Cir. 2023) (*en banc*). And while structural evidence suggests that § 908 and § 907 interact to inform and provide further context for the word "physician," it is still true that the language of § 908 distinguishes audiologists from physicians. It says that an audiogram is presumptive evidence of the level of hearing loss sustained only if conducted by a "certified audiologist or a physician who is certified in otolaryngology." 33 U.S.C. § 908(c)(13)(C). It does not say "audiologist or *other* physician." The structural interactions between these historical amendments to sections 907 and 908 would seem to exacerbate, rather than alleviate, the ambiguity presented by the plain text of the statute.

C

With text, structure, and history all indeterminate, we turn—as the Supreme Court has instructed us—to the purposes of the statute. *See Kisor v. Wilkie*, 139 S. Ct. 2400, 2424 (2019) (describing the traditional interpretive toolkit as "text, structure, history, and purpose"); *see also W. Refining Sw., Inc. v. FERC*, 636 F.3d 719, 727 (5th Cir. 2011) (observing that the court's interpretation of the statute at issue "is consistent with congressional intent" and "is in line with the purposes of the Act"). Importantly, inquiry into purpose cannot be used to contradict otherwise clear text. We look only **[—9—]** because the text, structure, and history all prove indeterminate, so the meaning of the words at issue in this case could be clarified by the aims of the statute. The Supreme Court has long recognized that some of the LHWCA's clear aims include "ensuring prompt payment to injured workers and of relieving claimants and their employers of the undue expense and administrative burden of litigating compensation claims." **{-251-}** *Pallas Shipping Agency, Ltd. v. Duris*, 461 U.S. 529, 538 (1983).

Achieving that aim requires that injured employees be able to get an accurate diagnosis. And the statute's amendment history suggests that the purpose of the physician-selection provision is to reduce the risk that employers will select physicians who say employees are in better health than they really are, so as to reduce the cost of medical treatments that might accompany a more fulsome diagnosis. In 1960, the LHWCA was amended "to provide that an injured employee shall have the right to select his own physician." Public L. 86-757, 74 Stat. 900 (Sept. 13, 1960). But the scope of that selection privilege was quite narrow: the statute provided that "The employee shall have the right to choose an attending physician from a panel of physicians to be named by the employer subject to [certain provisions]." *Id.* § 7(b). This is a far cry from the 1972 Amendments, which allow a much broader right to select a physician that is not constrained by the employer's screening of options, as the employer was able to do in the 1960 version of the law. *See* 86 Stat. 1254 (1972).

When Congress still authorized employers to select physicians for their employees, the care that those employees received sometimes suffered. *See, e.g.*, *Atl. & Gulf Stevedores, Inc. v. Neuman*, 440 F.2d 908, 910 (5th Cir. 1971) (an employee's necessary back surgery was delayed by months because the employer's hired doctors claimed the treatment was not required, which was proven incorrect when the employee sought surgery on his own accord). The mismatch in diagnoses and proposed treatments between an employee's **[—10—]** preferred physician and one hired by the employer is not just explainable by diverging financial interests, though. The doctor-patient relationship requires trust and confidentiality to facilitate the candid disclosure of sensitive health information. *Cf. Zadeh v. Robinson*, 928 F.3d 457, 476 (5th Cir. 2019) (Willett, J., concurring in part and dissenting in part) (concluding that, in the Fourth Amendment context, "the law strongly protects privacy in medicine").

All the purposes of the physician-selection provision discussed above would also seem to apply to an employee's selection of his or her own audiologist. The employer has a financial incentive in selecting audiologists who have a reputation of finding that an employee's hearing is not as impaired as the employee believes it to be. In the facts at hand, for example, Respondent Jones's preferred audiologist diagnosed him with a 17.2% hearing deficiency. The audiologist selected by the employer did not just disagree by a matter of a couple percentage points. He found that Jones's hearing-impairment level was 0%.

However, further examination of the statute's apparent purposes reveals that this conclusion about physician choice may not be so simple. Sections 908 and 907 work in tandem to provide employees with the tools for diagnosing and then treating hearing-relating injuries, respectively. Congress may have included audiologists among those who can *diagnose* hearing loss under § 908 while intentionally omitting audiologists from those who can *treat* such hearing loss under § 907 (which contains the physician-selection provision at issue). "It is not axiomatic that someone whose hearing is tested should be provided hearing aids, and the fact that Congress placed faith in the judgment of audiologists to determine the amount of hearing loss does not equate to faith in audiologists to prescribe care." Benefits Review Board No. 16-0690, Decision and Order on Motion for Reconsideration at 23 (Boggs, C.A.A.J., dissenting). Congress could believe that a **{-252-}** medical doctor **[—11—]** is better suited than an audiologist to look at the results of an audiologist-administered audiogram, as well as other relevant health information, and then determine the appropriate care for the patient.

Looking for congruence between the text of a portion of a statute and the purposes of the statute as a whole as expressed by its internal structure can sometimes resolve ambiguity. But here, this tool seems yet again to pull equally in both directions. Perhaps this is a good illustration of why we avoid "open-ended policy appeals and speculation about legislative intentions" that are not otherwise apparent from the text and structure of the statute alone. *Kisor*, 139 S. Ct. at 2442 (Gorsuch, J., concurring in the judgment).

* * *

We have exhausted all of our traditional tools of statutory construction. And yet "the relevant language, carefully considered, can yield more than one reasonable interpretation." *Pauley v. BethEnergy Mines, Inc.*, 501 U.S. 680, 707 (1991) (Scalia, J., dissenting). Whether audiologists are covered by the Act's physician-choice provision is therefore genuinely ambiguous.

III

Because the statute that Congress wrote is silent or ambiguous as to the legal issue raised by this case, we now "name *Chevron*, and apply its precedent." *Mexican Gulf Fishing Co. v. U.S. Dep't of Commerce*, 60 F.4th 956, 963 n.3, 11 Adm. R. 240, 242 n.3 (5th Cir. 2023); *see also Forrest Gen. Hosp. v. Azar*, 926 F.3d 221, 228

(5th Cir. 2019).[2] When an ambiguous statute is accompanied by lawfully **[—12—]** issued implementing regulations, "the court does not simply impose its own construction on the statute, as would be necessary in the absence of an administrative interpretation." *Chevron U.S.A. Inc. v. Nat. Res. Def. Council, Inc.*, 467 U.S. 837, 843 (1984) (footnote omitted). Instead, we look to the agency's lawfully promulgated regulation and defer to that interpretation if—but only if—"the agency's answer is based on a permissible construction of the statute." *Mexican Gulf Fishing*, 60 F.4th at 963, 11 Adm. R. at 242 (quoting *Huawei Techs. USA, Inc. v. FCC*, 2 F.4th 421, 433 (5th Cir. 2021)).

A

The LHWCA provides authorization for the Secretary of the Department of Labor to issue rules and regulations required to administer the provisions of the statute. 33 U.S.C. § 939(a). And we have held specifically that *Chevron* deference can apply to regulations that implement the LHWCA. *See Ceres Marine Terminal v. Hinton*, 243 F.3d 222, 227 (5th Cir. 2001). Therefore, we turn to the regulations to see if they are "reasonable." *Forrest Gen. Hosp.*, 926 F.3d at 228.

In 1977, the Agency interpreted the term "physician" to "include[] doctors of medicine (MD), surgeons, podiatrists, dentists, clinical psychologists, optometrists, chiropractors, and osteopathic practitioners within the scope of their practice as defined by State law." 20 C.F.R. § 702.404 **{-253-}** ("Physician defined"). The Agency defines the term not only by positively including examples of practitioners but also by excluding others: "Naturopaths, faith healers, and other practitioners of the healing arts which are not listed herein are not included within the term 'physician' as used in **[—13—]** this part." *Id.* And in 1985, after § 908 of the statute was relevantly amended to add the portion on hearing loss, the Agency promulgated a regulation on claims for loss of hearing that included references to audiologists and otolaryngologists. 20 C.F.R. § 702.441.

The Agency's interpretation of the statute fits neatly within the broad and narrow readings of the word "physician" that the traditional statutory interpretation methods revealed. *Cf. Kisor*, 139 S. Ct. at 2416 ("Note that serious application of those tools therefore has use even when a [statute] turns out to be truly ambiguous. The text, structure, history, and so forth at least establish the outer bounds of permissible interpretation."). The regulation includes many learned health care professionals, even though they are not all medical doctors. But the regulation draws the line at some point to prevent the term "physician" from sweeping in untrained or uncertified individuals who purport to exert a healing influence. These are the exact bounds discovered earlier, in Part II of the opinion.

B

Because the regulations are permissible under *Chevron*, we now see if they can relieve us from the ambiguity that the statute has left us with. *See Dominion Ambulance, L.L.C. v. Azar*, 968 F.3d 429, 434 (5th Cir. 2020) ("When a regulation is unambiguous, courts . . . simply apply the regulation's plain meaning."). Whether the regulations answer the question at hand is not immediately obvious, though. Although they provide a list of specific professions to be included in the definition of "physician," the regulations make no explicit mention of audiologists. However, a regulation "is not ambiguous merely because 'discerning the only possible interpretation requires a taxing inquiry.'" *Kisor*, 139 S. Ct. at 2415

[2] Although "*Chevron* has become something of the-precedent-who-must-not-be-named," it is the law "until and unless it is overruled by our highest Court." *Mexican Gulf Fishing*, 60 F.4th at 963 n.3, 11 Adm. R. at 242 n.3. That said, the judgment in this case is not conditional on *Chevron*'s longevity. *See Loper Bright Enters., Inc. v. Raimondo*, 45 F.4th 359, 10 Adm. R. 488 (D.C. Cir. 2022), *cert. granted*, --- S. Ct. ---, 2023 WL 3158352 (granting *certiorari* on whether *Chevron* **[—12—]** should be overturned). Even without according any deference to the agency's regulations, audiologists are properly understood as physicians under the LHWCA for the reasons discussed *infra*.

(quoting *Pauley*, 501 U.S. at 707 (Scalia, J., dissenting)). **[—14—]**

The full regulatory definition of "physician" is as follows:

> The term *physician* **includes doctors of medicine (MD), surgeons, podiatrists, dentists, clinical psychologists, optometrists, chiropractors, and osteopathic practitioners within the scope of their practice as defined by State law.** The term includes chiropractors only to the extent that their reimbursable services are limited to treatment consisting of manual manipulation of the spine to correct a subluxation shown by X-ray or clinical findings. Physicians defined in this part may interpret their own X-rays. All physicians in these categories are authorized by the Director to render medical care under the Act. **Naturopaths, faith healers, and other practitioners of the healing arts which are not listed herein are not included** within the term "physician" as used in this part.

20 C.F.R. § 702.404 ("Physician defined") (emphases added).

Huntington Ingalls argues that the regulation's limiting clause at the end of the definition requires that the list of examples appearing at the beginning must be exclusive. Because the limiting clause flatly says that "other practitioners of the healing arts which are not listed herein are not included within the term 'physician,'" and because audiologists are other practitioners of the healing arts, the company argues, **{-254-}** they are not "physicians" for purposes of the LHWCA.

This line of reasoning is mistaken. First, the list of examples of the beginning of the regulation says "includes," not "is limited to." And as we have held in the past, "the word 'includes' is usually a term of enlargement, and not of limitation." *DIRECTV, Inc. v. Budden*, 420 F.3d 521, 527 (5th Cir. 2005) (internal brackets and citation omitted). And second, the familiar semantic canon of *ejusdem generis* requires that the exclusionary clause at the end of the regulation be limited only to those other practitioners of the healing arts that are similar to naturopaths and faith healers. **[—15—]**

On *ejusdem generis*: that canon "applies when a drafter has tacked on a catchall phrase at the end of an enumeration of specifics, as in *dogs, cats, horses, cattle, and other animals*." Antonin Scalia & Bryan A. Garner, *Reading Law: The Interpretation of Legal Texts* 199 (2012). In Justice Scalia's example, the canon is required to determine the proper scope of the phrase "other animals" because that phrase is not defined. The text does not say "other mammalian animals," "other domesticated animals," or otherwise provide the relevant class. As a result, the reader must use his or her own reasoning to determine what level of generality the term "other animals" covers, based on context.

Likewise, the reader of the relevant regulation here does not know what kind of omitted practitioners are intended to be excluded from the "physician" category because the regulation does not define the relevant class. It says merely "other practitioners of the healing arts." 20 C.F.R. § 702.404. Thus, it would be appropriate as a matter of ordinary language to infer that the catchall phrase at the end of the list does not actually catch *all* other professions; it includes only other *similar* professions. The question, then, is whether audiologists are more akin to the explicitly included practitioners of the healing arts or closer in kind to the explicitly excluded practitioners.

The two named practitioners in the excluded list are "naturopaths" and "faith healers." As the Benefits Review Board found, "[a]udiologists are utterly antithetical to both." Benefits Review Board No. 16-0690, Decision and Order on Motion for Reconsideration at 16. A "naturopath" is a practitioner of naturopathy, which is a "theory of disease and system of therapy based on the supposition that diseases can be cured by natural agencies without the use of drugs." The New Shorter Oxford English Dictionary 1890 (3d ed. 1993). A faith healer "act[s] by faith and prayer, not drugs or other conventional medicine." *Id.* at 908. **[—16—]**

Audiologists, by contrast, are licensed by the State of Mississippi (where the employee in this case lives), and they engage in conventional medical treatment. They are analogous in many ways to optometrists, who are included as "physicians" in the regulatory definition. Optometrists, despite lacking a medical degree, are able to administer and interpret vision tests. And based on the results of those tests, optometrists can prescribe the appropriate corrective lenses that someone with impaired vision can use to bolster his or her ability to see. *What Is an Optometrist?*, Mississippi Optometric Ass'n (2019), https://www.mseyes.com/your-family-eye-doctor/what-is-an-optometrist/. Audiologists are similarly able to administer hearing tests, evaluate the resulting audiograms, and then use that information to fit a patient with hearing aids that are appropriately calibrated to the individual's level of auditory impairment. **{-255-}**

Because the plain meaning of the regulation includes audiologists, and because that regulation is entitled to *Chevron* deference, audiologists are included in § 907(b) of the LHWCA's use of the word "physician."

IV

In the alternative, we analyze the issue presented by assuming *arguendo* that the regulations are actually ambiguous. "*Chevron* deference (regarding ambiguous statutes) has a less-famous doctrinal cousin" under which a court provides some level of deference to an agency's reasonable interpretation of its own ambiguous regulation. *Forrest Gen. Hosp.*, 926 F.3d at 229. There are two levels of deference that may be appropriate in such a circumstance: *Skidmore* deference and *Auer* deference. *See Skidmore v. Swift & Co.*, 323 U.S. 134 (1944); *Auer v. Robbins*, 519 U.S. 452 (1997).

"When it applies, *Auer* deference gives an agency significant leeway to say what its own rules mean." *Kisor*, 139 S. Ct. at 2414, 2418. However, "that phrase 'when it applies' is important—because it often doesn't." *Id.* **[—17—]** A court should only use this stronger form of deference when an agency's interpretation: (1) is authoritative; (2) is based on its expertise; and (3) reflects the agency's "fair and considered judgment." *Kisor*, 139 S. Ct. at 2417 (quoting *Christopher v. SmithKline Beecham Corp.*, 567 U.S. 142, 155 (2012). If an agency interpretation does not meet these factors, then it is owed deference only so far as it is persuasive. *Skidmore*, 323 U.S. at 140.

A

The agency has interpreted its regulatory definition of "physician" as including audiologists. We therefore address the three requirements for *Auer* deference in turn and defer to the agency's interpretation only if it meets each necessary condition.

1

First is whether the agency's interpretation is authoritative, rather than merely a convenient litigating position. *Bowen v. Georgetown Univ. Hosp.*, 488 U.S. 204, 213 (1988). To be authoritative, the action need not come from the Secretary or his chief advisors. *Kisor*, 139 S. Ct. at 2416. In the past, "official staff memoranda" reported in the Federal Register have been considered authoritative, even if not officially approved by the agency head. *Id.* (quoting *Ford Motor Credit Co. v. Milhollin*, 444 U.S. 555, 566 n.9, 567 n.10 (1980)). But a speech made by "mid-level official" and an "'informal memorandum' recounting a telephone conversation between employees" have not counted as sufficiently authoritative. *Id.* at 2416–17. (citations omitted); *see also N.Y. State Dep't of Soc. Servs. v. Bowen*, 835 F.2d 360, 365–66 (D.C. Cir. 1987)).

Putting aside the Director's litigation materials, the two materials that could most plausibly be candidates for the "authoritative" agency view are a letter from the Occupational Health and Safety Administration and the Longshoreman's Manual. OSHA has indicated in a letter on a separate **[—18—]** regulation that audiologists are considered "physicians" for the purposes of treating hearing loss.[3] Perhaps it is for **{-256-}** this reason that although § 702.404 has never been formally amended to include audiologists, "[i]n practice, claimants have long been given their choice of audiologists to provide medical care for hearing loss." Benefits Review Board No. 16-0690, Decision and Order on Motion for Reconsideration at 3. This is positive evidence that the agency's position is not novel to this litigation. But it is not enough. The letter comes from the director of the Directorate of Enforcement Programs for OSHA, which is parallel to the Office of Workers' Compensation Programs in the Department of Labor's organization, but still a separate unit. *See* Opinion Letter, *supra* note 3. And although the letter does arguably equate audiologists with physicians, it concerns an unrelated regulation. The regulations at issue in this case make no reference to that OSHA program, so it is unclear how the OSHA program could be incorporated into the LHWCA or its implementing regulations.

The Longshore Procedure Manual, an official document, could also provide some evidence of the agency's authoritative views. The Manual "instructs that audiograms are presumptive evidence of the amount of hearing loss sustained if they are administered by a certified audiologist, physician, or a qualified technician under their supervision." Benefits Review Board No. 16-0690, Decision and Order on Motion for Reconsideration at 9. And as the Director put it in a letter responding to a public inquiry, "the fact that the Longshore Program has long accorded to their audiograms the same deference as those of physicians, indicates that the **[—19—]** Director has considered audiologists' reliability and expertise to be the same as physicians." *Id.* (quoting Dir. Letter Br. at 7, n.10).

However, the guidance provided by the Manual on this point is merely a parroting of the definition of "physician" that is provided in § 702.404. DLHWC Proc. Manual 5–0100, para. 4(1) https://www.dol.gov/agencies/owcp/dlhwc/lsProMan/ProMan#05-0100. This proves fatal. We have previously held that "an agency is not entitled to additional deference when its 'interpretation' of the statute simply repeats the statute's language." *La Union Del Pueblo Entero v. Fed. Emergency Mgmt. Agency*, 608 F.3d 217, 222 (5th Cir. 2010).

The Director's position is therefore not authoritative.

2

The second consideration is whether the interpretation implicates the Department's substantive expertise. An agency is at its strongest when the interpretation is within the bounds of its ordinary duty and implicates technical matters. *Kisor*, 139 S. Ct. at 2417. But other interpretive issues "fall more naturally into a judge's bailiwick," like the "elucidation of a simple common-law property term." *Id.*

The Director's position satisfies the substantive-expertise condition. The interpretation here is directly related to the Department's expertise—work-related injuries and the compensation and medical care that accompany them. Whether audiologists should be able both to assess and treat injuries or only to assess them is certainly more of a policy question and does not avail itself to judicial interpretation. As previously explored, the policy implications raised by that question are beyond the scope of our job and lead us only to ambiguous results. **[—20—] {-257-}**

3

The third and final consideration is whether the Director's interpretation is "fair and considered." *Id.* at 2417 (citation omitted). It should not be merely a "convenient litigating position," *id.*, nor should it be a new interpretation that "creates 'unfair surprise.'" *Id.* at 2418 (quoting *Long Island Care at Home, Ltd. v. Coke*, 551 U.S. 158, 170 (2007)). This is

[3] U.S. Dep't of Labor Occup. Safety & Health Admin., Opinion Letter on Definition of a Physician under 29 CFR 1910.95 and What Credentials Would Qualify a Person to Perform the Duties that Are Specifically Ascribed to Physicians by this Standard (May 10, 2016), *as published at* 2016 WL 6440727.

especially so when a disputed interpretation contradicts a prior one. *Id.* There is no indication here that the Department took a prior position contradictory to this one (*e.g.*, that it previously interpreted the regulation as excluding audiologists from the definition of physician). Nor is it a "convenient litigating position," as the manual and letter pre-existed litigation and take the same stance. Therefore, the Director's interpretation is likely "fair and considered."

* * *

Although the Director's interpretation might satisfy two of the three conditions needed for *Auer* deference, it fails to receive that heightened level of deference because it is not sufficiently authoritative. We therefore hold in the alternative that if the Director's position is to be granted any deference, it should receive only *Skidmore* deference.[4] Because we are persuaded by the text of the regulation itself that audiologists meet the definition of **[—21—]** "physician," applying *Skidmore* deference to the Director's same conclusion leads to an identical result.

V

Because an audiologist is a "physician" as that word is used in the Longshore and Harbor Workers' Compensation Act, the Benefits Review Board was correct to order that Clarence Jones had a right to select his own audiologist. Accordingly, we DENY the petition for review submitted by Huntington Ingalls, Inc.

---

[4] "This circuit follows the rule that alternative holdings are binding precedent and not obiter dictum." *Jarkesy v. SEC*, 34 F.4th 446, 459 n.9 (5th Cir. 2022) (quoting *Texas v. United States*, 809 F.3d 134, 178 n.158 (5th Cir. 2015)). The two holdings are as follows: First, under the plain meaning of the regulation, audiologists are physicians, so the agency's interpretation of its own regulation is not due any deference. Second, even if the regulation is ambiguous, the agency's interpretation of that regulation should receive only *Skidmore* deference—not *Auer* deference. Under either holding, the Benefits Review Board was correct to order that Clarence Jones had a right to select his own audiologist.

United States Court of Appeals
for the Fifth Circuit

No. 21-30761

BARROSSE
vs.
HUNTINGTON INGALLS, INC.

Appeal from the United States District Court for the Eastern District of Louisiana

Decided: June 12, 2023

Citation: 70 F.4th 315, 11 Adm. R. 299 (5th Cir. 2023).

Before **RICHMAN,** Chief Judge, and **HO** and **ENGELHARDT,** Circuit Judges.

[—1—] {-316-} **ENGELHARDT,** Circuit Judge: **{-317-}**

Federal law is the "supreme Law of the Land." U.S. CONST. art.VI. When a state law looks like it might conflict with a federal statute or regulation, courts consider preemption to see if the state law in question must yield. *Perry v. Mercedes Benz of N. Am., Inc.*, 957 F.2d 1257, 1261 (5th Cir.1992). Here, Defendant-Appellee argues that Plaintiffs-Appellants' state-law tort claims are preempted by the federal Longshore and Harbor Workers' **[—2—]** Compensation Act ("LHWCA" or "the Act"). But, under the specific facts of this case and applicable Supreme Court caselaw, they are not. We therefore REVERSE and REMAND.

I

A

Ronald Barrosse[1] worked for Defendant-Appellee Huntington Ingalls (formerly "Avondale") as a shipyard electrician from February 1969 to June 1977. In March 2020, Barrosse was diagnosed with mesothelioma. Following his diagnosis, he filed a state-law tort suit in the Civil District Court for the Parish of Orleans alleging that Avondale, among other defendants, caused Barrosse to contract mesothelioma by exposing him to asbestos in a negligent manner. Because Barrosse primarily worked on United States Navy ships when he was exposed, Avondale removed the case to federal district court under the federal officer removal statute. *See* 28 U.S.C. § 1442; *Latiolais v. Huntington Ingalls, Inc.*, 951 F.3d 286, 296, 8 Adm. R. 155, 161 (5th Cir. 2020) (en banc). Barrosse never claimed benefits under the LHWCA, which provides a no-fault compensation remedy to injured workers. 33 U.S.C. § 904.

Avondale moved for summary judgment. Relevant here, Avondale argued that Barrosse's state-law tort claims were preempted by the LHWCA because they directly conflicted with and frustrated the purposes of the Act. The district court agreed and held that the claims are preempted. *Barrosse v. Huntington Ingalls Inc.*, 563 F. Supp. 3d 541, 559 (E.D. La. 2021). Barrosse appeals. **[—3—]**

B

While cases about statutes typically begin with the text, recounting the development of federal maritime compensation law is necessary to understand the nuances presented in this case. In 1917, the Supreme Court "declared that States were constitutionally barred from applying their compensation systems to maritime injuries." *Sun Ship, Inc. v. Pennsylvania*, 447 U.S. 715, 717 (1980) (citing *S. Pac. Co. v. Jensen*, 244 U.S. 205 (1917)). After failed efforts to delegate compensation matters to the states, Congress passed the LHWCA in 1927 to provide compensation for maritime workers. *Id.* The original LHWCA expressly limited its application to those cases where state worker's compensation laws did not apply. *Id.* at 717–18.

But that limited application caused problems because it was unclear where "the **{-318-}** boundary at which state remedies gave way to federal remedies" was. *Id.* at 718. Injured workers had to guess whether to file a claim under state or federal law, and "the price of error was unnecessary expense and possible

[1] Barrosse unfortunately passed away mid-litigation, so his survivors substituted themselves as Plaintiffs-Appellants. To avoid confusion, they will collectively be referred to herein as "Barrosse."

foreclosure from the proper forum." *Id.* The Supreme Court responded with the creation of the so-called "twilight zone," an area of concurrent jurisdiction that applies on a case-by-case basis. *Id.* (discussing *Davis v. Dep't of Labor*, 317 U.S. 249, 253–56 (1942)).[2] Notably, it did so over a strong dissent which argued that the plain language of the Act "left no room for an overlapping dual system" of concurrent jurisdiction. *Davis*, 317 U.S. at 261 (Stone, C.J., dissenting). According to the dissent, the majority interpreted the LHWCA to "not mean what it says"—that "[i]f there is liability under the federal act, that liability is exclusive." *Id.* **[—4—]**

Nevertheless, the twilight zone prevailed. Among other cases, the Supreme Court decided *Hahn v. Ross Island Sand & Gravel Co.*, 358 U.S. 272, 273 (1959) (per curiam). In *Hahn*, the plaintiff brought a state-law tort claim. *Id.* Because the plaintiff was in the twilight zone and compensation "could have been, and in fact was, validly provided by [s]tate law,"[3] the LHWCA "did not bar" the claim. *Id.* (quotation marks omitted). Like *Davis*, *Hahn* was decided over a dissent which argued that the twilight zone's regime of concurrent jurisdiction extended only to "a state workmen's compensation act or the [LHWCA]," and not to torts. *Id.* at 274 (Stewart, J., dissenting).

"In 1972, Congress . . . extend[ed] the LHWCA landward beyond the shoreline of the navigable waters of the United States." *Sun Ship*, 447 U.S. at 719. Rather than "resurrecting the jurisdictional monstrosity" of pre-*Davis* longshore compensation law, the Supreme Court reaffirmed the twilight zone because it remained unclear where federal jurisdiction ended and state jurisdiction began, even though that point "is fixed upon land." *Id.* at 719–20. The upshot is that despite the text of the Act expressly providing that employer liability for injuries falling under its ambit is "exclusive and in place of all other liability of such employer to the employee . . . at law or in admiralty," the Supreme Court has limited that exclusivity to cases outside the so-called twilight zone. 33 U.S.C. § 905(a). **[—5—]**

C

The pertinent development of Louisiana compensation law is shorter, but just as relevant in this case of concurrent jurisdiction. Louisiana passed the applicable version of its Workers' Compensation Act ("WCA") in 1952. *See* La. Rev. Stat. § 23:1031.1 (1952). Like most workers' compensation statutes, the WCA gave an injured worker a remedy that was "exclusive of all other rights and remedies." *Id.* The pertinent portion of the statute took a schedule approach, only covering the diseases **{-319-}** listed in the statutory text. *See Rando v. Anco Insulations Inc.*, 16 So. 3d 1065, 1072–73 (La. 2009). If a disease was not listed, an afflicted worker could only bring a tort suit as neither the compensation nor the exclusivity provisions of the WCA applied. *Id.* at 1071.

Barrosse is one of those workers. Mesothelioma, the disease Barrosse suffered from, was not covered by the WCA until it was amended in 1975. *Id.; see Williams v. Lockheed Martin Corp.*, 990 F.3d 852, 864 (5th Cir. 2021). When survivors of a decedent bring state-law claims "based on asbestos exposure," we apply "the law in effect when the exposure occurred." *Savoie v. Huntington Ingalls, Inc.*, 817 F.3d 457, 464, 4 Adm. R. 225, 229 (5th Cir. 2016), *overruled on other grounds Latiolais*, 951 F.3d at 296 n.9, 8 Adm. R. at 161 n.9.[4] Barrosse's claims are based on alleged exposure, as

[2] The district court noted that "there appears to be no genuine [dispute] of material fact that this is a twilight zone case," and the parties do not contest that conclusion on appeal. *Barrosse*, 563 F. Supp. 3d at 556.

[3] This particular phrase is in reference to the pre-1972 version of the LHWCA, which extended LHWCA coverage only if the state does not—and could not—validly provide recovery. *See Newport News Shipbuilding & Dry Dock Co. v. Dep't of Labor*, 583 F.2d 1273, 1277 (4th Cir. 1978) (discussing the language and its subsequent removal). The district court held that the post-1972 version of the LHWCA applies here, and Barrosse does not challenge that holding on appeal. *Barrosse*, 563 F. Supp. 3d at 548–52.

[4] We do not address the district court's interpretation of *Savoie* or its holding that the post-1972 LHWCA applies to this dispute. Those issues are not presented here.

mesothelioma injuries in Louisiana are deemed to occur "at the time of significant exposure to asbestos, not later when [the] disease . . . manifest[s] itself." *Rando*, 16 So. 3d at 1083; *see Williams*, 990 F.3d at 865. Barrosse claims that his significant exposure first occurred vis-à-vis Avondale in 1969. Thus, the applicable version of the WCA does not cover the injury **[—6—]** he suffered. *See Rando*, 16 So. 3d at 1071.[5] As a result, Barrosse's *only* state-law remedy is a tort suit. *Id.*

The upshot of these parallel events and their timing[6] is that once Barrosse discovered his injury, he could seek relief under *either* the LHWCA *or* state tort law.[7] The question presented in this case is whether state tort law **[—7—]** is preempted by the LHWCA in the twilight zone under those circumstances.

II.

We review the district court's grant of summary judgment de novo and **{-320-}** affirm if "there is no genuine dispute as to any material fact and the movant is entitled to judgment as a matter of law." FED. R. CIV. P. 56(a); *Renfroe v. Parker*, 974 F.3d 594, 599 (5th Cir. 2020). Here, the sole issue is preemption, which "is a question of law." *Baker v. Farmers Elec. Co-op., Inc.*, 34 F.3d 274, 278 (5th Cir. 1994). "Preemption of state law may be the result of either express preemption, field preemption, or conflict preemption." *Wright v. Allstate Ins. Co.*, 415 F.3d 384, 389 (5th Cir. 2005).

Express preemption applies "[w]here Congress expresses an explicit intent to preempt state law." *Hetzel v. Bethlehem Steel Corp.*, 50 F.3d 360, 363 (5th Cir. 1995). "Conflict preemption applies (1) where complying with both federal law and state law is impossible; or (2) where the state law creates an unacceptable obstacle to the accomplishment and execution of the full purposes and objectives of Congress." *Janvey v. Democratic Senatorial Campaign Comm., Inc.*, 712 F.3d 185, 200 (5th Cir. 2013) (quotation omitted). Courts may not conduct "a freewheeling judicial inquiry into whether a state statute is in tension with federal objectives [because] such an endeavor would undercut the principle that it is Congress rather than the courts that preempts state law." *Chamber of Com. v. Whiting*, 563 U.S.

---

[5] The plaintiff in *Rando* was injured in 1970, but the 1952 WCA applied. *Rando*, 16 So. 3d at 1072.

[6] Condensing these developments, the following timeline emerges:

- 1927: Congress passes the LHWCA, providing workers' compensation remedies to maritime workers.
- 1942: The Supreme Court decides Davis, creating a regime of concurrent jurisdiction in twilight zone cases.
- 1952: Louisiana passes the applicable version of the WCA, which neither covers mesothelioma nor prohibits tort claims based on mesothelioma injuries.
- 1959: The Supreme Court decides Hahn, permitting a state-law tort claim in a twilight zone case when that tort claim was included in the state-law regime.
- 1969: Barrosse begins working for Avondale and suffers injury in the twilight zone for purposes of his present claims.
- 1972: Congress amends the LHWCA, expanding its coverage landward.
- 1975: Louisiana amends the WCA to cover mesothelioma injuries.
- 1980: The Supreme Court decides Sun Ship, reaffirming Davis and its twilight-zone progeny after the 1972 LHWCA amendment.
- 2020: Barrosse is diagnosed with mesothelioma and brings this suit.

[7] We do not address whether a plaintiff who brings a tort claim could subsequently obtain relief under the LHWCA. On at least one occasion, the Supreme Court has sanctioned LHWCA compensation *after* the beneficiary received state-law compensation, but only when the state payments were credited against LHWCA relief. *See Calbeck v. Travelers Ins. Co.*, 370 U.S. 114, 131 (1962) (upholding compensation payments under both the LHWCA and state law where the state payments were credited against the LHWCA payments so "no impermissible double recovery [wa]s possible"). Whether that holding extends to tort remedies is a question we leave for another day.

582, 607 (2011) (quotation omitted). For a state law to be conflict preempted, "a high threshold must be met." *Id.* (quotation omitted).

III.

Avondale argues that both express and conflict preemption bar Barrosse's claims. **[—8—]**

A

Express preemption does not apply. There is no dispute that this is a twilight zone case. *Id.* at 556. In the twilight zone, "although the LHWCA's exclusivity language would seem to express congressional intent to preempt state law, the Supreme Court has found that total preemption was not intended." *Hetzel*, 50 F.3d at 363.[8] Thus, despite the clear proclamation of exclusivity in the LHWCA's text that prohibits any liability "at law or in admiralty" for injuries covered by the Act, there is no express preemption here. 33 U.S.C. § 905(a).

Fundamental tension between the plain text of the Act and twilight-zone concurrent jurisdiction has been apparent and controversial from the very beginning. Indeed, *Davis* itself created the twilight zone over a dissent which argued that the twilight zone "is plainly not permissible" and "controverts the words of the statute," which "left no room for an overlapping dual system" of concurrent jurisdiction. *Davis*, 317 U.S. at 261–64 (Stone, C.J., dissenting). Avondale would have us agree, but a dissent is just that. Perhaps time and Supreme Court reconsideration will ultimately conclude that the twilight zone's creation was beyond "judicial competence," *id.* at 260, but until then, there is no express preemption in the twilight zone. *Hetzel*, 50 F.3d at 363.

B

Neither does conflict preemption apply under these circumstances. The Supreme **{-321-}** Court has recognized that LHWCA remedies exist **[—9—]** concurrently with state-law remedies, including at least some state-law tort claims, in the twilight zone. Consistent with that binding recognition, we cannot find that the limited and unusual circumstances that gave rise to Barrosse's state-law tort claims pose "an unacceptable obstacle to the accomplishment and execution of the full purposes and objectives of Congress." *Janvey*, 712 F.3d at 200. A contrary holding would, at least as far as Barrosse and similarly situated plaintiffs are concerned, have the LHWCA "supplant" rather than "supplement" state law by effectively eliminating the twilight zone and contradicting the Supreme Court's instruction in *Sun Ship*, 447 U.S. at 720. Indeed, Avondale concedes that if Barrosse's claims are preempted, his "exclusive remedy for any injury he suffered working for Avondale was—and is—available under the LHWCA." State law is nowhere to be found.

We begin our analysis by noting that existing caselaw is of little assistance. Numerous cases address LHWCA preemption of tort claims, but none address the situation before us—an injured employee, in the twilight zone, who declines to invoke the LHWCA but, under state law, is limited to a tort claim for relief.[9]

The most on-point case is *Hahn*, but *Hahn* neither prohibits nor endorses the claims at issue here. *Hahn* does not endorse claims like Barrosse's because it did not address a freestanding tort claim. The state statute in *Hahn* permitted employers to "elect[] to reject" the statute's "automatic compensation provisions," in which case an injured employee could bring "a negligence action for damages."

[8] It is apparent from context that the *Hetzel* panel was discussing express preemption despite using the phrase "total preemption." *See Hetzel*, 50 F.3d at 363. We clarify this point only to ensure that *Hetzel*'s imprecise language is not confused with "complete" preemption, an entirely different doctrine. *See Mitchell v. Advanced HCS, L.L.C.*, 28 F.4th 580, 585 n.2 (5th Cir. 2022).

[9] Some district court cases address a similar fact pattern but neither acknowledge nor analyze the complications presented by a concurrent-jurisdiction regime where the only state-law remedy is a tort claim. *See, e.g., Hulin v. Huntington Ingalls, Inc.*, 2020 WL 6059645, at *5–7 (E.D. La. Oct. 14, 2020).

Hahn, 358 U.S. at 273. Thus, **[—10—]** *Hahn* only sanctioned a state-law tort claim that was expressly contemplated by state statute. Here, Barrosse's tort claims arise under state law because they are *not* included in the relevant statute, i.e., the WCA. Barrosse cannot obtain automatic compensation for mesothelioma, but neither does the WCA's exclusivity provision apply to any tort claims he might bring for that injury. *Hahn* does not prohibit claims like Barrosse's either. Nothing in *Hahn* holds that tort claims are *only* permissible when expressly contemplated by state compensation statutes. *Hahn* clearly opens the door to at least some tort claims, but it is ultimately inapposite.

Avondale would nevertheless have us read *Hahn* to limit state-law tort claims in the twilight zone to claims "provided for by state workers' compensation law" as a sanction for failing to secure coverage. But *Hahn* doesn't say that, and the lone federal court of appeals case that Avondale cites for that proposition is distinguishable. In *Peter v. Hess Oil Virgin Islands Corp.*, the Third Circuit considered an injured worker's negligence action under Virgin Islands law. 903 F.2d 935, 936–37 (3d Cir. 1990). The employer had obtained coverage under *both* the LHWCA *and* the relevant Virgin Islands workers' compensation act. *Id.* at 953. The court held that "where an employer has obtained workmen's compensation coverage for its LHWCA employee under both [the] LHWCA and the state or territorial statute," tort claims are preempted. *Id.* On its own terms, *Peter* does not apply where, as here, an employer has obtained coverage under the LHWCA but *not* under a state or territorial statute. Thus, contrary to Avondale's **{-322-}** assertion at oral argument, permitting Barrosse's claims under these circumstances does not create a circuit split.[10] **[—11—]**

Other cases likewise do not bear on the question before us. Some permit claims against alleged third-party tortfeasors, not employers. *Norfolk Shipbuilding & Drydock Corp. v. Garris*, 532 U.S. 811, 819–20 (2001) (permitting general maritime negligence claim against a third party); *McLaurin v. Noble Drilling (US) Inc.*, 529 F.3d 285, 292–93 (5th Cir. 2008) (holding that plaintiff did not have a vessel negligence claim but could bring a state-law tort claim against the vessel owner as a third-party tortfeasor). Others address injuries that occurred on the Outer Continental Shelf, which is outside the twilight zone. *Hebron v. Union Oil Co.*, 634 F.2d 245, 246 (5th Cir. 1981) (per curiam); *Gaudet v. Exxon Corp.*, 562 F.2d 351, 354 (5th Cir. 1977); *see LeSassier v. Chevron USA, Inc.*, 776 F.2d 506, 509 (5th Cir. 1985) (noting that Outer Continental Shelf claims do not involve the twilight zone or any other "confusing concurrent jurisdictional realm").

Most of Avondale's cited cases concern plaintiffs attempting to obtain *both* LHWCA compensation *and* damages in tort. *See Hetzel*, 50 F.3d at 367; *Levene v. Pintail Enters., Inc.*, 943 F.2d 528, 530 (5th Cir. 1991) (plaintiff filed suit under the LHWCA); *Rosetti v. Avondale Shipyards, Inc.*, 821 F.2d 1083, 1084 (5th Cir. 1987) (plaintiff received LHWCA benefits from his nominal employer then sued his borrowing employer); *White v. Bethlehem Steel Corp.*, 222 F.3d 146, 148 (4th Cir. 2000) (same); *Langfitt v. Fed. Marine Terminals, Inc.*, 647 F.3d 1116, 1119 (11th Cir. 2011) (same); *In re Buchanan Marine, L.P.*, 874 F.3d 356, 362, 5 Adm. R. 100, 101 (2d Cir. 2017) (plaintiff received LHWCA benefits but filed a tort suit anyways). But an injured worker cannot eat his cake and have it too. Once a worker "receives LHWCA benefits," he "may not sue his employer under state law for any additional compensatory damages." *Jowers* **[—12—]** *v. Lincoln Elec. Co.*, 617 F.3d 346, 357 (5th Cir. 2010). Instead, once a worker "elect[s] the LHWCA remedy, he is bound by the provisions of the Act," including the exclusivity provision of § 905(a). *Hetzel*, 50 F.3d at 367. That comports with the Supreme Court's instruction that § 905(a)'s exclusivity provision "gains meaning only after a litigant has been found to occupy one side or the other of the doubtful jurisdictional line." *Davis*, 317 U.S. at 256; *see Sun Ship*, 447 U.S. at 722 n.4

[10] The district court supposed that Barrosse "could have sought compensation under Louisiana's Workers' Compensation Act." *Barrosse*, 563 F. Supp. 3d at 556. If that **[—11—]** were true, *Peter* would be applicable and potentially persuasive authority. But the district court's assumption was incorrect. *See Rando*, 16 So. 3d at 1071.

(clarifying that, in the twilight zone, § 905(a) "does not exclude remedies offered by other jurisdictions"); *see also Calbeck v. Travelers Ins. Co.*, 370 U.S. 114, 131 (1962) (upholding compensation payments under both the LHWCA and state law where the state payments were credited against the LHWCA payments, so "no impermissible double recovery [wa]s possible"); *Hahn*, 358 U.S. at 273 (holding that the exclusivity provision did not "prevent[] recovery" via a state-law tort claim). Barrosse did not engage in double-dipping. He has eschewed the LHWCA entirely and is only seeking compensation in tort.

Thus, even considering the cases raised by the parties and the district court, this is a *sui generis* case. We resolve this issue of first impression by holding that, on these facts and pursuant to binding jurisprudential authority, Barrosse's state-law **{-323-}** tort claims are not preempted. As a preliminary matter, we emphasize that the category of claims we address here is small. Our holding concerns only: 1) maritime workers; 2) injured in the twilight zone; 3) in Louisiana; 4) who neither seek nor obtain LHWCA compensation; and 5) whose injuries are not covered by the relevant version of the WCA.[11]

Recall that "[c]onflict preemption applies (1) where complying with both federal law and state law is impossible; or (2) where the state law creates **[—13—]** an unacceptable obstacle to the accomplishment and execution of the full purposes and objectives of Congress." *Janvey*, 712 F.3d at 200. But we may not conduct "a freewheeling judicial inquiry" to find such an obstacle, and the threshold for finding conflict preemption is "high." *Whiting*, 563 U.S. at 607. This dispute concerns only the second species of conflict preemption, so we look to whether the operation of state tort law in this case "creates an unacceptable obstacle" to the purpose of the LHWCA. *Janvey*, 712 F.3d at 200. And, in the twilight zone, the Supreme Court has interpreted the LHWCA to avoid "resurrecting the jurisdictional monstrosity that existed" prior to *Davis*. *Sun Ship*, 447 U.S. at 720. Thus, we consider conflict preemption with the understanding that the LHWCA "supplements, rather than supplants, state compensation law" and runs "concurrently with state remedies." *Id.*

The purpose that Barrosse's tort claims must not unacceptably obstruct is the "balance" between employer and employee wherein "[e]mployers relinquish[] their defenses to tort actions in exchange for limited and predictable liability," while "[e]mployees accept the limited recovery because they receive prompt relief without the expense, uncertainty, and delay that tort actions entail." *Morrison-Knudsen Constr. Co. v. Dep't of Labor*, 461 U.S. 624, 636 (1983) (citations omitted). Permitting Barrosse's claims upsets that balance to some extent. But conflict preemption is not triggered by ordinary incongruities or minor annoyances, only by "unacceptable obstacle[s]." *Janvey*, 712 F.3d at 200. Here, the Supreme Court has expressly carved out space for concurrent operation of often-asymmetrical state and federal law in the twilight zone, lessening any concern that obstacles posed by state law are "unacceptable." *Id.*; *see Sun Ship*, 447 U.S. at 723–25 (noting that "state remedial schemes" often differ from the LHWCA). **[—14—]**

Indeed, if tort claims themselves visited any inherent frustration on Congress' goals sufficient to trigger conflict preemption, the Supreme Court would have sided with the dissent in *Hahn*, which argued that permitting tort claims in the twilight zone would "frustrate th[e] very purpose" of the LHWCA. *Hahn*, 358 U.S. at 275 (Stewart, J., dissenting). But it did not. Given the limited circumstances permitting Barrosse's claims under Louisiana law, they pose little, if any, greater obstacle to congressional purpose than the category of tort claims permitted by *Hahn*. The only difference is that the Oregon legislature in *Hahn* *expressly* permitted negligence claims under certain *circumstances*, while the Louisiana legislature *implicitly* permitted negligence claims for certain *injuries* by excluding those injuries from the expressed schedule of covered diseases in the WCA. **{-324-}**

---

[11] The situation presented here, where a plaintiff's choices are the LHWCA or state-law tort, may arise under other states' laws. Whether such claims are preempted should be determined on a case-by-case and state-by-state basis, so our holding is limited.

What is more, that distinction simply reflects the differing policy choices of different states, a feature of any concurrent-jurisdiction regime. Accepting Avondale's arguments is, therefore, tantamount to eliminating concurrent jurisdiction in cases like Barrosse's.[12] We do not think that mesothelioma's exclusion from the pre-1975 WCA's schedule of covered diseases "mandate[s] the result that [Barrosse] can only seek recovery under the federal compensation scheme." *DiBenedetto v. Noble Drilling Co.*, 23 So. 3d 400, 406 (La. Ct. App. 2009).[13] Instead, because the LHWCA does not "supplant[]" state law, *Sun Ship*, 447 U.S. at 720, Barrosse may pursue the **[—15—]** remedy available to him under that law which, as state law applies here, is *only* a tort claim. *See DiBenedetto*, 23 So. 3d at 406.

The Supreme Court has already rejected the principal arguments to the contrary. Writing separately, Justices in *Davis* and *Hahn* criticized the twilight zone as illogical, contrary to the text, beyond the power of the judiciary to create, and unfair to employers who are deprived of the benefits of the LHWCA's quid pro quo and must instead secure compensation coverage under both federal and state law. *Hahn*, 358 U.S. at 275 (Stewart, J., dissenting) (characterizing the twilight zone as "illogic"); *Davis*, 317 U.S. at 259 (Frankfurter, J., concurring) (same); *id.* at 260–62 (Stone, C.J., dissenting) (arguing that recognizing the twilight zone is not "within judicial competence . . . [,] controverts the words of the statute," and "imposes an unauthorized burden on the employer" who will be subject to liability under state law). These 80-year-old objections have yet to overcome the twilight zone. We cannot hold that they do.

In sum, our conclusion that conflict preemption does not apply is supported by the existence of concurrent jurisdiction and the acceptable incongruity inherent therein, the Supreme Court's consistent rejection of arguments resisting that regime, the LHWCA's role of supplementing rather than supplanting state law, the limited category of claims at issue here, and the similarity between these claims and those the Supreme Court has already permitted in *Hahn*.

IV

The Supreme Court has recognized a twilight zone of concurrent jurisdiction, permitted by the LHWCA, in cases like this one. We are dutybound to interpret and apply the law consistent with that guidance. Here, that means preserving concurrent jurisdiction in the twilight zone and avoiding the resurrection of a "jurisdictional monstrosity" by allowing Barrosse's **[—16—]** state-law tort claims to proceed. *Sun Ship*, 447 U.S. at 720. We reiterate the highly unusual fact pattern that brought Barrosse to this point and reemphasize that our holding is narrow. It is only through the peculiar nature and application of Louisiana's pre-1975 worker's compensation statute, combined with the other characteristics of this case listed above, that Barrosse's claims survive preemption. We accordingly REVERSE **{-325-}** and REMAND for further proceedings consistent with this opinion.

---

[12] As noted above, Avondale effectively concedes this point.

[13] Although *DiBenedetto* is a state court case and not binding here, we find it persuasive as it is the *only* case that we or the parties are aware of that addresses the factual scenario before us head on. In *DiBenedetto*, the plaintiff was injured in Louisiana, in the twilight zone, before 1975, was diagnosed with mesothelioma, did not seek LHWCA benefits, and brought a tort suit. *Id.* at 404–05. Like Avondale, the defendants argued that the LHWCA preempted his claims. *Id.* at 404. The court held that it did not. *Id.* at 405.

United States Court of Appeals
for the Fifth Circuit

No. 22-30799

LOUISIANA STATE
vs.
NATIONAL OCEANIC & ATMOSPHERIC ADMIN.

Appeal from the United States District Court for the Eastern District of Louisiana

Decided: June 15, 2023

Citation: 70 F.4th 872, 11 Adm. R. 306 (5th Cir. 2023).

Before **SMITH**, **CLEMENT**, and **WILSON**, Circuit Judges.

[—1—] {-874-} WILSON, Circuit Judge: **{-875-}**

Before us is the narrow question of whether the district court erred in holding that, based on the summary judgment record, the State of Louisiana failed to establish standing to challenge a National Marine Fisheries Service **[—2—]** (NMFS) rule that requires certain shrimping vessels in Louisiana waters to use turtle excluder devices (TEDs). We affirm.

I.

A.

There have long been TED requirements for shrimping. In 1987, NMFS promulgated a rule requiring shrimp trawlers 25 feet or longer operating in offshore waters from North Carolina to Texas to install TEDs, subject to a few preconditions. *See* 52 Fed. Reg. 24,244 (June 29, 1987). Our circuit upheld that rule over Louisiana's challenge. *See State of La., ex rel. Guste v. Verity*, 853 F.2d 322, 324 (5th Cir. 1988). But the 1987 rule exempted skimmer trawlers and inshore shrimpers from its requirements, so long as the exempted vessels followed tow-time restrictions. 50 C.F.R. § 223.206(d)(2)(ii)(A)(3).

In 2012, NMFS proposed a more restrictive rule requiring TEDs for skimmer trawlers, 77 Fed. Reg. 27,411 (May 10, 2012), but withdrew it in 2013, 78 Fed. Reg. 9,024 (Feb. 7, 2013). In 2016, the agency proposed another rule, again largely requiring all skimmer trawlers to use TEDs regardless of length or whether they operated inshore. 81 Fed. Reg. 91,097 (Dec. 16, 2016). NMFS justified this newest iteration in part based on a conclusion that tow-time restrictions were "inherently difficult to enforce."

NMFS promulgated a tailored version of its proposed 2016 rule in December 2019 (the Final Rule). The Final Rule required TEDs on all skimmer trawlers over 40 feet, including those that operate inshore. *See* 84 Fed. Reg. 70,048 (Dec. 20, 2019). The Final Rule's environmental impact statement (EIS) estimates that:

> For the 1,047 vessels in the Gulf of Mexico that are expected to be affected by this regulatory action, the aggregate loss in gross revenue from shrimp loss is about $2.29 million, which represents about 2.9% of their gross revenue. Including the costs of purchasing TEDs, which are about $1.36 million, the **[—3—]** total adverse effect in the first year is about $3.65 million, which represents about 4.6% of their gross revenue in the aggregate.

The EIS projects that 178 vessels will shut down throughout the Gulf of Mexico as a result of these costs. Further, the EIS predicts a shrimp loss per vessel of 6.21%, with a total adverse effect of $3,482 per vessel in the first year in the Gulf of Mexico. These losses would be less in subsequent years, once TEDs are initially purchased and installed. Cumulatively, the **{-876-}** EIS forecasts that the "expected annual loss in food shrimp landings is approximately 870,000 lbs under this regulatory action," approximately 0.3% of all food shrimp processed in the Gulf.

According to NMFS, changes incorporated in the Final Rule compared to the proposed 2016 version reduced the number of vessels impacted by more than 80% and the total economic effect by 73%. Neither NMFS nor Louisiana has offered data specific to Louisiana's shrimping industry.

B.

The Final Rule was to go into effect on April 1, 2021, but on March 31, 2021, NMFS delayed the effective date to August 1, 2021, citing the COVID-19 pandemic as justification for the delay. On August 11, 2021, ten days after the rule's deferred effective date, Louisiana's Department of Wildlife and Fisheries (LDWF) sued NMFS[1] under the Administrative Procedure Act, challenging the Final Rule as arbitrary and capricious.[2] **[—4—]**

After denying Louisiana's request for a temporary restraining order, the district court preliminarily enjoined enforcement of the Final Rule in Louisiana inshore waters until February 1, 2022. In its order the court stated, in a footnote, that "'[t]he State of Louisiana ha[d] standing to sue in [its] quasi-sover[e]ign capacity because of its interest in and ownership of its marine resources.'" *Louisiana v. Dep't of Commerce*, 559 F. Supp. 3d 543, 548 n.19 (E.D. La. 2021) (quoting *State of La. ex rel. Guste v. Verity*, 681 F. Supp. 1178, 1181 (E.D. La. 1988), *aff'd*, 850 F.2d 211 (5th Cir. 1988)). The State did not seek an extension when the injunction expired.

Instead, Louisiana moved for summary judgment, focusing on the merits of its claims. NMFS opposed and filed a cross-motion for summary judgment. In its motion, NMFS defended the merits of the Final Rule but further asserted that Louisiana lacked standing to bring this action. In the State's last summary judgment brief (it both supported its motion and opposed NMFS's motion in the same filing), Louisiana devoted a mere two pages to standing.

The State urged that it had standing on four bases. First, citing *Verity*, it asserted that it had standing based on its "interest in and ownership of its marine resources." Louisiana cited no record evidence to support its assertion. Second, the State contended that it "suffer[ed] direct injury from the enforcement resources it will have to expend to comply with the [Final Rule]." Relatedly, Louisiana asserted that the Final Rule "undermine[d] the State's ability to enforce its existing laws by requiring the massive reallocation of resources away from other LDWF activities[, which] . . . places substantial pressure on the State to change its policies and enforcement priorities." For support, Louisiana relied on allegations in its complaint, referenced a declaration from Colonel Chad Hebert, with LDWF's enforcement division, and cited caselaw. Specifically, the State cited Hebert's statement that "[f]ull capacity for LDWF Enforcement staff and field agents is 234, however LDWF Enforcement is currently holding **[—5—]** 206 positions due to ongoing funding constraints." Finally, Louisiana asserted that it had *parens* **{–877–}** *patriae* standing "to vindicate the economic interests . . . of the entire State." Again, the State relied on its complaint and caselaw for support.

The district court granted NMFS's motion, holding that Louisiana had not carried its summary judgment burden to establish standing. The court rejected Louisiana's assertion that it had standing in its "quasi-sovereign" capacity because after the court entered the preliminary injunction, Louisiana had "made no attempt to show any injury to its marine resources resulting from the Final Rule." The court acknowledged that it had previously accepted "an interest in and ownership of its marine resources," *see Verity*, 681 F. Supp. at 1181, as a basis for standing at the preliminary injunction stage, but the court held that "at the summary judgment stage, more [was] required," *Louisiana v. Dep't of Commerce*, No. 21-CV-1523, 2022 WL 17251152, at *2 (E.D. La. Nov. 28, 2022) (citing *Lujan v. Defs. Of Wildlife*, 504 U.S. 555, 561 (1992)). The district court faulted Louisiana for citing "only to the allegations of its [c]omplaint

---

[1] Louisiana also sued the National Oceanic and Atmospheric Administration, Department of Commerce, and various administrators and secretaries in their official capacities. For ease of reference we focus, as the parties do, on NMFS as the principal defendant, as it promulgated the Final Rule.

[2] While the State, through LDWF, has vigorously pursued this action, to date, no shrimpers, presumably most directly impacted by the Final Rule, have attempted to intervene in this action.

[and] ma[king] no attempt to show any injury to its marine resources resulting from the Final Rule," *id.*, by offering evidentiary support for the State's alleged injury.

The district court also rejected Louisiana's arguments related to increased law enforcement costs and reallocation of resources. The court characterized Hebert's declaration as "insufficiently vague, speculative, and conclusory[.]" *Id.* at *3 (citing *Crane v. Johnson*, 783 F.3d 244, 252 (5th Cir. 2015)). Analogizing to *Crane*, the court found that, even considering Hebert's statements, "[t]here [was] no evidence of how the Final Rule will burden the LDWF or even any proof that it will not receive federal funding to offset that burden." *Id.* And the district court similarly rejected Louisiana's *parens patriae* argument, faulting the State for relying only on its complaint allegations and failing to "provide any evidence of economic harm to the State's economy caused by the Final Rule." *Id.* **[—6—]**

Louisiana timely appealed. We review only whether the district court erred in concluding that Louisiana lacked standing to challenge the Final Rule. It did not.

II.

On appeal, Louisiana asserts that it has standing because the Final Rule infringes on its sovereign, quasi-sovereign, and proprietary interests. *See Alfred L. Snapp & Son, Inc. v. Puerto Rico ex rel. Barez*, 458 U.S. 592 (1982). In *Alfred L. Snapp & Son*, the Supreme Court differentiated those three types of interests based on how a State is injured. *Id.* at 600–08. Sovereign interests are "based on [the State's] sovereign character." *Id.* at 601. The Court identified two kinds of sovereign interests: "First, the exercise of sovereign power over individuals and entities within the relevant jurisdiction—this involves the power to create and enforce a legal code, both civil and criminal; second, the demand for recognition from other sovereigns—most frequently this involves the maintenance and recognition of borders." *Id.* States have sovereign interests by virtue of their being co-sovereigns in our Nation's federalism.

Related, but distinct, quasi-sovereign interests "consist of a set of interests that the State has in the well-being of its populace." *Id.* at 602. "First, a State has a quasi-sovereign interest in the health and well-being—both physical and economic—of its residents in general. Second, a State has a quasi-sovereign interest in not being discriminatorily **{–878–}** denied its rightful status within the federal system." *Id.* at 607. Only the first is at play here.[3] In either case, a plaintiff-State may sue as *parens patriae*, i.e., in a **[—7—]** representative capacity, to vindicate an injury to a "sufficiently substantial segment of its population." *Id.* at 607.

Finally, a State may have proprietary interests sufficient to confer standing, much like a private litigant. After all, a State can enter into contracts, own land, and participate in business ventures. *See id.* at 601; *see also Chisholm v. Georgia*, 2 U.S. 419 (1793). "And like other such proprietors it may at times need to pursue those interests in court." *Alfred Snapp & Son*, 458 U.S. at 601–02. These proprietary interests have been extended, e.g., to a State's collection of excise tax revenues, at least as against other States. *See Wyoming v. Oklahoma*, 502 U.S. 437, 447–50 (1992). And we have held that a State suffered injury to a proprietary interest when a change in federal law would have required the State to issue additional driver's licenses at a loss. *Tex. v. United States*, 809 F.3d 134, 155 (5th Cir. 2015), *aff'd by an equally divided court*, 579 U.S. 547 (2016).

We examine the State's proffered interests and concomitant injuries as follows.

[3] The second type of quasi-sovereign interest centers on "ensuring that the State and its residents are not excluded from the benefits that are to flow from participation in the federal system." *Id.* at 608. "Federal statutes" create these "benefits" "that a [S]tate will obviously wish to have accrue to its residents." *Id.* Thus, there is a distinction between a State's sovereign interest in enforcing its own law and a State's quasi-sovereign interest in obtaining benefits under federal law on its residents' behalf.

III.

We review summary judgments *de novo*. *Norman v. Apache Corp.*, 19 F.3d 1017, 1021 (5th Cir. 1994). A party is entitled to summary judgment when "the movant shows that there is no genuine dispute as to any material fact and the movant is entitled to judgment as a matter of law." FED. R. CIV. P. 56(a). "[F]acts that are subject to genuine dispute are viewed in the light most favorable to [the non-moving party]." *Taylor v. Riojas*, 141 S. Ct. 52, 53 n.1 (2020) (per curiam).

We likewise review whether a plaintiff has Article III standing *de novo*. *Contender Farms, L.L.P. v. U.S. Dep't of Agric.*, 779 F.3d 258, 264 (5th Cir. 2015). As plaintiff, Louisiana bears the burden of establishing standing. *Tex. v. United States*, 50 F.4th 498, 513 (5th Cir. 2022). To do so, a plaintiff must "have (1) suffered an injury in fact, (2) that is fairly traceable to the **[—8—]** challenged conduct of the defendant, and (3) that is likely to be redressed by a favorable judicial decision." *Inclusive Cmtys. Project, Inc. v. Dep't of Treasury*, 946 F.3d 649, 655 (5th Cir. 2019) (quotation marks and citation omitted). Here, the major sticking point is whether Louisiana has presented evidence of an injury-in-fact that satisfies Article III.

Louisiana contends its sovereign interests are injured by the Final Rule's preemption of state laws, interference with Louisiana's enforcement of its own wildlife laws, and interference with the marine resources in the State's territorial waters (as well as with the State's regulation of those resources). Louisiana next argues that its quasi-sovereign interests in the economic well-being of its populace suffer injury because the Final Rule inflicts adverse economic consequences upon its citizens. Lastly, Louisiana asserts that the Final **{-879-}** Rule injures the State's proprietary interests because of increased LDWF enforcement costs.

A.

Casting a bit deeper into Louisiana's asserted sovereign interests, the State urges on appeal that it has standing based on: (1) "the Final Rule's preemption of state laws regulating the harvesting of shrimp in Louisiana waters"; (2) the rule's "interference with Louisiana's enforcement of its own wildlife laws"; (3) the State's "sovereign interest in the shrimp in its waters," *cf. Verity*, 681 F. Supp. at 1181;[4] and, relatedly, (4) Louisiana's interest in regulating those marine resources. The first and last grounds readily escape the net because Louisiana failed to raise these arguments **[—9—]** before the district court. The State's other asserted sovereign interests likewise yield no catch, for the reasons discussed in turn.

1. and 4.

Generally, "arguments not raised before the district court . . . cannot be raised for the first time on appeal," *Webster v. Kijakazi*, 19 F.4th 715, 720 (5th Cir. 2021) (quotation marks and citation omitted), "absent extraordinary circumstances," *Chevron USA, Inc. v. Aker Mar. Inc.*, 689 F.3d 497, 504 (5th Cir. 2012). However, "[a]n argument is not [forfeited] . . . if the argument on the issue before the district court was sufficient to permit the district court to rule on it." *Webster*, 19 F.4th at 720 (quotation marks and citation omitted).

Louisiana's contentions based on the Final Rule's preemption of state laws and its interference with the State's regulation of marine resources nowhere appear in the State's opposition to NMFS's motion for summary judgment. Nevertheless, Louisiana asserts that it did not forfeit either basis for standing because the State alleged in its complaint that it "sue[d] to vindicate its sovereign, quasi-sovereign, proprietary, and *parens patriae* interests." But alleging grounds for standing in a complaint is not the same as asserting—and substantiating—those theories when resisting summary judgment, because

[4] Specifically, the *Verity* district court held that "Louisiana ha[d] standing to sue in the quasi-sover[e]ign capacity because of its interest in and ownership of its marine resources." 681 F. Supp. at 1181. Louisiana adopted that characterization before the district court in this case but rebrands this species of interest as "sovereign" on appeal.

the district court cannot "rule on" mere allegations at the summary judgment stage of litigation. *Webster*, 19 F.4th at 720; *see also Chevron USA, Inc.*, 689 F.3d at 504. Louisiana therefore failed to preserve these grounds for standing by first adequately urging them in the district court.

Of course, there are exceptions to every rule. We have limited discretion to reach an issue first raised on appeal when it presents "a purely legal matter and failure to consider the issue will result in a miscarriage of justice." *Rollins v. Home Depot USA*, 8 F.4th 393, 398 (5th Cir. 2021) **[—10—]** (quotation marks and citation omitted). Louisiana urges us to exercise our discretion in this instance. Presuming the State's unpreserved bases for standing involve purely legal questions, we focus on whether extraordinary circumstances warrant doing so.

Louisiana maintains that it "had no reason to press the relevant argument[s] more specifically" at summary judgment because the district court had already determined that the State had standing in granting the preliminary injunction. The State thus "simply had no reason" to litigate the "standing issue more vigorously and raise[] the argument[s] more specifically." **{-880-}** While on the surface, Louisiana's position resonates somewhat—the district court had previously held the State had standing, after all—we discern no extraordinary circumstance that justifies consideration of the forfeited arguments.

Louisiana had the burden of establishing standing in the district court. *See Lujan*, 504 U.S. at 561. When NMFS cross-moved for summary judgment, in response to Louisiana's own dispositive motion, it argued that Louisiana lacked standing. Louisiana was therefore on notice that NMFS was contesting Louisiana's standing—and seeking summary judgment on that basis. *Cf. id.* (The elements of standing are "an indispensable part of the plaintiff's case, [such that] each element must be supported . . . with the manner and degree of evidence required at the successive stages of the litigation."). In the State's combined opposition to NMFS's motion and reply in support of its own, Louisiana engaged, briefly, on the standing issue. That the State failed to conjure all its grounds for standing for the district court's consideration is not itself an exceptional circumstance. And Louisiana offers no reason for its omission that rises to such a circumstance. Therefore, we discern no "miscarriage of justice," *Rollins*, 8 F.4th at 398, in declining to consider the Final Rule's purported preemption of state laws or **[—11—]** its interference with the State's regulation of its marine resources in evaluating Louisiana's standing.

2. and 3.

We turn now to the merits of Louisiana's preserved arguments: its *Verity*-based assertion that the State's interests in its natural resources are harmed by the Final Rule, and its contention that increased enforcement costs caused by the rule will pressure Louisiana to change its enforcement priorities. In the end, neither of these arguments nets standing for the State.

In *Verity*, the district court held that "the State of Louisiana ha[d] standing to sue in the quasi-sover[e]ign capacity because of its interest in and ownership of its marine resources." *See* 681 F. Supp. at 1181. Because we did not address standing in the appeal of that case, this court's decision "does not stand for the proposition that no [jurisdictional] defect existed." *Lefebure v. D'Aquilla*, 15 F.4th 650, 657 (5th Cir. 2021) (citation omitted). Regardless, assuming *arguendo* that *Verity* articulated a sovereign interest that could support standing, Louisiana's argument fails for lack of evidentiary support.

To resist summary judgment, Louisiana was required to present evidence of a "concrete and particularized invasion of a legally protected interest." *Sprint Commc'ns Co., L.P. v. APCC Servs., Inc.*, 554 U.S. 269, 273 (2008) (quotation marks and citation omitted). Under *Verity*, Louisiana's relevant interest is its ownership or trustee interest in its marine resources as "property" of the State. It follows that Louisiana must show an injury to those marine resources. But the State does not identify competent summary judgment evidence that substantiates any alleged injury that the Final

Rule inflicts on Louisiana's marine resources. On the contrary, under the Final Rule, less shrimp will be extracted from Louisiana waters and fewer turtles will ostensibly be caught inadvertently in shrimpers' nets. Besides, while Louisiana directs us to the Final Rule's EIS, which forecasts the impact on **[—12—]** shrimp harvests Gulf-wide, the State offers no evidence specific to *its own* shrimp harvests, in its own waters, much less an injury to its resources. We therefore agree with the district court that Louisiana "has made no attempt to show any injury to its marine resources resulting from the Final Rule," such that this argument fails. **{-881-}**

Louisiana also urges that "the Final Rule interferes with Louisiana's enforcement of its own wildlife and fisheries laws, and in so doing, places pressure on Louisiana to change those laws" thereby causing a separate injury to its sovereign interest. Louisiana tethers this argument to Colonel Hebert's declaration testimony that the Final Rule places "additional strain" on the LDWF's enforcement resources and relies on *Texas v. EEOC*, 933 F.3d 433, 447 (5th Cir. 2019), to support the notion that the Final Rule "pressures [Louisiana] to abandon its laws and policies."

This argument is necessarily contingent on a finding that the Final Rule will increase LDWF enforcement costs. Setting aside complaint allegations, the sum of Louisiana's proof on that score is drawn from Hebert's declaration. He states that additional enforcement duties triggered by the Final Rule "could substantially burden and interfere with LDWF Enforcement's ability to effectively perform its various other enforcement duties." He also avers that LDWF does not expect to receive "additional or commensurate" funding to defray the "additional LDWF Enforcement efforts." But Hebert's declaration does not explain the "pressure" this might bring to bear on Louisiana's sovereign prerogatives; i.e., the declaration does not "connect the dots" so as to create a genuine issue of material fact as to the State's ostensible sovereign injury. Instead, as further discussed in III.C. below, Hebert's testimony is couched in speculative, general language (the rule "*could*" burden LDWF) that is flatly belied by the Final Rule, which by its terms does not require Louisiana to enforce it, and unrefuted evidence from NMFS that demonstrates that the agencies **[—13—]** annually coordinate enforcement efforts, including funding to cover federal priorities. *See infra* n.6. Louisiana's lack of competent summary judgment evidence fatally undermines its assertion of standing on this basis.

B.

Next, we consider Louisiana's *parens patriae* argument, i.e., that the Final Rule injures its quasi-sovereign interests. The State correctly asserts that it has a quasi-sovereign interest in the general economic well-being of its residents. *See Alfred L. Snapp & Son*, 458 U.S. at 607. More specifically, Louisiana asserts that the Final Rule injures that interest because of the "significant adverse economic impact" the Final Rule will have on Louisiana's shrimping industry, a significant component of the State's economy. Still, Louisiana must show that any such injury affects "a sufficiently substantial segment of its population." *Id.* Louisiana falters on this requirement, again for lack of evidence.

In its opposition to NMFS's motion for summary judgment, Louisiana pointed to its complaint to substantiate its assertion that the Final Rule will affect a sufficiently substantial segment of Louisiana residents. But complaint allegations are insufficient at summary judgment because "pleadings are not summary judgment evidence." *Wallace v. Tex. Tech Univ.*, 80 F.3d 1042, 1047 (5th Cir. 1996) ("Once a summary judgment motion is made and properly supported, the nonmovant must go beyond the pleadings and designate specific facts in the record showing that there is a genuine issue for trial."). Moreover, while the Final Rule's EIS noted that the rule would adversely affect the shrimping industry across the Gulf of Mexico, Louisiana failed to provide evidence particularly substantiating the rule's impact on *its* shrimping industry or, ergo, "a sufficiently substantial segment of its population." *See Alfred L. Snapp & Son*, 458 U.S. at 607. **[—14—]** **{-882-}**

Nor does Louisiana's invocation of the "special solicitude" afforded States in the standing analysis, *see Texas*, 50 F.4th at 514, rescue this argument, or for that matter the State's other arguments. Special solicitude merely changes "the normal standards for redressability and immediacy," *id.* (citation omitted); it is not a standing shortcut when standing is otherwise lacking. In other words, it countenances some uncertainty as to both the efficacy of a judicial remedy and the *timing* of the injury alleged by a State. *See id.* But "special solicitude" does not absolve States from substantiating a cognizable injury, and neither the Supreme Court nor this court has held that it alters the requirements that the injury must be concrete and particularized. *See Massachusetts v. EPA*, 549 U.S. 497, 517–20 (2007); *Texas*, 50 F.4th at 514. The district court did not err in holding that Louisiana failed to support its standing based on a *parens patriae* theory.[5] **[—15—]**

C.

To finish, we consider whether Louisiana's alleged increased enforcement costs impinge on the State's proprietary interests. The State's argument is as follows: LDWF enforces laws relevant to the shrimping industry. Per Hebert, the Final Rule "could result in significant noncompliance from the shrimping industry." And while LDWF "will endeavor to enforce any and all regulations resulting from" the Final Rule, the additional enforcement duties imposed by the Final Rule "could substantially burden and interfere with LDWF Enforcement's ability to effectively perform its various other enforcement duties." Moreover, Hebert averred that LDWF does not expect to receive "additional and commensurate" funding from NMFS "despite the additional LDWF Enforcement efforts imposed by implementation of [the Final Rule]." As a result, the Final Rule "will result in additional strain on LDWF Enforcement resources," injuring Louisiana's proprietary interests.

NMFS counters that Hebert's declaration does not contain sufficient detail to create a genuine issue of material fact as to Louisiana's injury. Additionally, NMFS asserts that the Final Rule, by its terms, does not require Louisiana to enforce it, so any additional enforcement burden would be self-inflicted, especially because Louisiana could ask NMFS for additional funding to offset increased enforcement costs.

Louisiana's rejoinder is that, at summary judgment, the district court was required to consider Hebert's declaration in the light most favorable to the State. And **{-883-}** Louisiana asserts that in fact it is required to enforce the Final Rule, citing Louisiana Revised Statute § 56:493. That statute provides that "[t]he exclusive control of the shrimp fishery and the shrimp industry in Louisiana is vested in [LDWF], which shall enforce the laws regulating same." **[—16—]**

The district court rejected Louisiana's position, relying on *Crane v. Johnson*. We begin there.

[5] Additionally, it is dubious that Louisiana may maintain its *parens patriae* suit against the federal government at all. The D.C. Circuit has held that neither the APA nor *Massachusetts v. EPA* invalidates the "so-called *Mellon* bar, [under which] a State lacks standing as *parens patriae* to bring an action against the federal government." *Gov't of Manitoba v. Bernhardt*, 923 F.3d 173, 179 (D.C. Cir. 2019) (citing *Massachusetts v. Mellon*, 262 U.S. 447, 485–86 (1923) ("While the state, under some circumstances, may sue as *parens patriae* for the protection of its citizens, it is no part of its duty or power to enforce their rights in respect of their relations with the federal government." (cleaned up)). Indeed, the *Massachusetts v. EPA* Court explained that "there is a critical difference between allowing a State to protect her citizens from the operation of federal statutes (which is what *Mellon* prohibits) and allowing a State to assert its rights under federal law (which it has standing to do)." 549 U.S. at 520 n.17 (quotation marks omitted). There, Massachusetts did not "dispute that the Clean Air Act *applie[d]* to its citizens; it rather [sought] to assert its rights under the Act." *Id.* Here, Louisiana's *parens patriae* argument appears to fall in the first category, and not the second. Regardless, because the parties do not brief the nuanced applicability of the *Mellon* bar with any granularity, and our decision does not turn on it, we decline to address this point further.

In *Crane*, we considered Mississippi's challenge to the Deferred Action for Childhood Arrivals (DACA) program. 783 F.3d at 247. Mississippi urged that it had standing to challenge DACA as injurious to its proprietary interests. *Id.* at 252. In support, Mississippi relied on a 2006 report that showed that illegal aliens had cost the state over $25 million annually in social benefits. *Id.* Mississippi contended that because DACA allowed a certain class of those illegal aliens to remain in the state, the program caused the state to incur further costs. *Id.* Problematically, the report was from 2006, while the suit was filed in 2012. *Id.*

We affirmed the district court's conclusion that "Mississippi's alleged fiscal injury was purely speculative because there was no concrete evidence that Mississippi's costs had increased or [would] increase as a result of DACA." *Id.* We faulted Mississippi for failing to submit evidence that DACA-eligible immigrants resided in the state or would move to the state. *Id.* Noting that for Article III standing, Mississippi had to show a "concrete and particularized injury that [was] fairly traceable to DACA," we held that "Mississippi was required to demonstrate that the state [would] incur costs because of the DACA program." *Id.* (citation omitted). And we concluded Mississippi's alleged injury was purely speculative because it was "not supported by any facts[.]" *Id.*

While this case is not precisely on all fours with *Crane*, the same result obtains. Hebert's declaration is speculative on the material points, merely describing what "could" happen, and is thus insufficient by itself to forestall summary judgment. And while Hebert asserts that additional federal funding is not expected, so that the Final Rule will cost the State enforcement resources, Louisiana fails to provide sufficient facts, either through Hebert's **[—17—]** testimony or otherwise, to support those assertions. *See Ctr. for Biological Diversity v. EPA*, 937 F.3d 533, 545 (5th Cir. 2019) ("Article III demands more than such conclusory assertions."); *see also, e.g., Clark v. Am.'s Favorite Chicken Co.*, 110 F.3d 295, 297 (5th Cir. 1997) ("Unsupported allegations or affidavit or deposition testimony setting forth ultimate or conclusory facts and conclusions of law are insufficient to defeat a motion for summary judgment.").

By way of illustration, Hebert's assertion that LDWF will incur increased law enforcement costs as a result of the Final Rule is dependent upon LDWF's actually enforcing the Final Rule. Before the district court, Louisiana provided neither evidence nor argument in support of its assertion that it is required to enforce the Final Rule. If Louisiana's enforcement of the rule is discretionary, any increased enforcement costs would be self-inflicted and therefore insufficient to confer standing. *See Zimmerman v. City of Austin, Tex.*, 881 F.3d 378, 389 (5th Cir. 2018) ("[S]tanding cannot be conferred by a self-inflicted injury.").

Louisiana's belated argument on appeal that it is required to enforce the Final Rule under § 56:493, such that any increased enforcement costs would not be self-inflicted, does not change the calculus, for three reasons. First, Louisiana did not raise that argument before the district court, and "[a]rguments not raised in the district court will not be considered [on **{-884-}** appeal] absent extraordinary circumstances." *Chevron*, 689 F.3d at 504 (quotation marks and citation omitted). Additionally, NMFS represented during oral argument that it would offset costs incurred by the State in enforcing the Final Rule, and unrebutted record evidence supports that contention.[6] Thus, even if Louisiana is required by state law to enforce the **[—18—]** Final Rule, the record indicates that the State would suffer no cognizable injury because NMFS would provide commensurate funding to LDWF for its additional enforcement efforts.

[6] Emanuel Antonaras, the Assistant Director of the Southeast Division of NMFS's law enforcement arm, submitted a declaration describing the Joint Enforcement **[—18—]** Agreements (JEA) NMFS enters with States. Per Antonaras, LDWF and NMFS negotiate a JEA once a year that delineates coordinated enforcement efforts and provides funding to LDWF for federal enforcement priorities. For example, the 2020 JEA provided $293,538.40 to LDWF for coordinated TED enforcement.

Third, Louisiana cannot manufacture injury with a novel interpretation of a general state statute. There is nothing in the record to suggest that Louisiana has previously interpreted § 56:493 to require the State to enforce federal regulations.[7] Doing so now, in the context of this litigation, gives rise to self-inflicted injury, if it gives rise to injury at all. Louisiana's argument as to its proprietary injury therefore fails.[8]

* * *

Based on the record and procedural history of this case, the district court did not err in concluding that Louisiana failed to establish that it has standing to challenge the NMFS's Final Rule. The district court's summary judgment in favor of NMFS dismissing the State's claims is therefore

AFFIRMED.

---

[7] In fact, § 56:493 peacefully coexisted for years with now-repealed Louisiana Revised Statute § 56:57.2, which forbade LDWF from "enforc[ing] any federal law or regulation which requires any commercial or recreational fishermen to use TEDs in Louisiana waters until" several conditions had been satisfied.

[8] Nor is the anti-commandeering doctrine applicable. The doctrine applies when a *federal* law "directly command[s] the executive or legislative branch of a state government to act or refrain from acting without commanding private parties to do the same[.]" *Brackeen v. Haaland*, 994 F.3d 249, 299 (5th Cir. 2021) (en banc). The Final Rule, by its text, does not require Louisiana to "act or refrain from acting," and § 56:493, as a state statute, does not support any anti-commandeering argument.

United States Court of Appeals for the Fifth Circuit

No. 22-30488

JOHNSON vs. COOPER T. SMITH STEVEDORING CO.

Appeal from the United States District Court for the Middle District of Louisiana

Decided: July 14, 2023

Citation: 74 F.4th 268, 11 Adm. R. 315 (5th Cir. 2023).

Before **RICHMAN,** Chief Judge, and **STEWART** and **DOUGLAS,** Circuit Judges.

[—1—] {–270–} DOUGLAS, Circuit Judge:

Plaintiff Lester Johnson ("Johnson"), an injured maritime worker, appeals from the district court's grant of summary judgment to defendant Cooper T. Smith Stevedoring Company, Inc. ("Cooper") on his claims of Jones Act negligence, failure to pay maintenance and cure, unseaworthiness, and, alternatively, vessel negligence. The district court granted summary judgment after concluding that Johnson had not put forth evidence showing a genuine dispute of material fact concerning his seaman status or vessel negligence. We AFFIRM. **[—2—]**

I.

Cooper has a facility for midstream cargo operations near Darrow, Louisiana. At the Darrow facility, cargo operations occur while vessels are located midstream in the Mississippi River. In connection with its operations, Cooper owns and operates a weigh station vessel, the AMERICA, which is used to transfer bulk cargo from barges to oceangoing vessels. **{–271–}**

Cooper's Darrow facility hires longshoremen on a per-day basis through the local union hall to load and unload vessels. Johnson worked sporadically as a longshoreman for Cooper as early as 1998 and worked regularly for Cooper from 2008 through the date of his injury on June 22, 2018, never going more than a week and a half without working. Before his employment with Cooper, Johnson performed various jobs including operating a front-end loader and track hoe, flagging cranes, and loading barges.

According to Cooper, longshoremen like Johnson are not "assigned" to the AMERICA, are not its crewmembers, and "do not operate it, maintain it, clean it, fuel it, or perform any other functions similar to her crew," but instead are "instruct[ed]" to report to particular vessels "to identify the midstream location of the cargo barges and oceangoing vessels on which they will be working." In other words, Cooper gives longshoremen like Johnson assignments to cargo barges and oceangoing vessels that are limited to performance of "discrete tasks," after which their connections to the vessels end. Cooper also has full-time employees, which include crewmembers assigned to the AMERICA.

On the evening of June 22, 2018, Johnson was injured when he fell to the deck of the AMERICA from the deck of an adjacent cargo barge, the SCF 24122. On the night of the injury, Johnson reported to Cooper's Darrow **[—3—]** office and was transported from the landing dock to the AMERICA via crew boat. Johnson's job during that night's operations was inside the hold of the SCF 24112, operating a front-end loader to move cargo, soybean mill, into the AMERICA's "bucket," which would then move the cargo to the hold of an oceangoing vessel, the M/V XENIA. Cooper did not own or operate the SCF 24112 or the M/V XENIA.

After the cargo in the hold of the SCF 24112 had been unloaded, Johnson positioned the front-end loader to be removed from the cargo barge's hold by the AMERICA's winch and then climbed an aluminum ladder to exit the hold himself. The ladder was owned by Cooper and permanently stored on the AMERICA. On the deck of the barge, Johnson and another longshoreman, Joe Thomas, pulled the ladder out of the hold of the barge and attempted to place it in its storage "slot" on the AMERICA. Doing so was a routine task for Johnson and other longshoremen working for Cooper.

This time, however, Johnson slipped, fell, and landed headfirst on a catwalk on the AMERICA's deck, 13 feet below. Johnson testified that he and Thomas did not have any problem with the ladder, but that he slipped on "cargo"—meaning pieces of grain and grain dust—on the deck of the barge. He testified that cargo dust "gets all over the place" whenever vessels are being loaded or unloaded and that he saw cargo all over the barge when he got out of the hold the night of the accident.

Johnson suffered numerous personal injuries and was hospitalized because of his fall. Over the next year and half, he underwent multiple medical procedures (including two surgeries) and physical therapy. In connection with his injuries, Johnson collected workers' compensation benefits from Cooper pursuant to the Longshore and Harbor Workers' Compensation Act ("LHWCA"). **[—4—]**

Johnson filed suit against Cooper in federal district court in November 2020, alleging that he was a seaman and a member of the crew of the AMERICA, and bringing claims of Jones Act negligence, failure to pay maintenance and cure, and unseaworthiness (collectively, "seaman claims"). In the alternative, Johnson alleged that if he **{-272-}** was not a seaman and was covered by the LHWCA, then Cooper as vessel owner had been negligent pursuant to 33 U.S.C. § 905(b) and general maritime law. After discovery, Cooper moved for summary judgment, asserting that (1) Johnson was not a "seaman"; (2) there were no facts to support a vessel negligence claim under 33 U.S.C. § 905(b); and (3) Johnson's general maritime law negligence claim was barred by § 905(a)'s exclusivity provision. The district court granted the motion and dismissed Johnson's claims with prejudice. According to the district court, Johnson failed to cite to evidence that showed a genuine dispute of material fact as to whether he was a seaman and, alternatively, as to vessel negligence.

II.

"This court reviews de novo a district court's grant of summary judgment, applying the same standard as the district court." *Austin v. Kroger Tex., L.P.*, 864 F.3d 326, 328 (5th Cir. 2017) (citation omitted). Summary judgment is appropriate "if the movant shows that there is no genuine dispute as to any material fact and the movant is entitled to judgment as a matter of law." FED. R. CIV. P. 56(a). "A genuine [dispute] of material fact exists when the evidence is such that a reasonable jury could return a verdict for the non-moving party." *Austin*, 864 F.3d at 328 (citation omitted). "All evidence is viewed in the light most favorable to the nonmoving party and all reasonable inferences are drawn in that party's favor." *Id.* at 328–29 (citation omitted). **[—5—]**

"A party asserting that a fact cannot be or is genuinely disputed must support the assertion" by "citing to particular parts of materials in the record" or "showing that the materials cited do not establish the absence or presence of a genuine dispute." FED. R. CIV. P. 56(c). A party opposing summary judgment "must go beyond the pleadings and designate specific facts showing that there is a genuine issue for trial." *Little v. Liquid Air Corp.*, 37 F.3d 1069, 1075 (5th Cir. 1994) (en banc). "[C]onclusory allegations" and "unsubstantiated assertions" will not suffice. *Id.* (citations omitted).

III.

On appeal, Johnson challenges the district court's grant of summary judgment to Cooper on his seaman claims and his vessel negligence claim.[1] As explained below, after reviewing the

[1] Cooper also asserts that Johnson's general maritime law negligence claim is barred by the exclusivity provision of 33 U.S.C. § 905(a) because Cooper was his employer and secured payment of LHWCA compensation for his injury. "The liability of an employer" for LHWCA compensation "shall be exclusive and in place of all other liability of such employer to the employee . . . except . . . if an employer fails to secure payment of compensation as required by" the LHWCA. 33 U.S.C. § 905(a). The district court ruled that Johnson conceded this issue by failing to brief it and dismissed his general maritime law negligence claim as barred by § 905(a). Johnson's appellate brief likewise does not address Cooper's § 905(a) argument, and he has thus waived or abandoned the issue. *See Cavallini v. State Farm Mut. Auto Ins. Co.*, 44 F.3d 256, 260 n.9 (5th Cir. 1995); *McDowell v. Home Depot USA, Inc.*, 126 F.

record, we agree with the district court that Johnson failed to show a genuine dispute of material fact as to his claims. Cooper was therefore entitled to summary judgment.

A.

"The Jones Act grants 'a seaman' a cause of action against his employer in negligence." **{-273-}** *Sanchez v. Smart Fabricators of Tex., L.L.C.*, 997 **[—6—]** F.3d 564, 568–69, 9 Adm. R. 198, 200 (5th Cir. 2021) (quoting 46 U.S.C. § 30104).[2] "As the courts have often lamented, the term 'seaman' is not defined in the Jones Act." *In re Endeavor Marine Inc.*, 234 F.3d 287, 290 (5th Cir. 2000). Thus, it has largely fallen to the courts "to establish workable tests to define the word 'seaman.'" *Sanchez*, 997 F.3d at 569, 9 Adm. R. at 200.

To qualify as a "seaman," a maritime worker must satisfy a two-part test: he or she (1) "must contribute to the function of the vessel or to the accomplishment of its mission," and (2) "must have a connection to a vessel in navigation (or to an identifiable group of such vessels) that is substantial in terms of both its duration and its nature." *Endeavor Marine*, 234 F.3d at 290 (citing *Chandris*, 515 U.S. at 368)). Johnson claims that he is a seaman based on his connection to the AMERICA.

The first part of this test, the "threshold requirement" of whether a worker "does the ship's work," is "very broad." *Id.* (cleaned up). "'All who work at sea in the service of a ship' are *eligible* for seaman status." *Chandris*, 515 U.S. at 368 (quoting *McDermott Int'l, Inc. v. Wilander*, 498 U.S. 337, 354 (1991)) (emphasis in original). The parties and the district court all agree that Johnson meets the first part of the test, and so do we. Johnson's work loading and unloading cargo contributed to the mission of the AMERICA, as well as the various cargo barges and oceangoing vessels.

The second part of the test—whether the worker has a substantial connection to a vessel—has two elements: the worker's connection must be "substantial in terms of both [1] its duration and [2] its nature." *Sanchez*, 997 F.3d at 571, 9 Adm. R. at 202 (quoting *Chandris*, 515 U.S. at 368). For the duration **[—7—]** element, the "rule of thumb for the ordinary case" is that "[a] worker who spends less than about 30 percent of his time in the service of a vessel in navigation should not qualify as a seaman." *Chandris*, 515 U.S. at 371. Recently, in *Sanchez v. Smart Fabricators*, the en banc court refined this Circuit's test for the nature element. 997 F.3d at 573–74, 9 Adm. R. at 203–04. Post-*Sanchez*, we consider four factors when deciding whether a worker's connection to a vessel is substantial in nature: (1) the worker's exposure to "perils of the sea," meaning the hazards of a maritime working environment; (2) whether "the worker owe[s] his [or her] allegiance to the vessel, rather than simply to a shoreside employer"; (3) if his or her work is "sea-based or involve[s] seagoing activity"; and (4) whether "the worker's assignment to a vessel [is] limited to performance of a discrete task after which the worker's connection to the vessel end[s]," or whether he or she stays with the vessel. *Id.* at 574, 9 Adm. R. at 204.

Johnson's claim to seaman status founders on the duration element of the substantial-connection test. In opposing Cooper's motion for summary judgment in the district court, Johnson relied on two citations to his deposition testimony to establish that he was a seaman: (1) that he worked for Cooper for more than 20 years, and (2) that he took a crew boat provided by Cooper from the Darrow landing dock to the AMERICA on the night he was injured. The district court found this deposition testimony insufficient to create a genuine dispute of material fact as to the duration element. We agree. The fact that **{-274-}** Johnson performed longshoring work for Cooper for 20 years does not, without more, create a genuine dispute of material fact as to whether he had a connection to the AMERICA that was substantial in duration. Likewise, the

App'x 168, 170 (5th Cir. 2005) ("Where a claim is not briefed on appeal, it is abandoned.")

[2] In addition to damages for negligence under the Jones Act, seamen may also recover maintenance and cure and damages for unseaworthiness under the general maritime law. *See Chandris, Inc. v. Latsis*, 515 U.S. 347, 354 (1995).

fact that Johnson was transported by crew boat to the AMERICA on the night he was injured and was injured when he fell from an adjacent vessel on to the AMERICA is not enough to qualify him as a seaman. *See Chandris*, 515 U.S. at 363 (rejecting a "snapshot" test). A "more enduring relationship" with the AMERICA is required. *Id.* **[—8—]**

On appeal, Johnson attempts to bolster his claim to seaman status by citing to the declaration of Cooper's Director of Maintenance, James Gauthreaux, which describes Cooper's midstream operations. Relying on the declaration, Johnson's argument seems to be that because his longshore work for Cooper took place midstream in the Mississippi River and because the AMERICA is part of Cooper's midstream operations, we should infer that he had a connection to the AMERICA that was substantial in duration. Unfortunately for Johnson, however, nothing in Gauthreaux's declaration allows us to draw that inference.[3]

Assuming that this argument is not forfeited for failure to raise it in district court, *see Rollins v. Home Depot, USA*, 8 F.4th 393, 397–98 (5th Cir. 2021), the Gauthreaux declaration does not create a genuine dispute of material fact as to Johnson's status. The declaration establishes that longshoremen like Johnson performed their work for Cooper on vessels midstream and that Cooper used the AMERICA in connection with its midstream operations. But critically, the declaration is silent as to the duration of the connection that longshoremen like Johnson had with the AMERICA. Viewing the evidence in the light most favorable to Johnson, we simply do not know and cannot infer based on this record how often he reported to or worked on, around, in service of, or in connection with the AMERICA; there is a gap in the summary-judgment evidence that dooms his claim to seaman status. *See Little*, 37 F.3d at 1075 (explaining that "unsubstantiated assertions" do not satisfy nonmovant's summary **[—9—]** judgment burden); *cf. Endeavor Marine*, 234 F.3d at 291 (holding that crane operator who worked on a derrick barge had a connection to the vessel that was substantial in duration because he spent almost all his time working on the vessel in the 18 months prior to his accident).

Because Johnson did not show a genuine dispute of material fact as to whether he had a connection to the AMERICA that was substantial in duration, the district court was correct to grant summary judgment in Cooper's favor on Johnson's seaman claims, and we need not proceed to consider the nature prong of the substantial-connection test.

B.

In the alternative to his seaman claims, Johnson brought a claim against Cooper as owner of the AMERICA pursuant to the LHWCA, 33 U.S.C. § 905(b). The district court granted summary judgment to Cooper on this claim because Johnson failed to show a genuine dispute **{-275-}** of material fact as to vessel negligence. We agree.

Section 905(b) provides a cause of action to a person injured by "negligence of a vessel," with the caveat that "[i]f such person was employed by the vessel to provide stevedoring services, no such action shall be permitted if the injury was caused by the negligence of persons engaged in providing stevedoring services to the vessel." 33 U.S.C. § 905(b). In *Scindia Steam Navigation Co. v. De Los Santos*, 451 U.S. 156 (1981), the Supreme Court "outlined the three general duties shipowners owe to longshoremen." *Howlett v. Birkdale Shipping Co., S.A.*, 512 U.S. 92, 98 (1994) (citing *Scindia*, 451 U.S. at 167). Johnson contends that Cooper breached two of the *Scindia* duties: (1) the "turnover duty," which "relates to the condition of the ship upon the commencement of stevedoring operations";

[3] We also note that the section of Johnson's appellant brief that most forcefully argues that he had a connection to the AMERICA that was substantial in duration is tellingly short on record citations to support its factual assertions. *See* FED. R. APP. P. 28(a)(8) (requiring argument contain "citations to . . . parts of the record on which the appellant relies"); *see also Little*, 37 F.3d at 1075 (explaining that "unsubstantiated assertions" do not satisfy nonmovant's summary judgment burden).

and (2) the "active control" duty, which "provides that a shipowner must exercise reasonable care to prevent injuries to longshoremen in areas that remain under the **[—10—]** 'active control of the vessel'" during stevedoring operations. *Id.* (citing *Scindia*, 451 U.S. at 167–68).

Johnson failed to cite to any record evidence showing that Cooper breached either duty. *See* FED. R. CIV. P. 56(c) (explaining that a party must support assertion that there is a genuine dispute of material fact by "citing to particular parts of materials in the record" or "showing that the materials cited do not establish the absence or presence of a genuine dispute"); *Little*, 37 F.3d at 1075 (explaining that "conclusory allegations" and "unsubstantiated assertions" do not satisfy nonmovant's summary judgment burden). Nor could he, as an independent review of the record shows no evidence of vessel negligence. The district court was correct to grant summary judgment to Cooper on Johnson's § 905(b) claim.

IV.

As the district court stated in its ruling, summary judgment is about evidence. "We resolve factual controversies in favor of the nonmoving party, but only when there is an actual controversy, that is, when both parties have submitted evidence of contradictory facts. *We do not, however, in the absence of any proof, assume that the nonmoving party could or would prove the necessary facts.*" *Little*, 37 F.3d at 1075 (citing *Lujan v. Nat'l Wildlife Fed'n*, 497 U.S. 871, 888 (1990)) (emphasis in original). Because Johnson did not—and could not, based on his failure to put forth evidence—show a genuine dispute of material fact as to his claims, the district court's grant of summary judgment to Cooper is AFFIRMED.

United States Court of Appeals
for the Fifth Circuit

No. 22-20321

IN RE BOUCHARD TRANSP. CO.

Appeal from the United States District Court for the Southern District of Texas

Decided: July 25, 2023

Citation: 74 F.4th 743, 11 Adm. R. 320 (5th Cir. 2023).

Before **HIGGINBOTHAM, SMITH,** and **ENGELHARDT,** Circuit Judges.

[—1—] {-746-} SMITH, Circuit Judge:

Bouchard Transportation Company and its affiliates (collectively "Bouchard")—debtors in bankruptcy—prepared to sell some of their assets at an auction. Fearing the auction would go poorly, Bouchard solicited a "stalking horse bidder" to start the auction and set a floor price. In exchange, **[—2—]** Bouchard agreed to pay the stalking horse bidder a $3.3 million break-up fee and to reimburse expenses up to $1.5 million. The question is whether those payments were a permissible use of estate funds.

As the bankruptcy and district courts found, the stalking horse payments were lawful under both applicable provisions of the Bankruptcy Code—they provided an actual benefit to the estate and were issued in the reasonable exercise of business judgment. We accordingly affirm.

I.

A.

Bouchard, one of the largest petroleum shipping companies in the United States, filed for Chapter 11 bankruptcy in 2020. The United States Trustee for the Southern District of Texas created the Official Committee of Unsecured Creditors (the "Committee") to represent the interests of **{-747-}** the unsecured creditors. *See* 11 U.S.C. § 1102(a)(1).

During the bankruptcy, Bouchard went through two rounds of post-petition financing. It first opened a credit facility with Hartree Partners, LP ("Hartree"), but quickly defaulted. It then secured a second round of post-petition financing with JMB Capital Partners Lending, LLC ("JMB"). JMB's loan was secured by a variety of liens on Bouchard's shipping vessels. Using its new funds, Bouchard paid off the outstanding principal, interest, expenses, and fees owed to Hartree. But it still owed around $95 million to JMB (notwithstanding its prepetition debts).

After efforts to jump-start the business failed, Bouchard decided to sell some major assets. The court approved an auction, subject to a number of rules. Importantly, the court's bid-procedures order pre-authorized Bouchard to select a "stalking horse bidder." A stalking horse bidder is an initial bidder whose purchase offer is often negotiated in advance to guarantee a minimum sale price. Because the first bidder in an auction incurs significant **[—3—]** expense (including the cost of due diligence), a stalking horse bidder often haggles for bid protections, such as reimbursement for expenses or a "break-up fee" if it does not win the auction.[1] The bankruptcy court expressly authorized Bouchard to select a stalking horse bidder and to offer that bidder a break-up fee and expense reimbursement.

The selection of a stalking horse bidder was subject to several limitations. Any break-up fee could not exceed 3% of the purchase price, and any expense reimbursement was subject to a cap. If a stalking horse bidder was selected, Bouchard was required to notify the court and disclose the material terms of the deal. And other parties were permitted to object to the stalking horse agreement within three days of the notice. The auction was set for July 19, 2021, but the court required that a stalking horse bidder (if any) be selected by July 7.

Bouchard, however, struggled to generate interest in its vessels. It discussed the possibility of a stalking horse bidder with prospective purchasers, but no agreement was

[1] *See* David M. Holliday, Annotation, *Right to Recover Break-Up Fee Arising from Sale of Bankruptcy Estate Property*, 39 A.L.R. Fed. 2d 219 (2009).

reached by July 7. With the consent of the court, the deadline to select a stalking horse bidder was pushed back to July 11. Yet no agreements materialized. The deadline was delayed again to July 16. Still again, it was pushed back to 11:59 p.m. on July 18, just fifteen hours before the start of the auction.

Finally, after days of negotiations, Bouchard had two sale offers for its vessels: one from Hartree and one from Centerline Logistics ("Centerline"). The board met twice on July 18 to consider the options. Centerline's proposal was initially attractive, but the board had concerns that Centerline **[—4—]** would not be able to secure the financing necessary for the transaction. Centerline's bid was also not a stalking horse bid; Centerline wanted Bouchard to cancel the auction and accept its deal outright, which concerned the board. So Bouchard rejected their proposal.

That left Hartree's proposal. Hartree offered $110 million for 29 of the 31 vessels that secured JMB's financing facility. But it demanded a break-up fee of 3% of the purchase price ($3.3 million) and a maximum expense reimbursement of $1.5 million. Those fees would be paid even if Hartree did not submit the winning bid. Lastly, the proposal required any competitor to bid at least $500,000 more than **{-748-}** Hartree's offer (plus the value of the bid protections) to be successful.

After discussion, the board agreed to move forward with an auction with Hartree's offer as a stalking horse bid. Around 11 p.m. on July 18, the Bouchard notified the court that Hartree had been selected as a stalking horse bidder. It also disclosed that Hartree had been promised $4.8 million in bid protections as part of the purchase agreement. The Committee was informed of the negotiations and agreement with Hartree, but it filed no objections before the auction.

The auction started the next day. Shortly before it commenced, Bouchard learned that JMB also intended to bid on the vessels. After Hartree submitted its opening bid, Bouchard announced that a second bid would need to be a minimum of $115.3 million—Hartree's bid was $110 million, $4.8 million was owed in bid protections, and the minimum bid increment was $500,000. Then, JMB stated that it would bid exactly $115.3 million. Hartree declined to overbid, and JMB won the auction.[2] **[—5—]**

The Committee objected to the break-up fee and expense reimbursement three days later. It contended that the payments were administrative expenses under 11 U.S.C. § 503(b) and that Bouchard had failed to satisfy the statute's strict necessity standard. Bouchard countered that the fees were governed by 11 U.S.C. § 363(b), which allows payments related to an asset sale if they are spent in the reasonable exercise of business judgment.

B.

The bankruptcy court eventually approved the sale of the assets to JMB, but it withheld judgment on the legality of Hartree's bid protections. A few weeks after the auction, the bankruptcy court held a hearing to decide whether it was lawful for Bouchard to designate Hartree as the stalking horse bidder and to give Hartree bid protections. The hearing lasted for five hours, and the court heard testimony from three witnesses: (1) Richard Morgner, a director at Bouchard's investment bank; (2) Patrick Bartels, the independent director of Bouchard; and (3) Scott Levy, a partner at Hartree.

After the hearing, the bankruptcy court gave an oral ruling that the break-up fee and expense reimbursement were permitted, but it capped the expense reimbursement at $1 million (instead of the $1.5 million that Hartree had requested). It reasoned that, regardless of whether 11 U.S.C. § 503(b) or § 363(b) applied, the payments to Hartree were

[2] In accordance with the court's bid procedures order, Bouchard orally designated Hartree as the backup bidder in case closing negotiations between Bouchard and JMB fell **[—5—]** through. But the Committee disputes that on appeal.

lawful. The court thus ordered payment to Hartree on August 23, 2021.[3]

C.

The Committee appealed the Hartree order, and the district court **[—6—]** affirmed. *Official Comm. of Unsecured Creditors v. Bouchard Transp. Co. (In re Bouchard Transp. Co.)*, 639 B.R. 697, 702 (S.D. Tex. 2022). As a threshold matter, the court acknowledged that whether the bid protections were lawful was a mixed question of law and fact. *Id.* at 707. But it concluded that it did not matter whether the court employed *de novo* or deferential review. **{-749-}** Under either level of review, the bankruptcy court was correct to allow the fees. *Id.*

Like the bankruptcy court, the district court also declined to decide whether 11 U.S.C. § 503(b) or § 363(b) applied, as it found the payment law-ful under either provision. *Id.* at 712. If the administrative expense standard applied, the payment was necessary to secure a benefit to the estate—namely, to procure a valuable bid in the asset sale and to force JMB to bid higher than it otherwise would have. *Id.* at 718. If the business judgment rule applied, then Bouchard prevailed for similar reasons. Bouchard reasonably compensated Hartree in exchange for Hartree's serving as the stalking horse bidder. *Id.* at 721.

The Committee appeals again.

II.

In a bankruptcy appeal, we review the findings and conclusions of the bankruptcy court, not the district court. *See Official Comm. of Unsecured Creditors v. Moeller (In re Age Refining, Inc.)*, 801 F.3d 530, 538 (5th Cir. 2015). We generally review the bankruptcy court's conclusions of law *de novo* and its factual findings for clear error. *Id.* But the parties contest what level of review applies to the bankruptcy court's order permitting the break-up fee and expense reimbursement.

Whether the payments meet the statutory standard—either § 503(b) **[—7—]** or § 363(b)—is a quintessential "mixed" question of law and fact.[4] When reviewing a mixed question, we often choose the standard of review that best reflects which "judicial actor is better positioned" to make the decision. *Miller v. Fenton*, 474 U.S. 104, 114 (1985). That is, if the issue involves the interpretation of legal rules—a skill firmly within the bailiwick of an appellate court—we consider the issue *de novo*. *See U.S. Bank Nat'l Ass'n ex rel. CWCapital Asset Mgmt. LLC v. Vill. at Lakeridge, LLC*, 138 S. Ct. 960, 967 (2018). But if a dispute would "immerse [the court] in case-specific factual issues—compelling [it] to marshal and weigh evidence, make credibility judgments, and otherwise address . . . multifarious, fleeting, special, narrow facts that utterly resist generalization," we should defer to the court that did the factfinding. *Id.* (internal quotation marks and citation omitted).

The question in this case is firmly in the latter category. Whether the break-up fee and expense reimbursement provided an "actual" benefit to Bouchard under § 503(b), or whether the payments were a reasonable exercise of business judgment under § 363(b), are the kind of fact-intensive questions best directed to the bankruptcy court.[5] Indeed, the bankruptcy court ordered the payment to Hartree only after reviewing considerable record evidence and hearing five hours of witness testimony.

---

3 Notably, the court approved Bouchard's Chapter 11 reorganization plan three days later, on August 26, 2021.

4 *See Pullman–Standard v. Swint*, 456 U.S. 273, 289 n.19 (1982) (noting that mixed questions ask whether "the facts satisfy the statutory standard, or to put it another way, whether the rule of law as applied to the established facts is or is not violated").

5 The § 503(b) analysis is comparable to the mixed question in *Lakeridge*, 138 S. Ct. at 967–68. There, the Court reviewed for clear error whether a transaction was conducted at "arm's length." *Id.* at 969. Under § 503(b), we ask a similarly fact-bound question: whether a payment provided an "actual" and "necessary" benefit to a debtor in bankruptcy. Likewise, in *ASARCO, Inc. v. Elliott Mgmt. (In re ASARCO, L.L.C.)*, 650 F.3d 593, 603 (5th Cir. 2011), we applied clear-error review when we evaluated the propriety of reimbursements under § 363(b)'s business judgment rule.

Because the issues [—8—] are "primarily . . . factual," we review for clear {-750-} error. *Trendsetter HR L.L.C. v. Zurich Am. Ins. Co. (In re Trendsetter HR L.L.C.)*, 949 F.3d 905, 910 (5th Cir. 2020) (omission in original) (quoting *Lakeridge*, 138 S. Ct. at 967). We will affirm if the bankruptcy court's determinations are "plausible in light of the record." *Id.* (quotation omitted).

III.

Having settled the standard of review, we now decide whether the contested payments were lawful.

A.

In a Chapter 11 bankruptcy, fees related to the sale of assets are subject to court approval. 2 William L. Norton III, Norton Bankruptcy Law and Practice 3d § 44:28, Westlaw (database updated July 2023). That includes "the payment of bidding incentives to prospective purchasers," such as the break-up fee and expense reimbursement at issue here. *Id.* But there is a split of authority on what substantive standard a judge should use to decide whether such payments are permissible.

Some courts[6]—including the Third Circuit—use 11 U.S.C. § 503(b), under which estate funds can be used for "administrative expenses" if they are "the actual, necessary costs and expenses of preserving the estate." *Id.* § 503(b)(1)(A). "[T]o qualify as an 'actual and necessary cost' . . . a claim against the estate must have arisen post-petition and as a result of actions taken by the [debtor-in-possession] that benefitted the estate."[7] [—9—]

Other courts have instead relied on 11 U.S.C. § 363(b)(1), which governs the sale of estate property outside the ordinary course of business.[8] Section 363(b) incorporates the "business judgment standard" from corporate law. *ASARCO*, 650 F.3d at 601. A debtor-in-possession may sell its estate assets while satisfying its fiduciary duties if it gives "some articulated business justification for using, selling, or leasing the property." *Id.* (quotation omitted). That standard is less exacting and gives the debtor more discretion to sell assets (and pay fees) based on merely "sound business reasons." *See Cadle Co. v. Mims (In re Moore)*, 608 F.3d 253, 263 (5th Cir. 2010).

Unfortunately, *ASARCO*—our leading precedent on the issue—gives mixed signals about which provision applies to these facts. *ASARCO* also dealt with an asset sale in bankruptcy, but the debtor held a two-phase bidding process. After the first round, the debtor asked the court whether it could reimburse certain bidders for due diligence expenses they would incur in the next round of bidding. 650 F.3d at 597–98. The court held that § 363(b) was the governing provision because the debtor sought prospective authorization to reimburse bidders during an asset sale. *Id.* at 602. But it reasoned that § 503(b) would apply to entities that had already "incurred administrative expenses and wish to request payment from the estate." *Id.* at 601. {-751-}

This case is somewhere between the two situations that *ASARCO* described. On the one hand, this case is also an asset sale, and the debtor [—10—] sought court approval to reimburse a bidder before the auction began. That is similar to the facts of *ASARCO* and suggests that we should apply § 363(b). On the other hand, the court did not evaluate the specific request for a break-up fee and reimbursement until the after the auction when Hartree—a third party—had already expended resources. Per *ASARCO*, § 503(b)

---

[6] *See, e.g., Calpine Corp. v. O'Brien Env't Energy, Inc. (In re O'Brien Env't Energy, Inc.)*, 181 F.3d 527, 532 (3d Cir. 1999); *In re Reliant Energy Channelview LP*, 594 F.3d 200, 206 (3d Cir. 2010).

[7] *Nabors Offshore Corp. v. Whistler Energy II, L.L.C. (In re Whistler Energy II)*, [—9—] 931 F.3d 432, 441 (5th Cir. 2019) (quoting *Total Minatome Corp. v. Jack/Wade Drilling, Inc. (In re Jack/Wade Drilling, Inc.)*, 258 F.3d 385, 387 (5th Cir. 2001)) (first alteration in original).

[8] *See, e.g., ASARCO*, 650 F.3d at 602; *see also Official Comm. of Subordinated Bondholders v. Integrated Res., Inc. (In re Integrated Res., Inc.)*, 147 B.R. 650, 657 (S.D.N.Y. 1992) (not citing § 363(b) but applying the business judgment rule to a break-up fee arrangement).

should apply to a backward-looking request for reimbursement.

Because of that uncertainty, both the bankruptcy court and the district court found that the fees were lawful under either § 503(b) or § 363(b). We elect to do the same. This case does not require us to specify which provision of the bankruptcy code governs on these unique facts. Under either standard, the stalking horse payment was legal.

B.

We start with the more stringent provision: § 503(b). As the "claimant seeking administrative expenses," Hartree has the burden of proving that the break-up fee and expense reimbursement arose (1) "post-petition and as a result of actions taken by" Bouchard. *Whistler Energy II*, 931 F.3d at 441 (quoting *Jack/Wade Drilling*, 258 F.3d at 387). Hartree must also prove that the fees were (2) "actual" and (3) "necessary costs and expenses of preserving the estate." *Id.* (quoting § 503(b)(1)(A)). Hartree can satisfy each of those requirements.

1.

As a threshold matter, there was a postpetition agreement between Hartree and Bouchard. That is not a demanding requirement—all that the statute requires is that the expenses were incurred "as a result of actions taken" by the debtor, and that those actions occurred after bankruptcy. *Id.* (quoting *Jack/Wade Drilling*, 258 F.3d at 387). Bouchard signed a purchase agreement with Hartree, stipulating that Hartree would receive a break-up fee and reimbursement even if it was not the winning bidder at auction. And **[—11—]** it is undisputed that the agreement was reached after Bouchard had filed for bankruptcy.

The Committee insists that the Hartree asset purchase agreement was not enforceable until the bankruptcy court approved it, and therefore it was not a valid postpetition transaction. But the Committee reads the "post-petition agreement" requirement too strictly. The focus of the requirement is not so much on the *agreement*, but on its *postpetition* nature. The reason that a § 503(b) administrative expense must arise from a postpetition agreement is that claims for administrative expenses get priority over most other unsecured claims. *See Whistler Energy II*, 931 F.3d at 441–42 (citing 11 U.S.C. § 507(a)(2)). That priority encourages third parties to service the debtors' estate that would otherwise not do so out of fear that they might not get paid. But that incentive "is not required . . . when the relevant obligation pre-dates the bankruptcy." *Id.* at 442.

Therefore, an agreement for services in bankruptcy is enforceable even if the "post-petition business relationship [is] not . . . clearly defined." *Id.* at 442. For example, in *Whistler Energy II*, we upheld the payment of fees under § 503(b) where the debtor requested specific services and a counter-party voluntary performed them, even though there was no formal written agreement. *Id.* at 442–43. Here we have much more than that. Bouchard not only asked Hartree to serve as a stalking horse **{–752–}** bidder (a role it dutifully fulfilled), but the parties signed a purchase agreement to that effect.

And although the associated fees were dependent on court approval, that does not affect the postpetition nature of the transaction. Indeed, § 503(b) implicitly contemplates that debtors will incur postpetition administrative expenses before they seek court authorization.[9] It is unsurprising, **[—12—]** then, that the Third Circuit assumed that a valid postpetition transaction existed where a contract for break-up fees was contingent on approval by the court. *Calpine*, 181 F.3d at 529, 533.

That is the situation here. Hartree made a deal with a debtor in bankruptcy, carried out its half of the bargain, and now it wants its expenses paid. That is a postpetition transaction covered by § 503(b).

[9] "An entity may timely *file a request* for payment of an administrative expense, **[—12—]** . . . [and] [a]fter notice and a hearing, there shall be *allowed* administrative expenses." 11 U.S.C. § 503(a)–(b) (emphasis added).

2.

Furthermore, the break-up fee and expense reimbursement provided numerous benefits to the estate. *First*, by securing Hartree's participation as the stalking horse bidder, it helped Bouchard avoid a "naked" auction. When an auction begins with no known bidder, the debtor risks receiving no offers or being forced to sell its assets below market value. As Bouchard's investment banker testified, that concern animated the decision to negotiate with Hartree. With just hours to go before the sale, there was a real risk of a naked auction. By getting Hartree to set a floor price, Bouchard secured value for the estate.

The Committee responds that the risk of a naked auction was overblown. After all, at the same auction, Bouchard sold a different set of vessels to satisfy a pre-petition debt to Wells Fargo and did not use a stalking horse bidder. Those vessels—known as the "Wells Fargo collateral"—still fetched millions. Yet the Wells Fargo auction proves how dangerous a naked auction can be. Although the Wells Fargo collateral eventually sold, it went for approximately $30 million less than was needed to clear the associated debt. Bouchard wanted to avoid a similar scenario in the sale of the larger share of its vessels, so it spent a comparatively small amount of its money to **[—13—]** guarantee a minimum auction price.

The Committee says that the benefit of an initial bidder proves too much. The very definition of a stalking horse bid is one that sets the floor price at an action. If avoiding a naked auction is a *per se* "benefit" to the estate, then it will always be permissible to pay break-up fees to a stalking horse bidder. But we need not hold that avoiding a "naked" auction is beneficial in every case and at any price. For example, the *O'Brien* court held that offering break-up fees was unnecessary to avoid a naked auction where the bidders had other market incentives to come forward. *See* 181 F.3d at 537.

If there were such evidence here, the analysis would be different. But Bouchard produced evidence that it reached out to over 150 potential bidders, and yet, on the eve of the auction, it had no assurance that anyone would bid on its assets.[10] Because the risk of a poor auction was real, it **{-753-}** benefited from Hartree's generous stalking horse bid.

Still, the Committee insists that if the Hartree bid had been successful, it would have been bad for the estate. Although it was a substantial cash infusion, it would not have been enough to pay all of Bouchard's postpetition debts. And because of the nearly $5 million in bid protections, the estate would have been left with an outstanding administrative expense claim that it could not pay. On top of that, the unsecured creditors would receive no relief.

Yet the Committee ignores the fact that, in the absence of the Hartree bid, Bouchard faced the prospect of no viable bidders for most of its vessels. Although the Hartree purchase agreement cost the estate $5 million, that **[—14—]** cost is comparable to an insurance policy, under which avoiding a larger risk justifies small premiums. If Bouchard had received no bidders, it would have been far worse for the estate, resulting in paltry recovery for secured creditors and even less for unsecured creditors.

Second, the bid protections forced JMB to pay more for Bouchard's vessels than it otherwise would have. To win the auction, JMB had to bid $115.3 million, which added at least $500,000 in value to the estate, over and above Hartree's offer. Bouchard also maintains that selling the assets at that amount was essential to paying off its postpetition debts and confirming its Chapter 11 reorganization plan.

The Committee, however, contends that the bid benefited only JMB and certain senior creditors while providing no recovery for other creditors. But a benefit is still a benefit even if it helps only secured creditors. Although the Committee's loyalty to its interest group is

[10] And the only alternative to an auction—the Centerline purchase offer—lacked the requisite financing. The board understandably felt that its best option was proceeding with the auction with Hartree as the stalking horse bidder.

understandable, the fact that JMB's bid helped mainly priority creditors is not a reason to reject the administrative expenses. Unsecured creditors are in the back of the line, and sometimes that comes with downsides.

And again, we are not comparing JMB's bid to a perfect bid that made both the debtors and creditors completely whole. We are comparing JMB's bid to the alternatives: Hartree's stalking horse bid, or no bid for the vessels. The Committee itself contends that the former option was flawed, and JMB's bid was assuredly an improvement on that deal. It was $5.3 million more than Hartree's offer, which, once the $3.3 million break-up fee and $1 million capped expense reimbursement were subtracted, left $1 million for the estate above what Hartree would have provided.

Indeed, if no bidder had come forward for Bouchard's vessels, it may **[—15—]** have doomed Bouchard's chances of a Chapter 11 reorganization plan.[11] Bouchard did not have the money to repay its nearly $100 million in post-petition debts, so a Chapter 11 failure might have kicked the case into Chapter 7 and forced a complete liquidation. *See Koerner v. Colonial Bank (In re Koerner)*, 800 F.2d 1358, 1360, 1368 (5th Cir. 1986); *see also* 11 U.S.C. § 1112(b)(4)(M).

3.

The last requirement of § 503(b) is that the administrative expenses were "necessary" to secure the claimed benefit. Hartree demonstrated that as well. **{-754-}**

For starters, Hartree would not have served as the stalking horse bidder were it not for the break-up fee and expense reimbursement. The Committee speculates that Hartree could not have been induced by the break-up fee because it was contingent on court approval. The evidence in the record, however, suggests that Hartree fully expected it would get court approval. Indeed, the bankruptcy court had already pre-authorized a stalking horse bidder within the limitations in the Hartree purchase agreement.

The Committee points out that the Third Circuit held in *O'Brien* that break-up fees were unnecessary because the parties submitted bids with the full knowledge that the court might not approve a break-up fee. *O'Brien*, 181 F.3d at 537. But there, the court had already declined a break-up fee before the auction. *Id.* at 529. The bidders only hoped that the court would change its mind after the auction. **[—16—]**

Here, Hartree had not been previously denied fees. To the contrary, the court's bid procedures order explicitly contemplated break-up fees and reimbursement at the rate Hartree had requested. Furthermore, in *O'Brien*, there were strong incentives for the bidders to bid on the assets in the absence of a break-up fee. *Id.* at 537; *see also Reliant Energy*, 594 F.3d at 206–07 (conducting a similar analysis on similar facts). The Committee has not identified comparable incentives here. That makes it considerably more likely that the break-up fees incentivized Hartree.

The Committee's more persuasive suggestion is that, even if the break-up fee induced Hartree to bid in the first place, it did not induce JMB to top that bid. The Committee claims that "JMB had every incentive to submit a bid in the precise amount it submitted regardless of whether the Hartree Bid was submitted." That is because certain maritime lienholders and administrative expense claimants would get paid out before JMB. So in order for Bouchard to cover those payments plus its $95 million obligation to JMB, it needed a minimum of $115.3 million at the auction, regardless of what Hartree initially bid.

It does appear from the record that Bouchard needed at least $115.3 million to pay senior lienholders, professional fees, and its postpetition financers. The document prepared for Bouchard's board by Kirkland & Ellis

[11] The Committee avers that the Hartree stalking horse bid also did not provide enough money to avoid Chapter 7 conversion. But again, it would have been substantially worse for both the estate and creditors if Bouchard received less money at the auction than Hartree offered.

suggests as much, and Morgner (Bouchard's investment banker) testified to it in bankruptcy court. If Bouchard got less than $115.3 million, the senior lienholders and professionals would be paid first and JMB would not recover the full amount that Bouchard owed. On the other hand, $115.3 million was the exact amount needed to outbid Hartree and not one penny more. That suggests that JMB bid that number because it was trying to beat Hartree.

Both of those interpretations of the evidence are at least plausible. On clear-error review, there is no reason to reverse the bankruptcy court's fac- **[—17—]** tual finding. If anything, Bouchard and Hartree's theory is slightly more persuasive. Bouchard had no indication that JMB was going to bid on its vessels until Hartree was designated as the stalking horse bidder. And the agreement with Hartree added a $5 million administrative expense claim to the balance sheet that reduced JMB's recovery. Companies tend not to spend an extra $5 million if they do not have to.[12] Thus, Morgner **{-755-}** testified that JMB likely would not have bid as highly if it were not for the Hartree stalking horse bid. The bankruptcy court reasonably credited that testimony.

Considering the totality of the evidence, it is "plausible" both that Hartree's stalking horse bid created a benefit for the estate and that Hartree would not have served as the stalking horse bidder without the prospect of fees. It is also plausible that JMB only bid $115.3 million because it was forced to beat out Hartree. Therefore, the break-up fee and the expense reimbursement were "necessary" administrative expenses under § 503(b).

C.

Even if we were to apply § 363(b) instead of § 503(b), the result would be the same. Section 363(b) incorporates the business judgment rule, familiar to corporate law. *ASARCO*, 650 F.3d at 601. If the break-up fee and expense reimbursement were "necessary" to provide a benefit to the estate, then they easily satisfy a deferential reasonableness standard.

The Committee's primary rejoinder is that, even if the agreement was substantively reasonable, Bouchard failed appropriately to consider the con- **[—18—]** sequences of the Hartree purchase agreement. Given Bouchard's perilous financial straits, committing almost $5 million to Hartree was no small decision. And Hartree demanded that Bouchard reject certain charter agreements that would have cost Bouchard more money that it did not have. Based on the meeting minutes, it is unclear whether the board ever discussed those shortcomings specifically.

The individuals who were involved in the transaction, however, did not allege that the Hartree agreement was flawless. Instead, they testified to the bankruptcy court that they faced multiple flawed options. Bouchard could proceed with a "naked" auction and risk that a bidder would severely undervalue its vessels. It could accept the Centerline deal, even though the board had reason to doubt Centerline could finance the transaction and Centerline insisted that Bouchard cancel the auction and accept the deal on the spot. Or it could accept Hartree's stalking horse bid, paying more fees and reimbursement costs but guaranteeing a floor price at the auction. Given that trilemma, the stalking horse arrangement was the lesser of multiple evils.

Nor can the Committee seriously contend that Bouchard's leaders violated their fiduciary duty to inform themselves adequately and make a considered decision.[13] The process of finalizing the Hartree deal began on July 16, when Bouchard's board first met to discuss the

[12] Indeed, although JMB might not have recovered the full amount of its loan if it bid less than $115.3, any shortfall would have given JMB a deficiency claim against the estate for the difference. In that event, JMB would own the collateral outright and might still recoup all the money after Bouchard liquidated its other assets and paid off the deficiency claim.

[13] *See Aronson v. Lewis*, 473 A.2d 805, 812 (Del. 1984) ("[D]irectors have a duty to inform themselves, prior to making a business decision, of all material information reasonably available to them."), *overruled on other grounds*, *Brehm v. Eisner*, 746 A.2d 244, 254 (Del. 2000).

prospect of Hartree as a stalking horse bidder. According to the minutes, the board thoroughly discussed "the advantages and disadvantages of designating Hartree as the stalking horse bidder" at that time. Bouchard met again on July 17 to discuss the plan. Meanwhile, Bouchard and Hartree exchanged nine drafts of the **[—19—]** Hartree purchase agreement. Then, on July 18, the board considered a 24-page presentation on the bid. Only after two meetings on July 18 did Bouchard approve Hartree as the stalking horse bidder. **{–756–}**

True, as the Committee points out, the July 18 meetings lasted just forty minutes total. But because of the impending auction deadline, everything had to move quickly. To quote the district court, there is "no basis to conclude that the board did not thoroughly review the presentation and make a well-reasoned, careful decision to designate Hartree as the stalking-horse bidder." *Bouchard Transp.*, 639 B.R. at 721.[14] In signing the Hartree purchase agreement, Bouchard acted well within the bounds of reasonable business judgment. Section 363(b) does not require more.

IV.

Bouchard's payment to the stalking horse bidder is justified under either the stringent administrative-expense standard or the more relaxed business judgment rule. We AFFIRM the district court's judgment affirming the bankruptcy court's order that Bouchard pay Hartree a break-up fee and a capped expense reimbursement.

---

[14] There are also no allegations of self-dealing and the like, which might render a business judgment a breach of fiduciary duty.

United States Court of Appeals
for the Fifth Circuit

No. 22-30041

GREAT LAKES INS.
VS.
GRAY GROUP INVESTMENTS, L.L.C.

Appeal from the United States District Court for the Eastern District of Louisiana

Decided: August 1, 2023

Citation: 76 F.4th 341, 11 Adm. R. 329 (5th Cir. 2023).

Before **WIENER, HIGGINSON,** and **WILSON,** Circuit Judges.

[—1—] {-344-} **WILSON,** Circuit Judge: **{-345-}**

Hello, Dolly
Well, hello, Dolly
It's so nice to have you back where you belong . . . .[1]

Great Lakes Insurance, S.E. insured the Hello Dolly VI, a boat owned by Gray Group Investments, L.L.C. The Hello Dolly sank in Pensacola, **[—2—]** Florida, during a hurricane. Gray Group filed a claim under the insurance policy, Great Lakes denied coverage, and Great Lakes then sought a declaratory judgment that it properly did so. Ironically, the question largely turned on whether, contra her musical namesake, the Hello Dolly was "back where [she] belong[ed]," for purposes of coverage. The district court agreed with Great Lakes that she was not. We affirm.

I.

A.

Hurricane Sally struck the Gulf Coast in September 2020. In its path lay the Hello Dolly VI (hereafter, the Vessel), which was moored behind Gray Group's eponymous member Michael Gray's house in Pensacola. The Vessel sustained damage during the storm and sank at its mooring. The Vessel was insured under an insurance policy issued by Great Lakes. Great Lakes also insured several other watercraft within Gray Group's fleet under similar policies. Though the operative policy provided coverage for "named windstorms," Great Lakes denied coverage, asserting that Gray Group had breached several warranties.

Specifically, Great Lakes faulted Gray Group for breaching the "hurricane protection plan" (the HPP) that Gray Group had submitted in response to Great Lakes's "hurricane questionnaire" (the HQ). The HQ requested the Vessel's location during hurricane season and asked a series of questions regarding Gray Group's contingency plans in the event of a hurricane. In the HPP, Gray Group stated that the Vessel would be located at the Orleans Marina in New Orleans, Louisiana, and detailed the protective measures Gray Group would take when a hurricane approached.

The parties contest whether the HPP was incorporated by reference into the insurance policy, and, if so, whether Gray Group breached the HPP. **[—3—]** Before laying anchor there, we briefly chart the policy's incorporation clauses and the underlying documents at issue.

There are two incorporation clauses in the insurance policy. The first provides that "[t]his insuring agreement incorporates in full [Gray Group's] application for insurance[.]" The second states that "[t]his is a legally binding insurance document between [Gray Group] and [Great Lakes], incorporating in full the application form signed by [Gray Group]."

Gray Group submitted various documentation to facilitate underwriting for the policy at issue. Three such documents are particularly relevant: the "Application Form," the HQ, and the HPP. In the Application Form, Gray Group represented that the "primary mooring location of [the] Vessel . . . between July 1st [and] Nov[.] 1st" would be the Orleans Marina. In the HPP, Gray Group again named the Orleans Marina in response to the HQ's request for the "marina or residence **{-346-}** where [the] [V]essel [would be] located between

[1] From the Musical Production "HELLO DOLLY!" Music and lyrics by Jerry Herman, copyright 1963.

1st July and 1st November[.]" Whether the policy's incorporating clauses encompass these underwriting documents determines the seaworthiness of Gray Group's appeal.

B.

After denying coverage, Great Lakes sought a declaratory judgment that Gray Group breached the HPP by failing to evacuate the Hello Dolly VI to safe harbor, keep the Vessel fully manned, deploy the anchor, and moor the Vessel at the Orleans Marina. Gray Group countersued, contending that the HPP was not incorporated into the policy, and in any event, that Gray Group did not breach the HPP.

Gray Group moved for judgment on the pleadings. The district court denied the motion, holding that the phrase "application for insurance" was ambiguous because it could refer solely to the Application Form, or to a broader set of documents inclusive of the HQ and the HPP. Therefore, the **[—4—]** district court found that evidence outside the pleadings was necessary to determine the meaning of "application for insurance."

The parties then filed cross-motions for summary judgment. Great Lakes contended, *inter alia*, that regardless of whether the HPP was incorporated, the Application Form certainly was, and Gray Group misrepresented facts in the Application Form. Gray Group filed a motion to strike that argument. The district court granted Gray Group's motion because "Great Lakes did not allege any misrepresentation by Gray Group in its complaint."

However, the district court agreed with Great Lakes on its other points and granted it summary judgment. Specifically, the district court held that the phrase "application for insurance" was ambiguous but that extrinsic evidence showed that the parties intended "application for insurance" to encompass the HPP. Continuing the analysis, the court concluded that Gray Group's statement in the HPP that the Vessel was to be located at the Orleans Marina during hurricane season was also ambiguous. Again resorting to extrinsic evidence, the court found that the HPP meant that the Vessel would be moored at the Orleans Marina for the majority of hurricane season. The court determined that the HPP's "marina or residence" location constituted a warranty by Gray Group and found that the Vessel had not in fact been moored at the Orleans Marina for the majority of hurricane season. Gray Group had thus breached its warranty, justifying Great Lakes's denial of coverage.

Gray Group timely appealed, challenging the district court's denial of its motion for judgment on the pleadings as well as the court's summary judgment for Great Lakes. **[—5—]**

II.

We review a district court's ruling on a motion for judgment on the pleadings *de novo*. *Edionwe v. Bailey*, 860 F.3d 287, 291 (5th Cir. 2017). We apply the same standard to a district court's grant of summary judgment. *Springboards to Educ., Inc. v. McAllen Indep. Sch. Dist.*, 62 F.4th 174, 178 (5th Cir. 2023). Under New York law,[2] we review a district court's interpretation of an insurance policy *de novo*. *High Point Design, LLC v. LM Ins. Corp.*, 911 F.3d 89, 93 (2d Cir. 2018) (applying New York law).

A.

Gray Group's position is straightforward. It urges that "application for insurance" **{-347-}** is unambiguous—the clause refers only to the Application Form—and Great Lakes did not plead a breach of the Application Form. Thus, no need for extrinsic evidence, and the district court's analysis and judgment run aground. Alternatively, Gray Group posits that if "application for insurance" is ambiguous, then the clause is insufficient to incorporate an external document as a matter of law due to that ambiguity.

[2] The parties agree that New York law applies in this case.

Great Lakes takes a different tack, contending that Gray Group's responses to the HQ, through the HPP, were incorporated into the insurance policy through the "application for insurance." Per Great Lakes, "application for insurance" is ambiguous, but uncontroverted extrinsic evidence establishes that the parties intended the term to include the HPP.

So we must first consider (1) whether the term "application for insurance" is ambiguous, and, if so, (2) whether that ambiguity precludes incorporating by reference Gray Group's responses to the HQ via its HPP. **[—6—]**

1.

Under New York law, "an insurance contract is interpreted to give effect to the intent of the parties as expressed in the clear language of the contract." *Parks Real Estate Purchasing Group v. St. Paul Fire & Marine Ins. Co.*, 472 F.3d 33, 42 (2d Cir. 2006) (citation and quotation marks omitted). Whether an insurance contract is ambiguous is a question of law. *Id.* A contract is ambiguous when its terms "could suggest more than one meaning when viewed objectively by a reasonably intelligent person who has examined the context of the entire integrated agreement and who is cognizant of the customs, practices, usages and terminology as generally understood in the particular trade or business." *Id.* (citation and quotation marks omitted).

The Great Lakes insurance policy at issue "incorporat[es] in full the application form signed by [Gray Group]." The policy also "incorporates in full [Gray Group's] application for insurance[.]" Gray Group contends that both phrases refer to the same thing: the Application Form. Great Lakes counters that the phrase "application for insurance" plausibly includes more than just the Application Form—like, say, the documents Gray Group submitted during underwriting (including the HPP)—such that the policy's language is ambiguous.

We agree that the phrase "application for insurance" is ambiguous. The Application Form is clearly labeled as such, so the corresponding policy reference seems clear. But the "full" "application for insurance," slightly different nomenclature, implies a broader set of documents, including the Application Form *and* those Gray Group submitted during underwriting. The difference in verbiage is critical because under principles of contract interpretation, "[a] word or phrase is presumed to bear the same meaning throughout a text; a material variation in terms suggests a variation in meaning." *Landry's, Inc. v. Ins. Co. of the State of Pennsylvania*, 4 F.4th 366, **[—7—]** 370 (5th Cir. 2021) (quoting ANTONIN SCALIA & BRYAN GARNER, READING LAW 170 (2012)); *see also Two Farms Inc. v. Greenwich Ins. Co.*, 628 Fed. App'x 802, 805 (2d Cir. 2015) (applying New York rule that "a word used by the parties in one sense will be given the same meaning throughout the contract in the absence of countervailing reasons") (citation and quotation marks omitted)). Because "application for insurance" "could suggest more than one meaning" to a "reasonably intelligent person," *Parks Real Estate*, 472 F.3d at 42, the **{-348-}** term is ambiguous. So, we sail on to determine the effect of that ambiguity.

2.

The parties' disagreement as to the effect of the ambiguity is premised on competing understandings of New York's incorporation by reference doctrine. Gray Group posits that an incorporating clause must clearly identify an incorporated document; therefore, if the clause is unclear, it cannot effectuate a valid incorporation by reference. Essentially, Gray Group contends that if there is any ambiguity in what is incorporated, then the document in question is not. Great Lakes counters that the meaning of an ambiguous incorporating clause can be determined by extrinsic evidence, as with any other contractual provision. Therefore, a finding of ambiguity does not foreclose incorporation by reference—it merely shifts the issue to the factfinder. We agree with Great Lakes.

The Court of Appeals of New York has long recognized the concept of incorporation by reference. *See In re Bd. of Comm'rs of Washington Park*, 52 N.Y. 131, 134 (1873); *see also Tonnele v. Hall*, 4 N.Y. 140 (1850). Under

New York law, a document is incorporated into a contract if "(1) it is clearly identified in the agreement, and (2) the contract contains language that clearly communicates that the purpose of the reference is to incorporate the referenced material into the contract, rather than merely to acknowledge that **[—8—]** the referenced material is relevant to the contract." *Matter of Linn Energy, L.L.C.*, 927 F.3d 350, 353 (5th Cir. 2019) (citation and quotation marks omitted) ("New York courts use an objective standard, asking whether a reasonable person would understand the specific document to be incorporated by reference."). "[T]he paper to be incorporated into a written instrument by reference must be so referred to and described in the instrument that the paper may be identified beyond all reasonable doubt." *PaineWebber Inc. v. Bybyk*, 81 F.3d 1193, 1201 (2d Cir. 1996) (emphasis omitted) (quoting *Chiacchia v. Nat'l Westminster Bank USA*, 124 A.D.2d 626, 628 (N.Y. App. Div. 1986)). "[I]t must be clear that the parties to the agreement had knowledge of and assented to the incorporated terms." *Id.* (citation and quotation marks omitted). The doctrine "is grounded on the premise that the material to be incorporated is so well known to the contracting parties that a mere reference to it is sufficient." *Chiacchia*, 124 A.D. 2d at 628; *see also Orlander v. Staples, Inc.*, 802 F.3d 289, 295 n.6 (2d Cir. 2015).

For nearly as long as New York has recognized incorporation by reference, its Court of Appeals has allowed "[p]arol evidence . . . to prove the identity of the paper [that the parties attempted to incorporate]." *Bd. of Comm'rs of Washington Park*, 52 N.Y. at 134. New York courts have held that, generally, an ambiguity as to the identity of the incorporated document creates a fact issue. *See, e.g., Maines Paper & Food Serv., Inc. v. Keystone Assoc.*, 134 A.D. 3d 1340, 1342 (N.Y. App. Div. 2015) (weighing the evidence to determine whether the purportedly incorporated document was sufficiently identified in the executed contract); *Kenner v. Avis Rent A Car Sys., Inc.*, 254 A.D.2d 704, 704 (N.Y. App. Div. 1998) (holding that "[t]here is a triable issue of fact whether the oblique reference in the rental agreement to an otherwise unidentified 'rental document jacket' meets th[e] exacting standard [of incorporation by reference]"); *Chiacchia*, 124 A.D. 2d at 628 **[—9—]** ("Whether the paper encompassing the bank rules was referred to or described in the rental agreement such that it could be **{-349-}** identified beyond all reasonable doubt constitutes a question of fact precluding summary judgment."). But "[i]f the extrinsic evidence is 'so one-sided that no reasonable person could decide the contrary,' the court may resolve the ambiguity as a matter of law." *Jefferson Block 24 Oil & Gas, L.L.C. v. Aspen Ins. UK Ltd.*, 652 F.3d 584, 589 (5th Cir. 2011) (citation omitted) (applying New York law).

Gray Group relies on *Linn Energy* for the proposition that if a purportedly incorporated document is not "clearly identified in the agreement," 927 F.3d at 353, i.e., if the incorporating clause is unclear, then there is no valid incorporation. True, "the paper to be incorporated . . . by reference must be . . . identified beyond all reasonable doubt." *PaineWebber*, 81 F.3d at 1201 (quoting *Chiacchi*, 124 A.D. at 628). But that does not alter the general rule that a court may examine extrinsic evidence to ascertain the meaning of an ambiguous contract. *See Int'l Multifoods Corp. v. Commercial Union Ins. Co.*, 309 F.3d 76, 83 (2d Cir. 2002) ("If an ambiguity is found, the court may accept any available extrinsic evidence to ascertain the meaning intended by the parties during the formation of the contract." (cleaned up)) (applying New York law). Consistent with the New York cases discussed earlier, the general rule about consulting extrinsic evidence is as shipshape when ascertaining the meaning of an ambiguous incorporating clause as it is in any other context.

B.

Having surveyed the waterfront, we may cruise through the remaining issues on appeal. Gray Group urges that the district court erred by (1) denying its motion for judgment on the pleadings; (2) finding that the HPP was incorporated into the policy; and (3) concluding that the Vessel's **[—10—]** "marina or residence" location provided by Gray Group in the HPP was a warranty that required the Vessel to moor at the Orleans Marina for the majority of hurricane season.

1.

We affirm the district court's denial of Gray Group's motion for judgment on the pleadings.[3] "We evaluate a motion under Rule 12(c) for judgment on the pleadings using the same standard as a motion to dismiss under Rule 12(b)(6) for failure to state a claim." *Gentilello v. Rege*, 627 F.3d 540, 543–44 (5th Cir 2010). We thus must determine "whether, in the light most favorable to the plaintiff, the complaint states a valid claim for relief." *Id.* (citation and quotation marks omitted). As discussed above, the policy language at issue is ambiguous. While that is not dispositive as to whether the underwriting documents in question were validly incorporated by reference, it does mean that the scope of the policy's incorporating language turns on extrinsic evidence beyond the scope of the pleadings. Accordingly, the district court did not err in denying Gray Group's Rule 12(c) motion. **{–350–}**

2.

Next, we consider whether Gray Group's HPP, with its representation that the Vessel's "marina or residence" location during **[—11—]** hurricane season was the Orleans Marina, was included in the policy's ambiguous incorporation of Gray Group's "application for insurance." To remind, the full clause reads: "This insuring agreement incorporates in full [Gray Group's] application for insurance[.]" Under New York law, the burden rests on the insurer to prove that its interpretation of an ambiguous policy provision is correct. *Jefferson Block 24 Oil & Gas*, 652 F.3d at 589. "[T]he court may accept any available extrinsic evidence to ascertain the meaning intended by the parties during the formation of the contract [and] may resolve the ambiguity as a matter of law" "[if] the extrinsic evidence is so one-sided that no reasonable person could decide the contrary[.]" *Id.* (quotation marks and citation omitted).

The district court did not err in concluding that the HPP was incorporated into the policy. For starters, under a bolded header labeled "WARNING," the HQ, which prompted Gray Group's submission of the HPP, advised that "this declaration and warranty shall be incorporated in its entirety into any relevant policy of insurance." Gray Group's Fleet Risk Manager, Louis S. Crew, Jr., signed the HQ directly beneath that warning.

The parties' prior course of dealing removes any lingering doubt that Gray Group's "application for insurance" encompassed the HPP. In 2017, Great Lakes's underwriter notified Gray Group that another policy[4] then in force would expire in 15 days if Gray Group did not provide additional requested documentation, including a hurricane protection plan as to the insured watercraft. The underwriter followed up eight days later to remind Gray Group that the document remained outstanding and that failure to send it would void coverage. This exchange repeated itself in 2019, when Great **[—12—]** Lakes reminded Gray Group's broker that the requested hurricane protection plan "forms part of the policy." Additionally, Gray Group's Crew testified in his deposition that he "underst[oo]d that it [(the HPP)] would be incorporated into the policy."

Against this backdrop, the district court did not err in holding that the extrinsic evidence was "so one-sided that no reasonable person could decide" that the HPP was not incorporated into the policy. As it was properly

[3] Great Lakes argues that Gray Group failed to preserve its incorporation by reference argument in the district court. It is axiomatic that "[w]e will generally not countenance arguments not raised before the district court," *McManaway v. KBR, Inc.*, 852 F.3d 444, 455 (5th Cir. 2017), but Gray Group adequately raised the argument. Gray Group urged in its motion for judgment on the pleadings that "[t]he policy does not incorporate, attach, reference or ever mention the [HQ or the HPP]," and the district court noted that the incorporation argument was before it: "[Gray Group] moved for judgment on the pleadings under Federal Rule of Civil Procedure 12(c), arguing that the pleadings establish that the [HQ/HPP] was not a warranty because the agreement does not incorporate it . . . ."

[4] This policy covered a different boat owned by Gray Group, but it is undisputed that Gray Group's other vessels were insured under policies materially identical to the one at issue here.

incorporated, our next port-of-call is the interpretation of the HPP, and specifically the HPP's representation regarding the Vessel's "marina or residence" during hurricane season.

3.

In the HPP, Gray Group stated that the Orleans Marina was "the marina or residence where [the] [V]essel [would be] located between 1st July and 1st November." The district court concluded that this statement is ambiguous.[5] The court then relied on several email exchanges between the parties to ascertain its meaning. In 2019, Great Lakes's broker asked Gray Group's agent whether one of Gray Group's boats would be in the Bahamas or **{-351-}** Florida during hurricane season and explained that the information was important because if so, the premium would increase to account for the greater risk. Later in 2020, Gray Group's agent contacted Great Lakes's agent to ask if the same boat could travel to Florida and the Bahamas once hurricane season began. Great Lakes's agent responded:

> [The] application form showed that the[] mooring location during July to November would be Mississippi[,] and [the underwriters] rated the risks as such. If [a boat] change[d its] **[—13—]** mooring location to [the] Bahamas for the majority of hurricane season[,] then this must be re-rated. We rate on the assumption of where the vessel will be for the majority of the season.

The agent also stated that "[i]f [the boat] will spend the majority of that season in Mississippi[,] then the premium can stay the same[.]" In 2020, Great Lakes's underwriter again noted that "to amend the mooring location during the hurricane season" may require a premium increase.

Considering this evidence, the district court concluded that the HPP's representation regarding the Vessel's "marina or residence" location meant "the place where the [V]essel [was] to be moored the majority of hurricane season." We agree with the district court that the evidence establishes that the parties' contractual intent was that the Vessel be moored at the Orleans Marina for, if not the majority, at least some portion of hurricane season. We acknowledge that the email exchanges regarding the "mooring location" pertain to the Application Form, which requested the "primary mooring location" of the Vessel, and not the HQ or the HPP, which adduced "the marina or residence" where the Vessel would be "located" during hurricane season. Nevertheless, we conclude that the evidence also crystallizes the meaning of the HPP's representation about where the Vessel would be "located."

First, both the Application Form's request and the HPP substantively center on the Vessel's location during hurricane season. Whatever the distinctions between the "primary mooring location" and the "marina or residence" where the Vessel would be "located" during the season, Gray Group listed the Orleans Marina in response to both. At bottom, the extrinsic communications between the parties illuminate the parties' intent as to both the Application Form and the HPP: Great Lakes requested that Gray Group provide the marina where the Vessel would be located for the same reason it **[—14—]** requested its primary mooring location, *viz.*, because the insurer rated its policy premium "on the assumption of where the [V]essel [would] be for the majority of the season." *Cf. Chesapeake Energy Corp. v. Bank of New York Mellon Tr. Co., N.A.*, 773 F.3d 110, 116 (2d Cir. 2014) (rejecting proposed interpretation where "it cause[d] the word to carry different meanings in different iterations within the same contractual provision, indeed within the same sentence").

Inversely, Gray Group proffers no evidence to suggest a different interpretation of the HPP's representation. This dearth of proof to the contrary only buttresses the district court's interpretation of the HPP's language. *See Jefferson Block 24 Oil & Gas*, 652 F.3d at 589; *see also* FED. R. CIV. P. 56(c)(1)(A).

[5] We discern no error in the district court's determination that the HPP's representation as to where the Vessel would be located is ambiguous. And Gray Group does not contend otherwise.

Finally, and logically, the HPP's representation about the "marina or residence" where the Vessel would be "located" must mean *something*. Whether the provision means that the Vessel was to be located at the Orleans Marina "the majority of hurricane season," or for some lesser period, or for only intermittent docking, it is undisputed that the Vessel was *never* at the Orleans Marina during the 2020 hurricane **{–352–}** season. Thus, regardless of the precise requirement that the HPP imposed, Gray Group did not meet it. All that remains is to determine the effect of that lapse.

4.

The district court concluded that the HPP's representation regarding the Vessel's "marina or residence" location was a warranty such that Gray Group's breach of it voided the policy both under New York law and the terms of the policy. We consider only the latter justification and easily conclude that the district court did not err in its analysis.

The policy provides that: **[—15—]**

> Where any term herein is referred to as a 'warranty' or where any reference is made herein to the term 'warranted,' the term shall be deemed a warranty and regardless of whether the same expressly provides that any breach will void this insuring agreement from inception, it is hereby agreed that any such breach will void this policy from inception.

The HPP expressly identifies its contents, including the information in question, as warranties, providing that the insured "declare[s] that the particulars and answers in this form are correct and complete in every respect," and that "this declaration and warranty shall be incorporated in its entirety into any relevant policy of insurance." Therefore, under the terms of the policy, as validly augmented by the HPP, Gray Group warranted that the Vessel would be "located" at the Orleans Marina during hurricane season. Gray Group's breach of that warranty voided the policy *ab initio*, such that Great Lakes properly denied coverage.

III.

The Hello Dolly VI never got "back where [she] belong[ed]." Gray Group's representations to the contrary were validly incorporated into the policy as warranties, and Gray Group's breach of its warranties justified Great Lakes's denial of coverage when the Hello Dolly sank. Accordingly, the district court properly granted summary judgment for Great Lakes.

AFFIRMED.

United States Court of Appeals
for the Fifth Circuit

No. 22-30398

IFG PORT HOLDINGS, L.L.C.
vs.
LAKE CHARLES HARBOR & TERMINAL DIST.

Appeal from the United States District Court for the Western District of Louisiana

Decided: September 21, 2023

Citation: 82 F.4th 402, 11 Adm. R. 336 (5th Cir. 2023).

Before **GRAVES, HIGGINSON,** and **DOUGLAS,** Circuit Judges.

[—1—] {-404-} HIGGINSON, Circuit Judge: **{-405-}**

In 1979, Congress authorized Article III judges to refer civil cases to non-Article III magistrate judges "[u]pon consent of the parties." Federal Magistrate Act of 1979, Pub. L. No. 96-82, 93 Stat. 643, 643. Five years later, then-Judge Anthony Kennedy explained, writing for the *en banc* Ninth Circuit, that "consent of the parties is essential to the constitutionality of the Act." *Pacemaker Diagnostic Clinic of Am., Inc. v. Instromedix, Inc.*, 725 F.2d 537, 546 (9th Cir. 1984) (en banc). Shortly after, our court followed the lead of other circuits in upholding the constitutionality of consent-based **[—2—]** magistrate-judge referrals. *Puryear v. Ede's Ltd.*, 731 F.2d 1153, 1154 (5th Cir. 1984).

In this case, the parties consented to have their sprawling commercial dispute tried before a United States magistrate judge. But, allegedly unbeknownst to the defendant, the judge was longtime family friends with the lead trial lawyer for the plaintiff. Specifically, the lawyer had been a groomsman in the judge's own wedding, and the judge officiated the wedding of the lawyer's daughter three months before this lawsuit was filed. None of this information was disclosed to the defendant. After a twenty-day bench trial, the magistrate judge rendered judgment for the plaintiff, awarding $124.5 million, including over $100 million in trebled damages.

After the issuance of the judgment and award, the defendant learned about the undisclosed longstanding friendship and sought to have the magistrate-judge referral vacated. The district judge denied the request and denied discovery on the issue. The defendant now appeals.

We conclude that the facts asserted here, if true, raise serious doubts about the validity of the defendant's constitutionally essential consent to have its case tried by this magistrate judge. We therefore VACATE the district court's order. Because the facts are not sufficiently developed for us to decide whether the defendant's consent was validly given or whether vacatur of the referral is otherwise warranted, we REMAND to the district court for an evidentiary inquiry consistent with this opinion.

I.

This is an appeal from a judgment following a twenty-day bench trial before a magistrate judge. The case involves a years-long contract dispute between a commercial tenant, plaintiff-appellee IFG Port Holdings, LLC **[—3—]** ("IFG"), and its commercial landlord, defendant-appellant the Lake Charles Harbor & Terminal District, d/b/a the Port of Lake Charles ("the Port"). Following the trial, the magistrate judge entered judgment in favor of IFG and awarded it more than $124 million. The Port appeals.

A.

The Port sits on the corner of Contraband Bayou and a federal ship channel in Lake Charles, Louisiana. This dispute involves Berth 8, which sits at the very corner of the intersection of the two waterways. Starting around 2007, IFG and the Port began talks about IFG's desire to use Berth 8 to develop an export grain terminal **{-406-}** where vessels would load and unload cargo for shipment. In January 2008, IFG and the Port executed a Letter of Intent ("LOI"), which explained that the waterway alongside Berth 8 would need to be dredged to a lower depth than its current state. The dispute in this case revolves principally around the question of which party,

IFG or the Port, had the responsibility to secure the permitting necessary to complete the dredging.

In 2011, IFG and the Port executed the Ground Lease Agreement (the "Lease"), which provided that IFG would "arrange for and complete the initial dredging" to a depth of forty-two feet, but did not specify which party would obtain the necessary permitting from the U.S. Army Corps of Engineers.

IFG's facility was completed in July of 2015. But no permit had been issued for the necessary dredging, so the dredging had not happened. On August 6, 2015, IFG sent a letter to the Port stating that the waterway must be dredged to forty-two feet, and that, short of that depth, IFG's business capabilities would be "substantially limit[ed]." Noting that the Port had informed IFG that certain necessary soil testing and "the subsequent consent and permitting by relevant authorities" would take several months or longer, **[—4—]** IFG asserted that the "circumstances are beyond the control of IFG and are an event of Force Majeure as contemplated by the Lease."

On September 30, 2015, the Port responded with a letter (the "Default Notice") asserting that IFG was in breach of its obligations under the Lease. The Port wrote that "IFG was free to begin dredging Berth No. 8" as of January 1, 2012, and that "IFG chose to take no action or even discuss dredging relative to Berth 8 and Contraband Bayou until January 2015, a mere six months before the Rent Commencement Date." The Port stated that, "upon issuance of the required Corps permit amendment allowing for dredging to a depth of -42 feet MLG [mean low gulf], the dredging IFG is required to perform can proceed." The Port concluded that "the delays in the performance of IFG's dredging obligations . . . are totally within the control of IFG," and gave notice that IFG was in default of the Lease.

On January 29, 2016, IFG sued the Port in the U.S. District Court for the Western District of Louisiana. IFG alleged that the Port had breached the Lease and violated the Louisiana Unfair Trade Practices Act ("LUTPA"). IFG sought, *inter alia*, "[d]eclaratory relief finding that the alleged dredging default . . . [was] issued by the Port to IFG in error," an "injunction ordering the Port to withdraw all outstanding default notices against IFG and IFG's bank," an "injunction ordering the Port to proceed diligently to obtain the required amended dredging permit allowing IFG to dredge to 42 feet as required by the Lease," as well as "[a]ll monetary damages as may be appropriate and proven at trial including treble damages and attorney fees."

On January 27, 2017, the parties consented to have the case tried by a magistrate judge. On February 2, 2017, then-Chief Judge Dee Drell referred the case to Magistrate Judge Kathleen Kay. **[—5—]**

B.

Magistrate Judge Kay held a bench trial consisting of twenty days of trial testimony. Trial started on March 18, 2019 and ended on April 30, 2019. Twenty-three witnesses testified in total. On July 31, 2020, Magistrate Judge Kay issued a lengthy written order containing her findings of fact and conclusions of law.

In her written order, Magistrate Judge Kay found that the Port, *inter alia*, **{-407-}** "breached its contract with IFG . . . by failing to secure the appropriate permits that would allow IFG to complete its obligation to dredge to the depth designated in the contract by the time the facility opened in July of 2015." Magistrate Judge Kay found that while the Lease did not specify which party bore the obligation to acquire the permitting necessary for dredging, "the actions of the parties before execution of the [Lease] and after execution show clearly the Port knew these were its responsibilities." Magistrate Judge Kay therefore found the Port "liable to IFG for losses attributable to IFG's inability to market itself as a fully operational terminal and to load larger, deeper draft cargo vessels as was intended by its original business plan."

Magistrate Judge Kay found that IFG was entitled to lost-profits damages for each vessel "lost" by virtue of the Port's breach, *i.e.*, vessels that were "unable to be loaded for lack of proper depth at the IFG facility." Following post-trial briefing based on the appropriate formula for this calculation, Magistrate Judge Kay found that IFG's lost profits attributable to the Port's breach totaled $41,696,272.

Magistrate Judge Kay further found that the Port's conduct violated LUTPA, which proscribes "[u]nfair methods of competition and unfair or deceptive acts or practices in the conduct of any trade or commerce." LA. REV. STAT. § 51:1405(A). She listed nine "acts of conduct" by the Port **[—6—]** that she found "to be offensive to established public policy and to be immoral, unethical, oppressive, and unscrupulous resulting in substantial injuries to IFG." Magistrate Judge Kay found that the Port's "unscrupulous activities were engaged in purposely by the Port to cause IFG to abandon its project and leave the Port of Lake Charles."

Magistrate Judge Kay further determined that IFG was entitled to treble damages corresponding to IFG's lost profits starting from the date of an April 2016 written notice sent from the Attorney General to the Port, through August of 2019, when the lost-profits window closed. The trebled lost profits, plus the non-trebled lost profits, resulted in a damage award of $111,621,264.

Magistrate Judge Kay also ordered various other awards to IFG, including over $9 million in prejudgment interest and more than $3 million in attorney's fees. The ultimate award in favor of IFG totaled $124,531,652.

C.

After the issuance of Magistrate Judge Kay's order, the parties engaged in years of post-trial motion practice pertaining primarily to the question of diversity jurisdiction and the referral to the magistrate judge. Specifically, the Port asserted that IFG, as a limited liability company ("LLC"), had not sufficiently alleged the citizenship of its owner members and moved to dismiss for lack of subject-matter jurisdiction on that basis. The Port further alleged that it had uncovered a previously undisclosed relationship between Magistrate Judge Kay and William Monk, IFG's lead trial counsel, and accordingly moved to have the district judge vacate the referral to the magistrate judge. IFG prevailed on both the jurisdictional and magistrate-judge-referral disputes. These two issues, which remain live on appeal, are discussed in further detail *infra* Sections II and III, respectively. **[—7—]**

Magistrate Judge Kay entered judgment in favor of IFG on March 14, 2022, and a second judgment, awarding further attorney's fees and costs, on May 19, 2022. She denied the Port's final motion for a new trial on June 13, 2022. **{-408-}**

The Port appealed, raising challenges relating to subject-matter jurisdiction, the denial of its motion to vacate the referral to the magistrate judge, and various merits issues arising from the bench trial.

II.

The Port first raises a series of challenges relating to the district court's management of the parties' dispute regarding whether IFG had established subject-matter jurisdiction.

A.

While the Port stops short of affirmatively contending that this court lacks subject-matter jurisdiction, it attempts to raise doubts about it. We must first satisfy ourselves that we have jurisdiction before proceeding to the merits of the Port's other challenges. *See Steel Co. v. Citizens for a Better Env't*, 523 U.S. 83, 93-102 (1998). We therefore first address whether IFG has established federal jurisdiction. This court reviews *de novo* the determination that diversity jurisdiction exists. *Bynane v. Bank of N.Y. Mellon for CWMBS, Inc. Asset-Backed Certificates Series 2006-24*, 866 F.3d 351, 356 (5th Cir. 2017) (citation omitted).

IFG invokes diversity jurisdiction under 28 U.S.C. § 1332, which gives district courts jurisdiction over "all civil actions where the matter in controversy exceeds the sum or value of $75,000" and "is between citizens of different States," or "citizens of a State and citizens or subjects of a foreign state." *Id.* § 1332(a)(1)-(2). Diversity jurisdiction requires "complete **[—8—]** diversity," which means that "all persons on one side of the controversy [must] be citizens of different states than all persons on the other side." *McLaughlin v. Miss. Power Co.*, 376 F.3d 344, 353 (5th Cir. 2004) (per curiam) (citation omitted). The burden of establishing complete diversity rests on the party invoking federal jurisdiction. *Howery v. Allstate Ins. Co.*, 243 F.3d 912, 919 (5th Cir. 2001). "In making a jurisdictional assessment, a federal court . . . may look to any record evidence, and may receive affidavits, deposition testimony or live testimony concerning the facts underlying the citizenship of the parties." *Coury v. Prot*, 85 F.3d 244, 249 (5th Cir. 1996). "The court has wide, but not unfettered, discretion to determine what evidence to use in making its determination of jurisdiction." *Id.* (citation omitted).

It is undisputed that the Port is a Louisiana citizen, as it is a political subdivision created by statute. LA. REV. STAT. § 34:201 ("The Lake Charles Harbor and Terminal District is created as a political subdivision of the state . . . ."); *Moor v. Alameda Cnty.*, 411 U.S. 693, 717 (1973) ("[A] political subdivision of a State, unless it is simply 'the arm or alter ego of the State,' is a citizen of the State for diversity purposes." (citations omitted)). IFG is an LLC, and an LLC's citizenship for diversity purposes is determined by the citizenship of all of its members. *Harvey v. Grey Wolf Drilling Co.*, 542 F.3d 1077, 1080 (5th Cir. 2008). Accordingly, for complete diversity to exist, none of IFG's members may be citizens of Louisiana.

The Port first emphasizes that IFG did not adequately allege diversity in its pretrial pleadings. The Port is correct. To meet its burden of establishing complete diversity, a litigant must "distinctly and affirmatively allege the citizenship of the parties." *Smith v. Toyota Motor Corp.*, 978 F.3d 280, 282 (5th Cir. 2020) (cleaned up) (citation omitted). When LLCs are involved, the party invoking jurisdiction must "specifically allege the citizenship of every member of every LLC . . . involved **{-409-}** in [the] litigation." **[—9—]** *Id.* (quoting *Settlement Funding, LLC v. Rapid Settlements, Ltd.*, 851 F.3d 530, 536 (5th Cir. 2017)). Here, IFG did not allege the citizenship of its members in its initial complaint, nor in any of its amended or supplemental complaints filed before trial.[1] The jurisdictional allegations were therefore deficient at the pleading stage.

But this deficiency was cured by IFG's post-trial amendment. Under 28 U.S.C. § 1653, "[d]efective allegations of jurisdiction may be amended . . . in the trial or appellate courts." *Id.*; *see Howery*, 243 F.3d at 920 n.39 ("[P]rior to judgment, a party may amend its pleadings to allege omitted jurisdictional facts."). The Port acknowledges this rule but argues that the amended allegations are "generalized" and "remain[] defective." But the Port does not explain why this is so. The amended complaint includes a two-page exhibit fully alleging the citizenship of each owner-member of the LLC, as required by the case law. Nor does the Port otherwise cast doubt on or articulate any substantive challenge to IFG's foreign citizenship, which is supported by an ownership chart,[2] as well as multiple affidavits and their attachments.[3] Put differently, the Port does not seriously argue that diversity **[—10—]** is lacking. Because the record documents indicate that none of IFG's

[1] IFG alleged merely that the court "has subject matter jurisdiction over the claims made in this matter based on diversity of citizenship," and that "[c]omplete diversity exists because the Plaintiff and the sole Defendant to those claims share no common state of incorporation or principal place of business and Plaintiff's claims in this matter exceed $75,000." IFG's subsequent amendments to the complaint did not modify or add to this jurisdictional allegation.

[2] The chart lists the entities, sub-entities, and individuals that comprise IFG Port Holdings, LLC, and includes residence and citizenship information for each. None of the listed places—of residence, citizenship, or state of organization—is Louisiana.

[3] Before trial, IFG filed into the record two sworn and notarized affidavits from its CEO, attesting that (1) "[n]o individual owner of IFG, directly or indirectly, is a resident or citizen of the State of Louisiana," and (2) "[n]o juridical entity having any ownership interest in IFG Port Holdings LLC, at any level, is a resident of or has its principal place of business located within the State of Louisiana." After trial, IFG filed more affidavits, attesting to the citizenship, domicile, and, as applicable, principal places of business of the **[—10—]** people and entities comprising IFG as of January 29, 2016, when IFG filed its lawsuit. Again, the materials contain no evidence of Louisiana citizenship.

members was a citizen of Louisiana on the date this suit commenced, and because the Port offers no specific reason to doubt that IFG is not a citizen of Louisiana, we conclude that complete diversity exists.

B.

The Port relatedly requests that the case be remanded so the Port can take depositions relating to IFG's ownership. We reject this request. The party seeking jurisdictional discovery must "make clear which 'specific facts' he expects discovery to find." *Johnson v. TheHuffingtonPost.com, Inc.*, 21 F.4th 314, 326 (5th Cir. 2021) (citation omitted). The Port fails to do so. It seeks to cross-examine IFG's owners who submitted sworn affidavits attesting to IFG's citizenship, but it does not articulate what it expects a deposition of those affiants to uncover. The Port does not raise any credibility concerns regarding IFG's citizenship evidence, *compare Settlement Funding, LLC*, 851 F.3d at 537 (noting that the defendant "brought to this court's attention filings with the [SEC] that cast doubt on the accuracy of the [affidavit]" containing an LLC's citizenship allegations), nor does it contend that the **{–410–}** documents are facially deficient to carry IFG's burden to establish jurisdiction. The Port simply asks to continue probing so it can "ascertain" IFG's citizenship. This court has rejected litigants' attempts to conduct "jurisdictional fishing expedition[s]," *Johnson*, 21 F.4th at 326 (citation omitted), and we reject the Port's attempt to do so here.

C.

Finally, the Port asserts that IFG may not rely on sealed documents to establish diversity. Specifically, the Port contends that "[t]here is no legal **[—11—]** basis for a court sealing a complaint or exhibits concerning diversity," and that "[j]urisdiction cannot be asserted based on sealed documents." To the extent the Port contends that, as a general rule, jurisdictional facts cannot be established by material filed under seal, the Port cites no authority for this proposition, and we find none. Suggesting the contrary, district courts have relied on sealed material to find facts supporting diversity jurisdiction. *See, e.g., Madrid v. Galp Waters Ltd. P'ship*, No. 12-3252, 2014 WL 12539253, at *1 n.4 (S.D. Tex. June 6, 2014) (finding diversity jurisdiction based on the defendants' sealed "statement disclosing the citizenship of those persons composing [their] partnerships"); *Brandner v. State Farm Mut. Auto. Ins. Co.*, No. 17-454, 2017 WL 4678486, at *2 (M.D. La. Sept. 7, 2017), *report and recommendation adopted*, 2017 WL 4678217 (M.D. La. Oct. 17, 2017) (finding the amount in controversy required by § 1332 satisfied based on a proof-of-loss document filed under seal); *cf. Payton v. Entergy Corp.*, No. 12-2452, 2013 WL 5722712, at *12 n.7 (E.D. La. Oct. 21, 2013) (making specific citizenship findings in a sealed addendum, in the context of a CAFA diversity dispute under 28 U.S.C. § 1332(d)). Nothing in § 1332 suggests that this practice is a problem. In other words, the existence of jurisdiction is not undermined by the fact that certain supporting evidence is under seal.

However, the Port also argues that Magistrate Judge Kay abused her discretion in sealing the material related to IFG's citizenship. The Port asks us to unseal "[a]ll parts of the sealed record," including "IFG's amended complaint, its exhibit, all related pleadings, and the magistrate's order." In this sense, the Port does not attack the jurisdictional findings themselves and instead seeks only to have the jurisdiction-related materials unsealed. The Port is correct that the materials should be unsealed.

When a party seeks to file material under seal, the judge must "undertake a case-by-case, 'document-by-document,' 'line-by-line' balancing of 'the public's common law right of access against the interests **[—12—]** favoring nondisclosure'" and explain its sealing decision "at 'a level of detail that will allow for this Court's review.'" *Binh Hoa Le v. Exeter Fin. Corp.*, 990 F.3d 410, 419 (5th Cir. 2021) (quoting *United States v. Sealed Search Warrants*, 868 F.3d 385, 393, 397 (5th Cir. 2017)). A court errs "if it 'ma[kes] no mention of the presumption in favor of the public's access to judicial records' and fails to 'articulate any reasons that would support sealing.'" *Id.* (alteration in original) (quoting *SEC v. Van*

Waeyenberghe, 990 F.2d 845, 849 (5th Cir. 1993)).

The appellate record in this case is 40,705 pages long, and approximately 760 of those pages are sealed. It appears from the record—and the parties do not contend otherwise—that each sealed document filed by the parties was first subject to a motion to seal and a court order granting **{-411-}** the motion.[4] The orders—themselves unsealed—are generally either one-sentence text orders on the docket, or simple signoffs on the movants' proposed orders, containing no reasoning. The only reasoned decision regarding the decision to seal is the magistrate judge's March 2, 2022 order denying the Port's motion to unseal IFG's ownership chart.

We recently instructed that "courts should be ungenerous with their discretion to seal judicial records," *id.* at 418, and warned that "we heavily disfavor sealing information placed in the judicial record," *June Med. Servs., LLC v. Phillips*, 22 F.4th 512, 519-20 (5th Cir. 2022) (citation omitted). In light of these admonitions, it is clear that this record was over-sealed. The district judge and magistrate judge permitted sealing of essentially everything related to IFG's ownership, including not only the direct evidence of citizenship (*e.g.*, the affidavits, ownership chart, and identification **[—13—]** documents), but also all related motions, memoranda, and court orders. And until the Port sought to unseal the ownership chart, Magistrate Judge Kay's orders permitting sealing were unaccompanied by any explanation. These orders fail to acknowledge the public interest in access to judicial records and "fail[] to 'articulate any reasons that would support sealing.'" *Le*, 990 F.3d at 419 (citation omitted). These orders must be vacated.

One order requires separate treatment. As noted, Magistrate Judge Kay did issue a reasoned decision in denying the Port's motion to unseal IFG's ownership chart. In her order, Magistrate Judge Kay acknowledged the "presumed public interest in the transparency of judicial proceedings and open access to judicial records," and noted that the analysis proceeds case by case. But she concluded that disclosure of the sealed information would "impinge on the privacy interests of [IFG's] members." Magistrate Judge Kay further found that the information is of minimal interest to the public as it is relevant only to IFG's citizenship and not "the larger substantive issues in the case." Magistrate Judge Kay stated that, while she "would not endorse [a] blanket rule that would allow record documents related to citizenship . . . to be placed under seal in all circumstances," the circumstances surrounding this sealed material are "unique" because the Port contested IFG's citizenship after trial, when discovery had already concluded. Had the dispute played out before trial, Magistrate Judge Kay explained, "some or all of the information now placed in the record under seal might have been exchanged via written discovery or deposition, instead of being filed directly into the record." Ultimately, she credited IFG's "legitimate privacy interest" and denied the Port's request to unseal.

This particular ruling, therefore, at least dodges the biggest pitfalls flagged in *Le*: that the lower court must "mention . . . the presumption in favor of the public's access to judicial records" and articulate its reasons in support of sealing. *Id.* But Magistrate Judge Kay nonetheless erred in **[—14—]** concluding that sealing of this chart was warranted. The affidavit from IFG's CEO makes only a conclusory assertion that the chart is "competitively sensitive for IFG" and its owners and makes a vague reference to the chart's reflecting "certain tax considerations." Her order is similarly nonspecific, referring to undefined "privacy interests" of the LLC's owners. It is unclear why the ownership of this LLC is sensitive. There is no suggestion that sealing is necessary, for instance, to "protect[] trade secrets or the identities of confidential **{-412-}** informants." *Id.* IFG appears by all counts to be a normal private litigant, and its briefing on appeal does not suggest otherwise. It says in its brief merely that "a court may

[4] The apparent exception is Magistrate Judge Kay's own sealed orders, which the court was, of course, able to file under seal with no accompanying motion practice.

allow filings of materials containing sensitive business information under seal to prevent the competitive harm that could result from making them public." But IFG does not explain why the information is sensitive nor what "competitive harm" would result from unsealing. IFG's unspecified and unsubstantiated privacy concerns do not amount to "*compelling* countervailing interests" sufficient to warrant nondisclosure of presumptively public judicial records. *Id.* at 421 (emphasis added).

In light of the strong presumption against sealing judicial records, *see June Med.*, 22 F.4th at 519-22; *Le*, 990 F.3d at 421 (noting that sealings are "often unjustified" and "urg[ing] litigants and . . . judicial colleagues to zealously guard the public's right of access to judicial records . . . so 'that justice may not be done in a corner'" (citation omitted)), and finding that the presumption is not rebutted here, we vacate all of the sealing orders in this case, including the denial of the Port's motion to unseal. On remand, the district court shall reevaluate—with specific reasons and determinations as to each document, and with appreciation of the "arduous" standard for sealing, *June Med.*, 22 F.4th at 521—whether the material previously sealed in this case should remain under seal. *See id.* at 521-22 (vacating the district **[—15—]** court's sealing orders and issuing a limited remand to the district court to evaluate the orders "under the proper legal standards" within thirty days).[5]

* * *

The district court did not err in concluding that it had diversity jurisdiction nor in denying the Port further leave to continue conducting jurisdictional discovery into IFG's citizenship. We affirm as to these issues.

But the record generated throughout the jurisdictional dispute was over-sealed based on inadequate justification. We thus vacate the court's sealing orders and remand to the district court to determine, with appropriate reasons, to what extent the material currently maintained under seal should remain under seal. If no revised order issues within ninety days of issuance of mandate in this case, all sealed material in the case shall be unsealed.

III.

The Port also contends that the district judge erred in denying its motion to vacate the referral to Magistrate Judge Kay, on the basis that Magistrate Judge Kay did not disclose her longstanding friendship with IFG's lead trial counsel. We take up this issue next. **[—16—]**

A.

On January 29, 2016, this case was assigned to District Judge Patricia Minaldi **{-413-}** and Magistrate Judge Kathleen Kay. After Judge Minaldi took a leave of absence, the parties discussed with the magistrate judge the possibility of consenting to a trial before her. On January 27, 2017, counsel for the Port and IFG consented to have a magistrate judge "conduct all proceedings . . . including trial, the entry of final judgment, and all post-trial proceedings." The case caption on the consent form specified that the case was assigned to Magistrate Judge Kay. The following week, then-Chief Judge Drell referred the case to Magistrate Judge Kay.

At some unspecified time, Magistrate Judge Kay told the parties that the daughter of William Monk, IFG's lead trial counsel, was

[5] The Port repeatedly suggests that the material should be unsealed in part because jurisdiction is at issue. *See* Gray Br. 4 [ECF 80, 11] ("[B]ecause diversity jurisdiction involving an LLC is based on the citizenship of each of its members, there can be no legitimate claim that the corporate structure of the LLC is 'confidential.'"); *id.* at 5 [ECF 80, 12] (contending that "[t]his Circuit's rulings . . . reject the notion that such information is confidential," and citing a case requiring that citizenship be alleged in detail). But as explained above, we see no reason why the jurisdictional nature of the dispute would bear, in either direction, on the decision to seal. Our vacatur of the sealing orders is based not on the fact that the sealed material goes to jurisdiction, but instead on (1) the complete lack of explanation in the unreasoned orders, and (2) the weakness of the proffered privacy interests invoked in the one reasoned order.

one of her law clerks.[6] Magistrate Judge Kay told the parties that the law clerk would be screened off the case.

The bench trial ended on April 30, 2019, and Magistrate Judge Kay issued her reasons for judgment on July 31, 2020. The Port represents that Magistrate Judge Kay's order, ruling against the Port, "contained harsh language," characterizing the Port's conduct as, *inter alia*, "nefarious," "extortionary," and "sanctimonious." The Port asserts that the harshness **[—17—]** of the order "prompted [it] to investigate." The Port does not specify by what means it conducted this investigation.

On October 21, 2020, the Port filed a motion to vacate the referral to Magistrate Judge Kay. The Port attached an affidavit from its counsel, Matthew Mize, in support of the motion. Mize asserted that the Port's "investigation ultimately revealed that, not only did one of Mr. Monk's daughters work as a law clerk for Magistrate Judge Kay, as was disclosed; but also that:

(a) Mr. Monk had served as a groomsman in Magistrate Judge Kay's own wedding; and

(b) Magistrate Judge Kay had officiated the wedding of another of Mr. Monk's daughters approx.-imately three months prior to IFG filing the instant lawsuit on January 29, 2016."

Mize continued, "[T]he above events indicate and create the appearance of there being a longstanding personal relationship between Magistrate Judge Kay, Mr. Monk and his family." He asserted that, "[h]ad the above-listed events, and the complete nature of the relationship between the Monks and Magistrate Judge Kay been disclosed, the Port and its counsel simply would not have consented to the referral of this matter to Magistrate Judge Kay for trial." On November 10, 2020, the Port also moved for leave to conduct discovery to determine "the full extent of that relationship," including a deposition of Monk.

On January 15, 2021, District Judge Terry Doughty denied the Port's motion to vacate and denied discovery into the issue. Judge Doughty noted that the Port consented to the referral, and that it was undisputed that Magistrate Judge Kay **{-414-}** "neither coerced, strong-armed, or acted in any way improperly by offering counsel the options available to them once Judge Minaldi took a leave of absence, including the option to consent to proceed **[—18—]** before her." He further noted that Magistrate Judge Kay's rulings over the course of the litigation sometimes favored the Port and sometimes favored IFG, and that the Port had never before alleged that Magistrate Judge Kay's rulings evinced any bias. Judge Doughty explained that Magistrate Judge Kay's recusal list did not include Monk and that "some prior social and/or professional interactions" are common in "relatively small legal communities, such as Lake Charles." Analogizing to the recusal context, Judge Doughty stated that the personal relationship alleged in the affidavit "do[es] not create a mandatory obligation of recusal" and indeed "[is] not even significant enough, standing alone, to require disclosure." The district court further stated that "[t]he fact that the Port is now unhappy with [Magistrate Judge Kay's] factual findings and legal conclusions is not a basis to vacate the reference."

[6] There is no docket entry memorializing Magistrate Judge Kay's statement that her law clerk was Monk's daughter, so the precise timing and content of the statement are uncertain. The sequence of events as recounted in an affidavit from Matthew Mize (the Port's counsel) suggests that the discussion occurred some time after the parties consented to trial by the magistrate. Specifically, Mize first notes that the parties executed their consent agreement on January 27, 2017 and then states that, at a status conference held in chambers, Magistrate Judge Kay advised that her law clerk was Monk's daughter. The docket reflects that Magistrate Judge Kay held conferences on February 23, 2017 and September 12, 2017. But the minute entries address scheduling and make no mention of Magistrate Judge Kay's current employment of an immediate family member of Monk. That said, there is no dispute that this information was given and unobjected to.

B.

"Upon the consent of the parties, a full-time United States magistrate judge . . . may conduct any or all proceedings in a jury or nonjury civil matter and order the entry of judgment in the case . . . ." 28 U.S.C.A. § 636(c)(1). The court may vacate the referral of a civil matter to a magistrate judge "for good cause shown on its own motion, or under extraordinary circumstances shown by any party." 28 U.S.C. § 636(c)(4). Rule 73(b) of the Federal Rules of Civil Procedure contains an analogous provision. FED. R. CIV. P. 73(b)(3) ("On its own for good cause—or when a party shows extraordinary circumstances—the district judge may vacate a referral to a magistrate judge under this rule."). We review denials of motions to vacate a magistrate-judge referral for abuse of discretion. *Sanches v. Carrollton-Farmers Branch Indep. Sch. Dist.*, 647 F.3d 156, 171 (5th Cir. 2011) (citing *Lyn-Lea Travel Corp. v. Am. Airlines, Inc.*, 283 F.3d 282, 292 (5th Cir. 2002)). **[—19—]**

In *Carter v. Land Sea Services, Inc.*, we instructed that "a variety of factors" should guide a court's discretion in determining whether to permit withdrawal of consent to a trial by a magistrate. 816 F.2d 1018, 1021 (5th Cir. 1987). The court explained:

> Among the things a court may consider are: undue delay, inconvenience to the court and witnesses, prejudice to the parties, whether the movant is acting *pro se*,[7] whether consent was voluntary and uncoerced, whether the motion is made in good faith or is dilatory and contrived, the possibility of bias or prejudice on the part of the magistrate, and whether the interests of justice would best be served by holding a party to his consent.

Id. (internal citations omitted).

Here, although the Port and IFG dispute the conclusion that arises from application of the *Carter* factors, they agree that the factors constitute the appropriate framework for our analysis. We accept that the *Carter* factors guide our inquiry and thus proceed through those factors to assess whether Magistrate Judge Kay's nondisclosure of her longstanding friendship with IFG's trial counsel amounts to "extraordinary circumstances" **{-415-}** such that Judge Doughty abused his discretion in denying the Port's motion to vacate the referral. In so doing, we treat the uncontradicted assertions in the Mize affidavit as true but acknowledge the significant factual gaps in the record before us, and, indeed, conclude that this affidavit must be subject to adversarial treatment and district-court verification.

1. [—20—]

Our court in *Carter* instructs that courts are to assess whether the party's consent to the magistrate-judge referral "was voluntary and uncoerced." *Id.* The Port contends that its consent to have its case tried by Magistrate Judge Kay was vitiated by the nondisclosure of her relationship with Monk. Specifically, the Mize affidavit states that, if "the complete nature of the relationship between the Monks and Magistrate Judge Kay [had] been disclosed, the Port and its counsel simply would not have consented to the referral of this matter to Magistrate Judge Kay for trial."

We emphasize at the outset that party consent is the "touchstone of magistrate judge jurisdiction." *Anderson v. Woodcreek Venture Ltd.*, 351 F.3d 911, 914 (9th Cir. 2003). As courts of appeal across the country observed decades ago, the constitutionality of § 636(c) magistrate-judge referrals depends on the requirement that the parties give their consent.[8] *See Puryear*, 731 F.2d at 1154; Magistrate Judges Div., Admin. Off., U.S. Cts., *A Constitutional Analysis of Magistrate Judge Authority*, 150 F.R.D. 247, 306 n.3 (1993) (collecting cases). Congress, in passing the relevant provisions, agreed. In recommending that the consent-referral provisions pass, the Senate Judiciary Committee explained:

[7] The Port was represented by counsel. This factor is not relevant here, so we do not address it further.

[8] The constitutionality of consent-based referrals depends also on the "power of the district court to vacate the reference to the magistrate on its own motion." *Puryear*, 731 F.2d at 1154.

> The bill makes clear that the voluntary consent of the parties is required before any civil action may be referred to a magistrate. In light of this requirement of consent, no witness at the hearings on the bill found any constitutional question that could be raised against the provision.

S. REP. NO. 96-74, at 4 (1979). Consent to magistrate-judge jurisdiction is thus no formality; it is constitutionally essential. **[—21—]**

For these reasons, we reject IFG's attempts to downplay the significance of the voluntariness of party consent, which it calls "just one of several factors." Our opinion in *Carter* is clear that "when a party can show his consent was obtained involuntarily or through undue influence, § 636(c) requires the authorization of withdrawal." *Carter*, 816 F.2d at 1021 (citing *Boykin v. Alabama*, 395 U.S. 238 (1969)). This proposition is reinforced by the constitutional backdrop just described. We thus reiterate that, notwithstanding any other "factors," the *absence* of valid party consent to a magistrate-judge referral will end the inquiry. If an Article III court concludes that a party's consent to a trial by a magistrate judge was not validly given, it has no choice but to order that the referral be vacated. *See id.*; *see also Kofoed v. Int'l Bhd. of Elec. Workers, Loc. 48*, 237 F.3d 1001, 1004 (9th Cir. 2001) ("Where the magistrate judge has not received the full consent of the parties, he has no authority to enter judgment in the case, and any purported judgment is a nullity." (citation omitted)).

Having established that party consent under § 636(c) is a constitutional imperative, we turn now to the consent given in **{–416–}** this case. IFG contends that the Port's consent here was valid. IFG argues that the Port's consent was voluntarily given, as Magistrate Judge Kay did not "coerce" or "strong-arm" the parties into consenting to the referral. But, although there has been no suggestion that the Port was coerced into consenting to Magistrate Judge Kay's jurisdiction, IFG's argument answers only part of the question. It is of course critical that a party's consent to a magistrate-judge referral be *voluntary*, in that it is free from coercion or undue pressure. Appropriately, § 636 itself provides that a court's rules "for the reference of civil matters to magistrate judges shall include procedures to protect the voluntariness of the parties' consent." 28 U.S.C. § 636(c)(2). And Rule 73 of the Federal Rules of Civil Procedure contains a provision titled "Reminding the Parties About Consenting," which instructs that a "district **[—22—]** judge, magistrate judge, or other court official . . . must . . . advise [the parties] that they are free to withhold consent without adverse substantive consequences." FED. R. CIV. P. 73(b)(2). Again, here, there has been no suggestion that the Port's consent was induced by coercion or other influences that might compromise voluntariness.

But freedom from coercion alone does not render a party's consent constitutionally sufficient. Consent to a magistrate-judge referral—that is, a waiver of the right to an Article III adjudication—also cannot be valid if it is not given knowingly and intelligently. *See Wellness Int'l Network, Ltd. v. Sharif*, 575 U.S. 665, 685 (2015) ("emphasizing" that "a litigant's consent" to a non-Article III adjudication, "whether express or implied[,] must still be *knowing* and voluntary" (emphasis added)); *see also Norris v. Schotten*, 146 F.3d 314, 326 (6th Cir. 1998) (explaining that, in assessing a party's consent to a magistrate-judge referral, "[t]he record must show that the known right or privilege was waived by voluntary, *knowing*, and *intelligent* action" (emphasis added) (citations omitted)); *United States v. Dobey*, 751 F.2d 1140, 1143 (10th Cir. 1985) (upholding convictions following a jury trial before a magistrate judge because the defendants "consented to trial before a specifically designated magistrate and *knowingly* waived their right to trial before an Article III judge" (emphasis added)). Tellingly, in *Carter* we made repeated reference to the "knowing[ness]" of party consent. *Carter*, 816 F.2d at 1021 ("Once a right, even a fundamental right, is *knowingly* and voluntarily waived, a party has no constitutional right to recant at will." (emphasis added)); *id.* at 1022 (explaining that, there, the litigant's "consent was made *knowingly* and voluntarily" (emphasis added)). We thus make explicit what follows from the constitutional stakes of a party's waiver of his right to an Article III judge: A party's consent under § 636(c) to have its case tried by a non-Article III magistrate judge must be knowing. **[—23—]**

It is the Port's lack of knowledge that is at issue here. Neither party directs us to case law addressing whether a magistrate judge's nondisclosure of their longstanding friendship with lead, opposing counsel may undermine a party's consent to have that judge try its case. But we have no difficulty concluding that it may.

Consider even this incomplete record.

When the parties consented to the referral in 2017, the case had already been assigned to Magistrate Judge Kay. Indeed, the record reflects that Magistrate Judge Kay was involved in the consent conversation from the start. But when the parties discussed with Magistrate Judge Kay the possibility of consenting to a trial before her, neither Magistrate Judge Kay nor **{-417-}** Monk disclosed to the Port that there was a longstanding friendship between them. Puzzlingly, Magistrate Judge Kay saw it fit to advise counsel that Monk's daughter was her law clerk at the time—and that the daughter would be screened off the case—but she apparently stopped there. We presently must credit IFG's contention that this selective disclosure "left the impression that there was no other personal relationship with lead counsel."

Returning to knowingness, we must ask: Did the Port act knowingly when it agreed to have its multi-million-dollar dispute tried by a non-Article III judge who had an undisclosed longstanding friendship with counsel on the other side of the table? Would the Port have consented to have that non-Article III judge adjudicate this dispute if it knew that opposing counsel was a groomsman in the judge's wedding and that the judge officiated counsel's daughter's wedding mere months before this suit was filed? The Port says no, attesting in the Mize affidavit that, "[h]ad . . . the complete nature of the relationship between the Monks and Magistrate Judge Kay been disclosed, the Port and its counsel *simply would not have consented* to the referral of this matter to Magistrate Judge Kay for trial." **[—24—]**

Again, we do not have a complete factual record. Other than the Mize affidavit, the record contains no evidence of *what* disclosures were made, to *whom* they made, or *when*. The parties agree that Magistrate Judge Kay advised them that Monk's daughter was her law clerk, but there is no contemporaneous documentation even of this or when or how she was "walled" off from this case. Furthermore, the record contains no evidence beyond the Mize affidavit confirming the nature or extent of Magistrate Judge Kay's friendship with the Monks. Finally, and critically, although the Mize affidavit suggests that counsel did not learn about this friendship until after Magistrate Judge Kay's order and reasons, this assertion has not been subject to evidentiary testing and cross-examination.

These factual uncertainties preclude us from deciding, on this record, whether the Port's consent was knowingly and validly given. If, for instance, the facts alleged about this friendship (as deep and longstanding) are untrue, or if the friendship is otherwise distant—though it does not seem to be—then the nondisclosure may not render the Port's consent unknowing. Likewise, if the Port learned of the intimacy of the friendship *before* entry of judgment and chose to remain silent, then its consent would remain valid. *Roell v. Withrow*, 538 U.S. 580, 582 (2003) (holding that consent to a magistrate-judge referral "can be inferred from a party's conduct during litigation"). These hypotheticals serve not to exhaust the universe of possibilities but merely to illustrate why our record does not permit our dispositive determination of the issue.

2.

The parties also dispute whether these alleged facts demonstrate a "possibility of bias or prejudice on the part of the magistrate." *Carter*, 816 F.2d at 1021. IFG's central argument, echoing the district court, is that "friendships among judges and lawyers are common," especially in small **[—25—]** legal communities like Lake Charles. The Port, on the other hand, argues that Magistrate Judge Kay's friendship with the Monks was "deep" and "personal."

But as reflected by the parties' arguments, this is a highly fact-intensive inquiry. Because the district court conducted no evidentiary inquiry into the Port's assertions and denied the Port discovery on the issue, our appellate record on the friendship **{-418-}** consists *only* of the Mize affidavit. And the affidavit contains only those facts that we have now recounted many times: Monk's daughter was a law clerk for Magistrate Judge Kay around the time of consent (disclosed to the Port); Monk was a groomsman in Magistrate Judge Kay's wedding (not disclosed); and Magistrate Judge Kay officiated Monk's other daughter's wedding three months before this case was filed (not disclosed).

IFG would have us believe that the case law governing recusals under 28 U.S.C. § 455(a) sufficiently decides the issue. IFG is right to point out that our court's case law on judicial friendships, under the § 455 recusal standard, recognizes judges' friendships with lawyers. *See, e.g., Henderson v. Dep't of Pub. Safety & Corr.*, 901 F.2d 1288, 1295-96 (5th Cir. 1990) (holding that the disqualification criteria under § 455(a) were not met where the judge had known opposing counsel since counsel was a kid and the judge was friends with counsel's late father); *Travelers Ins. Co. v. Liljeberg Enters., Inc.*, 38 F.3d 1404, 1408, 1411-13 (5th Cir. 1994) (holding that a district judge did not abuse its discretion in denying recusal where the judge was a member of a social club where "several attorneys from two law firms representing Travelers . . . as well as the director of its parent company" were also members); *see also United States v. Murphy*, 768 F.2d 1518, 1537 (7th Cir. 1985) ("[I]n today's legal culture friendships among judges and lawyers are common."). **[—26—]**

But some authority, on different facts, points the other way. *See, e.g., In re Faulkner*, 856 F.2d 716, 718, 721 (5th Cir. 1988) (per curiam) (granting a petition for mandamus ordering that the district judge recuse himself because the judge was a cousin of a person involved in the transactions giving rise to an indictment, and their relationship was "more like that of 'brother and sister,'" and the cousin was the godmother of one of the judge's children); *United States v. Jordan*, 49 F.3d 152, 157 (5th Cir. 1995) (holding that a district judge abused her discretion in failing to recuse herself from a criminal case in light of an intense dispute between the defendant and a friend of the judge's); *United States v. Rechnitz*, 75 F.4th 131, 143, 148 (2d Cir. 2023) (holding that a district judge abused his discretion in failing to recuse in a criminal matter where the judge had "a close, near-paternal personal relationship" with a person involved in the criminal conduct before the court).

Of course, concerns of judicial impartiality are heightened in the context of bench trials. "When the judge is the actual trier of fact, the need to preserve the appearance of impartiality is especially pronounced." *Alexander v. Primerica Holdings, Inc.*, 10 F.3d 155, 166 (3d Cir. 1993).

Whatever these authorities might instruct, they do not decide this case, for two reasons. First, these cases arise in the separate and distinct legal context of recusals under § 455. The possibility of bias arising from a longstanding friendship, as informed by recusal law, is separate and distinct from the question of whether *nondisclosure* of a friendship casts doubt on the validity of an opposing party's *consent* to magistrate-judge jurisdiction in lieu of an Article III court. Put differently, even if a given friendship would not warrant recusal under § 455, it does not follow that *nondisclosure* of that friendship is constitutionally permissible under § 636(c). **[—27—]**

Second, these recusal authorities highlight what we have already explained is missing from this case: facts.[9] With no **{-419-}** information beyond the discrete facts alleged in

[9] ABA ethics guidance similarly emphasizes that this inquiry is fact-specific. As the ABA explained in its relatively recent Formal Opinion 488, addressing judges' social contacts in the judicial-ethics context, "[t]here may be situations . . . in which the judge's friendship with a lawyer or party is so tight that the judge's impartiality might reasonably be questioned." ABA Standing Comm. on

the Mize affidavit, we cannot reasonably assess the Port's contention that Magistrate Judge Kay's friendship with the Monks was, in fact, "deep" and "personal," nor can we dismiss the Port's concerns on the basis that "friendships among judges and lawyers are common."

3.

In *Carter*, we also instruct that attention be given to whether there was any "undue delay" in a party's request to have the magistrate-judge referral vacated. 816 F.2d at 1021. IFG and the district court emphasize that the Port's attempt to vacate the referral came four years after its consent to the referral and after completion of the trial. IFG notes that courts warn against "the risk of a full and complicated trial wasted at the option of an undeserving and opportunistic litigant." **[—28—]**

Factually, IFG is correct in the narrow sense that the Port's motion to vacate the referral long postdates its consent to the referral. But whether that delay is "undue" is a separate question. The basis of the Port's challenge is that it had no idea that IFG's counsel and Magistrate Judge Kay were longstanding friends. We cannot accept IFG's attribution of the years of "delay" to the Port, because both the judge *and IFG's counsel* knew all along of the friendship and its nondisclosure, and also because, again, unknown facts matter. The Port contends in the Mize affidavit that Magistrate Judge Kay's written reasons for judgment "prompted" its investigation, which in turn uncovered the friendship. Finding that there was no "undue" delay here rests critically on that asserted timeline being accurate. If the Port knew about the friendship all along, or even if it discovered it shortly before Magistrate Judge Kay issued her order, the "delay" factor would likely doom its claim now. (Again, those facts would also be fatal to the Port's "consent" arguments. *Roell*, 538 U.S. at 582).

Accepting the Port's timeline as true, the "undue delay" factor does not weigh against vacating the referral for factfinding.

4.

In *Carter*, we also asked the related question of whether the party's motion to vacate the referral "is made in good faith or is dilatory and contrived." 816 F.2d at 1021. IFG argues that the Port's challenge to the referral is not brought in good faith. It contends that the Port has raised the issue "simply because it was unhappy with the result of the trial." However, this issue, too, requires factfinding. The record indicates that the Port raised many objections **{–420–}** after Magistrate Judge Kay's written reasons issued. The motion to vacate was only one among many post-trial motions either attacking the fundamental power of the court to have heard the case—recall that the Port also moved to dismiss for lack of subject-matter jurisdiction— **[—29—]** or seeking leave to conduct discovery on various issues, which if granted would have had the effect of delaying the entry of final judgment against the Port. Of course, the fact that the Port's challenge emerged only after it lost the trial looms large. *See Sanches*, 647 F.3d at 172 ("Dissatisfaction with a magistrate judge's decision does not constitute 'extraordinary circumstances.'"). But again, if the Port in fact had no idea about Magistrate Judge Kay's longstanding friendship with the Monks and only found out about it once it sought an explanation for her "harsh language," then there is no basis to impugn the

---

Ethics & Pro. Resp., Formal Op. 488, *Judges' Social or Close Personal Relationships with Lawyers or Parties as Grounds for Disqualification or Disclosure* (2019), https://www.americanbar.org/content/dam/aba/administrative/professional_responsibility/aba_formal_opinion_488.pdf. "Whether a friendship between a judge and a lawyer or party reaches that point and consequently requires the judge's disqualification in the proceeding *is essentially a question of degree.*" *Id.* at 5-6 (emphasis added). "The answer," the ABA explained, "depends on the facts of the case." *Id.* at 6. And even if disqualification is not warranted, a "judge should disclose to the other lawyers and parties in the proceeding information about a friendship with a lawyer or party 'that the judge believes the parties or their lawyers might reasonably consider relevant to a possible motion for disqualification, even if the judge believes there is no basis for disqualification.'" *Id.* at 6 (quoting MODEL CODE OF JUD. CONDUCT r. 2.11 cmt. 5).

Port with bad faith. In this way, the "good faith" factor rises and falls alongside the "undue delay" factor—both depend on further factual development. If the Port's timeline is truthful, then the good-faith factor does not weigh against vacating the referral.

5.

We also assess "inconvenience to the court and witnesses." *Carter*, 816 F.2d at 1021. This factor does not require factual development. Vacating the referral would be hugely inconvenient to the parties and the witnesses. The bench trial in this case lasted for twenty days, and the record is north of forty thousand pages. Starting all over would require significant judicial resources. This factor weighs strongly against vacating the referral.

6.

The possible "prejudice to the parties," *id.*, quite plainly cuts both ways. Both parties would be prejudiced by the time and resources that would necessarily be spent in having to start all over. But IFG would be prejudiced moreover by the vacatur of the $124 million judgment awarded in its favor. We observe, however, that if the Port's contentions are true, any prejudice to IFG is, in significant regard, the product of its *own* inaction. Magistrate Judge Kay was not the only person in the room who is asserted to have held the undisclosed information; Monk could have easily made the disclosure, **[—30—]** and clarification, himself. IFG can hardly complain that its favorable award is now in jeopardy when IFG itself had the power to ensure disclosure of the friendship and thereby avoid this vulnerability on the back end. If the contentions in the Mize affidavit are true, the risk of starting all over arises, in part, from IFG's own silence. As to the Port, it would be prejudiced if the judgment stands, for the same reason: it is subject to a $124 million adverse judgment whose constitutional soundness it calls into question.

7.

Finally, subject to further evidentiary inquiry, the "interests of justice" may favor vacating the referral. Not only would justice be undermined by any undisclosed intimate friendship, but principles of fairness would be further strained if Monk, too, knew of such a relationship and at least acquiesced in its nondisclosure to the Port. In this regard, it is hard to overlook that Magistrate Judge Kay awarded Monk's client—and its lawyers—over $100 million in treble damages, contributing to a grand total of $124.5 million.

* * *

In sum, accepting, at present, the Port's uncontroverted facts as true, we have significant doubts about the knowingness and **{-421-}** validity of the Port's consent to have its case tried by Magistrate Judge Kay. Those same doubts compel the conclusion that the other *Carter* factors weigh in favor of vacating the referral. In light of the Port's assertions, we conclude that the district court abused its discretion in denying the Port's motion to vacate the referral and in denying the Port's request for discovery. We therefore VACATE the district court's order in full.

But we emphasize that critical facts remain untested or altogether undeveloped. The facts supporting our analysis thus far are contained only in an affidavit submitted by the Port's counsel. Below, IFG argued that the **[—31—]** affidavit was "legally insufficient," but stopped short of contesting its contents as untrue. On appeal, IFG remains silent as to the truth or falsity of the allegations. To decide whether the Port's consent to the magistrate judge was constitutionally valid, and whether vacatur of the referral is otherwise warranted, these factual gaps must be filled. We accordingly REMAND to the district court for an evidentiary inquiry into the issues we have identified. The district court's inquiry shall seek to determine the following facts, in addition to any other questions the district court deems appropriate in its assessment of this case:

(1) The extent and nature of Magistrate Judge Kay's friendship with Monk and his family;

(2) What information about these relationships Magistrate Judge

Kay disclosed to the parties and when these disclosures occurred;

(3) What precise steps the Port took upon its first discovery that a longstanding friendship existed, *i.e.*, what comprised its "investigation"; and

(4) When the Port first knew that Magistrate Judge Kay's relationship to Monk extended beyond her employment of Monk's daughter as her law clerk.

See United States v. Gemar, 65 F.4th 777, 781 (5th Cir. 2023) (remanding for an evidentiary hearing regarding possible juror bias in a criminal case where the juror failed to reveal his relationship with the defendant's wife during voir dire and the record was "silent" as to "obvious" questions concerning "what [the defendant] knew regarding [the juror] and when"); *In re Kensington Int'l Ltd.*, 353 F.3d 211, 223-25 (3d Cir. 2003) (remanding to a district judge for evidentiary development regarding a possible conflict of interest so the judge may decide whether to recuse). **[—32—]**

IV.

We are satisfied that federal subject-matter jurisdiction exists and the district court's conclusion in that regard is AFFIRMED. We also AFFIRM the district court's denial of the Port's request for jurisdictional discovery. We VACATE all sealing orders entered in this case and REMAND for the district court to decide, within ninety days of the issuance of mandate of this opinion, with specific reasons given, what sealed material, if any, shall remain under seal. If no revised order issues within ninety days of issuance of mandate, all sealed material in the case shall be unsealed.

We further VACATE the district judge's order denying the Port's motion to vacate the referral to the magistrate judge and denying the Port's request for discovery into the issues raised in the motion.[10] We **{-422-}** REMAND for factual development and further proceedings consistent with this opinion.

[10] The Port also raises a series of issues relating to the liability and damages findings following the bench trial in this case. Because it may be necessary to vacate the referral to the magistrate judge, we do not reach those issues.

United States Court of Appeals for the Fifth Circuit

No. 22-30371

CERTAIN UNDERWRITERS AT LLOYDS, LONDON vs. COX OPERATING

Appeal from the United States District Court for the Eastern District of Louisiana

Decided: October 13, 2023

Citation: 83 F.4th 998, 11 Adm. R. 351 (5th Cir. 2023).

Before **STEWART, DENNIS,** and **SOUTHWICK,*** Circuit Judges.

* Judge Southwick concurs in the judgment.

[—1—] {–1000–} PER CURIAM:

Certain Underwriters at Lloyds, London ("Lloyds") brought an intervenor complaint against Cox Operating LLC ("Cox") seeking to recover maintenance and cure benefits Lloyds paid to an injured seaman. Cox filed a motion for summary judgment, arguing that Lloyds bears responsibility for the payments under a protection and indemnity ("P & I") policy under which Cox is an assured. The district court agreed and granted **[—2—]** the motion. Lloyds timely appealed. Because the district court properly found that Lloyds is obligated to pay the maintenance and cure under the P & I policy, we AFFIRM.

I. Factual and Procedural Background

This intervenor suit arises from an underlying case whereby an injured seaman, James Michael Jones, sued Cox and his employer, nonparty Select Oilfield Services, LLC ("Select"). Jones brought claims of negligence and unseaworthiness based on injuries he sustained while employed by Select on a lift boat, the M/V SELECT 102, that Select time chartered to Cox. Jones, who was the captain of the M/V SELECT 102, sustained serious head injuries when he slipped and fell on a fixed saltwater platform owned by Cox. Select provided Jones's services as part of a Master **{–1001–}** Services Agreement ("MSA"), under which Select agreed to supply Cox with equipment, goods, and services to aid in the production of natural gas and oil.

Pursuant to the MSA, Select agreed to provide Cox with the M/V SELECT 102 lift boat, as well as a captain and crew to assist with Cox's oil and gas production in the Eloi Bay Field in St. Bernard Parish, Louisiana.[1] As relevant to this intervenor suit, Select also agreed to defend and indemnify Cox for "all [l]osses of every kind and character arising out of bodily injury, illness, death, property damage of [Select], arising out of, in connection with, incident to or resulting directly or indirectly from this Agreement or the provision of any Services, Goods, or Equipment provided under" the MSA, regardless of fault. To cover these indemnity obligations, Select agreed to procure insurance policies that included Cox as an additional assured and **[—3—]** contained waivers of subrogation in Cox's favor. To that end, Select obtained a general liability policy with U.S. Specialty Insurance Company ("USSIC"), and, as relevant to this appeal, a maritime P & I policy with Lloyds.

The P & I policy provided coverage for "all such loss and/or damage and/or expense as the [a]ssured shall as owners of the vessel named herein have become liable to pay," including "hospital, medical, or other expenses necessarily and reasonably incurred in respect of loss of life of, personal injury to, or illness of any member of the crew of the vessel." Select had the ability to add additional assureds and release from liability "others for whom the [a]ssured is performing operations," and added Cox as an additional assured under the policy. Lloyds, in turn, agreed to "waive all rights of subrogation against any parties so released." However, Lloyds also limited this waiver of subrogation by including a provision stating that "no party shall be deemed an [a]dditional [a]ssured or favoured with a waiver of subrogation on any vessel insured hereunder which is not actually engaged or involved in the intended operations at the time of loss[.]"

[1] On its website, Cox describes the Eloi Bay Field as being "[l]ocated in state waters of L[ousiana]." COX, ELOI BAY, https://coxoperating.com/footprint/eloi-bay/ (last visited October 12, 2023).

After Lloyds paid maintenance and cure to Jones under the P & I policy, Lloyds filed an intervenor complaint seeking to recoup those costs from Cox as the party at fault for Jones's injuries. Cox filed a motion for summary judgment, arguing that Lloyds's intervenor complaint should be dismissed because Lloyds had waived its subrogation rights under the P & I policy. The district court granted summary judgment in favor of Cox, determining that "[b]ecause Cox was named as an additional insured under the P&I policy and because Select released Cox from liability for Jones's injury, Lloyds has no right to recover from Cox through subrogation." The district court rejected Lloyds's argument that the limitation clause in the waiver of subrogation provision applied, finding that the M/V SELECT 102 was in fact "involved in the intended operations of the parties at the time **[—4—]** Jones was injured" since it was at the Eloi Bay Field to assist with Cox's operations, including the service platform, and "the M/V Select 102 was actually servicing the oil and gas production facility" on that day.

Lloyds now appeals the dismissal of its intervenor complaint, arguing that the district court erred in ruling in Cox's favor because the injury did not occur on the M/V SELECT 102 and thus was not covered by the P & I policy, or alternatively, **{-1002-}** falls within the clause limiting Lloyds's waiver of subrogation rights.

II. Standard of Review

We review a district court's grant of summary judgment de novo. *Tiblier v. Dlabal*, 743 F.3d 1004, 1007 (5th Cir. 2014). Summary judgment is proper "if the movant shows that there is no genuine dispute as to any material fact and the movant is entitled to judgment as a matter of law." FED. R. CIV. P. 56(a). "[T]his court construes 'all facts and inferences in the light most favorable to the nonmoving party.'" *McFaul v. Valenzuela*, 684 F.3d 564, 571 (5th Cir. 2012) (quoting *Dillon v. Rogers*, 596 F.3d 260, 266 (5th Cir. 2010)). The summary judgment movant bears the burden of proving that no genuine issue of material fact exists. *Latimer v. SmithKline & French Labs.*, 919 F.2d 301, 303 (5th Cir. 1990).

III. Discussion

A. The P & I policy covers Jones's maintenance and cure

The parties dispute whether the maintenance and cure Lloyds paid to Jones was covered by the P & I policy because Jones's injury did not take place on the M/V SELECT 102. Though the district court found that it was "undisputed" that Jones's maintenance and cure fell within the P & I policy, Lloyds vigorously denied before the district court, and maintains on appeal, **[—5—]** that Jones's maintenance and cure was not properly covered under the P & I policy.

Lloyds contends that the district court erred in finding Jones's injury to be covered under the P & I policy because the policy covered "only liabilities related to vessels that are scheduled under the policy" since the policy states that it provides coverage for "all such loss and/or damage and/or expense as the [a]ssured shall *as owners* of the vessel named herein have become liable to pay." The P & I policy includes coverage for claims asserted by Jones for "loss of life, injury, and illness," Lloyds's argument goes, and under Louisiana law[2] we must read this language in conjunction with the preceding paragraph that limits coverage to losses the assured acquires "as

[2] Given that there is no federal maritime rule governing the issues of whether Jones's maintenance and cure benefits are covered by the P & I policy or whether the limitation to the subrogation waiver applies here, this court applies Louisiana law as the state with the most substantial interest in the application of its state's laws to the interpretation of the P & I policy. *Naquin v. Elevating Boats, L.L.C.*, 817 F.3d 235, 238, 4 Adm. R. 221, 222 (5th Cir. 2016) ("In the absence of a specific and controlling federal maritime rule over this [marine insurance] dispute, we interpret this maritime insurance contract under Louisiana state law."). Select, the co-signatory of the P & I policy, is a Louisiana-based company, and the policy was executed to insure for risks associated with the provision of services on coastal waters of Louisiana, which is where Jones was injured.

owner"[3] of the M/V SELECT 102. *Naquin*, 817 F.3d at 239, 4 Adm. R. at 222–23 (under Louisiana law insurance contracts "must be interpreted in light of the other provisions so that each is given the meaning suggested by the contract as a whole").

Lloyds cites *Naquin* for the proposition that where an "as owner" clause to a P & I policy remains intact, coverage under the P & I policy only extends so far as there is a "causal operational relation between the vessel **[—6—]** and the resulting injury." *Id.* at 240, 4 Adm. R. at 223–24 (quoting **{-1003-}** *Lanasse v. Travelers Ins. Co.*, 450 F.2d 580, 584 (5th Cir. 1971)). Cox responds that *Naquin* is inapplicable because it only addressed liability coverage under a P & I policy, not an insurer's attempts to recoup maintenance and cure through subrogation. Indeed, *Naquin* involved a third-party complaint by a Jones Act employer against its insurers challenging the denial of liability coverage for a land-based incident. 817 F.3d at 237–8, 4 Adm. R. at 221–22. There, the court determined that the P & I insurer properly denied liability coverage because the employer was not liable, as owner of the covered vessel, for the land–based incident that caused the seaman's injury. *Id.* at 240, 4 Adm. R. at 223–24. Here, in contrast, Lloyds did not provide liability coverage under the P & I policy, and the issue instead is whether Jones became due maintenance and cure under the policy.

The court in *Naquin* relied on *Lanasse*, which called for "some causal operational connection between the vessel and the resulting injury" for the provision of maintenance and cure under a P & I policy to fall within a time charters' indemnity provision. 450 F.2d 580. Notably, the indemnity provision in the time charter in *Lanasse* only applied to damages "directly or indirectly connected with the possession, navigation, management, and operation of the vessel." *Id.* at 582 n.4.[4] Here, in contrast, the MSA's indemnity provision contained no such limitations, and explicitly applied to losses beyond the mere operation of the vessel to cover "all [l]osses of every kind and character arising out of bodily injury, illness, death, property damage" in connection with Select's services. **[—7—]**

Select bore the obligation to pay maintenance and cure to Jones as a shipowner whose seaman was injured while "in service of the vessel." Select thus became liable to pay Jones maintenance and cure precisely as the "owner" of the M/V SELECT 102. *Bertram v. Freeport McMoran, Inc.*, 35 F.3d 1008, 1013 (5th Cir. 1994) ("shipowner must pay maintenance and cure"); *Hernandez v. Bunge Corp.*, 01-1201 (La. App. 5 Cir. 4/10/02), 814 So. 2d 783, 791, *writ denied*, 2002-1551 (La. 9/30/02), 825 So. 2d 1193 ("Maintenance and cure is an obligation imposed upon a shipowner."); THOMAS J. SCHOENBAUM, ADMIRALTY AND MARITIME LAW, § 6– 28 (6th ed. 2022) (maintenance and cure is the "obligation of a shipowner who employs seamen to care for them if they are injured or become ill.").

Select's duty to provide Jones with maintenance and cure exists regardless of fault because Jones' injuries were sustained while he was in "service of his ship," and Select waived its right to recover any such costs from Cox under the indemnity provision of the MSA. *Warren v. United States*, 340 U.S. 523 (1951) (seaman entitled to maintenance and cure benefits when injured while on shore leave); *Noble Drilling Corp. v. Smith*, 412 F.2d 952, 958 (5th Cir. 1969) ("it would be unreasonable to say that a seaman working out from our shores in the Gulf of Mexico on a drilling platform, which his vessel has the function of servicing, is not also in the service of his ship"); *Cent. Gulf S. S. Corp. v. Sambula*, 405 F.2d

[3] While the "as owner" clause was deemed deleted with respect to any additional assureds under the P & I policy, additional assureds are nonetheless "not entitled to a broader scope of coverage than would be the owner."

[4] Judge Brown also cautioned that had the suit, which was between parties to a time charter, been a subrogation action brought by an insurer a "serious question" would arise as to whether the action would be barred by the anti-subrogation rule, under which "an underwriter cannot recover by way of subrogation against its own assured" where the policy includes an "explicit policy provision waiving subrogation." *Id.* at 585.

291, 296 (5th Cir. 1968) ("the vessel and her owners are liable, in case a seaman falls sick, or is wounded, in the service of the ship, to the extent of his maintenance and cure"); *Bertram*, 35 F.3d at 1013 (maintenance and cure "in no sense is **{-1004-}** predicated on the fault or negligence of the shipowner"). Given that Select has no right to seek reimbursement of Jones's maintenance and cure from Cox, Lloyds as a subrogated insurer, can have no greater rights as to Cox than Select as the subrogor. *Travelers Ins. Co. v. Impastato*, 607 So. 2d 722, 724 (La. App. 4th Cir. 1992) ("Under Louisiana law, a subrogated insurer acquires no **[—8—]** greater rights than those possessed by its subrogor and is subject to all limitations applicable to the original claim of the subrogor.").

Because Select was liable to pay Jones maintenance and cure as "owner" of the M/V SELECT 102, such benefits were covered by the P & I policy.

B. The limitation on Lloyds's waiver of subrogation does not apply

Having found that the P & I policy covered Jones's maintenance and cure, we next turn to the status of Lloyds's right to bring this subrogation action considering the waiver of subrogation rights provision[5] in the P & I policy.[6] The district court found that the M/V SELECT 102 was "engaged or involved in the intended operations" at the time of Jones's accident because "the M/V Select 102 and its crew were at the Eloi Bay Field to assist with Cox's operations there, including the service platform, and the M/V **[—9—]** Select 102 was actually servicing the oil and gas production facility on" the day Jones was injured.

Lloyds argues that the district court erred in finding that the vessel was engaged in its "intended operations" at the time of the Jones's incident because the "P & I Policy makes waiver of subrogation coextensive with coverage." Yet, having found that Jones's maintenance and cure was covered by the P & I policy, the waiver of subrogation clause also covers Cox as an additional assured under the policy. Lloyds insists that the district court's reasoning ignored the plain meaning of the limitation restricting coverage and the waiver of subrogation to "vessel operations," yet nowhere does the policy explicitly limit either coverage or the waiver of subrogation to "vessel operations." Instead, coverage extends to "all such loss and/or damage and/or expense as the [a]ssured shall as owners of the vessel named herein have become liable to pay," including "hospital, medical, or other expenses necessarily and reasonably incurred in respect of loss of life of, personal injury to, or illness of any member of the crew of the **{-1005-}** vessel." The P & I policy limits the waiver of subrogation where a vessel is "not actually engaged or involved in the *intended* operations at the time of loss." The policy thus limits the waiver of subrogation only where the vessel is not engaged in operations intended by the parties to the MSA at the time of the loss. *Doerr v. Mobil Oil Corp.*, 774 So.2d 119, 124 (La. 2000) (when the words of the insurance

[5] The "Blanket Additional Assureds and Waivers of Subrogation" provision in the P & I policy allowed Select to "name others for whom [Select] is performing work as [a]dditional [a]ssureds on this [p]olicy," release any additional assureds from liability, and required Lloyds to "waive all rights of subrogation against any parties so released [from liability by Select]." The provision also contained a limitation clause stating that "[n]otwithstanding the preceding provision, no party shall be deemed an [a]dditional [a]ssured or favoured with a waiver of subrogation on any vessel insured hereunder which is not actually engaged or involved in the intended operations at the time of loss[.]"

[6] The parties argue at length over whether Select's release of Cox in the MSA served to also waive Lloyds's subrogation rights as to Cox. Under Texas law, the law applicable to the MSA, "[s]ubrogation rights belong to the subrogated party and are waivable only by the insurer," so Select could not have waived Lloyds's subrogation rights through the MSA. *Halliburton Energy v. Ironshore Specialty Ins.*, 921 F.3d 522, 532 (5th Cir. 2019). Despite Select's agreement in the MSA to procure insurance that included a waiver of subrogation in Cox's favor, nowhere in the MSA does Select purport to waive subrogation rights on behalf of its insurer. Rather, Select agreed to support its indemnity obligations to Cox through an insurance policy in which Cox "is listed as an additional insured on and provided a written waiver of subrogation in [Cox's] favor."

contract "are unambiguous and the parties' intent is clear, the insurance contract will be enforced as written.") (citing LA. CIV. CODE ANN. art. 2046 (1985)).

The M/V SELECT 102 was involved in the operations intended by Select and Cox at the time of the incident—even if the vessel wasn't directly **[—10—]** involved in the incident.[7] Under the MSA, Select and Cox agreed that the intended operations of the vessel included "all services, labor and work performed by [Select] for the benefit of [Cox] or pursuant to [the MSA] or otherwise performed in connection with or without any Goods or Equipment, including delivery thereof," and it is undisputed that the MSA generally required Select to "assist with Cox's operations in the Eloi Bay Field." At the time of Jones's injury, the M/V SELECT 102 was engaged in its "intended operations" in the Eloi Bay as defined under the MSA, and Jones was serving Cox in his capacity as captain of the vessel. Even if there were ambiguity as to the term "intended operations," as included in the limitation on the waiver of subrogation, any such ambiguity is to be resolved "in favor of coverage." *Bonin v. Westport Ins. Corp.*, 2005-0886 (La. 5/17/06), 930 So. 2d 906, 911 (citations omitted); *Louisiana Ins. Guar. Ass'n v. Interstate Fire & Cas. Co.*, 630 So. 2d 759, 764 (La. 1994) ("ambiguous contractual provision is to be construed against the drafter, or, as originating in the insurance context, in favor of the insured.")

Because the M/V SELECT 102 was engaged in its "intended operations" at the time of Jones's injury and the limitation on the waiver of **[—11—]** subrogation does not apply, Lloyds waived its subrogation rights as to Cox.[8] The district court properly **{–1006–}** dismissed Lloyds's intervenor complaint.

IV. Conclusion

For the reasons set forth, we AFFIRM the district court's dismissal of Lloyds's intervenor complaint.

---

[7] Lloyds filed a 28(j) letter, arguing that cases applying the "active control duty" theory to negligence claims against vessel owners somehow means that the M/V SELECT 102 was not "actually engaged or involved in the intended operations at the time of the loss" as understood under the P & I policy. Under the "active control" doctrine, vessel owners have a "a duty to exercise reasonable care to prevent injuries to longshoreman working in areas remaining under the 'active control of the vessel' or when the vessel owner 'actively involves' itself in the cargo operations[.]" *Fontenot v. United States*, 89 F. 3d 205, 206 (5th Cir. 1996); *see also Scindia Steam Navigation Co. v De Los Santos*, 451 U.S. 156, 164 (1981) ("vessel [owner] may be liable if it actively involves itself in the cargo operations and negligently injures a longshoreman[.]) While negligence claims are subject to the "active control duty," *Manson Gulf, L.L.C v. Mod. Am. Recycling Serv., Inc.*, 878 F.3d 130, 134, 5 Adm. R. 331, 332 (5th Cir. 2017) (noting that "the Supreme Court clarified in *Scindia* that vessel owner liability sounds only in negligence"), maintenance and cure is "in no sense [] predicated on the fault or negligence of the shipowner." *Bertram*, 35 F.3d at 1013 (internal citation removed).

[8] Lloyds's claim is also barred by the anti–subrogation rule, under which "[a]n insurer cannot by way of subrogation recover against its insured *or an additional assured* any part of its payment for a risk covered by the policy." *Lloyd's Syndicate 457 v. FloaTEC, L.L.C.*, 921 F.3d 508, 521, 7 Adm. R. 240, 249 (5th Cir. 2019) (emphasis in original). It is undisputed that Cox was an additional assured under the P & I policy, and as discussed above, Jones's maintenance and cure was covered under the P & I policy. Lloyds attempts to evade the application of the anti-subrogation rule by pointing to cases that have found the rule to bar only subrogation suits that involved waivers of subrogation that did not contain the limitation contained in the P & I policy at issue here. However, the limitation on Lloyds's waiver of subrogation does not apply here because Jones's injuries arose while the vessel was engaged in the operations intended by the parties to the MSA.

United States Court of Appeals
for the Fifth Circuit

No. 22-30311

KENAI IRONCLAD CORP.
VS.
CP MARINE SERVS., LLC

Appeal from the United States District Court for the Eastern District of Louisiana

Decided: October 17, 2023

Citation: 84 F.4th 600, 11 Adm. R. 356 (5th Cir. 2023).

Before **HAYNES** and **ENGELHARDT,** Circuit Judges, and **DEGRAVELLES,** District Judge.*

* United States District Judge for the Middle District of Louisiana, sitting by designation.

[—1—] {-602-} **DEGRAVELLES,** District Judge:

Kenai Ironclad Corporation ("Kenai" or "Plaintiff") alleged that CP Marine Services, LLC, breached its contract to repair and convert Kenai's offshore supply vessel to a salmon fishing tender for use in Alaska. After Kenai expressed dissatisfaction with the work, the relationship deteriorated. **[—2—] {-603-}** Kenai alleged that, after paying its final invoice, it attempted to remove its vessel from CP Marine's shipyard, but as it did so, CP Marine and codefendant Ten Mile Exchange, LLC, ("TME") (collectively, "Defendants") rammed, wrongfully seized, detained, and converted Kenai's vessel for five days before finally releasing it.

After a five-day bench trial, the district court found that CP Marine did not breach its contract with Kenai but did wrongfully seize, detain, and convert the vessel. The court awarded punitive damages and attorney's fees for Defendants' bad faith and reckless behavior in ramming, seizing, and converting the vessel for five days.

Defendants appeal, arguing the trial court erred in (1) finding that they wrongfully arrested or detained Kenai's vessel; (2) finding that punitive damages were legally and factually justified; and (3) awarding prejudgment interest on the punitive damages award. After a careful review of the record, we hold that there was sufficient evidence to support the district court's finding that Defendants wrongfully seized, detained, and converted Plaintiff's vessel in a manner that warranted the imposition of attorney's fees and punitive damages. However, because the record is unclear as to certain aspects of the district court's award of punitive damages—namely, whether they were also intended, at least in part, to be compensatory and, if so, in what amount—we REMAND to the district court for clarification of its award.

FACTS AND PROCEDURAL HISTORY

In December 2018, Plaintiff Kenai orally contracted with Defendant CP Marine to repair, modify, and paint the M/V IRON DON, an offshore supply boat owned by Kenai that it intended to use as a salmon fishing tender in Alaska. Work began in January 2019. In January and February, Kenai's representatives repeatedly expressed concerns about the quality of the work **[—3—]** being performed and requested a written guarantee regarding the work's quality. CP Marine refused to give a guarantee.

Thereafter, CP Marine demanded immediate payment of outstanding invoices, which Kenai paid immediately. Then, Kenai's representatives decided to "end the working relationship with Defendants as soon as possible." CP Marine next demanded that Kenai's crew and equipment be immediately removed from the vessel and shipyard and threatened to charge a $1,000 per day storage fee if Kenai failed to comply. CP Marine further threatened to return the vessel from dry dock to the water and charge a $5,000 per day storage fee.

CP Marine had Jefferson Parish deputy sheriffs evict Kenai's crew from the vessel and then completed its work on same. On February 27, 2019, CP Marine sent Kenai a final invoice. Kenai's Austin Adler

> immediately wrote a check for the final invoice and delivered it to CP Marine, which CP marine deposited the same day. This payment satisfied all outstanding CP Marine invoices to

> Plaintiff. [ ] Adler called Plaintiff's bank to confirm that the check had cleared . . . [and] a representative from Plaintiff's bank confirmed that Defendant had cashed the check and that it cleared on February 28, 2019.

Six days later, on March 5, 2019, the vessel hired by Kenai to remove the IRON DON from the CP Marine shipyard (the M/V SUPER T) tied onto the IRON DON and began to leave the shipyard. As it was doing so, a vessel owned by TME, the M/V AUNT DI, "rammed" the SUPER T, pinned it and the IRON DON against the **{–604–}** bank, and thus prevented Kenai from retrieving its vessel. Joseph Dardar, a part owner of both TME and CP Marine, was at the wheel of the AUNT DI. Moreover, during this event, Dardar threatened Adler. **[—4—]**

The following day, while the IRON DON was still being detained in the CP Marine shipyard, TME "threatened Plaintiff by sending a $20,750 invoice from TME for ramming and detaining the IRON DON" and demanded payment within two days. At this point, Kenai had "no formal business relationship" with TME, and the invoice was sent "for the sole purpose of intimidating and threatening Plaintiff." Dardar admitted at trial that "he never intended to collect on this invoice and 'should never have sent it.'" "Plaintiff ultimately retrieved the IRON DON and left the CP Marine shipyard on March 11, 2019."

Kenai sued CP Marine and TME for breach of contract, wrongful vessel seizure, conversion, and tortious interference with contractual relations. After a five-day bench trial, the district court held that defendant CP Marine did not breach its oral contract and implied breach of warranty of workmanlike performance in connection with CP Marine's painting, repair, and modifications to the M/V IRON DON. The trial court held in part that "Plaintiff has not met its burden to show that Defendants' allegedly dilatory performance caused [the IRON DON's] late arrival in Alaska."

However, the district court also found that "Defendants acted with bad faith . . . [and] detained the [IRON DON] pursuant to an invalid maritime lien." The court awarded punitive damages measured by "the value of [the vessel's] missed contract days for the days that Defendants wrongfully detained the vessel." Specifically, the court stated it was awarding punitive damages in the amount of $17,580.50, measured by the vessel's daily rate of $3,516.10 times the five days the vessel was wrongfully detained, plus attorney fees, expenses, and court costs.

In addition, the court awarded "pre-judgment interest in accordance with La. R.S. § 9:3500 from March 5, 2019, to the date of judgment, and post-judgment interest in accordance with 28 U.S.C. § 1961(a)." Judgment was **[—5—]** entered on May 17, 2022, and Defendants timely appealed on May 25, 2022. Kenai did not.

The matter of the amount of attorney's fees to be awarded was referred to the magistrate judge. Although Kenai submitted attorney's fees totaling $78,017.68, the magistrate judge only recommended payment of $38,831.40, reflecting a downward adjustment due in part to Kenai's loss of its breach of contract claim.[1] On August 9, 2022, the district court adopted the magistrate judge's recommendation. Defendants separately appealed the district judge's adoption of the report and recommendation, but that appeal was dismissed for want of prosecution because Defendants failed to timely file a brief and record excerpts. *Kenai Ironclad Corp. v. CP Marine Servs., L.L.C.*, No. 22-30492, 2022 WL 18776210, at *1 (5th Cir. Dec. 7, 2022). The award of Kenai's attorney's fees is therefore final.

ISSUES ON APPEAL

Defendants' appeal raises the following issues: did the district court err (1) in finding

[1] The magistrate judge's report and recommendation and the district court's order adopting same were not made a part of the ROA. The ROA goes only to E.D. La. ECF No. 113, whereas these orders are E.D. La. ECF Nos. 116, 122.

that Defendants wrongfully seized, detained, and converted Kenai's vessel; (2) **{-605-}** in awarding punitive damages; or (3) in awarding prejudgment interest on the punitive damages award?

Resolution of the second issue turns on the proper relationship between punitive damages and compensatory damages, both generally under maritime law and in this case specifically. Sub-issues include: (a) whether the district court erred in awarding punitive damages exceeding the 1:1 punitive damage to compensatory damage ratio set by *Exxon Shipping Co. v. Baker*, 554 U.S. 471 (2008); (b) whether the district court erred as a matter of law in **[—6—]** awarding punitive damages in the absence of an explicit award of compensatory damages; and (c) if so, whether the district court's award nevertheless should be affirmed because it had a compensatory component, either because the award of attorney's fees was compensatory or because the punitive damage award itself was in part compensatory.

DISCUSSION

I. Did the district court err in finding Defendants wrongfully arrested and converted Kenai's vessel?

"To recover for wrongful arrest of a vessel, there must be (1) no bona fide claim of a maritime lien on the vessel and [(2)] a showing of bad faith, malice, or gross negligence [on the part] of the offending party." *Comar Marine, Corp. v. Raider Marine Logistics, L.L.C.*, 792 F.3d 564, 574–75, 3 Adm. R. 371, 377 (5th Cir. 2015) (citations and internal quotations omitted). "Whether a maritime lien exists is a question of law, reviewed de novo." *Id.* at 575, 3 Adm. R. at 377 (citations omitted). A district court's determination of bad faith, on the other hand, is "a conclusion of fact, which we review under the deferential clear error standard." *Id.*, 3 Adm. R. at 377 (citation omitted).

"[F]or a bench trial, . . . we will upset the district court's findings of fact only if we are 'left with the definite and firm conviction that a mistake has been committed.'" *Luwisch v. Am. Marine Corp.*, 956 F.3d 320, 326, 8 Adm. R. 181, 182 (5th Cir. 2020) (quoting *Barto v. Shore Constr., LLC*, 801 F.3d 465, 471, 3 Adm. R. 415, 416 (5th Cir. 2015)). "Moreover, and of particular relevance here, the clearly erroneous standard of review following a bench trial requires even 'greater deference to the trial court's findings when they are based on determinations of credibility.'" *Id.*, 8 Adm. R. at 182 (quoting *Guzman v. Hacienda Records & Recording Studio, Inc.*, 808 F.3d 1031, 1036 (5th Cir. 2015)). "Accordingly, '[w]e entertain a strong presumption that the court's findings must be sustained even though **[—7—]** this court might have weighed the evidence differently.'" *Id.*, 8 Adm. R. at 182 (quoting *Johnson v. Cenac Towing, Inc.*, 544 F.3d 296, 303 (5th Cir. 2008)).

The Federal Maritime Lien Act, 46 U.S.C. §§ 31341–31343, grants maritime liens to parties "providing necessaries to a vessel" and allows such parties to bring a civil action in rem to enforce the lien. *Id.* § 31342(a)(1)–(2). "'Necessaries' includes repairs, supplies, towage, and the use of a dry dock or maritime railway . . . ." *Id.* § 31301(4). Prior to Kenai's payment of its final invoice, CP Marine had a valid lien on the IRON DON. *See World Fuel Servs., Inc. v. MAGDALENA GREEN M/V*, 464 F. App'x 339, 341 (5th Cir. 2012) (quoting, *inter alia*, *Equilease Corp. v. M/V Sampson*, 793 F.2d 598, 602 (5th Cir. 1986) (en banc) (A maritime lien "arises when the debt arises . . . .")).

Because all amounts due had been paid with funds deposited in CP Marine's account six days prior, the district court did not clearly err in finding that no valid lien existed at the time the IRON DON was seized. Once the debt giving rise to the lien was paid, the lien ceased to exist. **{-606-}** *World Fuel Servs.*, 464 F. App'x at 341 ("Where, as here, the debt is repaid and satisfaction is acknowledged, the lien ceases to exist." (citing *Mullane v. Chambers*, 438 F.3d 132, 138 (1st Cir. 2006))). *See also Argos Ports (Hous.) LLC v. Kirby Inland Marine, LP*, 598 F. Supp. 3d 512, 519 (S.D. Tex. 2022) ("[A]ny claim T&T might have had would have been extinguished by payment.").[2]

Defendants argue that they seized the vessel because (a) Kenai's check had not cleared and (b) Dardar was concerned that Plaintiff might **[—8—]** cancel the check and remove the funds from CP Marine's account. The district court rejected this explanation because (a) Defendants had "produced no evidence that these check payments did not clear or were cancelled;" (b) Dardar's testimony lacked credibility; (c) the check had cleared on February 28, 2019; and (d) the funds had been in CP Marine's account for six days at the time the IRON DON was seized. On this record, ample evidence supports the district court's conclusion that well before the seizure, CP Marine's bill was paid in full, so there was no longer a valid lien.

Defendants also argue that the IRON DON was never arrested and thus could not have been arrested wrongfully. Contrary to the district court's finding that the AUNT DI "rammed" the SUPER T and endangered lives, "the evidence overwhelmingly shows that the bumping was controlled, safe and appropriate under the circumstances." According to Defendants, the bumping of the SUPER T was "initiated for a proper purpose," *i.e.*, "to create a pause in the unfolding events so they could be rationally discussed . . . ." Furthermore, there is no evidence that Defendants ever refused a request to return the IRON DON, and once the request was made on March 10, it was returned the next day.

Next, Defendants contend that Kenai did not prove that any arrest or detention was in bad faith: "the 'gravamen of the right to recover damages for wrongful [arrest] or detention of vessels.'" Defendants were "fully justified in the name of safety in stopping Kenai's effort to unilaterally remove the vessel from the shipyard . . . ." According to Defendants, the manner in which the SUPER T was removing the IRON DON was unsafe in that (a) it was being moved through a narrow channel, which imperiled CP Marine's hopper barge and dry dock, and (b) the removal attempt was reckless in that the attempt was being made with only a single vessel. **[—9—]**

Contrary to Defendants' argument, the record contains ample evidence that the IRON DON was wrongfully arrested and, indeed, rammed and pinned against the bank. This evidence includes the testimony of Jonathan Tingley, video evidence of the ramming, the testimony of Austin Adler, and even that of Joseph Dardar.[3] **{-607-}** Defendants' bad faith detention and conversion of the vessel is also supported by Defendants' intentional blocking of the canal for five days following the ramming.

Kenai presented sufficient evidence and testimony to support the trial court's finding that Defendants acted "in bad faith and with wanton disregard of the legal rights of Plaintiff." This evidence includes the backdrop against which the seizure occurred: the deterioration of the parties' relationship following Plaintiff's request for a written guarantee on the quality of the work and Defendants' refusal to provide same. It also includes (a) Defendants' demand that Plaintiff remove its personnel from the vessel and equipment from the shipyard although their presence had been a part of the original agreement; (b) Defendants' threat to charge

[2] *See also Bunkers Int'l Corp. v. M/V Wuchow*, No. 15-5221, 2016 WL 1161288, at *3 n.1 (E.D. La. Mar. 23, 2016) ("BIC's purported maritime lien would be extinguished if BIC received payment from China Navigation pursuant to its invoice."); *Maritrend, Inc. v. M/V SEBES*, No. 96–3140, 1997 WL 660614, at *2 (E.D. La. Oct. 23, 1997) ("the contractor acquires a maritime lien against the vessel until payment is satisfied").

[3] Although Defendants portray the contact as "the bumping of one tug into the other," Dardar admitted that he "laid up against him hard, and [Dardar] had a hold against him." Tingley described it as "extreme acceleration." After viewing the video, the district judge said, "[W]hat I'm seeing here is very troubling. The behavior here is very troubling." The court also stated, "[H]ow somebody goes to that extreme and puts life at stake because they think somebody owes them money is a very hard hurdle for me to overcome in my fact finding." We conclude that there was no clear error in the district court's assessment.

Plaintiff a storage fee of $1,000 per day if the equipment wasn't removed; (c) Defendants' threat to move the IRON DON from the dry dock to the water and thereafter charge $5,000 per day until it was removed because "[Dardar] wanted them off [his] property . . . to motivate them to get off [his] property"; (d) the AUNT DI's ramming of the SUPER T and the IRON DON, which the trial court found to be in "callous disregard for the safety of the people aboard the **[—10—]** vessels"; (e) Joseph Dardar's threat made during the course of the vessel's arrest that "[i]f I had my shotgun, you'd be dead"; (f) Defendants blocking the canal for five days following the seizure; (g) the district court's disbelief of Dardar's purported reason for holding the vessel (waiting for the check to clear); and (h) TME's billing Plaintiff for TME's wrongful seizure of the IRON DON on March 5, which the court found was "for the sole purpose of intimidating and threatening Plaintiff" and which Dardar later admitted was "inappropriate" and should never have been sent.

In conclusion, the district court did not clearly err in finding that Kenai's vessel was wrongfully seized and converted in bad faith and in reckless disregard of Kenai's rights.

II. Did the district court err in awarding punitive damages?

A. *Did the facts support such an award?*

General maritime law has long recognized the availability of punitive damages in the appropriate case. *Atl. Sounding Co. v. Townsend*, 557 U.S. 404, 414–15 (2009). As the Court in *Townsend* stated, "[P]unitive damages have long been available at common law[,] [and] . . . the common-law tradition of punitive damages extends to maritime claims." *Id.* at 414. *See also Exxon*, 554 U.S. 471.[4] "Punitive damages have long been an available remedy at common law for wanton, willful, or outrageous conduct," *Townsend*, 557 U.S. at 409, but have also been awarded when a defendant engaged in "reckless action," **[—11—]** that was "worse than negligent but less than malicious," *Exxon*, 554 U.S. at 510–11.[5] **{-608-}**

As summarized in the preceding section, Kenai presented sufficient evidence and testimony to support the district court's finding that Defendants' conduct was in bad faith, in callous disregard for the safety of the people aboard the vessels, and in reckless disregard of

[4] "[*Exxon*] and *Townsend* affirm that, as a general rule, punitive damages are available in appropriate cases under the general maritime law. Thus, punitive damage awards are generally proper in cases in admiralty jurisdiction." 1 Thomas J. Schoenbaum, *Admiralty & Maritime Law* § 5:10 (6th ed. 2022).

[5] The Court in *Townsend* noted that maritime punitive damages are available in a wide variety of circumstances as exemplified in maritime law's earliest cases, citing, for example, *Boston Manufacturing Co. v. Fiske*, 3 F. Cas. 957, 957 (Story, Circuit Justice, C.C. Mass. 1820) (No. 1,681) ("In cases of marine torts, or illegal captures, it is far from being uncommon in the admiralty to allow costs and expences, and to mulct the offending parties, even in exemplary damages, where the nature of the case requires it[.]"). *Townsend*, 557 U.S. at 411–12.

> In short, prior to enactment of the Jones Act in 1920, "maritime jurisprudence was replete with judicial statements approving punitive damages, especially on behalf of passengers and seamen." Robertson, Punitive Damages in American Maritime Law, 28 J. Mar. L. & Comm. 73, 115 (1997) (hereinafter Robertson); see also 2 Sedgwick § 599b, at 1156 ("Exemplary damages are awarded in Admiralty, as in other jurisdictions"); 2 J. Sutherland, Law of Damages § 392, p. 1272 (4th ed. 1916) ("As a rule a court of equity will not award [punitive] damages, but courts of admiralty will . . ." (footnote omitted)).

Id. at 412.

Townsend cited with approval Professor Robertson's article which discussed the general availability of punitive damages in admiralty. *Id.* Professor Robertson's article surveyed a variety of early maritime cases recognizing such awards. 28 J. Mar. L. & Com. at 88–115. Two such cases involved conversion, *id.* at 114–15, and one dealt with a steamboat that "deliberately rammed its rival, causing relatively slight property damage and no personal injuries," *id.* at 90.

Kenai's rights. Hence, the district court did not clearly err in finding facts sufficient to support an award of punitive damages. **[—12—]**

B. Was there legal error?

1. Is Exxon v. Baker's ratio absolute?

"A district court's damages award is a finding of fact, which this court reviews for clear error." *Comar Marine*, 792 F.3d at 574, 3 Adm. R. at 376 (quoting *Jauch v. Nautical Servs., Inc.*, 470 F.3d 207, 213 (5th Cir. 2006) (per curiam)). But, "[d]espite this court's typical deference to a district court's factual findings, 'a judgment based on a factual finding derived from an incorrect understanding of substantive law must be reversed.'" *Barto*, 801 F.3d at 471, 3 Adm. R. at 416-17 (quoting *Mobil Expl. and Producing U.S., Inc. v. Cajun Const. Servs., Inc.*, 45 F.3d 96, 99 (5th Cir. 1995)). Thus, this court reviews *de novo* the legal questions of whether *Exxon*'s 1:1 ratio applies in all maritime cases, and whether that ratio should have been applied by the district court, regardless of its specific factual findings as to Defendants' level of culpability and the amount of harm done to Kenai.

According to Defendants, *Exxon* held that "a 1:1 [punitive damage to compensatory damage] ratio . . . is a fair upper limit in such maritime cases." 554 U.S. at 513. Thus, Defendants argue, since no compensatory damages were awarded here, *any* punitive damage award impermissibly exceeds the ratio.

Plaintiff offers three reasons why Defendants' position is wrong. First, *Exxon*'s 1:1 ratio does not apply in this case because it only applies in cases involving gross negligence and only where the compensatory damages are significant. Here, Defendants' conduct was intentional and malicious, and the district court "limited [compensatory damages] to attorney's fees." Second, Plaintiff maintains that if *Exxon* does require compensatory damages as a prerequisite to an award of punitive damages, the attorney's fees awarded by the district court were compensatory. Finally, even if attorney's fees cannot be considered compensatory, the district court's punitive **[—13—]** damage award recognized and was measured by the harm that Plaintiff suffered from Defendants' five-day seizure and detention of its vessel. Thus, the punitive damage award "was, in fact, compensatory **{-609-}** – or at the very least, it had . . . a compensatory flavor[.]"

Regarding Plaintiff's first argument, this court has not had occasion to consider whether *Exxon*'s 1:1 ratio applies in all cases or only in cases "like" *Exxon,* involving "reckless action, profitless to the tortfeasor, resulting in substantial recovery for substantial injury[,]" and where the conduct was "worse than negligent but less than malicious." *Exxon*, 554 U.S. at 510–11. Nor, to our knowledge, have the other federal courts of appeal or district courts. Some state courts, however, have.

The majority of the cases that have squarely considered whether *Exxon* sets a hard rule applicable to all cases hold that it does not. *See, e.g., Clausen v. Icicle Seafoods, Inc.*, 272 P.3d 827, 835 (Wash. 2012), *cert. denied*, 568 U.S. 823 (2012) ("The *Exxon* case cannot be read as establishing a broad, general rule limiting punitive damage awards, primarily because nowhere in the opinion can such a rule be found."); *McWilliams v. Exxon Mobil Corp.,* 2012-1288 (La. App. 3 Cir. 4/3/13), 111 So. 3d 564, 579, *writ denied*, 2013- 1402 (La. 11/8/13), 125 So. 3d 451 (*Exxon* "did not establish a general rule pertaining to punitive damages, but rather, narrowly tailored that result to the unique case before it."); *Colombo v. BRP US Inc.*, 179 Cal. Rptr. 3d 580, 606 (Cal. Ct. App. 2014) ("[W]e conclude that the [C]ourt [in *Exxon*] did not intend to create . . . a bright-line rule limiting punitive damages to the amount of compensatory damages awarded to a plaintiff."); *Warren v. Shelter Mut. Ins. Co.*, 2016-1647 (La. 10/18/17), 233 So. 3d 568, 590 ("[W]e find the Court in *Exxon* was expressly attempting to set a 'fair upper limit' for punitive damages 'in cases with no earmarks of exceptional blameworthiness . . . .'" (quoting *Exxon*, 554 U.S. at 513)). In a Winter 2021 article surveying the **[—14—]** jurisprudence on this issue, Professor Thomas C. Galligan, Jr. summarized the case law as follows:

> To recap, virtually all of the courts that have meaningfully discussed the impact

of *Exxon*'s statement concerning the 1:1 ratio of punitive to compensatory damages have refused to treat it as a per se rule applicable in all admiralty cases. Rather than emphasizing the broad scope of Justice Souter's review of the relevant social science data on punitive damages, the lower courts have emphasized the limiting language in Justice Souter's opinion. That is, the lower courts have treated the 1:1 ratio as the precise holding of the *Exxon* case, a holding applicable to the facts before the Court. At most, the courts have treated *Exxon* as a rule for cases "like" *Exxon*. Those are cases where the defendant's conduct constituted recklessness or gross negligence and not worse, such as willful, wanton, malicious, arbitrary, capricious, or intentional wrongdoing. Additionally, *Exxon* was a case in which the damage was not difficult to detect—it was substantial and overt. It was also a case where the compensatory damages, fines and penalties, cleanup costs, and settlements of claims were substantial, even gargantuan. Moreover, *Exxon* was a case in which the defendant's behavior—not taking action to relieve a known, relapsed alcoholic of command of an oil tanker—was not motivated by profit.

Thomas C. Galligan, Jr., **{-610-}** *There Are More Things to Punitive Damages in Admiralty Than the 1:1 Ratio Set Forth in Exxon's Legal Philosophy*, 81 LA. L. REV. 395, 420–21 (2021).[6] **[—15—]**

Schoenbaum's treatise, on the other hand, states without elaboration that *Exxon* "ruled that 'a punitive to compensatory ratio of 1:1 . . . yields maximum punitive damages[ ]'" and that "[t]his ratio, the Court held, constitutes a 'fair upper limit' for maritime punitive damage awards." Schoenbaum, *supra*, at § 5:10. Schoenbaum cites for this proposition *Norfolk & Portsmouth Belt Line Railroad Co. v. M/V MARLIN*, No. 08-134, 2009 WL 1974298, at *4 (E.D. Va. Apr. 3, 2009), and *Priyanto v. M/S Amsterdam*, No. 07-3811, 2009 WL 1202888 (C.D. Cal. Apr. 30, 2009). But neither cited case dealt directly with the issue here: whether *Exxon*'s 1:1 ratio applies in all cases.[7]

Notably, Professor Galligan discusses *Norfolk & Portsmouth* at length. 81 LA. L. REV. at 407–09. He concludes that *Norfolk & Portsmouth* "essentially stands alone." *Id.* at 409. **[—16—]**

We hold that the majority position is the correct reading of *Exxon* for the following reasons. First, the language of *Exxon* itself strongly suggests that the 1:1 ratio applies, to use the words of the Court, in "cases like [that] one," 554 U.S. at 513, which was described as "a case of reckless action, profitless to the tortfeasor, resulting in substantial recovery for

[6] Galligan's article argues that the appropriate reading of *Exxon* is that it created a variable, multi-factor approach to punitive damages in maritime cases, rather than a universal 1:1 rule. The variable approach is supported by a careful reading of *Exxon* itself, **[—15—]** the desirability of flexibility in imposing punitive damages for purposes of adequate punishment and efficient deterrence, and the jurisprudence since Exxon. 81 LA. L. REV. at 395. *See also* Erin L. Brooks, *A Rule Old and New, Borrowed and Blue: Exxon Adapts State Punitive Liability Law to Craft New Interpretation in Admiralty*, 54 ST. LOUIS U. L.J. 357, 380 (2009) ("Under *Exxon*, punitive damages must only be limited in precise proportion to actual damages when the conduct is not exceptionally blameworthy (intentional, malicious, or driven for gain) or when it is without 'modest economic harm or [low] odds of detection.'") (citing *Exxon*, 554 U.S. at 513).

[7] For example, in *Norfolk & Portsmouth*, a maritime allision case, the court denied plaintiff's motion to amend its complaint to add a claim for damages pursuant to a Virginia punitive damage statute that provided for a "strict and inflexible [3:1] ratio of punitive damages to actual or compensatory damages . . . [which] automatically applied . . . ." 2009 WL 1974298, at *4. The court denied plaintiff's motion to amend because Virginia's "automatic punitive damage remedy in the form of triple damages is inconsistent with *Exxon*'s 1:1 ratio . . . and therefore conflicts with the general maritime law." *Id.* But while *Norfolk & Portsmouth* did not confront the precise issue of whether *Exxon* created a hard cap on all maritime punitive damage awards, it suggested in dicta that it did not. *See id.* at *3 (characterizing *Exxon*'s holding as, "*except for the most extreme cases*, the maximum permissible ratio is likely 1:1." (emphasis added) (citing *Exxon*, 554 U.S. at 514–15)).

substantial injury[,]" *id.* at 510–11. The court further defined Exxon's conduct as "worse than negligent but less than malicious." *Id.* at 510.

Second, there is nothing in the Supreme Court's subsequent maritime punitive damage cases suggesting that 1:1 is a hard and inflexible rule. In *Townsend*, decided a year later, the Court considered this an open question. *See Townsend*, 557 U.S. at 424 n.11 ("Nor have petitioners argued that the size of punitive damages awards in maintenance and cure cases necessitates a recovery cap, which the Court has elsewhere imposed. We do not decide these issues." (internally citing *Exxon*, 554 U.S. at 514–15)). **{–611–}**

Third, where the conduct is intentional and malicious, and the compensatory damages are small, imposing the 1:1 ratio would do little to serve the twin purposes of punitive damages: to punish the wrongdoer and deter his and others' similar future conduct. *Exxon*, 554 U.S. at 492 ("[T]he consensus today is that punitives are aimed not at compensation but principally at retribution and deterring harmful conduct.").

Defendants' conduct here, unlike that in *Exxon*, was intentional: the ramming of the SUPER T and its tow, the IRON DON. It was not done for purposes of safety but in anger. (*See, e.g.*, Dardar's threat that "[i]f I had my shotgun, you'd be dead."). The district court found that Defendants' conduct displayed "callous disregard for the safety of the people aboard the vessels" and was "in bad faith and with wanton disregard of the legal rights of Plaintiff." As reviewed above, there is no clear error in this finding. Furthermore, unlike *Exxon*, where the compensatory damages were massive, **[—17—]** the harm suffered by the five-day delay in the return of Kenai's vessel was relatively small.[8]

2. Do punitive damages require compensatory damages?

We need not resolve this issue now. As explained below, it is unclear whether the district court intended her award to be compensatory, at least in part. Because we remand to the district court for clarification on that issue, we pass on this thornier question.

3. Was this attorney's fee award compensatory?

Kenai contends that, even if a compensatory damage award is necessary in order to obtain punitive damages, the attorney's fees were awarded as compensatory damages. Defendants cite *Budinich v. Becton Dickinson & Co.*, 486 U.S. 196, 200 (1988) for the proposition that "[a]s a general matter . . . a claim for attorney's fees is not part of the merits of the action to which the fees pertain." Therefore, contend Defendants, the attorney's fees awarded by the district court were awarded as costs and not damages and cannot form a foundation for the award of punitive damages. Defendants maintain that *The Apollon*, 22 U.S. 362 (1824), relied on by Kenai, is inapposite in that here, unlike in *Apollon*, there was no proof of attorney's fees offered at trial.

While there is some basis for Kenai's position as a general proposition, it ultimately falls short under the law governing wrongful arrest and the facts **[—18—]** of this case. We have stated the following about the award of attorney's fees as damages in wrongful seizure cases:

> The reasons for the award of [such] damages are analogous to those in cases of malicious prosecution. The defendant is required to respond in damages for causing to be done through the process of the court that which would have been

[8] Awards of punitive damages are, of course, constrained by "[t]he Due Process Clause of the Fourteenth Amendment [which] prohibits the imposition of grossly excessive or arbitrary punishments on a tortfeasor." *State Farm Mut. Auto. Ins. Co. v. Campbell*, 538 U.S. 408, 416 (2003). *See also TXO Prod. Corp. v. Alliance Res. Corp.*, 509 U.S. 443, 446 (1993); *Wellogix, Inc. v. Accenture, L.L.P.*, 716 F.3d 867, 884–85 (5th Cir. 2013), *cert denied sub nom., Accenture, L.L.P. v. Wellogix, Inc.*, 573 U.S. 904 (2014); *Lincoln v. Case*, 340 F.3d 283, 292 (5th Cir. 2003).

> wrongful for him to do himself, having no legal justification therefor and acting in bad faith, with malice, or through a **{-612-}** wanton disregard of the legal rights of his adversary.

Frontera Fruit Co. v. Dowling, 91 F.2d 293, 297 (5th Cir. 1937).

Thus, by way of analogy, for common law malicious prosecution actions, "[c]ompensatory damages for tangible losses or harm normally include reasonable attorney fees and other expenses incurred in defending the wrongful criminal or civil litigation or avoiding or quashing abusive process . . . ." Dobbs, Hayden, & Bublick, *supra*, at § 596; *cf. also Hale v. Fish*, 899 F.2d 390, 403–04 (5th Cir. 1990) (reinstating § 1983 plaintiff's award of $25,000 "for the amount expended in his defense of the criminal charges against him").

Such awards are more properly categorized as compensatory damages only when they were incurred as "collateral legal expenses"—defined as attorneys' fee outlays incurred in some way *other* than the proceeding in which the attorneys' fee award is being sought . . . ." David W. Robertson, *Court-Awarded Attorneys' Fees in Maritime Cases: The "American Rule" in Admiralty*, 27 J. MAR. L. & COM. 507, 511 (1996) (emphasis added). However, many courts make such awards without drawing this distinction. *See id.* at 539 (citing, *inter alia*, *State Bank & Tr. Co. of Golden Meadow v. Boat D.J. Griffin*, 755 F. Supp. 1389 (E.D. La. 1991)).

Here, since the attorney's fees awarded were in connection with services rendered in this case, there was no other proceeding in which **[—19—]** attorney's fees were incurred and thus, no "collateral legal expenses." The magistrate judge's recommendation limited the attorney's fees in large measure to that part of the case dealing with the wrongful seizure (excluding the fees incurred in connection with the unsuccessful breach of contract claim). Still, the fees awarded were earned in this, not a collateral, proceeding and, therefore, may not properly be considered compensatory damages.[9]

4. Was the punitive damage award partly compensatory?

In connection with its argument on prejudgment interest, Kenai argues that the language and reasoning of the district court's award of punitive damages shows that the award was intended to be compensatory, at least in part. Defendants maintain the award was "entirely punitive" because "the district court found that Kenai suffered no damage from delay at CP Marine's shipyard."

In this case, the district court's ruling strongly suggests that the punitive damages award was intended, at least in part, to compensate Kenai for the five-day loss of its vessel:

> Although the Court finds that Defendants' performance was not dilatory and did not cause Plaintiff's late arrival in Alaska, *Defendants' wrongful detention of Plaintiff's vessel plainly delayed Plaintiff by five days*. Therefore, as a measure of punitive damages, the Court will award Plaintiff *the value of its missed contract days* for the days that Defendants wrongfully detained the vessel.

Here, the district court found that Defendants converted Plaintiff's vessel for five days. The district court's discussion of Defendants' bad faith **[—20—]** conduct in the court's Conclusions of Law is entitled "Wrongful Arrest and Conversion." **{-613-}**

"Under the general maritime law, as under the common law of torts, a person may be liable for certain intentional wrongs, such as conversion[.]" Schoenbaum, *supra*, at § 5:3 (citing *The Lydia* (*Hugh D. MacKenzie Co. v. Steamship Lydia*), 1 F.2d 18 (2d Cir. 1924)). The Fifth Circuit looked to the "landside context" for this maritime tort to define it as "the unlawful and wrongful exercise of

---

[9] We again note that Defendants' separate appeal of the attorney's fees award was dismissed for want of prosecution. *Kenai Ironclad*, 2022 WL 18776210, at *1. Thus, this award is final.

dominion, ownership or control over the property of another, to the exclusion of the same rights by the owner." *Goodpasture, Inc. v. M/V Pollux*, 602 F.2d 84, 87 (5th Cir. 1979) (citing *Bankers Life Ins. Co. v. Scurlock Oil Co.*, 447 F.2d 997, 1004 (5th Cir. 1971) (applying Texas law)). *See also 4 H Const. Corp. v. Superior Boat Works, Inc.*, 659 F. Supp. 2d 774, 780 (N.D. Miss. 2009), *aff'd*, 579 F. App'x 278 (5th Cir. 2014) (finding Mississippi state law of conversion relevant because its application "would not interfere with the uniformity or characteristic features of admiralty and maritime law[]"); Restatement (Second) of Torts § 222A (AM. L. INST. 1965) (defining "conversion" as "an intentional exercise of dominion or control over a chattel which so seriously interferes with the right of another to control it that the actor may justly be required to pay the other the full value of the chattel.").

Some courts have found that maritime law requires a finding of bad faith to establish conversion, at least in the context of wrongful attachment. *See Furness Withy (Chartering), Inc., Panama v. World Energy Sys. Assocs., Inc.*, 854 F.2d 410, 412 & n.6 (11th Cir. 1988). *See also Comar Marine*, 792 F.3d at 575 n.32, 3 Adm. R. at 377 n.32 (citing *Furness* with approval in describing burden of proving wrongful seizure and stating that it requires showing of bad faith). *See also* Restatement (Second) of Torts § 222A (identifying good faith as one of six "important" factors "[i]n determining the seriousness of the interference and the justice of requiring the actor to pay the full value"). Ultimately, the **[—21—]** exact contours of the maritime tort of conversion need not be defined here, as the district court correctly found that Defendants wrongfully exercised control over Kenai's vessel to Kenai's exclusion and that Defendants did so in bad faith.[10]

Defendants argue that despite the district court's finding that Defendants converted Kenai's vessel resulting in its loss of use for five days and despite the court's use of the vessel's daily rate as the measure of punitive damages, the court's award was in no way compensatory. While the district court's reference to the tort of conversion tends to support Kenai's position that the award is in part compensatory, there is some ambiguity in the trial court's decision. As a result, we remand for clarification. If the award was intended to be compensatory in part, the court should make clear its delineation of compensatory and punitive damages.

III. Did the district court err in awarding pre-judgment interest?

Defendants urge that the district court erred in awarding prejudgment interest, as it is not allowed under Louisiana law or **{-614-}** federal law.[11] Kenai responds that, while "prejudgment interest is not [generally] applicable to punitive damages awards under maritime cases[,]" the award here is actually **[—22—]** compensatory in nature, at least enough so to justify an award of prejudgment interest. Kenai points the panel to *Illinois Central Railroad Co. v. Texas Eastern Transmission Corp.*, 551 F.2d 943 (5th Cir. 1977), where the court affirmed pretrial interest on demurrage although the demurrage award was partly punitive in nature.

Defendants dispute Kenai's allegation that the punitive damages award was partly compensatory because "the district court found that Kenai suffered no damage from delay at CP Marine's shipyard." This, argue Defendants, is a critical fact that distinguishes *Illinois Central.*

---

[10] The district court called this an act of conversion, but there is some authority that this is perhaps more accurately called trespass to chattel. *See* Restatement (Second) of Torts § 222A cmt. c (distinguishing between two torts and explaining that conversion entitled plaintiff to "full value of the chattel" while trespass to chattel allows a plaintiff to "recover for the diminished value of his chattel because of any damage to it, *or for the damage to his interest in its possession or use*" (emphasis added)). Again, the exact contours of the tort need not be fully explored, as, either way, Kenai is entitled to compensation for the loss of use of its property.

[11] Defendants also argue that the district court's judgment did not grant prejudgment interest on the award of attorney's fees, but, to the extent that it did so, this was inappropriate. This is not before the court since the attorney's fee award was appealed separately and dismissed for want of prosecution.

> "As a general rule, prejudgment interest should be awarded in admiralty cases—not as a penalty, but as compensation for the use of funds to which the claimant was rightfully entitled." The district court has discretion to deny prejudgment interest "only when there are 'peculiar circumstances' that would make it inequitable for the losing party to be forced to pay prejudgment interest."

Comar Marine, 792 F.3d at 580, 3 Adm. R. at 381 (quoting *Noritake*, 627 F.2d at 728–29). *See also In re Signal Int'l, LLC*, 579 F.3d 478, 500 (5th Cir. 2009) (citing *Corpus Christi Oil & Gas Co. v. Zapata Gulf Marine Corp.*, 71 F.3d 198, 204 (5th Cir.1995)).

As discussed earlier, we are unable to resolve this issue because it is unclear whether the district court intended the punitive damages award to be in part compensatory. If, as in *Illinois Central*, it was intended to be partly compensatory, the district court's grant of prejudgment interest was appropriate. The case is remanded to the district court for clarification of this issue. **[—23—]**

CONCLUSION

In sum: we AFFIRM the district court's finding that Defendants wrongfully seized and converted Kenai's vessel in bad faith and in a manner egregious enough to warrant an award of punitive damages. We VACATE the district court's award of damages and REMAND on the limited basis of clarifying the court's award, specifying whether any part of the award was intended as compensatory damages and, if so, in what amount. In doing so, the district court should make whatever findings of fact and conclusions of law are necessary to arrive at its decision. Additional briefing of the parties is strongly encouraged. Whatever the decision of the district court, it will not be necessary for the parties to file a new notice of appeal in order to obtain appellate review of that decision. The parties need only file certified copies of the district court's ruling plus any supplementary briefs and materials. The matter will then be referred to this panel. *See United States v. Gaston*, 608 F.2d 607, 614 n.3 (5th Cir. 1979); *Chaney v. Schweiker*, 659 F.2d 676, 679 n.5 (5th Cir. 1981); *Royal Bank of Canada v. Trentham Corp.*, 665 F.2d 515, 519 (5th Cir. 1981).

United States Court of Appeals
for the Fifth Circuit

No. 22-30393

STREET
VS.
BP EXPLORATION & PROD., INC.

Appeal from the United States District Court for the Eastern District of Louisiana

Decided: October 20, 2023

Citation: 85 F.4th 266, 11 Adm. R. 367 (5th Cir. 2023).

Before **RICHMAN,** Chief Judge, and **SOUTHWICK,** and **OLDHAM,** Circuit Judges.

[—3—] **{-267-}** **SOUTHWICK,** Circuit Judge: **{-268-}**

These consolidated cases continue this court's saga of *Deepwater Horizon*. These plaintiffs argue the district court judge abused his discretion by failing to disqualify himself at their request. We conclude that any error was harmless and AFFIRM.

FACTUAL AND PROCEDURAL BACKGROUND

The issues surrounding *Deepwater Horizon* have been detailed in numerous appeals in this court. *See, e.g., In re Deepwater Horizon*, 728 F.3d 491, 494–97, 1 Adm. R. 280, 280–84 (5th Cir. 2013). We will only discuss the facts and procedural history pertinent to these 40 consolidated cases. The plaintiff in the lead case among the 40 is Corey Street. Counsel for all 40 appellants states that the "consolidated cases are nearly identical as far as the issues involved and the arguments presented to the lower court." We will refer to the parties as the Street plaintiffs, or, at times, just the plaintiffs.

Before these plaintiffs' cases were distributed to the district court, these cases were part of MDL 2179, the multi-district litigation proceeding before United States District Court Judge Carl J. Barbier in the Eastern District of Louisiana. Judge Barbier established what is known as the "B3 Bundle" within the overall litigation. The B3 Bundle included claims for personal injury and wrongful death due to exposure **{-269-}** to oil and/or other chemicals used during the response to the disaster. By a pre-trial order dated January 12, 2011, Judge Barbier ruled that claimants could intervene into the B3 Bundle Master Complaint by filing a "Short-Form Joinder." The Street plaintiffs **[—4—]** timely did so. After joining the Master Complaint, a class action settlement of the B3 claims was reached in May 2012 and approved by a final order filed on January 11, 2013. The Street plaintiffs timely opted out of the class settlement.

The Phase One trial established liability for the oil spill and took place from February 25 to April 17, 2013. The Street plaintiffs were parties to MDL 2179 and the Phase One trial that established liability of certain defendants for the oil spill. In this trial, the Stone Pigman law firm in New Orleans represented Cameron International, the manufacturer of the blowout preventer that failed and was alleged as a cause of the catastrophic BP Oil Spill. As a potential contributor to the spill, Cameron was directly adverse to the Street plaintiffs in the Phase One liability trial. The district court found that BP Exploration & Production Inc. and BP America Production Co. were "67%" responsible for the spill, and Transocean and Halliburton were responsible for the remainder. No liability was found as to Cameron, and the district court dismissed all claims against Cameron.

After the finding of liability in the Phase One trial, the Street plaintiffs were ordered to file individual lawsuits. These individual lawsuits named as defendants all parties found to be liable for causing the BP oil spill. A master complaint was drafted to cover claims for personal injuries, and no version of that master complaint has named Cameron as a party. Individual complaints were also filed, and none of the Street plaintiffs named Cameron. The Street plaintiffs alleged that exposure to substances associated with the spill caused various injuries. Thus, the Street plaintiffs have not alleged any liability against Cameron in the B3 litigation, as that question was resolved to finality in the separate Phase One trial. **[—5—]**

Following Judge Barbier's severance order, 85 B3 cases were assigned to District Judge Barry Ashe. Judge Ashe has been a federal district judge since 2018. Before his confirmation, he was a longtime partner at the Stone Pigman law firm. His history with Stone Pigman is a well-known fact among lawyers who practice in New Orleans. Upon having their cases assigned to Judge Ashe, no B3 plaintiff, including the Street plaintiffs, raised any objection to his consideration of their cases. Plaintiffs' counsel in this appeal, though, asserts he was unaware of Judge Ashe's background.

After the cases were assigned to him, Judge Ashe began issuing discovery orders, complete with schedules for expert reports and dispositive motion practice. For example, Judge Ashe held a scheduling conference in the current case on September 15, 2021. He gave the parties three months to amend their complaints and answers. Street was ordered to designate his experts by April 11, 2022. The district judge further ordered that all "pretrial motions, including dispositive motions and motions *in limine* regarding the admissibility of expert testimony, shall be filed and served in sufficient time to permit hearing thereon no later than June 2, 2022." This gave the parties more than nine months to conduct discovery in the 40 consolidated cases, in addition to the extensive information exchanges that had already occurred before the cases were severed from the MDL.

The Street plaintiffs, along with hundreds of other B3 plaintiffs, retained Dr. Jerald Cook as their causation expert. On **{-270-}** June 2, 2022, following discovery and briefing and consistent with the timeline set forth in the scheduling order, Judge Ashe excluded Dr. Cook's report in five B3 cases, including Street's, because Dr. Cook's "opinions on general causation d[id] not meet the *Daubert* standard of reliability." *See Daubert v. Merrell Dow* **[—6—]** *Pharms., Inc.*, 509 U.S. 579, 593–95 (1993). Those plaintiffs offered no admissible expert testimony regarding general causation. Therefore, Judge Ashe granted summary judgment to the BP defendants.

On June 17, 2022, a little more than two weeks after Judge Ashe began granting summary judgments following exclusion of Dr. Cook, Street's counsel moved to disqualify Judge Ashe in the five cases in which he had excluded Dr. Cook and in other cases where *Daubert* and summary judgment motions were still pending. These motions sought Judge Ashe's disqualification on two grounds: (1) he was a partner at Stone Pigman when other lawyers there represented Cameron in the Phase One trial, allegedly requiring disqualification under 28 U.S.C. § 455(b)(2); and (2) he previously represented Noble Energy, a company that allegedly "was and is a joint venture partner with the BP Defendants in numerous Gulf of Mexico oil lease transactions," thus potentially triggering disqualification under 28 U.S.C. § 455(a).

On June 30, 2022, while briefing regarding disqualification was ongoing, plaintiffs Street, Johns, Johnson, Macon, and Murray (all of whom are appellants here) appealed Judge Ashe's decisions excluding Dr. Cook's testimony and granting summary judgment to BP. Accordingly, on July 12, 2022, Judge Ashe concluded that, as to those five plaintiffs, he no longer had jurisdiction to decide their disqualification motions. On July 14, 2022, Judge Ashe denied the remaining disqualification motions as untimely and meritless.

In July 2022, after Judge Ashe and other judges began excluding Dr. Cook's testimony, hundreds of B3 plaintiffs moved to suspend the deadlines for dispositive motions. As relevant to these consolidated appeals, on July **[—7—]** 11, 2022, the plaintiffs other than Street, Johns, Johnson, Macon, and Murray — who already filed their notices of appeal — began moving to suspend Judge Ashe's deadlines for dispositive motions. These motions faulted BP for Dr. Cook's inability to offer admissible general-causation testimony, arguing that BP's and the federal government's failure to collect biomonitoring and dermal testing data prevented Dr. Cook from admissible testimony.

These challenges arose after a discovery dispute in another Eastern District of Louisiana case (not a B3 case), where the plaintiffs filed a "Back-End Litigation Option" claim and took a Rule 30(b)(6) deposition of a former BP employee. *See Torres-Lugo v. BP Expl. & Prod. Inc.*, No. CV 20-210, 2022 WL 2806420 (E.D. La. July 18, 2022). The many B3 plaintiffs who sought to extend their dispositive motion deadlines, including the Street plaintiffs, all invoked the *Torres-Lugo* discovery dispute as the basis for their requests. These requests were rejected by multiple district judges because the discovery dispute issue did not resolve the insufficiency of Dr. Cook's expert testimony to establish general causation. Judge Ashe concluded the same and rejected the requests. After that ruling, the Street plaintiffs filed disqualification motions, essentially identical to those previously denied, and these motions were likewise denied.

The Street plaintiffs timely appealed Judge Ashe's final judgments in BP's favor, and this court consolidated these 40 appeals. To be precise, 39 of the 40 cases **{-271-}** in this consolidated appeal used Dr. Cook as their expert. For those, Judge Ashe granted BP's *Daubert* motion to exclude and BP's motion for summary judgment. In the remaining appeal, Judge Ashe granted summary judgment to BP because that plaintiff neither filed an expert report nor opposed BP's motion for summary judgment. **[—8—]**

DISCUSSION

The Street plaintiffs do not challenge Judge Ashe's decision to exclude Dr. Cook's testimony under *Daubert*, nor do they raise any argument on the merits as to why his granting of summary judgment to BP was erroneous. In the briefing before this court, the two arguments raised were that Judge Ashe should have disqualified himself, and, in the alternative, that he should have extended the case-management deadlines. Plaintiff's counsel was unclear at oral argument whether he was abandoning the second issue. Later, when responding to BP's Federal Rule of Appellate Procedure 28(j) letter, Plaintiffs' counsel unambiguously abandoned it by stating that "the sole issue in this appeal [is] whether Judge Ashe should have recused himself." Thus, that is the only issue we address.

This court reviews the denial of a motion to disqualify under an abuse of discretion standard. *In re Hipp, Inc.*, 5 F.3d 109, 116 (5th Cir. 1993). The Street plaintiffs argue that Judge Ashe abused his discretion for not disqualifying himself under 28 U.S.C. § 455(b)(2) because he was a partner at Stone Pigman when it represented Cameron in the Phase One liability trial.

Section 455(b)(2) provides that a judge shall disqualify himself "[w]here in private practice[,] he served as [a] lawyer in the *matter in controversy*, or a lawyer with whom he previously practiced law served during such association as a lawyer concerning the matter, or the judge or such lawyer has been a material witness concerning it." (emphasis added). The Street plaintiffs argue Judge Ashe was *required* to recuse under this provision — that he had no discretion. They argue extensively that Judge Ashe's position at Stone Pigman was "exactly the adverse relationship that requires mandatory **[—9—]** disqualification." They do not, however, cite authority in support of their position.

Judge Ashe held that these motions to disqualify were all untimely. Nonetheless, he issued an order with his reasons for denying the motions, and he rejected the arguments as untimely and meritless.[1]

As to timeliness, Judge Ashe explained that his prior employment with Stone Pigman was so "widely known" that "[i]t is hard to believe that [these plaintiffs'] attorneys had no knowledge of these facts until two weeks after this Court granted motions for summary judgment dismissing other B3 cases." Indeed, the motions "came fourteen months after" these cases were assigned to Judge Ashe and were "based on facts that are generally public knowledge — and presumably even better known to lawyers long part of the *Deepwater Horizon* MDL." Judge Ashe further observed

[1] Judge Ashe's order denying the disqualification motions was issued in the case of plaintiff Carpenter, also an appellant, and all other orders adopted that discussion and ruling.

that four of the lawyers on the disqualification motions' signature blocks practiced in "the New Orleans area." Judge Ashe also faulted their failure to "explain how or why [these] attorneys only learned or acquired this information after these five other B3 cases were dismissed and judgment entered." He thus found that, in light of "the totality of the circumstances," **{-272-}** those motions "appear[ed] to be an attempt to manipulate the system and [were] not filed timely."

Judge Ashe also denied the disqualification motions as meritless. Specifically, he concluded that "Stone Pigman's representation of Cameron in **[—10—]** the phase one liability trial is sufficiently unrelated to the case presently before the [c]ourt as not to trigger the [§ 455(b)(2)] 'matter in controversy' requirement" because, among other reasons, "Cameron has never been a party to the B3 cases, and its liability has never been a question in these cases." According to Judge Ashe, the matter in controversy in the B3 cases "involves issues that are discrete, separate, and distinct from the issues handled by [Judge Ashe's] former partners."[2] The Street plaintiffs' claims, both in the district court and on appeal, "raise issues concerning causation and damages for [] personal injuries," not "what caused the oil spill and who was responsible." Accordingly, Judge Ashe observed, he "will not be asked to address the merits of any issue in which his former partners were involved." Judge Ashe explained that "[t]here is no indication that Noble was a party to any *Deepwater Horizon* litigation or had any involvement at all with that oil well," nor was he "even aware of Noble's joint ventures with BP when he represented Noble." He thus concluded that "a well-informed, thoughtful, and objective observer would not question [his] impartiality."[3]

The Street plaintiffs do not challenge the judge's actual impartiality on appeal. Instead, they rely solely on the "matter in controversy" language found in Section 455(b)(2) and argue that recusal was mandatory. Yet even mandatory recusal under Section 455(b)(2) can be harmless. We have expressed "confiden[ce] that [Section] 455(b) violations are also subject to the **[—11—]** doctrine of harmless error," not just Section 455(a) violations. *Patterson v. Mobil Oil Corp.*, 335 F.3d 476, 485 (5th Cir. 2003).

For possible harmlessness of a failure to recuse, we apply these factors: "(1) the risk of injustice to the parties in this case; (2) the risk that denial of relief will create injustice in other cases; and (3) 'the risk of undermining the public's confidence in the judicial process.'" *Id.* (quoting *Liljeberg v. Health Servs. Acquisition Corp.*, 486 U.S. 847, 864 (1988)).

Relevant facts include that Judge Ashe's 30-year association with Stone Pigman ended in 2018. That law firm's representation of Cameron occurred early in the *Deepwater Horizon* litigation a decade ago, and there is no evidence in the record that suggests lawyer Ashe worked on that litigation.

As to possible injustice to the parties, our review of the summary judgment granted in this case is *de novo*. *National Oilwell Varco, L.P. v. Auto-Dril, Inc.*, 68 F.4th 206, 216 (5th Cir. 2023). The Street plaintiffs do not even challenge the merits of the decision. Further, eight other district court judges have reached the same conclusion regarding the exclusion of Dr. Cook's testimony and the plaintiffs' failure to produce expert testimony complying with the strictures of *Daubert*.[4] There is no **{-273-}** basis for a belief that these consistent results

---

[2] Judge Ashe also conducted an analysis of impartiality under 28 U.S.C. § 455(a) and (b)(1), but neither of those bases for disqualification is raised on appeal.

[3] The Street plaintiffs do not brief any argument regarding Noble Energy.

[4] *Turner v. BP Expl. & Prod. Inc.*, 2022 WL 2967441, at *5 (E.D. La. July 27, 2022) (Africk, J.) (excluding Dr. Cook's testimony because he "fails to identify a particular chemical and corresponding dose to which [the plaintiff] was exposed"); *Barkley v. BP Expl. & Prod. Inc.*, 2022 WL 2342474, at *4 (E.D. La. June 29, 2022) (Barbier, J.) ("Dr. Cook fails to identify the dose of any such chemical that would result in the adverse health effects contained in his report, and his report is therefore unreliable and inadmissible."); *Harrison v. BP Expl. & Prod. Inc.*, 2022 WL 2390733, at *6 (E.D. La. July 1, 2022) (Morgan, **[—12—]** J.) ("Cook's expert report includes no identification of the necessary dose of exposure

have been the result of Judge Ashe's actions in this case. **[—12—]**

Finally, "the public's confidence in the judicial process" is not undermined once, after a review of the records in the consolidated cases before us on appeal, it can be seen that Judge Ashe has made the same rulings as his colleagues who have been presented with the same issues.

If Judge Ashe erred when he failed to recuse in these cases, that error was harmless. Nonetheless, as the arguments on this appeal support, potential conflicts of interest must be taken seriously by every member of the judiciary. The litigants and the public need to be confident in the impartiality of those who will decide legal disputes. This appeal is fair warning to each of us of the importance of assuring the reality and appearance of that impartiality.

AFFIRMED.

---

for any of Plaintiffs complained-of symptoms to manifest."); *Harris v. BP Expl. & Prod. Inc.*, 2022 WL 2789037, at *7 (E.D. La. July 15, 2022) (Vance, J.) ("Dr. Cook's failure to identify the level of exposure to a relevant chemical that can cause the conditions asserted in plaintiffs complaint renders his opinion unreliable, unhelpful, and incapable of establishing general causation."); *Hill v. BP Expl. & Prod. Inc.*, 2022 WL 4534747, at *6 (E.D. La. Sept. 28, 2022) (Vitter, J.) ("Dr. Cook does not even specify the exact chemicals that Plaintiff was allegedly exposed to, let alone provide evidence regarding the level of exposure at which Plaintiffs symptoms might manifest."); *see also Laster v. BP Expl. & Prod. Inc.*, 2022 WL 5165019, at *1 (E.D. La. Sept. 13, 2022) (Guidry, J.) ("[F]or the previous reasons cited by this Court as well as the seven other judges of this Court, both the *Daubert* Motion and the Motion for Summary Judgment shall be granted."); *Reed v. BP Expl. & Prod. Inc.*, 2022 WL 3099925, at *3 (E.D. La. Aug. 4, 2022) (Milazzo, J.) ("[F]or the same reasons articulated by Judges Ashe, Vance, Barbier, Morgan, and Zainey, the Court grants Defendants' *Motion in Limine*."); *Barksdale v. BP Expl. & Prod. Inc.*, 2022 WL 2789022, at *3 (E.D. La. July 15, 2022) (Zainey, J.) (excluding Dr. Cook's testimony "[f]or the same reasons given by Judges Vance, Barbier, Morgan, and Ashe").

United States Court of Appeals
for the Fifth Circuit

No. 22-30261

MARQUETTE TRANSP. CO. GULF-ISLAND, L.L.C.
vs.
NAVIGATION MARITIME BULGARE JSC

Appeal from the United States District Court for the Eastern District of Louisiana

Decided: December 4, 2023

Citation: 87 F.4th 678, 11 Adm. R. 372 (5th Cir. 2023).

Before **KING, JONES,** and **DUNCAN,** Circuit Judges.

[—1—] {-680-} JONES, Circuit Judge:

This action arises from a collision between the M/V STRANDJA and the M/V KIEFFER E. BAILEY on the Mississippi River. A jury found that **[—2—]** the owner of the KIEFFER E. BAILEY was not negligent with respect to the collision and awarded that vessel's owner $114,000 damages after finding that the STRANDJA's owner and **{-681-}** manager were negligent and that the STRANDJA's river pilot was grossly negligent. The noteworthy holding here is that Louisiana law governs the burden of proof for the pilot's error. Accordingly, we AFFIRM in part, VACATE in part, and REMAND for a new trial as to the M/V STRANDJA and its owners and pilot Johnson.

I. BACKGROUND

On the morning of January 3, 2019, the STRANDJA was anchored at the New Orleans General Anchorage, which is situated along the western side of the Mississippi River. The ship was facing upstream and was secured by both a port and starboard anchor.[1]

In preparation to return to sea, Captain Robert Johnson, a Louisiana state commissioned river pilot, boarded the vessel as its compulsory pilot. He requested that the STRANDJA's master, Captain Kiril Karapanov, instruct the crew to heave the port anchor. The process of heaving the port anchor at first pulled the ship's bow landward, to port. This landward movement was a natural result of the strain placed on the port anchor's chain during the heaving process. When the port anchor released from the river bottom, the strain shifted to the starboard anchor, which had not yet been raised. This shift in strain caused the bow to change course and begin drifting to starboard, into the middle of the river. As the crew began heaving the starboard anchor, the drift to starboard continued. The ship ultimately drifted approximately 300 feet outside the general anchorage. **[—3—]**

While the STRANDJA was heaving anchors, the KIEFFER E. BAILEY—an inland tugboat pushing a tow of six loaded barges—was headed downriver. It was navigating near the center of the river in preparation to pass an oceangoing vessel heading upriver that was approximately two miles downstream. The tug made multiple radio calls to the vessels in the area indicating its approach and its position in the river. No one from the STRANDJA responded to these calls or warned the KIEFFER E. BAILEY that the STRANDJA would be drifting into the middle of the river.

As the tug drew closer, it sounded a two-whistle signal, the internationally recognized signal that an approaching vessel intends to alter course to port to accomplish a starboard-to-starboard passing. On hearing this signal, Captain Johnson expected the tug to do just that—move to port to pass the STRANDJA and avoid a collision. Neither he nor Pilot Johnson thought the STRANDJA was in a position to avoid the collision itself because the ship's starboard anchor was still on the river bottom.

Nevertheless, when it became apparent that a collision was imminent, both vessels attempted to avoid the collision. The KIEFFER E. BAILEY steered hard away from the STRANDJA, toward the eastern side of the Mississippi river. The STRANDJA, for its part, put its engines in reverse. Despite these efforts, one of the KIEFFER E. BAILEY's barges

[1] With the bow as the point of reference, "port" means the left side of the ship and "starboard" means the right.

struck the STRANDJA's bulbous bow (a protrusion below the waterline at the front end of the ship). The collision damaged the barge and put a hole in the STRANDJA's bulbous bow.

The owner of the KIEFFER E. BAILEY, Marquette Transportation Company Gulf-Inland LLC, brought *in personam* claims against the owner of the STRANDJA, **{-682-}** Balkan Navigation Ltd, and the ship's manager, Navigation Maritime Bulgare JSC (together "Balkan"), under the federal court's diversity jurisdiction. Balkan asserted an *in personam* counterclaim against **[—4—]** Marquette and an *in rem* counterclaim against the KIEFFER E. BAILEY, both of which sounded in the court's admiralty jurisdiction. Marquette then amended its complaint to add *in rem* admiralty claims against the STRANDJA and impleaded Captain Johnson pursuant to Rule 14(c) of the Federal Rules of Civil Procedure.

The case proceeded to a jury trial over Balkan's objections. The jury determined that Marquette was not negligent; found Balkan negligent and Captain Johnson grossly negligent; concluded that Balkan and Captain Johnson were each 50% at fault; awarded Marquette $114,000 in damages; and awarded Balkan $0 in damages. Both Balkan and Captain Johnson appeal that judgment.

II. DISCUSSION

Captain Johnson and Balkan raise multiple issues on appeal. We conclude that the district court instructed the jury to apply the incorrect standard of proof for the claim against Captain Johnson. This error necessitates vacating the judgments as to Marquette's claims against both Captain Johnson and Balkan, even though we do not find any error in the trial of the claim against Balkan, considered alone. We affirm the judgment that Marquette was not liable for the accident.[2]

A. Subject Matter Jurisdiction

We begin by assessing subject matter jurisdiction. *See MidCap Media Finance, LLC v. Pathway Data, Inc.*, 929 F.3d 310, 313 (5th Cir. 2019). Marquette sued Balkan pursuant to the court's diversity jurisdiction. It therefore had the burden to plead each party's citizenship, including its own. **[—5—]** *Whitmire v. Victus, Ltd.*, 212 F.3d 885, 887 (5th Cir. 2000) (citation omitted). As a limited liability company, Marquette was required to plead the citizenship "of all of its members." *Harvey v. Grey Wolf Drilling Co.*, 542 F.3d 1077, 1080 (5th Cir. 2008). It failed to do this. It instead asserted only that it "is a Delaware limited liability company, having its principal place of business in Paducah, Kentucky." Marquette's jurisdictional allegations for diversity jurisdiction are therefore inadequate.

"Nevertheless, jurisdiction lies." *Ed & Fred Inc. v. Puritan Mar. Ins. U. Corp.*, 506 F.2d 757, 758 (5th Cir. 1975). All parties agree that Marquette's claims against Balkan fall within the court's admiralty jurisdiction as does one of the parties' counterclaims. Given that the claims arise from a collision on the Mississippi River, the parties are right to agree on this point. We thus have jurisdiction to hear this appeal. But on remand for new trial, Marquette will be required to amend its pleadings to state admiralty jurisdiction as the basis for its claims against Balkan. *See* 28 U.S.C. § 1653.

B. Captain Johnson's Appeal

Captain Johnson contends that the district court erred by determining that general maritime law preempted a Louisiana pilotage law and by admitting an accident reconstruction during trial. The first argument is correct. The second fails. **[—6—]**

1. Preemption

Louisiana law requires any "party seeking to hold a pilot acting under his **{-683-}** state commission issued in accordance with this Chapter liable for damages or loss occasioned

[2] Because we affirm the judgment that Marquette was not negligent, we do not reach Balkan's challenge to the jury's zero damages award.

by the pilot's errors, omissions, fault, or neglect" to "prove by *clear and convincing evidence* that the damages arose from the pilot's gross negligence or willful misconduct." LA. STAT. ANN. § 34:1137 (emphasis added). The district court held that this statute was preempted by general maritime law, which only requires a finding of ordinary negligence by a preponderance of the evidence. *See, e.g., Gavagan v. United States*, 955 F.2d 1016, 1022 (5th Cir. 1992); *see also* 1 Thomas J. Schoenbaum, ADMIRALTY AND MARITIME LAW § 5:5 (6th ed. 2022). Captain Johnson and amici curiae[3] argue this was error. We agree.[4]

Judicially crafted general maritime law preempts state laws that "prejudice the characteristic features of the maritime law" or "disrupt the harmony it strives to bring to international and interstate relations." *J. Ray McDermott & Co. v. The Vessel Morning Star*, 457 F.2d 815, 818 (5th Cir. 1972) (en banc); *see also East River S.S. Corp. v. Transamerica Delaval, Inc.*, 476 U.S. 858, 864, 106 S. Ct. 2295, 2298–99 (1986). Congress, however, has carved out an exception to this rule: "Except as otherwise provided in this subtitle, pilots in the bays, rivers, harbors, and ports of the United States shall be regulated only in conformity with the laws of the States." 46 U.S.C. **[—7—]** § 8501(a). The parties dispute whether LA. STAT. ANN. § 34:1137 falls within this exception.

"Prior to the ratification of the Constitution, the states regulated pilotage as sovereigns." *Gillis v. Louisiana*, 294 F.3d 755, 761 (5th Cir. 2002). The First Congress codified this power in the Lighthouse Act of 1789. *Id.* That statute has since been reenacted and recodified, most recently in Section 8501. *Id.* We have thus interpreted the statute "as an expression of Congress's general intent *not* to limit the power already held by the states unless otherwise provided by Congress." *Id.* (emphasis in original).

It is not in doubt that a state at the time of ratification could have passed a law regulating pilots' liability. No federal statute currently precludes such a regulation. And as amici explain, the limitation of pilots' liability serves as an essential cog in Louisiana's comprehensive pilotage regulatory system. *See* LA. STAT. ANN. tit. 34, ch. 6. Louisiana is also not alone in this regard. Other states include similar liability-limiting provisions in their pilotage regulatory systems. *See, e.g.*, ALASKA STAT. § 08.62.165 (liability cap in negligence actions); ME. STAT tit. 38, § 99-A (same); S.C. CODE ANN. § 54-15-350 (same); TEX. TRANSP. CODE § 66.083 (same); WASH. REV. CODE § 88.16.118 (same); *see also* 2 Thomas J. Schoenbaum, ADMIRALTY AND MARITIME LAW § 13:2 ("All the states bordering on the sea have laws establishing a comprehensive pilotage regulatory system."). We therefore have no difficulty in holding that this Louisiana law falls within the state's broad power to regulate pilotage. *See* LA. STAT. ANN. § 34:1137. **{-684-}**

The cases cited by Marquette are not to the contrary. In *Garrett v. Moore-McCormack Co.*, a seaman who had executed a release of liability brought a Jones Act personal injury claim in state court. 317 U.S. 239, 240– 41, 63 S. Ct. 246, 248–49 (1942). The state court, in assessing the validity of the release, applied a "clear, precise, and indubitable evidence" standard. *Id.* **[—8—]** at 242, 249. The Supreme Court reversed, as it held that the Jones Act's "uniformity requirement extends to the type of proof necessary for judgment." *Id.* No such uniformity requirement exists as to pilotage regulations. Congress instead has left this area in the states' capable hands. 46 U.S.C. § 8501(a); *see also* 2 Thomas J. Schoenbaum, ADMIRALTY AND MARITIME LAW § 13:1 (noting

[3] Amici are the Crescent River Port Pilots' Association, Inc., the New Orleans and Baton Rouge Steamship Pilots Association, and the Board of River Port Pilot Commissioners for the Port of New Orleans.

[4] Marquette suggests that Captain Johnson forfeited this argument because he failed to make a Rule 50 motion. To the contrary, Rule 51 of the Federal Rules of Civil Procedure only required Captain Johnson to object "on the record, stating distinctly the matter objected to and the grounds for the objection," which Captain Johnson did. *See Garcia-Ascanio v. Spring Indep. Sch. Dist.*, 74 F.4th 305, 308–09 (5th Cir. 2023).

the "irregular pattern of [pilotage] regulation" created by Congress's deference to state law).

In re Exxon Valdez, 270 F.3d 1215 (9th Cir. 2001), is also inapposite. That was a general maritime tort case; it did not address the scope of Section 8501 or involve a state statute regulating pilotage. Exxon argued "for a clear and convincing standard on various policy grounds." *Id.* at 1232. In the absence of statutory authority or precedent, the court rejected Exxon's arguments. *Id.* Here, in contrast, Louisiana law expressly provides for the application of the clear and convincing evidence standard in actions against pilots. LA. STAT. ANN. § 34:1137.

In sum, the district court incorrectly concluded that general maritime law preempted the burden of proof and the applicable negligence standard in LA. STAT. ANN. § 34:1137. The court therefore abused its discretion in instructing the jury that Marquette had the burden to prove gross negligence against Captain Johnson by only a preponderance of the evidence. *See EMJ Corp. v. Hudson Specialty Ins. Co.*, 833 F.3d 544, 550 (5th Cir. 2016). And in light of the contradictory evidence in the record, regarding the actions of STRANDJA and the pilot leading up to the collision, we cannot say that applying the lower standard of proof to Johnson's conduct in the jury interrogatory was harmless. *See Puga v. RCX Sols., Inc.*, 922 F.3d 285, 291– 92 (5th Cir. 2019); *see also Gardner v. Wilkinson*, 643 F.2d 1135, 1137 (5th Cir. 1981). We must vacate the judgment against Captain Johnson and remand for a new trial. **[—9—]**

2. Reconstruction testimony

Captain Johnson also challenges the admission of the accident reconstruction prepared by Marquette's witness, Steven Cunningham, in addition to the lay testimony Cunningham offered to authenticate the reconstruction. He argues (1) that the reconstruction was not properly authenticated, (2) that Cunningham testified as an expert and was therefore required to provide an expert report, and (3) that the reconstruction was not admissible as summary evidence.[5]

Marquette argues that Captain Johnson did not properly preserve these issues for appeal. This is true, but only to an extent. Before trial, Balkan filed a motion in limine seeking exclusion of the reconstruction. It argued in the motion that exclusion was appropriate because the reconstruction (1) was not authenticated, (2) was **{-685-}** inaccurate and misleading due to certain self-serving captions, (3) was not timely disclosed, and (4) could not be admitted without expert testimony. In a pretrial filing of his own, Captain Johnson incorporated the arguments from Balkan's motion, which was later granted in part.[6] The objections were also renewed in a proposed pretrial order that Captain Johnson and Balkan submitted jointly. In a separate pretrial filing, Captain Johnson objected to use of the reconstruction as a demonstrative, **[—10—]** this time not only incorporating but also summarizing the arguments from Balkan's motion in limine.

A "pre-trial objection is sufficient to preserve [an evidentiary] error for appellate review." *Mathis v. Exxon Corp.*, 302 F.3d 448, 459 (5th Cir. 2002). Captain Johnson's pretrial objections preserved the arguments contained in Balkan's motion in limine concerning authentication and expert testimony. But neither he nor Balkan argued below that the reconstruction was inadmissible summary evidence. That argument thus was not preserved for appeal.

[5] The reconstruction compiled by Cunningham consisted of three data sources: the STRANDJA's Voyage Data Recorder; the KIEFFER E. BAILEY's Rose Point Data; and Automatic Identification System data to verify the first two sources. Cunningham plotted these data onto Google Earth, synchronizing the sources as well as an overlay from the STRANDJA's audio. Cunningham also purported to confirm the reconstruction's accuracy using radar images.

[6] The district court ordered Marquette to remove the misleading captions and to authenticate the reconstruction by calling the individual who prepared it (Cunningham). It otherwise determined that the failure to timely disclose the reconstruction was harmless and that no expert testimony was required.

As to the preserved arguments, this court reviews a trial court's evidentiary rulings for abuse of discretion. "Evidentiary rulings, however, are also subject to harmless error review, so even if a district court has abused its discretion, we will not reverse unless the error affected the substantial rights of the parties." *Mahmoud v. De Moss Owners Ass'n, Inc.*, 865 F.3d 322, 327 (5th Cir. 2017) (internal quotation marks omitted).

Captain Johnson first argues that Cunningham's testimony did not adequately establish the reliability and accuracy of the process by which Cunningham created the accident reconstruction. *See* Fed. R. Evid. 901(b)(9). He also contends that Marquette was required to authenticate the reconstruction with expert testimony, which would require the filing of a pre-trial expert report.

Although the admission of the reconstruction raises important issues concerning the necessity for expert testimony, *see Doddy v. Oxy USA, Inc.*, 101 F.3d 448, 460 (5th Cir. 1996) ("[A] person may testify as a lay witness only if his opinions or inferences do not require any specialized knowledge and could be reached by any ordinary person."), any error by the district court in this respect was harmless. Neither Balkan nor Captain Johnson argued at or before trial that the reconstruction depicted the collision **[—11—]** inaccurately or that the data used to develop it were unreliable. In fact, Captain Johnson played the reconstruction video during his closing argument and used it to make substantive arguments to the jury. He also encouraged the jury to review the reconstruction during deliberations. Captain Johnson thus cannot plausibly argue on appeal that admission of the reconstruction affected his substantial rights.

The reconstruction issue will likely resurface when Marquette retries its claim against Captain Johnson. If it does, the district court should carefully consider whether it would be more appropriate for Cunningham to testify as an expert witness for purposes of authentication and offering an expert report pretrial.

C. Balkan's Appeal

Balkan contends that this case should not have been tried to a jury, that the evidence was insufficient to support the **{-686-}** jury's findings, and that the district court erroneously limited the testimony of Balkan's expert.[7] Each argument falls flat. Even so, we conclude that the claim against Balkan must be retried because of the error concerning the standard of proof for the claim against Captain Johnson.

1. Jury trial

Balkan first contends that the district court erred in trying this case to a jury where the only basis for jurisdiction was admiralty. This attempt to shoehorn a belated jurisdictional attack into a challenge to the district court's **[—12—]** employment of a jury is unavailing. Balkan moved to strike the jury demand two years before trial. Balkan did not argue in that motion that diversity of citizenship was lacking. It argued only that the amount-in-controversy requirement was not met and that, even if it was, Marquette had impliedly elected to proceed in admiralty based on the third-party demands it made in admiralty. Only on appeal does Balkan argue that the district court erred in denying the motion to strike because the absence of diversity deprived the court of a non-admiralty basis to hear the claims. Balkan forfeited this argument by not raising it below. *See Rollins v. Home Depot USA*, 8 F.4th 393, 397 (5th Cir. 2021).

Even if it did not forfeit the argument, Balkan does not have a constitutional right to a non-jury trial. *See Fitzgerald v. U.S. Lines Co.*, 374 U.S. 16, 20, 83 S. Ct. 1646, 1650 (1963) ("While this Court has held that the Seventh Amendment does not require jury trials in admiralty cases, neither that Amendment nor

[7] Balkan belatedly attempted to join Captain Johnson's appeal as to whether the district court properly admitted the testimony of Cunningham with respect to the reconstruction. As Balkan did not address this argument in its opening brief or expound upon it in either of its reply briefs, it is forfeited. *See SEC v. Hallam*, 42 F.4th 316, 327 (5th Cir. 2022).

any other provision of the Constitution forbids them."); *accord* Charles Alan Wright & Arthur R. Miller, FEDERAL PRACTICE AND PROCEDURE § 2317. Nor has Balkan argued how trial by jury adversely affected its substantial rights. Any error is therefore harmless. *See* 28 U.S.C. § 2111.

2. Evidentiary sufficiency

Balkan next argues that the jury erred in (1) finding that Marquette was not negligent and (2) awarding Marquette $114,000 in damages. Marquette responds that Balkan forfeited these arguments by failing to move for judgment as a matter of law under Rule 50(b) of the Federal Rules of Civil Procedure.

"[A] party who wishes to appeal on grounds of insufficient evidence must make a Rule 50(b) motion for judgment as a matter of law after the jury's verdict." *Downey v. Strain*, 510 F.3d 534, 543–44 (5th Cir. 2007) **[—13—]** (citing *Unitherm Food Sys., Inc. v. Swift-Eckrich, Inc.*, 546 U.S. 394, 400–01, 126 S. Ct. 980, 985–86 (2006)). "A postverdict motion is necessary because '[d]etermination of whether a new trial should be granted or a judgment entered under Rule 50(b) calls for the judgment in the first instance of the judge who saw and heard the witnesses and has the feel of the case which no appellate printed transcript can impart.'" *Unitherm*, 546 U.S. at 401, 126 S. Ct. at 985–86 (quoting *Cone v. W.V. Pulp & Paper Co.*, 330 U.S. 212, 216, 67 S. Ct. 752, 755 (1947)) (alteration in original). "[W]e lack power to address a claim not properly raised in a Rule 50(b) motion." *OneBeacon Ins. Co. v. T. Wade Weltch & Assocs.*, 841 F.3d 669, 680 (5th Cir. 2016). **{-687-}**

Balkan filed a Rule 50(a) motion at the close of Marquette's case-in-chief, contending that there was insufficient evidence for the jury to find that Balkan was negligent or that Marquette proved its damages. The district court denied that motion, and the record is clear that Balkan did not renew the motion after the jury returned its verdict. Consequently, we "lack power" to address Balkan's sufficiency of the evidence arguments concerning Marquette's negligence claim. *OneBeacon*, 841 F.3d at 680; *see also Thomas v. Hughes*, 27 F.4th 995, 1008 (5th Cir. 2022).[8] In its reply brief, Balkan implicitly concedes that it forfeited its challenge to the jury's award of damages to Marquette on Marquette's negligence claim against it.

Balkan also recognizes that it did not bring a Rule 50 motion as to its negligence counterclaim against Marquette. Marquette argues that, by **[—14—]** failing to do so, Balkan forfeited its challenge to the jury's finding that Marquette was not negligent. There is some support for forfeiture, *see U.S. v. Flintco, Inc.*, 143 F.3d 955, 967–68 (5th Cir. 1998), but we need not address it here. It is clear from the record that there was sufficient evidence for the jury to conclude that the KIEFFER E. BAILEY acted reasonably under the circumstances and that Marquette was therefore not negligent. The testimony of two of Marquette's experts, Captain Wayne Wilson and Captain Michael Berry, provided the necessary support. They testified that the pilot of the KIEFFER E. BAILEY, Captain Nobles, could not have reasonably anticipated that the STRANDJA would leave general anchorage and drift into the navigation stream, especially when the STRANDJA failed to provide notice of its intention to do so. This testimony supports a conclusion that the distance at which the KIEFFER E. BAILEY passed general anchorage was reasonable. Captain Berry also testified that Captain Nobles made prudent navigation decisions under the circumstances, including with respect to the speed at which the KIEFFER E. BAILEY was travelling. This evidence was sufficient to support the jury's finding that Marquette was not negligent.

[8] Some panels have reviewed for plain error even where the appellant failed to bring a Rule 50 motion. *See McLendon v. Big Lots Stores*, 749 F.3d 373, 375 n.2 (5th Cir. 2014) (unpublished) (collecting divergent cases). Even if the clear error standard applies, some evidence supports the jury's conclusion that Marquette sustained $114,000 in damages. *See Flowers*, 247 F.3d at 238; *see also Pizani v. M/V Blossom*, 669 F.2d 1084, 1088 (5th Cir. 1982) ("The plaintiff bears the burden of proof to show the amount, as well as the fact, of damages.").

3. Expert testimony

Balkan asserts that the district court abused its discretion in limiting the testimony of its liability expert, Captain A.J. Gibbs, regarding the lookout rule, the safe-speed rule, and the exchange between Master Karapanov and Captain Johnson about heaving the STRANDJA's anchors ("the master–pilot exchange").

An expert report must contain "a complete statement of all opinions the witness will express and the basis and reasons for them." FED. R. CIV. P. 26(a)(2)(B). Failure to disclose such an opinion precludes the proffering party from using that information "at a trial, unless the failure was **[—15—]** substantially justified or is harmless." FED. R. CIV. P. 37(c)(1). "A district court enjoys wide latitude in determining the admissibility of expert testimony, and the discretion of the trial judge and his or her decision will not be disturbed on appeal unless manifestly erroneous." *Johnson v. Thibodaux City*, 887 F.3d 726, 736 (5th Cir. 2018) (internal quotation marks and **{-688-}** citation omitted). "Even if we identify an abuse of discretion, the harmless error doctrine applies unless a substantial right of the complaining party was affected." *Id.* (internal quotation marks and citation omitted).

The safe-speed rule requires every vessel to "proceed at a safe speed so that she can take proper and effective action to avoid collision and be stopped within a distance appropriate to the prevailing circumstances and conditions." 33 C.F.R. § 83.06. The look-out rule requires every vessel to "maintain a proper look-out by sight and hearing" at all times to avoid collision. *Id.* § 83.05. The district court prevented Balkan from questioning Captain Gibbs about these rules after determining that Captain Gibbs's expert report did not express an opinion as to whether the KIEFFER E. BAILEY violated either one of them.

The district court did not abuse its discretion by limiting Captain Gibbs's testimony in this respect. Balkan's argument to the contrary relies on an excerpt of the expert report that, according to Balkan, expressed an opinion that both the safe-speed rule and the lookout rule were violated:

> 1. The Kieffer Bailey's operator failed to provide an independent lookout as prescribed by Rule 5
>
> 2. The Kieffer Bailey failed to comply with 33 CFR 165.810 (b) (2) When passing another vessel in motion, anchored, or tied up, a wharf or other structure liable to damage by collision, suction, or wave action, vessels shall give as much leeway as circumstances permit and reduce their speed sufficiently to preclude damage to the vessel or structure being passed. **[—16—]**
>
> . . . .
>
> The Kieffer Bailey had ample time to . . . to pass at a wider distance at a safer speed from the General Anchorage . . . .

In this excerpt, Captain Gibbs did not express an opinion that the safe-speed rule contained in 33 C.F.R. § 83.06 was violated. Although he stated a general opinion that the tug should have been traveling at a safer speed, his only reference to a rule concerning speed was not to § 83.06 but to § 165.810(b), which regulates navigation on a portion of the Mississippi River. Nor did Captain Gibbs unambiguously express an opinion that the KIEFFER E. BAILEY violated the lookout rule. To be sure, his report referred to § 83.05 and said that the KIEFFER E. BAILEY failed to provide "an independent lookout." But that rule does not require an *independent* lookout; it requires a proper lookout. And Captain Gibbs expressed no opinion in his report as to whether the KIEFFER E. BAILEY failed to provide a proper lookout. The decision of the district court to limit Captain Gibbs's testimony on these two rules thus was not an abuse of discretion.

Nor did the district court abuse its discretion with respect to Captain Gibbs's testimony on the adequacy of the master–pilot exchange, *i.e.*, the exchange between Master Karapanov and Captain Johnson before orders were given to heave the STRANDJA's anchors.

A line of questioning by Balkan about this exchange drew an objection from Marquette. But following an extended bench conference, Balkan indicated that it had no further questions on the topic. The district court thus did not limit the expert's testimony in any way that could have amounted to an abuse of discretion. **[—17—]**

4. Retrial

Despite the above conclusions, the district court's erroneous instruction concerning the standard of proof for the claim against Captain Johnson likely influenced **{-689-}** the jury's assessment of liability for the claim against Balkan. At the very least, this error had an impact on the jury's apportionment of fault between Captain Johnson and Balkan. On the other hand, it is not likely that the jury's exoneration of Marquette from negligence was influenced by the erroneous preponderance burden of proof as to Captain Johnson. As a result, we vacate the judgment and remand for a new trial on Marquette's claims against both Balkan and Captain Johnson, but we affirm the adverse judgment on Balkan's counterclaim against Marquette.

III. CONCLUSION

The judgment of the district court is AFFIRMED as to the finding that Marquette Transportation Company Gulf-Inland LLC was not negligent. The judgment of the district court against Balkan Navigation Ltd. and Navigation Maritime Bulgare JSC and Captain Robert Johnson is VACATED and the case is REMANDED in part for a new trial consistent with this opinion. Marquette is ORDERED, on remand, to amend its complaint within 14 days to allege admiralty jurisdiction as the jurisdictional basis for its claim against Balkan. *See* 28 U.S.C. § 1653.

This page intentionally left blank

United States Court of Appeals for the Seventh Circuit

United States Court of Appeals
for the Seventh Circuit

No. 22-2489

KREUZIGER
VS.
MILWAUKEE COUNTY, WIS.

Appeal from the United States District Court for the Eastern District of Wisconsin

Decided: February 13, 2023

Citation: 60 F.4th 391, 11 Adm. R. 382 (7th Cir. 2023).

Before **SYKES,** Chief Judge, and **WOOD** and **PRYOR,** Circuit Judges.

[—1—] {-392-} **SYKES,** Chief Judge: **{-393-}**

In the late 1930s, Milwaukee County built a dam on the Milwaukee River in Estabrook Park, an urban green space that runs along the east bank of the river where the City of Milwaukee borders suburban Shorewood **[—2—]** and Whitefish Bay. In 2017 the County transferred the dam to the Milwaukee Metropolitan Sewerage District for the purpose of removing it. Demolition was completed the following year.

With the dam removed, the water level immediately upstream fell by about four feet from its previous high-water mark. Brian Kreuziger owns a home along this stretch of the river, and the drop in the water level exposed a ten-foot swath of swampy land on his waterfront that used to be submerged. He sued the District and Milwaukee County, alleging that their removal of the dam amounted to a taking of his riparian right to the prior surface water level without just compensation. *See* U.S. CONST. amend. V; WIS. CONST. art. I, § 13. Ruling on cross-motions for summary judgment, the district judge entered judgment for the defendants, holding that Kreuziger had no property right to have the river remain at the previous level. We affirm.

I. Background

This case comes to us from a decision on cross-motions for summary judgment, so we construe the evidence and draw reasonable inferences in favor of Kreuziger as the party against whom the motion under consideration was made. *Gill v. Scholz*, 962 F.3d 360, 363 (7th Cir. 2020).

In 1937 Milwaukee County obtained a permit from the Wisconsin Public Service Commission to build a dam on the Milwaukee River, a navigable waterway, at a location near the northern border of Estabrook Park. According to the permit, the purpose of the dam was to promote "flood control, maintain[] normal water level under normal conditions, and ... provide recreational facilities." Shortly thereaf- **[—3—]** ter, the County built what became known as the "Estabrook Dam," and it owned and operated the dam from 1938 to 2017.

Starting in 1986, the County implemented seasonal drawdowns of the river, closing the gates in the spring and opening them in the fall. When the gates were closed, the river backed up, creating an artificial impoundment and raising the water level upstream. When the gates were opened in the fall, the upstream water level receded.

In September 2000 Kreuziger and his wife purchased a riverfront home immediately upstream from the dam in suburban Glendale. In 2009 the Wisconsin Department of Natural Resources ("DNR"), which manages the state's rivers, ordered the County to repair or abandon the Estabrook Dam. Years of political controversy and litigation ensued: upstream property owners, environmentalists, and county officials clashed over the fate of the dam. In 2017 the County obtained the DNR's permission to transfer the dam to the Milwaukee Metropolitan Sewerage District for the purpose of demolishing it. The District then applied for a permit to remove the dam. The DNR issued the permit, and the demolition was completed in 2018. **{-394-}**

After the dam was removed, the surface water level along Kreuziger's river frontage dropped by about four feet from the high-water mark typically experienced in the summer months when the dam's gates were closed. The new water level is roughly comparable to the traditional seasonal drawdowns in the fall when the gates were opened. The lower surface level of the river exposed a ten-foot strip of marshy land between Kreuziger's seawall and the water's edge that had previously been submerged. **[—4—]**

Kreuziger sued the District and Milwaukee County under 42 U.S.C. § 1983 invoking the Takings Clause of the Fifth Amendment to the United States Constitution and the Just Compensation Clause of the Wisconsin Constitution. He alleged that by removing the dam and thereby lowering the river's water level, the defendants took his riparian right to the previous water level and owed him compensation. In due course, the parties filed cross-motions for summary judgment. Kreuziger sought partial summary judgment on liability; the defendants argued that they had not taken anything because Kreuziger had no property right to the maintenance of the previous water level at or below the traditional high-water mark.

The judge denied Kreuziger's motion and entered judgment for the defendants. Relying on *United States v. Willow River Power Company*, 324 U.S. 499, 509–10 (1945), the judge determined that Kreuziger had no riparian right to the continuation of a particular surface water level along his river frontage; his interest in a higher water level was, at most, a convenience that must yield to the public's paramount interest in maintaining the state's navigable waterways.

II. Analysis

The Fifth Amendment to the United States Constitution provides that private property cannot "be taken for public use, without just compensation." U.S. CONST. amend. V. The Takings Clause applies to the States via the Fourteenth Amendment. *Kelo v. City of New London*, 545 U.S. 469, 472 n.1 (2005). Similarly, the Wisconsin Constitution bars the taking of private property for public use without just compensation. WIS. CONST. art. I, § 13. When the government takes **[—5—]** private property without paying for it, the aggrieved owner may sue immediately. *Knick v. Township of Scott*, 139 S. Ct. 2162, 2167 (2019) (overruling *Williamson Cnty. Reg'l Plan. Comm'n v. Hamilton Bank of Johnson City*, 473 U.S. 172 (1985), which had required plaintiffs to exhaust state remedies first).

To prevail on a federal takings-clause claim, an aggrieved property owner must make a threshold showing that the government has taken, either physically or by unduly onerous regulation, private property belonging to the plaintiff. *Conyers v. City of Chicago*, 10 F.4th 704, 710–11 (7th Cir. 2021), *cert. denied*, 142 S. Ct. 1669 (Apr. 18, 2022). Wisconsin law requires the same. *Adams Outdoor Advert. Ltd. P'ship v. City of Madison*, 914 N.W.2d 660, 664–65 (Wis. 2018).

Kreuziger argues that the defendants owe compensation for taking his riparian right to a higher water level on the river because their removal of the dam did nothing to improve navigation. His argument presumes that he has a property right to a particular water level at all. He does not.

In Wisconsin a riparian owner—that is, someone who owns land on a navigable waterway—has various riparian **{-395-}** rights, such as "the right to use the shoreline and have access to the waters ... [and] the right to have water flow to the land without artificial obstruction." *Movrich v. Lobermeier*, 905 N.W.2d 807, 813–14 (Wis. 2018) (cataloguing riparian rights) (quotation marks omitted). But riparian property rights are encumbered by and subordinate to the state's interest under the public-trust doctrine. Wisconsin holds the beds of its navigable lakes and rivers in trust for the benefit of the public, and riparian rights exist only insofar as they do not conflict with the public's interest in preserving navigable waters. *See R.W. Docks & Slips v. State*, 628 N.W.2d 781, 788 **[—6—]** (Wis. 2001). Riparian property owners cannot interfere with the public's navigation rights on the state's navigable lakes and rivers. *Doemel v. Jantz*, 193 N.W. 393, 398 (Wis. 1923).

"Navigation" is a term of art in this context and includes commercial transportation and noncommercial recreational activities, such as fishing, hunting, and boating. *Id.* at 395, 397. Accordingly, the public-trust doctrine is interpreted expansively to protect the public's interest in navigation, recreation, and the enjoyment of the scenic beauty of the state's lakes and rivers. *R.W. Docks & Slips*, 628 N.W.2d at 787–88.

Kreuziger insists that his bundle of riparian rights includes the right to have the river's water level remain unchanged. He says that Wisconsin recognized this right in *Smith v. Youmans*, 70 N.W. 1115 (Wis. 1897). There, a private dam operator sought to remove its 40-year-old dam, which had been built at the outlet of a lake where the water flowed into a stream connecting to another lake. *Id.* The dam's diversion of the natural water flow had the effect of raising the water level of the lake; removing it would have substantially lowered the lake's water level, thereby harming the property values of summer homes that had been built around the lake. *Id.* The Wisconsin Supreme Court blocked the removal of the dam because the other riparian owners had acquired by reliance an interest in maintaining the lake's water level. *Id.* at 1116.

Smith does not help Kreuziger. That case dealt with a clash of rights among *private* riparian owners. This case involves the government's interest in maintaining navigable waterways in the exercise of its responsibilities under the public-trust doctrine. **[—7—]**

The Supreme Court's decision in *Willow River* illustrates this distinction and is decisive here. Like this case, *Willow River* concerned the riparian rights of a Wisconsin riverfront property owner—there, a utility company that operated a hydroelectric plant on the St. Croix River using the waters of the river to generate power. 324 U.S. at 500. In 1938 the federal government built the Red Wing Dam on the upper Mississippi River, into which the St. Croix flows; the new dam altered the water level at the power company's property, diminishing the plant's capacity to generate electricity. *Id.* at 501. The power company claimed a riparian right to the previous water level and brought a takings suit seeking compensation from the United States.

The Court rejected the claim, observing that the company's interest in the river's surface water level was only "a privilege or a convenience, enjoyed for many years, permissible so long as compatible with navigation interests, but it is not an interest protected by law when it becomes inconsistent with plans authorized by Congress for improvement of navigation." *Id.* at 509. The Court confirmed that the riparian rights of the owners of property on navigable waterways "are subject **{-396-}** always to a dominant servitude in the interests of navigation and its exercise calls for no compensation." *Id.* When the government's regulatory authority conflicts with a riparian owner's interest in the surface level of a navigable waterway, the governmental interest is superior:

> Whatever rights may be as between equals such as riparian owners, they are not the measure of riparian rights on a navigable stream relative to the function of the Govern- **[—8—]** ment in improving navigation. Where these interests conflict[,] they are not to be reconciled as between equals, but the private interest must give way to a superior right, or perhaps it would be more accurate to say that as against the Government such private interest is not a right at all.

Id. at 510.

Put more succinctly, the riparian rights of waterfront property owners are subordinate to the government's authority to regulate navigable waterways under the public-trust doctrine. And the government's regulatory authority over navigable waterways is not limited to "navigation" in the commonly understood sense; rather, it broadly includes the authority to regulate in furtherance of other public interests such as recreation and environmental preservation. *R.W. Docks & Slips*, 628 N.W.2d at 787–88.

Kreuziger also suggests that he has a riparian right "to have water flow to the land without artificial obstruction." *Movrich*, 905 N.W.2d at 814 (quotation marks omitted). He asserts without authority that the water level the dam created is now the established water level and that removing the dam is equivalent to artificially obstructing water flow. But

Movrich is inapposite because it dealt with riparian owners' competing rights of access to a man-made lake. *See id.* It did not establish that government action *returning* a river to its natural course infringes a riparian owner's right to an artificial water level. *See id.*

In sum, Wisconsin holds in trust its navigable waters, including the land below the ordinary high-water mark of its **[—9—]** lakes and rivers, and "[t]he rights of riparian owners ... are qualified, subordinate, and subject to the paramount interest of the state and the paramount rights of the public in navigable waters." *R.W. Dock & Slips*, 628 N.W.2d at 788. The state legislature has delegated to the DNR substantial authority to administer this public trust. *Wis.'s Env't Decade, Inc. v. Dep't of Nat. Res.*, 271 N.W.2d 69, 72 (Wis. 1978). Kreuziger has not identified a case supporting his claim that he has a property right to the continuation of a particular surface water level along his river frontage. That's not surprising; rivers frequently ebb and flow, and lower water levels *as such* have never been held to implicate a taking. Quite the opposite—when a river recedes, a riparian owner's rights expand proportionally. *See Doemel*, 193 N.W. at 398. Because Kreuziger "had no private property right to" a particular water level in the river, he "cannot have suffered an unconstitutional taking." *R.W. Docks & Slips*, 628 N.W.2d at 787.

So Kreuziger's argument that removing the dam did not actually improve navigation is beside the point. He also argues that the judge erred by ignoring a disputed material fact—the degree to which removing the dam reduced the river's water level. But this dispute is also immaterial. No matter how much the river receded, Kreuziger had no right to have it remain at the previous high-water mark.

Finally, Kreuziger argues that the result here is "unjust, inequitable, and unconscionable" because the defendants have created an unowned,[1] unsightly strip of **{-397-}** land abutting **[—10—]** his property. Yet neither the Wisconsin Constitution nor the United States Constitution promises to "socialize all losses, but [only] those ... which result from a taking of property." *Willow River Power Co.*, 324 U.S. at 502; *E-L Enters. v. Milwaukee Metro. Sewerage Dist.*, 785 N.W.2d 409, 421 (Wis. 2010). Without an actual taking of property, a takings claim cannot succeed. *Willow River Power Co.*, 324 U.S. at 510; *R.W. Docks & Slips*, 628 N.W.2d at 787.

Kreuziger holds no right to have the Milwaukee River remain at the high-water level created by the Estabrook Dam. The defendants cannot have taken a right that he never had.

AFFIRMED

---

[1] Kreuziger says that the boggy strip of land is unowned, but what he seems to mean is that its ownership may be the subject of dispute. If the land is still part of the riverbed—that is, below the ordinary high-water **[—10—]** mark—then it is held in the public trust. *R.W. Docks & Slips v. State*, 628 N.W.2d 781, 787 (Wis. 2001). If the river has permanently receded, then the strip of land presumably belongs to him. *See Movrich v. Lobermeier*, 905 N.W.2d 807, 814 (Wis. 2018); *Doemel v. Jantz*, 193 N.W. 393, 398 (Wis. 1923) (noting that the owner of riverfront property owns to the thread of the stream, except that lands submerged by navigable rivers are subject to the public trust).

United States Court of Appeals
for the Seventh Circuit

No. 21-3145

LITTLE SANDY COAL CO.
VS.
COMMISSIONER OF INTERNAL REVENUE

Appeal from the United States Tax Court

Decided: March 7, 2023

Citation: 62 F.4th 287, 11 Adm. R. 386 (7th Cir. 2023).

Before **ROVNER, HAMILTON,** and **BRENNAN,** Circuit Judges.

[—1—] {-294-} **BRENNAN,** Circuit Judge:

This case requires us to interpret the research tax credit under Section 41 of the Internal Revenue Code. To claim the credit, a taxpayer must demonstrate, among other things, that at least 80 percent of its research activities for a business component constituted elements of a process of experimentation.

Taxpayer Little Sandy Coal Company, Inc., the parent of a shipbuilding company, claimed expenses for 11 vessels under **[—2—]** the tax credit. But the Commissioner of Internal Revenue disallowed the credit and assessed a tax deficiency. Taxpayer unsuccessfully challenged that decision in tax court.

We disagree with some aspects of the tax court's reasoning, but ultimately, Taxpayer claimed more tax credit than it could prove. Taxpayer did not offer a principled way to determine what portion of the employee activities for each vessel constituted elements of a process of experimentation, much less research activities. Instead, Taxpayer relied on arbitrary estimates and the newness of the vessels. So, we affirm.

I. Background

Taxpayer Little Sandy Coal Company, Inc. is the parent of a shipbuilding company, Corn Island Shipyard, Inc. (CIS), in southern Indiana. In the tax year ending in June 2014, Taxpayer claimed a tax credit under Section 41 of the Internal Revenue Code based on alleged qualified research expenses incurred for the design and construction of 11 first-in-class vessels—that is, vessels it had never built before. Taxpayer claimed employee wages, contract research expenses, and supply costs for the tax credit. After reviewing Taxpayer's tax return, the Commissioner of Internal Revenue disallowed the tax credit and assessed a tax deficiency as well as an accuracy-related penalty. **{-295-}**

Taxpayer then petitioned for redetermination by the United States Tax Court, which conducted a five-day bench trial. For purposes of trial, the parties agreed to treat two of the eleven CIS vessels as representative of the others. The two vessels were a tanker barge, known as Project 720 or the Apex 720 Tanker (Tanker), and a dry dock, known as Project 730 or the Detyens Dry Dock (Dry Dock). **[—3—]**

Vessel Development. At trial, the parties offered much testimony on the "iterative process" of designing and constructing vessels. CIS engineer, Brian Varner, and the Commissioner's expert, Kenneth Smith, each referred to the process as a "design spiral." They explained that vessel components were interdependent, so the design of some elements could not be determined until the designs of others were established. Changes in vessel weight and other metrics could trigger new calculations and designs for other parts, causing the development process to loop back to the drawing board. While engineers "tr[ied] to eliminate problems up front," the final design of some components could not be determined until construction. Varner explained that many of these design issues got "ironed out" as they built the ship, but they still had to feel "pretty comfortable with a design before … cutting steel." "Any repairs or modifications [could] become very costly very quickly."

Tanker. CIS based the design of the Apex Tanker on a previous tanker it had built, the Penn 80. But several elements were different. For example, CIS used three-dimensional modeling to redesign the stern notch, which attaches the Tanker to a pusher tug. The

Tanker also featured a towing bridle that was redesigned to minimize interference with other vessel components. Designing these components often required engineering. CIS's lead engineer and naval architect, Bud Johnson, performed an engineering calculation—called a "wind sail" calculation—to determine the appropriate size of the vessel's anchor. Others performed engineering calculations to test the strength of the ship's longitudinal elements and to design the tanker's vapor barrier system, a special coating to prevent corrosion. **[—4—]**

Some changes in the Apex Tanker's design, also determined through an iterative process, gave it greater cargo capacity than the Penn 80. After constructing the Tanker, CIS performed a deadweight survey to measure its water displacement, which indicates its cargo capacity. This displacement is a common contractual specification for vessels, and a sufficient variance can result in noncompliance with agreed-to terms. After analyzing CIS production employees' time records, one of its engineering technicians, Brian Meunier, estimated that 87% of the time those employees spent constructing the Tanker involved functions "tied directly to items" different from those of the Penn 80.

Dry Dock. A dry dock is a vessel that can partially submerge in water to raise a ship above water for repairs. CIS had never built a dry dock before it made the Detyens Dry Dock. As with the Tanker, CIS used engineering calculations and modeling to design the Dry Dock and to resolve problems. CIS drafted several versions of design drawings and performed calculations to test these designs.

One component, the outboard side plate, went through five design revisions. The safety deck also went through several versions, one of which involved raising the deck 18 inches to accommodate changes in the weight of the vessel. After building the Dry Dock, CIS conducted a partial raise-and-lower test to find out whether the Dry Dock properly submerged and rose. The client, Detyens, conducted a full raise-and-lower test after taking delivery. **{–296–}**

Expenses Claimed. For the Tanker, Taxpayer claimed the research tax credit on \$2,505,491 of production wages and **[—5—]** \$3,892,142 of supply costs.[1] And for the Dry Dock, Taxpayer claimed \$146,109 of production wages and \$1,943,265 of supply costs.

Taxpayer also claimed \$609,276 in nonproduction "estimated wage expenses" for the 11 vessels. These expenses were not broken out by vessel, but some of the wages were attributable to specific employees: \$173,996 to Bud Johnson, CIS's lead engineer and naval architect; \$126,734 to CIS's management, Don Foertsch, David Foertsch, and Alan Fleischmann; and \$56,895 to draftsmen, Dennis Gass, Kyle Harpenau, and Robert Kellems. Taxpayer calculated these nonproduction wages by applying to each employee's total wages an allocation percentage equal to the estimated portion of the employee's time spent on qualified research. Some trial witnesses testified that these estimates were reasonable. For example, Meunier testified that 60% is a "reasonable" allocation for the time Johnson spent on the design and development of the 11 vessels. David Foertsch similarly attested that the percentage estimations of time various employees spent on these vessels were "fair."

After trial, the tax court found that Taxpayer was not entitled to claim the research credit for any of the 11 vessels. The tax court upheld the tax deficiency and the accuracy-related **[—6—]** penalty. Taxpayer timely appealed to this court under I.R.C. § 7482(a)(1).

[1] Taxpayer also claimed \$17,504 in contract research expenses that are not at issue here. CIS paid Hayes Testing Labs to test some welds made in the Tanker's construction. The tax court found that this activity was excluded from the credit as the amounts CIS paid to Hayes were neither research nor experimental expenditures. Taxpayer did not address these expenses in its opening brief, so it waived argument on whether they are creditable. *Accident Fund Ins. Co. of Am. v. Custom Mech. Constr., Inc.*, 49 F.4th 1100, 1108 (7th Cir. 2022).

II. Statutory & Regulatory Framework

Before we consider the parties' arguments, we review the research tax credit and how it works. This includes examining what are qualified research expenses (including what qualifies as research); the Section 174 test, which allows research and experimental expenditures that taxpayers would otherwise capitalize to be deducted from taxable income; and the process of experimentation test and its components.

A. Research Tax Credit

Section 41 of the Internal Revenue Code provides a tax credit for 20% of "qualified research expenses" that exceed a prescribed base amount. I.R.C. § 41(a)(1). The statute is complex and has several nested definitions. We discuss only the relevant provisions.

Qualified Research Expenses. Qualified research expenses include "in-house research expenses" and "contract research expenses." § 41(b)(1). "[I]n-house research expenses" include "wages paid or incurred to an employee for qualified services" and "any amount paid or incurred for supplies used in the conduct of qualified research." § 41(b)(2)(A)(i)–(ii). "Qualified services" in turn "means services consisting of—(i) engaging in qualified research, or (ii) engaging in the direct supervision or direct support of research activities which constitute qualified research." § 41(b)(2)(B). Qualified research expenses are broad. They include, among other things, the cost of supplies used for qualified research as well as wages for direct supervision and support of qualified research. § 41(b)(2). Whether **{-297-}** such supply costs and wages are qualified **[—7—]** research expenses depends on whether the taxpayer has performed "qualified research" as defined in Section 41(d).

Qualified Research. To constitute qualified research, the research activities must satisfy four tests in Section 41(d)(1): (1) the Section 174 test, (2) the technological information test, (3) the business component test, and (4) the process of experimentation (or "substantially all") test. § 41(d)(1); *Union Carbide Corp. & Subs. v. Comm'r*, 97 T.C.M. (CCH) 1207, T.C. Memo. 2009-50, at *77 (2009), *aff'd*, 697 F.3d 104 (2d Cir. 2012). First, under the Section 174 test, the expenditures for the research must be deductible "research or experimental expenditures" under I.R.C. § 174. § 41(d)(1)(A). Second, the technological information test requires the research to be "undertaken for the purpose of discovering information ... which is technological in nature." § 41(d)(1)(B)(i). Third, under the business component test, the application of the research must be "intended to be useful in the development of a new or improved business component of the taxpayer." § 41(d)(1)(B)(ii). Fourth, substantially all of the research activities must constitute elements of a process of experimentation for the purpose of "(i) a new or improved function, (ii) performance, or (iii) reliability or quality." § 41(d)(1)(C), (3)(A).

These four tests are initially applied at the "business component" level. § 41(d)(2)(A); Treas. Reg. § 1.41–4(b)(2). "'[B]usiness component' means any product, process, computer software, technique, formula, or invention which is to be—(i) held for sale, lease, or license, or (ii) used by the taxpayer in a trade or business of the taxpayer." § 41(d)(2)(B). If a business component fails any of the qualified research tests, we follow the "shrinking-back rule" and apply the tests at the "most significant subset" of the business component. **[—8—]** § 1.41-4(b)(2). Failing that, the shrinking-back rule is applied to smaller subcomponents until "either a subset of elements of the product that satisfies the requirements is reached, or the most basic element of the product is reached and such element fails to satisfy the test." *Id.* Only the fourth "process of experimentation" test and indirectly the first test under Section 174 are in dispute here, so we elaborate on them, the latter first.

B. Section 174 Test

Section 174 allows research and experimental expenditures that taxpayers would otherwise capitalize to be deducted from taxable income. I.R.C. § 174(a)(1); *Union Carbide*, T.C. Memo. 2009-50, at *78. "The term *research or experimental expenditures*, as used in section 174, means expenditures incurred in connection with the taxpayer's trade or business which represent research and development costs in the experimental or laboratory sense." Treas. Reg. § 1.174-2(a)(1). "Expenditures represent research and development costs in the experimental or laboratory sense if they are for activities intended to discover information that would eliminate uncertainty concerning the development or improvement of a product." *Id.* And "[u]ncertainty exists if the information available to the taxpayer does not establish the capability or method for developing or improving the product or the appropriate design of the product." *Id.* "Whether an uncertainty exists is an objective test that depends on the information available to the taxpayer." *Union Carbide*, T.C. Memo. 2009-50, at *78 (citing *Mayrath v. Comm'r*, 41 T.C. 582, 590–91 (1964), *aff'd*, 357 F.2d 209 (5th Cir. 1966)).

"Because the taxpayer need only be uncertain as to 'the capability *or* method **{-298-}** ... *or* the appropriate design' of the **[—9—]** improvement, an uncertainty may exist even if the taxpayer knows that it is technically possible to achieve a goal but is uncertain of the method or appropriate design to use to reach that goal." *Id.* at *78 (quoting § 1.174-2(a)(1) (emphasis added)). "Whether expenditures qualify as research or experimental expenditures depends on the nature of the activity to which the expenditures relate, not the nature of the product or improvement being developed or the level of technological advancement the product or improvement represents." § 1.174-2(a)(1). In all cases, expenses deductible under Section 174 exclude "costs paid or incurred in the production of a product after the elimination of uncertainty." § 1.174-2(a)(2).

Uncertainty. It is critical to correctly frame "uncertainty" in Section 1.174-2 because, as explained later, this same concept undergirds the process of experimentation test. Generic uncertainty is inherent in constructing or manufacturing a product. That involves questions like: Will this tire fit? What kind of screws are needed to attach this panel? Or will this weld hold up this truss? But "uncertainty" in Section 174 means something more. "[D]eductions under section 174 are limited to 'expenditures of an investigative nature expended in developing the *concept* of a model or product,' as opposed to the construction or manufacture of the product itself." *Union Carbide*, T.C. Memo. 2009-50, at *79 (citation omitted) (quoting *Mayrath*, 41 T.C. at 590). Expenses incurred merely to determine whether a product is built to satisfy a client's desired specifications—without any indication that the expenses were incurred to improve or develop the concept of the product—do not qualify.

That is why the regulations exclude expenses for "ordinary testing or inspection of materials or products for quality **[—10—]** control (quality control testing)." § 1.174-2(a)(6)(i). Quality control testing refers to "testing or inspection to determine whether particular units of materials or products conform to specified parameters." § 1.174-2(a)(7). Still, "quality control testing does not include testing to determine if the design of the product is appropriate." *Id.* But the "design"—if expenditures for it are to be deducted under Section 174—cannot just be any design or modification to meet customer specifications. The design must be intended to remove the correct type of uncertainty: that related to the "development or improvement" of the product. § 1.174-2(a)(1).

We read "development" as used in Section 1.174-2(a)(1) to refer to more than mere construction (as in the common parlance of "real estate development"). The plain meaning of "development" is the "action or process of bringing something to a ... more advanced condition"— embracing the idea of "improvement"— but it can also mean general "change" or "progression by successive stages." *Development*, OXFORD ENGLISH DICTIONARY (3d ed. 2016), https://www.oed.com/view/Entry/51434?redirectedFrom=development#eid; *see also Develop*, WEBSTER'S THIRD NEW INTERNATIONAL DICTIONARY (1993) ("cause to increase or improve"). The former definition fits better in context. "Development," as used beside "improvement," implies an advancement in technology or product concept. *See* § 1.174-2(a)(1); ANTONIN SCALIA & BRIAN A.

GARNER, READING LAW 195 (2012) ("Associated words bear on one another's meaning (*noscitur a sociis*)."). Granted, whether expenses are deductible under Section 174 depends on activities covered by the expenditures, and not on the level of technological advancement. *See* § 1.174-2(a)(1). But while the degree of technological advancement may not matter, the **[—11—]** goal of the **{-299-}** research activity must still be development or improvement.

"The presence of uncertainty concerning the development or improvement of certain components of a product does not necessarily indicate the presence of uncertainty concerning the development or improvement of other components of the product or the product as a whole." § 1.174-2(a)(5). So even if research expenditures furthered the advancement of some parts of a product, other expenses to build other parts of that product may not be deductible under Section 174. Generic manufacturing or construction uncertainty for the other parts will not suffice. Put a different way, a manufacturer may not simply "add a few new bells and whistles" on a pre-existing product and claim uncertainty as to the whole. If summed up in one word, expenses deductible under Section 174 must be "investigative." *Union Carbide*, T.C. Memo. 2009-50, at *79 (quoting *Mayrath*, 41 T.C. at 590).

C. Process of Experimentation Test

The fourth test to constitute qualified research, the process of experimentation test, has two components: (1) substantially all the research activities must constitute elements of a process of experimentation, and (2) for a qualified purpose under Section 41(d)(3)(A). § 41(d)(1)(C). The Commissioner does not dispute the tax court's finding that CIS designed the Tanker and Dry Dock for proper purposes such as: "a new or improved function," "performance," or "reliability or quality." § 41(d)(3)(A). Only the "substantially all" fractional determination is in dispute.

Substantially All. By regulation, "[t]he substantially all requirement of section 41(d)(1)(C) ... is satisfied only if 80 **[—12—]** percent or more of a taxpayer's research activities, measured on a cost or other consistently applied reasonable basis ... constitute elements of a process of experimentation." Treas. Reg. § 1.41-4(a)(6). Accordingly, the "substantially all" fraction is:

$$\frac{\text{Research activities that constitute elements of a process of experimentation}}{\text{Research activities}}$$

See id.; § 41(d)(1)(C). The regulations explain what is meant by the generic denominator "research activities." The penultimate sentence of Section 1.41-4(a)(6) reads:

> Accordingly, if 80 percent (or more) of a taxpayer's research activities with respect to a business component constitute elements of a process of experimentation for a purpose described in section 41(d)(3), the substantially all requirement is satisfied even if the remaining 20 percent (or less) of a taxpayer's research activities with respect to the business component do not constitute elements of a process of experimentation for a purpose described in section 41(d)(3), *so long as these remaining research activities satisfy the requirements of section 41(d)(1)(A) and are not otherwise excluded under section 41(d)(4).*

§ 1.41-4(a)(6) (emphasis added).

This italicized portion clarifies that any non-"process of experimentation" research activities must "satisfy the requirements of section 41(d)(1)(A)" and not be "otherwise excluded under section 41(d)(4)." *Id.*; *see also Union Carbide*, T.C. Memo. 2009-50, at *80; *Suder v. Comm'r*, 108 T.C.M. (CCH) 354, T.C. Memo. 2014-201, at *17 (2014). An example in the **[—13—]** regulation reaffirms this requirement. § 1.41-4(a)(8), Ex. 4 (repeating italicized language above). Because Section 41(d)(1)(A) cross-references Section 174, the proper "substantially all" fraction becomes: **{-300-}**

Research activities that constitute
<u>elements of a process of experimentation</u>
Research activities not excluded under
Section 41(d)(4) and whose expenses are
deductible under Section 174

See § 1.41-4(a)(6).

Denominator. The "research activities" in the denominator must not be excluded under Section 41(d)(4) and expenditures for such activities must also be deductible under Section 174. Section 41(d)(4) excludes certain research activities from "qualified research" including: research conducted after the commercial production of a business component, § 41(d)(4)(A); research to adapt an existing business component to a particular customer's specifications, § 41(d)(4)(B); and research to duplicate an existing business component, § 41(d)(4)(C). We need not discuss the other exceptions. § 41(d)(4)(D)–(H).

Numerator—Elements of a Process of Experimentation. More importantly, the numerator—a subset of the denominator—also requires that the research activities "constitute *elements* of a process of experimentation." § 41(d)(1)(C) (emphasis added). Thus, the numerator is broad enough to encompass research activities that are not per se experimentation or testing. And "a process of experimentation is a process designed to evaluate one or more alternatives to achieve a result where the capability or the method of achieving that result, or the appropriate design of that result, is uncertain as of the beginning of the taxpayer's research activities." § 1.41–4(a)(5)(i). "A **[—14—]** process of experimentation ... involves the identification of uncertainty concerning the development or improvement of a business component ... ." *Id.* "The 'uncertainty' element of this test is essentially the same uncertainty as is required by the section 174 test, and the test may be satisfied even if the taxpayer is certain of either the capability or method of achieving the desired goal if the appropriate design of the desired result is uncertain at the outset." *Union Carbide*, T.C. Memo. 2009-50, at *80 (footnote omitted) (citing §§ 1.174-2(a)(1), 1.41–4(a)(5)(i)); *see also Siemer Milling Co. v. Comm'r*, 117 T.C.M. (CCH) 1196, T.C. Memo. 2019-37, at *8 (2019). As hinted earlier, our prior conclusions on "uncertainty" for the Section 174 test also apply for the process of experimentation test.

This raises the question: Is there daylight between the Section 174 and process of experimentation tests? The answer is "yes." While both tests are aimed at removing the same type of uncertainty concerning the development or improvement of a business component, the process of experimentation "test also imposes a more structured method of discovering information than section 174 requires and may not include all actions a taxpayer takes to resolve uncertainty." *Union Carbide*, T.C. Memo. 2009-50, at *80 (citing *Norwest Corp. & Subs. v. Comm'r*, 110 T.C. 454, 496 (1998) and *Eustace v. Comm'r*, 312 F.3d 905, 907 (7th Cir. 2002)). "A process of experimentation must fundamentally rely on the principles of the physical or biological sciences, engineering, or computer science." § 1.41–4(a)(5)(i). It "involves the identification of uncertainty concerning the development or improvement of a business component, the identification of one or more alternatives intended to eliminate that uncertainty, and the identification and the conduct of a process of evaluating the alternatives (through, **[—15—]** for example, modeling, simulation, or a systematic trial and error methodology)." *Id.*

This process requires the use of the scientific method to resolve the uncertainty. *Union Carbide*, T.C. Memo. 2009-50, at *81. By scientific method, we **{-301-}** mean "[a]n analytical technique by which a hypothesis is formulated and then systematically tested through observation and experimentation." *Id.* (citing *Scientific method*, BLACK'S LAW DICTIONARY (8th ed. 2004)). "To satisfy the process of experimentation test, the taxpayer should develop a hypothesis as to how a new alternative might be used to develop a business component, test that hypothesis in a scientific manner, analyze the results of the test, and then either refine the hypothesis or discard it and develop a new hypothesis and repeat the previous steps." *Id.* at *81.

A process of experimentation "must involve a methodical plan involving a series of trials to test a hypothesis, analyze the data, refine the hypothesis, and retest the hypothesis so that it constitutes experimentation in the scientific sense." *Id.* at *81; *Siemer Milling*, T.C. Memo 2019–37, at *8. "Testing and refining a hypothesis may involve determining the strengths and weakness of the alternative tested, whether and how the process could be further refined and improved, and whether other alternatives might be better suited for achieving the taxpayer's goal." *Union Carbide*, T.C. Memo. 2009-50, at *81 And while only one alternative need be identified and evaluated, a process of experimentation "generally should be capable of evaluating more than one alternative." *Id.*; § 1.41–4(a)(5)(i).

III. Discussion

With this factual background and statutory and regulatory overview, we move to analysis of the case. **[—16—]**

"Tax credits are a matter of legislative grace, are only allowed as clearly provided for by statute, and are narrowly construed." *United States v. McFerrin*, 570 F.3d 672, 675 (5th Cir. 2009) (citing *Stinson Est. v. United States*, 214 F.3d 846, 848 (7th Cir. 2000)); *see also VHC, Inc. v. Comm'r*, 968 F.3d 839, 841 (7th Cir. 2020). "In this case, as with all claimed tax credits, the taxpayer bears the burden of showing entitlement to the credit." *United Stationers, Inc. v. United States*, 163 F.3d 440, 443 (7th Cir. 1998). "A taxpayer claiming a credit under section 41 must retain records in sufficiently usable form and detail to substantiate that the expenditures claimed are eligible for the credit." § 1.41-4(d); *see also* I.R.C. § 6001; Treas. Reg. § 1.6001–1(a), (e). To the extent that the taxpayer's entitlement to the research tax credit turns on a legal interpretation, we review the tax court's legal determinations de novo. *Carter v. Comm'r*, 746 F.3d 318, 321 (7th Cir. 2014) (citation omitted). But as to findings of fact supporting that determination, including findings of evidentiary sufficiency, we review for clear error. *Wegbreit v. Comm'r*, 21 F.4th 959, 963 (7th Cir. 2021).

If a taxpayer can establish that qualified research occurred, we may estimate the qualified research expenses subject to the tax credit. *See McFerrin*, 570 F.3d at 679 (citing *Cohan v. Comm'r*, 39 F.2d 540, 544 (2d Cir. 1930)). But this estimate relates to Section 41(b), which is a separate—albeit related—inquiry from Section 41(d). Only after a taxpayer establishes that qualified research has occurred under Section 41(d) may we estimate, if needed, the amount of qualified research expenses under Section 41(b). *Shami v. Comm'r*, 741 F.3d 560, 568 (5th Cir. 2014) ("[T]he *Cohan* rule is not implicated unless the taxpayer proves that he is entitled to some amount of tax benefit."). Because Taxpayer failed to satisfy the process of **[—17—]** experimentation test in Section 41(d), we conclude that no qualified research expenses are creditable under Section 41(b).

To reach this conclusion, we explain where we agree with the tax court, we **{–302–}** review the pilot model production expenses, and then we review Taxpayer's failure of proof.

A. Where We Agree with the Tax Court

The tax court is correct in several of its conclusions.

"Substantially All" Fraction. The tax court properly construed the "substantially all" fraction for Section 41(d)(1)(C). As we did earlier, the tax court backed into the definition of the denominator, "research activities," by using the parameters that the regulations imposed on non-"process of experimentation" research activities. *See generally* § 1.41-4(a)(6) & (a)(8), Ex. 4. Recall that the correct fraction is research activities that constitute elements of a process of experimentation divided by research activities not excluded under Section 41(d)(4) and whose expenses are deductible under Section 174.

Novelty Approach. The tax court also rightly rejected Taxpayer's novelty argument, namely, that because the majority of the Tanker and Dry Dock was new, substantially all of the activities in designing the vessels constituted elements of a process of experimentation. As it did before the tax court, Taxpayer repeatedly emphasizes that the eleven vessels in question were first-in-class and that Taxpayer had never built a dry dock before. But the tax court correctly recognized that "Section 1.41-4(a)(6) ... requires that the substantially all test be applied in reference to activities—not physical elements of the business components being developed or improved." So **[—18—]** novelty of the business component cannot be the basis for measuring the proportion of research activities that constituted elements of a process of experimentation. *See* § 1.41-4(a)(6) ("substantially all of the activities must constitute elements of a process of experimentation").

This "feels new enough" approach was used in *Trinity Indus., Inc. v. United States*, 691 F. Supp. 2d 688 (N.D. Tex. 2010), *aff'd*, 757 F.3d 400, 2 Adm. R. 265 (5th Cir. 2014). That case also involved a shipbuilder who built several vessels, and the district court found the expenses incurred for two of six vessels to be qualified research expenses. *Id.* at 690, 694–97. For example, the district court found that research expenses incurred for "a very innovative special operations deployment craft ... designed to be very fast, undetectable, and able to fit on a C–5 cargo plane for rapid deployment" were qualified research expenses based on the vessel's novelty. *Id.* at 694. But like the stealth ship in question, the court evaded the mandate in Sections 41(d)(1)(C) and 1.41-4(a)(6) to determine whether the percentage of research activities exceed 80%. Rather, it used novelty as a shortcut. True, the regulation says courts may make this determination "on a cost or other consistently applied reasonable basis." § 1.41-4(a)(6). But the novelty of a business component is not one such "other consistently applied reasonable basis." *Id.* The *Trinity Industries* court said it did "not intend to enumerate everything about the [ship] that was new and required research expenditures." 691 F. Supp. 2d at 694. It was loath to follow the government's suggestion that "the [c]ourt should scour the records and determine which [expense] line items are for matters not properly considered [qualified research expenses]." *Id.* at 697. Instead, the district court used the heuristic of newness to bypass **[—19—]** statutory and regulatory directives. Like the tax court, we reject the novelty approach used in *Trinity Industries*.

Component-level Analysis. Taxpayer asserts that the tax court erred by applying the process of experimentation test at a subcomponent level as opposed to **{-303-}** the claimed business component level. But this gets it backward: The tax court explicitly applied the "substantially all" test at the business component—that is, vessel—level. In fact, the tax court said that it could not apply the shrinking-back rule contained in Section 1.41-4(b)(2) to see if the "substantially all" test is met for a subcomponent of either vessel. This was because Taxpayer had chosen an "all or nothing" strategy in claiming the development of entire vessels—as opposed to smaller components—as qualified research. So the court could not perform the Section 174 and process of experimentation tests underneath the vessel level, even though it observed that some of Taxpayer's activities with respect to certain subcomponents could involve a process of experimentation.

We recognize also that the Tanker's stern notch and towing bridle, as well as the Dry Dock's outboard side plate, among other elements, went through several design iterations. The research activities to develop these parts may very well constitute elements of a process of experimentation. But, as we revisit later, Taxpayer's documentation lacks the necessary detail to prove that. It is Taxpayer's burden to show entitlement to the research tax credit and to retain records to substantiate eligibility for the credit. *United Stationers*, 163 F.3d at 443; § 1.41-4(d); *see also* § 6001; § 1.6001–1(a), (e). Other taxpayers seeking to avail themselves of the research tax credit would be well-advised to document research activities **[—20—]** for subcomponents if they cannot demonstrate a process of experimentation at the business component level.

B. Pilot Model Production Expenses

While we agree with the tax court's ultimate conclusions, we disagree in part with its treatment of pilot model production expenses. As in the tax court, Taxpayer contends that the Tanker and Dry Dock are "pilot models," as defined by Section 1.174-2(a)(4). It argues therefore that production wages for making such models categorically qualify as research activities that constitute elements of a process of experimentation. The tax court did not determine that either vessel was a pilot model. Rather, for purposes of the "substantially all" analysis, the court alternatively assumed that the vessels were and were not pilot models. We follow this same approach. But first, we consider the interplay between pilot model production expenses and the components of the "substantially all" fraction.

1. Deductible Under Section 174

Assuming that the two vessels were pilot models, the tax court properly included pilot model production expenses into the denominator. "Pilot model" is a defined term for purposes of research expense deductibility under Section 174. It means "any representation or model of a product that is produced to evaluate and resolve uncertainty concerning the product during the development or improvement of the product." § 1.174-2(a)(4). So the creator's intent matters. And "pilot model" is included in the definition of "product." § 1.174-2(a)(3). Recall that "research or experimental expenditures" deductible under Section 174 include those expended for "activities intended to discover information that would **[—21—]** eliminate uncertainty concerning the development or improvement of a product." § 1.174-2(a)(1). Because pilot models by definition are "produced to evaluate and resolve uncertainty concerning the product during the development or improvement of the product," pilot model production expenses incurred prior to the elimination of uncertainty are deductible under Section 174. § 1.174-2(a)(2), (4). It **{-304-}** follows that pilot model production expenses are included in the denominator of the "substantially all" fraction. *Cf.* § 1.41–4(a)(6) ("so long as these remaining research activities satisfy the requirements of section 41(d)(1)(A)"—that is, Section 174).

This conclusion is buttressed by the examples provided in Section 1.174-2(a)(11). These examples also demonstrate that the way pilot model production expenses factor into the research and development process depends on the industry in question. Two of the examples illustrate the difference between pilot models for custom-made versus mass-produced products: In Example 3, a custom manufacturer, U, contracts to produce a custom machine based on a client's specifications. § 1.174-2(a)(11), Ex. 3. U incurs a total of $31,000 on the project, $10,000 of which is for "materials and labor to produce a model that is used to evaluate and resolve the uncertainty concerning the appropriate design." *Id.* $1,000 is for "using the model to test whether certain features can be integrated into the design of the machine." *Id.* "After uncertainty is eliminated, U incurs $20,000 to produce the machine for sale to the customer based on the appropriate design." *Id.* Of the $31,000, only "the $10,000 incurred to produce the model and the $1,000 incurred on design testing activities qualifies as research or experimental expenditures under section 174." *Id.* Example 3 states that expenses incurred in producing a model to resolve uncertainty concerning the appropriate **[—22—]** design of a custom-made product are deductible under Section 174. So the same expenses would also be included in the "substantially all" denominator. This example is analogous to the tailor-made shipbuilding industry in this case. But unlike in our circumstances, in the example the divide between pre-uncertainty and post-uncertainty expenses is well-defined.

In Example 5, a mass-production manufacturer, V, "incurs $5,000 to produce a number of models of the product that are to be used in testing the appropriate design before the product is mass-produced for sale." § 1.174-2(a)(11), Ex. 5. "Multiple models are necessary to test the design in a variety of different environments (exposure to extreme heat, exposure to extreme cold, submersion, and vibration)." *Id.* All $5,000 are deductible under Section 174. *Id.* Example 5 is the "crash test" scenario in which a manufacturer produces multiple pilot models and subjects them to a variety of tests in order to refine the product for mass production. This example also involves a definite separation between the "pilot" or developmental phase and the post-uncertainty production phase of a manufacturing project. The same is true for Examples 4 and 6, which involve the redesign of a product part and the development of a new part, respectively. *See* § 1.174-2(a)(11), Exs. 4, 6. In our case, the line at which uncertainty ends for each vessel is hazy, and that is problematic as a matter of proof for both the denominator and numerator of the "substantially all" fraction.

In Examples 7 and 8, the research is performed to develop a new line of product rather than to fulfill existing contractual obligations. § 1.174-2(a)(11), Exs. 7 (vertical take-off aircraft), 8 (new type of compressor blade for an aircraft engine). So all experimental expenses in producing and testing the models **[—23—]** are deductible expenses under Section 174. *Id.* Here, Taxpayer's alleged research activities were performed, first and foremost, to fulfill a contractual obligation. Now, that does not mean that a taxpayer cannot have a dual intent of contractual fulfillment and innovation. Taxpayer could have produced the Tanker and Dry Dock "to evaluate and resolve uncertainty concerning the product[s] during the **{-305-}** development or improvement of the product[s]." § 1.174-2(a)(4). That is, they could be pilot models. Ultimately, we need not resolve that question because, whether or not the vessels are pilot models, Taxpayer failed to demonstrate that the production and nonproduction wages for each vessel account for elements of a process of experimentation—the numerator in the "substantially all" fraction.

2. Elements of a Process of Experimentation

At this point, our analysis diverges from that of the tax court. In entertaining the possibility that the vessels were pilot models, the tax court also categorically excluded model production wages from the numerator of the "substantially all" fraction. That is, it found that pilot model production activities could not be an element of a process of experimentation. In so concluding, the tax court erroneously imported a distinction from Section 41(b)(2)(B) into the numerator of the fraction in Section 41(d)(1)(C). The court first observed the distinction that Section 41(b)(2)(B) draws between "direct support of research activities which constitute qualified research," § 41(b)(2)(B)(ii), and "qualified research," § 41(b)(2)(B)(i). Pilot model production, the court then reasoned, directly supported research activities but did "not have a close enough nexus to the testing to be considered qualified research in its own right." Accordingly, the tax court **[—24—]** concluded that activities in "direct support of research activities which constitute qualified research," § 41(b)(2)(B)(ii), including any pilot model production activities, are categorically not qualified research or elements of a process of experimentation.

Other courts have drawn similar distinctions. *E.g.*, *Shami*, 741 F.3d at 570 ("In short, the supervisor of the direct supervisor of employees who conduct qualified research is not himself engaged in qualified research."). The regulation expounding upon Section 41(b)—the scope of qualified research expenses—states, "direct support of research includes the services ... of a machinist for machining a part of an experimental model used in qualified research." § 1.41-2(c)(3)(ii). And Section 41(b)(2)(B)(ii) distinguishes direct support and supervision of qualified research from qualified research itself. So, it would make sense that pilot model production expenses have no part in the "qualified research" defined by Section 41(d). *See generally* ANTONIN SCALIA & BRIAN A. GARNER, READING LAW 167 (2012) (explaining the whole-text canon). While that reading may be sensible, it is incorrect for reasons we will explain.

Within the "substantially all" fraction in Section 41(d)(1)(C), we see the text justifying two options as to how we can treat activities that would qualify as "direct support" and "direct supervision" under Section 41(b)(2)(B)(ii). Either direct support and supervision activities should be considered in both the numerator and denominator of the fraction as Taxpayer proposes, or they should not be considered at all as the amicus curiae, the National Association of **[—25—]** Manufacturers, suggests.[2] The tax court took a third approach and suggested direct support

[2] We thank the National Association of Manufacturers for its well-reasoned and helpful amicus brief.

and supervision activities—more specifically, pilot model production activities—could be included in the denominator, but the court categorically excluded them from the numerator.[3] We **{-306-}** conclude that the first approach, advocated by Taxpayer, is correct.

If we were to rule for the second option—to carry over the Section 41(b) distinction between qualified research and direct support/supervision into Section 41(d)—then production activities that support qualified research would not belong in the "substantially all" fraction. For the reasons stated earlier, this approach is internally inconsistent. But applying the Section 41(b) distinction in Section 41(d) comes with more problems of its own. For one, neither the terms nor the concept of "direct support" or "direct supervision" appears in Section 41(d). **[—26—]**

More broadly, Section 41(b) and Section 41(d) address different subjects: Section 41(b) identifies the contours of qualified research *expenses* subject to the research tax credit under Section 41. It includes amounts spent on supplies for and wages in direct support or supervision of qualified research. § 41(b)(2)(A)(ii), (B)(ii). By contrast, Section 41(d) deals with qualified research *activities*. *See* § 41(d)(1)(C) ("research ... substantially all of the activities of which constitute elements of a process of experimentation"). The "substantially all" fraction in Section 41(d)(1)(C) excludes supply costs for research, but the denominator includes research activities not excluded under Section 41(d)(4) and whose expenses are deductible under Section 174. § 1.41-4(a)(6). So Section 41(d) is narrower in some respects, but broader in others, than Section 41(b). Qualified research expenses and qualified research are different—albeit related—concepts, and they have separate regulations explaining each. *See* §§ 1.41-2, 1.41-4. As explained next, importing a distinction from Section 41(b) into Section 41(d) presents conflicts with existing regulations expounding upon Section 41(d).

Nothing in the regulation explaining Section 41(d)—Section 1.41-4—explicitly addresses pilot models. Recall, though, that "pilot model" means "any representation or model of a product that is produced to evaluate and resolve uncertainty concerning the product during the development or improvement of the product." § 1.174-2(a)(4). And the "uncertainty" element of the process of experimentation test is the same as that of the Section 174 test. *Union Carbide*, T.C. Memo. 2009-50, at *80 (footnote omitted) (citing §§ 1.174-2(a)(1), 1.41-4(a)(5)(i)). If a pilot model, by definition, is produced to resolve the correct type of uncertainty, it would be odd that pilot model production activities should not constitute **[—27—]** research activities deductible under Section 174. So the second approach is at odds with the definition of "pilot model." Further, if the pilot model was used to evaluate alternatives as part of a "methodical plan involving a series of trials to test a hypothesis," the model production activities would also constitute elements of a process of experimentation. *Siemer Milling*, T.C. Memo 2019–37, at *8. This casts doubt on the tax court's third approach.

A deeper dive into Section 1.41-4 is helpful. Several examples within **{-307-}** Section 1.41-4(a)(8) explain what constitutes elements of a process of experimentation. One of the examples includes "design[ing]," "model[ing]," and "simulat[ing]"—not just "test[ing]"—alternative designs as part of the process of experimentation to eliminate uncertainties. § 1.41–4(a)(8), Ex. 4. This suggests that the

[3] Consider the practical import of the tax court's categorical exclusion of pilot model production expenses from the numerator. Under the tax court's reasoning, the more costly the production expenses for developing a pilot model, the less likely that a taxpayer can fulfill the "substantially all" test. Obviously, pilot model production expenses can vary widely depending on what is being modeled. For example, producing models of a plastic fork is much cheaper than making models of a fully functional automobile. If we include such model production expenses in the "substantially all" denominator but categorically exclude them from the numerator, as the tax court suggests, the satisfaction of the test would depend on how small the pilot model production expenses are relative to the non-production research expenses. It escapes reason why the "substantially all" test should depend on how expensive it is to produce the pilot model.

production of prototypes or pilot models can be an element of the process of experimentation. Example 3 concerns a food products manufacturer, X, who makes a large-shred version of a product. § 1.41–4(a)(8), Ex. 3. X, seeking to produce a fine-shred version of the product, machined several thinner blades as alternative designs to produce a fine-shred version of the food product. *Id.* X then systematically tested out these various blades. *Id.* Notably, the example does not distinguish the blade production activities from the testing activities in concluding that substantially all these activities constituted elements of a process of experimentation. *Id.* This example, too, tends to show that pilot model production expenses can be included in the "substantially all" numerator.

Given the regulation's apparent inclusion of some pilot model production activities in the numerator, we hold that those activities can be research activities (denominator) that **[—28—]** constitute elements of a process of experimentation (numerator). Our holding does not mean that any direct support or supervision activities may be considered in the "substantially all" fraction. Recall that an activity must be a *research* activity, whose expenses are deductible under Section 174, to make it into the fraction at all. *See* §§ 41(d)(1)(A), (C), 1.41-4(a)(6).

One more note about Example 3. The production of the fine-shred blades was an element of a process of experimentation because the blades were used in a "systematic trial and error process of analyzing various blade designs and materials to determine whether the new shredding blade must be constructed of a different material." § 1.41–4(a)(8), Ex. 3. And as discussed above, a process of experimentation "must involve a methodical plan involving a series of trials to test a hypothesis, analyze the data, refine the hypothesis, and retest the hypothesis so that it constitutes experimentation in the scientific sense." *Union Carbide*, T.C. Memo. 2009-50, at *81; *Siemer Milling*, 2019 WL 1598588, at *8. Just making a prototype model is not enough to pass the process of experimentation test. The model must be used to evaluate one or more alternatives using the scientific method. *See* § 1.41-4(a)(5)(i); *Union Carbide*, T.C. Memo. 2009-50, at *81. "To satisfy the process of experimentation test, the taxpayer should develop a hypothesis as to how a new alternative might be used to develop a business component, test that hypothesis in a scientific manner, analyze the results of the test, and then either refine the hypothesis or discard it and develop a new hypothesis and repeat the previous steps." *Union Carbide*, T.C. Memo. 2009-50, at *81. This is where Taxpayer failed as a matter of proof. **[—29—]**

C. Taxpayer's Failure of Proof

The tax court did not decide whether the two vessels were pilot models. Instead, it performed the "substantially all" analysis under alternative assumptions that the vessels were and were not pilot models. We follow the tax court's lead. Under either assumption, Taxpayer fails the "substantially all" test.

1. Assuming the Vessels are Not Pilot Models

Assuming the vessels are not pilot models, Taxpayer loses because it failed to show what, if any, portion of the activities **{-308-}** accounted for by the nonproduction wages constitutes elements of a process of experimentation. If none of the vessels are pilot models, then none of the production wages would be included in the "substantially all" fraction. This is because general production activities unconnected to "the elimination of uncertainty concerning the development or improvement of the product are not eligible under section 174." § 1.174-2(a)(2). So under our assumption, the fraction hinges entirely upon the nonproduction expenses: non-production wages that are for elements of a process of experimentation divided by nonproduction wages. As we mentioned earlier, the $609,276 in nonproduction wages are not broken down by vessel. So we are unable to perform the "substantially all" analysis at the business component level that Section 41(d)(2)(A) requires—that is, at the vessel level. But the lack of categorization is just the start. Taxpayer faces a more fundamental problem in that many of its nonproduction wages may account for non-research activities.

Taxpayer asks us to take on faith that the percentage allocations of each nonproduction employee's wages were only **[—30—]** for research activities that involved a process of experimentation. But Section 41(d) requires us to walk by sight, not by faith. Taxpayer has the burden to document that the activities accounted for by the nonproduction wages were elements of a process of experimentation. *United Stationers*, 163 F.3d at 443; § 1.41-4(d); *see also* § 6001; § 1.6001–1(a), (e). The regulations do not require records in any particular form, except that they must be "in sufficiently usable form and detail to substantiate that the expenditures claimed are eligible for the credit." § 1.41-4(d). And the "substantially all" test allows for the fraction to be measured "on a cost or other consistently applied reasonable basis." § 1.41-4(a)(6). So flexibility is built into the test. But shortcut estimates of experimentation-related activities will not suffice. Something more, such as documentation of time spent on such activities, is necessary. In any case, the tax court found as a matter of fact that much of the $609,276 in nonproduction wages accounted for non-research activities.

The tax court found that CIS's lead engineer and naval architect, Bud Johnson, spent much of his time involved in customer relations and management activities. And indeed, trial testimony supports that Johnson managed payrolls, took care of personnel issues, interfaced with clients, put together bids, and handled supply chain concerns. The father-and-son management team, Don and David Foertsch, were stipulated co-owners of Taxpayer, and the evidence did not demonstrate that they conducted much, if any, research activities apart from their management activities. Don Foertsch was copied on project-related emails, but none of the emails showed how his involvement was an element of a process of experimentation. He would meet with Johnson and David to review bids and ship designs. Taxpayer also alleged that Don assisted **[—31—]** with fabrication and production issues, but nothing documents how he did so. It seems Don played a supervisory role over research activities. David Foertsch's testimony regarding his efforts to "troubleshoot" the Tanker's towing bridle indicated that he may have engaged in some research activities that constituted elements of a process of experimentation. He also testified about his involvement in designing the stern notch. But, in the end, the record gave the tax court no means of determining the extent of time David spent on experimentation-related research activities.

Another member of management, Alan Fleischmann, was CIS's purchasing agent and responsible for assessing and obtaining **{-309-}** materials for shipbuilding projects. Meunier said Fleischmann worked with material vendors to procure ship parts that Johnson requested. Taxpayer's briefing similarly described Fleischmann's activities but also alleged he assessed material alternatives for functionality. Based on the record, the tax court found that at least some, if not a considerable portion, of Fleischmann's activities did not involve a process of experimentation. Finally, the tax court found that the draftsmen—Dennis Gass, Kyle Harpenau, and Robert Kellems—were not involved in a process of experimentation by "[s]imply drawing a design provided by an engineer." Indeed, Meunier attested that drafting work boils down to inputting specifications into a modeling program to create drawings. David Foertsch, too, testified that draftsmen simply took an engineer's calculations and produced the drawings. Without evidence of how the models they produced were used as part of a scientific method in evaluating alternative designs, the tax court had no basis to find that the nonproduction employees' activities were research activities **[—32—]** that constitute elements of a process of experimentation. We find no clear error in these factual determinations.

Like the tax court, we conclude that the record does not allow us to determine the percentage of nonproduction employee activities that constituted elements of a process of experimentation—even less, research activities. Even if we assumed that all $609,276 in nonproduction wages were deductible under Section 174 and so includible in the denominator, Taxpayer has failed to demonstrate what, if any part, of that number belongs in the numerator.

2. Assuming the Vessels Are Pilot Models

Assuming the vessels are pilot models, Taxpayer still does not prevail because it failed to show how such pilot models—that is, the entire vessels—were used in a process of experimentation. If the vessels are pilot models, the production expenses for them are included in the denominator.[4] *See supra* Section III.B.1. Then the "substantially all" fraction would be as follows: production and nonproduction wages that are elements of a process of experimentation divided by production and nonproduction wages. Remember that Taxpayer claimed the research tax credit on $2,505,491 and $146,109 of production wages for the Tanker and Dry Dock, respectively. Again, the fact that the $609,276 in nonproduction wages are not broken out by vessel presents a problem. We cannot **[—33—]** discern a way to factor these wages into the "substantially all" fraction without a breakdown by vessel.

The tax court addressed the issue by simply assuming that all the nonproduction wages were for the Tanker. The court also assumed that all $609,276 in nonproduction wages were for elements of a process of experimentation and categorically excluded pilot model production expenses from the numerator. Using this approach, the tax court found that, at best, the relevant fraction would be 19.6% ($609,276 ÷ ($609,276 + $2,505,491))—insufficient to satisfy the "substantially all" test. For the Dry Dock, the tax court also excluded pilot model production expenses from the numerator. But, instead of assuming that all $609,276 in nonproduction wages were for elements of a process of experimentation, the court **{–310–}** calculated the percentage of nonproduction wages that would need to be for the Dry Dock alone and included in the numerator in order to satisfy the "substantially all" test: 96% ($584,436 ÷ $609,276 and $584,436 = 0.8 ($584,436 + $146,109)). Because Taxpayer had not provided sufficient information to show its nonproduction employees' activities constituted elements of a process of experimentation, the tax court concluded that the Dry Dock also did not pass the "substantially all" test.

We cut a different path. Above, we concluded that the record does not allow us to determine the percentage of nonproduction wages that account for elements of a process of experimentation. We also concluded that much of the nonproduction wages account for non-research activities. Given these conclusions, we do not strain ourselves with the sequential assumptions made by the tax court. Because we are unsure what nonproduction expenses account for research activities, we simply exclude them from our "substantially all" **[—34—]** analysis. This is to Taxpayer's benefit because, under our previous conclusions, including the nonproduction expenses would only increase the denominator without any gains in the numerator.

So, whether Section 41(d)(1)(C) is satisfied comes down to whether substantially all of the pilot model production expenses are elements of a process of experimentation. Remember, the process of experimentation test is distinguished from the Section 174 test in that the former "imposes a more structured method of discovering information." *Union Carbide*, T.C. Memo. 2009-50, at *80 (citing *Norwest*, 110 T.C. at 496 and *Eustace*, 312 F.3d at 907). A process of experimentation "involves the identification of uncertainty concerning the development or improvement of a business component, the identification of one or more alternatives intended to eliminate that uncertainty, and the identification and the conduct of a process of evaluating the alternatives." § 1.41–4(a)(5)(i). The tax court found that Taxpayer had provided insufficient evidence to include the alleged pilot model production expenses for the Tanker and Dry Dock in the numerators of the respective fractions. We agree.

[4] Even if we reached a different conclusion as to whether pilot model production activities can constitute research activities and elements of a process of experimentation, *supra* Section III.B, the result would not change for Taxpayer. If the pilot model production expenses were not a factor in the "substantially all" fraction, then our analysis would be the same as that performed under the assumption that the vessels were not pilot models.

Tanker. The tax court began by rejecting Taxpayer's argument that the deadweight survey, conducted after the Tanker was built, established that the entire tanker was involved in a process of experimentation. But it also viewed with skepticism the Commissioner's argument that the survey was merely a quality control test that was not a process of experimentation or deductible research under Section 174. *See generally* §§ 1.174-2(a)(6)(i), 1.41-4(c)(5)(v). We do not share the tax court's hesitation on this point. The deadweight survey determines a vessel's water displacement, which indicates its **[—35—]** cargo capacity. Water displacement is a common contractual specification for vessels, and a sufficient variance can result in noncompliance with agreed-to terms. So the deadweight survey is closer to a quality control test that determines whether a customer's specifications have been met, § 1.174-2(a)(7), rather than a "methodical plan involving a series of trials to test a hypothesis, analyze the data, refine the hypothesis, and retest the hypothesis." *Union Carbide*, T.C. Memo. 2009-50, at *81; *Siemer Milling*, 2019 WL 1598588, at *8. No hypothesis was postulated, and no alternatives were evaluated. The test primarily addressed one question: Does the vessel conform to the customer's cargo requirements?

We do not doubt that Taxpayer encountered many uncertainties in building the Tanker. Plenty of trial testimony demonstrated that changes in one of several interdependent vessel components could trigger the redesign of other parts. But we **{–311–}** suspect that much of this design spiral addressed generic manufacturing uncertainty, rather than "investigative" uncertainty "in developing the *concept* of a model or product." *Union Carbide*, T.C. Memo. 2009-50, at *79 (quoting *Mayrath*, 41 T.C. at 590). The tax court found that Taxpayer had not established that post-fabrication testing was required to determine the design of every component of the Tanker that differed from its predecessor, the Penn 80. We agree and add that Taxpayer has not shown what expenses claimed for the whole Tanker were elements of a process of experimentation to remove uncertainty related to the "development or improvement" of the product. §§ 1.41-4(a)(5)(i), 1.174-2(a)(1). Sure, expenses incurred to iteratively design the Tanker's stern notch and towing bridle (among other parts) may have involved a process of experimentation. But Taxpayer failed to give us the means to apply the shrinking-back rule to apply the **[—36—]** "substantially all" test to any subcomponent of the Tanker. *See generally* § 1.41–4(b)(2). By choosing an "all or nothing" strategy, Taxpayer swung for the fences and missed. Assuming the Tanker is a pilot model, Taxpayer still failed to satisfy the "substantially all" test with respect to the Tanker.

Dry Dock. The tax court found that CIS's partial raise-and-lower test for the Dry Dock did not establish that the design of every element of the vessel remained uncertain, and thus constituted a process of experimentation. This raise-and-lower test, too, is less experimentation than it is a quality control test that establishes whether a customer's specifications have been met. § 1.174-2(a)(7). It merely ascertains whether a dry dock submerges and rises as designed and according to a customer's desired parameters. In fact, the client, Detyens—not CIS—conducted a full raise-and-lower test after taking delivery of the vessel at its shipyard. This supports the understanding that the raise-and-lower test confirmed the vessel's functioning as designed. Its primary function was not to test any hypothesis or evaluate alternatives CIS had in mind.

We recognize that the Dry Dock is the first one that CIS built. But we reiterate that the novelty of a business component is not a proper heuristic for the "substantially all" test. The test is applied in reference to research activities—not the business component being developed or improved. § 1.41-4(a)(6). We also acknowledge the many uncertainties Taxpayer encountered while building the Dry Dock. Surely, Taxpayer engaged in some research activities to address these uncertainties. But Taxpayer failed to document what, if any, of these activities involved a "methodical plan involving a series of trials to test a hypothesis, analyze the data, refine the hypothesis, and retest the hypothesis." *Union Carbide*, T.C. **[—37—]** Memo. 2009-50, at *81; *Siemer Milling*, 2019 WL 1598588, at *8. Taxpayer simply said the Dry Dock is first-in-class and did not document whether hypotheses and alternatives were tested and refined in a scientific manner. True, the Dry Dock's outboard side plate and safety deck, among other parts, went through several design iterations, the research activities for which could constitute elements of process of experimentation. But again, we are unable to apply the shrinking-back rule on such subcomponents for lack of documentation. *See generally* § 1.41–4(b)(2). Assuming the Dry Dock is a pilot model, Taxpayer also failed to satisfy the "substantially all" test with respect to the Dry Dock.

IV. Conclusion

For both vessels, Taxpayer failed to provide a principled way to determine the portion of employee activities that constituted elements of a process of experimentation. **{–312–}** Instead, Taxpayer offered arbitrary allocations for nonproduction employee wages that estimate the portion of the employee's time spent on qualified research. These allocations were not broken out by vessel and did not adequately document that nonproduction employees performed research activities which constitute elements of a process of experimentation. Taxpayer also claimed production employee wages, but similarly failed to show that the production activities accounted for by these wages were elements of a process of experimentation—even less, research activities. The pilot model argument does not help because, even assuming the vessels were pilot models, Taxpayer did not show why the alleged model production expenses belonged in the "substantially all" numerator. Taxpayer therefore failed to bear its burden to provide enough evidence for this court to calculate the "substantially all" **[—38—]** fraction "on a cost or other consistently applied reasonable basis." § 1.41-4(a)(6).

The lesson for taxpayers seeking to avail themselves of the research tax credit is to adequately document that substantially all of such activities were research activities that constitute elements of a process of experimentation. Generalized descriptions of uncertainty, assertions of novelty, and arbitrary estimates of time performing experimentation are not enough.

AFFIRMED.

United States Court of Appeals
for the Seventh Circuit

No. 22-2437

JARANOWSKI
VS.
INDIANA HARBOR BELT R.R. CO.

Appeal from the United States District Court for the Northern District of Indiana, Hammond Division

Decided: July 5, 2023

Citation: 72 F.4th 744, 11 Adm. R. 402 (7th Cir. 2023).

Before **HAMILTON, JACKSON-AKIWUMI,** and **LEE,** Circuit Judges.

[—1—] {-746-} HAMILTON, Circuit Judge:

Plaintiff-appellant Martin Jaranowski worked as a conductor for defendant-appellee Indiana Harbor Belt Railroad Company for twenty-two years. While operating a railroad switch in October 2020, plaintiff seriously injured his neck. He sued the railroad under the Federal Employers' Liability Act (FELA), 45 U.S.C. § 51 et seq., alleging that he was injured because the railroad failed to **[—2—]** maintain the switch properly. He accused the railroad of ordinary negligence and negligence per se based on alleged violations of Federal Railroad Administration (FRA) Track Safety Standards. *See* 49 C.F.R. Part 213. **{-747-}**

The district court concluded that Jaranowski had failed to present evidence that would support a finding that the railroad had actual or constructive notice of any defect in the switch before plaintiff was injured. The court granted summary judgment to the railroad on Jaranowski's claim for ordinary negligence and his claim for negligence per se, finding that the federal Track Safety Standards are violated only when a railroad has actual or constructive notice of track defects. We reverse. We agree with the district court that actual or constructive notice is required to violate the federal Track Safety Standards. We also find, however, that plaintiff presented sufficient evidence to create a genuine dispute as to whether the railroad at least should have known that the switch was defective before plaintiff was injured.

I. *Factual and Procedural History*

A. *Facts Relevant to Summary Judgment*

Plaintiff Jaranowski was employed as a conductor at Indiana Harbor Belt Railroad's Michigan Avenue Yard in East Chicago, Indiana. His duties included operating or "throwing" manually operated railroad switches. On October 26, 2020, while moving switch MA 27 from left to right, Jaranowski felt unexpected resistance in the switch followed by a strong pain in his neck and arm and tingling in his fingers. He was diagnosed with a spinal cord injury, and two months later, he underwent neck surgery. Jaranowski's injury **[—3—]** left him permanently unable to lift more than 20 pounds or to perform overhead work.

At the heart of a railroad switch is a lever about three feet long. By moving this lever, the operator is able to move short lengths of rail, which switch trains from one track to another. Switch MA 27 has such a lever with a handle at the end. The lever rests in a "switch keeper" when the switch is in a fixed and latched position. To operate the switch, the conductor disengages the latch with his foot, which releases tension and causes the lever to rise a few inches. Applying steady force, the conductor then walks the switch over to the opposite side and engages the latch to keep the switch in a fixed position. As the operator walks the switch from one side to the other, "switch points" in the rails are shifted into the desired position to switch trains from one track to another.

The railroad has a qualified track inspector inspect switch MA 27 monthly, as federal regulations require. *See* 49 C.F.R. § 213.235. Switch MA 27 was inspected on October 15, 2020, eleven days before Jaranowski was injured. The inspection report for that date noted no defect. Previous inspection reports of MA 27, going back to April 30, 2019, likewise showed no defect or issue with the switch. Jaranowski himself operated MA 27 without incident on October 22, four days before he was injured. Before throwing the switch on October 26, 2020, he looked at the switch points and saw no large debris in the points.

The day Jaranowski was injured, the railroad's director of safety, Eric Ritter, inspected switch MA 27. Ritter found that the switch was in good working condition, but his report noted that the amount of force required to operate the switch lessened substantially after he lubricated the switch as part of **[—4—]** his inspection. Pushing the handle down, for example, required 126 pounds of force before lubrication but only 55 pounds of force afterwards.

Plaintiff retained Alan Blackwell, a qualified track inspector, as an expert witness. Blackwell submitted a report and testified by affidavit in opposition to the railroad's motion for summary judgment. Blackwell identified several possible causes of Jaranowski's **{-748-}** injury. He noted that photographs of switch MA 27 taken by the railroad shortly after plaintiff's injury show debris, dirt, mud, ballast, and vegetation in the "tie cribs," which is where the connecting rod and switch rods are located. According to Blackwell, debris and vegetation in this location can interfere with the operation of the switch. The railroad's Ritter agreed that debris in the tie crib could affect the switch, and he testified that if he were to see a switch in the condition depicted in the photographs, he would order his crew to clean it up. Blackwell also noted that the photographs showed that the switch points were skewed and that fastenings that should keep the switch components in place were missing.

Blackwell personally inspected switch MA 27 on July 16, 2021, nine months after Jaranowski's injury. The day before his scheduled inspection, three maintenance workers for the railroad spent roughly 40 minutes cleaning and maintaining the switch. Ritter later explained that the railroad's crew knew the switch was going to be inspected and that they wanted to make sure it was in "good order." During his inspection, Blackwell noted that the switch appeared to have been recently lubricated and that there was no debris or vegetation in the tie cribs. Yet even after the clean-up and maintenance, and consistent with photographs taken after Jaranowski was **[—5—]** injured, Blackwell observed that the switch points were skewed and that several fastenings were loose or missing.

Blackwell also found excessive "lost motion" when the switch was moved from left to right, the same direction Jaranowski moved the switch when he was injured. "Lost motion" refers to a lag between movement of the switch handle and movement of the switch points in the rails. With lost motion, when the operator walks the switch handle from one side to the other, the switch points do not move right away. During his inspection, Blackwell discovered that the switch points on MA 27 did not move during the first half of the handle's journey. The switch points started to move only when the handle was at roughly a 90-degree angle. They completed their entire movement during the second half of the handle's journey. Blackwell explained that when switches are not properly maintained, they become difficult to operate, which means that the conductor must apply additional force to throw the switch, which in turn can lead to musculoskeletal injuries.

Blackwell concluded that the railroad had failed to provide a safe place for Jaranowski to work. He found that the railroad had failed to maintain switch MA 27 properly so that it could be operated without undue force and excessive lost motion. He also concluded that the railroad had failed to remove debris and vegetation from the tie cribs and that it failed to ensure fastenings were in place and secure. Blackwell further opined that the railroad had failed to perform detailed, monthly inspections "in a manner that ensured the switch was safe for operation." Finally, he concluded that the railroad had violated several federal Track Safety Standards. **[—6—]**

B. *Proceedings in the District Court*

Jaranowski sued Indiana Harbor Belt Railroad under the FELA, alleging that the railroad's negligence caused his injury. He accused the railroad of ordinary negligence and of negligence per se for its alleged violations of the federal Track Safety Standards.

The railroad moved for summary judgment, arguing that Jaranowski could not establish that the railroad had actual or constructive notice of any defect in switch MA 27. Under 28 U.S.C. § 636(c), the parties consented to adjudication by a **{-749-}** magistrate judge, who first granted the railroad's motion in part and denied it in part. *Jaranowski v. Indiana Harbor Belt R.R. Co.*, No. 2:20-cv-484, 2022 WL 2065022, at *1 (N.D. Ind. June 8, 2022). In that decision, the magistrate judge found that Jaranowski had not shown a genuine dispute of fact as to whether the railroad had actual or constructive notice that the switch was defective. The judge therefore concluded that the railroad was entitled to summary judgment on Jaranowski's claim of ordinary negligence. *Id.* at *4. Because the railroad's opening brief on summary judgment had not addressed Jaranowski's claim of negligence per se, the court took no action on that claim. *Id.* at *1 & n.2, and *4.

The railroad then moved for reconsideration of the district court's order. It argued that the federal Track Safety Standards are violated only when the railroad has actual or constructive notice of the violation. Because the court had already determined that Jaranowski could not establish that the railroad had such notice that MA 27 was defective, the railroad argued that it was also entitled to summary judgment on the claim for negligence per se. The magistrate judge agreed that notice is required to violate the federal Track Safety **[—7—]** Standards, and he granted summary judgment to the railroad on Jaranowski's remaining claim and entered final judgment for the railroad. *Jaranowski v. Indiana Harbor Belt R.R. Co.*, No. 2:20-cv-484, 2022 WL 3042236, at *3 (N.D. Ind. Aug. 2, 2022). Jaranowski has appealed on both claims.

II. *Analysis*

We review the district court's grant of summary judgment de novo, viewing the evidence and drawing all reasonable inferences in Jaranowski's favor. *Khungar v. Access Community Health Network*, 985 F.3d 565, 572 (7th Cir. 2021). Summary judgment is proper "if the movant shows that there is no genuine dispute as to any material fact and the movant is entitled to judgment as a matter of law." Fed. R. Civ. P. 56(a). A dispute about a material fact is genuine "if the evidence is such that a reasonable jury could return a verdict for the nonmoving party." *Anderson v. Liberty Lobby, Inc.*, 477 U.S. 242, 248 (1986). Substantive law determines which facts are material. *Id.*

Jaranowski makes two arguments on appeal. First, he argues that the evidence establishes a genuine dispute as to whether the railroad had actual or constructive notice that switch MA 27 was defective. Second, he contends that notice of a purported defect is not necessary to establish a violation of the federal Track Safety Standards that would establish negligence per se.

A. *Genuine Dispute as to Notice*

The FELA provides: "Every common carrier by railroad ... shall be liable in damages to any person suffering injury while he is employed ... for such injury or death resulting in whole or in part from the negligence of any of the officers, agents, or **[—8—]** employees of such carrier." 45 U.S.C. § 51. To prevail on his FELA claim, the plaintiff must prove "the traditional common law elements of negligence, including foreseeability, duty, breach, and causation." *Abernathy v. Eastern Illinois R.R. Co.*, 940 F.3d 982, 988, 7 Adm. R. 403, 405 (7th Cir. 2019), quoting *Fulk v. Illinois Central R.R. Co.*, 22 F.3d 120, 124 (7th Cir. 1994). To establish that his injury was foreseeable, the plaintiff "must show that the employer had actual or constructive notice" of the conditions he alleges were dangerous. *Holbrook v. Norfolk Southern Ry. Co.*, 414 F.3d 739, 742 (7th Cir. 2005). **{-750-}**

Because the Act was written "to offer broad remedial relief to railroad workers," the plaintiff's burden under the FELA is "significantly lighter than in an ordinary negligence case." *Holbrook*, 414 F.3d at 741–42. Under the FELA, "a railroad will be held liable where 'employer negligence played any part, even the slightest, in producing the injury.'" *Id.* at 742, quoting *Rogers v. Missouri Pacific R.R. Co.*, 352 U.S. 500, 506 (1957). Consequently, "a trial judge must submit an FELA case to the jury when there is even slight evidence of negligence." *Harbin v. Burlington Northern R.R. Co.*, 921 F.2d 129, 131 (7th Cir. 1990).

Viewed through the summary judgment lens, plaintiff's evidence would allow a reasonable jury to find that the railroad at least should have known that switch MA 27 was defective in one or more ways before plaintiff was injured. First, Blackwell, a certified track inspector with decades of experience, studied photographs of the switch taken soon after Jaranowski was injured and concluded that vegetation and debris in the tie cribs could have interfered with the switch's operation. The photographs show two plants, each roughly the height of the rail, as well as several water bottles, a cup, and other debris in the tie cribs. The railroad's own safety **[—9—]** director testified that if he had seen the switch in the condition depicted in the photographs, he would have ordered a crew to clean it up.

The railroad argues, however, that even if the vegetation interfered with the switch's operation, there is no evidence that the railroad knew or should have known of its presence. The switch was inspected eleven days before Jaranowski was injured, and that inspection report indicated no defects in the switch. The parties draw different conclusions from this fact. The railroad asks us to take the inspection report at face value, inferring that the switch was actually in good condition on the date of inspection, so that any defect in the switch must have arisen in the eleven days between the inspection and plaintiff's injury. Plaintiff argues, however, that a jury could conclude that the vegetation shown in the photographs could not possibly have grown in just eleven days. He insists that the only reasonable explanation, and certainly one reasonable explanation, is that the railroad's October 15th inspection just missed the problems because it was not performed with reasonable care.

In deciding a motion for summary judgment, the court does "not make credibility determinations, weigh the evidence, or decide which inferences to draw from the facts; these are jobs for a factfinder." *Johnson v. Advocate Health & Hospitals Corp.*, 892 F.3d 887, 893 (7th Cir. 2018), quoting *Payne v. Pauley*, 337 F.3d 767, 770 (7th Cir. 2003). Our only task is to determine whether there is a genuine dispute of material fact requiring a trial. *Id.* We conclude that a reasonable jury could accept Jaranowski's account of the facts and conclude that the railroad's prior inspection was performed without due care. **[—10—]**

The district court reasoned that vegetation in the tie cribs could not have provided notice to the railroad because, before operating the switch, Jaranowski checked to ensure that there was no large debris in the switch points. *Jaranowski*, 2022 WL 2065022, at *3. The court reasoned that if the vegetation did not put Jaranowski himself on notice before he operated the switch, the same vegetation could not have put the railroad on notice a few days earlier. *Id.* Keeping our focus on the standard for summary judgment, we respectfully disagree. Jaranowski was a conductor in the railroad's Transportation **{–751–}** department. He was not a qualified track inspector, and he was not trained to identify track defects. A reasonable jury could conclude that a trained inspector acting with reasonable care would discover defects that a conductor performing a brief scan might not.

Second, in addition to vegetation and debris in the tie cribs, plaintiff's expert Blackwell identified other defects in switch MA 27. The switch points were skewed, switch fastenings were loose or missing, and the switch operated with excessive lost motion. Again, the railroad argues that even if the switch was defective in the ways Blackwell describes, plaintiff has not presented evidence suggesting that the railroad knew or should have known of those defects. Plaintiff insists that the railroad should have discovered these defects during its regular inspections, and he argues a jury could infer that the inspections were performed negligently. It is true that inferences "that are supported by only speculation or conjecture will not defeat a summary judgment motion," *Carmody v. Board of Trustees of the Univ. of Illinois*, 893 F.3d 397, 401 (7th Cir. 2018), quoting *Design Basics, LLC v. Lexington Homes, Inc.*, 858 F.3d 1093, 1099 (7th Cir. 2017), but plaintiff here offers more. **[—11—]**

Plaintiff's expert Blackwell personally inspected switch MA 27 on July 16, 2021, one day after a three-person crew spent 40 minutes cleaning and maintaining the switch. The railroad's Ritter admitted that the crew was there to ensure the switch was in good condition before Blackwell's inspection, and the crew left the switch well lubricated and entirely free of debris and vegetation. Given Ritter's testimony, a reasonable jury could infer that the crew spent more time and effort cleaning and maintaining the switch before Blackwell's inspection than is spent on an ordinary switch inspection. Yet, even despite those unusual efforts, Blackwell still discovered missing fastenings, skewed switch points, and excessive lost motion. A jury could reasonably conclude that the railroad's October 15th inspection likewise should have discovered defects in the switch but did not. We thus find sufficient evidence to submit to a jury the question whether the railroad at least should have known before plaintiff's injury that switch MA 27 was defective.

B. *Notice and the Federal Track Safety Standards*

As an alternative theory of liability, Jaranowski argues that even if the railroad did not have actual or constructive notice of the defective switch, the defective switch established negligence per se because the track violated federal Track Safety Standards. In an FELA action, "the violation of a statute or regulation ... automatically constitutes a breach of the employer's duty and negligence *per se* and will result in liability if the violation contributed in fact to the plaintiff's injury." *Schmitz v. Canadian Pacific Ry. Co.*, 454 F.3d 678, 683 (7th Cir. 2006), quoting *Walden v. Illinois Central Gulf R.R.*, 975 F.2d 361, 364 (7th Cir. 1992). Although we have found a genuine factual dispute for trial on the issue of actual or constructive notice, **[—12—]** the negligence per se theory would, according to Jaranowski, call for jury instructions that do not require him to prove actual or constructive notice of the defective switch.

Jaranowski contends he can show negligence per se by showing violations of various Track Safety Standards that caused his injury. Specifically, he argues the evidence can show violations of 49 C.F.R. § 213.5(a) (requiring track owners to comply with Track Safety Standards or to halt operations on noncompliant track); **{-752-}** § 213.37(c) (requiring that vegetation on or near track be controlled so as not to interfere with rail workers' duties); § 213.133(a) (requiring that switch fastenings be intact and maintained so that components stay in place); § 213.135(e) (requiring that each switch be operable "without excessive lost motion"); and § 213.233(b) and (d) (requiring visual track inspections and immediate remedy of all defects).

The railroad contends that the federal Track Safety Standards are violated only when the owner of the track has actual or constructive notice of the alleged violation. We agree. Section 213.5(a) provides that any track owner who "knows or has notice that that track does not comply with the requirements of this part" shall bring the track into compliance or halt operations on the track. 49 C.F.R. § 213.5(a). Failure to do so may result in civil penalties imposed by the Federal Railroad Administrator. §§ 213.15(a) and 213.5(d).

In its final rule adopting the Track Safety Standards in 1998, the FRA explained that the Track Safety Standards are enforced only against a track owner "'who knows or has notice' that the track does not meet compliance standards." Track Safety Standards, 63 Fed. Reg. 33,992, 33,995 (June 22, 1998). Compared to other railroad safety regulations, this **[—13—]** knowledge element is "unique to the track regulations." *Id.* Generally, railroads are strictly liable if they fail to comply with FRA regulations. The final rule for the Track Safety Standards explained, however, that the FRA included a notice requirement for the track regulations because it recognized that railroads, even when exercising reasonable care, cannot prevent all track defects, which may occur suddenly due to changing traffic patterns or weather and may arise in remote areas. The regulation therefore provides that railroads "are held liable for non-compliance or civil penalties for only those defects that they knew about or those that are so evident the railroad is deemed to have known about them." *Id.*

Jaranowski acknowledges that the notice requirement in § 213.5 must be satisfied before the Federal Railroad Administrator may impose civil penalties, but he insists that a railroad's failure to comply with Track Safety Standards, when it results in employee injury, is actionable under the FELA even if the railroad lacked notice of the defect. He argues that the text of the track regulations at issue in this case, for example, 49 C.F.R. § 213.135(e), includes no notice requirement. That provision states: "Each switch stand and connecting rod shall be securely fastened and operable without excessive lost motion." 49 C.F.R. § 213.135(e). The final rule, however, distinguishes between track defects and violations of the Track Safety Standards. The rule explains that without the "knows or has notice" language found in § 213.5, "any defect found by an FRA inspector could be written as a violation," regardless of whether the railroad knew or should have known of the defect. 63 Fed. Reg. at 33,996. It is therefore a track defect if a switch operates with excessive lost motion, *see* 49 C.F.R. § 213.135(e), but it is not a violation of the Track Safety **[—14—]** Standards unless the railroad knew or should have known of that defect and failed to correct it.[1]

A railroad does not violate the federal Track Safety Standards unless it has actual or constructive notice of the alleged defect. To prevail on his claim of **{–753–}** negligence per se, Jaranowski must establish that the railroad violated a track regulation, which in turn requires him to show that the railroad had actual or constructive notice of the alleged defect. As we found above, however, there is sufficient evidence in the record for a reasonable jury to find that the railroad knew or should have known of defects in switch MA 27. Summary judgment should not have been granted to defendant on this claim.

Conclusion

Because the record shows a genuine dispute as to whether the railroad at least should have known that switch MA 27 was defective at the time plaintiff was injured, the judgment of the district court is REVERSED and the case is REMANDED to the district court for further proceedings consistent with this opinion.

---

[1] The Eleventh Circuit reached the same conclusion in a non-precedential decision. *Swoope v. CSX Transportation, Inc.*, 666 F. App'x 820, 823–24 (11th Cir. 2016).

United States Court of Appeals
for the Seventh Circuit

No. 22-1303

SMITH
VS.
CROUNSE CORP.

Appeal from the United States District Court for the Southern District of Indiana, New Albany Division

Decided: July 6, 2023

Citation: 72 F.4th 799, 11 Adm. R. 408 (7th Cir. 2023).

Before **RIPPLE, ROVNER,** and **BRENNAN,** Circuit Judges.

[—1—] {-801-} ROVNER, Circuit Judge:

Steven R. Smith sued Crounse Corporation for injuries he sustained while unloading coal from a barge owned by Crounse. The district court granted summary judgment in favor of Crounse, and we affirm. **{-802-}**

I.

Smith worked for Mulzer Crushed Stone ("Mulzer") as a Bobcat skid steer operator. Crounse had a contract with **[—2—]** Mulzer to provide barges for Mulzer to transport its crushed stone product. Crounse would deliver the barges to Mulzer, which would then clean the barges to its satisfaction, load the barges with Mulzer's crushed stone, deliver the stone product, clean the barges again to a "broom swept" state, and then release the barges back to Crounse. Crounse's barges were used by other companies to haul other materials, including coal. Barges carrying coal were sometimes released back to Crounse with as much as a foot of coal remaining in the bottom of the hopper. Mulzer and Crounse agreed that Mulzer would clear any remaining coal from the barges and sell it for Mulzer's own profit. This relieved Crounse of the duty of cleaning the barges before delivering them to Mulzer and benefited Mulzer with the sale of the reclaimed coal.

On April 24, 2017, Smith was tasked with clearing out the last foot of coal from Crounse barge #128 so that it could be loaded with Mulzer's crushed stone. To accomplish this task, Smith was operating a skid steer with a "blade" attached and positioned at its lowest height. Smith planned to use the blade to push coal from the back of the hopper to the front for removal, and then complete the job by removing any remaining coal with a push broom. While operating his skid steer at approximately five to eight miles per hour, the blade ran into an obstruction on the steel floor of the hopper. The skid steer came to an abrupt stop, propelling Smith forward. Smith's seatbelt failed and he was injured when he hit a safety bar on the skid steer.

The obstruction on the hopper floor turned out to be a "scab." The floor of the hopper is composed of strips of steel that are welded together at the seams. As a barge ages, the seams are subjected to various forces during loading and **[—3—]** unloading and sometimes split. At times, a piece of equipment catches the edge of a split seam and bends part of the steel strip upward, forming a scab. In this instance, Smith's skid steer ran into a scab approximately twelve to fourteen inches long, and a few inches tall. R. 34-9. The barge at issue was twenty-four years old.

Smith had been operating the skid steer for Mulzer for approximately ten months when the accident occurred. Although he had driven Bobcat skid steers in the past at other jobs, Mulzer employees Jonathon Mulzer and Jason Otterbach provided additional training to Smith in the use of the skid steer. Smith had never encountered a scab when cleaning a barge with a skid steer, but he learned after the accident that Jonathon Mulzer and Jason Otterbach had encountered this type of defect in barges before. They had discovered the defects that same way that Smith had: by driving a skid steer into a raised portion of hopper flooring. After the accident, Smith and his co-workers pushed the coal away from the area and saw the scab that had caused the skid steer to stop abruptly. Smith observed marks on the scab that he believed to have been caused by a sledgehammer. He averred that all of the damaged area appeared rusty and that there were no breaks or tears in the metal that looked "fresh." He opined that the hammer marks and the rust meant that the damage was old, and that the defect had been hammered down but not welded into place at some point in the past. After Smith's accident, other Mulzer employees hammered down the scab, and the coal was then cleared from the barge. A Mulzer employee then sent an email to Crounse's Traffic Department informing Crounse that there was "about a 12" to 14" scab **{-803-}** sticking up in the middle of the floor … that will need [to be] addressed sometime." According to the email, Mulzer **[—4—]** employees "bent it back down the best we could and will be able to load the barge. Might want to get it on a maintenance list sometime." R. 34-8. Mulzer did not inform Crounse that an employee had been injured as a result of running into the scab.

Crounse had procedures for regularly inspecting and repairing its barges. Every time a deckhand or engineer walked across barges that they were picking up or dropping off, they were directed to look for any damage that required repair. This inspection included any damage observed inside the hopper, on the hull of the barge, the winches, the deck fittings or any other areas of the barge. They also checked the barges for water leaks. If they found no damage, they made no report. If they found damage, they filed a damaged barge report. Crounse did not require employees to go into hoppers filled with a foot of coal dust to search for problems under the coal because it would not be safe to do so. Nevertheless, it was possible to detect split seams even in a barge loaded with coal. Employees inspecting barges were trained to look for water in the hull of the barge. Any water found would be pumped out, and an employee would then crawl the hull to determine where the water came from. This allowed Crounse to detect split seams from below the hopper where cargo was stored. Split seams are common on barges more than fifteen or twenty years old. Crounse asserted that damage that required immediate attention was always fixed at the first opportunity. That would include a floor scab that was protruding enough for equipment to become caught on it, or that was so extensive that it would cause rock or stone to leak down into the hull. Approximately eighty percent of damage was reported by Crounse employees conducting routine inspections, and **[—5—]** twenty percent was reported by third parties such as loading facilities.

Crounse did not consider the scab reported by Mulzer to be serious because the Mulzer email reporting it did not indicate that it was an urgent problem and did not reveal that anyone had been hurt as a result of this defect. Although split seams and scabs are common in barges of this age, Crounse's barge manager had never heard of anyone being injured by a split seam or scab in the eleven years he had been a barge manager. In the time period leading up to Smith's accident, Crounse had received no reports of damage to this barge, and the barge had last required repairs in December 2015. Nevertheless, after receiving the report from Mulzer, Crounse sent the barge for repairs in June 2017, and this seam, among others, was repaired within a few months of Smith's accident. Twenty-three days before Smith's accident, the barge had been cleaned by a blade without incident. The barge was also blade cleaned without incident only a few days before the June repairs were made. After Smith's accident and before the repairs were completed in June, the barge was used without any reported problems.

Nearly three years after the accident, Smith filed suit against Crounse for the injuries he sustained when his skid steer collided with the scab. He asserted claims for violations of section 905(b) of the Longshore and Harbor Workers' Compensation Act, 33 U.S.C. § 901, *et seq.*; general maritime law; and Indiana law. Following the completion of discovery, Crounse moved for summary judgment contending that: (1) there was no evidence that Crounse knew of or should have known of the scab defect at the time of the accident; (2) even if it had known of the defect, all parties were equally **[—6—]** aware that such a hazard could occur, and Mulzer determined how it **{-804-}** would go about the contractual task of cleaning the barge; and (3) Smith admitted that the seatbelt, the safety crossbar and the speed of the skid steer caused his injuries, all factors not within Crounse's turnover duties. The district court concluded that Smith lacked evidence that Crounse had actual knowledge of the defect or that it should have known of the defect in the exercise of ordinary care, and thus Smith failed to demonstrate that Crounse failed to comply with its turnover duties under *Scindia Steam Navigation Co. v. De Los Santos*, 451 U.S. 156 (1981). The court therefore granted summary judgment in favor of Crounse. Smith appeals.

II.

On appeal, Smith contends that the district court analyzed the duty owed by the vessel owner to longshoremen employees of a stevedore under the wrong standard. He also argues that the court improperly excluded the opinion testimony of a lay witness and failed to construe the facts in a light most favorable to the non-moving party. We review the district court's grant of summary judgment *de novo*, and we examine the record in the light most favorable to the party opposing judgment, in this case Smith, construing all reasonable inferences from the evidence in his favor. *Anderson v. Liberty Lobby, Inc.*, 477 U.S. 242, 255 (1986); *Horne v. Electric Eel Mfg. Co.*, 987 F.3d 704, 713 (7th Cir. 2021). Summary judgment is appropriate when there are no genuine disputes of material fact and the movant is entitled to judgment as a matter of law. Fed. R. Civ. P. 56(a); *Anderson*, 477 U.S. at 247–48; *Horne*, 987 F.3d at 713.

The Supreme Court explained the duties owed by vessel owners to longshoremen employees of stevedores under **[—7—]** section 905(b) in two seminal cases: *Scindia Steam Navigation Co. v. De Los Santos*, 451 U.S. 156 (1981); and *Howlett v. Birkdale Shipping Co.*, 512 U.S. 92 (1994). In *Scindia Steam*, the Court set out the general rule for liability of vessel owners under section 905(b):

> [T]he vessel owes to the stevedore and his longshoremen employees the duty of exercising due care "under the circumstances." This duty extends at least to exercising ordinary care under the circumstances to have the ship and its equipment in such condition that an expert and experienced stevedore will be able by the exercise of reasonable care to carry on its cargo operations with reasonable safety to persons and property, and to warning the stevedore of any hazards on the ship or with respect to its equipment that are known to the vessel or should be known to it in the exercise of reasonable care, that would likely be encountered by the stevedore in the course of his cargo operations and that are not known by the stevedore and would not be obvious to or anticipated by him if reasonably competent in the performance of his work.... The shipowner thus has a duty with respect to the condition of the ship's gear, equipment, tools, and work space to be used in the stevedoring operations; and if he fails at least to warn the stevedore of hidden danger which would have been known to him in the exercise of reasonable care, he has breached his duty and is liable if his negligence causes injury to a longshoreman.... It is also accepted that the vessel **[—8—]** may be liable if it actively involves itself in the cargo operations and negligently injures a longshoreman or if it fails to exercise due care to avoid exposing longshoremen to harm from **{-805-}** hazards they may encounter in areas, or from equipment, under the active control of the vessel during the stevedoring operation.

Scindia Steam, 451 U.S. at 166–67 (internal citation omitted).

The specific issue raised in *Scindia Steam* was the vessel's duty to longshoremen once cargo operations have begun. The Court noted that vessel owners are, to a certain extent, entitled to rely on stevedores to protect their longshoremen employees during cargo operations:

> We are of the view that absent contract provision, positive law, or custom to the contrary—none of which has been cited to us in this case—the shipowner has no general duty by way of supervision or inspection to exercise reasonable care to discover dangerous conditions that develop within the confines of the cargo operations that are assigned to the stevedore. The necessary consequence is that the shipowner is not liable to the

> longshoremen for injuries caused by dangers unknown to the owner and about which he had no duty to inform himself. This conclusion is plainly consistent with the congressional intent to foreclose the faultless liability of the shipowner based on a theory of unseaworthiness or nondelegable duty. The shipowner, within limits, *is* entitled to rely on the stevedore, and owes no duty to the **[—9—]** longshoremen to inspect or supervise the cargo operations.

Scindia Steam, 451 U.S. at 172.

The situation presented in *Scindia Steam* forced the Court to consider the limits of the vessel owner's reliance on the stevedore to keep its longshoremen employees safe. In that case, the ship's winch was malfunctioning, but the stevedore improvidently directed its longshoremen to continue using it. The Court concluded that, if the vessel owner knew of the defect in the winch and should have realized that the winch presented an unreasonable risk of harm to the longshoremen, then in some circumstances, the vessel owner would have a duty to intervene and repair the ship's winch. *Scindia Steam*, 451 U.S. at 175–76. This would be true, for example, if the vessel owner knew that the defect existed from the outset. The Court also noted that any contract between the stevedore and the vessel owner should also be considered if any provisions had bearing on the suit.

In *Howlett*, the Court addressed a vessel's turnover duty to warn of latent defects in the cargo stow and cargo area. *Howlett* involved a longshoreman who was injured when unloading cargo from the defendant's vessel. The cargo, which consisted of bags of cocoa beans, had been improperly placed on plastic sheets by the stevedore that loaded the bags. The vessel had supplied the plastic sheets to the loading stevedore. The plaintiff could not see the sheets, which were covered with dirt and debris, and he slipped and fell on a sheet, seriously injuring himself. The Court considered the scope of the vessel owner's duty to warn of latent hazards in the cargo stow, an analysis that depended in part on the vessel owner's duty to inspect for such defects. 512 U.S. at 94–96. **[—10—]**

The *Howlett* Court summarized the three general duties that shipowners owe to longshoremen:

> The first, which courts have come to call the "turnover duty," relates to the condition of the ship upon the commencement of stevedoring operations.... The second duty, applicable once stevedoring operations have begun, provides that a shipowner must exercise reasonable care to prevent injuries to longshoremen in **{-806-}** areas that remain under the "active control of the vessel." The third duty, called the "duty to intervene," concerns the vessel's obligations with regard to cargo operations in areas under the principal control of the independent stevedore.

Howlett, 512 U.S. at 98 (quoting *Scindia Steam*, 451 U.S. at 167–178) (internal citations omitted).

The turnover duty is at issue in Smith's appeal. The *Howlett* Court described that duty:

> A vessel must "exercise ordinary care under the circumstances" to turn over the ship and its equipment and appliances "in such condition that an expert and experienced stevedoring contractor, mindful of the dangers he should reasonably expect to encounter, arising from the hazards of the ship's service or otherwise, will be able by the exercise of ordinary care" to carry on cargo operations "with reasonable safety to persons and property." ... A corollary to the turnover duty requires the vessel to warn the stevedore "of any hazards on the ship or with **[—11—]** respect to its equipment," so long as the hazards "are known to the vessel or should be known to it in the exercise of reasonable care," and "would likely be encountered by the stevedore in the course of his cargo operations[,] are not known by the stevedore[,] and would not be obvious to or anticipated by him if reasonably

competent in the performance of his work."

Howlett, 512 U.S. at 98–99 (internal citations omitted). Howlett confined his claim to an allegation that the vessel owner failed to warn that the deck was covered with plastic rather than the paper and plywood that were ordinarily used when loading cocoa beans.

The Court concluded:

> [T]he vessel's turnover duty to warn of latent defects in the cargo stow and cargo area is a narrow one. The duty attaches only to latent hazards, defined as hazards that are not known to the stevedore and that would be neither obvious to nor anticipated by a skilled stevedore in the competent performance of its work. *Scindia Steam*, 451 U.S., at 167, 101 S.Ct., at 1622. Furthermore, the duty encompasses only those hazards that "are known to the vessel or should be known to it in the exercise of reasonable care." *Ibid.* Contrary to Howlett's submission, however, the exercise of reasonable care does not require the shipowner to supervise the ongoing operations of the loading stevedore (or other **[—12—]** stevedores who handle the cargo before its arrival in port) or to inspect the completed stow.

Howlett, 512 U.S. at 105.

With these standards in mind, we turn to the circumstances of Smith's injury. As Smith has pointed out, he was injured by a defect in the vessel, not a defect in the cargo stow. Nevertheless, that vessel defect was in the cargo area and was hidden by cargo (the remaining coal) that had been left behind by the last stevedore; in fact, Smith's employer was contractually obligated to remove that remaining cargo and clean the floor of the hopper. Smith has presented no evidence suggesting that Crounse had actual knowledge about the scab defect before the accident. Consequently, Crounse did not warn Mulzer or any of its employees about the scab. There is no dispute that Crounse charged its employees with regularly inspecting the barges and promptly reporting any problems. Crounse's corporate representatives testified that the company repaired serious problems as soon as it became aware of them. That included promptly fixing any scab that was protruding enough for **{-807-}** equipment to become caught on it. Crounse's inspections did not include requiring employees to go down into the remaining foot of coal/cargo and search for problems; such an inspection would require climbing in and out of the barge while it was moving up and down the river, a procedure that was not safe. Crounse also trained workers to check the hull for water leaks that could indicate split seam damage to the floor of the hopper.

Smith presented no evidence on industry standards for inspection of vessels and so the record contains no evidence that Crounse's inspection and repair procedures were inadequate, neglectful or failed to meet industry standards. Nor is there a **[—13—]** history of problems with Crounse's inspection procedures in the record. Although Smith had never encountered a defect of this type, there is no dispute that the two employees at Mulzer who trained Smith were aware that barges of this age could have split seams and scabs on the floor of the hopper. In fact, they had encountered defects of this sort in the past in the same manner that Smith did, by hitting them with a skid steer blade. Those encounters had not caused injuries, and the only Crounse employee to testify on the matter was not aware of any injuries caused by scabs in the eleven years that he had been employed there. The Mulzer trainers apparently had not passed on their knowledge of these types of defects to Smith.

Nevertheless, Smith contends that Crounse should have known of the defect or that the company had constructive knowledge of the scab and should have warned Mulzer. Specifically, Smith averred that the "scab appeared to be old damage. It did not have any tears or breaks in the metal that were fresh. All damage was rusty. The scab also had marks of prior repairs that showed it had been hammered down in the past, but had not been welded in place." R. 35-1. The district court ruled that, as a lay witness, Smith would be allowed to testify to his observations regarding the presence of rust or the appearance of marks on the scab. But the court would not admit Smith's opinions on whether the tears or breaks were "fresh" or "old damage," how long the rust had been present, or whether the scab had previously been repaired by being hammered down but not welded. We review the district court's decision to admit or exclude lay opinion for abuse of discretion. *Yancick v. Hanna Steel Corp.*, 653 F.3d 532, 547 (7th Cir. 2011). **[—14—]**

The court appropriately credited Smith's averments that rust was present and that he observed marks on the metal. But the court was well within its discretion in excluding Smith's lay opinion on the implications of these observations, such as whether the damage was old or fresh based on the rust and the marks on the metal, how the marks were created, or whether the scab had previously been hammered but not welded. The presence of corrosion or other marks on the metal and the inferences to be drawn from them are matters for expert rather than lay testimony, or so the district court could have reasonably concluded. A calculation of how fast corrosion would appear would likely depend on myriad factors that are the subject of expert rather than lay opinion. Federal Rule of Evidence 701 governs the admission of a lay witness's opinion testimony, which must be (a) rationally based on the witness's perception; (b) helpful to clearly understanding the witness's testimony or determining a fact in issue; and (c) not based on scientific, technical, or other specialized knowledge. *United States v. Eaden*, 37 F.4th 1307, 1312 (7th Cir. 2022). The district court reasonably found that the implications of rust or certain marks on the metal required scientific, **{-808-}** technical or specialized knowledge, requiring expert testimony. We see no abuse of discretion in that decision.

Smith had no personal knowledge of when the scab was created, how the marks that he observed were created, or whether Crounse or a third party had previously tried to repair the area with hammering or welding. He offered nothing other than speculation to support his opinion testimony. As is apparent from the actions of Mulzer employees on the day of Smith's accident, it is possible that a prior stevedore created the scab and then hammered it down in order to complete the job, without Crounse's knowledge. Indeed, immediately **[—15—]** before Crounse delivered the barge to Mulzer, another stevedore had loaded and then partially unloaded coal from the hopper and could have created the scab during that process. It is even possible that Smith created the scab when his skid steer blade hit a split seam. On this record, a jury would have to speculate about when the scab was created and whether Crounse would have had an opportunity to detect it before delivering the barge to Mulzer for cleaning.

Smith contends that the district court improperly weighed his credibility when it found his testimony "unpersuasive." It is clear from context, though, that the court was not weighing the evidence or deciding Smith's credibility but rather was excluding the opinion evidence because it was a matter for expert rather than lay testimony. No other evidence supported Smith's claim that the damage was old or existed at the outset, a point Smith sought to make to prove that Crounse should have known the defect was present when the vessel was turned over to Mulzer.

Smith also failed to produce evidence suggesting that Crounse should have known about the scab in the exercise of reasonable care. In fact, the evidence showed that Crounse's employees regularly inspected the barges, that no Crounse employee or third party had reported this defect, that the barge at issue had been cleaned with a blade by a skid steer without incident approximately three weeks before Smith's accident, and that the barge was used without incident for a few months after Smith's accident and before the seam in question was professionally repaired. Crounse's corporate representative testified that split seams were common on barges of this age and that persons operating skid steers in this environment would have known to proceed with caution. **[—16—]** Crounse was also unaware of any instance of a scab causing an injury, and Mulzer's own employees treated the issue as relatively minor, telling Crounse that it "[m]ight want to get it on a maintenance list sometime." Smith's own testimony that other

Mulzer employees had encountered scabs in similar situations supports Crounse's claim that the problem was one likely to be encountered by a stevedore in the course of cargo operations, and anticipated by him if reasonably competent in the performance of his work. There is no evidence in the record to the contrary. Under *Howlett* and *Scindia Steam*, the court therefore correctly concluded that Smith lacked evidence to hold Crounse liable for Smith's injuries under section 905(b).

Smith's remaining arguments to the contrary are unavailing. Smith asserts that the district court applied the standard for the vessel owner's duty regarding defects in the cargo stow rather than defects in the vessel itself. The court made no such error. The court ruled against Smith because he failed to provide evidence that Crounse knew of the defect or should have known of the defect in the exercise of ordinary care, the standard set forth for a vessel owner's turnover duty in **{-809-}** *Scindia Steam* and *Howlett. See Scindia Steam*, 451 U.S. at 167 ("The shipowner thus has a duty with respect to the condition of the ship's gear, equipment, tools, and work space to be used in the stevedoring operations; and if he fails at least to warn the stevedore of hidden danger *which would have been known to him in the exercise of reasonable care*, he has breached his duty and is liable if his negligence causes injury to a longshoreman.") (emphasis added); *Howlett*, 512 U.S. at 98–99 (same). As we just noted, Smith produced no evidence that Crounse's inspection and maintenance routines were **[—17—]** inadequate. The mere existence of the scab is not evidence that Crounse's procedures were neglectful.

Smith also argues that it was not merely his personal opinion that Crounse's inspections were inadequate but that the Supreme Court had decreed that the vessel's owner had a duty to inspect areas of the ship commensurate with its access and control. Again, although it is true that the Court stated that, between ports, the vessel's owner has a duty to inspect areas within its access and control, all of the evidence suggests that Crounse did so in a reasonable manner. The area under the remaining coal was not safely accessible while the vessel was in transit, and there is no evidence that Crounse could have discovered the scab before Smith's accident in the exercise of reasonable care. In addition to its frequent visual inspections, Crounse employees also regularly checked for water leaks that might indicate the presence of split seams, and there is no evidence in the record that Crounse failed to abide by this procedure or that this procedure did not meet the standard of reasonable care. Smith produced no evidence regarding industry standards, for example, to call into question the adequacy of Crounse's procedures in this situation. Summary judgment was therefore appropriate.

None of the cases relied upon by Smith alter this outcome. Smith cites *Matthews v. Ernst Russ S.S. Co.*, 603 F.2d 676 (7th Cir. 1979), as controlling the outcome here because the court there did not "agonize over what precisely the defendant therein knew and when the defendant knew it." Smith reads *Matthews* as holding that the vessel was implicitly charged with constructive knowledge of the flaws of a ladder where the vessel had allowed a state of disrepair arising from normal wear and tear over a period of time. But there is no holding **[—18—]** on constructive knowledge in *Matthews*. In that case, the vessel owner attempted to argue that it could not be held liable for the stevedore's use of a badly broken ladder because the dangers of using it were open and obvious. The court noted only that the jury was presented with sufficient evidence of the vessel owner's negligence without detailing that evidence. Smith reads too much into *Matthews*.

Nor is Smith aided by our analysis in *Cameron v. Consolidated Grain & Barge Co.*, 654 F.2d 468 (7th Cir. 1981). In *Cameron*, we reversed a jury verdict against a vessel owner and in favor of a longshoreman injured by a protrusion on the vessel because there was no evidence that the vessel owner had actual or constructive knowledge of the existence of the protrusion. Instead, the vessel owner produced evidence that, consistent with industry practice, it assigned the duty of inspecting the barges to barge cleaners and tugboat operators. The plaintiff's own expert testified that this practice was safe and reasonable so long as the inspectors were competent. The plaintiff produced no evidence that the inspectors were not competent. We noted that the record contained no evidence that the vessel owner should have known about the protrusion prior to the accident that injured the longshoreman:

> This is not a case in which the jury was compelled to choose between two conflicting **{-810-}** bodies of proof. Rather, the jury was confronted with [plaintiff's] unsupported assertions, on the one hand, and [the vessel owner's] proof to the contrary, on the other. [The vessel owner] proved that [the barge] was inspected in a reasonable and safe manner consistent with industry standards only three days prior to the accident and **[—19—]** that the inspection did not reveal the protrusion which caused [the plaintiff's] injury. [The plaintiff] offered no proof that the inspection was improper. [The vessel owner] also showed that the protrusion was not "wear and tear" but could have been caused by a single incident prior to [the plaintiff's] accident. ... He offered only his own testimony to show that the protrusion did not occur after the barge's arrival at Illinois Grain and nothing to show that it did not occur during towing. Absent proof that the inspection was improper or negligent or that the protrusion did not occur during or after the inspection, there simply was no evidence to support a finding of actual or constructive notice. Here the evidence showed only that [the vessel owner] took all reasonable steps to ensure that [the barge] was safe when it arrived[.]

Cameron, 654 F.2d at 472–73.

According to Smith, we can infer from *Cameron*'s holding of insufficient evidence what evidence would be sufficient to show constructive knowledge, including failure of inspection, knowledge of the hazard generally, testimony that the hazard is caused by wear and tear rather than a single unpredictable event, exclusive control by the defendant rather than a third party just prior to the accident, and evidence that the hazard existed at the outset of the plaintiff's encounter with the barge. According to Smith, all of that evidence is present here. But as we have just noted, Crounse did produce evidence of reasonable inspection and repair procedures, and Smith produced no evidence that these procedures were inadequate. **[—20—]** Although split seams are caused by wear and tear, the record contains uncontested evidence that scabs are created by unpredictable events when a piece of equipment such as a skid steer catches an edge of a split seam at great enough speed. In this case, the barge was under the control of the prior stevedore until Crounse delivered it to Mulzer, without a safe opportunity to inspect the bottom of the hopper that was covered with coal that Mulzer was contractually obligated to remove. Nor was there any competent evidence regarding how long the defect had existed when the barge was delivered to Mulzer. *Cameron* thus supports Crounse rather than Smith.

We have considered Smith's other arguments and find none persuasive. In the end, Smith produced no evidence demonstrating that Crounse knew or, in the exercise of reasonable care, should have known of the defect in the hopper floor. The district court correctly entered judgment in favor of Crounse.

AFFIRMED.

This page intentionally left blank

United States Court of Appeals for the Eighth Circuit

United States Court of Appeals
for the Eighth Circuit

No. 20-3671

UNITED STATES
VS.
MCKEE

Appeal from the United States District Court for the Western District of Missouri - Joplin

Decided: May 30, 2023

Citation: 68 F.4th 1100, 11 Adm. R. 418 (8th Cir. 2023).

Before **KELLY**, **ERICKSON**, and **GRASZ**, Circuit Judges.

[—1—] {-1101-} **KELLY**, Circuit Judge: **{-1102-}**

On July 19, 2018, 17 people were killed after *Stretch Duck 7*, a commercial tourism duck boat operating on Table Rock Lake in the Ozarks, sank during a storm. The government charged Kenneth Scott McKee, the captain of *Stretch Duck 7*, and Charles V. Baltzell and Curtis P. Lanham, managers of the duck boat company, with felony counts of "seaman's manslaughter" under 18 U.S.C. § 1115 and misdemeanor counts of operating a vessel in a grossly negligent manner under 46 U.S.C. **[—2—]** § 2302(b). In the 47-count second superseding indictment charging McKee, Baltzell, and Lanham (collectively, Defendants), the government alleged that the charged offenses occurred on "Table Rock Lake, a navigable water of the United States within the Western District of Missouri and within the admiralty jurisdiction of the United States." Defendants jointly moved to dismiss the indictment, arguing that it alleged only admiralty jurisdiction, and that the district court's admiralty jurisdiction does not extend to crimes occurring on Table Rock Lake because the lake is not "navigable" as a matter of law under Eighth Circuit precedent.

The district court[1] held a hearing on the motion, where the parties submitted evidence in writing pursuant to stipulation. On December 3, 2020, the district court granted Defendants' motion to dismiss, adopting a report and recommendation that concluded the prescriptive reaches of 18 U.S.C. § 1115 and 46 U.S.C. § 2302(b) are defined by admiralty law and do not cover the conduct alleged because Table Rock Lake does not fall under the court's admiralty jurisdiction.

The government now appeals the dismissal of the indictment. We have jurisdiction under 18 U.S.C. § 3731.

I.

We review a motion to dismiss an indictment de novo. *United States v. Metcalf*, 881 F.3d 641, 644 (8th Cir. 2018). "In doing so, we accept the allegations stated in the indictment as true, and ask whether they can form the basis of the charged offense." *United States v. Hansmeier*, 988 F.3d 428, 436 (8th Cir. 2021) (citation omitted). Where factual findings are required, we review them for clear error. *See United States v. Iron Crow*, 970 F.3d 1003, 1008 (8th Cir. 2020). **[—3—]**

II.

On appeal, the government argues that the district court erred in finding that 18 U.S.C. § 1115 and 46 U.S.C. § 2302(b) were enacted pursuant to Congress's authority to create and modify admiralty laws and thus reach only conduct occurring within the court's admiralty jurisdiction.[2] We address each statute in turn. **{-1103-}**

---

[1] The Honorable M. Douglas Harpool, United States District Judge for the Western District of Missouri, adopting the report and recommendation of the Honorable David P. Rush, Chief Magistrate Judge, United States District Court for the Western District of Missouri.

[2] The government also argues that because the district court found that it had subject matter jurisdiction to hear this case under 18 U.S.C. § 3231, it erred in further considering the prescriptive reach of the charged statutes under admiralty law. In the government's view, the district court's jurisdictional inquiry should have ended when it recognized that it had subject matter jurisdiction under § 3231. But the district court's jurisdictional inquiry did just that: The court concluded at the outset that it had subject matter jurisdiction over this case because the defendants were charged with "offenses against the laws of the United States." 18 U.S.C. § 3231. Its subsequent discussion about admiralty jurisdiction

A. 18 U.S.C. § 1115

Today, 18 U.S.C. § 1115 reads:

> Every captain, engineer, pilot, or other person employed on any steamboat or vessel, by whose misconduct, negligence, or inattention to his duties on such vessel the life of any person is destroyed, and every owner, charterer, inspector, or other public officer, through whose fraud, neglect, connivance, misconduct, or violation of law the life of any person is destroyed, shall be fined under this title or imprisoned not more than ten years, or both. **[—4—]**
>
> When the owner or charterer of any steamboat or vessel is a corporation, any executive officer of such corporation, for the time being actually charged with the control and management of the operation, equipment, or navigation of such steamboat or vessel, who has knowingly and willfully caused or allowed such fraud, neglect, connivance, misconduct, or violation of law, by which the life of any person is destroyed, shall be fined under this title or imprisoned not more than ten years, or both.

But the text of the seaman's manslaughter statute does not resolve the question raised in this appeal. The statute does not include a requirement that the offense occur within the admiralty jurisdiction of the United States. Nor does it contain an express element limiting its application to conduct that has an effect on interstate commerce.[3] *See United States v. Crenshaw*, 359 F.3d 977, 986 (8th Cir. 2004) (observing that statutory language such as "'engaged in, or the activities of which affect, interstate or foreign commerce' indicates that Congress intended a statute to extend to the outer limits of the Commerce Clause"). We turn, therefore, to the statute's legislative history and consider "the congressional purposes underlying the Act." *Offshore Logistics, Inc. v. Tallentire*, 477 U.S. 207, 220–21 (1986) (reviewing the legislative history of federal admiralty legislation addressing wrongful death remedies for survivors of persons killed on the high seas).

The earliest version of the seaman's manslaughter statute "appeared in 1838 as part of an act to prevent boiler explosions on steamboats plying 'the bays, lakes, rivers, or other navigable waters of the United States.'" *United States v. Allied* **[—5—]** *Towing Corp.*, 602 F.2d 612, 614 (4th Cir. 1979) (quoting Act of July 7, 1838, ch. 191, § 2, 5 Stat. 304, 304). The act was entitled, "An **{-1104-}** Act to provide for the better security of the lives of passengers on board of vessels propelled in whole or in part by steam." Act of July 7, 1838, ch. 191, 5 Stat. at 304. And § 12 of the act formed the predecessor of what is now 18 U.S.C. § 1115 and imposed liability on a "captain, engineer, pilot, or other person employed on board of any steamboat or vessel propelled in whole or in part by steam." *Id.*, § 12, 5 Stat. at 306. § 12 did not contain an express jurisdictional element tying it to one of Congress's enumerated powers, but other sections of the act contained language limiting their application to events occurring on the "navigable waters" of the United States. *Id.*, §§ 2–3, 5 Stat. at 304.

---

addressed a separate question—namely, whether 18 U.S.C. § 1115 and 46 U.S.C. § 2302(b) cover only those offenses that are committed on bodies of water that fall within the federal courts' admiralty jurisdiction, or whether the statutes' ambit is broader. *See United States v. Prado*, 933 F.3d 121, 132–38, 7 Adm. R. 92, 97–103 (2d Cir. 2019) (explaining the distinction between a court's subject matter jurisdiction, or "the question whether a case comes within the judicial power of the court," and questions of "jurisdiction" that instead concern the "scope, reach, or coverage" of a federal criminal statute).

[3] The government asserts that the elements of § 1115 "limit the persons that can be charged" under the statute "to those engaged in certain economic activities that have a substantial effect on interstate commerce," but it also agrees that the statute "lack[s] . . . a jurisdictional element." The statute uses the word "employed," and at least one court has interpreted that term to limit the scope of conduct to commercial activity. *See United States v. LaBrecque*, 419 F. Supp. 430, 437 (D.N.J. 1976). But there is nothing on the face of the statute to limit its application to commercial activity involving interstate commerce.

Over the next century, the provision that would become § 1115 was moved and revised several times. In 1874, seaman's manslaughter was codified in Title 70, "Crimes," in Chapter Three, "Crimes Arising Within the Maritime and Territorial Jurisdiction of the United States." *See* 70 Rev. Stat. § 5344 (1874); 18 Stat. 1037–38. This chapter prescribed several crimes, including murder, traditional manslaughter, and assault. *See* 70 Rev. Stat. §§ 5339, 5341, 5346; 18 Stat. 1038. As is relevant here, however, these criminal statutes were limited in reach to "the admiralty and maritime jurisdiction of the United States, and out of the jurisdiction of any particular state."[4] 70 Rev. Stat. § 5339; 18 Stat. 1038. § 5344—the seaman's **[—6—]** manslaughter statute—in contrast, had no such limitation. *See* 18 Stat. 1038. § 5344 was amended again in 1905 to add language regarding the criminal responsibility of "the owner or charterer of any steamboat or vessel" covered by the statute, but no changes were made to its prescriptive reach. Act of Mar. 3, 1905, ch. 1454, § 5, 33 Stat. 1023, 1025.

It was not until 1909 that Congress added language expressly restricting the reach of seaman's manslaughter to the special maritime and territorial jurisdiction. *See* Act of Mar. 4, 1909, ch. 321, § 282, 35 Stat. 1088, 1144. Seaman's manslaughter remained in a chapter entitled "Offenses Within the Admiralty and Maritime and the Territorial Jurisdiction of the United States." *Id.*, 35 Stat. at 1142. But that chapter was reconfigured, and the text regarding the special maritime and territorial jurisdiction was removed from individual sections. Instead, to avoid repetition, this limitation was placed in a separate section at the beginning of the chapter, and it applied to all of the "crimes and offenses defined in th[e] chapter." *Id.*, § 272, 35 Stat. at 1142. That introductory section stated in relevant part: "The crimes and offenses defined in this chapter shall be punished as herein prescribed: First. When committed on the high seas, or on any other waters within the admiralty **{–1105–}** and maritime jurisdiction of the United States and out of the jurisdiction of any particular State . . . ."[5] *Id.* Because seaman's manslaughter remained "in this chapter," its scope was now limited to the special maritime and territorial jurisdiction, even though that limitation had not been placed on any previous version of the statute. *See id.*, § 282, 35 Stat. at 1144. In 1926, the sections of the chapter were renumbered, but seaman's manslaughter was not revised. *See* 18 U.S.C. §§ 451, 461 (1926); 44 Stat. 498–99.

In 1948, seaman's manslaughter was moved to its current location at 18 U.S.C. § 1115. Act of June 25, 1948, ch. 645, § 1115, 62 Stat. 683, 757. It was at this point that Congress removed the special maritime and territorial jurisdiction limitation, and the statute essentially reads as it does today. The 1948 reviser's note **[—7—]** to § 1115 explained that the change was made to "restore[] the intent of the original enactments" in both the 1874 and 1905 versions by "mak[ing] this section one of general application." H.R. Rep. No. 80-304, at A91 (1947).

Our review of the statute's history leads us to the conclusion that the origins of seaman's manslaughter are in the admiralty jurisdiction of federal courts, see U.S. Const. art. III, § 2, and Congress's authority to pass legislation concerning matters that fall within that

[4] This limitation was akin to what is now known as "special maritime and territorial jurisdiction" and is a more limited jurisdictional area contained within the general admiralty jurisdiction. It does not include navigable waters within the general admiralty jurisdiction that are also within the territorial jurisdiction of a particular state. *See* 18 U.S.C. § 7 ("The term 'special maritime and territorial jurisdiction of the United States', as used in this title, includes: (1) The high seas, any other waters within the admiralty and maritime jurisdiction of the United States and out of the jurisdiction of any particular State, and any vessel belonging in whole or in part to the United States or any citizen thereof, or to any corporation created by or under the laws of the United States, or of any State, Territory, District, or possession thereof, when such vessel is within the admiralty and maritime jurisdiction of the United States and out of the jurisdiction of any particular State."). We use the phrase "special maritime and territorial jurisdiction" to refer to this early jurisdictional limitation even though it was not codified as such until later.

[5] Other limitations in this section are not relevant to our analysis here.

jurisdiction. *See Romero v. Int'l Terminal Operating Co.*, 358 U.S. 354, 361 (1959) (explaining that Article III "empowered Congress to revise and supplement the maritime law within the limits of the Constitution"); *Crowell v. Benson*, 285 U.S. 22, 39 (1932) ("[T]he general authority of the Congress to alter or revise the maritime law which shall prevail throughout the country is beyond dispute."). From 1874 until 1948, seaman's manslaughter was codified in a chapter of statutes addressing crimes committed "within the maritime and territorial jurisdiction of the United States." In 1905, Congress added language to clarify the criminal responsibility of corporate owners of vessels covered by the seaman's manslaughter statute, but nothing in the corresponding legislative history suggests lawmakers questioned the statute's admiralty-based jurisdictional scope. The year before the enactment of the 1909 version of the statute, the Special Joint Committee on the Revision of Laws submitted a report on revisions to the "Crimes" title, including revisions to the chapter entitled "Offenses within the Admiralty and Maritime Jurisdiction." H.R. Rep. 60-02, at 9–12 (1908). The report made no mention of seaman's manslaughter specifically. It did, however, cite to both an admiralty treatise and recent Supreme Court case law to emphasize that admiralty jurisdiction includes both civil and criminal maritime acts, and "that the admiralty jurisdiction over all navigable waters depends upon the Constitution and not upon any act of Congress." *Id.* at 12.

Furthermore, in the Congressional Record of 1908, senators discussed the reconfiguration of the chapter titled "Offenses within the Admiralty and Maritime Jurisdiction." 42 Cong. Rec. 1184 (1908). One senator expressed concern that the proposed revisions improperly expanded the jurisdiction of federal courts over **[—8—]** criminal conduct that was otherwise within the jurisdiction of the states. It was pointed out in response, however, that the introductory section to the revised chapter expressly limited the scope of the criminal statutes in the chapter—including seaman's manslaughter—to crimes committed in the special maritime and territorial jurisdiction **{–1106–}** of the United States. *Id.* at 1185–86. In short, all indications from the history of the seaman's manslaughter statute are that it was passed and revisited with attention to its scope. And that scope was, in turn, always defined by the reach of federal admiralty jurisdiction.

The most comprehensive analysis to date of the jurisdictional scope of § 1115 by a federal court appears in *Allied Towing*, where the Fourth Circuit similarly traced the statute's origins and development beginning in 1838 and reached a similar conclusion to ours today. 602 F.2d at 614–15. The court concluded that "[t]he history of § 1115 discloses . . . that Congress enacted this statute as an integral part of its regulation of the nation's maritime commerce," and that the statute therefore "reaches homicides committed anywhere within the general admiralty jurisdiction of the federal courts." *Id.* at 615. The court in *Allied Towing* pointed to the addition of a jurisdictional limitation to the seaman's manslaughter statute in 1909; the subsequent removal of that limitation in 1948; and the 1948 reviser's note as evidence that Congress intended the statute to cover the entirety of the general admiralty jurisdiction rather than the more limited special maritime and territorial jurisdiction. *Id.* at 614–15.[6]

The government views the significance of the 1948 revision differently. As the government sees it, Congress's removal in 1948 of the seaman's manslaughter statute's limitation to the special maritime and territorial jurisdictional is evidence of congressional recognition that the statute is a Commerce Clause enactment. And given the absence of any textual limitation related to admiralty and maritime **[—9—]** jurisdiction, the government posits, § 1115's ambit extends to any covered "misconduct, negligence, or inattention" on the part of any person "employed on any steamboat or vessel" that impacts interstate commerce, irrespective of

[6] The Fourth Circuit's understanding that § 1115's scope is defined by admiralty law is shared by the Sixth Circuit, the only other circuit court to consider § 1115's jurisdictional reach. *See Hoopengarner v. United States*, 270 F.2d 465, 470–72 (6th Cir. 1959) (discussing § 1115's scope in light of federal admiralty law).

whether that criminal conduct takes place on a body of water that otherwise falls within the federal courts' admiralty and maritime jurisdiction. But the regulation of interstate commerce outside the admiralty and maritime context is not mentioned in any of the historical materials concerning § 1115 that we have found. And despite the opportunity to do so, Congress has not added an interstate commerce element to the statute in its almost 200-year existence.

"[U]ntil relatively recently criminal Commerce Clause statutes tended overwhelmingly to contain jurisdictional elements" tying the covered conduct to interstate commerce. Margaret H. Lemos, *The Commerce Power and Criminal Punishment: Presumption of Constitutionality or Presumption of Innocence?*, 84 Tex. L. Rev. 1203, 1227 (2006). It was not until "the late 1960s" that Congress enacted "the first criminal statutes that prohibited conduct defined entirely without reference to interstate commerce." *Id.* In the absence of express jurisdictional elements, these newer statutes relied instead on congressional findings that the regulated conduct substantially affected interstate commerce. *Id.* The Supreme Court acknowledged these two approaches to legislating criminal Commerce Clause statutes in *United States v. Lopez*. 514 U.S. 549, 561–63 (1995). There, the Court found the fact that the Gun-Free School Zones Act contained neither a jurisdictional element nor **{-1107-}** congressional findings supported its ultimate conclusion that the statute did not fit within Congress's Commerce Clause authority. *See id.* at 561 ("§ 922(q) contains no jurisdictional element which would ensure, through case-by-case inquiry, that the firearm possession in question affects interstate commerce."); *id.* at 563 ("[T]o the extent that congressional findings would enable us to evaluate the legislative judgment that the activity in question substantially affected interstate commerce, . . . they are lacking here."). Thus, § 1115's lack of a jurisdictional element does not necessarily support the government's position that it must be a Commerce Clause statute. To the contrary, the statute's lack of either a jurisdictional **[—10—]** element or congressional findings tying it to interstate commerce means it does *not* look like a typical criminal Commerce Clause statute.

In support of its position, the government also cites cases where courts expressed the view that § 1115's original 1838 precursor "was enacted by congress in the proper exercise of its constitutional power 'to regulate commerce with foreign nations and among the several states.'" *LaBrecque*, 419 F. Supp. at 435 (quoting *United States v. Holtzhauer*, 40 F. 76, 78 (C.C.D.N.J. 1889)); *see United States v. Beacham*, 29 F. 284, 284 (C.C.D. Md. 1886) ("The authority for the statute is to be found in the constitutional grant of power to congress to regulate commerce among the several states."); *United States v. Jackson*, 26 F. Cas. 559, 561 (S.D.N.Y. 1841) ("[F]ull power to legislate over the subject in question is found in the authority to regulate commerce given by the constitution."). But none of these cases examined the origins of § 1115, which was enacted as part of a broader act regulating maritime travel, or considered the provision's subsequent legislative history, which involved the addition and removal of jurisdictional limitations indicating that Congress considered it to be an admiralty statute.

Moreover, that § 1115 implicates interstate commerce as a practical matter—specifically, by targeting the misconduct of those "employed on any steamboat or vessel"—is not surprising. "[T]he primary focus" of federal admiralty jurisdiction "is unquestionably the protection of maritime commerce." *Foremost Ins. Co. v. Richardson*, 457 U.S. 668, 674 (1982); *see Sisson v. Ruby*, 497 U.S. 358, 362 (1990) ("[P]rotecting commercial shipping is at the heart of admiralty jurisdiction . . . ."). And the purpose of § 1115's earliest precursor was, by its own terms, "to provide for the better security of the lives of passengers on board of vessels" traveling on "bays, lakes, rivers" and other channels of commerce. Act of July 7, 1838, ch. 191, § 2, 5 Stat. 304. Yet the fact that a federal criminal statute impacts or touches on maritime commerce does not mean that the statute's reach necessarily extends to any conduct that Congress could arguably regulate through its Commerce Clause power. **[—11—]**

And notably, the government alleged in its indictment that the charged offenses in this case occurred "within the admiralty jurisdiction of the United States." While it now argues that language is surplusage, *see, e.g., United States v. Thompson*, 6 F.4th 789, 795 (8th Cir. 2021) ("[M]ere surplusage [in an indictment] . . . may be disregarded if the remaining allegations are sufficient to charge a crime."), the indictment does not allege a connection between Defendants' conduct and interstate **{–1108–}** commerce, either.[7] We can find no case, and the parties alert us to none, where conduct occurring outside the general admiralty jurisdiction was prosecuted under § 1115.[8] We decline the government's invitation to expand the scope of a criminal statute without direction from Congress, and we conclude that the scope of § 1115 is defined by the reach of federal admiralty jurisdiction. *See Cleveland v. United States*, 531 U.S. 12, 24 (2000) ("We resist the Government's reading of [the statute] . . . because it invites us to approve a sweeping expansion of federal criminal jurisdiction in the absence of a clear statement by Congress."); *Bond* **[—12—]** *v. United States*, 572 U.S. 844, 857 (2014) ("The problem with this interpretation is that it would dramatically intrude upon traditional state criminal jurisdiction, and we avoid reading statutes to have such reach in the absence of a clear indication that they do." (citation omitted)).

B. 46 U.S.C. § 2302(b)

The government also argues that 46 U.S.C. § 2302(b) is a Commerce Clause statute. Enacted as part of the Motorboat Act of 1940, § 2302(b) makes it a class A misdemeanor for a person to "operat[e] a vessel in a grossly negligent manner that endangers the life, limb, or property of a person." Unlike § 1115, this statute includes an express reference to its prescriptive reach, which is defined and limited by admiralty jurisdiction. *See* 46 U.S.C. § 2301 ("[T]his chapter applies to a vessel operated on *waters subject to the jurisdiction of the United States*." (emphasis added)). We also note that the title of the act under which this statute was originally enacted refers to "the navigable waters of the United States," further reinforcing the conclusion that it was passed pursuant to Congress's admiralty authority. *See* Act of April 25, 1940, Pub. L. No. 76-484, 54 Stat. 163 ("An Act – [t]o amend laws for preventing collisions of vessels, to regulate equipment of certain motorboats on the navigable waters of the United States, and for other purposes."). We therefore reject the government's argument that § 2302(b) is a Commerce Clause enactment whose reach is not limited by the scope of federal admiralty jurisdiction.

III.

Because the government has failed to demonstrate that Congress enacted **{–1109–}** 18 U.S.C. § 1115 and 46 U.S.C. § 2302(b) pursuant to its power to regulate interstate

[7] The 28-page second superseding indictment does not mention interstate commerce even once. We also note that when the owners of *Stretch Duck 7* initiated a civil proceeding seeking exoneration from or limitation of liability for the accident at issue here, the government moved to intervene in the civil action to "present[] its position that Table Rock Lake . . . is a navigable water of the United States subject to . . . admiralty jurisdiction." Motion to Intervene, *In re Branson Duck Vehicles, LLC*, No. 18-03339, Doc. 73 at 1 (W.D. Mo. Jan. 18, 2019). The government represented that "[t]he grand jury returned the indictment [in the instant criminal case] under the admiralty jurisdiction of the United States," which was "premised on the fact that Table Rock Lake was a navigable water of the United States." *Id.* at 2. And the government reiterated that the "prosecution was brought under the admiralty jurisdiction of the United States." *Id.* at 5. The district court in the civil action denied the government's motion and ultimately dismissed the civil action for lack of admiralty jurisdiction. Order, *In re Branson Duck Vehicles*, No. 18-03339, Doc. 311 at 4-5 (W.D. Mo. Nov. 27, 2019).

[8] Even in the cases cited by the government where courts expressed the view that § 1115 was a Commerce Clause statute, the conduct at issue occurred on navigable-in-fact waters within the general admiralty jurisdiction. *See LaBrecque*, 419 F. Supp. at 431 (Atlantic Ocean); *Holtzhauer*, 40 F. at 78 (Newark Bay) *Beacham*, 29 F. at 285 (Chesapeake Bay); *Jackson*, 26 F. Cas. at 559 (East River).

commerce, we next consider whether the district court properly dismissed the charges against Defendants as outside the limits of the general admiralty jurisdiction. The government argues that the court's admiralty jurisdiction extends to crimes occurring on Table Rock Lake because the lake is presently navigable under the navigability-in-fact test. **[—13—]**

Article III, § 2 of the Constitution confers to the federal courts general subject matter jurisdiction over all admiralty and maritime cases involving waters that are navigable in fact. *Kaiser Aetna v. United States*, 444 U.S. 164, 171–72, 172 n.7 (1979). We have held that "the concept of 'navigability' in admiralty is properly limited to describing a present capability of waters to sustain commercial shipping." *Livingston v. United States*, 627 F.2d 165, 169–70 (8th Cir. 1980); *see id.* at 170 ("[A]bsent some present or potential commercial activity, there is no ascertainable federal interest that justifies frustrating the legitimate interests of the states in providing a forum and applying their law to regulate conduct within their borders." (citing *Adams v. Mont. Power Co.*, 528 F.2d 437, 439 (9th Cir. 1975)).

In its order dismissing the indictment, the district court here found that Table Rock Lake is not navigable for purposes of admiralty jurisdiction as a matter of law under our decision in *Edwards v. Hurtel*, 717 F.2d 1204 (8th Cir. 1983) (per curiam), *aff'd on reh'g*, 724 F.2d 689 (8th Cir. 1984) (per curiam). In *Edwards*, an injured boater sued another boater after their vessels collided on Table Rock Lake. 717 F.2d at 1205. The plaintiff brought claims under 28 U.S.C. § 1333 and invoked the court's admiralty jurisdiction. *Id.* In assessing whether Table Rock Lake was navigable in fact and therefore subject to admiralty jurisdiction, the district court took judicial notice of the following facts:

> The recreational nature of Table Rock Lake is generally known within the territorial jurisdiction of this Court. The lake has not been susceptible of use for commercial shipping and in fact has been used exclusively for recreational activities. Furthermore, there is no reasonable likelihood that Table Rock Lake will become or be made navigable in the near future.

Id. (cleaned up). On review, this court applied the judicially noticed facts to the navigability-in-fact standard and affirmed the district court's determination that Table Rock Lake was not navigable in fact. *Id.* **[—14—]**

Here, the government objects to the district court's reliance on *Edwards* as binding precedent regarding the status of Table Rock Lake and argues that the evidence of commercial activity on Table Rock Lake presented in this case establishes that the lake is navigable in fact. However, before deferring to *Edwards*, the district court reviewed all of the evidence submitted by the parties and found that the nature and frequency of commercial shipping on the lake had not substantially changed since the *Edwards* decision. Thus, the district court concluded that even if the *Edwards* precedent was not binding, it would still find that Table Rock Lake is not navigable in fact.

We detect no clear error in the district court's finding that the nature and frequency of commercial shipping on Table Rock Lake has not changed substantially since *Edwards*, and we agree with its conclusion that Table Rock Lake is not navigable in fact. The government points to mostly recreation-based commercial activity taking place on Table Rock Lake to **{-1110-}** argue that it functions as a highway of commerce and is thus navigable in fact. But under our precedent, "the concept of 'navigability' in admiralty is properly limited to describing a present capability of waters to sustain commercial shipping." *Livingston*, 627 F.2d at 169–70. Accordingly, evidence of recreational activity on the lake does not establish that it is navigable in fact. *See Edwards*, 717 F.2d at 1205 (finding Table Rock Lake non-navigable because it had "not been susceptible of use for commercial shipping and in fact ha[d] been used exclusively for recreational activities").

IV.

For the foregoing reasons, we affirm the district court's dismissal of the indictment. *See United States v. Love*, 20 F.4th 407, 411–12 (8th Cir. 2021) (explaining that because "federal jurisdiction over a particular place is a question of law," a district court "may take judicial notice that a place is within the special maritime and territorial jurisdiction of the United States and not submit that issue to the jury").

(Reporter's Note: Concurring opinion follows on p. 426).

[—15—] {-1110-} **GRASZ**, Circuit Judge, concurring:

The tragedy on Missouri's Table Rock Lake in July of 2018 is one of historic proportions and horrendous personal loss to the families involved. The issue before us, though, is whether it also gives rise to valid federal criminal charges. I agree that it does not. I write separately to emphasize the unique circumstances leading to my conclusion that the prescriptive reach of 18 U.S.C. § 1115—the so-called Seaman's Manslaughter Statute—is limited to the admiralty jurisdiction of the United States.

At its core, this case implicates principles of federalism. "Under our federal system, the 'States possess primary authority for defining and enforcing the criminal law.'" *United States v. Lopez*, 514 U.S. 549, 561 n.3 (1995) (quoting *Brecht v. Abrahamson*, 507 U.S. 619, 635 (1993)). And so we have "good reason to rely on a clear statement principle of statutory construction." *Raygor v. Regents of Univ. of Minn.*, 534 U.S. 533, 534 (2002). "When 'Congress intends to alter the usual constitutional balance between the States and the Federal Government, it must make its intention to do so unmistakably clear in the language of the statute.'" *Id.* (quoting *Will v. Michigan Dep't of State Police*, 491 U.S. 58, 65 (1989)). This is particularly true when it is done within the context of a criminal statute, where we apply the rule of lenity. *See Jones v. United States*, 529 U.S. 848, 858 (2000) (explaining "when [a] choice has to be made between two readings of what conduct Congress has made a crime, it is appropriate, before we choose the harsher alternative, to require that Congress should have spoken in language that is clear and definite" (quoting *United States v. Universal C.I.T. Credit Corp.*, 344 U.S. 218, 221–22 (1952))). So, the dispositive question here becomes whether Congress was sufficiently clear that it meant to extend criminal liability to non-navigable waters, something that historically was—with some delineated exceptions—within the States' jurisdictions.

Admittedly, the text of the statute could be read as suggesting Congress did intend to so expand criminal liability. After all, the statute is silent about jurisdictional limits. But under these unique circumstances, it is the very absence of *any* jurisdictional limit that creates ambiguity as to whether Congress intended such **[—16—]** a result. *See generally West v. Kerr-McGee Corp.*, 765 F.2d 526, 529 (5th Cir. 1985) **{-1111-}** ("When . . . a statute contains 'latent ambiguities' despite its superficial clarity, we turn to the statute's legislative history for guidance."); 2A *Sutherland Statutory Constr.* § 46:4 (7th ed.) (collecting cases discussing latent ambiguities). Indeed, Congress cannot enact criminal penalties unless the Constitution grants it such power. *See Torres v. Lynch*, 578 U.S. 452, 457 (2016). And, as the lead opinion explains, if Congress was acting pursuant to its power to regulate interstate commerce as the government suggests, one would expect to see either a jurisdictional element or congressional findings that the regulated conduct substantially affects interstate commerce.[9] *See also id.* (explaining "most federal offenses include, in addition to substantive elements, a jurisdictional one"). Neither is present here.

To the contrary, unless a jurisdictional limit is read into the text, 18 U.S.C. § 1115 would apply to the negligent operation of "vessels"[10] everywhere in the United States. An owner of a canoe or small fishing boat whose ordinary negligence results in a death on a farm pond in Nebraska could be charged with Seaman's Manslaughter under federal law. There is no basis to conclude that is what Congress

[9] And if we ignored this clue and assume Congress enacted the Seaman's Manslaughter Statute pursuant to its power to regulate interstate commerce, the absence of a jurisdictional element would seemingly mean there is no limit on the law's reach. *Lopez*, 514 U.S. at 562. This would compound the "legal uncertainty" inherent when Congress enacts legislation under the Commerce Clause because it would suggest there is no "judicially enforceable outer limits" to Congress' power to criminalize behavior. *Id.* at 566.

[10] *See United States v. Holmes*, 104 F. 884, 886 (N.D. Ohio 1900) (concluding the term "vessel" in what is now 18 U.S.C. § 1115 "includes every description of water craft . . . used, or capable of being used, as a means of transportation on water").

intended when it enacted the statute. **[—17—]**

The government attempts to avoid this absurdity by supplying and injecting additional verbiage into the statute—namely by adding "commercial" before "vessel." But this proposed solution suffers from a defect similar to that for which the government faults the district court's interpretation—adding to the plain text of the statute. Since either interpretation ultimately requires the court to add some sort of limiting language, it makes sense to interpret the statute with the assumption that Congress did not intend to disrupt the Constitution's federal-state balance. *See United States v. Bass,* 404 U.S. 336, 349–50 (1971). All this leads me to conclude § 1115's prescriptive reach is limited to the admiralty jurisdiction of the United States. Because admiralty jurisdiction is lacking here, dismissal of the indictments was appropriate.

(Reporter's Note: Opinion concurring in part and dissenting in part follows on p. 428).

[—17—] {-1111-} **ERICKSON,** Circuit Judge, concurring in part and dissenting in part:

On the issue of the navigable nature of Table Rock Lake, I note that while I may have reached different factual findings as to the underlying question of whether Table Rock Lake is presently capable of "sustaining commercial shipping," I agree that the district court committed no clear error in its findings and that those findings support the conclusion that Table Rock Lake is not navigable in fact.

The analysis on the defendants' motion to dismiss the indictment should have ended with the conclusion that jurisdiction exists under 18 U.S.C. § 3231. Even if subject matter jurisdiction hinges on which power Congress exercised when it enacted § 1115, I am convinced that the Congress enacted § 1115 under its Commerce Clause {-1112-} power and I respectfully dissent as to the charged offenses under § 1115.

Section 3231 grants federal district courts jurisdiction over "all offenses against the laws of the United States." 18 U.S.C. § 3231. When a court has jurisdiction over a federal criminal case pursuant to § 3231, that is the "beginning and the end of the 'jurisdictional' inquiry." *United States v. White Horse*, 316 F.3d 769, 772 (8th Cir. 2003) (quoting *Hugi v. United States*, 164 F.3d 378, 380 (7th Cir. [—18—] 1999)) (dismissing the defendant's assertion that indictment was fatally flawed when it lacked a supposedly jurisdictional element because that element was only "relevant to the matter of proof but irrelevant on the matter of jurisdiction"). The district court's determination that it had subject matter jurisdiction over this case under § 3231 ended the jurisdictional question.

This is not an international waters case where Congress's authority to regulate may be questionable. *See United States v. Prado*, 933 F.3d 121, 136–38, 7 Adm. R. 92, 100–03 (2d Cir. 2019) (discussing the reach of the Maritime Drug Law Enforcement Act in extraterritorial waters). By considering the statute's prescriptive reach, and whether the indictment met the requisite elements of § 1115, the district court and majority conflated merits questions with the jurisdictional question. *See United States v. Cotton*, 535 U.S. 625, 631 (2002) (explaining courts have "jurisdiction of all crimes cognizable under the authority of the United States" and objections to an indictment "go[] only to the merits of the case" (citation omitted)). If the analysis is properly limited to jurisdiction, the § 1115 charges should not have been dismissed on jurisdiction grounds.

Even if we were required to look beyond § 3231, a district court does not need to have admiralty jurisdiction to hear a criminal case under 18 U.S.C. § 1115 because the text of the statute demonstrates that § 1115 was enacted under Congress's Commerce Clause power. Equally telling, nothing in the text of the statute indicates it was enacted pursuant to Congress's admiralty powers.

Cases decided contemporaneously with § 1115's statutory precursor from 1838 recognized the statute "was enacted by [C]ongress in the proper exercise of its constitutional power 'to regulate commerce.'" *United States v. Holtzhauer*, 40 F. 76, 78 (C.C.D.N.J. 1889) (discussing Act of July 7, 1838, ch. 191, § 12, 5 Stat. 304, 306). *See also United States v. Beacham*, 29 F. 284, 284 (C.C.D. Md. 1886) (same); *United States v. Jackson*, 26 F. Cas. 559, 561 (S.D.N.Y. 1841) (same). [—19—]

The history of the alterations of § 1115 and its statutory predecessors does not appear to me to be helpful to establish which power Congress used to enact the original 1838 law. And the other laws enacted alongside what would later become § 1115 do not undermine the statute's commercial language and the contemporaneous understanding that the statute was an exercise of Congress's commerce power. *See, e.g., United States v. Jackson*, 26 F. Cas. 559, 561 (S.D.N.Y. 1841).

For these reasons, I would reverse the district court's dismissal of the indictment.

United States Court of Appeals
for the Eighth Circuit

No. 21-3366

LANCASTER
vs.
BNSF RY. CO.

Appeal from the United States District Court for the District of Nebraska - Lincoln

Decided: August 2, 2023

Citation: 75 F.4th 967, 11 Adm. R. 429 (8th Cir. 2023).

Before **SHEPHERD**, **STRAS**, and **KOBES**, Circuit Judges.

[—1—] **{-968-}** **KOBES**, Circuit Judge:

James Lancaster, a former BNSF Railway Company employee, died from lung cancer in 2018. Rebecca Lancaster, on behalf of her late husband's estate, brought this wrongful death action against BNSF under the Federal Employers' Liability Act (FELA), alleging James's cancer was caused by his exposure to toxins **[—2—]** at work. The district court[1] excluded Lancaster's expert witness testimony and granted summary judgment to BNSF. We affirm. **{-969-}**

I.

James worked for BNSF for 33 years. In 2016, he was diagnosed with lung cancer and died less than two years later. Lancaster sued, alleging that James's cancer was caused by his exposure to diesel exhaust, silica dust, and asbestos at work. To prove her case, Lancaster hired two expert witnesses: Dr. Neil Zimmerman and Dr. Ernest Chiodo. Dr. Zimmerman was retained to give an opinion on, among other things, James's work-related exposures, while Dr. Chiodo was supposed to give an opinion that the alleged exposures caused James's cancer. BNSF moved to exclude both experts. The district court denied the motion as to Dr. Zimmerman but excluded Dr. Chiodo. Because Lancaster could not prove causation without Dr. Chiodo, the district court granted summary judgment to BNSF. Lancaster appeals the exclusion of Dr. Chiodo's expert testimony and the resulting grant of summary judgment.

II.

We review the exclusion of expert testimony for an abuse of discretion, "and will only reverse if its decision was based on an erroneous view of the law or a clearly erroneous assessment of the evidence." *Trost v. Trek Bicycle Corp.*, 162 F.3d 1004, 1008 (8th Cir. 1998) (citation omitted).

FELA allows a plaintiff to recover by showing that the railroad's negligence played *any* part in causing his or her injury. *Rogers v. Mo. Pac. R.R. Co.*, 352 U.S. 500, 506 (1957). "Because the type of injury [James] suffered had no obvious origin"—like a broken leg from being struck by a car—"expert testimony is **[—3—]** necessary to establish even that small quantum of causation required by FELA." *Brooks v. Union Pac. R.R. Co.*, 620 F.3d 896, 899 (8th Cir. 2010) (citation omitted). Despite FELA's relaxed causation standard, expert testimony must still meet *Daubert*'s and Federal Rule of Evidence 702's requirements for admissibility. *See Claar v. Burlington N. R.R. Co.*, 29 F.3d 499, 503 (9th Cir. 1994); *Wills v. Amerada Hess Corp.*, 379 F.3d 32, 47 (2d Cir. 2004).

Under *Daubert*, district courts must make a "preliminary assessment of whether the reasoning or methodology underlying [an expert's] testimony is scientifically valid and of whether that reasoning or methodology properly can be applied to the facts in issue." *Daubert v. Merrell Dow Pharms., Inc.*, 509 U.S. 579, 592–93 (1993) (discussing Fed. R. Evid. 702). "Among the factors to consider is whether the 'expert testimony proffered in the case is sufficiently tied to the facts of the case that it will aid the jury in resolving a factual dispute.'" *Concord Boat Corp. v. Brunswick Corp.*, 207 F.3d 1039, 1055 (8th Cir. 2000) (quoting *Daubert*, 509 U.S. at 591). "[A]ny step that

[1] The Honorable John M. Gerrard, Senior United States District Judge for the District of Nebraska.

renders the analysis unreliable renders the expert's testimony inadmissible. This is true whether the step completely changes a reliable methodology or merely misapplies that methodology." *In re Wholesale Grocery Prods. Antitrust Litig.*, 946 F.3d 995, 1001 (8th Cir. 2019) (citations omitted).

The district court found that Dr. Chiodo's opinion lacked a reliable foundation because it was premised on a misunderstanding of Dr. Zimmerman's expert report. *See* Fed. R. Evid. 702 (explaining that testimony must be "based on sufficient facts or data"). Dr. Chiodo thought that Dr. Zimmerman's report concluded that James was exposed to above-background rates of asbestos, diesel exhaust, and silica dust.[2] But as the district court **{-970-}** pointed out, Dr. Zimmerman only opined that James had **[—4—]** above-background exposure to silica dust and that James had the *potential* for exposures to diesel combustion fumes[3] and asbestos.

As a result, the district court found Dr. Chiodo's methodology for proving causation unreliable. To prove specific causation[4] between James's exposures and cancer, Dr. Chiodo performed a differential etiology, a test where the expert "rule[s] in" all scientifically plausible causes of injury, and then "rule[s] out" the least plausible causes until the most likely cause remains. *Johnson v. Mead Johnson & Co.*, 754 F.3d 557, 560 n.2 (8th Cir. 2014). The district court found the differential etiology unreliable because it "ruled in" asbestos and diesel combustion fumes as plausible causes of James's lung cancer, but didn't rule them out despite the lack of evidence of exposure. *See Barrett v. Rhodia, Inc.*, 606 F.3d 975, 980 (8th Cir. 2010) (explaining that "the proponent must show that the expert's reasoning or methodology was applied properly to the facts at issue").

While the factual basis of an expert opinion generally goes to its credibility rather than its admissibility, *Hartley v. Dillard's, Inc.*, 310 F.3d 1054, 1061 (8th Cir. 2002), expert testimony that is "speculative, unsupported by sufficient facts, or contrary to the facts of the case" is inadmissible, *Marmo v. Tyson Fresh Meats, Inc.*, 457 F.3d 748, 757 (8th Cir. 2006). *See also Hartley*, 310 F.3d at 1061 (explaining that an expert opinion that is "so fundamentally unsupported that it can offer no assistance to the jury" should be excluded (citation omitted)). **[—5—]**

There is no direct evidence that James was exposed to asbestos[5] or diesel combustion fumes.[6] Even if a jury could infer that James had been exposed, there is no evidence of the level of exposure. While a quantifiable amount of exposure is not required to find causation between a toxic exposure and injury, *see Bonner v. ISP Techs., Inc.*, 259 F.3d 924, 931 (8th Cir. 2001), there must be, at a minimum, "evidence from which the factfinder can conclude that the plaintiff was exposed to

[2] "I take [Dr. Zimmerman's] opinion that Mr. Lancaster was exposed to silica, asbestos[,] and diesel exhaust above and beyond what the average person would be exposed to[,] to then formulate my opinions about general causation and about specific causation." Chiodo Dep. at 54:6–11.

[3] Although Lancaster alleged that diesel exhaust exposure was a cause of James's cancer, Dr. Zimmerman determined that diesel exhaust—referring to exhaust coming out of a locomotive engine—is not an issue in this particular case. He instead examined potential exposure to diesel combustion fumes from rope burning. Like the district court, we assume Dr. Chiodo's references to diesel exhaust refer to diesel combustion fumes.

[4] That is, that the exposures *did in fact* cause James's cancer. *See Junk v. Terminix Int'l Co.*, 628 F.3d 439, 450 (8th Cir. 2010).

[5] "Q: You would agree with me that you don't know if Mr. Lancaster had any exposure to asbestos from work in buildings at the railroad, correct? A: That's correct . . . ." Zimmerman Dep. at 63:17–20. "Q: So as we sit here today, is it fair to say that you also cannot testify that if Mr. Lancaster had exposure to asbestos, it exceeded the appropriate exposure limits for the relevant time period? A: That's correct." *Id.* at 65:24–66:3.

[6] "[T]here is no evidence of any level of exposure to Mr. Lancaster being exposed to products of combustion from burning diesel fuel." Zimmerman Dep. at 94: 4–6. "Q: Therefore, sir, is it correct that you cannot sit here and provide testimony that any potential exposure to diesel fuel combustion products by Mr. Lancaster exceeded an exposure limit or even a proposed exposure limit; is that fair? . . . . A: Yes, because there—as I said, we don't know what his exposure was." *Id.* at 96:4–11.

levels of that agent that are known to cause the kind of harm that the plaintiff **{–971–}** claims to have suffered," *Wright v. Willamette Indus., Inc.*, 91 F.3d 1105, 1107 (8th Cir. 1996). There is no such evidence here. *See Bland v. Verizon Wireless, (VAW) L.L.C.*, 538 F.3d 893, 898 (8th Cir. 2008) (holding there was "simply too great an analytical gap" to support admissibility where expert lacked knowledge of the degree of plaintiff's exposure to toxin (citation omitted)).

Still, Dr. Chiodo relied on the assumption that James was exposed to above-background levels of asbestos and diesel combustion fumes for his differential etiology. As a result, his opinion is speculative at most. *See Concord*, 207 F.3d at 1057 (holding that "[b]ecause of the deficiencies in the foundation of the opinion, the expert's resulting conclusions were mere speculation" (citation omitted)).

The district court did not abuse its considerable discretion by determining that Dr. Chiodo's opinion lacked a sufficient foundation and that, in turn, his **[—6—]** methodology for proving causation was unreliable.[7] *See Wholesale Grocery*, 946 F.3d at 1003 (holding that the district court did not abuse its discretion by excluding an expert's testimony, given that the factual assumption underlying the application of the expert's methodology was "insufficiently validated," so his opinion was "ultimately speculative").

III.

Having decided that the district court did not abuse its discretion in excluding Dr. Chiodo's testimony, we conclude that the district court did not err in in granting BNSF's motion for summary judgment[8] because Lancaster cannot otherwise establish causation. We affirm.

---

[7] The district court had additional grounds for excluding Dr. Chiodo's testimony, but we decline to reach those as its decision was sufficient on this basis. *Wholesale Grocery*, 946 F.3d at 1001 ("Under *Daubert*, any step that renders the analysis unreliable renders the expert's testimony inadmissible." (citation omitted)).

[8] We review grants of summary judgment *de novo*, *see Odom v. Kaizer*, 864 F.3d 920, 921 (8th Cir. 2017), and will affirm if "there is no genuine dispute as to any material fact and the movant is entitled to judgment as a matter of law," Fed. R. Civ. P. 56(a).

This page intentionally left blank

United States Court of Appeals for the Ninth Circuit

United States Court of Appeals
for the Ninth Circuit

No. 21-35185

METLAKATLA INDIAN COMMUNITY
VS.
DUNLEAVY

Appeal from the United States District Court for the District of Alaska

Decided: January 31, 2023 (Amended Opinion)

Citation: 58 F.4th 1034, 11 Adm. R. 434 (9th Cir. 2023).

Before **FLETCHER, RAWLINSON,** and **OWENS,** Circuit Judges.

[—4—] {-1036-} FLETCHER, Circuit Judge:

Since time immemorial, members of the Metlakatlan Indian Community ("the Community") and their Tsimshian ancestors have inhabited the coast of the Pacific Northwest and fished in its waters. In 1887, at the invitation of President Grover Cleveland, the Community relocated from British Columbia, Canada, to the Annette Islands in what was then the United States Territory of Alaska. In 1891, Congress passed a statute (the "1891 Act") recognizing the Community and establishing the Annette Islands Reserve as its reservation. **[—5—]**

In 1916, President Woodrow Wilson proclaimed that the Metlakatlans' reservation extends 3,000 feet from the shoreline of the Annette Islands, and that the Metlakatlans have an exclusive right to fish within the reservation boundaries (the "Proclamation"). After the Proclamation, the Metlakatlans continued to fish, as they always had, both in the waters immediately surrounding the islands and in waters far from the islands' shores. In subsequent years, courts, federal agencies, and the Territory of Alaska acknowledged with approval that the Metlakatlans fished in their traditional off-reservation waters. **{-1037-}**

In 1972, Alaska amended its constitution to authorize the State to restrict the entry of new participants into commercial fisheries in state waters. Pursuant to the amendment, Alaska enacted a statute creating a limited entry program for commercial fishing. In 2020, in response to Alaska's attempt to subject the Metlakatlans to its limited entry program, the Community sued Alaskan officials in federal district court. The Community contended that the 1891 Act grants to the Community and its members the right to fish in the off-reservation waters where Community members have traditionally fished. The district court disagreed, holding that the Act provides no such right.

We reverse. We hold that the 1891 Act grants to the Community and its members a non-exclusive right to fish in the off-reservation waters where they have traditionally fished.

I. Historical Background

Community members are descendants of the Tsimshian people indigenous to the Pacific Northwest. Tsimshian fishermen long followed the fish runs along the coast and in **[—6—]** the rivers of what is now British Columbia, establishing temporary villages to obtain fish for subsistence, use in cultural practices, and trade. Marjorie M. Halpin & Margaret Seguin, *Tsimshian Peoples: Southern Tsimshian, Coast Tsimshian, Nishga, and Gitksan, in 7 Handbook of North American Indians* 267, 268–71, 281 (Wayne Suttles & William Sturtevant eds., 1990). Historical sources indicate that they fished as far north as 50 miles from the Annette Islands in what is now the State of Alaska.

In 1862, a group of Tsimshians joined a lay Anglican missionary, "Father Duncan," in establishing a coastal community at Metlakatla, British Columbia. *See* Andrew Martindale et al., *Bending but Unbroken: The Nine Tribes of the Northern Tsimshian Through the Colonial Era, in Power, Political Economy, and Historical Landscapes of the Modern World* 251, 270 (Christopher R. DeCorse ed., 2019); Halpin & Seguin, *supra*, at 281. The name Metlakatla—a Tsimshian word that means "place beside calm water"—reflects a relationship with rivers and the sea that, for Tsimshian peoples, centers on fishing as the "bedrock of the Tsimshian culture and way of life." Professor Brian Hosmer observed:

> [Tsimshian cultural stories] reveal[] a great deal about the way Tsimshians understand their world. Away from human beings, salmon live as people, in villages, with chiefs, organizing their lives around the annual runs, which appeared to them as cottonwood leaves. It is only when the humans and salmon are in contact that salmon "people" take on their familiar form. Their relationship is reciprocal. Salmon **[—7—]** runs would continue only so long as humans remain faithful to rituals . . .

Brian C. Hosmer, *American Indians in the Marketplace: Persistence and Innovation Among the Menominees and Metlakatlans, 1870-1920* 115 (1999).

The Tsimshians who gathered at Metlakatla began a communal commercial fishing enterprise. *Id.* at 149. In 1884, the Community established a fish cannery. The cannery turned out 8,300 cases of canned fish in its first year of operation. *Id.* at 183.

In the 1880s, Canada began to impose a reserve system throughout Tsimshian territory, dividing tribal land into allotments to be distributed to individual tribal families. Martindale, *supra*, at 274. In 1883 and 1884, Canada placed Metlakatla under the ambit of its Indian Act and appointed an agent to oversee community affairs. Hosmer, *supra*, at 191. At the same time, non-Indian **{–1038–}** fishermen and canneries began to compete with the Metlakatlans. *See id.* at 193. Before the Canadian provincial court, the Metlakatlans advocated for recognition of their aboriginal territorial rights and their attendant resource rights. *See id.* at 198; Peter Murray, *The Devil and Mr. Duncan: A History of the Two Metlakatlas* 184–87 (1985). After the provincial Supreme Court denied the Metlakatlans such recognition, Metlakatla's tribal council authorized Father Duncan to travel to Washington, D.C., to attempt to secure land for the Metlakatlans in the Territory of Alaska. Hosmer, *supra*, at 198; Murray, *supra*, at 190.

In March 1887, a group of five Metlakatlans traveled to the Territory of Alaska in search of a new home. Susan Neylan, *"Choose Your Flag": Perspectives on the* **[—8—]** *Tsimshian Migration from Metlakatla, British Columbia, to New Metlakatla, Alaska, 1887, in New Histories for Old: Changing Perspectives on Canada's Native Pasts* 196, 198 (Theodore Binnema & Susan Neylan eds., 2007). The group chose the nearby Annette Islands because of the islands' easy access to waters with abundant fish. *Alaska Pac. Fisheries v. United States*, 248 U.S. 78, 88 (1918) ("[The Metlakatlans] looked upon the islands as a suitable location . . . because the fishery adjacent to the shore would afford a primary means of subsistence and a promising opportunity for industrial and commercial development."); Neylan, *supra*, at 211; Brief for Appellant at 11, *Metlakatla Indian Cmty., Annette Islands Rsrv. v. Egan*, 363 U.S. 555 (1960) (No. 326) ("[The Metlakatlans] specifically selected the Annette Islands because of their fishing potential."). At the invitation of President Cleveland, the remainder of the 823 Metlakatlans followed on August 7, 1887. 21 Cong. Rec. 10092 (1890); Neylan, *supra*, at 199; Hosmer, *supra*, at 200; Nat'l Surv. of Hist. Sites & Bldgs., U.S. Dep't of the Interior & Nat'l Park Serv., *Alaska History: 1741-1910*, at 127, 209 (1961). Years later, reflecting on the migration, Metlakatlan Rod Davis recounted,

> When we landed in . . . Alaska, now, at the time it was a nice beautiful day. How well I remember that day; it was bright and sunny, and there was a lot of fish. We camped at one of the creeks on Saturday night . . . and in those days that creek was just loaded with salmon, pink salmon. There must have been millions of them in that creek. How well I remember.

Neylan, *supra*, at 211. **[—9—]**

After moving to the Annette Islands, the Metlakatlans continued to fish throughout the waters of Southeast Alaska. *See* Hosmer, *supra*, at 200–01. In 1891, four years after the Metlakatlans moved to the islands, Congress passed the 1891 Act, recognizing the Metlakatlan Indian Community and establishing the Annette Islands as the Community's reservation. The Act, later codified as amended at 25 U.S.C. § 495, provided:

> That until otherwise provided by law the body of lands known as Annette Islands, situated in Alexander Archipelago in Southeastern Alaska, on the north side of Dixon's entrance, be . . . set apart as a reservation for the use of the Metlakahtla [sic] Indians, and those people known as Metlakahtlans [sic] who have recently emigrated from British Columbia to Alaska, and such other Alaskan natives as may join them, to be held and used by them in common, under such rules and regulations, and subject to such restrictions, as may [be] prescribed from time to time by the Secretary of the Interior.

Act of Mar. 3, 1891, ch. 561, § 15, 26 Stat. 1101 (1891). **{-1039-}**

After Congress established the reservation, Community members continued to fish where they had always fished, both in the waters immediately surrounding the reservation and in the waters miles away. Hosmer, *supra*, at 203, 205. Reports by federal agencies and federal officials documented Metlakatlans fishing up to 50 miles from the reservation. Jefferson F. Moser, U.S. Comm'n of Fish & **[—10—]** Fisheries, *The Salmon and Salmon Fisheries of Alaska: Report of the Operations of the United States Fish Commission Steamer Albatross for the Year Ending June 30, 1898*, at 63, 68 (1899) (identifying sites at Quadra Bay and Moira Sound); Jefferson Moser, U.S. Comm'n of Fish & Fisheries, *The Salmon and Salmon Fisheries of Alaska: Report of the Alaskan Salmon Investigations of the United States Fish Commission Steamer Albatross in 1900 and 1901*, at 298 (1902) (identifying sites at Home Stream, Tamgas, Quadra Bay, Karta Bay, Kithraum, Peter Johnson, Nowiskay, Old Johnson, Kegan, and Kagahine); George R. Tingle, Inspector of Salmon Fisheries, Special Agent Div., U.S. Treasury Dep't, *Report on the Salmon Fisheries in Alaska, 1896*, at 5, 21 (1897) (identifying sites at Naha Bay, Karta Bay, and Kah Shakes Cove); *see* Hosmer, *supra*, at 203 (concluding that these practices "provid[e] convincing evidence that they did not equate immigration with a relinquishing of their aboriginal resource rights"). Father Duncan's letters corroborate these reports, documenting Metlakatlan fishing throughout the southern Alaska panhandle. Hosmer, *supra*, at 205.

Fishing at these off-reservation locations supplied a cannery that Metlakatlans established on the reservation in 1891. This cannery replaced the cannery they had established at Metlakatla, British Columbia, before they moved to the Annette Islands. Moser, *1900 and 1901*, *supra*, at 297–98; Hosmer, *supra*, at 201–02. By 1900, the cannery had annual output of more than 17,000 cases of cans. Moser, *1900 and 1901*, *supra*, at 298. By 1912, total production reached nearly 300,000 cases. Hosmer, *supra*, at 201. Metlakatlans also continued to rely on fish for cultural practices, including feasts for observances of birth, marriage, death, and other important life transitions **[—11—]** entailing consuming, giving, and exchanging fish. According to Professor Hosmer, the Metlakatlans "successfully picked up and relocated, hardly missing a beat." *Id.* at 204.

In 1915, the Secretary of the Interior promulgated regulations establishing an elected Community council with authority to enact local ordinances for the reservation, and allowing Community members to obtain federal permits for the use of salmon traps in waters adjacent to the Annette Islands. *See Metlakatla Indian Cmty., Annette Islands Rsrv. v. Egan*, 369 U.S. 45, 48 (1962).

In 1916, President Wilson proclaimed that the waters 3,000 feet from the shoreline of the Annette Islands were reserved for the exclusive use of the Metlakatlans. The Proclamation provides:

> Now, therefore, I, Woodrow Wilson, President of the United States of America, by virtue of the power in me vested by the laws of the United States, do hereby make known and proclaim that the waters within three thousand feet from the shore lines at mean low tide of

> Annette Island, Ham Island, Walker Island, Lewis Island, Spire Island, Hemlock Island, and adjacent rocks and islets, located within the area segregated by the broken line upon the diagram hereto attached and made a part of this proclamation; also the bays of said islands, rocks, and islets, are hereby reserved for the benefit of the Metlakahtlans [sic] and such other Alaskan natives **{-1040-}** as have joined them or may join them in residence on these islands, **[—12—]** to be used by them under the general fisheries laws and regulations of the United States as administered by the Secretary of Commerce.

Proclamation No. 1332, 39 Stat. 1777–78 (Apr. 28, 1916).

The Department of the Interior promulgated the Proclamation as a regulation at 25 C.F.R. § 241.2. The Community's cannery operations were thereafter organized under the aegis of the Annette Island Packing Company. *See Territory v. Annette Island Packing Co.*, 6 Alaska 585 (D. Alaska 1922), *aff'd*, 289 F. 671 (9th Cir. 1923), *cert. denied*, 263 U.S. 708 (1923).

In 1916, shortly before President Wilson issued the Proclamation, non-Indians had placed a fish trap 600 feet off the shore of the reservation. The United States brought suit in the district court for the Territory of Alaska, seeking an injunction that would require removal of the trap. The court granted the injunction. It wrote:

> In passing [the 1891 Act], Congress must be held to have known (what every one else knew) that the Indians of Alaska are fisher folk and hunters and trappers, and largely, if not entirely, dependent for their livelihood upon the yield of such vocations. It must be held to have known that without the food yield of the sea these Indians could not survive, for the Annette Islands would not of themselves, "as land," afford a subsistence for a community of souls; there being little or no agricultural land on the islands, or for that matter in all Southeastern Alaska. **[—13—]**

United States v. Alaska Pac. Fisheries, 5 Alaska 484, 486–87 (D. Alaska 1916).

The Supreme Court affirmed. In *Alaska Pacific Fisheries*, 248 U.S. at 89, the Court held that the 1891 Act establishing the reservation granted an exclusive right to Metlakatlans to fish in the "fishing grounds" "adjacent" to the Annette Islands. The Court wrote:

> After their settlement and before the reservation was created, the Indians . . . adopted a form of self-government suited to their needs . . . and constructed and installed an extensive establishment where they canned salmon for the market. The purpose of creating the reservation was to encourage, assist and protect the Indians in their effort to train themselves to habits of industry [and] become self-sustaining . . . . Evidently Congress intended to conform its action to their situation and needs.

Id. at 88–89. In affirming the injunction requiring the removal of the non-Indians' fish trap, the Supreme Court relied only on the 1891 Act. It did not rely on, or even mention, the 3,000-foot boundary established by President Wilson's 1916 Proclamation. *See also Egan*, 369 U.S. at 49 ("In 1918, without reference to the proclamation, this Court upheld the right of the Metlakatlans to exclude others from the waters surrounding their islands on the ground that these waters were included within the original reservation by Congress." (citing *Alaska Pacific Fisheries v. United States*, 248 U.S. 78)). **[—14—]**

After the Supreme Court's decision in *Alaska Pacific Fisheries*, Metlakatlans continued to fish in the off-reservation waters where they had always fished. An internal Department of the Interior report in 1920 recounted that "Metlakatla natives did, as they have from time immemorial, go beyond the [reservation's] limit[s] to seine fish." The Territory of Alaska acknowledged the geographical extent of the Metlakatlans' traditional fishing grounds in a tax dispute arising out of the Community's commercial fishing. In its answer to **{-1041-}** the Secretary of the Interior's complaint-in-intervention, Alaska wrote:

> [T]he right of the inhabitants of said Annette Island[s] reserve to catch fish outside of the reserve . . . has always been and is now recognized by the [Secretary of the Interior] and by the Government of the United States, and such right is and at all times has been claimed by the said Metlakatla people.

Answer to Complaint in Intervention, at 5, *Territory v. Annette Island Packing Co.,* 6 Alaska 585 (No. 2023-A). In deciding the tax dispute, the territorial court noted that fish for the Metlakatlan cannery were "secured from any waters" and that, in 1919, the cannery had processed "approximately 130,000 salmon caught by Indian residents of Metlakahtla [sic] outside of the Annette Indian reserve and its reserved waters." *Annette Island Packing Co.,* 6 Alaska at 592 (agreed statement of facts).

Congress granted statehood to Alaska in 1958. Pub. L. No. 85-508, § 6(e), 72 Stat. 339, 340 (1958). In 1972, Alaskans adopted a constitutional amendment that authorized the State to limit the entry of new participants **[—15—]** into commercial fisheries in Alaskan waters. Alaska Const. art. VIII, § 15. In 1973, pursuant to that amendment, Alaska instituted a "limited entry" program to regulate commercial fishing. Alaska Stat. § 16.43.010.

In recent years, changing conditions have threatened fish stocks available to the Community. Community members primarily fish for salmon. Migratory fish such as salmon are subject to changes in their migratory routes in response to environmental conditions, including climate change. Non-Indian commercial fishing practices in the State-managed fishing areas surrounding the Community's exclusive zone have put a substantial strain on Community fish yields. State-managed fisheries sometimes intercept salmon before they return to the Community's exclusive zone. Community members also fish for herring. The Community has adopted a management strategy that has increased the exclusive zone's herring biomass to more than 20,000 tons—one of the largest herring stocks in Southeast Alaska. However, when herring leave the exclusive zone, Alaska's limited entry program restricts access to the herring by Community members.

II. Proceedings Below

On August 7, 2020, the Community sued Alaskan officials in federal district court, alleging that Alaska's limited entry program illegally restricts Community members' right to fish outside the reservation boundaries. The Community's complaint seeks (1) a declaration that "Congress' reservation of the Annette Islands Reserve for the Metlakatla Indian Community included the non-exclusive right to fish in waters adjacent to the Reserve currently designated as Districts 1 and 2, free from unreasonable interference by the defendants, and that such **[—16—]** right has not been revoked or diminished"; and (2) "a permanent injunction barring the defendants from asserting jurisdiction over the Community and its members inconsistent with the Community's reserved fishing rights, and from otherwise unreasonably interfering with the Community's reserved fishing rights."

Defendants moved to dismiss the complaint for failure to state a claim under Rule 12(b)(6). The Community opposed the motion and requested oral argument. The district court denied the request for oral argument and granted the motion to dismiss. The court determined that the Community failed to state a claim for relief because, in the view of the court, the 1891 Act did not reserve off-reservation fishing **{-1042-}** rights for the Community and its members.

The Community timely appealed. For the reasons that follow, we reverse.

III. Standard of Review

We review de novo a dismissal for failure to state a claim under Rule 12(b)(6). *United States v. Washington,* 853 F.3d 946, 961 (9th Cir. 2017). We review de novo questions of statutory interpretation. *Confederated Tribes of Chehalis*

Indian Rsrv. v. State of Washington, 96 F.3d 334, 340 (9th Cir. 1996). We review for abuse of discretion a decision to grant or deny permanent injunctive relief, but we review de novo the underlying legal conclusions on which the district court based its decision. *United States v. Oregon*, 470 F.3d 809, 810 n.2 (9th Cir. 2006). **[—17—]**

IV. Discussion

A. Indian Canon of Construction

Statutes that touch upon federal Indian law "are to be construed liberally in favor of the Indians, with ambiguous provisions interpreted to their benefit." *Swinomish Indian Tribal Cmty. v. BNSF Ry. Co.,* 951 F.3d 1142, 1156 (9th Cir. 2020) (quoting *Montana v. Blackfeet Tribe of Indians,* 471 U.S. 759, 766 (1985)); *Chehalis,* 96 F.3d at 340 ("Courts have uniformly held that treaties, statutes[,] and executive orders must be liberally construed in favor of establishing Indian rights."). Statutes that create reservations, like treaties and executive orders, "are interpreted as the Indians would have understood them." *Chehalis,* 96 F.3d at 342 (citing *Parravano v. Babbitt,* 70 F.3d 539, 544 (9th Cir. 1995), *cert. denied,* 518 U.S. 1016 (1996)); *Puyallup Indian Tribe v. Port of Tacoma,* 717 F.2d 1251, 1257 n.6 (9th Cir. 1983), *cert. denied,* 465 U.S. 1049 (1984) ("This principle of treaty construction applies with equal force to statutes passed for the benefit of Indians and to executive orders." (citations omitted)). A right will be inferred when that right supports a purpose for which a reservation was established. *Winters v. United States,* 207 U.S. 564, 576–77 (1908). Because the purposes of reservations are often unarticulated in a statute, treaty, or executive order, we consider "the circumstances surrounding their creation[] and the history of the Indians for whom they were created." *Chehalis,* 96 F.3d at 342 (citing *Colville Confederated Tribes v. Walton,* 647 F.2d 42, 47 (9th Cir. 1981)), *cert. denied,* 454 U.S. 1092 (1981). "We also consider their need to maintain themselves under changed circumstances." *Colville,* 647 F.2d at 47. These interpretive principles "are rooted in the unique trust relationship between the United States and the Indians." **[—18—]** *Oneida Cnty. v. Oneida Indian Nation of New York State,* 470 U.S. 226, 247 (1985).

B. Implied Off-Reservation Rights

The Indian canon requires us to infer rights that support a reservation's purpose. The seminal case is *Winters v. United States,* in which the Court found implied water rights that supported the purpose of the Fort Belknap Reservation. 207 U.S. at 576–77. The reservation had been created by an agreement between the United States and the Gros Ventre and Assiniboine Tribes. *Id.* at 565. The purpose of the reservation was to encourage the Tribes to give up their "nomadic" way of life and to become farmers. *Id.* at 576. No provision was made in the agreement for water to irrigate the arid land on the reservation. The Court chose "between two inferences[—]*one* **{–1043–}** *of which would support the purpose of the agreement* and the other impair or defeat it." *Id.* at 577 (emphasis added). The Court chose the former inference on the ground that the agreement creating the reservation should be construed to imply a right to water for irrigation in order not to "defeat the declared purpose" of the agreement. *Id.*

In *Arizona v. California,* 373 U.S. 546 (1963), the Court inferred a right to irrigation water from the Colorado River for five Indian reservations. One of the reservations had been created by statute; the other four had been created by executive order. *Id.* at 596. Citing *Winters,* the Court held that all five reservations had implied rights to water for irrigation. *Id.* at 599–600. The Court affirmed the Special Master, who had concluded "that the water was intended *to satisfy the future as well as the present needs* of the Indian Reservations and ruled that enough water was reserved to irrigate all of the practicably irrigable acreage **[—19—]** on the reservations." *Id.* (emphasis added); *see also United States v. New Mexico,* 438 U.S. 696, 702 (1978) ("Where water is necessary to fulfill the very purposes for which a federal reservation was created, it is reasonable to conclude, even in the face of Congress' express deference to state water law in other areas, that the United States intended to reserve the necessary water.").

We have applied the *Winters* implied-rights rule in several cases in this circuit. In *Colville*, 647 F.2d at 45, an agreement between the United States and the tribes established a reservation in eastern Washington. We construed the purposes of the reservation broadly: "The specific purposes of an Indian reservation . . . were often unarticulated. The general purpose, to provide a home for the Indians, is a broad one and must be liberally construed." *Id.* at 47 (footnotes omitted). We wrote: "Congress intended to deal fairly with the Indians by reserving waters without which their lands would be useless." *Id.* We held that there was an implied right not only to water for irrigation, but also to water for streams for spawning trout. We wrote:

> Providing for a land-based agrarian society, however, was not the only purpose for creating the reservation. The Colvilles traditionally fished for both salmon and trout. Like other Pacific Northwest Indians, fishing was of economic and religious importance to them. . . . The Tribe's principal historic fishing grounds on the Columbia River have been destroyed by dams. The Indians have established replacement fishing grounds in Omak Lake **[—20—]** by planting a non-indigenous trout. . . . [P]reservation of the tribe's access to fishing grounds was one purpose for the creation of the Colville reservation. Under the circumstances, we find an implied reservation of water . . . for the development and maintenance of replacement fishing grounds.

Id. at 48 (citations omitted).

In *United States v. Adair*, 723 F.2d 1394, 1397–98 (9th Cir. 1983), a treaty established a reservation for the Klamath Tribe in eastern Oregon. The treaty promised that the Tribe would have the right to "hunt, fish, and gather on their reservation," *id.* at 1398, but did not mention any right to water. A purpose of the reservation was to "secure to the Tribe a continuation of its traditional hunting and fishing" way of life. *Id.* at 1409. Because game and fish on the reservation depended on a continuous flow of water from the Williamson River, we held that there was an implied right under the treaty to an amount of river water that would ensure an adequate amount of game and fish for the Tribe. **{–1044–}** *Id.* at 1411; *see also Washington*, 853 F.3d at 965 ("[E]ven if Governor Stevens had made no explicit promise, we would infer . . . a promise to 'support the purpose' of the Treaties. . . . [T]he Tribes' right of access to their usual and accustomed fishing places would be worthless without harvestable fish.").

Our sister circuit endorsed the application of the *Winters* framework to the context of off-reservation fishing rights in *United States v. Michigan*, 653 F.2d 277 (6th Cir. 1981). The Sixth Circuit affirmed the district court's holding that a treaty reserved for the Sault Ste. Marie Tribe **[—21—]** of Chippewa Indians of Michigan and Bay Mills Indian Community implied non-exclusive fishing rights in certain areas of the Great Lakes. *United States v. Michigan*, 471 F. Supp. 192, 253, 258 (W.D. Mich. 1979), *aff'd*, 653 F.2d 277. The district court concluded that the historical evidence "demonstrat[ed] that the Indians were absolutely dependent upon fishing for subsistence and their livelihood" such that "they would not have relinquished their right to fish in the ceded waters of the Great Lakes." *Id.* at 253. Applying *Winters*, the district court held that the treaty "impliedly reserved a right to fish commercially and for subsistence" in those areas of the Great Lakes because (1) the treaty lacked "language expressly relinquishing the aboriginal right of the . . . Indians to fish in the . . . waters"; (2) at the time of the treaty, "commercial fishing was essential to the livelihood of these Indians and for them to have relinquished fishing rights would have been tantamount to agreeing to a systematic annihilation of their culture, and perhaps of their very existence"; (3) the tribes and the federal government "were aware that the Indians had no way of sustaining themselves in Michigan except by fishing"; and (4) "the Indians did not understand the treaty to limit their right to fish." *Id.* at 257–58.

C. The Community's Off-Reservation Fishing Right

The question before us is not the existence of implied fishing rights of the Community. In *Alaska Pacific Fisheries*, 248 U.S. at 88–89, the Supreme Court answered this threshold question when it inferred a fishing right from the 1891 Act, relying on that right to affirm an injunction against a non-Indian fish trap 600 feet from the shore of the Community's reservation. We thus know from *Alaska Pacific Fisheries* that there is an implied fishing right stemming from the 1891 Act. The question before us is the **[—22—]** scope of that right. A central purpose of the reservation, understood in light of the history of the Community, provides the answer.

As described above, since time immemorial Metlakatlans have fished outside the boundaries of their current reservation. Before the arrival of European settlers, they fished throughout the waters of Southeast Alaska for ceremonial purposes, for personal consumption, and for trade. Shortly before they came to the Annette Islands, Metlakatlans established a commercial fish cannery to adapt their mode of trade to modern conditions. When Metlakatlans moved to the islands in the late 1880s at the invitation of President Cleveland, they did so with the understanding that they would be able to support themselves by fishing, as they had always done. Indeed, soon after moving to the reservation, the Community set up a new cannery—supplied by off-reservation fishing—and quickly increased production in the following years. When Congress passed the 1891 Act establishing the Metlakatlans' reservation, it did so with the expectation that the Metlakatlans would continue to support themselves by fishing. *Id.* at 89 ("The purpose of creating the reservation was to encourage, **{-1045-}** assist[,] and protect the Indians in their effort to . . . become self-sustaining . . . . Without [fishing rights] the [Community] could not prosper."). That is, Congress passed the Act with the expectation not only that Metlakatlans would catch fish for ceremonial purposes and personal consumption, but that they would also pursue the commercial fishery that had provided, and continued to provide, essential economic support for the Community. Congress clearly contemplated that Metlakatlans would continue to fish off-reservation toward those ends. Congress also expected fishing to **[—23—]** support the Community not only at the time the reservation was created, but in the future. In the words of the Supreme Court in *Arizona v. California,* fishing "was intended to satisfy the future as well as the present needs" of the Community. 373 U.S. at 600; *see also Alaska Pac. Fisheries*, 248 U.S. at 89 ("Congress intended to conform its action to their situation and needs.").

We therefore hold that the 1891 Act preserved for the Community and its members an implied right to non-exclusive off-reservation fishing in the traditional fishing grounds for personal consumption and ceremonial purposes, as well as for commercial purposes. Because this case comes to us on appeal from a ruling on a Rule 12(b)(6) motion, we remand to the district court to allow further proceedings to determine whether the Community's traditional off-reservation fishing grounds included the waters within Alaska's Districts 1 and 2.

D. Arguments Made by Alaska

Alaska argues that distinguishing features of the Community's reservation require us to analyze the Metlakatlans' right differently from the rights of members of other tribes. Alaska presented a substantially similar argument to the Supreme Court over sixty years ago in *Egan*. There, Alaska argued: "The nature of the Metlakatlan 'reservation' cannot be too strongly emphasized. It is not, and has never been treated as what is normally termed an Indian reservation. . . . It is only necessary to . . . apply relevant legal theory—not theories which may be applicable to Indian reservations elsewhere, set up under different terms, and given different historical treatment." Brief for Appellees at 44–45, *Metlakatla Indian Cmty. v. Egan*, 369 U.S. 45 (1961) (No. 2). The **[—24—]** Court declined to ascribe analytical significance to the different set of circumstances surrounding the creation of the Community's reservation, and so do we.

Here, Alaska first asks us to distinguish between statutes and executive orders, contending that an implied right should not be found in a statute, such as the 1891 Act, whose text is "utterly silent" about such a right. The distinction Alaska asks us to draw does not exist in the case law. As Professor Phil Frickey observed:

> [M]any federal Indian law decisions, especially those dealing with developments since the mid-nineteenth century, turn not on treaty language, but on the text of seemingly more mundane instruments of law, such as statutes, executive orders, and federal regulations. For example, millions of acres of Indian lands are located on reservations established by executive order. This difference in form should not, however, substantially alter judicial methodology. Some of these non-treaty enactments embody agreements with tribes that would have been handled by treaty in former eras. Many of the rest embody unilateral alterations of prior treaties. In any event, because all are constitutive in nature—all adjust a sovereign-to-sovereign, structural relationship **{-1046-}** based on Chief Justice Marshall's understanding of the earliest colonial practices prior to the negotiation of any treaty—the canon should apply to them, too. Consistent with this notion, the Court **[—25—]** has drawn no fundamental interpretive distinction between reservations established by statute or executive order and those protected by treaty.

Philip P. Frickey, *Marshalling Past and Present: Colonialism, Constitutionalism, and Interpretation in Federal Indian Law*, 107 Harv. L. Rev. 381, 421–22 (1993) (footnotes omitted); *see also* James T. Campbell, Aurelius*'s Article III Revisionism: Reimagining Judicial Engagement with the* Insular Cases *and "The Law of the Territories"*, 131 Yale L. J. 2542, 2637 (2022) ("The Court has declined to distinguish between treaty and nontreaty agreements with the federal government, subjecting both to interpretive rules that are designed to vindicate those promises . . . . That interpretive approach flows from a meaningful interrogation of historical practice . . . ." (footnotes omitted)).

The case law reflects this principle. The Court in *Arizona v. California* dealt with implied rights to water for tribes on five reservations. 373 U.S. at 596. One of the reservations was created by statute; the others were created by executive order. The Court drew no distinction between the two types of legal instruments. *See id.* at 598–600. In *Puyallup Indian Tribe*, 717 F.2d at 1257 n.6, we wrote that the Indian canon, while often applied to treaties as a matter of historical coincidence, also "applies with equal force to statutes passed for the benefit of Indians and to executive orders." Later, in *Parravano*, 70 F.3d at 544, we wrote that "[t]he rule of construction applicable to executive orders creating Indian reservations is the same as that governing the interpretation of Indian treaties." And in *Chehalis*, 96 **[—26—]** F.3d at 340, we recognized that the Indian canon applies "uniformly" to "treaties, statutes[,] and executive orders."

The type of legal instrument that establishes a reservation thus makes no difference to our inquiry into a tribe's attendant resource rights. Because the Indian canon is rooted in the trust relationship between the federal government and Indian tribes, *see Oneida Indian Nation*, 470 U.S. at 247, and because federal recognition of an Indian tribe institutionalizes that relationship, *see* Cohen's Handbook of Federal Indian Law § 3.02[3] (Nell Jessup Newton ed., 2017), it does not matter which type of document provides such recognition or establishes a reservation. *See also Seminole Nation v. United States*, 316 U.S. 286, 296–97 (1942).

Second, Alaska argues that the Community is foreclosed from claiming an implied right to off-reservation fishing because Metlakatlans "had no aboriginal claims to preserve." However, as discussed above, Metlakatlans and their Tsimshian ancestors asserted and exercised a right to fish in these waters since time immemorial. In passing the 1891 Act, Congress "confirmed the continued existence of th[is] right[]." *Adair*, 723 F.2d at 1414.

Third, Alaska asks us to distinguish between the Community and tribes that were forced off of all or part of their original lands, where those tribes gave up their original lands in exchange for explicit and/or implicit appurtenant off-reservation rights. In the view of Alaska, because the United States provided the Annette Islands to the Community as a gift rather than pursuant to an exchange, the United States did not intend the 1891 Act to provide any implicit off-reservation rights. **[—27—] {–1047–}**

There is nothing in the case law indicating that implied rights are only found in instances where there has been an exchange. Indeed, it is difficult to characterize the creation of many reservations as resulting from any sort of genuine "exchange." *See Choctaw Nation v. Oklahoma*, 397 U.S. 620, 631 (1970) (observing that these legal arrangements were often "imposed upon [the Indians] and they had no choice but to consent"); *Hagen v. Utah*, 510 U.S. 399, 422 n.1 (1994) (Blackmun, J., dissenting) (noting the "unequal bargaining power when agreements were negotiated"). The Supreme Court has recently emphasized, "[I]n order to create a reservation it is not necessary that there should be a formal cession or a formal act setting apart a particular tract. It is enough that from what has been there results a certain defined tract appropriated to certain purposes." *McGirt v. Oklahoma*, 140 S. Ct. 2452, 2475 (2020) (alteration in original) (quoting *Minnesota v. Hitchcock*, 185 U.S. 373, 390 (1902)). As the Supreme Court wrote in *Egan*, 369 U.S. at 52, "The words 'set apart as a reservation,' appearing in the statute creating the Annette Islands Reserve, are substantially the same as used in numerous other statutory reservations." The Court noted that reservations secured by other legal instruments, such as treaties, are "sometimes phrased in terms of a gift or assignment rather than a reservation of land." *Id.*

Fourth, Alaska argues that the legislative history of the 1891 Act "demonstrates a lack of intent to convey off-reservation fishing rights." Alaska argues:

> The Senate's understanding of the Metlakatlans' history was "well-known." The Senate understood that Father Duncan sought Congress's "consent" to allow these **[—28—]** *immigrants* to continue to live on the Annette Islands. And Congress gave that consent after considering that the Metlakatlans had formed what senators believed was a *model Christian community*. . . . The congressional record says nothing about fishing rights, much less some sort of prioritized off-reservation fishing rights for the Metlakatlans.

(emphases added). Neither the fact that the Metlakatlans were "immigrants," nor the fact that they had formed what the Senators believed was a "model Christian community" is relevant to the question whether Congress expected the Metlakatlans to support themselves through off-reservation fishing. The Metlakatlans did, in fact, immigrate to the Annette Islands from British Columbia, but the Supreme Court has told us that this is legally irrelevant. The Court wrote in *Alaska Pacific Fisheries*: "True, the Metlakahtlans [sic] were foreign born, but the action of Congress has made that immaterial here." 248 U.S. at 89. Further, the Senate's understanding of the religious beliefs of Community members tells us nothing about the means by which Congress expected them to support themselves.

E. Regulation

Alaska's limited entry program, as currently administered, is incompatible with the Metlakatlans' off-reservation fishing rights. Fishing had always been, and continues to be, the heartbeat of the Community. Congress' intent in the 1891 Act was that the Metlakatlans would have off-reservation fishing rights that would "satisfy the future as well as the present needs" of the Community. *Arizona*, 373 U.S. at 600. Any regulation by **[—29—]** Alaska of off-reservation fishing by the Community must be consistent with such rights. **{–1048–}**

Conclusion

We hold that the 1891 Act reserves for the Metlakatlan Indian Community an implied right to non-exclusive off-reservation fishing in the areas where they have fished since time immemorial and where they continued to fish in 1891 when their reservation was established. We reverse the decision of the district court and remand for further proceedings consistent with this opinion.

REVERSED and REMANDED.

United States Court of Appeals
for the Ninth Circuit

No. 21-35985

UPPER SKAGIT INDIAN TRIBE
vs.
SAUK-SUIATTLE INDIAN TRIBE

Appeal from the United States District Court for the Western District of Washington

Decided: May 1, 2023

Citation: 66 F.4th 766, 11 Adm. R. 445 (9th Cir. 2023).

Before **IKUTA** and **COLLINS,** Circuit Judges, and **FITZWATER,*** District Judge.

* The Honorable Sidney A. Fitzwater, United States District Judge for the Northern District of Texas, sitting by designation.

[—6—] {–767–} **IKUTA,** Circuit Judge: **{–768–}**

The Upper Skagit Indian Tribe (the Upper Skagit tribe) claims that the usual and accustomed fishing areas of the Sauk-Suiattle Indian Tribe (the Sauk tribe) under a 1974 decision do not include the Skagit River, and therefore that decision did not authorize the Sauk tribe to open salmon fisheries on that river. We conclude that the district court intended to omit the Skagit River from the Sauk tribe's usual and accustomed fishing areas.

I

A

This case is a subproceeding arising out of *United States v. Washington*, 384 F. Supp. 312 (W.D. Wash. 1974) (*Final Decision I*). In *Final Decision I*, Judge George Boldt resolved disputes arising from the 1855 Treaty of Point Elliot, in which tribes in the area covered by the treaty agreed to convey most of their tribal land to the United States, in exchange for retaining their rights of taking fish "at usual and accustomed grounds and stations." Treaty of Point Elliott art. v, 12 Stat. 927 (Apr. 11, 1859). *Final Decision I* defined the term "usual and accustomed grounds and stations" to include "every fishing location where members of a tribe customarily fished from time to time at and before treaty times, however distant from the then usual habitat of the tribe, and whether or not other tribes then also fished in the same waters." 384 F.Supp. at 332. In a lengthy and detailed opinion, Judge Boldt determined many of the usual and accustomed fishing places where tribes fished before the treaty. We refer to a tribe's usual and accustomed grounds **[—7—]** and stations, as defined in the findings of facts included in *Final Decision I*, and a 1991 modification of that decision, *United States v. Washington*, 18 F. Supp. 3d 1172, 1213 (W.D. Wash. 1991), as the tribe's "U&As."

Recognizing that a single decision could not resolve every future dispute over tribal fishing rights, *Final Decision I* included an injunction retaining jurisdiction to implement the decision. 384 F. Supp. at 413–20. The injunction provided that any of the parties "may invoke the continuing jurisdiction of the court" to make one of seven types of determinations. *Id.* at 419. The parties to *Final Decision I* have most frequently invoked the court's jurisdiction for the determinations listed in paragraphs 25(a)(1) and 25(a)(6).[1] Paragraph 25(a)(1) allows tribes to invoke the court's jurisdiction to determine "[w]hether or not the actions, intended or effected by any party . . . are in conformity with [*Final Decision I*] or this injunction." *Id.* Paragraph 25(a)(6) allows tribes to invoke the court's **{–769–}** jurisdiction to determine what was left unsaid by *Final Decision I*—"the location of any of a tribe's usual and accustomed fishing grounds [U&As] not specifically determined by [*Final Decision I*]." *Id.* The court first exercised its continuing jurisdiction shortly after issuing *Final Decision I*, when it determined the U&As of several tribes whose U&As were not "specifically determined" in *Final Decision I*. *See United States v. State of Wash.*, 459 F. Supp. 1020, 1028 **[—8—]** (W.D. Wash. 1978),

[1] These paragraphs were previously termed paragraphs 25(a) and 25(f), but were renumbered by *United States v. Washington*, 18 F. Supp. 3d 1172, 1213 (W.D. Wash. 1991), which modified *Final Decision I*. Paragraph 25 prescribes procedural steps a tribe must take to invoke the court's jurisdiction to open a new subproceeding.

aff'd, 645 F.2d 749 (9th Cir. 1981) (*Final Decision II*).

B

The dispute in this case relates to the meaning of Finding of Fact 131 in *Final Decision I,* which defines the Sauk tribe's U&As as follows:

> The usual and accustomed fishing places of the Sauk River Indians at the time of the treaty included Sauk River, Cascade River, Suiattle River and the following creeks which are tributary to the Suiattle River—Big Creek, Tenas Creek, Buck Creek, Lime Creek, Sulphur Creek, Downey Creek, Straight Creek, and Milk Creek. Bedal Creek, tributary to the Sauk River, was also a Sauk fishing ground. (Ex. USA-29, p. 13; Ex. MS-10, p. 3, l. 1-6).

Final Decision I, 384 F. Supp. at 376.

The parenthetical at the end of Finding of Fact 131 refers to two exhibits. The first exhibit, USA-29, p. 13, refers to an expert report prepared by Dr. Barbara Lane regarding the fisheries of the Sauk tribe (the Lane Report). In general, *Final Decision I* relies heavily on Dr. Lane's conclusions. In *Final Decision I,* Judge Boldt stated that "the reports of Dr. Barbara Lane . . . have been exceptionally well researched and reported and are established by a preponderance of the evidence," 384 F.Supp. at 350, that they are "authoritative and reliable," *id.*, and that they are not "controverted by any credible evidence in the case," *id.* Finding of Fact 131 is materially identical to Dr. Lane's Conclusion Five in the **[—9—]** Lane Report.[2] The second reference, "Ex. MS-10, p. 3, l. 1-6," refers to an excerpt from the testimony of James Enick, a member of the Sauk tribe, which is described below. *See infra* at 14–16.

The Sauk tribe's U&As in Finding of Fact 131 include rivers and creeks that are tributaries to the Skagit River, but do not include the Skagit River itself. Therefore, fish migrating to the Sauk tribe's U&As must travel on the Skagit River, which is part of the U&As for the Upper Skagit tribe and the Swinomish Indian Tribal Community (the Swinomish tribe). For several years, the Sauk tribe has taken the position that the Upper Skagit tribe and the Swinomish tribe should alter their fishing practices so that more fish reach the Sauk tribe's U&As. These tribes have not agreed to do so, however. This dispute came to a head at the start of the 2020 fishing season, when the Sauk tribe issued a fishing regulation that permitted its tribal members to harvest Coho salmon in two areas that include a portion of the main stem of the Skagit River between the confluence of the Cascade River and Rocky Creek.

In response to the Sauk tribe's regulation, the Upper Skagit tribe invoked the **{-770-}** continuing jurisdiction of the district court pursuant to paragraph 25 of *Final Decision I,* and sought an emergency order requiring the Sauk tribe to close **[—10—]** its fishery. The district court denied the motion for a temporary restraining order but granted the Upper Skagit tribe's request to open a new subproceeding. The Upper Skagit tribe then filed a motion for summary judgment requesting a determination that the Sauk tribe has no U&As in the Skagit River, and so the fishing regulation violated *Final Decision I.* The district court granted the Upper Skagit tribe's summary judgment motion under paragraph 25(a)(1). It concluded that Judge Boldt intentionally omitted the Skagit River from the Sauk tribe's U&As and therefore the Sauk tribe's attempts to open fisheries in the mainstem of the Skagit River were not in conformity with *Final Decision I.* The Sauk tribe appealed.

---

[2] Conclusion Five in the Lane Report states:

> The principal fisheries of the Sauk Indians included Sauk River, Cascade River, Suiattle River and the following creeks which are tributary to the Suiattle River—Big Creek, Tenas Creek, Buck Creek, Lime Creek, Sulphur Creek, Downey Creek, Straight Creek, and Milk Creek. Bedal Creek, tributary to the Sauk River was also a Sauk fishing ground.

II

We have jurisdiction under 28 U.S.C. § 1291. *Muckleshoot Tribe v. Lummi Indian Tribe*, 141 F.3d 1355, 1357 (9th Cir. 1998) (*Muckleshoot I*). We review de novo the district court's entry of summary judgment in favor of the Upper Skagit tribe and its interpretation of *Final Decision I*. *See Tulalip Tribes v. Suquamish Indian Tribe*, 794 F.3d 1129, 1133, 3 Adm. R. 577, 579 (9th Cir. 2015).

As with any other judicial decision, a court must interpret *Final Decision I* "so as to give effect to the intention of the issuing court." *Muckleshoot I*, 141 F.3d at 1359 (citing *Narramore v. United States*, 852 F.2d 485, 490 (9th Cir. 1988)). In determining Judge Boldt's intent, a court begins by reviewing the language used in the decision. *See Muckleshoot Indian Tribe v. Lummi Indian Nation*, 234 F.3d 1099, 1100–01 (9th Cir. 2000) (*Muckleshoot II*). Because "[o]pinions, unlike statutes, are not usually written with the knowledge or expectation that each and every word may be the subject of searching analysis," we do not follow statutory **[—11—]** canons of construction with their focus on "textual precision" when interpreting judicial opinions. *United States v. Muckleshoot Indian Tribe*, 235 F.3d 429, 433 (9th Cir. 2000) (*Muckleshoot III*). Rather, a court reads the language of the decision in the context of the decision as a whole and the entire record before Judge Boldt, "augmented only by evidence of contemporaneous understanding of ambiguous terms." *Upper Skagit Indian Tribe v. Washington*, 590 F.3d 1020, 1025 n.9 (9th Cir. 2010). The court "may resolve conflicting inferences and evaluate the evidence to determine Judge Boldt's intent." *Id.*

When a moving party invokes the district court's jurisdiction under paragraph 25(a)(1), it bears the burden of establishing that its interpretation of *Final Decision I* is consistent with Judge Boldt's intent. *See Tulalip Tribes*, 794 F.3d at 1133, 3 Adm. R. at 579. The moving party must carry this burden regardless whether it claims that a contested area is part of its own U&As, or that a contested area is not part of another tribe's U&As. *See id.*, 3 Adm. R. at 579. We have sometimes described a subproceeding under paragraph 25(a)(1) as involving "a two-step mode of analysis." *Id.*, 3 Adm. R. at 579; *see also Upper Skagit*, 590 F.3d at 1023.

At step one, a court uses the standard tools for interpreting precedent, starting with the text of the applicable Finding of Fact and considering the language at issue in the context of the Final Decision as a whole. A court also considers the record evidence before Judge Boldt, *see Muckleshoot III*, 235 F.3d at 432, along with any other evidence raised by the moving party that sheds light on Judge Boldt's understanding of geography at the time, *see Upper Skagit*, 590 F.3d at 1024–25. At this **{-771-}** step, we have upheld a "district court's decision [as] correctly interpret[ing] Judge Boldt's opinion on the basis of **[—12—]** information known to Judge Boldt and the words he chose." *Muckleshoot II*, 234 F.3d at 1101. However, "whether the text [of a Finding of Fact] is unambiguous or not," a court must understand the Finding of Fact "in light of the facts of the case," *Muckleshoot III*, 235 F.3d at 433, and so may proceed to step two to determine whether the moving party has carried "the burden of showing that there was no evidence in the record before Judge Boldt," that favors the non-moving party's contrary interpretation of the Finding of Fact in a way that would undermine the moving party's theory of Judge Boldt's intent. *See Tulalip Tribes*, 794 F.3d at 1133, 3 Adm. R. at 579 (citation and quotation marks omitted).[3]

[3] *See id.* at 1133–35, 3 Adm. R. at 579–81 (holding that, at step two, the moving party failed to carry its burden of showing that the contested area was excluded from the non-moving party's U&As because the evidence before Judge Boldt demonstrated that the non-moving party had fished in the contested area); *see also Upper Skagit Indian Tribe v. Suquamish Indian Tribe*, 871 F.3d 844, 849–50 (9th Cir. 2017) (holding that, at step two, the moving party met its burden of showing that the contested area was excluded from the non-moving party's U&As because the non-moving party presented only general evidence of travel through waters adjacent to the contested area, which did not undermine the moving party's interpretation of Judge Boldt's intent.)

In sum, in undertaking this two-step inquiry, the district court must determine whether the moving party has carried its burden of showing that its interpretation of the Finding of Facts is consistent with Judge Boldt's intent. If so, the moving party is entitled to judgment as a matter of law. *See Upper Skagit*, 590 F.3d at 1023, 1026. In contrast, if the moving party's interpretation is not consistent with Judge Boldt's intent, the court must dismiss the moving party's claim. *See Tulalip Tribes*, 794 F.3d at 1135–36, 3 Adm. R. at 580–81. **[—13—]**

III

A

We now turn to Finding of Fact 131, which determined the Sauk tribe's U&As. The Upper Skagit tribe argues that this finding clearly and unambiguously establishes Judge Boldt's intent not to include the Skagit River in the Sauk tribe's U&As. *See Suquamish*, 871 F.3d at 848.

We agree. The text of Finding of Fact 131 does not include the Skagit River. Instead, it lists the Suiattle River and nine creeks which flow into the Sauk River and Cascade River. It also lists the Sauk River and the Cascade River, which flow into the Skagit River. Despite including three rivers, it does not list the Skagit River. Judge Boldt's inclusion of the Skagit River in the Upper Skagit tribe's U&As, *see Final Decision I*, 384 F. Supp. at 379, and in the Swinomish tribe's U&As, *Final Decision II*, 459 F. Supp. at 1049, while omitting it from the Sauk tribe's U&As, indicates that his omission was intentional, *see United States v. Lummi Indian Tribe*, 235 F.3d 443, 452 (9th Cir. 2000). Had Judge Boldt intended to include the Skagit River in the U&As of the Sauk tribe, "he would have used that specific term, as he did elsewhere." *Id.*

The Lane Report, on which Judge Boldt heavily relied, reinforces our conclusion. Conclusion Five of the Lane Report, which is substantially identical to Finding of Fact 131, did not include the Skagit River as one of the Sauk tribe's fishing grounds. Elsewhere, the Lane Report stated that "some of the [Sauk tribal members], if not most" continued to live "along the Sauk and Suiattle rivers where their descendants still reside," and were "distinguished **{–772–}** from the residents of the main Skagit River." This evidence strongly suggests that the Sauk tribe did not fish in the Skagit **[—14—]** River itself, which further supports our conclusion that Judge Boldt did not intend to include it.

B

The Sauk tribe disagrees with our conclusion. It argues that Finding of Fact 131 is ambiguous in the context of *Final Decision I* as a whole and the evidence in the record, and we cannot reliably determine Judge Boldt's intent. The Sauk tribe raises four arguments to support this claim. We address each argument in turn.

1

First, the Sauk tribe argues that Finding of Fact 131 is ambiguous because it lists rivers and creeks that are tributaries to the Skagit River, raising the inference that Judge Boldt intended to include the Skagit River as well. We cannot draw such an inference because Judge Boldt expressly included both the Skagit River and its tributaries in his determination of the Swinomish tribe's U&As, *Final Decision II*, 459 F. Supp. at 1049. Judge Boldt's inclusion of rivers and tributaries in other tribes' U&As strongly indicates that Judge Boldt did not intend to include a river by reference to its tributaries alone; rather, he listed a river and its tributaries when he intended to include both. Therefore, we reject the Sauk tribe's argument that Finding of Fact 131's list of tributaries undermines our conclusion that Judge Boldt's intent is clear.

2

Second, the Sauk tribe points to a transcript of the testimony of James Enick (a member of the Sauk tribe) in September 1973 regarding his knowledge of the Sauk tribe's fishing locations. The transcript stated: **[—15—]**

> Q: What were the areas where your tribe traditionally fished?

A: Wherever the people were, but mostly on the Sauk River, the whole river, and all the streams coming into the river, that's where the Indians fished.

Q: Where has the Sauk-Suiattle Tribe lived?

A: Up and down the Skagit River and the Sauk River mostly.

According to the Sauk tribe, the excerpt indicates that the Sauk tribe fished "[w]herever the people were," meaning wherever tribal members lived, and that the Sauk tribe lived "[u]p and down the Skagit River." Therefore, according to the Sauk tribe, Sauk tribal members must have fished "[u]p and down" the Skagit River. The Sauk tribe notes that Judge Boldt incorporated this testimony by including a parenthetical reference to "Ex. MS-10, p. 3, l. 1-6" at the end of Finding of Fact 131. The Sauk tribe argues that the inclusion of this parenthetical, which incorporates Enick's 1973 testimony by reference, makes Finding of Fact 131 ambiguous and raises the inference that Judge Boldt intended to include the Skagit River in the Sauk tribe's U&As.

We disagree. First, Enick's testimony does not state that the Sauk tribe fished on the mainstem of the Skagit River, and so is not evidence that the river was part of the Sauk tribe's U&As. Moreover, in identifying the Sauk tribe's fishing areas elsewhere in his testimony, Enick states that the Sauk tribe fished "mostly on the Sauk River, the whole river, and all of the streams coming into the river." This testimony is consistent with Finding of Fact 131, which also includes **[—16—]** the Sauk River and a tributary to the river. Second, although the Sauk tribe puts weight on Judge Boldt's reference to this excerpt in **{-773-}** the parenthetical at the end of Finding of Fact 131, that reference indicates only that Judge Boldt was aware of this testimony, yet nevertheless chose not to include the Skagit River in his findings.

We therefore conclude that Enick's testimony is not evidence showing that Judge Boldt meant to include the Skagit River in the U&As, and therefore does not change our conclusion that Judge Boldt's intent is clear.

3

Next, the Sauk tribe argues that the Sauk River and the Cascade River are part of the Sauk tribe's U&As, and that the most likely path of travel between the Sauk River and Cascade River is the Skagit River. According to the Sauk tribe, this raises the inference that the Sauk tribe traveled and fished on the Skagit River, which is evidence that Judge Boldt intended to include the Skagit River as part of the Sauk tribe's U&As.

In making this argument, the Sauk tribe relies on our cases analyzing U&As describing large marine areas between distant geographic anchor points. For example, Finding of Fact 46 of *Final Decision I* provided that "the usual and accustomed fishing places of the Lummi Indians at treaty times included the marine areas of Northern Puget Sound from the Fraser River south to the present environs of Seattle." 384 F. Supp. at 360. We held that this Finding of Fact was "ambiguous, because it does not delineate the western boundary of the Lummi's usual and accustomed grounds and stations." *Lummi Indian Tribe*, 235 F.3d at 449. **[—17—]**

We nevertheless discerned that even though the Finding of Fact did not mention Admiralty Inlet (a marine "passageway along the west side of Whidbey Island") by name, Judge Boldt intended to include it "within the 'marine areas of Northern Puget Sound from the Fraser River south to the present environs of Seattle'" because "Admiralty Inlet would likely be a passage through which the Lummi would have traveled from the San Juan Islands in the north to the 'present environs of Seattle.'" *Id.* at 450, 452; *see also Tulalip Tribes*, 794 F.3d at 1133, 3 Adm. R. at 579 (holding that U&As described as "the marine waters of Puget Sound from the northern tip of Vashon Island to the Fraser River" were ambiguous).

The Sauk tribe's reliance on these cases is misplaced. For example, unlike the finding of fact determining the Lummi's U&As, Finding of Fact 131 does not ambiguously describe marine areas between two distant geographic anchor points. Instead, Finding of Fact 131 describes specific rivers and tributaries, and does not describe any area extending between the Sauk River and Cascade River, or indicate that Judge Boldt intended to include a path of travel between those rivers. Therefore, the Sauk tribe's "path of travel" theory does not make Judge Boldt's intent unclear, or constitute evidence that Judge Boldt intended to include the Skagit River in the Sauk tribe's U&As.

4

Finally, the Sauk tribe relies on scattered statements throughout *Final Decision I* and the Lane Report evidencing that the Sauk tribe historically fished in the Skagit River.

First, the Sauk tribe points to statements suggesting that Sauk tribal members lived near the Skagit River. For instance, Finding of Fact 129 states that the Sakhumehu tribe **[—18—]** (predecessor to the Sauk tribe) resided in a village located at the confluence of the Sauk River and Skagit River and that the historical residence of the Sauk tribe was on "the upper reaches **{-774-}** of the Skagit River System." *Final Decision I*, 384 F. Supp at 375. Further, Dr. Lane's summary of her report states that the "principal fisheries" of the Sakhumehu "were the headwaters of Skagit River including Baker River, Sauk River, and the smaller creeks which belonged to that water system."

The Sauk tribe also points to evidence that individual Sauk tribal members had access to the Skagit River. For instance, Finding of Fact 129 indicates that Sauk tribal members sometimes married Upper Skagit tribal members. *Final Decision I*, 384 F. Supp. at 375–76. The Lane Report stated that "some of the Sauk people went to the Cascades on the Skagit River to fish and to Baker River to fish with Upper Skagit friends and relatives there."

Further, the Sauk tribe points to Finding of Fact 132, which states that the tribe "traveled to the saltwater in order to procure marine life unavailable in their own territory." *Id.* at 376. Because the rivers listed in the Sauk tribe's U&As do not connect to the saltwater, the Sauk tribe argues that the tribe must have traveled on the Skagit River to the ocean.

Finally, the Sauk tribe relies on Dr. Lane's general statement that "Indian fisheries existed at all feasible places along a given drainage system from the upper reaches of the various tributary creeks and streams, down the main river system to the saltwater."

None of these statements undermines our conclusion that Judge Boldt's intent was clear, or shows that Judge Boldt intended to include the Skagit River in the U&As contrary to the plain text of Finding of Fact 131. Neither the **[—19—]** statement that a Sauk village is located at the confluence of the Sauk and Skagit Rivers, nor that Sauk tribal members resided on the upper reaches of the Skagit River system, is evidence of U&As on the mainstem of the Skagit River. Likewise, Dr. Lane describes headwaters as distinct from the main part of a river, so the presence of the Sauk tribe's principal fisheries in the headwaters of the Skagit River does not establish U&As on the mainstem of the river. Nor does evidence that *some* Sauk tribal members fished with friends and relatives on the Skagit River establish U&As for the tribe. As *Final Decision I* made clear, "occasional and incidental [fishing] was not considered to make the marine waters traveled thereon the usual and accustomed fishing grounds of the transiting Indians." 384 F. Supp. at 353. The statement that the Sauk tribe traveled to the saltwater, without more, does not establish customary fishing on the Skagit River to support U&As on it. Finally, Dr. Lane's general statement about Indian fisheries is not sufficiently specific to the Sauk tribe to inform Judge Boldt's intent regarding the Sauk tribe's U&As.

IV

We conclude that Judge Boldt did not intend to include the Skagit River in the Sauk tribe's U&As. *See Tulalip Tribes*, 794 F.3d at 1133, 3 Adm. R. at 579. Because there is no ambiguity as to Judge Boldt's intent, we affirm the district court's holding that the Upper Skagit tribe was entitled to summary judgment.

AFFIRMED.

United States Court of Appeals
for the Ninth Circuit

No. 21-35812

SWINOMISH INDIAN TRIBAL COMMUNITY
VS.
LUMMI NATION

Appeal from the United States District Court for the Western District of Washington

Decided: September 11, 2023
Amended: October 3, 2023

Citation: 80 F.4th 1056, 11 Adm. R. 452 (9th Cir. 2023).

Before **IKUTA** and **COLLINS,** Circuit Judges, and **FITZWATER,*** District Judge.

* The Honorable Sidney A. Fitzwater, United States District Judge for the Northern District of Texas, sitting by designation.

[—8—] {-1058-} **COLLINS,** Circuit Judge: **{-1059-}**

This is the latest proceeding in a long-running case regarding Indian fishing rights in certain waters in Washington State. The governing law is a 1974 decree issued by Judge George Boldt of the U.S. District Court for the Western District of Washington, which settled various competing tribal rights arising from, *inter alia*, the 1855 Treaty of Point Elliott. We have interpreted that 1974 decree many times since its issuance, and these appeals call upon us to do so once again.

This proceeding was instituted by three Indian tribes who sought a ruling that the recognized fishing rights of the Lummi Nation ("the Lummi") under the 1974 decree do not extend to certain areas. Specifically, the current dispute centers on a single line in the decree recognizing that "the usual and accustomed fishing places" in which the Lummi have fishing rights "include[] the marine areas of Northern Puget Sound from the Fraser River south to the present environs of Seattle, and particularly Bellingham Bay." *United States v. State of Washington*, 384 F. Supp. 312, 360 (W.D. Wash. 1974) ("*Final Decision I*"). For the reader's convenience, the Fraser River, Seattle, and Bellingham Bay are shown here:[1] **[—9—] {-1060-}**

[—10—]

The question is whether the specific waters in dispute here—namely, the sheltered waters

[1] These physical maps are taken from the Bureau of Land Management's webpage, at https://webmaps.blm.gov/program_apps/BLM_Natl_Recreation_Opportunities/. We may properly take judicial notice of maps produced by a government agency for the limited purpose of elucidating, for the reader, the general locations of the relevant geographic areas. *Montana Green* **[—9—]** *Party v. Jacobsen*, 17 F.4th 919, 927 (9th Cir. 2021). We have added markers for relevant geographic points in large font for the reader's convenience.

east of Whidbey Island and south of Fidalgo Island—fall within the Lummi's historical fishing territory. For the reader's convenience, the approximate location of the disputed waters is shown here: **{-1061-}**

[—11—]

The district court ruled against the Lummi, holding that the disputed waters are not part of their historical fishing waters under the 1974 decree. We affirm.

I

A

In 1854 and 1855, Isaac Stevens, Governor of what was then Washington Territory, signed a series of treaties with the Indian tribes of the Pacific Northwest. One of those treaties was the 1855 Treaty of Point Elliott.[2] Under the treaty's terms, **{-1062-}** the signatory tribes agreed to "cede, relinquish, and convey to the United States" much of their tribal land. Treaty of Point Elliott, art. I, 12 Stat. 927 (1859). But the tribes retained their "right of taking fish at usual and accustomed grounds and stations," which the Treaty "secured to said Indians in common with all citizens of the Territory." 12 Stat. at 928. The Treaty did not specify, however, the precise location of those "usual and accustomed" fishing waters. *Id.*

More than a century later, the questions left open by the various Stevens treaties sparked complex litigation in the U.S. District Court for the Western District of Washington between Indian tribes, the State of Washington, various non-Indian fishermen, and the United States. In February 1974, District Judge George Boldt, who presided over that litigation, issued a wide-ranging decree to settle the parties' competing claims to "treaty right fishing" across the various **[—12—]** waterways between the state capital and the Canadian border, some 135 miles to the north. *Final Decision I*, 384 F. Supp. at 327. Judge Boldt's decree purported to fix the location of "some," though "by no means all," of the "usual and accustomed fishing places" historically frequented by various Indian tribes in waters "of the State of Washington west of the Cascade Mountains and north of the Columbia River drainage area." *Id.* at 327–28, 333. This area covered more than 100 nautical miles and included "the American portion of the Puget Sound watershed, the watersheds of the Olympic Peninsula north of the Grays Harbor watershed, and the offshore waters adjacent to those areas." *Id.* at 327–28. Judge Boldt's wide-ranging decree was substantially affirmed by this court, *United States v. State of Washington*, 520 F.2d 676, 693 (9th Cir. 1975), and ultimately by the Supreme Court, *Washington v. Washington State Commercial Passenger Fishing Vessel Ass'n*, 443 U.S. 658, 685–87 (1979).[3] **[—13—]**

[2] Others included the Treaty of Medicine Creek, 10 Stat. 1132 (1855); the Treaty of Point No Point, 12 Stat. 933 (1859); the Treaty of Neah Bay, 12 Stat. 939 (1859); and the Treaty with the Yakamas, 12 Stat. 951 (1859). Each treaty included similar language regarding Indian fishing rights in "usual and accustomed" areas. *See Final Decision I*, 384 F. Supp. at 331.

[3] The Supreme Court initially denied certiorari, 423 U.S. 1086 (1976), leaving our court's affirmance intact. However, when the Washington Supreme Court subsequently adopted a different reading of

Judge Boldt recognized, however, that a single decree could not definitively resolve every future dispute over tribal fishing rights anywhere in western Washington. *Final Decision I* therefore reserved the district court's continuing jurisdiction in two circumstances relevant here. First, any of the parties to the 1974 decree could invoke the district court's continuing jurisdiction to determine "whether or not the actions, intended or effected by any party (including the party seeking a determination) are in conformity with Final Decision # I." *Final Decision I*, 384 F. Supp. at 419. Second, any of the parties could request that the district court determine "the location of any of a tribe's usual and accustomed fishing grounds not specifically determined by Final Decision # I." *Id.* These two sources of retained jurisdiction appear, respectively, in Paragraphs 25(a)(1) and 25(a)(6) of the current, amended **{-1063-}** version of Judge Boldt's 1974 permanent injunction.[4] In effect, Paragraph 25(a)(1) allows the district court to adjudicate present-day disputes about what the 1974 decree really said. Paragraph 25(a)(6) allows the district court to adjudicate disputes about what the 1974 decree left *un*said—that is, historical fishing rights the 1974 decree did not purport to address at all.

In the nearly 50 years since Judge Boldt's 1974 decree, the Indian tribes of Washington State have often invoked the district court's continuing jurisdiction under Paragraph 25 to settle overlapping tribal claims to historical fishing waters. This court, in turn, has often been called upon to review the 1974 decree in the exercise of its appellate jurisdiction over the district court. The task of interpreting the occasionally **[—14—]** cryptic terms of a decades-old decree, itself based on a sometimes thin record of anthropological evidence regarding the practices of Indian tribes more than a century earlier, has not always proved to be an easy one. Nonetheless, it remains the task we have today.

B

This appeal involves a dispute among several Indian tribes over the waters east of Whidbey Island, a land formation that stretches approximately 37 miles north-to-south across Puget Sound. The disputed waters include Skagit Bay, directly south of the Swinomish Reservation; the Saratoga Passage between Whidbey Island and Camano Island; Port Susan, a bay separating Camano Island from the mainland; Holmes Harbor, a cove at the southern end of Whidbey Island; and Possession Sound, near the mainland city of Everett.

With respect to the core dispute on appeal, the parties are the Swinomish Indian Tribal Community; the Tulalip Tribes; the Upper Skagit Indian Tribe; and the Lummi Nation.[5] All four tribes bear respective rights under the Treaty of Point Elliott, as recognized in Judge Boldt's decrees,[6] and the primary issue on

---

the Stevens treaties, the U.S. Supreme Court granted review of various federal and state decisions presenting that treaty interpretation issue. 443 U.S. at 672 & n.19, 674. The U.S. Supreme Court agreed with Judge Boldt that the treaty phrase "in common with all citizens of the Territory" referred to a group-based "right to take a [certain] share of each run of fish that passes through tribal fishing areas," rather than a mere "personal right to attempt to land fish" on the part of each individual tribal member, no different from the right to fish of any other citizen of Washington State. *Id.* at 674, 679; *see also Final Decision I*, 384 F. Supp. at 343; *Upper Skagit Indian Tribe v. Washington*, 590 F.3d 1020, 1022 (9th Cir. 2010). The Court, however, made certain modifications to the formula Judge Boldt used to calculate the tribal share of the fishing catch. 443 U.S. at 687–89.

[4] These provisions, previously termed 25(a) and 25(f), were renumbered in a 1993 order amending paragraph 25 of the 1974 decree. *See United States v. Washington*, 18 F. Supp. 3d 1172, 1213 (W.D. Wash. 1993) (compiling various orders in the overall matter from 1991–1993).

[5] For purposes of this case, the Lummi also include "the Semiahmoo and Samish Indians who were subsumed under the Lummi designation." *Final Decision I*, 384 F. Supp. at 360.

[6] For the Swinomish, see *Swinomish Indian Tribal Cmty. v. BNSF Ry. Co.*, 951 F.3d 1142, 1146 (9th Cir. 2020); *United States v. Washington*, 459 F. Supp. 1020, 1039 (W.D. Wash. 1978). For the Lummi, see *United States v. Lummi Nation*, 876 F.3d 1004, 1007, 5 Adm. R. 443, 443–44 (9th Cir. 2017); *Final Decision I*, 384 F. Supp. at 360. For the Upper Skagit, see *Upper Skagit Indian Tribe v.*

appeal concerns the **[—15—]** fishing rights of the Lummi. Specifically, the Lummi Nation—which, in a line of cases over the past two decades, has successfully persuaded this court to recognize the tribe's historical fishing rights in certain waters to the *west* of Whidbey Island, *see United States v. Lummi Nation*, 876 F.3d 1004, 1011, 5 Adm. R. 443, 446 (9th Cir. 2017); *United States v. Lummi Indian Tribe*, 235 F.3d 443, 453 (9th Cir. 2000)—would like to fish in the waters *east* of Whidbey Island as well. The Lummi are opposed in this endeavor by certain tribes who currently fish east of Whidbey Island: the Swinomish, the Tulalip, and the Upper Skagit. Under the 1974 decree, one tribe's "usual and **{-1064-}** accustomed" fishing grounds are not legally exclusive of another's—that is to say, multiple tribes may, as a purely legal matter, have overlapping "usual and accustomed" fishing grounds. *Final Decision I*, 384 F. Supp. at 332, 417. But since the overall tribal catch is limited to "50 percent of the harvested fish from runs passing through [tribes'] off-reservation" usual and accustomed fishing grounds, *Upper Skagit Indian Tribe v. Washington*, 590 F.3d 1020, 1022 (9th Cir. 2010), each tribe has a practical incentive, via proceedings like the one before us, to eliminate fishing competition from other tribes in overlapping waters.

In October 2019, the Swinomish, Tulalip, and Upper Skagit filed a joint "Request for Determination" in the District Court for the Western District of Washington, invoking that court's continuing jurisdiction under Paragraph 25(a)(1) of Judge Boldt's 1974 permanent injunction. The requesting tribes claimed that the Lummi, who planned to open a crab fishery east of Whidbey Island, **[—16—]** had no fishing rights in that area under the 1974 decree. The tribes asked the district court for "a declaration to that effect," as well as an injunction "prohibiting Lummi from issuing regulations purporting to open any portion" of the disputed area "to Lummi fishing and prohibiting Lummi from fishing for any species in any portion" of the area.

The parties filed cross-motions for summary judgment. The Swinomish's motion asked the court to declare that "the usual and accustomed fishing places" of the Lummi "do not include the secluded waters to the east of Whidbey Island" and to grant "permanent injunctive relief enjoining Lummi from fishing or authorizing its members to fish for any species" in the disputed waters. The Upper Skagit's motion asked the court "to grant summary judgment in its favor by declaring that the area previously adjudicated to be the usual and accustomed grounds" of the Lummi Nation does not include the disputed "waters east of Whidbey Island." The Tulalip's motion asked the court to "prohibit the Lummi Nation . . . from engaging in any fishing for finfish or shellfish" in the disputed waters; the Tulalip "also move[d] for a permanent injunction enjoining Lummi and its fishers from engaging in any fishing in the named Region."

The Lummi's motion, for its part, asked the court to "dismiss[] the Request for Determination" filed by the Swinomish, Upper Skagit, and Tulalip, and to "rul[e] that the Lummi's usual and accustomed fishing grounds and stations," as determined by Judge Boldt's 1974 decree, *do* "include marine areas . . . to the east of Whidbey Island," including all five of the specific areas in dispute here.

C

The district court held for the Swinomish, Tulalip, and Upper Skagit, stating that the disputed waters were not **[—17—]** included in Judge Boldt's "determination of Lummi's usual and accustomed fishing grounds and stations." The district court consequently denied the Lummi Nation's motion for summary judgment, granted summary judgment in part to the Swinomish, Upper Skagit, and Tulalip, and declared the matter closed on September 20, 2021.[7] The Lummi filed a timely notice of appeal three days later.

Lundgren, 138 S. Ct. 1649, 1651 (2018); *Final Decision I*, 384 F. Supp. at 379. For the Tulalip, see *Greene v. United States*, 996 **[—15—]** F.2d 973, 975 (9th Cir. 1993); *United States v. Lummi Indian Tribe*, 841 F.2d 317, 317 (9th Cir. 1988); *United States v. Washington*, 459 F. Supp. at 1039.

[7] Summary judgment was granted only "in part" because the district court denied, as unnecessary,

On October 1, however, the Jamestown S'Klallam Tribe and Port Gamble S'Klallam Tribe (collectively, "S'Klallam") made an appearance. The S'Klallam filed a motion for reconsideration asking the district court to "reconsider and amend certain **{-1065-}** language" from its summary judgment order. The S'Klallam objected "particularly" to language in the district court's order that, in the S'Klallam's view, could be construed to imply that additional tribes, other than the Lummi, might have fishing rights in certain waters *west* of Whidbey Island where the S'Klallam claim fishing interests. In the S'Klallam's view, the district court should have made clearer that only the *Lummi*, and not Indian tribes more generally, were covered by the challenged language in the district court's order. The S'Klallam asked the court to "delete or reframe the [relevant] sentences to make clear the only precedent or law of the case created here is how *Lummi*," not *other* tribes, fished west of Whidbey Island.

The district court denied the S'Klallam's motion for reconsideration in a brief order. The district court concluded that, because the Lummi had timely filed an appeal to our court, the district court had already lost jurisdiction over the **[—18—]** case (and hence jurisdiction to adjudicate the S'Klallam's motion for reconsideration). "[E]ven if the Court had jurisdiction to consider the motion for reconsideration," the district court continued, "the Court would deny the motion."

The S'Klallam then filed a timely notice of appeal seeking to "cross-appeal" the district court's original order of September 20, "as well as appeal" the court order denying the S'Klallam's October 1 motion for reconsideration.

II

As noted above, this case asks us to determine the meaning of Judge Boldt's 1974 statement that the usual and accustomed fishing places of the Lummi Indians, at the time of the Treaty of Point Elliott in 1855, included "the marine areas of Northern Puget Sound from the Fraser River south to the present environs of Seattle, and particularly Bellingham Bay." *Final Decision I*, 384 F. Supp. at 360. Before addressing the meaning of that phrase, we first clarify the general principles that we have developed to interpret Judge Boldt's decrees—a set of principles we have often referred to as the "*Muckleshoot* framework," after a series of cases involving that Tribe.[8]

A court reviewing Judge Boldt's 1974 decree pursuant to Paragraph 25(a)(1) is interpreting a prior judicial decree and, as such, is carrying out what is ultimately a legal inquiry. *See United States v. DAS Corp.*, 18 F.4th 1032, **[—19—]** 1040 (9th Cir. 2021). In conducting that inquiry, we have explained, a reviewing court should construe the decree "so as to give effect to the intention of the issuing court"—*i.e.*, Judge Boldt—at the time the decree was written. *Muckleshoot Tribe v. Lummi Indian Tribe*, 141 F.3d 1355, 1359 (9th Cir. 1998) (citation omitted). "We have sometimes described a subproceeding under paragraph 25(a)(1) as involving a 'two-step mode of analysis.'" *Upper Skagit Indian Tribe v. Sauk-Suiattle Indian Tribe*, 66 F.4th 766, 770, 11 Adm. R. 445, 447 (9th Cir. 2023) ("*Sauk-Suiattle*") (citation omitted). We recently described that two-step inquiry as follows:

> At step one, a court uses the standard tools for interpreting precedent, starting with the text of the applicable Finding of Fact and considering the language at **{-1066-}** issue in the context of the Final Decision as a whole. A court also

the three tribes' requests for "permanent injunctive relief beyond that provided in the underlying case."

[8] Specifically, the referenced framework derives its name from three of our prior cases: *Muckleshoot Tribe v. Lummi Indian Tribe*, 141 F.3d 1355 (9th Cir. 1998); *United States v. Muckleshoot Indian Tribe*, 235 F.3d 429 (9th Cir. 2000); and *Muckleshoot Indian Tribe v. Lummi Indian Nation*, 234 F.3d 1099 (9th Cir. 2000). We have further developed that framework in a series of subsequent cases. *See generally Upper Skagit Indian Tribe v. Sauk-Suiattle Indian Tribe*, 66 F.4th 766, 11 Adm. R. 445 (9th Cir. 2023).

> considers the record evidence before Judge Boldt, along with any other evidence raised by the moving party that sheds light on Judge Boldt's understanding of geography at the time. At this step, we have upheld a district court's decision as correctly interpreting Judge Boldt's opinion on the basis of information known to Judge Boldt and the words he chose. However, whether the text of a Finding of Fact is unambiguous or not, a court must understand the Finding of Fact in light of the facts of the case, and so may proceed to step two to determine whether the moving party has carried the burden of showing that there was no evidence in the record before Judge Boldt, that favors the non-moving party's contrary **[—20—]** interpretation of the Finding of Fact in a way that would undermine the moving party's theory of Judge Boldt's intent.

Id. at 770–71, 11 Adm. R. at 447 (simplified). The goal of both steps of "this two-step inquiry" is to "determine whether the moving party has carried its burden of showing that its interpretation of the Finding of Facts is consistent with Judge Boldt's intent." *Id.* at 771, 11 Adm. R. at 448.

Because fishing rights under the relevant treaties generally turn on the usual and accustomed fishing grounds ("U&A") of a particular tribe at the relevant time in history, the disputes presented to us under Paragraph 25(a)(1) of the decree typically involve a disagreement over the meaning of Judge Boldt's findings of fact concerning the historical U&A of the relevant tribes. In particular, we have frequently been confronted with claims in which one tribe has invoked Paragraph 25(a)(1) to obtain an affirmative ruling that a competing tribe has *not* been granted certain fishing rights under that decree.

To the extent that the moving tribe seeks a ruling that Judge Boldt's findings as to a competing tribe's U&A do *not* cover a particular area, the fact that the decree's text does not unambiguously exclude the particular area from the competing tribe's U&A is not the end of the matter. If the text of the relevant findings is susceptible to the moving party's interpretation that the competing tribe was excluded from the area, the moving party can carry its burden (at step two) by showing that there was no evidence before Judge Boldt that the competing tribe "fished or traveled through the contested areas." *See Upper Skagit Indian Tribe v. Suquamish Indian Tribe*, 871 F.3d 844, 848 (9th Cir. 2017) ("*Suquamish*") (simplified). **[—21—]**

That characterization of the burden applicable in that specific context flows directly from the nature of the underlying inquiry. Judge Boldt's 1974 decree stated that, for a fishing area to be "usual and accustomed," the tribe in question must have fished in that area on more than an "occasional and incidental" basis. *Final Decision I*, 384 F. Supp. at 353, 356. Mere travel through a set of waters was, in Judge Boldt's view, not sufficient to render a body of water a "usual and accustomed" fishing place for the traveling tribe. Although "[m]arine waters were . . . used as thoroughfares for travel by Indians who trolled en route," this sort of "occasional and incidental trolling was not considered to make the marine waters traveled thereon the usual and accustomed fishing grounds of the transiting Indians." *Id.* at 353; *see also United States v. Lummi Indian Tribe*, 841 F.2d 317, 320 (9th Cir. 1988) (stating that "travel through an area and incidental trolling are not sufficient to establish an area as a usual and accustomed fishing ground"). Because Judge Boldt must be understood to have followed his own announced standards in making **{–1067–}** his factual findings as to the various tribes' U&As, it follows that, if the record contains "*no evidence*" that the competing tribe "fished or traveled through the contested areas," *Suquamish*, 871 F.3d at 848 (simplified) (emphasis added), in a manner that "was more than 'incidental' or 'occasional,'" *United States v. Muckleshoot Indian Tribe*, 235 F.3d 429, 435 (9th Cir. 2000), then an ambiguous U&A finding concerning that competing tribe's fishing rights simply cannot be construed as including those contested areas. In other words, because Judge Boldt should not be understood to have made a finding that the record could not support under the standards he himself articulated, a moving party which carries its specific step-two burden under the *Muckleshoot* framework is **[—22—]** entitled to a determination under Paragraph 25(a)(1) that the competing tribe's U&A does not extend to the contested areas.

Our decision in *United States v. Muckleshoot Indian Tribe*, 235 F.3d 429, illustrates how this two-step inquiry works. There, three tribes invoked Paragraph 25(a)(1), seeking a determination that the language of "Finding 76" in the 1974 decree, which concerned the U&A of the Muckleshoot tribe, "does *not* include any areas outside Elliott Bay." *See id.* at 431 (emphasis added). The relevant language of Finding 76 stated that the Muckleshoot's U&A extended, "secondarily," to locations "in the saltwater of Puget Sound." *Id.* (quoting *Final Decision I*, 384 F. Supp. at 367) (emphasis omitted). After evaluating all of the relevant record evidence before Judge Boldt, we concluded that there was no evidence in the 1974 record "that the Muckleshoot's ancestors had U&A fishing grounds beyond Elliott Bay." *Id.* at 435. Thus, to the extent that the referent of "saltwater of Puget Sound" was ambiguous, the three moving tribes had shown that there was no evidence to support construing that phrase as extending beyond Elliott Bay. *Id.* We therefore affirmed the district court's summary judgment affirmatively holding that "the Muckleshoot's U&A under Finding 76 was limited to Elliott Bay." *Id.* at 432.

III

Applying this *Muckleshoot* framework here and reviewing de novo, *see Tulalip Tribes v. Suquamish Indian Tribe*, 794 F.3d 1129, 1133, 3 Adm. R. 577, 579 (9th Cir. 2015) ("*Tulalip Tribes*"), we conclude that the district court correctly held that the Swinomish, Tulalip, and Upper Skagit carried their burden to warrant a ruling, under Paragraph 25(a)(1), that **[—23—]** Judge Boldt's "determination of Lummi's usual and accustomed fishing grounds and stations" did not extend to the disputed waters at issue here.

A

We have previously held that, as to waters *west* of Whidbey Island, Finding of Fact 46—the paragraph of Judge Boldt's decree determining the scope of the Lummi Nation's historical fishing grounds—is ambiguous, requiring us to "examine the record before Judge Boldt to clarify his intent." *United States v. Lummi Nation*, 876 F.3d 1004, 1009, 5 Adm. R. 443, 445 (9th Cir. 2017) ("*Lummi III*"); *see United States v. Lummi Nation*, 763 F.3d 1180, 1187, 2 Adm. R. 489, 494 (9th Cir. 2014) ("*Lummi II*"); *United States v. Lummi Indian Tribe*, 235 F.3d 443, 449 (9th Cir. 2000) ("*Lummi I*"). Considering Finding of Fact 46 in the relevant context, *see also Sauk-Suiattle*, 66 F.4th at 770–71, 11 Adm. R. at 446–48, we reaffirm that conclusion today as to the waters *east* of Whidbey Island.

1

We begin with the decree's text.

Finding of Fact 45 states: "The Lummis had reef net sites on Orcas Island, San Juan Island, Lummi Island and Fidalgo **{–1068–}** Island, and near Point Roberts and Sandy Point. . . . They trolled the waters of the San Juan Islands for various species of salmon." *Final Decision I*, 384 F. Supp. at 360. Finding of Fact 14 states that these "Lummi reef net sites in Northern Puget Sound," among others, "are examples of some Indian usual and accustomed fishing grounds and stations in marine waters." *Id.* at 353. The boundaries of "Northern Puget Sound" are not defined in the decree. Finding of Fact 46—the key finding at issue in this case—states: "In addition to the reef net locations listed above, the usual and accustomed **[—24—]** fishing places of the Lummi Indians at treaty times included the marine areas of Northern Puget Sound from the Fraser River south to the present environs of Seattle, and particularly Bellingham Bay." *Id.* at 360.

Three points are worth noting about this last statement. First, if "the marine areas of Northern Puget Sound from the Fraser River south to the present environs of Seattle" included—as the Lummi argue—every single area of water between "the Fraser River" and "the present environs of Seattle," it is not clear why Judge Boldt would have listed the Lummi "reef net locations" in the San Juan Islands as a separate, distinct fishing ground. *Final Decision I*, 384 F. Supp. at 360. After all, the San Juan Islands—just like the separately listed reef net locations in marine waters at "Point Roberts," "Lummi Island," "Sandy Point," and "Fidalgo Island"—are located between the Fraser River and Seattle. Yet Finding of Fact 46 states that "[*i*]*n addition to*" their usual and accustomed fishing places at those locations, the Lummi's usual and accustomed fishing places *also* included "the marine areas of Northern Puget Sound from the Fraser River south to the present environs of Seattle." *Id.* (emphasis added). Where Judge Boldt used separate terms to refer to separate bodies of water, this court (naturally) understands him to have been referring to separate bodies of water. *Lummi I*, 235 F.3d at 451–52. So too would an ordinary reader, who could reasonably conclude that the waters around the listed reef net locations—despite their geographic position in waters directly between the Fraser River and Seattle—must not be part of "the marine areas of Northern Puget Sound from the Fraser River south to the present environs of Seattle." *Final Decision I*, 384 F. Supp. at 360. But if not all waters between the Fraser River and Seattle are included in that general description, which waters are? **[—25—]**

Second, the geographic width of the U&A recognized in Finding of Fact 46 is left undefined. More precisely, to the extent that the language might arguably be read as referring to some sort of path "from" the Fraser River "to" Seattle, the general words are unilluminating as to the width of any such path. *Final Decision I*, 384 F. Supp. at 360. Those words could be referring to all waters anywhere on the map between any portion of the Fraser River and Seattle—a usage akin to the phrase "from sea to shining sea." Finding of Fact 46 could also be referring to a narrower nautical path or paths traced southward "from" the Fraser River, through northern Puget Sound, "to" Seattle. The decree itself, however, does not explain.

Finally, if Judge Boldt had intended to recognize Lummi fishing rights in every single body of water between the Fraser River and Seattle, it is not clear why he would have used the distinctive operative phrase "the marine areas of Northern Puget Sound from the Fraser River south to the present environs of Seattle." If, in other words, Judge Boldt really used the term "Northern Puget Sound" to mean all waters north of Seattle and south of any portion of the Fraser River as the crow flies—as the Lummi argue—Judge Boldt could simply have said that the Lummi's **{–1069–}** usual and accustomed fishing grounds were "Northern Puget Sound," or he could have used other similarly broad language. Why, then, the idiosyncratic phrasing?

2

The answer lies in an expert report concerning the history and practices of the Lummi Nation, authored by an anthropologist, Dr. Barbara Lane. Judge Boldt relied heavily on Dr. Lane's report, which was entered into the 1974 trial record as Exhibit "USA-30," in authoring his **[—26—]** findings regarding the Lummi; indeed he cited the report 11 times in the space of five paragraphs. (Judge Boldt also extensively cited a second report of Dr. Lane's, entered into evidence as "USA-20," which more broadly summarized her conclusions concerning all "Coast Salish and Nootkan speaking peoples residing west of the Cascade Mountains in the geographic area" at issue in *Final Decision I.* Judge Boldt cited that broader report at least 35 times in the course of drafting the decree.) Judge Boldt praised Dr. Lane's reports as "exceptionally well researched and reported," found their conclusions "established by a preponderance of the evidence," and declared them "authoritative and reliable summaries of relevant aspects of Indian life in the case area at and prior to the time of the treaties."[9] *Final Decision I*, 384 F. Supp. at 350.

[9] The "case area" is the area covered by Judge Boldt's decree: "that portion of the State of Washington west of the Cascade Mountains and north of the Columbia River drainage area," including "the American portion of the Puget Sound watershed, the watersheds of the Olympic Peninsula

Indeed Judge Boldt's endorsement of Dr. Lane's findings was so thoroughgoing that he incorporated many of her findings about the Lummi directly into his decree, often with minimal (or no) modification. Here are a few examples:

- **Dr. Lane**: "The single most valuable fish resource was undoubtedly the sockeye, which the Semiahmoo, Lummi, and Samish were able to intercept in the Straits on their annual migration from the ocean to the Fraser River." **[—27—]**
    - **Judge Boldt**: "The single most valuable fish resource was undoubtedly the sockeye, which the Lummis were able to intercept in the Straits on the annual migration of the sockeye from the ocean to the Fraser River." *Final Decision I*, 384 F. Supp. at 360.
- **Dr. Lane**: "Springs, silvers, and humpback were also taken with gill nets and springs were harpooned near the mouth of the Nooksack River," and "[s]teelhead were taken by harpoon at the mouth of Whatcom Creek and . . . in basketry traps."
    - **Judge Boldt**: "These Indians also took spring, silver and humpback salmon and steelhead by gill nets and harpoons near the mouth of the Nooksack River, and steelhead by harpoons and basketry traps on Whatcom Creek." *Final Decision I*, 384 F. Supp. at 360.
- **Dr. Lane**: "When nature did not provide optimum conditions, the reefnetters artificially created them."
    - **Judge Boldt**: "When nature did not provide optimum reef conditions the Indians artificially created them." *Final Decision I*, 384 F. Supp. at 360.

It is quite clear, in other words, that many of Judge Boldt's findings regarding the Lummi were copied, sometimes word-for-word, from Dr. Lane's expert report. Where Judge Boldt borrowed language directly **{-1070-}** from Dr. Lane's reports— **[—28—]** reports he expressly declared "authoritative and reliable"—we think a rebuttable presumption is warranted that Judge Boldt intended to adopt the meaning and scope that that language possessed in the reports, and that the parties would have shared that understanding at the time of decision. *See Final Decision I*, 384 F. Supp. at 350.

3

That point is crucial to understanding the statement of Judge Boldt's at issue in this case, regarding the Lummi Nation's usual and accustomed fishing areas. Dr. Lane's report on the Lummi covered this topic directly. Under the headline "USUAL AND ACCUSTOMED FISHING AREAS," Dr. Lane first outlined what she viewed as the Lummi Nation's "home territory," which included a set of "traditional fishing areas" that "extended from what is now the Canadian border south to Anacortes," on the north side of Fidalgo Island. (None of these areas are within the disputed waters at issue here.) Dr. Lane then made her *only* specific mention of Lummi fishing outside their home territory. "In addition to the home territory discussed to this point, Lummi fishermen were accustomed, at least in historic times, and probably earlier, to visit fisheries *as distant as the Fraser River in the north and Puget Sound in the south*" (emphasis added).

That comment concluded Dr. Lane's findings describing the U&A of the Lummi. She then listed a series of numbered "CONCLUSIONS" that summarized the contents of the report as already described. Conclusion 4, which closely tracks the phrasing of the statement at the center of this case, is the Conclusion relevant here. In Conclusion 4, Dr. Lane summarized her earlier statement about Lummi fishing outside the tribe's home territory. Dr. Lane repeated that in **[—29—]**

---

north of the Grays Harbor watershed, and the offshore waters adjacent to those areas." *Final Decision I*, 384 F. Supp. at 328.

addition to their "traditional fisheries" in their home territory north of Fidalgo Island, the Lummi also utilized other fisheries "*from the Fraser River south to the present environs of Seattle*" (emphasis added). This is, of course, precisely the same language Judge Boldt eventually used in the decree itself. And Judge Boldt cited, in using those words, the precise pages on which those same words appear in Dr. Lane's report. *See Final Decision I*, 384 F. Supp at 360 (citing Ex. USA-30, pp. 23–26).

The confusion in this case, we think, can be traced back to Dr. Lane's original finding—namely, that the Lummi "visit[ed] fisheries as distant as the Fraser River in the north and Puget Sound in the south." In using that phrase, Dr. Lane was merely describing the maximum north-south distance that the Lummi traveled to fish. The Lummi argue that Dr. Lane's reference to "Puget Sound in the south" refers to the east-of-Whidbey-Island waters disputed in this case, but that is wrong. By using the phrase "Puget Sound in the south," Dr. Lane was referring to the waters south of Admiralty Inlet, in the vicinity of Seattle. We know that because, when summarizing the relevant finding in her subsequent Conclusion 4, Dr. Lane used "the present environs of Seattle" as a synonym for her earlier reference to "Puget Sound in the south." In other words, Dr. Lane's original finding described the farthest two geographic points to which the Lummi ever traveled to fish: "Fraser River in the north" and "Puget Sound in the south," *i.e.*, the waters close to what is now Seattle. Dr. Lane's numbered Conclusion 4 then summarized her earlier finding, using slightly different words but repeating the same substance: "Other fisheries in the Straits and bays from the Fraser River south to the present environs of Seattle were utilized." **[—30—]**

Viewed in this context, Dr. Lane's report concluded that the Lummi used various unspecified fisheries in the waters **{–1071–}** between the Fraser River and Seattle. Consider for clarity a parallel sentence with more familiar locations. "Other cities in the States and lands from Seattle east to the present environs of New York were visited" means that the visitor ranged as far as Seattle and New York, and also visited at least some other cities in between. It does *not* mean that the visitor spent time in every single city between New York and Seattle. Especially given the context of Dr. Lane's earlier finding—which described the Lummi as fishing in locations "*as distant as*" the Fraser River and "Puget Sound in the south," which she used to mean the waters near Seattle—it is clear Dr. Lane was *not* saying that the Lummi fished in *every single area of water between the Fraser River and Seattle*. Nor would (indeed, could) Judge Boldt have understood her to be saying so. Dr. Lane said simply that, outside the Lummi's home territory, "[o]ther fisheries in the Straits and bays from the Fraser River south to the present environs of Seattle were utilized." Dr. Lane's report did not specify where those fisheries were, and she did not provide a citation for the conclusion that Lummi fishers ranged as far as the Fraser River and Seattle.

4

Judge Boldt's translation of Dr. Lane's language into his decree magnified, rather than resolved, the confusion. First, Judge Boldt directly copied Dr. Lane's language about Lummi fishing grounds outside their historical home territory—*i.e.*, that the Lummi had visited various unspecified fishing areas in the marine waters "from the Fraser River south to the present environs of Seattle." *Final Decision I*, 384 F. Supp. at 360. Next, Judge Boldt blended in Dr. Lane's separate findings about the Lummi Nation's **[—31—]** traditional, home-water fishing grounds in what Judge Boldt apparently viewed as "Northern Puget Sound," including the tribe's historical center of gravity north of Whidbey Island, near "Bellingham Bay." *Id.* Evidently intending to emphasize the home-water nature of Bellingham Bay as described in Dr. Lane's report, Judge Boldt stated that the Lummi "particularly" fished there. And he concluded by adding, at the beginning of the sentence, the phrase "the marine areas of Northern Puget Sound." *Id.* However, the phrase "Northern Puget Sound" is not defined in the 1974 decree. Nor is the term "marine," which typically appears to refer to saltwater, but occasionally seems to connote open waters over which long-distance travel would have occurred—a usage that here would match the distinction Judge Boldt seems to have drawn between "the marine areas of Northern Puget Sound" and the saltwater passageways between and among the San Juan Islands, where the Lummi had reef net locations. *See Final Decision I*, 384 F. Supp. at 353 ("Marine waters were also used as thoroughfares for travel by Indians who trolled en route," although "[s]uch occasional and incidental trolling was not considered to make the marine waters traveled thereon the usual and accustomed fishing grounds of the transiting Indians").

The result is a cobbled-together, patchwork sentence containing three elements: (1) "the marine areas of Northern Puget Sound," (2) "from the Fraser River south to the present environs of Seattle," and (3) "particularly Bellingham Bay." *Final Decision I*, 384 F. Supp. at 360. Except for Bellingham Bay, which is clearly identified as a Lummi usual and accustomed fishing ground, the remaining two elements provide little clarity. "Northern Puget Sound" has no defined boundaries in the decree, so it is difficult to tell whether Judge Boldt considered any waters east of Whidbey **[—32—]** Island to fall within the term's scope in 1974. Even if he did, the unusual remaining term, "from the Fraser River south to the present environs of Seattle," is copied **{–1072–}** directly from Dr. Lane's report, where it operated as a diffuse reference to a set of unidentified fishing waters and plainly did not include every single body of water between the Fraser River and Seattle. Nor, despite Judge Boldt's use of directional "from" and "to" language, does the decree clarify whether it is referring to a particular path of nautical travel from one point to the other—much less what that path (or paths) might be.

It is, in short, fundamentally ambiguous—even after reading the language of Finding of Fact 46 in light of the record evidence before Judge Boldt at the time of decision—whether Judge Boldt and the parties, in 1974, would have understood "the marine areas of Northern Puget Sound from the Fraser River south to the present environs of Seattle, and particularly Bellingham Bay," to include any waters east of Whidbey Island. 384 F. Supp. at 360. We must—as in all three *Lummi* cases preceding us—turn to further examination of the record evidence before Judge Boldt.

B

We proceed to step two of the *Muckleshoot* framework. As we have noted, here, the Swinomish, Tulalip, and Upper Skagit moved for a determination, under Paragraph 25(a)(1), that the Lummi's U&A, as described in Finding of Fact 46 of the decree, does *not* include the disputed waters east of Whidbey Island. These tribes' burden under step two, accordingly, is to show that there was no evidence in the record before Judge Boldt of historical Lummi fishing in the disputed waters beyond what would be merely incidental or occasional. *Sauk-Suiattle*, 66 F.4th at 771, 774, 11 Adm. R. 447–48, 450; *Suquamish*, 871 F.3d at 848; *Tulalip Tribes*, 794 F.3d at 1133, 3 Adm. R. at 579. We think **[—33—]** the moving parties have met that burden here. Indeed, there is no record evidence that the Lummi historically fished in waters east of Whidbey Island.

1

The Lummi point to a few excerpts from the 1974 trial record, but all of them are either irrelevant or entirely speculative.

First, the Lummi point out that Dr. Lane's report contained a map listing a lone Lummi reef net site off the *western* side of Fidalgo Island: **{–1073–}**

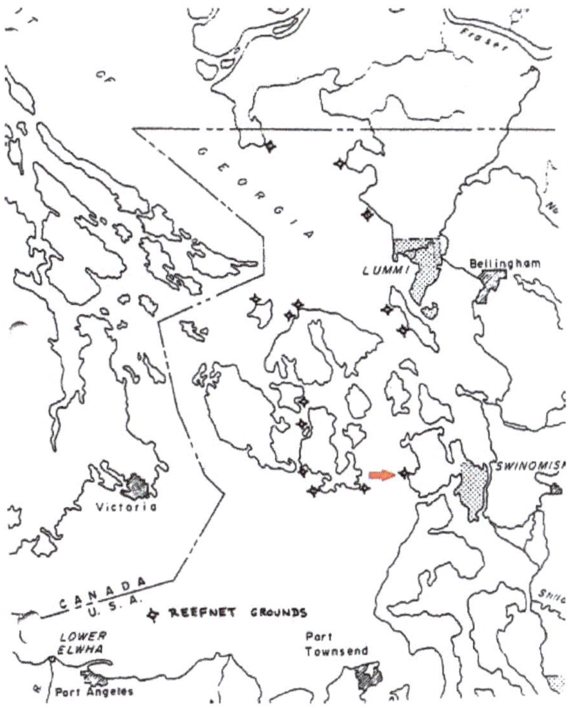

[—34—]

This reef net site is plainly not within the disputed east-of-Whidbey-Island waters, and we consequently see nothing to be gained from it.

Second, the Lummi point to an exhibit in the 1974 trial record—*viz.*, Exhibit PL-94w. Exhibit PL-94w is a confusingly worded affidavit from the late 19th century, submitted as part of the case that eventually became *United States v. Alaska Packers' Ass'n*, 79 F. 152 (C.C.D. Wash. 1897). That case involved "a suit by the United States and certain Indians of the Lummi tribe for an injunction against the Alaska Packers' Association . . . to protect the Lummi Indians in the right to take salmon, by their ancient and primitive means of fishing, *in the waters adjacent to Point Roberts*," an area far to the north of the waters disputed here. *Id.* at 153 (emphasis added). In June 1895, B.N. McDonough, a 60-year-old "Indian Trader" who had lived on or near the Lummi Reservation since 1871, submitted an affidavit in the case. McDonough stated that "during all the time I have known these [I]ndians they have fished at all points in the lower Sound and wherever the run of fish was greatest and the salmon were most easily taken including Point Roberts." McDonough did not explain what he meant, in 1895, by "the lower Sound," and the only specific geographic reference he made in conjunction with the term was to Point Roberts, some 40 miles to the north of the waters at issue in this case. McDonough also stated that the Lummi "have always fished at all the usual fishing places within many miles of their Reservation including Point Roberts and Vill[a]ge Point." Again, McDonough did not explain what these "usual fishing places" were, and Village Point is located on Lummi Island in Lummi home waters, far to the north of Whidbey **{–1074–}** and Fidalgo Islands. (Dr. Lane's summary report, in fact, described these two locations quite **[—35—]** precisely: "The principal fisheries of the Lummi included the reef-net locations for sockeye at Point Roberts, Village Point, off the east coast of San Juan Island as well as other locations in the San Juan Islands.") McDonough's affidavit is, in short, no evidence at all of Lummi fishing east of Whidbey Island and south of Fidalgo Island.

Third, the Lummi point to a single sentence from the 1973 trial testimony of a Lummi tribal elder named Forrest "Dutch" Kinley. Kinley was born around 1913, nearly six decades after the Treaty of Point Elliott. He had worked in fishing since he was around 12 years old—sometime in the early 1920s—and at one point served as chairman and a member of the Lummi tribal council. Kinley testified extensively on various topics regarding the Lummi tribe; indeed, the transcript of his testimony runs more than 90 pages. The Lummi point to a single page of this extensive transcript where, on redirect examination, Kinley testified that "I have fished in the Straits, I have fished *in Whidby Island south* and into the Canadian border" (emphasis added). When asked whether this and other fishing was "as a Lummi Indian at your usual and accustomed places," Kinley answered "Yes."

This fragment of transcript is patently insufficient to show historical Lummi fishing rights east of Whidbey Island, for at least two reasons. First, the parties agree that Judge Boldt did not cite Kinley's testimony at all in Finding of Fact 46. There is consequently no way to know, unlike in the case of Dr. Lane's reports, what Judge Boldt thought about

Kinley's testimony (if he thought about it at all). Second, there is no way to know what Kinley meant by his confusing statement that he had fished "in Whidby Island south." Kinley could have meant, quite uncontroversially, that he fished south of Whidbey Island in the "environs of **[—36—]** Seattle," the maximum range point of Lummi fishing described in Dr. Lane's report and in Judge Boldt's decree. Kinley could also have meant that he fished somewhere near the western coast of Whidbey Island, "south" of the Lummi reefnets in the San Juan Islands. There is absolutely no evidence that by fishing "in Whidby Island south," Kinley meant fishing in the waters *east* of Whidbey Island. Any inference to the contrary is entirely speculative.

Finally, the Lummi rely on an extraordinarily thin chain of inference from two statements by Dr. Lane regarding Lummi trade practices. Dr. Lane wrote that the Lummi "apparently imported various fibers and grasses from upriver Skagit and flint from Puget Sound." She also stated that the "imports" of the Semiahmoo people, whom Judge Boldt described as "subsumed" within the Lummi for purposes of the Treaty (*Final Decision I*, 384 F. Supp. at 360), included "[f]lint from Puget Sound and woven root hats from the West Coast." From these two isolated statements, the Lummi draw the following chain of inferences: (1) the Lummi traded fish and clams for "woven root hats" and "imported various fibers and grasses from upriver Skagit"; (2) "[b]ecause the Skagit River empties into waters disputed here," the Lummi must have traveled to the area surrounding the mouth of the Skagit River, on "the mainland shore on the eastern side of the disputed waters," to obtain the aforementioned "woven root hats" and "various fibers and grasses"; and (3) this travel, in turn, "confirms Lummi's travel (and fishing) throughout" the disputed waters. This speculative line of reasoning is unavailing.

For one thing, Dr. Lane describes the Lummi as having "imported" the land-based goods in question. This importation **{-1075-}** process *could* have taken the form of Lummi traders traveling to visit the Skagit; it could also have **[—37—]** occurred via Skagit traders traveling to visit the Lummi; or trade between the two areas could have occurred via middlemen from neither tribe. There is simply no way to know on this record. Second, even if the Lummi *did* trade by traveling to the mouth of the Skagit River, there is no evidence in the record that, upon their (hypothetical) arrival, the Lummi ever *fished* there—much less for any period of time sufficient to create "usual and accustomed" fishing grounds. *See Final Decision I*, 384 F. Supp. at 353, 356 (fishing must have been more than "occasional and incidental" to qualify an area as a "usual and accustomed" fishing ground). The Lummi's chain of inferences is entirely speculative and ungrounded in the record, as the district court in this case correctly observed.

In sum, there is no evidence in the record before Judge Boldt that the Lummi ever held usual and accustomed fishing grounds in waters east of Whidbey Island and south of Fidalgo Island. Nor did Judge Boldt mention, anywhere in the text of his description of historical Lummi fishing waters, the specific waters east of Whidbey Island at issue in this case. We thus conclude that, under the 1974 decree, the Lummi have no usual and accustomed fishing rights in those waters.

2

The record evidence cited by Judge Boldt in Finding of Fact 46 suggests, if anything, the opposite: that Lummi fishing was confined to areas west and, in particular, north of Whidbey Island.

Exhibit PL-94e is another 1895 affidavit in the *Alaska Packers* case, this time from a man named George Sknoughton. Sknoughton stated that he was a Lummi Indian who was 60 years old at the time of the affidavit; he was **[—38—]** therefore born around 1835, and would have been approximately 20 years old at the time of the Treaty of Point Elliott. Sknoughton explained that the Lummi at treaty times "got most of their fish at Point Roberts," a location some 40 miles to the north of the disputed waters here, and that "at no other place in the waters near the reservation did the sockeye salmon run [in] such large quantities or were they so easily caught."

Exhibit PL-94u is an 1895 affidavit from Harry Sewalton, who identified himself as a 65-year-old "member of the Lummi Tribe of Indians." According to Sewalton, "the main part of the food supply of the Lummi Indians since my boyhood" was taken at the reef adjacent to Point Roberts. Sewalton explained that "Point Roberts reef and the Reef at Vill[a]ge Point on Lummi Island . . . are the *only* two reefs in the waters of said County or in the Lower Sound upon which the said Lummi Indians can take salmon with hand or lift nets" (emphasis added).

Exhibit G-26 is a section of an untitled and undated report by an unknown author. The report states that "[t]he area claimed by the Indians who designate themselves as the Lummi Tribe of Indians and the San Juan Tribe of Indians includes the sites of autonomous Indian villages along the coastal region *north* of Puget Sound proper, around Bellingham, Lummi and Birch Bays, and on some of the islands of the San Juan Archipelago" (emphasis added). "Settlement of the northern area" inhabited by these Indians, according to the author, differed considerably from that in the "southern part of the basin" where "Seattle, Tacoma, and Olympia" were located.

Finally, we note that in spring 1973, the Washington Reef Net Owners Association served interrogatories **[—39—]** requesting the Lummi Nation to identify "*in full all locations* which are claimed to be its 'usual and **{–1076–}** accustomed fishing places and stations within and contiguous to the western portion of the State of Washington'" (emphasis added). The Lummi's answer repeated verbatim Dr. Lane's statement that "[t]he traditional fishing areas" extended "from what is now the Canadian border south to Anacortes"; the Lummi then cited a series of locations drawn directly from Dr. Lane's reports. These included Haro and Rosario Straits, "the salt waters contiguous to the San Juan Islands," Point Roberts, Lummi Island, Fidalgo Island, Birch Bay, Village Point, Cherry Point, and various reef-net locations in the San Juan Islands. These are essentially the same areas identified by Dr. Lane in her description and map of Lummi fishing locations—which makes perfect sense, because the Lummi specifically identified Dr. Lane as the source of their information regarding historical reef-net fishing. None of the areas the Lummi identified in 1973 are east of Whidbey Island; indeed, none are remotely near the "present environs of Seattle." The Lummi did state that "[t]here were, in addition, other important fisheries," but the Lummi did not name any of them, so that general statement is of no use. We find it telling that, asked directly to identify "in full all locations" claimed to be their "usual and accustomed" fishing grounds in 1973, the Lummi mentioned *no* fishing locations east of Whidbey Island and south of Fidalgo Island. The Lummi had the opportunity to claim such locations at trial and did not. **[—40—]**

C

Our precedent is in accord with these conclusions.

1

The most on-point case, and one involving two of the same bodies of water at issue here, is *Upper Skagit Indian Tribe v. Washington*, 590 F.3d 1020 (9th Cir. 2010) ("*Upper Skagit*"). That case involved a dispute between the Upper Skagit and the Suquamish as to whether Saratoga Passage and Skagit Bay—two of the bodies of water east of Whidbey Island at issue here—fell within the scope of yet another of Judge Boldt's vaguely worded classifications: "the marine waters of Puget Sound from the northern tip of Vashon Island to the Fraser River including Haro and Rosario Straits, the streams draining into the western side of this portion of Puget Sound and also Hood Canal." *Id.* at 1023 (quoting *Final Decision I*, 384 F. Supp. at 1049). As in this case, the waters at issue in *Upper Skagit* were east of Whidbey Island, and the statement of Judge Boldt's at issue in the case concerned "the marine waters of Puget Sound" between a southern anchor point and the Fraser River. (There, the southern anchor point was Vashon Island, which lies directly to the southwest of Seattle, the anchor point in this case. We see no relevant difference between these two anchor points; both are located due south of the disputed east-of-Whidbey-Island waters.)

Faced with a comparable (and equally vague) description of "the marine waters of Puget Sound" between a southern anchor point and "the Fraser River," the *Upper Skagit* court turned (just as we turn) to the record evidence before Judge Boldt. The *Upper Skagit* court found dispositive the fact that "[t]here is no evidence in the record before Judge Boldt that the Suquamish fished or traveled in the waters on the eastern **[—41—]** side of Whidbey Island, particularly in Saratoga Passage or Skagit Bay." 590 F.3d at 1025. (The same, as we have explained, is true of the Lummi in this case.) Moreover, "[a]lthough Lane's Report showed that several areas on the *west* shores of Area Four comprised Suquamish's on-reservation territory and fishing locations, there was no evidence from Lane or otherwise that the *east* shores of Area Four, as well as Skagit Bay and Saratoga Passage," were included. *Id.* (emphasis added). (Much the same is, as **{-1077-}** we have explained, true here: Dr. Lane's report contained a map showing a Lummi fishing site on the *west* shores of Fidalgo Island, but none on the *eastern* shores of the disputed waters.) Finally, when Judge Boldt "intended to include an area, it was specifically named"; thus, the fact that "Judge Boldt neglected to include Skagit Bay and Saratoga Passage in the Suquamish's U&A supports our conclusion that he did not intend for them to be included." *Id.* (The same is again true in this case; the fact that Judge Boldt named three areas outside the Whidbey-Fidalgo Island chain—the San Juan Islands, Bellingham Bay, and Seattle—but did not name any waters east of Whidbey Island, suggests that he did not intend to include them.) Ultimately, the *Upper Skagit* court concluded, the Suquamish U&A did not include the contested waters east of Whidbey Island. *Id.* at 1026. We reach precisely the same conclusion, regarding an analogous U&A description, in this case.

The Lummi attempt to distinguish *Upper Skagit* on the ground that the court referenced a 1975 bench ruling from Judge Boldt, and that no such bench ruling is present in the record of this case. We see no legally relevant distinction. The *Upper Skagit* court merely noted that Judge Boldt's ruling from the bench further confirmed the absence of any record evidence of tribal fishing by the Suquamish in the **[—42—]** disputed east-of-Whidbey-Island waters. 590 F.3d at 1025. We conclude that there is a similar lack of record evidence here.

If anything, *Upper Skagit* is the harder case. There, Judge Boldt's description was not limited to the undefined area of "northern" Puget Sound, as it is here; he instead described the Suquamish U&A as simply including, without qualification, "the marine waters of Puget Sound." 590 F.3d at 1023. Nonetheless, we declined to read into that language, in the absence of any record evidence, an inference that waters east of Whidbey Island were included. *Id.* at 1026. We reach the same conclusion here, and on easier facts. As the district court in this case correctly observed, if "Suquamish's U&A was determined to be ambiguous as to whether it included Skagit Bay and Saratoga Passage," then there is "no reason that Lummi's *more restrictive* U&A should unambiguously include the Disputed Waters" (emphasis altered).

2

Our 2017 decision in *Lummi III*, 876 F.3d 1004, 5 Adm. R. 443, is likewise in accord. In that case, we "examine[d] the record before Judge Boldt to clarify his intent" regarding a particular "nautical path" traced "from the San Juan Islands to Seattle" in *Lummi I*, 235 F.3d at 452. *See Lummi III*, 876 F.3d at 1009–10, 5 Adm. R. at 445–46. We concluded that Judge Boldt had meant to include waters along that "nautical path" in the Lummi's usual and accustomed fishing territory. *Id.* at 1009–10, 5 Adm. R. at 445–46 (citation omitted). That nautical path does not cut through any waters east of Whidbey Island, so neither *Lummi I* nor *Lummi III* governs the waters at issue in this case.

The Lummi nonetheless urge us to read *Lummi III* to stand for the broad proposition that a court may infer Lummi **[—43—]** fishing rights in *any* area of Puget Sound between the Fraser River and Seattle through which the Lummi might, at some point, have traveled. We have never held that, and we decline to do so now. And for good reason: that limitless holding would be inconsistent with both the text of the decree and well-established precedent. **{-1078-}**

Again, Judge Boldt's decree clearly states that, although "[m]arine waters were . . . used as thoroughfares for travel by Indians who trolled en route," this sort of "occasional and incidental trolling *was not considered to make the marine waters traveled thereon the usual and accustomed fishing grounds of the transiting Indians.*" 384 F. Supp. at 353 (emphasis added). Judge Boldt plainly did not believe that the possibility of travel in disputed waters was sufficient to support a finding of U&A fishing there. He stated precisely the opposite. Accordingly, we cannot, when reading ambiguous language in the decree, understand Judge Boldt to have violated his own cardinal principle for discerning usual and accustomed fishing grounds (*i.e.*, by recognizing fishing rights for the Lummi in waters east of Whidbey Island, where, as we have explained, there is no record evidence that such fishing ever occurred). *See Suquamish*, 871 F.3d at 848; *Tulalip Tribes*, 794 F.3d at 1133, 3 Adm. R. at 579; *see also Sauk-Suiattle*, 66 F.4th at 771, 774, 11 Adm. R. at 447–48, 450. Since we have thrice concluded (today makes four) that Judge Boldt's vague description of the Lummi's U&A is ambiguous, that same admonition applies here and precludes the Lummi's sweeping argument. *See Lummi III*, 876 F.3d at 1008–09, 5 Adm. R. at 444–45; *Lummi II*, 763 F.3d at 1187, 2 Adm. R. at 494; *Lummi I*, 235 F.3d at 449.

The Lummi's limitless reading of *Lummi III* suffers from an additional flaw—namely, that it would render *Lummi III* directly inconsistent with *Upper Skagit*, 590 F.3d 1020, in which we *declined* to infer fishing rights east of Whidbey **[—44—]** Island from materially identical language in another of Judge Boldt's U&A descriptions. *Id.* at 1023, 1026. As we have said, the two cases are, properly understood, perfectly consistent. *Lummi III* concluded, after "examin[ing] the record before Judge Boldt to clarify his intent," that Judge Boldt had meant to include waters along a specific west-of-Whidbey-Island "nautical path" in the Lummi's historical fishing territory. 876 F.3d at 1009–10, 5 Adm. R. at 445–46. *Upper Skagit* concluded, after engaging in the same sort of inquiry, that Judge Boldt had *not* meant to include certain east-of-Whidbey-Island waters in the Suquamish's historical fishing territory. 590 F.3d at 1023, 1026. We apply in this case the same standards we applied in *Lummi III* and *Upper Skagit*. We have "examine[d] the record before Judge Boldt to clarify his intent" regarding a set of waters as to which the decree is ambiguous. *Lummi III*, 876 F.3d at 1009, 5 Adm. R. at 445. Because there is no evidence in that record of historical Lummi fishing east of Whidbey Island, we decline to read the decree to grant the Lummi fishing rights east of Whidbey Island. *See Sauk-Suiattle*, 66 F.4th at 771, 774, 11 Adm. R. at 447–48, 450; *Suquamish*, 871 F.3d at 848; *Tulalip Tribes*, 794 F.3d at 1133, 3 Adm. R. at 579.

IV

The remainder of the dispute before us is easily resolved. The S'Klallam Tribe has filed a cross-appeal for the sole purpose of objecting to what it views as "damaging and erroneously broad statements" in the district court's summary judgment order that, in the S'Klallam's view, appear to suggest that many Indian tribes fished in waters *west* of Whidbey Island, where the S'Klallam claim fishing interests. Specifically, the S'Klallam express concern about two sentences of the "current language in the district court decision": first, the district court's statement that "the Ninth Circuit . . . previously determined that the waters west of **[—45—]** Whidbey Island served as the primary thoroughfare for tribes traveling between the Fraser River and the environs of Seattle," and second, the district court's statement that these waters were "the main north-south thoroughfare" for tribes transiting through Puget Sound en route to Seattle. In the S'Klallam's view, this language incorrectly implies that "*other* tribes," in addition to the Lummi, now have leeway to "also claim the western **{-1079-}** route as their primary route" for fishing and travel (emphasis added). The S'Klallam's concern appears to be that an unknown number of other tribes may seize on the district court's language to attempt to justify increased fishing west of Whidbey

Island, potentially leading to new incursions upon the "S'Klallam U&A on the west side of Whidbey Island." The S'Klallam ask us to make "modifications to the district court's order" in response; in other words, they request that we delete (or change the phrasing of) the passages to which the S'Klallam object. The S'Klallam take no position, however, on whether we should affirm or reverse the underlying judgment in the dispute between the Lummi and the Swinomish, Tulalip, and Upper Skagit; indeed, they concede that their desired modifications to the district court's order "may or may not reverse the outcome."

Generally speaking, a litigant may "appeal only if the judgment gives him less relief than he considers himself entitled to"; he "cannot appeal a judgment merely because there are passages in the court's opinion that displease him," even if those passages may "come back to haunt him in a future case." *Abbs v. Sullivan*, 963 F.2d 918, 924 (7th Cir. 1992). In any event, we have already concluded, in the ordinary course of deciding the dispute between the Lummi and the Swinomish, Tulalip, and Upper Skagit, that neither *Lummi III* nor *Upper Skagit* stands for the proposition that **[—46—]** all tribes (indeed, any tribe besides the Lummi) traveled and fished west of Whidbey Island. (The district court explained much the same in its order denying reconsideration.) Nor, as we have just explained, do our cases stand for the proposition that the mere possibility of travel through disputed waters is sufficient to support a grant of U&A rights there—a principle Judge Boldt directly rejected and we likewise have never accepted. Having already clarified both points in the S'Klallam's favor in the ordinary course of disposing of the Lummi's appeal, we consider the S'Klallam's appeal moot.

We decline to address the parties' dispute regarding whether the Lummi may initiate a future subproceeding *under Paragraph 25(a)(6)*, which addresses a separate basis for jurisdiction not presented to the district court in this case. *Cf. Muckleshoot Indian Tribe v. Tulalip Tribes*, 944 F.3d 1179 (9th Cir. 2019). We do not understand that question to have been resolved by the district court and we decline to address it in the first instance on appeal. *Merritt v. Countrywide Fin. Corp.*, 759 F.3d 1023, 1035 (9th Cir. 2014).

V

The district court's grant of summary judgment to the Swinomish, Tulalip, and Upper Skagit is AFFIRMED. The S'Klallam's cross-appeal of the district court's grant of summary judgment is DISMISSED AS MOOT. The S'Klallam's appeal of the district court's denial of the S'Klallam's motion for reconsideration is likewise DISMISSED AS MOOT.

United States Court of Appeals for the Ninth Circuit

No. 22-35195

WESTERN TOWBOAT CO.
vs.
VIGOR MARINE, LLC

Appeal from the United States District Court for the Western District of Washington

Decided: October 31, 2023

Citation: 85 F.4th 919, 11 Adm. R. 469 (9th Cir. 2023).

Before **FLETCHER, PAEZ,** and **VANDYKE,** Circuit Judges.

[—4—] {-921-} **FLETCHER,** Circuit Judge: **{-922-}**

Vigor Marine, LLC ("Vigor") hired Western Towboat Co. ("Western") to tow a drydock from Seattle, Washington, to Ensenada, Mexico, where it was to be broken down for scrap. While off the coast of California, the drydock was damaged in a storm. In an attempt to bring the drydock to shelter in Monterey Bay, Western's tug towed the drydock into the Monterey Bay National Marine Sanctuary (the "Sanctuary"). While in the Sanctuary, the drydock capsized and sank. Because the drydock sank in the Sanctuary, the parties were exposed to liability under the National Marine Sanctuaries Act of 1972 ("NMSA"), 16 U.S.C. §§ 1431–45c-1.

Western sued Vigor in federal district court in admiralty. Western sought to recover the towing fee under its contract with Vigor, and a declaratory judgment that it would not be liable for any damages or penalty sought by the government **[—5—]** under the NMSA. Vigor counterclaimed, claiming breach of contract and negligence by Western.

The district court took great care in its handling of this case. The court determined that any decision on the issue of liability under the NMSA would be premature and dismissed for lack of subject matter jurisdiction all claims under the NMSA. *Western Towboat Co. v. Vigor Marine, LLC* (*Western Towboat I*), 544 F. Supp. 3d 1100, 1113–16 (W.D. Wash. 2021). Neither party appeals that dismissal. The court granted partial summary judgment to Vigor, holding that Western had been negligent as a matter of law in allowing the drydock to sink in the Sanctuary. *Id.* 1126–28. After a trial on the remaining issues, the court denied both parties' contract claims and held that both had been negligent. In a comparative negligence analysis, the court found that Vigor was sixty percent negligent and Western was forty percent negligent. Limiting Vigor's recovery to forty percent of the $100,000 not reimbursed by Vigor's insurance, the district court awarded Vigor $40,000. *Western Towboat Co. v. Vigor Marine, LLC* (*Western Towboat III*), 575 F. Supp. 3d 1318, 1339 (W.D. Wash. 2021).

Both parties appealed. We affirm in all respects but one. We vacate the award of prejudgment interest to allow recalculation by the district court.

I. Background

Vigor is a commercial shipyard in Washington State. It owned a drydock, YFD-70, constructed in 1945. A drydock is a floating enclosed basin that allows cleaning or repairing parts of a ship that would ordinarily be underwater. *Dry Dock, International Maritime Dictionary* (2d ed. 1961). The ship enters the drydock through open gates while the **[—6—]** drydock is partially submerged. The gates are then closed and the water is pumped out of the drydock, leaving the entire ship exposed. *Id.*

In 2013, Vigor hired Heger Dry Dock, Inc. ("Heger") to perform an ultrasonic gauging survey of YFD-70. An ultrasonic gauging survey evaluates the steel's thickness. The purpose of the survey was to determine the drydock's continuing commercial viability. The survey showed impaired longitudinal stiffeners and "heavy corrosion" of portions of the drydock.

In 2015, the pump, two reach rods, and a valve broke on the drydock. Due to the cost of repair, Vigor determined it was no longer economical to maintain the drydock. Vigor sold the drydock to Amaya Curiel Corp. ("Amaya") for scrapping at a shipyard in Ensenada, Mexico. Due to dock constraints in Ensenada,

Amaya and Vigor agreed to have the drydock towed to Ensenada **{-923-}** rather than transported on the deck of a ship.

YFD-70 could be towed in two different configurations. First, it could be towed in a single piece, without disassembling the drydock. Second, its end sections could be separated and stacked on the center section, resulting in a three-piece tow. If a drydock is towed in the open ocean, high waves cause structural stress—"hogging" and "sagging." Such stress is reduced in a three-piece tow. U.S. Navy guidance specific to YFD-70 provides, "The dock has been designed to facilitate towing at sea. When towed, the end sections are stowed on the center section." U.S. Navy, *Floating Dry Docks YFD-68, YFD-69, YFD-70, YFD-71: General Information and Operating Manual* 4 (1944).

To replace YFD-70, Vigor arranged for a sister drydock that was subject to the same Navy guidance to be towed **[—7—]** through the ocean from Portland to Seattle. To determine whether that drydock, YFD-69, could be towed safely, Vigor hired Heger to conduct an engineering study. Heger did multiple computer simulations, towing YFD-69 in both the one-piece and three-piece configurations. Based on the simulations, Heger determined that YFD-69 could be towed in either configuration, with different restrictions depending on which configuration was used.

Western is a maritime towing company predominantly operating in Alaska and Washington. One of Vigor's naval architects, Daniel Keen, contacted Western's president, Bob Shrewsbury, for a price quotation to tow YFD-70 from Seattle to Ensenada. Despite the drydock's condition, Shrewsbury testified that he felt Western could tow it "at the right time of the year and in decent conditions."

Vigor and Western entered into a Standard Towage Agreement (the "Tow Agreement"). The agreement provided that Western would tow the drydock for $142,800 plus the cost of fuel (the "contractual fee"). The agreement provided that the tow would start on or about October 7, 2016. However, the agreement provided that the tow depended on favorable weather conditions. If favorable weather conditions did not exist by November 7, 2016, either party could reschedule the tow dates.

Vigor prepared YFD-70 for towing. As part of the preparation, Vigor hired Captain Richard Shaw from Bowditch Marine, Inc. to conduct a marine warranty survey and provide tow recommendations. Shaw found that Vigor had improved YFD-70 structurally and had outfitted it with proper equipment in preparation for the tow. He concluded that the tug and drydock were suitable for an ocean tow from **[—8—]** Seattle to Ensenada if there were a favorable weather forecast.

Shaw recommended restrictions designed to minimize stress on the drydock. He recommended that the tow avoid seas with wave heights of greater than eight to ten feet, and that the tug not leave any safe port or sheltered water without first determining that the weather forecast conformed to these restrictions. Shaw made no recommendation whether the drydock should be towed in one or three pieces.

Shaw's survey was the only examination of the drydock in preparation for the tow. Vigor did not tell Shaw about Heger's 2013 ultrasonic gauging survey of the drydock. Neither Heger nor any other firm was asked to perform an engineering study on YFD-70 comparable to the study that had been performed on YFD-69 prior to its tow from Portland to Seattle.

A tow plan provides recommendations to a tug captain on how to perform a voyage. Western created a tow plan for the YFD-70, which it amended after receiving **{-924-}** Shaw's report. The plan provided that an ocean-going tug, OCEAN RANGER, with Captain Stephen McGavock as master, would tow YFD-70 out of Puget Sound and past Cape Flattery, into the ocean. The tug would then go south along the coast to Mexico. McGavock testified at trial there were no realistic ports of refuge between Cape Flattery and San Francisco.

After an initial delay due to unfavorable weather conditions, the OCEAN RANGER left Seattle on October 17, 2016. On October 19 and

20, while near the mouth of the Columbia River, the tug and tow encountered winds of twenty-five knots and wave heights between ten and twelve feet. The tug and tow made it through this weather without **[—9—]** incident and continued south. On October 21 and 22, off the coast of southern Oregon, waves reached as high as thirteen to fifteen feet. The tug and tow again made it through without incident. On October 24, a "major wind event" occurred between Point Arena and Bodega Bay, north of San Francisco, with wind speeds of over thirty knots and waves heights more than eleven feet. On October 25, waves and wind remained high from Point Reyes to San Francisco.

On October 25, while slightly north of San Francisco, McGavock noticed that the drydock had a port bow list. He contacted Shrewsbury, who in turn consulted Keen, Vigor's naval architect. Shrewsbury and Keen suggested that the best course of action might be to bring the drydock into San Francisco Bay. However, as the condition of the drydock deteriorated, McGavock believed it was unsafe to do so as it could sink and block the shipping channel into San Francisco Bay.

McGavock also expressed concern to Shrewsbury about the drydock sinking in the Greater Farallones National Marine Sanctuary west of San Francisco Bay. The tug and tow left the Farallones Sanctuary in an attempt to reach Monterey, south of San Francisco Bay. On the evening of October 25, McGavock brought the tow into the Monterey Bay Sanctuary. Darkness and fog made it difficult to assess the condition of the drydock. McGavock maintained the OCEAN RANGER's position in the Sanctuary that night, with a plan to assess the situation in the morning. At the time, McGavock believed the drydock would stay afloat until morning.

At about two in the morning of October 26, the fog cleared enough to allow the crew to see that the drydock's condition had worsened. Soon thereafter, the drydock began **[—10—]** to capsize. McGavock dumped the tow line and released the drydock in order to save the OCEAN RANGER and its crew. The drydock sank in the Sanctuary.

On January 19, 2021, the United States National Oceanic and Atmospheric Administration sent a letter to Vigor, Western, and Amaya informing them that YFD-70 had sunk in the Monterey Bay Sanctuary. According to the letter, the three could be responsible for damage to the Sanctuary, costs to assess the damage, and civil penalties under 16 U.S.C. § 1437(d).

In an attempt to mitigate damages, Vigor paid for a survey to locate the sunken drydock and assess damage to the Sanctuary. The survey cost $351,980.14. Combined with related expenses, Vigor calculated its costs to be $415,441.67. On advice of counsel, Western declined to cooperate with mitigation efforts.

II. Procedural History

Western filed suit against Vigor in district court for the Western District of Washington in admiralty. Vigor answered and counter-claimed.

The parties brought cross motions for summary judgment. Western claimed that **{-925-}** Vigor breached the Tow Agreement by failing to render a seaworthy tow and failing to pay for services rendered. Vigor claimed that Western had breached the Tow Agreement by failing to render reasonable assistance when the drydock developed a list. The district court denied summary judgment on both claims, holding that there were disputed material facts that needed to be resolved. *Western Towboat I*, 544 F. Supp. 3d at 1117, 1119. Vigor also argued that Western was negligent in allowing the drydock to sink in the Marine Sanctuary. The **[—11—]** court granted partial summary judgment on this issue, holding that Western had been negligent as a matter of law. *Id.* at 1125–28.

After a five-day bench trial, the district court ruled against Western on its claim for breach of contract, holding that Western had "breached its duty of prudent seamanship" in agreeing to perform the tow in mid-October. *Western Towboat III*, 575 F. Supp. 3d at 1337. The court also ruled against Vigor on its counterclaim for breach of contract, holding that Western had rendered reasonable assistance. *Id.* at 1338. The court further held that Vigor was negligent in failing to exercise diligence in rendering a seaworthy tow to Western. *Id.* at 1338–39. Applying comparative negligence analysis, the court found that Western was forty percent negligent because it had undertaken the tow in October and then allowed the drydock to sink in the Sanctuary rather than somewhere else. *Id.* at 1339. It found Vigor sixty percent negligent for failing to tender a seaworthy drydock. *Id.*

Vigor had been compensated by its insurance company for all of its mitigation expenditures except for a $100,000 deductible. In a post-trial ruling, the district court declined to apply the collateral source rule, holding that Western was not liable for Vigor's expenditures in excess of its non-reimbursed deductible. *Western Towboat Co. v. Vigor Marine, LLC* (*Western Towboat II*), 566 F. Supp. 3d 1095, 1101 (W.D. Wash. 2021). The district court awarded Vigor $40,000, based on Western's forty percent comparative negligence. *Western Towboat III*, 575 F. Supp. 3d at 1339.

Both parties appealed. **[—12—]**

III. Standards of Review

We review de novo summary judgment rulings. *Devereaux v. Abbey*, 263 F.3d 1070, 1074 (9th Cir. 2001) (en banc). Summary judgment is appropriate if, when "viewing the evidence in the light most favorable to the nonmoving party, there is no genuine dispute as to any material fact." *Zetwick v. Cnty. of Yolo*, 850 F.3d 436, 440 (9th Cir. 2017) (internal quotation marks omitted). Factual findings of a district court sitting in admiralty, including comparative negligence findings, are reviewed for clear error. *In re White Cloud Charter Boat Co.*, 813 F.2d 1513, 1517 (9th Cir. 1987). The application of the collateral source rule is reviewed de novo. *United States v. City of Twin Falls*, 806 F.2d 862, 873 (9th Cir. 1986), *rev'd on other grounds by Ass'n of Flight Attendants, AFL-CIO v. Horizon Air Indus., Inc.*, 976 F.2d 54, 551-52 (9th Cir. 1992). We review a district court's award of prejudgment interest for abuse of discretion. *Alkmeon Naviera, S.A. v. M/V Marina L*, 633 F.2d 789, 797 (9th Cir. 1980).

IV. Discussion

The parties raise a number of arguments on appeal. We analyze them in turn.

A. Grant of Partial Summary Judgment to Vigor

The district court granted partial summary judgment against Western, holding as a matter of law that Western was **{-926-}** negligent in allowing the drydock to sink in the Monterey Bay Marine Sanctuary. The district court wrote:

> [T]he record only indicates Western's intention that the OCEAN RANGER wait in deeper water until daylight, without regard to **[—13—]** where the vessel sat in relation to the boundaries of the Marine Sanctuary. Despite Western's recognition that the Drydock was sinking as the OCEAN RANGER headed away from San Francisco Bay, the record reflects no understanding by Western that the Drydock was inside a marine sanctuary at the time it sank, nor any awareness as to the practical consequences—whether legal, environmental, or economic—of releasing the tow line in that location.

Western Towboat I, 544 F. Supp. 3d at 1127 (internal citations omitted).

On reconsideration, the district court recognized that there was evidence that McGavock knew he was in the Sanctuary. But it reaffirmed its holding that Western was unaware of the consequences of allowing the drydock to sink in the Sanctuary. It therefore left intact its partial summary judgment against Western. *See Western Towboat Co. v. Vigor Marine, LLC*, No. C20-0416-RSM, 2021 WL 2584911, at *2 (W.D. Wash. June 23, 2021) ("[I]t remains undisputed that Captain McGavock failed to understand the hazards presented by that sanctuary to a tug towing a sinking drydock.").

Western argues that there were material issues of fact that precluded the grant of partial summary judgment. We agree with the district court that there was no evidence in the record that anyone at Western, including McGavock, was aware of the legal consequences of allowing the drydock to sink in the Monterey Bay Marine Sanctuary. We therefore affirm the grant of partial summary judgment to Vigor. **[—14—]**

B. Collateral Source Rule

Vigor sought recovery of the $415,441.67 it spent in seeking to mitigate the damages that Vigor, Western, and Amaya might owe to the federal government under the NMSA. The district court held that claims relating to future potential damages and penalties owed to the government under NMSA were so speculative that the court had no subject matter jurisdiction over them. *Western Towboat I*, 544 F. Supp. 3d at 1114–15. The parties do not dispute that conclusion. However, Vigor's expenditures to mitigate damages were not speculative.

Vigor was reimbursed by its insurance carrier for all but $100,000 of its expenditures. Vigor argued under the collateral source rule that reimbursement from Western should be calculated based on the full $415,441.67. The district court held that the collateral source rule did not apply, and that any reimbursement from Western should be calculated based only on the $100,000 for which Vigor was out of pocket. *Western Towboat II*, 566 F. Supp. 3d at 1101. We agree.

The collateral source rule allows a tortfeasor to be assessed the full amount of damages when the victim receives compensation from a source collateral to the tortfeasor. *Gypsum Carrier, Inc. v. Handelsman*, 307 F.2d 525, 534 (9th Cir. 1962). The collateral source rule applies in admiralty cases. *The Atlas*, 93 U.S. 302, 310 (1876); *Gypsum Carrier*, 307 F.2d at 535. The rule applies only to money received from a "wholly independent" source. *Dillingham Tug & Barge Corp. v. Collier Carbon & Chem. Corp.*, 707 F.2d 1086, 1091 (9th Cir. 1983) (internal quotation marks omitted). To determine if a source is wholly independent, we look to "'the purpose and nature of the fund **[—15—]** and **{-927-}** of the payments,' and not merely at their source." *Russo v. Matson Nav. Co.*, 486 F.2d 1018, 1020 (9th Cir. 1973) (quoting *Gypsum Carrier*, 307 F.2d at 534 n.31).

Vigor's insurance policy was not a wholly independent source. The Tow Agreement required Vigor to purchase insurance, and Western determined its contractual fee based in part on Vigor's doing so. As the district court correctly noted, agreed payments to Vigor were calculated "pursuant to insurance policies that Vigor was required to procure under the Towing Agreement." *Western Towboat II*, 566 F. Supp. 3d at 1101. The collateral source rule therefore does not apply.

C. Comparative Negligence

After trial, the district court held that neither Western nor Vigor could recover for breach of the Tow Agreement. However, with respect to Vigor's $100,000 out-of-pocket expenditures in seeking to mitigate damages, it held that both Western and Vigor could be held liable for negligence.

The district court held that both Western and Vigor were negligent. Western was negligent in two respects. First, "Western's negligence led to the Drydock sinking inside the marine sanctuary when it breached its duty to navigate." *Western Towboat III*, 575 F. Supp. 3d at 1338. Second, "Western's negligence in agreeing to undertake the specialty tow in mid-October with only one realistic port of refuge after Cape Flattery contributed to the Drydock's sinking." *Id.* Vigor was negligent in failing to exercise diligence "in tendering a seaworthy vessel to Western." *Id.* Vigor also "caused the Drydock to undertake a voyage where it would likely hit conditions in excess of weather conditions the 71-year-old Drydock could withstand. Vigor's decision therefore contributed to the Drydock's sinking when it hit **[—16—]** the unpredicted storm on October 24." *Id.* The court held that Western was forty percent negligent and that Vigor was sixty percent negligent. *Id.* at 1339.

Western and Vigor both argue that the district court erred in its comparative negligence analysis, but we find no clear error.

D. Other Objections

1. Prejudgment Interest

The district court awarded prejudgment interest on the $40,000 award against Western, running from the date the drydock sank rather than from the date Vigor made its expenditures. *Western Towboat III*, 575 F. Supp. 3d at 1339. Western objects, contending that interest should run from the date of the expenditures. Vigor does not dispute that interest should run from the date of the expenditures.

Instead, Vigor argues that the invited error doctrine applies on the ground that Western submitted the proposed final judgment containing the interest award to which it objects. *See, e.g., Sovak v. Chugai Pharm. Co.*, 280 F.3d 1266, 1270 (9th Cir. 2002). However, in its Findings of Fact and Conclusion of Law, the district court selected the wrong date for calculating prejudgment interest. After the district court did so, Western submitted its proposed final judgment using that date. Western thus did not invite the error. We vacate and remand to allow the district court to recalculate the prejudgment interest based on the correct date.

2. Hold Harmless Agreement

Section 8 of the Tow Agreement provided that the parties "shall be separately responsible for, and shall indemnify and hold harmless each other from and against . . . all loss, **[—17—]** damage, expenses, **{-928-}** claims, liabilities and suits arising out of or relating to property owned by it." The district court held that this provision requires the parties to hold each other harmless only for injury to "their own property." *Western Towboat I*, 544 F. Supp. 3d at 1121. That is, "parties are responsible for claims arising out of or relating to their own property such that Vigor is barred from recouping loss of the Drydock, but not from recouping costs incurred as a result of Western's negligent injury to third parties." *Id.*

Western argues to us that "the parties specifically agreed in the Tow Agreement not to seek a negligence recovery for any insurance deductible." Vigor spent the non-reimbursed $100,000 in an attempt to mitigate damages potentially owed to the United States—a third party to the Tow Agreement. In making its hold harmless argument under the agreement, Western does not challenge the district court's ruling that the hold harmless provision does not apply to claims brought by third parties. Western has therefore waived the argument that it cannot be required to reimburse Vigor for all or part of its $100,000 deductible. *See Greenwood v. F.A.A.*, 28 F.3d 971, 977 (9th Cir. 1994).

3. Percentage Share of Contractual Fee

Section 1(A) of the Tow Agreement provides Western shall be paid, even if the tow is lost, "except to the extent" the loss arises from Western's negligence. Western argues that under this provision it is entitled to sixty percent of the contractual fee because it was only forty percent at fault.

Western never made this argument to the district court. We generally do not entertain arguments on appeal that were not presented to the district court. *Villanueva v. California*, 986 F.3d 1158, 1164 n.4 (9th Cir. 2021). Western has given no reason why we should do so in this case. **[—18—]**

V. Conclusion

For the reasons provided above, we affirm the district court in all respects by one. We vacate the award of prejudgment interest and remand for calculation based on the correct date. The parties shall bear their own costs on appeal. *See* Fed. R. App. P. 39(a)(4).

AFFIRMED in part, VACATED in part, and REMANDED.

(Reporter's Note: Opinion dissenting in part follows on p. 475).

[—18—] {-928-} VANDYKE, Circuit Judge, dissenting in part:

I agree with the majority that Western waived its appeal argument about being owed a partial contract fee. But the majority is incorrect that Western waived the argument that under the tow agreement the parties agreed to hold each other harmless for any portion of the other's insurance deductible. As the majority acknowledges, Western argued in its opening brief that section 8 of the agreement requires the parties to "look solely" to their own insurance for coverage of "any" and "all" losses they might incur, including payment of their own insurance's deductibles. Western's argument that any and all deductible payments for a party's insurance coverage were the "sole[]" responsibility of the party who purchased that insurance necessarily includes any deductible payments paid out because of claims brought by third parties. Because Western's section 8 argument is both correct and not waived, I would hold that Western does not owe Vigor any compensation for Vigor's deductible payment and would not reach many of the remaining issues the majority unnecessarily decides. I thus respectfully dissent in part. **[—19—] {-929-}**

I. Western Towboat Waived the Argument as to the Partial Recovery of the Contract Fee by Not Raising It Before the District Court.

The majority correctly concludes that Western waived its argument about recovering part of its contract fee. Western argued in district court that it is owed the entirety of its contract fee, and on appeal it now instead argues only that it is owed a portion of that fee comparable to Vigor's share of the negligence that resulted in the drydock sinking. This is an entirely new argument made under section 1(A) of the agreement, and as the majority correctly observes, this court generally does not consider arguments raised for the first time on appeal. *Villanueva v. California*, 986 F.3d 1158, 1164 n.4 (9th Cir. 2021).

II. Western Did Not Waive the Argument that It Cannot Be Required to Reimburse Vigor for All or Part of Its Insurance Deductible.

I disagree, however, with the majority's conclusion that Western waived a challenge to the district court's ruling that section 8 of the towing agreement holds the parties harmless only for injury to their own property, i.e., not for claims brought by third parties. Across four pages of its opening brief, Western argued that the district court was wrong, because section 8 contains a knock-for-knock provision that requires the parties to "look solely" to their insurances for coverage of *any* losses they might incur "rather than maintain claims against each other based on negligence or fault." And Western specifically argued that this global reciprocal hold harmless rule expressly applies to "*all* ... deductibles ... applicable to such insurance." (Emphasis added). **[—20—]**

The majority appears to find great import in the fact that Western argued that "the parties specifically agreed in the Tow Agreement not to seek a negligence recovery for any insurance deductible," without expressly explaining that by saying "*any* insurance deductible" it really meant "any"—and thus includes an insurance deductible paid out as a result of a claim brought by a third party. But finding waiver based on that is wholly unwarranted. If section 8 universally holds the parties reciprocally harmless for "*any* insurance deductible" paid by the other party, as Western expressly argued, it necessarily holds the parties harmless for the subset of insurance deductibles paid as a result of third-party claims. That is inherent in the plain meaning of "any," which means "every" or "at all." *The Merriam-Webster Dictionary* 47 (1990). Using the majority's flawed and illogically parsimonious reasoning, one might just as well conclude that when Western made its universal argument about the contract's allocation of responsibility for paying "any" deductible, it neglected to argue that "any insurance deductible" includes deductibles paid out on Tuesdays, or deductibles paid out if the drydock were to sink in water deeper than 100 feet. "Any" and "all" means what everyone knows those words mean, and Western therefore did not waive the argument that the district court erred in requiring Western to reimburse Vigor for part of Vigor's deductible.

III. Because Section 8 Contains a Pertinent and Dispositive Knock-for-Knock Provision, I Would Hold that Western Owes Nothing to Vigor and Would Not Reach the Other Three Issues the Majority Decides.

Because the majority concludes that Western waived its argument about Vigor's responsibility for its own insurance deductible, the majority never decides that argument. I **[—21—]** would, and I would conclude **{-930-}** that Western is correct that section 8 holds it harmless for any portion of Vigor's insurance deductible.

The plain text of section 8 allows for no other conclusion. Start with section 8(A), where the parties note that:

> It is the intent of the parties that the insurance identified in this section cover *all* losses, damages, liabilities and suits incident to the services being provided, and that the parties shall look *solely* to such insurances ... rather than maintain claims against each other based upon negligence or fault. To that end, the parties agree to procure and maintain the following insurances, to promptly submit and prosecute all claims against such insurances, *and to look solely to such insurances for recovery.*

(Emphases added). Section 8(A) makes clear that the insurances identified in subsequent subsections should cover "all" losses incident to the drydock tow, and that the parties must "look solely" to those insurances for recovery of losses.

Section 8(B) then makes clear that the parties are each responsible for their own deductibles for the insurances they are required to purchase under the contract, including policies for "pollution and environmental liability insurance, including coverage for damages [and] cleanup and restoration costs." Then section 8(B)(3) states clearly: the party "required to procure and maintain an insurance as above shall be *solely* responsible for the payment of *all* ... deductibles ... applicable to such insurance." (Emphases **[—22—]** added). In other words, section 8(B) expressly provides that Vigor is *solely* responsible for *all* deductibles it might have to pay out under its own required environmental liability insurance policy that covered its site survey of the marine sanctuary.

The contract language is clear enough, and there is nothing inappropriate about the parties' agreement thus allocating responsibility. Such knock-for-knock provisions have long been common in contracts for various risky maritime undertakings. *See* Graydon S. Staring, *Meting out Misfortune: How the Courts Are Allotting the Costs if Maritime Injury in the Eighties*, 45 La. L. Rev. 907, 917 (1985). And because proper analysis of Western's unwaived argument about Vigor's insurance deductible disposes of many of the other issues addressed by the majority, rendering analysis of those issues superfluous, I would not decide those unnecessary issues in this published opinion.

First, the majority affirms in section IV(A) of its opinion the district court's grant of partial summary judgment against Western on the issue of whether Western was negligent in allowing the drydock to sink in the marine sanctuary. But because the only money that Vigor is out of pocket is its $100,000 insurance deductible, and section 8 of the contract precludes Vigor from recovering compensation from Western for that deductible payment regardless of whether Western was negligent, the majority addresses that issue unnecessarily.

Second, the majority affirms in section IV(B) of its opinion the district court's holding that the collateral source rule does not apply to all the roughly $415,000 Vigor spent seeking to mitigate any damages the United States might be owed under the National Marine Sanctuary Act, 16 U.S.C. **[—23—]** § 1431, on the grounds that Vigor's insurance proceeds were not wholly independent from Western. *See Dillingham Tug & Barge Corp. v. Collier*

Carbon & Chem. Corp., 707 F.2d 1086, 1088 (9th Cir. 1983).

The majority correctly notes that determining whether or not the proceeds are wholly independent requires this court to look to "the purpose and nature **{-931-}** of" the proceeds, as well as to their "source." *See Russo v. Matson Nav. Co.*, 486 F.2d 1018. 1020 (9th Cir. 1973). That typically includes examining at least whether the insurance policy provides for waiver of subrogation, lists the tower as a second insured, or contains other terms written for the tower's benefit. 2 Thomas J. Schoenbaum, Admiralty and Maritime Law § 12:9 (2d ed. 2022); George W. Nowell, *Subrogation: Selected Bars, Waivers and Pitfalls*, 7 U. of S.F. Maritime L.J. 421, 459–60 (1995) (additional considerations). The examination of the policy language must be punctilious because public policy concerns unique to the towing industry strictly limit towers' ability to offset *any* liability for their negligence via outside insurance. *Bisso v. Inland Waterways Corp.*, 349 U.S. 85, 91 (1955); *McLean v. Runyon*, 222 F.3d 1150, 1156 (9th Cir. 2000); *see* Charles S. Donovan, *Exculpatory and Benefit of Insurance Clauses in Towage and Pilotage*, 70 Tulane L. Rev. 605, 605–06 (1995).

Yet the parties agree that the record does not even identify the *source* of the proceeds, that is, which particular insurance policy paid Vigor. The district court sprang over that gap in the record with a "logical leap" to "surmise" that the paying policy must be one whose terms not only mirror what section 8 requires but are also limited in all relevant ways to *only* what section 8 requires. The majority adopts that same approach, but it need not do so. We need not even reach the question of whether the collateral source rule **[—24—]** applies here because the valid knock-for-knock provision in section 8 of the contract precludes Vigor from obtaining any compensation from Western. I therefore would not reach the issue.

Third, the majority holds in section IV(C) of its opinion that the district court did not commit clear error when it apportioned liability for negligence with respect to Vigor's deductible expenditure 40 percent to Western and 60 percent to Vigor. Again, that is unnecessary given that section 8 renders any such division irrelevant. Whether Western is 99 percent or 1 percent contributorily negligent, under the parties' agreement it owes Vigor nothing for Vigor's own insurance deductible.

Finally, the majority's conclusion that the district court's erred in calculating prejudgment interest is correct. But it is also unnecessary, because if the majority had properly addressed the contract's assignment of responsibility for paying insurance deductibles, Western would owe Vigor nothing, and thus owe no prejudgment interest.

United States Court of Appeals
for the Ninth Circuit

No. 22-35978

IDAHO CONSERVATION LEAGUE
vs.
POE

Appeal from the United States District Court for the District of Idaho

Decided: November 20, 2023

Citation: 86 F.4th 1243, 11 Adm. R. 478 (9th Cir. 2023).

Before **WARDLAW** and **SMITH**, Circuit Judges, and **HINKLE,*** District Judge.

* The Honorable Robert L. Hinkle, United States District Judge for the Northern District of Florida, sitting by designation.

[—4—] {-1244-} SMITH, Circuit Judge:

This appeal raises questions of statutory interpretation concerning the Clean Water Act (CWA), 33 U.S.C. § 1311(a). For several years, Shannon Poe engaged in instream suction dredge mining in Idaho's South Fork Clearwater River (the South Fork) without a National Pollutant Discharge Eliminating System (NPDES) permit. Plaintiff Idaho Conservation League (ICL) sued Poe, arguing that he violated the CWA each time he operated a suction dredge on the South Fork without an NPDES permit. Poe countered that (1) his suction dredge mining did not add pollutants to the South Fork and therefore did not require an NPDES permit, and (2) even if his suction dredge mining did add pollutants, those pollutants are "dredged" or "fill" material regulated exclusively pursuant to Section 404, not Section 402, of the CWA. The district court granted summary judgment to ICL. Poe appeals the judgment as to liability. We affirm.

STATUTORY AND REGULATORY BACKGROUND

Congress enacted the CWA "to restore and maintain the chemical, physical, and biological integrity of the Nation's waters." 33 U.S.C. § 1251(a). The CWA "categorically prohibits any discharge of a pollutant from a point source without a permit." *Comm. to Save Mokelumne River v. E. Bay Mun. Util. Dist.*, 13 F.3d 305, 309 (9th Cir. 1993). "[D]ischarge of a pollutant" is **{-1245-}** defined as the "addition of any pollutant to navigable waters from any point source . . . ." 33 U.S.C. § 1362(12). The CWA defines "pollutant" broadly to include "dredged spoil," "solid waste," "rock," "sand," and "industrial . . . waste discharged into water." 33 **[—5—]** U.S.C. § 1362(6). A point source is "any discernible, confined and discrete conveyance . . . ." 33 U.S.C. § 1362(14). Navigable waters are defined as "the waters of the United States . . . ." 33 U.S.C. § 1362(7). The CWA does not define what constitutes the "addition" of a pollutant. *See* 33 U.S.C. § 1362.

Before discharging any pollutant, one must obtain a permit from either the Environmental Protection Agency (the EPA) or the Army Corps of Engineers (the Corps). *See* 33 U.S.C. §§ 1311(a), 1342, 1344. The NPDES permitting program (also referred to as Section 402 permitting) authorizes the EPA to issue permits "for the discharge of any pollutant, or combination of pollutants," on the condition that the discharge will otherwise comply with the CWA. 33 U.S.C. § 1342(a)(1). Section 404 of the CWA authorizes the Corps to issue permits "for the discharge of dredged or fill material . . . ." 33 U.S.C. § 1344(a). When a discharge requires a Section 404 permit, it does not require a Section 402 permit. *See* 33 U.S.C. § 1342(a)(1); 40 C.F.R. § 122.3(b). The CWA does not define "discharge of dredged material" or "dredged material." *See* 33 U.S.C. §§ 1342, 1362.

FACTUAL AND PROCEDURAL BACKGROUND

Suction dredge mining is a method of placer mining that uses a floating watercraft device with a pump to suck water, riverbed sands, and minerals through a nozzle. The water and riverbed material are run through a "sluice box," where gold and other heavy metals are separated out. Water, sand, and minerals are then discharged back into the river, along with sediments and other pollutants. Dredging creates tailing piles behind the dredge, where larger and heavier processed riverbed materials are discarded and settle to the **[—6—]** river bottom nearby. Tailing piles can rise to the surface level of the river and can span most of the river's width.

Dredging overburden and bedrock involves dismantling the riverbed by dislodging and moving rocks and boulders, and breaking up tightly bound sediments using the miner's hands, the dredge nozzle, and other tools, like crowbars. The resulting holes can be several feet deep under the riverbed.

During the 2014, 2015, and 2018 dredge seasons, Poe suction dredge mined forty-two days on the South Fork, a navigable water located in north-central Idaho. Poe never obtained an NPDES permit pursuant to Section 402 of the CWA.

On August 10, 2018, ICL sued Poe, alleging that Poe was violating the CWA by failing to obtain an NPDES permit while dredging and discharging sediment and other pollutants in the South Fork. On December 21, 2018, Poe filed a motion to dismiss arguing that (1) the district court lacked subject matter jurisdiction because, in part, ICL's 2017 and 2018 notice letters were not sent via certified mail as required by the CWA and its implementing regulations; and (2) ICL lacked standing to the bring the suit in the first instance. The district court denied the motion.

ICL then moved for summary judgment on liability. Poe cross-moved for summary judgment. On June 4, 2021, the district court granted summary judgment to ICL, concluding that (1) Poe's suction dredge mining added pollutants to the South Fork, thereby requiring an NPDES permit under Section 402 of the CWA; and (2) the processed material discharged from Poe's suction dredge mining was a pollutant, not dredged or fill material, requiring **{-1246-}** an NPDES permit under Section 402 of the CWA rather than a permit under Section 404. The court thereafter enjoined Poe from **[—7—]** suction dredge mining in the South Fork without a valid CWA Section 402 permit and imposed a $150,000 civil penalty. Poe appeals the judgment as to liability.

JURISDICTION AND STANDARD OF REVIEW

We have jurisdiction pursuant to 28 U.S.C. § 1291. We review de novo a district court's decision to grant summary judgment. *Lopez v. Smith*, 203 F.3d 1122, 1131 (9th Cir. 2000) (en banc). We "must determine whether, viewing the evidence in the light most favorable to the nonmoving party, there are any genuine issues of material fact and whether the district court correctly applied the relevant substantive law." *Id.* Summary judgment is appropriate where "there is no genuine dispute as to any material fact and the movant is entitled to judgment as a matter of law." Fed. R. Civ. P. 56(a).

ANALYSIS

I. Dumping Suction Dredge Mining Waste into the South Fork Is an "Addition" of Pollutants Pursuant to the CWA.

To establish a violation of the CWA's NPDES requirements, "a plaintiff must prove that defendant[] (1) discharged, i.e., added (2) a pollutant (3) to navigable waters (4) from (5) a point source." *Comm. to Save Mokelumne River*, 13 F.3d at 308. The parties dispute the first element—whether Poe's suction dredge mining "added" a pollutant to the South Fork.

What amounts to the "addition" of a pollutant is not defined under the CWA. "It is well settled that the starting point for interpreting a statute is the language of the statute itself." *Olympic Forest Coal. v. Coast Seafoods Co.*, 884 F.3d 901, 905 (9th Cir. 2018) (quoting *Gwaltney of* **[—8—]** *Smithfield, Ltd. v. Chesapeake Bay Found., Inc.*, 484 U.S. 49, 56 (1987)). "When interpreting a statute, we first use the 'traditional tools of statutory construction,' to determine whether Congress directly addressed the 'precise question at issue.'" *Id.* (quoting *Chevron, U.S.A., Inc. v. Nat. Res. Def. Council, Inc.*, 467 U.S. 837, 843 n.9 (1984)). "If the precise question at issue is addressed, then the 'unambiguously expressed intent of Congress controls.'" *Id.* (quoting *Chevron*, 467 U.S. at 843). Where a statute is ambiguous, courts defer to the reasonable interpretation of the agency charged with administering that statute. *See Chevron*, 467 U.S. at 844.

Since the 1970s, the EPA has interpreted the CWA as prohibiting discharges from placer mining sluice boxes unless done in compliance with a Section 402 permit. *See Trustees for Alaska v. EPA*, 749 F.2d 549, 552–53 (9th Cir. 1984) (reviewing the EPA's issuance of Section 402 permits to gold placer miners in 1976 and 1977). In 1988, the EPA adopted industry-wide regulations setting effluent limitations for Section 402 permits for gold placer miners, including gold mining from floating dredges. *See* 40 C.F.R. § 440.140.

In *Rybachek v. EPA*, 904 F.2d 1276 (9th Cir. 1990), miners challenged these regulations, arguing that placer mining does not cause the "addition" of a pollutant. We rejected that argument. We noted that "resuspension" of streambed materials "may be interpreted to be an addition of a pollutant under the Act," and we deferred to the EPA's reasonable interpretation that such activity constitutes the "addition" of a pollutant under the CWA. *Id.* at 1285–86 (first citing **{-1247-}** *Avoyelles Sportsmen's League, Inc. v. Marsh*, 715 F.2d 897, 923 (5th Cir. 1983) (stating that "[t]he word 'addition,' as used in the definition of the term 'discharge,' **[—9—]** may reasonably be understood to include 'redeposit'"); and then citing *United States v. M.C.C. of Florida, Inc.*, 772 F.2d 1501, 1506 (11th Cir. 1985) (action of digging up sediment and redepositing it on sea bottom by boat propellers constitutes an addition of pollutants), *vacated and remanded on other grounds*, 481 U.S. 1034 (1987)). We further explained: "Because the EPA has been charged with administering the [CWA], we must show great deference to the Agency's interpretation of the Act. We especially defer where the Agency's decision on the meaning or reach of the [CWA] involves reconciling conflicting policies committed to the Agency's care and expertise under the Act." *Id.* at 1284 (citation omitted).

Poe's mining activities fall squarely within the scope of *Rybachek*. Undisputed evidence in the record, including photos and descriptions of Poe's dredge operating on the South Fork, shows that he "excavate[d] the dirt and gravel" in the river using a high-pressure blaster nozzle, "extract[ed] any gold" and other heavy metals, and "discharge[d] the dirt and other non-[heavy metal] materials into the water." *See id.* at 1285. That is, Poe engaged in placer mining "subject to regulation under the [CWA]." *Id.* Poe, therefore, "added" pollutants to the South Fork. *See id.* ("[W]e will not strike down the EPA's finding that placer mining discharges pollutants within the meaning of the Act."); *see also Borden Ranch P'ship v. U.S. Army Corps of Engineers*, 261 F.3d 810, 814 (9th Cir. 2001) (reaffirming *Rybachek*, which "held that removing material from a stream bed, sifting out the gold, and returning the material to the stream bed was an 'addition' of a pollutant'"), *aff'd*, 537 U.S. 99 (2002).

In response, Poe argues that (1) *Rybachek* is no longer good law in light of subsequent Supreme Court decisions or, in the alternative, (2) the court should not apply *Chevron* **[—10—]** deference and overrule *Rybachek*. Neither argument is persuasive.

Poe suggests that the Supreme Court has, since *Rybachek*, twice confirmed the "commonsense interpretation" of the CWA—i.e., that a person does not illegally discharge a pollutant unless he or she adds new material from the outside world. *See S. Fla. Water Mgmt. Dist. v. Miccosukee Tribe of Indians*, 541 U.S. 95 (2004); *L.A. Cnty. Flood Control Dist. v. Nat. Res. Def. Council, Inc.*, 568 U.S. 78 (2013). That is, according to Poe, *Miccosukee Tribe* and *L.A. County* eviscerate the logic of *Rybachek*. But these cases are both distinguishable from *Rybachek* and inapposite here. In *Miccosukee Tribe*, polluted water was removed from a canal, transported through a pump station, and deposited into a reservoir a short distance away. *See* 541 U.S. at 98–99. The Court held that pumping polluted water from, and back into, the same body of water, without more, "cannot constitute an 'addition' of pollutants." *Id.* at 109–10 ("As the Second Circuit put it in *Trout Unlimited*, if one takes a ladle of soup from a pot, lifts it above the pot, and pours it back into the pot, one has not 'added' soup or anything else to the pot." (citing *Catskill Mountains Chapter of Trout Unlimited, Inc. v. City of N.Y.*, 273 F.3d 481, 492 (2d Cir. 2001) (cleaned up)). In *L.A. County*, the Court held that "the flow of water from an improved portion of a navigable waterway into an unimproved portion of the very same waterway does not qualify as a discharge of pollutants under the CWA." 568 U.S. at 83. In both cases, polluted water was transferred from one **{-1248-}** location to another within the same waterbody.

Here, by contrast, Poe excavated rocks, gravel, sand, sediment, and silt from the riverbed. Poe punched holes in the riverbed by excavating through layers of riverbed down **[—11—]** to the bedrock. Poe then processed the materials by running them through the sluice on his dredge, and then discarded the waste material into the water. This added a plume of turbid wastewater to the South Fork. These materials were not already suspended in the water; they were previously deposited in the riverbed. Poe's dredging was therefore not simple water transfer.

As the district court correctly observed,

> Poe's reliance on [*L.A. County* and *Miccosukee Tribe*] misses the point. Suction dredge mining does not simply transfer water (what the above cases address); to the contrary, it excavates rock, gravel, sand, and sediment from the riverbed and then *adds* those materials back to the river—this time, in suspended form.

See also EPA, 2018 Response to Comments Idaho Small Suction Dredge General Permit (GP) ("If, during suction dredging, only water was picked up and placed back within the same waterbody . . . , no permit would be necessary. However, in suction dredging, bed material is also picked up with water. Picking up the bed material is in fact the very purpose of suction dredging—the bed material is processed to produce gold. This process is an intervening use that causes the addition of pollutants [rock and sand, see CWA § 502(6)] to be discharged to waters of the United States. As a result . . . an NPDES permit is required for the discharge from this activity." (alteration in original) (citation omitted)). Thus, *Miccosukee Tribe* and *L.A. County* do not disturb our holding in *Rybachek*, which remains good law. **[—12—]**

In addition, or in the alternative, Poe asks us not to apply *Chevron* deference and to overrule *Rybachek*. Specifically, Poe argues that (1) the ordinary meaning of "addition" under the CWA is clear, making *Chevron* deference inappropriate, (2) *Chevron* should not be applied where a statute may subject individuals to criminal penalties, and (3) *Chevron* should not be applied where the EPA has taken inconsistent positions on the meaning of "addition" under the CWA. Adopting any of these theories would require us to depart from our ruling in *Rybachek*. A three-judge panel may depart from controlling circuit precedent only if "our prior circuit authority is clearly irreconcilable with the reasoning or theory of intervening higher authority." *Miller v. Gammie*, 335 F.3d 889, 893 (9th Cir. 2003) (en banc). "[T]he 'clearly irreconcilable' requirement 'is a high standard.'" *Fed. Trade Comm'n v. Consumer Def., LLC*, 926 F.3d 1208, 1213 (9th Cir. 2019) (quoting *Rodriguez v. AT&T Mobility Servs. LLC*, 728 F.3d 975, 979 (9th Cir. 2013)). "[I]f we can apply our precedent consistently with that of the higher authority, we must do so." *Id.*

As explained above, *Rybachek*'s holding regarding placer mining is not irreconcilable, let alone "clearly irreconcilable," with *L.A. County* or *Miccosukee Tribe*'s holdings regarding the transfer of water within a single waterbody. We therefore follow *Rybachek* on the issues raised by Poe and hold that Poe's instream suction dredge mining constitutes the "addition" of a pollutant under the CWA. **[—13—]**

II. The Processed Material Discharged from Instream Suction Dredge Mining is a Pollutant that Requires a Section 402 Permit.

Poe also argues that, even if his suction dredge mining adds pollutants to the South Fork, the waste discharged from his operation constitutes "dredged" or "fill material" over which the Corps has exclusive **{-1249-}**

permitting authority.[1] Poe makes this argument pursuant to (1) the ordinary meaning of "dredged material" under the CWA and (2) the ordinary meaning of the Corps' own regulatory definition of "dredged material." Neither argument is persuasive.

Under the CWA, pollution discharges require a Section 402 permit from the EPA, unless the discharge is "dredged or fill material" requiring a Section 404 permit from the Corps. *See* 33 U.S.C. §§ 1342, 1344; 40 C.F.R. § 122.3; *Coeur Alaska, Inc. v. Se. Alaska Conservation Council*, 557 U.S. 261, 274 (2009). The terms "dredged material" and "discharge of dredged material" are not defined under the CWA. *See* 33 U.S.C. § 1362; *Olympic Forest Coal.*, 884 F.3d at 905 ("It is well settled that the starting point for interpreting a statute is the language of the statute itself."). Nor does the statute define whether material that is dredged from navigable water remains "dredged material" after it has been processed. That is, nothing in the CWA says that once a material has been dredged, it remains a dredged material forever. If, as the district court explained (citing *EOMA*, 445 **[—14—]** P.3d 251, 257 (2019)), processing dredged material can change its character, the text of the statute does not identify the point at which the processed material becomes a pollutant other than dredged material that is subject to the EPA's rather than the Corps' permitting authority. The CWA therefore does not, in plain terms, address the question presented here.

We next look to the regulations promulgated to implement the Act. *See Coeur Alaska*, 557 U.S. at 277–78 (explaining that, if the text of the CWA is ambiguous, courts look to the agencies' implementing regulations and, if those regulations are ambiguous, to the agencies' interpretation and application of their regulations to determine what the CWA means)). The CWA regulations define "dredged material" as "material that is excavated and dredged from waters of the United States," but offer no further explanation of the term. *See* 33 C.F.R. § 323.2(c). Like the CWA, the regulations do not specifically address the question of which agency has the authority to permit the discharge of dredged material that has been processed, such as the leftover waste material that is discharged during suction dredge mining.

Absent clear direction from either the CWA or the regulations promulgated thereunder, we look to the agencies' interpretation and application of those regulations. *See Coeur Alaska*, 557 U.S. at 277–78; *Kisor v. Wilkie*, 139 S. Ct. 2400, 2415–18 (2019). The EPA and Corps have long agreed that when materials are dredged from a waterbody and are subsequently processed, they are no longer dredged materials and have become industrial waste, rock, sand, or other CWA pollutants regulated under Section 402.[2] For **[—15—]** example, in their 1986 memorandum of agreement, the EPA and the Corps agreed that "placer mining wastes" were the type of "pollutant" discharged in "liquid, semi-liquid, or suspended form" subject to Section 402, not Section 404. Memorandum of **{-1250-}** Agreement Concerning Regulation of Discharge of Solid Waste Under the Clean Water Act, 51 Fed. Reg. 8871, 8872 (March 14, 1986). A 1990 Regulatory Guidance Letter from the Corps states that once "dredged material" is "subsequently processed to remove desired elements, its nature has been changed" and "it is no longer dredged material" regulated under Section 404. U.S. Army Corps of Engineers, *Regulation of Waste Disposal from In-Stream Place Mining*, Regulatory Guidance Letter 88-10 (July 28, 1990), https://usace.contentdm.oclc.org/utils/getfile/collection/p16021coll9/id/1386; *see also* U.S. Army Corps of Engineers, *Regulatory Guidance Letters*, https://www.usace.army.mil/Missions/Civil-

[1] The Oregon Supreme Court recently addressed this issue. *See E. Or. Mining Ass'n v. Dep't of Env't Quality*, 445 P.3d 251, 274 (2019) (*EOMA*) (deferring to the "EPA's and the Corps' reasonable conclusion that the EPA (or its state delegate) has the authority to issue a permit under section 402 for all the processed waste discharged as a result of suction dredge mining"). We find *EOMA* well-reasoned and persuasive and substantially follow its analysis, as did the district court.

[2] The district court included a more detailed account of the regulatory history, which Poe does not contest on appeal.

Works/Regulatory-Program-and-Permits/Guidance-Letters (noting that, "unless superseded by specific provisions of subsequently issued regulations or guidance, the content provided in [Regulatory Guidance Letters] generally remains valid after the expiration date"). The Corps explained: "The raw materials associated with placer mining operations are not being excavated simply to change their locations as in a normal dredging operation, but rather to obtain materials for processing, and the residue of this processing should be considered waste."

As the district court noted, "whatever patchwork of permitting authority has existed over time, from *at least 2013* (via the general permitting process, initiated in 2010 and after notice and comment), it is *the EPA* that has required a Section 402 permit for suction dredge mining." "This fact, **[—16—]** coupled with the overall approach to and assignment and acceptance of responsibilities under the EPA's and the Corps' interpretation of the applicable regulations to suction dredge mining . . . , confirms that the agencies have taken an official position and made a fair and considered judgment, based on its substantive expertise, that the operation of a suction dredge results in the discharge of processed wastes, thus requiring Section 402 permits." We therefore defer to the agencies' reasonable interpretation of the CWA and implementing regulations that the processed material discharged from Poe's suction dredge mining is a pollutant, not a dredged or fill material, and requires an NPDES permit under Section 402 of the CWA. *See Kisor*, 139 S. Ct. 2400.

Poe's arguments to the contrary are unavailing. Principally, citing the dissent in *EOMA*, Poe argues that (1) the text of Section 404 itself is enough to settle the case: suction dredge mining does "dredge" material, and, in a literal sense, that material is then "discharged" into the water, and (2) the Corps' regulation defining "dredged material" is not genuinely ambiguous as to the question over whether instream suction dredge mining is regulated under Section 404 once ordinary interpretive methods have been applied. However, as explained above, even if the material starts as dredged material, that fact does not settle the issue of whether material that was dredged remains "dredged material" after it has been processed. Poe processed the materials dredged from the riverbed when he ran them through the sluice on his dredge, extracted heavy metals and other materials, and discharged the remaining waste and sediments into the South Fork.

In any event, the meaning of the CWA and implementing regulations remains sufficiently ambiguous that deference to the agencies' official joint conclusion is appropriate. *See* **[—17—]** *Coeur Alaska*, 557 U.S. at 277–78. As the Oregon Supreme Court noted, "[b]oth the statutes and the regulations are genuinely ambiguous on [this] question." *EOMA*, 445 P.3d at 270. The concern here "is not with the navigability of the water body, a concern that falls within the Corps' expertise; rather, **{-1251-}** the concern is with the health of the water body, a concern that lies at the heart of the EPA's expertise. The Corps and the EPA reasonably could conclude that the EPA was better suited than the Corps to make th[e]se types of water quality decisions." *Id.* at 272.

CONCLUSION

For the foregoing reasons, the district court's grant of summary judgment to ICL is **AFFIRMED**.

This page intentionally left blank

United States Court of Appeals for the Eleventh Circuit

United States Court of Appeals
for the Eleventh Circuit

No. 21-11733

SERENDIPITY AT SEA, LLC
vs.
UNDERWRITERS AT LLOYD'S OF LONDON SUBSCRIBING TO POLICY NUMBER 187581

Appeal from the United States District Court for the Southern District of Florida

Decided: January 4, 2023

Citation: 56 F.4th 1280, 11 Adm. R. 486 (11th Cir. 2023).

Before **PRYOR,** Chief Judge, **ROSENBAUM,** and **MARCUS,** Circuit Judges.

[—2—] {-1281-} MARCUS, Circuit Judge:

This appeal arises out of an insurance dispute involving a yacht, the Serendipity, that was destroyed by Hurricane Dorian, a Category 5 storm, that slammed into Great Abaco Island in the Bahamas. Serendipity at Sea, LLC ("Serendipity, LLC"), a holding company created by Mikael Sean Oakley and Jacqueline English ("the Oakleys") to manage the Serendipity, sued Underwriters at Lloyd's of London Subscribing **{-1282-}** to Policy Number 187581 ("Lloyd's") for breach of contract after Lloyd's denied the Oakleys' insurance claim for the damage Hurricane Dorian caused to the Serendipity. In denying that it had breached the contract, Lloyd's argued that it was not liable because Serendipity, LLC did not employ a full-time licensed captain in violation of the policy's Captain Warranty, and that the breach increased the hazard to the yacht because a licensed captain would have operated the vessel back to Florida when Hurricane Dorian formed and was forecast to hit the Bahamas. **[—3—]**

The district court granted summary judgment in favor of Lloyd's under Federal Rule of Civil Procedure 56(f). It found that the Captain Warranty was unambiguous; that Serendipity, LLC breached the agreement by failing to hire a full-time licensed captain; and that the breach increased the hazard posed to the Serendipity based on the purportedly undisputed testimony of Captain Thomas Danti, an expert hired by Lloyd's.

While we agree with the district court's conclusion that Serendipity, LLC breached the Captain Warranty, a disputed question of material fact remains about whether the breach increased the hazard posed to the vessel. Thus, we reverse the district court's grant of summary judgment in favor of Lloyd's and remand the case to the district court for further proceedings consistent with this opinion.

I.

The relevant facts -- for purposes of summary judgment -- are these. The Oakleys own a 61-foot Viking Princess yacht named the Serendipity, which they manage through their holding company, Serendipity, LLC. The Oakleys insured the yacht through a SeaWave Yacht Insurance Policy (the "Policy"). They used an insurance broker, USI Insurance Services, LLC, to secure the Policy, which was underwritten by Lloyd's.

The Policy contained two warranties: a Captain Warranty and a Crew Warranty. It is the Parties' disagreement over how to interpret the Captain Warranty that brought them to court. The **[—4—]** Captain Warranty in effect in 2015 "[w]arranted a full time licensed captain is employed for the maintenance and care of the vessel and is aboard while the vessel is underway. Michael [sic] Sean Oakley is permitted to operate the vessel without the Captain aboard." The Captain Warranty in effect in each subsequent renewal period (and when the loss occurred) omitted the second line; it only "[w]arranted a full time licensed captain is employed for the maintenance and care of the vessel and is aboard while underway." A separate provision of the Policy also stated that "[i]t is agreed that the person in charge of and in control of ***Your Boat*** while making way or under way shall only be ***You*** or others as may be permitted by the terms and conditions of this ***Contract***."

Despite the slight variations of the Captain Warranty, all Parties agree that Oakley was allowed to drive the boat without a captain present. They disagree, however, about what the Captain Warranty required of Serendipity, LLC when the vessel was not underway. As a preview: Serendipity, LLC believed it only needed to have a captain "on call" to assist as needed with the vessel, while Lloyd's believed that the Policy required Serendipity, LLC to hire a captain to care for the Serendipity "full time."

The Policy also contained a Crew Warranty, but it proved far less controversial. It said only that "[c]overage is provided for [1] full time paid crew." It is relevant for our purposes because the Oakleys believed that the Captain Warranty was intended **{–1283–}** to function the same as the Crew Warranty: Oakley said in his deposition **[—5—]** that he thought the Captain Warranty was intended to protect the Oakleys from liability if Captain Connelly "slipped and fell or hurt" himself. In other words, Oakley understood the warranty as intended "to protect any captain that was on board operating the vessel," providing additional coverage like the Crew Warranty did.

Because of the Captain Warranty, the Oakleys were required to list a "captain of the vessel" on their insurance application. And so they listed William Scott Connelly ("Captain Connelly"), a family friend. But in addition to being a friend of the Oakleys, Captain Connelly is also a retired captain. While he used to operate marine vessels as his main profession, since his retirement he no longer "[got] to captain vessels on a regular basis, as [he] once did." But, as he put it in an affidavit, he was "always available" to help the Oakleys when they needed him.

On or about July 27, 2019, Oakley drove the Serendipity from Cape Canaveral, Florida to Great Abaco Island in the Bahamas. Two friends joined him for the voyage, which took about eleven hours. The month prior, Oakley had made significant and expensive improvements to the Serendipity, to the tune of $100,000 or so. He received a certificate of insurance from their broker, USI, in order to make the repairs, and he told USI about his plan to take the Serendipity to the Bahamas at that time.

When the Serendipity arrived in the Bahamas, Oakley and a licensed captain, Captain Trevor Lightbourne, docked the yacht behind a home known as the Pink Paradise. Oakley also updated **[—6—]** the cameras around the dock to a high-tech brand. Oakley returned home to Florida in early August. While he was gone, Captain Lightbourne and another licensed captain, Captain Stanley McIntosh, checked in on the Serendipity.

All was well for a few weeks. But on August 23, 2019, a storm started brewing in the Atlantic Ocean. The same day that the storm was announced, Oakley consulted with Captains Lightbourne and McIntosh and determined that the safest place for the Serendipity to weather the storm, which was predicted to hit Central Florida, was in the Bahamas. Captains Lightbourne and McIntosh secured the vessel to the dock, with Oakley directing the preparation using the cameras.

By August 26, 2019, the storm -- now named Dorian -- was forecast to hit Puerto Rico as a tropical storm. It was a particularly erratic storm, however, and the forecast changed quickly and frequently. On August 29, 2019, Dorian was predicted to bypass the Bahamas and hit Central Florida directly. But forecasters remained uncertain about when and where exactly the storm would make landfall. On the afternoon of August 30, 2019, Dorian became a Category 3 hurricane. Only seven hours later, it strengthened into a devasting Category 5 hurricane. It made landfall on Great Abaco, where the Serendipity was docked. The Serendipity was destroyed.

Serendipity, LLC subsequently filed an insurance claim for the damage. But its claim was denied on February 19, 2020. In the **[—7—]** denial letter, a representative of Lloyd's explained that the Policy "warranted that a licensed captain is employed and is aboard while the vessel is underway," but that Oakley "moved the boat to the Bahamas and there was no licensed Captain aboard for that voyage."

Serendipity, LLC sued Lloyd's in Florida state court on February 14, 2020. Lloyd's removed the matter to the United States

District Court for the Southern District of Florida asserting diversity jurisdiction **{-1284-}** on March 10, 2020. Serendipity, LLC's initial complaint raised two counts against Lloyd's for breach of contract and bad faith. Serendipity, LLC has since amended its complaint several times. The operative complaint, the Fourth Amended Complaint, brings one count against Lloyd's for breach of contract, and two counts against the insurance broker, USI, for breach of fiduciary duty and negligence.

The Parties filed cross motions for summary judgment, and the district court denied them all following a Report and Recommendation from a magistrate judge. But at the same time it denied the cross motions for summary judgment, the district court directed Serendipity, LLC to file a brief addressing "the issue of whether Plaintiff's breach of the Captain Warranty 'increased the hazard within the control of the insured,' Fla. Stat. § 627.409(2)" in accordance with Federal Rule of Civil Procedure 56(f). Serendipity, LLC filed its response on April 20, 2021 and Lloyd's replied the next day. Serendipity, LLC largely ignored the instructions of the **[—8—]** district court and spent much of its brief addressing breach. To the extent the brief addressed the hazard issue, it mainly addressed it in relation to breach. That is, Serendipity, LLC argued that an "increased risk" required a "material breach" and because "Mr. Oakley was authorized to operate the boat without a captain on board . . . his bringing the boat to the Bahamas without incident, was authorized and not a breach." Serendipity, LLC added, however, that "[t]he vessel was not in jeopardy with Mr. Oakley as the captain" because Oakley "was highly experienced operating the subject vessel and similar vessels" and "had extensive experience navigating to and from and within the Bahamas."

For its part, Lloyd's offered an expert, Captain Danti, to opine on the hazard issue. Based on Captain Danti's testimony, the district court granted summary judgment in favor of Lloyd's under Federal Rule of Civil Procedure 56(f). The district court concluded that Serendipity, LLC had "produced no evidence to rebut this testimony, and thus the record is clear that [Serendipity, LLC]'s breach of the Captain Warranty increased the hazard within the control of the insured." And so it entered final judgment in favor of Lloyd's.

This timely appeal followed. **[—9—]**

II.

A.

We carried one jurisdictional issue with this case: "[W]hether there is a final and appealable order in light of the voluntarily stipulated dismissal without prejudice, which does not appear to have been signed by [Lloyd's]." We conclude that there is. Serendipity, LLC's claims against USI were properly dismissed under Federal Rule of Civil Procedure 41(a)(2). That rule provides, in relevant part, that "an action may be dismissed at the plaintiff's request only by court order, on terms that the court considers proper." Fed. R. Civ. P. 41(a)(2). While the Parties cited Federal Rule of Civil Procedure 41(a)(1)(A)(ii) in their Joint Stipulation, they appeared to have contemplated additional action by the district court, consistent with Rule 41(a)(2), and the district court did take further action by entering an order dismissing USI. The dismissal of USI met the requirements of Rule 41(a)(2), and the only claim remaining in this matter when the district court entered summary judgment in favor of Lloyd's was Serendipity, LLC's breach of contract claim against Lloyd's. Accordingly, Serendipity's appeal of that decision provides us with a final decision from the district court to review. *See* 28 U.S.C. § 1291; *see also* **{-1285-}** *World Fuel Corp. v. Geithner*, 568 F.3d 1345, 1348 (11th Cir. 2009) (explaining that a final decision is "one that ends the litigation on the merits and leaves nothing for the court to do but execute its judgment" (quotation marks and citation omitted)). **[—10—]**

B.

We review the district court's grant of summary judgment *de novo*, applying the same legal standards as the district court. *Penley v. Eslinger*, 605 F.3d 843, 848 (11th Cir. 2010). A motion for summary judgment is properly granted when "there is no genuine dispute as to any material fact and the movant is entitled to judgment as a matter of law." Fed. R. Civ. P. 56(a); *see also Richmond v. Badia*, 47 F.4th 1172, 1179 (11th Cir. 2022).

On appeal, Serendipity, LLC argues that the Captain Warranty is ambiguous and vague, and that under the reading of the warranty most favorable to it -- the reading that we are required to adopt under binding Florida law, *see Roberson v. United Servs. Auto. Ass'n*, 330 So. 2d 745, 746 (Fla. 1st DCA 1976) -- there was no breach. Serendipity, LLC also argues that even if there was a breach, the breach did not justify denial of coverage under the Policy because it did not "increase the hazard" posed to the Serendipity by Hurricane Dorian. If the breach did not "increase the hazard," the Policy remained enforceable and Lloyd's was required to pay, absent some other breach or excuse for nonpayment.

Our first task, then, is to determine whether the Captain Warranty is ambiguous. And there is no better place to begin than with the language of the warranty. The warranty said, in its entirety, that the policy "[w]arranted a full time licensed captain is employed for the maintenance and care of the vessel and is aboard while underway." Serendipity, LLC claims this language is vague **[—11—]** and ambiguous for a number of reasons, which it presented as a list of hypothetical questions to the district court (e.g., "what exactly is a 'full time licensed captain,'" "what is considered 'full time,'" "is the captain employed 'full time' if he is only aboard while the vessel is 'underway'"?).

Under Florida law, which we are *Erie*-bound to apply in this diversity action, *see Erie R.R. Co. v. Tompkins*, 304 U.S. 64 (1938), "[a]n insurance contract is ambiguous if it is susceptible to two or more reasonable interpretations that can fairly be made." *Dahl-Eimers v. Mut. of Omaha Life Ins. Co.*, 986 F.2d 1379, 1381 (11th Cir. 1993); *see also Travelers Indem. Co. v. PCR Inc.*, 889 So. 2d 779, 785 (Fla. 2004) ("Policy language is considered to be ambiguous . . . if the language is susceptible to more than one reasonable interpretation, one providing coverage and the other limiting coverage." (quotation marks and citation omitted)). "In interpreting an insurance contract, we are bound by the plain meaning of the contract's text." *State Farm Mut. Auto. Ins. Co. v. Menendez*, 70 So. 3d 566, 569 (Fla. 2011).

"If the language used in an insurance policy is plain and unambiguous, a court must interpret the policy in accordance with the plain meaning of the language used so as to give effect to the policy as it was written." *Travelers*, 889 So. 2d at 785. But a provision is not ambiguous "simply because it is complex or requires analysis." *Penzer v. Transp. Ins. Co.*, 29 So. 3d 1000, 1005 (Fla. 2010) (citation omitted). And courts should not "put a strained and **[—12—]** unnatural construction on the terms of a policy." *Southern-Owners Ins. Co. v. Eason Rhodes & Assocs., LLC*, 872 F.3d 1161, 1164 (11th Cir. 2017) (citation omitted). If there is genuine ambiguity, however, **{–1286–}** "[i]nsurance policies are construed liberally in favor of the insured and strictly against the insurer." *Roberson*, 330 So. 2d at 746.

We turn now to the interpretations of the Captain Warranty that Serendipity, LLC offers. First, Serendipity, LLC's most preferred interpretation: that the Captain Warranty provided additional coverage to the Oakleys in the event a hired captain was injured while aboard the vessel. This interpretation is patently unreasonable because it is belied by the text of the warranty. There is no reading of "[w]arranted a full time licensed captain is employed for the maintenance and care of the vessel and is aboard while underway" that expands coverage for personal injuries suffered by a captain on the vessel. Indeed, there is no reading that does not require Serendipity, LLC to hire a full-time licensed captain in some capacity. And we cannot "put a strained and unnatural construction" on the warranty to read it this way. *See Southern-Owners*, 872 F.3d at 1164. Had the Captain Warranty said the same thing the Crew Warranty says -- "[c]overage is provided for [1] full time paid crew" -- this argument may have held more water. But as it stands, this argument fails under the plain text of the warranty.

Nevertheless, we are persuaded that the Captain Warranty is otherwise ambiguous. We say this because there is more than one reasonable way to read the plain language of its text. *See Dahl-* **[—13—]** *Eimers*, 986 F.2d at 1382 ("Ordinary rules of construction require us, first, to assess the natural or plain meaning of the policy language."). The Captain Warranty is ambiguous about what it means by the phrase "a full time licensed captain is employed." One reasonable interpretation is that Serendipity, LLC is required to hire a person whose full-time profession is that of a captain but who only works for Serendipity, LLC part time. The full-time captain could work over forty hours per week as a captain, but only work, say, five hours each week on the Serendipity and forty hours each week as a captain somewhere else. Another reasonable interpretation is that Serendipity, LLC must hire a person to work on the Serendipity exclusively as a full-time captain's job -- as in a typical nine-to-five arrangement. The word "full time" is not defined anywhere in the Policy, which "does not create ambiguity per se," but nevertheless lends support to the conclusion that the Captain Warranty is ambiguous. *See id.*

In the end, though, the fact that the warranty may have been ambiguous does not save Serendipity, LLC because under *any* reasonable interpretation of its text, Serendipity, LLC failed to fulfill its obligations. Under any reasonable interpretation of the Policy, Serendipity, LLC was required to hire a licensed captain either to care for the Serendipity full time, or whose full-time job was as a licensed captain. Plainly, Serendipity, LLC did neither.

Oakley testified in his deposition that he "hired many, many people to work on the boat; but did we ever hire a full-time captain? **[—14—]** No. The -- the full-time captain was me." This concession is fatal to Serendipity, LLC's argument; all agree that Oakley was not a licensed captain during the relevant period, and Serendipity, LLC makes no attempt to argue that Oakley himself satisfied the warranty. Instead, Serendipity, LLC says that Captain Connelly filled the role. But Captain Connelly neither worked full time on the Serendipity nor worked full time as a licensed captain during the period the Policy was in effect. It is true that Captain Connelly submitted an affidavit explaining that he was "always available to assist in any way [he] c[ould]." **{-1287-}** He went on to explain, however, that he "was paid for [his] services with dinners and attending cruises with [the Oakleys]." This is not compensation for full-time work. But still more problematic, Captain Connelly disclosed that he was *retired* from his job as a captain by the time the Oakleys purchased the Serendipity; he swore in his affidavit that he is "retired, and [doesn't] get to captain vessels on a regular basis, as [he] once did." Under even the most charitable reading of the Captain Warranty, this was not what the Policy required, and the district court correctly concluded that there had been a breach.

C.

Our inquiry does not end there, however. In order to escape coverage, Lloyd's must prove not only that Serendipity, LLC breached the Captain Warranty, but also that the breach "increased the hazard" posed by Hurricane Dorian to the Serendipity. The district court concluded that the record "demonstrate[d] that there **[—15—]** is no genuine dispute of fact that the failure to employ a full-time licensed captain did indeed increase the hazard." In support, the district court explained that Serendipity, LLC "produced no evidence to rebut" the testimony of Lloyd's' expert witness, Captain Danti, who concluded that any licensed captain would have driven the Serendipity back to Cape Canaveral before Hurricane Dorian struck the Bahamas. We disagree.

1.

Before explaining why a material dispute of fact remains on the issue of hazard, we pause to explain why we believe the argument was properly presented to the district court. "It is well settled that issues not raised in the district court in the first instance are forfeited." *Douglas Asphalt Co. v. QORE, Inc.*, 657 F.3d 1146, 1152 (11th Cir. 2011). So "if a party hopes to preserve a claim, argument, theory, or defense on appeal, [it] must first clearly present it to the district court, that is, in such a way as to afford the district court an opportunity to recognize and rule on it." *Juris v. Inamed Corp.*, 685 F.3d 1294, 1325 (11th Cir. 2012) (citation omitted).

Lloyd's suggests that Serendipity, LLC may have forfeited its argument that the breach did not increase the hazard because it did not "produce any facts to rebut the testimony of Captain Danti that the absence of a full time captain employed for the maintenance and care of the vessel increased the risk or hazard to the vessel" in the district court. Alternatively, Lloyd's suggested at oral argument that Serendipity, LLC forfeited the argument by not **[—16—]** raising it a second time to the district court in response to the district court's order requiring briefing under Rule 56(f). We are not persuaded by either argument.

"There is no burden upon the district court to distill every potential argument that could be made based upon the materials before it on summary judgment." *Resol. Tr. Corp. v. Dunmar Corp.*, 43 F.3d 587, 599 (11th Cir. 1995) (en banc). And we will not require the district court to undertake the proverbial hunt for the Red October submarine in the Atlantic Ocean[1] in order to find a disputed issue of fact in the summary judgment record. But, contrary to the position taken by Lloyd's, we see no need to hunt here. **{-1288-}**

It was apparent throughout Serendipity, LLC's Motion for Summary Judgment and its Statement of Material Facts that it disputed the testimony in Captain Danti's report. More precisely, it was apparent that Serendipity, LLC disputed a meteorological fact (the Dooley SeaWeather report) that formed the basis of Captain Danti's report -- a meteorological fact of which Captain Danti did not possess any particular expertise. Beginning with the introduction in its Motion for Summary Judgment, Serendipity, LLC explained that

> [O]n August 27, 2019, Hurricane Dorian began forming and was initially predicted to hit Florida. As such, **[—17—]** Mr. Oakley believed the M/Y Serendipity to be safer in the Bahamas. (Exhibit 3 [sic], Combined Weather Reports[2]). Further, he believed that it would not be safe or reasonable to return to Florida and potentially face the storm in the open sea.

Then, in a section of its Motion for Summary Judgment titled "Plaintiff Did Not Breach Any Aspect of the Hurricane Plan by Bringing the Vessel to the Bahamas," Serendipity, LLC claimed that "[b]ased on the information available at the time, Mr. Oakley determined that the vessel would be safer in the Bahamas" and that "[i]t would have been an *unnecessary hazard* to attempt to move the vessel hours before the Hurricane struck and risk facing the storm in the open sea." Any way you read it, this argument cuts directly to the hazard issue, even though the argument was placed under the wrong topical heading. **[—18—]**

In addition, just above the section of Serendipity, LLC's Motion titled "None of the Alleged Breaches by Plaintiff Served to Increase the Insurance Hazard of Defendant Underwriters," -- but still not under the correct topical heading -- Serendipity, LLC pointed out that it "had initially appeared that Florida would be hit more severely by the storm" and attempting to navigate the vessel to Cape

---

[1] *See* The Hunt for Red October (Paramount Pictures 1990) (based on Tom Clancy, *The Hunt for Red October* (1984)).

[2] In response to Serendipity, LLC's Motion for Summary Judgment, but not on appeal, Lloyd's objected to these reports because they "present[] alleged facts in a manner that would not be admissible at trial" in that they have not been authenticated by a witness. Lloyd's argument missed the mark for two reasons. First, the reports appear in newspaper articles, and newspaper articles are self-authenticating. *See* Fed. R. Evid. 902(6). And second, even if inadmissible in the form presented, these weather reports are properly considered on summary judgment because they could easily be reduced to admissible form at trial. *See Smith v. Marcus & Millichap, Inc.*, 991 F.3d 1145, 1156 n.2 (11th Cir. 2021). This Court has explicitly held that this is true with respect to newspaper articles. *See Church of Scientology Flag Serv. Org., Inc. v. City of Clearwater*, 2 F.3d 1514, 1530 (11th Cir. 1993).

Canaveral from the Abacos "could have exposed the vessel and human life to greater risk." In this location, the district court would not have been required to scour the record to find Serendipity, LLC's position on whether any breach increased the hazard.

Most significantly, however, for our purposes, Serendipity, LLC directly disputed Captain Danti's testimony in its Statement of Material Facts, which additionally served as its response to Lloyd's Statement of Material Facts. Paragraph 59 of Lloyd's Statement provides: "This change in mooring location [from Cape Canaveral to the Bahamas], *substantially increased the risk* to the Subject Vessel during the hurricane season. . . ." In turn, ¶ 59 of Serendipity, LLC's response reads this way: "Hurricane Dorian was at that time predicted to hit Cape Canaveral, the primary location for the subject vessel. It wasn't till hours before it hit Paradise Cay, that any prediction said it would hit the Abacos." So, directly in response to **{–1289–}** Lloyd's claim that Serendipity, LLC's conduct "substantially increased the risk to the Subject Vessel," -- *i.e.*, increased the hazard -- Serendipity, LLC responded that Dorian was not predicted to hit the Abacos until hours before the yacht was destroyed. **[—19—]**

The argument continued in ¶ 63 of Serendipity, LLC's Statement of Material Facts. There, Serendipity, LLC claimed that "[a]t th[e] stated time frame [between August 24, 2019 and August 30, 2019], the hurricane was still predicted to hit Florida's coast line and not yet predicted to hit the Abacos. Trying to relocate the boat would have been a reckless endeavor."

Then, finally, in ¶ 66 of Serendipity, LLC's Statement of Material Facts, Serendipity LLC directly disputed the critical predicate fact upon which Captain Danti's report relied. That paragraph summarized, verbatim, some of the testimony of Captain Danti: "Based on the forecast information obtained by Dooley Sea-Weather, there is no question that a licensed Captain assigned to M/Y Serendipity would have made the decision to evacuate." Serendipity, LLC expressly disputed this fact, arguing that it "contradicts the weather reports that existed at that time," challenging the idea that "personal interpretations by lay people take precedence over licensed meteorologists," and then specifically referencing the weather reports in Exhibit 9, which show Hurricane Dorian consistently forecast to hit Cape Canaveral, including on August 30, 2019 -- the day the Serendipity was destroyed.

Moreover, in a footnote in his Report and Recommendation, the magistrate judge expressly said that he reviewed "the materials filed in connection with the motions," including Plaintiff's Statement of Material Facts. He also cited to Plaintiff's Statement of Material Facts on one occasion in his Report and **[—20—]** Recommendation, strongly suggesting that he was at least aware of the facts averred therein, including those found in ¶¶ 59, 63, and 66. So, in our view, Serendipity, LLC's argument was presented to the district court in its Motion for Summary Judgment and accompanying Statement of Material Facts. And our caselaw cannot be read to require Serendipity, LLC to reraise the same argument the district court rejected a second time in response to the district court's Rule 56(f) order. *See Browning v. AT&T Paradyne*, 120 F.3d 222, 225–26 (11th Cir. 1997) (finding an argument properly preserved when raised on summary judgment before a district court judge, even though the argument was not reraised in subsequent summary judgment briefing before a magistrate judge after the parties consented to magistrate jurisdiction); *cf. Belevich v. Thomas*, 17 F.4th 1048, 1051 n.1 (11th Cir. 2021) (concluding that "[b]ecause the [defendants] adequately presented their non-statutory defenses in their second amended answer and in their opposition to [plaintiff's] motion for a protective order, they have preserved these issues for appeal" even though the arguments were not reraised during summary judgment).

2.

At last, we come to the heart of this appeal -- whether a material dispute of fact remains about whether Serendipity, LLC's failure to hire a full-time licensed captain increased the risk to the Serendipity posed by Hurricane Dorian. We conclude that it does.

Under Florida law, **[—21—]**

> A breach or violation by the insured of a warranty, condition, or provision of a wet marine or transportation insurance policy, contract of insurance, endorsement, or application does not void the policy or contract, or constitute a defense **{-1290-}** to a loss thereon, unless such breach or violation increased the hazard by any means within the control of the insured.

Fla. Stat. § 627.409(2). "The statute is designed to prevent the insurer from avoiding coverage on a technical omission playing no part in the loss." *Pickett v. Woods*, 404 So. 2d 1152, 1153 (Fla. 5th DCA 1981). The question of whether an insured increased the hazard is typically a question of fact for the jury. *Pearl Assur. Co. v. S. Wood Prods. Co.*, 216 F.2d 135, 136 (5th Cir. 1954).[3]

Serendipity, LLC offers five reasons its breach did not increase the hazard:

> 1) two licensed captains were physically present with the Serendipity in the days leading up to Dorian hitting the Abaco; 2) Mr. Oakley was in regular communications with Captains McIntosh, Lightbourne and Connelly and the Cape Marina in the days and hours leading up to Dorian hitting the Abaco, and all **[—22—]** determined that it was best to leave the Vessel where it was; 3) Captains McIntosh and Lightbourne secured the Vessel with assistance from crew, and Mr. Oakley observed and oversaw the process via live video camera; 4) Captain Lightbourne stayed in the Pink Paradise, therefore a licensed Captain **was** with the Vessel at the time Dorian hit; 5) the suggestion that anyone, given Dorian's record-breaking unpredictability, changing nature and wind velocity, would have been able to predict Dorian's path to avoid Dorian in the days leading up to August 30 is ludicrous.

Lloyd's does not address any of these arguments directly. Instead, it claims that Serendipity, LLC offered no evidence to rebut Captain Danti's testimony that Serendipity, LLC's failure to employ a full-time licensed captain increased the hazard to the vessel. The district court agreed with the position taken by Lloyd's; it found that Serendipity, LLC "ha[d] produced no evidence to rebut [Captain Danti's] testimony," making the record "clear that [Serendipity, LLC]'s breach of the Captain Warranty increased the hazard within the control of the insured."

In our view, however, both Lloyd's and the district court failed to consider the ample evidence that we have already cited in the record creating a genuine dispute of fact about whether Serendipity, LLC's breach increased the hazard -- that Hurricane Dorian was consistently predicted to hit Central Florida, and that it would **[—23—]** have been "an unnecessary hazard to attempt to move the vessel" on account of Hurricane Dorian's strength and unpredictability. Serendipity, LLC supported this claim by attaching news articles and weather reports covering Hurricane Dorian's path as an exhibit to its Motion. And, again, Serendipity, LLC also clearly disputed Captain Danti's testimony in its Statement of Material Facts. It wrote, in no uncertain terms, that Captain Danti's testimony "contradicts the weather reports that existed at that time" and cited Exhibit 9 in support. This evidence plainly contradicts Captain Danti's testimony. We therefore cannot conclude, as the district court did, that Serendipity, LLC "produced no evidence to rebut [Captain Danti's] testimony."

A jury may well credit Captain Danti's testimony over the weather reports offered by Serendipity, LLC. But that is a credibility determination for the jury to make. The district court erred in granting summary **{-1291-}** judgment for Lloyd's when a disputed question of material fact remains about whether

---

[3] Decisions of the former Fifth Circuit issued before October 1, 1981, constitute binding precedent in the Eleventh Circuit. *Bonner v. City of Prichard*, 661 F.2d 1206, 1209 (11th Cir. 1981) (en banc).

Serendipity, LLC's breach of the Captain Warranty increased the hazard posed to the Serendipity by Hurricane Dorian.

Accordingly, we **REVERSE** the district court's order granting final summary judgment in favor of Lloyd's and **REMAND** this case to the district court for further proceedings.

United States Court of Appeals for the Eleventh Circuit

No. 20-14315

UNITED STATES vs. MOREL

Appeal from the United States District Court for the Southern District of Florida

Decided: March 23, 2023

Citation: 63 F.4th 913, 11 Adm. R. 495 (11th Cir. 2023).

Before **PRYOR,** Chief Judge, and **ROSENBAUM** and **MARCUS,** Circuit Judges.

[—2—] {-914-} **PRYOR,** Chief Judge:

Francisco Morel challenges his convictions for cocaine possession on two grounds: that the trial judge should not **{-915-}** have instructed the jury about the elements of conspiracy after Morel's cross-examination of a witness and that there was legally insufficient evidence for his convictions. But the district court accurately explained a legal term that a witness misunderstood. And under the prudent-smuggler doctrine, the jury had sufficient evidence to find that Morel had the *mens rea* required for his convictions. We affirm.

I. BACKGROUND

Federal agents arrested Morel as part of a bust of a cocaine-trafficking operation that involved the *Sea Hunter*, a 54-foot fishing vessel. Federal officers tracked the *Sea Hunter* on its return from the Dominican Republic, where it had been loaded with cocaine, to a house on the coast of southern Florida. The house was uninhabitable, with no running water, and there was no sign that anyone was living there. Federal officers who had been monitoring the *Sea Hunter* approached when they saw people begin to unload the ship. They arrested three of Morel's co-defendants, Gregorio Martinez, Luis Carlos Melendez, and Garibaldo Paulino, at the ship. They arrested co-defendant Rafael Gracesqui hiding under a **[—3—]** parked car. And they arrested Morel inside the house and Joel Moreno Rosario outside of it.

On board the *Sea Hunter*, officials found over 400 kilograms of cocaine organized into hundreds of bricks. Based on Paulino's estimates at trial, the *Sea Hunter* transported roughly $11.6 million of cocaine. There was so much cocaine involved in the transaction that the *Sea Hunter* smelled of cocaine.

A grand jury indicted all six men on four counts. Count one charged conspiracy to import cocaine, 21 U.S.C. § 963, count two charged importation of cocaine, *id.* § 952(a), count three charged conspiracy to possess cocaine with the intent to distribute it, *id.* § 846, and count four charged possession of cocaine with intent to distribute it, *id.* § 841(a)(1).

Morel and Martinez pleaded not guilty and proceeded to trial, where Paulino and Moreno testified against them. Morel did not call any witnesses of his own or testify, so his challenge to his conviction turns on the sufficiency of the prosecution's case.

The officers who surveilled the *Sea Hunter* and arrested Morel and his co-defendants testified about the surveillance and bust of the *Sea Hunter*. The prosecution also called a Homeland Security agent, who testified that Morel received a message that gave Morel, who lived in Orlando, the address 1395 Brickell Avenue, Miami the day before the *Sea Hunter* docked in Fort Lauderdale. Paulino had separately met with co-defendant Melendez at the 1395 Brickell Avenue location to discuss offloading the cocaine on **[—4—]** the morning the *Sea Hunter* docked. Melendez told Paulino that, just before he met with Paulino, he had been waiting for some other people who were going to help "pick up the drugs" from the *Sea Hunter*. The Homeland Security agent also testified that the GPS records connected to Morel's cell phone established that its holder traveled from 80 miles north of Miami to the 1395 Brickell Avenue address the day before the *Sea Hunter* arrived in Florida.

Cooperating witnesses Paulino and Moreno testified that Morel would have been at the house only if he had been a trusted and knowledgeable member of the conspiracy. Moreno was the navigator on the *Sea Hunter* on its trip to the Dominican Republic and back. Soon after Moreno arrived at the house in Fort Lauderdale aboard the *Sea Hunter*, Morel arrived carrying a bucket of oil for which the passengers on the boat had called. Moreno and Morel rested in the house together briefly, **{-916-}** but they did not discuss the *Sea Hunter*'s cargo.

When Moreno testified that he did not know Morel before they met at the house, Morel's counsel asked Moreno, "[Y]ou're not alleging that you conspired with Mr. Morel in this case[?]" Moreno said, "No." The district court held a sidebar conference in which the prosecution requested an instruction about the requirements of conspiracy. Morel's counsel objected that mid-trial instructions would prejudice his cross-examination, but the district court agreed with the prosecution's request. Moreno had also earlier testified that he did not "conspire[] directly" with Martinez. **[—5—]**

After the prosecution on redirect elicited from Moreno that he erroneously believed that to "conspire" with someone, one had to know the individual personally, the district court explained that members of a conspiracy do not have to know each other:

> [G]enerally speaking, under the law, a conspiracy is an agreement by two or more persons to commit an unlawful act. . . . Every member of the conspiracy becomes the agent or partner of every other p[erson]. The Government does not have to prove that all of the people named in the indictment were members of the plan or that those who were members made any kind of formal agreement. The heart of the conspiracy is the making of the unlawful plan itself. . . . A person may become a conspirator without knowing all the details of the unlawful plan or the names and identities of all the other alleged conspirators.

The next day, Moreno testified that although he did not know Morel before Morel arrived with the oil, he was not worried because he "thought that everything was in the family."

Paulino provided further testimony regarding Morel's role in the conspiracy. Paulino testified that he was in frequent contact with Melendez—with whom Morel waited at the house—about the details of the conspiracy and that Paulino, Moreno, and Melendez specifically discussed drug trafficking and referred to cocaine in particular. When Paulino arrived at the house and did not recognize Morel, he asked Melendez what Morel was doing there and "if it was clear for [him] to be there." As Paulino explained, "we[] **[—6—]** [were] trying to mak[e] a drug transaction, so I didn't want to put myself to, you know, expose myself to anybody there that . . . [didn't] belong there." Melendez confirmed that "friends" sent Morel over, so Paulino did not leave, but he testified that he would have fled if he had not been assured that Morel was "clear."

Paulino also explained that Morel was part of a conversation about securing oil for the *Sea Hunter* and volunteered to retrieve the oil because he knew what type was needed. According to Paulino, Morel was hired as a driver for the conspiracy and knew where the cocaine was to be transported after unloading; he even had the address in his phone's GPS. When the *Sea Hunter* arrived, Paulino and Melendez boarded and began to unload the drugs from a hidden compartment. And when Paulino became tired during that process, he asked Melendez if Morel and Martinez—who were inside the house—were going to help. Melendez told him to bring Morel and Martinez from the house onto the *Sea Hunter* to help unload the cocaine. Morel did not do so only because he was still away retrieving oil for the *Sea Hunter*.

After the prosecution rested, Morel moved for a judgment of acquittal based on insufficient evidence. The district court denied the motion. After the jury convicted Morel of counts three and four, Morel again moved for acquittal and for a new trial based on the lack of evidence. The **{-917-}** district court denied these motions in a written opinion. The district court sentenced Morel to 82 months of imprisonment and five years of supervised release. Martinez was acquitted. **[—7—]**

II. STANDARDS OF REVIEW

This Court reviews a decision to give jury instructions during trial for abuse of discretion. *United States v. McCoy*, 539 F.2d 1050, 1064 n.22 (5th Cir. 1976) (Wisdom, J.). We likewise "review the denial of a motion for a new trial for abuse of discretion," but we review any issues not raised in the district court for plain error. *United States v. Spoerke*, 568 F.3d 1236, 1244 (11th Cir. 2009) (citation omitted). Under plain-error review, we can reverse only if the error is plain, affects substantial rights, and "seriously affects the fairness, integrity, or public reputation of the judicial proceeding." *United States v. Bobal*, 981 F.3d 971, 975 (11th Cir. 2020) (citation omitted). And we review a denial of a motion for acquittal *de novo* when the defendant made the same challenge in the district court. *United States v. Almanzar*, 634 F.3d 1214, 1221 (11th Cir. 2011). We must affirm the conviction "unless no rational trier of fact could have found the essential elements of the crime beyond a reasonable doubt." *Id.* (citation omitted).

III. DISCUSSION

We divide our discussion into two parts. First, we explain that the district court did not abuse its discretion when it gave a jury instruction during Moreno's testimony. Second, we explain that sufficient evidence supported the jury's finding that Morel knew that the contraband on the *Sea Hunter* was cocaine. **[—8—]**

A. The District Court Did Not Abuse Its Discretion When It Gave a Corrective Instruction During Moreno's Testimony

The district court did not abuse its discretion when it intervened to prevent a misunderstanding of the law of conspiracy that Morel's counsel invited. As we have explained, "[a] trial judge is more than a referee to an adversarial proceeding. Indeed, the judge may question witnesses, comment on the evidence, and *interrupt the trial in order to correct an impropriety*." *United States v. Harris*, 720 F.2d 1259, 1261 (11th Cir. 1983) (emphasis added). "The judge's participation is limited only by the need to remain impartial." *Id.* at 1262.

A witness, Moreno, used the legal term "conspiracy" incorrectly. He implied that he had to personally know Morel to "conspire" with him. *Cf. United States v. Reeves*, 742 F.3d 487, 498 (11th Cir. 2014). The district court intervened to explain what the legal term meant. Without that intervention, the jury could have been confused about the significance of the facts to which Moreno testified. And the district court gave a curative instruction only after the prosecution's redirect examination made clear that the witness testified based on a misunderstanding of the word "conspire." It was not a departure from neutrality for the district judge to discharge his fundamental duty to "determine the law" and "instruct the jury on the law." *See United States v. Brown*, 996 F.3d 1171, 1183 (11th Cir. 2021) (en banc) (citations omitted).

This curative instruction was far from an impermissible, unfair instruction that one party's evidence is not to be believed. *See,* **[—9—]** *e.g., United States v. Fischer*, 531 F.2d 783, 786 (5th Cir. 1976) (reversing because the trial judge remarked to the jury that "someone obviously didn't tell the truth from the witness stand in this case" and hinted at the testimony the judge had in mind). The district court did not instruct the jury that Moreno lied or that he conspired **{-918-}** with Morel but instead left those questions to the jury. The district court only clarified the law.

Morel does not deny that the district court gave accurate instructions. Instead, he argues that the district court departed from its obligatory neutrality by *sua sponte* instructing the jury on the law of conspiracy after having allowed co-defendant Martinez's counsel to ask an indistinguishable question about "conspir[ing]" without a clarifying instruction. We disagree.

To the extent that Morel complains that the prosecution did not object to his trial counsel's question about "conspir[ing]," Morel misunderstands the role of the trial judge. If a party fails to object to testimony at trial, he can forfeit a challenge to that testimony and become obliged to prove plain error on appeal to obtain relief. *See United States v. Turner*, 474 F.3d 1265, 1275 (11th Cir. 2007). But the prosecutor's failure to object did not mean that the trial judge, as "the governor of the trial for the purpose of assuring its proper conduct and of determining questions of law," *Quercia v. United States*, 289 U.S. 466, 469 (1933), *could* not intervene *sua sponte*. And the prosecution, in any event, had requested at the earlier sidebar that the district court give the jury a curative **[—10—]** instruction. The district court did so only after the witness explained his erroneous understanding of a conspiracy.

Morel also argues that the district court was "inconsistent[]" because it allowed Martinez's counsel to ask Moreno whether he "conspired directly" with Martinez but issued clarifying instructions after Morel's counsel attempted a similar inquiry. This argument misses the point. The instruction was correct. If Martinez's counsel's line of questioning likewise should have been followed by a clarifying instruction, that error might have prejudiced the prosecution, but it would not affect Morel's rights. Any unfair advantage to Martinez would not be an unfair disadvantage to Morel. And the jury would have understood the curative instruction that the district court later gave to apply to the entirety of Moreno's testimony, not only his examination by Morel's counsel. After all, the district court prefaced its instruction with the phrase "generally speaking, under the law," and we presume jurors follow their instructions. *See Almanzar*, 634 F.3d at 1223.

Morel concedes that he did not mention this jury instruction in his motion for a new trial, so he must establish that it was plain error not to grant him a new trial on that basis. *Spoerke*, 568 F.3d at 1244. Morel's case for plain error fails at the first step: there was no error. **[—11—]**

B. Sufficient Evidence Supported the Finding that Morel Knew the Sea Hunter *Transported Cocaine.*

Morel challenges the legal sufficiency of the evidence for his convictions on the ground that the prosecution did not prove he had the requisite *mens rea* for his convictions. Specifically, he argues that the prosecution did not provide sufficient evidence from which the jury could infer that he knew that he was conspiring to possess *cocaine* in particular. Based only on the evidence at trial, Morel contends, he "could have just as easily thought that [*Sea Hunter*]'s cargo was contraband other than drugs, like guns or counterfeit currency or cigarettes."

Morel's challenge fails under the prudent-smuggler doctrine. *United States v. Duenas*, 891 F.3d 1330, 1334 (11th Cir. 2018); *see United States v. Cruz-Valdez*, 773 F.2d 1541, 1547 (11th Cir. 1985) (en banc) ("[A] prudent smuggler is not likely to suffer the presence of unaffiliated bystanders."). **{-919-}** Although he also marshals other challenges to his possession convictions, he failed to challenge one of the bases for conviction presented to the jury, so we affirm the district court on the basis Morel does not challenge.

Morel's two convictions—one for conspiracy to possess cocaine with the intent to distribute it and the other for cocaine possession with the intent to distribute it—share the element that he had to know that the substance in the *Sea Hunter* was cocaine. For his conspiracy conviction, the prosecution had to prove beyond a reasonable doubt that Morel "knew the essential nature of the conspiracy," including the type of contraband at issue. *United States v.* **[—12—]** *Ohayon*, 483 F.3d 1281, 1291 (11th Cir. 2007). And for his possession conviction, the prosecution had to prove that Morel knew what substance he possessed. *See* 21 U.S.C. § 841(a)(1); *United States v. Iglesias*, 915 F.2d 1524, 1527 (11th Cir. 1990).

The jury can infer knowledge from circumstantial evidence, and a jury may reasonably infer that "a prudent smuggler is not likely to suffer the presence of unaffiliated bystanders." *Duenas*, 891 F.3d at 1334 (quoting *Cruz-Valdez*, 773 F.2d at 1547). That is, "when the orchestrator of a conspiracy vests substantial trust in an associate to contribute to the scheme, a jury may infer the associate's knowing participation" and that "the smuggler will likely apprise him of the transaction's essential details, including the nature of the contraband involved." *Id.*

The prudent-smuggler doctrine forecloses Morel's challenge to his convictions based on a lack of *mens rea.* Morel's testifying co-conspirators established that Morel was communicating and working closely with at least Melendez, and Paulino testified that Melendez knew that he was participating in a conspiracy to traffic cocaine. Paulino met with Melendez at 1395 Brickell Avenue before the *Sea Hunter* arrived to discuss the offloading of the cocaine. At that time, Melendez told Paulino he was coordinating with other members of the conspiracy. Morel's phone records show that he received the same 1395 Brickell Avenue address, and GPS data from Morel's cellphone confirm that it arrived at that address shortly before the *Sea Hunter* docked in South Florida. A reasonable jury could infer that Melendez and Morel met at 1395 Brickell **[—13—]** Avenue and discussed what they were trafficking. Further, on the night the *Sea Hunter* arrived, when Paulino tired of unloading the cocaine, Melendez told him that he should bring the men from inside the house, including Morel, to help. Morel was away getting oil at the time, but Martinez complied with the request. Melendez would not have invited Morel onto the *Sea Hunter* to help unload cocaine if he were not a trusted co-conspirator, especially because the men who were unloading the cocaine could see what was in the packages they were transferring.

Morel was also privy to the time and remote location of the drug shipment and its eventual destination. Paulino testified that he would not have tolerated the presence of an outsider at the scene of the crime. Moreno likewise testified that he understood everyone at the house to be "in the family." The prosecution did not rely on Morel's mere presence at the crime scene to prove that he knew what contraband he was helping to traffic. *Cf. United States v. Louis*, 861 F.3d 1330, 1334–35 (11th Cir. 2017) (holding the evidence legally insufficient when the defendant had a legitimate pre-existing reason to be at the location of the contraband and there was little evidence of *mens rea* apart from presence at that location). As the district court explained when it denied Morel's **{–920–}** motions, a jury could have reasonably found that Morel's co-defendants would not have invited Morel to the secluded location of their docking at the critical moment of unloading if he were not a knowledgeable member of the conspiracy. The jury was also entitled to infer that Morel would not have been entrusted with driving the **[—14—]** cocaine to its next destination without knowing what he was assigned to drive.

Morel's argument—that he traveled across Florida to participate in a multi-million-dollar criminal plan without being privy to what contraband he was going to transport—makes little sense. The jury was entitled to reject it. We cannot set aside either of his convictions on the ground that insufficient evidence established the *mens rea* for his crimes.

Morel also argues that because the cocaine was in the *Sea Hunter* and he was in the house, there was no evidence that he had actual or constructive possession of the cocaine. He argues that he did not directly control the cocaine, nor did he have "dominion" over it or the *Sea Hunter* as required for constructive possession. *See Iglesias*, 915 F.2d at 1528. But the jury was also instructed that it could convict Morel for aiding and abetting the others' conspiracy to possess and their possession of the cocaine. Morel does not argue that the jury was not entitled to convict on this theory, so "he is deemed to have abandoned any challenge of that ground, and it follows that the judgment is due to be affirmed." *Sapuppo v. Allstate Floridian Ins. Co.*, 739 F.3d 678, 680 (11th Cir. 2014).

IV. CONCLUSION

We **AFFIRM** the judgment of conviction.

United States Court of Appeals
for the Eleventh Circuit

No. 21-14509

TRAVELERS PROPERTY CAS. CO. OF AM.
VS.
OCEAN REEF CHARTERS LLC

Appeal from the United States District Court for the Southern District of Florida

Decided: June 23, 2023

Citation: 71 F.4th 894, 11 Adm. R. 500 (11th Cir. 2023).

Before **NEWSOM, LUCK,** and **TJOFLAT,** Circuit Judges.

[—2—] {-896-} **TJOFLAT,** Circuit Judge: **{-897-}**

This is the second time this Court has considered this insurance coverage dispute between Travelers Property Casualty Company of America ("Travelers") and Ocean Reef Charters LLC, ("Ocean Reef"), a Florida Limited Liability Company. Ocean Reef owned a 92-foot yacht, the *M/Y My Lady*, which was destroyed during Hurricane Irma in September 2017. Ocean Reef had a $2 million insurance policy with Travelers covering property damage to the yacht. One of the *My Lady*'s representatives for Ocean Reef with respect to the boat, Richard Gollel, moored the yacht to a dock behind his Pompano Beach, Florida residence as the hurricane approached. But the yacht was destroyed by what registered as a Category 4 storm.

Travelers tried to avoid paying for the loss by preemptively seeking a declaratory judgment that the policy did not cover the loss because Ocean Reef did not have a full-time, licensed captain **[—3—]** and crew for the yacht during the hurricane, as required under warranties in the insurance policy. It brought the declaratory action in the Western District of New York, alleging that Ocean Reef had an office and its principal place of business in Rochester, New York.[1] Under New York state law, an insured forfeits coverage by violating a marine insurance warranty, regardless of whether the violation had any effect on the accident.[2] The same is true under federal admiralty law as applied to at least some marine insurance warranties. *Travelers Prop. Cas. Co. of Am. v. Ocean Reef Charters LLC*, 996 F.3d 1161, 1167–68, 9 Adm. R. 377, 380–82 (11th Cir. 2021).

The Western District of New York granted Ocean Reef's motion to transfer the case to the Southern District of Florida under 28 U.S.C. § 1404(a). The Court found venue proper in the Southern District of Florida because the convenience of witnesses favored Florida, New York bore little connection to the dispute, and, for the purposes of considering the motion to transfer, the **[—4—]** choice-of-law analysis favored applying Florida law rather than New York law. After the transfer, Ocean Reef—relying on Florida law—counterclaimed for damages on the theory that Travelers breached the insurance contract by refusing to cover the loss. It claimed it had a right to recover the policy maximum, as no deductible applied because the accident was a total loss of the yacht. Ocean Reef also sought declaratory judgments that the warranties did not preclude coverage. Under Florida law, an insured remains covered for an accident despite violating a **{-898-}** policy warranty, unless the violation "increased the hazard by any means within the control of the insured." Fla. Stat. § 627.409(2).

On cross-motions for summary judgment, the District Court granted summary judgment for Travelers, agreeing with it that federal law

[1] The Travelers insurance policy for the *My Lady* stated Ocean Reef was in care of Gollel's company, Richard Gollel & Co., Inc., which has a Rochester, New York address.

[2] *See Com. Union Ins. Co. v. Flagship Marine Servs., Inc.*, 190 F.3d 26, 31–32 (2d Cir. 1999) (discussing how, "[u]nder . . . the law of most states," including New York, "warranties in maritime insurance contracts must be strictly complied with, even if they are collateral to the primary risk that is the subject of the contract, if the insured is to recover" (citing N.Y. Ins. L. § 3106(c))). "However, unlike New York and the majority of states, Florida does not require strict compliance with all warranties, but it does preclude recovery where the 'breach or violation increased the hazard by any means within the control of the insured.'" *Id.* at 32 (quoting Fla. Stat. § 627.409(2)).

applied, and that Ocean Reef therefore forfeited its insurance coverage. On appeal, we reversed, holding that under *Wilburn Boat Co. v. Fireman's Fund Insurance Co.*, 348 U.S. 310, 75 S. Ct. 368 (1955), Florida law applied because we did not find that any "entrenched federal maritime rules governing captain or crew warranties" existed. *Travelers*, 996 F.3d at 1169, 1171, 9 Adm. R. at 383, 384. That meant Travelers would have to prove on remand that the failure to retain a full-time captain "play[ed] [a] part in the loss" under Florida's anti-technical statute.[3] *Id.* at 1170, 9 Adm. R. at 383 (quoting parenthetically *Pickett v. Woods,* 404 So. 2d 1152, 1153 (Fla. 5th Dist. Ct. App. 1981)). **[—5—]**

On remand, because Travelers offered no expert witness—such as a licensed captain competent to speak to the issue—to prove that the lack of a full-time captain and crew played a role in the destruction of the yacht during Irma, the District Court granted summary judgment to Ocean Reef. We affirm.

I.

A.

Ocean Reef first obtained insurance from Travelers for the *My Lady* in 2014. Coverage under that plan ran from October 10, 2014, through October 10, 2015. Ocean Reef renewed its policy for two more terms, so that in September 2017, it was covered by a policy running from October 10, 2016, through October 10, 2017. The policy covered Ocean Reef for up to $2,000,000 of property damage.

Ocean Reef's insurance policy had contained two express warranties since Ocean Reef first insured the *My Lady* with Travelers in 2014. One was called the "Captain Warranty." The Captain Warranty provides:

> It is warranted you employ a professional captain for the yacht shown on the Declarations Page of this policy. Such captain shall be employed full time and approved by us. We will pay up to $1,500 for the cost of hiring a replacement captain, approved by us, if **[—6—]** your captain is unable to perform his regular duties due to a medically certified cause.

The other warranty was called the "Crew Warranty." The Crew Warranty provides:

> You employ 1 full time or part time professional crew for your yacht shown on the Declarations Page of this policy. We also provide coverage for any additional, temporary crew you employ.

Travelers initially issued the insurance policy with the Captain and Crew Warranties only after Ocean Reef amended its application to represent that it would employ Jason Gabriel—a professional, licensed captain—as the full-time captain. Gabriel resigned later that year. Ocean Reef then hired Captain Michael McCall—another licensed, professional captain—in January 2015. Captain McCall accompanied Gollel and his family on a two-week trip to the Bahamas shortly after he began his duties. He remained captain of the *My Lady* until April 2015, though he noted in **{-899-}** his deposition that he did not consider the role a "full-time assignment" after the Bahamas trip.

The parties generally dispute the extent to which Ocean Reef complied with the Captain and Crew Warranties between April 2015 and September 2017; they also dispute Travelers' willingness to pay out claims in prior cases when Ocean Reef was non-compliant. Travelers paid a claim for damages to the yacht caused by a lightning strike in 2016, though it now claims it only "honored" the claim "after Ocean Reef provided proof that it had a pro- **[—7—]** fessional, full-time licensed captain[,] albeit one not previously submitted to Travelers for approval." The captain when lightning struck the boat was Captain Daniel Tam. Ocean Reef claims that, in paying out this

[3] Florida Statute § 627.409(2) is a "so-called 'anti-technical statute.'" *Travelers,* 996 F.3d at 1164, 9 Adm. R. at 378. The statute "was 'designed to prevent the insurer from **[—5—]** avoiding coverage on a technical omission playing no part in the loss.'" *Id.* at 1170, 9 Adm. R. at 383 (quoting parenthetically *Pickett v. Woods,* 404 So. 2d 1152, 1153 (Fla. 5th Dist. Ct. App. 1981)).

claim, "Travelers did not rely on the retroactive approval alone, and it was irrelevant," because Travelers' internal documents discussing the claim provided that Travelers also "determined that the 'capt[ain] was not material to this loss.'" (quoting a note by the Travelers adjuster assigned to review the claim). Ocean Reef says this note meant Travelers covered the loss because it knew "Florida's anti-technical statute" applied.

On the other hand, Travelers denied a claim for the loss of a jet ski that was stolen from the yacht in June 2017 while the *My Lady* was in the Bahamas. Travelers denied coverage "because the Vessel did not have a professional, licensed captain approved by Travelers at the time of the theft." Ocean Reef does not dispute the facts surrounding the denial of coverage for the theft of the jet ski. By August 2017, a Travelers underwriter had emailed management recommending that the company not renew Ocean Reef's coverage—which would expire on October 10, 2017—due to a "very shady" claims history.[4] Travelers then sent Ocean Reef a "notice of nonrenewal of insurance" dated August 14, 2017. **[—8—]**

Hurricane Irma approached Florida in early September 2017. On September 4, Gollel contacted Captain McCall—the former captain—to see if he could retake the helm as "temporary captain" of the *My Lady* during the storm. McCall said he was in Provincetown, Massachusetts, but would track the storm forecasts and fly down to move the yacht if appropriate.

The following afternoon, McCall called Gollel back.[5] McCall testified at his deposition that he "told him that after looking at the latest forecast, that [he] didn't see a safe place to take the boat." The hurricane forecast had changed, and it was projected "to go close to south Florida and then turn and go straight up the east coast." Gollel "agreed and told [McCall] that he had called a marina close by and he was waiting to hear back from them."

On September 6, Gollel then had his insurance agent reach out to Travelers' agent to request Travelers' permission to move his yacht, even though, per the email, Gollel was "in between captains." The email said Gollel was "requesting to be able to move the vessel himself, to a safe harbor in the vicinity, for the approaching Hurricane Irma." The email said **{-900-}** Gollel "has been boating his whole life" and ultimately wanted advice on whether he should instead "leave it where it is & just secure it with additional lines, bumpers, etc." **[—9—]**

Travelers' agent responded that evening by emailing Gollel's agent that she had "not yet heard back from [T]ravelers" about Gollel moving the boat himself and "would say to not move the boat until we have confirmation from the carrier. The insured is already in breach of warranty by not having a full-time captain so we don't want to chance it." Travelers' agent then reached back out on the morning of September 7 to inform Gollel's agent that Travelers had "requested an updated hurricane plan as this will need to go to home office for approval prior to anyone other than the [full-time] captain operating the boat."

Later that morning, Gollel's agent responded to Travelers' agent. She said: "[T]he insured is leaving the vessel docked where it is usually docked in lieu of moving it to inside the [Intracoastal waterway] where he feels it will be safer & suffer less damage." She then asked if there was "any way" the agent could get Travelers' underwriting department "on the phone quickly to see if they would prefer he move the vessel." Early that afternoon, Travelers' agent relayed the following from the insurer: "Given the impending weather threat and short notice given by the insured, the policy cannot be changed." Gollel explained in

[4] The email read: "Per discussions with Tom & Joe, I was told we should look to non-renew this account due to a very shady 2016 claim. I was told [that] the PWC theft is also suspect and when the first claim happened the Capt. said he was not full time and then he was, according to Joe, it just seems very shady." The email also noted the yacht had "a 655% loss ratio" due to the claims described above.

[5] McCall testified in his deposition that he made the last phone call regarding temporary service as captain three days after the first call, but that he had no reason to dispute his phone records showing a call the following day.

his deposition that he thought the nearby Intracoastal waterway would be a "more protected" place during the storm—presumably meaning "more protected" from waves and wind.

Gollel ended up securing the yacht to the dock behind his residence before the hurricane struck. His two sons assisted. Gollel testified at his deposition that they "tied the boat up with extra **[—10—]** ropes," positioned "extreme commercial bumpers between the boat and the dock," and "disconnected the anchor and chained the boat to a secure tree." They also secured loose items. They tied the yacht to ten concrete pilings that "ran perpendicular to the dock," and then to two "dolphin pilings" that were adjacent to the dock.

Hurricane Irma struck between September 10 and 11. During the storm, the *My Lady* sank. The parties describe the sinking's cause differently but generally agree that a mooring pile came loose, the boat hit Gollel's cement sea wall—which caused the hull to break—and it sank. The boat sustained enough damage to amount to a "total loss" under Ocean Reef's policy.

B.

Within a day after the hurricane, Ocean Reef submitted a claim for coverage of the loss of the *My Lady* and requested that Travelers front the money for raising the yacht out of the water. Travelers considered this request, and then informed Gollel on September 21 that it would front the money for raising the vessel but would still investigate whether it would cover the loss. Travelers then sent Ocean Reef a "reservation of rights" letter dated September 25, 2017, informing Ocean Reef that it reserved the right to deny coverage and to seek reimbursement for fronting the cost of raising the yacht out of the water.

On September 26, Travelers filed for a declaratory judgment in the Western District of New York—where it claimed Ocean Reef's principal place of business was located. The action sought a **[—11—]** declaration that Ocean Reef failed to comply with the Captain and Crew Warranties, and that the *My Lady*'s sinking was therefore not covered.

On November 9, 2017, Travelers sent Gollel a letter indicating it would continue **{-901-}** to front the money to finish raising and securing the vessel, but that it declined coverage for his claim because he failed to comply with the Captain Warranty and Crew Warranty. The letter also noted that Travelers had filed for a declaratory judgment in the Western District of New York "in support of th[e] Declination."

* * *

As indicated *supra*, Travelers likely engaged in a strategy to avoid the application of Florida's anti-technical statute, Fla. Stat. § 627.409(2). Under that statute, it would need to prove that the lack of a full-time captain and crew played a material role in the *My Lady*'s sinking to avoid paying Ocean Reef. On the other hand, under the federal rule that applies to some marine insurance warranties, *Travelers*, 996 F.3d at 1167–68, 9 Adm. R. at 380–82, "and the law of most states," including New York, "warranties in maritime insurance contracts must be strictly complied with, even if they are collateral to the primary risk that is the subject of the contract, if the insured is to recover." *Com. Union Ins. Co. v. Flagship Marine Servs., Inc.*, 190 F.3d 26, 31–32 (2d Cir. 1999) (citing N.Y. Ins. L. § 3106(c)). When the Western District of New York granted Ocean Reef's motion to transfer the case to the Southern District of Florida, it found—for **[—12—]** the purposes of that order—that "the choice-of-laws analysis disfavors New York and favors the State of Florida, which appears to have more relevant contacts." Travelers had to know that Florida law may apply, even if *Wilburn Boat*'s framework causes "confusion" as to which marine insurance warranties fall under federal rules requiring strict compliance. *See Travelers*, 996 F.3d at 1167–68, 9 Adm. R. at 380–82. The following reviews the evidence each side gathered about the accident.

* * *

In October 2017, Gollel spoke with Captain McCall. McCall then emailed Gollel and Lisa Steinhoff, a manager at Ocean Reef. The email explained McCall's arrangement with Gollel as Irma approached:

> I Captain Mike McCall was hired by Mr. Gollel on September 5 thru September 15 2017 as temporary Captain. At that time I was on another boat in New England but was going to make arrangements to fly down. Due to uncertainty of where to move the boat, Hurricane forecast, and miscommunications with Mr. Gollel I never made the arrangements and therefore [was] not present at the time.

Ocean Reef never compensated Captain McCall for this temporary captain assignment.

Neither party disclosed Captain McCall as an expert witness. So, at trial, he could only testify based on his "personal knowledge." Fed. R. Evid. 602. Any opinions he might give would need to be "rationally based on" his first-hand observations and **[—13—]** "not based on scientific, technical, or other specialized knowledge." Fed. R. Evid. 701(a), (c).

When Travelers deposed Captain McCall, it asked him about his prior experience preparing various boats for hurricanes as their captain. It also asked, in various ways, whether it is "generally" better to move a boat out of the path of a hurricane. The following exchange illustrates:

> **Travelers' Counsel**: Would you leave a vessel like the *My Lady* tied up to a concrete bulkhead during the storm that was anticipated?
>
> **McCall**: If that was the only option, yes.
>
> **Travelers' Counsel**: If there was—would there be an[y] preferable options that you can think of to leaving a vessel tied to a concrete bulkhead in the conditions that you were anticipating? **{-902-}**
>
> **McCall**: Yes. To move the vessel.
>
> **Travelers' Counsel**: What sort of locations would you consider to be a better option?
>
> [intervening objection to form]
>
> **McCall**: A long ways away from where the storm was projecting to hit.

McCall also noted that whether the Ocean Reef Marina would be "an appropriate place to leave the *My Lady* during hurricane conditions" would "depend[] on the conditions" and the particular circumstances of the storm. **[—14—]**

McCall then clarified on cross-examination by Ocean Reef's counsel that using straps and ropes to secure a boat would be "typical" when moving a boat out of a storm's path was not a viable option. He also said that he did not "see a good option . . . for moving [the *My Lady*] to avoid the storm entirely" because the storm was forecasted to move up the East Coast, where he had previously considered moving it.

Travelers did not disclose an expert witness for its case-in-chief to discuss what a captain would have done with the *My Lady* during Irma. On January 28, 2019, however, Travelers disclosed a rebuttal expert, Captain Joseph Ahlstrom, notifying Travelers that "Captain Ahlstrom may be called to rebut any testimony that Ocean Reef Charters LLC had a full-time, professional captain at any relevant time." It made this disclosure assuming a federal strict-compliance rule applied.

On February 25, 2019, Ocean Reef disclosed Captain Thomas Danti and Allister Dredge, a marine surveyor, as expert witnesses. They attached both experts' reports to the disclosure. The disclosure included both experts' qualifications, their opinions, and the bases for their opinions. *See* Fed. R. Civ. P. 26(a)(2). Captain Danti opined, after interviewing Gollel and inspecting the site, that the "storm preparations by Mr. Gollel met the standard of care of a professional Mariner." He also opined that "[t]he main cause of the vessel's damage was unforeseeable failure of a mooring pile." So, "[t]he lack of a full time captain would not have prevented the **[—15—]** yacht [from] becoming a total loss." Danti's bottom-line conclusion was: "There was no increase[d] hazard in risk to the vessel by not having a full time captain at the time of the incident."

Dredge, the surveyor, also opined that the damage to the yacht was a "constructive total loss," as repairs would cost $2.5 million.

Captain Danti fleshed out his opinion when Travelers' counsel deposed him. Danti answered various questions about moving boats away from hurricanes. The upshot of his answers was that there is "no magical formula" to preparing for a hurricane "except to try to do the best you can to protect your vessel in a particular location. So you have to take that into consideration, the size of the vessel, where it's located, how congested it is in the area," along with the weather conditions and how the vessel could be secured.

Captain Danti also discussed how finding an available place for a boat as a hurricane approaches can be challenging. He noted that, "if you go down any of the canals in Florida today, you'll see that they're all developed, that the ability to even put a boat in the mangroves has gone away because of development." As to the Intracoastal waterway, it "is very congested today, loaded with private docks and private yachts and is very limited as far as any locations that may be applicable for use that I know of." And as to whether hauling a boat out of the water is better than securing it in the water, he explained that "[t]he vessels that were damaged during Hurricane Irma in the islands, a lot of those boats were hauled out of the water **{-903-}** and then once the storm came through, it was like a domino effect." **[—16—]**

Travelers had thirty days from Ocean Reef's submission of Captain Danti's report on February 25, 2019, to disclose expert "evidence [that was] intended solely to contradict or rebut evidence on the same subject matter." Fed. R. Civ. P. 26(a)(2)(D)(ii). Thirty days from then was March 27, 2019. In a letter postmarked on April 1, 2019, Travelers mailed Ocean Reef a report—with March 29, 2019, as the date in the header—by Captain Ahlstrom purporting to rebut Captain Danti's opinions. In it, Ahlstrom opined, "Any competent captain would have recognized that the *My Lady* was in a perilous position moored behind Mr. Gollel's house at Hillsboro Inlet and needed to be relocated to a more sheltered location." He also opined that, "[d]uring the hurricane, the vessel pushed on pilings and the cement seawall[,] exactly the risk a competent captain would have recognized and sought to avoid by moving the vessel."

* * *

After we remanded the case for consideration under Fla. Stat. § 627.409(2), the parties held an unreported status conference on June 8, 2021. The District Court did not reopen discovery, and neither party claims it requested that the Court do so. Ocean Reef then renewed its motion for summary judgment and renewed a motion it had filed along with its first motion for summary judgment.[6] In the latter motion, Ocean Reef moved to either (1) strike Captain Ahlstrom's rebuttal report as untimely and beyond the initial disclosure—that he would rebut evidence offered to show **[—17—]** Ocean Reef had employed a full-time captain; or (2) preclude Travelers from calling Captain Ahlstrom to testify in its case-in-chief, and thereby exclude the report from consideration for summary judgment purposes.

Travelers responded to Ocean Reef's motion on Ahlstrom's report by making two arguments pertinent to this appeal. One was titled, "Travelers Timely Disclosed Captain Ahlstrom as its Expert, and any Delay in Producing Captain Ahlstrom's Rebuttal Report was Harmless" under Federal Rule of Civil Procedure Rule 37. *See* Fed. R. Civ. P. 37(c)(1) ("If a party fails to provide information or identify a witness as required by Rule 26(a) or (e), the party is not allowed to use that information or witness to supply evidence on a motion, at a hearing, or at a trial, unless the failure was substantially justified or is harmless."). It argued that even if it sent Ocean Reef the report too late, the delay was "hardly time for any prejudice to Ocean Reef." Travelers "alternatively pray[ed] for a brief extension of the expert disclosure deadline to

[6] Ocean Reef also argued in its renewed motion for summary judgment that Travelers could not meet its burden with a rebuttal expert.

bring its service of Captain Ahlstrom's report into compliance with Rule 26(a)(2)(D)(ii)," which provides the 30-day deadline for disclosure of expert rebuttal evidence. The second argument was titled, "Captain Ahlstrom's Report is Proper Rebuttal Testimony," meaning "Ocean Reef's Motion" to strike the report "should be denied because Captain Ahlstrom's report squarely rebuts Mr. Danti's opinions."

The District Court granted Ocean Reef's motion to exclude Ahlstrom from testifying in Travelers' case-in-chief and then **[—18—]** granted summary judgment for Ocean Reef because Travelers lacked competent evidence to prove its case under Florida law. The District Court held that Ocean Reef was "entitled to $2 million—the full coverage amount of the Vessel . . . in case of complete loss." As to Ahlstrom's report, the **{-904-}** Court only reached the issue of whether to exclude Ahlstrom from testifying in Travelers' case-in-chief but did not strike the report as untimely and implicitly assumed that it was proper rebuttal evidence, even if it went beyond the scope of Travelers' initial, January 2019 disclosure. This appeal followed.

II.

We review the District Court's grant of summary judgment *de novo*. *Penley v. Eslinger*, 605 F.3d 843, 848 (11th Cir. 2010). Summary judgment is proper when "there is no genuine dispute as to any material fact and the movant is entitled to judgment as a matter of law." Fed. R. Civ. P. 56(a). A party can show there is no genuine dispute of material fact by "showing that the materials cited do not establish the absence or presence of a genuine dispute, or that an adverse party cannot produce admissible evidence to support the fact." Fed. R. Civ. P. 56(c)(1)(B).

Travelers bore the burden of proof under Florida law. *See infra*, Part II.A. In moving for summary judgment, Ocean Reef bore "the initial responsibility of informing the district court of the basis for its motion," and then Rule 56 "mandate[d] the entry of summary judgment, after adequate time for discovery and upon **[—19—]** motion, against" Travelers if it "fail[ed] to make a showing sufficient to establish the existence of an element essential to [its] case, and on which [it would] bear the burden of proof at trial." *Celotex Corp. v. Catrett*, 477 U.S. 317, 322–23, 106 S. Ct. 2548, 2552–53 (1986). "'In such a situation, there [could] be 'no genuine issue as to any material fact,' since a complete failure of proof concerning an essential element of the nonmoving party's case necessarily renders all other facts immaterial.'" *Grange Mut. Cas. Co. v. Slaughter*, 958 F.3d 1050, 1057 (11th Cir. 2020) (quoting *Celotex*, 477 U.S. at 322–23, 106 S. Ct. at 2552). For the reasons discussed in *Travelers Property Casualty Co. of America v. Ocean Reef Charters LLC*, 996 F.3d 1161, 9 Adm. R. 377 (11th Cir. 2021), Florida law applies.

This case boils down to two issues. One is whether, under Florida's anti-technical statute, the insurance company must prove that the breach of the Captain Warranty "contribute[d] to" the *specific* accident. *Pickett*, 404 So. 2d at 1153. Travelers claims that all it must show is that the lack of a full-time captain *generally* makes vessels more susceptible to damage from hurricanes. Under Travelers' theory, Florida law does not require it to prove that Ocean Reef's noncompliance with the Captain Warranty actually caused *this* accident to any extent.

The second, related issue is whether, in meeting its burden of proof under Florida law, Travelers needed to introduce expert testimony in its case-in-chief about what would have been different if Ocean Reef had complied with the applicable warranties. Trav- **[—20—]** elers argues it could show that the lack of a full-time captain increased the hazard to the *My Lady* during Hurricane Irma without an expert witness in its case-in-chief. Instead, it claims it could meet its burden with lay testimony by Gollel that he wanted to move the *My Lady* as Hurricane Irma approached, and so-called "hybrid fact-expert witness testimony" by Captain McCall. Appellant's Br. at 23. Travelers also claims, "the District Court's decision to grant Ocean Reef's [motion] to the [sic] limit the testimony of Travelers' expert (Captain Ahlstrom) solely to rebuttal and, in turn, employ the general rule that the testimony of a rebuttal expert cannot be used to avoid summary judgment was an abuse of discretion." Appellant's Br. at 37.

Travelers is wrong on all counts. We address each issue in turn. **{–905–}**

A.

The Florida anti-technical statute we must apply provides:

> A breach or violation by the insured of a warranty, condition, or provision of a wet marine or transportation insurance policy, contract of insurance, endorsement, or application does not void the policy or contract, or constitute a defense to a loss thereon, unless such breach or violation increased the hazard by any means within the control of the insured.

Fla. Stat. § 627.409(2). "The statute is designed to prevent the insurer from avoiding coverage on a technical omission playing no part in the loss." *Pickett*, 404 So. 2d at 1153. Whether an insured **[—21—]** increased the hazard by noncompliance with a warranty "is typically a question of fact for the jury." *Serendipity at Sea, LLC v. Underwriters at Lloyd's of London Subscribing to Pol'y No. 187581*, 56 F.4th 1280, 1290, 11 Adm. R. 486, 493 (11th Cir. 2023) (citing *Pearl Assurance Co. v. S. Wood Prods. Co.*, 216 F.2d 135, 136 (5th Cir. 1954)).[7]

The Florida District Court of Appeal discussed the significance of the state's anti-technical statute in *Pickett*. There, an insurance company tried to avoid covering a claim for a death in a plane crash.[8] *Pickett*, 404 So. 2d at 1152–53. The insurer claimed that the loss was not covered because the policy did not apply to an insured "who operates or permits the operation of the aircraft, while in flight, unless its airworthiness certificate is in full force and effect." *Id.* at 1152. After the jury found, on a special verdict form, that the plane lacked a valid airworthiness certificate during the accident, the trial court entered judgment for the insurance company. *Id.*

The Florida District Court of Appeal reversed and remanded. The court explained that, "[f]rom the facts as stated" by the insured, "the crash was due to pilot error," as "the plane flew **[—22—]** into the ground while attempting to land in bad weather." *Id.* at 1153. The crash was not, however, "the result of any malfunction," so "the failure to have a valid airworthiness certificate did not contribute to the accident." *Id.* The court held that the anti-technical statute "should apply and prevent the insurance company from relying on the exclusion to deny coverage" if the trial court found on remand that the breach did not increase the hazard to the plane. *Id.* The court emphasized that if the insurer's "interpretation" of the anti-technical statute "were accepted, it would actually be to the insurer's advantage that the insured failed to renew the airworthiness certificate. In such event, the insurer would collect a premium but would have no exposure to risk because the policy would no longer be effective." *Id.*

We recently applied Florida's anti-technical statute in a case involving the destruction of a yacht during Hurricane Dorian. *See Serendipity at Sea*, 56 F.4th at 1282, 11 Adm. R. at 486–87. There, the insurer, not the insured, hired Captain Danti as an expert witness. *Id.*, 11 Adm. R. at 486. The insurer claimed Captain Danti offered "undisputed testimony" that the insured's **{–906–}** failure to "employ a full-time licensed captain in violation of the policy's Captain Warranty" increased the hazard to the yacht. *Id.*, 11 Adm. R. at 486. In essence, he opined that a full-time captain would have moved the boat away from the Bahamas—where the yacht was moored,

[7] Decisions of the former Fifth Circuit issued before October 1, 1981, constitute binding precedent in the Eleventh Circuit. *Bonner v. City of Prichard*, 661 F.2d 1206, 1209 (11th Cir. 1981) (en banc).

[8] The decedent had originally planned "to return [home] by commercial airline to Daytona Beach from a golfing trip in North Carolina." Tracie S. Boone, Case Note, Pickett v. Woods, *404 So. 2d 1152 (Fla. 5th DCA 1981)*, 10 Fla. St. U. L. Rev. 737, 741 (1983) (citing Appellant's Initial Br. at 5, *Pickett*, 404 So. 1152 (No. 80-1112)). He changed his mind and "accepted a ride home in a friend's Cessna 310," a propeller plane, "and played nine more holes of golf." *Id.*

and where the hurricane hit head on—and back to Cape Canaveral, the yacht's primary mooring location. *Id.* at 1287, 11 Adm. R. at 490. The District Court found Captain Danti's opinion on the matter undisputed because the insured did not offer an opposing expert and granted summary judgment to the insurer. *Id.*, 11 Adm. R. at 490. **[—23—]**

We reversed the District Court because we found Captain Danti's expert opinion relied on facts about which there was reasonable dispute. *See id.* at 1288, 11 Adm. R at 491–92. Specifically, we explained that the insured cited weather reports in its motion for summary judgment that showed Hurricane Dorian was unpredictable, and that as of the day before the storm hit the Bahamas—where the yacht was moored—it was projected to hit Cape Canaveral, not the Bahamas. *Id.* at 1283, 1289, 11 Adm. R. at 487, 492. That undermined Captain Danti's opinion that a full-time captain would have moved the yacht from the Bahamas to Cape Canaveral. *See id.* at 1287–89, 11 Adm. R. at 490–93. So, there was a genuine factual issue for the jury as to whether the lack of a full-time captain increased the hazard to the yacht. *Id.* at 1290–91, 11 Adm. R. at 493–94.

The rule from these cases is clear: to meet its burden under Florida's anti-technical statute, the insured must show that, under the circumstances of the specific accident at issue, the breach of the warranty had some material effect on the loss. Otherwise, the insurer could "avoid[] coverage on a technical omission playing no part in the loss." *Pickett*, 404 So. 2d at 1153.

B.

The next question is whether Travelers has admissible evidence that raises a genuine issue of material fact about whether the lack of a full-time captain or crew played a material role in causing the *My Lady*'s sinking. Because Travelers did not disclose an expert to testify in its case-in-chief, it lacks evidence from which a jury could reasonably find in its favor. **[—24—]**

The effect of Ocean Reef's failure to retain a full-time captain and crew leading up to and during Hurricane Irma is exactly the kind of issue that requires expert testimony. The question is hypothetical. Discussing what *would have* happened if a captain *were* in charge of the *My Lady* during Hurricane Irma necessarily requires hypothesizing. "And the ability to answer hypothetical questions is '[t]he essential difference' between expert and lay witnesses." *United States v. Henderson*, 409 F.3d 1293, 1300 (11th Cir. 2005) (citation omitted) (alteration in original).

As Rule 701 provides, a lay witness could not competently offer an opinion on what a captain would have done with the *My Lady* if one were in charge. Federal Rule of Evidence 701, Opinion Testimony by Lay Witnesses, states:

> If a witness is not testifying as an expert, testimony in the form of an opinion is limited to one that is:
>
> (a) rationally based on the witness's perception;
>
> (b) helpful to clearly understanding the witness's testimony or to determining a fact in issue; and
>
> (c) not based on scientific, technical, or other specialized knowledge within the scope of Rule 702.

Fed. R. Evid. 701.

So, a lay witness can only speak to what he in fact observed. Rule 701 permits opinions, but only those "rationally based on **{-907-}** the **[—25—]** witness's perception" that help clarify the lay witness's actual observations, and which do not rely "on scientific, technical, or other specialized knowledge." *Id.* A lay witness cannot offer a hypothesis about what caused the *My Lady* to sink or what professional captains or crews might have done to change the outcome. Indeed, the question here is what *experts* would have done differently to avoid the accident.

Travelers' attempts to avoid this fundamental problem with its case-in-chief do not work. There is no such thing as "hybrid fact-expert witness testimony" in the sense that Travelers claims. Appellant's Br. at 23. Of course, a properly disclosed and qualified expert can testify as both an expert and a fact witness. But the Advisory Committee's note to the 2000 amendment to Rule 701—the amendment that added Rule 701(c)—explicitly says that the amendment was designed to "eliminate the risk that the reliability requirements set forth in Rule 702 will be evaded through the simple expedient of proffering an expert in lay witness clothing." Fed. R. Evid. 701 advisory committee's note to 2000 amendment. And so, "[b]y channeling testimony that is actually expert testimony to Rule 702, the amendment also ensures that a party will not evade the expert witness disclosure requirements set forth in Fed. R. Civ. P. 26 and Fed. R. Crim. P. 16 by simply calling an expert witness in the guise of a layperson." *Id.*

True, a lay witness who has a job requiring expertise may acquire first-hand, "particularized knowledge" of probative facts **[—26—]** while performing her duties. *Id.* For example, a physician's observation of a patient's injury during treatment is permissible lay testimony (assuming it is otherwise admissible). *See Henderson*, 409 F.3d at 1300. But a hypothesis about causation is outside a lay witness's competency, even if the lay witness happens to have the expertise to draw such conclusions.[9] *See id.*; *see* **{-908-}** *also* 4 *Weinstein's Federal Evidence* § 701.03[1] (2023) ("Regardless of the degree to which **[—27—]** a witness's lay opinion is based on specialized knowledge, it seems clear that the witness's personal perception will remain a fundamental prerequisite to admissibility.").

---

[9] There is some gray area between lay and expert testimony when the lay witness has expertise and used that expertise to make first-hand observations. For example, in *Henderson*, we noted that a treating physician's "diagnosis of the injury itself, that [the victim's] jaw was fractured, would be permissible lay testimony." 409 F.3d at 1300. But we have not held that any treating physician can testify as a lay witness about any diagnosis she made while treating the patient. The plain language of Federal Rule of Evidence 701(c) prohibits lay opinions "based on scientific, technical, or other specialized knowledge within the scope of Rule 702." Fed. R. Evid. 701. A diagnosis requiring more complex diagnostic reasoning than that required to notice a broken jaw may fall under Rule 701(c)'s prohibition. *See* Stephen A. Saltzburg et al., 3 *Federal Rules of Evidence Manual* § 701.02[7] (Matthew Bender 12th ed.) ("When the [treating] physician testifies that the plaintiff was coughing and running a fever, this is lay witness testimony governed by Rule 701. However, if the physician also testifies that he diagnosed the patient as having Reactive Airways Dysfunction Syndrome caused by exposure to a toxic chemical, then this is testimony based on scientific, technical, or other specialized knowledge and must be qualified under Rule 702.") (citing *Williams v. Mast Biosurgery USA, Inc.*, 644 F.3d 1312, 1317–18 (11th Cir. 2011)). We also note that the Tenth Circuit cases we cited for the so-called "treating physician" doctrine, under which "[a] treating physician is not considered an expert witness if he or she testifies about observations based on personal knowledge, including the treatment of the party," *Davoll v. Webb*, 194 F.3d 1116, 1138 (10th Cir. 1999), both predated the 2000 **[—27—]** amendment to Rule 701. The other case was *Weese v. Schukman*, 98 F.3d 542 (10th Cir. 1996).

In *Williams v. Mast Biosurgery USA*, we summarized "our discussion" of the treating physician doctrine in *Henderson* as follows: "[W]hen a treating physician's testimony is based on a hypothesis, not the experience of treating the patient, it crosses the line from lay to expert testimony, and it must comply with the requirements of Rule 702." 644 F.3d at 1317–18. We also emphasized that "[t]he testimony of treating physicians presents special evidentiary problems that require great care and circumspection by the trial court," *id.* at 1316, and "that trial courts [must] be vigilant in ensuring that the reliability requirements set forth in Rule 702" are not "'evaded through the simple expedient of proffering an expert in lay witness clothing.'" *Id.* at 1317 (quoting *Henderson*, 409 F.3d at 1300 (quoting Fed. R. Evid. 701 advisory committee's note to 2000 amendment)).

Here, the issue is what *would have* happened *if* the *My Lady* had a captain, a hypothetical that McCall cannot speak to as a lay witness. In an appropriate case, we should clarify when a lay witness goes too far in discussing observations that he made using his expertise.

Accordingly, Captain McCall—whom Travelers did not disclose as an expert witness—could not provide his opinion on what would have happened to the *My Lady* if a licensed, professional captain were employed full-time. He could discuss the weather forecasts he observed and relate what Gollel asked of him. But those facts would leave the jury to speculate about what a captain would have done differently to avoid the storm under the specific circumstances of this case. **[—28—]**

Nor does evidence of Gollel's subjective desire to move the *My Lady* before the hurricane change the equation. Gollel, who is not a professional captain, thought his yacht might have been safer somewhere else. But where the yacht would have actually been safer was not within the competence of a nervous boat-owner as the storm approached.

Finally, Travelers cannot rely on potential testimony from Captain Ahlstrom to avoid summary judgment because it only disclosed him as a rebuttal expert. If the case went to trial, Travelers would first present its case-in-chief as plaintiff. It would need to prove that the lack of a captain had some material effect on the *My Lady*'s demise. It would not have an expert to present in its case-in-chief. After it rested, Ocean Reef would move for judgment as a matter of law under Rule 50 of the Federal Rules of Civil Procedure. The District Court would grant the motion because "a reasonable jury would not have a legally sufficient evidentiary basis to find for" Travelers. Fed. R. Civ. P. 50(a)(1). We can therefore grant summary judgment for Ocean Reef because Travelers does not have a legally sufficient case to present.

III.

Travelers' remaining argument is that the District Court abused its discretion in refusing to consider Captain Ahlstrom's report for summary judgment purposes. Specifically, Travelers argues that it was "effectively seeking to use a rebuttal expert as a primary expert, [which] was akin to a motion to add or substitute an expert." Appellant's Br. at 39. Travelers emphasizes that after **[—29—]** remand, the burden of proof flipped in that it had to prove the lack of a full-time captain played a role in the accident. So, Travelers claims the District Court "should have employed its discretion to allow Travelers a modicum of flexibility to adjust to that change (at the time Ocean Reef filed and Travelers responded to Ocean Reef's Motion to Strike Captain Ahlstrom) by allowing Travelers some flexibility with regard to Captain Ahlstrom's use as an expert." *Id.* at 38. Travelers claims there was "'good cause' to re-designate or effectively substitute Captain Ahlstrom as Travelers' primary expert in this case." *Id.* at 38–39 (quoting **{-909-}** Fed. R. Civ. P. 16(b)(4) ("A schedule may be modified only for good cause and with the judge's consent.")).

When reviewing the District Court for abuse of discretion, we must affirm unless the District Court made a legal error—such as "appl[ying] an incorrect legal standard" or "follow[ing] improper procedures in making a determination"—or made "clearly erroneous" factual findings. *Equal Emp. Opportunity Comm'n v. Eberspaecher N. Am. Inc.*, 67 F.4th 1124, 1130 (11th Cir. 2023) (internal quotation marks and citation omitted). The District Court did not consider a motion to redesignate Captain Ahlstrom as an expert for Travelers' case-in-chief because Travelers did not file one. In its response to Ocean Reef's motion to exclude Captain Ahlstrom's report, Travelers asked the District Court not to strike Ahlstrom's rebuttal report as untimely. And it argued that his report rebutted Captain Danti's opinions as if it did not have the burden of proof or did not need an expert to meet that burden. The District Court did not strike the report. But Travelers did not move the Court to **[—30—]** redesignate Ahlstrom as a case-in-chief expert. And the District Court correctly applied Rule 56 by refusing to consider rebuttal evidence as evidence that could meet Travelers' burden of proof. We will not reverse the District Court for failing to *sua sponte* rescue Travelers' case.

IV.

All told, without expert testimony about what a professional captain would have done differently to avoid harm to the *My Lady* during Hurricane Irma, the jury would have had to speculate to find for Travelers under Florida's anti-technical statute. And we see no need to give Travelers another bite at the apple. The District Court's grant of summary judgment is

AFFIRMED.

United States Court of Appeals
for the Eleventh Circuit

No. 21-13850

SKANSKA USA CIVIL SOUTHEAST INC.
vs.
BAGELHEADS, INC.

Appeal from the United States District Court for the Northern District of Florida

Decided: August 2, 2023

Citation: 75 F.4th 1290, 11 Adm. R. 512 (11th Cir. 2023).

Before **BRANCH** and **GRANT,** Circuit Judges, and **SCHLESINGER,*** District Judge.

* The Honorable Harvey E. Schlesinger, United States District Judge for the Middle District of Florida, sitting by designation.

[—3—] {-1297-} **GRANT,** Circuit Judge: **{-1298-}**

Hurricane Sally hit Pensacola Bay with a vengeance in September 2020, and 28 barges moored in the Bay were not spared. The barges slammed around the Bay after their moorings snapped, leading to significant damage—including to the Pensacola Bay Bridge, which was closed for months. Skanska, the construction company that owned the barges (and was working on replacing the Bay Bridge) faced hundreds of potential lawsuits. Some were directly related to property damage, but most were economic loss claims from nearby businesses that lost customers during the months-long closure of the bridge.

Skanska filed what are called petitions for limitation of liability, one for each of its 28 barges. These petitions invoked the Limitation Act, a federal law that allows the owner of a maritime vessel to limit its damages in a negligence suit to the combined **[—4—]** value of the vessel and its cargo—but only where the owner has neither privity nor knowledge of the negligent acts at issue. After extensive discovery and a bench trial, the district court decided that Skanska could not limit its liability because its own corporate officials were responsible for the negligent acts that led to the barges getting loose in the storm. And once it decided that no limitation of damages could apply, it dismissed the Limitation Act petitions—freeing the claimants to pursue litigation in state court.

Skanska says the district court acted too fast, because the Limitation Act entitles it to more than a decision on limitation of damages (the denial of which it does not contest). It claims that the Limitation Act required the district court to decide whether it was liable to each and every claimant and only *then* to determine whether it had a right to limit that liability. Here, it says, that would have meant dismissing the economic loss claims because it had no duty as the owner of the barges to prevent that sort of indirect damage.

Skanska's approach would turn the Limitation Act on its head, and our precedents have already rejected it. We have been clear that the purpose of the Act is limitation, not exoneration. And the statute's text is equally clear—we see no mandate to enforce the two-step process that the company insists is necessary. The Limitation Act allows a federal court to take over all negligence claims to preserve the vessel owner's right to limit its liability and then proportionally distribute the available assets to the successful claimants. But only to the extent necessary to protect the right to **[—5—]** limitation; it does not create an independent right to have the full merits of each **{-1299-}** individual claim decided in federal court when no limitation is available.

Skanska also disputes several of the district court's other decisions, including multiple evidentiary rulings, the conclusion that it committed negligent acts when it left the barges in the Bay, and the imposition of spoliation sanctions for the destruction of cellphone data. Here too we disagree. We see no reversible error in the district court's evidentiary rulings, its findings of fact, or its spoliation sanctions. We therefore affirm the district court.

I.

A.

Pensacola is a city in the westernmost part of the Florida panhandle. It is known for its access to beaches, which attract both locals and tourists from across the country. But Pensacola Bay separates the actual city of Pensacola from the area's major beaches (and from several smaller towns such as Gulf Breeze). Pensacola remains connected to its beaches thanks to the Pensacola Bay Bridge—a roughly three-mile bridge across the Bay that has existed in some form since the 1930s.

Around 2010, the bridge needed replacing. Skanska USA Civil Southeast Inc.—which is wholly owned by Skanska USA, Inc.—won a contract to build two new spans and then to destroy **[—6—]** the old bridge.[1] Those tasks required construction barges—lots of them. Skanska had a hurricane preparedness plan for the project. If winds of 58 miles per hour or greater were expected within the next 72 hours, the plan called for the construction barges to be moved to Butcherpen Cove on the south side of the Bay, a process that would take at least 30 hours.

The first major warning sign of Hurricane Sally came on Thursday, September 10, 2020, five days before Skanska's barges began to break loose. That's when the National Hurricane Center issued its notice of a potential storm. Skanska had 55 barges working on the project, and the record does not show that anyone at Skanska was yet aware of the notice. The next day, the National Hurricane Center issued Advisory 1 about what it then called "Tropical Depression 19." Though it projected that the storm would most likely land at the border between Louisiana and Mississippi, Pensacola Bay fell in the possible 5-day path. Still no sign that Skanska was aware of the storm.

By Saturday morning, that had changed. The National Hurricane Center's 72-hour report showed a 16% chance that winds of 58 miles per hour or greater would reach Naval Air **[—7—]** Station Pensacola (a few miles west of the bridge) by Tuesday. Skanska decisionmakers conferenced on Saturday afternoon. By that point, the storm had been upgraded to Tropical Storm Sally and forecasters thought it would be a hurricane by Monday evening. The storm was still projected to make landfall near the Louisiana-Mississippi border—but Pensacola Bay remained on the outskirts of the storm's three-day probable path. Skanska management decided to begin preparations to move and secure the barges if necessary. But—in part because of logistical issues with moving the barges over the weekend—the group largely took a "wait **{-1300-}** and see" approach and agreed to meet again the next morning.

By then, Sunday, the National Hurricane Center had issued a tropical storm warning for the panhandle coast. The 72-hour forecast was slightly better than it had been on Saturday, but it still showed a 9% chance that winds of 58 miles per hour or greater would hit Naval Air Station Pensacola by Wednesday. Skanska began moving its barges, but decided not to take them all the way to Butcherpen Cove. Instead, it moored the barges to various pipe pilings in the Bay—generally within 500 feet of the bridge. Most, but not all, of the barges were tied down by Monday morning, which is also when Tropical Storm Sally was upgraded to Hurricane Sally and the Governor of Florida issued a State of Emergency for the greater Pensacola area. By Monday afternoon, Pensacola Bay was squarely within the hurricane warning zone. **[—8—]**

On Tuesday morning, Naval Air Station Pensacola reported winds from 15–26 miles per hour, with gusts reaching almost 45 miles per hour. Skanska's barges began to break loose in the Bay, and multiple barges crashed into the bridge. At first, Skanska tried to secure its unmoored barges, but by Tuesday evening it was too dangerous to continue the recovery attempts. On Wednesday, when Hurricane Sally passed through the Bay, it brought winds from 47 to 74 miles per hour, with gusts as high

[1] The district court sat in admiralty and made findings of fact after a bench trial. "When reviewing the judgment of a district judge sitting in admiralty with no jury, we may not set aside the court's findings of fact unless they are clearly erroneous." *Dresdner Bank AG v. M/V Olympia Voyager*, 446 F.3d 1377, 1380 (11th Cir. 2006). So—other than those findings of fact that Skanska challenges, which we review for clear error—we take all of the district court's findings of fact as true.

as 92 miles per hour—causing even more barges to slip their moorings. In the end, 28 barges came loose, slamming into the bridge and other property along the Bay's edge.[2] The bridge was closed to traffic for many months because of the damage. This dramatically increased the amount of time it took to get between Pensacola and the towns and beaches on the other side of the Bay.

B.

In short order, Skanska found itself facing state-court lawsuits—many lawsuits—about the damage caused by its barges. Seeking both to limit its liability and to consolidate the multiplying claims in a single forum, Skanska initiated proceedings in federal district court under the Limitation Act. The core of that Act is relatively simple: when a vessel causes "loss, damage, or injury by **[—9—]** collision" without the vessel owner's "privity or knowledge," the owner's liability is limited to the value of the vessel and its pending freight. 46 U.S.C. § 30523.

To initiate a limitation proceeding, a vessel owner brings a civil action and deposits the value of the vessel and its freight with the district court. *Id.* § 30529; Fed. R. Civ. P. Supp. Admiralty & Mar. Claims (Supplemental Rules) F(1), F(2), F(9). This creates a single equitable proceeding about the damage caused by the vessel. All other litigation about the incident—whether in state or federal court—must "cease." 46 U.S.C. § 30529(c); Supplemental Rule F(3); *Beiswenger Enters. Corp. v. Carletta*, 86 F.3d 1032, 1036 (11th Cir. 1996). At the same time, those injured by the vessel retain rights under the "saving to suitors" clause. 28 U.S.C. § 1333. That clause, which accompanied the original grant of admiralty jurisdiction to federal district courts, ensures that federal admiralty jurisdiction does not eliminate traditional remedies, including state jury **{-1301-}** trials. *Lewis v. Lewis & Clark Marine, Inc.*, 531 U.S. 438, 443–46, 453–55 (2001).

Between December 2020 and March 2021, Skanska filed 28 petitions for exoneration or limitation of liability—one for each barge that broke loose during the storm. Following Skanska's unopposed motion, all 28 proceedings were consolidated.[3] The consolidated proceedings followed standard Limitation Act **[—10—]** procedure: Skanska deposited the value of each of the barges with the district court, initiating a Limitation Act proceeding for each barge, and the court enjoined the filing or prosecution of all related proceedings in other courts. Parties alleging that they had suffered harm from the loose barges then filed claims in the consolidated proceeding, generally with "reservation of rights to proceed in state court."

Some of these claims came from people and entities whose property was directly damaged by the barges—the United States, for example, alleged that multiple barges caused millions of dollars of damage when they allided with property at Naval Air Station Pensacola. But most of the filings came from businesses claiming not direct physical damage, but economic loss suffered after the closure of the Pensacola Bay Bridge. As an example, the top-line plaintiff here is Bagelheads, Inc., a bagel shop immediately next to the bridge on the Pensacola side. It says it suffered more than $90,000 in damages from the bridge outage because the dramatic increase in travel time from Pensacola to the beach and to the residential towns on the other side of the bridge cut the shop's sales by 35%. And Bagelheads was not alone—hundreds of similar claims followed. Skanska moved to dismiss these claims from the limitation proceeding, arguing that it owed no duty to any party whose property did not suffer direct physical damage from the barges.

---

[2] The district court mentioned 27 barges that broke loose. But Skanska initiated Limitation Act proceedings for 28 barges, and on appeal, both parties refer to 28 barges as having broken loose. We adopt the parties' characterization that 28 barges broke loose for clarity, but we do not hold one way or the other whether the district court's finding that 27 barges broke loose was erroneous.

[3] Twenty-two of the proceedings were consolidated in an order on February 15. The remaining six proceedings were filed on March 26 and were treated as part of the consolidated proceeding.

The district court entered a scheduling order setting a deadline for claimants to join the proceeding and directing all **[—11—]** claimants to join in two amended master complaints—one for direct property damage and one for economic damage arising from the bridge outage. The court also announced a bifurcated bench trial. First, the court would consider whether Skanska was entitled to limitation of liability. That involved deciding whether the accident was caused by any negligent acts and, if so, whether Skanska had privity or knowledge of the negligence. Next—but only if that first inquiry showed that Skanska had a right to limit its liability—the parties would conduct damages discovery and the court would schedule any necessary further proceedings. Neither Skanska nor the claimants objected to this scheduling order.

In the end, over 1,000 claimants joined the proceedings—more than 900 of whom alleged economic loss damages from the bridge outage. After the window closed for new filings, Skanska renewed its motion to dismiss the economic loss claims. The court deferred consideration of that issue, in part to better protect the claimants' right to litigate in the forums of their choice if Skanska were denied limitation.

During discovery, Skanska sought evidence about the claimants' storm preparations, including extensive discovery from the United States Navy about steps it had taken at the nearby naval air station. A magistrate judge handling pretrial issues held that the Navy's preparations were of **{-1302-}** minimal relevance because it operated seagoing vessels (not barges) and that Skanska's discovery of the Navy was not proportional to the needs of the case. *See* Fed. R. Civ. P. 26(b). Despite that discovery order, Skanska requested **[—12—]** depositions from fifteen individuals under the control of the United States Navy, and the magistrate judge granted the Navy a protective order.

After discovery, the district court conducted a five-day bench trial on two issues: Skanska's negligence and Skanska's right to limit its liability. Yet again, an evidentiary dispute arose. Skanska examined a tugboat captain who had two barges moored to a wharf in Pensacola Bay during Hurricane Sally, with the court repeatedly warning Skanska's counsel that his questions about the captain's personal experience up to and during the hurricane were mostly irrelevant and directing him to get to the point. After about 14 minutes, the court dismissed the captain, but Skanska was allowed to proffer the rest of his testimony, which showed that the captain would have testified about his experience with storms and about his decision to moor his barges in Pensacola Bay during Hurricane Sally.

The district court ultimately concluded that Skanska had acted negligently. It began with "the *Louisiana* rule," which creates a rebuttable presumption that a vessel is negligent when it collides with a stationary object. *See In re Skanska USA Civil Se. Inc.*, 577 F. Supp. 3d 1302, 1313–14 (N.D. Fla. 2021) (citing *Bunge Corp. v. Freeport Marine Repair, Inc.*, 240 F.3d 919, 923 (11th Cir. 2001)); *The Louisiana*, 70 U.S. (3 Wall.) 164, 173 (1866). The court rejected Skanska's assertion that it was "caught off guard" by the storm and found that Butcherpen Cove would have been a safer place to moor the barges. 577 F. Supp. 3d at 1314–18. The "only surprise" to **[—13—]** Skanska, the court said, "was that its unreasonable choice to discount—or even ignore—the clear warnings of an approaching tropical storm turned out to have harsh consequences." *Id.* at 1322.

The court quickly rejected Skanska's "perfunctory" argument that it lacked privity or knowledge of the negligent acts, pointing out that those acts "sprung wholly from executive decision-making that resulted in the failure to take reasonable measures to protect its barges from the impending storm." *Id.* at 1324. It then dismissed Skanska's petitions for exoneration from or limitation of liability and dissolved the injunction barring prosecution of all related litigation. *Id.* The court never ruled on Skanska's motion to dismiss the economic loss claims.

C.

Along with the adverse verdict, Skanska was sanctioned for spoliating electronic evidence under Rule 37(e); the data from five out of thirteen discovery custodians' cell phones was destroyed. Even with an active litigation hold and actual litigation, Skanska did not back up the relevant employees' cell phones. Nor did it suspend its ordinary cell phone data destruction policies.

Two phones were deliberately reset according to Skanska's ordinary employee departure procedures when their owners left the company. Another was somehow "disabled" and became inaccessible after the owner left Skanska. Yet another was allegedly lost overboard. And still another had all text messages deleted under disputed circumstances. **[—14—]**

The district court ruled that Skanska "acted with the intent to deprive" the claimants of the cell phone data and sanctioned **{-1303-}** the company under Rule 37(e)(2).[4] The court emphasized that it saw no cogent explanation, apart from bad faith, for Skanska's systematic failure to make *any* effort to preserve cell phone data until at least seven months after the litigation hold was (technically) in place. So it made two adverse inferences against Skanska and ordered it to pay the claimants' costs and attorneys' fees for the sanctions motion.

Skanska appeals both the district court's final judgment and its sanctions order, and we consolidated the appeals. Skanska also moved to stay the dissolution of the district court's injunction pending appeal to prevent the lawsuits from proceeding against it in state court, but we denied its request.

II.

We begin by addressing Skanska's core argument—that the district court violated the Limitation Act by failing to first adjudicate the full merits of the claims before deciding whether its liability could be limited. In particular, we consider Skanska's argument that it was entitled to have the economic loss claims dismissed, which would have barred the claimants from bringing **[—15—]** those claims in another forum. We review questions of law about the scope of the Limitation Act de novo. *See Dresdner Bank AG v. M/V Olympia Voyager*, 446 F.3d 1377, 1381 (11th Cir. 2006). And we review the district court's decision to dismiss the entire Limitation Act proceeding for abuse of discretion. *See Lewis*, 531 U.S. at 454.

A.

The Limitation Act is a difficult statute. It was written in 1851 to address economic realities that are unrecognizable today.[5] *Lewis*, 531 U.S. at 446–47. And it was "badly drafted even by the standards of the time." *Id.* at 447 (quoting 2 T. Schoenbaum, *Admiralty and Maritime Law* 299 (2d ed. 1994)). Of course, that does not change this Court's job—we apply the law as it exists, no matter how poorly it may have aged. But, keenly aware of the inscrutability of this statute, we offer relevant background about the basic history and substance of the Act (and its implementing rules), the petitioner's ability to demand exoneration, the **[—16—]** injunction against ongoing litigation, and the Act's relationship with the equally mysterious saving to suitors clause.

[4] The claimants' spoliation motion was referred to a magistrate judge, who issued the opinion sanctioning Skanska. But the district court denied Skanska's objections to the order and "wholly concur[red]" with the magistrate judge, so we refer to the magistrate judge's order as coming from the district court for clarity.

[5] Nearly fifty years ago, our predecessor Court referred to the Act as "hopelessly anachronistic"—largely because it was a creative way to limit liability "in an era before the corporation, with its limited shareholder liability, had become the standard form of business organization and before the present range of insurance protection was available." *Univ. of Tex. Med. Branch at Galveston v. United States*, 557 F.2d 438, 441, 454 (5th Cir. 1977). It also quoted a leading 1950s admiralty treatise that said the Act "has been due for a general overhaul for the past seventy-five years." *Id.* at 441 & n.3 (quoting Grant Gilmore & Charles L. Black, Jr., *The Law of Admiralty* 677 (1st ed. 1957)). If Gilmore and Black were right, then we are at 141 years and counting.

First, the history. In 1851, Congress thought the American shipping industry was disadvantaged as compared to its foreign competitors. *See Lewis*, 531 U.S. at 446–47. Unlike their counterparts in England, American courts did not limit the potential liability of vessel owners. *See generally* Joseph C. Sweeney, **{-1304-}** *Limitation of Shipowner Liability: Its American Roots and Some Problems Particular to Collision*, 32 J. Mar. L. & Com. 241, 243–52 (2001). Congress stepped in, enacting the Limitation Act "to encourage ship-building and to induce capitalists to invest money in this branch of industry." *Lewis*, 531 U.S. at 446 (quoting *Norwich Co. v. Wright*, 80 U.S. (13 Wall.) 104, 121 (1872)). To that end, the Act limits a vessel owner's liability for any "loss, damage, or injury by collision . . . done, occasioned, or incurred, without the privity or knowledge of the owner." 46 U.S.C. § 30523(b).[6] And "consistent with the statutory purpose to protect innocent investors, 'privity or knowledge' generally refers to the vessel owner's personal participation in, or actual knowledge of, the specific acts of negligence or conditions of unseaworthiness which caused or contributed to the accident." *Suzuki of Orange Park, Inc.* **[—17—]** *v. Shubert*, 86 F.3d 1060, 1064 (11th Cir. 1996).[7] In other words, the Act limits the liability of vessel owners who were not in some sense responsible for the specific negligent acts or conditions of unseaworthiness that caused the accident. *Id.*

If a vessel owner is entitled to limitation, then its liability is limited to the post-accident value of the vessel and its pending freight. 46 U.S.C. § 30523(a); *Tug Allie-B, Inc. v. United States*, 273 F.3d 936, 939 (11th Cir. 2001). That means that the owner's *total* loss—its liability plus the loss from the accident itself—will be no greater than the value of the vessel and its cargo. The Act also recognizes that multiple would-be plaintiffs might need to share in these limited funds, so it provides that—if the funds are insufficient to pay all claims—injured parties will be "paid in proportion to their respective losses." 46 U.S.C. § 30525(1).

When courts first began to apply the Limitation Act, they encountered a major problem: it had no procedures. In the Supreme Court's first case about the Act, the Court observed that it was "reduced to the dilemma of inferring that the legislature has **[—18—]** passed a law which is incapable of execution." *Norwich*, 80 U.S. (13 Wall.) at 123. So the Court took matters into its own hands, promulgating rules of admiralty to implement the Act. *Lewis*, 531 U.S. at 447 (citing Supplementary Rules of Practice in Admiralty, 80 U.S. (13 Wall.) xii–xiv (1872)). A vessel owner seeking limitation of liability would deposit the value of his interest in the vessel and its freight before the court. *Id.* Then, the district court would order all claimants to appear. *Id.* If the vessel owner was entitled to limitation, the court would distribute the limited fund among the claimants. *Id.* at 448.

Congress eventually codified the basic bond posting procedure for the Limitation Act, and the Supreme Court over time has amended and restyled the limitation rules. **{-1305-}** *See* 46 U.S.C § 30529; Supplemental Rule F. But the same basic structure remains, and the Act's procedures are still primarily implemented by court rule rather than statute.

One of those procedures is the injunction against existing litigation. When a Limitation Act petition is filed, the district court enjoins the prosecution of all pending litigation that overlaps with the subject matter of that

[6] While this appeal has been pending, Congress restructured and renumbered the codified Limitation Act and limited the extent to which the Act applies to certain small passenger vessels. James M. Inhofe National Defense Authorization Act for Fiscal Year 2023, Pub. L. No. 117–263, § 11503, 136 Stat. 2395, 4130–31 (2022).

[7] Linguistically, the idea of a vessel owner having "privity or knowledge" of specific "negligent acts" is a little awkward; ordinarily, one thinks of privity as being with *actors*, not of *acts*. But the meaning of this clause can be clarified by thinking about the archetypical case of limitation: a nineteenth century shipowner whose ship was thousands of miles away, completely outside of his control, when the crew unexpectedly acted negligently. In such cases, the vessel owner might be in a formal sense in privity with the negligent *actors*, but would not be thought to have had "privity or knowledge" of the crew's specific negligent acts.

petition. 46 U.S.C. § 30529(c); Supplemental Rule F(3). A pause in other litigation about the incident is necessary to protect the limitation fund—after all, the plaintiffs' combined damages may well exceed the value of the vessel and its cargo. But if one or more plaintiffs received final judgments in other litigation that exceeded this value, then the vessel owner's right to limit its liability would be meaningless. **[—19—]** Here, the injunction stopped lawsuits like the one the bagel shop filed in Florida state court—but only while the limitation petitions were pending. Skanska's objection is that the district court dissolved the injunction and allowed the lawsuits to proceed.

Finally, we discuss the complicated relationship between the Limitation Act and the saving to suitors clause. *See* 28 U.S.C. § 1333. That clause falls not in the Limitation Act, but in the general grant of admiralty jurisdiction to the federal district courts. *Id.* It gives federal district courts "original jurisdiction, exclusive of the courts of the States" of any "civil case of admiralty or maritime jurisdiction." *Id.* But it does so while "saving to suitors in all cases all other remedies to which they are otherwise entitled." *Id.* Both this grant of federal jurisdiction and the clause's corresponding protection of suitors have existed in some form since the Judiciary Act of 1789. *Lewis*, 531 U.S. at 443–44 (citing Judiciary Act of 1789, ch. 20, § 9, 1 Stat. 73, 77). The Supreme Court has "theorized that the saving to suitors clause was 'inserted, probably, from abundant caution,'" so that the grant of admiralty jurisdiction was not wrongly understood to eliminate "'the concurrent remedy which had before existed'"—state tort lawsuits. *Id.* at 444 (quoting *N.J. Steam Navigation Co. v. Merchs.' Bank of Bos.*, 47 U.S. (6 How.) 344, 390 (1848)). This clause, then, makes it clear that the existence of federal admiralty jurisdiction (which offers no jury right) does not generally keep plaintiffs from seeking relief in other forums—perhaps forums that *do* offer a jury trial. *See id.* at 445–46, 454–55; *see also, e.g.*, *Suzuki*, 86 F.3d at 1063. **[—20—]**

Make no mistake—"tension exists between the saving to suitors clause and the Limitation Act." *Lewis*, 531 U.S. at 448. The former protects the right to a jury trial. *Id.* at 445–46, 454–55. The latter creates a proceeding with no jury trial and stays all litigation in any other forum—including where a jury trial would be available. *Id.* at 448. In light of these somewhat contradictory provisions, the district court is charged with safeguarding a vessel owner's right to have the question of limitation adjudicated in federal court while simultaneously ensuring that claimants retain their choice of forum under the saving to suitors clause.

Both this Court and the Supreme Court have repeatedly grappled with this interplay. *See, e.g.*, *Offshore of the Palm Beaches, Inc. v. Lynch*, 741 F.3d 1251, 1257–59, 2 Adm. R. 536, 539–42 (11th Cir. 2014); *Lewis*, 531 U.S. at 448–56; *Suzuki*, 86 F.3d at 1063–64; *Beiswenger*, 86 F.3d at 1036–40; *Lake Tankers Corp. v. Henn*, 354 U.S. 147, 150–54 (1957); **{-1306-}** *Langnes v. Green*, 282 U.S. 531, 541–44 (1931). At least a few clear principles have emerged. To start, a vessel owner has an "absolute right to claim the Act's liability cap, and to reserve the adjudication of that right in the federal forum." *Beiswenger*, 86 F.3d at 1037 (quotation omitted). This guarantee means that a primary duty of the limitation court is to ensure that outside lawsuits do not undermine its exclusive authority to decide limitation. And if that right to limitation cannot be adequately protected with other lawsuits proceeding elsewhere, the limitation court may adjudicate the merits of the entire controversy—which means deciding both liability and limitation. *Lewis*, 531 U.S. at 454. But if the right to litigate and enforce limitation in federal court *is* protected, the **[—21—]** saving to suitors clause counsels in favor of giving plaintiffs their choice of forum. *Id.* at 454–55. In that case, the district court has "discretion to stay or dismiss Limitation Act proceedings to allow a suitor to pursue his claims in state court." *Id.* at 454.

B.

With this background, we can address Skanska's argument that the Limitation Act requires a federal court to decide whether it owed a duty to each and every claimant—or, to put it another way, Skanska's argument that it had a right to be exonerated in federal court.

Skanska primarily leans on a two-step procedure that we have said is "typical" in a Limitation Act case: "First, the court must determine what acts of negligence or conditions of unseaworthiness caused the accident. Second, the court must determine whether the shipowner had knowledge or privity of those same acts of negligence or conditions of unseaworthiness." *Beiswenger*, 86 F.3d at 1036 (quoting *Hercules Carriers, Inc. v. Florida*, 768 F.2d 1558, 1563–64 (11th Cir. 1985)); *see also, e.g., Farrell Lines, Inc. v. Jones*, 530 F.2d 7, 10 (5th Cir. 1976); *Hartford Accident & Indem. Co. v. S. Pac. Co.*, 273 U.S. 207, 214–15 (1927); *Providence & N.Y. S.S. Co. v. Hill Mfg. Co.*, 109 U.S. 578, 595 (1883).[8] Skanska reads these cases as creating a mandatory order of decision for nearly all Limitation Act cases. And, in Skanska's telling, that mandatory first **[—22—]** step includes a decision on *every* element of negligence—duty, breach, injury, and actual and proximate cause—for *every* claimant. So, Skanska claims, the district court violated this order of decision by reaching the question of privity and knowledge before fully adjudicating its liability to each claimant.

This Court has already rejected Skanska's rigid reliance on the "typical" Limitation Act procedure. We have held that if it is "impossible under any set of circumstances for the vessel owner to demonstrate the absence of privity or knowledge," then "the admiralty court may decide the privity or knowledge issue without first deciding the liability issue." *Suzuki*, 86 F.3d at 1064. Although *Suzuki* articulated a summary judgment standard, the same basic principle logically applies at every stage of the proceedings, including after a trial.[9] Once it is apparent that the vessel owner cannot establish a lack of **{-1307-}** privity or knowledge, then limitation is not at issue. And if limitation is not at issue, then "the basis for granting exoneration vanishes." *Id.* (quoting *Fecht v. Makowski*, 406 F.2d 721, 723 (5th Cir. 1969)). So whenever the court finds that the vessel owner cannot establish a lack of privity or knowledge, it is appropriate to dismiss the petition to protect the claimants' rights under the saving to suitors clause—even if that means forgoing (in part or in entirety) a decision on the vessel owner's liability. **[—23—]**

This is consistent with decades of Limitation Act law about claimants' saving to suitors clause rights. The Act does "not create a freestanding right to exoneration from liability in circumstances where limitation of liability is not at issue." *Lewis*, 531 U.S. at 453. It is about limitation of liability, not immunity from liability or the exclusivity of the federal forum. *Lake Tankers*, 354 U.S. at 152–53. Courts should thus "give effect to both the Limitation Act and the saving to suitors clause whenever possible" and "damage claimants must be allowed to litigate the vessel owner's negligence in state court, 'where it is apparent that limitation cannot be granted.'" *Beiswenger*, 86 F.3d at 1037; *Suzuki*, 86 F.3d at 1063 (quoting *Fecht*, 406 F.2d at 722).[10]

Here, Skanska's "perfunctory" claim that it lacked privity or knowledge straightforwardly failed (indeed, Skanska did not even appeal the district court's finding that the company had privity or knowledge). After all, the decision not to move the barges to safety was made by Skanska executives, and when a corporation owns a vessel, "the privity and knowledge of corporate managers vested with discretionary

[8] All published cases of the former Fifth Circuit decided before the close of business on September 30, 1981, are precedent in this Circuit. *See Bonner v. City of Prichard*, 661 F.2d 1206, 1207 (11th Cir. 1981) (en banc).

[9] The district court declined to apply *Suzuki* at summary judgment, holding that it was still possible at that point in the litigation for Skanska to show a lack of privity or knowledge. But clearly, after trial, the court determined that Skanska could not meet its burden to show a lack of privity or knowledge.

[10] Skanska claims that *Beiswenger* identifies the only instances in which district courts may depart from the two-step Limitation Act procedure. But *Beiswenger* did not attempt to identify every scenario where procedural flexibility is appropriate. To the contrary, we read *Beiswenger* as blessing procedural creativity by district courts in order to give effect to both the clause and the Limitation Act "whenever possible." *See* 86 F.3d at 1037.

authority is attributed to the corporation." *Suzuki*, 86 F.3d at 1065 (quotation omitted). Once it was clear that Skanska had privity or knowledge of any negligent acts that caused **[—24—]** the barges to damage property, it was equally clear that the company had no right to limit its liability. So there was no continued need for a limitation proceeding. The district court thus did not abuse its discretion by dismissing the consolidated proceedings.[11]

While we can resolve this case on precedent alone, the text of both the Limitation Act and its rules point in the same direction. The operative provisions of the Limitation Act do not mention exoneration. *See* 46 U.S.C. §§ 30501–30530. The only source of positive law that even plausibly supports Skanska's argument is Rule F's statement that a vessel owner "may demand exoneration from as well as limitation of liability." Supplemental Rule F(2). **{-1308-}** But this argument misses the mark. The rule's history clarifies its narrow scope. The limitation rules' exoneration language was added to clarify that, unlike under the "very onerous" English rules, an American vessel owner did not need to concede liability in order **[—25—]** to seek limitation of liability. *Lewis*, 531 U.S. at 447–48 (quotation omitted). In light of this history, we see no reason to think that this language does anything more than preserve the right to contest liability while also seeking limitation; it certainly does not "create a freestanding right to exoneration from liability in circumstances where limitation of liability is not at issue." *Id.* at 453.

Even if there were evidence that Rule F somehow expanded vessel owners' rights to a federal forum, we would not be able to read it that way. Judicially promulgated rules cannot "abridge, enlarge or modify any substantive right." 28 U.S.C. § 2072; *see also In re Tidewater Inc.*, 249 F.3d 342, 347 (5th Cir. 2001) (rejecting an aggressive reading of Rule F on this ground). Any tension between the judicially adopted rules and the congressionally enacted saving to suitors clause must be resolved in the clause's favor. No matter how Skanska frames its argument, it simply has no right to a federal forum beyond the question of limitation.[12] **[—26—]**

As a last resort, Skanska points to dicta saying that the Act and its rules protect vessel owners from "being harassed by litigation in other tribunals" which could lead to the "subversion of the whole object and scheme of the statute." *Providence & N.Y. S.S. Co.*, 109 U.S. at 594–95; *see also, e.g., Hartford*, 273 U.S. at 215–16. But the Court has long-since abandoned this dicta. For example, in *Lake Tankers*, "the Court explicitly rejected the argument that the Limitation Act protects the vessel owner against a multiplicity of suits." *Beiswenger*, 86 F.3d at 1039 (citing *Lake Tankers*, 354 U.S. at 153–54). If limitation is not implicated, the Court noted, there is no reason why a vessel owner "should be treated

[11] The parties dispute, for what it is worth, whether the district court even departed from the two-step procedure. Although the court did not determine every element of negligence for every claimant, it did decide that Skanska's negligence in not moving the barges to Butcherpen Cove caused the damage to the bridge and other property struck by the barges. The claimants argue that this finding was enough to show what "acts of negligence caused the accident," satisfying the first step of the two-step procedure, while Skanska argues that nothing short of a full adjudication of every element of negligence for every individual claimant will do. But we think that this debate misses the point; it does not matter whether the district court followed the ordinary two-step procedure. All that matters is that Skanska's right to have limitation adjudicated in federal court was protected—and it was.

[12] None of this is to say that the two-step approach articulated in many Limitation Act cases is obsolete. After all, it is an intuitive way to approach the problem. "Without negligence there can be no privity or knowledge," because the vessel owner's privity or knowledge must be of a particular negligent act. *Farrell Lines Inc.*, 530 F.2d at 10 n.1 (quoting 3 *Benedict on Admiralty*, § 41, p. 5-5). So it makes sense that courts often decide negligence (either in part or in full) before deciding privity or knowledge. At the same time, courts should not overread our discussions of the "typical" Limitation Act case, including the occasional use of the word "must" when discussing the steps of that procedure. "The language of an opinion is not always to be parsed as though we were dealing with language of a statute." *Nat'l Pork* **[—26—]** *Producers Council v. Ross*, 143 S. Ct. 1142, 1155 (2023) (alteration adopted and quotation omitted).

any more favorably than an airline, bus, or railroad company." *Lake Tankers*, 354 U.S. at 153. To be sure, if Congress wishes to protect vessel owners from a multiplicity of suits, it can always expand the Limitation Act and contract the saving to suitors clause. But in the meantime, courts and litigants alike must respect the relationship between these laws.

Neither Skanska's appeals to procedure nor its gestures to policy sway our conclusion that the district court did not abuse its discretion in dismissing Skanska's limitation petitions without fully addressing the question of Skanska's liability. Yes, Skanska had the right to have the question of limitation adjudicated in federal court. And the question of limitation *was* adjudicated in federal court. But **[—27—]** that is as far as it goes. Once the district court decided that Skanska was not entitled to **{-1309-}** limitation, it correctly dismissed the case so that the claimants could pursue remedies in whichever forums that they chose.[13]

III.

Skanska also challenges two evidentiary rulings: the order limiting its discovery of the Navy's preparations during Hurricane Sally and the court's mid-testimony dismissal of Captain Towne at trial.[14] "We review a district court's evidentiary rulings for abuse of discretion." *Great Lakes Ins. SE v. Wave Cruiser LLC*, 36 F.4th 1346, **[—28—]** 1353, 10 Adm. R. 394, 397 (11th Cir. 2022). And "even a clearly erroneous evidentiary ruling will be affirmed if harmless." *Id.*, 10 Adm. R. at 397 (quotation omitted). An error is harmless unless "it affects the substantial rights of the parties" such that the reviewing court cannot confidently say that "the judgment was not substantially swayed by the error." *Furcron v. Mail Ctrs. Plus, LLC*, 843 F.3d 1295, 1304 (11th Cir. 2016) (quotation omitted).

Starting with the Navy, under Rule 26(b), parties may only obtain discovery that is both "relevant" and "proportional to the needs of the case." Fed. R. Civ. P. 26(b)(1). The magistrate judge's discovery order limited discovery relating to the Navy because it was irrelevant *and* because it was not proportional. On appeal, Skanska only argues that its proposed discovery was relevant—it never explains why the burdens were proportional to the benefits. Skanska has therefore forfeited any challenge to proportionality, so we affirm. *See Sapuppo v. Allstate Floridian Ins. Co.*, 739 F.3d 678, 681 (11th Cir. 2014).[15]

As for Captain Towne, the district court heard nearly fifteen minutes of his testimony while repeatedly urging Skanska's counsel to get to the point. It then considered the captain's testimony via a one-sided proffer, and it explicitly stated that the full testimony would not have affected its decision. Any exclusion **[—29—]** of relevant evidence that the captain might have offered was harmless.

---

[13] Skanska fleetingly briefs another procedural argument, saying that the district court violated Federal Rule of Civil Procedure 12(i) by failing to rule on its 12(b)(6) motion. If Skanska wished to argue that Rule 12(i) required the district court to address the motion to dismiss before the first phase of the bifurcated trial, then it needed to raise that issue before the first phase of the bifurcated trial. It did not do so, instead raising the issue for the first time in post-judgment motions. We review issues not timely raised before the district court only for plain error, and rarely in civil cases. *See SEC v. Diversified Corp. Consulting Grp.*, 378 F.3d 1219, 1227 & n.14 (11th Cir. 2004). "Under the civil plain error standard, we will consider an issue not raised in the district court if it involves a pure question of law, and if refusal to consider it would result in a miscarriage of justice." *Burch v. P.J. Cheese, Inc.*, 861 F.3d 1338, 1352 (11th Cir. 2017) (quotation omitted). Refusing to consider this argument does not result in a miscarriage of justice, and we therefore do not consider it.

[14] Skanska says that the order denying discovery of the Navy led them to believe that the court would not allow discovery of other parties. It now argues that, because this constructively denied additional discovery, the entire discovery process was defective. But it goes without saying that Skanska cannot challenge a hypothetical ruling of the district court. We therefore review only the two specific evidentiary rulings that Skanska appeals.

[15] Because we affirm the limitation of the discovery as non-proportional, we do not address whether the information Skanska sought was relevant.

IV.

Moving to the factual basis for the district court's final judgment, Skanska challenges the finding that it did not exercise **{-1310-}** reasonable care.[16] For maritime tort cases, "we rely on general principles of negligence law" and have consulted "in particular the Restatement (Second) of Torts" to discern these general principles. *Tesoriero v. Carnival Corp.*, 965 F.3d 1170, 1178, 8 Adm. R. 463, 466–67 (11th Cir. 2020) (quotations omitted). Whether the defendant's conduct violated the standard of care is a question of fact. *See* Restatement (Second) of Torts § 328C cmt. b (Am. L. Inst. 1965). Because the district court sat in admiralty without a jury, we review its findings of fact for clear error. *Dresdner Bank*, 446 F.3d at 1380. A factual finding is clearly erroneous if "the entirety of the evidence leads the reviewing court to a definite and firm conviction that a mistake has been committed." *Id.*

The core of the district court's analysis was simple: Under the *Louisiana* rule, Skanska bore the burden of disproving a presumption that it failed to exercise reasonable care. Throughout the weekend, the National Hurricane Center's weather forecasts showed a 9–16% chance of 58 mile per hour or greater winds hitting Pensacola Bay. According to Skanska's own hurricane **[—30—]** preparedness plan, these wind speeds warranted moving the barges to Butcherpen Cove. Skanska's inability to get its barges to Butcherpen Cove before high winds arrived was one of two things: a deliberate choice or the consequence of a failure to act more quickly. Either way, the court explained, Skanska left its barges in a less safe location than Butcherpen Cove—and its gamble backfired with disastrous consequences. Given the substantial damage that the barges could do to others if the wind unmoored them, the court found that a reasonable company facing a 9–16% chance of these winds would have moved the barges. Thus, the court held, Skanska acted unreasonably by leaving the barges by the bridge.

This conclusion was not clearly erroneous. Skanska does not attempt to show that the district court's finding that there was a 9–16% chance of high winds hitting the Bay was incorrect. Nor does it present us with evidence that a reasonable company would have left its barges by the bridge notwithstanding those odds of high winds. Indeed, it fails to engage with the factual findings of the lower court, instead repeating its arguments below about how its preferred weather reports did not show that a hurricane was more likely than not to hit Pensacola Bay until Monday morning (without ever suggesting exactly how likely the storm was to hit the Bay) and emphasizing the difficulty of moving the barges over the weekend. This argument is non-responsive to the district court's finding that reasonable care required Skanska to take **[—31—]** precautions even with a 9–16% chance of high winds in the Bay. Skanska has failed to show reversible error.[17]

V.

Finally, Skanska challenges spoliation sanctions it received under Rule 37(e)(2) for the destruction of the data from five of its custodians' cell phones. We review that decision for abuse of discretion. **{-1311-}** *Tesoriero*, 965 F.3d at 1177, 8 Adm. R. at 465. In the spoliation context, this Court has often articulated our abuse of discretion review as asking whether the district court "has made a clear error of judgment, or has applied the wrong legal standard." *Mendez v. Wal-Mart Stores E., LP*, 67 F.4th 1354, 1361 (11th Cir. 2023) (quotation omitted). But we see no difference between this formulation of the

---

[16] We do not read the district court as having decided whether Skanska violated any duty to any particular claimant. So Skanska is still free to argue in state court that it did not owe a duty to the economic loss claimants.

[17] Relatedly, Skanska challenges the district court's factual finding that its hurricane preparedness plan was triggered at all. But we agree with the district court that the core inquiry is "whether the decision to demobilize the barges near the bridge was reasonable," making the question of whether Skanska's plan was triggered largely beside the point. *In re Skanska USA Civil Se. Inc.*, 577 F. Supp. 3d at 1317. In any event, the court's interpretation of the plan was not clear error.

abuse of discretion standard and our articulations of that standard in other contexts. *See, e.g., Callahan v. United Network for Organ Sharing*, 17 F.4th 1356, 1360 (11th Cir. 2021) ("A district court abuses its discretion when it applies an incorrect legal standard, follows improper procedures in making the determination, makes findings of fact that are clearly erroneous, or commits a clear error of judgment." (quotations omitted)). Accordingly, as is typical for this Court's abuse of discretion review, we review the district court's **[—32—]** legal conclusions de novo and its subsidiary factual findings for clear error. *Common Cause Ga. v. Georgia*, 17 F.4th 102, 107 (11th Cir. 2021). That means that we review the district court's conclusion that Skanska acted in bad faith—a factual finding—for clear error. *Cf. Mar. Mgmt., Inc. v. United States*, 242 F.3d 1326, 1331 (11th Cir. 2001).

A.

Spoliation sanctions are often imposed under the broad discretion of the district court, which has inherent power to "manage its own affairs and to achieve the orderly and expeditious disposition of cases." *Flury v. Daimler Chrysler Corp.*, 427 F.3d 939, 944 (11th Cir. 2005). But sometimes other sources of federal law provide more specific authority.

Rule 37(e) from the Federal Rules of Civil Procedure is one such example. It was adopted in 2006 and modified in 2015 in response to the explosion of electronic discovery. 2015 Committee Notes on Rule 37(e). The Rule seeks to balance the centrality of electronic information to modern litigation with the almost always substantial (and sometimes unnecessary) costs of preserving electronic data. *Id.*

By its text, Rule 37(e) creates a two-tiered sanctions regime—with lesser sanctions under Rule 37(e)(1) and more severe sanctions under Rule 37(e)(2). Both parts of the rule share two preconditions: (1) "electronically stored information that should have been preserved in the anticipation or conduct of litigation" was "lost because a party failed to take reasonable steps to preserve **[—33—]** it" and (2) that information "cannot be restored or replaced through additional discovery." The requirements diverge after that. Rule 37(e)(1) sanctions are centered on the *effect* of a violation; they apply only where lost electronic evidence causes "prejudice to another party," which then justifies sanctions "no greater than necessary to cure the prejudice." Rule 37(e)(2) sanctions, on the other hand, look more to the *cause* of the violation. They require a finding that "the party acted with the intent to deprive another party of the information's use in the litigation." If so, the court is justified in imposing more severe sanctions: adverse jury instructions, and even dismissal or default judgment. Fed. R. Civ. P. 37(e)(2). What's more, Rule 37(e)(2) sanctions do not require "any further finding of prejudice." 2015 Committee Notes on Rule 37(e)(2). "This is because the finding of intent required by the subdivision can support not only an inference that the lost information was unfavorable to the party that intentionally destroyed it, but also an inference that the opposing party was prejudiced by the loss of information that would have favored its position." *Id.*

This is the first time we have had reason to thoroughly consider Rule 37(e)(2). In **{–1312–}** previous cases, we have suggested or assumed, but never held in a published opinion, that the Rule's "intent to deprive" standard is the same as the "bad faith" standard our Court has used in other spoliation contexts. *See ML Healthcare Servs., LLC v. Publix Super Mkts., Inc.*, 881 F.3d 1293, 1308 (11th Cir. 2018); *Ala. Aircraft Indus., Inc. v. Boeing Co.*, No. 20-11141, 2022 WL 433457, at *15 (11th Cir. Feb. 14, 2022) (unpublished). Here, the **[—34—]** district court and both parties have assumed that "intent to deprive" and "bad faith" are the same.

We now explicitly agree: the "intent to deprive another party of the information's use in the litigation" is the equivalent of bad faith in other spoliation contexts. Fed. R. Civ. P. 37(e)(2). In this Circuit's spoliation precedents, bad faith "generally means destruction [of evidence] *for the purpose of hiding* adverse evidence." *Tesoriero*, 965 F.3d at 1184, 8 Adm. R. at 471 (emphasis added) (quotation omitted). This standard is more than mere negligence and aligns with both the text and advisory committee notes for Rule 37(e)(2). *See id.* at 1184–86, 8 Adm. R. at 471–73; Rule 37(e)(2); 2015 Committee Notes on Rule 37(e)(2). The phrase "intent to deprive" naturally requires that the spoliator has a "purpose of hiding adverse evidence" from other parties. And the advisory committee notes explain that "intent to deprive" is more than negligence or even gross negligence. 2015 Committee Notes on Rule 37(e)(2). So rather than adopt a new law of spoliation from scratch for Rule 37(e)(2) sanctions, we will borrow our identical and well-trodden standard of "bad faith." *See also EEOC v. Jetstream Ground Servs., Inc.*, 878 F.3d 960, 965–66 (10th Cir. 2017) (conducting a similar analysis).[18] **[—35—]**

B.

We now review the district court's imposition of Rule 37(e)(2) sanctions. It is not entirely clear whether Skanska challenges Rule 37(e)'s first requirement, that information that "should have been preserved in the anticipation or conduct of litigation" was "lost because a party failed to take reasonable steps to preserve it." Skanska concedes that it was "probably negligent." But it also seems to suggest in its briefs that its preservation failures could be excused because it may not have reasonably anticipated litigation.

The facts reveal that argument's folly. To start, within days of Hurricane Sally, Skanska's in-house counsel had orally informed employees of an evidence retention policy. And about a month later, counsel sent a formal legal hold letter about the Pensacola Bay Bridge incident. Litigation started just a few weeks after that. But even with an active litigation hold—and then active litigation—Skanska did not back up its employees' cell phones. **{-1313-}** Nor did it suspend its ordinary cell phone data destruction policies—not even **[—36—]** for known electronic data custodians. It was, as we see it, entirely predictable that cell phone data would be needed for litigation, and that some of that data would be lost.

Next, Skanska more directly challenges the applicability of Rule 37(e)'s second condition that the information could not have been "restored or replaced through additional discovery." It argues that, because discovery of other Skanska employees included some of the text messages and because the claimants were able to depose the five custodians whose data was destroyed, nothing was actually lost.

The district court was not moved; nor are we. While some of the lost text messages were discoverable through other Skanska employees' text messages, others were not. And it should go without saying that deposing workers well after an event is not a perfect substitute for reviewing their contemporaneous text messages.

Finally, Skanska challenges the district court's finding that it acted in bad faith when it failed to back up the custodians' text messages and suspend its destruction policies. The court found a "lack of any cogent explanation" for Skanska's complete failure to make any effort to preserve the destroyed cell phones. *In re Skanska USA Civil Se. Inc.*, 340 F.R.D. 180, 189 (N.D. Fla. 2021). It focused in particular on how the company "took no action" to educate its custodians and administrators about the litigation hold and "made no effort" to collect its custodians' cell phone data until at

---

[18] We reject, however, the applicability of the so-called "*Flury* factors" to a Rule 37(e) analysis. *See Mendez*, 67 F.4th at 1362 n.9 (recognizing that this question was unresolved). *Flury* was decided before Rule 37(e) was written, and that opinion borrowed from Georgia spoliation law because of a lack of federal Circuit precedent on the precise issue in that case and because the parties and the district court had relied upon Georgia law. *See Flury*, 427 F.3d at 944–45. **[—35—]** But there is no reason to believe that Rule 37(e) borrows from Georgia spoliation law. And one of the *Flury* factors, prejudice to the defendant, is specifically disclaimed as a consideration for Rule 37(e)(2) sanctions by the Advisory Committee. *See Flury*, 427 F.3d at 945; 2015 Committee Notes on Rule 37(e)(2). So while we hold that the fourth *Flury* factor—bad faith—is the same as "intent to deprive," courts should not look to the five *Flury* factors (or, for that matter, factors from other tests in different contexts) when interpreting Rule 37(e). The right things to consider are the rule's text, the advisory committee notes, and our spoliation caselaw analyzing bad faith.

least seven months after the litigation hold was in place. *Id.* at 188–89. **[—37—]** And it highlighted other egregious discovery behavior by Skanska, like its representation to the court that "no documents relating to Skanska's storm preparations or efforts has [sic] been deleted or destroyed"—a representation made before Skanska had even bothered to check if its custodians' cell phone data was still available. *Id.* at 189 (alteration adopted and quotation omitted). In the district court's view, bad faith was the only thing that explained the company's actions.

If our review were de novo, this would be a close question. On the one hand, we find Skanska's utter failure to implement even the most basic data-protection safeguards egregious—so egregious that an inference of bad faith is easy to make. On the other, this is not a case with direct evidence of bad faith; it is also plausible from this record that Skanska was "just" grossly negligent.

But we review the district court's finding of bad faith for clear error. And an inference of bad faith here was not clear error. Skanska can provide no reasonable explanation for its conduct other than to plead negligence. True enough, much of the evidence was destroyed through "routine" document destruction policies. But a hands-off implementation of an ordinary corporate destruction policy is not a silver bullet. We have already explained that we would be "highly skeptical" of a claim that evidence was unintentionally destroyed "pursuant to a routine policy" after a request that the evidence be preserved. *Tesoriero*, 965 F.3d at 1186, 8 Adm. R. at 473. We will not second guess the district court's skepticism in those very circumstances. **[—38—]**

Our conclusion is further confirmed by the advisory committee notes to Rule 37(e). The reasonableness of evidence preservation efforts depends in part on "the party's sophistication with regard to litigation in evaluating preservation efforts." 2015 Committee Notes on Rule 37(e). Skanska is a sophisticated entity—a multinational company tasked with completing a construction contract worth nearly $400 million. Skanska USA even boasts **{-1314-}** on its website that it is "one of the largest, most financially sound construction and development companies in the U.S." Even so, Skanska did not bother to take the most fundamental of precautions—starting with backing up the custodians' cell phones and suspending its policy of wiping those phones. And the company is not being held liable for a failure of imagination—Skanska had an active litigation hold, but took no steps to implement it.

Finally, Skanska argues that—as a per se rule—a finding of bad faith premised on circumstantial evidence requires an "affirmative act" by the spoliating party.[19] But that argument flouts both the text of Rule 37 and our bad-faith caselaw. As we have explained, the rule provides for sanctions when "electronically stored information that should have been preserved in the anticipation or conduct of litigation is lost because a party *failed to* **[—39—]** *take reasonable steps to preserve it*." Fed. R. Civ. P. 37(e) (emphasis added). Failure to act can thus—by definition—be a violation of Rule 37.

Our caselaw on spoliation also shows that failures to act can be just as harmful as affirmative acts of destruction. In *Flury*, we affirmed sanctions after the spoliating party "failed to preserve" a vehicle that the other party wished to inspect, "inexplicably ignored" requests for the location of the vehicle, and "allowed the vehicle to be sold for salvage without notification to defendant of its planned removal." 427 F.3d at 943, 947, 945. These are failures to act—not affirmative actions. Even so, it "is no surprise that we found bad faith on those facts." *Tesoriero*, 965 F.3d at 1185, 8 Adm. R. at 472.

So too here. Skanska's passivity does not change the basic fact that the evidence was destroyed. Given that other circumstances pointed to a reasonable inference of bad faith

[19] In Skanska's defense, the district court framed its inquiry into "bad faith" by applying a test that asked whether Skanska had committed an "affirmative act." *In re Skanska*, 340 F.R.D. at 188. But we may affirm the court's ultimate finding of bad faith on any ground supported by the record. *In re Feshbach*, 974 F.3d 1320, 1328 (11th Cir. 2020).

by Skanska, it is irrelevant whether an act or a failure to act directly caused the spoliation. The court's finding of bad faith thus was not clear error, and its imposition of Rule 37(e)(2) sanctions was not an abuse of discretion.

* * *

Under the Limitation Act, Skanska had a right to have the issue of limitation litigated by a federal court. That's exactly what Skanska got. The claimants now have the right to determine where any subsequent litigation about the damage caused by Skanska's barges during Hurricane Sally will occur. And Skanska has failed **[—40—]** to show any other reason why the district court's dismissal of its petitions should be reversed.

We **AFFIRM** both the district court's dismissal of the Limitation Act proceedings and its sanctions order.

United States Court of Appeals for the Eleventh Circuit

No. 22-11569

WILLIS
vs.
ROYAL CARIBBEAN CRUISES, LTD.

Appeal from the United States District Court for the Southern District of Florida

Decided: August 14, 2023

Citation: 77 F.4th 1332, 11 Adm. R. 527 (11th Cir. 2023).

Before **ROSENBAUM**, **BRANCH**, and **BRASHER**, Circuit Judges.

[—2—] {–1333–} **BRANCH**, Circuit Judge:

Judith Willis brought a three-count maritime negligence action against Royal Caribbean Cruises, Ltd. ("Royal Caribbean") after she fell aboard one of its cruise ships. She alleged that during the ship's muster drill,[1] a Royal Caribbean employee rushed her down a set of stairs—causing her to fall and severely injure her neck.

The district court granted summary judgment in favor of Royal Caribbean. First, on Count I (general negligence) and Count II (negligent failure to warn), the district court found that Willis failed to show that Royal Caribbean had notice of the dangerous conditions that allegedly caused her fall. Second, on Count III (general negligence against Royal Caribbean for its employee's conduct under a theory of vicarious liability), the district court determined that Willis put forth insufficient evidence of medical causation.[2]

On appeal, Willis argues that these conclusions were erroneous and asks us to reverse. After careful review, and with the benefit of oral argument, we conclude that Willis failed to adduce sufficient medical evidence to satisfy proximate cause. And because proximate cause must be satisfied for each of her three **[—3—]** negligence-based claims to prevail, we affirm the district court's grant of summary judgment to Royal Caribbean.

I. Background

A. Factual Background

On May 4, 2019, Willis was a passenger aboard the *Anthem of the Seas*, a Royal **{–1334–}** Caribbean cruise ship. Shortly after the ship departed, Willis—like all passengers—was required to participate in a muster drill. As part of the drill, Willis was directed to the ship's Royal Theater. According to Willis, once she reached the theater, a Royal Caribbean employee, Valeriya Artyushenko, rushed Willis through the seat-finding process which caused her to fall down a set of steps:

> [Royal Caribbean Counsel]: What happened when you arrived at the theater?
>
> [Willis]: Well, they swiped us in . . . . So we went in and [Artyushenko] comes up to me and says, You're late. Hurry up. Get a seat.
>
> So I felt, you know, she was attacking me. So I said all right. And I went to the edge of the steps, and I looked around. I said, where are the seats? There were tons of people there.
>
> So she said, follow me. She really had an attitude. So I held on, and I went down. And she said go in there. She points to a place. I went over there, and there **[—4—]** was a pole. And then there was like 6 inches room, and then there was the next banister, the hand.
>
> I said, I can't fit in there. She said—I'm fat, you know. I can't. So she said go in there. I said I can't go in there. I can't climb. I'm old. I'm fat. So she says, oh,

[1] Muster drills are safety exercises that cruise lines are required to conduct.

[2] The district court noted that the lack of evidence on medical causation was an additional reason to grant summary judgment on Counts I and II.

come on, follow me. So I held on again, and I stepped down and I went down. I don't know what happened. I went down. She was rushing me.

In her amended complaint and throughout her deposition testimony, Willis emphasized that she fell because she was rushed by Artyushenko even though Artyushenko knew that Willis's age and weight limited her physical abilities. In fact, Willis specifically disclaimed other potential causes; she noted that her view of the steps was not blocked, the lighting was sufficient for her to see, she did not slip on any liquid or foreign substance, and the steps did not surprise her (*i.e.*, she knew she was about to go down steps—she just fell once she started descending them).

According to Willis, the fall "injured her neck, lower back, both arms and hips." The medical evidence she provided at the district court level, however, focused primarily on her neck injury.[3] That evidence included her deposition testimony that she hurt her neck, an MRI of her neck from June 2019 (roughly one month after **[—5—]** her fall),[4] and a one-paragraph letter from her treating physician that read:

> [Willis] has been a patient in this medical practice since 2012. She has been seen on a regular basis because of a number of comorbid medical illnesses. During that period of time there had been no complaint of neck pain until her visit on June 19, 2019. During that visit she did describe a fall that occurred while being on a cruise and related having been seen by an orthopedic surgeon who had requested an MRI of the cervical spine because of pain which she had been suffering from since her fall. The MRI did indeed show multi-level disc disease of the cervical spine. There had never been any prior radiologic study of the spine to my knowledge to which any comparison could be made. I hope this information has been helpful.

B. Procedural History

Willis initially sued Royal Caribbean in March 2020, but then moved to stay the **{-1335-}** case pending completion of her medical treatment. The district court granted Willis's motion and stayed the case. In September 2021, the district court granted Willis's motion to reopen the case, and she filed an amended complaint, which became the operative complaint in this case. **[—6—]**

The operative complaint asserted claims for general negligence, negligent failure to warn, and negligence for Artyushenko's conduct under a theory of vicarious liability. After answering and asserting affirmative defenses, Royal Caribbean filed (1) an omnibus motion in limine that sought to exclude evidence of three prior incidents that Willis sought to introduce to prove that Royal Caribbean was on notice that injuries like hers could occur aboard its ships, and (2) a motion for summary judgment. The district court granted the motion in limine in part, determining that the three prior incidents that Willis pointed to were not "substantially similar" to Willis's fall such that they were inadmissible. Then, the district court granted summary judgment in favor of Royal Caribbean, focusing—in pertinent part—on the fact that Willis lacked medical expert testimony which the district court understood to be required when a plaintiff's complained-of injury is not readily observable.[5] **[—7—]**

---

[3] On appeal, Willis focuses exclusively on her neck injury.

[4] The MRI indicated that Willis had some disc herniations (C4-C5; C5-C6) and some bulging discs (C6-C7; C7-T1) in her spinal column.

[5] More specifically, as to proximate cause, Willis pointed to (1) her deposition testimony that she hurt her neck, (2) an MRI of her neck from June 2019, and (3) the one-paragraph letter from her treating physician. Royal Caribbean responded that her physician's letter did not "actually opine on whether [Willis's] fall on the cruise caused the injury to her neck" and that expert testimony is required to establish medical causation for conditions that are "not readily observable" under Eleventh Circuit precedent. The district court found that Willis's physician's letter did not adequately address causation because it simply stated that Willis had neck pain and noted that there had not been previous studies of her neck. In other words, the district court understood the evidence to show that Willis had a neck injury, but not show when that

Willis appeals.

II. Standard of Review

"We review *de novo* a district court's grant of summary judgment, applying the same legal standards as the district court." *Chapman v. AI Transport*, 229 F.3d 1012, 1023 (11th Cir. 2000) (en banc). This familiar standard dictates that "[t]he court shall grant summary judgment if the movant shows that there is no genuine dispute as to any material fact and the movant is entitled to judgment as a matter of law." Fed. R. Civ. P. 56(a).

III. Discussion

Willis puts forth three arguments. First, she argues that the district court erred in excluding the prior incident evidence she sought to introduce. Second, on the issue of medical causation, she argues that the district court erred procedurally—by prematurely shifting the summary judgment burden from Royal Caribbean to her—and substantively—by wrongfully determining that she did not present sufficient evidence. Third, she argues that the district court erred in determining that she did not present sufficient evidence in support of her vicarious liability claim.

We start our analysis by jumping straight to Willis's second argument (medical causation) because causation is an element required by each of her three negligence-based claims. We conclude that Willis fails to provide sufficient evidence to create a **[—8—]** genuine dispute of material fact as to medical causation and, therefore, we affirm the district court's grant **{–1336–}** of summary judgment to Royal Caribbean.[6]

A. Medical Causation

The district court found that Royal Caribbean was "entitled to summary judgment on all claims . . . for which causation is an essential element" (*i.e.*, each of Willis's claims) because Willis "has not borne her burden of bringing forth medical expert evidence opining on the issue of causation." Willis argues that the district court erred in making this determination because she put forth three pieces of evidence that were sufficient to satisfy her burden regarding medical causation: (1) her deposition testimony that she hurt her neck when she fell, (2) the June 2019 MRI showing injuries to her neck, and (3) the one-paragraph letter from her treating physician that referenced her neck injury.[7] We agree with the district court and conclude that Willis's evidence is insufficient.

---

injury began or whether that injury was caused by her fall on the **[—7—]** ship. As such, the district court determined that Willis had not "borne her burden of bringing forth medical expert evidence opining on . . . causation."

[6] In light of this conclusion, we need not analyze Willis's first argument (prior incident evidence). Even if she were to prove that the district court's "substantial similarity" analysis—which undergirded its decision to partially grant Royal Caribbean's motion in limine—constituted an abuse of discretion, it would not change our ultimate conclusion in light of her failure to satisfy the causation requirement.

[7] Willis also argues that the district court prematurely shifted the summary judgment burden from Royal Caribbean to her because Royal Caribbean had not yet "negate[d]" an element of her claim. Willis misstates the fundamental **[—9—]** legal principle. The correct principle is simply that "[t]he moving party bears the initial burden to show the district court, by reference to the materials on file, that there are no genuine issues of material fact that should be decided at trial." *Clark v. Coats & Clark, Inc.*, 929 F.2d 604, 608 (11th Cir. 1991). "Only when that burden has been met does the burden shift to the non-moving party to demonstrate that there is indeed a[n] . . . issue of [material] fact that precludes summary judgment." *Id.* But when the non-moving party bears the burden of proof on an issue at trial, the moving party need not "support its motion with affidavits or other similar material *negating* the opponent's claim" in order to discharge this initial responsibility. *Celotex Corp. v. Catrett*, 477 U.S. 317, 323 (1986) (emphasis in original). Instead, the moving party may simply "point out to the district court that there is an absence of evidence to support the nonmoving party's case." *Rice-Lamar v. City of Ft. Lauderdale*, 232 F.3d 836, 840 (11th Cir. 2000) (alterations adopted). Royal Caribbean satisfied this requirement and met its initial burden—it showed the district court that Willis could not prove the causation element because she lacked medical expert testimony that opined on the cause of her neck injury. Willis's argument that Royal Caribbean had to do more is incorrect.

As an initial matter, "[m]aritime law governs actions arising from alleged torts committed aboard a ship sailing in navigable **[—9—]** waters." *Guevara v. NCL (Bahamas) Ltd.*, 920 F.3d 710, 720, 7 Adm. R. 476, 481 (11th Cir. 2019). Along with our judicially created body of maritime law, we "rely on general principles of negligence law" in analyzing a maritime tort case. *Id.*, 7 Adm. R. at 481 (quotation omitted); *Tesoriero v. Carnival Corp.*, 965 F.3d 1170, 1178, 8 Adm. R. 463, 466 (11th Cir. 2020) ("For maritime tort cases in particular, we rely on general principles of negligence law." (quotation omitted)). Those general principles, of course, require a plaintiff to show that "(1) the defendant had a duty to protect the plaintiff from a particular injury; (2) the defendant breached that duty; (3) the breach actually and proximately caused the plaintiff's injury; and (4) the plaintiff suffered actual harm." *Chaparro v. Carnival Corp.*, 693 F.3d 1333, 1336 (11th Cir. 2012). **[—10—]**

The third element (causation) requires a plaintiff to show that "the breach actually and proximately caused the plaintiff's **{-1337-}** injury." *Yusko v. NCL (Bahamas), Ltd.*, 4 F.4th 1164, 1167–68, 9 Adm. R. 403, 404 (11th Cir. 2021); *see also Comcast Corp. v. Nat'l Ass'n of Afr. Am.-Owned Media*, 140 S. Ct. 1009, 1014 (2020) ("It is textbook tort law that a plaintiff seeking redress for a defendant's legal wrong typically must prove but-for causation." (quotation omitted)); *Lexmark Int'l, Inc. v. Static Control Components, Inc.*, 572 U.S. 118, 132 (2014) ("For centuries, it has been a well established principle of [the common] law, that in all cases of loss, we are to attribute it to proximate cause, and not to any remote cause." (quotation omitted)).

Our analysis of the causation question in this appeal boils down to the following question: What does a plaintiff need to show to prove causation in a maritime negligence claim involving non-observable medical injuries?

The district court understood our law to require medical expert testimony to prove causation for non-observable medical injuries. That interpretation is understandable because we have relied on such a rule in our unpublished case law. *See, e.g., Rivera v. Royal Caribbean Cruises Ltd.*, 711 F. App'x 952, 954 (11th Cir. 2017) (unpublished) ("When the causal link between alleged injuries and the incident at issue is not readily apparent to a lay person, expert medical testimony as to medical causation is typically required."). And, relying on our unpublished case law, this rule has become well-accepted and oft-applied among district courts in our Circuit. *See, e.g., Mann v. Carnival Corp.*, 385 F. Supp. 3d 1278, 1285 (S.D. Fla. **[—11—]** Apr. 22, 2019) ("Courts have recognized that soft-tissue injuries, such as lower back pain are not a readily observable medical condition[] and, therefore, expert testimony as to the cause of such injuries is required." (quotation omitted)); *Landivar v. Celebrity Cruises, Inc.*, 584 F. Supp. 3d 1150, 1159–60 (S.D. Fla. Feb. 8, 2022) ("Only expert testimony can support a finding of medical causation if the causal connection between the breach and the harm is not readily observable or susceptible to evaluation by lay persons." (quotation omitted)); *Taylor v. Royal Caribbean Cruises Ltd.*, 437 F. Supp. 3d 1255, 1261 (S.D. Fla. Feb. 4, 2020) ("In cases where injuries are not readily observable or susceptible to evaluation by lay persons, expert testimony is required to establish medical causation." (quotation omitted)). This body of case law, however, does not bind our instant analysis. *Lenis v. U.S. Att'y Gen.*, 525 F.3d 1291, 1292 n.3 (11th Cir. 2008) ("Because these opinions were unpublished . . . they have no precedential value."); *Washington v. Rivera*, 939 F.3d 1239, 1244 n.8 (11th Cir. 2019) ("[D]istrict court opinions are not binding precedent.").

Tracing this rule back to its roots, we find that our unpublished cases (as well as the district court cases in our Circuit) generally cite *Allison v. McGhan Medical Corporation*, 184 F.3d 1300 (11th Cir. 1999), for the rule that non-observable injuries require medical expert testimony to prove causation. *See, e.g., Rivera*, 711 F. App'x at 954–55. *Allison*, however, interpreted Georgia's substantive negligence law—rather than common law negligence or maritime negligence. 184 F.3d at 1320 (applying Georgia law and concluding that because whether "breast implants can and did **[—12—]** cause systemic disease in Allison is not a natural inference that a juror could make through human experience," medical expert testimony was necessary in order to prove causation). Thus, before we cement the non-observable injury rule from **{–1338–}** *Allison* in our maritime law, we make sure that such reliance is proper.

Without a controlling maritime principle, as is the case here, "courts may apply state law provided that the application of state law does not frustrate national interests in having uniformity in admiralty law." *Coastal Fuels Mktg., Inc. v. Fla. Express Shipping Co., Inc.*, 207 F.3d 1247, 1251 (11th Cir. 2000); *see also Steelmet, Inc. v. Caribe Towing Corp.*, 779 F.2d 1485, 1488 (11th Cir. 1986) ("One must identify the state law involved and determine whether there is an admiralty principle with which the state law conflicts, and, if there is no such admiralty principle, consideration must be given to whether such an admiralty rule should be followed."). Looking to Florida negligence law,[8] we find the same rule: non-readily observable injuries require expert medical evidence to prove causation. *See Crest Prods. v. Louise*, 593 So. 2d 1075, 1077 (Fla. 1st DCA 1992) ("Lay testimony is legally insufficient to support a finding of causation where the medical condition involved is not readily observable." (quotation omitted and alteration adopted)); *see also Wausau Ins. Co. v. Tillman*, 765 So. 2d 123, 124 (Fla. 1st DCA **[—13—]** 2000) (collecting cases). Thus, we wind up with the rule we started with—*Allison*'s conclusion that non-readily observable injuries require medical expert testimony to prove causation. 184 F.3d at 1320.

There is no indication that this rule would "frustrate national interests in having uniformity in admiralty law." *Coastal Fuels*, 207 F.3d at 1251. In fact, other states in our Circuit follow this rule, or one similar. The non-readily observable injury rule is a fixture of Georgia law (as covered in this opinion). *See, e.g., Allison*, 184 F.3d at 1320. And Alabama courts have applied it as well, but not in the causation context. *See, e.g., Cajun Operating Co. v. Elijah*, 163 So. 3d 1037, 1041 (Ala. Civ. App. 2014) ("Although some injuries that are observable to the jury do not require expert evidence to permit the jury to determine that the injuries are permanent, vision injuries such as the nonobservable complaints raised by Elijah are not matters of common knowledge from which a layperson could infer their permanence.").

Accordingly, we formally recognize in the maritime context that non-readily observable injuries require medical expert testimony to prove causation. *Tesoriero*, 965 F.3d at 1178, 8 Adm. R. at 465 ("[I]n the absence of an established federal maritime rule, we may borrow from a variety of sources in establishing common law admiralty rules to govern maritime liability where deemed appropriate." (quotation omitted)).

With the law established, we turn back to Willis's injury and her supporting causation evidence. While her complaint **[—14—]** references her injuries in only general terms (*e.g.*, "Plaintiff was injured about Plaintiff's body and extremities"), she later provided sworn testimony that her lawsuit is based on injuries to her neck:

> [Royal Caribbean Counsel]: Can you tell me what injuries you're claiming to have suffered in the accident on the [cruise ship] in May of 2019?
>
> [Willis]: What injuries? Well, I hurt my neck. I'm told I have herniated discs, **{–1339–}** and I have something leaning on a nerve. I hurt my neck, the discs in my neck.
>
> . . .
>
> [Royal Caribbean Counsel]: Okay. Any other injuries that you're claiming aside from your neck pain that radiates to your head, shoulders, and arms?

[8] According to Willis's complaint, Royal Caribbean has its principal place of business in Florida and "[t]he acts of [Royal Caribbean] set out in th[e] [c]omplaint occurred in whole or in part in this county and/or state." Florida law is further appropriate because neither party disputes the application of Florida law. *Coastal Fuels*, 207 F.3d at 1252 n.1.

[Willis]: And back, top back.

[Royal Caribbean Counsel]: Top of your back?

[Willis]: Not from that accident.

Neither party disputes that her complained-of neck injury is a non-observable injury.

Her first two pieces of evidence (her own testimony about her neck injury and the MRI itself) are clearly not medical expert testimony and thus are not sufficient to establish proximate cause. Willis herself is not a medical expert. Similarly, her MRI—although performed by a medical doctor who noted, among other things, that Willis had disc herniations and bulging discs in her neck—does not touch on anything other than the condition of her **[—15—]** neck and, therefore, cannot be considered an expert explanation regarding *causation*. Willis's final piece of evidence, her physician's letter, lacked any discussion of, or reference to, causation of her neck injury altogether. While the letter creates a baseline (*i.e.*, Willis had been seen on a regular basis without complaining of neck pain prior to the incident) and analyzes the MRI to state that it "show[s] multi-level disc disease of the cervical spine," nothing links Willis's disc disease to her fall on the cruise ship. The letter simply lacks the necessary specificity to establish proximate cause as it pertains to non-readily observable injuries like Willis's neck injury.[9] And because proximate cause is a necessary element for Count I (general negligence) and Count II (negligent failure to warn), the district court correctly granted summary judgment.

B. Vicarious Liability

Finally, the district court determined that because Willis was unable to adduce evidence sufficient to create a genuine issue of material fact as to causation, Willis's vicarious liability claim (Count III) also necessarily failed. Because vicarious liability still requires causation, *see Yusko*, 4 F.4th at 1167–68, 9 Adm. R. at 404, and Willis lacks evidence to satisfy that element, her claim that the district court **[—16—]** erred in holding that she did not present sufficient evidence in support of her vicarious liability claim is a non-starter.[10] **{-1340-}**

IV. Conclusion

The district court got it right. We conclude, after clarifying our law, that the district court was correct in determining that Willis failed to adduce sufficient evidence to create a genuine issue of material fact as to medical causation because she had no medical expert opinion evidence regarding the proximate cause of her non-observable neck injury. Thus, each of Willis's three negligence-based claims necessarily failed and the district court correctly granted summary judgment to Royal Caribbean.

AFFIRMED.

---

[9] Willis's additional argument that she should have been permitted to testify as to damages misses the mark because, as analyzed above, it is clear that she cannot satisfy the other necessary elements of her negligence-based claims. *See generally Sorrels v. NCL (Bahamas) Ltd.*, 796 F.3d 1275, 1279–80, 3 Adm. R. 659, 659–60 (11th Cir. 2015) (listing the four elements, each of which a plaintiff must satisfy, in order to prevail on a claim under maritime negligence law).

[10] Willis argues that notice (which the district court determined she was unable to satisfy because her prior incident evidence was not "substantially similar" to her factual situation) is not a required element of vicarious liability, so her claim should be allowed to proceed. *See Yusko*, 4 F.4th at 1167, 9 Adm. R. at 404 ("[T]he notice requirement does not—and was never meant to—apply to maritime negligence claims proceeding under a theory of vicarious liability."). But the lack of a notice requirement does not matter in this case because Willis still has to show that the injury was caused by the actions of Artyushenko, and at that point she runs into the same problem analyzed above.

United States Court of Appeals for the Eleventh Circuit

No. 21-12702

UNITED STATES
vs.
HURTADO

Appeal from the United States District Court for the Middle District of Florida

Decided: December 20, 2023

Citation: 89 F.4th 881, 11 Adm. R. 533 (11th Cir. 2023).

Before **GRANT, TJOFLAT,** and **CARNES,** Circuit Judges.

[—2—] {-885-} PER CURIAM:

All panel members agree that the judgment of the District Court is due to be affirmed. The only disagreement arises from defining the holding of a particular prior panel precedent that relates to one of the issues that is raised in this appeal. For reasons explained in Judge Carnes's concurring opinion, which is joined by Judge Grant, the two of them do not join the last two paragraphs of Part IV.A. of Judge Tjoflat's opinion. As a result, those two paragraphs do not reflect the views of this Court in this case. The views of this Court on that matter are the ones expressed in the concurring opinion of Judge Carnes.

[—2—] {-885-} TJOFLAT, Circuit Judge: **{-886-}**

The United States Coast Guard apprehended Asdrubal Quijada Marin and Juan Carlos Acosta Hurtado—as well as five other co-defendants—aboard a motor vessel, the *Zumaque Tracer*, in the Caribbean Sea. Marin and Acosta Hurtado were convicted after a bench trial in the Middle District of Florida for (1) conspiracy to possess with intent to distribute five kilograms or more of cocaine while aboard a vessel subject to the jurisdiction of the United States and (2) possession with intent to distribute five kilograms or more of cocaine on a vessel subject to the jurisdiction of the United States, pursuant to the Maritime Drug Law Enforcement Act (the MDLEA). *See* 46 U.S.C. §§ 70503(a), 70506(a)–(b); 21 U.S.C. § 960(b)(1)(B)(ii). **[—3—]**

On appeal, Marin and Acosta Hurtado appeal the denial of several pre-trial motions. Marin appeals the denial of a motion to dismiss the indictment for lack of jurisdiction. Acosta Hurtado appeals the same. Acosta Hurtado additionally appeals the denials of: (1) a motion to suppress evidence, because he alleges the stop and search of the *Zumaque Tracer* violated the Fourth Amendment; (2) a motion to dismiss the indictment, based on unnecessary delay; and (3) a motion to dismiss the indictment, because of outrageous government conduct. After careful review of the record and with the benefit of oral argument, we find these challenges unpersuasive and accordingly affirm the District Court's judgments.

I.

The issues on appeal were addressed in a pre-trial evidentiary hearing. We therefore take the substantive facts leading up to Acosta Hurtado and Marin's indictment from the evidence in the record at that time and the witnesses presented at that hearing. Some of the facts also come from a certificate submitted by the Government from United States Coast Guard Commander David M. Bartram as designee of the Secretary of State (the Certificate).[1] By and large, the parties do not dispute the facts. **[—4—]**

A.

On August 12, 2019, a British vessel with a United States law enforcement detachment spotted the motor vessel *Zumaque Tracer*, a roughly 260-foot vessel, anchored in international waters between Aruba and

[1] We treat a certificate of someone designated by the Secretary of State to act on the part of the Department of State, as was Commander Bartram here, the same as a certificate of the Secretary of State himself. *See United States v. Hernandez*, 864 F.3d 1292, 1299, 5 Adm. R. 477, 479 (11th Cir. 2017) 46 U.S.C. § 70502(d)(2) ("The response of a foreign nation to a claim of registry . . . is proved conclusively by certification of the Secretary of State *or the Secretary's designee*." (emphasis added)).

Venezuela.[2] The *Zumaque Tracer* flew a Republic of Cameroon flag. The British vessel engaged in right-of-approach questioning. Right-of-approach questioning is authorized by international law and can be conducted by a law enforcement vessel in international waters as a matter of course. **{-887-}** *The Marianna Flora*, 24 U.S. 1, 10–11, 11 Wheat. 1, 5–6 (1825). Right-of-approach questioning aims at ascertaining the nationality of a vessel traveling in international waters. *See United States v. Marino-Garcia*, 679 F.2d 1373, 1385 (11th Cir. 1982) ("Under international law, the Coast Guard has the authority to approach an unidentified vessel in order to ascertain the vessel's nationality.").

The United States law enforcement personnel on board the British vessel reported the results of the right-of-approach questioning to District Seven—the United States Coast Guard district responsible for coordinating and commanding action in the Caribbean Sea—in Miami. Generally, the Coast Guard districts **[—5—]** immediately command assets in their jurisdictional waters and report up to Coast Guard headquarters. Through the right-of-approach questions, the Coast Guard learned that the master of the *Zumaque Tracer*—Marin—claimed Cameroonian registry, the vessel had been anchored for twenty-one days with an engine problem, the vessel was not transmitting on Automated Information Systems (AIS),[3] and the vessel only had a crew of seven. After engaging in their deliberative process and based on the information it had received from the British vessel, District Seven determined that the *Zumaque Tracer* was suspicious and warranted boarding. District Seven, therefore, "requested to invoke the Article 17 process through Coast Guard headquarters," which involves the "Government of the United States . . . reach[ing] out to the . . . flag state and ask[ing] for permission to . . . exercise law enforcement authority on behalf of the flag state."[4] The Coast Guard received no response **[—6—]** for many days, during which the British vessel monitored the anchored *Zumaque Tracer* and awaited further direction.[5]

Having waited multiple days with no response from Cameroon granting permission to board, the British vessel had to move on. A vessel with the Dutch Coast Guard, again containing a United States Coast Guard detachment, assumed monitoring duties while the United States continued to await permission to act on its suspicions from Cameroon. On August 20, 2019, the *Zumaque Tracer* weighed anchor and entered the territorial waters of Venezuela—where the United States lost contact with the vessel—and

---

[2] The Certificate states:

> On August 12, 2019, U.S. law enforcement personnel detected the motor vessel ZUMAQUE TRACER at anchor in approximate position 12-22.72 N, 070-14.42 W, approximately 2.5 nautical miles west of Aruba's territorial sea limit and 3 nautical miles from Venezuela's territorial sea limit, seaward of the territorial sea of any State.

[3] According to witness testimony, AIS is a "feature that transmits the vessel's position, course, speed, [and] operational . . . character, meaning [whether the vessel is] underway, or anchored." AIS signals can be received by other vessels and stations ashore. Its uses involve avoiding collisions with other vessels and allowing the vessel to be found in case of distress. But AIS also allows a vessel to be found by law enforcement vessels. Having no functioning AIS, therefore, could allow a vessel to avoid detection, but would also risk the safety of the vessel and any vessel that may come within close proximity to it.

[4] The Certificate states:

> On August 13, 2019, under Article 17 of the United Nations Convention Against Illicit Traffic in Narcotic Drugs and Psychotropic Substances of 1988, the Government of the United States requested that the Government of the Republic of **[—6—]** Cameroon verify the vessel's registry and, if confirmed, grant permission to stop, board, and search the vessel.

[5] When a Coast Guard or allied vessel monitors a suspected vessel while awaiting further instruction from the appropriate district, the law enforcement vessel does not necessarily stay directly adjacent to the suspected vessel. According to the District Seven Coast Guard commander at the evidentiary hearing, a Coast Guard vessel can be as far as three miles away, keeping "eyes" on the suspected vessel across the horizon or via radar.

the Dutch vessel continued its patrol duties elsewhere.

At some point over the next ten days, having been unable to order the boarding and search of what the Coast Guard believed to be a suspicious vessel, District **{-888-}** Seven sent the Coast Guard cutter *Northland* to patrol a section of the Caribbean Sea where the cutter might find the *Zumaque Tracer* after it emerged from Venezuelan territorial waters. On August 30, 2019, the *Northland* encountered **[—7—]** the *Zumaque Tracer* in international waters, roughly 180 nautical miles south of Haiti.[6]

The *Northland* engaged in right-of-approach questioning, revealing the following suspicious aspects of the vessel in addition to what the Coast Guard already knew from the previous right-of-approach questioning. First, the *Zumaque Tracer* was pointed 285 degrees true (north northwest), which would eventually cause the vessel to arrive at land around northern Honduras or Grand Cayman. Yet, the vessel claimed to be headed for Panama, much further to the south. Second, the *Zumaque Tracer* said it had come from Venezuela—where it allegedly conducted repairs—but the vessel appeared to be in the same bad shape observed earlier in August.[7] Marin also claimed—again—that the purpose of the vessel's voyage—this time to Panama—was for repairs. Third, the *Zumaque Tracer* was in a known narcotics-ferrying corridor of the **[—8—]** Caribbean. Fourth, the *Zumaque Tracer* had only a crew of seven—all of Venezuelan nationality, and none of whom were on deck. The minimum manning crew for this vessel was nine crewmembers. The *Northland* was of roughly the same size and had a crew of about ninety-five people. Fifth, the AIS on board the *Zumaque Tracer* was still off; in fact, Marin—the master of the vessel—claimed to not even know how to use it or what AIS was. International standards require ships of 300 gross tons or more to use AIS; the *Zumaque Tracer* had a gross weight of over 2,500 tons. Sixth, the *Zumaque Tracer* had trouble maintaining a steady course. Seventh, despite being a cargo vessel, the *Zumaque Tracer* apparently had no cargo on board nor any equipment with which to handle cargo.

Again, the *Northland* communicated these findings to District Seven. District Seven in turn communicated with Coast Guard headquarters, requesting to invoke the Article 17 process to board the *Zumaque Tracer*. Coast Guard headquarters presumably requested that the Republic of Cameroon grant the United States permission to engage in law enforcement activities on Cameroon's behalf by boarding and searching the *Zumaque Tracer*. This time, a response—in the affirmative—arrived fairly quickly and Coast Guard headquarters authorized District Seven to order the *Northland* to stop, board, and search the *Zumaque Tracer*.[8] In so **[—9—]** permitting the **{-889-}** United States Coast Guard to board and search the *Zumaque Tracer*, Cameroon confirmed that the vessel was indeed registered as a Cameroonian vessel.

[6] The Certificate says, "On August 30, 2019, U.S. law enforcement personnel relocated ZUMAQUE TRACER at approximate position 15-03.4 N, 074-36.3 W, approximately 205 nautical miles southeast of Kingston, Jamaica and seaward of the territorial sea of any State."

[7] The *Zumaque Tracer* had multiple holes that were visibly taking on water, including a six-by-ten-foot hole on the back left of the vessel. Eventually, the *Northland* crew would learn the following. The vessel was equipped with three generators, but only one was working—the others having been disassembled for parts—and it was only able to power part of the ship. Further, the vessel had two engines. One was not running, and the other had started leaking cooling water—risking overheating—during the *Northland*'s boarding and had to be turned off. The *Zumaque Tracer* was discovered to have a dewatering pump on board that needed active attention and was keeping the vessel afloat. The vessel also lacked fresh food, water, and sanitary devices.

[8] The Certificate says, "On August 21, 2019, the Government of the Republic of Cameroon confirmed that ZUMAQUE TRACER was registered in Cameroon, and granted permission for U.S. law enforcement personnel to stop, board, and search the vessel." It is unclear whether Cameroon was asked for **[—9—]** permission again on August 30. Either way, *before* United States law enforcement personnel stepped foot on the *Zumaque Tracer*, the government of Cameroon had given permission for a search of the vessel on its behalf.

A boarding team from the *Northland* eventually boarded the *Zumaque Tracer* where the team engaged in a three-step search. First, the team confirmed the identity and nationality of the vessel. Second, the team performed an initial safety sweep—including mustering the crew—to ensure the vessel was safe for Coast Guard personnel to be aboard. Third, the team searched for evidence of criminal activity.

On August 31, 2019, the search crew from the *Northland* found 140 bales of what appeared to be cocaine inside wing tanks—typically filled to ballast the ship—in the engine room.[9] Two consecutive field tests revealed that at least one of the bales indeed contained cocaine. The *Northland* crew passed this information along to District Seven, which informed Coast Guard headquarters, which requested that Cameroon waive jurisdiction over the crew of the *Zumaque Tracer*.

District Seven also instructed the *Northland* to treat the seven crew members of the *Zumaque Tracer* as detainees and bring them back to the *Northland*. The *Northland* crew was not able to **[—10—]** transfer the contraband until September 3 due to a hurricane in the area. The boarding of the *Zumaque Tracer* ended on the same day. On September 5, the *Zumaque Tracer* sank, having taken on too much water—its dewatering pump likely having become disabled without active attention.

Throughout September and October, District Seven inquired about the status of the jurisdiction waiver at least four times. Additionally, the United States government reiterated its request that Cameroon waive jurisdiction on September 19.

While waiting for word from Cameroon, the *Zumaque Tracer* crew remained handcuffed to the decks of various Coast Guard vessels.[10] They were housed under a shelter, ate the same meals as the crew of the *Northland*, were allowed bathroom breaks and showers, and were seen by a Coast Guard medical officer twice a day. Because they were at sea, however, the crew had no contact with family, attorneys, or a judge. While on board the various Coast Guard vessels, the *Zumaque Tracer* crew were neither read their *Miranda* rights nor interrogated.[11] In total, while awaiting a response from Cameroon, the *Zumaque Tracer* crew was transferred between approximately five different Coast Guard vessels before finally being brought ashore to the United States. **[—11—]**

District Seven later learned—on October 12—that Cameroon had deleted the *Zumaque Tracer* from its registry on September 18, 2019.[12] Coast Guard authorities **{-890-}** that same day "granted a statement of no objection to assimilate the vessel to without nation status" and considered the United States to have jurisdiction over the crew. The vessel on which the *Zumaque Tracer* crew was detained made for Puerto Rico on the same day, arriving in the late morning of October 18. Upon arriving in Puerto Rico, federal agents took into custody the crew of the *Zumaque Tracer*, having been indicted on October 16.[13] The crew were then processed by Customs and Border Protection in San Juan, Puerto Rico and flown

---

[9] The Certificate says the amount of cocaine retrieved weighed "approximately 4,225 kilograms."

[10] The *Northland* passed the seven *Zumaque Tracer* crewmembers to a different Coast Guard vessel around September 13.

[11] *Miranda v. Arizona*, 384 U.S. 436, 86 S. Ct. 1602 (1966).

[12] The Certificate says:

> Subsequently, the Government of the United States received through law enforcement channels a Cameroon vessel registry deletion certificate dated September 18, 2019, for the ZUMAQUE TRACER. The deletion certificate specified that the Government of the Republic of Cameroon had permanently deleted ZUMAQUE TRACER from its vessel registry and could no longer fly the Cameroonian flag due to the vessel's illicit drug trafficking activity described in the preceding paragraphs that had been reported to the Government of the Republic of Cameroon by the Government of the United States.

[13] A grand jury in the Middle District of Florida indicted Marin, Acosta Hurtado, and the five other crew members for conspiracy to possess and knowingly and intentionally possessing with intent to distribute five or more kilograms of cocaine in violation of 46 U.S.C. §§ 70503(a), 70506(a)–(b).

to Tampa, arriving around 5:00 P.M. on Friday, October 18. Only afterwards were the crew read their rights and questioned. On **[—12—]** Monday morning, they were arraigned in Tampa. That same day, the president of Cameroon consented to the United States's exercise of jurisdiction over the crew of the *Zumaque Tracer*. Cameroon reaffirmed its consent to jurisdiction in writing on October 24.

B.

Relevant to this appeal, Marin filed a motion to dismiss the indictment challenging jurisdiction under the MDLEA on January 15, 2020. Acosta Hurtado moved to adopt the motion at a hearing before the magistrate judge on January 22. The magistrate judge granted the motion to adopt. Marin also filed a motion to suppress evidence, which encompassed the cocaine found on board the *Zumaque Tracer*, on January 15. Again, Acosta Hurtado moved to join the motion. The magistrate judge granted Acosta Hurtado's motion to join in an order on January 27. Acosta Hurtado additionally filed a motion to dismiss based on violations of Federal Rules of Criminal Procedure 5 and 48, as well as unnecessary pre-indictment delay and due process violations on March 17.

A magistrate judge held a day long evidentiary hearing on March 5 addressing, in relevant part, the motions to dismiss and suppress. The Government presented evidence and examined witnesses, including the commander of District Seven at the time of the *Zumaque Tracer*'s interdiction as well as crew members who were on the *Northland* on August 30. The various defense attorneys for the defendants cross-examined the Government's witnesses but did not present any affirmative evidence. **[—13—]**

On April 24, the magistrate judge issued a Report and Recommendation that, in relevant part, recommended the District Court deny the motions to dismiss and suppress. The District Court accepted the magistrate judge's recommendation in an order on November 6.

Eventually, on May 7, 2021, the District Court held a short bench trial for Marin and Acosta Hurtado. The District Court adjudicated them guilty of conspiracy to possess and actual possession with intent to distribute five kilograms or more of cocaine while aboard a vessel subject to the jurisdiction of the United States pursuant to a stipulation with the Government. The District Court subsequently sentenced Marin and Acosta Hurtado to a term of imprisonment.[14] Marin and Acosta Hurtado timely appealed. **[—14—] [—15—] {-891-}**

---

[14] Acosta Hurtado stipulated to the following:

> IT IS HEREBY AGREED BY AND BETWEEN the United States of American and the defendant, Juan Carlos Acosta Hurtado, by and through his attorney, Jorge Leon Chalela, Esq, that the following statements are true and that no evidence need be presented by the United States at trial or in any further proceedings regarding the same:
>
> 1. On or about July 31, 2019, the U.S. Coast Guard Cutter (USCGC) NORTHLAND located the motor vessel (M/V) ZUMAQUE TRACER, a 256 foot Cameroon flagged coastal freighter, in the international waters of the Caribbean Sea, approximately 200 nautical miles southeast of Kingston, Jamaica on a northwesterly course towards Grand Cayman. The defendants, Asdrubal Quijada Marin, Juan Carlos Acosta Hurtado, Rafael Antonio Querales Grafe, Edwin Ramon Marcano Morales, Juan Carlos DiazMorales, Henry Jose Marquez, and **[—14—]** Jose Rafael Perez Colina were the seven crew members of the M/V.
>
> 2. The NORTHLAND conducted right of approach questioning to determine and verify the nationality of the ZUMAQUE TRACER. During the right of approach questioning, defendant Asdrubal Quijada Marin, identified himself as the master of the vessel and claimed that the purpose of the voyage was to transit to its next port of call in Panama.
>
> 3. During the Coast Guard's subsequent search of the M/V, the boarding team located and seized 143 bales containing approximately 4,225 kilograms of cocaine concealed in the vessel's aft wing ballast tanks.

II.

We review a motion to dismiss an indictment for an abuse of discretion. *United States v. Castaneda*, 997 F.3d 1318, 1325 (11th Cir. 2021). This Court, however, reviews a denial of a motion to dismiss an indictment de novo if the asserted ground is outrageous government conduct. *Id.* While we review subject matter jurisdiction de novo, we review for clear error a district court's factual findings underlying its jurisdiction decision. *United States v. Iguaran*, 821 F.3d 1335, 1336, 4 Adm. R. 457, 457 (11th Cir. 2016) (per curiam). Finally, the denial of a motion to suppress involves mixed questions of law and fact. *United States v. Spivey*, 861 F.3d 1207, 1212 (11th Cir. 2017). This Court reviews a district court's factual findings for clear error and the application of the law to those facts de novo. *United States v. Gonzalez-Zea*, 995 F.3d 1297, 1301 (11th Cir. 2021).

III.

A.

The MDLEA prohibits certain acts while "on board a covered vessel." 46 U.S.C. § 70503(a). The definition of covered vessel includes "a vessel subject to the jurisdiction of the United States." *Id.* § 70503(e). The MDLEA further defines a vessel subject to the jurisdiction of the United States multiple ways. Two definitions are relevant for purposes of this appeal, each providing a potential route to jurisdiction over the crew of the *Zumaque Tracer*: (1) "a vessel without nationality" and (2) "a vessel registered in a foreign nation if that nation has consented or waived objection to the **[—16—]** enforcement of United States law by the United States." *Id.* § 70502(c)(1).

The statute further defines each of these routes. One way a vessel could be "without **{-892-}** nationality" is if the vessel's "master or individual in charge makes a claim of registry that is denied by the nation whose registry is claimed." *Id.* § 70502(d)(1)(A). Consent or waiver by a flag nation "may be obtained by radio, telephone, or similar oral or electronic means" and "is *proved conclusively* by certification of the Secretary of State or the Secretary's designee." *Id.* § 70502(c)(2) (emphasis added). Because we decide that Cameroon properly consented to United States jurisdiction over the crew of the *Zumaque Tracer*, we need not address whether jurisdiction could be exercised under the first route—characterizing the *Zumaque Tracer* as a vessel without nationality once its registration was deleted.

"[T]his Court has 'interpreted the "on board a vessel subject to the jurisdiction of the United States" portion of the MDLEA as a congressionally imposed limit on courts' subject matter jurisdiction.'" *Iguaran*, 821 F.3d at 1336, 4 Adm. R. at 457 (quoting *United States v. De La Garza*, 516 F.3d 1266, 1271 (11th Cir. 2008)). Additionally, we frequently entertain jurisdictional challenges under the MDLEA. *See, e.g.*, *United States v. Nunez*, 1 F.4th 976, 984, 9 Adm. R. 385, 388 (11th Cir. 2021); *United States v. Cabezas-Montano*, 949 F.3d 567, 588, 8 Adm. R. 364, 374 (11th Cir. 2020); *United States v. Hernandez*, 864 F.3d 1292, 1298, 5 Adm. R. 477, 478–79 (11th Cir. 2017); *Iguaran*, 821 F.3d at 1336, 4 Adm. R. at

---

4. On November 6, 2020, this Court [the District Court] entered an Order that proper jurisdiction existed in this case over the objections of the defense.

5. The defendant, Juan Carlos Acosta Hurtado, willingly agreed to transport approximately more than 5 kilograms of cocaine aboard the M/V ZUMAQUE TRACER with his codefendants and others. The purpose of this agreement was to smuggle this cocaine through international waters and distribute the cocaine to other persons. The defendant knew that the bales onboard the M/V ZUMAQUE TRACER and seized by the U.S. Coast Guard contained five or more kilograms of cocaine and knew that the planned voyage was a drug smuggling venture.

Marin stipulated to the same. Though both stipulations state that the *Zumaque Tracer* was interdicted on July 31, this is clearly a scrivener's error since the overwhelming weight of the record points to interdiction occurring on August 30.

457; *United States v. Tinoco*, 304 F.3d 1088, 1112 (11th Cir. 2002). **[—17—]**

Though Marin and Acosta Hurtado can challenge jurisdiction—and this Court will entertain that challenge—they have limited standing to do so, as will soon become clear. We begin with the text of the MDLEA itself. "Jurisdiction of the United States with respect to a vessel subject to this chapter is not an element of an offense." 46 U.S.C. § 70504. Additionally:

> A person charged with violating section 70503 of this title . . . does not have standing to raise a claim of failure to comply with international law as a basis for a defense. A claim of failure to comply with international law in the enforcement of this chapter may be made only by a foreign nation. A failure to comply with international law does not divest a court of jurisdiction and is not a defense to a proceeding under this chapter.

Id. § 70505. So, even though Marin and Acosta Hurtado can challenge jurisdiction, the potency of any such challenge is very limited.

B.

We do not patrol the world's oceans, asserting jurisdiction over wrongdoers wherever they may be found regardless of citizenship or flag of nationality. *See Marino-Garcia*, 679 F.2d at 1380 ("To insure the principle of freedom of the seas, international law generally prohibits any country from asserting jurisdiction over foreign vessels on the high seas."). To do so would create an untenable fish-eat-fish environment governed only by *realpolitik* on the high seas. In such an environment, the same way that our **[—18—]** Coast Guard could seize a vessel registered in a foreign nation, take its foreign citizens to the United States, and prosecute them under United States law, an unfriendly nation could do the same to Americans on board a United States-flagged vessel. This is how Marin and Acosta Hurtado would like to characterize what happened to them, but it is not quite true.

On the other hand, the opposite approach—limiting our Coast Guard to only patrolling United States waters or approaching only vessels flying the United States flag—risks transforming international waters into aquatic avenues for piracy, and illegal smuggling of illicit drugs, weapons, and humans. This portrait, much like that above, also does not reflect reality. **{-893-}** *See id.* at 1382 ("Vessels without nationality are international pariahs. They have no internationally recognized right to navigate freely on the high seas.").

The real law—provided by treaties,[15] the MDLEA, and international law—strikes a balance between no free navigation and **[—19—]** lawlessness. Relevant to this appeal, this law includes allowing law enforcement vessels to engage in right-of-approach questioning. This questioning allows nations to identify the pariahs of the sea. *See id.* Vessels without nationality (or those that claim multiple nationalities) are pariahs in part because they effectively attempt to secede from all lawful authority (or evade particular authorities) merely by being in international waters. For that same reason, the law allows a nation, as the MDLEA allows the United States, to exercise jurisdiction over a stateless vessel in international waters. If it did

---

[15] It is worth noting that the Republic of Cameroon has not signed the two potentially relevant treaties here. *See* Convention on the High Seas, *opened for signature* Apr. 29, 1958, 13 U.S.T. 2312; United Nations Convention Against Illicit Traffic in Narcotic Drugs and Psychotropic Substances, *opened for signature* Dec. 20, 1988, 28 I.L.M. 493. This in no way affects our analysis:

> Even absent a treaty or arrangement, the United States could, under the "protective principle" of international law, prosecute foreign nationals on foreign vessels on the high seas for possession of narcotics. The protective principle permits a nation to assert jurisdiction over a person whose conduct outside the nation's territory threatens the nation's security or could **[—19—]** potentially interfere with the operation of its governmental functions.

United States v. Romero-Galue, 757 F.2d 1147, 1154 (11th Cir. 1985).

otherwise, the law would allow a ship-full of people to become sovereign on their own accord; being subject to no territorial jurisdiction and no flag state jurisdiction. *See id.* ("[F]lagless vessels are frequently not subject to the laws of a flag-state. As such, they represent 'floating sanctuaries from authority' and constitute a potential threat to the order and stability of navigation on the high seas." (citation omitted)). These allowances all go to striking the balance between the two extremes above.

The flag of a nation gives occupants of that vessel protection of a sort by the law of the flag nation. But if a flag nation waives jurisdiction or consents to another nation's jurisdiction, the wrongdoing crew must be held to answer to the nation that caught them in an illicit act in international waters—otherwise they would answer to no sovereign and no law. In operating on a ship with a **[—20—]** certain nation's flag, the crew risks that the flag nation will consent to jurisdiction by another. To leave such a crew answerable to no nation—neither an uninterested flag state nor an apprehending state—risks creating the same dystopian seas as would leaving stateless vessels or vessels that claim multiple flags untouchable.

C.

The MDLEA's jurisdictional provision reflects this same principle in allocating much of the jurisdictional determination to the executive branch—the branch of the federal government responsible for foreign relations. "[T]he MDLEA's jurisdictional provisions allocate power between the courts and the executive as to which of the two will be responsible for complying with U.S. obligations under the international law of criminal jurisdiction." *Hernandez*, 864 F.3d at 1303–04, 5 Adm. R. at 483. That is why a certification by the Secretary of State or his designee serves as *conclusive proof* of jurisdiction. In relying on the certificate, the judicial branch acknowledges that "the statutory requirements for MDLEA prosecution in U.S. courts have been met, while **{-894-}** recognizing that any further jurisdictional complaint over that U.S. prosecution is to be handled by the executive branch, nation-to-nation, in the international arena." *Id.* at 1304, 5 Adm. R. at 483; *see also Tinoco*, 304 F.3d at 1108 ("[T]he jurisdictional requirement [of the MDLEA] was inserted into the statute as a diplomatic courtesy to foreign nations and as a matter of international comity in order to avoid 'friction with foreign nations.'" (quoting *United States v. Gonzalez*, 776 F.2d 931, 940 (11th Cir. 1985))). **[—21—]**

Here, the Government submitted the Certificate finding jurisdiction. Our analysis could probably stop there. But Cameroon also validly waived jurisdiction. The fact that formal waiver did not occur until after the crew of the *Zumaque Tracer* arrived in the United States and were indicted is of no moment. The MDLEA limits the United States's courts' subject matter jurisdiction, but the MDLEA's jurisdictional provision is, importantly, not a right of criminal defendants. Rather, it is a tool to make sure courts protect comity among nations—protection that is already ensured by the Certificate. Cameroon green-lit the prosecutions of Marin, Acosta Hurtado, and their co-defendants. The timing of that green light is irrelevant. It does not offend Cameroon's sovereignty for the United States to prosecute the *Zumaque Tracer*'s crew because Cameroon has waived its claim of jurisdiction.

This Court said the following regarding the timing of consent to board a vessel by the United States Coast Guard: "What is important is that the [flag nation] ratified the decision to board before this case came to trial. The timing of the consent makes no constitutional difference since evidence obtained from a boarding premised on anticipated consent which never materializes would have to be excluded." *United States v. Reeh*, 780 F.2d 1541, 1547 (11th Cir. 1986). The same is true with jurisdiction. At any point between when the United States began asserting jurisdiction over Marin and Acosta Hurtado and when Cameroon consented to the United States's exercise of jurisdiction, Cameroon could have decided to exercise its own jurisdiction. At that point, the prosecution **[—22—]** could have been stopped and the defendants extradited to Cameroon. But that is all hypothetical, because Cameroon *did* consent.

In holding that flag nation consent to United States jurisdiction is valid even if given after prosecution has begun, we appear to be in good company with our sister circuits. *See United States v. Bustos-Useche*, 273 F.3d 622, 627 (5th Cir. 2001) ("The only statutory prerequisite to the district court's jurisdiction under [the MDLEA] is that the flag nation consent to the enforcement of United States law before trial."); *United States v. Juda*, 46 F.3d 961, 966 (9th Cir. 1995) ("We have held, however, that when MDLEA jurisdiction is premised on consent of the flag nation, such consent relates back to activity that occurred prior to consent."); *United States v. Greer*, 285 F.3d 158, 175 (2d Cir. 2002) ("[The MDLEA's] jurisdictional element may be satisfied by consent provided any time before trial.").

D.

Marin also argues that Cameroon could not have consented to jurisdiction when it did because, by October 21, the *Zumaque Tracer* had been deleted from the Cameroonian registry. Marin's Br. at 20. Thus, Cameroon would have had no jurisdiction to waive at that point. We reject this argument because it admits the *Zumaque Tracer* was stateless after the registry deletion—still providing for jurisdiction under the MDLEA. This is so because there was no other nation that could have had **{-895-}** jurisdiction over the vessel. Under Marin's reading—no Cameroon jurisdiction, but also not stateless—the *Zumaque Tracer* would be one of those **[—23—]** floating pariahs, immune from any law. International law does not allow this.

We hold that the District Court properly exercised jurisdiction over Marin and Acosta Hurtado under the MDLEA.

IV.

Next, Acosta Hurtado—and only Acosta Hurtado—appeals the denial of the motion to suppress. He asserts the District Court should have suppressed pieces of evidence such as the cocaine found aboard the *Zumaque Tracer*, his post-*Miranda* statement procured after arriving in the United States, and his identity because they were all fruit of an unconstitutional search and seizure.

A.

As a threshold question, we must determine if the Fourth Amendment even applies to Acosta Hurtado. The United States Supreme Court says no. In *United States v. Verdugo-Urquidez*, the Supreme Court held that the Fourth Amendment does not apply to people who are not United States citizens or resident aliens and who are searched or seized by United States law enforcement outside the United States. 494 U.S. 259, 274–75, 110 S. Ct. 1056, 1066 (1990). In so holding, the Supreme Court explicitly stated that its reasoning applied to law enforcement interdictions in international waters: "There is likewise no indication that the Fourth Amendment was understood by contemporaries of the Framers to apply to activities of the United States directed against aliens in foreign territory or in international waters." *Id.* at 267, 110 S. Ct. at 1061. According to the Supreme Court, foreign nationals found abroad **[—24—]** lack the requisite connections to this country to be considered part of "the people" protected by the Fourth Amendment. As a Venezuelan citizen found to be committing a crime in international waters, Acosta Hurtado cannot claim the protections of the Fourth Amendment.

This Court has recently—and firmly—held that the Fourth Amendment does not apply to those in Acosta Hurtado's shoes. In *Cabezas-Montano*, a case involving a vessel interdicted by the United States Coast Guard in international waters, 949 F.3d at 580, 8 Adm. R. at 366–67, a panel of this Court explicitly held that "the Fourth Amendment does not apply to searches and seizures (arrests) by the United States of a non-citizen/non-resident alien *arrested in international waters or a foreign country*." *Id.* at 593, 8 Adm. R. at 378.

Under the prior panel precedent rule, however, "each succeeding panel is bound by the holding of the first panel to address an issue of law, unless and until that holding is overruled en banc, or by the Supreme Court."[16] *United States v. Smith*, 201 F.3d 1317, 1322 (11th Cir. 2000) (quoting *United States v. Hogan*, 986 F.2d 1364, 1369 (11th Cir. 1993)). This is true even of erroneous precedent. *See United States v. Steele*, 147 F.3d 1316, 1317–18 (11th Cir. 1998) (en banc) ("Under our prior precedent rule, a panel cannot overrule a prior one's holding even [if] convinced it is wrong."). **[—25—]**

Tinoco—decided twelve years after *Verdugo-Urquidez* and eighteen years before **{-896-}** *Cabezas-Montano*—involved a foreign vessel with a crew of foreign citizens stopped in international waters. *See Tinoco*, 304 F.3d at 1091–93. On appeal, a panel of this Court considered "whether evidence concerning the cocaine seized by the Coast Guard should have been suppressed at trial under the Fourth Amendment." *Id.* at 1116. The *Tinoco* Court proceeded to analyze the Coast Guard's stop of the vessel under a reasonable suspicion framework, "conclud[ing] that the district court did not err in ruling that the Coast Guard acted consistently with the Fourth Amendment when it stopped and boarded the vessel in this case."[17] *Id.* Though decided twelve years after *Verdugo-Urquidez*, the *Tinoco* Court did not address that case and came to an inconsistent conclusion. It is also worth noting that the *Cabezas-Montano* Court did not address *Tinoco* in holding that the Fourth Amendment did not apply to the defendants in that case.

True, *Tinoco* does not explicitly hold that the Fourth Amendment applies to foreign nationals interdicted in international waters. But *Tinoco* holds that the district court did not err in finding that the Coast Guard's behavior conformed with the Fourth Amendment. And *Tinoco*, not *Cabezas-Montano*, is this Circuit's first holding on that particular issue of law. We therefore must **[—26—]** follow *Tinoco* despite its erroneous application of the Fourth Amendment.

B.

Nevertheless, the *Northland*'s stop and search of the *Zumaque Tracer* did not violate the Fourth Amendment, so the District Court did not err in denying the defendants' motion to suppress evidence. With no Fourth Amendment violation, there can be no fruit of a Fourth Amendment violation. Under *Tinoco*'s erroneous Fourth Amendment analysis (similar to the analysis this Court used prior to *Verdugo-Urquidez*), law enforcement ships need only reasonable suspicion—not probable cause—to stop and search a vessel on the high seas. *See Tinoco*, 304 F.3d at 1116; *United States v. Padilla-Martinez*, 762 F.2d 942, 950 (11th Cir. 1985).

"To determine whether a suspicion was reasonable, we evaluate the totality of the circumstances surrounding the stop, including the collective knowledge of all officers involved in the stop." *United States v. Bishop*, 940 F.3d 1242, 1249 (11th Cir. 2019). In determining reasonable suspicion, law enforcement personnel may make "common sense conclusions." *United States v. Cortez*, 449 U.S. 411, 418, 101 S. Ct. 690, 695 (1981). And reasonable suspicion can exist even if each observation "alone is susceptible of innocent explanation." *United States v. Arvizu*, 534 U.S. 266, 277, 122 S. Ct. 744, 753 (2002); *see also Reeh*, 780 F.2d at 1544 ("[I]t is also well established that circumstances completely consistent with legal conduct may still amount to reasonable suspicion."). "Probable cause 'is not a high bar,'" *Dist. of Columbia v. Wesby*, 138 S. Ct. 577, 586 **[—27—]** (2018) (citation omitted); by sheer force of logic, reasonable suspicion must be even lower.

Considering the totality of the collective knowledge from all of the Coast Guard decisionmakers in late August 2019, there was certainly reasonable suspicion that the *Zumaque Tracer* was engaged in illegal

[16] "The holding of a case comprises both 'the result of the case and those portions of the opinion necessary to that result.'" *United States v. Caraballo-Martinez*, 866 F.3d 1233, 1244 (11th Cir. 2017) (quoting *United States v. Kaley*, 579 F.3d 1246, 1253 n.10 (11th Cir. 2009)).

[17] We pause to note the brief alternative holding that follows the Fourth Amendment analysis. The *Tinoco* Court held in the alternative that "even if reasonable suspicion had not been present," the crew "effectively abandoned the [cocaine] and thus have no Fourth Amendment standing to challenge the seizure." *Tinoco*, 304 F.3d at 1117.

activity. The Coast Guard knew that (1) **{-897-}** the AIS was not on (and the master of the vessel did not know how to use it), (2) the *Zumaque Tracer* should have been repaired in Venezuela and was not, (3) the vessel's purported destination made no sense, (4) the *Zumaque Tracer* was not outfitted for cargo as its nature would have suggested, (5) the vessel had a dangerously small crew, (6) the *Zumaque Tracer* was having trouble maintaining a steady course, and (7) the vessel was in a known drug smuggling corridor. Together, these observations went well beyond reasonable suspicion. Additionally—and perhaps more importantly—the Coast Guard obtained Cameroon's permission to board and search the vessel.

C.

Acosta Hutado errs in asserting that each individual observation that builds into reasonable suspicion must constitute evidence of crime. Not only do courts analyze reasonable suspicion based on the totality of the circumstances, but each individual observation can be innocuous, and certainly need not itself be *evidence of crime*. For instance, it may not be illegal to drive down the freeway with a bumper sticker that says, "I sell drugs," but a state trooper would be foolish to overlook such an observation if other **[—28—]** circumstances suggest the car might contain drugs. The bumper sticker goes to reasonable suspicion.

Acosta Hurtado also makes a staleness argument. But the information on the ground—or water—was refreshed when the *Northland* encountered the *Zumaque Tracer*. The suspicious observations before boarding that day were therefore as fresh as could be. If the staleness argument only goes to the staleness of Cameroon's consent, this argument is meritless. Foreign nation consent is not like a warrant. Permission to board and search is a function of the flag nation's sovereignty, not of United States criminal procedure. Unlike a warrant, which must be specific, permission to board and search is general. The odds of stale information spoiling a good warrant does not neatly apply to general permission to board and search a foreign nation's vessel.

We therefore hold that the District Court did not err in denying the motion to suppress evidence based on a Fourth Amendment violation.

V.

In addition to the Fourth Amendment challenge, Acosta Hurtado alone raises an unnecessary delay argument under due process and Federal Rules of Criminal Procedure 5 and 48.[18] **[—29—]**

A.

"To establish a violation of a defendant's Fifth Amendment rights, the defendant must show that 'pre-indictment delay caused him actual substantial prejudice and that the delay was the product of a deliberate act by the government designed to gain a tactical advantage.'" *United States v. Gayden*, 977 F.3d 1146, 1150 (11th Cir. 2020) (quoting *United States v. Foxman*, 87 F.3d 1220, 1222 (11th Cir. 1996)). Whether or not Acosta Hurtado was prejudiced by the admittedly long delay between initial detainment on board the *Northland* and indictment, he cannot satisfy the second prong. Acosta Hurtado provides nothing but "conclusory assertions about the [G]overnment's timeline" **{-898-}** that suggests the United States held him and his co-defendants at sea intentionally to gain a tactical advantage over him. *Id.* In fact, the most likely reason for the delay from the record seems to be that the Coast Guard was truly making a good faith effort to avoid the jurisdictional problem discussed above. Further, Acosta Hurtado and his co-defendants remained uninterrogated the entire time they were on the Coast Guard vessels, so it is unclear what tactical advantage the United States could have possibly obtained over them.

[18] The District Court ruled that arguments regarding the challenges under the Federal Rules of Criminal Procedure contained in Acosta Hurtado's motion to supplement his motion to dismiss were untimely. We do not weigh in on the timeliness question because the arguments are obviously meritless.

B.

Not only does Acosta Hurtado not have a constitutional unnecessary delay claim, his challenge under the Rules of Criminal Procedure fares no better:

> This Court[, in *United States v. Purvis*,] held that various factors are considered in determining whether a **[—30—]** delay was unnecessary, including: (1) the distance between the location of the defendant's arrest in international waters and the U.S. port he was brought to; (2) the time between the defendant's arrival at the U.S. port and his presentment to the magistrate judge; (3) any evidence of mistreatment or improper interrogation during the delay; and (4) any reason for the delay, like exigent circumstances or emergencies.

Cabezas-Montano, 949 F.3d at 591, 8 Adm. R. at 377 (citing 768 F.2d 1237, 1238–39 (11th Cir. 1985)).[19]

The first factor weighs in favor of Acosta Hurtado. It was a multi-day journey from where the *Zumaque Tracer* was interdicted to San Juan, but not a forty-eight-day journey—forty-eight days counting from September 3, when the search of the vessel ended, to October 21, when the defendants saw a magistrate.

The second factor weighs against Acosta Hurtado. The crew of the *Zumaque Tracer* arrived in the United States on a Friday. They had to be processed by Customs and Border Protection. From San Juan, they were flown to Tampa—the federal district where they had already been indicted by a grand jury two days prior—and arrived at 5 P.M., the end of the business day. The defendants saw a magistrate the very next opportunity: Monday morning. *Cf. County of Riverside v. McLaughlin*, 500 U.S. 44, 57, 111 S. Ct. 1661, 1670 (1991) (requiring defendants to be brought **[—31—]** before a magistrate judge for a probable cause determination within forty-eight hours after *a warrantless arrest*, unlike here where defendants were arrested pursuant to an indictment and warrant).

The third factor also weighs against Acosta Hurtado. None of the crew were interrogated and all evidence points to them having been treated humanely—eating the same food as the *Northland*'s crew and being provided showers, a toilet, and medical care. The testimony at the evidentiary hearing suggests the amenities on the *Northland* (even for detainees) were superior to those on the *Zumaque Tracer*.

The fourth factor weighs against Acosta Hurtado. The reason for the delay was clearly that the Coast Guard did not think it had jurisdiction to bring the defendants to the United States. In other words, the Coast Guard's goal of acting lawfully caused the delay. The "allegation that the government deliberately and tactically delayed in order to forum shop is pure speculation and unsupported by any record evidence." *Cabezas-Montano*, 949 F.3d at 592, 8 Adm. R. at 377. Again, Acosta Hurtado provides only conclusory **{-899-}** assertions that the delay was to gain a tactical advantage. He provides zero evidence to support those assertions.

Not only does Acosta Hurtado not show that the District Court erred under the *Purvis* framework, dismissing this indictment would not comport with the policy behind Rule 5. "[T]he purpose of Rule 5(a) is to prevent oppressive police interrogations and other 'third-degree' tactics before bringing the accused in front of an officer of the court." *Id.* at 591, 8 Adm. R. at 376. To argue that such tactics or **[—32—]** interrogations happened here would be to blatantly ignore the record. In analyzing Rule 5, the Supreme Court has said, "[t]he duty enjoined upon arresting officers to arraign 'without unnecessary delay' indicates that the command does not call for mechanical or automatic obedience." *Mallory v. United States*, 354 U.S. 449, 455, 77 S. Ct. 1356, 1359–60 (1957). Rather, "delay must not be of a nature to give opportunity for the extraction of a confession." *Id.* at 455, 77 S. Ct. at 1360. The delay here had nothing to do with extracting a

[19] It is worth noting that *Cabezas-Montano*, though on plain error review, involved a 49-day delay. 949 F.3d at 591–92, 8 Adm. R. at 376–78.

confession, and dismissing this indictment would do nothing to deter bad law enforcement tactics. The only thing it might deter is the Coast Guard carefully waiting for jurisdiction, but we would not want to encourage that change.[20]

C.

Acosta Hurtado appears to make a few other arguments that go to delay. None of them persuade us. First, he says that rather than (1) prematurely bring the *Zumaque Tracer* crew to the United States before Cameroon consented to United States jurisdiction or (2) waiting for forty-eight days at sea, the United States should have brought the crew to Cameroon for prosecution. This argument does not hold water. Rather than proceed with caution—as the Coast Guard did here—Acosta Hurtado suggests that the United States should do the following: sail across an ocean on a Coast **[—33—]** Guard *warship* into the territorial waters of another nation without permission to give them seven detainees over whom the nation has expressed no interest in exercising jurisdiction. To read the argument is to see its absurdity. Acosta Hurtado rejoins that the United States could have received permission to bring the *Zumaque Tracer* crew to Cameroon. But Cameroon was not responding to the United States's request for consent or waiver, which implicitly already asked if Cameroon wanted to exercise jurisdiction over the defendants. How could requesting another way—"can we bring these defendants to Cameroon for you to exercise jurisdiction?"—have elicited any quicker a response?

Acosta Hurtado also argues that he was prejudiced by the delay because it caused him to confess—post-*Miranda*—"admitting of knowledge of the presence of the contraband under joint and constructive possession circumstances and of the conspiracy to possess with the intent to distribute." Acosta Hurtado Br. at 42. None of this changes the analysis, however, because Acosta Hurtado *stipulated to the same facts even more directly* over a year later on the advice of the same counsel he has on appeal.[21] **{–900–}**

We therefore hold that the District Court did not err in denying Acosta Hurtado's motion to dismiss based on unnecessary delay arguments. **[—34—]**

VI.

Finally, Acosta Hurtado raises an outrageous government conduct claim. "Outrageous conduct is only a potential defense in this circuit because neither the Supreme Court nor this Court has ever found it to actually apply and barred the prosecution of any case based on it." *Castaneda*, 997 F.3d at 1324 ("Like the fabled creature Sasquatch, this defense has entered the common consciousness and is mentioned from time to time. Some claim to have caught fleeting glimpses of it in the remote backwoods of the law, but its actual existence has never been confirmed."). Acosta Hurtado points to nothing in the intervening two years between *Castaneda* and now that would change that assessment.

In theory, "[o]utrageous government conduct occurs when law enforcement obtains a conviction for conduct beyond the defendant's predisposition by employing methods that fail to comport with due process guarantees." *United States v. Jayyousi*, 657 F.3d 1085, 1111–12 (11th Cir. 2011) (internal quotation marks omitted) (quoting *United States v. Ciszkowski*, 492 F.3d 1264, 1270 (11th Cir. 2007)). In other words, law enforcement would need to somehow cause the defendant to engage in criminal conduct. Acosta Hurtado points to nothing to suggest as much in his circumstance. Any alleged outrageous conduct took place after Acosta Hurtado committed his crime.

[20] Here, it is hard to imagine how a Rule 48 challenge for delay can help Acosta Hurtado. We have already analyzed how the delay does not warrant dismissal, and Rule 48 is discretionary. A "court *may* dismiss an indictment . . . if unnecessary delay occurs." Fed. R. Crim. P. 48(b) (emphasis added).

[21] Acosta Hurtado also asserts that "this Court presumes our delay as 'unnecessary'" based on Judge Rosenbaum's concurrence in *Cabezas-Montano*. Acosta Hurtado Br. at 40. It goes without saying, but concurring and dissenting opinions in this Circuit do not constitute precedential law.

Other than the entrapment-like circumstances, "the defense can only be invoked in the rarest and most outrageous circumstances," when the government conduct "violate[s] that **[—35—]** fundamental fairness, shocking to the universal sense of justice, mandated by the due process clause of the fifth amendment." *United States v. Haimowitz*, 725 F.2d 1561, 1577 (11th Cir. 1984) (quotation marks and citations omitted). Acosta Hurtado points to nothing that fits the bill. As already discussed, the delay was far from outrageous, and the crew were treated humanely in detention. In fact, this Court has not blinked an eye in the past at the practice of housing detainees on the decks of Coast Guard vessels under some sort of shelter, with or without restraints. *See Purvis*, 768 F.2d at 1239 (detainees kept handcuffed on the deck of a Coast Guard vessel); *Nunez*, 1 F.4th at 983 (detainees kept on the deck of a Coast Guard vessel, possibly shackled).

Acosta Hurtado has not found Sasquatch, or—more appropriately here—the Kraken. The *Zumaque Tracer* sunk as a result of the mundane—disrepair—not a sea monster. Likewise, with the exception of a delay attributable to Cameroon, Acosta Hurtado's detention was fairly run-of-the-mill, not a result of outrageous government conduct.

Accordingly, the District Court's judgments are

AFFIRMED

(Reporter's Note: Concurring opinion follows on p. 547).

[—1—] {–900–} **CARNES,** Circuit Judge, joined by **GRANT,** Circuit Judge, concurring:

We concur in the judgment of the Court in this case, which affirms the judgment of the district court. We also join in all of Judge Tjoflat's opinion except for the discussion in the last two paragraphs of Part IV.A. Those two paragraphs reflect his view of the panel decision in *United States v. Tinoco,* 304 F.3d 1088, 1116–17 (11th Cir. 2002). He believes *Tinoco* held that Fourth Amendment protections extend to noncitizens and nonresidents in foreign territory or on a ship in international waters, **{–901–}** and "thereby came to an inconsistent conclusion" from *Verdugo-Urquidez,* 494 U.S. 259 (1990), which held that they do not. *See* Lead Op. at 24–26.

If *Tinoco* held what Judge Tjoflat believes it did, it would be inconsistent with the decision in *Verdugo-Urquidez,* which preceded *Tinoco.* The Supreme Court held in *Verdugo-Urquidez* that the Fourth Amendment does not apply to searches and seizures of property owned by noncitizen, nonresidents located in another country. *See* 494 U.S. at 261 ("The question presented by this case is whether the Fourth Amendment applies to the search and seizure by United States agents of property that is owned by a nonresident alien and located in a foreign country. We hold that it does not.").

But *Tinoco* is not inconsistent with *Verdugo-Urquidez.* What Tinoco did is affirm the denial of a motion to suppress made on Fourth Amendment grounds when there was reasonable suspicion that a foreign crew was violating the laws of the United States and **[—2—]** the defendants lacked Fourth Amendment standing. *Tinoco,* 304 F.3d at 1116–17. That does not implicate *Verdugo-Urquidez's* holding.

The *Tinoco* opinion had no occasion to address whether the same actions would have violated the Fourth Amendment if there had been no reasonable suspicion to believe that the foreign crew had been violating the laws of the United States. It did not purport to hold anything about that different scenario. A holding that X + 1 (search of a foreign ship in international waters plus reasonable suspicion) does not violate the Fourth Amendment is not inconsistent with a holding that X alone (search of a foreign ship in international waters without reasonable suspicion) also does not violate it.

The *Tinoco* opinion does say that "the district court did not err in ruling that the Coast Guard acted consistently with the Fourth Amendment when it stopped and boarded the vessel in this case." *Id.* at 1116. But that does not mean the *Tinoco* decision must have *held,* as our colleague fears, that the Fourth Amendment applies to searches of foreign crew members on a foreign ship outside the territorial waters of the United States. *See* Lead Op. at 26. The quoted statement does not mean that because it is dicta, not a holding.

Our circuit law is rock-solid and clear as a mountain stream that the only statements in, or parts of, an opinion that are holdings are those that are necessary to the result of the decision that the opinion accompanies. *See, e.g., United States v. Gillis,* 938 F.3d 1181, **[—3—]** 1198 (11th Cir. 2019) ("The holding of a case comprises both the result of the case and those portions of the opinion necessary to that result.") (quotation marks omitted); *Auto. Alignment & Body Serv., Inc. v. State Farm Mut. Auto. Ins. Co.,* 953 F.3d 707, 725 (11th Cir. 2020) ("Our statement . . . in [an earlier case] was not necessary to the decision we reached, so it is not part of our holding."); *Castillo v. Fla., Sec'y of DOC,* 722 F.3d 1281, 1290 (11th Cir. 2013) ("[B]ecause those statements in [an earlier] opinion are not necessary to the result in that case . . . they are not the holding of the decision."); *see also Ingram v. Comm'r of Soc. Sec. Admin.,* 496 F.3d 1253, 1265 (11th Cir. 2007) ("[J]udicial opinions do not make binding precedents; judicial decisions do.").

Statements that are not necessary to the result are dicta. *See, e.g., United States v. Shamsid-Deen,* 61 F.4th 935, 949 n.1 (11th Cir. 2023) ("Because the statement . . . was not necessary to the result in that case, it was dicta."); *Rambaran v. Sec'y, Dep't of Corrs.,* 821 F.3d 1325, 1333 (11th Cir. 2016) ("[T]he statement is dicta **{–902–}** because it was not necessary to the result in [the earlier case].");

Powell v. Thomas, 643 F.3d 1300, 1304–05 (11th Cir. 2011) ("As we've said, dicta is defined as those portions of an opinion that are not necessary to deciding the case then before us, whereas holding is comprised both of the result of the case and those portions of the opinion necessary to that result by which we are bound.") (quotation marks omitted).

And neither we nor anyone else is required to follow dicta, not even a few steps down the decisional path. *See also, e.g., Pretka* **[—4—]** *v. Kolter City Plaza II, Inc.*, 608 F.3d 744, 762 (11th Cir. 2010) ("We are not required to follow dicta in our own prior decisions. Nor for that matter is anyone else.") (citation omitted); *Welch v. United States*, 958 F.3d 1093, 1098 (11th Cir. 2020) ("Dicta is not binding on anyone for any purpose."); *United States v. Pickett*, 916 F.3d 960, 966 (11th Cir. 2019) (same); *Edwards v. Prime, Inc.*, 602 F.3d 1276, 1298 (11th Cir. 2010) ("We have pointed out many times that regardless of what a court says in its opinion, the decision can hold nothing beyond the facts of that case. All statements that go beyond the facts of the case . . . are dicta. And dicta is not binding on anyone for any purpose.") (citations omitted).

The result of the appeal in the *Tinoco* case was a ruling that the district court correctly denied the motion to suppress and therefore the convictions were due to be affirmed. 304 F.3d at 1116–17, 1125. In the course of reaching that ruling and result, the panel opinion did not state that the Fourth Amendment applies to searches and seizures involving noncitizen, nonresidents outside the territorial jurisdiction of the United States.[1] But even if the **[—5—]** *Tinoco* opinion had said that it does, that statement would not have been necessary to the result in the appeal. It wouldn't have been necessary to the result because there was reasonable suspicion to justify the search and seizure in *Tinoco* anyway; and the defendants in that case also lacked statutory standing to raise the issue.

Reasonable suspicion that a search will turn up contraband is enough to justify a search and seizure of a foreign ship and its crew in international waters. *United States v. Williams*, 617 F.2d 1063, 1089 (5th Cir. 1980) (en banc) ("We have held that the Coast Guard undoubtedly had grounds for a reasonable suspicion that they would find contraband in the hold of the [foreign vessel in international waters]. Therefore, the search satisfied the requirements of the [F]ourth [A]mendment."); *United States v. Reeh*, 780 F.2d 1541, 1546–47 (11th Cir. 1986) ("These considerations have led us to apply the 'reasonable suspicion' standard, not probable cause, to boardings of foreign vessels in international waters."); **{-903-}** *United States v. Glen-Archila*, 677 F.2d 809, 813 (11th Cir. 1982) (stopping a vessel on the high seas does not violate the Fourth Amendment if there is reasonable suspicion that it is engaged in smuggling contraband into the United States). And the *Tinoco* panel found there was reasonable suspicion aplenty. *Tinoco*, 304 F.3d at 1116 **[—6—]** (explaining why "it is clear that the Coast Guard had reasonable suspicion to believe that the vessel here was engaged in illegal smuggling activities").

Not only that, but the defendants in *Tinoco* also lacked statutory standing to challenge the search and seizure on Fourth Amendment grounds. *See id.* at 1117 ("Alternatively, even if reasonable suspicion had not been present,

[1] At most, the *Tinoco* panel assumed for purposes of that case that the Fourth Amendment applied, because it didn't make any difference since the Coast Guard had reasonable suspicion to believe the ship was carrying illegal drugs, which is enough by itself for the search to pass muster under the Fourth Amendment. Assuming away unnecessary issues or questions to decide a case on easier or more efficient grounds is a basic part of Judging 101. We all do it with some regularity. And as we have explained when presented with assumptions about the law that prior panels made in the course of deciding an appeal: "assumptions are not holdings" for purposes of the prior precedent rule. *United States v. Jackson*, 55 F.4th 846, 853–54 (11th Cir. 2022), *cert. granted,* **[—5—]** 143 S. Ct. 2457 (2023); *accord, Brown v. Electrolux Home Prods., Inc.*, 817 F.3d 1225, 1239 (11th Cir. 2016) ("Such assumptions are not holdings."); *cf. Brecht v. Abrahamson*, 507 U.S. 619, 631 (1993) ("[S]ince we have never squarely addressed the issue, and have at most assumed" a position on it, "we are free to address the issue on the merits" without regard to stare decisis).

[the] challenge to the suppression motion still would fail. This is because the cocaine was seized by the Coast Guard after it was thrown into the ocean by the vessel crew members. The crew members . . . effectively abandoned the contraband and thus have no Fourth Amendment standing to challenge the seizure."). The *Tinoco* panel rejected the defendants' claim on that additional basis as well.

So the same result would have occurred in *Tinoco*, even if the Fourth Amendment did apply to searches and seizures of foreign vessels and their crews in international waters. It follows that nothing the *Tinoco* panel opinion said, or implied, about the Fourth Amendment's application to searches and seizures of foreign crews and ships outside the territorial jurisdiction of the United States was necessary to the rejection of the Fourth Amendment claim and affirmance of the convictions in that case. There is no Fourth Amendment *holding* in *Tinoco*, other than it is not violated where the Coast Guard, acting on reasonable suspicion that a ship is carrying contraband to the United States, searches the ship and its crew. That is not inconsistent with the Supreme Court's earlier **[—7—]** holding in *Verdugo-Urquidez* that the Fourth Amendment does not apply at all to such searches.

This Court should continue doing what the panel did in *United States v. Cabezas-Montano*, 949 F.3d 567, 594, 8 Adm. R. 364, 378–79 (11th Cir. 2020). Which is to apply the Supreme Court's *Verdugo-Urquidez* decision as though there was no *holding* in the *Tinoco* case about whether Fourth Amendment protections apply to foreign crew aboard foreign vessels in international waters. Which there wasn't.

This page intentionally left blank

United States Court of Appeals for the District of Columbia Circuit

United States Court of Appeals for the District of Columbia Circuit

No. 21-1249

INTERNATIONAL ORG. OF MASTERS, MATES & PILOTS
vs.
NATIONAL LABOR RELATIONS BD.

On Petition for Review of an Order of the National Labor Relations Board

Decided: March 3, 2023

Citation: 61 F.4th 169, 11 Adm. R. 552 (D.C. Cir. 2023).

Before **HENDERSON** and **PILLARD**, Circuit Judges, and **EDWARDS**, Senior Circuit Judges.

[—2—] {-172-} EDWARDS, Senior Circuit Judge: **{-173-}**

Since 1981, the International Organization of Masters, Mates & Pilots, ILA, AFL-CIO ("the Union" or "IOM"), has been the lawful bargaining agent for the Licensed Deck Officers ("LDOs") on four container ships that carry goods between ports in California and Hawaii. The LDOs are licensed by the Coast Guard and they include a master, first (or "chief"), second, and third officers (also called "mates") on each of the four ships. For four decades, the Union has negotiated with a series of successor companies that have owned the vessels to reach collective bargaining agreements covering the LDOs. In 2015, The Pasha Group purchased the ships, and its wholly owned subsidiary, Sunrise Operations, LLC ("Sunrise"), now operates the vessels and is the most recent successor employer of the LDOs.

In 2017 and 2018, the Union sought information from Sunrise regarding the LDOs on the four vessels. Sunrise refused to provide the information sought by the Union and then refused to participate in arbitration at the Union's headquarters in Maryland, as required by the parties' collective bargaining agreement. The Union filed unfair labor practice **[—3—]** ("ulp") charges with the National Labor Relations Board ("Board" or "NLRB"). The Board's General Counsel then filed a complaint alleging that Sunrise had violated sections 8(a)(1) and 8(a)(5) of the National Labor Relations Act ("NLRA" or "Act"), 29 U.S.C. § 158(a)(1), (5), when it failed to provide information to the Union and declined to participate in arbitration proceedings in Maryland.

A hearing on the ulp charges was held before an Administrative Law Judge ("ALJ"). The judge found, *inter alia*, that the Union was the LDOs' exclusive bargaining representative; that Sunrise had admitted that it recognized the Union as such, as had three predecessor employers who owned the vessels before Pasha and Sunshine; and that because the LDOs who were second and third mates were employees, not supervisors under Section 2(11) of the NLRA, 29 U.S.C. § 152(11), the LDOs' bargaining unit was an appropriate "mixed" unit of statutory employees and supervisors. The ALJ thus rejected Sunrise's claim that it had no duty to bargain with the Union under Section 8(a)(5) of the NLRA because the LDO unit consisted entirely of supervisors. Given that Sunrise and its predecessors had recognized and bargained with the Union on behalf of the LDOs, and that the Union retained majority support among the bargaining unit employees, the ALJ concluded that Sunrise had violated the NLRA by refusing to provide the Union with the information that it had sought and by failing to abide by an agreement requiring the parties to meet for arbitration proceedings in Maryland.

Sunrise filed exceptions with the NLRB to contest the ALJ's decision. The employer's principal argument before the ALJ was that all of the LDOs were in fact supervisors and, therefore, the LDOs did not constitute an appropriate bargaining unit under the Act. Sunrise pressed this same argument in its exceptions to the Board. A 2-1 majority of the **[—4—]** Board ruled against the Union, but it never addressed the issue raised by Sunrise, *i.e.*, whether the Board lacked jurisdiction because all of the LDOs were *in fact* supervisors. Instead, the Board majority held that it had no jurisdiction to hear the case because, as the Board saw it, Sunrise *believed* that all **{-174-}** of the LDOs were supervisors. In the majority's view, it did not matter whether, as the ALJ found, the second and third mates were not supervisors. According to the majority, what mattered was that when Sunrise and its predecessors voluntarily recognized the Union as the unit's bargaining representative, they did not *believe* that the LDO unit was a "mixed" unit.

It is clear that the majority opinion for the Board purports to decide this case without regard to the parties' principal claims presented to the ALJ, and it rests on a position that was never advanced by Sunrise either before the ALJ or in its exceptions to the Board. Sunrise never argued that the disposition of this case should turn on the employer's *subjective beliefs* about whether the LDOs were supervisors. And we can find no case in which the Board or a reviewing court has held that an employer's *unannounced beliefs* about workers' supervisory status determines whether the Board has jurisdiction to enforce the NLRA.

For the reasons explained below, we find that the Board's holding in this case lacks support in the record, defies established law, and creates a new rule without reasoned justification. It thus fails substantial evidence review and is arbitrary and capricious for want of reasoned decision making. We therefore grant the petition for review, vacate the Board's decision, and remand the case for reconsideration consistent with this opinion. **[—5—]**

I. Background

A. Statutory and Regulatory Background

Under the NLRA, labor organizations like IOM "can achieve the status of a majority collective bargaining representative through either Board certification or voluntary recognition by the employer[.]" *Raymond F. Kravis Ctr. for Performing Arts, Inc. v. NLRB*, 550 F.3d 1183, 1188 (D.C. Cir. 2008). Section 8(d) of the Act requires an employer and a recognized union representative "to meet at reasonable times and confer in good faith with respect to wages, hours, and other terms and conditions of employment, or the negotiation of an agreement, or any question arising thereunder, and the execution of a written contract incorporating any agreement reached if requested by either party." 29 U.S.C. § 158(d). This means that the employer and the union bargaining agent have a mutual obligation to "confer in good faith with respect to any question arising under [the parties' collective bargaining agreement]." *NLRB v. Acme Indus. Co.*, 385 U.S. 432, 436-37 (1967) (cleaned up). The duty to bargain also requires an employer to provide information that is needed by a recognized union for the proper performance of its duties as the employees' bargaining agent. *Id.* at 435-36.

A "supervisor" is not an "employee" entitled to protection under the NLRA. 29 U.S.C. § 152(3) (excluding "supervisor[s]" from definition of employee). Statutory supervisors are those with authority to act "in the interest of the employer" to carry out or "effectively to recommend" at least one of twelve enumerated activities, provided that the exercise of that authority requires "the use of independent judgment." 29 U.S.C. § 152(11); *see NLRB v. Health Care & Ret. Corp.*, 511 U.S. 571, 573-74 (1994). The twelve activities are: "to hire, transfer, suspend, lay off, recall, promote, **[—6—]** discharge, assign, reward, or discipline other employees, or responsibly to direct them, or to adjust their grievances, or effectively to recommend such action." 29 U.S.C. § 152(11).

The Board looks beyond mere labels or job descriptions to determine supervisory **{–175–}** status. *See, e.g., G4S Regulated Sec. Sols*, 362 NLRB 1072, 1073, 1074 n.9 (2015); *Dole Fresh Vegetables, Inc.*, 339 NLRB 785, 785 (2003). And the party asserting supervisory status bears the burden of proof on the point. *See NLRB v. Ky. River Cmty. Care, Inc.*, 532 U.S. 706, 710-12 (2001).

B. The Parties' Dispute

In 1981, the Union on behalf of the LDOs who were working aboard the four container ships signed a collective bargaining agreement ("CBA") with one of the companies that was a predecessor to Sunrise. The CBA describes LDOs as follows:

> The Master is the [LDO] in command of the vessel at all times, subject to the lawful directives of the Company.
>
> The Chief Officer is the Head of the Deck Department and as such, performs supervisory duties outlined in this agreement. In addition, he performs the duties of the Master as necessary in the Master's absence.
>
> The Second Officer is the Navigating Officer and, subject to the direction of the Master, is in charge of all navigational equipment, and is responsible for maintaining charts, publications, and navigational equipment, in accordance with all pertinent navigation regulations and statutes .... **[—7—]**
>
> The Third Officers stand a regular navigation watch at sea and assist in the normal operation of the vessel as directed by the Department Head.

Joint Appendix ("J.A.") 369. The CBA explains, *inter alia*, that "[t]he Parties agree that the duties of the [LDOs] . . . shall be maintained as supervisory and professional" and notes that LDOs are tasked with "the shipboard supervision" of certain maintenance and cargo activity. J.A. 369, 370.

The Pasha Group purchased the four ships in 2015, retaining a majority of the Union-represented LDOs who were employed aboard the ships. The Pasha Group assured the Union that it would assume and abide by the 1981 CBA and recognize the Union as the LDOs' exclusive bargaining representative. It agreed that it would "not engage in activities . . . calculated to undermine" the Union's status. J.A. 362. Although the employer has been variously described as The Pasha Group, Pasha Hawaii, SR Holdings, and Sunrise, the Union has routinely interacted with Sunrise. The ulp complaint in this case asserts that Sunrise violated the NLRA by failing or refusing to provide information to the Union, by delaying the provision of such information, and by repudiating a CBA provision that required arbitration to occur in Maryland. Petitioner's Br. 1-2, 9. And Sunrise has entered an appearance as Intervenor before this court (as the employer of the LDOs).

C. Proceedings Before the ALJ

In response to the complaint filed by the Board's General Counsel, Sunrise raised several affirmative defenses. None of the defenses rested on a claim that Sunrise or its predecessors always *believed* that the LDOs in the bargaining unit included only supervisors. Rather, Sunrise's principal claim was that the **[—8—]** Board lacked jurisdiction over this case because all of the LDOs in the bargaining unit are *in fact* supervisors. The NLRB General Counsel and the Union countered that "the second and third mate officers are *employees*, not supervisors under Section 2(11)." J.A. 41 (emphasis added). A second and third mate testified that they did not perform any NLRA Section 2(11) supervisory functions for Sunrise. J.A. 202-11, 227-32. And Counsel for the Union testified that the Union had never stipulated to the supervisory **{-176-}** status of all LDOs in any of the approximately 50 ulp charges it had filed in the last two decades. J.A. 95-96.

The ALJ conducted a fact-intensive inquiry – including an assessment of disciplinary records, on-board technological advancements that had routinized the roles of second and third mates, and other evidence – and found that the LDOs comprise a mixed unit of statutory employees and supervisors. Sunrise had not been compelled by law to recognize the mixed unit, but the ALJ found that it was clear from the record that Sunrise opted to do so. Accordingly, the ALJ concluded that the NLRB had jurisdiction over the case. The ALJ additionally held that Sunrise violated the NLRA by refusing to timely provide relevant information to the Union, and by refusing to meet in Maryland for arbitration proceedings as required by the parties' CBA.

The ALJ also offered detailed responses to each of Sunrise's allegations regarding the supervisory status of second and third mates. *First, the ALJ rejected Sunrise's claims that certain LDO responsibilities transform all LDOs into supervisors.* Sunrise had argued that second and third mates are supervisors "by law" when they serve as Officers of the

Watch, referring to a role outlined by the International Safety Management Code. The ALJ disagreed, finding that in this role, second and third mates' "use of independent judgment and **[—9—]** discretion is circumscribed by the master's standing orders, and the Operating Regulations[.]'" J.A. 41 (quoting *Chevron Shipping Co.*, 317 NLRB 379, 381 (1995)). More broadly, the ALJ found that in carrying out each of their responsibilities, second and third mates must: "(1) follow the Master's established orders or seek clarification from the superior on duty on handling any particular situation, or (2) adhere to the established protocols found in [Sunrise's] Safety Management Administration policies." J.A. 41. In no role did the second and third mates perform "any supervisory functions as set forth in Section 2(11) of the [NLRA]" over other employees. J.A. 42.

Second, the ALJ rejected Sunrise's claim that all LDOs evaluate unlicensed crew. The ALJ found that Sunrise failed to proffer a single example of second and third mates asserting disciplinary responsibilities over unlicensed crew. For instance, the ALJ found no proof in the record that second and third mates ever issued disciplinary letters to other employees. The ALJ concluded that none of the responsibilities of second and third mates in their relationships with unlicensed crew required independent judgment or satisfied other indicia of supervisory status.

Third, the ALJ rejected the testimony of a Sunrise Officer as to his knowledge regarding whether Sunrise's LDOs were supervisors. The ALJ tellingly said: "I accord [the officer's] testimony very little weight since it constitutes mainly opinion evidence. In fact, [he] has no independent or expert knowledge regarding the supervisory status of [Sunrise's] LDOs much less Section 2(11)'s standards for evaluating one's supervisory status. Simply put, [Sunrise] has failed to show that its LDOs are supervisors under the Act." J.A. 42.

In sum, the ALJ concluded that Sunrise failed to meet its "burden of proving [all LDOs'] supervisory status," J.A. 41. **[—10—]** Instead, the ALJ found that "the evidence clearly shows that [Sunrise]'s second and third mate officers perform duties that are routine in nature and do not perform any supervisory functions as set forth in Section 2(11) of the Act." J.A. 42. As explained below, the Board did not dispute any of the ALJ's findings.

Finally, the ALJ rejected Sunrise's argument that the Board lacked jurisdiction **{-177-}** over this case because the Union was never certified by the NLRB as the exclusive bargaining representative of the LDOs. The ALJ properly noted that certification is not the only way to prove majority-support status. J.A. 42 (citing *Barrington Plaza & Tragniew, Inc.*, 185 NLRB 962, 963 (1970), *enforced in part,* 470 F.2d 669 (9th Cir. 1972). The ALJ explained that:

> The issue . . . is not whether the unit is appropriate or whether the Board could have initially certified the unit under the Act. . . . Rather, it is whether the employer voluntarily agreed to recognize . . . a "mixed" unit. . . . [W]here an employer has consented to a bargaining unit that includes supervisors, the [Board] properly may find the employer guilty of an unfair labor practice with respect to that bargaining unit. . . . It is undisputed that [Sunrise] voluntarily recognized the Union as the exclusive bargaining representative of the LDOs on the four vessels. . . . [T]he 1981 collective-bargaining agreement (as modified by successive [agreements]) remained in force when [Sunrise] acquired the vessels, and George Pasha assured the Union that [Sunrise] would assume and abide by the collective-bargaining agreement.

J.A. 25-26 (citations omitted). **[—11—]**

Notably, Sunrise never argued to the ALJ, nor did it offer evidence to support any claim that either it or the predecessor employers always *believed* that the LDOs constituted a supervisors-only unit.

D. Sunrise's Exceptions to the Board

Sunrise filed exceptions to the ALJ's decision, claiming for the first time that "[t]here is no dispute that since at least 1981, the parties' collective bargaining agreement unambiguously states the parties' mutual intent and understanding that the [LDO]s—including the Second and Third Mates—*are* statutory Supervisors." Petitioner's Br. 18 (citation omitted) (emphasis added). However, Sunrise did not argue that any subjective understanding that Sunrise or its predecessors may have had about the supervisory status of the LDO unit would, in and of itself, strip the Board of jurisdiction over the case.

In response to Sunrise's exceptions, the Union contended that the parties had never agreed that LDOs were part of an all-supervisors unit. *Id.*

E. The Findings of the Board Majority

In response to Sunrise's exceptions, a two-member majority of the Board determined that it "need not engage in an analysis of whether individuals in the several LDO classifications possess any of the supervisory indicia enumerated in Section 2(11) of the [NLRA]." J.A. 5. The majority accepted the ALJ's findings that Sunrise had recognized the Union, agreed to the CBA, and refused to provide information or arbitrate pursuant to the terms of the CBA. The majority did not dispute the ALJ's factual findings that the second and third mates *are in fact* employees, not **[—12—]** statutory supervisors. And the majority did not contest the settled law that an employer is bound by its voluntary recognition of a mixed unit of employees and supervisors. The majority simply dismissed the complaint without passing on the merits of the ulp charges, ruling that because Sunrise always *believed* that the bargaining unit consisted only of statutory supervisors, it had no duty to bargain with the Union. The majority held that Sunrise's apparent *belief* stripped the Board of jurisdiction over the case.

Pointing to the majority opinion's lack of any "support in the [NLRA] or its policies, in Board or judicial precedent, or in the record in this case," the dissenting member **{-178-}** of the Board predicted the majority's decision would "sink" on judicial review. J.A. 6, 11. The Union now petitions for review.

II. ANALYSIS

A. Standard of Review

"Judicial review of NLRB determinations in unfair labor practice cases is generally limited, but not so deferential that the court will merely act as a rubber stamp for the Board's conclusions. Board orders will not survive review when the Board's decision has no reasonable basis in law or when the Board has failed to apply the proper legal standard. A Board's decision will also be set aside when it departs from established precedent without reasoned justification or when the Board's factual determinations are not supported by substantial evidence." *Titanium Metals Corp. v. NLRB*, 392 F.3d 439, 445-46 (D.C. Cir. 2004) (cleaned up); *see also Hawaiian Dredging Constr. Co., Inc. v. NLRB*, 857 F.3d 877, 881 (D.C. Cir. 2017). Substantial evidence "'means such relevant evidence as a reasonable mind might accept as adequate to support a **[—13—]** conclusion.'" *Micro Pac. Dev. Inc. v. NLRB*, 178 F.3d 1325, 1329 (D.C. Cir. 1999) (citation omitted). We are obligated to assess the "'whole record,'" including "'whatever in the record fairly detracts from'" the NLRB's decision. *Tenneco Auto., Inc. v. NLRB*, 716 F.3d 640, 647 (D.C. Cir. 2013) (quoting *Universal Camera Corp. v. NLRB*, 340 U.S. 474, 488 (1951)).

Furthermore, "judicial deference is not warranted where the Board fails to adequately explain its reasoning, or where the Board leaves critical gaps in its reasoning." *David Saxe Prods., LLC v. NLRB*, 888 F.3d 1305, 1311 (D.C. Cir. 2018) (cleaned up). When the Board fails to explain or acknowledge its deviation from established precedent, we vacate its decision as arbitrary and capricious. *See Manhattan Ctr. Studios, Inc., v. NLRB*, 452 F.3d 813, 816 (D.C. Cir. 2006).

B. The Board Erred in Purporting to Decide an Issue That Was Never Raised With the ALJ

"It is a basic tenet of administrative law that each party to a formal adjudication must have a full and fair opportunity to litigate the issues to be decided by the agency," *Trident Seafoods,*

Inc. v. NLRB, 101 F.3d 111, 116 (D.C. Cir. 1996), because otherwise, "the record developed with regard to that issue will usually be inadequate to support a substantive finding in [the proponent's] favor," *id.* The law is clear that "notice adequate to provide a fair opportunity to defend on [an] issue" must "occur[] *before* the record is closed," and that the Board generally should not consider significant issues that the parties failed to raise. *Id.*; *see Collective Concrete, Inc. v. NLRB*, 786 F. App'x 266, 267 (D.C. Cir. 2019) (declining to review issues not presented to the ALJ); *Chicago Local No. 458-3M v. NLRB*, 206 F.3d 22, 24 n.1 (D.C. Cir. 2000) (an issue that "the parties did not litigate . . . before the ALJ" was "not properly before the court"). **[—14—]**

Here, Sunrise alleged that all LDOs are *in fact* supervisors. As explained above, the ALJ reviewed the record and concluded that second and third mates are *in fact* statutory employees, not supervisors. The Board disregarded Sunrise's allegations, ignored the ALJ's principal findings, and gave no heed to controlling precedent in purporting to hold that it lacked jurisdiction because Sunrise *believed* it had consented to a unit "consisting entirely of supervisors excluded from coverage under the [NLRA]." J.A. 5. Neither **{-179-}** the litigants nor the ALJ were on notice that the Board would focus on this issue. More fundamentally, no party had the opportunity to present evidence before the ALJ regarding Sunrise's *beliefs*, and the ALJ never considered the matter. The greatest irony is that the Board majority either accepted as accurate the ALJ's findings or did not dispute any of the ALJ's principal conclusions.

When the Board majority departed from the case that had been presented to the ALJ and focused instead on a significant issue that had never been raised before the ALJ, it arbitrarily and inexcusably denied the parties a full and fair opportunity to be heard on the merits of the ulp charges. This alone is grounds to reverse the Board decision. There is more, however.

C. The Board Created a New Rule That Lacks Reasoned Justification

Beyond disregarding the case presented to the ALJ, the Board majority decided this case based on a rule untethered to established law, the parties' claims, and the record. Neither the Board nor any reviewing court has ever found that an employer's unannounced *belief* about the supervisory status of employees determines the Board's jurisdiction. If anything, Board precedent suggests the opposite. *See Gratiot Cmty.* **[—15—]** *Hosp.*, 312 NLRB 1075, 1075 n.2 (1993); *Arizona Elec. Power Coop., Inc.*, 250 NLRB 1132, 1133-34 (1980). And nothing in the NLRA instructs the Board to consider parties' *beliefs* as part of its jurisdictional analysis. Furthermore, what the Board majority *surmised* that Sunrise *believed* is not what Sunrise argued that it believed before the ALJ. Indeed, Sunrise did not make any arguments before the ALJ about its subjective beliefs. In particular, it never argued before the ALJ or the Board that its subjective beliefs should play a dispositive role in the Board's jurisdictional analysis. Therefore, the Board effectively decided this case not only on a new rule of law but on a position never fathomed by the ALJ or the parties.

While "[a]gencies are free to change their existing policies," they must "provide a reasoned explanation for the change." *Encino Motorcars, LLC v. Navarro*, 579 U.S. 211, 221 (2016); *see NLRB v. CNN Am., Inc.*, 865 F.3d 740, 748 (D.C. Cir. 2017) (declining to enforce a Board order that "appear[ed] to be inconsistent with its precedents, without addressing those precedents or explaining why they do not govern"); *see also Dupuy v. NLRB*, 806 F.3d 556, 562 (D.C. Cir. 2015). The explanation "must at least display awareness that [the Board] is changing position and show that there are good reasons for the new policy." *Encino Motorcars*, 579 U.S. at 221 (cleaned up); *see FCC v. Fox Television Stations, Inc.*, 556 U.S. 502, 515 (2009). And it must acknowledge that "longstanding policies may have engendered serious reliance interests that must be taken into account," as failure to do so renders the new rule arbitrary and capricious. *Dep't of Homeland Security v. Regents of Univ.*

of Calif., 140 S. Ct. 1891, 1913 (2020) (cleaned up).

Under the Board's new rule, employees may lose the protections of the NLRA not because they are *in fact* uncovered by the Act, but because their employer asserts a *belief* that they **[—16—]** are supervisors. Although the ALJ found, and the Board did not dispute, that the second and third mates *are in fact* employees covered by the NLRA, the Board majority found that the LDOs have no enforceable rights under **{-180-}** the NLRA to be free from ulps simply because some members of the Board assumed that the employer always *believed* that all LDOs were supervisors. Apart from finding no support in established law, the rule makes little sense. If allowed to stand, the Board's new rule might easily destabilize established bargaining relationships and encourage unseemly strategic litigation. The rule propounded in the majority opinion would allow any employer or union to challenge the jurisdiction of the Board (and thereby aim to deny employees their rights under the Act) simply by asserting that company or union representatives *believed* all workers in the bargaining unit did not meet the statutory definition of an "employee."

The Board adopted its new rule with no regard for the parties' reliance interests. The Board did not consider the sweeping impact of its new rule or explain why existing case law does not govern. It did not acknowledge – much less justify – its adoption of a new rule, and it afforded the affected parties no opportunity to address it or offer relevant evidence. Thus, we are left with no choice but to vacate the Board's arbitrary and capricious decision for want of reasoned decision making.

D. The ALJ's Findings of Fact Are Uncontested and Thus Dispositive

There can be no doubt that determining supervisory status requires a heavily fact-intensive analysis of the record to determine *actual*, not believed, exercises of authority. *See Jochims v. NLRB*, 480 F.3d 1161, 1168 (D.C. Cir. 2007). As discussed above, after meticulously reviewing disciplinary records, testimony, and other evidence, the ALJ found that **[—17—]** second and third mates are *in fact* statutory employees because they "have no authority to hire/fire, discipline or recommend discipline, transfer, lay off, promote or suspend, schedule, reschedule, recall or assign any LDOs." J.A. 41. The ALJ found that Sunrise voluntarily agreed to bargain with the Union as the LDOs' bargaining agent and "admitted that it recognized the Union as the exclusive collective-bargaining representative for the LDOs." J.A. 42. Accordingly, the ALJ reasonably concluded that the LDOs form an "appropriate bargaining unit" over which "the Board retains jurisdiction." J.A. 42.

No party has questioned the ALJ's finding that the 1981 CBA is still in effect and that the parties voluntarily agreed to it. Nor has any party attempted to undermine the ALJ's finding that Sunrise is an employer within the meaning of NLRA Section 2(2) and the Union is a labor organization within the meaning of NLRA Section 2(5). Indeed, the Board itself left untouched the ALJ's finding that second and third mates *are* employees within the meaning of NLRA Section 2(3). Thus, on the record before us, the LDO unit *is in fact* a voluntarily recognized mixed bargaining unit protected by the NLRA. The Board's decision to stray from that record and rest its holding on what the majority surmised about Sunrise's *beliefs* cannot stand.

E. The Board Majority's Attempt to Justify Its Position Cannot Withstand Scrutiny

The Board majority began its analysis by acknowledging NLRB precedent establishing that an employer has a duty to bargain with a voluntarily recognized "mixed" bargaining unit. J.A. 25 (citing *Union Plaza Hotel & Casino*, 296 NLRB 918 (1989), *enforced sub nom. E.G. & H. Inc. v. NLRB*, 949 F.2d 276 (9th Cir. 1991)). The majority opinion does not question the controlling law that, after voluntarily recognizing a mixed **[—18—]** unit, an employer **{-181-}** may neither invoke the mixed nature of the unit as a defense to any ulp charge, nor assert that the Board would not have certified the unit in the first place. However, the majority opinion effectively casts aside this controlling case law because, in its view, the ALJ failed to "address the threshold question of what type of unit [Sunrise] voluntarily recognized." J.A. 26. It holds that because Sunrise somehow failed to understand that the LDO unit was mixed, it did not consent to a mixed unit. In attributing this *belief* to Sunrise, the majority presents arguments and offers findings that no party raised or addressed in the hearing before the ALJ. The justifications offered to bolster the majority opinion are plainly specious.

First, the Board majority attempted to ground its "threshold question" analysis in NLRB precedent. But the sole case it discussed – *Virginia Mason Hospital* – provides no support for its position. 357 NLRB 564 (2011). *Virginia Mason* neither discusses parties' beliefs about workers' supervisory status nor suggests that an employer may avoid a present bargaining obligation by belatedly asserting a mistaken belief about a bargaining unit's composition. *See generally id.* Indeed, we can find no case law, and the Board offers nothing, suggesting that Sunrise should be excused for its alleged error. Rather, case precedent is clear that when parties execute a collective bargaining agreement "with full knowledge of the nature of the present duties" of all those covered by the contract, parties are bound by the agreement. *Arizona Elec. Power Coop.*, 250 NLRB at 1133. Sunrise is charged with knowledge of the duties of its employees. *See id.* Sunrise's purported mistaken belief does not controvert the evidence in the record regarding the actual character of LDOs' work as employees, not supervisors. **[—19—]**

The Board majority opinion also asserts that the parties must have *believed* all LDOs are supervisors because the text of the CBA refers to LDOs' duties as "supervisory." J.A. 26. But case precedent makes clear that merely labelling a position supervisory does not transform an employee into a supervisor for the purposes of the NLRA. *See Oakwood Healthcare, Inc.*, 348 NLRB 686, 688, 690 n.24 (2006). "Job descriptions, job titles, and similar paper authority, without more, do not demonstrate supervisory authority." *G4S Regulated Sec. Sols.*, 362 NLRB at 1072-73 (cleaned up). Contrary to the majority opinion, the Board was not free to ignore its duty to engage in a fact-intensive analysis to determine the actual status of second and third mates, and these employees are not "supervisors" merely because the CBA uses the term descriptively. Notably, the CBA does not state that the parties intended for the LDOs to be treated as statutory supervisors under Section 2(11) of the Act, nor does it recite or refer to the statutory criteria for determining supervisory status. And there is nothing in the record to suggest that Sunrise said or did anything that would have put the Union on notice that Sunrise supposedly *believed* that the unit consisted only of statutory supervisors and that the parties' relationship was not governed by the NLRA.

The Board majority opinion also surmises that the parties' collective bargaining relationship must have always existed "outside the aegis of the [NLRA]," based on three findings: (1) the Union had not, until now, "invok[ed] the [NLRA] or involv[ed] the Board" in the parties' 40-year relationship, J.A. 26; (2) federal courts in the 1970s and '80s found – and the Union itself once argued – that all LDOs are supervisors, J.A. 26 & n.7, 27; and (3) the Union was never certified under the **{–182–}** NLRA. These arguments are unpersuasive. **[—20—]**

First, as amici explain, "the absence of Board charges could be evidence that a collective bargaining relationship is working as the statute intended rather than that the union believed the workers have no statutory rights." Amicus Br. 18. In other words, a lack of ulp charges or other NLRB involvement does not prove that the NLRA is inapplicable.

Second, the supervisory status of LDOs aboard ships in the 1970s and '80s is irrelevant here, where the ALJ specifically found – based on the record *in this case* – that some LDOs are employees. And even if the facts of the cited cases had any bearing here, the Board majority inexplicably ignored countervailing evidence that technological advances in the last several decades have transformed the roles of LDOs.

Third, the law is clear that an employer is bound by its acceptance of a labor agreement for a mixed unit *even if* the unit is one that the

NLRB would not have certified in a Board-conducted election. *See Loomis Armored US, Inc.*, 364 NLRB No. 23 (2016). Employers seeking to renege on bargaining obligations cannot simply point out that a Section 9 election never occurred; instead, they must establish a good faith reasonable doubt about the union's continuing majority support. *Allentown Mack Sales and Serv., Inc. v. NLRB*, 522 U.S. 359, 364, 372 (1998). This is true where, as here, the employer assumed a CBA as a successor employer. *See Fall River Dyeing & Finishing Corp. v. NLRB*, 482 U.S. 27, 44 (1987).

The majority opinion also suggests that the "practicalities of operating large vessels on the open seas" lends support to its finding that Sunrise only "consented to a supervisory unit." J.A. 26. The opinion notes, for example, that the LDOs worked and slept separately from unlicensed crewmembers. J.A. 26. However, the majority's reliance on cherry-picked practices is **[—21—]** based on its erroneous conflation of maritime practices and labor law. Pointing to crewmembers' sleeping arrangements – or even pointing to authority they may have wielded "to demand obedience" from other officers – simply "doesn't answer the questions posed by the 2(11) indicia of supervisory status." *Brusco Tug & Barge*, 359 NLRB 486, 493 (2012), *aff'd* 696 F. App'x 519 (D.C. Cir. 2017).

Finally, it is worth noting that it is implausible to imagine that Sunrise would not have adopted the same position as the Board majority if the employer thought there was any truth to the claim that it always *believed* that the LDO unit consisted of only supervisors. If Sunrise had truly *believed* that all LDOs aboard its own ships were supervisors and thought this *belief* was a significant consideration, we assume that Sunrise would have tried to press the point before the ALJ. It did not. Rather, Sunrise claimed only that the LDOs are *in fact* supervisors, a position that not even the Board majority opinion embraces.

III. CONCLUSION

On the record before us, we find that the Board's position, as reflected in the Board majority opinion, lacks support in the record, defies established law, and creates a new rule without reasoned justification. It therefore fails substantial evidence review and is arbitrary and capricious for want of reasoned decision making. We also find that the arguments advanced by Sunrise find no support in the record or in controlling precedent. We therefore grant the petition for review, vacate the Board's decision, **{-183-}** and remand the case for reconsideration consistent with this opinion.

So ordered.

United States Court of Appeals
for the District of Columbia Circuit

No. 21-1137

MATSON NAVIGATION CO.
vs.
UNITED STATES DEP'T OF TRANSP.

On Petitions for Review of Orders of the U.S. Department of Transportation and On Appeals from the United States District Court for the District of Columbia

Decided: August 15, 2023

Citation: 77 F.4th 1151, 11 Adm. R. 561 (D.C. Cir. 2023).

Before **WILKINS**, **RAO**, and **PAN**, Circuit Judges.

[—2—] **{-1154-}** **RAO**, Circuit Judge:

This case begins and ends with jurisdiction, which we lack under the Hobbs Act. The United States Maritime Administration ("MARAD") approved a shipping company's request to replace two vessels operating in the Pacific trade within the Maritime Security Program. Matson Navigation Co., a competitor in the Pacific, petitions for review of the replacements. As a source of jurisdiction, Matson points to the Hobbs Act, under which we have original jurisdiction over some acts of MARAD. But we have Hobbs Act jurisdiction only when a "party aggrieved" files a timely petition for review.

Matson was not a "party" to the replacement proceedings for either vessel, and we therefore deny the petitions for direct review. We also reverse two orders of the district court, consolidated with these petitions, that held jurisdiction over Matson's claims under the Administrative Procedure Act ("APA") was exclusive in the court of appeals. Because we **[—3—]** lack jurisdiction under the Hobbs Act, Matson's APA claims were appropriately brought to the district court in the first instance, and we remand for further proceedings.

I.

A.

Matson is an American shipping company that has been providing freight carrier services in the Pacific since 1882. Matson's vessels carry cargo from the West Coast of the United States to ports in Asia, Hawaii, Guam, and the Northern Mariana Islands, to name a few. One of Matson's competitors in the region is APL, a shipping company organized in Delaware and owned by a French corporation.

APL participates in the Maritime Security Program ("MSP"). The MSP provides annual payments to the owners of vessels that are made available for use "by the United States for national defense or military purposes in time of war or national emergency." 46 U.S.C. § 53102(b)(4)(A); *see also id.* § 53107. The purpose of the MSP is to "maintain a United States presence in international commercial shipping" that can be activated in a crisis. *Id.* § 53102(a). MARAD, an agency within the Department of Transportation, oversees the MSP by determining vessel eligibility, **{-1155-}** entering into operating agreements, and approving "replacement" vessels for the MSP fleet. *Id.* §§ 53102, 53103, 53105(f); *see also* 46 C.F.R. § 296.1.

MSP vessels must trade exclusively in foreign commerce with one important exception. Vessels approved before 2018[1] **[—4—]** and "replacement" vessels may trade in "mixed" foreign and domestic trade with designated islands in the Pacific.[2] *See* 46 U.S.C. § 53105(a)(1)(A) (explaining MSP

[1] Congress tightened the requirements for MSP vessels engaging in domestic trade in the National Defense Authorization Act for 2018. Pub. L. No. 115-91, § 3503, 131 Stat. 1283, 1911 (2017). Except a **[—4—]** carveout for replacements, only vessels approved before the Act may engage in "mixed" domestic and foreign trade. *See* 46 U.S.C. § 53105(a).

[2] In the United States, domestic shipping is heavily regulated. For example, under the Jones Act, a vessel may not engage in the transportation of merchandise "between points in the United States to which the coastwise laws apply" unless several requirements are met. 46 U.S.C. § 55102(b). And the vessel must be "wholly owned by citizens of the United States," *id.* § 55102(b)(1), and "built in the United States," *id.* § 12112(a)(2)(A).

vessels must trade "exclusively in the foreign commerce or ... in mixed foreign commerce and domestic trade allowed under a registry endorsement"); *id.* § 53105(a)(2) ("[I]n the case of a vessel, other than a replacement vessel ..., first covered by an operating agreement after ... 2018, the vessel shall not be operated in the transportation of cargo between points in the United States and its territories either directly or via a foreign port."). Because new vessels participating in the MSP cannot engage in trade with domestic islands in the Pacific, it is valuable for a new vessel to be approved as a "replacement."

MARAD, in conjunction with the Secretary of Defense, may approve the replacement of a vessel with another vessel eligible to be included in the MSP fleet. *Id.* § 53105(f). To be eligible for participation in the MSP, a vessel must be owned and operated by United States citizens as defined by section 50501. *Id.* § 53102(c)(1); *see also id.* § 50501 (defining entities "deemed citizens of the United States"). The vessel must be "self-propelled" and suitable for "national defense" purposes. **[—5—]** *Id.* § 53102(b)(3)–(4). And the vessel must provide "transportation in foreign commerce." *Id.* § 53102(b)(2).

Replacement approvals are handled informally between MARAD and the MSP contractor. Neither the statute nor the regulations provide for intervention by third parties in these proceedings. *See* 46 C.F.R. § 296.30; 46 U.S.C. § 53105(f).

B.

This case involves two replacement vessels. APL requested approval of the HERODOTE as a replacement for the GUAM, a vessel operating in the Pacific.[3] MARAD approved the replacement in 2021, and the HERODOTE began carrying cargo originating in the United States to Saipan. The agency does not ordinarily provide public notice that an MSP contractor has applied to replace one vessel with another, and so Matson was unaware of the proceedings. When it learned of the approval, Matson asked MARAD to provide the administrative record so Matson could contest the approval. MARAD refused.

Matson filed an APA challenge against MARAD in district court pursuant to 28 U.S.C. § 1331, arguing that approval of the HERODOTE was arbitrary, capricious, **{–1156–}** and contrary to law. At the same time, Matson also filed a petition for direct review in our court pursuant to the Hobbs Act. The district court dismissed the APA challenge, holding the Hobbs **[—6—]** Act vested exclusive jurisdiction in the court of appeals, and Matson appealed.

In June 2022, MARAD approved the DAKAR to replace another APL vessel operating in the Pacific, the AGATE. Because of litigation involving the SAIPAN, an earlier replacement for the AGATE,[4] MARAD informed Matson that APL was seeking to replace the SAIPAN with an unnamed vessel. MARAD initially provided no details to Matson about the replacement vessel, but invited Matson to submit comments. In its comments, Matson argued that MARAD had violated the Due Process Clause, the APA, and various regulations by not turning over more information about the replacement proceedings. Matson also maintained the new ship was an ineligible replacement under the MSP because it engaged in domestic trade and because the SAIPAN had been operating

[3] Matson previously contested the 2015 approval of the GUAM as a replacement vessel. Matson's challenge reached our court, and we dismissed for lack of jurisdiction under the Hobbs Act because Matson's petition was untimely. *Matson Navigation Co. v. DOT*, 895 F.3d 799, 801, 804, 6 Adm. R. 491, 494 (D.C. Cir. 2018).

[4] Matson also contested approval of the SAIPAN as a replacement vessel in 2016. We dismissed Matson's challenge to the SAIPAN for lack of jurisdiction under the Hobbs Act because MARAD's order did not invoke section 50501. *Matson Navigation*, 895 F.3d at 805, 6 Adm. R. at 495. The district court vacated approval of the SAIPAN and remanded the issue to MARAD. *Matson Navigation Co. v. DOT*, 471 F. Supp. 3d 60, 62–63 (D.D.C. 2020). APL eventually stopped seeking approval for the SAIPAN because its age made it ineligible for the MSP. *See* 46 U.S.C. § 53102(b)(3). The parties dispute whether the DAKAR is replacing the AGATE or the SAIPAN.

unlawfully. In total, Matson submitted 24 pages of comments and 38 exhibits. Matson also requested to intervene and fully participate in the proceedings.

In its order approving the DAKAR as a replacement vessel, MARAD responded to Matson's comments but rejected the request to intervene and fully participate. Matson filed suit again under the APA, in the district court pursuant to 28 U.S.C. § 1331 and in our court pursuant to the Hobbs Act. Matson **[—7—]** moved for a preliminary injunction, but the district court denied Matson's motion, holding the Hobbs Act granted the court of appeals exclusive jurisdiction. Matson filed an interlocutory appeal. We granted the parties' request to consolidate the four dockets regarding the DAKAR and HERODOTE: the two Hobbs Act petitions filed in this court, the interlocutory appeal from the denial of a preliminary injunction, and the appeal from a dismissal for lack of jurisdiction.

II.

Matson petitions for direct review under the Hobbs Act, which provides a "party aggrieved by [a] final [agency] order may, within 60 days after its entry, file a petition to review the order in the court of appeals wherein venue lies." *Id.* § 2344. The Hobbs Act enumerates covered agency actions, which include "all rules, regulations, or final orders of ... the Secretary of Transportation issued pursuant to section 50501." *Id.* § 2342(3). "Implementation of the [MSP] has been delegated by the Secretary of Transportation to [MARAD]." 46 C.F.R. § 296.1. Matson claims MARAD's approvals of the HERODOTE and the DAKAR were issued pursuant to section 50501, which defines "[e]ntities deemed citizens of the United States," one of the eligibility criteria for participation in the MSP. 46 U.S.C. § 50501; *see also id.* § 53102(c). We do not reach the merits of Matson's claim because Matson was not a "party aggrieved" by APL's replacement proceedings, and we lack jurisdiction under the Hobbs Act.

To determine whether a petitioner is a "party aggrieved" under the Hobbs Act, we apply "two successive steps." **{-1157-}** *Water Transp. Ass'n v. ICC*, 819 F.2d 1189, 1192 (D.C. Cir. 1987). First, a petitioner is "aggrieved" when the traditional analysis for Article III standing is satisfied—namely the petitioner "has suffered an injury in fact traceable to the [agency's] ruling and **[—8—]** redressable by a decision" of our court. *Id.* at 1193. Second, we consider whether the petitioner was a "part[y] to the underlying agency proceedings." *ACA Int'l v. FCC*, 885 F.3d 687, 711 (D.C. Cir. 2018). We "must read 'party' as referring to a party before the agency, not a party to the judicial proceeding." *Simmons v. ICC*, 716 F.2d 40, 43 (D.C. Cir. 1983). This reflects the "special judicial review provisions of the Hobbs Act," in which Congress specified a petitioner must be a "party aggrieved," rather than a "*person* aggrieved" as in the APA's judicial review provision enacted just four years earlier. *Id.* (emphasis added). Giving "meaning to that apparently intentional variation," a petitioner must acquire "party" status before the agency in order to invoke jurisdiction under the Hobbs Act. *Id.*

The prerequisites to being a "party" will depend in part on the nature of the agency proceedings because the Hobbs Act provides for review of a variety of agency actions, including "rules, regulations, [and] final orders." *See* 28 U.S.C. § 2342(3). We have said the level of participation necessary to be a "party" depends on the formality of the proceedings. *Ohio Nuclear-Free Network v. NRC*, 53 F.4th 236, 239 (D.C. Cir. 2022); *see also Simmons*, 716 F.2d at 43 (explaining that when agency proceedings are not "structured" so "at least some persons may acquire party status," there are "other means to assure, where appropriate," that an "order will be directly appealable" under the Hobbs Act). When intervention before the agency is required, review "will be denied to those who did not seek—or who sought but were denied—leave to intervene." *Ohio Nuclear-Free Network*, 53 F.4th at 239 (cleaned up). In informal proceedings, however, a petitioner may be considered a "party" after making a "full presentation of views" before the agency. *Water Transp. Ass'n*, 819 F.2d at 1193. "[D]e minimis participation is insufficient." *S. Pac. Transp. Co. v. ICC*, 69 F.3d 583, 587 (D.C. Cir. 1995) (cleaned up). **[—9—]**

Even assuming that MARAD's orders approving the HERODOTE and the DAKAR were issued pursuant to section 50501 and that Matson was "aggrieved" as a competitor to APL's replacement vessels, Matson was not a "party" to the MARAD proceedings and therefore we lack jurisdiction over Matson's Hobbs Act petitions.

A.

We first consider MARAD's order approving the HERODOTE as a replacement vessel under the MSP. "MARAD has always handled MSP participant requests for approval of a replacement vessel as informal matters between MARAD, in consultation with the [Department of Defense], and the MSP participant." Email from Joseph O. Click, Lead Attorney, Maritime Support Programs, to Mark A. Perry & Brian Burgess, Attorneys for Matson Navigation Co. (Sept. 1, 2021). MSP contractors send a request for approval to the Maritime Administrator. There is no formal mechanism for third parties to submit comments or intervene. Matson admits it did not participate, in any way, in the 2021 MARAD proceedings about whether the HERODOTE should be approved as a replacement vessel. Matson did not seek to intervene and did not otherwise present its views to the agency. In fact, Matson complains it was unaware the replacement proceedings were happening at all. After learning of the HERODOTE's approval, Matson requested the administrative record, but MARAD refused. **{-1158-}**

Because it was in the dark about the proceedings, Matson made no presentation of its views to the agency, much less the full presentation necessary to being a "party aggrieved." We therefore lack jurisdiction over Matson's Hobbs Act petition challenging MARAD's 2021 approval of the HERODOTE as a replacement vessel. **[—10—]**

B.

With respect to the approval of the DAKAR as a replacement vessel, Matson managed some participation in the MARAD proceedings. In 2021, APL requested approval to replace the AGATE. Because Matson had successfully sued MARAD in district court for approving the SAIPAN as a replacement for the AGATE in 2016, and the court had "requested that MARAD keep Matson apprised of developments," the agency informed Matson about the replacement application. *See* Email from Joseph O. Click to Mark A. Perry & Brian Burgess. Although MARAD declined to provide Matson with detailed information about the replacement, because of "the unique circumstances" of the long-running lawsuit against MARAD over the AGATE, the agency invited Matson to "submit any comments with respect to the vessel application" within two weeks. *Id.* This was unusual for what is normally a bilateral process between the MSP contractor and the agency.

Matson submitted 24 pages of comments and 38 exhibits to MARAD. Matson maintained that the agency had violated the Due Process Clause, the APA, and MARAD's regulations by not allowing Matson to participate fully. Additionally, Matson argued, on the merits, that the new ship was ineligible under the MSP because it engaged in domestic trade and was ineligible as a replacement because the vessel being replaced had been operating unlawfully. Finally, Matson asked to "intervene" and "fully participate" in the proceedings. MARAD allowed APL to submit a response.

MARAD approved the DAKAR in May 2022, responding to Matson's comments and APL's response, but rejecting Matson's attempts to "intervene" and "fully participate" in the proceedings. MARAD stated that for "informal adjudications" **[—11—]** like the replacement proceedings, only "minimal procedural requirements" are necessary. According to MARAD, it had "provided Matson with a significant opportunity to appear before the agency and present its views," but allowing third parties to intervene would "convert the MSP vessel replacement process into an adversarial proceeding" and "only disrupt[] what has heretofore been an informal process that has operated smoothly and relatively expeditiously." Although MARAD rejected Matson's request to participate more fully, the agency responded to and rejected several of Matson's comments on the merits.[5]

Matson's limited participation in the DAKAR's approval did not make Matson a "party" to the agency proceedings for the purposes of the Hobbs Act. First, MARAD refused to turn the replacement approval process into a formal proceeding. Although MARAD permitted Matson to submit limited comments, the agency explicitly rejected Matson's request to intervene. And we have held that a petitioner is not a party when intervention is sought but denied. *Ohio Nuclear-Free Network*, 53 F.4th at 239. Intervention is the process by which a non-party *becomes* a party to a **{–1159–}** proceeding. *See generally Broidy Cap. Mgmt. LLC v. Muzin*, 61 F.4th 984, 990 (D.C. Cir. 2023) ("Parties to the record include the original parties and those who have become parties by intervention.") (cleaned up). Ordinarily, an individual denied intervention "is not a party." *Defs. of Wildlife v. Perciasepe*, 714 F.3d 1317, 1328 (D.C. Cir. 2013) (cleaned up). Matson never became a "party" under the Hobbs Act because its request to intervene was denied. *Ohio Nuclear-Free Network*, 53 F.4th at 239. In fact, Matson **[—12—]** acknowledges that "MARAD refused to allow Matson to intervene and fully participate in the DAKAR proceedings." Reply Br. 5. Matson may separately claim MARAD's denial of intervention was unlawful, but it has not done so in the petition before this court.

Second, Matson did not make a "full presentation of views" before MARAD. In its comments, Matson argued the agency had acted unlawfully by denying the opportunity to "fully participate." Matson pointed out that it did not have the requisite information to present all its views, including "timely copies of any submissions, applications, correspondence, or other communications" to the agency. In addition, Matson was not provided with the "how, when[,] and why" of APL's decision to operate the DAKAR, or even the technical specifications of the vessel like "size, type, and age." In no way was the 2022 replacement proceeding an "adversarial" one. Rather, it was an administrative application process between APL and MARAD. Matson played a limited outside role and submitted comments within the narrow scope permitted by MARAD. Because Matson did not, and was not allowed to, fully present its views in the DAKAR proceedings, Matson was not a "party" within the meaning of the Hobbs Act.

While we have held that less formal participation may sometimes be sufficient for "party" status, those cases are distinguishable from the facts here. For example, in *Water Transportation Association*, the agency "did not call for formal intervention" and instead "solicited general protests." 819 F.2d at 1193. "Given the informality of th[e] proceeding," we found the petitioner participated fully by submitting a protest and therefore had "party status." *Id.* There, the petitioner had full access to information about the proceedings, and so was able to present a full protest to the agency's action. *Id.*; *see also ACA Int'l*, 885 F.3d at 711 (finding the petitioner had achieved party **[—13—]** status by commenting on another's request for a declaratory ruling from the agency because the petitioner had "expressed support" for the request and "address[ed] certain additional issues," similar to the process of "submitting comments ... in the context of a rulemaking") (cleaned up).

By contrast, Matson tried to participate fully and was prevented from doing so. The agency action here was not a rulemaking in which a person could participate by submitting comments; nor did the agency provide information about the proceedings and allow third parties to make a general protest. As MARAD has explained, replacement proceedings under section 53105(f) have always been informal and bilateral, between the MSP Contractor and the agency, without adversarial participation or public comments. There is no process for intervention and no specific procedures the agency must follow. *See* 46 C.F.R. § 296.30 (explaining simply that the

[5] MARAD disagreed with Matson's claims that the DAKAR's trade with Saipan rendered it ineligible under the MSP, that the DAKAR could not replace the AGATE because the AGATE was ineligible, that the DAKAR violated MARAD's "heel-to-toe" policy for replacement, and that the DAKAR was not commercially viable.

vessel owner can seek replacement). Here, Matson was able to make limited comments, with limited information about the proceeding, as a matter of administrative grace. Matson's participation was so limited, it argued the proceedings violated the APA and the Constitution. Accordingly, Matson was not a "party" before MARAD under the Hobbs Act and we lack jurisdiction **{–1160–}** to review Matson's petitions for review.

III.

Our lack of jurisdiction under the Hobbs Act also dispenses with Matson's two appeals from the district court. In Matson's challenges to the DAKAR and HERODOTE proceedings under the APA, the district court held that the court of appeals had exclusive jurisdiction under the Hobbs Act. Because this was error, we reverse and remand both cases to the district court to consider the merits of Matson's claims. **[—14—]**

* * *

Whether a case begins in district court or is eligible for direct review in our court is a policy decision that is for "Congress rather than us to determine." *Simmons*, 716 F.2d at 43. The important thing is clarity. As Matson's counsel stated at oral argument, the company is just "trying to get review." Because sending limited comments based on limited information to an informal agency proceeding does not confer "party" status under the Hobbs Act, that review starts in the district court.

We therefore dismiss the two petitions for review under the Hobbs Act; we reverse the district court's denial of a preliminary injunction in the challenge to the 2022 approval order; and we reverse the dismissal of the 2021 approval order. We remand to the district court for further proceedings consistent with this opinion.

So ordered.

United States Court of Appeals for the Federal Circuit

United States Court of Appeals
for the Federal Circuit

No. 21-2326

FISHERMEN'S FINEST, INC.
vs.
UNITED STATES

Appeal from the United States Court of Federal Claims

Decided: February 8, 2023

Citation: 59 F.4th 1269, 11 Adm. R. 568 (Fed. Cir. 2023).

Before **MOORE,** Chief Judge, **DYK** and **CHEN,** Circuit Judges.

[—2—] {-1270-} CHEN, Circuit Judge: **{-1271-}**

This case involves commercial fishing within the United States' Exclusive Economic Zone[1] (EEZ). Fishermen's Finest, Inc.; Fishermen's Finest Holdings, LLC; North Pacific Fishing, Inc.; U.S. Fishing, LLC; and America's Finest Fishing, LLC (collectively, FFI) appeal a decision by the United States Court of Federal Claims (Claims Court) dismissing their Fifth Amendment takings claim for lack of a cognizable property interest in certain fishing endorsements, licenses, and permits, separate from or appurtenant to their fishing vessels. Because (i) our precedent establishes that fishing permits and licenses issued pursuant to the Magnuson–Stevens Fishery Conservation and Management Act (the Magnuson–Stevens Act) are revocable privileges, rather than compensable property interests, *Conti v. United States*, 291 F.3d 1334, 1341–42 (Fed. Cir. 2002); *Am. Pelagic Fishing Co. v. United States*, 379 F.3d 1363, 1373–76 (Fed. Cir. 2004); (ii) subsequent amendments to the Magnuson–Stevens Act and the National Marine Fisheries Service's (Fisheries Service) regulations did not then create compensable property rights in fishing permits or licenses; and (iii) there is no inherent right in vessel **[—3—]** ownership to fish within the EEZ, *Am. Pelagic*, 379 F.3d at 1382–83, we *affirm*.

BACKGROUND

A. Statutory And Regulatory Scheme

Congress enacted the Magnuson–Stevens Act in 1976 as part of "[a] national program for the conservation and management of the fishery resources of the United States." 16 U.S.C. § 1801(a)(6) (1976). "Congress explicitly assumed sovereign rights and exclusive fishery management authority over all fish in the EEZ[, which] indisputably encompasses all rights to fish in the EEZ." *Am. Pelagic*, 379 F.3d at 1378 (internal quotation marks omitted); *see also* 16 U.S.C. § 1811(a) (1994) ("[T]he United States claims, and will exercise in the manner provided for in this chapter, *sovereign rights and exclusive* fishery management *authority over all fish* . . . within the [EEZ]." (emphases added)). The Magnuson–Stevens Act's plain language indicates that no claim or entitlement to compensable property rights are conferred with fishing privileges issued thereunder. 16 U.S.C. § 1853(d)(3)(D) (2000) ("An individual fishing quota or other limited access system authorization . . . *shall not create*, or be construed to create, *any right, title, or interest* in or to any fish before the fish is harvested." (emphases added)); *see also Am. Pelagic*, 379 F.3d at 1379 ("[T]here is no language in the statute to the effect that any fishing privileges that are granted pursuant to the Magnuson[-Stevens] Act **{-1272-}** vest in their owners a property right protected by the Fifth Amendment."); *Conti*, 291 F.3d at 1342 n.6 ("[T]he language certainly suggests that since the permit does not confer any cognizable property right to harvest fish, the [Magnuson–Stevens Act] creates no property right in the permit.").

The Fisheries Service regulates fisheries in the EEZ. *See N.C. Fisheries Ass'n, Inc. v. Gutierrez*, 550 F.3d 16, 17 (D.C. Cir. 2008). Pursuant to the Magnuson–Stevens Act, the Fisheries Service has promulgated regulations, having **[—4—]** the force and effect of law, that establish various licensing and permitting

[1] The EEZ consists of a zone extending 200 nautical miles from the baseline from which the breadth of the United States' territorial sea is measured. Proclamation No. 5030, 48 Fed. Reg. 10,605 (Mar. 10, 1983); *see also* 16 U.S.C. § 1811(a) (1992).

requirements to govern fishing activities in the Gulf of Alaska (GOA) and the Bering Sea and Aleutian Islands (BSAI) management areas (collectively, Management Areas). *See* 50 C.F.R. § 679.1 (1996); 50 C.F.R. § 679.4 (2021); *see also Conti*, 291 F.3d at 1336 (citing 16 U.S.C. §§ 1854–1855 (2000)); 16 U.S.C. §§ 1854–1855 (2012).

In 2007, Congress amended the Magnuson–Stevens Act to expand on then-existing individual fishing quotas by establishing national criteria for quota-based fishing programs, known as limited access privilege programs, and authorizing the quota-based fishing permits and licenses at issue in FFI's Fifth Amendment takings claim. *See* S. REP. NO. 109-229, at 1 (2006); Magnuson–Stevens Fishery Conservation and Management Reauthorization Act of 2006, Pub. L. No. 109-479, sec. 303A, 120 Stat. 3575, 3586– 93 (2007) (codified at 16 U.S.C. § 1853a); *see also* 16 U.S.C. § 1853(d) (2000) (individual fishing quotas). FFI's claim involves four different permitting, licensing, and endorsement requirements for fishing in the Management Areas: (1) Federal Fisheries Permit; (2) License Limitation Program license; (3) Amendment 80 Quota Share permit; and (4) fishery endorsements. *See* J.A. 73 ¶ 11.

First, a Federal Fisheries Permit (FFP) is required for a vessel to fish in the Management Areas. *See* 50 C.F.R. § 679.4(b)(1) (2021). The Fisheries Service issues FFPs to particular vessels, for a particular time period, and for specific types of authorized operations within the Management Areas. *Id.* § 679.4(b)(1)–(3). "An FFP . . . is not transferable or assignable and is valid only for the vessel for which it is issued." *Id.* § 679.4(b)(6). And although an FFP is necessary for any fishing activity in the Management Areas, it does not grant harvest privileges on its own. *See generally id.* § 679.4(b). **[—5—]**

Second, a License Limitation Program (LLP) license is also required for a vessel to harvest or process fish in the Management Areas. *Id.* § 679.4(k)(1)(i). Each LLP license designates the specific areas that may be fished, the specific categories of fish that may be harvested, the specific manner in which vessels may be operated, and the specific types of vessel and gear that may be utilized. *Id.* An LLP license may be transferred from one fishing company to another, so long as certain eligibility criteria are met. *Id.* § 679.4(k)(7). However, each LLP license may be transferred only once per calendar year, *id.* § 679.4(k)(7)(vi), and an LLP license's various designations are not severable, *id.* § 679.4(k)(7)(viii). An LLP license is also a prerequisite for obtaining a Quota Share (QS) permit. *See id.* § 679.4(o)(1)(vi).

Third, the QS permits relevant here are associated with the Amendment 80 (A80) limited access privilege program. After Congress amended the amended Magnuson–Stevens Act, the Fisheries Service promulgated regulations to implement the A80 limited access privilege program, allocating fishing quotas for six species of non-pollock groundfish in the BSAI management area: Pacific ocean perch, Atka mackerel, flathead sole, Pacific cod, rock **{–1273–}** sole, and yellowfin sole. *See* Fisheries of the Exclusive Economic Zone Off Alaska; Allocating Bering Sea/Aleutian Islands Fishery Resources; American Fisheries Act Sideboards, 72 Fed. Reg. 52,668, 52,671 (Sept. 14, 2007) [hereinafter A80 Final Rule] (codified at 15 C.F.R. pt. 902 and 50 C.F.R. pt. 679). The A80 program seeks to remedy wasteful discarding of certain harvested fish by allocating a portion of available groundfish to certain vessels, allowing vessel operators to "fish in a slower and less wasteful fashion," increase efficiency, and reduce waste. *See* A80 Final Rule at 52,668–70. Each year, the Fisheries Service "allocate[s] an amount of [A80] species available for harvest," and then assigns a portion of that allowable catch—i.e., Quota **[—6—]** Share—to each A80 vessel based on their historic participation in the A80 program. *See id.* at 52,671–72.

The Fisheries Service approves certain vessels—designated A80 vessels—for participation in the A80 program, *see id.* at 52,671, and non-A80 vessels are prohibited from catching A80 species, 50 C.F.R. § 679.7(o)(1)(i) (2021). An A80 QS permit may be assigned to either a particular A80 vessel or a particular LLP license. 50 C.F.R. § 679.4(o)(1)(ii) (2021). The A80 QS permit may be transferred, but the conditions applicable to such a transfer will depend on whether the permit is assigned to a vessel or an LLP license, *see id.* § 679.90(e), and the Fisheries Service must approve any request to transfer an A80 QS permit, *id.* § 679.90(f).

Fourth, a vessel must obtain a fishery endorsement to engage in commercial fishing activities. 46 U.S.C. § 12113(b)(1); *see also id.* § 12102(a) (specifying that "a vessel may engage in a trade only if the vessel has been issued . . . an endorsement for that trade"). A fishery endorsement is issued only to vessels that satisfy certain statutory requirements—e.g., compliance with a "built in the United States" requirement. *Id.* § 12113(a); *see also* 46 C.F.R. § 67.21(b)(1). If, at any point, a vessel ceases to comply with applicable requirements, its fishery endorsement becomes invalid. 46 U.S.C. § 12135.

B. Procedural Background

FFI is a collection of related Washington State companies. J.A. 73 ¶ 10. Until 2014, FFI owned two vessels— *American No. 1* and *U.S. Intrepid*—with the necessary fishery endorsements, FFPs, LLP licenses, and A80 QS permits to operate in the Management Areas. *See* J.A. 73 ¶ 10; J.A. 73–74 ¶ 11; J.A. 78 ¶ 28; J.A. 81 ¶¶ 39–40. FFI's LLP licenses and A80 QS permits were issued pursuant to the Magnuson–Stevens Act. **[—7—]**

In November 2014, FFI retained Dakota Creek Industries, Inc. (Dakota Creek) to construct a new fishing vessel— *America's Finest*. J.A. 80 ¶ 37. In early 2017, the Fisheries Service approved (1) FFI's purchase of an LLP license and a QS permit (originally associated with another fishing vessel known as *Defender*) from another fishing company. J.A. 81 ¶ 39. FFI also obtained approval to (1) designate *America's Finest* as a replacement vessel for *American No. 1* and transfer the latter's LLP license and A80 QS permit to the former and (2) designate *American No. 1* as a replacement vessel for *Defender* and transfer the latter's LLP license and A80 QS permit to the former. J.A. 81–82 ¶¶ 40–41; J.A. 73–74 ¶ 11. However, in March 2017, Dakota Creek informed FFI that foreign steel was used in the construction of *America's Finest*. J.A. 82 ¶ 42. Accordingly, the Coast Guard, which oversees vessel documentation, determined that *America's Finest* was noncompliant with 46 U.S.C. § 12113(a)'s "built in the United States" requirement and therefore ineligible to receive the requisite fishery endorsements **{-1274-}** to operate in the Management Areas. J.A. 67–77 ¶ 23; J.A. 83 ¶ 43.

Dakota Creek then lobbied Congress for a waiver to the "built in the United States" requirement for *America's Finest*, J.A. 83 ¶ 44, and Congress subsequently passed the Frank LoBiondo Coast Guard Authorization Act of 2018, Pub. L. No. 115-282, 132 Stat. 4192 (Coast Guard Act). Section 835 thereof granted a waiver so that *America's Finest* could harvest and process fish in the Management Areas. *See id.* sec. 835(a)–(b). However, section 836 of the Coast Guard Act limited the amount of A80 groundfish and non-A80 fish that FFI's vessels could collectively harvest and process in the Management Areas. *See id.* sec. 836(a)(1)(A)–(B). These "sideboards," which do not apply to harvesting outside of the GOA management area and expire in 2024, restrict FFI's three vessels (i.e., *U.S. Intrepid*, *America's Finest*, and *American No. 1*), any replacement vessels thereto, and any vessel assigned the **[—8—]** *Defender*'s LLP license, to the collective, historic harvesting and processing figures of those vessels from 2012 to 2017. *See id.* sec. 836(a)–(b). FFI interprets these sideboards as restricting its three vessels to the *U.S. Intrepid* and *American No. 1*'s historical figures, depriving FFI of any increased capacity from acquiring the *Defender*'s LLP license and QS permit and building *America's Finest*. *See* J.A. 93–94 ¶¶ 70–71.

FFI then filed a claim with the Claims Court, alleging that the Coast Guard Act's sideboards amounted to an unlawful, uncompensated taking that (1) deprived FFI of the full scope of its rights under its endorsements, licenses, and permits; and (2) devalued its vessels. J.A. 71–72 ¶¶ 3–5. The government moved to dismiss. *Fishermen's Finest, Inc. v. United States*, 155 Fed. Cl. 576, 591 (2021). Relying on our decisions in *Conti* and *American Pelagic*, the Claims Court dismissed FFI's complaint for failure to state a claim, concluding that: (i) the express language of the Magnuson–Stevens Act indicated "congressional intent not to confer any right, title, or interest, and to preserve the government's authority to revoke privileges enjoyed in" fishing licenses and permits issued pursuant to the Magnuson–Stevens Act, *id.* at 601–02; (ii) FFI's licenses and permits did not have the essential characteristics of compensable property—i.e., transferability and the right to exclude others, *id.*; and (iii) FFI "do[es] not have a cognizable property interest in the right to conduct commercial fishing activities in any part of the EEZ," *id.* at 606–07.

FFI timely appealed. We have jurisdiction pursuant to 28 U.S.C. § 1295(a)(3).

DISCUSSION

I

When reviewing a dismissal for failure to state a claim, we "must accept as true all the factual allegations in the complaint and we must indulge all reasonable inferences **[—9—]** in favor of the non-movant." *Conti*, 291 F.3d at 1338 (citation omitted). Whether the Claims Court properly dismissed a complaint for failure to state a claim is a question of law that we review independently and without deference. *Id.* For Fifth Amendment takings claims, "[w]e review de novo the existence of a compensable property interest." *Hardy v. United States*, 965 F.3d 1338, 1344 (Fed. Cir. 2020).

II

The Fifth Amendment to the United States Constitution provides that private property "shall not be taken for public use without just compensation." U.S. Const. amend. V, cl. 4. Courts must evaluate two prongs in determining whether a **{-1275-}** government action constitutes a taking: "First, the court determines whether the claimant has identified a cognizable Fifth Amendment property interest that is asserted to be the subject of the taking. Second, if the court concludes that a cognizable property interest exists, it determines whether that property interest was 'taken.'" *Acceptance Ins. Cos. v. United States*, 583 F.3d 849, 854 (Fed. Cir. 2009) (collecting cases).

As to the first prong, "[i]t is well settled that existing rules and understandings and background principles derived from an independent source, such as state, federal, or common law, define the dimensions of the requisite property rights for purposes of establishing a cognizable taking." *Id.* at 857 (internal quotation marks omitted). However, where a "claimant fails to demonstrate the existence of a legally cognizable property interest, the court[']s task is at an end." *Am. Pelagic*, 379 F.3d at 1372. Our precedent establishes that fishing permits and licenses issued pursuant to the Magnuson–Stevens Act are revocable privileges, rather than compensable property interests, *see Conti*, 291 F.3d at 1341–42, and there is no inherent, cognizable property interest in the use of vessels for fishing within the EEZ, *see Am. Pelagic*, 379 F.3d at 1382–83. **[—10—]**

In *Conti*, a claimant alleged that the government limited his rights under a swordfish permit, issued pursuant to the Magnuson–Stevens Act, without compensation. 291 F.3d at 1339. We observed *inter alia* that the Magnuson–Stevens Act expressly states that any limited access authorization system "shall not create, or be construed to create, any right, title, or interest in or to any fish," 16 U.S.C. § 1853(d)(3)(D), (d)(2)(A) (2000), and that the government may limit or terminate any particular fishing permit system "without compensation to holders of any limited access system permits," *id.* § 1853 (d)(2)(A). *See Conti*, 291 F.3d at 1342 & n.6. Moreover, the "absence of crucial indicia of a property right"—i.e., transferability and exclusivity—"coupled with the government's irrefutable retention of the right to suspend, revoke, or modify" fishing permits "compel[led] the conclusion" that fishing permits are revocable privileges, rather than compensable property. *See id.* at 1341–42.

Likewise in *American Pelagic*, we rejected an argument that the "government could not refuse to issue or reissue, revoke, modify, or suspend" fishing privileges issued pursuant to the Magnuson–Stevens Act absent the commission of "specified 'offense[s]' or for failure to pay a penalty." *See* 379 F.3d at 1373–74. The claimant alleged that Congress "took" its right to use its vessel for fishing by canceling its fishery permits and authorization letter. *Id.* at 1374 n.15. We explained, however, that the Fisheries Service's regulations "preserved the government's right to deny or sanction the permits and authorization letter issued" by specifically stating that nothing precluded "sanction or denial of a permit for reasons not relating to enforcement." *Id.* at 1374 (quoting 15 C.F.R. § 904.301(a) (1987)). In sum, under *Conti* and *American Pelagic*, FFI has no cognizable property interest in its fishing permits, licenses, and endorsements. **[—11—]**

III

Attempting to overcome our precedent in *Conti* and *American Pelagic*, FFI argues those cases were decided before Congress amended the Magnuson–Stevens Act in 2007, which, in FFI's view, altered the nature of fishing endorsements, licenses, and permits such that they now bear the traditional hallmarks of compensable **{-1276-}** property[2]—i.e., transferability, exclusivity, and irrevocability. *See* Appellants' Br. 4, 23–31, 34–39; Appellants' Reply Br. 2; Oral Arg. 2:48–3:36. We disagree. Consistent with our holdings in *Conti* and *American Pelagic*, the language of the amended Magnuson–Stevens Act and the Fisheries Service's regulations maintain FFI's LLP licenses and QS permits as non-compensable, revocable privileges.[3]

Even though *Conti* and *American Pelagic* were decided before the Magnuson–Stevens Act was amended, neither the amended Magnuson–Stevens Act nor the Fisheries Service's subsequent regulations governing limited access privilege programs (e.g., the A80 program) made FFI's fishing licenses and permits compensable property. The amended Magnuson–Stevens Act continues to expressly **[—12—]** state that "[l]imited access privilege, quota share, or other limited access system authorization . . . *shall not create*, or be construed to create, *any right, title, or interest* in or to any fish before the fish is harvested by the holder." 16 U.S.C. § 1853a(b)(4) (2012) (emphasis added). Authority makes clear that such language suggests that the Act does not create a Fifth Amendment property interest in the licenses and permits to engage in fishing. *See Conti*, 291 F.3d at 1342 n.6 (stating that although the Magnuson–Stevens Act's "disavowal of the permit's creation of 'any right, title, or interest in . . . any fish' . . . is not facially commensurate with a statement that the law does not create any right, title, or interest in the *permit*[,] . . . to the extent that the right to harvest and thus possess fish in the fishery is inextricably tied to the possession of a permit, the language certainly suggests that" the Act "creates no property right in the permit." (emphases modified and first ellipses in original) (quoting 16 U.S.C. § 1853(d)(3)(D) (2000)); *see also United States v. Fuller*, 409 U.S. 488, 489, 494 (1973).

Moreover, the Magnuson–Stevens Act's statutory language— both before and after amendment—informs the public's expectations and forms the "existing rule or background principle of federal law that inhered in [FFI]'s title to [its] vessel[s]." *See Am. Pelagic*, 379 F.3d at 1379 (cleaned up) (quoting *Lucas v. S.C. Coastal Council*, 505 U.S. 1003, 1029–30 (1992)). Indeed, FFI concedes that compensable property rights, if any, must be established by the Magnuson–Stevens Act. *See* Oral Arg. at 9:28– 10:02. As with the statutory language of the Magnuson–Stevens Act that we analyzed in *Conti* and *American Pelagic*, there is nothing in the plain language of the amended Magnuson–Stevens Act that creates

[2] "The rights to sell, assign, or otherwise transfer are traditional hallmarks of property." *Conti*, 291 F.3d at 1341.

[3] Although FFI contends that it has a cognizable property interest in "the combination of licenses, permits and endorsements, including Amendment 80 QS and Amendment 80 LLPs," Appellants' Reply Br. 10, its substantive arguments focus on the characteristics of its LLP licenses and QS permits, *see, e.g.*, Appellants' Br. 20 (arguing that "FFI has a compensable property interest in its permits and licenses"). FFI presents no arguments as to how its fishing endorsements, other than being a prerequisite for using LLP licenses and QS permits, impart compensable property rights.

a compensable property right in fishing licenses or permits. On its face, § 1853a(b)(4)'s "express statutory language . . . prevent[s] the formation of a protectable property interest." *See Members of Peanut Quota Holders Ass'n v. United States*, 421 F.3d 1323, 1330 (Fed. Cir. 2005). **[—13—]** **{-1277-}**

Similarly, consistent with the Magnuson–Stevens Act, the Fisheries Service's regulations expressly provide that LLP licenses and A80 QS permits "are *neither a right to the resource nor any interest* that is subject to the 'takings' provision of the Fifth Amendment to the U.S. Constitution." *See* 50 C.F.R. § 679.4(a)(8) (2017) (emphasis added); *see also* 50 C.F.R. § 679.4(a)(8) (2006) (same). Indeed, the Department of Commerce's regulatory notice regarding the A80 program reiterated that QS permits "confer[] a privilege, not a property right, and [are] not subject to compensation." *See* A80 Final Rule at 52,696–97. The Fisheries Service's regulations further undercut any expectation that FFI might have to compensable interests in its fishing licenses or permits. In sum, the amended Magnuson–Stevens Act and the Fisheries Service's regulations make clear that fishing permits and licenses are not compensable. *See Conti*, 291 F.3d at 1341–42; *Am. Pelagic*, 379 F.3d at 1373– 76.

We reject FFI's contention that, despite the Magnuson–Stevens Act's clear expression that there are no compensable property rights in fishing permits and licenses, its LLP licenses and A80 QS permits are compensable because, under the amended Magnuson–Stevens Act, they are transferable, exclusive, and irrevocable. *See* Appellants' Br. 20–34 (citing 16 U.S.C. § 1853a(b)(2),(c)(7)). As an initial matter, we note that FFI concedes that, if its LLP licenses and QS permits are freely revocable by the government, they confer no cognizable property interests.[4] *See* Oral Arg. 3:55–4:30, 8:10–8:49. The Magnuson–Stevens Act—both before and after amendment—decrees that fishing permits and licenses are so revocable: "[L]imited access privilege[s], quota share[s], or other limited access system authorizations . . . may be *revoked, limited, or modified at any time* in accordance with this chapter" and "*shall* **[—14—]** *not confer any right of compensation* to the holder . . . if it is revoked, limited, or modified." 16 U.S.C. § 1853a(b)(2)–(3) (2012) (emphasis added); *accord id.* § 1853(d)(3)(B)–(C) (2000) (similar); *see also Conti*, 291 F.3d at 1341–42; *Am. Pelagic*, 379 F.3d at 1373–74.

FFI's contention that 16 U.S.C. § 1853a(b)(2)'s "in accordance with this chapter" language limits the government's power to revoke, modify, or limit licenses and permits issued under the Magnuson–Stevens Act to specifically enumerated situations involving enforcement or overall management is unconvincing. *See* Appellants' Reply Br. 15–18. We read that language to mean that licenses and permits may be revoked, modified, or limited in a manner that is not inconsistent with the Magnuson–Stevens Act. *See Ysleta Del Sur Pueblo v. Texas*, 142 S. Ct. 1929, 1942–43 (2022) (interpreting "in accordance with" in a different statute to mean consistent with). In fact, the legislative history for the 2007 amendments to the Magnuson–Stevens Act indicate that Congress intended to "re-affirm existing law relating to [individual fishing quotas] that a [limited access privilege program] is a permit that may be *revoked or limited at any time* without right to compensation." S. REP. NO. 109-229, at 26 (emphasis added). Congress's suggestion that "permit[s] . . . *could also* be revoked or modified for any failure to comply with the program or if the system is found to have jeopardized the sustainability of the stock or the safety of fishermen" suggests that revocation or modification is not limited to such circumstances. *See id.* (emphasis added); *see also, e.g.*, 16 U.S.C. § 1858(g) (setting forth permit sanctions for certain prohibited acts). Simply **{-1278-}** put, there is no express language or other indication of congressional intent to limit Congress's legislative power to revoke, modify, or limit privileges granted under the Magnuson–Stevens Act. *See Conti*, 291 F.3d at 1341–42; *Am. Pelagic*, 379 F.3d at 1373–74. As such, the Coast Guard Act's limitation on FFI's aggregate catch totals did not amount to any taking **[—15—]** of

[4] *See* discussion *supra* note 3.

compensable property.[5] Because FFI concedes that the revocability issue is dispositive, Oral Arg. 3:55–4:30, 8:10–8:49, we need not reach its arguments regarding the remaining characteristics of compensable property—i.e., transferability and exclusivity.[6]

We are also unpersuaded by FFI's argument that subjecting its fishing licenses and permits to taxation or liens by the Internal Revenue Service (IRS) or liens under maritime law overrides Congress's express intent that such licenses and permits are non-compensable property. *See* Appellants' Br. 39–41. The IRS taxes both non-compensable, government-issued privileges and compensable property. *See Internal Revenue Serv. Notices of Levy on Undelivered Com. Dep't Fishing Quota Permits*, 19 U.S. O.L.C. 23, 1995 WL 944019, at *4 (1995) ("Despite the recognition that *licenses and permits are* considered[] privileges and *not rights* . . . courts nonetheless treat them as property subject to levy. . . ." (emphases added)). In other **[—16—]** words, taxation does not transform non-compensable privileges—e.g., fishing endorsements, LLP licenses, and QS permits—into compensable property, contrary to congressional intent. FFI's reliance on maritime law, specifically, *Gowen, Inc. v. F/V Quality One*, 244 F.3d 64 (1st Cir. 2001), is also unavailing. In *Gowen*, the First Circuit held that federal fishing permits under the Magnuson–Stevens Act are "appurtenances" of a vessel and subject to maritime liens due to the value such permits contribute to the vessel. *See id.* at 67. *Gowen*, however, was silent as to whether the permits are themselves compensable property. Regardless, value alone does not transform a revocable, non-compensable privilege into a compensable property interest. *See Fuller*, 409 U.S. at 493 (holding that "the value added to fee lands by a revocable permit authorizing the use of neighboring lands that the Government owns" is not compensable under the Fifth Amendment); *see also Conti*, 291 F.3d at 1340–41 (holding that revocable fishing permits under the Magnuson–Stevens Act are not compensable because to hold otherwise would compensate "a claimant for 'the value of a right that the Government . . . can grant or withhold as it chooses'" (alteration in original) (quoting *Fuller*, 409 U.S. at 493)).

In sum, the Magnuson–Stevens Act, as amended, forecloses FFI's claim, and we hold that FFI's LLP licenses and A80 QS permits were subject to revocation, modification, **{-1279-}** or limitation by Congress. The Coast Guard Act's sideboards that Congress placed on FFI's vessels are consistent with the revocable nature of FFI's fishing licenses and permits. We therefore agree with the Claims Court that FFI did not possess any cognizable property interests in its LLP licenses and A80 QS permits.

IV

FFI also argues that the Coast Guard Act's sideboards deprived it of a property interest in using its vessels to harvest and process fish. Appellants' Br. 45–46. We disagree. **[—17—]** FFI does not have a compensable property interest in using its vessels to harvest and process fish in the Management Areas.

In *American Pelagic*, we rejected a claimant's similar assertion that it had a property right in its fishing permits and authorizations "appurtenant to the use and operation of [its] fishing vessel" to harvest or process fish in the EEZ. 379 F.3d at 1372–73. Because Congress, via the Magnuson–Stevens Act, "assumed 'sovereign rights and exclusive fishery management authority over all fish' in

[5] Furthermore, consistent with our regulatory analysis in *American Pelagic*, the A80 regulations at issue here expressly state that "quota shares, permits, or licenses represent *only a harvesting privilege that may be revoked or amended* subject to the requirements of the [Magnuson- Stevens Act] and other applicable law." 50 C.F.R. § 679.4(a)(8) (2017) (emphasis added). Under the A80 program, the government retained the right to revoke, suspend, or modify fishing privileges. *See id.* § 679.4(a)(7), (8); *see also* 15 C.F.R. § 904.300 (2017); *id.* § 904.1(c)(24).

[6] FFI separately argues that because Congress singled it out for special restrictions, this case implicates fairness concerns underlying the Takings Clause. *See* Appellants' Br. 37–39. But such considerations may go to whether a property was "taken," not to whether it was cognizable property in the first place. *See E. Enters. v. Apfel*, 524 U.S. 498, 537 (1998).

the EEZ," which "indisputably encompasses all rights to fish in the EEZ," the ability to harvest and process fish in the United States' sovereign waters is not a right inherent to vessel ownership, even of permitted, licensed vessels. *Id.* at 1378–79, 1381. The right to fish in the EEZ is not "one of the sticks in the bundle of property rights that [are] acquired with title." *Id.* at 1382–83.

Here, the Coast Guard and the Fisheries Service issued and approved fishing endorsements, LLP licenses, and A80 QS permits that allowed FFI's vessels to harvest and process fish from the Management Areas. Without these government-issued privileges, FFI does not have an inherent right to use its vessels to harvest or process fish in the Management Areas, as FFI itself recognizes. *See* Appellants' Reply Br. 10 ("[I]t is the *combination* of licenses, permits and endorsements, including Amendment 80 QS and Amendment 80 LLPs, which *allows FFI to fish* in [the Management Areas]." (second emphasis added)); Appellants' Br. 7 (contending that "new entrants *must acquire* an existing vessel, license, and endorsements" (emphasis added)). As such, FFI does not have a compensable interest as to the use of its vessels to harvest and process fish in the Management Areas. *See Am. Pelagic*, 379 F.3d at 1381 ("Because the right to use the vessel to fish in the EEZ was not inherent in its ownership of the [vessel], [claimant] did not suffer the loss of a property interest for purposes of the Takings Clause when its [fishing] permits were revoked."); **[—18—]** *see also Mitchell Arms, Inc. v. United States*, 7 F.3d 212, 217 (Fed. Cir. 1993) (concluding that the right to sell assault weapons in domestic commerce was merely a "collateral interest," incidental to gun ownership, that was not protected by the Fifth Amendment and not "a right inherent in [claimant]'s ownership of [property]").

Although the Coast Guard Act limits FFI's ability to use its vessels, FFI may nonetheless continue to operate its vessels in the Management Areas. Any expectation that FFI might have had in using its vessels to harvest or process fish arise from government-issued permits, licenses, and endorsements that were always subject to revocation, modification, and limitation. *See Am. Pelagic*, 379 F.3d at 1382–83.

CONCLUSION

We have considered FFI's remaining arguments and do not find them persuasive. For the foregoing reasons, the Claims Court did not err in dismissing FFI's takings claim for lack of a cognizable property **{–1280–}** interest. We therefore affirm the Claims Court's dismissal.

AFFIRMED

This page intentionally left blank

Tables of Authority

This page intentionally left blank

Table of Cases

This page intentionally left blank

Table of Cases[1]

Page

A

[1] Cases named solely after ships, *see, e.g.*, *The Pennsylvania*, 86 U.S. (19 Wall.) 125 (1873), are alphabetized under the letter "T." Cases where the United States is the plaintiff are alphabetized by defendant under the letter "U."

B

C

D

E

F

G

H

I

J

K

L

M

N

O

P

Q

R

S

T

U

V

W

Y

Z

This page intentionally left blank

Table of Statutes and Rules

This page intentionally left blank

Table of Statutes and Rules[1]

Page

Treaties/International

Federal

Constitution

Miscellaneous

[1] As cited in the opinions reported.

Statutes

RULES

REGULATIONS

STATE

Index

This page intentionally left blank

INDEX

PAGE

A

B

C

D

E

F

G

H

I

J

L

M

N

P

Q

R

S

U

W

www.ingramcontent.com/pod-product-compliance
Lightning Source LLC
LaVergne TN
LVHW070905210926
848482LV00017B/996
* 9 7 9 8 9 9 6 4 2 9 5 0 9 *